FIT FOR BUSINESS:
TRANSFORMING HR IN THE PUBLIC SECTOR

David Vere and Lynne Butler

The Chartered Institute of Personnel and Development is the leading publisher of books and reports for personnel and training professionals, students, and all those concerned with the effective management and development of people at work.
For full details of all our titles, please contact the Publishing Department:
Tel: 020 8612 6204
E-mail: publish@cipd.co.uk

To view and purchase all CIPD titles:
www.cipd.co.uk

For details of CIPD research projects:
www.cipd.co.uk/research

FIT FOR BUSINESS: TRANSFORMING HR IN THE PUBLIC SECTOR

David Vere and Lynne Butler

THE DEVELOPMENT PARTNERSHIP

A CIPD Research Report

First published 2007

Cover and text design by Sutchinda Rangsi-Thompson
Typeset by Curran Publishing Services
Printed in Great Britain by Short Run Press

British Library Cataloguing in Publication Data
A catalogue record for this book is available from the British Library

ISBN-13 978 1 84398 192 3

Chartered Institute of Personnel and Development
151 The Broadway, London SW19 1JQ

Tel: 020 8612 6200
Website: www.cipd.co.uk

Incorporated by Royal Charter. Registered charity no. 1079797.

CONTENTS

List of figures and tables vi

Foreword vii

Executive summary viii

1 **Introduction** 1

2 **Context** 3

3 **Our starting point** 9

4 **Goals** 11

5 **Results** 17

6 **Performance** 25

7 **Technique** 31

8 **Teamwork** 37

9 **Fitness** 43

10 **Physique** 49

11 **Conclusions** 59

Appendix 1. Forty questions for HR 61

Appendix 2. Baseline questions from the first *Fit for business* report 63

Notes 67

LIST OF FIGURES AND TABLES

Figure 1.	The building blocks of strategic HR	6
Figure 2.	The DWP HR value model	19
Figure 3.	Relative importance of people outcomes	21
Figure 4.	Relative importance of HR activities	21
Figure 5.	Supporting people-performance management	27
Figure 6.	HR working with the business	39
Figure 7.	DWP professional standards	47
Figure 8.	DWP HR professional development programme	47
Figure 9.	Drivers and barriers to change in HR	51
Figure 10.	The 'three legged stool'	52
Figure 11.	DWP shared services model	54
Figure 12.	HM Revenue and Customs HR services model	54
Figure 13.	RB Kingston HR operating model	55
Figure 14.	Food Standards Agency HR structure	55

Table 1.	The *Fit for business* themes: the key questions	ix
Table 2.	Participating organisations	2
Table 3.	Priorities for HR leaders and chief executives	5
Table 4.	Sequence of HR design issues	6
Table 5.	The consortium agenda	9
Table 6.	Measuring the effectiveness of rostering action	20
Table 7.	National Audit Office HR scorecard	23
Table 8.	Cabinet Office HR management maturity index	24
Table 9.	HR skill sets	45
Table 10.	Evolution of HR roles	51
Table 11.	Employees and HR organisation	56
Table 12.	HR service criteria in Leeds City Council	57

FOREWORD

The pressures on the public sector to improve services while reducing costs continue to be intense. This presents the HR function with some of the biggest challenges it has ever faced, to both support the process of transformation by becoming more strategic and demonstrate added value with fewer staff. The 'choice' agenda, which implies continuing competition by the private and voluntary sectors to deliver public services, means competition also in the ability to manage staff effectively. So how are HR departments shaping up?

This is a report on the second action-learning consortium of public sector employers with which the CIPD has been associated. The report on the first consortium, *Fit for business*, published in 2005, described what nine organisations in central and local government were doing to build a strategic HR function. This second report picks up where the first left off and charts the progress of another group of nine public sector organisations, two years on.

What state is the public sector in to meet the challenge from the private sector, and what contribution is HR making? The report maps a great deal of activity by people in the HR function, directed towards restructuring the function and increasing its effectiveness. But it also makes clear that a great deal remains to be done. Key messages are:

- HR needs to work more closely with senior managers to build strong leadership and develop organisation-wide talent.

- Senior managers need to help HR identify key business priorities and focus on what needs to be done to achieve them.

- There is a big issue for HR in developing the skills to act strategically, instead of hoping that the labour market will supply the necessary talent.

- The HR agenda currently seems to neglect employee engagement, though this is critical to achieving high performance.

One underlying theme of the report is that HR cannot succeed in becoming more strategic by its own unaided efforts. The problems it is seeking to tackle are essentially organisational issues that demand the ongoing attention of permanent secretaries, central government and local authority chief executives. Do they recognise the need for effective HR input on the major changes required across the organisation, or are they relying on buying in help from outside?

The strength of this report is that it contains an objective account of how HR in each of the nine organisations that took part in the consortium is tackling the challenges it faces, and the lessons being learned along the way. Each chapter includes practical 'learning points' and lists a series of questions for HR. The report is a powerful tool that can be used by other public sector employers, most of whom face very similar issues.

The CIPD is very grateful to David Vere and Lynne Butler who not only wrote the report but led the consortium and supported its members. The Institute is pleased to have been associated with the project and believes that further action-research of this kind can make a useful contribution to increasing understanding of how the HR function is changing, as well as providing practical support to members in negotiating those changes.

EXECUTIVE SUMMARY

This research report describes the experience and learning gained by organisations in an action-learning consortium of nine public sector organisations that worked together from 2006–7 to develop a more strategic approach to HR. The central and local government organisations that took part were: British Transport Police, the Crown Office and Procurator Fiscal Service, the Department for Work and Pensions, the Food Standards Agency, the Health and Safety Executive, HM Revenue and Customs, Leeds City Council, National Audit Office and the Royal Borough of Kingston.

THE CONTEXT

Public sector organisations remain under continued pressure to provide better services with fewer resources at a time of increasing expectations from stakeholders, customers and taxpayers. There is also a major push to extend the choice of service delivery options, which is likely to lead to further partnership with the private and third sectors. Responding to these tough challenges means finding better ways to deliver services. This means changing organisational structures, systems and processes and developing workforce skills. To really make a sustained difference to organisational performance these changes must also be underpinned by a new performance culture.

For the consortium organisations this context offered significant opportunities for HR to make a real impact on the business, but only if it could engage strategically and help shape and implement change to create the performance culture required.

STRATEGIC HR

Our first *Fit for business* report described many of the changes being introduced to make HR more strategic and start to contribute to the performance agenda. During the second consortium many of these changes were still being embedded. HR is still implementing significant change within the function while striving to make a greater contribution to wider organisational change.

Placing clear responsibility for people management within the line was at the heart of changes in the last consortium, with consequent changes for the role of HR. A frequent issue for consortium members this time was how to manage the HR/manager relationship to achieve better people management and business results. For us this relationship is the fulcrum for the performance culture required.

A TRANSFORMATION ROUTE MAP

What has also become increasingly clear in the second consortium is the need to look again at the most suitable route to follow to achieve HR transformation. Our reflections suggest that too much of the transformation has been driven by changes in the HR operating model as a goal in itself rather than a reflection of what the business needs. This model has to be explained to the business instead of being a reflection of it. So our report this time follows a structure based on what we feel is a more appropriate route map to build strategic HR, based on the seven themes from our first report (see Table 1).

The learning from the consortium is described in each section under these themes, and some important lessons emerged.

Goals and results

Organisational results in the public sector depend on the effective management of people and performance, so a key goal for organisations is to ensure that they undertake these responsibilities well. HR needs to work more closely with senior managers to develop strong leadership and organisational talent, build a modern infrastructure to support good people management, and create a culture where high performance is rewarded. HR needs to be credible and confident to get a seat at the strategy table.

HR measurement continues to challenge HR organisations given the complexity of the HR system and the variable scope of its

Table 1 ✣ The *Fit for business* themes: the key questions

Theme	Description	Questions addressed by this consortium
Goals	What the organisation is aiming to achieve. The people outcomes needed to bring this about.	What needs to be in place for strategic HR to become a reality?
Results	How to measure success in delivering the people outcomes the business needs.	How do we demonstrate the value that HR is adding to the business?
Performance	What people managers and their teams need to do to deliver the people outcomes.	How do we ensure that effective people management practice is enacted through the line?
Technique	The HR services and activities required to enable delivery of the people outcomes.	What should HR be doing to add real value?
Teamwork	How HR works with people managers to implement those activities.	How should HR best engage with the business and work in partnership?
Fitness	The capabilities HR practitioners need to work with the business in this way.	How can we build the competence and confidence of the HR function?
Physique	The way HR should be organised to deliver this capability.	How can we best embed HR operating models and processes?

responsibilities to achieve outcomes. This calls for a balanced set of HR measures to capture the complete HR contribution in terms of service quality, enabling change, setting direction and delivering business results.

Performance focus, teamwork and technique

The desire of HR to be strategic is more likely to be realised when there is organisational 'buy in', sufficient HR and management capability and employee support for it to take on that role. To achieve this HR must show itself to be credible and confident by delivering on the 'basics' first and engaging well with customers at all levels of the business.

The shift of HR from a 'policing' role to a more facilitative one means evolving new ways of working with managers to ensure they fulfil their people-management responsibilities. HR must also increase its contribution to the management of change and organisational development through greater business partnership. Finally HR has to be especially effective in delivering the 'big' HR initiatives with the potential to make a long-lasting impact on business performance.

HR fitness

This transformed HR environment also calls for new HR skills and behaviours and fresh approaches to develop and acquire them. Action here is vital to sustain a capable, confident HR function in the longer term that can continue to support the business flexibly. HR also needs to communicate better with its four principal customer groups by using easily accessible language with minimal jargon and ensuring HR policies and other guidance are straightforward.

HR physique

It is essential to attend to practical details when adapting and embedding a new HR delivery model and related processes. Evaluation of how these new arrangements are working is also critical to ensure that they continue to support the needs of the business and delivery of HR strategy.

There are still questions about strategic HR in the public sector that need to be answered, and we believe that further collaborative action along consortium lines would help to provide the answers. The experience and learning from the second *Fit for business* consortium led us to believe that there is real progress in HR transformation, but still more to do. We concluded that:

- HR and senior managers need to collaborate to create the performance culture and build the right infrastructure to support effective people management.
- To really add value it is essential for HR to identify the people issues that will make the greatest difference to business performance and act on those above all else. These are the activities that HR should be measuring.
- To achieve such focus will mean adopting radical approaches and making some tough people-management choices, otherwise business impact is likely to be minimal.
- The HR reform agenda seems to neglect employee engagement – except indirectly through emphasis on diversity and fair treatment policies and practices. Engaging employees is too important to the performance culture to be neglected.
- HR can be unduly insular and defensive. It needs to be more open minded and take more opportunities to learn from HR practitioners elsewhere and business colleagues. The

contacts made with these people were among the key benefits of the consortium and a collaborative approach. So the message is still to get out more – even more.

- A big issue for HR is still how to develop the skills and confidence to act strategically in areas such as business partnering, organisation development (OD) and change management. Investment in continued professional development is vital.

- The HR operating model (that is, the structure) is still a major preoccupation for organisations but it is not the answer – although it must be right for your organisation. To often the shape of the operating model drives the HR transformation agenda. HR transformation needs to be business driven. Ultimately HR must be fit for purpose – and hence fit for business.

INTRODUCTION 1

- **This chapter outlines the background to the *Fit for business* consortium and the approach involved.**
- **Nine public sector organisations participated in the consortium.**
- **The report highlights seven themes which cover the key elements to be considered in transforming the HR function.**

In October 2005, we published our research report *Fit for business: building a strategic HR function in the public sector,*[1] which described how nine public sector organisations had sought to build a more effective HR function. These organisations had worked together in an action-learning consortium to tackle specific projects and share their experiences in developing a more strategic approach to HR.

In October 2006, a second action-learning consortium was established, again with nine organisations, to work together and continue to develop this strategic approach to HR. This report describes the experience and learning gained by those organisations – putting strategic HR into practice.

THE CONSORTIUM APPROACH

The nine public sector organisations in the second consortium were all engaged in major programmes of business change, with consequent changes in their approach to HR issues. These organisations were at different points in a spectrum of models and approaches to HR, and so their comparative experience was particularly worthwhile in a consortium context. Within the consortium, each organisation focused on a particular issue of importance within its HR change programme, and agreed to share its learning about that work.

To stimulate and inform these projects and the participating organisations' wider change programme, consortium members undertook a series of consortium learning activities. The aim was to share experience and good practice and highlight learning for the benefit of public sector organisations more generally by drawing on HR experts and practitioners from both the public and private sector. Overall we believe this is a unique and innovative approach of value to not only the organisations and individuals involved but also the wider HR community.

PARTICIPATING ORGANISATIONS

The nine participating organisations and their projects are set out in Table 2.

THEMES FOR THE REPORT

In this report we have summarised the lessons learnt by these organisations in addressing these issues and taking forward their overall HR reform agenda. To provide continuity with our last report, our findings are described under the seven *Fit for business* themes and address some important questions about strategic HR in practice.

- *Goals*: What needs to be in place for strategic HR to become a reality?
- *Results*: How do we demonstrate the value that HR is adding to the business?
- *Performance*: How do we ensure that effective people-management practice is enacted through the line?
- *Technique*: What should HR be doing to add real value?
- *Teamwork*: How should HR best engage with the business and work in partnership?
- *Fitness*: How can we build the competence and confidence of the HR function?
- Physique: How can we best embed HR operating models and processes?

Table 2 ✣ Participating organisations

Organisation	Project goal
British Transport Police	Develop an action plan to implement elements of police workforce modernisation
Crown Office and Procurator Fiscal Service	Determine the role of the new HR business partners
Department for Work and Pensions	Develop a cost-effective methodology for identifying and measuring the contribution of HR to business outcomes
Food Standards Agency	Bring about a sustained improvement in performance management across the Agency
Health and Safety Executive	Create a business-driven learning and development strategy
HM Revenue and Customs	Develop a practical guide for line managers to help them deal with a range of common performance-management issues
Leeds City Council	Establish the services that HR should provide for the business and a suitable HR organisation for the future
National Audit Office	Develop a service level agreement and metrics for a restructured HR organisation
Royal Borough of Kingston upon Thames	Establish a programme to develop senior women managers

STRUCTURE OF THE REPORT

In the report, we first discuss the changing context for the work of HR in organisations, particularly in the public sector. We then set out the starting point for the work of the consortium, based on an initial benchmark of issues for the organisations involved, and then describe our main findings under each of the seven *Fit for business* themes, highlighting:

- the key questions that were addressed by consortium organisations
- the principles or theory that underpinned their approach
- examples of what was done
- the experience and lessons that emerged
- concluding questions HR professionals should ask themselves.

FORTY QUESTIONS FOR HR

The 40 questions for HR that arise from the report are contained in Appendix 1.

HOW TO USE THE REPORT

Each section of the report covering the seven themes is designed to be free standing, so readers can dip into the sections that are of interest to them or relate to an issue for their organisation.

SUPPORT TO THE CONSORTIUM

The consortium received support from the CIPD, the Public Sector People Managers Association (PPMA) and the Improvement and Development Agency (IDeA). We are also grateful to all of those who spoke at the six consortium learning events or hosted a consortium visit. Most thanks of all go to those individuals in the participating organisations whose hard work, willingness to learn and readiness to share their experiences provided the material for our report.

CONTEXT 2

- **This chapter sets out the organisational context for the work of the consortium and the challenges faced by member organisations.**
- **It sets out the change context in central and local government, covering the key themes of performance, delivery, efficiency, better service, leadership and staff capability.**
- **The chapter also draws out the implications of this context for the HR function and the agenda of HR issues to be addressed and how the *Fit for business* themes help organisations tackle these issues.**

Two years on from our first *Fit for business* report, the challenges facing public sector organisations continue to be about better delivery with constrained resources, set against the increasing expectations of stakeholders, customers or taxpayers. This means that the public sector is continually seeking better ways to deliver, with consequent changes in structure, systems and processes as well as the skills required of employees and managers. There is now also a major push to extend the choice of service delivery options, which is likely to lead to greater partnership with the private and third sectors. The ability to manage significant cultural shift is critical to future success. Overall this presents a significant change agenda. One of the key questions for the organisations within the consortium was how HR could best contribute to this change agenda whilst continuing to consolidate change in the HR function. The consortium comprised organisations from central and local government (including the police service), each of which had its own particular set of challenges to tackle.

CENTRAL GOVERNMENT CAPABILITY REVIEWS

As part of the latest phase of the government's transformation efforts, central government departments are being subjected to scrutiny to assess how well placed they are to meet the demands that will be placed on them in future. These 'capability reviews' aim to make departments work better and assess their effectiveness on 10 specific aspects within three broad areas of 'capability': leadership, strategy and delivery.

To date 14 out of 17 departments have been reviewed. The aim is to judge the capability they require to meet three key tasks, described as:

- tough delivery outcomes to be achieved with fewer resources
- the need to anticipate and respond to a rapidly changing world and delivery environment, with new technologies, demographic changes and the impact of global events on domestic priorities
- challenging and demanding stakeholders and customers, increasingly expecting excellent public services and demanding more.[2]

Each report has identified between three and five areas for action for the department concerned, and the overall results show a need for further development under four themes:

- *Leadership*: Leaders need to apply passion, pace and direction to sustain delivery and provide coherence in approach across departmental business.
- *Business models*: It is important to find the most suitable model to deliver results effectively to customers through diverse delivery chains, partnership models and contractual arrangements.
- *Delivery and performance*: Customer demands must be met through really effective performance management, understanding of customer needs and focus on value for money.
- *Skills, capacity and capability*: It is necessary to make the most of the people in the organisation against headcount reductions and efficiency savings by improved leadership, effective talent management, skills development and performance management.

THE CHANGE AGENDA

The consequent changes now being introduced in central government organisations include:

- changes to organisational structures and governance arrangements

- continuing implementation of e-enabled processes to streamline service to customers, pool information and achieve resource economies
- increased use of diverse delivery arrangements through contracting, partnership working and collaboration across sectors
- an increase in the priority being given to the development of improved Civil Service leadership
- greater emphasis on optimising talent and the improvement of Civil Service skills, reflected in the Professional Skills for Government programme
- continued reduction in headcount, as well as reducing corporate overheads and transferring resources to the front line.

The nature of central government often means that there are still HR initiatives 'imposed' by the centre which may or may not fit with the priorities of each organisation at that point. So there are still many examples of HR action being policy rather than business driven.

The consequence of all this change for these organisations has been a real impact on the morale of staff, which is evident in a deterioration of staff survey assessments of the quality of leadership and people management, career development opportunities, communications and the way performance is managed. This has all added to the HR agenda and placed additional demands on the HR function.

LOCAL GOVERNMENT

Local councils face some key challenges over the next few years if they are to meet the requirements of the Local Government White Paper (2006) and sustain the high performance needed to maintain four-star Comprehensive Performance Assessment (CPA) ratings from the Audit Commission. These challenges include:

- implementing efficiencies from the Gershon Review
- enhancing the role of councils in local communities
- improving services to citizens and communities
- developing greater customer focus
- working in partnership
- managing performance
- working in new regional structures.

Although local government has been very successful in achieving efficiencies to date, the tightening of public sector resources requires further cost reductions. This means local government needs to consider more radical ways of working such as large-scale restructuring, and to review professional roles and existing working practices while ensuring it continues to improve the way it works with communities and customers.

According to a recent IDeA report, *The future shape of local authorities' workforces* (2007), many councils are now reviewing their plans with a view to more collaborative working and the need to develop shared services for a wide range of support services, including HR and payroll. However little attention has so far been given to what this would mean for their workforce strategies. This structural change is likely to lead to a gradual headcount reduction in directly employed staff over the next three years, leaving a small but better-paid professional elite within each support service

In addition to making efficiency savings, the Cabinet Office and the Treasury are expecting much greater market testing and open competition in local government, particularly where council services are rated as 'poor'.

These challenges are being addressed through the local government national pay and workforce strategy with the following themes:

- developing the organisation
- developing leadership
- developing workforce skills and capability
- resourcing local government
- pay and rewards.

Recent national research by Local Government Association Research (LGAR)[3] suggests that this strategy is having a positive impact on people management and performance in the sector. At present 82 per cent of councils have people or workforce strategies and 85 per cent of the local government workforce is covered by the 'Investors in People' standard. Councils have also managed to reverse negative recruitment trends. However, many councils report major skills gaps, and these are likely to hamper their ability to implement and improve strategic HR. Skills gaps include:

- change management and organisational development
- business process redesign and analysis
- performance management
- people management.

So although progress is encouraging there is still some way to go.

In 2005 the Public Sector People Managers Association (PPMA) commissioned research with chief executives in local government called *How can HR help chief executives sleep at night?* The aim of this research was to determine whether HR leaders and chief executives felt they were facing the same challenges and helping each other with the same priorities, and explore what they could personally do to ensure a productive relationship. PPMA was also interested to establish if there was anything PPMA, the Society for Local Authority Chief Executives (SOLACE) or others could do to support both parties to ensure they were working to common goals. The top five quoted issues from the research are set out in Table 3.

Table 3 Priorities for HR leaders and chief executives

Ranking	For HR leaders	For chief executives
1	Equal pay and conditions. Single status. Competitive market salaries. Pay and reward – not paying staff to sit around for 20 years.	Pay review.
2	Finance. Funding.	Budget pressure and gaining sustained funding. Budgetary control and reductions. Generating new income.
3	Change/transformation. Engaging staff in change. Improving culture and morale. Organisation change.	Creating a learning organisation within and from others. Coping with changing environment. Achieving culture change.
4	Leadership development. Getting managers to manage people. Junior management skills development. Restructuring.	Building new management team. Reorganisation of management structure. Leadership skills.
5	Organisational development. Building for the future – capability, capacity and competency frameworks. Workforce and skills planning and development, including member development. Capability of HR.	Redesign of services and workforce required to underpin improvements. Skills issues and infrastructure. Succession planning.

Five themes appeared to be the most consistent issues at the top of both chief executives' and HR leaders' agendas: equal pay, finance, culture change, leadership development and organisational development. There were also a reassuring number of common issues and objectives shared between HR leaders and the chief executives in the research overall.

THE CHALLENGE FOR HR

In this context there are significant opportunities for HR to make a real impact on the business. The challenge for HR is to be engaged at a strategic level in the design of change and to contribute fully to its implementation. The important question is whether the HR function can reach beyond concern for HR organisation, issues and policies to making a real contribution to business decisions. This in turn depends on HR delivery of the core business and getting the basics right.

Building strategic HR

Our first report described many of the changes being introduced with the aim of making HR more strategic, and in the current consortium many of these changes have still to bed down and demonstrate real results. So they are changes that are not proven. This often means an HR function that is still preoccupied with its own internal change agenda. As a result HR risks losing sight of organisation-wide change in its efforts to put its own house in order. We have increasingly come to the conclusion that the approach to strategic HR – *Fit for business* – needs to be based on a different route map than hitherto. Figure 1 illustrates the ingredients of the model.

Far too often the approach has been HR-centric rather than business-centric. To implement strategic HR for the business means ideally addressing the HR design issues in the sequence shown in Table 4.

HR and the line

At the heart of the changes reported upon last time was a 'shift in responsibility' for people issues from HR back into the line: that is, to where those responsibilities should have resided in the first place. This shift has yet to settle in. Indeed many managers in consortium organisations do not accept the shift and continue to expect HR to deal with people issues – and not just the tough people problems. Frequently the issue for the consortium organisations this time was the respective roles of HR and the line (or perhaps more accurately 'people managers') and how best to manage the interface between the two. These new roles and the relationship are being tested in handling each of the major people issues on the HR agenda: namely, headcount reductions, talent management, skills development, performance management and leadership development.

Ultimately the aim of the change in the HR operating model was to create a new and more effective partnership between HR and people managers to deliver better people management and thereby achieve business results. What impact this has had on each organisation so far is hard to judge. Our experience in the consortium suggests there is still some way to go before HR is consistently regarded as a true strategic business partner.

Figure 1 ❖ The building blocks of strategic HR

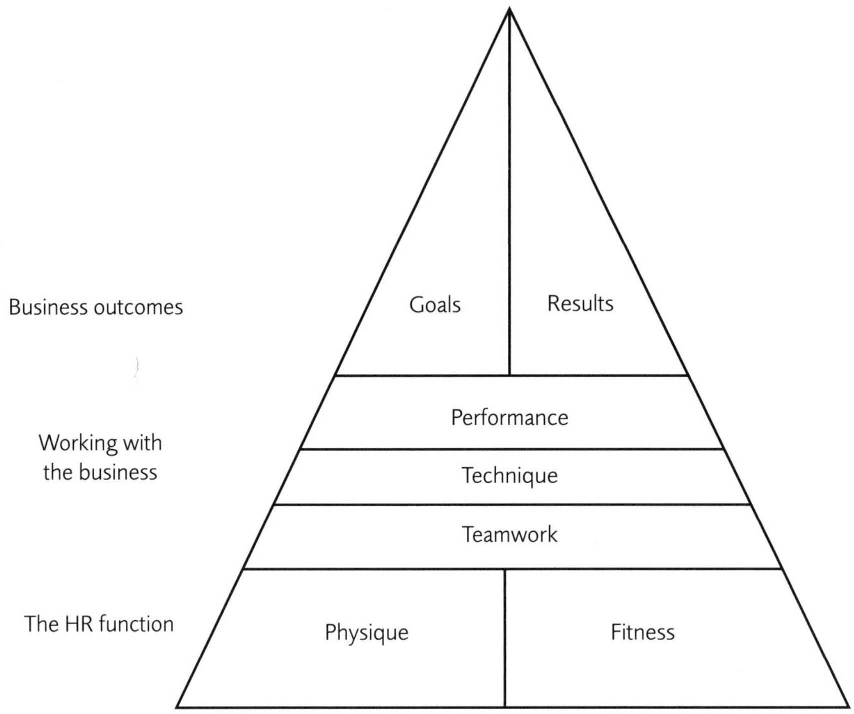

Table 4 ❖ Sequence of HR design issues

Business outcomes	
Goals	What the organisation is aiming to achieve The people outcomes needed to bring this about
Results	How to measure success in delivering the people outcomes the business needs
HR working with the business	
Performance	What people managers and their teams need to do to deliver the people outcomes
Technique	The HR services and activities required to enable delivery of the people outcomes
Teamwork	How HR works with people managers to implement those activities
The HR function	
Physique	The way HR should be organized to deliver this capability
Fitness	The capabilities HR practitioners need to work with the business in this way

A NEW APPROACH FOR HR

Each section of our report explores how this new relationship is being developed and the practical means through which an effective partnership for results can be achieved. The essence of this new approach involves HR:

- Making a more strategic contribution by focusing on issues for the business rather than the function, on business results and outcomes not HR policies.
- Working with top leaders to create and implement a performance culture and provide authentic leadership to create the climate for better results.
- Seeking to enact HR policies effectively via people managers – with the aim that managers manage and HR advises.
- Delivering a much better, more efficient HR service to the business, to agreed standards. This means getting the basics right in the key areas of recruitment, resourcing, development, employee relations and HR advice.
- Creating a more professional and sustainable HR function with the skills to be effective and the confidence to contribute in these new ways.
- Making sure that HR is in a position to demonstrate and measure its contribution – and justify its existence.

OUR STARTING POINT 3

- **This chapter sets out an agenda of issues that consortium members tackled under the seven *Fit for business* themes.**
- **The themes are: Goals, Results, Performance, Technique, Teamwork, Fitness and Physique.**
- **Each theme is discussed in the following chapters.**

At the outset, we asked the organisations participating in the consortium to benchmark themselves against the learning points from the first *Fit for business* report. We did this by asking questions about the degree to which they felt HR in their organisation was 'fit for business'. The questions we used are set out in Appendix 2.

The areas where consortium members most frequently identified scope for improvement are summarised in Table 5. Their work addressing these issues within the consortium now provides many practical examples of how this agenda can be met.

We believe these issues reflect the wider public sector picture. In the following sections we have captured this new learning for the benefit of other public sector organisations (and indeed organisations more generally) that are still wrestling with them.

Table 5 ❖ The consortium agenda

Goals
- Clarity within HR as to how it should best add value to the business.
- Helping managers in the business understand the meaning of strategic HR and what it can do for them.
- HR engaging strategically with the organisation.

Results
- HR focusing its efforts on the outcomes it has to deliver for the organisation.
- Developing a strategy process to align HR and business priorities.

Performance
- People managers embracing responsibility for HR issues in their team and developing their capability accordingly.
- People managers still overly dependent on HR to resolve people issues.
- Setting a climate for better people and performance management through exemplary top management.

Technique
- Tackling strategic people issues for the business.
- Providing an efficient, high-quality service to the business.

Teamwork
- Making clear the mutual expectations between HR personnel and their business partners at the top of the organisation and with people managers.
- Being clear what each HR relationship delivers for the organisation.

Fitness
- HR adapting flexibly to changing organisational needs.

Physique
- Line managers understanding their role in the new HR operating framework.
- Ensuring HR gets out into the business more and networks externally.

GOALS 4

Objects of effort or ambition; destination.

- **This chapter discusses the elements that need to be in place to make strategic HR a reality.**
- **It describes what we mean by strategic HR; this includes being focused on business priorities, defining HR roles to deliver organisational success and add value, engaging differently with the organisation and an organisational desire for HR to contribute in this way.**
- **Strategic HR requires a credible HR function, management buy in, capable people managers, effective access to HR services, a clear business strategy and a linked strategic HR agenda.**

FLASHBACK

Learning points from *Fit for business I*

- The HR team needs to understand what being strategic means in their **particular** organisation.
- The organisation needs a sufficiently well-developed business strategy to enable the HR priorities to be identified.
- Strategy is as much about the strategy process as its content.
- Strategic HR content is about the vertical and horizontal alignment, impact and comprehensiveness of HR activities.
- Working strategically means engagement, credibility, confidence and capability – working in partnership with the business.
- Managers in the business also need to know what strategic HR looks like.

FAST FORWARD TO THE PRESENT ➡

Learning points from *Fit for business II*

- HR must be focused primarily on the business priorities in order to determine the people contribution needed to achieve them.
- HR should be prepared and equipped to operate at both a strategic and operational level; both are equally essential to organisational success.
- HR has to deliver on the 'basics' first, ensuring it meets customer needs, in order to earn its place as a credible strategic partner.
- There is a real tension between the desire of HR to be strategic and the readiness of the people in the organisation to allow HR to take on this role.
- HR is too often inward looking. To be aware of opportunities, proactive and responsive to change, HR needs to build a good intelligence network both inside and outside the organisation.

WHAT ARE THE CRITICAL HR ISSUES OF STRATEGIC IMPORTANCE TO THE BUSINESS?

There is now widespread acknowledgement among senior managers and HR professionals in public sector organisations that effective people management is the essential factor in improving business performance. This covers managing transformation and change, performance management, improving leadership and the development of talent. So whilst it is clear that HR needs to raise its game to help organisations address these issues, the debate continues about how HR can **best** intervene and contribute at a more strategic level than before.

At we identified in our first *Fit for business* report, being strategic is:

> *the means chosen to achieve objectives for the recruitment, development, motivation and reward of people that contribute directly to the achievement of the strategic goals of the organisation. ... Being strategic is important because it ensures that HR is making a full contribution to what the organisation is trying to achieve.*

Being strategic means that HR needs to align and support the business in the achievement of its goals. This means HR being very clear about and focused on the business priorities in the organisation and how people should contribute to achieving them. In practice it means that HR should undertake a variety of roles at both strategic and operational level to achieve business outcomes and deliver value, both of which are equally important to ensure organisational success. How HR undertakes these roles is critical. HR needs to be outward looking and proactive, not passive, in the way it supports the business.

In the first *Fit for business* report we discussed how HR needed to engage in a different way with the organisation, be business focused and support the organisation to achieve its aims rather than constraining it. This view still holds, but in the second consortium members have found an increasing tension between the desire of HR to be strategic and the readiness of the organisation for it to take on this role. This reflects the capability of HR but also the degree to which managers understand what HR can offer.

WHAT NEEDS TO BE IN PLACE FOR HR TO BE STRATEGIC?

Experience in the consortium has shown that for strategic HR to work well there should be a strong belief in the organisation that HR can deliver a high-quality service. There also needs to be a good people-management infrastructure that will support the HR goals of the organisation. Otherwise there is a risk that a move to so called 'strategic HR' has a negative impact on both organisational productivity and employee morale because managers and employees will not have the support they need to perform well, and will get bogged down in people issues.

Consortium members have found that HR needs the competence and confidence to earn its place as a strategic partner carving out a clear role for itself that is well understood by everyone. Managers also need to recognise the importance of their role in managing people and be willing and able to take this on. So both managers and HR professionals need to change the way they operate within the new HR framework. A formal statement of mutual responsibilities can be really helpful in establishing the baseline whilst still allowing flexibility in the HR–manager relationship. Whatever delivery model is adopted, a shift to strategic HR will also have an impact on employees. They are likely to have more limited direct access to HR and depend more on their line managers as well as take more personal responsibility for their own performance.

Breaking previous patterns of behaviour and instilling new ones can be challenging for HR, managers and employees. This behavioural change therefore needs to be factored into any move to strategic HR and managed well. All three groups will need extra support to change behaviour, so this shift may work better if the process is gradual and takes proper account of how all HR activities will be managed. Otherwise HR may find itself 'thinly stretched' by still undertaking a significant operational role responding to day-to-day queries from line managers, whilst also trying to develop and deliver a strategic input to wider business issues such as restructuring. This 'stretch' could undermine both the strategic and the operational contribution.

Experience among consortium members has suggested six factors that need to be in place for HR functions to be strategically effective:

- a credible, capable HR function that is well led, outward looking and responsive to customer feedback
- senior management 'buy in' and understanding of what good people management and strategic HR look like
- sufficient line management 'buy in' and capability to manage people well without day-to-day support from HR
- the information and means for managers and employees to access readily and make proper use of operational HR services
- a well-formed business strategy that sets outs the organisational priorities, goals and outputs and is shared by all
- a clear strategic HR agenda which identifies the key people priorities that support the business strategy, how these will be addressed and by whom.

HOW DOES HR DEVELOP AND RETAIN CREDIBILITY?

In undertaking their projects, consortium HR staff have engaged fully with senior managers and line managers to understand their needs and identify the best way to take new initiatives forward. Although many senior managers and some line managers do have a good understanding of strategic HR and the benefits of working in partnership at this level, there can be an HR 'credibility gap' which hampers the development of more productive working relationships. This is because HR is often perceived as not having the leadership capability, solutions focus and change management skills required; not delivering well on the 'basics'; communicating in a language business does not understand; or being insufficiently customer focused.

It is therefore important for HR to request regular feedback from their customers in a variety of ways. HR should then ensure any arising issues are tackled quickly – adjusting the way services are delivered or addressing shortfalls in HR capability. This is particularly important so that HR delivery models evolve to a design that is appropriate whilst the positive aspects of the existing HR service are retained.

When HR is credible it is far better placed to persuade senior managers of the value of good people management and strategic HR action. With better 'buy in' at this level HR can strengthen its strategic position further by influencing business planning and wider organisational culture at an early stage. This helps HR to 'break free' from unhelpful stereotypes of its role and establish itself as the guardian of corporate health. The emphasis then becomes the prevention of people problems rather than treating their symptoms.

HOW CAN HR FACILITATE TRANSFORMATION AND CHANGE?

Facilitation of transformation and change is increasingly seen as a central part of the HR role: the 'change agent'. So is improving performance management and developing leadership capability. Consortium members were often managing a number of these activities simultaneously.

> The Food Standards Agency has embarked on a process of establishing a new business strategy with a much greater emphasis on business performance management to deliver results for stakeholders, partners and consumers. At the heart of this approach are the processes of effective business planning, performance monitoring and the management of individual performance. In line with this approach the Agency has recently revised its performance-management system and placed much greater emphasis on effective people management. This is being reinforced through a leadership programme for the senior managers in the Agency, and this has stimulated a dialogue about better management leading to a more consistent approach to people issues across the organisation.

Members also reported that the need to develop greater organisational capacity and retain good staff meant there was an increased emphasis on talent management, particularly to fill top-level roles or attract new entrants.

> The goal of the project at the Royal Borough of Kingston was to establish a network for senior women to develop their confidence and skills and ultimately increase their representation at the top level in the organisation.

To respond to the challenge of change and anticipate what needs to happen in the future, HR needs a good intelligence network inside and outside the organisation. This is critical for building organisational capability to respond to future workforce challenges as well as strengthening the contribution of the HR function. Internally it means HR using both formal and informal mechanisms to really engage with managers and employees at all levels. This helps to ensure that HR staff have a good understanding of business issues and up-to-date information, and are then able respond appropriately, for example in supporting downsizing or restructuring.

> The Inland Revenue and HM Customs and Excise merged to become HM Revenue and Customs (HMRC) two years ago. One of the key priorities for the new organisation is to achieve significant efficiency savings and performance improvements over the next two years. HR is engaged in a

transformation programme to help merge the culture of these two organisations, drive up performance and reduce the size of its workforce.

HMRC has prepared a new People Strategy setting out its HR priorities under six themes:

- leadership
- skills
- engagement and communications
- being a leader in UK HR
- workforce change
- driving great performance.

The last theme seeks to equip line managers with the right skills and attitudes – as well as establish processes and policies – to achieve high performance and maximise the individual contribution of staff. The HR Strategy and Policy team has established a series of projects and initiatives to create the right climate for better performance. It has engaged widely across the organisation, particularly with line managers, to map existing practice and culture, and to identify what needs to be done to merge the cultures of these two organisations successfully.

To manage and implement ongoing change calls for a strong focus on priorities so that HR can act quickly and deploy its resources flexibly. HR also needs to be able to 'sell' the benefits of change to both its own staff and the organisation, particularly line managers.

Leeds City Council HR is moving from a decentralised, functional model to a shared HR services model in 2007. As part of the consultation process, HR managers identified some key benefits that could be used to help 'sell' the new HR Service across the Council. These were as follows:

Benefits to managers

The new HR Service would:

- address managers' concerns better and still deliver the basics ('shop window stuff' such as annual leave, employment contracts, sickness, and making sure learning and development needs from appraisals are met)
- offer a more consistent approach to tackling HR issues
- offer more help with business/workforce planning if HR is involved earlier in the planning cycle.

Benefits to HR

The new HR Service would:

- offer more career progression and greater opportunity for HR staff to develop capability as experts
- provide a bigger HR community
- share best practice and learning and avoid reinvention of the wheel
- provide greater economies of scale
- have greater recognition
- be a more powerful force in the council as one service with greater power to influence and guide
- help the organisation move away from department identity/silo working to being 'one council'
- consolidate trade union consultation
- provide a good example to the rest of the council of how to work differently.

Many consortium members are establishing shared services projects as part of wider organisational change programmes that require better understanding of the interface between HR, IT and Finance. This shows an increasing need for the people involved to work holistically and have a sound knowledge of organisational design and development. Some members felt that the complexity of these programmes could make projects challenging for them to deliver and implement on schedule. HR may therefore need to do more to ensure it maintains a focus on priorities and delivery of clear outcomes against the tide of operational issues. This suggests advantages in a separation of strategic from operational HR. It also emphasises the need for HR staff to develop more formal project and change management skills.

In central and local government HR also needs to be proactive in identifying good practice and building productive relationships outside the organisation. This is particularly important to help manage the increasing trend for partnership working with other organisations (eg, between neighbouring local authorities and also between local authorities and primary care trusts) or managing external contractors (eg, where HR services are outsourced). It often means HR taking a leading role in facilitating joint delivery of services.

SUMMARY

There is continuing debate about how HR can best work strategically to add value to the business. Whichever approach it adopts, HR needs to ensure that it suits the context and supports the achievement of organisational goals. The desire of HR to be strategic is more likely to be realised when there is organisational 'buy in' and sufficient HR and management capability and employee support for it to take on that role. To do this HR must show itself to be credible and confident by first delivering on the 'basics' and second engaging with customers at all levels of the business. To be proactive and respond to change, it is also critical that HR builds good networks both inside and outside the organisation to bring in external learning and expertise.

QUESTIONS FOR HR

1. Does your HR function have a clear strategic role that is well understood across the organisation? If not, how can you bring about this understanding?
2. How often do you review the degree to which your HR function is supporting and aligned with the goals of your organisation? How do you do this?
3. How do you make sure that your HR function develops and retains credibility in the organisation?
4. What are the drivers requiring your HR function to be more strategic? How can you use these to influence others to take on their people-management responsibilities in your organisation?
5. What are the barriers that prevent your HR function from being strategic? What can you do to overcome these barriers?
6. Does your HR function have all the information and internal networks it needs to act strategically? If not, how can you make sure that you acquire them?
7. At what point does your HR function become involved in designing and implementing change or transformation in your organisation? What effect does this have on the ability of HR to influence the organisation?
8. How often do you review the way your HR function works with external partners and identify how these partners add value to your strategic HR contribution? Which external partners add the most value? What other external partners do you need?

RESULTS 5

Outcome of something; satisfactory outcomes; list of winners.

- **This chapter describes an approach to demonstrating the added value of HR to the business.**
- **Recognising the difficulty of some aspects of measurement, it illustrates how to align business and HR outcomes and describes a process for identifying suitable measures for an HR strategy.**
- **It also explores the range of measures needed to capture HR impact, service delivery, HR learning and efficiency.**

FLASHBACK

Learning points from *Fit for business I*

- A coherent strategy mapping process enables vertical and horizontal alignment of HR.
- HR has to focus on the outcomes that it has to deliver to the organisation.
- HR measures should assess the extent to which outcomes are delivered or the factors that cause them to be delivered are in place.
- Both senior managers and the HR team need to measure and then manage what matters.

FAST FORWARD TO THE PRESENT ➡

Learning points from *Fit for business II*

- Setting up a **joint** process that enables HR and line managers to align people management with business outcomes will ensure HR delivers what the organisation requires.
- A balanced set of HR measures is needed so that all aspects of the HR contribution are recognised by the business – both outcomes and quality of service.
- HR measures should concentrate on those issues that make the most difference to business results.
- Benchmarking HR with other organisations should be treated with caution, given the range of HR operating models in place.

In our last report we described approaches being used to align HR measures to business goals through the creation of a strategy map and the implementation of a balanced HR scorecard. We also highlighted that fact that in many organisations there is a tendency to measure what HR is doing now and what can be measured easily rather than assessing the impact of HR activities on business performance. In the current consortium the further development of measures has been driven from two directions:

- identifying the people outcomes HR has to deliver to achieve business outcomes
- capturing the *breadth* of the HR contribution.

THE CHALLENGE OF MEASUREMENT

In an environment where all functions of the business are under scrutiny for their efficiency and effectiveness, HR in particular needs to be able to clearly demonstrate added value. Yet there are some inherent difficulties in doing this. First and foremost, responsibility for the delivery of many HR outcomes is shared between employees, managers and HR. For example, developing staff capability requires employee commitment, line manager support and learning options from HR. So whilst HR might measure these aspects, it cannot always be held wholly accountable for their achievement. Second, the causal relationship between HR and business performance is not always clear-cut and can be difficult to trace. For example, job performance is affected not only by the capability of the employees and the quality of their management but also by policies, procedures and technology. Third, the data to measure the HR contribution is not always readily available and the costs of collection could exceed the benefits – although e-HR systems make such data more readily available.

Within the consortium, three organisations focused on aspects of measurement of HR value. The Department for Work and Pensions (DWP) sought to put in place a more effective mechanism for aligning HR and business outcomes. The Food Standards Agency wished to continue to develop its HR balanced scorecard, illustrated in the previous report. The National Audit Office wished to define service standards for HR and define a basket of HR measures covering all aspects of the HR service. In each case there were common features to their approach to developing HR measures.

ALIGNMENT OF BUSINESS AND HR OUTCOMES

As we have emphasised, to make a strategic contribution, HR needs to be clear what the business as a whole is seeking to achieve – the outcomes for the organisation. These outcomes may often be clearly expressed in strategic or business plans and in performance targets, but the HR outcomes that contribute to those results may be taken for granted, vague or not aligned. So it is necessary to clarify the link between HR and business outcomes by discussion with business managers, especially as they are the ones who manage the people who need to deliver those outcomes.

So for example, arranging staff rosters so that customers can be contacted in the early evenings is a key HR outcome if the Child Support Agency is to meet its case resolution target. Managers are responsible for the employees who do this, but HR policies and action can significantly affect achievement of the aim. Exploration of the options to organise the roster was essential if that HR outcome was to be delivered. This means that there often needs to be discussion of choices between different HR activities that could deliver the same outcome to decide which will make the greatest impact. So alignment is not just about what HR can do but about what it could do that would best achieve the business outcome. Providing a framework for this dialogue to take place was the essence of the work carried out by the DWP as it wanted to test a better process for deciding on HR action and measures of success. Figure 2 shows the HR value model that lies behind this process.

Figure 2 ✣ The DWP HR value model

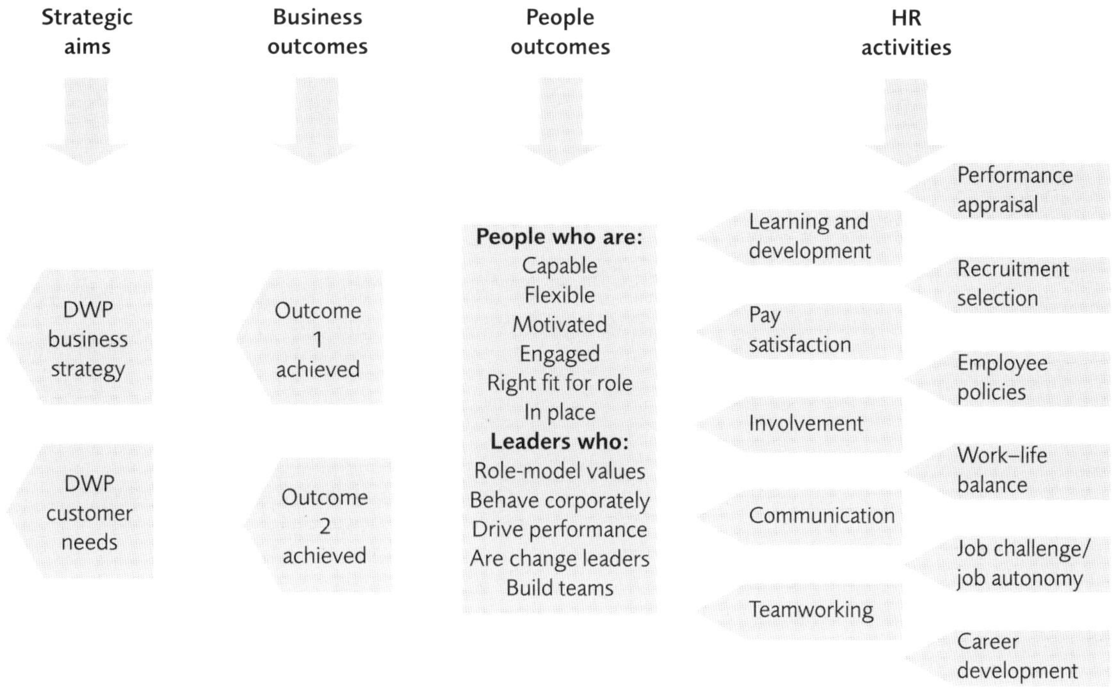

DEPARTMENT FOR WORK AND PENSIONS: MEASURING THE HR CONTRIBUTION TO BUSINESS RESULTS

The DWP sought to determine the causality and alignment of four elements:

- *Business outcomes*: what does the business need to achieve? These outcomes are defined in the Secretary of State's targets and annual business plans – required at a national, business, regional or local level – focusing on delivery to customers. Such outcomes might also describe the future state of the business or the cultural characteristics to be established through a change programme, such as the current CSA Operational Improvement Plan.
- *People outcomes*: what are the people factors or outcomes that will ensure the delivery of the business outcomes? This includes the number of people required, where and when; their skills, capabilities and attitudes; and the way they are organised and led.
- *HR activities*: what are the HR activities required to deliver these people outcomes? What are the recruitment, learning and development, leadership and management activities required?
- *HR measures*: how will we judge if these HR activities have been successful? How can we measure the results we want from these HR activities?

This was achieved through a discussion of seven questions by a group of line managers and their HR partners:

Step 1: What are the key business outcomes or targets?

Step 2: What is the precise people contribution to achieve each business outcome (eg, capability, motivation, job opportunity, line management)?

Step 3: What factors constrain or enable the people contribution (eg, technology, organisation, processes and systems, policy)?

Step 4: Which HR activities best deliver the people contribution (eg, resourcing, L&D, business partner support, line management)?

Step 5: What do we judge to be the relative contribution of these HR activities?

Step 6: How do we measure the HR contribution?

Step 7: What have we learned from this process?

The critical success factors for this approach to be effective are:

- Engage operational managers in the discussion from the outset. They are the ones who are clear about business outcomes; they know what people outcomes they need and HR needs their buy in to demonstrate HR value.
- Ensure you have access to the source data on the business outcomes required.
- Approach each stage in the discussion with on open mind. Consider what is possible, not just what we do at the moment.
- Map the outputs of each stage of the discussion so that all participants can see them, to ensure common understanding and buy in.
- Generate the output quickly and move on to the next stage; momentum will be lost if it takes three weeks to write up the results.

The outputs from this process include an agreed, clear statement of the people outcomes required from HR and their relative importance to achieving the result, as illustrated in Figure 3 for the delivery of Jobcentre Plus business outcomes for customers.

Outputs from the process also include a statement of the best set of HR activities required to deliver each of these people outcomes, which can form the basis for an HR strategy and an action plan to achieve each outcome. The discussion then needs to establish what factors will be used to judge whether the HR activities are successful. This provides the basis for the business-linked HR performance measures that can be used in the HR scorecard. Figure 4 shows the HR activities needed to bring about an improvement in performance management in the Child Support Agency and Table 6 shows the measures to be used to judge the success of the approach to rostering described above.

This approach can be used to help HR and the business to:

- focus HR effort on business activities
- engage business managers in the discussion of how HR should contribute to business results and gain their commitment to the plans that result
- take a fresh look at what HR is doing for the business
- help identify HR measures geared to the people outcomes required rather than to what HR can measure
- require HR and the business to take decisions on priorities and make choices between scarce HR and business resources.

This can be done as a means of considering the overall HR strategy, HR support to a particular change programme or HR action to support a particular business activity. In each case it enables HR and the business to work together at a strategic level.

Table 6 ✣ Measuring the effectiveness of rostering action

Outcome	Measure
Adequate, appropriate coverage across all working hours	Staff attend to agreed work patterns Adequate coverage for incoming calls No staff attend work outside business hours
Staff are motivated to deliver improved customer service	Sickness absence level Attrition rates/voluntary exits Staff attitude survey engagement index Grievances compared with RFC (request for change) Grievances when instructed to change working pattern

Figure 3 ◆ Relative importance of people outcomes

Jobcentre Plus: The relative importance of each people factor to the outcome	1	2	3	4	5	6
	Required		Important		Critical	
Team members						
1. Get in the right people – competence, attitude, fit						■
2. Reflect the customer community			■			
3. Competent people					■	
4. Commitment						■
5. Actually being there						■
6. Customer focus				■		
7. Compliance			■			
8. Flexibility				■		
Team leaders						
9. Motivational leadership						■
10. Accountability			■			
11. Customer/business/performance focus						■
12. Innovative			■			
13. Corporate and networked – not cynical				■		
14. Change leadership					■	

Figure 4 ◆ Relative importance of HR activities

What is the relative importance of each HR activity to deliver the people outcomes? – Performance management and coaching	1	2	3	4	5	6
	Required		Important		Critical	
1. Upskilling of line managers: process and packages (ie, assessments, mentors, learning, line mgt role)				■		
2. Hands on HRBP support (ie, dialogue, assessment, guidance, support, options, etc)				■		
3. Analysing performance data and highlighting issues			■			
4. Support for managing TU relations and clarifying the relationship at area level			■			
5. Managing the business hours change (status, legal position, enacting change, implementation plan)						■
6. Policy clarity		■				
7. Having difficult conversation about contracts, rostering and performance management					■	
8. Creating the new culture (phone-based, team, performance management, rostering, etc)				■		

MEASURING THE HR CONTRIBUTION

For many organisations, a balanced HR scorecard derived from a business scorecard is the best means to capture the breadth of the HR contribution. The classic scorecard combines a performance or financial perspective, a stakeholder or customer perspective, a process perspective and a learning and growth perspective. This can be used for the business as a whole or for the HR function. In both the Food Standards Agency (FSA) and National Audit Office (NAO), these perspectives were adapted so that they include measures which cover the four HR perspectives set out below, linked to the priorities for the business.

HR impact on the business *The outcomes HR delivers to the business*	**HR delivery to customers** *The service HR provides to its internal customers*
HR process efficiency *The way the HR function runs its business*	**HR learning and growth** *The development of HR function capability and improvement of its performance*

The experience of developing the measures now being used by the NAO and FSA under the four perspectives shows that it is essential that HR measures are:

- Broad in scope, covering all HR aspects: service delivery and quality as well as HR outcomes.
- From a range of sources: e-HR data, HR process data, line data, staff attitude surveys and so on, and both qualitative and quantitative.
- In areas where the line also has a contribution to make, but which are still important for HR to know about.
- Focused on the priority issues for each organisation. These might include headcount reduction, continued professional development, diversity, retention of particular grades of staff and speed of recruitment – but will be different for each organisation. The important thing is to measure what matters to you.
- Relatively few in number.
- Readily and regularly reported by the HR function.
- Allocated clear responsibility for their fulfilment: an owner for each measure is required whether within HR or in the line.

As an illustration, the measures developed by the NAO are set out in Table 7.

MEASUREMENT IN CONTEXT: HR MATURITY

The development of an HR measurement framework should be seen as part of the wider HR reform agenda because the measures can be used both to reflect change and to drive improvement. As has often been said: 'what you measure is what you manage.' Our experience shows that most organisations are on a journey when it comes to the development of measures, and this reflects the degree of strategic HR transformation. This approach has been extremely well captured by the HR Management Maturity Matrix created by the Cabinet Office to help central government organisations assess the development of their HR system.

The level of maturity reflects four aspects of HR contribution (Table 8). Operational excellence and service quality provide the platform of credibility from which HR can support business change effectively and play a part in the direction and influence of business strategy. This in turn provides the basis to build the workforce and workplace practices that build capability for business delivery.

The consortium experience has shown that the nine organisations involved are seeking to improve HR effectiveness in all four of these quadrants at the same time, although most have some way to go in the last quadrant to establish an accepted framework of HR practice and to manage HR as a whole system.

SUMMARY

HR measurement continues to provide a challenge to HR organisations, given the complexity of the HR system and the variable scope of its responsibilities to achieve outcomes. An effective dialogue between HR and the line can enable the alignment of HR action and outcomes with business outcomes and provide the basis for HR strategy, action plans and measures. Equally it is important for HR to have in place a balanced set of HR measures to capture the complete HR contribution in terms of service quality, enabling change, setting direction and delivering business results. Overall the development of measures is an evolutionary process that both follows and can also stimulate the pace of HR transformation.

Table 7 ✣ National Audit Office HR scorecard

HR impact on the business

Workforce
No of staff in post
Location of staff
Front line v support staff ratios
% women leaders/managers
% ethnic minority staff
% staff with a disability

HR resourcing
Turnover %
Retention %
Audit principal refreshment
Trainee time ratio
Financial staffing ratio
CCAB staffing ratio
Career managers
Contracting out
Staff utilisation

Corporate performance
ICAEW quality assurance reviews
LSE/Oxford VFM quality score
Financial audit outputs v target
VFM outputs v target

Workforce competence, commitment and engagement
Staff attitudes
% of qualified staff
% of CPD target
Sickness absence average days pa
No of disciplinary cases
No of formal complaints
No of tribunal cases

Health and Safety
No of reported H&S occurrences

HR delivery to customers

HR service quality (SLA targets)
Timeliness of response to email/enquiries/meetings
Online HR self-service availability
Timely delivery of HR transactions
Scores on HR customer survey

Recruitment
General recruitment v targets
Graduate recruitment v targets

Professional development
ICAEW pass rates
No of days development per employee pa
No of days development per leader pa
Average expenditure on employee development pa

Performance management
% staff with minimum number of assessment reports
% of staff with appraisals completed and confirmed by 31 March
% of staff with assignment plans agreed by 31 May
% of staff with a PDP by 30 June
% formal appeals against appraisal ratings

Business management
HR provides regular, timely and accurate data to the business
HR provides comprehensive annual report to the business

HR process efficiency

Overhead
Ratio of HR staff/all staff
Ratio of HR costs/total running costs

Processes
Average time taken to recruit
Average cost of a recruit
HR process accuracy

HR learning and growth

Learning
% professionally qualified HR staff
No of days professional development pa

Refreshment
HR secures appropriate balance between retention of experience and engagement of fresh talent (% of HR staff resigning and replaced)

Commitment and engagement
Staff attitude data for the HR function

Note: Measures in italics are public sector audit agencies' recommended benchmark figures.

Table 8 Cabinet Office HR management maturity index

Operational excellence and service quality	Enabling business change
HR provides value for money by defining and achieving excellent operational efficiency and service. It has excellent and consistent practices in all key transactional processes and relationships with users. Good performance indicated by: • Service Level Agreements in place and continuously improved to ensure: – the costs of key transactions are in an acceptable range – managers and employees get the service they need. • Line and HR roles are clear. • Data requirements are understood and met. • Casework is defined. • Policy is simplified.	*HR adds value by refining its policies, services and skills to help ensure business change. It understands how to use HR to influence specific business outcomes.* Good performance indicated by: • Evidence of early involvement in initiation of, and common approach across, change programmes. • Change readiness is measured. • Civil Service policies refined to be fit for purpose. • Change managers get the support they need. • Readiness/availability of HR expertise.
Directing/influencing strategy development	**Building capability for business delivery**
HR creates value by ensuring that timely and reliable people information is the key driver of the organisation's ambitions and customer-facing strategy. It facilitates top team effectiveness. Good performance indicated by: • Evidence of how HR has contributed to the generation of strategic options. • Bringing future workforce challenges/solutions to the table • Challenging strategic choices through: - identification of workforce readiness - generating options - acting as a coach/catalyst to an effective/aligned top team.	*HR drives value by ensuring that key business targets are achieved through relevant workforce and workplace practices. It ensures that people plans are integrated into business planning and budgeting.* Good performance indicated by: • A clear framework of HR practice to build organisational capability. • Evidence of HR strategy/plans being integrated with capability reviews/business planning and budgeting. • HR uses corroborative evidence to support workforce hypotheses. • HR is managed as a whole system.

QUESTIONS FOR HR

1. How does your HR function engage with the business to determine what outcomes HR needs to deliver and how?
2. How do you decide which HR activities are best able to deliver the HR outcomes that you require?
3. How do you judge the quality of service that HR provides to the business? Are these standards set out explicitly for your customers?
4. Do you have a measurement framework that captures the breadth of HR contribution to business results and how is this used?
5. Are clear accountabilities established for the delivery of HR performance between the HR function, line managers and employees?

PERFORMANCE 6

Carrying out, doing; notable feat; achievement under test.

- **This chapter discusses the ways to build effective people management capability across the organisation.**
- **It describes the role required of people managers, why this is difficult for some managers and how to build people management culture, commitment, capability and confidence.**
- **It also describes the very valuable role HR can play in building people management capability and putting effective people management in place.**

FLASHBACK

Learning points from *Fit for business I*

- Better people management means managers embracing responsibility for HR issues in their team.
- Managers need support to be equipped to address the difficult aspects of management, but also need to be weaned off dependency on the HR team.
- The climate for better management must be set by exemplary management at the top.
- The HR team needs to put in place a range of mechanisms to support better management – single initiatives will not work.
- The organisation needs an agreed view of what better management looks like in its own context.

FAST FORWARD TO THE PRESENT ➡

Learning points from *Fit for business II*

- Better people management means tackling the four 'C's: organisational culture and people manager commitment, capability and confidence.
- Public sector organisations have some way to go to develop a performance-management culture and consequently their people remain sceptical of their organisation's commitment to it, especially in the way poor performance is dealt with.
- A performance culture needs to be built on the personal action of those at the top. Leaders need to set clear expectations for their individual business units and foster good people management.
- Effective people-performance management requires a comprehensive development programme for managers at all levels if it is to be improved and sustained.
- HR needs to adapt its approach to provide the right support to help people managers manage, and to develop its own capabilities to do so.
- A lot can be achieved through the production of practical guidance on how to deal with the key aspects of performance management, based on best people-management practice not HR policy and procedures.

THE ROLE OF PEOPLE MANAGERS

Organisational results in the public sector depend on the quality of people management. The transformation programmes in HR described in this report presume an increasingly important role for people managers. In essence the goal is to ensure people managers fulfil their responsibilities and enact strategic HR policies to develop leaders, build skills and capability, develop talent, manage performance and deliver business results. This is important because ultimately it is people managers who deliver the people outcomes in the way they manage their people. In the consortium the main preoccupation of member organisations was how people management could be done better and how people managers could become more self-sufficient and less dependent on HR. In our chapter on Technique we highlight the importance of the four 'C's: culture, commitment, competence and confidence. In seeking to deliver improved performance, consortium organisations sought to tackle all of these aspects to create better people management.

Continuing research at Bath University on *Understanding the people and performance link* – sponsored by the CIPD – highlights the four ways that managers contribute to delivery of high performance:

- implementing HR policies correctly – appraisal, recruitment, development, attendance management, diversity
- enacting HR policies – carrying them out with enthusiasm and commitment
- front-line leadership – communicating to the team and individuals, responding to suggestions, treating people fairly and handling operational problems
- controlling employees' work – supervision, monitoring work quality, delegation, distribution of work and dealing with team issues.

THE CHALLENGE FOR PEOPLE MANAGERS

We have already highlighted the continually increasing emphasis on delivery with fewer resources and the need to ensure every individual is contributing fully. Performance management is thus a critical issue for all public sector organisations, yet all the evidence suggests that the public sector is very poor at doing this. For example, most of the organisations in the consortium conduct regular staff attitude surveys and in nearly every case the principal concerns are about the quality of leadership, the management of change and the weakness of arrangements to deal with poor performance. For example only 10 per cent of staff in the Food Standards Agency felt that it dealt well with poor performance, 45 per cent were neutral and the balance felt that it did not. Yet in this organisation, as in many others, the performance-management system identifies less than 1 per cent of staff as underperforming or needing significant development. This fact also has morale implications as many employees feel that they have to 'carry' others at a time of real pressure. Similar issues are evident in the DWP, HMRC and the Health and Safety Executive (HSE).

Tackling performance management is in many ways the acid test of the new HR operating models as it is here that most can be done to ensure business delivery targets are met – on the assumption that HR recruits the right people (which is why streamlining recruitment is another transformation priority). Traditionally, poor performance has been 'somebody else's problem' and that usually meant HR. Yet in the new operating models, HR has fewer staff to tackle these issues and it is expected that managers will take ownership instead. Hence the new HMRC culture of 'the manager decides and HR supports'. Understandably many managers feel they do not have the expertise to deal with what may be infrequent problems and so they still expect advice from HR. If the performance culture is lacking they can also see other managers not tackling these issues, so the reaction is understandably 'why should I?'

So it is for HR to help put in place the infrastructure to support better people-performance management shown in Figure 5 below.

CREATING A PEOPLE-MANAGEMENT CULTURE

At the heart of action to tackle these issues is the need to create a performance-management culture – broadly expressed – because this as much about business as it is about people performance. Practical experience from the consortium shows that this culture can be created in a number of ways.

We conducted research in the Food Standards Agency to determine what creates a performance-management culture. The research showed it is stimulated by:

- visible leadership at the top – meaning executive management board members
- the quality of personal leadership and management demonstrated by the people at the top
- an emphasis on the vision and values of the business unit (directorate, division, branch or national office)
- clear statements of what is expected of people in that unit
- open and two-way communication with staff – from top to bottom of the unit
- a strong sense of teamwork and community in the unit, fostered through a clear sense of unit identity
- a readiness amongst managers and leaders to give praise and recognise individual contributions or good performance
- equally, a similar readiness to give honest feedback and let people know if they need to improve or change – and people seem clearer about the high standards expected in that context
- an equal readiness to tackle weaknesses in management performance by managers' managers
- investment of time in unit development events and away days where management issues feature regularly on the agenda – with the goal of continuously improving business and people management and performance.

As part of the consortium learning programme we visited the RAF Division of the Ministry of Defence Joint Service Command and Staff College to look at the development of people management in a very different context. This was to challenge our thinking and see what could be learned in an environment where high performance is critical. From this exercise we gained valuable insights into the military culture where people are truly valued as a key asset and where there is a high level of investment in training and development to meet service needs. Developing strong leadership is regarded as key to the RAF performance

Figure 5 ✣ Supporting people-performance management

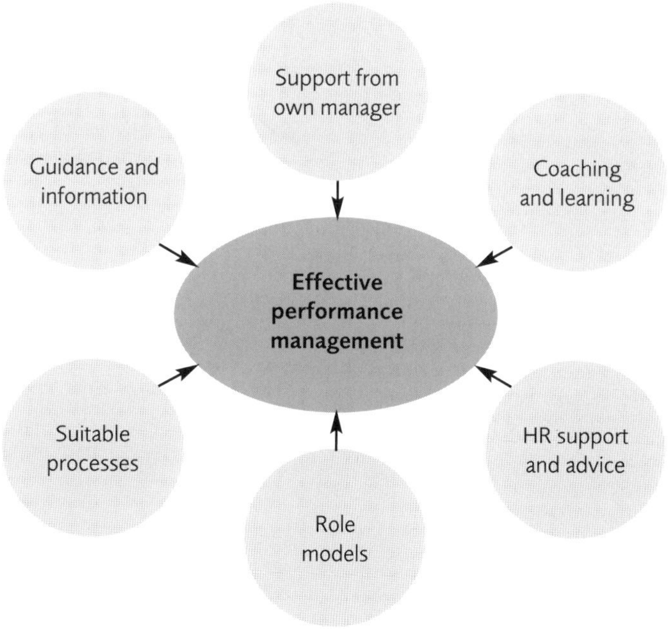

culture, and this links strongly both with the CIPD research at Bath University (*Understanding the people and performance link*) and our findings in the FSA.

Consortium members visited the RAF Division of the Joint Service Command and Staff College (JSCSC) at Shrivenham to find out how junior RAF officers are trained to manage people, how they are motivated to lead their teams and how these activities link to personnel and military strategy. The college is part of the Defence Academy – the UK Ministry of Defence's Higher Educational Institution. The aim of JSCSC is to provide command and staff training at junior, advanced and higher levels for all three services to a world-class standard.

As a military force the RAF has a very different ethos and culture from civilian organisations, but in developing people to achieve strategic goals there are many similarities.

There is a strong sense of duty and vocation. The RAF is a close-knit community with tradition and esprit de corps. People management is regarded as integral to the achievement of RAF strategy, and personnel and development policies are constructed to contribute to the delivery of this goal. The strategy aims to develop personnel who are agile, adaptable and capable. Workforce planning and development is much longer term than in civilian organisations as officers join the RAF for commissions of between five and 25 years.

> *The primary role of an officer is to command. As part of their duties officers are expected to plan, think, and operate at the tactical, operational or strategic levels as appropriate; to make decisions and understand their ramifications; and to give direction and deliver results. ... Overall officers must be able to shape their environment and not merely manage within it.*
>
> *Extract from The Officers' Career Management Strategy*

As the Director of the RAF Division, put it: 'Effective people management is regarded as everyone's business and is part of everything we do.'

Our learning from this visit was that:

- Leadership is highly valued and there is a strong emphasis on developing leadership at all levels across the RAF. This is regarded as the most cost-effective way to improve operational effectiveness.
- A good officer has high-quality technical skills and leads, manages and develops all staff in his or her team well. You are not judged to be a good officer/leader unless you do all of these.
- The approach used to manage performance (called the mission command approach) emphasises the importance of clarity about what needs to be done, and why it is essential to effective operations. The commanding officer has to make the intent clear and allocate sufficient resources, and then it is up to subordinates to fulfil this intent. This involves acceptance of risk, trust in subordinates' judgement and learning from experience.
- There is a strong focus on annual appraisal. Officers are given extensive training on how to do this effectively as it is key to officer promotion and postings.
- There is high investment of time and money in educating/training and developing the talent of staff to deliver now and in the future.
- The Junior Officers' Command and Staff Course (JOC) is part of a wider officer command and staff training programme. A key part of the JOC (three weeks' duration) is to study and be able to recognise a variety of approaches to leadership. Other aspects of the course include: development of analytical skills, effective speaking, leadership of change, interview techniques, appraisal and media skills.
- Mentoring is also often used to develop leadership.
- There is active management of officer talent and careers. Although officers can express preferences, their careers are primarily managed and structured to meet service needs.

THE RIGHT SUPPORT FROM HR

The new HR models involve reduced handholding from HR and increased people-manager accountability. That being said, best practice HR provides the right level of appropriate support through HR advisers and business partners. There is some debate about whether this is an appropriate role for business partners as it is not 'strategic'. Consortium experience would suggest that it is not right for business partners to take responsibility for dealing with these issues personally, but that they may appropriately coach managers to do so.

Best practice in the consortium shows HR support to managers should comprise:

- straightforward performance-management arrangements that place the emphasis on manager–employee dialogue and coaching
- active engagement by the manager's manager to ensure the people manager is not left to deal with issues alone
- clear and accessible procedures and guidance and practical tips for managers
- expert HR staff willing to coach managers through difficult issues so they become self-sufficient

- consistent HR advice, rather than a different view from each HR person, especially as this removes the temptation for managers to shop around until they get the advice they want
- HR staff offering support rather than citing the 'correct procedure'
- universal and thorough training in performance-management processes, especially the skills of listening and coaching
- a balanced approach between employee representation and line manager support from HR in tackling the most contentious issues.

PEOPLE-MANAGEMENT CAPABILITY

The starting point for the development of people-management capability is generally seen to be in the area of leadership and management development. All consortium organisations have programmes for initial management training, training in specific skills and leadership programmes. But the evidence is that this is generally patchy and not always mandatory; the good managers attend but not 'those who really need it'. An effective people manager programme should provide opportunities for continuing management development at the different management levels.

A PEOPLE-MANAGEMENT CAPABILITY PROGRAMME

- initial management induction (preparation for the first management role)
- first line management (for people in their first management role)
- specific management skills – feedback, coaching, handling conflict, dealing with performance issues, setting objectives
- managing managers (middle management)
- leadership development
- senior leaders' programmes
- management self-assessment and 360 degree feedback against management standards conducted on a regular basis.

Accreditation of leadership and management programmes reinforces the notion that people management is a profession just like others. The key to all such development is to ensure it takes place early enough to prevent bad habits setting in or the avoidance of difficult people issues due to lack of capability or confidence.

Such a core programme needs to be complemented by one-to-one coaching by the line manager (whose coaching skills will also need to be developed to enable this) or peer coaching where this might offer effective support to explore day-to-day management issues – especially from more experienced peers. Opportunities can also be developed for action learning and management projects outside the leadership programme.

There is also a need for managers to have access to regular seminars on management topics, as well as surgery sessions with HR or experienced managers where managers facing difficult or new issues could talk through a proposed approach and seek advice. This should include basic employment law and HR policy updates, for example on recent age legislation, bullying and harassment, grievance arrangements and diversity.

Organisations continue to underinvest in people-management capability despite the clear evidence of its benefits and the clear costs of poor people management.

BUILDING MANAGER CONFIDENCE: PRACTICAL GUIDANCE FOR MANAGERS

A significant factor in dealing with performance issues is the confidence of the manager to hold difficult conversations. In building manager capability, action to build confidence is therefore an essential ingredient.

Our work with HM Revenue and Customs focused on the development of a practical guide for all managers. The aim of this project was to develop a practical mini-toolkit (called BOOST) to help managers tackle performance issues more effectively, particularly underperformance, and to help them with moderation of assessments in the HMRC performance-management process. The emphasis was on giving managers more confidence in dealing with performance issues, providing ideas of how to build good relationships with employees (including praising and rewarding good performance) and helping managers encourage all employees to contribute more actively to improvement in HMRC.

BOOST

HMRC Guide to managing performance

Contents:

- the importance of the managers' role in helping staff perform well
- the joint responsibility of managers and staff for managing performance
- building good relationships
- giving feedback
- acknowledging good performance

- helping staff develop
- engaging staff in continuous improvement
- tackling underperformance
- making effective use of appraisal.

BUILDING HR SUPPORT FOR BETTER PEOPLE PERFORMANCE

To support the action by people managers, HR needs to provide and be seen to provide consistent, prompt, expert advice and hands-on support to individual managers as required. Action to achieve this could include:

- setting standards for HR service, captured in the form of an SLA
- conducting a focused skills audit of those staff in HR who provide advice
- identifying professional development and training requirements for HR staff
- ensuring staff in advisory roles are equipped to provide the expected service
- offering surgeries or seminars to update managers or discuss current issues
- continuing to build on the business partner relationships to provide facilitation and support to develop line management effectiveness
- monitoring HR customer service through regular surveys of the line management clients.

Following the recent merger of the Inland Revenue and Customs and Excise, the HMRC HR team established an HR Task Force to help managers use new policies to improve performance. The Task Force is made up of carefully selected staff who run customised events on request for managers on any performance issue.

This initiative has been very highly rated by managers because it involves:

- just-in-time solutions which are customer focused
- discussion fora to help managers think how they can act as a group to take a more consistent approach to performance management
- exercises and scenarios to generate discussion
- good presenters
- inspired leadership.

SUMMARY

Organisational results in the public sector depend on the effective management of people and performance, so a key goal for organisations is to ensure that people managers enact these responsibilities well. The public sector has not been effective at tackling people and performance issues, so improvement in this area is a priority. HR needs to work with senior managers to develop strong leadership, build a modern infrastructure to support good people management and create a culture where high performance is rewarded. For some organisations this may mean adopting radical approaches and taking difficult decisions about the way that that people are managed, otherwise changes to the status quo are likely to be minimal. It means providing the right support to enable managers to manage their people and putting in place a comprehensive development programme focusing on building both manager capability and confidence. HR also needs to provide practical support and make explicit what is expected of managers.

QUESTIONS FOR HR

1. Who sets the climate for people management in your organisation? Who needs to change their behaviour to send the right signals?
2. What style does your HR team adopt in engaging with people managers to deal with difficult performance issues?
3. What do you need to do to establish a professional people-management development programme for your people managers?
4. What practical guidance do you have to help managers hold those difficult conversations?
5. Is better people performance at the heart of everything your HR function does?

TECHNIQUE 7

Means of achieving one's purpose; mode of artistic execution.

- **This chapter describes how HR can add real value to the organisation.**
- **It discusses the strategic business issues where HR effort is currently being focused and the need for HR to deliver on basic service, support line managers and employees, and build their capability.**
- **It also describes the crucial role of HR in managing change and making a difference on the big issues: performance, leadership, talent and capability.**

FLASHBACK

Learning points from *Fit for business I*

- Adding value through HR means achieving organisational goals through better motivation, commitment and morale of people with the right capabilities for the future.
- The HR function also adds value by providing efficient services to the organisation.
- HR people need a single-minded focus on these outcomes for the organisation.
- Success means action not rhetoric.

FAST FORWARD TO THE PRESENT ➡

Learning points from *Fit for business II*

- HR organisations that recognise the importance of high-quality service to their top management, line management and employee customers are continuing their efforts to improve the quality, consistency and reliability of the HR service within new HR structures.
- In the new HR environment, effective people management depends fundamentally on line management capability, but changes in HR structures require the creation of different forms of advice and support to ensure managers' new requirements are met.
- HR should provide practical tools and advice to help managers manage, as well as providing support and coaching to build manager capability.
- At the strategic level the HR contribution should be focused on effective support for change and tackling organisation-wide people issues.
- The specific areas where HR needs to make a difference at a strategic level are: developing effective, authentic leadership; building employee capability and developing talent; managing performance to deliver results; building diversity; and updating the employee deal to build loyalty, commitment and improve morale.
- Within organisations there is a continuing appetite for ideas, information and good practice in addressing these issues, and HR organisations need to strengthen their own capability to handle them.

WHAT TO DO?

An important question at the outset is how HR decides where to focus its effort: how to make the choices on what to do. This question needs to be considered alongside the role people managers are expected to play, described in the last chapter. Within the consortium organisations the HR agenda is being driven by several internal factors:

- The organisational drive for better delivery means an emphasis on leadership direction, staff capability and better performance management.
- The drive for efficiency and headcount reductions creates a significant resourcing and redeployment agenda, but also a need to tackle poor performance; leaner organisations cannot afford passengers.
- The organisational change agenda creates the need for better leadership, change management, new skills and greater employee engagement, coupled with flexibility;
- All three of these create a challenging employee relations agenda to maintain morale and commitment during continuing change.

As in all organisations, the HR agenda in the public sector is also being driven by age and diversity legislation. Unlike the private sector however, the public sector HR agenda is also driven by centrally derived initiatives to ensure the public sector is an exemplary employer, which may or may not align with the priorities of that particular organisation at that point. They may be important but strategic HR means making choices – perhaps doing things in phases rather than all at once.

SERVICE QUALITY: GETTING THE BASICS RIGHT

As we have mentioned, HR needs to ensure it gets the basics right, particularly following transformation efforts supposedly designed to increase HR contribution, improve service and reduce costs. In organisations that have adopted the three-tier approach of e-HR, service centres and business partners, each of those should be making an improved contribution to HR service. To ensure this is the case, several of the consortium organisations are putting in place service statements or service-level agreements to clarify the standards that can be expected by people managers and employees. The focus is on speed, accuracy and simplicity of transactions handled through e-HR or service centres; the timeliness, quality and consistency of HR advice; and the level of business partner engagement, delivery of change and support to people managers.

The National Audit Office has one of the smaller HR organisations within the consortium and has made changes to its structure and service to match wider changes in the management of people in the organisation. In an effort to improve the quality of people management, especially staff development and performance management, the Office has concentrated responsibility for these functions into 25 'development manager' roles in line units for all non-managerial audit staff. Each development manager spends 40 per cent of his or her time performing these functions for their group of staff. To improve the quality of service to employees and managers, the HR team has created a small service centre to handle all the day-to-day HR transactions not now conducted on their e-HR system, PARIS. To set standards for the delivery of HR services, the HR team has published a service level agreement (SLA) against which its future performance will be judged. The contents of the SLA are set out below.

NAO HR service level agreement: contents

- How HR supports the business aims of the Office.
- What we aim to provide for each of our customers.
- HR resourcing targets – covering retention, absence, staffing numbers, diversity etc.
- The HR structure and service portfolio.
- HR customer service standards:
  - access methods
  - contact points
  - service availability
  - response times
  - confidentiality
  - quality of service.
- Roles and responsibilities for HR in the NAO: development managers, managers, employees, HR.
- Resolving problems.
- Contacts for HR services.
- HR reporting.

SERVICE TO PEOPLE MANAGERS: THE HEART OF HR

Implicit in the HR changes under way is a transfer of responsibility for people issues to line or people managers. This is a transfer that has not been generally welcomed by managers as it is seen as HR offloading its responsibilities to them – not popular at a time of already increasing demands on managers as individuals anyway. It coincides with consortium organisations placing greater emphasis on performance management, talent management and skills development, and the consequent role of managers in bringing these about. So in HMRC and the FSA the HR teams were seeking to provide better support to managers in addressing these issues. The new HR 'technique' was to discover what managers needed to be able to do to fulfil their new role and then put those arrangements in place. Both organisations consulted extensively with managers to determine the barriers to effective people management and how they could be overcome.

Building better people managers

Our discussions with managers in the FSA revealed that the issues could be captured in the four 'C's of effective people management:

- The *culture* of management in the organisation, business unit or team. This culture is something we found is set from the top of the organisation, so embedding a new performance culture needs to start there too.
- The *commitment* of individual managers to people management. Individuals given a management role do not always welcome it, but in many professionally staffed organisations this comes with promotion. HR has a real challenge to bring round such people to want to manage, so structural solutions like allowing them to specialise rather than manage, or recruiting staff who are really committed to managing people may be the answer.
- The *competence* of people managers. This has long been recognised as important, but the quality of management development is still very patchy in organisations. The answer is to establish and maintain progressive management development programmes reinforced by good-quality guidance and suitable HR advice.
- The *confidence* of people managers. On many difficult HR issues managers may have no prior experience of dealing with the problem, either because they are inexperienced or because it is a new problem. This is where coaching support is needed from peers, line managers or HR. But too often HR will recite the procedures rather than provide the hands-on coaching needed. This needs experienced HR people – not always available in the service centre – and frequently this is a role taken up by business partners close to managers instead.

ENABLING CHANGE

The establishment of the business partner network in organisations has proved a particularly effective mechanism to support change. Many business partners have been recruited from an organisational development or learning and development background and so are well equipped and inclined to support change. That being said, a great deal of this is implementing changes to HR activities and policies rather than business-driven change – where HR tends to be brought in after the change has been designed. HR needs to do more to increase its credibility and active involvement in organisation development (OD) from the outset. The main benefit of a business partner team that is located in the business unit has been to work as part of the business unit management team advising on and facilitating change. This has been particularly the case in the DWP in its business-restructuring and headcount-reduction programmes, and similarly in the HMRC. The Crown Office and Procurator Fiscal Service sees a major part of its business partner role as being a change agent to bring about operational changes in each procurator fiscal area. Equally business partners are being used as an organisation-wide resource to address some of the strategic HR priorities described at the start of this section.

TACKLING THE BIG HR ISSUES

On every HR agenda are issues to do with leadership, talent, skills, performance management and diversity, and each organisation has a set of programmes to tackle them. However, the success of organisations in achieving real change to meet the goals of these programmes seems very varied. Much of the learning in the consortium has involved new ways to tackle these issues with a more effective partnership between HR, line managers and employees. Part of this reflects the fact that many HR organisations now have the strategic capability in the business partner, learning and development or organisational development teams to support such action. In addition, organisations are getting more adept at handling such programmes and continue to learn to do it better.

The work in the consortium highlighted some important learning for HR about delivering effective strategic change:

- The issue needs to be on the strategic business agenda and managers must see how action will improve business results: that is, there needs to be a sound business case for the initiative. HR managers need to be able to demonstrate the return on the planned investment.
- The change needs to have the active backing of those at the top of the organisation, so it is for the HR director to gain the commitment of the top team and engage them in a practical way in taking the work forward. There is a noticeable difference in this aspect where the chief executive is committed to HR issues; the climate for HR change is much more positive. So a strong partnership between chief executive and HR director is essential.
- HR needs to engage managers in the design of change programmes from the outset (or, if this is business-driven change, HR needs to be involved at the outset).
- The programme needs to be framed in the language of the business to have real meaning and achieve 'buy in' for all parties; if there is too much HR jargon, this will be a turn off.
- Project and programme-management skills are crucial to ensure the programme is well planned and resourced and risks are assessed and managed. The consortium experience showed that projects frequently ran behind schedule so these skills are at a premium. This means ensuring a good project plan is in place and results are measured.
- As in all change programmes the importance of communication is paramount to explain, engage and commit people to the programme.
- In this respect the crucial role that HR can play is to ensure that employees are fully engaged in the design and implementation of the change.
- HR needs to draw on others' experience and learning. Too often HR starts from scratch rather than looking outwards and drawing on experience elsewhere, and for this reason the consortium was felt to be especially valuable.
- HR needs to recognise areas where it is more cost effective to buy in expertise, so it needs to know how to use consultants well.
- Equally where HR does look outside it needs to be wary of adopting others' ideas lock, stock and barrel without adapting them to the organisation's own circumstances.

SUMMARY

To make an effective strategic contribution, HR needs to be active in a wider range of areas and to fulfil different roles than previously, albeit in areas that clearly contribute to business results. Essential in all of this is for HR to deliver high-quality transactional and advisory services to people managers and employees. It also means that HR needs to evolve new ways of working with managers to ensure they enact their people-management responsibilities. HR must also make a major contribution in managing change, as increasingly it can offer organisational development capability through business partnerships. Finally HR needs to be especially effective in delivering the 'big' HR initiatives with the potential to make a long-lasting business impact.

Like other police forces, the British Transport Police (BTP) has been considering options for workforce modernisation. This is an initiative that has the full support of the Home Office, HM Inspectorate of Police and the Association of Chief Police Officers. It aims to optimise workforce resources and achieve the most effective balance between police and civilian staff in the performance of police service functions. A number of police services across England and Wales have run pilot projects to test different ways to carry out police work. BTP wanted to explore the possibilities for modernising the work in transport policing. The HR team explored the options open to BTP based on the ideas in the national workforce pilots and business issues in transport policing where workforce modernisation could potentially achieve results. The approach involved exploring options, obtaining commitment from senior officers to test out these ideas, and then engaging local line managers in the development of specific options for the service. Experience showed that the operational imperatives in BTP were not as strong as in some of the other areas where modernisation pilots were taking place, and also the results of the pilots were not proven for the particular BTP context. BTP is now seeking to align modernisation work more directly with current workforce issues affecting business results, such as the shortage of sergeants.

QUESTIONS FOR HR

1. What is on your HR agenda at the moment and is it making a difference to business results?
2. How do you judge the quality of service you provide to customers? Is this made explicit to those customers?
3. To what extent are managers good 'people managers', and how is HR supporting the development of their capabilities so that they can be self-sufficient 'people managers'?
4. Does HR have a leading role in change in the organisation and how are you making a difference? If not, what is it that limits your ability to get engaged?
5. What role does HR have in OD? What more can you do to increase your involvement?
6. How successful have the 'big HR' changes been in your organisation? What can you learn from that experience about doing it better in future?
7. Who are the leading practitioners in the topics where your HR function is trying to make a difference? Have you talked to them and what did you learn?

TEAMWORK 8

Combined effort; organised cooperation.

Partner: one of a pair of dancers or players on the same side in a game.

- **This chapter discusses how HR should best engage with the business by working in partnership.**
- **It highlights the different needs of HR customers and how best to engage with each.**
- **The importance of better communication with the business is highlighted, as is the way to build relationships with each of its customers.**

FLASHBACK

Learning points from *Fit for business I*

- HR needs to develop a relationship tailored to each of its partners in the business and be clear what each relationship delivers for the organisation.
- Mutual expectations between the HR team and their partners need to be explicit and understood.
- Sound processes need to be in place and used to ensure effective joint working.
- HR needs to be visible throughout the organisation.

FAST FORWARD TO THE PRESENT ➡

Learning points from *Fit for business II*

- HR needs to really engage with people managers to create a shared agenda so that people management is more integrated into both strategic planning and day-to-day business.
- The move from a 'policing' to a more facilitative role for HR calls for a significant shift in approach and behaviours among HR professionals.
- Working jointly with the business to develop HR strategy and policy and generally implement solutions to people issues is critical for ensuring that the measures taken are relevant, practical and ultimately successful.
- HR needs to use easily accessible language that keeps jargon to a minimum.
- It is important for HR to establish real partnerships with customers, otherwise a strategic HR function may be regarded as remote from the business.

HR CUSTOMERS

In the first *Fit for business* report we highlighted how a strategic HR function needs to differentiate its relationship with its four principal customer groups (see Figure 6):

- the board/senior management team
- business units and service areas
- line managers
- employees.

Experience in the current consortium has underlined the continuing importance of developing the quality of these relationships further and clarifying what each delivers for HR and for the organisation. Consortium members reported an ongoing shift in the role of HR from a traditional directive or 'policing' role to an increasingly facilitative one with the three management groups.

WHAT PARTNERSHIP MEANS IN PRACTICE

In practical terms, this change requires HR to work in closer partnership with managers at all levels across the organisation to ensure that people management is more integrated into business life at both the strategic and day-to-day level, by sharing ownership of issues and solving business problems. HR also needs to work in close partnership when updating and implementing changes to HR policies and systems, to ensure these are understood and meet customer needs.

By showing it can partner successfully in a range of contexts HR is much more likely to be invited to help address the 'big' strategic issues from the outset. This is particularly important when it comes to managing change as it means that HR is much better placed to gain 'buy in' from managers and employees in successful design and implementation.

To make this work HR has to ensure the mutual expectations between itself and its business partners at the top of the organisation and with people managers are very clear. HR also needs to be prepared to 'let go' of its previous roles and approaches and adapt a working style suited to context and situation that will help find practical solutions to people problems. For example, HR may work alongside managers by coaching 'at the shoulder' to build their confidence and resolve issues together as a team; for more confident managers partnership may mean HR adopting more of an advisory role and pointing out the risks of adopting a particular approach. In HMRC this is summed up as: 'HR supports – the manager decides'.

This significant shift in working style may be a challenge for some HR professionals, and they may need support to develop new skills and behaviours to ensure these partnerships really work.

THE IMPORTANCE OF GETTING THE LANGUAGE RIGHT

In both the public and private sectors, poor communication is widely cited as the key barrier to good working relationships and to effective change. In the public sector HR is often criticised, particularly by people managers, for producing policies and documents that are overcomplex with too much jargon. This is often driven by an HR desire to cover every eventuality and make sure managers 'do it right' – as if there were always only one right way. If it is going to work in greater partnership and improve its strategic profile then HR must do more to use the same language as the business and keep jargon to a minimum, otherwise it risks being 'sidelined'. This means taking the time to really understand issues from the customers' perspective, and then communicating with them in ways that they can understand and relate to.

THE POWER OF PARTNERSHIP AND EFFECTIVE COMMUNICATION

Working in greater partnership with the different customer groups across the business provides very good opportunities to improve mutual understanding and develop better, more natural communication channels. If HR is able to make the best of these

Figure 6 ◆ HR working with the business

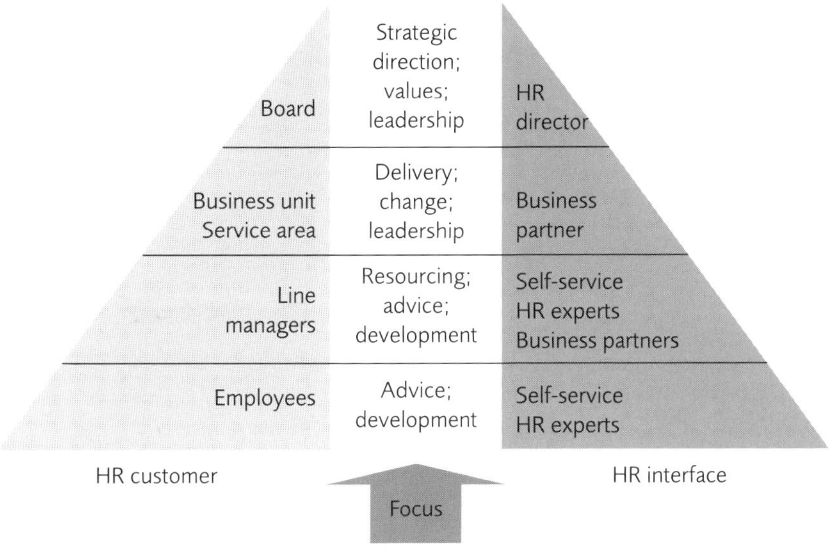

opportunities it may score some 'quick wins', and it is also much more likely to enhance its reputation as a credible strategic partner that can really enable the organisation to achieve its goals.

At the Royal Borough of Kingston the HR team has used this partnership approach very successfully as a first step to improve representation of women at a senior level in the organisation.

Currently only five out of 35 senior officers in the borough are female. Kingston wants to increase representation of women at this level by promotion from within and through external appointments. This action is regarded as important to ensure it makes the most of organisational talent and optimises service delivery to the local community. While 80 per cent of the staff are female, only 39 per cent of middle managers are women.

As part of a wider strategy to tackle this problem, HR began by consulting to find out the key issues from a range of perspectives, to identify possible solutions and to ensure 'buy in' to future action. It commissioned external research across the organisation to determine the barriers to the promotion of women to senior roles and what would help to overcome them.

A key issue that emerged was that women often lacked self-confidence and were not always willing to put themselves forward for promotion to more senior positions due to lack of experience in wider organisational roles. One recommendation from the research meant HR invited all female middle managers to a lunchtime event to establish support for a network that would provide a supportive environment and a forum to tackle their career issues. The publicity for this was deliberately designed to exclude jargon and really 'sell' the idea to managers in the target group.

The launch event included a short talk by the chief executive giving his full support, as well as input from HR and a talk by a successful female entrepreneur from a local business. There was also an opportunity for participants to work in small groups to decide on the key priorities for the network, topics for the first year, when and where activities should take place and how the network should be organised. This event was very well attended by women from the target group. There was great enthusiasm and overwhelming support for the establishment of a women's network, which now meets quarterly.

HR currently chairs the team running the network with help from a group of managers who are members. Each has volunteered to serve for a six-month stint. At the second meeting network members voted on a name for their network which is called 'Fast Forward'. The approach adopted by the HR team has certainly got this initiative off to a very positive start.

As part of its wider change programme, the HR Strategy and Policy Team at HM Revenue and Customs has worked in partnership with managers and staff across a range of its business directorates to develop and pilot a new, very practical, mini-toolkit for managers called BOOST (its contents were described in Chapter 6, Performance).

The underlying rationale for BOOST was that it would:

- be based on current HMRC performance-management policies and processes
- be founded on the new role envisaged for managers in HMRC
- be based on some underlying key principles, reflecting HMRC values and sound management practice
- take managers through a step-by-step approach to tackling performance issues in clear, accessible language
- suggest how and when to reward good performance
- provide advice on how to encourage all employees to contribute more actively to improvement at HMRC
- signpost more detailed sources of information and advice in HMRC to help them tackle each issue.

Following very positive feedback during piloting with managers, BOOST is currently being rolled out to all 17,000 managers and their people – a total of over 95,000 employees.

Our work with the Food Standards Agency focused on what was needed in the organisation to make performance management effective; the specific aim was to bring about a sustained improvement in performance management across the Agency and develop more effective working between HR and line managers.

The Agency engaged in a dialogue with people managers at each of the main levels between the chief executive and heads of branch, the lowest unit of organisation. The focus was on how they managed, the barriers to effective people management, what help they needed to be better people managers, and what could be done to strengthen the performance-management culture generally. The value of this approach was that it stimulated a dialogue on people management across the organisation which was reinforced by a top leader's programme going on at the same time. One clear output of this dialogue was a clear statement of effective management that could form a 'charter for good management'.

Effective managers

- are clear what they want to achieve
- explain that in a compelling way – are inspiring
- take time to get to know people
- establish good rapport with staff
- listen actively and show empathy
- are visible and have regular face-to-face contact with staff
- keep staff informed and 'in the loop'
- encourage staff to speak up and contribute
- are aware of the capabilities of different staff, what they can do and their preferences
- know what motivates each individual
- reach out and offer help and advice
- take the time to coach staff
- appreciate each person's contribution, say thank you and pass this feedback up the line
- don't make assumptions about individuals' capacity and capability but discuss these matters with them
- give clear instructions on tasks to explain what is required
- ensure people are well occupied and given interesting and challenging work to do.

SUMMARY

The quality of the relationships that HR develops with each of its four principal customer groups is critical to increasing its visibility and credibility as a strategic partner. Shifts in the HR role from a 'policing' to a more facilitative one means that it often needs to adopt a different working style and develop new skills and behaviours. This can be challenging. When working in partnership at strategic level, HR has to strike the right balance so that it is not perceived as 'too hands on' or 'too remote' by its customer groups. This can be a hard task for HR to manage but there can be real benefits. HR needs to do more to communicate well with customers by using language that is easily accessible and uses minimal jargon, and ensuring HR policies and other guidance documents are straightforward to use. Although there is still some way to go it is clear that when HR works in well in partnership and uses the language of the business, it can make a more positive contribution to helping the organisation deliver its goals.

QUESTIONS FOR HR

1. What does the business partnership between HR and its customers mean in your organisation?
2. Does HR speak the language of HR or of the business?
3. What recent examples do you have of HR really engaging with people in the organisation? What was done differently as a result?

FITNESS 9

Well adapted or suited for purpose; qualified, competent, worthy.

- **This chapter discusses how consortium organisations are building the capability and confidence of the HR function.**
- **It identifies the changing capabilities required of HR people and how these capabilities can best be developed and deployed.**
- **This is illustrated through the different approaches being adopted for HR professional development.**

FLASHBACK

Learning points from *Fit for business I*

- Strategic HR capability means understanding the business and establishing productive relationships with managers across the organisation.
- Crucial to the ability of HR to deliver is the ability to be flexible and adapt.
- These abilities are more important in the strategic HR context than HR expertise.
- Building capability through external recruitment can only be a short-term solution; longer-term capability needs to be built in-house.

FAST FORWARD TO THE PRESENT ➡

Learning points from *Fit for business II*

- Increasing pressure to improve performance across the business is driving HR to enhance HR service quality by developing better service channels, introducing SLAs and using sharper business metrics as well as developing the capability of its own staff.
- The new roles in transformed HR organisations call for new, well-structured programmes to develop HR capability and create new career paths.
- CIPD development routes for HR staff are becoming more flexible in order to meet new and emerging role requirements.
- There are continuing questions about the most appropriate role for business partners to add value, and the best way to acquire people with the right capabilities for the role.
- The strong link between effective people management and business performance means that managing and developing HR talent should be a key business priority.

THE DRIVE TO IMPROVE HR CAPABILITY AND CONFIDENCE

Increasing pressure from the business to raise its game is driving consortium members to take action on a number of fronts to provide better, more strategic HR services to support people managers and deliver HR action for business results.

HR is taking action to develop the quality of HR service by:

- Defining new and emerging roles within the HR function and fitting these into the overall HR delivery model.
- Explaining how these roles work in practice to both HR staff and management. This was particularly important for new roles in HR shared-service models such as business partners and HR advisers; examples include Leeds City Council and the Crown Office and Procurator Fiscal Service (COPFS).
- Developing SLAs to give clear information about the HR services being delivered and clarify the division of roles between HR and the line. This aims to provide greater service consistency, especially when HR services are being reorganised; examples include the NAO and COPFS.
- Using sharper metrics to show how HR adds value to the organisation and provide feedback to HR on how it is performing and what needs to improve; examples include the NAO, FSA and DWP.
- Managing and developing HR staff talent within the function to ensure it has a sustainable future.

CHANGING SKILL SETS AND BEHAVIOURS FOR HR STAFF

CIPD offered the consortium some broad observations on the development of HR careers across both the public and private sectors:

- Traditional careers still exist, but there are fewer generalist roles.
- There are more 'parachutists' – HR directors without an HR background who subsequently move on to other roles.
- 'Zig-zaggers' – line managers who move into business partner roles and then back to the line – are becoming more common.
- Roles are more strategic; HR is moving from directive to facilitative decision making.
- There are more 'business partners' helping managers achieve their goals.
- There are more consultants/portfolio workers.
- Specialist roles are developing, available as third-tier support from the centre.
- Role boundaries are blurring, with many different titles and blends of HR roles emerging.
- There are fewer opportunities for progress and more lower-level roles due to increasing use of e-HR and service centres.

To respond to these changes CIPD is reviewing how it defines levels of HR practice (ie, potential membership grade profiles) and its related professional standards. CIPD is also developing more flexible routes to membership that still maintain the existing professional rigour. The experience of consortium members broadly reflected these observations. One exception was that there was currently much less evidence of line managers moving into business partner roles, and external recruitment remains the main source of new business partners. However, members could foresee more line recruits in future if suitable mechanisms were put in place to develop their HR skills and support transition. This option is currently being considered by the CIPD.

The changing, more strategic nature of HR calls for a broader skill set and different behaviours, especially to pursue a senior career in HR because this combines traditional HR knowledge with wider business acumen. Table 9 summarises the suggested strategic HR skill sets drawn up by CIPD, the Civil Service (Professional Skills for Government), and David Ulrich and Wayne Brockbank in their book *The HR value proposition*. As can be seen, there is considerable overlap between them, though the Civil Service skill set has more explicit reference to change management than the other two. This reflects the significance of the HR role in supporting the Civil Service changes mentioned in Chapter 2.

DEVELOPING HR CAREERS

Consortium members recognised the importance of having capable, confident HR staff to support HR service delivery as part of a wider strategy to improve their service quality. They were concerned about how changes in HR structures and roles (particularly HR shared services) might affect the ability of their staff to develop the broad range of skills needed (as outlined in Table 9) to progress to more senior HR positions.

The role of the business partner, which is at the heart of the transformed HR delivery model, presented members with three issues:

- defining the new role to ensure that both HR staff and management were clear about what it entailed and how it would contribute to the business
- identifying individuals to fill business partner roles from within HR or from outside the organisation
- ensuring a supply of high-quality staff to fill these roles in the future.

There was considerable variation in the actual level of activity in the consortium to address broader HR skills issues and fill specific roles (eg, business partners). Within the consortium DWP had made significant progress by developing a comprehensive HR professional development framework (further details are given later in this chapter).

There are cultural and practical issues to overcome when introducing new ways of managing HR staff development and progression.

At Leeds City Council, HR managers highlighted the following HR career issues during consultation on their new HR delivery model:

- how to replicate the informal learning that currently happens in mixed teams of HR staff at different levels, particularly how staff in entry HR and administrative roles will progress to higher-level HR work
- how to become a true learning organisation and capture knowledge of those who leave or retire, as well as share existing good practice
- the importance of being realistic with HR staff about what is expected of them and what is possible with the resources available.

The use of role rotation across HR was proposed as one approach to give greater flexibility and provide broader work experience, but HR managers were not really sure if this would work in practice as in the past departments had been reluctant to release people. Some thought this might be less of an issue with more pooled resources in the new HR Service. Other ideas that were put forward to help with HR staff development included:

- conducting a skills audit to identify the current skills base and any gaps

Table 9 HR skill sets

CIPD	The Civil Service	Ulrich and Brockbank
Personal drive	Building personal credibility	Personal credibility
Business awareness	Knowing the business	Business knowledge
Broad HR experience	HR expertise Knowing the business	HR technology HR delivery
Influencing skills	Personal credibility Acting as change agent	Personal credibility
Strategic thinking	Knowing the business Acting as change agent Demonstrating HR expertise	Strategic contribution
CIPD qualifications and learning	HR expertise	Business knowledge
	Acting as change agent	

- setting up more structured networking opportunities
- producing a newsletter to keep HR staff's professional knowledge up to date and encourage information exchange
- running action-learning sets.

Some managers said that future HR job descriptions should be less rigid than in the past and be more competency based. It was suggested that assessment centres would be an appropriate way to recruit staff to new roles, particularly business partners.

At Leeds City Council these matters are now being considered as a key part of the implementation plan for the new HR Service.

CIPD RESEARCH INTO HR CAREERS

Concerns about HR careers in a changing environment are not just confined to the public sector. Structural change was also raised as an issue in the CIPD research report in 2005, *HR: Where is your career heading?*, where HR professionals (in both public and private sectors) indicated that shared services, over-specialisation and staying in one organisation were significant barriers to HR career progression.

Research participants stated that in future they believed qualifications would be regarded as of less importance to HR professionals than they are now, while specialist experience, experience outside HR and in different organisations, strategic thinking and consultancy skills were all seen as of growing importance. Respondents cited the following factors as important for getting to the top in HR:

- personal drive, ambition and business awareness (regarded as the most important single factors)
- being on a formal training scheme for the first HR job
- being a generalist rather than a specialist
- having a degree
- being older
- working for a number of different organisations
- having had a significant number of career steps
- having been in HR for more than 10 years
- having international experience
- working for a large organisation.

What is clear is that HR now faces some tough challenges to adopt new approaches to manage and develop HR talent against a backdrop of change in HR and the wider organisation.

The Department for Work and Pensions is the largest employer in central government and has 2,500 people in its HR function. It has adopted a very holistic, structured approach to how it manages and develops HR capability to fill key roles in shortage areas (such as business partners) and ensure that staff can be deployed flexibly to meet changing service demands now and in the future.

The DWP has developed its own high-level HR professional development framework across the organisation including:

- professional standards
- functional groups
- core roles
- career paths.

Although these are being developed specifically for its own use, the DWP is working closely with the Cabinet Office, the National School for Government and other departments to ensure consistency with the overall direction of HR in the Civil Service.

The DWP has used the CIPD and Civil Service skills sets (see Table 9 above) to develop its own HR professional standards at four levels whilst at the same time integrating Professional Skills for Government and CIPD skills definitions (see Figure 7). The levels are foundation, development, professional, director, and the skill areas are:

- customer focus
- deploying HR expertise
- organisational development
- personal effectiveness.

In addition, functional subgroups have been defined and each has its own role-specific standards and development pathways, which align with the DWP's service delivery model.

Although the DWP has a common HR service delivery model for all the agencies within the DWP family, it has chosen not to create a single definitive list of roles to which every agency has to adhere. Instead its preferred option has been to identify the common or core roles critical to the delivery of HR services. These core roles:

- support the DWP skills strategy (role clustering)
- enable specification and definition of generic role profiles
- support the professional development programmes
- underpin succession planning and talent management.

Figure 7 ❖ DWP professional standards

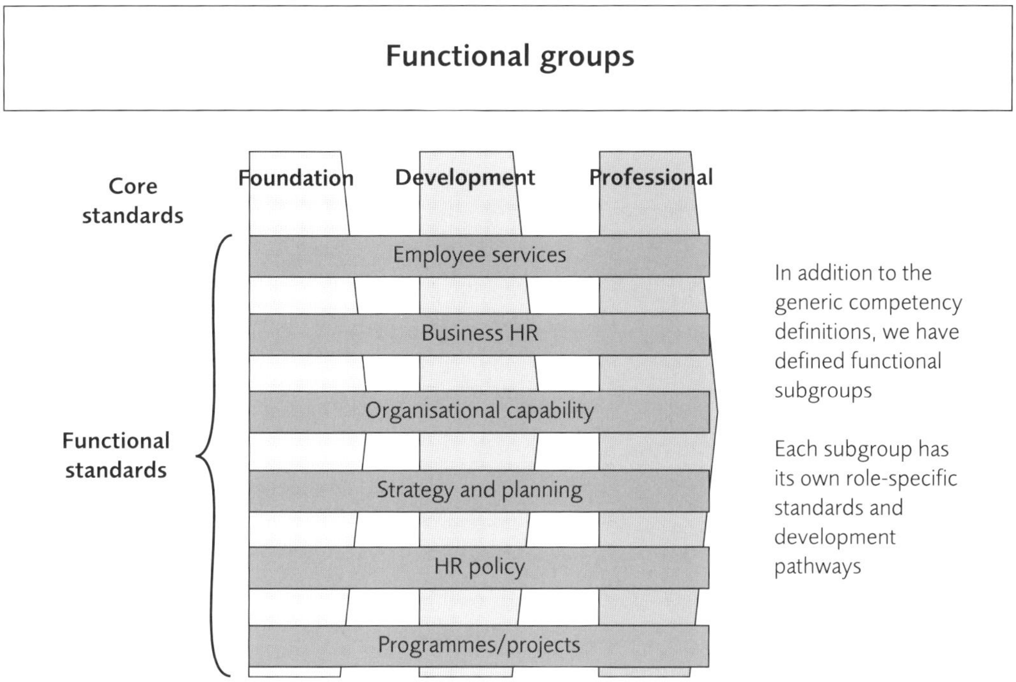

Figure 8 ❖ DWP HR professional development programme

Programme levels

HR foundation *Developing HR underpinning skills and competencies of HR professionalism*			
Induction: Diagnostics/skills assessment; Learning to learn; Service delivery model	Core skills *Core HR delivery skills – Level 1*: Facilitation – influencing; Communication – presentation	HR expert *Delivering HR in DWP*: A 'taster' of HR within DWP; Components of HR; Delivering an integrated service	CPD: Development pathway; Further learning; Solutions; CPD networks
HR development *Developing advanced HR skills and competencies*			
Induction: Diagnostics; Skills assessment; Learning to learn	Core skills *Core HR delivery skills – Level 2*: Consultancy – Adv presentation – Problem solving – Adv influencing; Adv facilitation	HR expert *Delivering business solutions*: Organisational diagnosis; Change and culture; HR measures	Induction: Development pathway; Project/Resourcing/Analysis; CPD networks
HR professional *Developing the PSG (level 3) HR standards*			
Induction: Diagnostics; Skills assessment; Development plan	Core skills *Core HR delivery skills – Level 3*: Adv consultancy – Leadership and strategic thinking – Strategic influencing – Adv facilitation	HR expert *Business transformation in action*: Change leadership; Strategic change management; Organisational development	Induction: CPD networks/Job rotation; OGD mentoring

Each programme level follows a similar schedule of activity:

- The development of core skills; each level builds on the previous one and becomes more sophisticated.

- HR expert modules begin at foundation level and describe how each element of HR works together to deliver business solutions through to business transformation and change leadership at the professional level. These HR expert modules use case studies in a workshop setting to help the participants apply the core and HR expert skills, using self-learning which includes:
  - action-learning sets
  - online learning modules
  - a management report
  - recommended reading
  - the delivery of presentations to internal and external groups.

The DWP HR professional framework is still being refined and formatted. Talent management and succession planning are already in place. Discussions about accreditation are already under way with CIPD.

SUMMARY

Improving HR capability and confidence is about taking action to crystallise how HR services are to be delivered in future and then taking a structured and managed approach to developing the talent of HR staff. The transformed HR environment calls for different skills sets at both strategic and operational level, and new ways of developing and acquiring them. This can be challenging with all of the other pressures on HR, but action is vital to sustain a capable, confident HR function in the longer term that can continue to flexibly support the business.

QUESTIONS FOR HR

1. What are the key challenges you face in developing and managing talent for your HR function?
2. Do you know your current HR capabilities and where you need to develop these further? How will you do this?
3. What performance frameworks do you currently have in place to improve HR capability and confidence?
4. What performance frameworks will you need in future?
5. What will your successful, confident HR function look like?

PHYSIQUE 10

Bodily structure, organisation, physical shape.

- **This chapter discusses how best to embed the different HR operating models introduced by organisations.**
- **It emphasises the need for clarity in HR roles and the pros and cons of different models.**
- **It also looks at the implementation issues in introducing new HR operating models, such as changing processes, explaining roles, clarifying service standards and improving access and communications.**

FLASHBACK

Learning points from *Fit for business I*

- Designing the HR organisation is about ensuring the best fit for each organisation and its environment.
- An effective HR delivery model is derived from the best balance of HR expertise, business focus, service quality and technology.
- Delivering the new structure requires the simultaneous adaptation to their new roles of the HR function and its customers in the line.
- HR needs to be close to the line to understand their needs; the message is 'get out more'.

FAST FORWARD TO THE PRESENT ➡

Learning points from *Fit for business II*

- HR needs to ensure that its new role is understood and bought into by senior managers.
- HR should have a clearly stated rationale for the chosen delivery model and the way this enables HR to best help the organisation achieve its goals.
- HR delivery models must remain flexible to ensure a continuing match between HR and business requirements.
- A well-structured approach to implementing and embedding new HR delivery models is essential if HR is to be seen as credible and exemplary in handling transition and change
- HR should evaluate regularly how the HR operating model is working to ensure it remains fit for purpose
- Each different customer group needs to be well informed about and understand what HR services are on offer and how best to access them easily if the new delivery models and processes are to work properly
- So, to keep the HR model closely in tune with business needs, the message is for HR to 'get out even more'.

DEVELOPING HR MODELS THAT ENABLE THE ORGANISATION TO ACHIEVE ITS GOALS

To add value HR needs to really understand the organisational context, business drivers and the business strategy. It should equally be clear about its own capability and be realistic about what it can offer with the resources at its disposal. From this understanding HR will be in a strong position to agree with senior managers what they expect from HR, and to adopt a viable HR strategy and a suitable delivery model to enable the organisation to achieve its goals. By adopting this holistic approach HR can ensure that there is a clear rationale or business case for what it needs to do, the delivery model adopted and each HR process (ie, the how) that then flows from it.

An essential part of understanding organisational context includes an awareness of the key drivers and barriers for change and how these impact on HR transformation. Figure 9 shows the drivers and barriers for changing the shape of HR functions that the consultants Reach HR suggest are the crucial ones.

These factors generally mirror the experience within the consortium. The reasons for members adopting new HR delivery models and processes were to:

- support and facilitate change across the organisation
- ensure a better HR 'fit' with the wider organisational business model
- improve overall HR service quality and strategic capability
- reduce HR staffing overall
- focus on transactional services and efficiency.

ROLE CLARITY

In their latest book, *The HR value proposition*,[4] Ulrich and Brockbank propose the following updated framework for HR professionals to achieve greater role clarity and add maximum value to the organisation:

- HR leader – credible to their own function and the organisation
- strategic partner – helping managers to achieve their goals
- functional expert – designing and delivering HR practices to deliver individual competence and organisation capability
- human capital developer – building the workforce of the future
- employee advocate – making sure that the employer–employee relationship is one of reciprocal value.

These roles have been developed from the four roles that Ulrich presented in *Human Resource champions* in 1997 in response to changes in leading HR practice and to address his critics.[5] Table 10, taken from *People Management* magazine,[6] shows how these roles have evolved:

ROLE VERSUS STRUCTURE

It is important to note that Dave Ulrich did not set out to define a specific HR *structure* when he developed the original four HR roles. Nevertheless many organisations in both the public and private sector have adopted an HR shared service structure based on these roles. This model, often called the 'three legged stool', is shown in Figure 10.

Figure 9 ✣ Drivers and barriers to change in HR

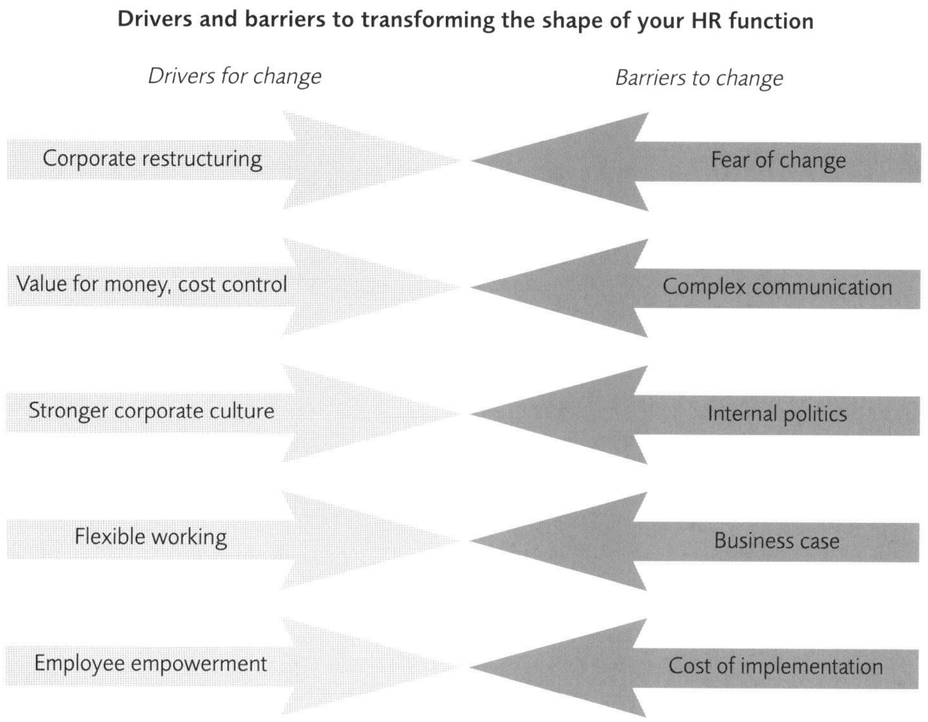

Table 10 ✣ Evolution of HR roles

Mid-1990s	Mid-2000s	Evolution of thinking
Employee champion	Employee advocate (EA) Human capital (HC) developer	EA focuses on the needs of today's employee; HC focuses on preparing employees to be successful in future
Administrative expert	Functional expert	HR practices are central to HR value. Some HR practices are delivered through administrative efficiency (such as technology of process redesign) and others through policies, menus and interventions
Change agent	Strategic partner	Being a strategic partner has multiple dimensions: business expert, change agent, strategic HR planner, knowledge manager and consultant
Strategic partner	Strategic partner	As above
	Leader	Being an HR leader required functioning in each of these four roles, however being an HR leader also has implications for leading the HR function, collaborating with other functions, setting and enhancing the standards for strategic thinking and ensuring corporate governance

Figure 10 ❖ The 'three legged stool'

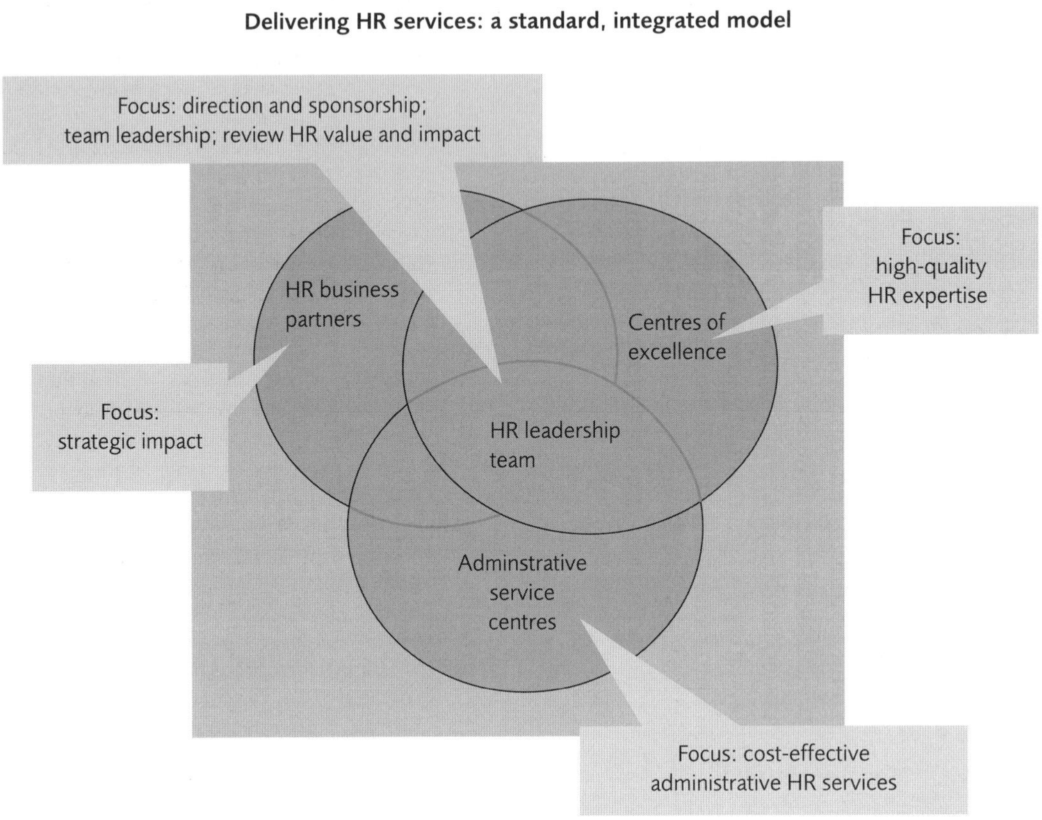

Variants of this model have been adopted by larger central government organisations in the consortium (eg, DWP, HMRC and HSE). Others are in the process of moving to variations of this model (NAO, COPFS and Leeds City Council). However some member organisations have chosen to keep to a more integrated model where the majority of HR activities are undertaken by a central functional HR team (BTP, FSA, Royal Borough of Kingston). The factors that have influenced the choice of models adopted have included:

- The degree of pressure on HR organisations to achieve cost and headcount reductions. This factor seems stronger the larger the organisation.
- The availability of information systems able to support e-HR. For some of the consortium members considerable investment in such systems is either well under way or planned shortly; others are not yet resourced to do so.
- The level of drive from within the HR function – especially at HR director level – to improve the effectiveness of HR and grasp a more strategic HR role.
- The readiness of managers in the organisation to take on 'devolved HR'. This is a function of attitude, commitment and the level of manager capability.
- Achieving the best balance between what the organisation might expect from the HR function and what HR could deliver.

As in our first report, we still see no evidence that top management or line customers in each organisation are demanding these changes. On the contrary, many are resistant to the changes even at the highest level, where they continue to demand a highly personalised HR service. This suggests that HR has not sold to senior management the model on which hopes of defensible staffing reductions in HR depend.

There was also no real evidence of organisations in the consortium specifically incorporating the full range of the five roles suggested by David Ulrich into any of their current delivery models. That being said, the latest adopters of the business partner model such as COPFS are envisaging a role which encompasses all of the change agency/strategic partner roles described. The role description for the COPFS business partner is set out in the box below:

COPFS BUSINESS PARTNER: MAIN RESPONSIBILITIES:

The main responsibilities of the business partner role cover:

- *HR planning*: Develop an area or unit HR plan to ensure that the unit has the right people in the right place with the right skills to deliver business results now and in future. This would cover staffing levels, recruitment plans, development needs, talent management, and action to achieve diversity and performance-management standards and expectations. Assist in the development of local strategies to implement the COPFS people strategy. Develop plans to identify and address the issues affecting morale within the service, including the development of strategies to respond to staff survey results.

- *Building people-management capability*: Advise and help area or unit managers to deliver results by making the best use of the people they have. This would cover job-based leadership and management development (through advice, training and coaching) and the operation of staff attendance and performance-management processes. It would also include delivery and implementation of organisation-wide HR initiatives for developing management and leadership capability, and generally improving performance management. The goal is to ensure managers are committed, competent and confident in their people-management role.

- *Developing managers*: Coach, mentor and support local managers through the performance-management cycle, in the development of people-management skills and techniques generally, and develop local strategies to tackle individual poor performance.

- *HR advice*: Specific advice, guidance and coaching to help individual managers deal with (and more importantly, learn to deal with) people issues such as developing talent, persistent absence, poor performance, discipline or grievances, and to develop action plans to deal with individual cases.

- *Problem solving*: Help the area or unit tackle more pervasive resourcing or people-management issues by finding solutions to the problem within the area/unit. This means responding promptly and flexibly to people issues. It could include specifying local recruitment campaigns and working with the HR resourcing team, local development or team events, action (with central HR) to fill hard-to-fill vacancies, or address pervasive absence or retention issues in particular teams or offices (but generally not individual cases).

- *Change management*: Advise on the people aspects of the design of change and lead/contribute to implementation of area, unit or corporate change programmes. Work alongside the Crown Office business change and IT teams from the outset in the design of major change programmes. The team would also be available to contribute to the design of and lead the implementation of corporate HR initiatives.

- *HR policy development*: Work with HR to develop suitable policies and processes to support the business in future. Lead policy development work in own areas of expertise, if that expertise is not available within central HR.

- *HR management*: Work as part of the HR management team. Provide reports to the HR director and to management board or the area fiscals group on HR issues in their area of responsibility.

- *Professional HR advice*: Keep up to date with developments in the HR profession to ensure proven HR practice is applied for the benefit of the organisation.

HR delivery models being used or adopted in the consortium fell into two broad categories:

- *Shared HR services*: a model based on the adoption of the 'three legged stool' with HR activities split between transformational and transactional teams, with web-enabled self-service for managers and employees, an HR service centre, a network of business partners and a strategy and policy team (although this model is often attributed to Dave Ulrich, in a recent CIPD interview he does not take credit for it). Variants of this model being used in HMRC and the Department for Work and Pensions are shown in Figures 11 and 12.

- *Functional model*: a centralised model with HR activities split into functional teams. Different adaptations of this approach being used in the Royal Borough of Kingston and the FSA are shown in Figures 13 and 14.

The smaller organisations on the whole have tended to maintain more of a functional model, as the level of transactional work is not always sufficient to make shared services cost effective. That being said, some of the smaller organisations have adopted parts of the model. For example the NAO has established a shared services team to deal with most of the routine HR transactions that cannot be dealt with online. COPFS has established a recruitment team to seek to achieve efficiencies in its HR service. So as a minimum, HR organisations are focusing on measuring the efficiency of transactional services with well-defined customers, and using standards and metrics to stimulate better service delivery.

Table 11 summarises the delivery models either in place or being adopted by consortium members, shown in the context of their employees and HR headcount.

Figure 11 ✣ DWP shared services model

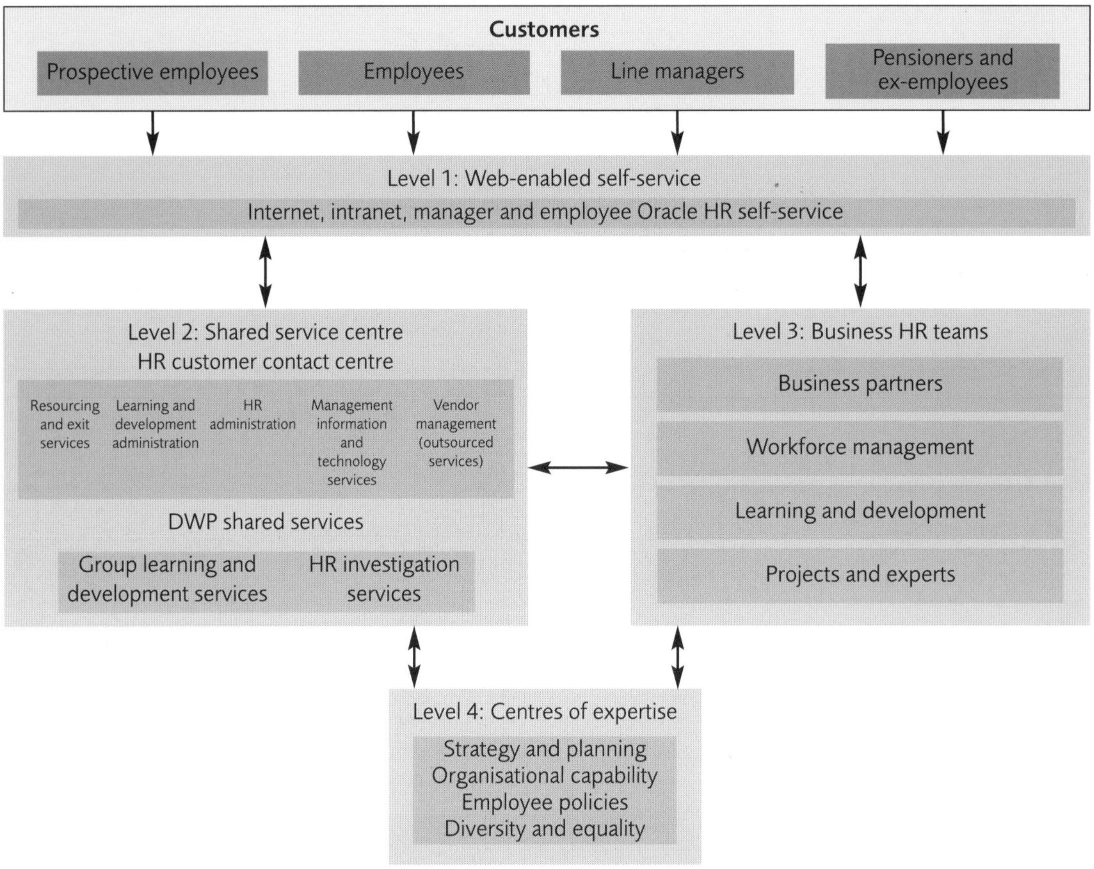
Customers
Prospective employees
Employees
Line managers
Pensioners and ex-employees
Level 1: Web-enabled self-service
Internet, intranet, manager and employee Oracle HR self-service
Level 2: Shared service centre
HR customer contact centre
Resourcing and exit services
Learning and development administration
HR administration
Management information and technology services
Vendor management (outsourced services)
DWP shared services
Group learning and development services
HR investigation services
Level 3: Business HR teams
Business partners
Workforce management
Learning and development
Projects and experts
Level 4: Centres of expertise
Strategy and planning
Organisational capability
Employee policies
Diversity and equality

Figure 12 ✣ HM Revenue and Customs HR services model

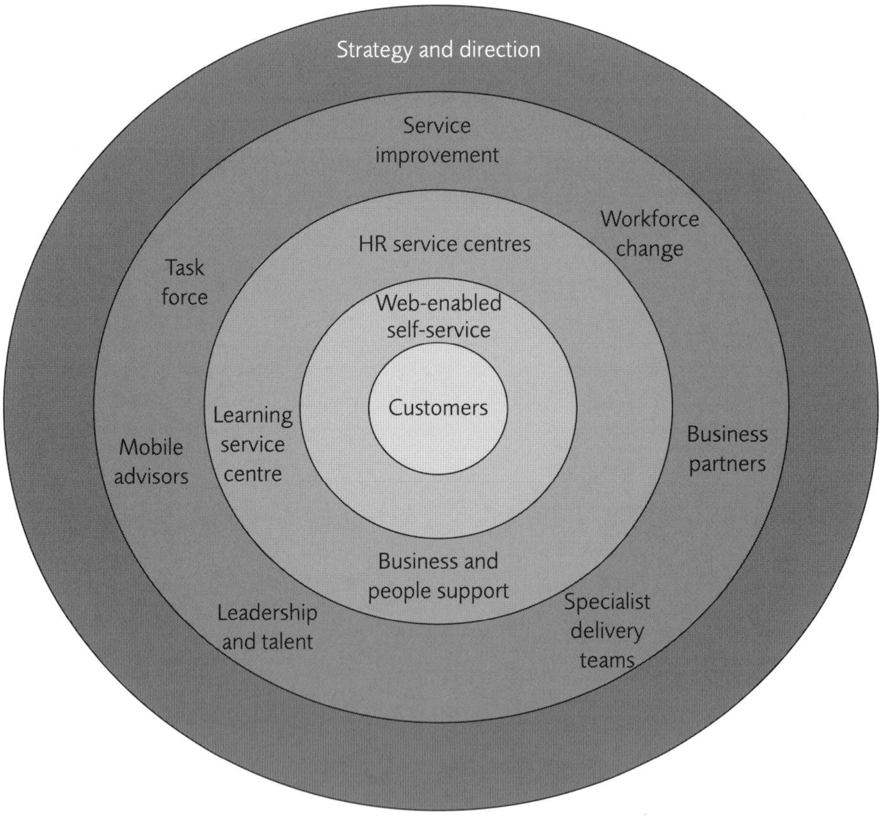
Strategy and direction
Service improvement
Workforce change
Task force
HR service centres
Web-enabled self-service
Customers
Learning service centre
Mobile advisors
Business partners
Business and people support
Leadership and talent
Specialist delivery teams

Figure 13 ◆ RB Kingston HR operating model

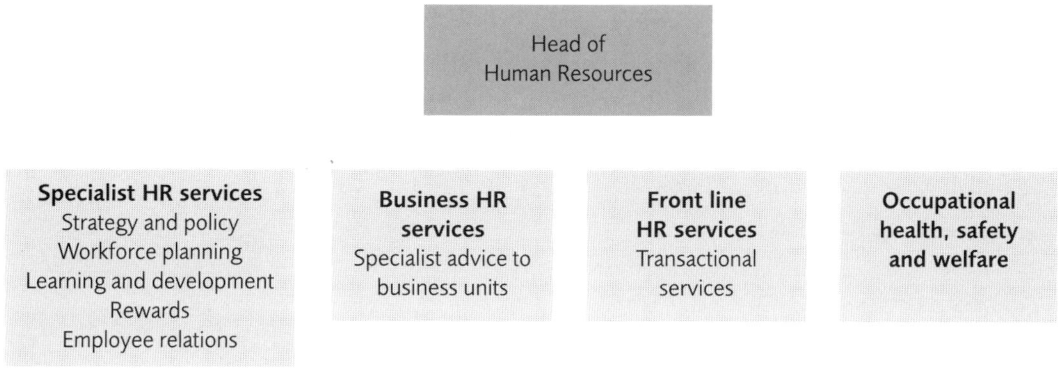

Figure 14 ◆ Food Standards Agency HR structure

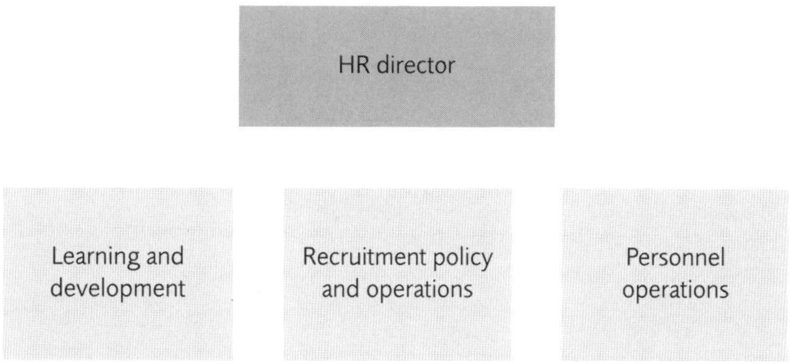

OVERCOMING PRACTICAL ISSUES IN IMPLEMENTATION

Planning for the implementation of new HR delivery models has been a critical part of the change process, requiring a structured, methodical approach. Consortium members highlighted the importance of getting the new HR service off to a good start by thinking through implementation issues and how the new model and processes would be judged by customers (issues of critical importance to them) to avoid initial problems with service credibility. The shared services model in particular has suffered from some lack of role clarity at the outset with consequent overlaps between the different legs of the stool. Many managers view the remoteness and impersonality of service centres as a reduction in service quality. They have looked instead to the local business partner to provide the face-to-face service expected.

The key practical issues that consortium members faced when adopting and embedding new HR delivery models and processes were how to:

- adopt delivery models that were flexible enough to match changes in business strategy and organisational structure
- understand the current HR processes, decide what needs to change and then design new streamlined processes
- ensure effective working links between different parts of the HR function to provide a 'seamless' and consistent service
- ensure appropriate communication and ease of access for all employees to HR services and self-service through telephony and IT
- educate managers and staff to use different services and sources of advice
- evaluate the strategic and operational effectiveness of HR delivery models and processes
- develop the appropriate HR behaviours and skills to make the model work.

Table 11 ✣ Employees and HR organisation

Organisation	Organisation size	HR-function size	HR delivery model in place or in process of adopting
British Transport Police	3,406 (2,773 police officers; 254 special constables; 1,379 police staff)	210	Functional
Crown Office and Procurator Fiscal Service	1,600	34	Functional plus shared HR recruitment service
Department for Works and Pensions	108,040	2,526	Shared HR service
Food Standards Agency	750	26	Functional
Health and Safety Executive	3,174	115	Shared HR service
HM Revenue and Customs [HR and L&D]	95,096	1,822	Shared HR service
Leeds City Council	14,321	314	Shared HR service
National Audit Office	900	26	Functional plus shared HR service
Royal Borough of Kingston	4,436	38	Centralised, functional with payroll outsourced
Total staff in the consortium	**231,723**	**5,111**	

Consultation with HR managers at Leeds City Council identified the following issues as critical to ensuring effective implementation of the new HR Service:

- There must be clear buy in from top managers.
- Details of the rationale for the change should be communicated to all staff in the council.
- Senior managers need to make it very clear that a central part of a manager's role is people management. Recruitment to management roles should be based on ability and commitment to manage people rather than technical merit.
- It is important to preserve what is good in HR now and enhance the quality of the service provided overall.
- The transition period will be critical as managers will be cynical and HR needs to 'hit the ground running' to maintain credibility.
- If the new HR service does not work well then directorates and managers may do 'their own thing' and this may make more work for HR.
- Phased implementation of different HR services across the Council should be considered.
- HR needs to manage organisational expectations of what the new service can deliver.
- Communication of change and scheduled implementation will be key; explanation of business partner roles to managers in particular should be a priority.
- Because of differences in the current way services are delivered across current directorates, the new HR service will involve less of a change for some managers.

HOW HR PROCESSES NEED TO CHANGE WITH THE NEW WAYS OF WORKING

HR needs to ensure its customers' requirements are taken on board (eg, senior managers, service managers, line managers and employees) in order to address practical implementation issues effectively. This means that before designing or updating the service specification HR needs to consult with its own staff and customer groups to identify the HR processes that work well, the ones that do not, and why. It can then determine what needs to be retained and what needs to change to ensure HR delivers and sustains a high-quality service suited to need.

At Leeds City Council consultation with managers identified the most important criteria for their new service. These are set out in Table 12. Managers identified quality and consistency of HR advice and easy access to HR staff as things they particularly valued and wished to retain in their new service. The HR team at Leeds City Council used this feedback to help them define the specification for the new HR Service and also to decide how best to communicate and implement the change effectively so that managers and employees have real 'buy in'.

PROVIDING A 'SEAMLESS' AND CONSISTENT SERVICE

To ensure greater consistency of approach, HR needs to define the key responsibilities of HR teams and ensure that staff really understand their role in delivering a high-quality service to customers. HR must make sure managers understand their responsibilities and the importance of their role too, giving them support where necessary. The ongoing shift of people management from HR to the line means that managers are expected to take a more active role in what have previously been regarded as HR activities (eg, recruitment, and managing disciplinary and grievance procedures). In HMRC this new relationship is summed as 'HR supports – the manager decides'. In the NAO a service-level agreement (SLA) has been set up to define the basic split of responsibilities between HR and the line and help ensure greater consistency of service.

Although the HR–manager interface is critical, HR must understand how it interacts with other support services such as Finance and IT so that it can make sure that its new services fully integrate with them. For example, it is particularly important to ensure that both technology and processes are compatible across the organisation when introducing e-HR otherwise any service efficiencies can easily be lost. Several of the consortium organisations, such as DWP, HMRC, NAO and HSE, are now using integrated HR and finance or resource management systems.

EFFECTIVE COMMUNICATION AND ACCESS TO HR SERVICES

Good communication channels are vitally important, so HR also needs to put suitable mechanisms in place for effective information exchange and division of responsibilities between the different HR teams as well as with senior managers, managers and employees. Making sure that all staff, particularly line managers, are very clear about the benefits of the new model and how it will work in practice will also help raise the profile and credibility of HR during the transitional period. This is being done by identifying frequently asked questions and providing answers, running briefing sessions and giving practical examples in straight-forward guidance. These activities do not need to be elaborate to be effective.

Employees and managers also require easy access to HR services. This means HR taking account of those without access to PCs and those with limited IT skills or other special needs as well as properly explaining the system to make sure every one of the mainstream customers knows how and when to use the new delivery models and processes.

CUSTOMER EDUCATION

A key part of planning and embedding a new delivery model is for HR to ensure that its own staff, managers and other staff have the right skills and behaviours to make it work. For example, HR may need to support managers through coaching, training or briefing sessions to give them more confidence in developing effective staff relationships and tackling performance problems as soon as they arise.

Table 12 ◆ HR service criteria in Leeds City Council

Criterion	Rationale
Quick and easy to access	Managers know where to go for information and how this will be provided and when
Accurate	Avoid basic administrative errors, for example in contracts or payroll
Not bureaucratic	Make it easy and quick to select and recruit staff
High quality	HR staff give advice based on good technical knowledge of HR issues and appropriate policies and procedures
Consistent	Managers do not get different answers on policy or procedures depending on whom they talk to in HR
Responsive	HR staff engage with managers to help them solve a problem rather than saying 'No'

Employee engagement is critical to ensuring that organisations perform effectively, and there is an increasing trend for employees to be given more personal responsibility for their own performance and the way they manage their work. So employees will also benefit from training and briefing on how to access services via their line managers and HR.

Knowing how to make effective use of HR services is essential for everyone in the organisation to help them perform well. It is something that should be built into staff induction and included in appraisal training and briefings as a matter of course.

HOW ARE THE NEW DELIVERY MODEL AND PROCESSES WORKING?

Finally, mechanisms need to be put in place to gather feedback from HR staff and managers to assess how the new HR organisation is working both on an operational level (ie, on a day-to-day basis) and at a strategic level. Developing a set of HR measures to establish a baseline and then track progress is therefore an essential part of this process. For further details of HR measurement see Chapter 5, Results.

SUMMARY

HR needs a good understanding of the business to adopt and embed HR delivery models and processes that really enable the organisation to achieve its goals. It is essential to pay attention to the practical details when adapting and embedding a new HR delivery model and processes to ensure that HR credibility is maintained, otherwise HR's ability as a strategic partner may be called into question. Evaluation of how the new HR delivery model and processes are working is also critical to ensure that they continue to support the needs of the business and delivery of HR strategy.

QUESTIONS FOR HR

Consultants Reach HR posed the following five questions to consortium members to help them select an appropriate HR delivery model and make it work well in their organisations:

1. Responsibility. How much of the proposed transformation impact is within your personal area of responsibility?
2. Effective or efficient. What organisational goal is the change supporting?
3. Appetite. What is the appetite both within and outside HR for the transformation you are considering?
4. Capability. Are your systems and processes capable of making any new delivery model a success?
5. Human capital. What is the likely aptitude and attitude of the HR/payroll staff to any change?

Other questions to be considered are:

6. How do you make sure that all of your customers know what HR services are on offer and how they can access them?
7. What processes do you have in place to gather feedback from HR staff and customers to monitor and evaluate how your current HR delivery model and processes are working at operational and strategic level?

CONCLUSIONS 11

- **This chapter draws together our conclusions from the consortium work.**
- **It emphasises the importance of HR focusing on the things that contribute directly to organisational results, engaging with business managers in doing so.**
- **It is also critical for the HR function to develop HR talent and build future capability.**
- **It is the responsibility of top managers to ensure they use HR successfully to support the delivery of results.**

- Real progress but more to do ...

From our work in the second consortium, we have drawn a number of conclusions about progress in HR transformation since *Fit for business I*.

MESSAGES FOR HR TEAMS IN THE PUBLIC SECTOR

Being strategic is as much about what you don't do as what you do. Public sector HR is still trying to do everything, including taking on centrally imposed initiatives that are not always relevant to each organisation at that moment. It is important to identify the key HR issues that will make the difference to business performance and address them first. These are also the activities that HR should concentrate on measuring.

The powerful link between organisational results in the public sector and the effective management of people and performance means that a key goal for organisations is to ensure that they enact these responsibilities well. To make this happen and be truly 'fit for business' HR needs to work more closely with senior managers to develop strong leadership and wider organisational talent, build a modern infrastructure to support good people management and create a culture where high performance is rewarded. The HR reform agenda seems to neglect employee engagement – except indirectly through emphasis on diversity and fair treatment policies and practices. The strong link between employee engagement and high performance means that this should now be a key area for HR action.

If there are issues which are hampering progress, HR needs to identify these and work with senior mangers to tackle them. There is a joint responsibility here and if senior managers are not taking this on board then HR needs to do more to persuade them.

Getting the basics right is essential to get HR a seat at the strategy table. The HR service generally needs to be much more consistent and of better quality to ensure HR has a credible role as business partner and strategic adviser.

Whilst HR is engaging more with business managers, it needs to be more outward facing and customer focused; some consortium projects were still too HR centric and managers were not always consulted when changes were being planned. HR must also be prepared to do more to 'sell' the benefits of good people management to ensure that the organisation achieves its goals.

This means HR has to know how to engage with managers in analysing business issues, not just HR issues per se. The language HR uses also needs to be made still more accessible to customer groups, with jargon kept to a minimum.

HR needs to add real value – to make a difference to business issues and help find creative solutions – by looking afresh at current HR solutions.

HR should also be more open minded and take opportunities to learn from others – one of the key benefits of a consortium and a collaborative approach. So get out even more is still the message.

There is still a big issue for HR in developing the skills to act strategically, such as business partnering skills, OD and change management. Too often HR departments look to the labour market (where there are a strategic skills shortage and a business partner pay-bidding war) rather than looking longer term at building sustainable capability internally. Changing HR roles mean that organisations urgently need to devise more structured programmes to develop HR capability and create new career paths.

The HR operating model (ie, the structure) is still a major preoccupation for organisations but it is not a universally applicable answer. It must be the right fit for your organisation – and if the transformed HR model is not seamless it could mean a worse not better service for its customers

MESSAGES FOR SENIOR PUBLIC SECTOR MANAGERS

Central and local government organisations have some significant challenges to address in the next few years. Developing the right culture and people-management practices that reward and support high performance will be critical to helping organisations address them. Senior managers have a key role in this process. For some organisations this may mean adopting radical approaches and taking some tough people-management decisions, as otherwise changes to the status quo are likely to be minimal.

Senior managers need to consider how they can best work with HR to achieve positive outcomes in their organisations, so this means identifying the key business priorities and focusing on what needs to be done to achieve them.

Experience in the consortium has shown that it tends to be HR rather than senior managers that is pushing for a more strategic approach to people management. It is also up to senior mangers to identify what is hampering progress towards the key organisational goals and take action to rectify them.

SOME OUTSTANDING QUESTIONS ...

We believe the consortium has provided a further wealth of experience in tackling the transformation agenda and generated a great deal of learning for members that we are sharing in this report. But there is so much more to do. The questions we and consortium members would still like an answer to are:

1. Do the new delivery models deliver better service and increase HR added value?

2. What would really help HR work more successfully with the business?

3. How can HR demonstrate added value?

4. How can HR develop credible strategic HR professionals for the future?

5. How do managers learn to use HR strategically?

6. What else can be done to help develop a suitable environment in organisations that will enable HR to be truly strategic?

Another consortium might provide some of the answers.

APPENDIX 1
FORTY QUESTIONS FOR HR

GOALS

1. Does your HR function have a clear strategic role that is well understood across the organisation? If not, how can you bring about this understanding?

2. How often do you review the degree to which your HR function is supporting and aligned with the goals of your organisation? How do you do this?

3. How do you make sure that your HR function develops and retains credibility in the organisation?

4. What are the drivers requiring your HR function to be more strategic? How can you use these to influence others to take on their people-management responsibilities in your organisation?

5. What are the barriers that prevent your HR function from being strategic? What can you do to overcome these barriers?

6. Does your HR function have all the information and internal networks it needs to act strategically? If not, how can you make sure that you acquire them?

7. At what point does your HR function become involved in designing and implementing change or transformation in your organisation? What effect does this have on the ability of HR to influence the organisation?

8. How often do you review the way your HR function works with external partners, and identify how these partners add value to your strategic HR contribution? Which external partners add the most value? What other external partners do you need?

RESULTS

9. How does your HR function engage with the business to determine what outcomes HR needs to deliver and how?

10. How do you decide which HR activities are best able to deliver the HR outcomes that you require?

11. How do you judge the quality of service that HR provides to the business? Are these standards set out explicitly for your customers?

12. Do you have a measurement framework that captures the breadth of HR contribution to business results? How is this used?

13. Are clear accountabilities established for the delivery of HR performance between the HR function, line managers and employees?

PERFORMANCE

14. Who sets the climate for people management in your organisation? Who needs to change their behaviour to send the right signals?

15. What style does your HR team adopt in engaging with people managers to deal with difficult performance issues?

16. What do you need to do to establish a professional people-management development programme for your people managers?

17. What practical guidance do you have to help managers hold those difficult conversations?

18. Is better people performance at the heart of everything your HR function does?

TECHNIQUE

19. What is on your HR agenda at the moment, and is it making a difference to business results?

20. How do you judge the quality of service you provide to customers? Is this made explicit to those customers?

21. To what extent are managers good 'people managers', and how is HR supporting the development of their capabilities so that they can be self-sufficient 'people managers'?

22. Does HR have a leading role in change in the organisation and how are you making a difference? If not, what is it that limits your ability to get engaged?

23. What role does HR have in OD? What more can you do to increase your involvement?

24. How successful have the 'big HR' changes been in your organisation? What can you learn from that experience about doing it better in future?

25. Who are the leading practitioners in the topics where your HR function is trying to make a difference? Have you talked to them and what did you learn?

TEAMWORK

26. What does the business partnership between HR and its customers mean in your organisation?

27. Does HR speak the language of HR or of the business?

28. What recent examples do you have of HR really engaging with people in the organisation? What was done differently as a result?

FITNESS

29. What are the key challenges you face in developing and managing talent for your HR function?

30. Do you know your current HR capabilities and where you need to develop these further? How will you do this?

31. What performance frameworks do you currently have in place to improve HR capability and confidence?

32. What performance frameworks will you need in future?

33. What will your successful, confident HR function look like?

PHYSIQUE

34. How much of the proposed transformation impact is within your personal area of responsibility?

35. What organisational goal is the change supporting?

36. What is the appetite both within and outside HR for the transformation you are considering?

37. Are your systems and processes capable of making any new delivery model a success?

38. What is the likely aptitude and attitude of the HR/payroll staff to any change?

39. How do you make sure that all of your customers know what HR services are on offer and how they can access them?

40. What processes do you have in place to gather feedback from HR staff and customers to monitor and evaluate how your current HR delivery model and processes are working at operational and strategic level?

APPENDIX 2
BASELINE QUESTIONS FROM THE FIRST *FIT FOR BUSINESS* REPORT

Table ◆ Appendix 2

Yes	Themes and questions	No
	1. GOALS **The strategic role of HR**	
	Does the organisation have a sufficiently well-developed business strategy to enable the HR priorities to be identified?	
	Are HR priorities aligned to support each of the business priorities?	
	Is the HR team clear about how it is adding value to the business?	
	Do managers in the business know what strategic HR means to them?	
	Is a strategic planning process embedded in the organisation?	
	Does HR play a full part in that process?	
	Do HR initiatives and activities reinforce or cut across one another?	
	Does HR work strategically? This means engagement with top management, credibility with line managers, confidence to contribute, business understanding and HR capability – in partnership with the business.	
	2. PHYSIQUE **Organisation of the HR function**	
	Is the HR organisation designed to align and work with the business?	
	Has an effective HR delivery model been established, based on the best balance of HR expertise, business focus, service quality and technology?	
	If the structure has changed, how far have the HR function and its customers in the line adapted to their new roles?	

Table ❖ Appendix 2 continued

Yes	Themes and questions	No
	Is HR close to the line and does it understand line managers' needs?	
	Is HR out and about in the business and does it understand what the business issues are?	
	3. TECHNIQUE **HR adding value**	
	Is HR helping to achieve organisational goals through supporting and encouraging line managers to improve the motivation, commitment and morale of people with the right capabilities for the future?	
	Does the HR function add value by providing efficient services to the business?	
	Do HR people have commitment and a single-minded focus on these outcomes for the organisation?	
	Does HR focus on action not words?	
	4. FITNESS **A capable and confident HR team**	
	Does HR understand the business and have productive relationships with managers across the organisation?	
	Is HR flexible and does it adapt to organisational changes?	
	Is HR building its strategic capability and leadership for the future?	
	5. TEAMWORK **Working with the other organisational players**	
	Does HR have a relationship that is tailored to each of its partners in the business?	
	Is HR clear what each relationship delivers for the organisation?	
	Are mutual expectations between the HR team and its partners made explicit and understood?	
	Are sound processes in place and used to ensure effective joint working with the line?	
	Is HR visible throughout the organisation?	
	6. PERFORMANCE **Enabling managers to release performance**	
	Do managers embrace responsibility for HR issues in their team?	
	Do managers get support in addressing the difficult aspects of management, and staff performance and attendance issues?	
	Are managers overly dependent on HR to resolve people problems?	
	Is a climate for better management set by exemplary management at the top?	

Table ❖ Appendix 2 continued

Yes	Themes and questions	No
	Does the organisation/HR team have in place a range of mechanisms to support better leadership and management?	
	Does the organisation have an agreed view of what better leadership and management and leadership look like in its own context?	
	7. RESULTS **The contribution HR makes to the organisation**	
	Does HR focus all its efforts on the outcomes it has to deliver to the organisation?	
	Is there a coherent strategy process enabling vertical and horizontal alignment of HR to the business?	
	Does HR measure the extent to which outcomes are delivered or the factors that contribute to them being delivered?	
	Do both senior managers and the HR team measure and then manage HR issues that matter?	

NOTES

1. CIPD (2005). Available at www.cipd.co.uk/Bookstore/_catalogue/HRPractice/1843981521.htm.

2. Civil Service Capability Reviews (March 2007) *Capability reviews tranche 3: Findings and common themes. Civil Service – strengths and challenges*. Cabinet Office.

3. Local Government Association (2007) *Pay and Workforce Strategy Survey 2006*. Available at http://www.lgar.local.gov.uk/lgv/core/page.do?pageId=24761.

4. David Ulrich and Wayne Brockbank (2005) *The HR value proposition*. Boston, Mass.: Harvard Business School Press.

5. David Ulrich (1997) *Human Resource champions*. Boston, Mass.: Harvard Business School Press.

6. David Ulrich and Wayne Brockbank (2005) Role call, *People Management*. 16 June. pp24–28

Street by Street

GW01149936

LONDON

Extended Coverage of the Capital

5th edition April 2010

Original edition printed May 2001

Enabled by Ordnance Survey This product includes map data licensed from Ordnance Survey® with the permission of the Controller of Her Majesty's Stationery Office. © Crown copyright 2010. All rights reserved. Licence number: 100021153.

The copyright in all PAF is owned by Royal Mail Group plc.

RoadPilot® Information on fixed speed camera locations provided by RoadPilot © 2010 RoadPilot® Driving Technology.

Published by AA Publishing (a trading name of AA Media Limited, whose registered office is Fanum House, Basing View, Basingstoke, Hampshire RG21 4EA. Registered number 06112600)

Produced by the Mapping Services Department of The Automobile Association. (A03956)

A CIP Catalogue record for this book is available from the British Library.

Printed by Oriental Press in Dubai

Ref: MX039w

Key to map pages ii–iii

Key to map symbols iv–1

Enlarged map pages 2–19

Main map pages 20–181

Index – towns & villages 182

Index – streets 183–259

Index – featured places 260–280

Acknowledgements 280

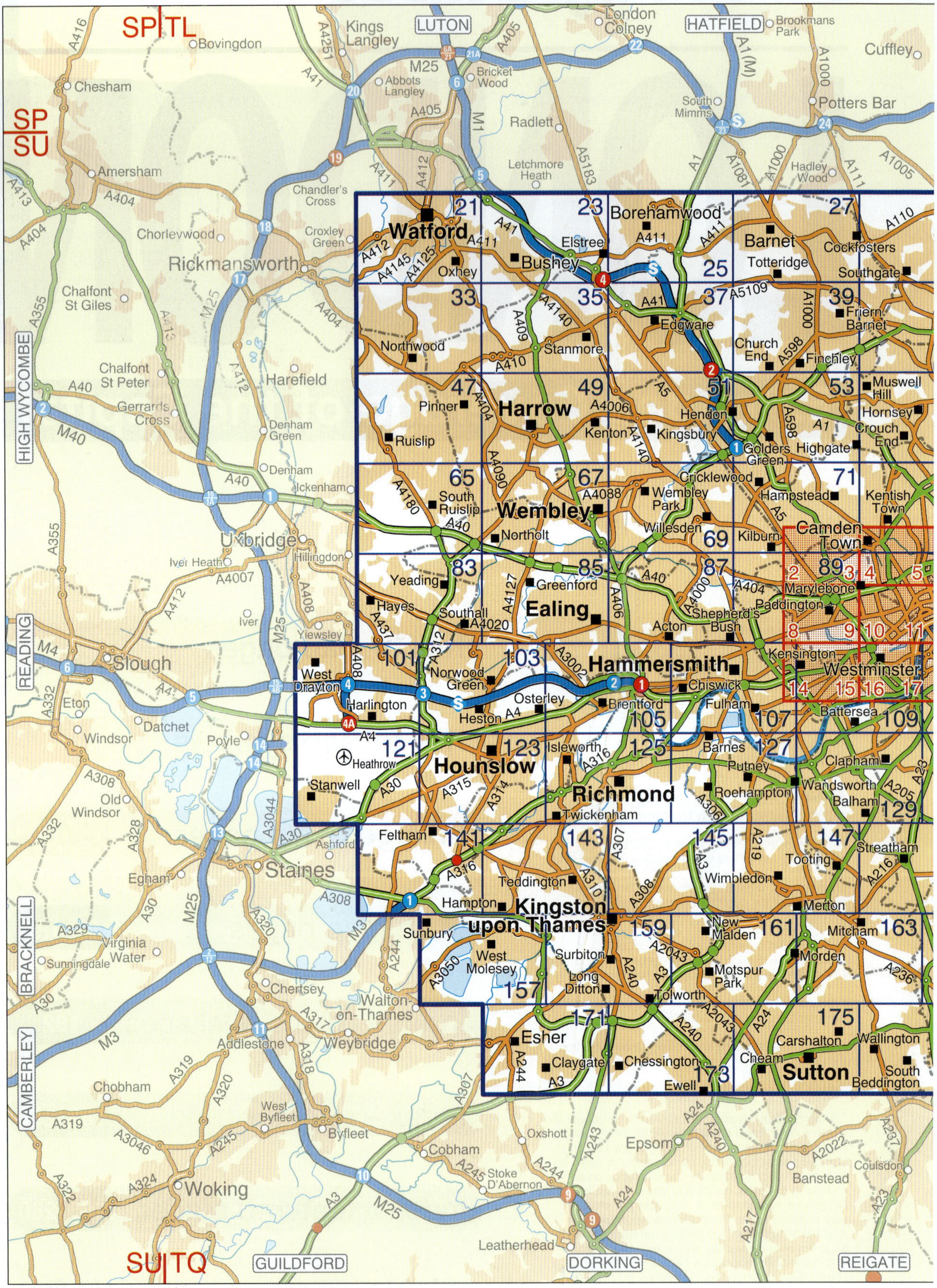

Scale of enlarged map pages 1:10,000 6.3 inches to 1 mile

0 1/4 miles 1/2 3/4

0 1/4 1/2 kilometres 3/4 1 1 1/4

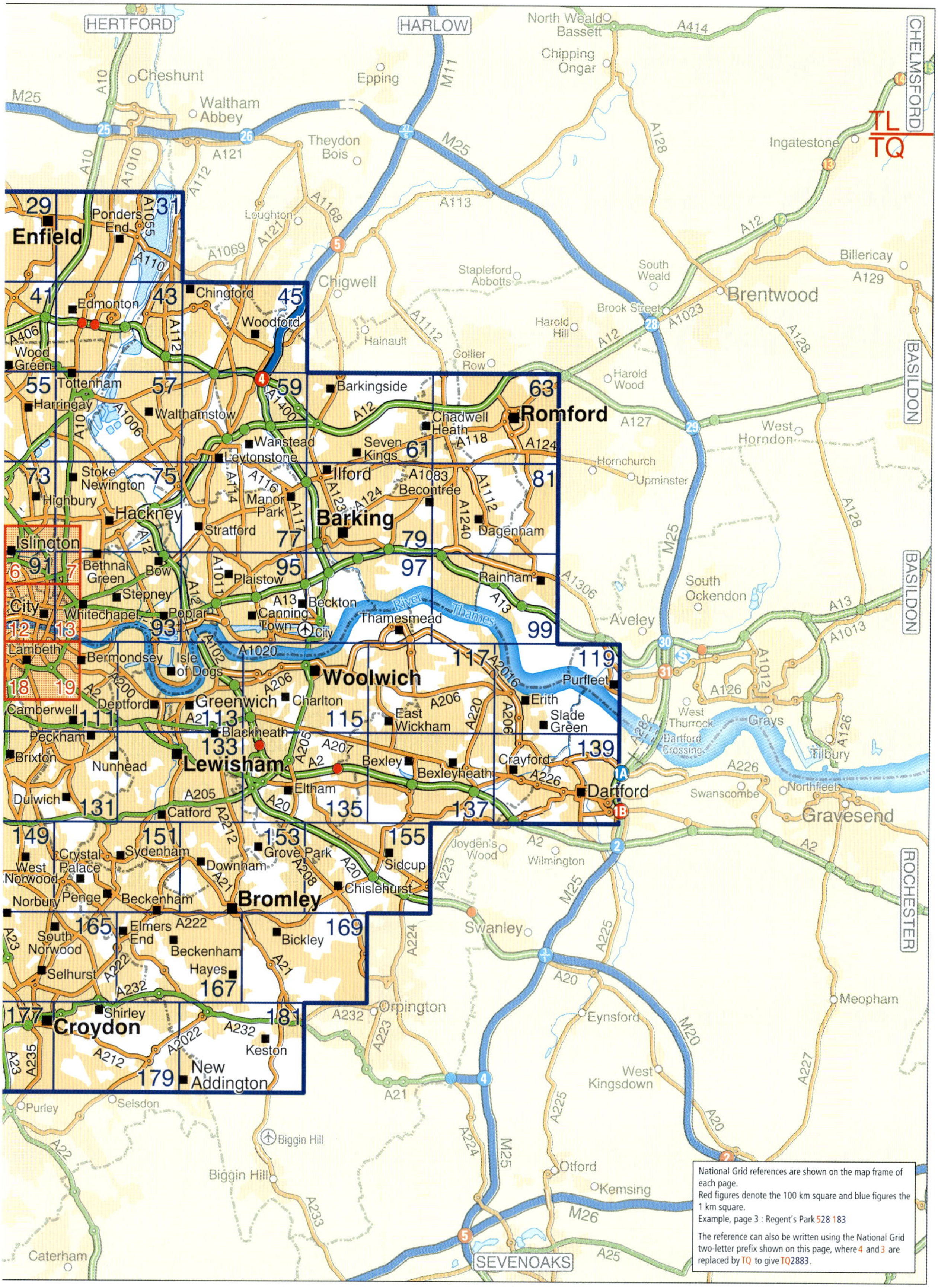

National Grid references are shown on the map frame of each page.
Red figures denote the 100 km square and blue figures the 1 km square.
Example, page 3 : Regent's Park 528 183

The reference can also be written using the National Grid two-letter prefix shown on this page, where 4 and 3 are replaced by TQ to give TQ2883.

4.2 inches to 1 mile

Scale of main map pages 1:15,000

0 | 1/4 | miles | 1/2 | 3/4 | 1

0 | 1/4 | 1/2 | kilometres | 3/4 | 1 | 1 1/4 | 1 1/2 | 1 3/4

Symbol	Description
Junction 9	Motorway & junction
Services	Motorway service area
	Primary road single/dual carriageway
Services	Primary road service area
	A road single/dual carriageway
	B road single/dual carriageway
	Other road single/dual carriageway
	Minor/private road, access may be restricted
	One-way street
	Pedestrian area
	Track or footpath
	Road under construction
	Road tunnel
30 V	Speed camera site (fixed location) with speed limit in mph or variable
40 V	Selection of road with two or more fixed camera sites; speed limit in mph or variable
50 50	Average speed (SPECS™) camera system with speed limit in mph
P	Parking
P+	Park & Ride
	Bus/coach station

Symbol	Description
	Railway & main railway station
	Railway & minor railway station
	Underground station
	Docklands Light Railway (DLR) station
	London Overground station
	Light railway & station
	Preserved private railway
LC	Level crossing
	Tramway
	Ferry route
	Airport runway
	County, administrative boundary
	Congestion Charging Zone *
	Charge-free routes through the Charging Zone
	Low Emission Zone (LEZ) (visit **theaa.com** for further information)
93	Page continuation 1:15,000
7	Page continuation to enlarged scale 1:10,000
	River/canal, lake, pier
	Aqueduct, lock, weir
465 Winter Hill	Peak (with height in metres)

* The AA central London congestion charging map is also available

Woodland

Park

Cemetery

Built-up area

Industrial / business building

Leisure building

Retail building

Other building

City wall

A&E Hospital with 24-hour A&E department

PO Post Office, public library

Tourist Information Centre, seasonal

Petrol station, 24 hour
Major suppliers only

Church/chapel

Public toilets, with facilities for the less able

PH Public house
AA recommended

Restaurant
AA inspected

Madeira Hotel — Hotel
AA inspected

Theatre or performing arts centre

Cinema

Camping
AA inspected

Caravan site
AA inspected

Camping & caravan site
AA inspected

Golf course

Theme park

Abbey, cathedral or priory

Castle

Historic house or building

Wakehurst Place (NT) — National Trust property

Museum or art gallery

Roman antiquity

Ancient site, battlefield or monument

Industrial interest

Garden

Garden Centre
Garden Centre Association Member

Garden Centre
Wyevale Garden Centre

Arboretum

Farm or animal centre

Zoological or wildlife collection

Bird collection

Nature reserve

Aquarium

Visitor or heritage centre

Country park

Cave

Windmill

Distillery, brewery or vineyard

2
Iverson Road
B520
Kilburn High Road
Loveridge Road
West Hampstead Station
West Hampstead Station
Blackburn Rd
Works
A
B
C
D
E
F
70
71
Broadhurst Gardens
Broadhurst Cl
Finchley Road Stn
Eye Clinic
Holy Trinity CE Primary School
Sumpter Close
Canfield Pl
Edgware Coll
Finchley Road
Netherwood St
Linstead St
Lowfield Rd
Kylemore Rd
Gladys Rd
Hilltop Road
West Hampstead Clinic
Compayne Gardens
Fairhazel Gardens
Canfield Gardens
Greencroft Gardens
Broadhurst School
Surgery
Naseby Cl
Marston Close
Fairfax Road
Fairfax Pl
Goldhurst Terrace
Belsize Road
Palmerston Road
Hemstal Road
Cleve Road
West End Lane
Priory Road
Dynham Road
Cotleigh Road
Kingsgate Primary School
Woodchurch Road
Tricycle Theatre
Tricycle
Dunster Gdns
Streatley Road
Buckley Road
Callcott Road
Drakes Ctyd
Messina Avenue
Kingsgate Road
Gascony Avenue
Grange Place
Smyrna Road
Mazenod Avenue
Kings Gardens
St Eugene de Mazenod RC Primary School
Acol Road
Wavel Ms
St Mary's Ms
Aberdare Gardens
Goldhurst Terrace
Coleridge Gardens
Hilgrove Road
Alexandra Road
Eresby Place
Queensgate Place
Kingsgate Pl
Christ Church Brondesbury CE J&I Sch
A4003
B510
Quex Road
St Marys Kilburn Prim Sch
Abbot's Place
Abbey Road
Belsize Road
B509
Jack Taylor School
Langtry Walk
Ainsworth Way
Boundary Road
Rowley Way
Loudoun Road
Kilburn Square
College of North West London
Victoria Road
Victoria Ms
Birchington Road
Mutrix Road
Bransdale Close
Hermit Pl
Priory Terrace
Kingsley Road
Kenilworth Road
Tennyson Road
Douglas Road
Glengall Road
Hazelmere Road
Esmond Road
Charteris Road
Charteris Road Sports Centre
Algernon Road
NW6
Kilburn High Road Station
Kilburn Vale
Kilburn Place
B507
Abbey Medical Centre
Ben Uri Gallery, London Jewish Museum of Art
Langtry Road
Mortimer Crs
Mortimer Place
Springfield Road
Clifton Hill
Rutland Ms
Belgrave Gdns
Bolton Road
KILBURN
Donaldson Rd
Lynton Road
Honiton Road
Brondesbury Road
Brondesbury Villas
Mallard Cl
Kilburn Bridge
A5
Coventry Cl
Greville Road
Greville Place
Kilburn Priory
Marriott Hotel
Carlton Hill
St John's Wood
Blenheim Road
Marlborough Day Hospital
Marlborough Place
Carlton Hill
B451
Alpha Pl
Kilburn Park Station
Cambridge Avenue
Oxford Road
Tollgate Gardens
Primary School
Gorefield Place
St Marys RC Primary School
Chichester Road
Surgery
School
Naima Jewish Preparatory School
Kilburn Park Road
Maida Vale
Randolph Gdns
Andover Place
Hillside Cl
Blenheim Ter
New London Synagogue
Langford Pl
The Lane
Aubrey Place
Abbey Gardens
Eliot Ms
Queen's Park Station
Albert Road
Denmark Road
Canterbury Road
Canterbury Ter
Princess Road
Peel Precinct
School of Islamic Republic Iran
Granville Road
Surgery
Randolph Avenue
St Georges RC School
Hamilton Terrace
Abercorn Place
Abercorn School
Alma Square
Hill Road
Salusbury Rd
Carlton Vale
B413
Kilburn Park Junior School
St Lukes CE Primary School
Carlton V
Nelson Cl
Stafford Rd
Paddington Recreation Ground
Maida Vale
North West London Medical Centre
Hamilton Gdns
Abercorn Wk
Wellesley Ct
Marban Rd
Fernhead Road
Ashmore Road
Carlton Vale Infant School
Bradiston Road
Malvern Road
Saltram Crescent
Surgery
Cambridge Rd
Denholme Rd
88
College
Oxley Rd
Malvern Ms
Hampton Close
Park Bus Cen
B414
Paddington Recreation Ground Athletics Track
Pavilion
The Lanark Medical Centre
Elgin Ms
Maida Vale Station
Surgery
Lanark Road
Randolph Avenue
Vale Close
Hall Road
Crompton
Hamilton Terrace
Fordingley Road
Shirland Road
Portnall Road
Riverton Cl
Stuart Rd
Essendine Primary School
Morshead Road
Grantully Road
Ashworth Road
Biddulph Rd
Maida Vale Medical Cen
Spanish & Portuguese Synagogue
Sutherland Av
St Josephs RC Primary School
Surgery
Shirland Mews
Lydford Road
Elmfield Way
Warlock Road
Portgate Cl
Coryton Path
Barnsdale Rd
Errington Rd
Walterton Road
Chippenham Road
Lanhill Rd
Crittleton Rd
Wymering Road
Widley Road
City of Westminster College
Elgin Avenue
Lauderdale Road
W9
Paddington Bowling & Sports Club
Castellain Road
BBC Studios
Delaware Road
Warrington Crescent
Randolph Crs
Clifton Road
Randolph Av
Lanark Road
Kennet Rd
Queen Elizabeth II School
A404
Secondary School
Oakington Rd
Edbrooke Road
Elgin Avenue
Shirland Road
Westbourne Green
8
Goldney Road
Chantry Cl
Fermoy Road
Hormead Rd
Formosa St
Warwick Av
Primary School
Elnathan Ms
Clifton Gardens
Warwick Avenue Station
Little Venice Medical Centre
Aldsworth Cl
Downfield Cl
Barnwood Cl
Surrendale Place
Sutherland Avenue
1 grid square represents 250 metres
School
Police
A404 Harrow Road

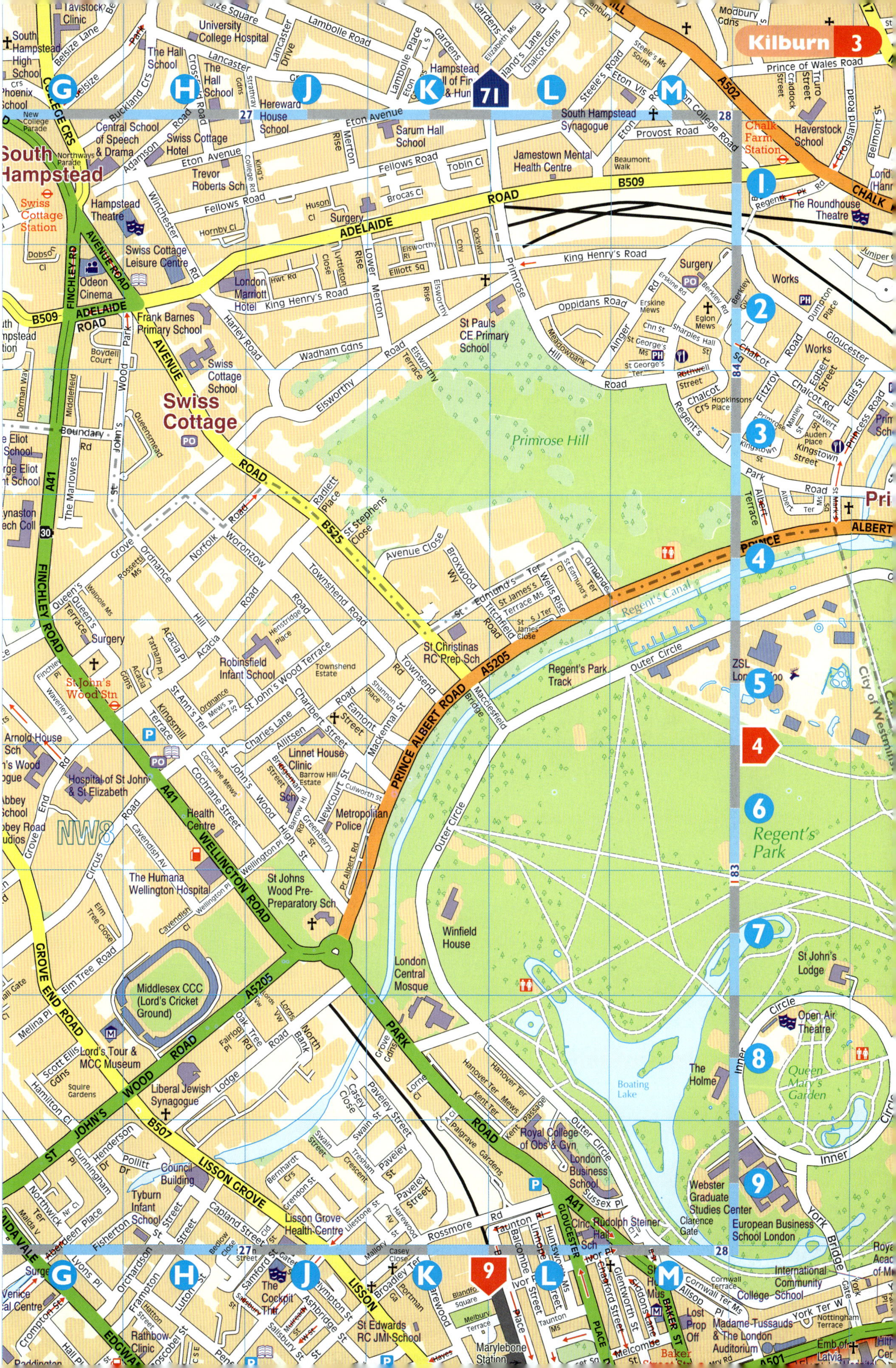

Kilburn 3
South Hampstead
Swiss Cottage
Swiss Cottage Station
Primrose Hill
Regent's Park
Regent's Canal
NW8
Finchley Road
Adelaide Road
Avenue Road
Wellington Road
Prince Albert Road
Park Road
Lisson Grove
Grove End Road
St John's Wood Road
Eton Avenue
Fellows Road
King Henry's Road
Elsworthy Road
Outer Circle
Inner Circle
Chalk Farm Station
The Roundhouse Theatre
Hampstead Theatre
Swiss Cottage Leisure Centre
Odeon Cinema
London Marriott Hotel
St Paul's CE Primary School
St John's Wood Stn
Hospital of St John & St Elizabeth
The Humana Wellington Hospital
Middlesex CCC (Lord's Cricket Ground)
Lord's Tour & MCC Museum
Liberal Jewish Synagogue
London Central Mosque
Winfield House
Boating Lake
The Holme
Open Air Theatre
Queen Mary's Garden
St John's Lodge
Regent's Park Track
ZSL London Zoo
Royal College of Obs & Gyn
London Business School
Rudolph Steiner Hall
Webster Graduate Studies Center
European Business School London
International Community College School
Madame Tussauds & The London Auditorium
Marylebone Station
Baker St
The Cockpit Thtr
St Edwards RC JMI School
Lisson Grove Health Centre
Metropolitan Police
St Johns Wood Pre-Preparatory Sch
Robinsfield Infant School
St Christinas RC Prep Sch
Linnet House Clinic
University College Hospital
Central School of Speech & Drama
Swiss Cottage Hotel
Sarum Hall School
Jamestown Mental Health Centre
South Hampstead Synagogue
Haverstock School
Frank Barnes Primary School
Swiss Cottage School
Council Building
Tyburn Infant School
A41
A5205
B509
B525
B507
A502
A501
4
9
71

4
A
B
C
D
E
F
1
2
3
4
5
6
7
8
9
72
3
10
CAMDEN TOWN
Primrose Hill
Regent's Park
NW1
Camden Market
Camden Lock
Chalk Farm Station
Haverstock School
Chalcot School
Holy Trinity in St Silas
London Zendo (Hannya Temple)
The Roundhouse Theatre
CHALK FARM RD
HAWLEY RD
KENTISH TOWN ROAD
CAMDEN ROAD
ROYAL COLLEGE STREET
ST PANCRAS WAY
Camden Road Station
Camden Town Station
CAMDEN HIGH ST
PKWY
London Capital College
Mornington Sports & Fitness Cen
The Cavendish School
Odeon
Holiday Inn
Primrose Hill School
Cecil Sharpe House
PRINCE ALBERT A5205 ROAD
Regent's Canal
Outer Circle
ZSL London Zoo
City of Westminster
Camden
The British American Drama Academy
North Bridge House Prep School
The Jewish Museum
DELANCEY ST A503
Mornington Crescent Stn
Camden Thr
CROWNDALE ROAD
Crowndale Hlth Cen
Richard Cobden Primary School
Ampthill Square Medical Centre
Regent's Park Barracks
Christ Church School
HAMPSTEAD ROAD
National Temperance Hospital
Thistle Hotel
Maria Fidelis Convent School
Ibis Hotel
Medical Cen
Police Station
Camden People's Thtr
University of Westminster
Euston Tower
Univ of Westminster Euston Centre
Royal College of Physicians
St John's Lodge
Open Air Theatre
Queen Mary's Garden
Inner Circle
Chester Road
Boating Lake
Holme
London Business School
Graduate Studies Center
European Business School London
Clarence Gate
Cumberland Gate
Gloucester Gate
Royal Academy of Music
Regent's Park Stn
Great Portland St Stn
Warren Street Stn
EUSTON ROAD
University Coll Hosp
Royal Nat Orthopaedic Hospital
MARYLEBONE ROAD
BAKER ST
TOTTENHAM
1 grid square represents 250 metres

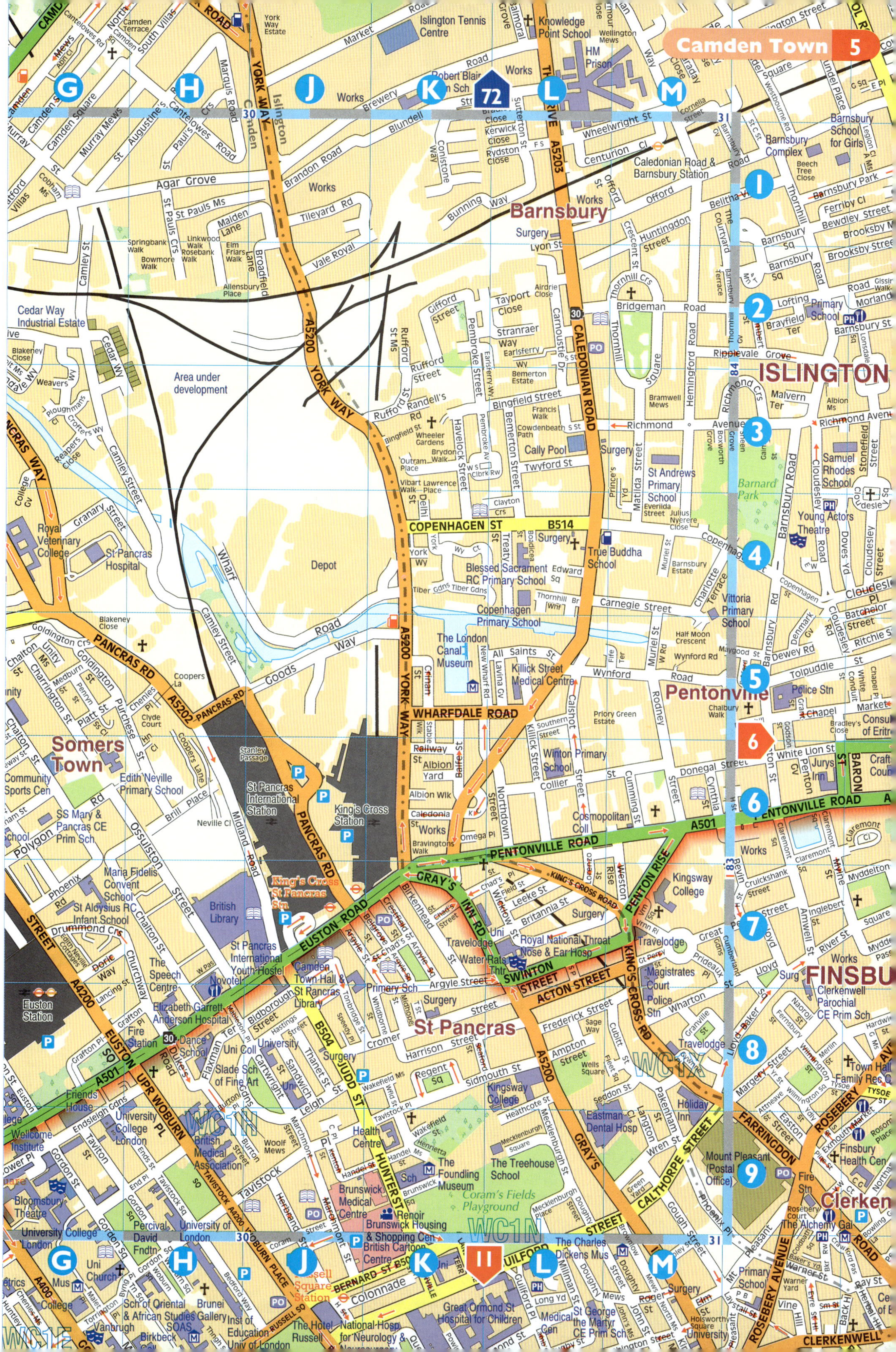
Barnsbury
ISLINGTON
Pentonville
Somers Town
St Pancras
FINSBURY
Clerkenwell
Islington Tennis Centre
Knowledge Point School
HM Prison
Caledonian Road & Barnsbury Station
Barnsbury Complex
Barnsbury School for Girls
Cedar Way Industrial Estate
Area under development
Depot
Royal Veterinary College
St Pancras Hospital
The London Canal Museum
Copenhagen Primary School
Blessed Sacrament RC Primary School
Killick Street Medical Centre
Winton Primary School
St Pancras International Station
King's Cross Station
King's Cross St Pancras Stn
British Library
St Pancras International Youth Hostel
Camden Town Hall & St Pancras Library
Elizabeth Garrett Anderson Hospital
Euston Station
Slade Sch of Fine Art
Wellcome Institute
British Medical Association
University College London
The Foundling Museum
Coram's Fields Playground
Brunswick Medical Centre
Brunswick Housing & Shopping Cen
Great Ormond St Hospital for Children
Kingsway College
Eastman Dental Hosp
Mount Pleasant (Postal Office)
Vittoria Primary School
Samuel Rhodes School
Young Actors Theatre
Barnard Park
St Andrews Primary School
True Buddha School
Maria Fidelis Convent School
Edith Neville Primary School
SS Mary & Pancras CE Prim Sch
The Speech Centre
Bloomsbury Theatre
Clerkenwell Parochial CE Prim Sch
Royal National Throat Nose & Ear Hosp
Magistrates Court
YORK WAY
CALEDONIAN ROAD
PENTONVILLE ROAD
EUSTON ROAD
PANCRAS RD
GRAY'S INN RD
KING'S CROSS RD
COPENHAGEN ST
WHARFDALE ROAD
FARRINGDON
ROSEBERY AVENUE
WC1H
WC1N
WC1X

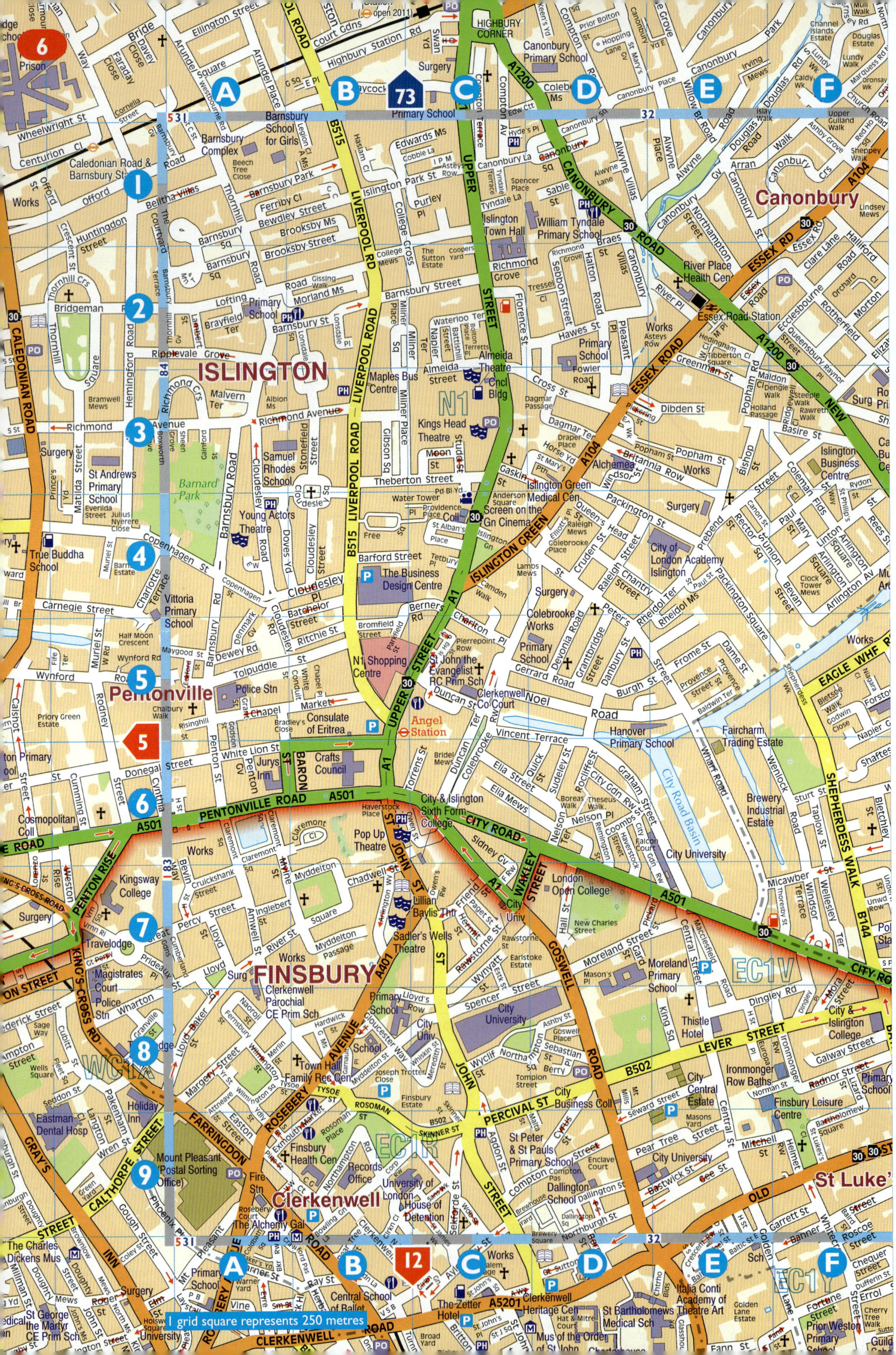
6
73
5
12
A
B
C
D
E
F
1
2
3
4
5
6
7
8
9
ISLINGTON
Pentonville
FINSBURY
Clerkenwell
Canonbury
St Luke's
N1
EC1V
EC1R
WC1X
EC1Y
CALEDONIAN ROAD
LIVERPOOL ROAD
UPPER STREET
ESSEX RD
CANONBURY ROAD
NEW NORTH ROAD
PENTONVILLE ROAD
CITY ROAD
ST JOHN ST
ROSEBERY AVENUE
GOSWELL ROAD
KING'S CROSS RD
FARRINGDON ROAD
CLERKENWELL ROAD
SHEPHERDESS WALK
EAGLE WHF RD
PERCIVAL ST
LEVER STREET
OLD STREET
GRAY'S INN ROAD
ISLINGTON GREEN
HIGHBURY CORNER
Highbury Station Rd
Caledonian Road & Barnsbury Sta
Barnsbury Complex
Barnsbury School for Girls
Islington Town Hall
William Tyndale Primary School
Almeida Theatre
Kings Head Theatre
Samuel Rhodes School
Young Actors Theatre
St Andrews Primary School
True Buddha School
Vittoria Primary School
Barnard Park
Essex Road Station
River Place Health Cen
Islington Green Medical Cen
City of London Academy Islington
N1 Shopping Centre
Angel Station
Crafts Council
Consulate of Eritrea
Police Stn
Hanover Primary School
City Road Basin
Faircharm Trading Estate
Brewery Industrial Estate
City & Islington Sixth Form College
Pop Up Theatre
Sadler's Wells Theatre
Lillian Baylis Thr
City Univ
London Open College
City University
Moreland Primary School
Kingsway College
Travelodge
Magistrates Court
Police Stn
Clerkenwell Parochial CE Prim Sch
Finsbury Health Cen
Mount Pleasant Postal Sorting Office
Eastman Dental Hosp
City Business Coll
St Peter & St Pauls Primary School
Dallington School
Finsbury Leisure Centre
Ironmonger Row Baths
Thistle Hotel
The Charles Dickens Mus
St George the Martyr CE Prim Sch
Central School of Ballet
The Zetter Hotel
Clerkenwell Heritage Cen
Italia Conti Academy of Theatre Art
St Bartholomews Medical Sch
1 grid square represents 250 metres

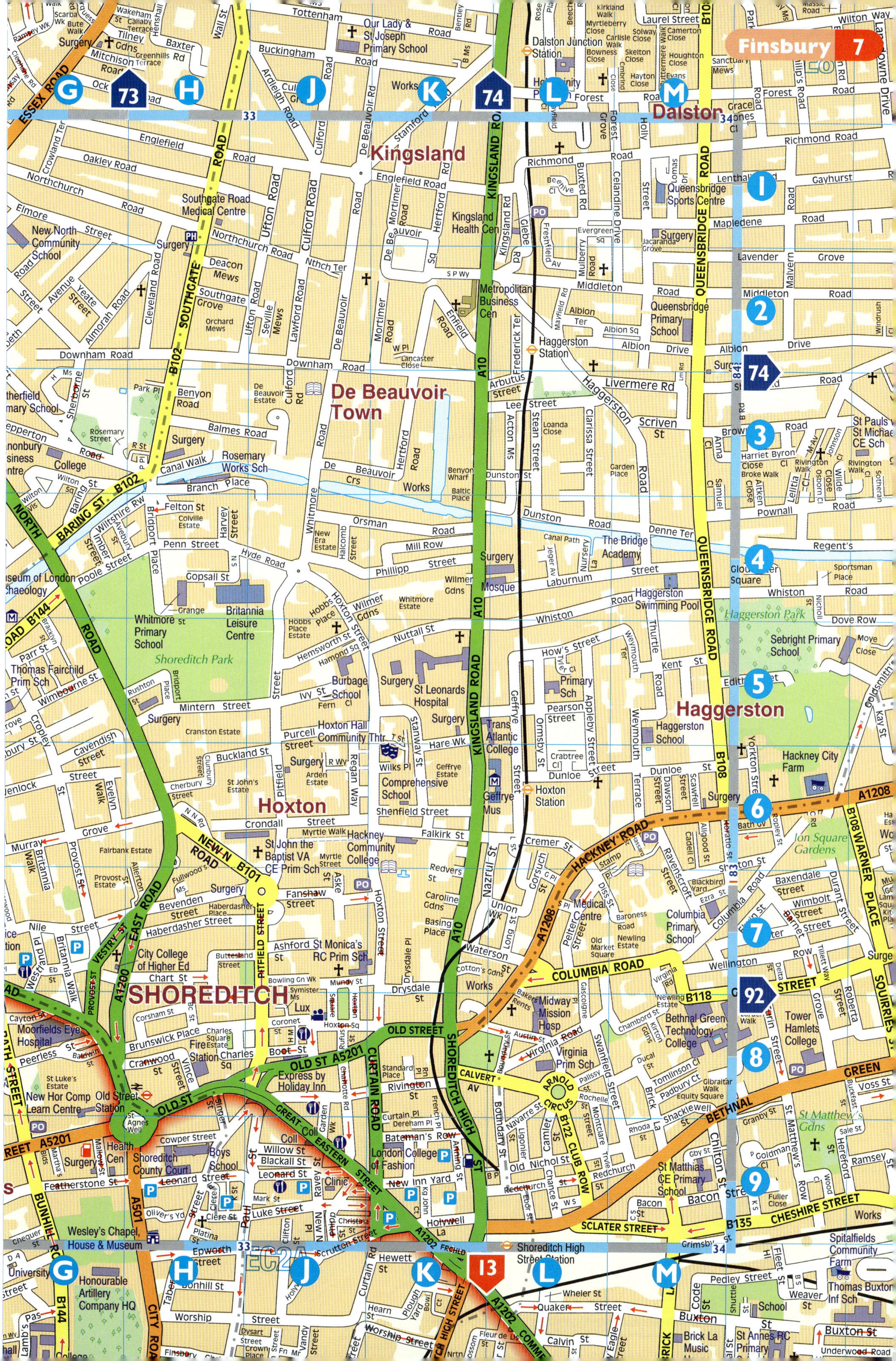
Dalston
Kingsland
De Beauvoir Town
Haggerston
Hoxton
SHOREDITCH
Dalston Junction Station
Haggerston Station
Hoxton Station
Old Street Station
Shoreditch High Street Station
KINGSLAND ROAD
QUEENSBRIDGE ROAD
SOUTHGATE ROAD
NEW NORTH ROAD
EAST ROAD
CITY ROAD
HACKNEY ROAD
COLUMBIA ROAD
OLD STREET
GREAT EASTERN STREET
CURTAIN ROAD
SHOREDITCH HIGH STREET
BETHNAL GREEN
CHESHIRE STREET
SCLATER STREET
CALVERT AV
ARNOLD CIRCUS
BOUNDARY STREET
CLUB ROW
WARNER PLACE
SQUIRRIES STREET
BUNHILL ROW
ESSEX ROAD
BALLS POND ROAD
PITFIELD STREET
A10
A1208
A1200
A5201
A501
A1202
B102
B101
B108
B118
B122
B135
B144
A1208
73
74
92
13
33
34
G
H
J
K
L
M
I
2
3
4
5
6
7
8
9
Englefield Road
Northchurch Road
Downham Road
Balmes Road
Whitmore Road
Hertford Road
De Beauvoir Road
Mortimer Road
Culford Road
Ufton Road
Stamford Road
Richmond Road
Middleton Road
Albion Drive
Livermere Rd
Scriven St
Dunston Road
Laburnum Street
Whiston Road
Hyde Road
Nuttall St
Mintern Street
Falkirk St
Crondall Street
Fanshaw Street
Haberdasher Street
Nile Street
Provost St
Vestry St
Rivington St
Old Nichol St
Redchurch St
Virginia Road
Hackney City Farm
Haggerston Park
Shoreditch Park
Regent's Canal
Queensbridge Sports Centre
Kingsland Health Cen
Metropolitan Business Cen
Britannia Leisure Centre
Haggerston Swimming Pool
Geffrye Mus
Hoxton Hall Community Thtr
St Leonards Hospital
Moorfields Eye Hospital
Wesley's Chapel, House & Museum
Honourable Artillery Company HQ
Bethnal Green Technology College
Tower Hamlets College
London College of Fashion
City College of Higher Ed
Spitalfields Community Farm
Ion Square Gardens
St Matthew's Gdns
Whitmore Primary School
Haggerston School
Columbia Primary School
Virginia Prim Sch
Sebright Primary School
Comprehensive School
Holiday Inn Express
EC2A

8
2
14
88
W9
A
B
C
D
E
F
1
2
3
4
5
6
7
8
9
25
26
Westbourne Green
Bayswater
Kensington Gardens
HARROW ROAD
SHIRLAND ROAD
WESTWAY
A40
A404
A4207
A4206
A402
A4205
A5
B414
B413
B415
B405
B411
B450
CLIFTON GARDENS
WARWICK AV
Warwick Avenue Station
Westbourne Park Station
Royal Oak Station
Bayswater Stn
Queensway Station
Notting Hill Gate Stn
WESTBOURNE PK RD
CHEPSTOW ROAD
WESTBOURNE GROVE
PORCHESTER RD
QUEENSWAY
BISHOP'S BRIDGE ROAD
GLOUCESTER TER
CLEVELAND TER
LEINSTER TER
BAYSWATER ROAD
NOTTING HL GATE
KENSINGTON PARK ROAD
PEMBRIDGE VILLAS
PEMBRIDGE RD
HOLLAND PK AV
KENSINGTON CHURCH
PALACE GDNS TER
CT WESTERN ROAD
PARK ROAD
Westbourne Park Villas
Paddington Community Hospital
Paddington Academy
Paddington Bowling & Sports Club
Westminster Academy
Westbourne Green Sports Complex
Warwick Estate
Little Venice
Canal Cafe Theatre
Fire Station
Grand Union Canal
Council Building
Whiteleys Shopping Centre
Porchester Leisure Cen
Queens Ice Rink & Bowl
Hallfield Estate
Hallfield Clinic
Hallfield Infant School
Emb of Liberia
Emb of Slovak Republic
Emb of Lebanon
Emb of Nepal
Emb of Russian Federation
Emb of Philippines
Emb of Uzbekistan
Emb of Greece
High Comm of Guyana
Kensington Palace State Apartments & Royal Ceremonial Dress Collection
Round Pond
The Broad Walk
Ladbroke Square Gardens
Holland Park School
Kensington & Chelsea College
Police Station
Surgery
Coronet
Gate Thtr
Lancaster Gate
Porchester Gate
Black Lion Gate
Orme Sq Gate
London Toy & Model Mus
Thistle Hotel
1 grid square represents 250 metres

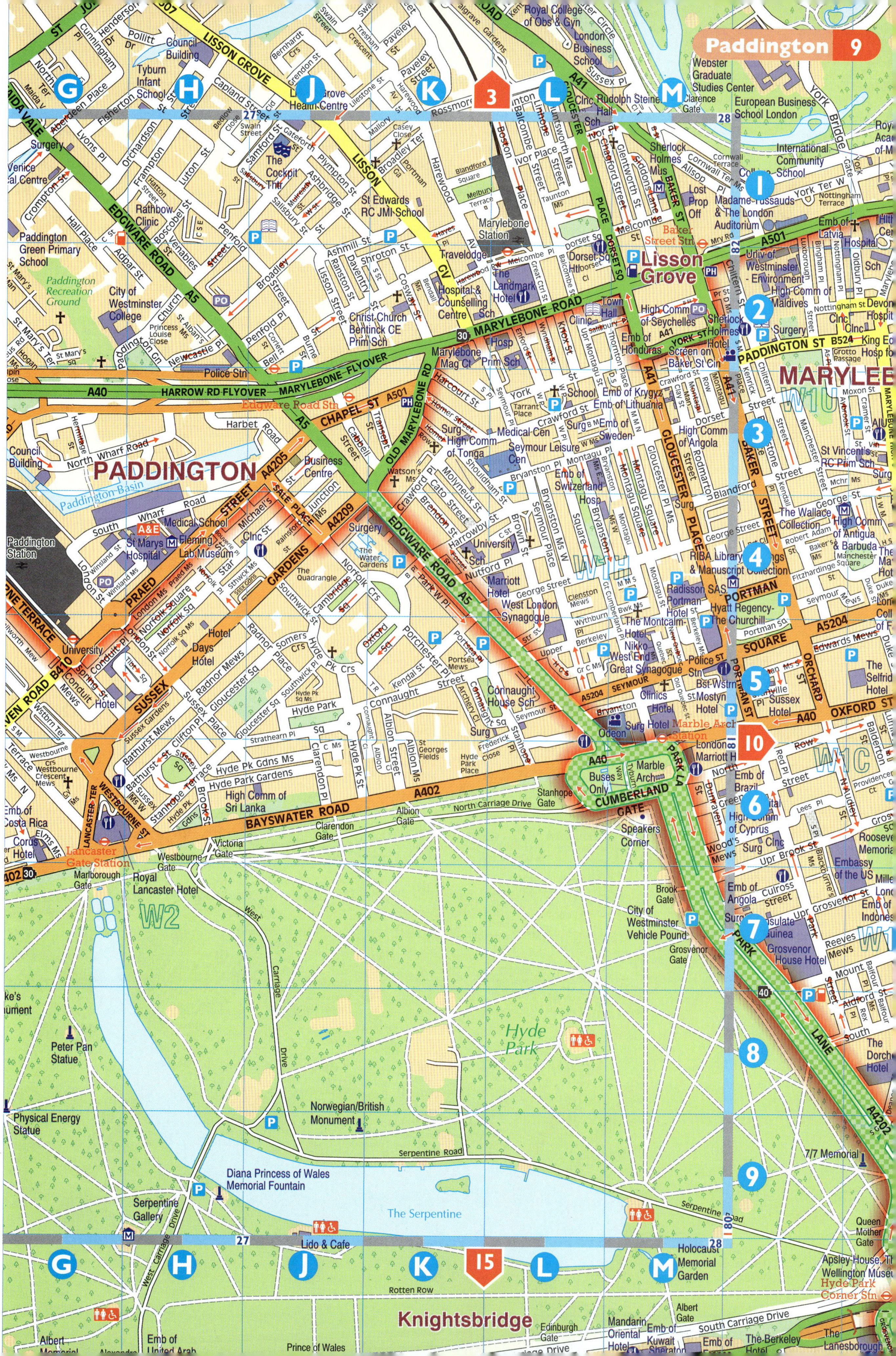
PADDINGTON
Lisson Grove
MARYLEBONE
Knightsbridge
Hyde Park
The Serpentine
Diana Princess of Wales Memorial Fountain
Paddington Basin
Paddington Station
Marylebone Station
Edgware Road Stn
Baker Street Stn
Marble Arch Station
Lancaster Gate Station
Hyde Park Corner Stn
EDGWARE ROAD
MARYLEBONE ROAD
MARYLEBONE FLYOVER
HARROW RD FLYOVER
BAYSWATER ROAD
OXFORD ST
PARK LANE
PRAED ST
SUSSEX GARDENS
LISSON GROVE
BAKER STREET
GLOUCESTER PLACE
PORTMAN SQUARE
CUMBERLAND GATE
SEYMOUR PL
Speakers Corner
Peter Pan Statue
Physical Energy Statue
Norwegian/British Monument
Serpentine Gallery
Lido & Cafe
Serpentine Road
Rotten Row
North Carriage Drive
West Carriage Drive
7/7 Memorial
Holocaust Memorial Garden
Madame Tussauds
The London Auditorium
Sherlock Holmes Mus
St Marys Hospital
Fleming Lab Museum
Royal Lancaster Hotel
City of Westminster College
W2
W1H
W1C
W1U
G
H
J
K
L
M
1
2
3
4
5
6
7
8
9
10
15
27
28

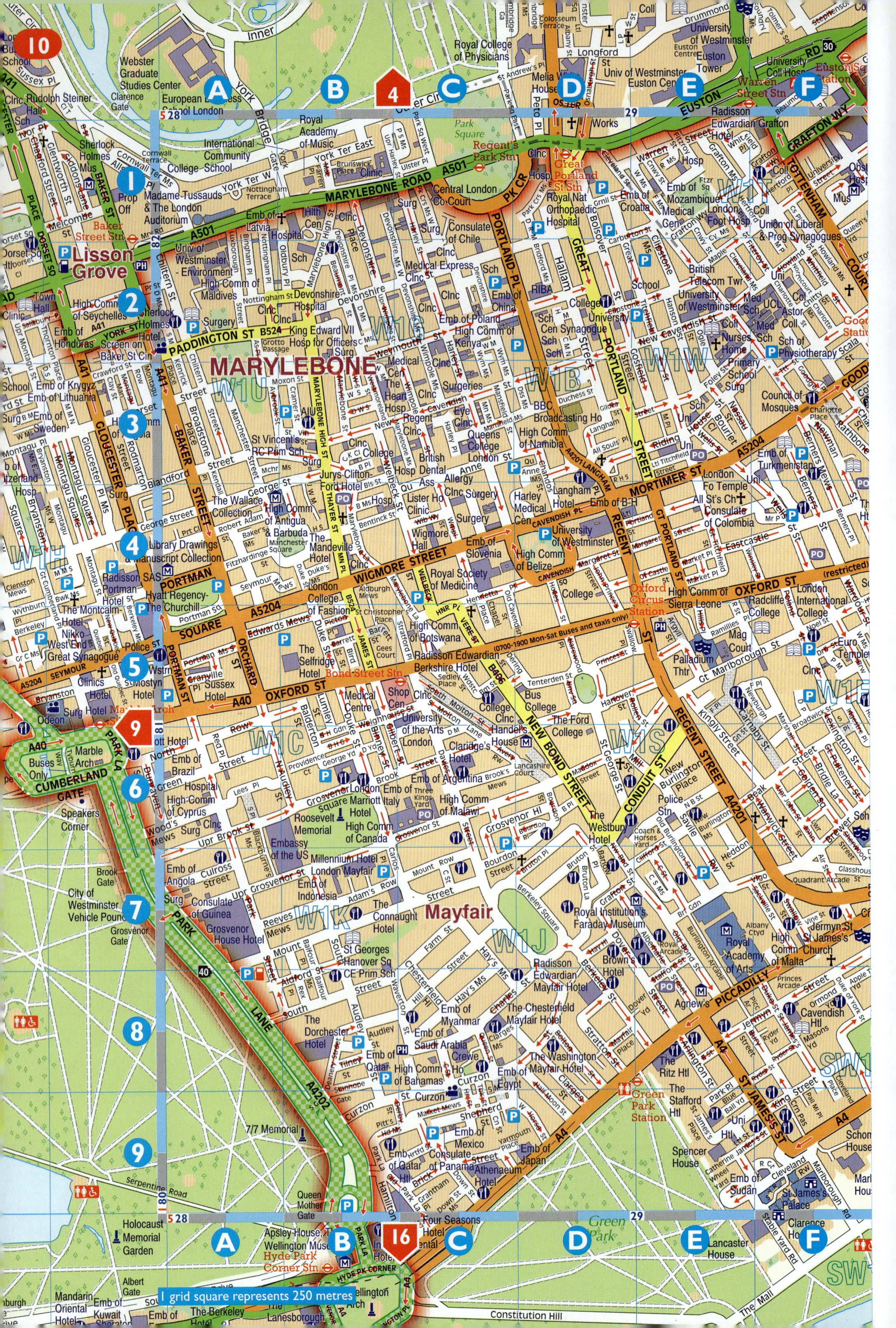

10
4
9
16
A
B
C
D
E
F
1
2
3
4
5
6
7
8
9
MARYLEBONE
Mayfair
Lisson Grove
W1U
W1G
W1B
W1W
W1H
W1C
W1K
W1J
W1S
W1T
W1F
SW1
MARYLEBONE ROAD
A501
EUSTON
GRAFTON WY
TOTTENHAM COURT
PADDINGTON ST
BAKER STREET
GLOUCESTER PLACE
PORTMAN SQUARE
ORCHARD ST
OXFORD ST
WIGMORE STREET
MARYLEBONE HIGH ST
PORTLAND PL
GREAT PORTLAND
REGENT ST
REGENT STREET
NEW BOND STREET
CONDUIT ST
MORTIMER ST
PICCADILLY
PARK LANE
A4202
CUMBERLAND GATE
A40
A4
A5204
A4201
Marble Arch
Baker Street Stn
Regent's Park Stn
Great Portland St Stn
Warren Street Stn
Euston Sq Station
Oxford Circus Station
Bond Street Stn
Green Park Station
Hyde Park Corner Stn
Madame Tussauds & The London Auditorium
Royal Academy of Music
Royal College of Physicians
Univ of Westminster
The Wallace Collection
Royal Society of Medicine
Royal Institution's Faraday Museum
Royal Academy of Arts
The Dorchester Hotel
The Ritz Htl
St James's Palace
Apsley House: The Wellington Museum
Speakers Corner
Serpentine Road
7/7 Memorial
Holocaust Memorial Garden
Green Park
Constitution Hill
The Mall
Lancaster House
Clarence House
Marlborough House
Spencer House
Berkeley Square
Grosvenor House Hotel
Embassy of the US
1 grid square represents 250 metres

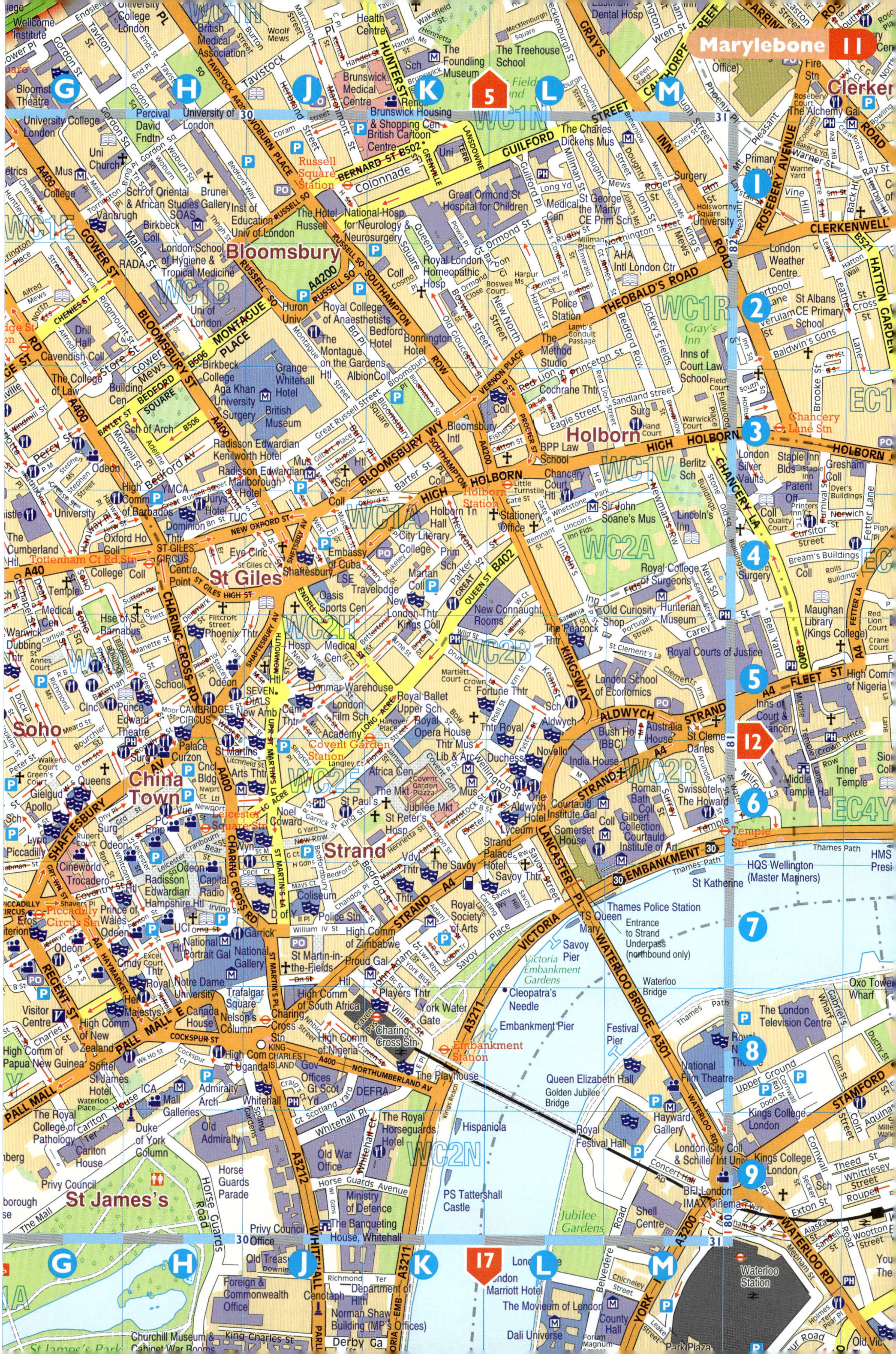
Bloomsbury
Holborn
St Giles
Soho
China Town
Strand
St James's
Covent Garden Station
Russell Square Station
Holborn Station
Chancery Lane Stn
Temple Stn
Embankment Station
Charing Cross Stn
Piccadilly Circus Stn
Tottenham Ct Rd Stn
Leicester Square Stn
Waterloo Station
Piccadilly
Oxford St
New Oxford St
Shaftesbury Av
Charing Cross Rd
Kingsway
Aldwych
Strand
High Holborn
Theobald's Road
Gray's Inn Road
Southampton Row
Bloomsbury Wy
Gower St
Tottenham Court Rd
Regent St
Haymarket
Pall Mall
The Mall
Whitehall
Victoria Embankment
Waterloo Bridge
Waterloo Rd
Stamford St
Fleet St
Clerkenwell Road
Rosebery Avenue
Guilford St
Bernard St
British Museum
Univ of London
Lincoln's Inn
Royal Courts of Justice
Somerset House
National Gallery
National Portrait Gal
Trafalgar Square
Nelson's Column
Royal Festival Hall
Queen Elizabeth Hall
National Film Theatre
Cleopatra's Needle
Embankment Pier
Festival Pier
Savoy Pier
Hispaniola
The Banqueting House, Whitehall
Horse Guards Parade
Old Admiralty
Ministry of Defence
Foreign & Commonwealth Office
Department of Health
Norman Shaw Building (MP's Offices)
Thames Police Station
Thames Path
HQS Wellington (Master Mariners)
The Foundling Museum
The Treehouse School
Great Ormond St Hospital for Children
London School of Economics
King's College London
The London Television Centre
Waterloo Bridge
WC1H
WC1N
WC1E
WC1B
WC1R
WC1V
WC1A
WC2A
WC2H
WC2B
WC2E
WC2R
WC2N
EC1
EC4Y
G
H
J
K
L
M
1
2
3
4
5
6
7
8
9
5
17

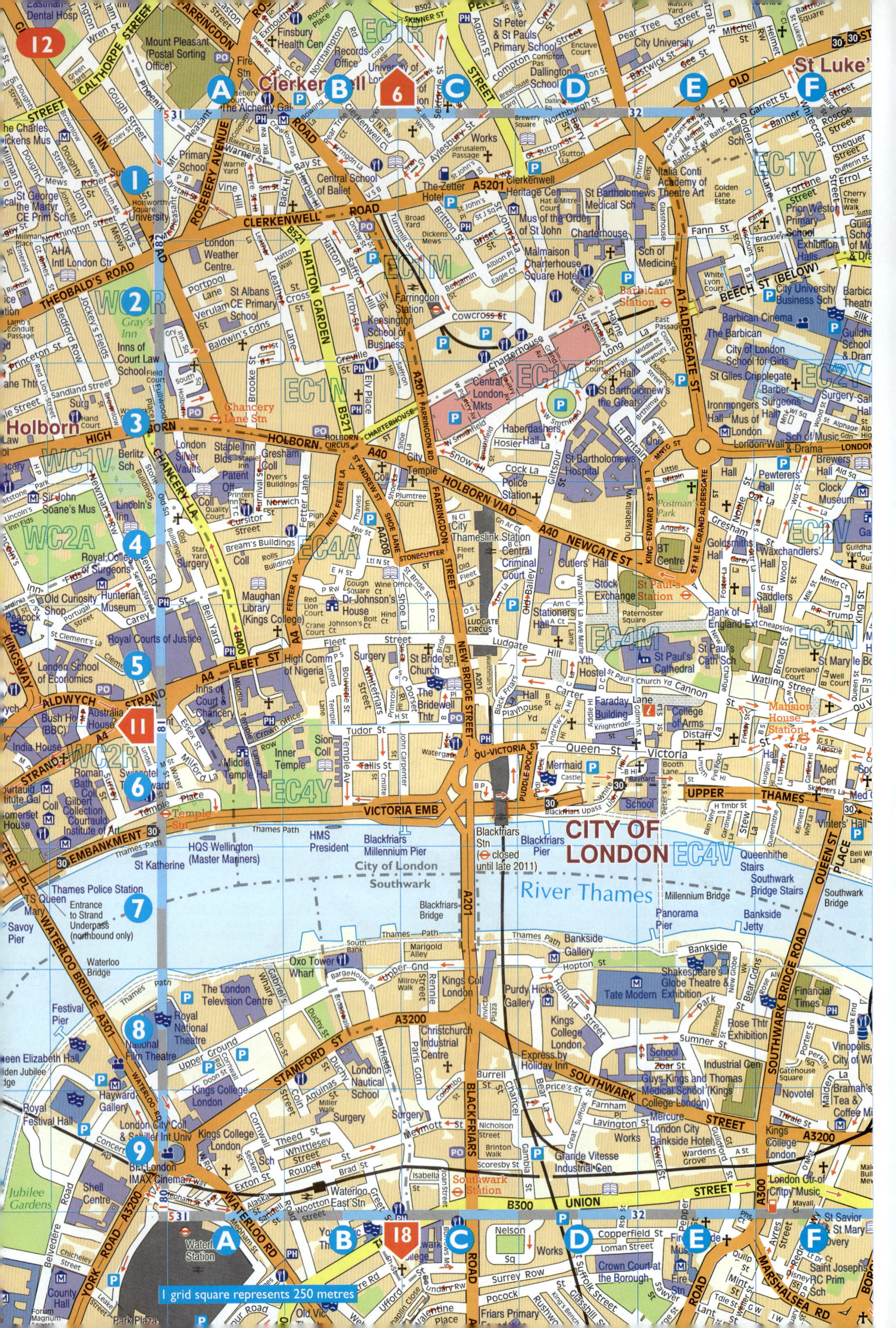
12
6
11
18
Clerkenwell
Holborn
St Luke's
CITY OF LONDON
River Thames
EC1R
EC1M
EC1N
EC1A
EC1Y
EC2Y
EC2V
EC4A
EC4M
EC4N
EC4Y
EC4V
WC1R
WC1V
WC2A
WC2R
Mount Pleasant (Postal Sorting Office)
Finsbury Health Cen
Records Office
Clerkenwell Road
Theobald's Road
Rosebery Avenue
Farringdon Road
Hatton Garden
Holborn Viad
Newgate St
Aldersgate St
Chancery La
Fleet St
Strand
Aldwych
Kingsway
Victoria Emb
Upper Thames St
Queen Victoria St
Cannon St
Southwark Street
Southwark Bridge Road
Stamford St
Waterloo Rd
Waterloo Bridge
Blackfriars Bridge
Blackfriars Rd
Union Street
Farringdon Station
Barbican Station
Chancery Lane Stn
St Paul's Station
Mansion House Station
Temple Stn
Blackfriars Stn (closed until late 2011)
Southwark Station
Waterloo East Stn
Waterloo Station
Gray's Inn
Lincoln's Inn
Sir John Soane's Mus
Royal Courts of Justice
London School of Economics
Bush Ho (BBC)
Australia House
Somerset House
Courtauld Institute of Art
Middle Temple Hall
Inner Temple
Central London Mkts
St Bartholomew's Hospital
The Barbican
Barbican Cinema
Museum of London
St Paul's Cathedral
Stock Exchange
Central Criminal Court
Thameslink Station
HMS President
HQS Wellington (Master Mariners)
Thames Police Station
Blackfriars Millennium Pier
Millennium Bridge
Tate Modern
Shakespeare's Globe Theatre & Exhibition
Royal National Theatre
National Film Theatre
Queen Elizabeth Hall
Royal Festival Hall
Hayward Gallery
BFI London IMAX Cinema
Oxo Tower Wharf
The London Television Centre
Kings College London
Bankside Gallery
Financial Times
Jubilee Gardens
1 grid square represents 250 metres

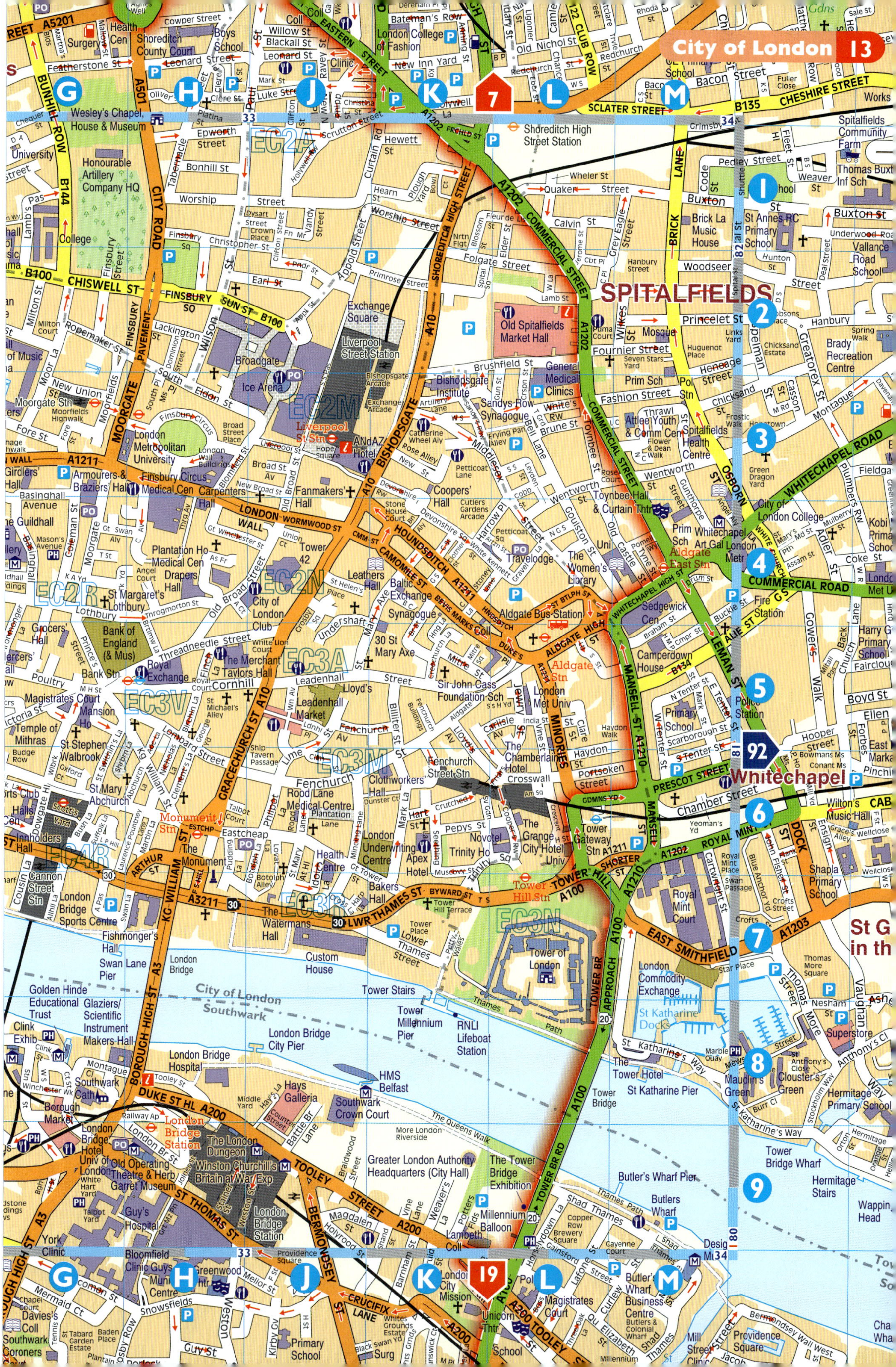
SPITALFIELDS
Whitechapel
EC2A
EC2M
EC2N
EC2R
EC3A
EC3V
EC3M
EC4R
EC3R
EC3N
Shoreditch High Street Station
Old Spitalfields Market Hall
Liverpool Street Station
Exchange Square
Broadgate
Ice Arena
Bank of England (& Mus)
Royal Exchange
Lloyd's
Leadenhall Market
Tower 42
Aldgate Bus Station
Tower of London
Tower Bridge
London Bridge
London Bridge Station
London Bridge City Pier
HMS Belfast
Hays Galleria
Southwark Crown Court
Greater London Authority Headquarters (City Hall)
The Tower Bridge Exhibition
St Katharine Dock
London Commodity Exchange
Tower Millennium Pier
RNLI Lifeboat Station
Custom House
Golden Hinde Educational Trust
Guy's Hospital
The London Dungeon
Winston Churchill's Britain at War Exp
Old Operating Theatre & Herb Garret Museum
Wesley's Chapel, House & Museum
Honourable Artillery Company HQ
London Metropolitan University
Toynbee Hall
Whitechapel Art Gal
Tower Gateway Stn
Tower Hill Stn
Aldgate Stn
Aldgate East Stn
Monument Stn
Cannon Street Stn
Moorgate Stn
Barbican
CITY ROAD
BISHOPSGATE
COMMERCIAL STREET
COMMERCIAL ROAD
WHITECHAPEL ROAD
CHESHIRE STREET
SCLATER STREET
CHISWELL ST
LONDON WALL
HOUNDSDITCH
FENCHURCH ST
CANNON ST
LWR THAMES ST
EAST SMITHFIELD
TOOLEY STREET
BOROUGH HIGH ST
TOWER BRIDGE RD
MINORIES
MANSELL ST
LEMAN ST
PRESCOT STREET
ROYAL MINT ST
GRACECHURCH ST
KING WILLIAM ST
MOORGATE
BUNHILL ROW
BRICK LANE
SHOREDITCH HIGH STREET
THAMES
City of London
Southwark
7
19
92
33
34
81
80
G
H
J
K
L
M
1
2
3
4
5
6
7
8
9

14
8
107
108
A
B
C
D
E
F
1
2
3
4
5
6
7
8
9
Round Pond
Kensington Palace State Apartments & Royal Ceremonial Dress Collection
Emb of Russian Federation
St Mary Abbots Church Hall
Emb of Romania
Emb of Israel
Royal Garden Hotel
Milestone Hotel
Emb of Netherlands
Queens Gate
Royal College of Art
KENSINGTON ROAD
Holland Park
King George VI Youth Hostel
Holland House
Holland Park Theatre
Commonwealth Institute
Leighton House Museum
Queen Elizabeth College
Kensington & Chelsea College
Holland Park School
Emb of Greece
Kensington & Chelsea Town Hall
KENSINGTON HIGH ST
High Street Kensington Stn
Heythrop College
Scarsdale Place Medical Centre
Emb of Armenia
Copthorne Tara Hotel
Thomas London Independent Day Sch
KENSINGTON
W8
SW5
SW7
SW10
Emb of Paraguay
Emb of Bahrain
Emb of Morocco
Emb of Thailand
Superstore
David Lloyd Leisure Centre
CROMWELL ROAD
A4
Gloucester Rd Stn
Millennium Bailey's Htl
The Bentley Kempinski Hotel
South Kensington
The Kensington Clinic
Cromwell Hospital
The Rockwell Hotel
Marriott Hotel
London Academy of Music & Dramatic Art
International Medical Cen
Earl's Court
Earl's Court Station
K+K Hotel George
Twenty Nevern Square Hotel
Earl's Court Exhibition Centre
West Brompton Station
West Brompton
Brompton Medical Centre
Bousfield Primary School
BOLTON GARDENS
The Boltons
REDCLIFFE GARDENS
FINBOROUGH ROAD
OLD BROMPTON ROAD
A3218
A3220
WARWICK ROAD
EARL'S COURT RD
West Kensington Station
Gibbs Green Special School
Avon Trading Estate
Imperial College of Science
Ibis Hotel
Normand Croft Community School
LILLIE ROAD
NORTH END ROAD
FULHAM ROAD
Chelsea & Westminster Hosp
Emb of Guatemala
Brompton Cemetery
Leisure Centre
Farm Lane Trading Est
Key Arts Centre
1 grid square represents 250 metres

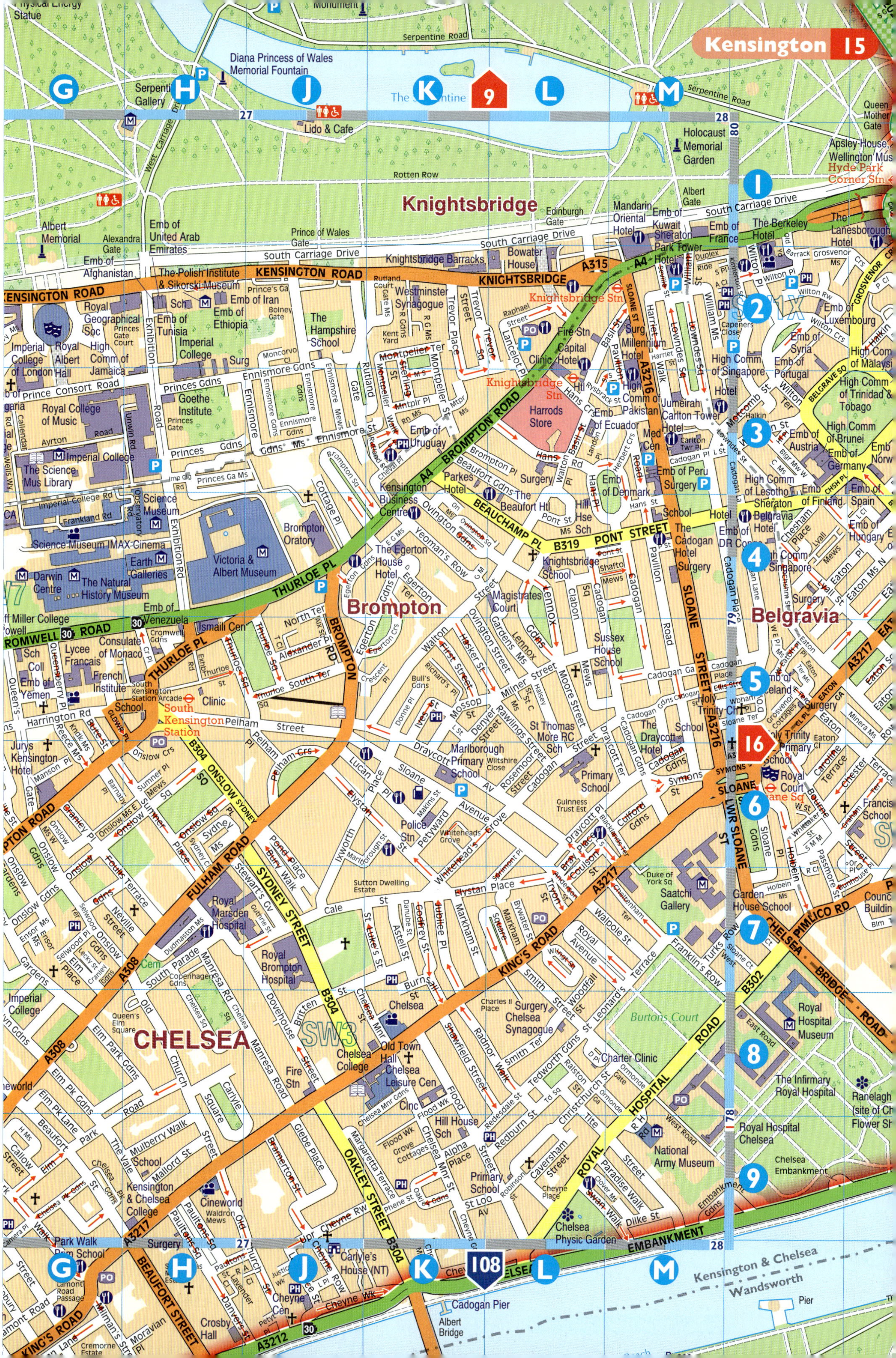
Knightsbridge
Brompton
Belgravia
CHELSEA
SW3
SW1X
Kensington Road
Knightsbridge
Brompton Road
Thurloe Pl
Cromwell Road
Fulham Road
King's Road
Sloane Street
Pont Street
Beauchamp Pl
Sydney Street
Oakley Street
Royal Hospital Road
Chelsea Bridge Road
Pimlico Rd
Embankment
Beaufort Street
Onslow Sq
Sloane Sq
South Carriage Drive
Serpentine Road
Rotten Row
The Serpentine
Diana Princess of Wales Memorial Fountain
Serpentine Gallery
Lido & Cafe
Albert Memorial
Holocaust Memorial Garden
Apsley House, Wellington Mus
Hyde Park Corner Stn
Royal Albert Hall
Imperial College
Royal College of Music
Science Museum
Science Museum IMAX Cinema
The Natural History Museum
Victoria & Albert Museum
Brompton Oratory
Harrods Store
Knightsbridge Stn
South Kensington Station
Sloane Square Stn
Royal Court
Saatchi Gallery
Royal Brompton Hospital
Royal Marsden Hospital
Chelsea College
Chelsea Physic Garden
Burtons Court
Royal Hospital Museum
National Army Museum
Royal Hospital Chelsea
Ranelagh Gardens (site of Chelsea Flower Show)
Cadogan Pier
Albert Bridge
Carlyle's House (NT)
Crosby Hall
Kensington & Chelsea
Wandsworth
A4
A315
A3216
A3217
A308
A3212
B304
B302
B319
16
108

Serpentine Road
7/7 Memorial
Holocaust Memorial Garden
Queen Mother Gate
Apsley House, The Wellington Museum
Hyde Park Corner Stn
Hyde Pk Corner
Wellington Arch
InterContinental Hotel
Four Seasons Hotel
Green Park
Constitution Hill
South Carriage Drive
The Lanesborough Hotel
The Berkeley Hotel
Mandarin Oriental Hotel
Sheraton Park Tower Hotel
Emb of Kuwait
Emb of France
Knightsbridge
Queen Victoria Memorial
Buckingham Palace
Buckingham Palace Gardens
The Queen's Gallery
Birdcage Walk
Wellington Barracks
Lancaster House
Clarence House
St James's Palace
The Mall
European School of Economics
The Halkin Hotel
Emb of Ireland
Grosvenor Place
Emb of Luxembourg
Emb of Syria
Emb of Turkey
High Comm of Malaysia
High Comm of Singapore
Emb of Portugal
High Comm of Trinidad & Tobago
Emb of Cote d'Ivoire
High Comm of Brunei
Emb of Austria
Emb of Germany
Emb of Norway
St Peter's Church
Belgrave Sq
Emb of Ecuador
Emb of Peru
Emb of Denmark
Jumeirah Carlton Tower Hotel
Millennium Hotel
Comm of Pakistan
Emb of Spain
Emb of Finland
Emb of Hungary
Emb of Belgium
Emb of Bolivia
High Comm of Lesotho
Sheraton Belgravia Hotel
Emb of DR Congo
High Comm of Singapore
Pont Street
The Cadogan Hotel
Belgravia
Eaton Square
Eccleston St
Hobart Pl
London Tourist Board
Emb of Albania
Goring Hotel
Victoria Pal Thtr
Apollo Victoria Thtr
Victoria St
Bressenden Pl
The Royal Mews
Buckingham Gate
51 Buckingham Gate (Hotel)
Westminster City Sch
Westminster City Hall
Westminster Cathedral
St Vincent de Paul RC Prim Sch
Choir School
High Comm of Swaziland
Westminster Thtr
Victoria Station
Victoria Bus Stn
Thistle Hotel
Victoria Pl Shop Cen
Victoria Rail/Air Terminal
UK Passport Office
Buckingham Palace Road
Wilton Road
Vauxhall Bridge Road
Victoria Park Plaza Hotel
Italian Hosp
Victoria Medical Cen
Rochester Row
Queen Mother Sports Cen
Warwick Sq
Belgrave Rd
Pimlico
Days Inn
Express by Holiday Inn
Lupus Street
Pimlico Academy
Churchill Gardens Primary School
St Gabriels CE Primary School
Gloucester Street
Inchbald School of Design
Police Station
Victoria Coach Station
Victoria Coach Sta (arrivals)
The Colonnades Shopping Centre
Emb of Iceland
Holy Trinity CE Primary School
Royal Court Thtr
Sloane Sq Stn
Francis Holland School
Sussex House School
Cadogan Gdns
Sloane Street
Lwr Sloane St
The Draycott Hotel
Primary School
Duke of York Sq
Saatchi Gallery
Garden House School
Pimlico Rd
Council Building
St Barnabas CE Prim Sch
Ebury Bridge Road
Ebury Bridge
Abbots Manor Estate
Chelsea Bridge Road
Royal Hospital Museum
The Infirmary Royal Hospital
Ranelagh Gardens (site of Chelsea Flower Show)
Royal Hospital Chelsea
Chelsea Embankment
National Army Museum
Burtons Court
Charter Clinic
Royal Hospital Road
Franklin's Row
Turks Row
Royal Avenue
Chelsea Physic Garden
Embankment
Council Building
The Lister Hospital
Grosvenor Road
Grosvenor Bridge
Chelsea Bridge
Kensington & Chelsea
Wandsworth
Thames Path
Pier
Chelsea Bridge Gate
Queenstown Road
Tideway Industrial Estate
SW1X
SW1W
SW1E
SW1V
SW1
1 grid square represents 250 metres
10
15
109
A B C D E F
1 2 3 4 5 6 7 8 9
528
29

St James's Park
Birdcage Walk
Horse Guards Parade
Whitehall
Parliament St
Victoria Emb
Westminster Pier
Westminster Station
Bridge Street
Westminster Bridge Rd
Big Ben
Westminster Bridge
Palace of Westminster Houses of Parliament
Westminster Abbey
Parliament Sq
Abingdon Street
Victoria Tower Gardens
City of Westminster
Lambeth
London Eye
County Hall
Waterloo Station
Waterloo Rd
York Road
Lambeth Palace Road
Archbishop's Park
Lambeth Palace
Lambeth Bridge
Museum of Garden History
St Thomas Hospital
Florence Nightingale Museum
Westminster Br Rd
Lambeth North Stn
Kennington Road
Imperial War Museum
Horseferry Road
Marsham Street
Millbank
Tate Britain
Millbank Tower
Albert Embankment
Vauxhall Bridge
Vauxhall Bridge Rd
Vauxhall
Vauxhall Station
Kennington Lane
Kennington Oval
Harleyford Rd
Wandsworth Rd
Nine Elms Lane
Parry St
Grosvenor Road
Pimlico Station
Pimlico Gardens
River Thames
Surrey County CC (The Oval)
Oval Station
Kennington
Lambeth High Street
Black Prince Rd
Tyers Street
Durham St
Thames Path
Westminster
SW1P
SE11
WC2N
Westminster Cathedral RC Prim Sch
St James's Park Stn
St George's Sq
Covent Garden Flower Market
New Scotland Yard
Home Office
Department of Trade & Industry
Dept for Transport
Old Admiralty
Foreign & Commonwealth Office
Ministry of Defence
Treasury
18
109
110

18
12
17
110
A
B
C
D
E
F
1
2
3
4
5
6
7
8
9
531
32
Waterloo Station
Jubilee Gardens
Shell Centre
IMAX Cinema
Young Vic Theatre
Old Vic Theatre
THE CUT
UNION
B300
Southwark College
Nelson Sq
Friars Primary Foundation School
Crown Court at the Borough
Fire Brigade Mus
County Hall
Park Plaza County Hall Hotel
Westminster Bridge Park Plaza Hotel
Johanna Primary School
Waterloo Health Centre
Lambeth North Stn
WESTMINSTER BR RD
A3202
LAMBETH
Morley College
Metropolitan Hospital
St George's Cathedral
South Bank University
BOROUGH ROAD
London South Bank University
Eden College
Elephant & Castle Stn
Council Building
Geraldine Mary Harmsworth Park
Imperial War Museum
Newington
IWM Annexe
London College of Communication
Metropolitan Tabernacle
Elephant & Castle Shopping Centre
Elephant & Castle Leisure Cen
Inner London Sessions Ho (Crown Court)
Newington Gardens
SE1
NEW KENT RD
A201
Archbishop's Park
Lambeth Palace
A3203
LAMBETH RD
Walnut Tree Walk Primary School
KENNINGTON ROAD
A23
The Michael Tippett School
London College of FE
Archbishop Sumners CE Prim Sch
SE11
Lillian Baylis School
St Thomas Childrens Day Hospital
KENNINGTON LANE
A3204
NEWINGTON BUTTS
KENNINGTON PARK ROAD
Kennington Station
Lambeth County Court
City & Guilds of London Art School
Keyworth Primary School
Crampton Primary School
Walworth Town Hall
Walworth Museum
The Cumming Museum
Tibetan Buddhist Centre
WALWORTH ROAD
A215
St Pauls CE Primary School
Robert Browning Primary School
Police Stn
Walworth
Oval Business Centre
Westminster Business Square
St Marks CE Prim School
Henry Fawcett Primary School
Surrey County CC (The Oval)
KENNINGTON OVAL
HARLEYFORD RD
DURHAM ST
Archbishop Tenison's School
Oval Ho-Thtr
Aspen House School
John Ruskin Primary School
Kennington Centre
1 grid square represents 250 metres

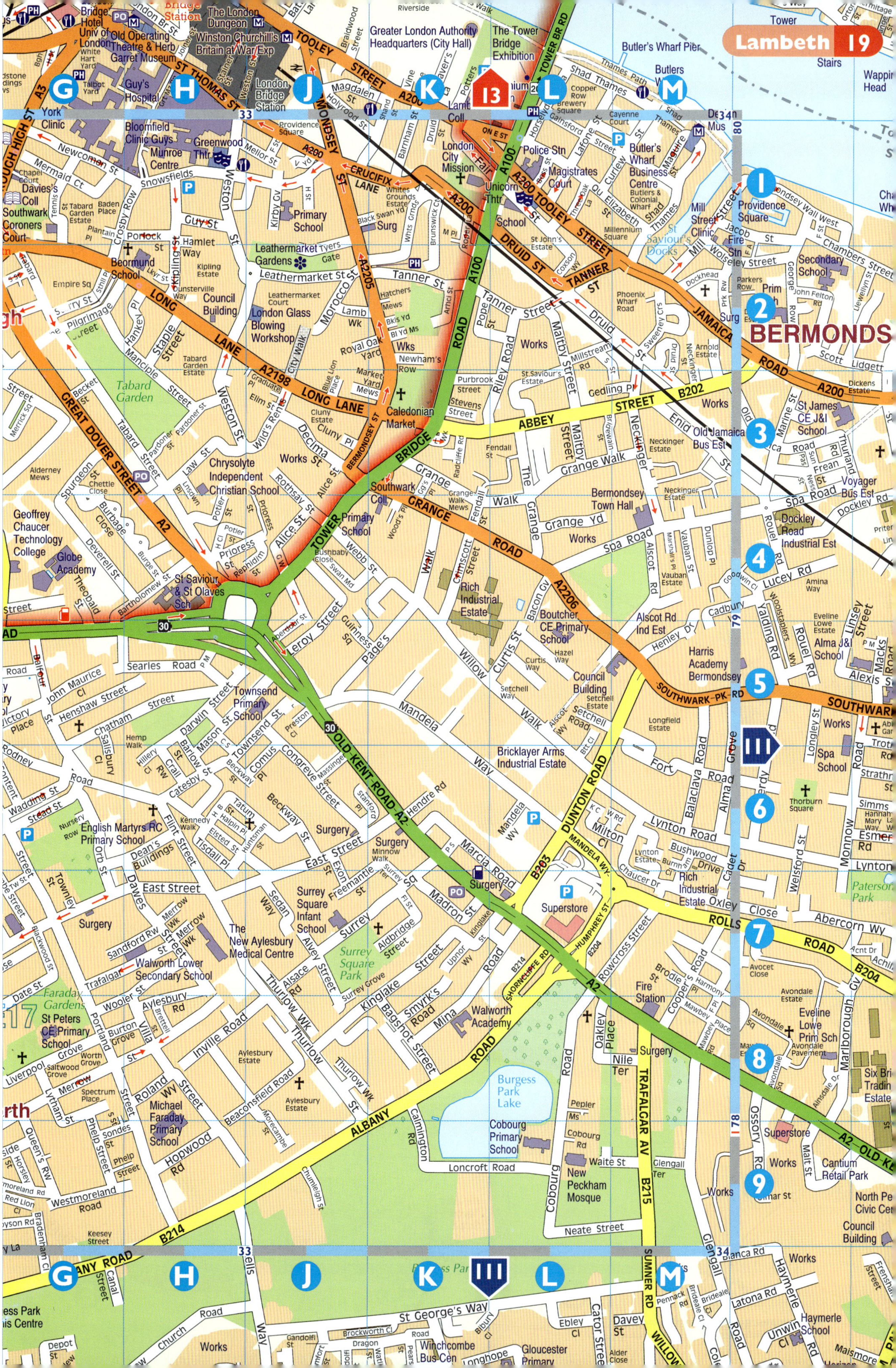
Tooley Street
Greater London Authority Headquarters (City Hall)
The Tower Bridge Exhibition
Tower Bridge Rd
Butler's Wharf Pier
Butlers Wharf
Shad Thames
Guy's Hospital
London Bridge Station
St Thomas St
The London Dungeon
Winston Churchill's Britain at War Exp
Old Operating Theatre & Herb Garret Museum
Univ of London
Bridge Hotel
York Clinic
Bloomfield Clinic Guys
Munroe Centre
Greenwood Thtr
Snowsfields
Weston St
Bermondsey St
Crucifix Lane
Druid St
Tanner St
Police Stn
Magistrates Court
Unicorn Thtr
London City Mission
Butler's Wharf Business Centre
Millennium Square
Providence Square
Jamaica Road
Bermondsey
Leathermarket Gardens
Leathermarket St
London Glass Blowing Workshop
Long Lane
Great Dover Street
Tabard Garden
Beormund School
Council Building
Caledonian Market
Abbey Street
Tower Bridge Road
Grange Road
Grange Walk
Bermondsey Town Hall
Spa Road
Neckinger
Southwark Coll
Chrysolyte Independent Christian School
Geoffrey Chaucer Technology College
Globe Academy
St Saviour & St Olaves Sch
Rich Industrial Estate
Boutcher CE Primary School
Alscot Rd Ind Est
Harris Academy Bermondsey
Southwark Park Rd
Spa School
Dockley Road Industrial Est
Lucey Rd
Old Kent Road A2
Bricklayer Arms Industrial Estate
Mandela Way
Dunton Road
Townsend Primary School
English Martyrs RC Primary School
East Street
Surrey Square Infant School
Surrey Square Park
The New Aylesbury Medical Centre
Walworth Lower Secondary School
Walworth Academy
St Peters CE Primary School
Faraday Gardens
Michael Faraday Primary School
Albany Road
Burgess Park Lake
Cobourg Primary School
Loncroft Road
New Peckham Mosque
Trafalgar Av
Rolls Road
Abercorn Wy
Superstore
Six Bridges Trading Estate
Cantium Retail Park
North Peckham Civic Centre
St George's Way
Camberwell Road
Aylesbury Estate
Westmoreland Road

WATFORD
West Watford
Holywell
Cassiobury Park
Watford Station
Croxley Station
Cassiobury J&I Schools
West Herts College (Watford Campus)
Watford Grammar School for Boys
West Herts Golf Club
Golf Course
Old Merchant Taylors Sports Club
Malvern Way School
Chater Infant School
St Anthonys RC Primary School
Westfield Community Tech College
Laurance Haines School
Holywell School
Merchant Taylors School
Moor Park Industrial Estate
Wolsey Business Park
Byfleet Industrial Estate
Vale Industrial Estate
Industrial Estate
Hampermill Lake
River Colne
Grand Union Canal
Oxhey Hall
WD18
RICKMANSWORTH ROAD A412
WATFORD RD
HEMPSTEAD RD A411
TOLPITS LANE
A4145
HAGDEN LANE
VICARAGE ROAD
Rousebarn Lane
Little Green Lane
Cassiobury Park Avenue
Swiss Avenue
Shepherds Road
Whippendell Road
Sydney Road
Ascot Road
Greenhill Crescent
Caxton Way
Dwight Road
Croxley View
Scammell Way
Charlock Way
Mildred Avenue
Kensington Av
Kings Av
Baldwins Lane
Sycamore Road
Valley Walk
Beechcroft Av
Oakleigh Drive
Gade Avenue
Cassiobury Drive
Parkside Drive
1 grid square represents 500 metres

32

WD24
Watford Junction Station
Colonial Business Park
Holly Industrial Park
Ind Est
Synagogue
Watford United
Bedford Street
ST. ALBANS ROAD
A412
Station Rd
Col Court
The Medical Centre
Health Centre
Police Station
Mag Court
St John's Rd
Woodford Road
Orphanage Rd
Works
Link Rd
Radlett Road
Rhodes Way
A4008
Highwood Primary School
Superstore
Business Centre
Friars Way
Avenue
Scottswood Rd
Park Avenue
Bushey Mill Lane
Hartspring Sports Centre
Surgery
Recreation Ground
River Colne
Ver-Colne Valley Walk
STEPHENSON WAY
Golf Course
Queens School
Metropolitan Bushey
ALDENHAM ROAD
B462
BEECHEN GROVE
Business Cen
Clarendon Rd
Sotheron Rd
Estcourt Road
Gladstone Road
Pal Theatre
Indoor Market
Telephone Exchange
Hotel
The Harlequin Shopping Cen
Primary School
Rec Ground
UPTON RD
Western House Hotel
CASSIO RD
EXCHANGE RD
VICARAGE RD
High Street
Market Street
Surgery
Watford High Street Stn
Mosque
Watford Grammar Sch for Girls
Field Infant Sch
Museum
Waterfields Retail Park
Superstore
WATERFIELDS WAY
A411
Walton Road
Greatham Road Industrial Estate
Bushey Hall Golf Club
Bushey Grove Leis Cen
Longwood School
Hall Road
Water Lane
International University
Royal Connaught Dr
The Avenue
Heathfield Road
Woodlands Road
Belmont Road
Silverdale Rd
Hillside Road
Grange Road
Watford FC & Saracens RFC (Vicarage Road Stadium)
Watford General Hospital
Vicarage Road Cemetery
Field Junior Sch
Theatre
Gazelda Industrial Est
Colne Valley Retail Park
Watford Arches Retail Park
Colne Bridge Retail Park
LWR HIGH ST
DALTON WAY
WIGGENHALL ROAD
Fisher Industrial Estate
Cardiff Road Industrial Estate
Oxhey Park
Bushey Hall Swimming Pool
Falconer Special School
Bushey Manor Junior School
Bushey & Oxhey Infant School
Bushey Hall School
Bushey Mus & Art Gallery
CHALK HILL
LONDON ROAD
Bushey Health Centre
Sacred Heart RC Primary School
Haydon Hill
A4178
DEACONS HILL
A4125
Oxhey
Bushey Station
PINNER ROAD
Works
Riverside Road
Eastbury Road
Cedar Road
Kingsfield Road
Bromet Primary School
Brookside Road
Thorpe Crs
Woodwaye
Nancy Downs
Watford Heath
Oxhey Avenue
Sherwoods Road
Lowson Grove
Elm Avenue
BROOKDENE AVENUE
B4542
Raglan Gardens
Oaklands
Hillcroft Crescent
Highlands
Oxhey Park Golf Centre
The Pathway
Anthony Cl
PRESTWICK
Golf Course
South Oxhey Playing Fields
Oxhey Warren
The Hill
Courtway
Avenue
OXHEY
Watford Heath
Carpenders Park
F
G
H
J
K
I
1
2
3
4
5
6
7
11
12
13
22
33
94
95
96
97

Letc Heat
Patchetts Green
Superstore
CP House Business Centre
Hartspring Sports Centre
Hartspring Industrial Park
HARTSPRING LA
B462
Pegmire Lane
Hilfield Lane
Bushey Mill Lane
Metropolitan Police Bushey Sports Ground
Queens School
ALDENHAM ROAD
Bushey Jewish Cemetery
Little Bushey Lane
Ramada Hotel
Sandy Lane
A41
M1
Hilfield Lane
International University
Finch Lane
Farm Way
Harvest Rd
Cornfield Rd
Girtin Rd
Turner Rd
Mostyn Road
Harcourt Rd
Great Grove
Meadow Road
Bushey Meads School
Meadow Wood School
Rossway Dr
Bournehall J&I School
Bushey Hall Swimming Pool
Falconer Special School
Bushey Hall School
Bushey Mus & Art Gallery
Falconer Rd
Herkomer Rd
Melbourne Road
Clapgate Rd
Herne Road
Little Reddings Primary School
Coldharbour Lane
Cooks Md
Chiltern Avenue
Oundle Avenue
Pentland Rd
The Birches
Kg George Av
HIGH STREET
ROAD
WD23
Bushey Golf & Country Club
Golf Course
Haydon Hill
BUSHEY
Coombe Rd
Richfield Road
Council Building
St Hildas School
Ashfield Junior School
Police Station
Merry Hill Infant School
A411
SPARROWS HERNE
ELSTREE RD
Bushey & District Synagogue
St Margarets School
Merry Hill Road
Merry Hill
Hooper Ms
Wren Crs
Comyns
Rose Lawn
Warren Road
Downalong
Giant Tree Hl
California Lane
HIGH ROAD
Primary School
Rutherford Way
Windmill Street
Windmill Lane
Bushey Heath
Rosary Priory H School
Immanuel College
Caldecote Gdns
Tate Gdns
Allard Crs
Finucane Rise
Gleed Av
Hartsbourne Road
Hartsbourne Primary School
A4140
MAGPIE HALL RD
Abercorn Dell
22
21
34
513
14
15
97
96
95
94
1 grid square represents 500 metres

hmore
F
G
H
J
16
17
18
Aldenham Road
The Orch
Aldenham Preparatory School
Wards Lane
Slades Farm
North Medburn Farm
Butterfly Lane
Elstree Golf & Country Club
Golf Cou
The Haberdashers Askes School
Elstree Aerodrome
Aldenham Road
Watling Street
Tykes Water Lake
Hogg Lane
Dagger Lane
Home Farm
Hilfield Park Reservoir
Aldenham Road
24
Allum
Aldenham Country Park
Allum Cem
Elstree Hill Nth
Dagger Lane
Aldenham Reservoir
Potters Ms
The Bartons
Surgery
Elstree
Lands' End
St Nicholas Cl
St Nicholas School
Roman Rd
New Rd
Synagogue
Watford Road
Schubert Rd
Britten Cl
Rodgers Cl
Delius Cl
Beethoven Rd
Elgar Close
Sullivan Way
Coates Rd
Summer Gv
Fortune La
A411
Hilfield La South
Caldecote Lane
A411 Elstree Road
Elstree Road
A411
Lismarrine Industrial Park
M1
A5183
Elstree Hill South
Centennial Avenue
Caldecote Hill
A409
Paynesfield Rd
Arden Close
Heathbourne Road
A41
Elstree Hl S
Wg Fm Cl
Brockley Hill Farm
Hertfordshire
M1
Junction 4
Royal National Orthopaedic Hospital
Stanmore Common
35
K
Padelford La
Capel Crs
Nutt Gv
A5
A41
Lane
1
2
3
4
5
6
7
94
95
96
97

BOREHAMWOOD
WD6
Elstree
Deacons Hill
Golf Course
Allum Lane Cemetery
Elstree & Borehamwood Station
Boulevard 25 Retail Park
Metropolis Centre
Elstree Studios
Kinetic Business Centre
Harkness Industrial Est
West Herts Business Centre
Manor Place Industrial Estate
Superstore
Borehamwood FC
St Teresa's School
Fairbrook Medical Cen
Council Building
Haberdashers RUFC
Meryfield Primary School
Middle School
Monksmead School
Yavneh College
Summerswood Primary School
Holmshill School
Oaklands College
Innkeeper's Lodge
Thrift Farm Lane
St Nicholas School
Synagogue
Corus Hotel
Bury Farm
Broadfields Primary School
Days Hotel
London Gateway (Scratchwo
SHENLEY ROAD B5378
ALLUM LANE B5378
ELSTREE WY A5135
BARNET LANE A411
ELSTREE HILL SOUTH
M1
A41
Hertfordshire County
Barnet
London Loop
Edgwarebury Lane
23
30
36
A B C D E
1 2 3 4 5 6 7
518 19 20
97 96 95 94
1 grid square represents 500 metres

F
G
H
J
21
22
23
I
2
3
4
5
6
7
97
96
95
94
Fold Farm
BARNET BY-PASS
Grace Cl
Ealing Cl
Studio Wy
Pinewood Cl
Kelly Cl
Mason Cl
Borehamwood Industrial Park
York Crs
30
Elstree Way
ROWLEY LA
ROWLEY LA
Works
Road
Road
Warwick
Holiday Inn
NEWARK GREEN
Newark Gn
Kensington Way
Rowley Lane
Corfe Cl
K Wy
Cft Ct
D Ct
Powys Ct
Kenilworth Primary School
Kenilworth Drive
Buckingham Road
Norfolk Gardens
Buckingham Road
Drive
Tempsford Avenue
Wansford Park
Easton Gdns
Rye Cl
Warren Cl
Howard Drive
Balmoral Drive
Knebworth Pth
Cr Cl
Way
Saffron Green Primary School
70
A1
ROWLEY LANE
Hertfordshire County
Barnet
Paddock Lane
Rowley Green
Golf Course
Laings Sports Ground
Rowley Lane
Arkley Golf Club
Woodlands Farm
Arkley Lane
High
Old Fo
Grimsdyke Crescent
Galley Lane
Wood S
Field End
Oaklands Lane
Stonecroft
Barnet Rd
Vyse Close
Arkley View
Arkley Drive
Barnet Rd
BARNET ROAD
26
Carrington Close
Chartridge Close
Hazel Mead
Garthland Drive
Endersby Road
North Close
Escot Way
Den Close
Raebarn Gardens
West Close
Quinta Drive
Saddlers Cl
Hedgerow La
A411
Rowley Green Road
St Peter's Close
Rycroft Crescent
Hackforth Close
Farm Close
Brett Road
Hill Close
Arkley
Ripon Way
Monkswood Gardens
Ely Gdns
Nicoll Way
Richmond Close
Stangate Crs
Ripon Way
Dacre Gdns
Drive
Clydesdale Cl
Halter Close
Stirling Industrial Cen
Works
Dales Rd
Farriers
Percheron Rd
Shetland Close
Retail Park
Stirling Way
BARNET LANE
Meadowbanks
Kates Cl
Meadowlands
Glebe Lane
Lynford Close
Windmill La
Dingle Close
Barnet Rd
Rockways
Dr
Wylo
Brickfield La
Barnet Gate
A411 BARNET ROAD
Winifred Cl
Chantry Cl
Chantry Close
Barnet Gate Lane
B552
A1
Hyver Hill
Hyver Hall
BARNET WAY
May's Lane
May's Lane
Althorp Cl
London Loop
HENDON WOOD LANE
Hendon Wood La
Service Area
Golf Course
Totteridge Green
A5109
TOTTERIDGE COMMON
K
Totteridge Common
37
Crown Close
Nan Clark's Lane
Mill Hill County High School
Mill Hill
(BARNET

Monken Hadley
High Barnet
Hadley
Chipping Barnet
BARNET
Ducks Island
Underhill
Totteridge
Totteridge Green
EN5
N20
ST ALBANS ROAD
GREAT N RD
A1000
HADLEY GN
HIGH ST
WOOD STREET
A411
BARNET HILL
GT NORTH RD
TOTTERIDGE COMMON
A5109
TOTTERIDGE VILLAGE
Old Fold Manor Golf Club
Monken Hadley CE Primary Sch
St Martha Senior School
Camlet Way
Dury Rd
Hadley Wood
Christ Church CE Primary School
Cemetery
Foulds School
Queen Elizabeths Boys School
The Spires Shopping Centre
St Marthas Jun Sch
Surgery
Works
King George's Field
London Loop
Barnet Trading Estate
Theatre Sch
The Bull Theatre
Police Station
Queen Elizabeth Leisure Centre
Queen Elizabeths Girls School
Barnet Museum
Barnet College
Mag Court
High Barnet Station
Barnet Hospital Chest Clinic
Barnet General Hospital
A&E
Old Court House Rec Gnd
St Catherines RC School
Barnet Health Centre
Odeon
Barnet Hill JMI School
Whitings Hill Primary Sch
Underhill Infant School
Barnet FC (Underhill)
Playing Field
Grasvenor Avenue Infant School
Ravenscroft School
Golf Course
Oaklands Road
White Orchards
The Pastures
Ellern Mede School
South Herts Golf Club
St Andrews CE JMI School
Totteridge Common
Wellhouse Lane
Galley Lane
Mays Lane
Barnet Lane
Dollis Valley Drive
Leeside
Manor Road
Hillside Gardens
Sutton Crescent
Chesterfield Rd
Grange Avenue
Horseshoe Lane
Lime Gv
Northcliffe Dr
Harmsworth Way
Pine Grove
25
38
1 grid square represents 500 metres

EN4
Monken Hadley Common
Enfield
Barnet
Golf Course
Bakers Hill
Hadley Common
East Barnet School
Livingstone Primary School
Westbrook Crescent
Lawton Road
Castlewood Road
Northfield Rd
Linthorpe Road
Grove Road
Games Road
Fairgreen
Cockfosters Road
Cockfosters Sports Ground
Southgate Compton CC
Trent Park Cemetery
Cockfosters Station
Cromer Road Primary School
Potter's Road
Lytton Road
Fordham Road
Park Road
Crescent Road
Victoria Road
Margaret Road
East Barnet Road
A110
Red Rose Trading Estate
County Court
New Barnet Stn
New Barnet
Lyonsdown School
Somerset Road
Richmond Road
Gloucester Road
Greenhill Park
Barnet Synagogue
Eversleigh Road
Longmore Avenue
B193
Brookhill Road
East Barnet Health Cen
Cockfosters
Cat Hill
Museum of Domestic Design & Architecture
Chestnut Grove
East Barnet School
Oakland CP School
Primary School
St Marys CE Primary School
Trent CE Primary School
Pleasant Way
Lyonsdown Road
Lyonsdown Avenue
Meadow Works
Cherry Hill
Great North Road
A1000
Lyttelton Road
Willenhall Avenue
Northumberland Road
Holyrood Road
Calton Road
Netherlands Road
The Hook
Cranbrook Road
Trading Estate
Oakleigh Park Station
East Barnet
Pymmes Brook Trail
Church Hill Primary School
Church Farm Swimming Pool
Friern Mount Drive
Langton Avenue
Temple Avenue
Chandos Avenue
Old Owens Sports Ground
Oakleigh Park North
Oakleigh Park South
Oakleigh Avenue
Downland Close
Works
Great Bushey Drive
Oak Tree Dr
West Hill Way
Totteridge & Whetstone Stn
Whetstone
Oakleigh Road
A109
Oakleigh Park
Sacred Heart RC JMI School
Primary School
Russell Road
Russell Lane
B1453
Barnet College
Haslemere Av
Derwent Av
Church Hill
Parkside Gdns
Woodfield Drive
Health Cen
Surgery
F
G
H
J
K
1
2
3
4
5
6
7
28
39
26
27
28
97
96
95
94

A
B
C
D
E
1
2
3
4
5
6
7
27
40
Middlesex University (Trent Park Campus)
Trent Country Park
Snakes Lane
Golf Course
Trent Park Cemetery
Cockfosters Sports Ground
Southgate Compton CC
Cockfosters Station
COCKFOSTERS ROAD
A111
Trent CE Primary School
Trent Park Golf Club
ENFIELD RD
A110
Oakwood Station
Westpole Avenue
Southgate School
Sussex Way
BRAMLEY ROAD
Oakwood Medical Cen
CAT HILL
Museum of Domestic Design & Architecture
Chicken Shed Theatre
De Bohun Primary School
Salcombe Preparatory School (Infants)
Middlesex University (Cat Hill Campus)
CHASE SIDE
Oakwood
Oakwood Park
Merryhills Drive
Lonsdale Drive
South Lodge Drive
Prince George Avenue
Sheringham Avenue
Merrivale
Cowper Gardens
Fairway
Reservoir Rd
Primary School
Oakwood Park Rd
Fountains Crs
Monkfrith Primary School
Salcombe Prep School (Juniors)
Synagogue
West Grove Prim School
Ivy Road
Sir Thomas Lipton Memorial Hospital
N14
St Andrews CE Primary School
Southgate Leisure Cen
Southgate Stn
Osidge JMI School
OSIDGE LANE
B1453
Barnet College
RUSSELL LANE
Brunswick Park JMI School
Ashmole Centre
Ashmole School
Southgate College
HIGH STREET
THE BOURNE
Queen Elizabeth's Drive
Grovelands Priory Hospital
Bourneside Sports Club
Osidge
Pymmes Brook Trail
1 grid square represents 500 metres

Enfield Town
ENFIELD
World's End
Grange Park
Winchmore Hill
Southgate
Lower Edmonton
SLADES HILL
A110 WINDMILL HILL
CHURCH STREET
CECIL RD
LONDON ROAD
A105 PARK AVENUE
VILLAGE ROAD
RIDGE AVENUE
GREEN LANE
A1005
Enfield Golf Club
Golf Course
Bush Hill Park Golf Club
Grange Park Primary School
Merryhills Primary School
Merryhills Clinic
Chase Side Primary School
Enfield County School
Grammar School (Upper)
Palace Gardens Shopping Centre
Enfield Chase Station
Enfield Town Stn
Grange Park Station
Winchmore Hill Station
Moor Primary School
Highfield Primary School
Winchmore School
Edmonton Lower School
Edmonton Cemetery
Winchmore Hill CC
Enfield CC
St Annes Cath High Sch for Girls
St Georges RC Primary School
North London Nuffield Hospital
St Johns Senior School
Comfort Hotel
Town Park
New River
Chaseville Clinic
Ridge Ho Clinic
Winchmore Hill Clnc
Police Station
Civic Cen
Sports Ground
Preparatory School
N21
Old Park Avenue
Bush Hill
The Grangeway
Green Dragon Lane
Grange Park Avenue
Vicar's Moor Lane
Sherbrook Gardens
Houndsden Road
Eversley Crescent
Chaseville Park Road
Glenbrook S
Uplands Way
Cranleigh Gdns
Vera Avenue
Church Hill
Park View
Broad Walk
Woodcroft
Highfield Rd
Fernleigh Road
Woodberry Av
Lytton Av
Ford's Grove
Firs Park Avenue
Halstead Road
Bury Street
Chase Green Avenue
Culloden Road
Gordon Road
Parsonage Lane
Baker Street
Silver St
Essex Road
Uvedale Road
Walsingham Road
B154
A105
F
G
H
J
K
1
2
3
4
5
6
7
30
41
31
32
33
94
95
96
97

30
Forty Hill
Enfield
EN1
Enfield Playing Fields
Queen Elizabeth Stadium
David Lloyd Sports Centre
Carterhatch Lane
Southbury Road
A110
A10
Great Cambridge Road
Hertford Road
A1010
Ponders End
Bush Hill Park
Bush Hill Park Stn
Southbury Station
Enfield Town Stn
Lincoln Road
Main Av
Village Road
A105 Park Avenue
London Road
Church Street
Nightingale Road
Enfield College
Middlesex University (Enfield Campus)
Martinbridge Industrial Estate
Great Cambridge Industrial Est
Haslemere Business Centre
Northgate Business Centre
Queensway Business Cent
Bush Hill Park Recreation Ground
George Spicer Primary School
Kingsmead School
Suffolks Primary School
Galliard Primary School
Houndsfield Primary School
Edmonton Upper School
Edmonton Lower School
Raglan Junior Sch
Churchfield Primary School
Starksfield Primary School
Salisbury School
Turin Grove School
N9
29
40
42
Edmonton
Edmonton Cemetery
A
B
C
D
E
1
2
3
4
5
6
7
33
34
35
94
95
96
97
1 grid square represents 500 metres

Brimsdown
EN3
Brimsdown Station
Osborne Road
Green Street
Mollison Av
A1055
King George V Reservoir
William Girling Reservoir
Lea Valley Road
A110
Meridian Way
Ponders End Station
Sewardstone Road
A112
Kings Head Hill
Mansfield Hill
Waltham Way
A1037
Lee Valley Campsite
Mill Lane
Leaside Business Centre
Plaza Business Centre
Sovereign Business Centre
Watermill Business Centre
Enterprise Works
Ponders End Industrial Estate
Trafalgar Trading Est
Mill River Trading Estate
Alexandra Business Centre
Valley Link Business Est
Riverside Industrial Est
Redburn Industrial Est
Lee Valley Leisure Complex, Athletics Centre & Golf Club
Lee Valley Camping & Caravan Park
Odeon
Golf Course
Durants Park
Brimsdown Infant School
St Marys RC Primary School
Alma Primary School
Middlesex University
Yardley Primary School
Chingford Foundation School
Chingford RFC
Ridgeway Hotel
Horizon Business Cen
Dominion Business Pk
Pymmes Brook Trail
Lea Valley Walk
River Lea or Lee
Enfield
Essex County
B169
The Ridgeway
43

20
46
A
B
C
D
E
1
2
3
4
5
6
7
508
09
10
94
93
92
91
Northwood Preparatory School
Merchant Taylors School
Sandy Lodge Road
Askew Road
Sandy Lodge Lane
East Drive
The Dell
Sandy Lodge Golf Club
Moor Park Station
Golf Course
PO
Wolsey Road
North Approach
Main Av
Pembroke Road
Main Avenue
Russell Rd
South Approach
Astons Road
Thornhill Rd
Russell
Bedford Rd
Ormonde Rd
Temple Gdns
Moor Park
Anson Walk
Old Gannon Cl
Oxford Cl
Russell Cl
Nevill Cl
Heathside Rd
Heathside Cl
Batchworth Lane
Farm Rd
Ebury Cl
Treetops Cl
St Martins
Grove Farm Park
Hertfordshire County
Hillingdon
Langton Gv
Kewferry Road
Kewferry Drive
Mezen Cl
Grove Road
Moor Park Road
Thirlmere Gdns
Halland Way
Rickmansworth Road A404
Gateway
Holy Trinity School
High Elms Cl
Hill Road
Sherborne
Wildwood
Sunshine House School
Woodridge Way
Sandy Way
Dene Rd
Trinity Cl
London School of Theology
Foxdell
Woodlea Gv
College Way
The Hall School
The Avenue
Cygnet Cl
Langland Cl
Green Lane B469
HA6
Denville Hall
Northgate
Northwood College
Surgery
Police Station
Northwood United Synagogue
Maxwell Road
Lingfield Road
Murray Road
Greenhays Cl
Northbrook Dr
Highfield Road
Northwood Golf Club
Golf Course
NORTHWOOD
Rickmansworth Road
Silverwood Cl
Links Way
Copse Wood Way
Nicholas Way
Rogers Ruff
Broadwalk
Oak Glade
Fringewood Cl
A4180 Ducks Hill Road
Manor House Drive
Teal Drive
Hills Lane
New Farm Lane
Chestnut Av
Haste Hill Golf Club
Northwood Hills
Northwood Cemetery
Northwood FC
Westbury Road
The Roughs
Bishops Avenue
Crofters Road
The Fairway
Bourne End Road
Farm Way
Woodfield Av
Heron Wk
Eastbury Farm JMI School
Eastbury
Ross Wy
Wildacres
Batchworth Lane
Davenham Avenue
Ardross Av
Shelley Close
Holbein Gate
Eastgrade
Eastbury Avenue
St Mary's Avenue
Grosvenor Road
Parkside Road
Altair Way
Avior Dr
Capella Rd
Orion Way
Valency Cl
Canopus Wy
Vega Crs
Apollo Av
Adhara Rd
Sirius Rd
Atria Rd
The Lee
Wellesley Av
Frithwood Avenue
Morgan Cl
Kirby Cl
Kings Dr
Chartwell Rd
Canterbury Cl
Rofant Road
Eastbury Road
Kiln Way
Pines Cl
St Helens School
Carew Rd
Maycock Gv
Frithwood Prim School
Northwood Pinner Liberal Synagogue
Little St Helens School
Madison Bowl
Northwood Stn
Forge Lane
Hallowell Road
Hawes Close
Chester Road
Bennett Cl
Roy Road
Barker Cl
Reginald Road
Watford Road
Brookdene Drive
Elgood Av
Green Lane
Gatehill Rd
Church Rd
Townsend Way
Emmanuel Road
Hillside Infant School
Northwood Way
Hillside
Hillside Rise
Hillside Crescent
Hilliard Road
Addison Way
Acre Way
Northwood Way
Northwood & Pinner Community Hosp
A4125 High Street
A404 Pinner Road
Works
Jasmin Cl
Robina Cl
Windsor
Oakdale Av
Briarwood Drive
Ferndown
Stanley Road
Hampermill
Vivian Close
Sandy Lane A4125
Hayling Rd
Ashburnham Dr
Dumfries Cl
Brampton Rd
Bramshot Way
Oxhey Ri Close
The Woods
Mountview
Ravenswood Pk
Willow End
Woodgate Crs
Gatehill Rd
Wieland Rd
Elgood Av
Gate End
Shefton Ri
1 grid square represents 500 metres

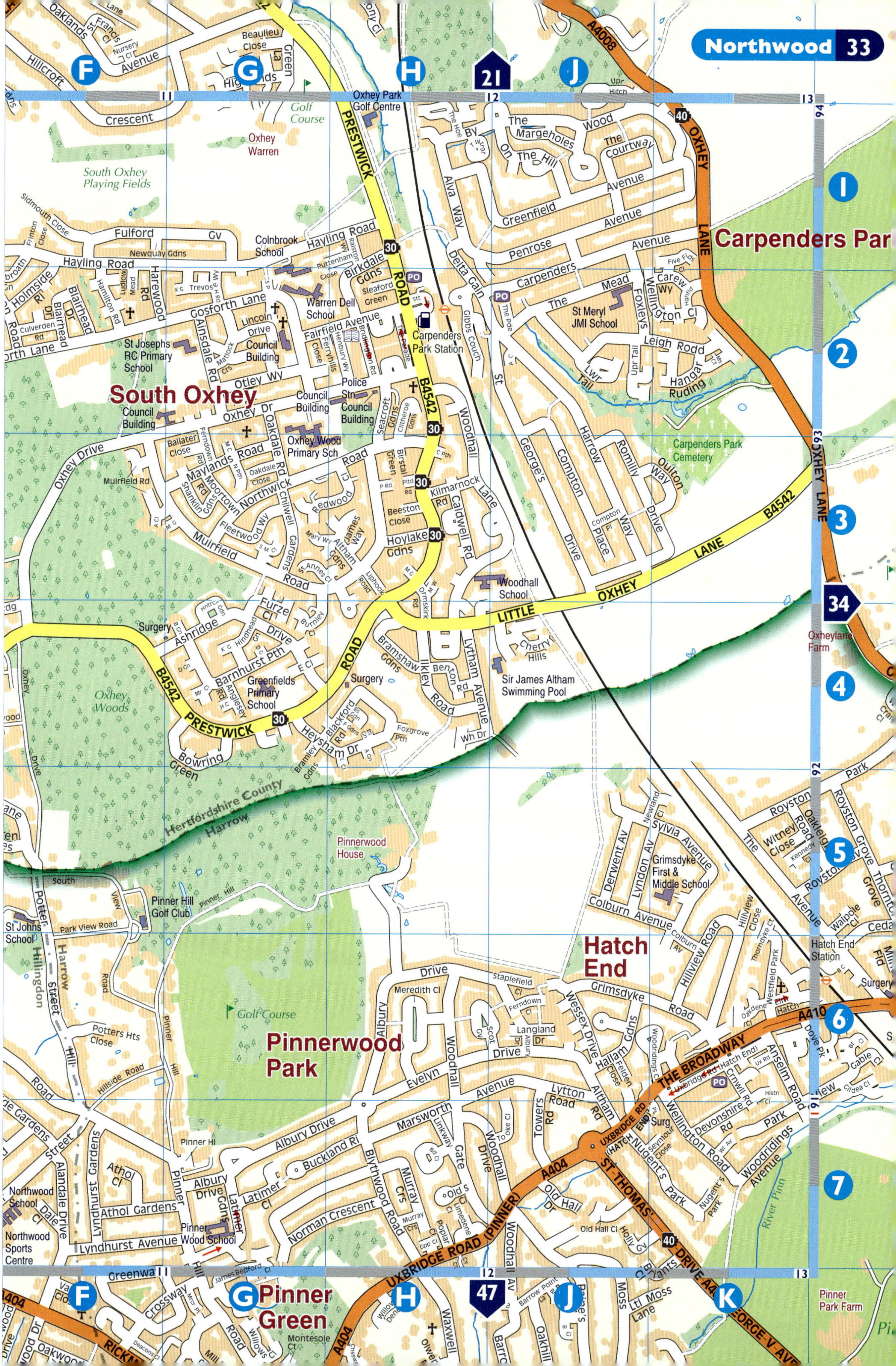
South Oxhey
Carpenders Park
Hatch End
Pinnerwood Park
Pinner Green
South Oxhey Playing Fields
Oxhey Warren
Golf Course
Oxhey Park Golf Centre
Colnbrook School
Warren Dell School
St Josephs RC Primary School
Council Building
Police Stn
Oxhey Wood Primary Sch
Carpenders Park Station
St Meryl JMI School
Carpenders Park Cemetery
Woodhall School
Sir James Altham Swimming Pool
Greenfields Primary School
Surgery
Oxhey Woods
Hertfordshire County
Harrow
Pinnerwood House
Pinner Hill Golf Club
St Johns School
Grimsdyke First & Middle School
Hatch End Station
Oxheylane Farm
Northwood School
Northwood Sports Centre
Pinner Wood School
Pinner Park Farm
River Pinn
Prestwick Road
Little Oxhey Lane
Oxhey Lane
Hayling Road
Oxhey Drive
Uxbridge Road (Pinner)
The Broadway
St Thomas' Drive
Grimsdyke Road
Woodhall Drive
Albury Drive
Fulford Gv
Gosforth Lane
Muirfield Road
Ashridge Drive
Carpenders Avenue
Penrose Avenue
Greenfield Avenue
A4008
A410
A404
B4542

Merry Hill
arpenders Park
Hertfordshire County
Harrow
Harrow Weald Common
Grim's Dyke Hotel
The Kiln
Golf Course
Grims Dyke Golf Club
Oxheylane Farm
OXHEY LANE
A4008
Old Redding
Ass House La
COMMON ROAD
A409
MAGPIE HALL RD
A4140
Westwood School
Hartsbourne Road
Hartsbourne Primary School
Hartsbourne Av
Prowse Avenue
Finucane Rise
Allard Crs
Giant Tree Hi
Downalong
Warren Road
Rose Lawn
Peterborough & St Margaret's School
Clamp Hill
Brookshill Drive
Brookshill Av
BROOKSHILL
Timbers Clinic
Harrow Weald Pk
Harrow College
Harrow Weald Cemetery
Bannister Stadium
Roger Bannister Sports Ground
John Rumney Playing Fields
Birch Pk
Ross Close
UXBRIDGE ROAD (HARROW WEALD)
A410
UXBRIDGE RD (HARROW
Belfield Av
West Drive
Lakeland Cl
Royston Park Road
Royston Grove
Clonard Way
Oakmeade
Hazelcroft
Rowlands
Highbanks Rd
Saddlers Close
Cedar Drive
Pinewood Av
Oxhey La
The Lawns
Furham Field
Sherington Av
Hatch End Station
Surgery
UXBRIDGE RD (HATCH END)
Superstore
Hatch End Swimming Pool
Harrow Arts Centre
Hatch End High School
Tillotson Road
Langton Rd
Woodlands F&M School
Hutton Wk
Mepham Crs
Chicheley Road
Stafford Rd
Cedars Manor School
Boxtree Drive
Belsize Road
Hutton Lane
Colmer Place
Blackwell Cl
Weighton Road
High Road
A409 HIGH ROAD
Harrow Weald
Kynaston Close
Fontwell Cl
Monro Gdns
Lorraine Pk
College Avenue
Medical Centre
Winston Ct
Shaftesbury School
St Teresa RC First & Middle School
Long Elmes
Old Millhillians Sports Ground
Wyevale Garden Centre
Headstone La Station
Headstone Lane
Augustine Road
Courtenay Avenue
Carmelite
Hampden Road
Windsor Road
Elmes
Stanhope
Sefton Av
Pinner Park Farm
Parkfield Aven
Brinsley Road
Toorack Road
Nicola Cl
Salvatorian College
Sacred Heart Language College
Whitefriars Dr
1 grid square represents 500 metres
A B C D E
1 2 3 4 5 6 7
22 33 48
513 14 15
94 93 92 91

Junction 4
Royal National Orthopaedic Hospital
23
Stanmore Common
Bentley Priory
The Common
Warren Lane
Wood Lane
Brightwen Gv
Samuel Close
Capel Crs
Harrow RFC
Brockley Hill
A5
A41
Edgware Way
Barnet
Harrow
Nutt Gv
Cleopatra Close
Julius Caesar Way
Augustus Close
Flora Close
Fauna Close
Priory Drive
Priory Cl
Park La
Springfield Close
Hilltop Wy
Fallowfield
Aylwards Rise
Aylmer Cl
A4140
Stanmore Hill
Pine Cl
Dennis Lane
Eaton Close
Hall Farm Cl
Spring Lake
Old Forge Cl
Heriots Cl
Adelaide Cl
St Johns Church of England Sch
Embry Way
Embry Close
Surgery
Green Lane
Halsbury Cl
Kingsgate Gdns
Rec Gnd
Tennis Club
The Broadway
Dennis Gdns
Valencia Road
Knightsbridge Road
Kerry Av
Glanleam Road
Stanmore Synagogue
London Road
A410
Snaresbrook Dr
Stanmore Station
Westbere Dr
Pangbourne Dr
Merrion Avenue
Craigweil Dr
Sandymount Avenue
Aylward First & Middle Schools
Dalkeith Grove
North London Collegiate School
Bentley Wood Girls School
Flecker Close
Bridges Rd
Masefield Avenue
Chenduit Way
Sitwell Gv
Binyon Crs
Brockhurst Cl
Uxbridge Rd
White Orchards
Dearne Close
Oldfield Close
Winscombe Wy
Holland Wk
Old Lodge Way
Church Road
HA7
STANMORE
Elm Park
Haig Rd
Marsh Lane
Malcolm Ct
Nelson Road
Du Cros Drive
Peters Cl
Wychwood Avenue
Cheyneys Avenue
Howberry Road
Jellicoe Gdns
Conway Close
The Chase
Kenneth Gardens
Robb Rd
Goodhall Close
Trenchard Cl
Temple Md Close
Leavesden Rd
Gordon Av
Georgian Close
Stanmore College
Old Church La
The Ridgeway
Silverston Wy
Lansdowne Road
Barn Crs
Gas Works
Old Church Lane
Rosedale Cl
Wolverton Rd
Stanmore Golf Club
Golf Course
Winston Cl
Woodlands Dr
Chartley Avenue
Cairn Wy
Holme Wy
Kenton Lane
Drummond Dr
Alton Av
Hwy
The Drive
Woodcroft Av
Weald Middle School
Weald Rise
Chestnut Dr
The Avenue
Mountside
Three Mdw Ms
Vernon Drive
St Edmunds Drive
Hermitage Way
Beverley Gardens
Curzon Av
Felbridge Av
College Hill Rd
Connaught Rd
Dryden Rd
Kenton
Adderley Rd
Church Lane
Golf Cl
Abercorn Road
Sports Ground
Whitchurch Middle School
Stanburn First School
Belmont Lane
Wemborough Road
Honister Pl
Honister Close
Honister Gdns
Acorn Close
Coledale Drive
Braithwaite Gardens
St Andrews Park
Bromefield
Bush Gv
Lyon Meade
Bush Grove
Honeypot Lane Centre
Honeypot Lane
B461
Longcrofte Rd
Cornbury Road
Watersfield Wy
Donnefield Avenue
Surgery
Honeypot Business Centre
Wigton Gdns
Dalston Gardens
Honeypot La
Aldridge Av
Bellamy Dr
Weston Dr
Wetheral Dr
Kynance Gdns
Crowshott Av
Lamorna Cl
Ladycroft Walk
Annesmere Gardens
Pearcey Av
Fisher Road
Belmont First School
Belmont
St Josephs RC First & Middle School
York Avenue
Kenton Avenue
Clifton Av
Grange Avenue
Culver Grove
Derwent Crs
Burnell Gardens
Park High School
Broadcroft Avenue
Carisbrooke Close
Fairways
49
36
16
17
18
30
40
F
G
H
J
K
I
2
3
4
5
6
7

36
A
B
C
D
E
24
50
35
1
2
3
4
5
6
7
Farm
Edgwarebury Cemetery
Broadfields Primary School
Days Hotel
Luther Close
Luther
Morley Crescent
Bushfield Crescent
Meadfield
Springwood Crs
Burrell Close
Hartland Close
Hartland
Drive
Franklyn Gardens
Harrowes Meade
Bullescroft Road
Rosh Pinah School
Glengall Rd
Aldridge Avenue
Kenilworth Road
Marlborough Av
Warwick Av
Harcourt Avenue
Fairmead Crescent
Bellamy Close
Edgwarebury Park
Edgwarebury Lane
Parsons Gv
Wolmer Gdns
Blackwell Gdns
Broadfields Avenue
Windsor Av
Lynford Gardens
Parnell Cl
Tashbar of Edgware Prim Sch
Holland House Sch
Surg
Broadhurst Av
Edgware United Synagogue
EDGWARE WAY (WATFORD BY-PASS)
Riverdene
EDGWARE WAY (WATFORD BY-PASS)
HILL
Newlands Close
Grantham Close
Pipers Gn Lane
Hamlyn Close
Brockley Avenue
SPUR ROAD A410
London Academy
Surgery
Lacey Dr
LONDON ROAD
Snaresbrook Dr
Court Dr
Stone Grove
The Spinney
Brockley Cl
Tintagel Drive
Pangbourne Dr
Westbere Dr
Aylward First & Middle Schools
Edgware Reform Synagogue
STONE GROVE
Green Lane
Hillside Gardens
Sterling Avenue
Glendale Avenue
Ranelagh Cl
Ashcombe Gdns
Fairview Wy
Edgwarebury Lane
Mowbray Rd
Hazel Gdns
Hillcrest Avenue
The Grove
Priory Field Drive
Highview Avenue
Highview Gardens
Upcroft Av
Stoneyfields Lane
Edgware
The Drive
The Rise
HA8
Orchard Dr
Surgery
Oakleigh Gdns
Park Grove
Harrods Gn
Savoy Cl
Shelley Cl
Edgware Jewish Primary School
A5100
HALE LANE
Cloister Gdns
Heather Walk
Surgery
Penshurst Gardens
St Margarets Road
Farm Road
Orchard Crs
Stone Grove Park
The Lake
Dalkeith Grove
Queen's Cl
Heronsgate
Masorti Synagogue
STATION ROAD
Brook Av
Lovatt Cl
Meadow Gdns
West Way
Deansbrook Infant School
Hale
DEAN'S LANE
North London Collegiate School
Dukes Av
Powell Close
Canons Drive
The Basin
Yeshurun Synagogue
Edgware Station
Bus Station & Depot
Broadwalk Shopping Centre
Chestnut Av
Cavendish Dr
Sharp Sports Cen
War Mem
Clnc
Edgware Junior School
Parkfield Close
Fairfield Av
Fairfield Crs
Banstock Rd
Dryfield
Walter Walk
Crispin Rd
A5109
Dorset Drive
The Forum
Infant School
Police Stn
Woodstead Gv
Canons Park
Canons Park Station
Boys' Club
Heming Road
Littlefield Rd
Edgware FC & Wealdstone FC
Menorah Grammar School
Langham Gdns
WHITCHURCH LANE
B461
Torbridge Close
Whitchurch Av
Winton Gdns
Chandos Crs
The Drizen Sch
Works
A5109 DEANSBROOK RD
Blood Transfusion Centre
TA Centre
Edgware Community Hospital
Buckingham Gdns
Buckingham Road
Chandos Recreation Ground
Bransgrove Rd
Little Stanmore
Bacon Lane
Northolme Gdns
Oak Lodge Medical Centre
HONEYPOT LANE
Little Stanmore First & Middle School
Honeypot Business Cen
Krishna-Avanti Primary Sch
William Ellis Sports Ground
Broadway Clnc
BURNT OAK BROADWAY
A5
Burnt Oak Station
Watling Medical Centre
Barnfield Primary School
Middlesex School of Comp Medicine
Works
Camrose Avenue
St David's Dr
St Bride's Av
Haverford Wy
Oakleigh Avenue
The Highlands
Market Lane
Back Lane
Canons High School
Whistler Gdns
Mollison Wy
Millfield Road
Raeburn Road
Hogarth Road
Broadcroft Avenue
Wigton Gdns
Dalston Gardens
A41
1 grid square represents 500 metres

Highwood Hill
Mill Hill
NW7
Burnt Oak
TOTTERIDGE COMMON
A5109
HIGHWOOD HILL
MARSH LANE
WATFORD WAY (BARNET BY-PASS) A1
BARNET BY-PASS
DAWS LANE B1461
HALE LANE
A5100
SELVAGE LANE
A41
M1
THE BROADWAY
THE RIDGEWAY
HAMMERS LANE
GREAT NORTH WAY (BARNET BY-PASS)
Junction 2
FIVE WAYS JUNCTION
Mill Hill County High School
Mill Hill Golf Club
Courtland JMI Sch
Fairway Primary School
Northway School
St Marys Abbey
Belmont (Mill Hill Prep School)
St Pauls CE Primary School
St Joseph's RC College
Mill Hill School
St Vincents RC Prim Sc
Rhode Farm Clinic
Goodwyn School
The Homoeopathic Health Cen
Wyevale Garden Centre
Mill Hill Park
St Martins School
Mathilda Marks Kennedy Primary School
Paradise Swimming Pools
Mill Hill Broadway Station
Mill Hill Synagogue
Mill Hill Cemetery
Mill Hill Industrial Estate
Pentavia Retail Park
Copthall School
Dollis Infant School
Barnet Copthall Pool
Golf Course
Barnet Copthall Stadium
The Metro Golf Centre
Hasmonean High School Girls Site
The Annunciation RC Junior School
Granard Business Cen
Woodcroft Primary School
Watling Clinic
Goldbeaters Primary School
Business Training & Solutions
Barnet Coll
Grahame Park J&I School
Grahame Park Health Cen
Hurricane Trading Centre
Police Station
Primary School
Royal Air Force
25
38
51
F
G
H
J
K
1
2
3
4
5
6
7
21
22
23
91
92
93
94

TOTTERIDGE
Ellern Mede School
Chestnut
26
A5109
Totteridge Common
Totteridge Village
TOTTERIDGE VILLAGE
A5109 TOTTERIDGE
Pine
Harmsworth Way
Grove
South Herts Golf Club
The Close
St Andrews CE JMI School
N20
Willow End
Elmstead Cl
Greenway Close
Totteridge CC
Southway
Coppice Walk
Laurel
Lynton
Woodridge Primary School
Southover
Chiddingfold
Arlington
Framfield Cl
Northiam
Shortgate
Michleham Down
Woodside Park
Woodside Park Golf Club
Twinehan Green
The Mill Hill CC
Burtonhole Lane
Golf Course
Hillview Road
Burtonhole Cl
Eleanor Crescent
St Vincents La
St Vincents RC Sch
St Vincents Lane
Rhodes Farm Clinic
37
RIDGEWAY
High St
Hollies End
Vinries
Mount School
Millfield Hill
B552
Partingdale Lane
Reading Way
Charles Sevright Drive
Henry Darlot Dr
Holmes
Peacock Cl
Roberts Road
Lidbury Rd
Price Cl
Kelly Rd
Drew Av
Twinn Rd
Approach La
Lullington
Pycombe Corner
Chanctonbury Way
Rodmell Slope
Cissbury Ring North
Garth
Offham Slope
Wolstonbury
Cissbury Ring South
Singleton Scarp
Argyle
Saddlescombe Wy
Poynings Wy
Steynings Wy
Walmington Fold
Folkington Corner
Cissbury
Linkside
Golf Course
Westlinton Close
Mill Hill Cemetery
Woodcote Avenue
Rushden Gdns
Bittacy Park Av
Bittacy Rise
Bittacy Cl
Curry Rise
Bray Rd
Road
Frith Lane
Chesterfield Road
Westbury
Nethercourt Av
Fursby Avenue
Brookfield Cres
Brookfield Av
Melden Cl
Moreton Close
PO
Salcombe Gdns
Engel Park
BITTACY HILL B552
Bray Wy
Walden
Sanders La
Bittacy
Surgery
Brookfield
Finchley Golf Club
Finchley Lawn Tennis Club
Brent Way
West Avenue
Hamilton Wy
Penstemon Cl
Finchley Wy
The Dr
Surgery
Road
Pursley
Dollis Infant School
Sanders Lane
Grants Cl
Colebrook Close
Shirwell Cl
Mill Hill East Stn
Bittacy Business Centre
Tav Av
Marwood Dr
Bradshaw
Stockford Ave
New Rd
Oakgene Pk
Lansdowne Road
Grosvenor Rd
Eversleigh Road
Elm Park Road
Gordon Road
Nether Street
Nether Cl
Howcroft Crescent
Wentworth
Hendon Golf Club
Barnet Copthall Pool
Golf Course
Ashley Lane
Osborn Gdns
Aberdare Gardens
Devonshire Crs
Devonshire Road
Lee Rd
Vineyard Avenue
Abercorn Road
Frith Court
Mallow Mead
Links Vw
B1462
Sellers Hall Close
Cornwall Av
Falkland Av
The Grove
Oakhampton Rd
Hendon Crematorium
B1462 DOLLIS RD
Thornfield Av
St Marys CE Primary School
Dollis Av
Crescent Rd
NETHER ST
Shopping Precinct
Finchley Central Synagogue
Finchley Central Stn
FIN
N3
Barnet Copthall Stadium
The Metro Golf Centre
Golf Course
Hendon Cemetery
Christ's College Playing Fields
Claremont Pk
Lyndhurst Gardens
Grass Park
Clifton Av
Church Crs
Dollis Pk
Park
Telephone Exchange
Victoria Hall
Victoria Av
County Court
REGENT'S PK RD
Works
Holders Hill
ROAD
Hendon Avenue
Rectory Close
Arcadia Avenue
Station
Lichfield
Chur
WAY (BARNET BY-PASS)
Hilltop
Ashley
52
Turnberry Cl
Linksway
HOLDERS HILL
Cyprus Gardens
St Mary's Av
Cyprus Av
Freston Pk
Works
Rathgar Close
HENDON LANE
GRAVEL HILL
Pardes House & Beis Yaakov Sch
Spencer Cl
Avenue House Museum
Avenue House Grounds
Playing Fields
Manor Av
1 grid square represents 500 metres
A
B
C
D
E
1
2
3
4
5
6
7
523
24
25
94
93
92
91

Oakleigh Park
Whetstone
Totteridge & Whetstone Stn
OAKLEIGH ROAD NORTH
A109
RUSSELL LANE
B1453
Sacred Heart RC JMI Sch
Primary School
Police Stn
Superstore
Queenswell J&I School
Golf Course
North Middlesex Golf Club
FRIERN BARNET
B550
Ravens Lawn Tennis Club
Friary Park
FRIERN BARNET
Finchley Cath High School
North London International School
The North London Hospice
Woodside Park International School
Woodside Park Station
Noam Prim Sch
Woodside Pk Synagogue
Torrington Clnc
Park Health Cen
Archgate Business Cen
Finchley Industrial Cen
N12
Northside Primary School
Grammar School
Finchley Progressive Synagogue
Barnet Coll
Wren Academy
North London Int Sch
St Johns CE Primary School
Friern Barnet School
Colney Hatch
COLNEY HATCH LANE
KINGSWAY
WOODHOUSE ROAD
A1003
North Finchley
Woodhouse College
Superstore
HIGH ROAD
A1000
BALLARDS LANE
A598
West Finchley Stn
Moss Hall Junior School
Finchley Reform Synagogue
Summerside JMI School
The Compton School
Compton Sports Centre
Wingate & Finchley FC
David Lloyd Leisure
Finchley Lido Leisure Centre
Vue Cinema
Finchley Memorial Hospital
Our Lady of Lourdes RC Prim Sch
Victoria Park
N CIRCULAR RD
A406
St Pancras & Islington Cemetery
Islington Crematorium
Greenfields Special School
Coppetts Wood Hospital
Coppetts Wood Primary Sch
Manorside Primary School
Tudor Prim Sch
Coldfall Wood
Surgery
FINCHLEY
27
40
53

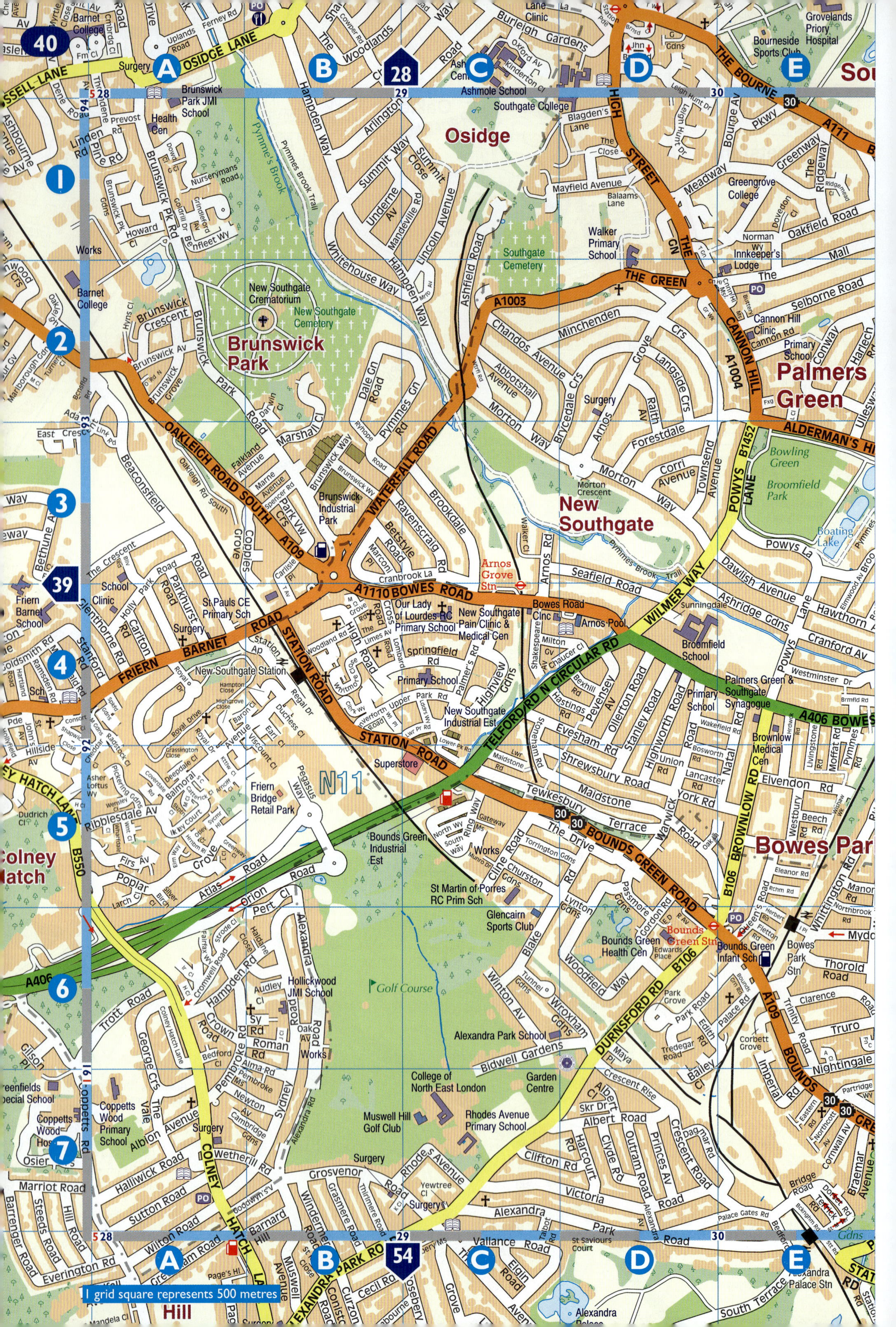

40
28
39
54
A
B
C
D
E
1
2
3
4
5
6
7
Osidge
Osidge Lane
Brunswick Park
New Southgate Crematorium
New Southgate Cemetery
Southgate Cemetery
Southgate College
Ashmole School
Barnet College
Brunswick Park JMI School
Brunswick Industrial Park
Oakleigh Road South
Waterfall Road
A1003
A1110 Bowes Road
Friern Barnet Road
Station Road
New Southgate Station
Arnos Grove Stn
Arnos Pool
New Southgate
Palmers Green
Bowes Park
Bowling Green
Broomfield Park
Boating Lake
Alderman's Hill
The Green
High Street
Cannon Hill
A1004
The Bourne
A111
Grovelands Priory Hospital
Bourneside Sports Club
Walker Primary School
Greengrove College
Wilmer Way
Telford Rd N Circular Rd
A406
Powys Lane
B1452
Brownlow Rd
B106
Bounds Green Road
Bounds Green Stn
Bowes Park Stn
Broomfield School
Palmers Green & Southgate Synagogue
Friern Bridge Retail Park
Superstore
N11
Bounds Green Industrial Est
Golf Course
Muswell Hill Golf Club
College of North East London
Alexandra Park School
Rhodes Avenue Primary School
Hollickwood JMI School
Coppetts Wood Primary School
Colney Hatch
Colney Hatch Lane
B550
Durnsford Rd
Alexandra Palace Stn
1 grid square represents 500 metres

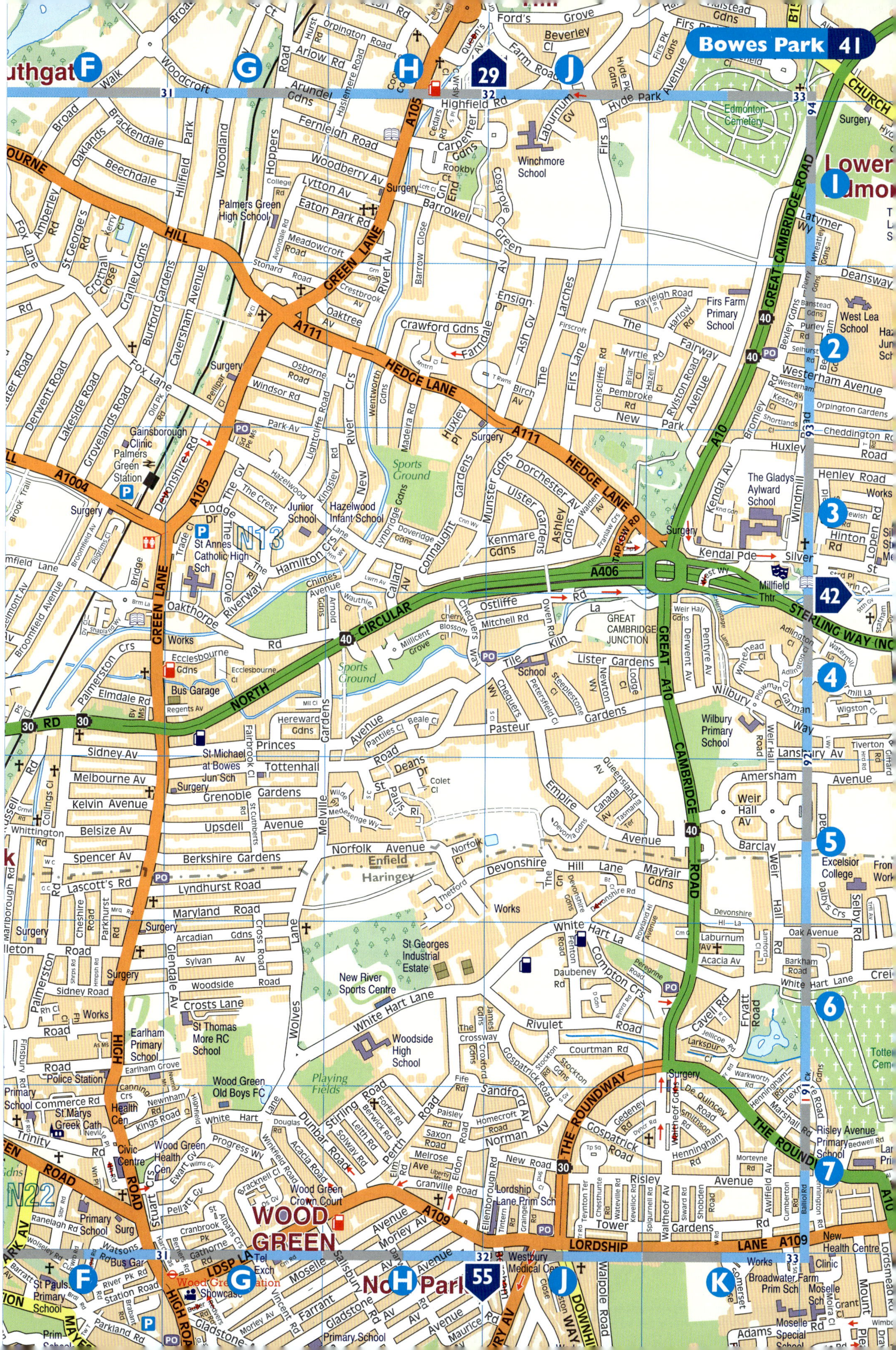

Bowes Park 41
29
42
55
Southgate
Lower Edmonton
Edmonton Cemetery
Winchmore School
Palmers Green High School
Firs Farm Primary School
West Lea School
The Gladys Aylward School
Junior School
Hazelwood Infant School
St Annes Catholic High Sch
Gainsborough Clinic
Palmers Green Station
Sports Ground
Millfield Thtr
GREAT CAMBRIDGE JUNCTION
Wilbury Primary School
St.Michael at Bowes Jun Sch
Excelsior College
Enfield
Haringey
St.Georges Industrial Estate
New River Sports Centre
Woodside High School
Playing Fields
Earlham Primary School
St Thomas More RC School
Wood Green Old Boys FC
Police Station
Commerce Rd
St.Marys Greek Cath
Civic Centre
Wood Green Health Cen
Wood Green Crown Court
WOOD GREEN
Lordship Lane Prim Sch
Risley Avenue Primary School
Broadwater Farm Prim Sch
Moselle Sch
Moselle Special School
Westbury Medical Cen
St Pauls Primary School
Wood Green Station
Showcase
Bus Garage
N13
N22
A105
A111
A406
A10
A1004
A109
GREEN LANE
HEDGE LANE
NORTH CIRCULAR RD
GREAT CAMBRIDGE ROAD
HIGH ROAD
THE ROUNDWAY
LORDSHIP LANE
STERLING WAY
Hyde Park Avenue
Highfield Rd
Fernleigh Road
Woodberry Av
Lytton Av
Eaton Park Rd
Barrowell Green
Crawford Gdns
Farndale
Ensign Dr
Ash Gv
Larches
Firs Lane
Rayleigh Road
Fairway
Westerham Avenue
Orpington Gardens
Cheddington Rd
Huxley Pl
Henley Road
Hinton Rd
Kendal Pde
Silver
Dorchester Av
Ulster Gardens
Kenmare Gdns
Munster Gdns
Connaught Gardens
Lynbridge Gdns
Madeira Rd
Wentworth Gdns
River Av
Osborne Road
Windsor Rd
Park Av
Fox Lane
Caversham Avenue
Burford Gardens
Cranley Gdns
Derwent Road
Lakeside Road
Grovelands Road
Devonshire Rd
Hazelwood Lane
Hamilton Crs
Oakthorpe Rd
Ecclesbourne Gdns
Elmdale Rd
Palmerston Crs
Ostliffe Rd
Mitchell Rd
Lister Gardens
Pasteur Gardens
Wilbury Way
Lansbury Av
Amersham Avenue
Weir Hall Av
Barclay
Sidney Av
Melbourne Av
Kelvin Avenue
Belsize Av
Spencer Av
Lascott's Rd
Princes Av
Tottenhall Rd
Grenoble Gardens
Upsdell Avenue
Berkshire Gardens
Norfolk Avenue
Devonshire Hill Lane
Mayfair Gdns
Lyndhurst Road
Maryland Road
Arcadian Gdns
Sylvan Av
Woodside Road
Crosts Lane
White Hart Lane
Rivulet Road
Courtman Rd
Compton Crs
Daubeney Rd
Laburnum Av
Acacia Av
Oak Avenue
Barkham Road
Cavell Rd
Fryatt Road
Larkspur Cl
Gospatrick Road
Henningham Rd
Waltheof Gdns
De Quincey Road
Sandford Av
Norman Av
Granville Road
Lordship
Tower Gardens
Risley Avenue
Dunbar Road
Stirling Road
Acacia Road
Progress Wy
Pellatt Gv
Catherine Rd
Cranbrook Pk
Moselle Av
Farrant Av
Gladstone Av
Morley Av
Maurice Av
Parkland Rd
Station Road
Bus Garage
Walpole Road
Downhills Way
Adams Rd
Mount Pleasant Rd

42
30
41
56
A
B
C
D
E
1
2
3
4
5
6
7
33
34
35
Lower Edmonton
EDMONTON
Upper Edmonton
N9
N18
N17
Edmonton Cemetery
Church Street
B154
Great Cambridge Road
Starksfield Primary School
Churchfield Primary School
Surgery
Fire Station
Hospital
Latymer All Saints CE Primary School
The Latymer School
Northern Avenue
Deansway
West Lea School
Hazelbury Junior School
Westerham Avenue
Orpington Gardens
Cheddington Rd
Huxley Road
Henley Road
The Gladys Aylward School
Pymmes Park
Silver Street Station
Silver Street Medical Cen
Sterling Way (North Circular)
A406
A&E
North Middlesex Hospital
Sterling Way Clnc
Bridgport Road
Shaftesbury Road
Langhedge Lane Industrial Est
Excelsior College
Frontier Works
Peacock Est
Gibson Business Centre
Peacock Industrial Est
Haringey Sixth Form Centre
White Hart Lane Station
Creighton Road
White Hart Lane
Tottenham Cemetery
Risley Avenue Primary School
Lancasterian Prim Sch
Bruce Castle Park
Bruce Castle Museum
Lordship Lane
Magistrates Court
The Roundway
A10
A109
Health Centre
Clinic
Broadwater Farm Prim Sch
Moselle Sch
Bruce Grove
High Road
A1010
Fore Street
The Broadway
The Green
Edmonton Green Stn
Shopping Cen
Haringey Arts Cncl
Police Stn
Edmonton Leisure Centre
Pymmes Brook Trail
Tottenham Park Cemetery
Fleecefield Primary Sch
Brettenham Prim Sch
Youth Centre
Angel Road Station
Angel Rd
Conduit Lane
Lea Valley Trading Est
Crispin Industrial Cen
The London Make-Up Academy
Superstore
Gas Works
Glover Dr
Leeside Road
Hotspur Industrial Est
Northumberland Park Industrial Est
Leeside Trading Est
Leeside Works
Mowlem Trading Est
Unicorn Works
Northumberland Park Station
Watermead Way
Meridian Way
A1055
Montagu Rd
B137
Tottenham Hotspur FC (White Hart Lane)
The Gibson Business Cen
Wingate Trading Est
Northumberland Park Sch
Lea Valley Primary School
St Pauls & All Hallows CE Jun Sch
The Royal London Est
Lea Trading Est
Triumph Trading Est
Lake Business Cen
Sunrise School
Primary School
Poynton Road
Rosebery Ind Park
Lockwood Reservoir
Eldon Infant School
Eldon Junior School
Phoenix Academy
Enfield FC
Claverings Industrial Est
Pegamoid Road
Second Av Industrial Estate
1 grid square represents 500 metres

Edmonton 43
Golf Course
Horizon Business Cen
Dominion Business Pk
Pickett's Lock
Pymmes Brook Trail
Lock La
Lee Park Way
Lea Valley Walk
Ardra Rd
Works
Nobel Road
River Lea or Lee
Waltham Way
Church Road
Silverthorn Gardens
Lambourne Gdns
Eatons Md
Lawrence Hill
Ridgeway Hotel
B169
Nevin
Peel Cl
Wellington Prim Sch
Walmer Cl
Wellington Av
Heriot Av
Lansdowne Rd
Leadale Avenue
Chingford Avenue
Brindwood Road
Priory Close
Rectory Close
Priory Avenue
Chingford Mount Cemetery
Gunners Gv
Heathcote Gv
Cherrydown Close
Cherrydown Avenue
Middleton Close
Middleton Avenue
Hurst Av
Churchill Terrace
Alpha Road
Salisbury Rd
Mount Av
Templeton Avenue
Medical Centre
Marmion Cl
Marmion Avenue
Brook Crs
Larkswood Primary Sch
New Road
Windsor Rd
Russell Road
A1009 Hall Lane
Hall Lane
A1037
Old Church
A112
Chingford Health Centre
Works
Albert Av
Normanshire Drive
Larkswood Road
Larkswood Playing Fields
Chase Lane Primary School
Surgery
Chingford Industrial Cen
Hampton Rd
Soper Cl
Frankland Road
Kingsley Gdns
Burnham Road
Sinclair Road
Westward Road
Maple Avenue
Ainslie Wood Road
Ainslie Wood Gdns
Underwood Road
Ainslie Wood Primary School
Royston Avenue
Rolls Park Av
Cranston Gdns
Coningsby Gdns
Woodside Gdns
Cooks Ferry Roundabout
A406
Walthamstow Avenue
Hawley Rd
Stonehill Business Park
Stonehill Business Cen
Harbet Rd
Hastingwood Trading Est
Ravenside Retail Park
Works
Lea Valley Trading Estate
Shadbolt Avenue
Lee Valley Watersports Centre
Enfield
Haringey
Banbury Reservoir
Burnside Av
George Rd
Leonard Rd
Frances Rd
Primary School
Superstore
Higham Station Avenue
United Synagogue
Marlborough Road
Nelson Road
Bellamy Rd
Selwyn
Rowden Road
Loxham Rd
Rushcroft Road
Rushcroft School
Selwyn Primary Sch
Higham's Park
Chingford Mount Road
Chingford Road A112
Trinity Way
Avenue Industrial Est
Morrison Av
North Circular
Superstore
Express by Holiday Inn
Empress Av
Grove Pk Av
Crooked Billet Roundabout
Wadham Road
Wadham Av
Folly La
Peacock Cl
Kimberley Industrial Est
Walthamstow Academy
Britannia Sports Ground
B179
Billet Works
William Morris School
Banbury Road
Swift Cl
Cogan Av
Cooper Av
Lawrence Av
McEntee Av
Billet Road
Sinnott Rd
Durban Rd
Stow Crs
Cheney Rw
Cecil Rd
Chapel End Infant School
Knebworth Avenue
Primary School
Lyne Crs
Whittingham Community Primary School
Fair View Cl
Millfield Av
Carlton Road
Douglas Av
Penrhyn Avenue
Junior School
Kitchener Road
Beresford Road
Roberts Road
Wadham Lodge Sports Centre
Brookscroft Road
Brettenham Road
Surgery
Sutton Road
Lee Close
Hecham Cl
Manor Road
Warwick Road
Countess Rd
Worcester Road
Gloucester Road
Mayfield Rd
Clarence Rd
Lancaster Rd
Mount Pleasant Rd
Rodney Pl
Priors Croft
Tennant Ter
Surgery
Lockwood Wy
Higham Hill
Chingford Road
Chapel End Infant School
Sir George Monoux College
Fulbourne Road
Bridge End
Victoria Rd
Works
31
44
57
50

44
43
58
Chingford
Friday Hill
Chingford Hatch
Hale End
Highams Park
Woodford
South
A
B
C
D
E
1
2
3
4
5
6
7
38
39
40
93
92
91
THE RIDGEWAY
KING'S ROAD
WHITEHALL ROAD
A110
LARKSHALL ROAD
B160
B146
FRIDAY HILL
NEW ROAD
HATCH LA
A1009
CHINGFORD LANE
WOODFORD GREEN
HIGH RD A104
A104
A1009
BROADMEAD ROAD
WOODFORD NEW ROAD
A1199
HIGH RD WOODFORD GN
WINCHESTER ROAD
NORTH CIRCULAR
SOUTHEND ROAD (NORTH CIRCULAR)
FULBOURNE ROAD
SOUTHEND ROAD
A406
A503
B169
Mayfield Rd
Elmfield Rd
Endlebury
Simmons Lane
Weale Road
Wittenham Way
Dale View Avenue
Dale View Crs
Gunners Gv
Colvin Gardens
Heathcote Gv
Larkshall Business Centre
Heathcote School
Manor Farm Drive
Normanton Pk
Bernwell Rd
Chingdale Road
Courtland Av
Rosslyn Avenue
Whitehall Lane
Almonds Ave
Bancrofts School
Chiltern Way
Woodside Road
Mornington Road
Montrose Close
High School
St Antonys RC Primary School
Trinity Catholic Lower High School
Golf Course
Woodford Golf Club
Woodford Green Primary School
Larkswood Playing Fields
Jubilee Sports Ground
Ropers Avenue
Castle Avenue
Falmouth Av
Nightingale Av
Forest Glade
Sunnydene Av
Sheredan Rd
Clivedon Rd
Centenary Walk
Henry's Avenue
Beechwood Drive
Charter Road
Nesta Road
Woodford County High School Girls
Woodford Green Prep School
Handsworth Avenue
Handsworth Hlth Clinic
Highams Park Station
Highams Park Primary School
Special School
Brookfield House School
Armstrong Av
Hollywood Way
Oak Hill
Forest Drive
Selwyn Avenue
Cavendish Rd
Selwyn Primary Sch
Rushcroft School
Beech Hall
Malvern Avenue
Hale End Road
St Aubyns School
Empress Av
Fuller's Road
Derby Road
Chelmsford Road
St Alban's Road
Abbotsford Gardens
St Ronans Crescent
Prep Sch
South Woodford Health Cen
Churchfields J&I School
The Synagogue
Winston House
Wadham Road
Chapel End Infant School
Wadham Lodge Sports Centre
Bridge End
Forest View Road
Longacre Road
Trevose Road
Pentire Road
Primary School
Whitefield School & Leisure Centre
Eastwood Rd
George Lane
Grove
Elmhurst Drive
Odeon
Bremer Secondary Sch
Ainslie Wood Primary School
Underwood Road
Surgery
1 grid square represents 500 metres

Buckhurst Hill
Woodford Wells
Woodford Green
Woodford Bridge
Buckhurst Hill Station
Roding Valley Station
Woodford Station
Buckhurst Hill Primary School
Guru Gobind Singh Khalsa College
Holly House Private Hospital
Loyola Preparatory Sch
Lord's Bushes
New Barns Farm
Old Bancroftians FC
West Hatch High School
St Johns RC Special School
Innkeeper's Lodge
Ray Lodge Primary School
Ashton Playing Fields Track
Madeira Grove Clinic
Woodbridge High Sch & Language Coll
Redbridge Drama Centre
Roding Primary School
Glade Primary School
Caterham High School
Wells Primary School
Council Building
Cemetery
Essex County
Redbridge
PALMERSTON RD
RODING LANE
HIGH ROAD
BROADMEAD ROAD
CHIGWELL ROAD
MANOR RD
NORTH CIRCULAR ROAD
Junction 4
M11
A104
A121
A1009
A113
B170
IG9
IG8
59

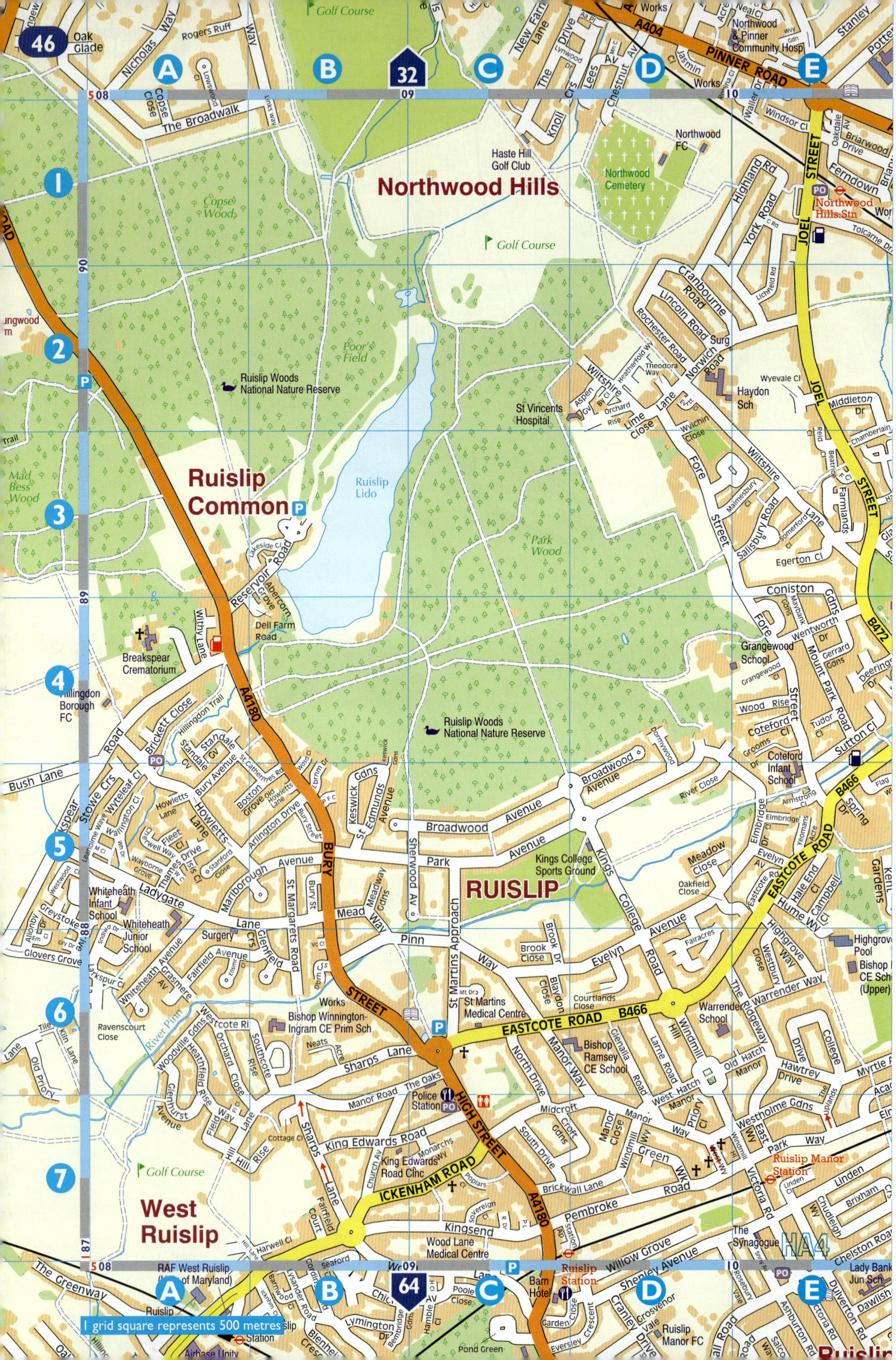
Northwood Hills
Ruislip Common
RUISLIP
West Ruislip
Ruislip Woods National Nature Reserve
Ruislip Lido
Poor's Field
Copse Wood
Mad Bess Wood
Park Wood
Golf Course
Haste Hill Golf Club
Northwood Cemetery
Northwood FC
Northwood Hills Stn
Northwood & Pinner Community Hospl
PINNER ROAD
A404
JOEL STREET
B472
A4180
BURY STREET
HIGH STREET
EASTCOTE ROAD
B466
ICKENHAM ROAD
Broadwood Avenue
Park Avenue
Pinn Way
Ladygate Lane
Kings College Road
Kings College Sports Ground
Reservoir Road
Dell Farm Road
Breakspear Crematorium
Hillingdon Borough FC
Bush Lane
Stowe Crs
Whiteheath Infant School
Whiteheath Junior School
Glovers Grove
St Martins Approach
St Martins Medical Centre
Bishop Winnington-Ingram CE Prim Sch
Bishop Ramsey CE School
Warrender School
Grangewood School
Coteford Infant School
Haydon Sch
St Vincents Hospital
Police Station
King Edwards Road Clinc
Wood Lane Medical Centre
Ruislip Station
Ruislip Manor Station
Ruislip Manor FC
RAF West Ruislip
Barn Hotel
Pembroke Road
Kingsend
Sharps Lane
Manor Road
Willow Grove
Shenley Avenue
Victoria Rd
The Synagogue
HA4
Highgrove Pool
Lady Bank Jun Sch
Golf Course
Ravenscourt Close
River Pinn
Cranbourne Road
Lincoln Road
Rochester Road
Wiltshire Lane
Fore Street
Mount Park Road
Coniston Gdns
Egerton Cl
Middleton Dr
Farmlands
Windsor Cl
Ferndown
Tolcarne Dr
Highland Rd
York Road
The Broadwalk
Rogers Ruff
Nicholas Way
Oak Glade
1 grid square represents 500 metres
32
64

Pinner Green
Pinner
Eastcote Village
Eastcote
North Harrow
Rayners Lane
HA5
Pinner Station
Eastcote Station
Rayners Lane Station
Pinner Park Farm
Pinner New Cemetery
Cemetery
RICKMANSWORTH ROAD
UXBRIDGE ROAD
A404
PINNER GREEN
CUCKOO HILL
B466
EASTCOTE ROAD
HIGH ROAD
GEORGE V AVENUE
A404 GEORGE V AVENUE
ST THOMAS' DRIVE
Northwood School
Northwood Sports Centre
Harlyn School
West Lodge Middle School
Innellan Ho Sch
Mayfield Sch
MS Business Centre
Pinner & District Synagogue
Cecil Park Clinic
Pinner Medical Centre
Reddiford School
Tudor Lodge Hotel
Eastcote Health Centre
Cannon Lane First School
Heathfield School
Eastcote Industrial Estate
Canada Ho Business Cen
Newnham Junior School
Moriah Jewish Day School
Longfield Primary School
Buckingham College Prep School
Regent College London
Harrow Town CC
Eastcote CC
Newton Farm First & Middle School
Roxbourne First School
Harrow
Hillingdon
The Roxbourne
33
48
65
30
40
F
G
H
I
J
K
1
2
3
4
5
6
7
11
12
13
87
88
89
90

48
34
47
66
A
B
C
D
E
1
2
3
4
5
6
7
513
14
15
90
89
88
87
Wyevale Garden Centre
Middle School
Pinner Park Farm
Pinner Park
George V Avenue
Pinner Pk Av
Parkfield Avenue
Surgery
Barrett Way Industrial Est
Waverley Industrial Est
Whitefriars Trading Estate
Tudor Enterprise Park
Salvatorian College
Sacred Heart Language College
Whitefriars F&M Sch
Medical Centre
High Road A409
High St
Police Stn
Pinner Park Primary School
Holmwood Close
Harrow Heritage Museum
Headstone Manor Recreation Ground
Headstone
Pinner New Cemetery
Nower Hill High School
Harrow Crown Courts
Headstone Drive
Harrow & Wealdstone Station
Caryl Thomas Clnc
Civic Centre
Marlborough First & Middle School
Civic Medical Cen
St John Fisher RC First & Middle Sch
Kingsfield Avenue
Old Lyonian Sports Ground
Pinner View Medical Centre
Alpha Prep School
Alpha Preparatory School
Norbury First & Middle School
North Harrow Station
St Andrews School
Pinner Road
A404
Harrow Cemetery
HARROW
Quality Hotel
St Georges Shopping Centre
Crescent Hotel
A4005
Greenhill
St Ann's Shopping Cen
Vue Cinema
College Road
Harrow-on-the-Hill Station
West Harrow Station
Vaughan First & Middle School
The Harold Macmillan Medical Cen
Middlesex New Synagogue
Harrow College
Bus Village
Grove Fields
St Anselms RC Primary School
Harrow School
Longfield Primary School
Imperial Drive
A4090
West Harrow Recreation Ground
West Harrow
Whitmore High School
Whitmore Road
Shaftesbury Avenue
Marshall Medical Cen
Bessborough Road
A312
Lower Road
John Lyon School
Rayners Lane Station
Harrow Town CC
Grange First School
Shaftesbury Medical Centre
HA2
Roxeth
Roxeth Hill
Council Building
Police Stn
First & Middle School
Bowden House
Newton Farm First & Middle School
Archdale Business
Lowlands Road
High Street
B458
Harrow the Hill
North Harrow
1 grid square represents 500 metres

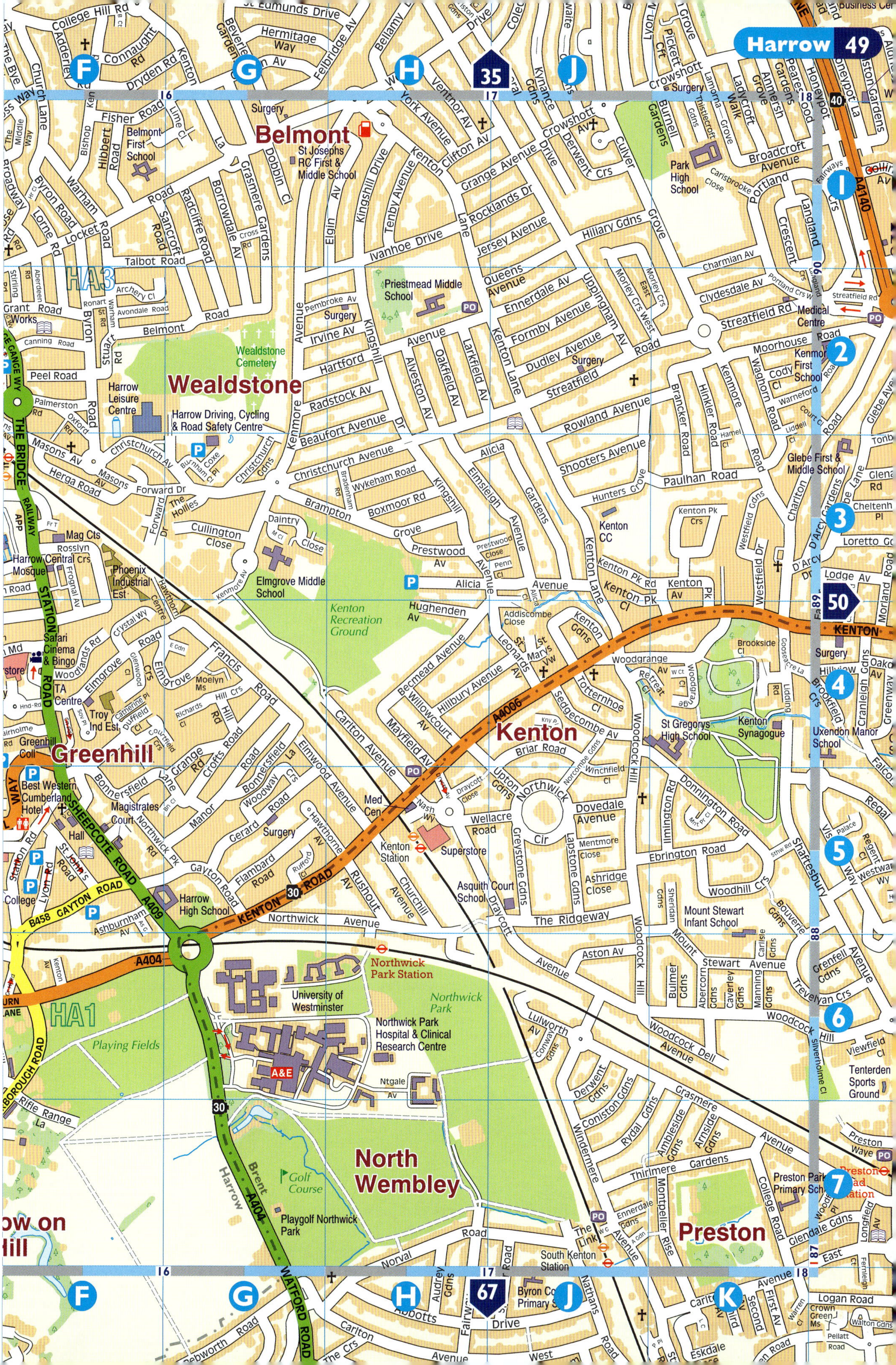
35
50
67
F
G
H
J
I
K
2
3
4
5
6
7
16
17
18
HA3
HA1
Belmont
Wealdstone
Greenhill
Kenton
North Wembley
Preston
Wealdstone Cemetery
Harrow Leisure Centre
Harrow Driving, Cycling & Road Safety Centre
Priestmead Middle School
St Josephs RC First & Middle School
Belmont First School
Park High School
Elmgrove Middle School
Kenton Recreation Ground
Kenton CC
Kenton First School
Glebe First & Middle School
St Gregorys High School
Kenton Synagogue
Uxendon Manor School
Harrow High School
Asquith Court School
Mount Stewart Infant School
Preston Park Primary School
Tenterden Sports Ground
Mag Cts
Harrow Central Mosque
Phoenix Industrial Est
Safari Cinema & Bingo
TA Centre
Troy Ind Est
Greenhill Coll
Best Western Cumberland Hotel
Magistrates Court
University of Westminster
Northwick Park Hospital & Clinical Research Centre
A&E
Northwick Park
Northwick Park Station
Playing Fields
Golf Course
Playgolf Northwick Park
Kenton Station
Superstore
Med Cen
South Kenton Station
Medical Centre
Surgery
Kenton Road
Kenton Lane
Kenton Pk Rd
Kenton Pk Cl
Station Road
Sheepcote Road
Gayton Road
Northwick Avenue
The Ridgeway
Woodcock Hill
Woodcock Dell Avenue
Preston Road
Watford Road
Harrow
Brent
Kingshill Drive
Kenmore Avenue
Streatfield Road
Uppingham Av
Shaftesbury Av
Belmont Road
Christchurch Avenue
Brampton Grove
Alicia Avenue
Elmsleigh Avenue
Carlton Avenue
Mayfield Av
Donnington Road
Ebrington Road
Woodhill Crs
Trevelyan Crs
Grasmere Avenue
Thirlmere Gardens
Windermere Avenue
Norval Road
Abbotts Drive
Logan Road
A404
A409
A4006
A4140
B458

50
36
49
68
Middlesex School of Comp Medicine
Works
Wigton Gdns
Honeypot La
Dalston Gardens
Pearswood Gardens
Amherst Gardens
Broadcroft Avenue
Portland Crescent
Langland Crs
Fairways
Collins Av
Taunton Way
Dean Drive
Camrose Av
Camrose Avenue
Bridgewater Gdns
Canons High School
Tiverton Road
Turner Road
Whistler Gdns
Cotman Gdns
Tenby Road
Tenby Rd Clinic
Raeburn Road
Hogarth Road
Constable Gdns
Stag Lane First School
Gainsborough Gardens
Mollison Way
Mollison
William Ellis Sports Ground
Broomgrove Gardens
Greencourt Av
Axholme Av
Chase
Oakleigh Avenue
The Highlands
De Havilland Rd
Lawrence Crs
Holyrood Gdns
Stag Lane
Redhill Dr
Limesdale Gdns
Holmstall Avenue
Burnt Oak Broadway
Burnt Oak Station
Watling Medical Centre
Barnfield Primary School
Back Lane
Millfield Road
Honeypot Medical Centre
Streatfield Rd
Medical Centre
Kenmore Park First School
Cody Cl
Warneford
Waghorn Road
Reynolds Drive
Calder Gdns
Brinkburn Gardens
Beverley Drive
Carlisle Road
Capitol Ind Park
Capitol Way
Colindale Business Park
Capitol Industrial Park
Queensbury Station
Queensbury
Superstore
Lowther Road
Everton Drive
Honeypot Lane
A4140
Esoldo Wy
Beverley Drive
Dryburgh Gdns
Wimborne Dr
Tewkesbury Gdns
Tintern Avenue
Fairway Avenue
Byron Av
Milton Av
Girton Avenue
Surgery
Bowman Trading Est
Winchester
Sandhurst
Eton Grove
Rugby Road
Stag Lane Medical Cen
Glebe Avenue
Glebe Crs
Glebe First & Middle School
Tonbridge Crs
Glenalmond Rd
Cheltenham Pl
Loretto Gdns
Shrewsbury Avenue
Malvern Gardens
Winchester Road
Ruth Cl
St Bernadettes RC Prim Sch
Mary Cl
Kingsbury Hospital
Honeypot Lane
Cowbridge Rd
Repton Rd
Princes Avenue
Grosvenor Crs
Kingsbury High School
Roe Green Junior School
Bacon Lane
Roe Lane
Goldsmith La
Grove Park School
Hay Lane School
Elmwood Crs
Kingsbury High School
D'Arcy Gardens
Westfield Dr
Lodge Av
Radley Gdns
Morland Road
Newnham Wy
Farrer Rd
Kenton Road
Clifton Road
Paul's Avenue
Ruskin Gdns
Pinecroft
Winckley Cl
Orchard Gv
Elmcroft Gdns
Berkeley Road
Brampton Road
Manor Cl
Sutherland Ct
Roe Green Park
Bacon Lane
Stubbs Cl
Fairfields Crs
Highfield Avenue
Surgery
Clinic
Salehurst Cl
Kinross Cl
Leybourne Rd
Kenton Lane
Old Kenton Lane
Sedum Cl
Larkspur Cl
Sri Saddhatissa International Buddhist Temple
Kingsbury
Kenton Synagogue
Brookside
Hillview Av
Oakdale Av
Claremont Av
Cranleigh Gdns
Greenway
Brookfield Crs
Uxendon Manor School
Claremont High Sch
Chapman Cl
Melbury Road
Dorchester Way
Kingsbury Rd
Kingsbury Station
Crundale Avenue
Mersham Dr
Valley Drive
Kingsbury Green Primary School
Kingsbury
Pipers Green
Woodland Close
Lewgars Av
St Robert Southwell RC Prim Sch
Fryent Country Park
Falcon Way
Vine Cl
Lindsay Drive
Ormesby Way
Preston Hill
Parnells Sports Ground
Wyndale Av
Waltham Av
Regal Way
Vista Way
Imperial Way
Branksome Way
The Garth
The Mall
Jewish Free School
Michael Sobell Sinai School
Sandy La
Robin Grove
Fryent Way
Shaftesbury Av
Westward Wy
Tylers Ga
Belvedere Wy
Bush Hl Rd
Surgery
Vane Close
Page Cl
Shakespeare Dr
Tookey Close
Arnold Cl
Boycroft Av
Tunworth Close
Bowcombe Cl
Carlisle Gdns
Manning Gdns
Avenue
Grenfell Gdns
Trevelyan Crs
Preston Hill
Kinch Gv
Wilson Cl
Wilson Dr
Ledway Drive
Fryent Country Park
Salmon St
Bush Grove
Laburnum Gv
Holly Gv
Maple Gv
Sycamore Grove
Mallard Way
Alington Crescent
Merley Ct
Cock Hill
Viewfield Cl
Tenterden Sports Ground
Toley Av
Oxenpark Av
Ravenscroft Avenue
Uxendon Hill
Wentworth Hill
Wykeham Hill
West Hill
West Cl
Alverstone Rd
Beverley Gdns
Preston Road
Preston Waye
Preston Road Station
Uxendon Crs
The Avenue
Beverley Gardens
Brampton Grove
Charlton Rd
Barn Hill
Barn Rise
Salmon Street
Lavender Avenue
Langdon Dr
Rossdale Drive
Glenwood Gv
Holden Av
Dimsdale Dr
Hill Drive
Kingsmere Park
Dunster Drive
Deanscroft Avenue
Church Lane
Hill Dr
Saltcroft Cl
Pilgrims Wy
Swinton Cl
College Road
Woodford Pl
Glendale Gdns
Longfield
East Hill
Carlton Av
Elmstead Avenue
Midholm
Logan Road
Aylands Cl
Crown Green
Hillview Cl
Marifields
Corrington Rd
Eversley Avenue
The Crossways
Wickliffe Gdns
Greenhill Way
The Paddocks
Adams Cl
Greenhill
The Mount
Salmon St
Tudor Gardens
St Nicholas School
Walk
Second Av
First Av
Third
1 grid square represents 500 metres

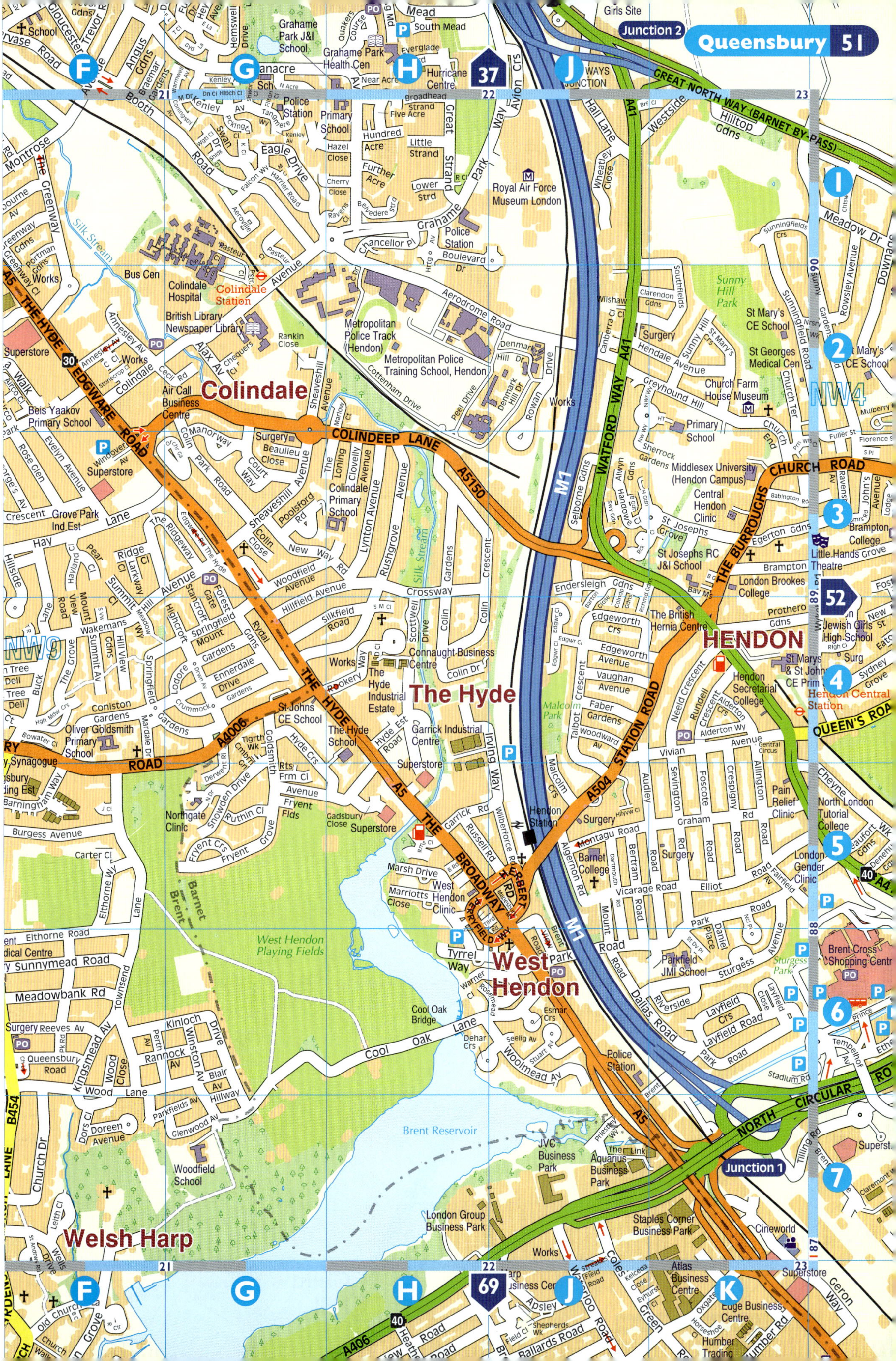

Queensbury 51
Junction 2
Colindale
Colindale Station
Colindale Hospital
British Library Newspaper Library
Metropolitan Police Track (Hendon)
Metropolitan Police Training School, Hendon
Royal Air Force Museum London
Grahame Park J&I School
Grahame Park Health Cen
Hurricane Centre
Great North Way (Barnet By-Pass)
Edgware Road
The Hyde
Colindeep Lane
A5150
Watford Way
A41
M1
Sunny Hill Park
St Mary's CE School
St Georges Medical Cen
Church Farm House Museum
NW4
Church Road
The Burroughs
Middlesex University (Hendon Campus)
Central Hendon Clinic
St Josephs RC J&I School
London Brookes College
Hendon
The British Hernia Centre
Jewish Girls High School
Hendon Secretarial College
Hendon Central Station
Queen's Road
Station Road
A504
Hendon Station
Barnet College
The Hyde
NW9
Silk Stream
Malcolm Park
Garrick Industrial Centre
The Hyde School
St Johns CE School
Oliver Goldsmith Primary School
A4006
Road
Synagogue
Northgate Clinic
West Hendon Playing Fields
The Broadway
West Hendon
West Hendon Clinic
Brent Reservoir
Cool Oak Bridge
Cool Oak Lane
Welsh Harp
Woodfield School
JVC Business Park
Aquarius Business Park
Staples Corner Business Park
London Group Business Park
North Circular Road
Junction 1
Cineworld
Brent Cross Shopping Centre
North London Tutorial College
London Gender Clinic
Parkfield JMI School
Sturgess Park
Dallas Road
Atlas Business Centre
Edge Business Centre
Superstore
A406
Police Station
37
52
69
21
22
23
F
G
H
J
I
K
1
2
3
4
5
6
7

Holders Hill
38
Hendon
Finchley Central Stn
NW4
NW11
N3
Hendon Central Station
Brent Cross Station
Golders Green Station
Golders Green
Child's Hill
Brent Cross Shopping Centre
Hendon Park
Recreation Ground
Golders Green Crematorium
Jewish Cemetery
GREAT NORTH WAY (BARNET BY-PASS)
HENDON LANE A504
FINCHLEY LANE A504
CHURCH ROAD
NORTH CIRCULAR ROAD A406
REGENT'S PARK ROAD A598
FINCHLEY ROAD A598
GOLDERS GREEN ROAD
BRENT STREET
QUEEN'S ROAD
PARSON STREET B552
HOLDERS HILL ROAD B552
BRENT CROSS FLYOVER
A504 EAST END ROAD
HENDON WAY
A41
A502
51
70
1 grid square represents 500 metres

East Finchley
Hampstead Garden Suburb
Fortis Green
Highgate
North End
Hampstead Heath
N2
N6
39
54
71
HIGH ROAD
A1000
NORTH CIRCULAR ROAD
EAST END ROAD
LYTTELTON ROAD
AYLMER ROAD
FORTIS GREEN
A504
GREAT NORTH ROAD
CHERRY TREE HILL
ARCHWAY ROAD
NORTH HILL
HAMPSTEAD LANE
B519
SPANIARDS ROAD
NORTH END ROAD
East Finchley Station
St Marylebone Crematorium
East Finchley Cemetery
The Jewish Museum
Finchley CC
Christs College Finchley
Brookland Junior School
Bishop Douglass RC School
Martin Primary School
Finchley Youth Theatre
Phoenix
The Kerem School
Hampstead Garden Suburb Synagogue
Henrietta Barnett School
Golders Hill Health Centre
Annemount School
Highgate Golf Club
Golf Course
Hampstead Golf Club
Kenwood House
Spaniards Inn
Highgate School
Highgate Junior School
Highgate Private Hospital
Blanche Nevile School
Coll of Fuel Technology
Athlone House Hospital
Fortismere School
Muswell Hill Synagogue
Tetherdown Primary School
King Alfred School
Middlesex University
Golders Green Health Centre
Coldfall Wood
Police Station
Haringey
Barnet
Camden

54
40
53
72
A
B
C
D
E
1
2
3
4
5
6
7
28
29
30
87
88
89
90
Muswell Hill
N10
Alexandra Palace
Alexandra Palace Ice Rink
Alexandra Park
Alexandra Palace Stn
Middlesex University
Reservoir
Filter Beds
Fortis Green
Cranley Gardens
Highgate Wood
Queen's Wood
HORNSEY
N8
Crouch End
Highgate
N6
Upper Holloway
N19
Highgate Cemetery
Waterlow Park
Highgate Station
Archway Stn
Alexandra Park Road
Colney Hatch Lane
Queens Av
Fortis Gn Rd
A504 Muswell Hill
Priory Road
Priory Rd
A1201 Park Road
Muswell Hill Road
Southwood La
Archway Road
A1 Archway
North Hill
B519
B550
North Road
Hampstead Lane
Highgate High Street
Highgate Hill
Hornsey Lane
B540
Crouch End Hill
Hornsey Rise
The Broadway
A103 Tottenham Lane
Crouch Hill
Wood Vale
Shepherd's Hill
Priory Gardens
Claremont Road
Avenue Road
Coolhurst Rd
Park Av South
Middle Lane
Muswell Hill Broadway
Grosvenor Road
Victoria Road
Alexandra Park Road
Dukes Avenue
Woodland Gardens
Onslow Gardens
Connaught Gardens
Summersby Rd
Queen's Wood Road
Etheldene Avenue
Tetherdown
Ante Natal Clinic
Police Station
Odeon Cinema
Hornsey Central Hospital
Park Road Palace Clinic
Swimming Centre
Highgate Wood School
Coleridge Primary School
St Aloysius College
Channing Sch
Whittington Hospital
Middlesex University
Archway Leisure Centre
1 grid square represents 500 metres

WOOD GREEN
Noel Park
West Green
Downhills Park
Harringay
Hornsey Vale
Stroud Green
Finsbury Park
N22
N4
N15
LORDSHIP LANE A109
HIGH ROAD A105
WESTBURY AVENUE
A1080 WESTBURY AV
DOWNHILLS WAY
DOWNHILLS ROAD
TURNPIKE LANE
GREEN LANES A105
WEST GREEN ROAD A504
PHILIP LANE
ST ANN'S ROAD B152
SEVEN SISTERS ROAD A503
WIGHTMAN ROAD B138
HORNSEY PARK ROAD B138
CHURCH LANE
TOTTENHAM LANE
STROUD GREEN ROAD
ENDYMION ROAD B150
TOLLINGTON PARK
AMHURST PARK
MANOR ROAD
LORDSHIP PARK
Wood Green Station
Turnpike Lane Station
Hornsey Station
Harringay Station
Harringay Green Lanes Stn
Manor House Station
Seven Sisters
Crouch Hill Station
Finsbury Park Station
Shopping City
Cineworld
Showcase
Coronet
Asylum Medical Centre
College of North East London
St Ann's General Hospital
Finsbury Park Track
Woodbery Down Centre Health Centre
Finsbury Park Synagogue
Watersports Centre
Crusader Industrial Estate
Arena Estate
Hornsey Secondary School for Girls
Weston Park Primary School
Belmont Infant School
Aarotya Medical Centre
Park View Academy
Chestnuts Primary School
Police Station
St Marys RC Junior School
Germal College
Thtr for Mankind
Euro Way School London
Woodberry Down Community Primary
Sir Thomas Abney Primary School
Yeshivo Horomo Talmudical College
Beis Rochel D'S Girls School
Bnois Jerusalem Girls School
Grazebrook Primary School
Olympia Industrial Est
Booster Cushion Thtr
Gas Works
Trading Estate
Hornsey Coroners Court Public Mortuary
Police Stn
New River Village
Broadwater Farm Prim Sch
Moselle Special School
Westbury Medical Cen
Lordship Lane Prim Sch
Wood Green Crown Court

56
42
55
74
TOTTENHAM
Tottenham Hale
South Tottenham
Stamford Hill
Upper Clapton
STOKE
N17
N15
N16
LORDSHIP LANE
BRUCE GROVE
HIGH RD
HIGH ROAD
STAMFORD HILL
MONUMENT WAY
THE HALE
HALE ROAD
BROAD LA
BROAD LANE
FERRY LANE
FOREST ROAD
WATERMEAD WAY
PHILIP LANE
WEST GREEN ROAD
SEVEN SISTERS ROAD
ST ANN'S ROAD
AMHURST PARK
CLAPTON COMMON
MANOR ROAD
A10
A503
A504
A107
B152
B153
Lockwood Reservoir
Warwick Reservoir
Walthamstow Marsh Nature Reserve
Springfield Park
Down Lane Recreation Ground
Milmead Industrial Cen
Tottenham Hale Station
Tottenham Hale Retail Park
Fountayne Business Centre
High Cross Centre
City of London Business College
Seven Sisters Station
Stamford Hill Stn
Bruce Grove Stn
Bruce Castle Museum
Tottenham Grn Leisure Cen
Town Hall
College of North East London
South Tottenham District Synagogue
Crowland Primary School
Copper Mills Works
Coppermill Lane
Lea Valley Walk
Ferry Lane Primary School
Abney Park Cemetery
Walthamstow Marsh
1 grid square represents 500 metres

WALTHAMSTOW
Higham Hill
E17
E10
Upp
BLACKHORSE LANE
BLACKHORSE ROAD
FOREST ROAD
HOE STREET
CHINGFORD ROAD
LEA BRIDGE ROAD
MARKHOUSE ROAD
CHURCH ROAD
HIGH ROAD
LEYTON GREEN ROAD
BILLET
A503
A112
A1006
A104
Blackhorse Road Station
Walthamstow Central Station
Walthamstow Queens Road Stn
St James St Stn
Leyton Midland Road Station
Uplands Business Park
Forest Trading Estate
Highams Lodge Business Cen
Willowfield Adult Education Centre
Coppermill Primary School
Low Hall Sports Ground
Forest Business Park
Leyton Industrial Village
Roxwell Trading Park
Lee Valley Ice Centre
Dorma Tdg Park
Lea Park Trading Est
Leyton FC
Cemetery
Community Centre
Leisure Centre
Kelmscott School
Lloyd Park Centre
William Morris Gallery
Waltham Forest Theatre
Sir George Monoux College
Waltham Forest Pool & Track
Waltham Forest Magistrates Court
Waltham Forest College
Council Building
Chapel End Infant School
Holy Family Technology College
The Hiltongrove Business Centre
Cinema
Vestry House Mus
Superstore
Leyton Leisure Centre
Leyton Youth Sports Ground
George Mitchell School
Riverley Prim School
St Josephs RC Junior Sch
Thomas Gamuel Prim Sch
St Saviours CE Primary School
Barn Croft Primary School
Mission Grove Primary School
Alpha Business Cen
Islamic Shaksiyah Foundation Sch
St James's Health Cen
Coroners Court
Willow Brook Primary
Lammas School
St Josephs Catholic Jn School
Orient Ind Park
Eastgate Bus Pk
Burwell Ind Est
Industrial Estate
Whittingham Community Primary School
Winns Primary School
Forest Road Medical Cen
Police Station
St Marys CE Primary Sch
School for Girls
Hillyfield Prim Sch
RC Prim Sch
Sybourn Infant School
Junior School
Fire Stn
Walthamstow
57
43
58
75
30
36
37
38
88
89
90
F
G
H
I
J
K
1
2
3
4
5
6
7

58
44
76
57
A
B
C
D
E
1
2
3
4
5
6
7
38
39
40
90
89
88
87
Upper Walthamstow
South Woodford
Leytonstone
E18
E11
Forest Road
A503
A104
A406
A114
A12
A11
A112
A113
A1199
A106
B160
B167
Fulbourne Road
Wood Street
Woodford New Road
Lea Bridge Road
Whipps Cross Road
Hollybush Hill
New Wanstead
Snaresbrook Road
Bush Road A114
Blake Hall Road
Leyton Green Road
Cambridge Park Road
Southend Road
George Lane
Grove Green Rd
Gainsborough Rd
Church Lane
High Road Leyton
Hermon Hill
Walthamstow Business Cen
Frederick Bremer Secondary Sch
Whitefield School & Leisure Centre
Waltham Forest College
Woodside Primary School
Hyland House School
Forest Prep School
Snaresbrook Crown Court
Snaresbrook Station
Wood Street Station
Whipps Cross Hospital
Leyton VI Form College
Leyton Leisure Centre
Leytonstone Stn
Leytonstone High Road Stn
Leyton Midland Road Station
Leyton Youth Sports Ground
Norlington Sch
Gwyn Jones Primary School
Leytonstone Mosque
Police Cadet School
Police Station
Superstore
Surgery
Works
1 grid square represents 500 metres

Redbridge Drama Centre
Gordon Road
Roycroft Close
Fieldhouse Close
Works
Maybank Road
Chigwell
F
G
H
45
J
Glade Primary School
Barrington Close
Cheriton Avenue
(NORTH CIRCULAR ROAD)
Junction 4
Raven Road
Violet Rd
Primrose Rd
Kensington Drive
Rivington Avenue
Summit Drive
Westview Drive
Lechmere Approach
Roding Lane
Chalgrove Crs
Marston Road
Wensleydale
Atherton
Harewood Drive
Heathcote Ave
Caterham High School
Caterham
Cottesmore Av
Kirkland
Viaduct
Daisy Rd
George Lane
Oakdale Infant Sch
Oakdale Junior Sch
Granville Road
Woodville Road
Rose Av
A113
Portman Dr
Woodford Trading Est
Embroidery World Business Centre
Unity Trading Estate
Peel Place
Coburg Gdns
Vienna Cl
Ewellhurst Road
St Clair Close
IG5
Clayhall Avenue
Clayhall
Stradbroke Grove
Clayhall Clnc
Old Mill Court
Chigwell Road
B168
Pulteney Road
Pelham Road
Brinkworth Road
Marlborough
Marlands
Surgery
Chadacre Avenue
Mellows Road
Dymchurch Cl
Tiverton
Rushden
Parkhill Primary School
Southend Road A1400
Anderson Road
Hatton School
Animal Cemetery
PDSA Hospital
BUPA Roding Hospital
Woodford Bridge Rd
Beal High School
Stoneleigh Road
Herent Drive
Lord Avenue
Abbotsford Gardens
Wernett Road
Monkswood Gdns
Earlswood Gdns
Hill
Alexandra Rd
Sherwood Av
Southview Drive
Cadogan Gardens
Onslow Gardens
Charnwood
Lancaster Avenue
Monmouth Avenue
Admirals Close
Hurstwood Av
North Circular Road
Roding Lane South
Carswell Close
Lodge Hill
Clayhall Park
Parkview Gardens
Cranbourne
Ashbourne Avenue
Colvin Gdns
Nightingale Prim Sch
Victory Road
Wanstead Hospital
Whitney Av
Lakeside Av
Leigh Avenue
Torquay Gardens
Babbacombe Gdns
Widecombe Gardens
Coniston Gdns
Derwent Gdns
Longwood Gardens
Hedgeley
Rodney Road
Elmcroft
Lorne Gdns
Devonport Gardens
Works
Merrivale Avenue
Peakerton Avenue
Falmouth Gardens
Braintree Avenue
Keswick
Brantwood Gardens
Grasmere Gardens
Beehive Preparatory School
Highwood
Beechwood
60
Rutland Rd
Warwick Rd
Hereford Road
Buckingham Rd
Eaton Rise
Laura Cl
Mighell Avenue
Fowey Avenue
Tryfan Close
Bergholt Av
Redbridge Prim Sch
IG4
College Gdns
Ridgeway Gardens
Grangeway Gardens
Gosford Gdns
Gosford Primary School
Somersby Gdns
A1400 Woodford Avenue
Collinwood
Glenwood
Eastway
Grosvenor Rd
Nightingale Lane
Cowley Rd
Leicester Road
Park
Gloucester Road
Eaton Manor RFC
Preston Drive
A406
Vista Drive
Fairmead Gdns
Edwina Gdns
Hollycliffe Gardens
Elmhurst Gardens
Windermere Gardens
Danehurst Gdns
Inglehurst Gardens
Wycombe Road
Avery Gdns
Beehive Lane
Ethelbert Gdns
Gants Hill
Gants Hill Station
Travelodge
Grove
The Avenue
Kendon Cl
Elm Hall Gdns
Reydon Av
Redbridge
50
Rosemary Drive
Redbridge
Margaret Way
Redbridge Station
A12
Eastern Avenue
40
High St
Gardner Cl
Eastern Avenue A12
Wigram Road
Corbett Rd
River Close
West
Wanstead Leisure Centre
Wanstead Station
Chester Rd
Mansfield Road
Oak Hall Rd
Redbridge
Wanstead High School
Studley Drive
Evanston Gardens
Castle Drive
Surgery
Castleview Gardens
Preston Gdns
Hillview Crs
Clarence Avenue
St Helen's Road
Cranbrook Rise
B192
Ilford Synagogue
Cranbrook
5
Draycot Road
St Mary's Av
Langley Drive
Langley Crs
Warren Drive
Colebrooke Drive
Royston Gdns
Carlisle Gdns
Stonehall Avenue
Wanstead
Ripon Gdns
Canterbury
Worcester Gdns
Hereford Gdns
Gloucester Gardens
Lincoln Gardens
Chelmsford Gdns
Cranbrook Primary School
St George's Road
St Andrew's Road
Vaughan Gardens
Cowley Road
6
WANSTEAD
Overton Drive
Wanstead Golf Club
The Warren Dr
Raynes Avenue
Lincoln Island
Wanstead CC
Wanstead Park
North Circular Road
A406
The Drive
Chichester Gdns
Rochester Gdns
Exeter Gdns
Infant Sch
Highlands Prim Sch
Stanhope Gardens
Sackville Gdns
Seymour Gdns Medical Centre
Kensington Gardens
Endsleigh Gdns
De Vere Gardens
Ranelagh Gardens
Redcliffe Gardens
Cavendish Gdns
A123
7
Golf Course
Aldersbrook
Woodlands Avenue
Aldersbrook Primary School
Northumberland Av
Aldersbrook Cty Sec Sch
Ilford Golf Club
Belgrave
Brading
Harpenden Road
Wanstead Park
Clavering Road
Arran Drive
Herongate Road
Margaret's
Surgery
41
42
77
43
K
Courtland
Mayfair
Empress
Golf Course

60
59
78
A
B
C
D
E
1
2
3
4
5
6
7
43
44
45
90
89
88
87
IG1
IG2
IG5
IG6
Fullwell Cross
Barkingside
Aldborough Hatch
Clayhall
Gants Hill
Newbury Park
Cranbrook
Valentines Park
Clayhall Park
Barkingside Cemetery
Redbridge Sports Centre
Fairlop Station
Fullwell Cross Health Cen
King Solomon High School
Starch House Lane
Hyleford Leavers Unit School
Pool & Rec Cen
Ilford County High School
Mossford Green Primary School
Gilbert Colvin Primary School
Clore Tikva Sch
Parkhill Primary School
Police Station
Ilford Jewish Primary School
Barkingside FC
Barkingside Station
Superstore
Fullwood Primary School
Geanes Junior School
Infant School
Lower Sch
Primary Sch
Infant Sch
Oaks Park High School
South West Essex Reform Synagogue
Newbury Park Station
Gants Hill Station
Gants Hill Medical Cen
Valentine High School
Ilford Synagogue
Health Centre
Express by Holiday Inn
Seven Kings High School
Downshall Primary School
St Aidans RC Primary School
Canon Palmer RC High School
Seven Kings Health Cen
Seven Kings
Seymour Gdns Medical Centre
Apex Prim Sch
Cranbrook College
Prep Sch
High Sch
Park Sch
New Rush Hall School
Ilford Retail Park
Ilford Swimming Pool
Council Bldgs
Buckingham Road Cemetery
William Torbitt J&I School
Works
Surgery
HIGH STREET
CRANBROOK ROAD
WOODFORD AVENUE
BEEHIVE LANE
EASTERN AVENUE
A123
A12
A1400
A118
B192
Fullwell Avenue
Basildon Avenue
Clayhall Avenue
Fremantle Rd
Mossford Green
Tanners Lane
Station Rd
Horns Road
Perrymans Farm Road
Ley Street
Wards Road
Lynn Road
Clifton Road
Benton Road
Vicarage Lane
Bradford Road
Cameron Road
Eastern Avenue
Valentines Road
Ilford Lane
Aldborough Road
Meads Lane
Balfour Road
1 grid square represents 500 metres

F
G
H
J
K
I
2
3
4
5
6
7
46
47
48
90
89
88
87
Fairlop Waters
Hainault Farm
Seven Kings Water
Redbridge
Barking and Dagenham
Painters Road
Hainault Road
Red House Farm
Billet Road
Little Heath
Little Heath School
St James Gardens
A12
EASTERN AVENUE
40
50
Newton Industrial Est
King George Hospital
A&E
Redbridge College
Newbridge School
Grove Primary School
Chadwell Heath Lane
Chadwell Heath
Marks Gate Junior Sch
Hlth Service Clinic
RM6
62
Seven Kings Park
Newbury Park (United) Synagogue
Farnham Green Primary School
BARLEY LANE
B177
The Chadwell Heath Found Sch
Gove Farm Retail Park
Superstore
Chadwell Primary Sch
A118
HIGH ROAD
Chadwell Heath Station
Chadwell Heath Leisure Cen
Barley Lane Primary Sch
Goodmayes Retail Park
Goodmayes Station
GOODMAYES ROAD
Eastcourt Independent School
Ilford Prep School
London Coll of Science & Tech
IG3
Kings Private Clinic
Al-Noor Primary School
A1083
GREEN LANE
Henry Green Primary School
Chadwell Heath Industrial Park
St Vincents RC Prim Sch
79
Eastern Avenue
Applegarth Drive
Ramsgill Drive
Aldborough Road North
Bawdsey Avenue
Freshwell Avenue
Rochford Avenue
Tendring Way
Second Av
Third Av
Somerville Road
Canon Avenue
Havering Gardens
Norbury Gdns
Tolworth Gardens
Portland Gdns
Percival Gardens
Hall Road
Gresham Drive
Langham Dr
Priestley Gdns
Primrose Avenue
Eccleston Crescent
Percy Road
Atholl Rd
Douglas Rd
Epsom Road
Meads Lane
Mayfield Road
Gibson Road
Palmer Rd
Freshwater Road
Valence Avenue
West Rd
Junction Rd
Overton Drive
Uplands Road
Arneways Av
Rosehatch Av
Roles Grove
Kingston Cl
Fenman Gdns
Kinfauns Road
Castleton Road
Express Drive
Ashgrove Road
Vernon Road
Felbrigge Road
Surgery
Works

A
B
C
D
E
1
2
3
4
5
6
7
48
49
50
90
89
88
87
Marks Gate
Chadwell Heath
RM6
RM7
61
80
Works
Collier Row FC
Northgate Ind Park
Crownfield Primary School
Collier Row Lane
B174
Mowbrays Road
Mawney Rd
Redriff Road
Walmer Close
Dunster Cl
Dover Cl
Surgery
Percy Rd
Hainault Road
Abbotts Cl
Birch Road
Birch Close
Forest Road
Silver Way
Epping Close
Essex Road
Burleigh Cl
Essex Close
Marlborough Road
Blandford Close
Crownmead Wy
Winston Close
Mawney Road
Cross Road
Hart Lane
Vanguard Close
Barnham Close
Linley Crs
Hubbinet Ind Est
King George Cl
Susan Cl
Beaufort Cl
Blenheim Cl
Eastern Avenue
Poplar Street
Cedar Rd
Willow St
Beech St
Vine St
Lime Cl
Oak St
Pretoria Road
Mildmay Rd
Barkwood Close
Palm Rd
Billet Road
Kingston Hill Avenue
Whalebone Lane North
A1112
Barking and Dagenham
Havering
Marks Gate Junior School
Hlth Service Clinic
Cemetery
Thatches Grove
Rose Lane
Padnall Rd
Crabtree Avenue
Longhayes Av
Roles Gv
Sheepcotes Road
Warren Farm
Eastern Avenue West
A12
Melbourne Gdns
Tolworth Gardens
Portland Gdns
Adelaide Gdns
Geneva Gardens
Pemberton Gdns
Warren Comprehensive School
Warren Sports Centre
Warren Junior School
North Rd
Morley Road
Kelly Way
The Cl
South Road
West Rd
Mayfair Av
Alexandra Road
Edward Road
Lee Av
Mill Lane
Willow Road
Ashton Gardens
Sylvan Av
Gordon Road
Albany Road
Hainault Road
Kings Avenue
High Road
A118
London Road
Furze Infant School
Salcombe Drive
Saville Road
Grantham Gdns
Bennett Rd
Wadeville Av
Farrance Road
Woodlands Av
Chadwell Heath Leisure Cen
Works
Japan Rd
Back Lane
Eric Rd
Cecil Rd
Eustace Road
Junction Rd W
Kenneth Road
Burlington Gdns
Heath Road
Broomfield
Mirravale Trading Estate
Coppen Road
Crow Lane
Rosslyn Av
Chadwell Heath Station
Selinas Lane
Freshwater Road
Works
Superstore
Eldenwall Industrial Estate
Purland Cl
Stanley Avenue
Torrington Road
Mount Road
Gray Av
Brendon Road
Albert Rd
James Av
Temple Avenue
Grosvenor Road
Whalebone Lane South
All Saints Catholic School & Technology College
Cornshaw Road
Lymington Road
Chadwell Heath Industrial Park
Turnage Road
Winifred Road
Gerald Rd
Ross Avenue
Tenterden Road
Fordyke Rd
Lamberhurst Rd
Green Lane
A1083
Inskip Road
Surgery
Bentry Road
Stockdale
Laburnum Health Centre
Stour Rd
Wood Lane
A124
Dagenham Civic Centre
Gosfield Road
Terling Road
Wood Lane Sports Centre
Barton Av
Meadow Road
Bell House Road
Rush Green Road
Romford Cemetery
Legon Av
Viking Business Centre
Danes Road
Bernard Rd
Beechfield Gardens
Maldon Rd
Crowlands Primary School
Norfolk Road
Cromer Rd
Sheringham
Kimberley Av
Ainsley Av
Derby Av
Lessington Av
Burlington Avenue
Crowlands Avenue
Jutsums Lane
Weald Way
Eddy Close
Bridport Av
St Edwards CE Comprehensive School
Southern Way
Jubilee Avenue
Recreation Av
Richards Avenue
Spring Gdns
Seabrook Gardens
Vignoles Rd
Goldsmith Avenue
1 grid square represents 500 metres

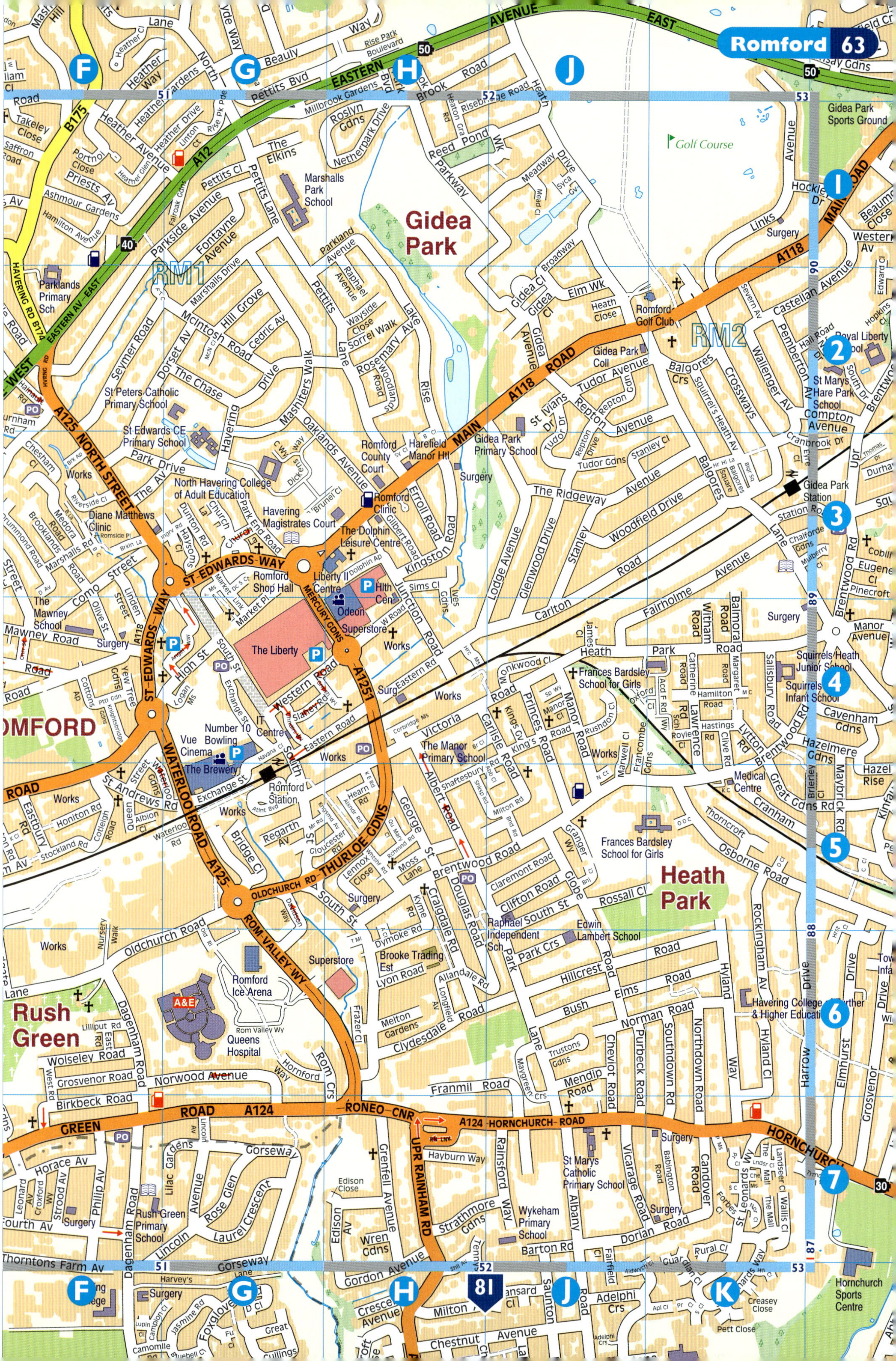
Gidea Park
Heath Park
Rush Green
ROMFORD
RM1
RM2
EASTERN AVENUE
AVENUE EAST
MAIN ROAD
A118
A12
A125 NORTH STREET
ST EDWARDS WAY
WATERLOO ROAD
A125
ROM VALLEY WY
A124
ROAD
GREEN
HORNCHURCH ROAD
RONEO CNR
UPR RAINHAM RD
OLDCHURCH RD
THURLOE GDNS
MERCURY GDNS
A1251
The Liberty
Liberty II Centre
Odeon
Romford Shop Hall
Romford Station
Gidea Park Station
Romford Golf Club
Golf Course
Gidea Park Sports Ground
Marshalls Park School
Parklands Primary Sch
St Peters Catholic Primary School
St Edwards CE Primary School
North Havering College of Adult Education
Havering Magistrates Court
The Dolphin Leisure Centre
Romford County Court
Romford Clinic
Gidea Park Coll
Gidea Park Primary School
Royal Liberty School
St Marys Hare Park School
Squirrels Heath Junior School
Squirrels Heath Infant School
Frances Bardsley School for Girls
The Manor Primary School
Raphael Independent Sch
Edwin Lambert School
Havering College of Further & Higher Education
Romford Ice Arena
Queens Hospital
A&E
Brooke Trading Est
Vue Cinema
Number 10 Bowling
The Brewery
St Marys Catholic Primary School
Wykeham Primary School
Rush Green Primary School
Hornchurch Sports Centre
Medical Centre
Surgery
Superstore
Works
Diane Matthews Clinic
The Mawney School
Marshalls Drive
Mashiters Walk
Oaklands Avenue
Lodge Avenue
Glenwood Drive
Woodfield Drive
Balgores Lane
Brentwood Road
Victoria Road
Albert Road
South Street
Oldchurch Road
Dagenham Road
Norwood Avenue
Birkbeck Road
Wolseley Road
Grosvenor Road
Clydesdale Road
Brentwood Road
Heath Drive
Harrow Drive
Osborne Road
Mawney Road
Como Street
Park Drive
The Chase
Pettits Lane
Pettits Blvd
Parkside Avenue
Carlton Road
The Ridgeway
Tudor Avenue
Castellan Avenue
Crossways
Wallenger Av
Pemberton Av
Compton Avenue
Eastern Rd
Exchange St
Market Pl
High St
Western Road
Gorseway
Thorntons Farm Av
Gordon Avenue
Milton Av
Chestnut Avenue
Adelphi Crs
Dorian Road
Vicarage Road
Northdown Road
Southdown Rd
Purbeck Road
Cheviot Road
Norman Road
Elms Road
Hillcrest Road
Bush Road
Framnil Road
Clifton Road
Claremont Road
Douglas Road
Craigdale Rd
Lyon Road
Melton Gardens
Rom Valley Wy
Cranham Rd
Great Gdns Rd
Rockingham Av
Hyland Way
Elmhurst Drive
50
40
30
81
51
52
53
87
88
89
90
F
G
H
J
K
I
2
3
4
5
6
7

West Ruislip
Ruislip Manor
Ruislip Gardens
North Hillingdon
Ickenham Manor
Northolt Aerodrome
UB10
HA4
46
82
Golf Course
RAF West Ruislip (Univ of Maryland)
Ruislip Golf Club
West Ruislip Station
Airbase Unity Elementary School
Ickenham Clinic
Compass Theatre
Ickenham Station
The Douay Martyrs RC School
Glebe Primary School
Sacred Heart RC Primary School
Ruislip RFC
Pond Green
Barn Hotel
Ruislip Station
Ruislip Manor FC
The Synagogue
Lady Bank Jun Sch
Ruislip High School
Ruislip Gardens Station
Ruislip Gardens Primary School
Works
Wood Lane Medical Centre
Gutteridge Wood
Hillingdon Trail
Dog Rose Ramble
Oak Farm Infant School
Ryefield Primary School
Old Abbotsonians RFC
Swakeleys School
Ickenham Road
High Road Ickenham
Long Lane
Western Avenue
A40
A437
A4180
B466
West End Road
Wood Lane
Pembroke Road
Brickwall Lane
Willow Grove
Shenley Avenue
Victoria Road
The Greenway
Glebe Avenue
Austins Lane
Sussex Road
Tavistock Road
Burnham Av
Milverton Drive
Crosier Way
Herlwyn Avenue
Westfield Way
Roxburn Way
Beechwood Av
Cornwall Road
Torrington Road
Sidmouth Drive
Bromley Crescent
Trevor Crs
Bedford Road
Clyfford Road
Lea Crs
Stafford Road
Granville Road
Richmond Avenue
Merton Avenue
Windsor Avenue
Lynhurst Crescent
Leybourne Road
Sutton Court Road
Charville Lane
Shenley Avenue
1 grid square represents 500 metres

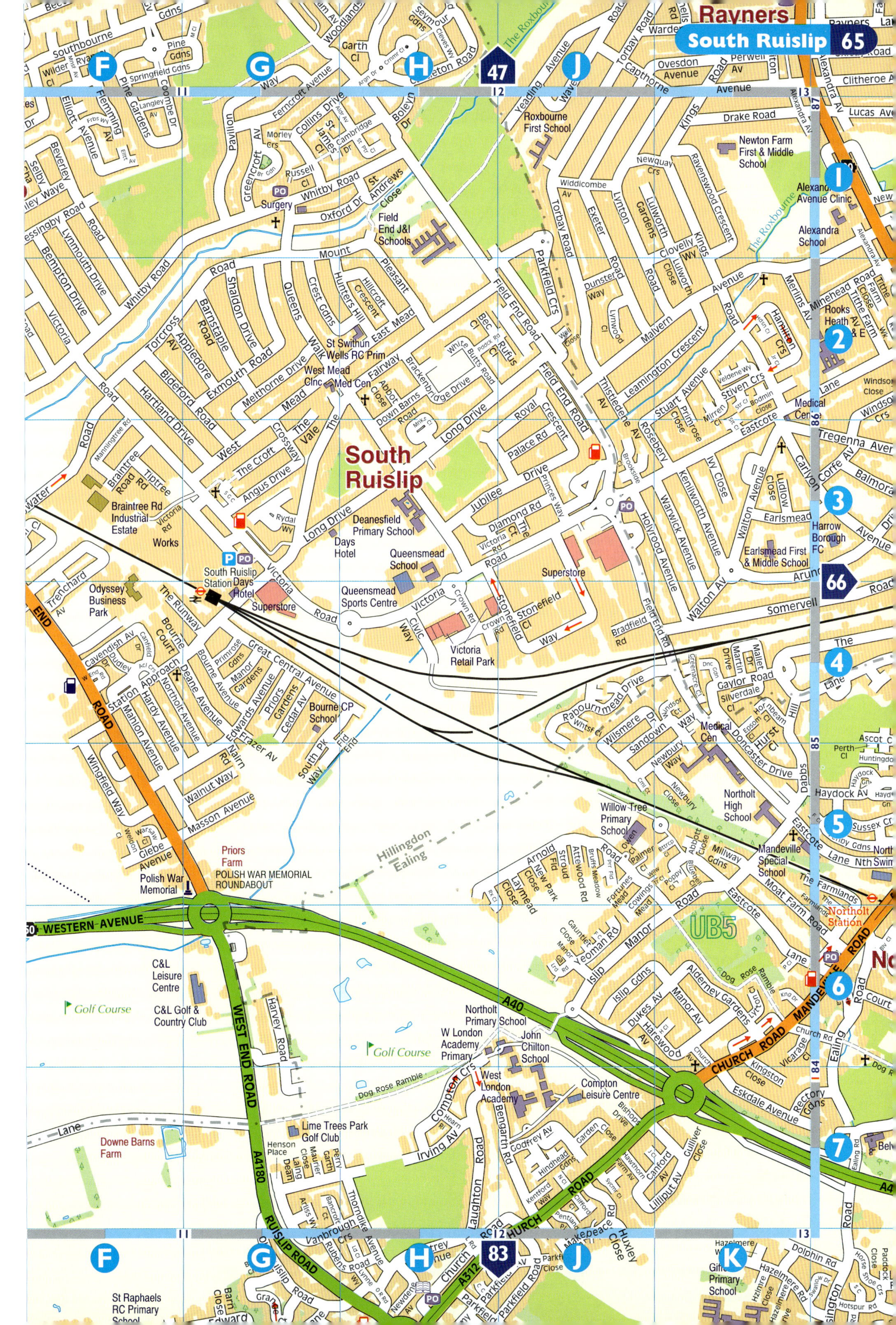
Rayners
South Ruislip
Northolt
Victoria Road
Field End Road
Long Drive
Whitby Road
Mount Pleasant
Queens Walk
West Mead
Station Approach
West End Road
Western Avenue
Ruislip Road
Church Road
Mandeville Road
Eastcote Lane
Victoria Retail Park
Queensmead School
Queensmead Sports Centre
Deansfield Primary School
Field End J&I Schools
St Swithun Wells RC Prim
Days Hotel
Superstore
Odyssey Business Park
Braintree Rd Industrial Estate
Works
Bourne CP School
Roxbourne First School
Newton Farm First & Middle School
Alexandra Avenue Clinic
Alexandra School
Rooks Heath H & E
Earlsmead First & Middle School
Harrow Borough FC
Medical Cen
Northolt High School
Willow Tree Primary School
Mandeville Special School
Northolt Station
Northolt Primary School
W London Academy Primary
John Chilton School
West London Academy
Compton Leisure Centre
C&L Leisure Centre
C&L Golf & Country Club
Golf Course
Lime Trees Park Golf Club
Downe Barns Farm
Priors Farm
POLISH WAR MEMORIAL ROUNDABOUT
Polish War Memorial
Hillingdon
Ealing
UB5
A40
A4180
A312
Gifford Primary School
St Raphaels RC Primary School
South Ruislip Station
Surgery
47
66
83
F
G
H
J
K
1
2
3
4
5
6
7
11
12
13
84
85
86
87

66
48
65
84
A
B
C
D
E
1
2
3
4
5
6
7
HA2
Rayners Lane
Oxleay Road
Clitheroe Avenue
Lucas Avenue
Scott Crs
Eliot Drive
Swift Cl
Coles Crescent
Newton Farm First & Middle School
Alexandra Avenue Clinic
Alexandra School
Newton Close
Roxbourne Medical Centre
Eastleigh Avenue
Sandringham Crs
Rooks Heath AV Coll B & E
Eastcote Lane Cem
South Harrow
Roxeth
Archdale Business Cen
Franklins Ms
Works
Stanley Road
Sherwood Road
Shaftesbury Medical Centre
John Lyon School
Harrow School
Harrow on the Hill
Middle Road
First & Middle School
ROXETH HILL
A4005
Council Building
Police Stn
Cowen Avenue
St Dominics Sixth Form College
Bowden House Clinic
Wendela Ct
Fircroft Gdns
The Purcell School
Orley Farm School
Harrow Fields Gardens
South Harrow Station
NORTHOLT ROAD
A312
Northolt Road Clinic
Middle School
Roxeth Gv
Wood End Av
Westwood Av
Paddocks Close
Northolt Park Station
ALEXANDRA AVENUE
Windsor Close
Windsor Crs
Medical Centre
Tregenna Avenue
Balmoral Road
Harrow Borough FC
Earlsmead First & Middle School
Earlsmead
Arundel
Somervell Road
The Heights
Harrow
Ealing
Acock Grove
Halsbury Road
Clauson Avenue
Reading Road
Russell Road
Killowen Avenue
East End Way
Wood End Way
Greenwood Prim Sch
Wood End J&I Schools
Dimmock Drive
Ealing Northern Sports Centre
Bedser Drive
Bannister Close
Sudbury Hill Station
Cavendish Avenue
Harrow CC
Tyrell Cl
South Vale
GREENFORD ROAD
Greenford Green Clinic
Ennismore Avenue
Horsenden Primary School
Berkeley Av
Surgery
PETT'S HILL
A4090
WHITTON AV WEST
Newmarket Avenue
Petts Hill Primary School
Wood End Lane
Newnham Gdns
Barnabas Medical Cen
Currey Rd
Wadham Gardens
Malden Avenue
Rugby Av
Oldfield Lane North
Haydock Av
Southwell Close
Sussex Crescent
Lewes Close
Mandeville Special School
Nth Swimarama
MANDEVILLE ROAD
Innkeeper's Lodge
Ribblesdale Av
Castle Road
Carr Road
Blenheim Road
Lancaster Road
Girton Close
The Fairway
Worcester
Rothesay Av
Clare Road
Hadden Way
Auriol Drive
Oldfield Lane North
Northolt Station
Northolt
Belvue Close
Sandringham Rd
Court Farm Rd
Summit Rd
Belvue Business Cen
Ockham Dr
Grand Union Canal
Dog Rose Ramble
Kingston Close
Eskdale Avenue
Rectory Gdns
Belvue School
Rowdell Road
Taunton Road
Derby Road
Greenford Industrial Estate
Halifax Road
Bridport Road
Field Way
Bristol Road
Kelvin Ind Est
Superstore
Fairway Dr
Allington Cl
Station Approach
Birkbeck Avenue
Rockware Business Cen
Greenford Station
Uneeda Drive
Greenpark Way
Works
Rockware Avenue
Bennetts Avenue
Lyon Way
Ingram Way
Downing Drive
A40
WESTERN AVENUE
Oldfield Primary School
Greenford Rd Medical Cen
Dolphin Rd
Hazelmere
Union Road
Evesham Close
Chesterton Close
Melrose
Darlington Drive
1 grid square represents 500 metres

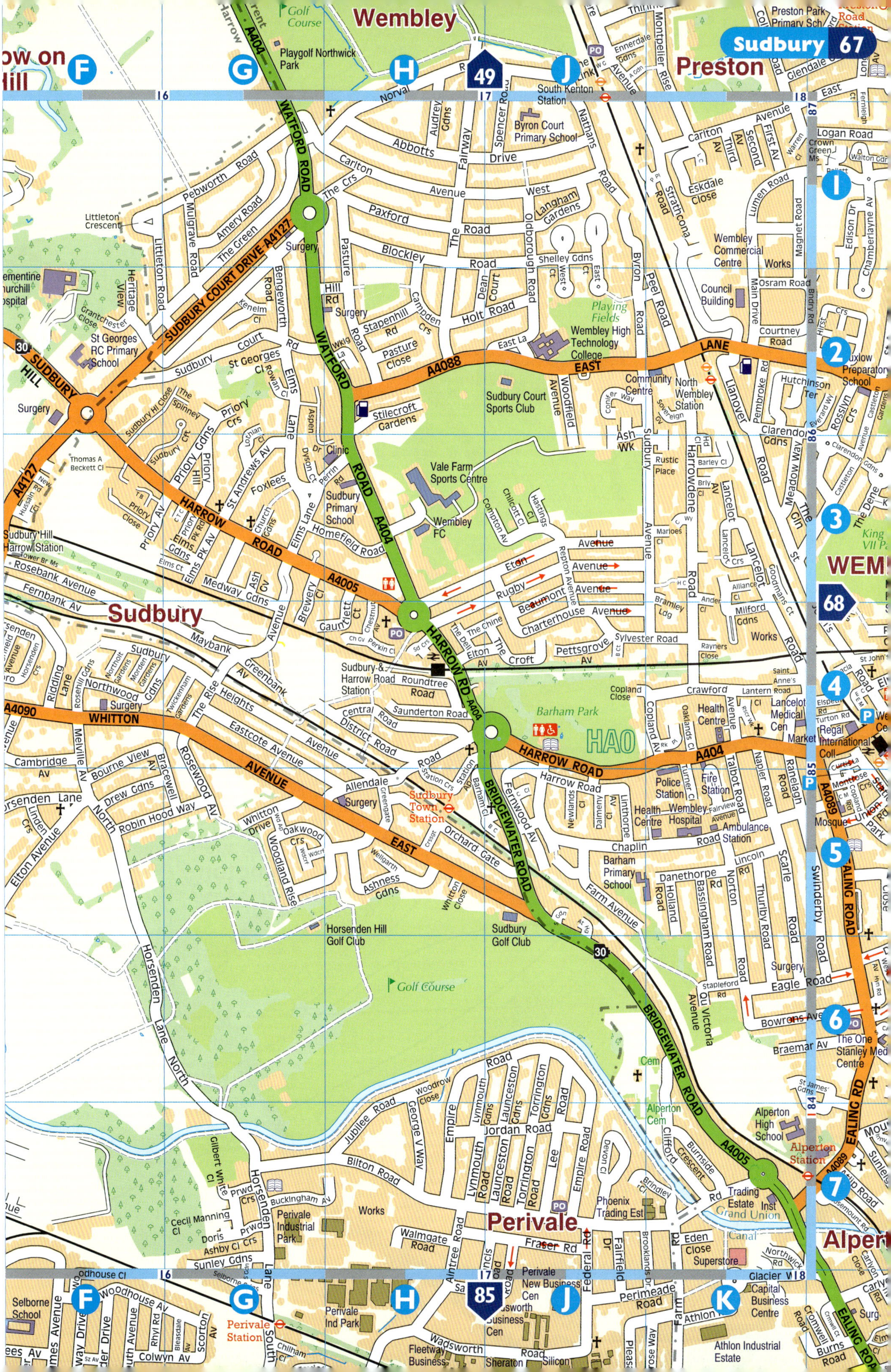
Wembley
Preston
Sudbury
Perivale
Alperton
HA0
49
68
85
F
G
H
J
K
1
2
3
4
5
6
7
16
17
18
84
85
86
87
Playgolf Northwick Park
Golf Course
South Kenton Station
Byron Court Primary School
Preston Park Primary Sch
Watford Road
A404
Norval
Audrey Gdns
Spencer Road
Fairway
Abbotts Drive
Carlton Avenue
The Crs
Paxford
West
Langham Gardens
Blockley
The Road
Oldborough Road
Shelley Gdns
Nathans Road
Byron Road
Peel Road
Strathcona Road
Eskdale Close
Carlton Av
Second Av
Third Av
First Av
East
Logan Road
Lumen Road
Magnet Road
Edison Dr
Chamberlayne Av
Wembley Commercial Centre
Works
Osram Road
Main Drive
Bridge Road
Council Building
Courtney Road
Playing Fields
Wembley High Technology College
East La
East Lane
A4088
Holt Road
Dean Court
Stapenhill Rd
Campden Crs
Pasture Close
Pasture Road
Hill Rd
Surgery
Pebworth Road
Mulgrave Road
Amery Road
The Green
Sudbury Court Drive A4127
Littleton Crescent
Littleton Road
Heritage View
Clementine Churchill Hospital
Grantchester Close
St Georges RC Primary School
Kenelm Cl
Bengeworth Road
St Georges Cl
Court
Rowan Cl
Elms Lane
Rd
Sudbury Hill
Sudbury
Surgery
A4127
The Spinney
Sudbury Hl Close
Priory Crs
Priory Gdns
Priory Hill
Priory Av
Priory Close
Thomas A Beckett Cl
Sudbury Ct
St Andrews Av
Foxlees
Church Gdns
Elms Pk Av
Elms Gdns
Elms Ct
Harrow Road
A4005
Sudbury Hill Harrow Station
Tower Br Ms
Rosebank Avenue
Fernbank Av
Medway Gdns
Ash Gv
Brewery Cl
Gauntlett Ct
Chestnut Av
Aspen Dr
Dyson Ct
Perrin Rd
Clinic
Sudbury Primary School
Homefield Road
Stilecroft Gardens
Sudbury Court Sports Club
Woodfield Avenue
Vale Farm Sports Centre
Wembley FC
Compton Av
Chilcott Cl
Hastings Cl
Community Centre
Conifer Way
North Wembley Station
Sovereign Cl
Ash Wk
Sudbury Avenue
Rustic Place
Harrowdene Road
Barley Cl
Lancelot Avenue
Lancelot Crs
Lancelot Road
Llanover Road
Pembroke Rd
Hutchinson Ter
Clarendon Gdns
Meadow Way
The Gln
Rosslyn Crs
Castleton Av
Castleton Gardens
The Dene
King Edward VII Pk
Buxlow Preparatory School
WEM
Eton
Rugby
Beaumont
Charterhouse
Avenue
Repton Avenue
Marloes Cl
Bramley Lodge
Goodwins Ct
Milford Gdns
Works
Alliance Cl
Rayners Close
Sylvester Road
Pettsgrove Av
The Dell
The Chine
The Croft
Elton Av
Maybank
Greenbank Av
Heights
The Rise
Sudbury & Harrow Road Station
Roundtree Road
Saunderton Road
Central Road
District Road
Perkin Cl
Sudbury Gardens
Northwood Gdns
Northolt Gardens
Morden Gardens
Twickenham Gardens
Rosehill Gdns
Ridding Lane
Horsenden Crs
A4090
Whitton Avenue
Whitton Drive
Cambridge Av
Melville Av
Bourne View
Drew Gdns
Braemar Av
Rosewood Av
Robin Hood Way
Horsenden Lane
Linden Crs
Elton Avenue
Eastcote Avenue
Allendale Road
Station Crs
Station App
Sudbury Town Station
Surgery
Greenholme
Oakwood Crs
Woodland Rise
Orchard Gate
Ashness Gdns
Wellgarth
Whitton Close
Copland Close
Copland Av
Barham Park
Crawford Avenue
Health Centre
Oaklands Ct
Lantern Road
Saint Anne's Road
Lancelot Medical Cen
Market
Harrow Road
A404
Bridgewater Road
Barham Cl
Fernwood Av
Newlands Cl
Dalmeny Av
Linthorpe
Police Station
Fire Station
Wembley Hospital
Health Centre
Ambulance Station
Talbot Road
Napier Road
Ranelagh Road
Regal International Coll
Mosque
Chaplin Road
Barham Primary School
Farm Avenue
Danethorpe Rd
Holland Road
Bassingham Road
Norton Road
Lincoln Rd
Thurlby Road
Scarle Road
Swinderby Road
Ealing Road
A4089
Eagle Road
Surgery
Stapleford Rd
Bowrons Ave
Braemar Av
Victoria Avenue
The One Stanley Medical Centre
Horsenden Hill Golf Club
Golf Course
Sudbury Golf Club
Cem
Alperton Cem
Clifford Road
Burnside Crescent
Alperton High School
Alperton Station
Jubilee Road
Woodrow Close
George V Way
Bilton Road
Empire Road
Lynmouth Gdns
Lynmouth Road
Launceston Gdns
Launceston Road
Torrington Gdns
Torrington Road
Jordan Road
Lee Gdns
Devon Cl
Bringley Cl
Phoenix Trading Est
Trading Estate
Grand Union Canal
Works
Buckingham Av
Gilbert White Cl
Perivale Industrial Park
Cecil Manning Cl
Doris Ashby Cl
Sunley Gdns
Horsenden Lane South
Walmgate Road
Aintree Road
Fraser Rd
Federal Rd
Fairfield Rd
Brooklands Dr
Eden Close
Superstore
Northwick Rd
Glacier Way
Perivale New Business Cen
Perimeade Road
Capital Business Centre
Athlon Road
Athlon Industrial Estate
Woodhouse Cl
Woodhouse Av
Selborne School
Perivale Station
Perivale Ind Park
Wadsworth Business Cen
Wadsworth Road
Fleetway Business
Sheraton
Silicon
Cromwell Road
Burns Road
Rhyl Rd
Colwyn Av
Scorton Av
Ealing Road

68
50
67
86
A
B
C
D
E
1
2
3
4
5
6
7
Preston Park Primary Sch
Preston Road Station
WEMBLEY
Wembley Park
Tokyngton
Alperton
HA9
Wembley Stadium
Wembley Arena
Conference Centre
Exhibition Halls
Wembley Stadium Station
Wembley Park Station
Wembley Central Station
Alperton Station
Stonebridge Park Station
Preston Manor School
Preston Medical Centre
Wembley Synagogue
Buxlow Preparatory School
Wembley Primary School
King Edward VII Park
Park Lane Primary School
Lancelot Medical Cen
Regal International Coll
Copland Specialist Science College
St Josephs RC J&I School
Central Square Shopping Centre
Playing Fields
Elsley Primary School
Oakington Manor School
Chalkhill Primary School
Wembley Stadium Industrial Estate
Wembley Park Business Cen
MSP Business Cen
Towers Business Park
Hallmark Trading Estate
Cannon Trading Est
Metro Trading Cen
Olympic Trading Estate
Olympic Ind Est
Olympic Retail Park
Wembley Stadium Ind Estate
Quality Hotel
Ibis Hotel
Bingo Hall
Market Area
Stadium Business Cen
Stadium Retail Park
Stadium Industrial Est
Adams Bridge Bus Cen
Pop In Business Cen
Tokyngton Community Centre
British Transport Police Stn
Sports Ground
Coll of North West London
St Christophers Sch
Gower House School
St Nicholas School
Hazeldene Medical Cen
St Raphaels Way Medical Cen
Bridge Park Business & Leisure Centre
The Princess Royal Distribution Centre
Our Lady of Lourdes RC Prim Sch
The Stonebridge Primary Sch (London Welsh School)
Townsend Industrial Estate
Mill Trading Estate
Grand Union Industrial Estate
Northfields Industrial Estate
Abbey Industrial Estate
Lyon Park Infant School
Alperton Community School
Alperton High School
The One Stanley Medical Centre
Capital Business Centre
Grand Union Canal
River Brent
FORTY AVENUE
FORTY LANE
WEMBLEY PARK DRIVE
PARK LANE
EMPIRE WAY
BRIDGE ROAD
HIGH ROAD
HARROW RD
EALING ROAD
SOUTH WAY
GREAT CENTRAL WAY
WEMBLEY HILL ROAD
SALMON ST
TUDOR GARDENS
BRENTFIELD
NORTH CIRCULAR ROAD
A4088
A4089
A479
A404
A406
A4140
A4005
B4557
1 grid square represents 500 metres

Wembley Park 69
Junction 1
Welsh Harp
Woodfield School
London Group Business Park
Staples Corner Business Park
Cineworld
Harp Business Centre
Atlas Business Centre
Edge Business Centre
Humber Trading Estate
NORTH CIRCULAR ROAD
A406
EDGWARE
Dollis Hill
Braincroft Primary School
John Kelly Girls Technology College
Menorah High School for Girls
Evans Bus Cen
Junior School
Oxgate Gardens
Dollis Hill Lane
Gladstone Park Gardens
Torah Temimah Primary School & Synagogue
Brent Arts Council
The Stables Gallery & Art Centre
Gladstone Park
Wykeham Primary School
St Margarets Clitherow RC Prim Sch
NEASDEN LA
A4088
Neasden
Dudden Hill Lane
Gladstone Medical Centre
The Grange Mus
Drury Way Industrial Estate
GREAT CENTRAL WAY
B4557
Superstore
Central Business Cen
Brent Trading Estate
Neasden Station
Falcon Park Industrial Est
Brent Child & Family Clnc
Burnley Road Clnc
Dollis Hill Station
Gladstone Park Prim Sch
Helena Road Clinic
Coll of North West London
Cygnus Business Cen
Trading Cen
Dudden Hill
Chapman Park Industrial Est
Community Centre
WILLESDEN
HIGH ROAD
A407
Brent Magistrates Court Ho
Brentfield Medical Centre
Mitchell Brook Primary School
Hindu Temple
Swaminarayan School
Brentfield Primary School
Church End Medical Centre
Primary School
Cobbold Est
Trojan Business Cen
Bus Depot
St Andrew & St Francis CE JMI Sch
Medical Cen
Police Stn
Junior School
Superstore
Synagogue
Islamic Coll for Advanced Studies
Church End
World Spiritual University
Willesden New Cemetery
Fire Stn
Willesden Centre for Health & Care
Roundwood Park
Newfield Primary School
St Andrews School
Donnington Primary School
Willesden Green
Belvedere Day Hospital
Capital City Academy
Willesden Sports Stadium
Willesden Sports Centre
Cardinal Hinsley College
Convent of Jesus & Mary Lang Coll
HILLSIDE
A404
CRAVEN PK RD
MANOR PK ROAD
NW10
Stonebridge Shop Cen
Craven Park Medical Cen
Health Cen
College
Police Stn
Harlesden
Harlesden Station
Willesden Co Court
B4492
ACTON LANE
51
70
87

Junction 1
70
52
69
88
A
B
C
D
E
1
2
3
4
5
6
7
Child's Hill
Cricklewood
Brondesbury
Willesden Green
Brondesbury Park
KILBURN
Kensal Rise
Queen's Park
NW2
NW6
Barnet
Camden
A5 EDGWARE ROAD
CRICKLEWOOD BROADWAY
A5 SHOOT-UP-HILL
CRICKLEWOOD LANE
HENDON WAY
FINCHLEY ROAD
CHICHELE ROAD
WALM LANE
WILLESDEN LANE
IVERSON ROAD
KILBURN HIGH RD
BRONDESBURY ROAD
A407
A41
A4003
B520
B451
B510
Recreation Ground
Hendon FC
Claremont Way Industrial Estate
Claremont Primary School
Cricklewood Trading Estate
Childs Hill Primary School
Granville Road Industrial Estate
Torah Vodaas
All Saints CE Primary School
Welbeck Clinic
Greenfield Medical Centre
Cricklewood Station
Broadway Retail Park
Britannia Bus Cen
Crown Moran Hotel
The Mosque & Islamic Centre of Brent
Hampstead School
Hampstead Cemetery
The Hampstead School of Art
The Open University
Shomrei Hadath Synagogue
Anson Primary School
Cricklewood Synagogue
Mulberry House Sch
Walm Lane Clinic
Willesden Green Station
Convent of Jesus & Mary Inf Sch
London Welsh School
Council Building
Islamic Coll for Advanced Studies
Emb of Senegal
Cricket Ground
South Hampstead CC
MPR Eurotots School
North West London Jewish Primary School
Brondesbury College for Boys
Malorees Junior School
Queens Park Community School
Brondesbury Park Station
Al Sadiq & Al-Zahra High School
Islamia Girls School
Cemetery
Christ Church Brondesbury CE J&I Sch
Brondesbury Station
Kilburn Station
West Hampstead Station
Tricycle Theatre
Kingsgate Primary School
St Eugene de Mazenod RC Prim School
Coll of North West London
Kilburn Park Stn
St Marys RC Primary School
Willesden Sports Stadium
Willesden Sports Centre
Mill Lane Medical Cen
Solent Road Health Cen
1 grid square represents 500 metres

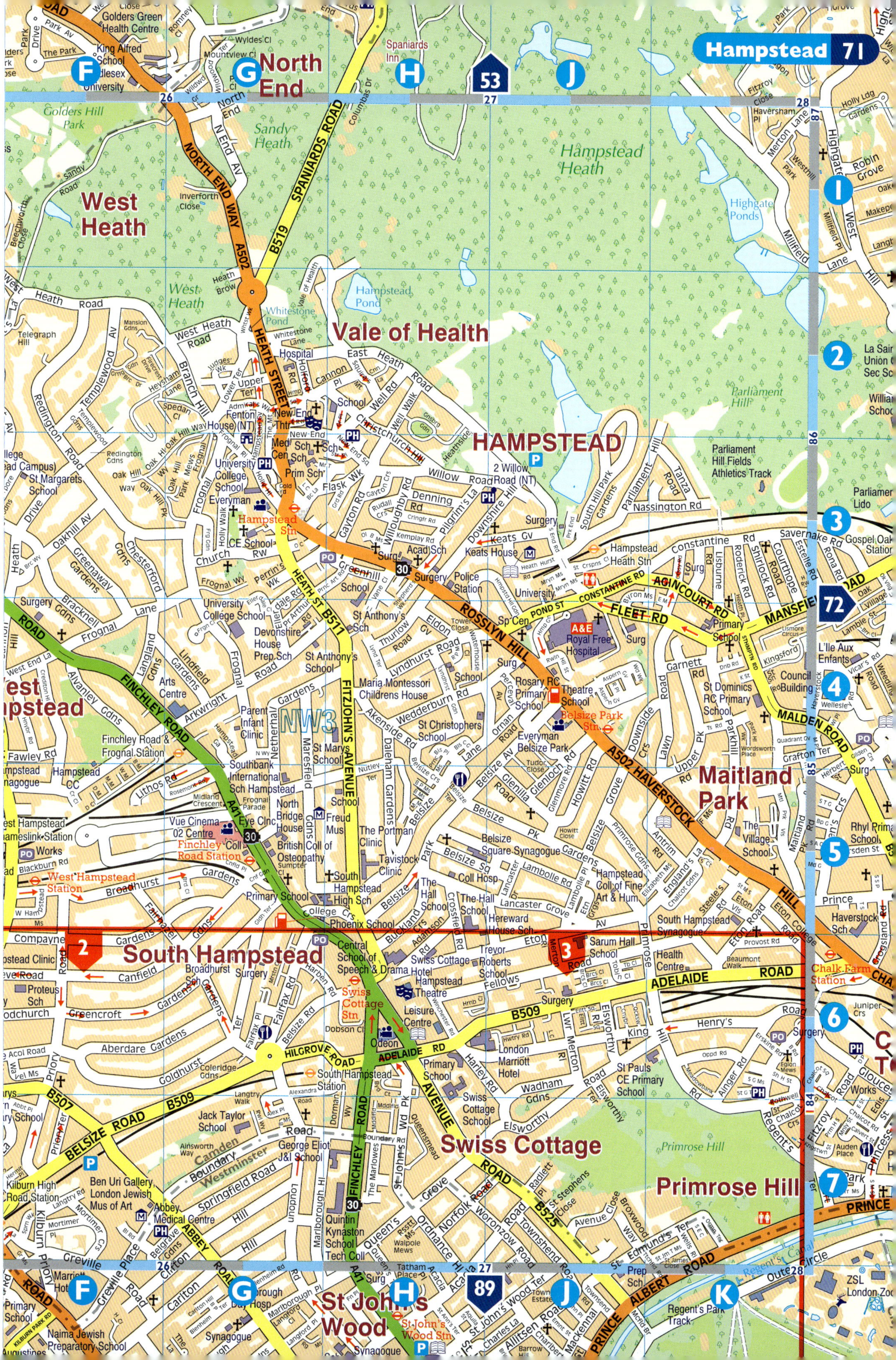
North End
West Heath
Sandy Heath
Hampstead Heath
Golders Hill Park
Highgate Ponds
Vale of Health
Hampstead Pond
Whitestone Pond
HAMPSTEAD
Parliament Hill
Parliament Hill Fields Athletics Track
Parliament Lido
NORTH END WAY
SPANIARDS ROAD
HEATH STREET
ROSSLYN HILL
FITZJOHN'S AVENUE
FINCHLEY ROAD
HAVERSTOCK HILL
FLEET RD
AGINCOURT RD
ADELAIDE ROAD
BELSIZE ROAD
HILGROVE ROAD
MALDEN ROAD
PRINCE ALBERT ROAD
Hampstead Stn
Belsize Park Stn
Hampstead Heath Stn
Finchley Road Stn
Swiss Cottage Stn
South Hampstead Station
West Hampstead Station
Chalk Farm Station
St John's Wood Stn
Royal Free Hospital
Keats House
Maitland Park
South Hampstead
Swiss Cottage
Primrose Hill
St John's Wood
NW3
Spaniards Inn
Golders Green Health Centre
King Alfred School
Middlesex University
Regent's Park
Regent's Canal
ZSL London Zoo
Camden
Westminster

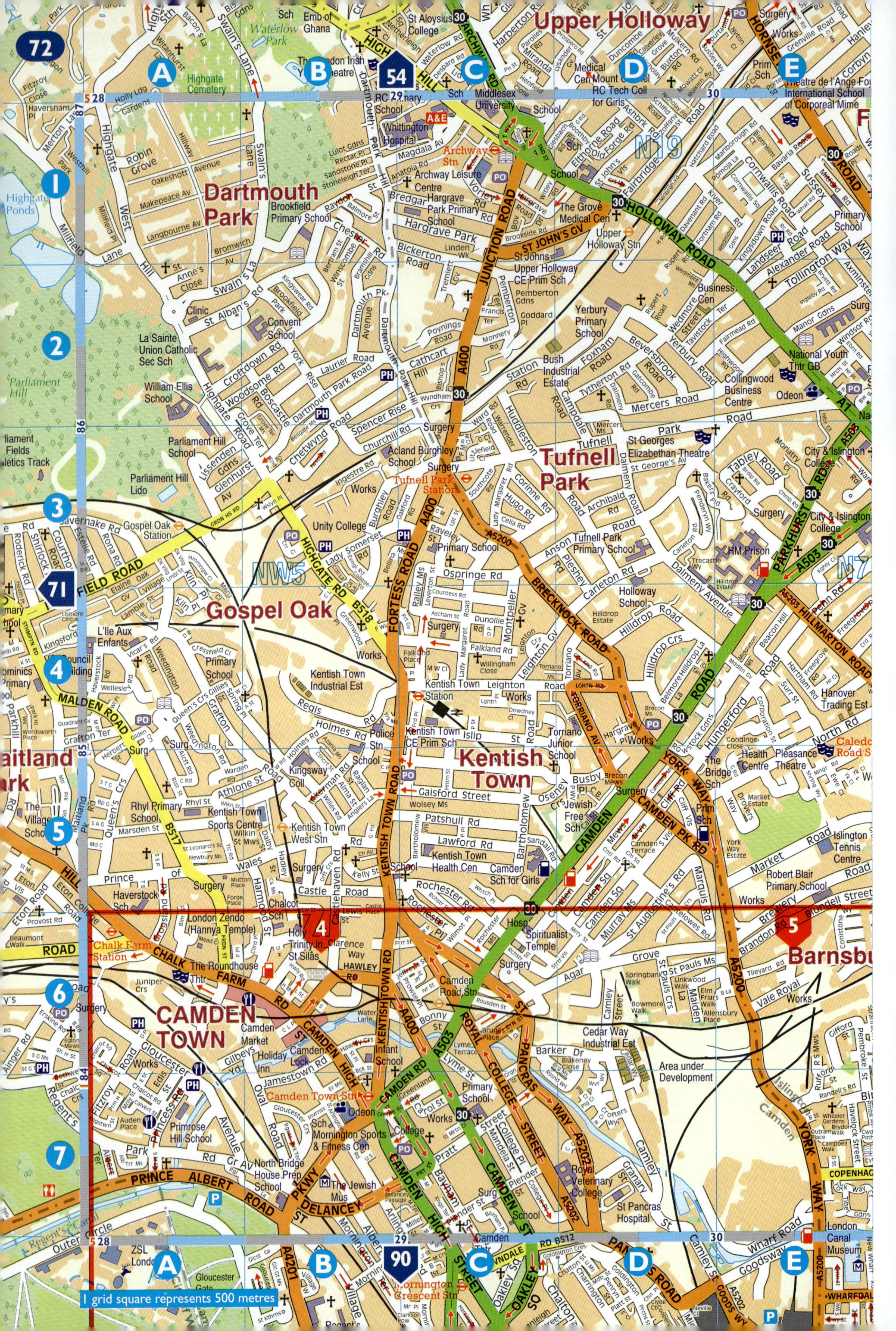

72
54
71
4
5
90
A
B
C
D
E
1
2
3
4
5
6
7
Upper Holloway
Dartmouth Park
Tufnell Park
Gospel Oak
Kentish Town
CAMDEN TOWN
Barnsbury
N19
NW5
N7
Highgate Cemetery
Highgate Ponds
Parliament Hill
Waterlow Park
Archway Stn
Upper Holloway Stn
Tufnell Park Station
Gospel Oak Station
Kentish Town Station
Kentish Town West Stn
Camden Road Stn
Camden Town Stn
Chalk Farm Station
Mornington Crescent Stn
Whittington Hospital
HM Prison
Royal Veterinary College
St Pancras Hospital
Holloway Road
Junction Road
Fortess Road
Kentish Town Road
Camden Road
Brecknock Road
Highgate Road
York Way
Camden High Street
Royal College Street
Pancras Way
Chalk Farm Road
Prince Albert Road
Parkway
Agar Grove
Hillmarton Road
Parkhurst Road
Tufnell Park Road
Dartmouth Park Hill
Swain's Lane
Highgate West Hill
Gordon House Road
Malden Road
Regent's Canal
London Canal Museum
Camden Market
1 grid square represents 500 metres

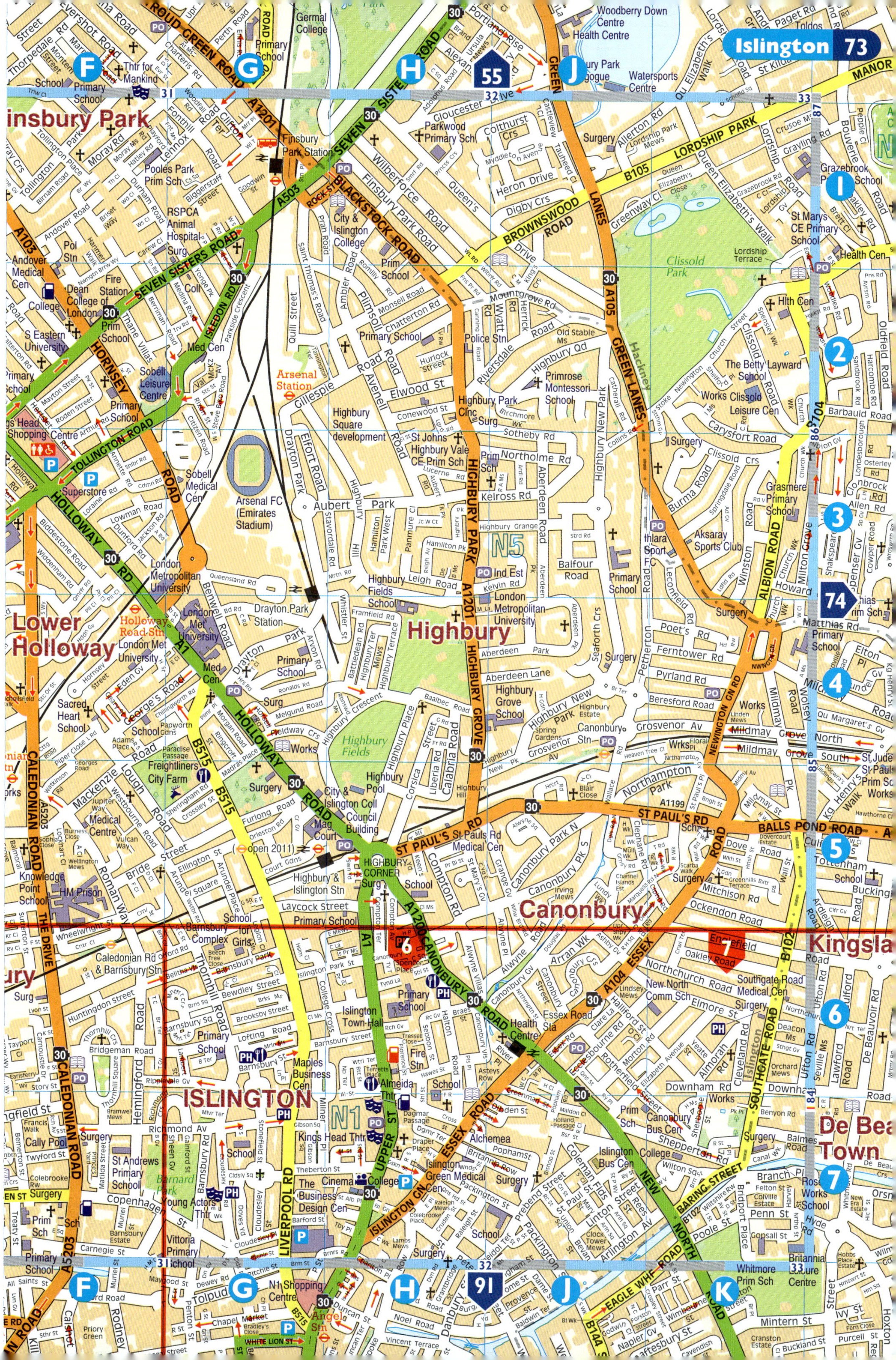
Finsbury Park
Lower Holloway
Highbury
Canonbury
ISLINGTON
Kingsland
De Beauvoir Town
Highbury Fields
Clissold Park
Arsenal FC (Emirates Stadium)
Finsbury Park Station
Arsenal Station
Drayton Park Station
Holloway Road Stn
Highbury & Islington Stn
Canonbury Stn
Angel Stn
SEVEN SISTERS ROAD
BLACKSTOCK ROAD
BROWNSWOOD ROAD
GREEN LANES
LORDSHIP PARK
HORNSEY ROAD
TOLLINGTON ROAD
HOLLOWAY ROAD
HIGHBURY PARK
HIGHBURY GROVE
ST PAUL'S RD
BALLS POND ROAD
CANONBURY ROAD
ESSEX ROAD
UPPER ST
LIVERPOOL RD
CALEDONIAN ROAD
NEW NORTH ROAD
SOUTHGATE ROAD
NEWINGTON GN RD
ALBION ROAD
BARING STREET
City & Islington College
London Metropolitan University
Islington Town Hall
HM Prison
Freightliners City Farm
N1
N5
F
G
H
J
I
K
1
2
3
4
5
6
7
55
74
91
31
32
33

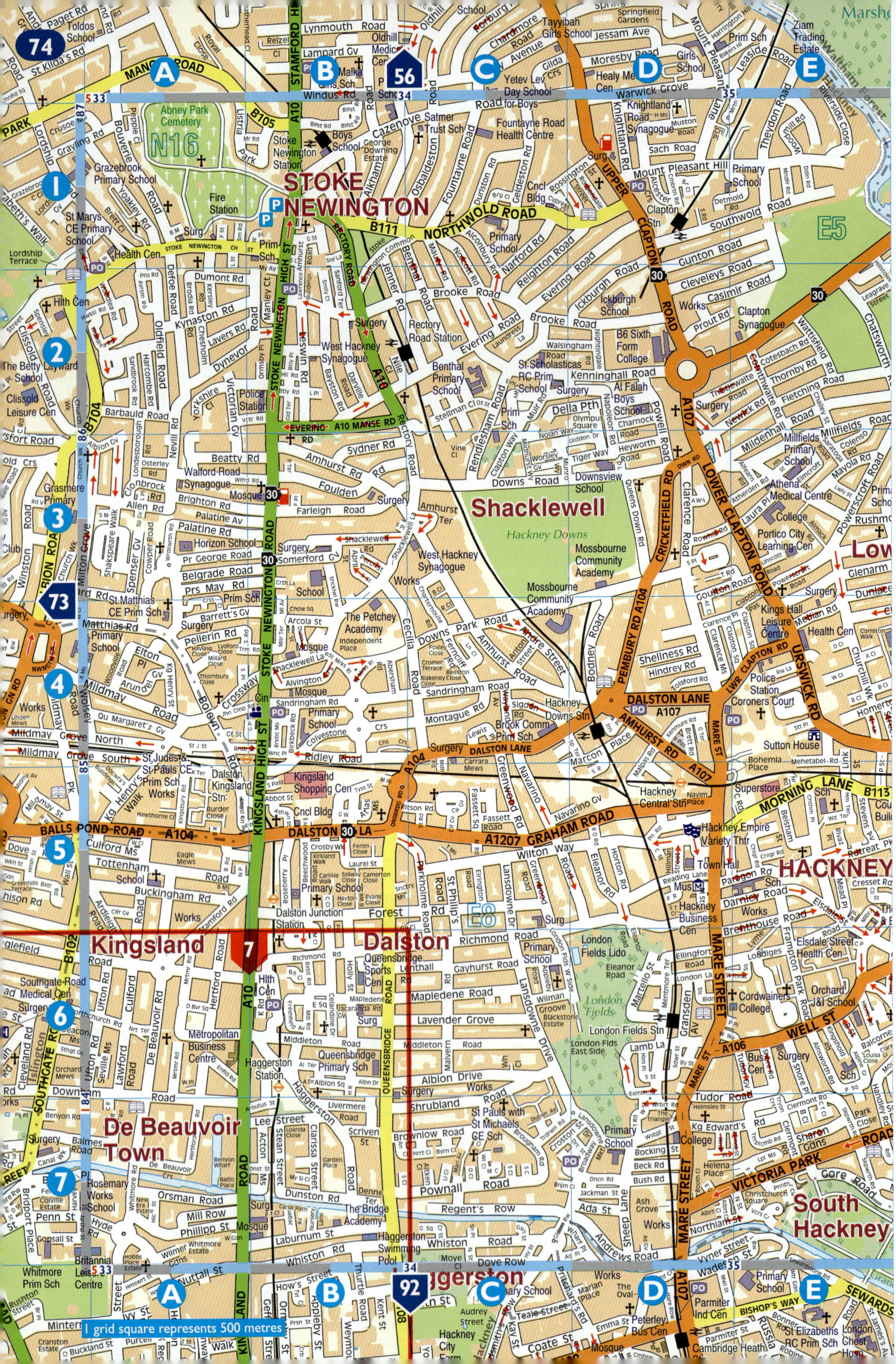
74
56
A
B
C
D
E
1
2
3
73
4
5
6
7
92
STOKE NEWINGTON
Shacklewell
Hackney Downs
HACKNEY
Kingsland
Dalston
De Beauvoir Town
South Hackney
Haggerston
Abney Park Cemetery
N16
E5
E8
STAMFORD HILL
STOKE NEWINGTON HIGH ST
STOKE NEWINGTON ROAD
KINGSLAND HIGH ST
NORTHWOLD ROAD
UPPER CLAPTON ROAD
LOWER CLAPTON ROAD
AMHURST RD
DALSTON LANE
BALLS POND ROAD
A1207 GRAHAM ROAD
MARE STREET
MORNING LANE
WELL ST
VICTORIA PARK ROAD
QUEENSBRIDGE ROAD
SOUTHGATE ROAD
PEMBURY RD A104
CRICKETFIELD RD
URSWICK RD
RECTORY ROAD
MANOR ROAD
SEWARDSTONE RD
Mount Pleasant Hill
1 grid square represents 500 metres

Lea Bridge
Hackney Marsh
Clapton Park
Lower Clapton
Temple Mills
Hackney Wick
Homerton
Old Ford
Stratford Marsh
Victoria Park
Lea Valley Ice Centre
Fairways Business Park
Leyton Business Centre
Orient Ind Park
Leyton Orient FC (Matchroom Stadium)
Superstore
New Spitalfields Market
Hackney Sports Centre
Homerton University Hospital
Mandeville Primary School
Cardinal Pole RC School
Gainsborough Primary School
Vision College of Technology
Hackney Wick Station
Victoria Park Industrial Cen
Cardinal Pole RC Secondary Lower School
Olympic site under development
Stratford International Station
Pudding Mill Lane Station
Crown Close Business Cen
Axis Business Centre
Vanguard Trading Est
Marsh Gate Business Centre
Lauriston Primary School
Roman Indoor Mkt
LEA BRIDGE ROAD
HOMERTON ROAD
MARSH HILL
HIGH STREET
WICK ROAD
EASTWAY
RUCKHOLT ROAD
HIGH ROAD LEYTON
VICTORIA PARK ROAD
CASSLAND ROAD
GROVE ROAD
OLD FORD ROAD
PARNELL ROAD
CHAPMAN ROAD
EAST CROSS ROUTE
BLACKWALL TNL NORTHERN AP
A12
A106
A102
B112
B118
B119
Thames Path
Lee Navigation
River Lea or Lee
E9
E10
57
76
93

76
58
75
94
Leytonstone
LEYTON
Forest Gate
Stratford New Town
STRATFORD
Stratford Marsh
E15
Cemetery
Olympic site under development
Channel Tunnel Rail Link
Westfield Stratford City development (due to open spring 2011)
Stratford International Station
Stratford Station
Stratford Shopping Centre
Leytonstone High Road Stn
Leyton Stn
Forest Gate Station
Plaistow Station
Orient FC Stadium
Superstore
Drapers Sports Ground
West Ham Park
Ramgarhia Sikh Gurdwara Temple
Atherton Leisure Centre
Cathall Leisure Centre
Langthorne Health Centre
Langthorne Hosp
Newham Training & Ed Ctr
Uni of E London
County Court
Police Stn
Ibis Hotel
Axis Business Centre
Vanguard Trading Est
Marsh Gate Business Centre
Heron Industrial Estate
The British American Academy
Connaught School for Girls
Davies Lane Primary School
Tom Hood School
Jenny Hammond Prim Sch
Maryland Prim Sch
Earlham Primary School
Park Primary School
Rokeby School
Odessa Infant School
College of Bus & Tech
Quwwat Ul Islam Girl's School
St Bonaventure's School
HIGH ROAD LEYTON
GROVE GREEN ROAD
HARROW ROAD
DAMES ROAD
CHOBHAM ROAD
LEYTON ROAD
LEYTONSTONE ROAD
WATER LANE
ROMFORD ROAD
VICARAGE LA
ANGEL LANE
EASTERN ROAD
BROADWAY
HIGH ST
WEST HAM LANE
CARPENTERS ROAD
PORTWAY
NEW PLAISTOW RD
PLAISTOW RD
STOPFORD ROAD
CENTRE ROAD
RUCKHOLT RD
MANOR ROAD
A12
A11
A112
A106
A118
B161
B164
B165
A114
1 grid square represents 500 metres

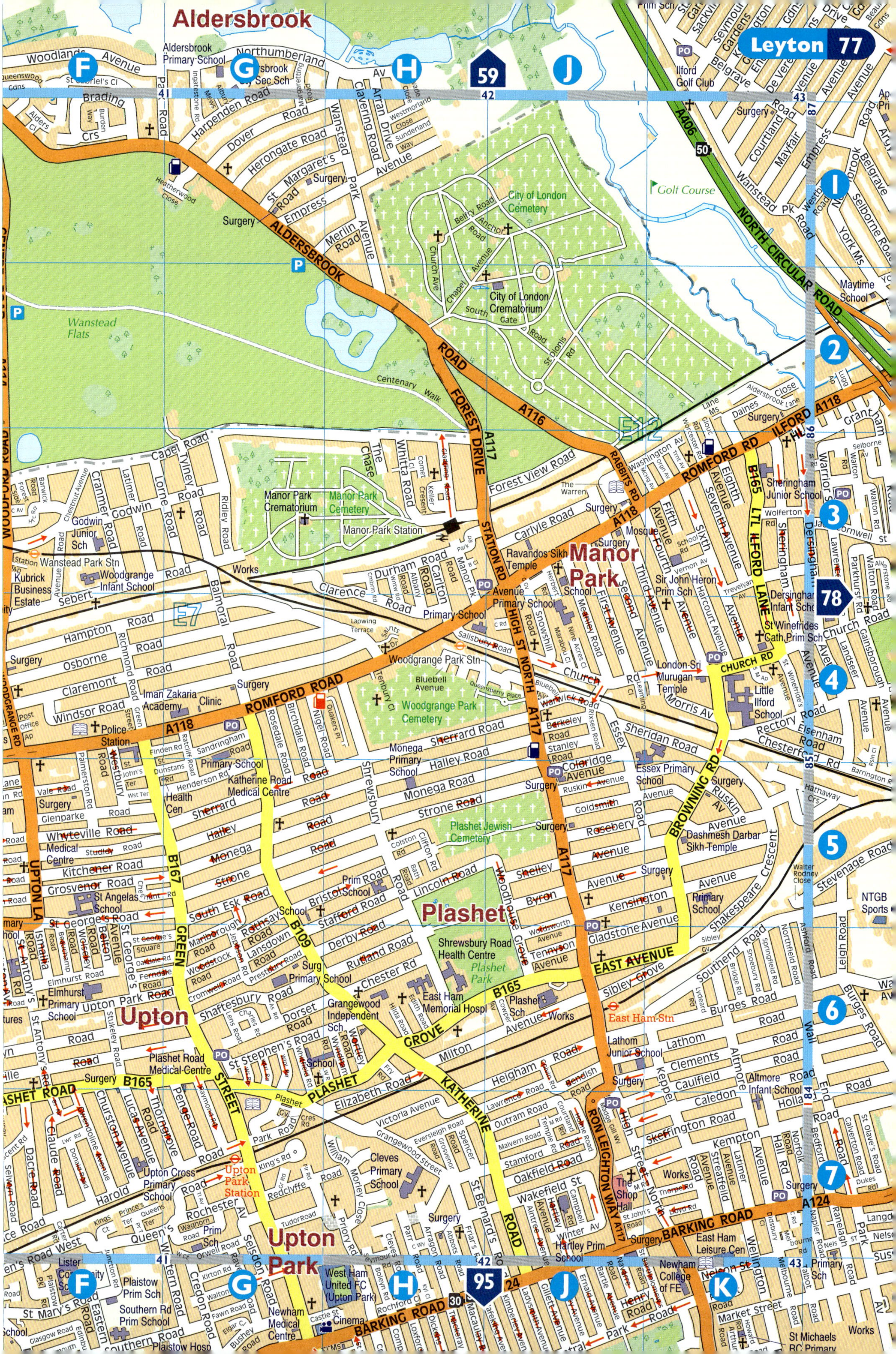
Leyton 77
59
78
95
Aldersbrook
Aldersbrook Primary School
Wanstead Flats
City of London Cemetery
City of London Crematorium
Golf Course
NORTH CIRCULAR ROAD
ALDERSBROOK ROAD
FOREST DRIVE
Centenary Walk
A116
A117
A118
A406
Manor Park Crematorium
Manor Park Cemetery
Manor Park Station
Manor Park
STATION RD
HIGH ST NORTH
ROMFORD ROAD
Woodgrange Park Cemetery
Woodgrange Park Stn
Wanstead Park Stn
E7
E12
Plashet
Plashet Park
Plashet Jewish Cemetery
Shrewsbury Road Health Centre
East Ham Memorial Hospl
East Ham Stn
Upton
Upton Park Station
Upton Park
West Ham United FC (Upton Park)
GREEN STREET
B167
B165
B109
PLASHET ROAD
KATHERINE ROAD
RON LEIGHTON WAY
BARKING ROAD
A124
EAST AVENUE
BROWNING RD
LTL ILFORD LANE
UPTON LA
WOODGRANGE RD
Little Ilford School
Sheringham Junior School
Newham College of FE
East Ham Leisure Cen
NTGB Sports
Maytime School
Dashmesh Darbar Sikh Temple
London Sri Murugan Temple
Ravandos Sikh Temple
Upton Cross Primary School
Cleves Primary School
Grangewood Independent Sch
Newham Medical Centre
Plaistow Hosp
Plaistow Prim Sch
Southern Rd Prim School
St Michaels RC Primary

78
60
77
96
40
A
B
C
D
E
1
2
3
4
5
6
7
543
44
45
84
85
86
87
ILFORD
Little Ilford
Loxford
BARKING
Wallend
IG1
NORTH CIRCULAR ROAD
HIGHBRIDGE ROAD
A406
A118
A1083
A123
A124
GREEN LANE
HIGH ROAD
ILFORD HILL
CHAPEL RD
WINSTON WAY
ILFORD LANE
FANSHAWE AVENUE
LONGBRIDGE ROAD
NORTHERN RELIEF RD
LONDON ROAD
ABBEY RD
ST PAULS RD
ILFORD LTL A118
CHURCH RD
River Roding
Ilford Station
Barking Station
The Exchange
The Bus Cen
Kenneth More Theatre
Ilford Retail Park
New Rush Hall School
Buckingham Road Cemetery
Cricklefield Stadium
Ilford Swimming Pool
South Park
South Park Terrace
SS Peter & Pauls RC Primary School
Gordon Infant School
Woodlands J&I School
Loxford School of Science & Technology
South Park Clinic
Barking Abbey Comprehensive School (Lower)
Barking Park
Uphall Primary School
Northbury Primary School
Jamia Mosque
Singh Sabha Temple
NTGB Sports Ground
The Vicarage Field Shopping Cen
Health Clinic
Magistrates Court
Superstore
Barking Abbey Industrial Est
St Margarets Primary School
St Josephs RC Primary School
Abbey Sports Centre
Medical Cen
Gascoigne Primary School
Ripple Infant School
Hopewell School
Fresh Wharf Est
Seven Kings
Seven Kings Health Cen
Canon Palmer RC High School
Cranbrook College
Ilford Medical Cen
Cleveland Prim Sch
Sheringham Junior School
Little Ilford School
St Winefrides Cath Prim Sch
Altmore Infant School
Maytime School
Winston Way Prim Sch
Apex Prim Sch
Park Sch
Prep Sch
High Sch
The Orchard Health Cen
Langdon School
1 grid square represents 500 metres

Goodmayes
Goodmayes Park
Becontree Primary School
Fair Cross
Becontree
Castle Green
Parsloes Park
Mayesbrook Park
Mayesbrook Park Arena
University of East London
Barking FC
Barking Abbey Leisure Centre
Barking Abbey Comprehensive School (Upper)
Barking Abbey School
Manor Infant School
Barking Hospital
Upney Station
Becontree Station
Rippleside Cemetery
Barking Ind Park
Alfreds Way Industrial Est
Renwick Industrial Estate
Dorothy Barley Primary School
East Barking Centre
Childs Welfare Clinic
St Teresa RC Primary School
Roding Prim Sch
The Sydney Russell School
Keith Davis Cue Sports Club
Cambell Primary School
Monteagle Primary School
The Jo Richardson Community School
Goresbrook Leisure Centre
Barking RUFC
Eastbury Primary School
Mayespark Primary School
Valence Primary Sch
Valence House Mus & Library
Becontree Hospital
Henry Green Primary School
St Vincents RC Prim Sch
Southwood Prim Sch
GREEN LANE
GOODMAYES LANE
LONGBRIDGE ROAD A124
PORTERS AVENUE A1153
BENNETT'S CASTLE LANE B191
LODGE AVENUE A1153
RIPPLE ROAD A13
RIPPLE ROAD A123
Becontree Avenue
Goresbrook Road
Ivyhouse Road
Hedgemans Road
Rugby Road
Sheppey Road
Woodward Road
Bevan Avenue
Keir Hardie Way
Woodbridge Road
Mayesbrook Road
Valence Avenue
Valence Circus
Felbrigge Road A1083
IG3
IG11
RM8
61
80
97

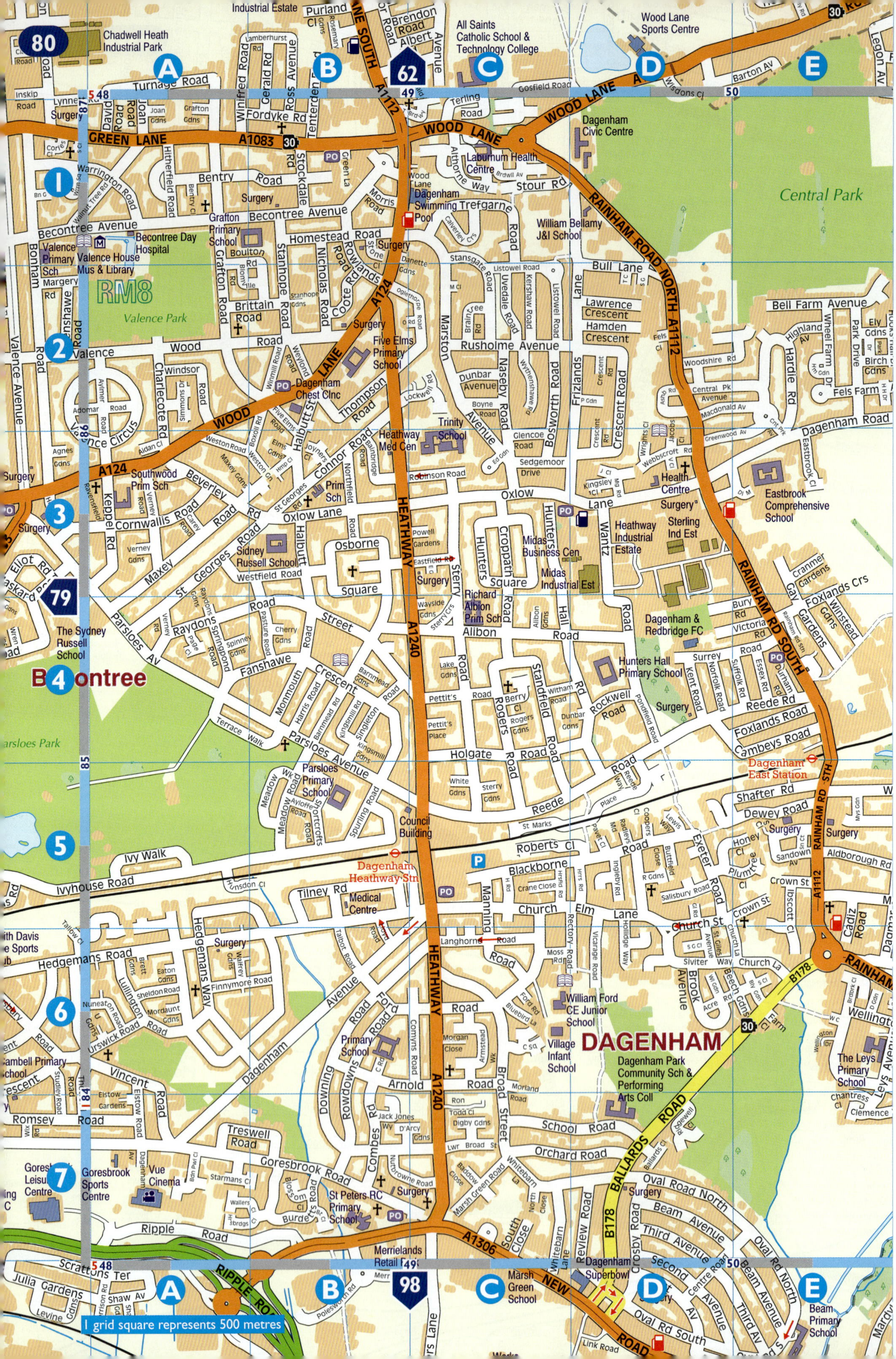

80
Chadwell Heath Industrial Park
Industrial Estate
Purland Cl
Brendon Road
All Saints Catholic School & Technology College
Wood Lane Sports Centre
62
A
B
C
D
E
548
49
50
Turnage Road
Gosfield Road
Green Lane
A1083
Wood Lane
A1112
Dagenham Civic Centre
Laburnum Health Centre
Central Park
Rainham Road North A1112
Warrington Road
Bentry Road
Becontree Avenue
Becontree Day Hospital
Valence Primary Sch
Valence House Mus & Library
RM8
Valence Park
Grafton Primary School
Homestead Road
Dagenham Swimming Pool
Trefgarne Road
Stour Rd
William Bellamy J&I School
Bull Lane
Lawrence Crescent
Hamden Crescent
Bell Farm Avenue
Rusholme Avenue
Five Elms Primary School
Dagenham Chest Clnc
Valence Circus
A124
Heathway
A1240
Trinity School
Heathway Med Cen
Sedgemoor Drive
Oxlow Lane
Health Centre
Eastbrook Comprehensive School
Heathway Industrial Estate
Sterling Ind Est
Midas Business Cen
Midas Industrial Est
Dagenham Road
Southwood Prim Sch
Sidney Russell School
79
The Sydney Russell School
Becontree
Parsloes Park
Parsloes Avenue
Parsloes Primary School
Richard Alibon Prim Sch
Alibon Road
Dagenham & Redbridge FC
Hunters Hall Primary School
Rainham Rd South
Dagenham East Station
Council Building
Dagenham Heathway Stn
Ivyhouse Road
Ivy Walk
Medical Centre
Church Elm Lane
Hedgemans Road
William Ford CE Junior School
Village Infant School
DAGENHAM
Dagenham Park Community Sch & Performing Arts Coll
The Leys Primary School
Ballards Road
B178
Goresbrook Sports Centre
Vue Cinema
St Peters RC Primary School
Goresbrook Road
Ripple Road
A1306
Merrielands Retail Pk
98
Marsh Green School
Dagenham Superbowl
New Road
Oval Road North
Beam Avenue
Beam Primary School
1 grid square represents 500 metres

63
99
Elm Park
South Hornchurch
RM10
RM
Eastbrookend Country Park
Eastbrook End Cemetery
Harrow Lodge Park
Hornchurch Sports Centre
The Albany School
Barking College
Rush Green Primary School
Wykeham Primary School
Catholic Primary School
Abbs Cross Sch & Arts Coll
Aylof Primary School
Dunningford Primary School
Elm Park Station
Kings Estate
Rosewood Medical Centre
The RJ Mitchell Prim Sch
John Perry Prim Sch
Scargill Jun Sch
Scargill Inf Sch
St Albans RC JMI School
Brittons School Technology College
Whybridge Infant School
Whybridge Junior School
Health & Welfare Clinic
Albyns Farm
Bretons
Works
Barking & Dagenham
Havering
Beam River
UPPER RAINHAM ROAD
RAINHAM ROAD
A125
A1112
DAGENHAM RD
Dagenham Road
Thorntons Farm Av
Gorseway
Valentines Way
Eastbrook Drive
The Chase
Warren Drive
Woodcote Avenue
Northwood Avenue
Elm Park Avenue
Woburn Av
St Andrews Avenue
Windermere Avenue
Carnforth Gardens
Maylands Av
Coronation Dr
South End Road
Maybank Avenue
Cavendish Crs
Mungo Park Road
Simpson Road
Ford Lane
Grove Park Road
Avelon Road
Hayes Dr
Airfield Way
Western Avenue
Auriel Av
Goring Road
Manor Road
Beamway
Canberra Crs
Frederick Road
Lowen Road
Nelson Road
Stanley Road
North Road
Blacksmith's Lane
Alexandra Road

64
101
A
B
C
D
E
1
2
3
4
5
6
7
508
09
10
83
82
81
80
Hillingdon Heath
HAYES
Hayes End
Wood End Green
Wood End
UB11
Old Abbotstonians RFC
Swakeleys
Abbotsfield School
Highfield School
Works
Charville Primary School
Hedgewood School
Brook House FC
Hayes Park J&I School
Grange Park Junior School
Grange Park Clinic
Mellow Lane School
Pronto Trading Estate
Uxbridge Co Court
The Beck Theatre
Hayes CC
The Hayes Manor School
Rosedale College
Hayes Stadium Sports Centre
Dr Tripletts School
Uxbridge College
Junior Sch
McMillan Clinic
Hayes FC
Hayes Social & Sports Club
Golf Course
Stockley Park Golf Club
Stockley Park Business Centre
Silverdale Industrial Estate
Minet Clinic
Hayes Pool
Rec Gnd
Sikh Temple
Rostrever Gardens
Caxton Trading Estate
Crown Trading Centre
Botwell RC Prim Sch
Betam Rd
Clayton
Provident
Sutton Court Road
Charville Lane
Dog Rose Ramble
Sharvel
Hillingdon Trail
Yeading Brook
Lawrence Rd
Gainsborough Road
Hayman Crs
Raeburn Rd
Hoppner Road
Harrow View
Mellow Lane East
Kingshill Avenue
Kingshill Cl
Bury Avenue
Goshawk Gardens
Grosvenor Road
Lansbury Drive
Weymouth Road
Dorset Avenue
Adelphi Crs
Bradenham Rd
Portland Road
Exmouth Rd
Raynton Dr
Fairholme Crs
Leamington Place
Park Lane
Mansfield Dr
Frogmore Avenue
Frogmore Gardens
Balmoral Dr
Derwent Drive
Hurstfield Crs
Woodrow Avenue
Whittington Avenue
Gledwood Dr
Gledwood Av
Balmoral Road
Marvell Ave
Chaucer Av
Spencer Av
Shakespeare
Warley Avenue
Belmore Av
Coleridge Way
Uxbridge Road
UXBRIDGE R
Addison
Craven Close
Swift Cl
Acacia Avenue
Church Road
Rectory Road
Manor Road
Hesa Avenue
Harrow View
Hemmen Lane
Freemans Lane
Central Avenue
Orchard Road
Judge Heath Lane
Church Walk
Botwell Lane
Botwell Common Road
Compton Road
Forris Avenue
Moray Avenue
Coldharbour Lane
Birchway
Minet Drive
Hunters Grove
Fairdale Gdns
Pump Lane
Printinghouse Lane
Golden Crs
Lannock Road
Sycamore Avenue
Juniper Way
Barra Hall Road
Beechwood Av
Princes Pk La
Dawley Road
DAWLEY ROAD
A437
Bolingbroke Way
Furzeground Way
The Square
Roundwood Av
Longwalk Road
Grand Union Canal Wk
Uxbridge Road
New Road
Fountain
Hayes End Dr
Hayes End Rd
Newport Rd
Church Rd
Middleton
Wood End Green Road
Queens Road
Grange Road
Wood End
Albion Road
Leven Way
Cromwell Road
Tudor Road
Bishops Road
York Avenue
Kingsway
Saxony Pde
Hanover
Stuart Crs
Normandy Drive
Victoria Road
Cranmer Road
North Rd
B465 WEST DRAYTON ROAD
Green Lane
Harlington Road
HARLINGTON ROAD
Dawley Av
Cherry Grove
Pole Hill Road
Marlborough Road
Nelson Rd
Charles Street
Westbourne Road
Collingwood Road
Sibley Ct
Haig Rd
Dickens Av
Gould's Gn
Corwell Lane
Hewens Road
Heath Rd
Star Road
Purkis Cl
Surgery
1 grid square represents 500 metres

Yeading
Hayes Town
SOUTHALL
UB4
UB1
65
84
102
Downe Barns Farm
St Raphaels RC Primary School
Downe Manor Primary School
Yeading Medical Centre
Viking Primary School
Belmore Primary School
Barnhill Community High School
Brookside Primary School
The Willows School
Superstore
Gifford Primary School
Greenford Sports Centre
Lady Margaret Primary School
Durdans Park School
Cranleigh Gardens Industrial Estate
Yeading Primary School
Yeading Junior School
The Warren Medical Centre
Lombardy Retail Park
Elystan Business Cen
Hayes Bridge Retail Park
Houston Business Park
Brook Industrial Est
Guru Nanak Sikh Secondary School
Guru Nanak Sikh Primary School
Yeading FC
Blair Peach Primary School
Minet J&I School
Pump Lane Industrial Est
Trading Est
Guru Nanak Medical Cen
Medical Centre
Hambrough Primary Sch
Villiers High School
Southall & West London Coll
Middle School
Arches Business Cen
Hindu Temple
Fire Station
Police Station
Dog Rose Ramble & Hillingdon Trail
Yeading Brook
Grand Union Canal
Grand Union Canal Wk
THE PARKWAY
A312
RUISLIP ROAD
B455
UXBRIDGE ROAD
A4020
THE BROADWAY
SOUTH ROAD
A3005
CHURCH ROAD
A180
Kingshill Avenue
Yeading Lane
Glencoe Road
Ashford Avenue
Berwick Avenue
Lady Margaret Road
Greenford Avenue
Beaconsfield Road
Hillingdon
Ealing

84
66
83
103
A
B
C
D
E
1
2
3
4
5
6
7
WESTERN AVENUE
GREENFORD
Dormer's
Wells
Hanwell
UB6
UB1
RUISLIP ROAD
B455
A4127
GREENFORD ROAD
UXBRIDGE ROAD
A4020
Grand Union Canal
River Brent
Belvue School
Kelvin Ind Est
Greenford Rd Medical Cen
Oldfield Primary School
South Greenford Station
Perivale Park Athletics Track
Perivale Park Golf Club
Golf Course
Coston Primary School
E Betham CE Primary School
Greenford Synagogue
Greenford Sports Centre
Greenford High School
Crossmead Primary School
Surgery
Stanhope Prim Sch
Portland House Medical Centre
Our Lady of the Visitation RC Prim
Cardinal Wiseman RC School (Technology & Art College)
Brentside High School
Brentside Primary School
Greenford Park Cemetery
Lady Margaret School
Mayfield Primary School
Greenford Avenue Medical Centre
Allenby Primary School
Dormers Wells High School
Dormers Wells Leisure Centre
Medical Centre
Kings Avenue Medical Centre
Brent Valley Golf Club
West Middlesex Golf Club
Dormers Wells Junior School
Hindu Temple
Fire Station
Police Station
Tutorial College of W London
Villiers High School
Southall Park
Barrett Ind Park
Windmill Business Centre
Works
Ealing Hospital
St Marks Primary School
Hanwell Stn
Great Western Ind Park
Southall Stn
Arches Business Cen
Middlesex Business
Three Bridges Business
1 grid square represents 500 metres

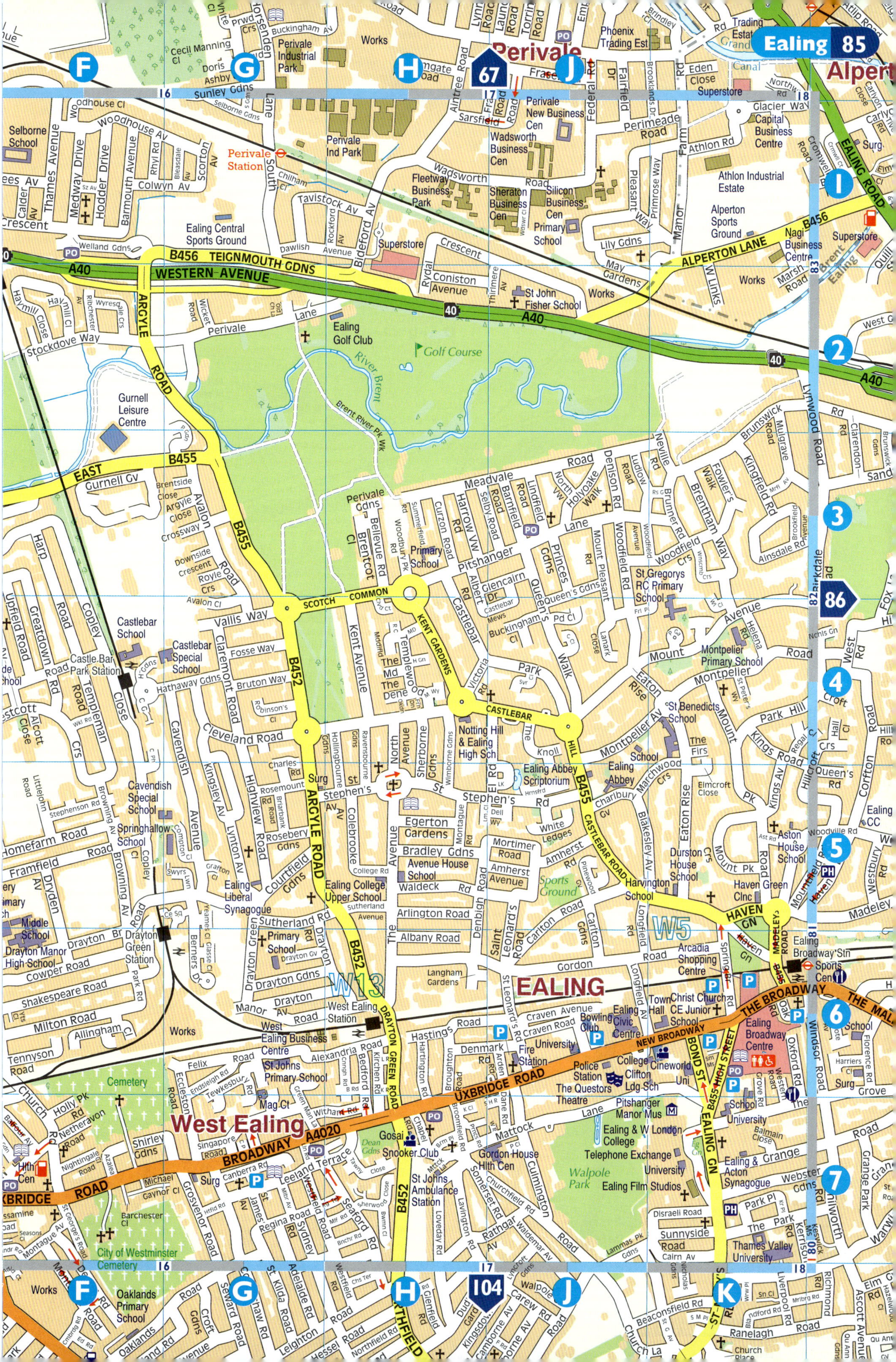

Perivale
67
F
G
H
J
16
17
18
Perivale Industrial Park
Works
Phoenix Trading Est
Perivale New Business Cen
Wadsworth Business Cen
Perivale Ind Park
Perivale Station
Selborne School
Thames Avenue
Medway Drive
Hodder Drive
Barmouth Avenue
Colwyn Av
Scorton Av
Sunley Gdns
Woodhouse Av
Tavistock Av
Fleetway Business Park
Sheraton Business Cen
Silicon Business Cen
Primary School
Perimeade Road
Athlon Rd
Athlon Industrial Estate
Alperton Sports Ground
Capital Business Centre
Glacier Way
Superstore
Ealing Road
Grand Union Canal
Alpert
1
2
3
4
5
6
7
Ealing Central Sports Ground
B456 TEIGNMOUTH GDNS
A40 WESTERN AVENUE
Bideford Av
Superstore
Crescent
Coniston Avenue
Thirlmere Av
St John Fisher School
Works
ALPERTON LANE
B456
Nagi Business Centre
Lily Gdns
May Gardens
Pleasant Way
Primrose Way
Manor Farm
W Links
Brent
River Brent
ARGYLE ROAD
Perivale Lane
Ealing Golf Club
Golf Course
Brent River Pk Wk
Stockdove Way
Gurnell Leisure Centre
EAST
B455
Gurnell Gv
Lynwood Road
Brunswick Road
Mulgrave Rd
Kingfield Rd
Brentham Way
Fowler's Walk
Neville Rd
Denison Rd
Ludlow Rd
Holyoake Walk
Meadvale Road
Lindfield Rd
Barnfield Rd
Selby Road
Harrow Vw
Curzon Road
Perivale Gdns
Bellevue Rd
Brentcot Cl
Primary School
Pitshanger Lane
Princes Gdns
Mount Pleasant Rd
Woodfield Rd
Woodfield Crs
St Gregorys RC Primary School
Ainsdale Rd
86
SCOTCH COMMON
KENT GARDENS
Castlebar Rd
Queen's Gdns
Buckingham Cl
Avenue
Helena Rd
Montpelier Primary School
Mount Avenue
Montpelier Road
B455
Harp Road
Upfield Road
Greatdown Rd
Copley Cl
Castlebar School
Castle Bar Park Station
Castlebar Special School
Templeman Road
Vallis Way
Fosse Way
Bruton Way
Hathaway Gdns
Claremont Road
B452
Cleveland Road
Kent Avenue
The Dene
Templewood
CASTLEBAR HILL
Victoria Rd
Park Rd
Eaton Rise
St Benedicts School
Park Hill
Kings Road
Notting Hill & Ealing High Sch
Ealing Abbey Scriptorium
Knoll Rd
Ealing Abbey
School
Montpelier Av
Marchwood Crs
The Firs
Elmcroft Close
Aston House School
Woodville Rd
Queen's Rd
Corfton Rd
Ealing CC
Cavendish Special School
Springhallow School
Cavendish Avenue
Kingsley Av
Lynton Av
Highview Road
Rosemount Rd
Rosebery Gdns
Hollingbourne Gdns
St Stephen's Av
Stephen's Rd
Colebrooke Av
Egerton Gardens
Bradley Gdns
Avenue House School
Waldeck Rd
Mortimer Road
Amherst Avenue
White Ledges
Sports Ground
CASTLEBAR ROAD
Charlbury Gv
Blakesley Av
Eaton Rise
Durston House School
Mount Pk Road
Haven Green Clnc
Homefarm Road
Framfield Road
Dryden Av
Browning Av
Middle School
Drayton Manor High School
Drayton Br Road
Drayton Green Station
Cowper Road
Shakespeare Road
Milton Road
Allingham Cl
Tennyson Road
Ealing Liberal Synagogue
Courtfield Gdns
Sutherland Rd
Primary School
Drayton Gdns
Drayton Green Rd
ARGYLE ROAD
Ealing College Upper School
Arlington Road
Albany Road
Langham Gardens
Harvington School
HAVEN GN
MADELEY RD
W5
Arcadia Shopping Centre
Ealing Broadway Stn
Sports Cen
THE BROADWAY
THE MALL
W13
EALING
Gordon Road
Manor Road
West Ealing Station
Works
West Ealing Business Centre
St Johns Primary School
Alexandria Road
DRAYTON GREEN ROAD
Hastings Road
Craven Avenue
Craven Road
Bowling Club
Ealing Civic Centre
Town Hall
Christ Church CE Junior School
Ealing Broadway Centre
Oxford Rd
Windsor Road
NEW BROADWAY
Fire Station
University
Police Station
The Questors Theatre
College
Clifton Lodge Sch
Cineworld
Uni
BOND ST
B455 HIGH STREET
EALING GN
Cemetery
West Ealing
BROADWAY
A4020
UXBRIDGE ROAD
Pitshanger Manor Mus
Ealing & W London College
Telephone Exchange
University
Ealing Film Studios
Walpole Park
Mattock Lane
Gordon House Hlth Cen
Snooker Club
St Johns Ambulance Station
Gosai
Leeland Terrace
Ealing & Acton Synagogue
Grange Road
Webster Gdns
Hlth Cen
Shirley Gdns
Barchester Cl
City of Westminster Cemetery
Grosvenor Road
Regina Road
Sydney Road
Seaford Rd
Culmington Road
Disraeli Road
Sunnyside Road
Cairn Av
Thames Valley University
The Park
Lammas Pk Gdns
K
104
Works
Oaklands Primary School
Oaklands Rd
Seward Road
St Kilda Road
Adelaide Rd
Leighton Rd
Northfield Rd
Carew Rd
Beaconsfield Rd
Ranelagh Road
Liverpool Rd
Richmond Rd
Ascott Avenue

86
68
85
105
Alperton
Park Royal
Lower Place
West Acton
Acton
NORTH CIRCULAR ROAD
WESTERN AVENUE
HANGER LANE
EALING ROAD
GUNNERSBURY AVENUE
UXBRIDGE RD
HIGH ST
HORN LANE
PARK ROYAL ROAD
ACTON LANE
THE BROADWAY
THE MALL
A40
A406
A4020
A4000
B456
Hanger Lane Station
Park Royal Stn
North Ealing Station
West Acton Station
Ealing Broadway Stn
Ealing Common Stn
Acton Main Line Station
Central Middlesex Hospital
A&E
Acton Hospital
Ealing Common
Pavilion Barclays Sports Ground
The Shamrock Sports Club
Ellen Wilkinson School for Girls
West Acton Primary School
West Twyford Primary School
The Japanese School
Twyford CE High School
Acton Superbowl
Vue Cinema
Crowne Plaza
Travelodge
Lakeside Drive
Cumberland Avenue
Coronation Road
Queensbury Road
Abbey Avenue
Westfields Road
Churchfield
Creffield
Mill Hill Rd
River Brent
Grand Union Canal Walk
1 grid square represents 500 metres

Harlesden
College Park
Old Oak Common
East Acton
Shepherd's Bush
Wormwood Scrubs Park
Kensal Green Cemetery
London West Crematorium
Acton Park
NW10
W12
69
88
106
Harlesden Station
Willesden Junction Station
North Acton Station
East Acton Stn
Acton Central Station
Kensal Station
Grand Union Canal
Grand Union Canal Walk
Euro Freightliner Terminal
The New Business Centre
Kingham Industrial Est
Cumberland Park Industrial Estate
Gateway Industrial Est
Star Works
Apex Industrial Est
Hythe Road Industrial Estate
Hogarth Industrial Estate
North Pole Depot
Superstore
Oakwood Business Centre
Bush Industrial Estate
Acton Business Centre
Park Royal Business Centre
Pilot Industrial Centre
Victoria Industrial Estate
Chase Road Trading Estate
Ramada Encore Hotel
North Acton Business Park
Mitre Bridge Ind Park
Little Wormwood Scrubs Recreation Park
Linford Christie Stadium
HM Prison Wormwood Scrubs
Hammersmith Hospital
Queen Charlotte's & Chelsea Hospital
Burlington Danes School
Old Oak Primary School
John Perryn Primary School
Phoenix High School
Bentworth Primary School
BBC Media Village
BBC Television Centre
QPR FC (Loftus Road Stadium)
Janet Adegoke Leisure Centre
Bromyard Leisure Centre
King Fahad Academy
Barbara Speake Theatre School
East Acton Primary School
Shepherd's Bush CC
Acton Park Industrial Est
Acton Park Industrial Est
Furness Primary School
Princess Frederica CE J&I School
Willesden Sports Centre
Cardinal Hinsley College
Wormholt Park Prim Sch
Canberra Primary School
Commonwealth Av Primary School
Old Oak Common La
Victoria Rd A4000
Scrubs Lane
Harrow Rd A404
High St Harlesden
Manor Pk Road
Westway A40
Uxbridge Road A4020
The Vale
Wood Lane
Hammersmith & Fulham

88
70
87
107
A
B
C
D
E
1
2
3
4
5
6
7
Willesden Sports Centre
Park
KILBURN
Cemetery
Queen's Park
Kensal Rise
Kensal Green
Kensal Rise Station
Kensal Green Station
West Kilburn
Kilburn Park Stn
Queens Park Station
BRONDESBURY ROAD
HARVIST ROAD
KILBURN LANE
CARLTON VALE
KILBURN PARK ROAD
HARROW ROAD
MORTIMER RD
CHAMBERLAYNE
LADBROKE GROVE
Grand Union Canal Walk
Superstore
Canal Way
Kensal Town
Westbourne Green
Westbourne Park Station
W10
North Kensington
ST QUINTIN AVENUE
NORTH POLE RD
WESTWAY
A40
Ladbroke Grove Stn
WESTBOURNE PARK RD
CHEPSTOW ROAD
PEMBRIDGE VILLAS
Notting Hill
Notting Hill Gate Stn
Latimer Road Station
W11
WOOD LANE
White City Station
Wood Lane Station
BBC Television Centre
W12
Shepherd's Bush
Westfield London
WEST CROSS ROUTE
Shepherd's Bush Market Station
Holland Park Stn
HOLLAND PARK AVENUE
UXBRIDGE ROAD
Kensington Park Rd
Kensington Church
Holland Park
W8
1 grid square represents 500 metres

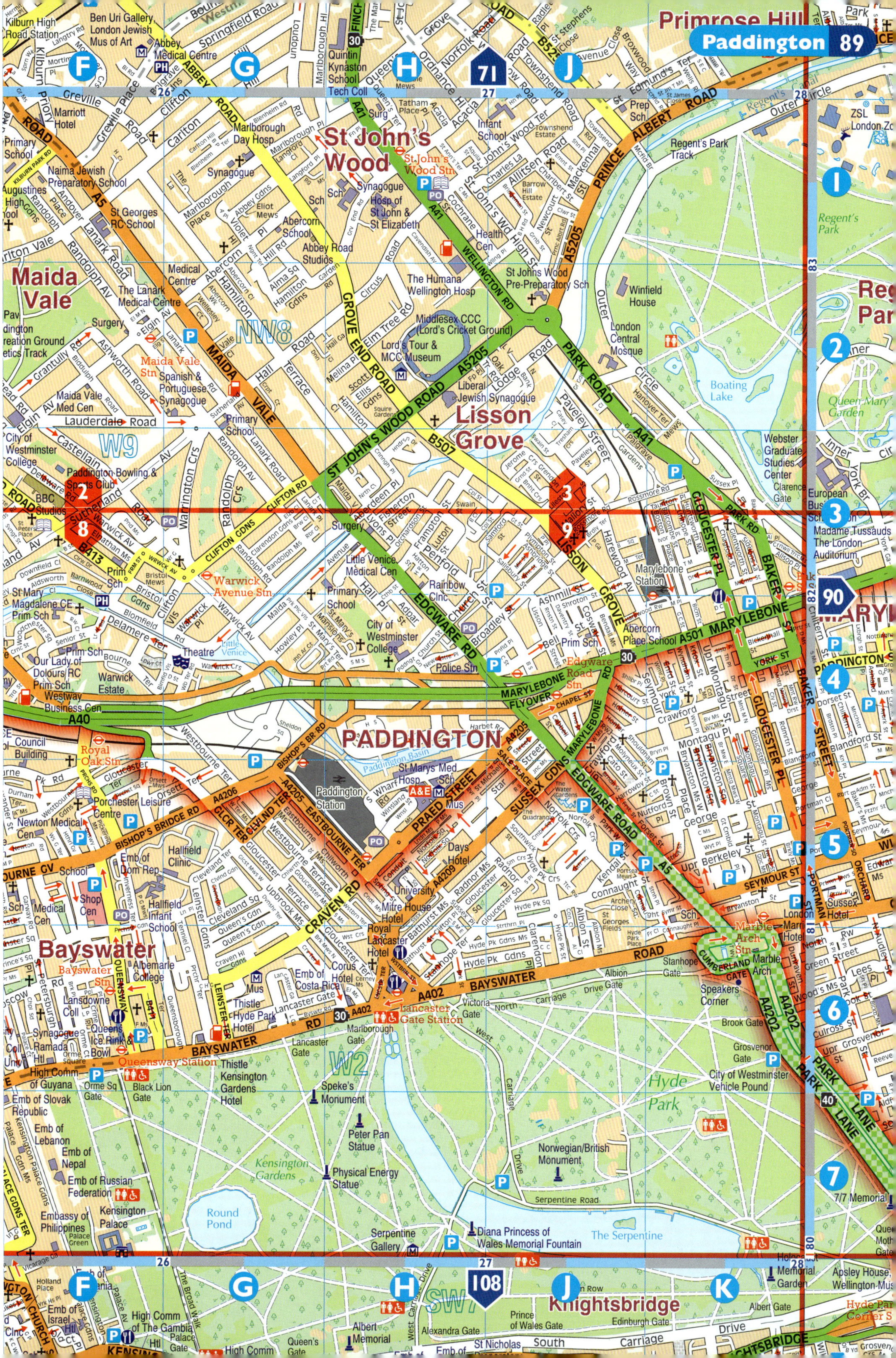

Primrose Hill
St John's Wood
Maida Vale
Lisson Grove
PADDINGTON
Bayswater
Knightsbridge
Regent's Park
Hyde Park
Kensington Gardens
The Serpentine
Round Pond
Boating Lake
NW8
W9
W2
SW7
71
90
108
PRINCE ALBERT ROAD
MAIDA VALE
GROVE END ROAD
ST JOHN'S WOOD ROAD
PARK ROAD
EDGWARE ROAD
MARYLEBONE FLYOVER
A501 MARYLEBONE
BAKER STREET
GLOUCESTER PL
PRAED STREET
SUSSEX GDNS
BISHOP'S BRIDGE RD
BAYSWATER
BAYSWATER ROAD
PARK LANE
CLIFTON GDNS
ABBEY ROAD
WELLINGTON RD
Paddington Station
Marylebone Station
Lord's Tour & MCC Museum
Marble Arch
Speakers Corner
Diana Princess of Wales Memorial Fountain
Serpentine Gallery
Lancaster Gate Station
Queensway Station
Bayswater Stn
Warwick Avenue Stn
Maida Vale Stn
St John's Wood Stn
Edgware Road Stn
Royal Oak Stn
Marble Arch Stn
London Central Mosque
Winfield House
Speke's Monument
Peter Pan Statue
Physical Energy Statue
Norwegian/British Monument
Albert Memorial

90
89
72
109
A
B
C
D
E
1
2
3
4
5
6
7
Prince Albert Road
ZSL London Zoo
Gloucester Gate
Regent's Park
Cumberland Gate
Queen Mary's Garden
Inner Circle
Outer Circle
Chester Road
Camden Thtr
Mornington Crescent Stn
Camden High Street
Crowndale Rd
Eversholt St
Hampstead Road
Albany Street
Somers Town
St Pancras International Station
King's Cross Station
King's Cross St Pancras Stn
British Library
Euston Station
Euston Road
Euston Square Station
Warren Street Stn
University Coll Hosp
University College London
Great Portland St
Regent's Park Stn
Madame Tussauds & The London Auditorium
Marylebone Road
MARYLEBONE
Baker St
Gloucester Pl
Marylebone High St
Wigmore Street
Cavendish Pl
Portland Place
New Cavendish St
Mortimer Street
Goodge St Stn
Tottenham Court Road
Tottenham Court Road Station
Gower Street
Petrie Museum of Egyptian Archaeology
Univ of London
Russell Square Stn
Russell Sq
Bloomsbury
British Museum
Bloomsbury Way
New Oxford St
St Giles
Oxford Street
A40 (Restricted)
Oxford Circus Stn
Bond Street Stn
Marble Arch Stn
Marble Arch
Park Lane
Emb of the US
Grosvenor Square
Mayfair
New Bond Street
Regent Street
Soho
Shaftesbury Av
Charing Cross Road
Leicester Square Stn
Covent Garden Stn
The Mkt
Strand
Piccadilly
Piccadilly Circus
Piccadilly Circus Stn
Green Pk Station
Royal Acad of Arts
St James's St
Pall Mall
Haymarket
National Gallery
Nelson's Column
Cockspur St
Northumberland Av
Charing Cross Stn
Whitehall
Horse Guards Parade
St James's Palace
St James's
The Mall
7/7 Memorial
Apsley House The Wellington Museum
Hyde Park Corner
Constitution Hill
Queen Victoria Memorial
Churchill Museum & Cabinet War Rooms
Westminster
Victoria Embankment
Ministry of Defence
Dukes Hotel
Sofitel St James Hotel
1 grid square represents 500 metres

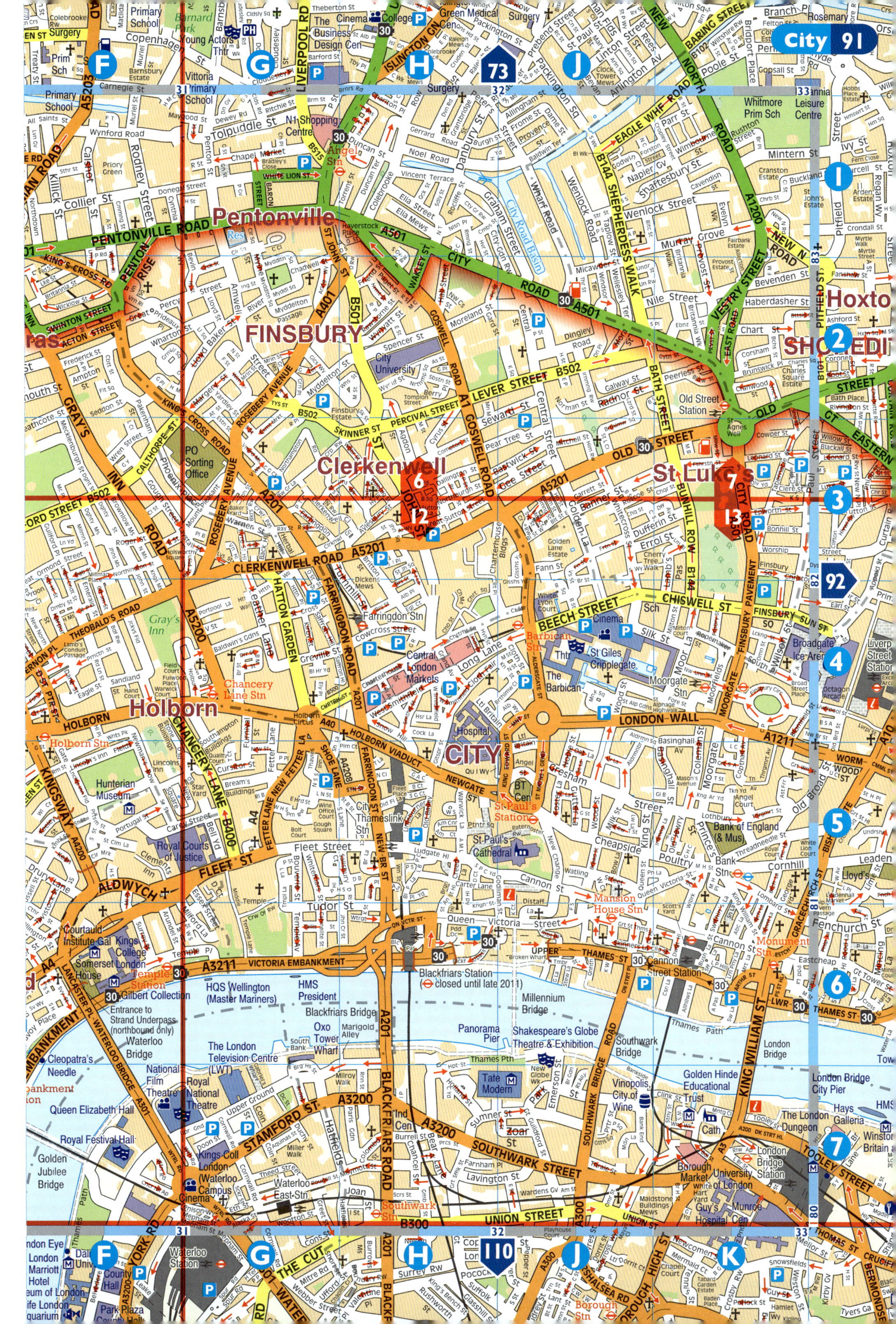
Pentonville
FINSBURY
Clerkenwell
St Luke's
Holborn
CITY
Hoxton
SHOREDITCH
PENTONVILLE ROAD
CITY ROAD
CLERKENWELL ROAD
OLD STREET
BEECH STREET
CHISWELL ST
LONDON WALL
HOLBORN VIADUCT
NEWGATE
FLEET ST
ALDWYCH
VICTORIA EMBANKMENT
UPPER THAMES ST
STAMFORD ST
SOUTHWARK STREET
UNION STREET
BLACKFRIARS ROAD
FARRINGDON ROAD
GOSWELL ROAD
KINGSWAY
CHANCERY LANE
KING WILLIAM ST
EAGLE WHF ROAD
SHEPHERDESS WALK
LEVER STREET
Barbican
St Paul's Cathedral
Bank of England & Mus
Blackfriars Bridge
Millennium Bridge
Southwark Bridge
London Bridge
Waterloo Bridge
Tate Modern
Shakespeare's Globe Theatre & Exhibition
Royal Festival Hall
National Theatre
Somerset House
Royal Courts of Justice
Central London Markets
Farringdon Stn
Old Street Station
Blackfriars Station (closed until late 2011)
Cannon Street Station
Waterloo Station
London Bridge Station
Southwark Stn
Borough Stn
Holborn Stn
Temple Station
Chancery Lane Stn
Mansion House Stn
Monument Stn
St Paul's Station
Barbican Stn
Moorgate Stn
Thames

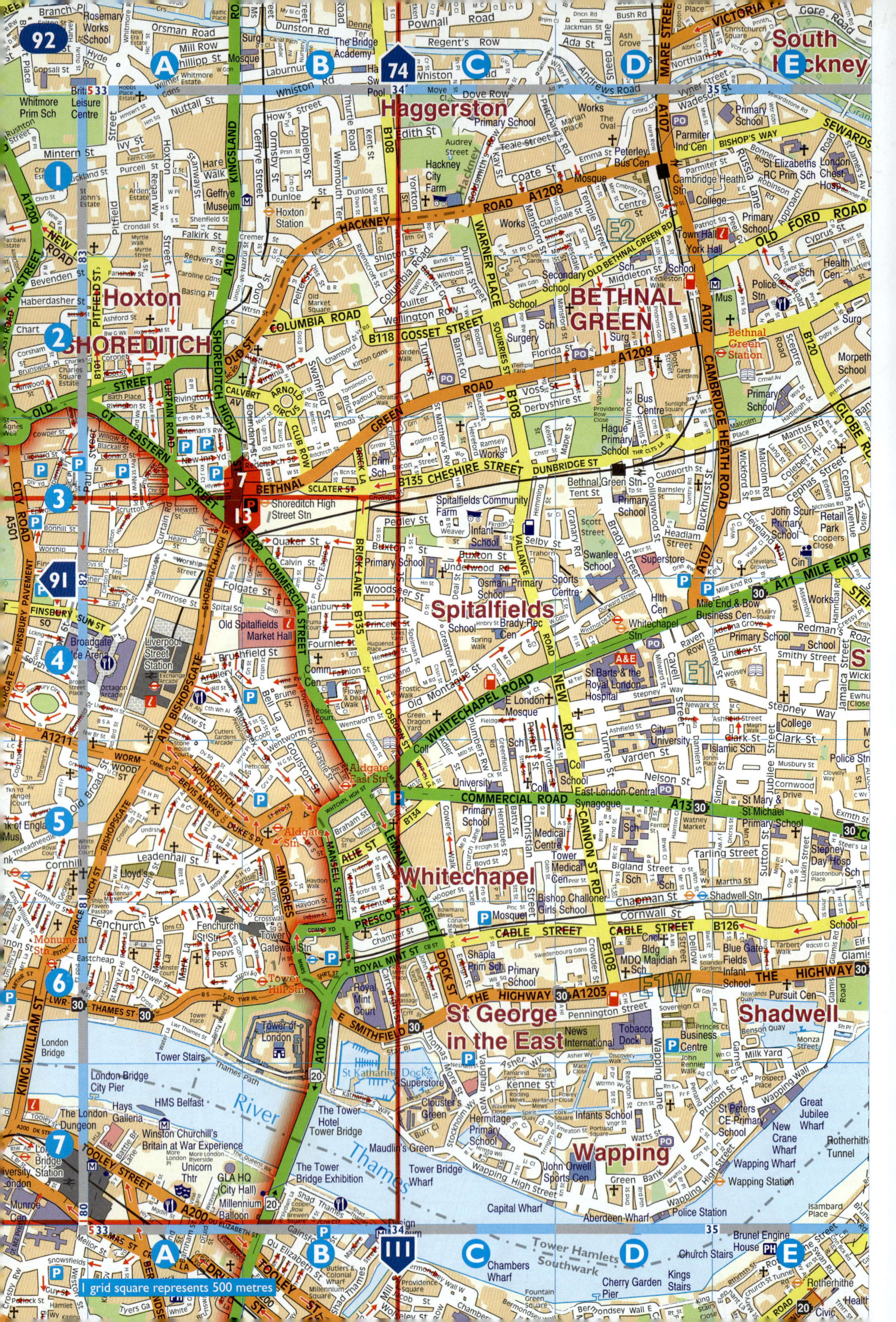

92
74
91
111
A
B
C
D
E
1
2
3
4
5
6
7
Haggerston
South Hackney
Hoxton
SHOREDITCH
BETHNAL GREEN
E2
Spitalfields
Whitechapel
E1
St George in the East
E1W
Shadwell
Wapping
River Thames
HACKNEY ROAD
OLD BETHNAL GREEN RD
CAMBRIDGE HEATH ROAD
MARE STREET
VICTORIA
BISHOP'S WAY
OLD FORD ROAD
COLUMBIA ROAD
GOSSET STREET
BETHNAL GREEN ROAD
CHESHIRE STREET
DUNBRIDGE ST
SCLATER ST
SHOREDITCH HIGH ST
KINGSLAND
NEW NORTH ROAD
OLD STREET
GT EASTERN STREET
CITY ROAD
FINSBURY PAVEMENT
BISHOPSGATE
COMMERCIAL STREET
BRICK LANE
WHITECHAPEL ROAD
NEW RD
COMMERCIAL ROAD
MILE END RD
CABLE STREET
THE HIGHWAY
ROYAL MINT ST
MANSELL STREET
LEMAN STREET
MINORIES
FENCHURCH ST
KING WILLIAM ST
TOOLEY STREET
WAPPING HIGH STREET
Hackney City Farm
Geffrye Museum
Hoxton Station
Shoreditch High Street Stn
Liverpool Street Station
Old Spitalfields Market Hall
Aldgate East Stn
Aldgate Stn
Tower Gateway Stn
Tower Hill Stn
Tower of London
Tower Bridge
St Katharine Docks
London Bridge City Pier
HMS Belfast
The London Dungeon
Winston Churchill's Britain at War Experience
GLA HQ (City Hall)
The Tower Bridge Exhibition
Bethnal Green Station
Shadwell Stn
Wapping Station
Rotherhithe Tunnel
Tower Hamlets
Southwark
Cherry Garden Pier
Royal London Hospital
East London Central Synagogue
Tobacco Dock
News International
London Bridge
Monument Stn
Tower Stairs
Capital Wharf
Chambers Wharf
1 grid square represents 500 metres

Globe Town
BOW
Bromley
Mile End
Bow Common
STEPNEY
Limehouse
POPLAR
Canary Wharf
Tower Hamlets
Southwark
GROVE ROAD
OLD FORD ROAD
ROMAN ROAD
B119
BURDETT ROAD
A1205
A11
MILE END ROAD
BOW ROAD
COMMERCIAL ROAD
A13
EAST INDIA DOCK ROAD
WEST INDIA DOCK RD
LIMEHOUSE LINK
WESTFERRY RD
WESTFERRY CIRC
BLACKWALL TNL NORTHERN AP
ST PAUL'S WAY
BEN JONSON ROAD
DEVONS ROAD
DEVAS ST
SALTER ROAD
Mile End Stadium
Mile End Park
Cemetery
Queen Mary College
Limehouse Stn
Bow Road Stn
Mile End Stn
Bromley by Bow Station
Devons Rd Stn
Langdon Pk Stn
Stepney Green Station
Poplar Station
West India Quay Station
Canary Wharf Station
Heron Quays Station
South Quay Station
Pudding Mill Lane Station
Westferry Stn
Museum in Docklands
Billingsgate Fish Market
Canary Riverside
Surrey Docks
Rotherhithe Street
75
94
112
36
37
38
80
81
82
83
F
G
H
J
K
I
1
2
3
4
5
6
7
E3
E14

94
76
93
113
E15
E14
Mill Meads
Plaistow
South Bromley
Blackwall
River Thames
River Lea or Lee
Tower Hamlets
Greenwich
Newham
Blackwall Reach
Bugsby's Reach
The O2
Blackwall Basin
Poplar Dock
A118 HIGH STREET
BLACKWALL TUNNEL NORTHERN APPROACH
A102
A13
EAST INDIA DOCK ROAD
BARKING ROAD
NEWHAM WAY
A1011 MANOR ROAD
STEPHENSON STREET
A1020 LOWER LEA CROSSING
SILVERTOWN WAY
ASPEN WAY
A102 BLACKWALL TUNNEL
A1206
PRESTON'S ROAD
COTTON STREET
NEW PLAISTOW RD
PLAISTOW RD
A112 HIGH ST
A124
B125 ABBOTT ROAD
Abbey Road Station
West Ham Station
Plaistow Station
Bromley by Bow Station
Star Lane Station
Canning Town Station
East India Station
Blackwall Station
All Saints Stn
Poplar Station
Royal Victoria Station
West Silvertown Station
North Greenwich Station
Pumping Station
The British American Drama Academy
Channelsea Business Centre
PCMS London
Kingsland College of Business Studies
Three Mills Heritage Centre
Invicta Industrial Estate
Hedges & Butler Estate
East London RUFC
East London Crematorium
East London Cemetery
Memorial Recreation Ground
London Contemporary Dance School
Barratt Industrial Park
Datapoint Business Cen
Pylon Trading Estate
Industrial Estate
London Chinese Dance School
Blackwall Trading Estate
Culloden Primary School
London Esthetique
London International College
London Natural Therapy School
The Rathbone Education Cen
Balaam Leisure Centre
Royal Victoria Docks Watersports Centre
Crowne Plaza
Billingsgate Fish Market
Greenshields Industrial Est
Minerva Works
Gas Works
Travelodge
Tunnel Avenue Trading Est
Wood Wharf Business Park
Manor Road
Barking Road
Woolwich Road
Victoria Dock Rd
Grange Road
Howard's Road
London City Airport Link
The David Beckham
I grid square represents 500 metres

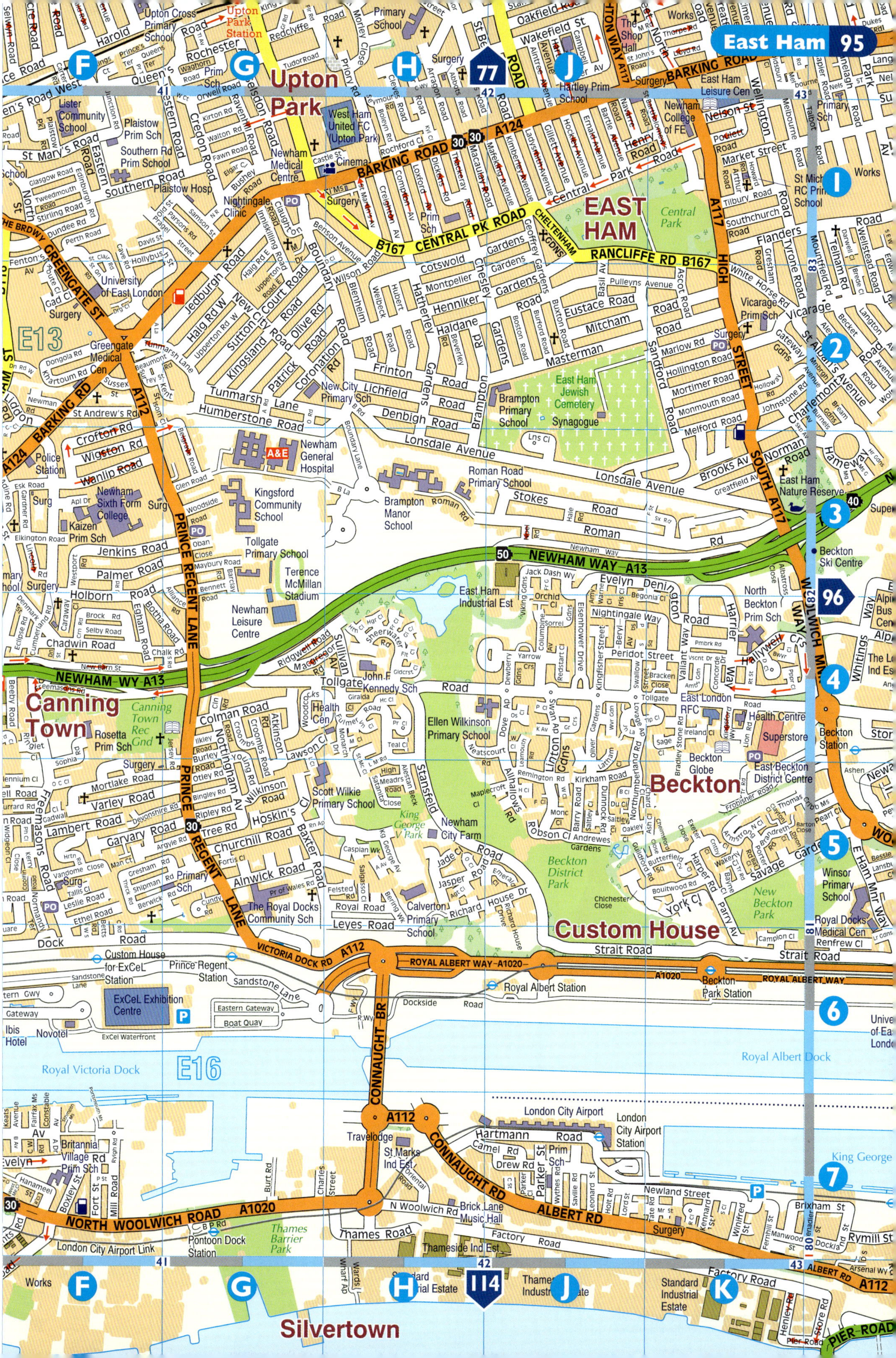
Upton Park
EAST HAM
E13
Canning Town
Beckton
Custom House
E16
Silvertown
BARKING ROAD A124
CENTRAL PK ROAD
B167
RANCLIFFE RD B167
HIGH STREET SOUTH A117
GREENGATE ST
BARKING RD A124
PRINCE REGENT LANE
A112
NEWHAM WAY A13
NEWHAM WY A13
WOOLWICH MR WAY
VICTORIA DOCK RD
ROYAL ALBERT WAY A1020
CONNAUGHT BR
CONNAUGHT RD
ALBERT RD
NORTH WOOLWICH ROAD A1020
PIER ROAD
West Ham United FC (Upton Park)
Newham General Hospital
University of East London
East Ham Jewish Cemetery
Central Park
Brampton Manor School
Kingsford Community School
Tollgate Primary School
Terence McMillan Stadium
Newham Leisure Centre
East Ham Industrial Est
East Ham Nature Reserve
Beckton Ski Centre
North Beckton Prim Sch
Beckton District Park
New Beckton Park
Beckton Globe
East Beckton District Centre
Beckton Station
Beckton Park Station
Royal Albert Station
Custom House for ExCeL Station
Prince Regent Station
ExCeL Exhibition Centre
Royal Victoria Dock
Royal Albert Dock
London City Airport
London City Airport Station
Pontoon Dock Station
Thames Barrier Park
London City Airport Link
King George V Park
Newham City Farm
Ellen Wilkinson Primary School
Scott Wilkie Primary School
The Royal Docks Community Sch
Calverton Primary School
Winsor Primary School
Royal Docks Medical Cen
Newham Sixth Form College
Rosetta Prim Sch
Canning Town Rec Gnd
St Marks Ind Est
Thameside Ind Est
Standard Industrial Estate
Brick Lane Music Hall
Travelodge
Novotel
Ibis Hotel
41
42
43
F
G
H
I
J
K
1
2
3
4
5
6
7
77
96
114

96
78
95
115
Wallend
Creekm
A124
A406
A13
A1020
A117
NORTH CIRCULAR ROAD
ALFRED'S WAY
NEWHAM WAY
ROYAL DOCKS ROAD
WOOLWICH MNR WAY
WOOLWICH MANOR WAY
ROYAL ALBERT WAY
ALBERT ROAD
SOUTH
STREET
E6
Sussex Road
Langdon School
Langdon Crs
St Michaels RC Primary School
Market Street
Southchurch Road
Flanders Road
Tyrone Road
Vicarage Prim Sch
Vicarage
St Alban's Avenue
Gooseley Lane
Folkestone Rd
Wellstead Road
Mountfield Rd
Telham Rd
Norman Road
Hameway
East Ham Nature Reserve
Superstore
Beckton Triangle Retail Park
Gateway Retail Park
Claps Gate Lane
Eric Clarke Lane
Jenkins Lane
Spur Road
Showcase Newham Cinema
Abbey Wharf Industrial Estate
Abbey Park Industrial Est
Fresh Wharf
St Pauls Rd
Sports Centre
Medical Cen
Gascoigne Primary School
The Orchard Health Cen
New England Industrial Est
Works
River Road Business Park
Katella Trading Est
River Road Business Park
Cromwell Business Cen
Waverley Gdns
Westminster Gdns
River Road
Lyon Business Park
Barking Creek
Beckton Ski Centre
Eastbury Road
Alpine Bus Cen
GX Superbowl
Alpine Way
The London Ind Estate
Roding Road
London Ind Park
Whitings Way
Superstore
Gallions Reach Shopping Park
Armada Way
Health Centre
Superstore
Beckton Station
East Beckton District Centre
Stonewall
Cygnet Clinic
Beckton
Gallions Primary School
Oxleas
Covelees Wall
Savage Gardens
New Beckton Park
Winsor Primary School
Royal Docks Medical Cen
Renfrew Cl
Strait Road
Cyprus Station
Cyprus Place
Gallions Reach Station
Armada Wy
Atlantis Av
Magellan Bvd
Albert Basin Wy
Basin Ap
University of East London
University Way
Royal Albert Dock
King George V Dock
King George V Station
Brixham St
Rymill St
Woodman St
Fishguard Wy
Gallions Reach
Newham
Greenwich
Margaret or Tripcock Ness
Miles Drive
Battery Rd
Ridge Close
Pier Rd
1 grid square represents 500 metres

Castle Green
Thamesmead 97
79
98
116
Barking Ind Park
Community School
Goresbrook Leisure
Goresbrook Sports
Ripple Road
A13
Alfreds Way Industrial Est
Renwick Industrial Estate
Renwick Road
Box Lane
Works
Scrattons Ter
Julia Gardens
Levine Gdns
Morrison Rd
Shaw Av
Crescent
Maybury Road
Wivenhoe Road
Roxwell Road
Crouch Av
Roycraft Avenue
Bastable Avenue
Thames View Clinic
Thames View J&I School
Stanley Avenue
Curzon Crs
Alderman Av
Stern Close
Keel Close
Choats Road
Blessing Way
Wanderer Drive
Sovereign Road
Gt Galley Close
Skillion Business Park
Riverside Industrial Est
Thames Road
Estuary Cl
Twine Cl
River Road Business Park
Radford Way
Crossness Road
Gallions Cl
Bankside Park Industrial Est
Shearwater Cl
Marine Dr
Anchor Cl
Marine Drive
Galleons Drive
Creek Road
Creekmouth Industrial Park
River Road
Long Reach Road
Works
Trafalgar Business Centre
Anglian Industrial Estate
Balmoral Trading Estate
Buzzard Creek Industrial Estate
Atcost Road
River Road
Works
River Thames
Barking and Dagenham
Newham
Bexley
Greenwich
Cross Ness
Barking Reach
Birkdale Close
St Andrews Cl
Lytham Cl
Riverside Golf Club
Woburn Cl
Cherbury Close
Longworth Cl
Golf Cours
Voyagers Cl
Thamesbank Place
Copperfield Rd
Watersmeet Way
Dolphin Cl
Fairway
Summerton Way
Castillion Primary School
Manordene Road
Crossway
Kingfisher Close
Walsham Rd
Wroxham Rd
Greenhaven Dr
Nickelby Cl
Thamesmead
Thamesmead Leisure Centre
Primary School
Superstore
Thamesmere Dr
Thamesmead Shopping Centre
Central Way
Central Wy
Carlyle Road
Bishop John Robinson CE Prim School
Goldcrest Close
Crossway
Kinder Cl
Haldane Road
Twin Tumps Way
Tawney Rd
Titmuss Avenue
Police Station
Tripcock Point Development Site
Waldstock Rd
Hutchins Road
Hawksmoor Primary School
Windrush Prim Sch
Crowden Way
Glendale Way
Jubilee Primary School
Poplar Pl
Green Chain Walk
Eastern Way
Belvedere Road
Waterside Drive
Barnham Drive
Newmarsh Rd
Woolwich Polytechnic School
SE28
Bentham Road
Austen Close
Byron Cl
Owen Cl
Disraeli Cl
Discovery Prim Sch
Marathon Wy
Battery Rd
Pitfield Crs
Roman Sq
Sorrel Cl
Epstein Rd
St Margaret Clitherow RC Primary School
Sunset Road
Eastern Way
Birchmere Bus Park
Ampleforth Road
Binsley Wk
Hartslock Dr
Portmeadow Wk
Seacourt Road
Southlake
St Brides Close
The Busin

Goresbrook Leisure
98
Goresbrook Sports Centre
Vue Cinema
Starmans Cl
Goresbrook Road
St Peters RC Primary School
Surgery
Ripple Road
80
A1306
South Close
Marsh Green Road
Whitebarn Lane
Review Road
B178
Oval Road North
Beam Avenue
Dagenham Superbowl
Crosby Road
Second Avenue
First Avenue
Centre Road
Third Av
Oval Rd South
Oval Rd S
Beam Primary School
Merrielands Retail Park
Merrielands Crs
Scrattons Ter
Julia Gardens
Levine Gdns
Morrison Rd
Shaw Av
Shaw Gdns
RIPPLE ROAD
Polesworth Rd
Marsh Green School
NEW ROAD
A1306
Link Road
Sierra Drive
Sierra Dr
E Entrance
Mardyke Cl
Lower Mardyke
NEW
RM9
Works
Dagenham Dock Station
LC
Chequers Lane
Avenue
A13
Choats Manor Way
Thames Gateway Park
Breach Lane
Kent Avenue
Ford Industrial Park
Lake Road
Thames Avenue
Works
Choats Road
Pascoe La
Rob
Hindmans Way
Power Station
Consul
A13
Courier
Works
Industrial Estate
Hindmans Way
Kent Av
Thunderer Road
Fiesta Drive
Hornchurch Marshes
97
Works
Perry Road
Works
River Thames
Ness
Halfway Reach
St Andrews
Lytham Cl
Riverside Golf Club
Woburn Cl
Summerton Way
Cherbury Close
Longworth
Golf Course
Courtland Gro
Fleming Way
Chadwick
Bayliss Av
Wallace Cl
Works
EASTERN WAY
Road
A2016
Norman Road
Works
Capital Industrial Est
Crabtree Manorway North
Fisher's Way
Fordgate Business Park
A
B
C
D
E
1
2
3
4
5
6
7
548
49
50
83
82
81
80
117
30
A2016
ERN WAY
MANORWAY
Anderson Way
Jenningtree Way
Mulberry
Way
Erith Marshes
East
The Business
St Brides Close
St Edmunds Cl
Green Chain Wk
Drive
1 grid square represents 500 metres

Hornchurch
RAINHAM
F
G
H
J
K
81
118
51
52
53
83
82
81
80
1
2
3
4
5
6
7
Lowen Road
Frederick Road
Newtons Primary School
Walden Av
Askwith Rd
Spencer Road
Manser Road
Surgery
Betterton Road
Spinney Cl
Karen Cl
Maytree Cl
Nelson Road
Stanley Road
North Road
Hood Rd
Trafalgar Rd
Whybridge Close
Blake Cl
Blacksmith's Lane
Health & Welfare Clinic
Stanhope Rd
Victory Rd
A125
RAINHAM RD
RAINHAM ROAD
Wymark Cl
Neptune Cl
Knightswood Road
Collingwood Rd
Christchurch Avenue
Edmund Road
Hubert Rd
Tree Lane
Edwin Close
Cherry Tree La
Philip Road
Queens Gdns
Fordview Industrial Estate
Works
ROAD
Suttons Business Park
New Zealand Way
Dunedin Road
Queenstown Gdns
Evansdale
La Salette RC Prim Sch
Rainham Trading Estate
Mudlands Estate
A1306
NEW ROAD
Dovers Corner Industrial Estate
Ind Est
Creekside
BRIDGE RD
B1335
Consul Av
Consul Avenue
Marsh Avenue
Manor Way
Marsh Way
Manor Way Business Cen
Road
Penny Cl
Stirling Close
Wentworth Way
Anchor Dr
Davies Cl
Glebe Road
Police Station
Farm
Parsonage
Rainham Village Primary School
Glenwood Av
Ashwood Av
Hawthorn Av
Waverley Rd
South Road
Upminster Road
Pkwy
Cloister Cl
West Cl
East Cl
Martin Dr
Brights Av
Ingrebourne Road
Wantz La
Baillie Cl
Arterial Av
Orchard Av
Vincent Rd
Glen
Lamb's
Rainham Hall (NT)
St Helens Ct
Cowper Road
Melville Road
Ferro Rd
PO
Surg
BROADWAY
Surgery
WENNINGTON ROAD
Rainham Station
LC
Capstan Dr
Lamson Road
Ferry Lane Industrial Est
Lamson Rd
Albright Industrial Estate
Denver Industrial Estate
Palliser Dr
Ellis Av
Findon Gdns
Venette Cl
Wilfred Av
Elizabeth Rd
Brookway
Penerley Road
Beechwood Gdns
Rothbury Av
Southbury Av
South Hall Drive
Eastwood Drive
B1335
Chafford Sports Complex
Chafford School
Primary School
Ingrebourne River
Blackwater Cl
Creek Way
Star Business Centre
Thamesview Business Centre
Barlow Way S
Barlow Way
Barlow Way South
Lorimar Business Cen
Salamons Way
Frog Lane
Marsh Way
Fairview Industrial Centre
Ferry Lane
A13
Denver Industrial Estate
Industrial Estate
KP Estate
Frog Island
Jenningtree Point
Rainham Marshes
Rainham Marshes RSPB Reserve
Coldharbour Lane
Belvedere Industrial Centre
Works
A13

West Drayton
Harmondsworth
Sipson
UB7
TW6
Heathrow
M4
Junction 4
Junction 4a
HOLLOWAY LANE
SIPSON ROAD
STOCKLEY ROAD
A408
A3044
HATCH LANE
BATH ROAD
A4
Harmondsworth Lane
Sipson Lane
Northern Perimeter Rd (West)
Warwick Rd
Fairway Avenue
Porters Way
Thornton Av
Cherry Lane
Crowne Plaza
Novotel
Holiday Inn
Thistle Hotel
West Drayton Cemetery
West Drayton Prim Sch
Police Station
Heathrow Primary School
Longmead Primary School
Cherry-Lane Primary School
Airport Gate Business Centre
Chambers Business Park
Fire & Ambulance Station
Iron Bridge Road North
Grand Union Canal Wk
Duke of Northumberland's River
Moorland Road
Skyport Dr
Zealand Av
Pinglestone Close
Blunts Avenue
A
B
C
D
E
1
2
3
4
5
6
7
506
07
80
79
78
77
1 grid square represents 500 metres

120

Stockley Park Business Centre
The Square
Rostrever Gardens
Lannock Road
Hayes Pool
Central Avenue
Rec Gnd
Silverdale Industrial
Birchway
82
Temple
Warnford Industrial Estate
Caxton Trading Estate
Botwell RC Prim Sch
Crown Trading Centre
Swallowfield Wy
Speedway Industrial Est
Rigby Lane
Works
Aberglen Industrial Estate
Betam Rd
Kestrel Way
Adler Ind Est
Clayton Road
Printinghouse Lane
Fairview Industrial Est
Frogmore Industrial Est
Blyth Rd
Hayes & Harlington Station
Cranford Park Primary School
Pump Lane
Pump Lane Industrial Est
Trading Est
Provident Ind Est
Argent Cen Ind Est
Chailey Ind Est
Silverdale Ind Est
Regent Business Cen
Peter James Business Cen
Halls Business Cen
Johnsons Industrial Estate
Trinity Trading Est
Grand Union Canal Wk
DAWLEY ROAD
A437
UB3
N HYDE RD
NORTH HYDE RD
Keith Road
Squirrels Trading Estate
Nestle's Avenue
North Hyde Gardens
Bull's Bridge
Superstore
Bullsbridge Industrial Estate
THE PARKWAY
A312
Bourne Avenue
Glamis Crs
Waltham Avenue
Colbrook Av
Wentworth Crs
Skipton Drive
Carnarvon Drive
Elers Road
Elers Clinic
Pinkwell Avenue
Pinkwell La
Pinkwell Primary School
Harlington Community School
Millington Road
Station Road
Monmouth Road
Crowland Avenue
Woolacombe Wy
Croyde Avenue
Cleave Avenue
Bedwell Gardens
Cranford Drive
Cranford Park Junior School
Laburnum Rd
Coronation Rd
Hillborne Road
Roseville
Watersplash Lane
Comfort Inn
M4
60
Junction 3
102
Medical Centre
High Street Harlington
Victoria Lane
Hudson Road
Imperial College Athletic Ground
William Byrd School
Sipson Lane
Gravel Works
Hillingdon Hounslow
Cranford Park
Cranford Lane
Shortlands
Harlington
Works
West End Lane
Pennine Wy
High St Harlington
Little Elms
Radisson Edwardian Hotel
Marriott Hotel
Sheraton Skyline Hotel
Holiday Inn
Ibis Hotel
Cranford
The Cedars Primary School
Cranford Community College
The Hartlands
Quinton Close
Eton Road
Saunton Av
Oxford Av
Winchester Road
Malvern Road
Windsor Park Rd
Park Lane
BATH ROAD
40
World Business Cen Heathrow
Newall Road
Northrop Road
Northern Perimeter Rd
Northern Perimeter Road
Cranford Lane
Heathrow
Surgery
Berkeley Avenue
Wave Avenue
Meadowbank Gdns
Byron Avenue
Chaucer Avenue
Airport
121
Business Park
F G H J K
08 09 10
1 2 3 4 5 6 7
80 79 78 77

102
83
101
122
A
B
C
D
E
1
2
3
4
5
6
7
SOUTHALL
North Hyde
Heston
UB2
TW5
M4
A312
A4
A30
A3005
THE PARKWAY
MERRICK ROAD
SOUTH ROAD
Junction 3
Heston Services
Golf Course
Airlinks Golf Club
Air Links Industrial Estate
Grand Union Canal
Hillingdon
Ealing
Hounslow
Hortus Road
Southall Stn
Arches Business Cen
Featherstone Industrial Est
Dilloway Industrial Est
Dokal Industrial Est
Western Road
Western International Market
Bullsbridge Industrial Estate
International Trading Est
Brent Park Industrial Estate
Balfour Business Cen
Pump Lane Industrial Est
Regent Business Cen
Peter James Business Cen
Halls Business Cen
Trinity Trading Est
Houston Business Park
Guru Nanak Sikh Primary School
Guru Nanak Sikh Secondary School
Beaconsfield Road
Featherstone Prim School
Norwood Green Junior School
Norwood Green Infant School
Wolf Fields Primary School
Havelock Primary School
Hambrough Primary Sch
Southall & West London Coll
Middle School
The Mosque
Endsleigh Industrial Est
Witley Industrial Est
Wentworth Road
Convent Way
The Common
Ringway
N Hyde Lane
North Hyde La
Spitfire Way
Southall Lane
Cranford Community College
The Cedars Primary School
Berkeley Primary School
Springwell Infant School
Springwell Junior School
Heston Park
Heston Ind Mall
The Andrew Ewing Prim School
Parkway Trading Estate
Travelodge
North Road
Cranford Lane
Vicarage Farm Rd
Great West Road
Bath Rd
Wellington School
1 grid square represents 500 metres

Heston 103
Tutorial College of W London
Villiers High School
Southall Park
Knowsley Avenue
Argyll Av
Park
Morland Gdns
ROAD
A4020
Works
Brentvale Av
Blackmore Av
Windmill Business Centre
Iron Br Cl
Alexander Cl
Ellis Rd
84
Park Road
F
G
H
J
13
14
15
Great Western Ind Park
Collett Way
Jackson Way
Dean Way
Armstrong Way
Armstrong Wy
WINDMILL LA
A4127
Navigator Drive
Chevy Rd
Chaucer Clinic
A&E
Ealing Hospital
Walker Cl
A3002
BOSTON RD
Works
St Marks Primary School
Green Lane
Bishop's Rd
St Mark's Road
St Dunstan's Road
Rosebank Road
Park
Grange Rd
Humes Avenue
Mallard Cl
St Margaret's Road
Osterley Vw Rd
Studley Grange Rd
Middlesex Business Cen
Three Bridges Business Centre
Grand Union Canal Walk
Rd
The Bridge Business Cen
Quaker La
Hunt Rd
Waterside Rd
Hillary Rd
Wylie Rd
Gregory Rd
Sybil Elgar School
Glade
Cookham Cl
Works
LANE
Wolsey Cl
Road
Poplar Av
Osterley RFC
Havelock
The Waterside Trading Cen
Grand Union Canal Wk
Belvedere Rd
Trumpers
2
Boston Business Park
River Brent Business Park
Three Bridges Primary School
Melbury Avenue
TENTELOW
WINDMILL
The Aviary
Shaftesbury Avenue
Stour Av
Minterne Av
Ealing
Hounslow
Norwood Green
Blandford
Dorset Av
Sherborne Av
Wimborne Av
Manston Av
Cranborne Avenue
St Marys Av
St Marys Cl
LANE
79
River Brent
3
M4
NORWOOD ROAD
A4127
Norwood Gn Rd
St Marys Av
Osterley Lane
104
Alleyn Pk
Green Wk
The Lawn
Osterley Lane
Boundary Cl
Osterley Lane
WINDMILL LANE
B454
Golf Course
60
4
Wyevale Garden Centre
Osterley Park & House (NT)
78
Wyke Green Golf Club
Ferraro Cl
Biscoe Cl
Wheatlands
Old Cote Drive
Wheatlands
Osterley Park
Ashley Dr
Jersey Road
5
SYON LANE
Grasshoppers RFC
Crowntree Close
Lingwood Gardens
Wood Lane
Heston Junior School
Heston Infant School
Heston Community Sports Hall
Heston Community School
Osterley
Herm Close
Jersey Road
Bassett Gdns
Thistleworth Cl
Thornbury
Jersey Road
Ridgeway Rd North
Great W Rd
St Mary's Crs
40
6
GREAT WEST ROAD
Brunel University (Osterley Campus) Track
CHURCH ROAD
Eldon Av
Hogarth Gdns
Sonia Gardens
Sutton Hall Rd
Sark Cl
HESTON
Alderney Avenue
Jersey Rd
Surgery
Lulworth Av
Stucley Rd
Pevensey Cl
Penwerris Av
Cranmore Av
Bassett Gardens
Osterley Av
Osterley Station
40
Thornbury Av
Campion House College
Isleworth & Syon School for Boys
Ridgeway
Brunel University
Caroline Cl
Church Rd
St Andrew's Cl
Borough Rd
Sutton Road
Guernsey Cl
Channel Cl
Camborne
UPR SUTTON LA
RD
Lime Tree Rd
Jersey Rd
40
Spring Grove
Kilberry Close
Deborah Cl
Osterley Rd
Osterley Crs
Highfield Rd
College Road
Wood Lane
Musgrave Rd
LAMPTON
JERSEY
Brackendale Cl
Spring Gv
Surgery
Lampton
Gresham Road
Palmerston Rd
Oakley Cl
Aplin Way
Crown Court
7
North Dene
Great W Rd
Berwyn Av
Lampton Av
Lampton School
Harris Cl
Sutton Dene
Neville Cl
Brookwood Rd
LAMPTON ROAD
Farnell Hse Medical Centre
SPRING
Addison Av
Taylor Cl
Spencer Rd
Burlington Rd
Eversley Crs
Ashton House Sch
Vincent Rd
Witham Rd
GROVE ROAD B363
The Harvard
Grove
West Thames College
Grove Rd
Parkland Gv
Hotel
Works
Herbert Pl
Surgery
London Road
Metro Industrial Centre
Crawford
Isleworth Station
B363
K
Primary
Civic Centre
Avonwick Rd
Sunnycroft
Elmsworth Av
Denbigh Rd
Alexandra
Kingsley Rd
Tiverton Road
Kingsley Av
123
Worton Gdns
Drive
Primary School
Clifton Rd
Sidmouth
Castle
TW7

104
UXBRIDGE ROAD
85
St Johns Ambulance Station
B452
Walpole Park
Ealing Film Studios
University
Acton Synagogue
Disraeli Road
Sunnyside Road
Thames Valley University
City of Westminster Cemetery
Works
Oaklands Primary School
BOSTON ROAD
NORTHFIELD AVENUE
SOUTH EALING RD
ST MARY'S RD
Grange Primary School
Church Place
Ranelagh
Beaconsfield Rd
South Ealing Stn
Elthorne Park High School
Elthorne Sports Centre
Boston Business Park
River Brent Business Park
River Brent
Fielding Primary School
Northfields Station
Windermere Road
Devonshire Rd
Overdale Rd
B455
B4491 LITTLE EALING LANE
POPE'S
Ealing Park Health Cen
South Ealing Cemetery
Primary School
Laurel Clinic
King Fahad Academy (Girls Upper School)
Boston Manor Station
A3002
Boston Manor Road
WINDMILL ROAD
EALING ROAD
Lawrence Rd
Occupation La
Chestnut Av
Gunnersbury Catholic Sch
Reynard Mills Trading Estate
Our Lady & St Johns RC Prim Sch
Casualty Plus Clinic
MANOR ROAD
M4
40
103
WINDMILL LANE
Golf Course
Wyevale Garden Centre
B454
Wyke Green Golf Club
Centaurs RFC
Centaurs Business Centre
Grasshoppers RFC
SYON LANE
Superstore
Brentford Stn
BRENTFORD
Brentford School for Girls
St Paul's CE Primary School
Great West Trading Estate
Brentford End
TW8
Rock Works
Brentford Business Cen
Holiday Inn
HALF ACRE
Police Station
County Court
Transport Avenue
A4
Great W Rd
Brunel University (Osterley Campus) Track
Syon Lane Station
The Green School
SPUR ROAD
LONDON ROAD
A315
A310
Marlborough Primary School
Butterfly House
Syon House
Wyevale Garden Centre
Brentwaters Business Park
River Thames
Hounslow
Richmond upon Thames
Boathouse
TW7
West Thames College
Metro Industrial Centre
Isleworth Station
Smallberry Green Primary School
Isleworth Town
124
A&E
W Middlesex University
Queen Charlotte's Cottage
1 grid square represents 500 metres

Brentford 105
Acton
HIGH ST
86
Acton Hospital
Reynolds Sports Centre
Acton High School
GUNNERSBURY LA
A4000
Acton Town Station
Mill Hill Rd
Elm Avenue
The Falcons School for Girls
Crosslands Av
Evelyn Gv
Kingsbridge Av
Carbery Av
Boddington Gdns
Baronsmede
Old Actonians Sports Club
B4491
LANE
Gunnersbury Park Museum
Gunnersbury Park
A406 GUNNERSBURY AV
Princes Avenue
Park Drive
The Ridgeway
Triangle Way
Acton Lane Medical Cen
ACTON LANE
BEACONSFIELD RD
Berrymede Junior Sch
Infant Sch
Bollo Br Rd
Rowley Ind Park
South Acton Stn
Works
International School of London
Gunnersbury Cemetery
Chiswick Business Park
Chiswick Park Station
Bell Industrial Est
Superstore
Claypords Hospital
Lionel Road Primary School
Junction 2
Junction 1
Chiswick Moran Hotel
CHISWICK HIGH RD
A315
CHISWICK HIGH RD
106
HEATHFIELD TER
A3000
Heathfield Ho Sch
W4
Gunnersbury Station
WELLESLEY RD
Capital Int Way
Brentford Fountain Leisure Centre
Kew Bridge Station
Green Dragon Lane
Green Dragon Primary School
Kew Bridge Steam Museum
Musical Museum
KEW BR RD
EALING ROAD
Travelodge
Watermans Arts, Cinema & Theatre Centre
CEDARS ROAD
GREAT WEST RD
Chiswick Village
Infant School
Kew Bridge
KEW ROAD
A205
Strand-on-the-Green
Thames Path
River Thames
Kew Green
Kew Palace
Princess of Wales Conservatory
Royal Botanic Gardens, Kew
Kew
Royal Botanic Gardens Kew School
Palm House
The Queens CE Primary School
The National Archives
Strand Drive
MORTLAKE ROAD
Kew Retail Park
Kew Gardens Stn
Marlborough Trading Estate
Broomfield House Sch
Unicorn School
Chiswick Station
University of Westminster
Grove Park Road
Primary School
125
North Sheen
Mortlake Crematorium
Chiswick Bridge
SW14
Evolution House
Temperate House
Pavilion Restaurant
A316
F
G
H
J
K
I
2
3
4
5
6
7

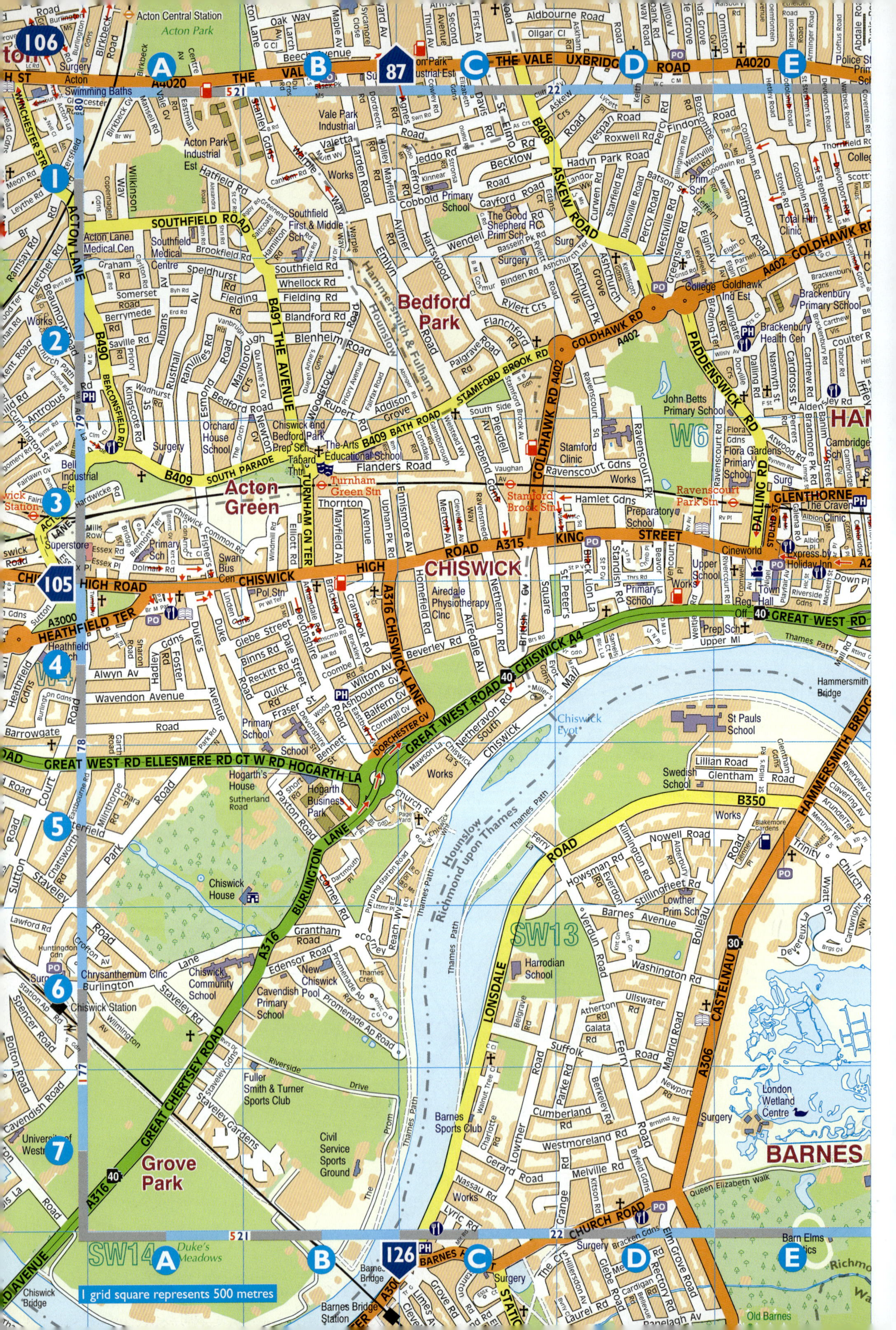
106
87
105
126
A
B
C
D
E
1
2
3
4
5
6
7
Acton Central Station
Acton Park
THE VALE
UXBRIDGE ROAD
A4020
Acton Swimming Baths
Vale Park Industrial Est
Acton Park Industrial Est
Askew Road
SOUTHFIELD ROAD
Southfield First & Middle Sch
Southfield Primary School
ACTON LANE
Acton Lane Medical Cen
Southfield Medical Centre
Bedford Park
Hammersmith & Fulham
Hounslow
B491 THE AVENUE
B490 BEACONSFIELD RD
Cobbold Primary School
The Good Shepherd RC Prim Sch
Askew Road
GOLDHAWK RD
A402 GOLDHAWK RD
A402
Goldhawk Ind Est
Brackenbury Primary School
Brackenbury Health Cen
PADDENSWICK RD
John Betts Primary School
W6
STAMFORD BROOK RD
B409 BATH ROAD
B409 SOUTH PARADE
Chiswick and Bedford Park Prep Sch
The Arts Educational School
Flanders Road
Stamford Clinic
Ravenscourt Gdns
Flora Gardens Primary School
Acton Green
Turnham Green Stn
TURNHAM GN TER
Stamford Brook Stn
Ravenscourt Park Stn
GLENTHORNE RD
The Craven Clinic
Bell Industrial Est
Superstore
CHISWICK HIGH ROAD
A315
KING STREET
CHISWICK
Airedale Physiotherapy Clnc
Preparatory School
Primary School
Cineworld
Holiday Inn
Town Hall
A3000
HEATHFIELD TER
A316 CHISWICK LANE
GREAT WEST RD
A4
40
Thames Path
Hammersmith Bridge
Chiswick Eyot
St Pauls School
Swedish School
B350
HAMMERSMITH BRIDGE
GREAT WEST RD ELLESMERE RD GT W RD HOGARTH LA
DORCHESTER GV
Hogarth's House
Hogarth Business Park
BURLINGTON LANE
A316
Chiswick House
Grantham Road
Chrysanthemum Clnc
Burlington
Chiswick Community School
Cavendish Primary School
Chiswick Station
Hounslow
Richmond upon Thames
Thames
SW13
Harrodian School
LONSDALE
Lowther Prim Sch
CASTELNAU
A306
30
London Wetland Centre
BARNES
Fuller Smith & Turner Sports Club
Civil Service Sports Ground
Barnes Sports Club
GREAT CHERTSEY ROAD
Grove Park
University of West
SW14
Duke's Meadows
CHURCH ROAD
Barnes Bridge
Barnes Bridge Station
Chiswick Bridge
Queen Elizabeth Walk
Barn Elms
Old Barnes
1 grid square represents 500 metres
521
22
80
79
78
77

Westfield London
Shepherd's Bush Station
Holland Park Avenue
Uxbridge Road
Shepherd's Bush Empire
West 12 Shopping & Leisure Cen
Holland Road
Holland Park
Holland House
Kensington & Chelsea College
Holland Park School
King George VI Youth Hostel
Holland Park Theatre
Commonwealth Institute
Leighton House Museum
High St Kensington Stn
KENSINGTON
Kensington (Olympia) Stn
Olympia
Kensington High St
Addison Road
Warwick Gdns
Pembroke Rd
Earls Ct Rd
West Cromwell Rd
Brook Green
HAMMERSMITH
Shepherd's Bush Road
Hammersmith Rd
Kings Mall Shopping Cen
Hammersmith Stn
Flyover
Talgarth Road
West Kensington
West Kensington Station
Barons Court Station
Hammersmith Cemetery
Queen's Club
Charing Cross Hospital
Earl's Court
Earl's Court Exhibition Centre
West Brompton Stn
Lillie Rd
North End Road
Fulham Palace Road
FULHAM
Fulham Cemetery
Dawes Road
Fulham Broadway Stn
Walham Green
Parsons Green Stn
Parsons Green
New King's Road
Harwood Rd
Wandsworth
Fulham FC (Craven Cottage)
Barn Elms Sports Centre
Hammersmith & Fulham
Richmond upon Thames
Thames Path
W8
W14
SW6
88
108
127

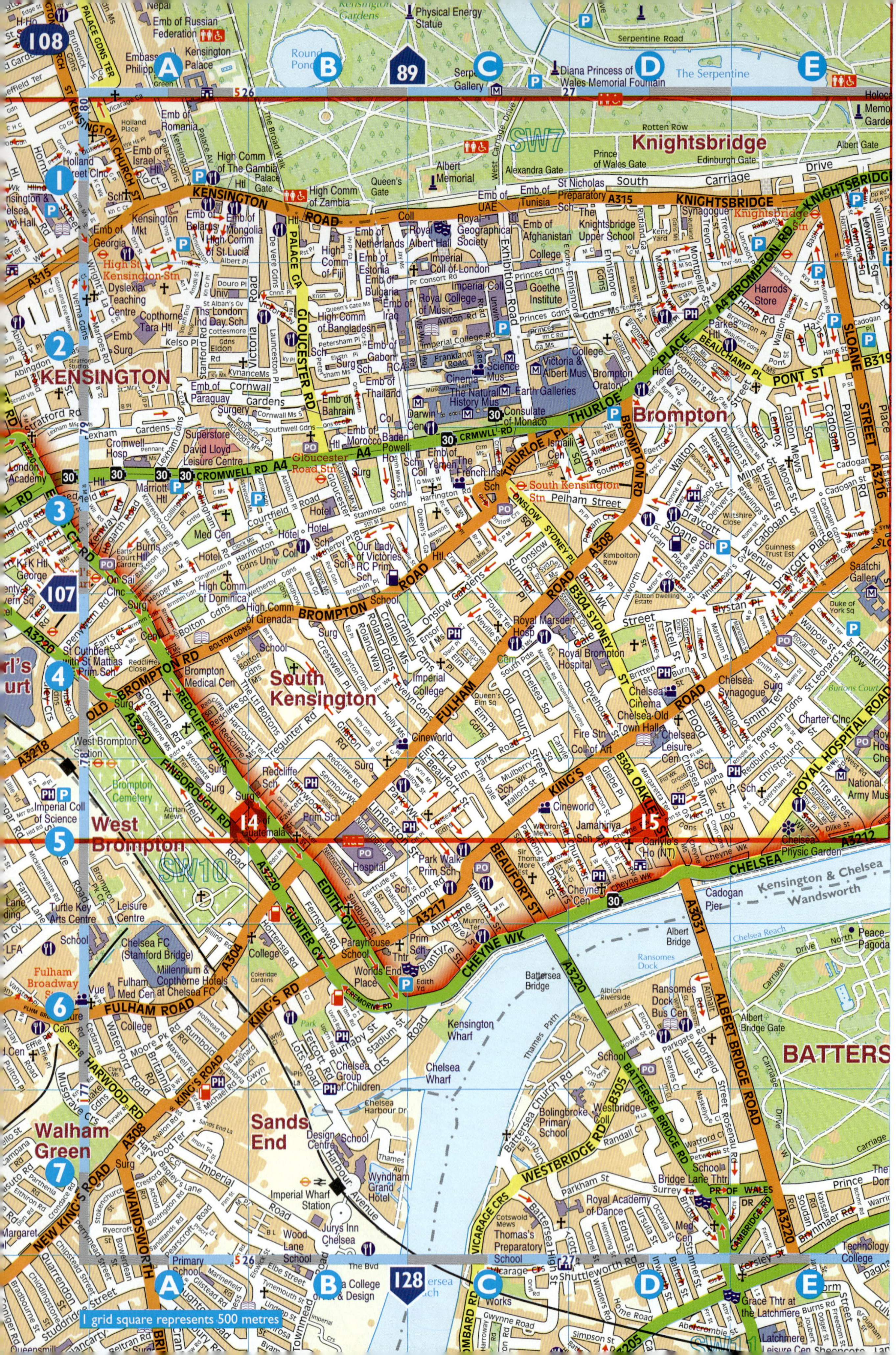

Knightsbridge
Kensington
Brompton
South Kensington
West Brompton
Walham Green
Sands End
Batters
SW7
SW10
Kensington Palace
Emb of Russian Federation
Round Pond
Physical Energy Statue
Serpentine Road
The Serpentine
Diana Princess of Wales Memorial Fountain
Serp Gallery
Rotten Row
Prince of Wales Gate
Edinburgh Gate
Albert Gate
Albert Memorial
Alexandra Gate
Queen's Gate
The Broad Walk
Carriage Drive South
Kensington Road
Knightsbridge
Royal Albert Hall
Royal Geographical Society
Royal Coll of Music
Imperial Coll of London
Imperial College Rd
Exhibition Road
Science Mus
Victoria & Albert Mus
Natural History Mus
Brompton Oratory
Harrods Store
Knightsbridge Stn
Brompton Rd
Beauchamp Pl
Pont St
Sloane Street
High St Kensington Stn
Gloucester Road Stn
South Kensington Stn
Cromwell Rd A4
Cromwell Hosp
Earl's Court Rd
Thurloe Place
Pelham Street
Fulham Road
Royal Marsden Hosp
Royal Brompton Hospital
Chelsea Old Town Hall
King's Road
Oakley St
Cheyne Wk
Chelsea Physic Garden
Royal Hospital Road
National Army Mus
Saatchi Gallery
Duke of York Sq
Carlyle's Ho (NT)
Chelsea Embankment
Cadogan Pier
Albert Bridge
Albert Bridge Road
Battersea Bridge
Battersea Bridge Rd
Kensington Wharf
Chelsea Wharf
Chelsea Harbour Dr
Imperial Wharf Station
Brompton Cemetery
Redcliffe Gdns
Finborough Rd
Edith Gv
Gunter Gv
Chelsea FC (Stamford Bridge)
Fulham Broadway
Fulham Road
Harwood Rd
Wandsworth Bridge Rd
New King's Road
Westbridge Rd
Vicarage Crs
Ransomes Dock
Peace Pagoda
Chelsea Reach
Kensington & Chelsea
Wandsworth
108
89
107
128
14
15
A
B
C
D
E
1
2
3
4
5
6
7
1 grid square represents 500 metres

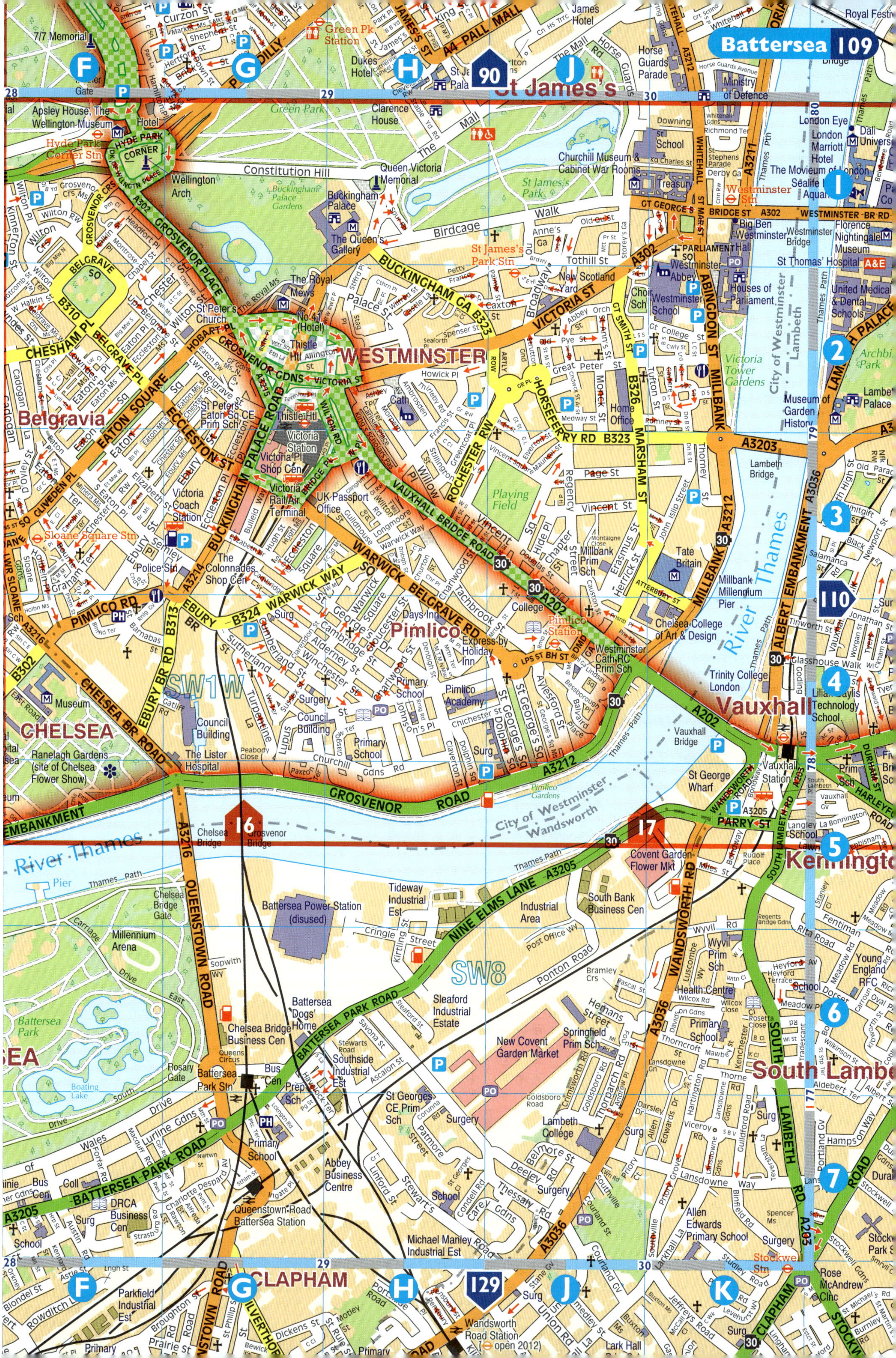

St James's
Green Park
Constitution Hill
Buckingham Palace
St James's Park
Westminster
Belgravia
Pimlico
Chelsea
Vauxhall
Kennington
South Lambeth
Clapham
Battersea Park
Battersea Power Station (disused)
River Thames
Grosvenor Road
Nine Elms Lane
Battersea Park Road
Queenstown Road
Wandsworth Road
Vauxhall Bridge Road
Victoria Station
Victoria Coach Station
Houses of Parliament
Westminster Abbey
Big Ben
Lambeth Bridge
Vauxhall Bridge
Chelsea Bridge
Grosvenor Bridge
Tate Britain
New Covent Garden Market
SW1W
SW8

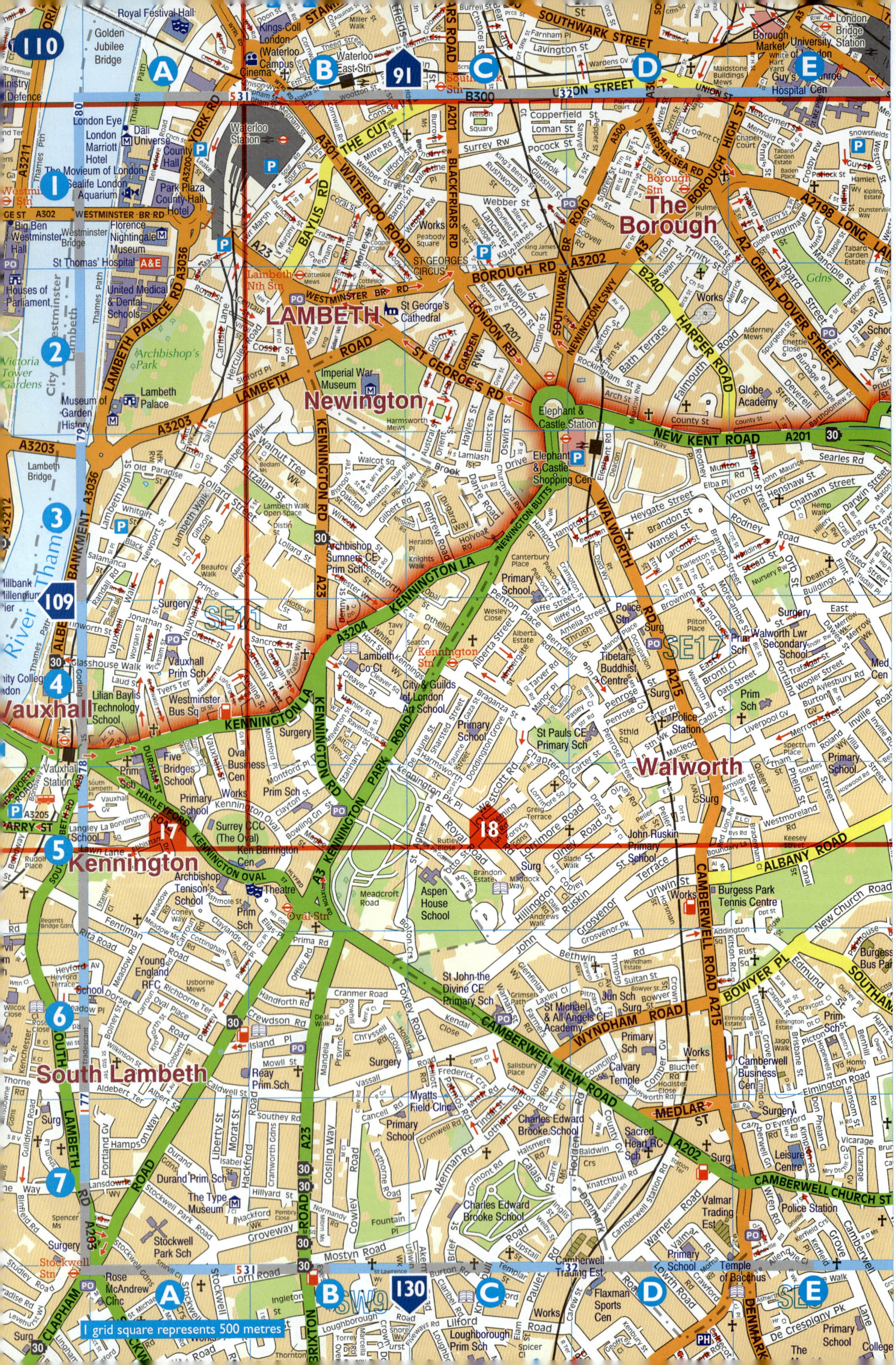

110
91
109
130
Royal Festival Hall
Golden Jubilee Bridge
Waterloo East Stn
Southwark Street
Union Street
London Bridge Station
Borough Market
Guy's Hospital
London Eye
London Marriott Hotel
The Movieum of London
Sealife London Aquarium
Waterloo Station
The Cut
Waterloo Road
Blackfriars Rd
Borough High St
Marshalsea Rd
Westminster Br Rd
Big Ben
Westminster Bridge
Florence Nightingale Museum
St Thomas' Hospital
Houses of Parliament
County Hall
Park Plaza County Hall Hotel
Baylis Rd
St Georges Circus
Borough Rd
The Borough
Long Lane
Great Dover Street
Lambeth Nth Stn
Westminster Br Rd
LAMBETH
St George's Cathedral
Lambeth Palace Rd
Lambeth Rd
St George's Rd
London Rd
Newington Cswy
Harper Road
Archbishop's Park
Lambeth Palace
Imperial War Museum
Newington
Museum of Garden History
Victoria Tower Gardens
Elephant & Castle Station
Elephant & Castle Shopping Cen
New Kent Road
Lambeth Bridge
Albert Embankment
Kennington Rd
Kennington La
Newington Butts
Walworth Rd
River Thames
SE11
SE17
Kennington Stn
City & Guilds of London Art School
Vauxhall
Vauxhall Station
Kennington Park Road
Kennington Park
Walworth
Albany Road
Burgess Park
Kennington
Kennington Oval
Oval Stn
Surrey CCC (The Oval)
Camberwell New Road
Camberwell Road
Wyndham Road
Bowyer Pl
South Lambeth
South Lambeth Rd
Clapham Road
Brixton Road
Medlar St
Camberwell Church St
Denmark Hill
Stockwell Stn
Stockwell Park Sch
The Type Museum
Charles Edward Brooke School
Aspen House School
Camberwell Trading Est
Temple of Bacchus
Flaxman Sports Cen
SW9
SE5
1 grid square represents 500 metres

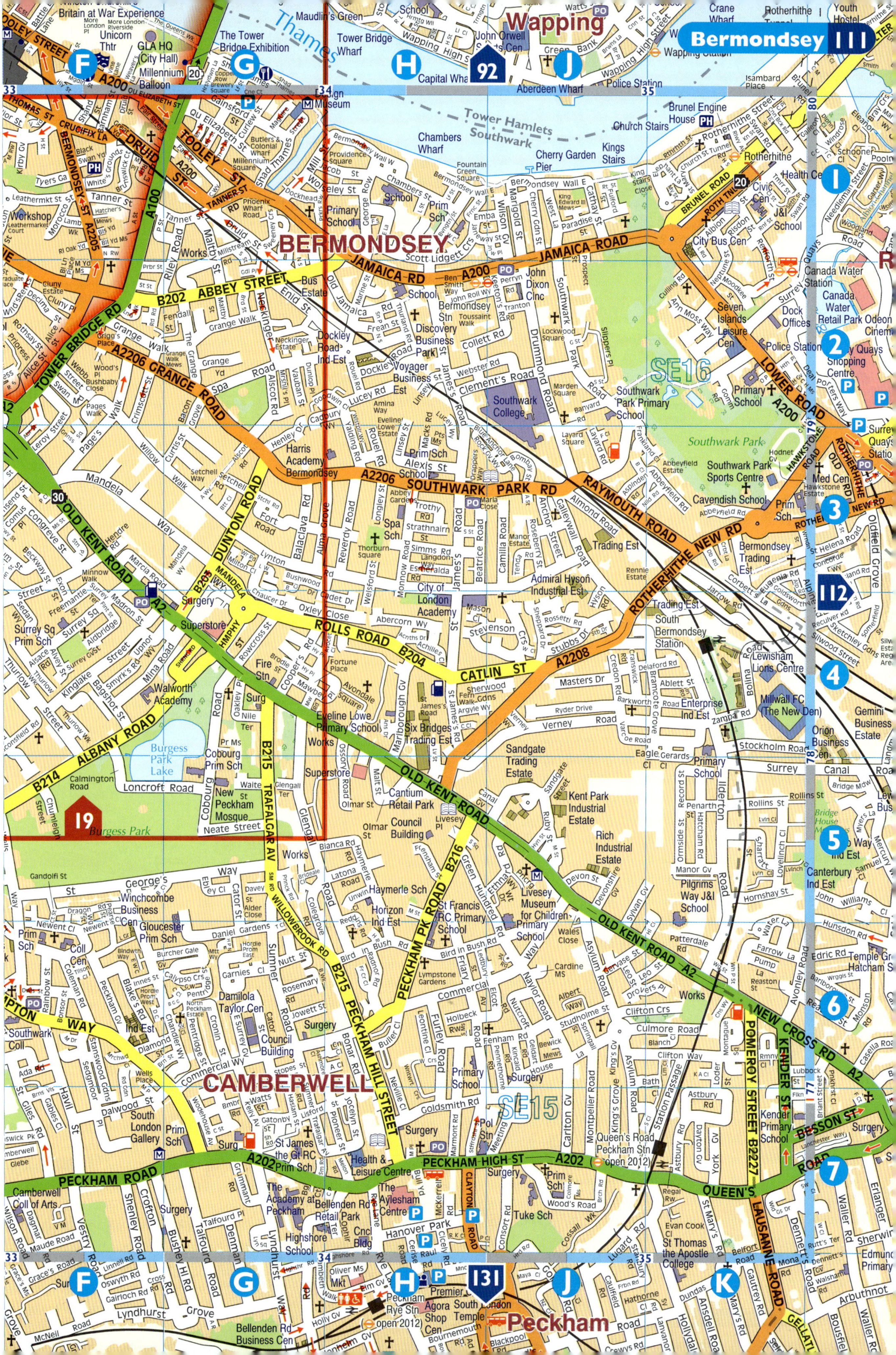
Wapping
BERMONDSEY
CAMBERWELL
Peckham
SE16
SE15
Thames
Tower Hamlets
Southwark
Britain at War Experience
GLA HQ (City Hall)
Millennium Balloon
The Tower Bridge Exhibition
Tower Bridge Wharf
Capital Wharf
Aberdeen Wharf
Police Station
Design Museum
Chambers Wharf
Cherry Garden Pier
Kings Stairs
Church Stairs
Brunel Engine House
Rotherhithe
Canada Water Station
Canada Water Retail Park
Odeon Cinema
Surrey Quays Shopping Centre
Surrey Quays Station
Southwark Park
Southwark Park Primary School
Southwark Park Sports Centre
Cavendish School
Southwark College
City Bus Cen
Bermondsey Stn
Discovery Business Park
Voyager Business Est
Harris Academy Bermondsey
Bermondsey Trading Est
Admiral Hyson Industrial Est
City of London Academy
South Bermondsey Station
Lewisham Lions Centre
Millwall FC (The New Den)
Gemini Business Estate
Orion Business Centre
Sandgate Trading Estate
Kent Park Industrial Estate
Rich Industrial Estate
Six Bridges Trading Est
Cantium Retail Park
Burgess Park Lake
Burgess Park
Walworth Academy
New Peckham Mosque
Livesey Museum for Children
Camberwell Coll of Arts
South London Gallery
Peckham Stn
Peckham Rye Stn
Queen's Road Peckham Stn
Bellenden Rd Retail Park
Bellenden Rd Business Cen
The Academy at Peckham
The Aylesham Centre
Highshore School
St Thomas the Apostle College
Kender Primary School
Canterbury Ind Est
TOOLEY ST
JAMAICA ROAD
ABBEY STREET
GRANGE ROAD
TOWER BRIDGE RD
LOWER ROAD
SOUTHWARK PARK RD
RAYMOUTH ROAD
ROTHERHITHE NEW RD
OLD KENT ROAD
ROLLS ROAD
CATLIN ST
DUNTON ROAD
ALBANY ROAD
TRAFALGAR AV
WILLOWBROOK RD
PECKHAM HILL STREET
PECKHAM PK ROAD
PECKHAM ROAD
PECKHAM HIGH ST
QUEEN'S ROAD
NEW CROSS RD
BESSON ST
POMEROY STREET
LAUSANNE ROAD
CLAYTON ROAD
A200
A2
A202
A2206
A2208
B202
B204
B215
B216
B2227
F
G
H
J
K
I
1
2
3
4
5
6
7
19
20
30
33
34
35
92
112
131

112
93
111
132
Rotherhithe
Rotherhithe Tunnel
Youth Hostel
Salter Road
Fisher Athletic FC
Bacon's College
Horn Stairs
Nelson Dock Museum
Lawrence Wharf
Canary Wharf Pier
Thames Path
River House Montessori Sch
Heron Quays Station
Canary Wharf
Canary Wharf Stn
Citigroup Tower
South Colonnade
Wood Wharf
Business Centre
Redriff Prim Sch
Surrey Docks Health Cen
Durands Wharf
Trinity Business Cen
Surrey Docks Farm
West India Pier
Millennium Harbour
Limehouse Reach
South Quay Station
South Quay Plaza
Marsh Wall
St Johns RC Primary School
Alfred Salter Prim Sch
Mulberry Business Cen
Quebec Industrial Estate
Canada Water Station
Canada Water Retail Park
Odeon Cinema
Hollywood Bowl
Associated Newspapers Off
Dock Offices
Surrey Quays Shopping Centre
Surrey Quays Leisure Park
Redriff Road
Greenland Dock
Surrey Docks Watersports Centre
Howland Quay
Rope Street
New Caledonian Wharf
Helsinki Sq
New Atlas Wharf
Greenland Pier
South Lock
Tower Hamlets
Southwark
Lewisham
Primary School
Old Bellgate Wharf
Barkantine Clinic
Seven Mills Primary Sch
Tiller Cen (Swimming Baths)
Tiller Leisure Cen
Daily Telegraph
Dockland Sailing & Watersports Centre
Poplar Business Park
Guardian Newspapers
Enterprise Business Park
Glengall Bridge
Crossharbour Station
Millwall Docks
Millwall
Westferry Road
Lower Road
Surrey Quays Station
Plough Way
Hawkstone Road
Rotherhithe New Rd
Southwark Park Sports Centre
Bermondsey Trading Est
Woodcroft Works
Cannon Wharf Bus Cen
Grove Medical Cen
Grove St
Diploma Works
Pepys Park
Victoria Wharf Industrial Estate
Deptford Park Primary School
Deptford Park
Deptford Park Business Cen
Convoy's Wharf
The Space Arts Centre Cinema
Landing Stage
Borthwick Wharf
River Thames
Burrells Wharf
Fire Station
Morecambe St
Spindrift Avenue
Trundley's Road
Silwood Estate Regeneration Area
Lewisham Lions Centre
Millwall FC (The New Den)
Gemini Business Estate
Orion Business Cen
Stockholm Rd
Surrey Canal Road
Deptford Bus Cen
Deptford Trading Est
Evelyn St
DEPTFORD
SE8
Charlotte Turner Primary School
Greenwich Reach
Millennium Quay
Deptford Creek
Creek Road
Goldsmiths University
Bellerbys College
Lewisham Business Cen
Elizabeth Trading Est
Folkestone Gardens
Juno Way Ind Est
Industrial Estate
Canterbury Ind Est
Parkside Business Est
The Kingfisher Medical Cen
Arklow Trading Est
Sanford Street
Edward St
Pagnell St
Deptford Stn
Albany Cen & Theatre
Deptford Church Street
Laban Centre
Trading Est
Greenwich Cen Business Park
Faircharm Trading Est
Arts Centre
Novotel
Norman Rd
Greenwich High Road
Temple Grove Hatcham Sch
Superstore
SE14
New Cross Sports Arena
New Cross Station
New Cross Gate Stn
New Cross Rd
Deptford Broadway
Greenwich Coroners Office
Lewisham College
Deptford Bridge Station
Blackheath Rd A2
Besson St
Kender St
Pomeroy Street B2227
St James CE Primary School
Goldsmiths University of London
Haberdashers Askes Hatcham Coll
New Cross Gate
Amersham Rd
Florence Road
Lewisham Way
Brookmill Rd
Edmund Waller Primary School
New Cross
Malpas Road
St Johns
St Johns Stn
Lausanne Road
1 grid square represents 500 metres
A
B
C
D
E
1
2
3
4
5
6
7
536
37

GREENWICH
Greenwich Park
SE10
Blackheath
SE3
Cubitt Town
ISLE OF DOGS
Mudchute Park
The O2
North Greenwich Station
Blackwall Tunnel
Blackwall Reach
Bugsby's Reach
Thames Path
Tunnel Avenue Trading Est
Delta Wharf
The David Beckham Academy
Millennium Way
Gas Works
John Harrison Way
Millennium Prim Sch
Greenwich Odeon
Bugsby's Way
Woolwich Road
Trafalgar Road
Romney Road
Blackwall Lane
Creek Road
Cutty Sark
Cutty Sark Station
Gypsy Moth IV
Greenwich Pier
Greenwich Foot Tunnel
Old Royal Naval College
Trinity College of Music
University of Greenwich
National Maritime Museum
The Queens House
Flamsteed House Museum
Old Royal Observatory Greenwich
Ranger's House
The Wernher Collection at Ranger's House
Greenwich Theatre & Art Gallery
Maze Hill Station
Westcombe Park Station
Charlton Way
Shooters Hill Rd
Blackheath Hill
Hyde Vale
Royal Hill
Greenwich Station
Vanbrugh Park
Stratheden Road
Shooters Hill Road
Prince of Wales Rd
Westcombe Park Road
Blackheath Preparatory School
Blackheath Business Estate
Morden College Homes
Manor Brook Medical Centre
Millennium Wharf
Island Gardens Station
Mudchute City Farm
George Greens School
Manchester Road
Cubitt Town Infant School
Angerstein Business Park
Brocklebank Industrial Estate
Maritime Industrial Estate
West Silvertown Station
Greenshields Industrial Est
Minerva Works
The Heart of Greenwich development
Lawrence Trading Estate
East Greenwich Christ Church CE Prim Sch
Invicta Primary School
John Roan Lwr Sch
Blackheath High Senior School
Trinity Hospital
Meridian Prim Sch
Ibis Hotel
Council Building
The Fan Museum
Greenwich Cinema
Conduit House
St Ursulas Convent School
Maze Hill
Charlton Road
Dover
Lewisham
94
113
114
133

114
95
113
134
Silvertown
North Woolwich
River Thames
Thames Barrier
Newham
Greenwich
Woolwich Reach
Thames Barrier Information & Learning Centre
New Charlton
Charlton
SE7
SE3
Kidbrooke
Silvertown Station
Greenshields Industrial Est
London City Airport
Pontoon Dock Station
Standard Industrial Estate
Thameside Industrial Estate
Factory Road
Albert Rd
North Woolwich Road
A1020
Anchorage Point Industrial Estate
Riverside
Lombard Trading Estate
VIP Trading Estate
Ropery Business Park
Stone Lake Retail Park
Ashleigh Commercial Estate
Meridian Trading Estate
Maritime Industrial Estate
Greenwich Industrial Estate
Angerstein Business Park
Brocklebank Industrial Estate
Bugsby's Way
A2052
Anchor & Hope Lane
Woolwich Road
A206
Woolwich Church St
Harlinger Street
Dockyard Industrial Est
Woolwich Dockyard Stn
Charlton Stn
Westcombe Park Station
Charlton Athletic FC (The Valley)
Maryon Wilson Park
Little Heath B210
Hillreach B210
Museum of the Artillery in the Rotunda
Charlton Park Rd B210
The Village
Charlton House
Charlton Park
Charlton Cemetery
Charlton School
Queen Elizabeth Hospital
Meridian Sports Club
Woolwich Common
Academy Road
Charlton Road B210
Old Dover Road
Shooters Hill Road A207
Sun in Sands Roundabout
Hornfair Park
Charlton Lido
Charlton Manor Junior School
Cherry Orchard Primary School
Blackheath RFC (The Rectory Field)
Blackheath Bluecoat School
Our Lady of Grace RC Prim Sch
Invicta Primary School
Wricklemarsh Road
Kidbrooke Park Primary School
Kidbrooke School
Broad Walk
Mayday Gardens
Morden College Homes
Long Lane AFC
A205
A2
1 grid square represents 500 metres

96
135
116
F
G
H
J
I
K
1
2
3
4
5
6
7
43
44
45
80
79
78
77
King George V Station
Galleons Reach
Albert Rd
A112
A117
Pier Road
Woolwich Foot Tunnel
Woolwich Ferry
WOOLWICH
Waterfront Leisure Centre
Firepower Royal Artillery Museum
Royal Arsenal
Woolwich High St
A206
Beresford St
John Wilson St
Woolwich New Road
Wellington St
B210
Grand Depot Rd
A205
Woolwich Common
Woolwich New Road
Military Barracks
Plumstead Road
Plumstead Station
Plumstead High Street
Pettman Crescent
Western Way A2016
Magistrates Court
Woolwich Crown Court
HM Prison Belmarsh
West Thamesmead Business Park
Boughton Road
Hadden Road
Heronsgate Primary School
Whinchat Road
Erebus Drive
Harden's Manorway
Cadogan Road
Wellington Av
Tom Cribb Road
Gateway Bus Cen
Greenwich Community College
Woolwich Arsenal Station
Town Hall
University
Mag Ct
Prim Sch
Education
Outdoor Market
Indoor Market
Theatre
SEHA Hindu Temple
Mulgrave Primary School
Cncl Bldg
County Court
Bingo
Plumstead
SE18
Plumstead Common Rd
Plumstead Common
Shree KS Swaminarayan Temple
Plumstead Manor School
Heavitree Rd
St Margarets CE Prim Sch
Community College
Negus Sixth Form Centre
Greenslade Primary School
Winn Common Road
Timbercroft Primary School
Rockliffe Manor Primary School
Conway Medical Cen
Conway Primary School
Waterside Prim Sch
St Patricks RC Primary School
Foxfield Prim Sch
St Peters RC Primary School
Eglinton Prim Sch
Junior School
Shooters Hill Post 16 Campus
Eaglesfield School
Shooters Hill Golf Club
Golf Course
Shooters Hill
Dover Road
A207
Memorial Hospital
Primary School
Eltham Common
Cemetery
Griffen Manor School
Nightingale Pl
Genesta Road
Nithdale Road
Dallin Road
Eglinton Hill
Red Lion Lane
Donaldson Road
Occupation Lane
Cleanthus Road
Eaglesfield Road
Kinlet Road
Ashridge Crs
Garland Rd
Swingate Lane
Welton Road
Chelsworth Drive
Macoma Road
Tuam Road
Wickham Street
Chaucer Road
Edison Grove
Bexley Rd
Greenwich

116
97
115
136
SE28
SE2
DA16
A
B
C
D
E
1
2
3
4
5
6
7
546
547
180
179
178
177
Abbey Wood
Plumstead Common
East Wickham
West Heath
Western Way
Eastern Way
A2016
A2041
A206
A209
B213
Harrow Manor Way
Knee Hill
McLeod Road
Basildon Road
Bostall Hill
Woolwich Road
Wickham Lane
Discovery Prim Sch
St Margaret Clitherow RC Primary School
Birchmere Bus Park
Broadreach College
West Thamesmead Business Park
Kellner Road
Nathan Way
Sewell Road
Cookhill Road
Finchale Road
Felixstowe Road
Mottisfont Road
Abbey Wood School
St Thomas a' Becket RC Primary Sch
Edington Rd
Lyndean Industrial Estate
Primary School
Industrial Estate
Godstow Road
Yarnton Way
Wolvercote Road
Lensbury Way
Overton Road
Abbey Primary School
Southlake Primary School
Hartslock
Seacourt Road
Clinic
Superstore
Alsike
Fendyke Road
Rushdene
Abbey Wood Station
Abbey Grove
Abbey Wood Road
Lesnes Abbey
North Rd
Marmadon Road
Bracondale Road
Birkdale Road
Blithdale
Brookdene Road
Benares Road
Manton Rd
Myrtledene Rd
Federation Rd
Fuchsia St
Commonwealth Way
Willrose Crs
Mitchell Close
Primary School
Police Stn
Leisure Cen
Council Building
Granite St
Plumstead High Street
Saunders Road
Gatling Rd
Surgery
The Dell
Bastion Road
Glendown Rd
Old Pk Rd
Hurst La
Harvel Crs
Priory Dr
Green Chain Walk
Greenwich
Bexley
Abbey (rems of)
Bostall Woods
Longleigh Lane
St Joseph's Annexe
Burcharbro Road
Amberley
Heath Avenue
Winn Common Road
King's Highway
Bleak Hill Lane
Revell Rise
Gilbourne Rd
Kingsdale Road
Rockliffe Manor Primary School
Timbercroft Primary School
Camdale Road
Southland Rd
Woolwich Cemetery
St Pauls RC School
Superstore
Alliance Road
Woodbrook Road
Plumstead Cemetery
Pinecroft
Patricia Court
Langley Road
Hadlow Road
First Avenue
Lansdowne Avenue
Madison Crs
Primary School
Plymstock Road
Sidmouth Road
Budleigh Crescent
Okehampton Crescent
Axminster Crescent
Stevens Park
St Michaels CE Primary School
Brixham Road
Preston Drive
Berkeley Avenue
Mayfair Avenue
Surgery
Brampton Road
Abbott's
King
Highmead
Edison Grove
Griffen Manor School
Dryden Road
Glenmore Road
Green Chain Walk
Wickham Street
Daren Rd
Anthony Road
Linton Cl
Wickham Lane
East Wickham Primary School
Berwick Road
Welling School
Wrotham Road
Swanley Road
Normanhurst Avenue
Wickham Street
Cemetery
Exeter Rd
Leigh Pl
Graves Yard Industrial Estate
Balliol Road
Somerhill Road
Elsa Road
Farnham Road
Brampton Primary School
Holmesdale Road
1 grid square represents 500 metres

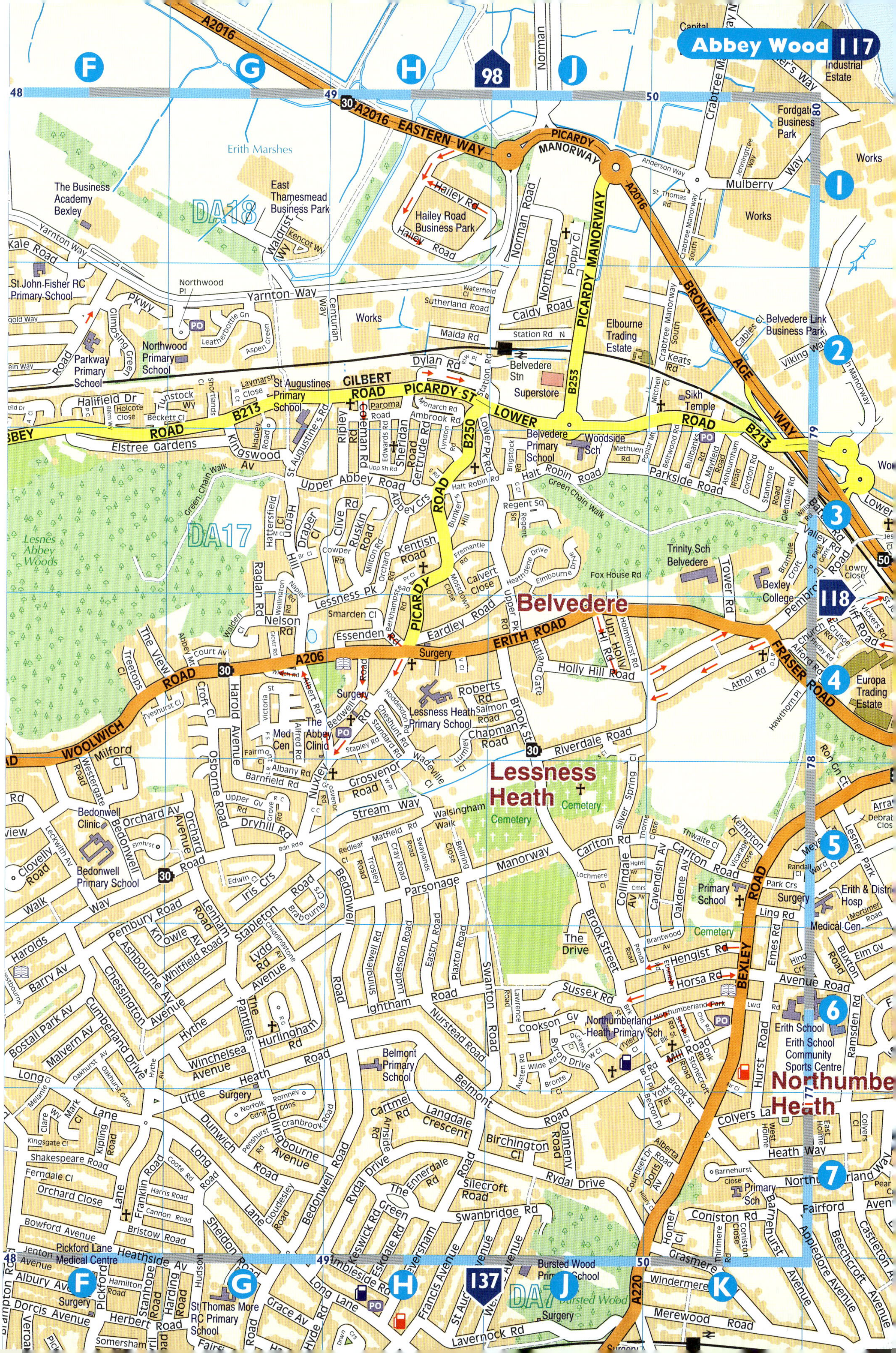
F
G
H
98
J
48
49
50
A2016
EASTERN WAY
PICARDY MANORWAY
Erith Marshes
DA18
The Business Academy Bexley
East Thamesmead Business Park
Hailey Road Business Park
Hailey Rd
Norman Road
North Road
Caldy Road
Poppy Cl
BRONZE AGE WAY
Crabtree Manorway South
Mulberry Way
Works
Fordgate Business Park
Industrial Estate
Anderson Way
Jenningtree Way
Yarnton Way
Kale Road
St John Fisher RC Primary School
Northwood Pl
Parkway Primary School
Northwood Primary School
Centurion Way
Sutherland Road
Waterfield Cl
Maida Rd
Station Rd
Belvedere Stn
Superstore
B253
Elbourne Trading Estate
Belvedere Link Business Park
Viking Way
Dylan Rd
GILBERT ROAD
PICARDY ST
LOWER ROAD
B213
St Augustines Primary School
Sikh Temple
Halifield Dr
Tunstock Wy
Beckett Cl
Holcote Close
Laymarsh Close
Elstree Gardens
Kingswood Av
Belvedere Primary School
Woodside Sch
Parkside Road
Upper Abbey Road
Halt Robin Road
Green Chain Walk
B250
PICARDY ROAD
DA17
Lesnes Abbey Woods
Trinity Sch Belvedere
Fox House Rd
Bexley College
Tower Rd
118
Belvedere
ERITH ROAD
A206
WOOLWICH ROAD
Lessness Pk
Nelson Rd
Raglan Rd
Heron Hill
Kentish Road
Calvert Close
Eardley Road
Essenden Rd
Surgery
Holly Hill Road
FRASER ROAD
Europa Trading Estate
Athol Rd
Lessness Heath Primary School
Roberts Rd
Chapman Road
Brook St
Riverdale Road
The Abbey Clinic
Lessness Heath
Cemetery
Milford Cl
Bedonwell Clinic
Bedonwell Primary School
Orchard Av
Osborne Road
Grosvenor Road
Stream Way
Walsingham Walk
Manorway
Carlton Road
Parsonage
Bedonwell Road
Pembury Road
Lenham Road
Knowle Av
Whitfield Road
Ashbourne Av
Chessington Avenue
Stapleton Road
Lydd Rd
Avenue
Hurlingham Rd
The Pantiles
Winchelsea Avenue
Hythe Avenue
Shinglewell Rd
Huddleston Road
Eastry Road
Plaxtol Road
Swanton Road
Nurstead Road
Belmont Primary School
Belmont Road
Northumberland Heath Primary Sch
Primary School
Bexley Road
Erith School
Erith School Community Sports Centre
Northumberland Heath
Erith & District Hosp
Medical Cen
Ling Rd
Park Crs
Hengist Rd
Horsa Rd
Sussex Rd
The Drive
Brook Street
Cumberland Drive
Bostall Park Av
Malvern Av
Long Lane
Heath Road
Little Heath
Dunwich Road
Hollingbourne Avenue
Langdale Crescent
Cartmel Rd
Birchington Cl
Dalmeny Road
Rydal Drive
Silecroft Road
Swanbridge Rd
Kipling Road
Shakespeare Road
Orchard Close
Franklin Road
Bristow Road
Bowford Avenue
Pickford Lane Medical Centre
Heathside Av
Hudson Road
St Thomas More RC Primary School
Bursted Wood Primary School
Bursted Wood
Crasmere Rd
Windermere Road
Merewood Road
Lavernock Rd
Coniston Rd
Barnehurst Road
Appledore Avenue
Fairford Avenue
Heath Way
Colyers La
A220
137
DA7
K
Harolds Road
Barry Av
Clovelly Road
Medical Centre
Albury Av
Dorcis Avenue
Herbert Road
Somersham Rd
1
2
3
4
5
6
7
77
78
79
80

118
99
117
138
A
B
C
D
E
1
2
3
4
5
6
7
551
52
80
79
78
77
Belvedere Industrial Estate
Fordgate Business Park
Works
Mulberry
Belvedere Link Business Park
Viking Way
Church Manorway
B213
Works
Lower Rd
Corinthian Manorway
Galleon Close
Battle Rd
Lowry Close
Sandcliff Road
Vickers Rd
St John's Rd
A2016
West Street
Chandlers Dr
Chichester Wh
Winifred Road
Maximfeldt Rd
Tower Rd
Fraser Road
Church Rd
Cross Rd
Alford Rd
Athol Rd
Hawthorn Pl
Europa Trading Estate
Hamlet International Industrial Estate
Erith Station
Ind Park
Cricketers Cl
Riverside Swimming Centre
Erith High St
Library & Mus
Saltford Cl
Erith
Erith Playhouse
Erith Reach
Coldharbour Lane
Coldharbour
Havering
Bexley
Erith Rands
A206
A220
30
50
Pier Road
Wharfside Cl
Colebrk St
Superstore
James Watt Way
Wheatley Ter Road
Business Centre
Crescent Road
Manor Road
Health Cen
Erith High St
Queens Road
Christ Church Av
Victoria Road
Arran Close
Debrabant Close
Park Crescent
Christ Church Primary School
Lesney Park Road
Erith & District Hosp
Surgery
Medical Cen
Avenue Road
Erith Stadium
Erith Sports Centre
DA8
Thanet Road
South Road
Compton Pl
Alexandra Rd
Reddy Road
Betsham Road
Springhead Road
Aperfield Road
Cornwallis Close
Raleigh Close
Frobisher Rd
Turpin Lane
Works
Bilton Road
Manford Industrial Estate
Ray Lamb Way
Canada Rd
Durlun Way
Sandpiper Dr
Longreach Rd
Beacon Rd
Jenningtree Rd
Widgeon Rd
Hilden Dr
Brompton Dr
Hollywood Way
Festival Close
Church Trading Estate
Slade Green Primary School
Howbury Centre
Slade Green Road
Richmer Rd
Alderney Road
Bexley Road
Ling Rd
Emes Rd
Buxton Road
Elm Gv
Broadoak Rd
Frinsted Rd
Valence Rd
Stelling Rd
Hemsted Rd
Birling Rd
Brasted Rd
Twigg Cl
Larner Rd
Waterhead Close
Badlow Cl
Arthur St
Nursery
Page Crs
Pearsewood Road
Northend Primary School
North End Trading Est
Health Centre
Medical Centre
Colyers Lane
Myrtle Close
Selkirk Drive
Doyle Close
Brendon Close
Erith School
Erith School Community Sports Centre
Northumberland Heath
Hurst Road
Colyers La
Heath Way
Northumberland Way
Normandy Primary School
Pear Tree Cl
Fairford Avenue
Barnehurst Close
Barnehurst Avenue
Primary Sch
Iston Rd
Appledore Avenue
Beechcroft Avenue
Castleton Avenue
Downbank Avenue
Edenbridge Road
Pennine Way
Chiltern Close
Hurstwood Avenue
Northend Road
Cloudesley Rd
Newbery Road
Scott Crs
Bridge Road
Cayden Rd
Power Ind Estate
North End
Slade Green Station
Forest Road
Elm Road
Larkswood Cl
Hazel Road
Cedar Rd
Willow Road
Leycroft Gdns
Slade Green FC
Moat Lane
Oak Rd
Slade Green
Hazel Dr
Rodeo Cl
Fern Cl
Whitehall Lane
Lane Green
Dale View
Lincoln Road
Sun Ct
Howbury
Works
Venners Cl
Eversley Avenue
Ravensworth Cl
Lincoln Cl
Works
1 grid square represents 500 metres

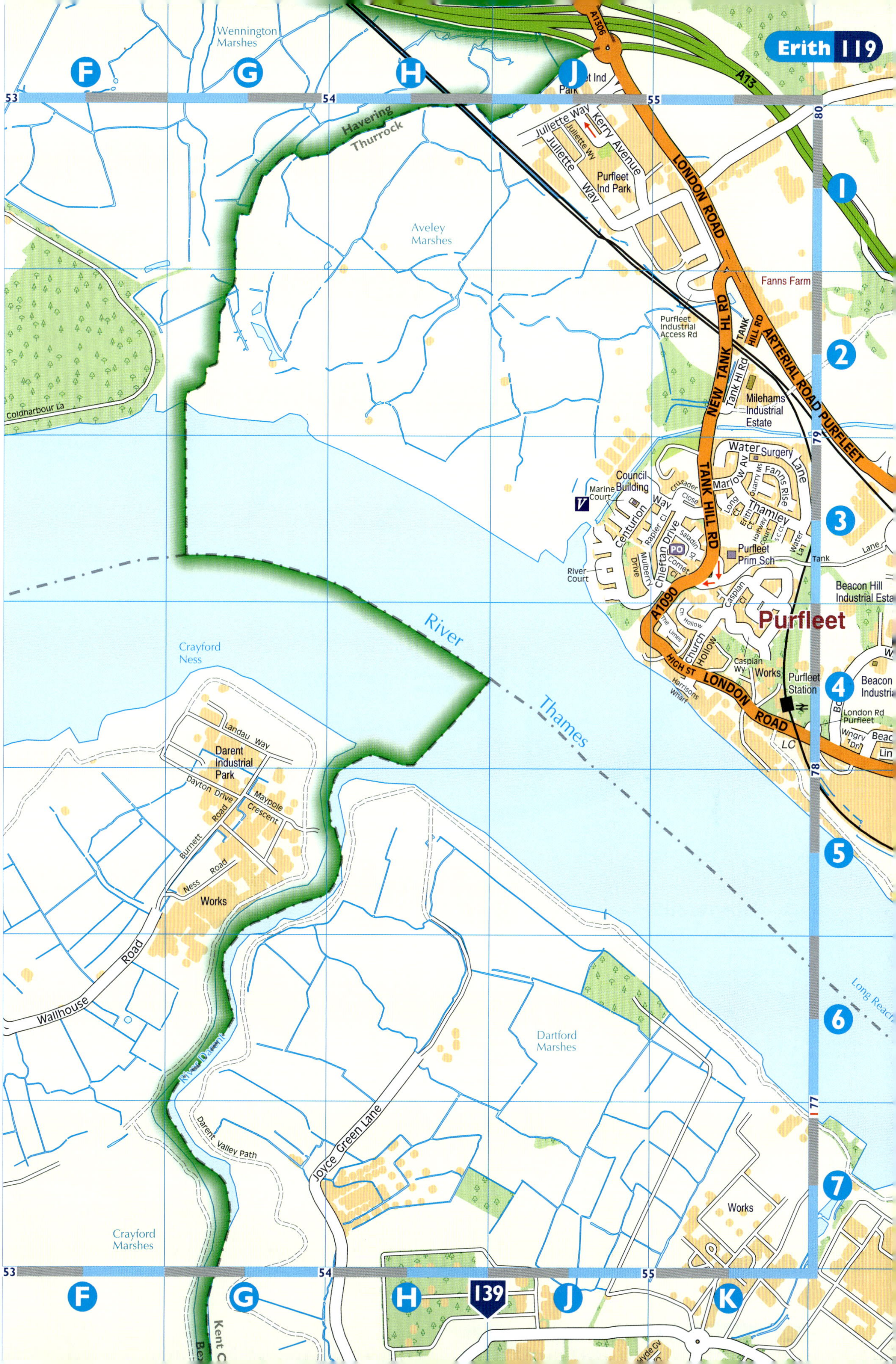
Wennington Marshes
Havering
Thurrock
Aveley Marshes
Juliette Way
Juliette Wy
Kerry Avenue
Purfleet Ind Park
London Road
A1306
A13
Fanns Farm
Purfleet Industrial Access Rd
New Tank Hl Rd
Tank Hill Rd
Arterial Road Purfleet
Tank Hl Rd
Milehams Industrial Estate
Water Lane
Surgery
Marlow Av
Fanns Rise
Quarry Ms
Thamley
Long Ct
Erith Ct
Halfway Court
Water La
Council Building
Marine Court
Crusader Close
Centurion Way
Rapier Cl
Saladin
Chieftan Drive
Mulberry Drive
Comet
PO
Purfleet Prim Sch
River Court
Tank Lane
Beacon Hill Industrial Esta
A1090
Caspian Cl
Ch Hollow
The Limes
Church Hollow
Purfleet
Caspian Wy
Works
Purfleet Station
High St
Harrisons Wharf
London Road
Beacon Industri
London Rd Purfleet
Wngry Dr
LC
Coldharbour La
River Thames
Crayford Ness
Landau Way
Darent Industrial Park
Dayton Drive
Maypole Crescent
Road
Burnett
Ness Road
Works
Wallhouse Road
Long Reach
Dartford Marshes
River Darent
Darent Valley Path
Joyce Green Lane
Works
Crayford Marshes
Kent
Hyde Gv
139
F G H J I 2 3 4 5 6 7 K
53 54 55 80 79 78 77

120
100
A
B
C
D
E
1
2
3
4
5
6
7
TW6
Heathrow
Perimeter Rd (West)
Northern Perimeter Rd
Fire & Ambulance Station
Terminal 5
D'Albiac House
Airbus Coach Station
Terminal 1
Heathrow Terminals 1 & 3 Stn
Bus & Coach Stn
Arrivals
Terminal 3
Departures
Control Tower
Queen's Building
Viewing Area
Terminal 2 redevelopment
Heathrow World Cargo Centre
Terminal 4
Heathrow Terminal 4 Stn
Southern Perimeter Road
Southampton Rd E
Tunnel Link Road
Sealand Road
Shoreham Road (West)
Shoreham Road (East)
Sandringham Rd
Riverside Road
Bedfont Road
Court Farm Industrial Estate
Blackburn Trading Estate
Longford River
Hillingdon
Hounslow
Stanwell
Stanwell Burial Ground
St Marys CE Junior School
St Annes County Primary School
St Davids Health Centre
Town Farm Primary School
West Bedfont
East Bedfont
Long Lane
Clockhouse Industrial Estate
Staines Rd
London Road A30
Ashford Sports Club
Ashford Cemetery
Superstore
Town Lane B378
B3003
1 grid square represents 500 metres

Northern Perimeter Rd
Northern Perimeter Road
Airport
Heathrow Terminals 1, 2 & 3 Stn
Eastern Perimeter Rd
Eastern Business Park
Esher Crs
Eastchurch Rd
Exeter Wy
Exeter Rd
Vanguard Wy
Ensign Cl
Eastchurch Road
Electra Av
Elmdon Rd
Eastern Perimeter Road
Envoy Avenue
Jurys Inn
Viscount Way
British Airways Museum
Works
Lithgow's Rd
Hatton Rd
Hatton Cross Stn
Hatton
Faggs Rd
Green Man Lane
Dockwell Close
St Theresa's Road
St Anthony's Wy
Faggs Road
Hatton Gn
Myrtle Av
Hatton Road
Wellington Rd
Great South-West Road
Perimeter Road
Cain's Lane
Orchard Av
Unwin Av
Edward Rd
Hatton Road
The Marjory Kinnon School
Surgery
Bedfont J&I School
Hazelmere Cl
Marriott Cl
Heathrow Terminal 4 Stn
Swindon Rd
Southern
Sheffield Rd
Snowdon Road
Swansea Road
Shrewsbury Road
Shrewsbury Rd
Seven Seas Rd
Scarborough Rd
A30
The Gardens
Hillingdon
Hounslow
Cranford Infant School
Cranford Junior School
Byron Avenue
Chaucer Avenue
River Crane
Sun Life Trading Estate
Girling Way
Causeway
A312
Heron Wy
Hasler Industrial Estate
Armadale Rd
Superstore
Cemetery
Faggs Road
Dukes Gn Av
Dukes Gn Avenue
Central Way
Works
Clive Road
Minimax Close
Surgery
Pentelow Gdns
Kingston Av
Longford Avenue
Richmond Av
Peninsular Cl
Northumberland Crs
Target Cl
Staines Road
A315
Staines Rd
Ruskin Av
Burns Avenue
Shaftesbury Avenue
Rosslyn Av
Buckingham Av
Harlington Road
Gladstone Av
Shakespeare Avenue
Cassiobury Avenue
Longford Community School
Letchworth Av
Feltham & Hounslow Borough FC
Feltham Athletics Arena
TW14
Bedfont Lane
B3377
Bedfont La
Dorchester Dr
Bethany Waye
Gould Rd
Warfield Rd
Colonial Rd
Imperial Rd
Bedfont Health Clinic
Montrose Rd
Horsham Rd
Bedfont Cl
Hatton Road
Benedict Dr
West Road
East Road
North Rd
Page Road
Lewin Terrace
New Road
Stanwell Rd
Longleat Wy
Pates Mnr Dr
Burlington Cl
Staines Road
St Mary's Drive
Surgery
Spinney Drive
West View
Natalie Cl
Grovestile Waye
Beech Road
Cedar Rd
Grove Village Medical Cen
Kilross Rd
Southville Road
Southville Close
Southville Crs
Monarch Cl
Oak Way
Ash Gv
Watermead
Sandy Dr
Elsworth Close
Bowden Close
Beattie Cl
Westmacott Dr
Walker Cl
Southville Infant School
Chandlers Close
Trevithick Cl
Waterloo Cl
Westmacott Drive
Derwent Cl
Fruen Road
Tachbrook Rd
Shore Cl
Hawkes Rd
Westminster Cl
Ashmead Rd
Southern Av
Proctors Cl
Sandycombe Rd
Locomotive Dr
Station Est Rd
New Road
Feltham Station
Travelodge
Cardinal Rd Infant Sch
Victoria Rd
A244
Hatchett Rd
Bedfont Green Cl
Dudley Road
Elm Road
Sherborne Rd
Peacock Avenue
Fairholme Primary School
Manor Rd
Fawns Rd
Bedfont Lakes Office Park
Bedfont Cemetery
Bedfont Road
Industrial Estate
Edward Pauling School
Padstow Wk
Hanover Av
Guildford Av
Superstore
Surgery
Bedfont Lakes
101
122
140
50
F
G
H
J
K
1
2
3
4
5
6
7
08
09
10
73
74
75
76

102
122
121
141
A
B
C
D
E
1
2
3
4
5
6
7
Hounslow West
North Feltham
TW4
Hounslow Heath
Golf Course
Reservoir
A4
A30
A312
A315
A3063
A3006
A244
B3377
SOUTH-WEST ROAD A30
Bath Rd
Great West Rd
STAINES ROAD
WELLINGTON ROAD NORTH
WELLINGTON ROAD SOUTH
HANWORTH ROAD
HARLINGTON ROAD WEST
HARLINGTON ROAD EAST
HOUNSLOW ROAD
FAGG'S ROAD
CAUSEWAY
BEDFONT LA
NEW ROAD
UXBRIDGE RD
Hounslow West Station
Cranford Junior School
Cranford Infant School
Heathrow International Trading Est
Sun Life Trading Estate
Wallbrook Business Cen
Maple Grove Business Cen
North Feltham Trading Est
River Gardens Business Cen
Dockwell's Industrial Est
Tamian Industrial Est
Freehold Industrial Cen
Superstore
Works
The Beavers Comm Prim Sch
Hounslow Heath Infant School
Hounslow Heath Jun Sch
Logan Prim Sch
Lascar Works
Jamia Mosque
Hounslow CC
Wellington School
New Brentford Cemetery
Hounslow Heath Golf Club
Sheridan Court
Wraysbury Close
The Heathland School
Feltham & Hounslow Borough FC
Feltham Athletics Arena
Sparrow Farm Infant School
Sparrow Farm Junior School
Hounslow Cemetery
Mill Farm Business Park
South West Middlesex Crematorium
Feltham Station
Travelodge
Cardinal Rd Infant Sch
Junior School
Cineworld
St Lawrence Business Cen
Feltham Community College
Crane Park Island
Surgery
Surgeries
1 grid square represents 500 metres

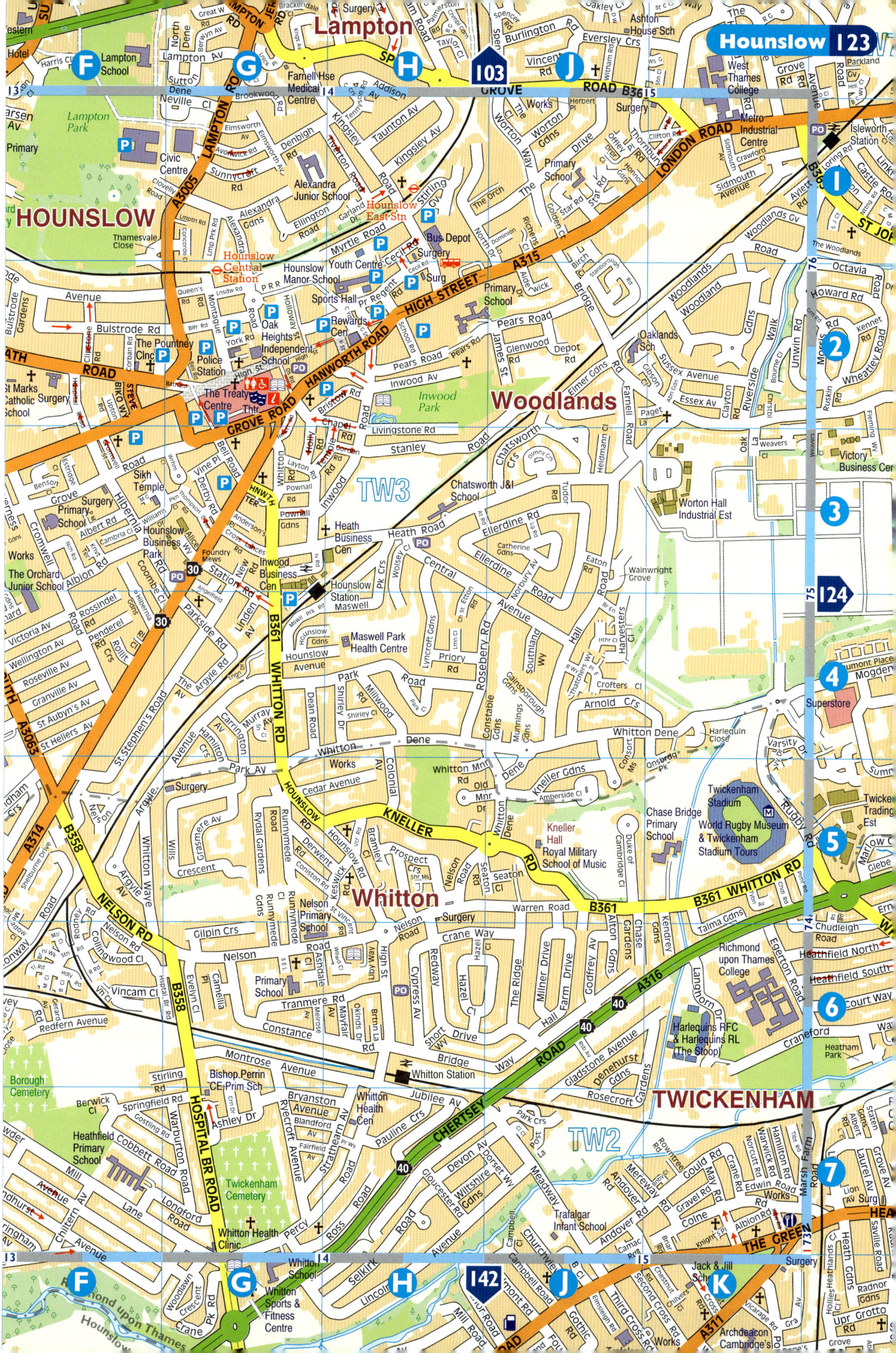
Lampton
HOUNSLOW
Woodlands
Whitton
TWICKENHAM
TW3
TW2
Lampton Park
Lampton School
Hounslow Central Station
Hounslow East Stn
Hounslow Station
Whitton Station
Isleworth Station
Inwood Park
Twickenham Stadium
World Rugby Museum & Twickenham Stadium Tours
Twickenham Cemetery
Borough Cemetery
Kneller Hall Royal Military School of Music
Richmond upon Thames College
Harlequins RFC & Harlequins RL (The Stoop)
The Treaty Centre
Worton Hall Industrial Est
Victory Business Cen
Superstore
HIGH STREET
LONDON ROAD
GROVE ROAD
HANWORTH ROAD
CHERTSEY ROAD
B361 WHITTON RD
KNELLER RD
HOSPITAL BR ROAD
NELSON RD
THE GREEN
103
124
142
F G H J K
1 2 3 4 5 6 7

124
104
123
143
TW7
TW1
ISLEWORTH
St Margarets
Cole Park
Old Deer Park
Syon Park
Golf Course
Royal Mid-Surrey Golf Club
Richmond Lock
Twickenham Bridge
Richmond Bridge
River Thames
Thames Path
Hounslow
Richmond upon Thames
Isleworth Station
Metro Industrial Centre
West Thames College
Smallberry Green Primary School
Isleworth Town Primary School
W Middlesex University Hosp
Isleworth Cem
Snowy Fielder Waye
Brewery Mews Bus Centre
Convent School
The Blue Sch
Prim Sch
Victory Business Cen
Isleworth Recreation Centre
Waterside Business Cen
Primary School
University
Rambert School
Superstore
Ivybridge Retail Park
Twickenham Trading Est
Twickenham Rugby Museum
Primary School
Junior School
Moormead
Recn Ground
St Margarets Business Centre
Infant School
St Mary's Junior School
Marble Hill Park
Marble Hill House
Orleans House Gallery
Twickenham Park Health Cen
Cambridge Park Bowling & Sports Club
Bingham Hotel
Richmond Theatre
Richmond Green
Richmond Magistrates Court
Pools on the Park
Community College
Richmond FC
Film House
Riverside Museum
Odeon
Richmond upon Thames College
Heatham Park
Richmond Community College
Acorn Medical Cen
Civic Centre
Council Building
Oak Lane Medical Cen
Mary Wallace Theatre
Eel Pie Island
Twickenham Stn
St Margaret's Stn
Deutsche Schule
Ham House & Garden (NT)
The Russell School
Strathmore School
Queen Charlotte's Cottage
Wyevale Garden Centre
Boathouse
ST JOHN'S ROAD
TWICKENHAM RD
SOUTH STREET
RICHMOND ROAD
ST MARGARET'S RD
LONDON RD
THE AVENUE
CHERTSEY ROAD
A316 TWICKENHAM ROAD
WHITTON RD
WHITTON ROAD
ST MARGARET'S RD
CROWN RD
RICHMOND ROAD
BRIDGE ST
HILL RISE
HEATH ROAD
THE GREEN
KING ST
ARRAGON ROAD
A310
A3004
A305
B363
1 grid square represents 500 metres

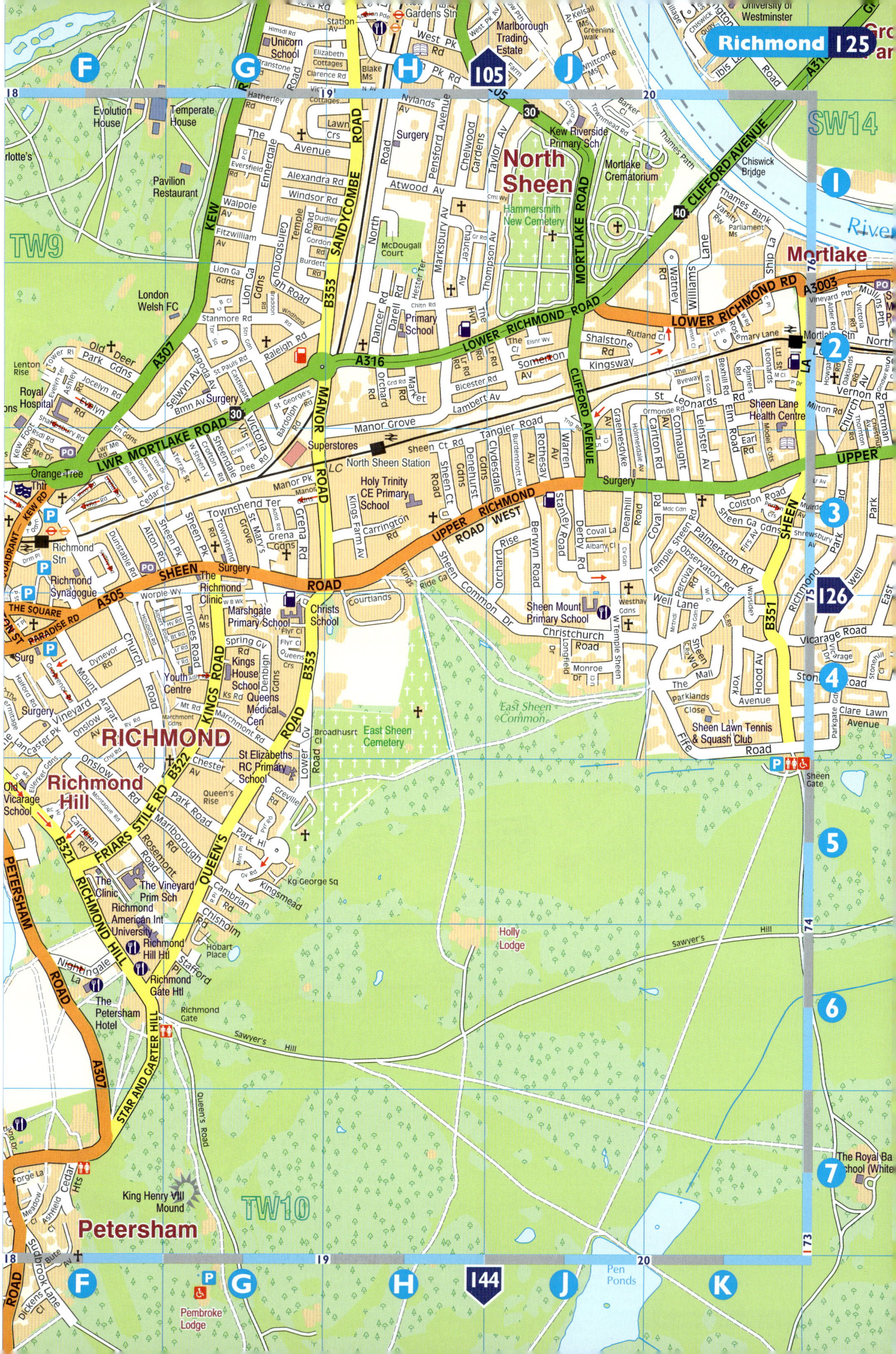
North Sheen
Mortlake
RICHMOND
Richmond Hill
Petersham
TW9
TW10
SW14
LWR MORTLAKE ROAD
LOWER RICHMOND ROAD
UPPER RICHMOND ROAD WEST
SHEEN ROAD
MANOR ROAD
SANDYCOMBE ROAD
KEW ROAD
MORTLAKE ROAD
CLIFFORD AVENUE
KINGS ROAD
QUEEN'S ROAD
FRIARS STILE RD
RICHMOND HILL
STAR AND GARTER HILL
PETERSHAM ROAD
PARADISE RD
THE SQUARE
A307
A316
A305
A3003
B353
B321
B322
B351
Hammersmith New Cemetery
Mortlake Crematorium
East Sheen Cemetery
East Sheen Common
North Sheen Station
Richmond Stn
Mortlake Stn
Kew Riverside Primary Sch
Holy Trinity CE Primary School
Sheen Mount Primary School
Marshgate Primary School
Christs School
St Elizabeths RC Primary School
Queens Medical Cen
Richmond Synagogue
Richmond American Int University
The Vineyard Prim Sch
Richmond Hill Htl
Richmond Gate Htl
The Petersham Hotel
Richmond Gate
Sheen Gate
Pen Ponds
Holly Lodge
Pembroke Lodge
King Henry VIII Mound
Sawyer's Hill
Sheen Lawn Tennis & Squash Club
Sheen Lane Health Centre
London Welsh FC
Royal Hospital
Chiswick Bridge
Thames Bank
River
Evolution House
Temperate House
Pavilion Restaurant
Unicorn School
Marlborough Trading Estate
Superstores
Courtlands
Kg George Sq
Hobart Place
Youth Centre
Old Vicarage School
The Royal Ballet School (White
F
G
H
J
K
I
1
2
3
4
5
6
7
18
19
20
73
74
75
76
105
126
144

126
Grove Park
A
B
C
D
E
106
BARNES
SW14
Duke's Meadows
Chiswick Bridge
River Thames
Barnes Bridge
Barnes Bridge Station
Mortlake
MORTLAKE HIGH STREET
THE TERRACE
BARNES HIGH ST
CHURCH RD
STATION ROAD
Barn Elms Athletics Track
Old Barnes Cemetery
Putney Lower Common Cemetery
Barnes Common
MILL HILL ROAD
ROCKS LANE
QUEEN'S RIDE
Barnes Station
Mortlake Stn
St Mary Magdalens Prim Sch
Westfields Primary School
Barnes Primary School
Barnes Hospital
Mortlake Cem
Sheen Lane Health Centre
UPPER RICHMOND ROAD WEST
UPPER RICHMOND ROAD
A205
A306
A3003
B349
B306
Rosslyn Park RFC
East Sheen Primary School
Paddock School
Sheen School
Sheen Sports Centre
The Roehampton Priory Hospital
Roehampton University (Southlands College)
National Tennis Centre
Roehampton
Roehampton University (Digby Stuart College)
Sacred Heart Catholic Primary School
East Sheen
125
Lawn Tennis Club
Sheen Gate
Roehampton University (Froebel College)
Grove House (Froebel College)
Queen Mary's University Hospital
Douglas Bader Foundation
SW15
Granard Primary School
Ibstock Place School
South Thames College
Roehampton Gate
Richmond Park Golf Club
ROEHAMPTON LANE
Roehampton Recreation Centre
Roehampton University (Whitelands College)
Roehampton Church School
Royal Hospital & Home
Westmoor Community Clinic
Richmond upon Thames
Wandsworth
Beverley Brook
The Royal Ballet School (White Lodge)
Golf Course
Primary School
KINGSTON
Putney Vale Crematorium
Putney Vale Cemetery
Richmond Park National Nature
145
1 grid square represents 500 metres
1
2
3
4
5
6
7

F
G
H
J
K
107
128
146
23
24
25
1
2
3
4
5
6
7
Barn Elms Sports Centre
Barn Elms Water Sports Centre
Fulham FC (Craven Cottage)
Bowls Club
Imperial College
The Moat School
All Saints CE Primary School
Fulham Palace
Museum of Fulham Palace
Bishops Park
Preparatory School
Church Gate
Putney Bridge
Putney Bridge Station
Ranelagh Gardens
Works
Parsons Green
Peterborough Primary School
Queensmill School
Sulivan Primary School
Hurlingham House
Hurlingham Business Park
Hurlingham Private School
River Thames
Thames Path
WANDSWOR
Riverside Quarter
Wandsworth Park
Northfields Prospect Business Cen
Express by Holiday Inn
Osier Ind Est
Ferrier Industrial Estate
B306 LOWER RICHMOND ROAD
All Saints CE Primary Sch
Putney Leisure Centre
Putneymead Medical Centre
Our Lady of Victories RC Prim
Shopping Centre
Felsham Rd
PUTNEY BRIDGE AP
A219 PUTNEY BRIDGE AP
PUTNEY HIGH ST
PUTNEY BRIDGE ROAD
UPPER RICHMOND RD
A205
Lion House School
Arts Theatre
Putney Stn
School of Art
Wandsworth County Court
East Putney Station
PUTNEY
South Thames College
Merlin School
Putney High Sch
St Josephs Primary School
The Roche School
ARMOURY WY
WANDSWORTH HIGH ST
Police Station
Best Western Lodge Hotel
Ashcroft Technology Academy
College
WEST HILL A3
Fire Station
Southside Shopping Centre
Arndale Health Centre
The Southfields Clnc
Wandle Recreation Centre
SW18
Wandsworth Trading Estate
King George's Park
BUCKHOLD RD
A217
MERTON RD A218
Royal Hospital for Neuro-Disability
West Hill
Putney Heath
TIBBET'S RIDE
WIMBLEDON PARK SIDE
Prospect House Sch
Ronald Rose Primary Sch
Our Lady Queen of Heaven RC Prim
Tudor Lodge Health Cen
John Paul II RC School
Southmead Primary School
Theatre of the Dispossessed
Linden Lodge School
Saint Cecilias CE Sch
Primary School
Grammar School
Sheringdale Primary School
Merton Road Industrial Estate
Riverside Business Centre
Southfields Station
Southfields
Southfields Community College
Albemarle Primary
Wimbledon Park
Southdean Gardens

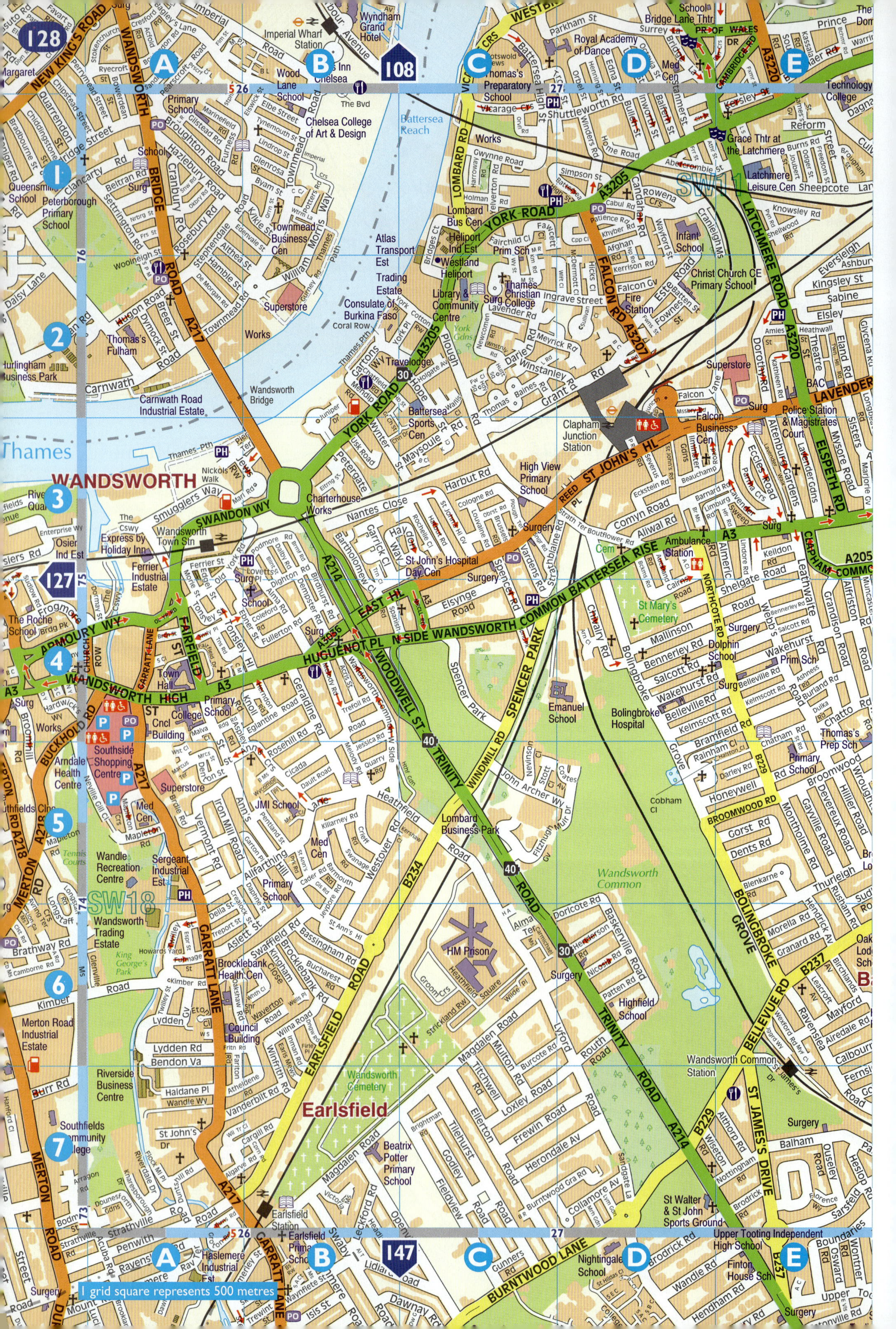

128
108
127
147
A
B
C
D
E
1
2
3
4
5
6
7
WANDSWORTH
Thames
Battersea Reach
SW11
SW18
Earlsfield
Clapham Junction Station
Wandsworth Town Stn
Wandsworth Common
Wandsworth Common Station
Earlsfield Station
Wandsworth Cemetery
HM Prison
Southside Shopping Centre
Wandsworth Bridge
Imperial Wharf Station
Wyndham Grand Hotel
Chelsea College of Art & Design
Royal Academy of Dance
Grace Thtr at the Latchmere
Latchmere Leisure Cen
Technology College
Carnwath Road Industrial Estate
Hurlingham Business Park
Thomas's Fulham
Peterborough Primary School
Queensmill School
Townmead Business Cen
Atlas Transport Est
Trading Estate
Consulate of Burkina Faso
Lombard Bus Cen
Heliport Ind Est
Westland Heliport
Library & Community Centre
Thames Christian College
Battersea Sports Cen
High View Primary School
Christ Church CE Primary School
Infant School
Falcon Business Cen
Police Station & Magistrates Court
Charterhouse Works
Express by Holiday Inn
Ferrier Industrial Estate
Osier Ind Est
The Roche School
Town Hall
Cncl Building
Wandle Recreation Centre
Sergeant Industrial Est
Wandsworth Trading Estate
King George's Park
Merton Road Industrial Estate
Riverside Business Centre
Southfields Community College
Brocklebank Health Cen
Council Building
JMI School
St John's Hospital Day Cen
Emanuel School
Bolingbroke Hospital
St Mary's Cemetery
Ambulance Station
Dolphin School
Wakehurst Prim Sch
Thomas's Prep Sch
Lombard Business Park
Highfield School
Beatrix Potter Primary School
St Walter & St John Sports Ground
Upper Tooting Independent High School
Finton House Sch
Nightingale School
Haslemere Industrial Est
WANDSWORTH BRIDGE ROAD
NEW KING'S ROAD
YORK ROAD
SWANDON WY
WANDSWORTH HIGH
ARMOURY WY
FAIRFIELD
GARRATT LANE
EARLSFIELD ROAD
TRINITY ROAD
WINDMILL RD
SPENCER PARK
N SIDE WANDSWORTH COMMON
BATTERSEA RISE
ST JOHN'S HL
FALCON RD
LATCHMERE ROAD
LAVENDER
BOLINGBROKE GROVE
BELLEVUE RD
ST JAMES'S DRIVE
BURNTWOOD LANE
MERTON ROAD
BUCKHOLD RD
HUGUENOT PL
EAST HL
WOODWELL ST
1 grid square represents 500 metres

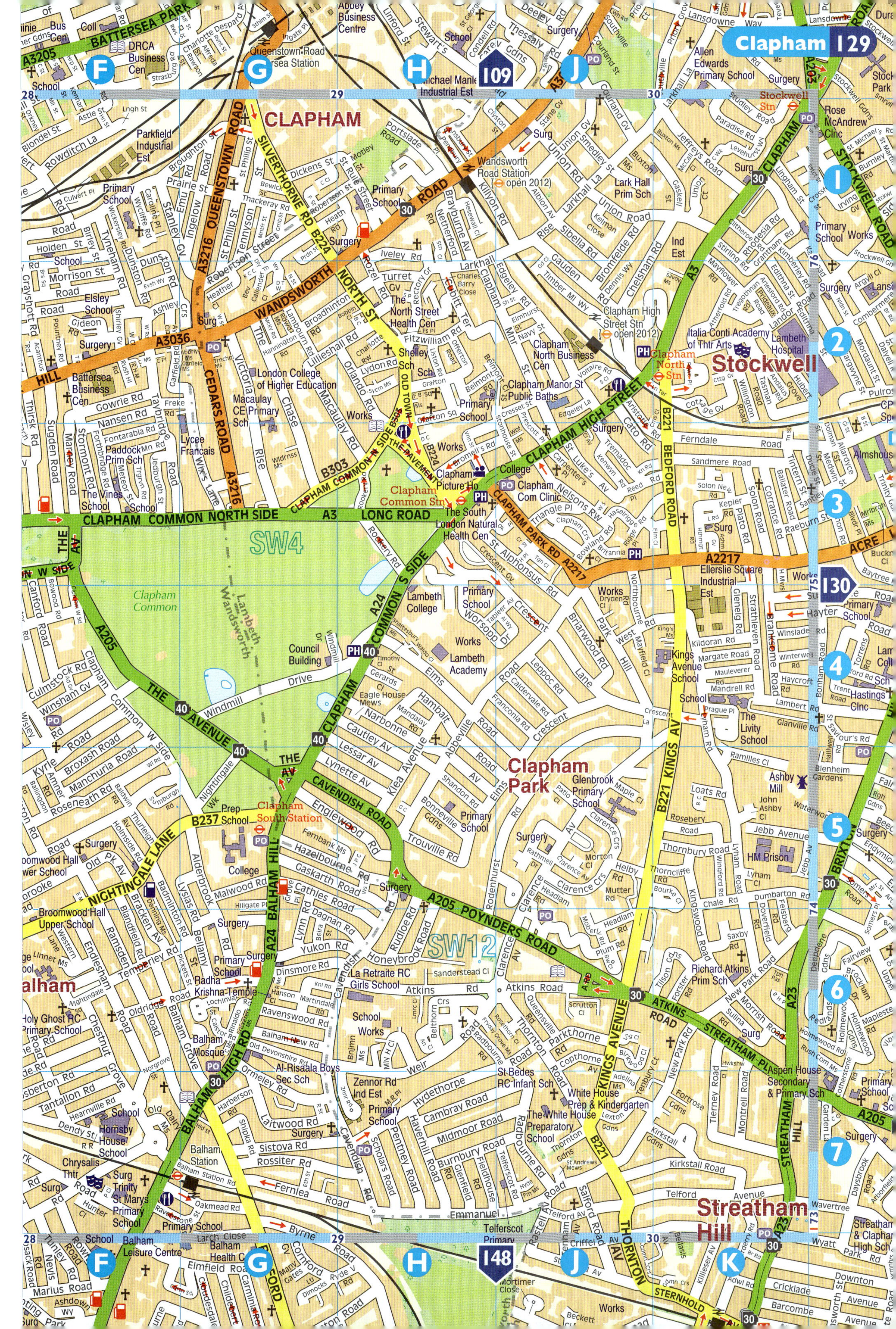
CLAPHAM
Stockwell
Clapham Park
Streatham Hill
Balham
SW4
SW12
Clapham Common
109
130
148
Battersea Park Rd
Queenstown Road
Queenstown Road Battersea Station
Wandsworth Road Station (open 2012)
Clapham High Street Stn (open 2012)
Clapham North Stn
Clapham Common Stn
Clapham South Station
Stockwell Stn
Balham Station
Wandsworth Road
Silverthorne Rd
Queenstown Road
Cedars Road
North St
Clapham Common North Side
Long Road
Clapham Common S Side
Clapham High Street
Clapham Park Rd
Bedford Road
Kings Av
Kings Avenue
The Avenue
Windmill Drive
Cavendish Road
Poynders Road
Nightingale Lane
Balham Hill
Balham High Rd
Atkins Road
Streatham Pl
Streatham Hill
Brixton Hill
Clapham Road
Stockwell Road
Old Town
The Pavement
Lambeth
Wandsworth
Lambeth College
Lambeth Academy
Clapham Picture Ho
Clapham Manor St Public Baths
Clapham North Business Cen
Italia Conti Academy of Thtr Arts
Lambeth Hospital
The South London Natural Health Cen
London College of Higher Education
Macaulay CE Primary Sch
Lycee Francais
Paddock Prim Sch
The Vines School
Battersea Business Cen
Parkfield Industrial Est
DRCA Business Cen
Michael Manley Industrial Est
Allen Edwards Primary School
Clapham Com Clinic
Ellerslie Square Industrial Est
Kings Avenue School
The Livity School
Hastings Clnc
Glenbrook Primary School
HM Prison
Richard Atkins Prim Sch
Aspen House Secondary & Primary Sch
Broomwood Hall Upper School
Radha Krishna Temple
Balham Mosque
Al-Risaala Boys Sec Sch
La Retraite RC Girls School
St Bedes RC Infant Sch
White House Prep & Kindergarten
The White House Preparatory School
Hornsby House School
Chrysalis Thtr
Trinity St Marys Primary School
Balham Leisure Centre
Balham Health C
Streatham & Clapham High Sch
Ashby Mill
A3205
A3216
A3036
A3
A24
A205
A2217
A23
B221
B237
B303
B224
B222
A203
F
G
H
J
K
I
2
3
4
5
6
7
28
29
30
73
74
75
76

130
110
129
149
A
B
C
D
E
1
2
3
4
5
6
7
SW9
SE5
SE24
SW2
BRIXTON
Stockwell
Herne Hill
Knight's Hill
Tulse Hill
Streatham
West Dulwich
Brockwell Park
Ruskin Park
Belair Park
CAMBERWELL CHURCH ST
CHAMPION PK
DENMARK HILL
COLDHARBOUR
ATLANTIC ROAD
ACRE LANE
BRIXTON ROAD
BRIXTON HILL
STOCKWELL ROAD
CLAPHAM ROAD
EFFRA RD
TULSE HILL
NORWOOD ROAD
DULWICH ROAD
RAILTON ROAD
MILKWOOD ROAD
HALF MOON LANE
VILLAGE WAY
HERNE HILL
CROXTED ROAD
THURLOW PARK ROAD
CHRISTCHURCH ROAD
King's College Hospital
Kings College School of Medicine & Dentistry
The Maudsley Hosp
HM Prison
Herne Hill Stadium (Cycle Centre)
Brixton Stn
Herne Hill Station
Tulse Hill Station
West Dulwich Station
North Dulwich Station
Loughborough Junction Stn
Denmark Hill Stn (reopen 2012)
A203
A2217
A215
A2216
A204
A205
A23
A2199
B223
1 grid square represents 500 metres

Brixton 131
Peckham
East Dulwich
Dulwich Village
Nunhead
Honor Oak
SE22
Peckham Road
Peckham Rye
Peckham Rye Park
Peckham Rye Stn
East Dulwich Rd
A2214
A2216
B219
B238
Grove Vale
Dog Kennel Hill
Lordship Lane
East Dulwich Stn
Dulwich Hamlet FC
Dulwich Hospital
Dulwich Leisure Centre
Dulwich Park
Dulwich Picture Gallery
Dulwich College
Dulwich Common
Forest Hill Road
Honor Oak Park
London Road
Nunhead Lane
Evelina Road
Gellatly Rd
Nunhead Stn
Cemetery
Camberwell New Cemetery
Old Cemetery
Golf Course
Aquarius Golf Club
Harris Girls Academy
The City of London Academy
Waverley Lower Secondary School
The Horniman Museum & Gardens
Horniman Primary School
Southwark Sports Ground
Marlborough CC
Forest Hill Station
Premier Cinema
Bellenden Rd Business Cen
St Thomas the Apostle College
Alleyns Junior School
St Anthonys RC Primary School
Goodrich J&I School
St Francesca Cabrini Primary School
Fairlawn Primary School
Malham Road Industrial Est
132
150
F G H J K
1 2 3 4 5 6 7
33 34 35

132
112
131
151
A
B
C
D
E
1
2
3
4
5
6
7
New Cross Gate
New Cross
St Johns
Nunhead
Ladywell
Brockley
Honor Oak
Honor Oak Park
Forest Hill
SE4
SE23
Haberdashers Askes Hatcham Coll
Goldsmiths University of London
Edmund Waller Primary School
Haberdashers Askes Hatcham College
Crossways Academy
Brockley Cross Business Cen
Lewisham College
Thurston Industrial Est
Lewisham Bridge Primary School
Meadowgate Sch
Prendergast School
Hilly Fields Medical Centre
Ladywell Cemetery
Ladywell Stn
University Hospital
Brockley Stn
Crofton Park Station
Honor Oak Park Station
Honor Oak Crematorium
Camberwell New Cemetery
Aquarius Golf Club
Ivydale Primary School
Brockley Way
Southwark
Lewisham
Crofton Leisure Centre
Prendergast Ladywell Fields College
Ladywell Arena
Ravensbourne River
Holbeach Primary School
Catford Bridge Station
Catford Station
St Dunstans College
Phoenix Leisure Centre
Rushey Green Prim Sch
Catford Cricket & Sports Club
Catford Trading Estate
Rathfern Primary School
Stillness Primary School
St William of York Prim Sch
Jenner Health Cen
Malham Road Industrial Est
Forest Hill Station
LOAMPIT HILL
THURSTON RD
LEWISHAM WAY
MALPAS ROAD
B218
B2142 DRAKEFELL ROAD
GELLATLY RD
ADELAIDE AV
B236 LADYWELL ROAD
BROCKLEY ROAD
HONOR OAK PARK
STONDON PK
BROCKLEY RI
STANSTEAD ROAD
A205
CATFORD ROAD
A212 CATFORD HILL
RUSHEY GN
LEWISHAM HIGH ST
A21
BROMLEY ROAD
WALDRAM PK RD
536
37
30
1 grid square represents 500 metres

Blackheath
Blackheath Park
LEWISHAM
Hither Green
Lee
CATFORD
SE3
SE13
SE12
113
134
152
BLACKHEATH HILL
SHOOTERS HILL RD
PR OF WALES RD
B212
A2
LEWISHAM RD A21
MOLESWORTH ST
A21
LEE TERRACE
BELMONT HILL
B220
LEE HIGH ROAD
A20
ELTHAM ROAD
A2212 BURNT ASH ROAD
BURNT ASH HILL
WESTHORNE AVENUE
BROWNHILL ROAD
A205
ST MILDREDS ROAD
BARING ROAD
A2212
LEE ROAD B212
MONTPELIER RW
ROYAL PDE
TRANQUIL V
Blackheath Stn
Lewisham Centre
Clock Tower
AMF Bowling
Superstore
St Matthew Academy
Christ the King Sixth Form College
All Saints CE Primary Sch
Camden Ho Clinic
Blackheath High School GDST
Prep School
Blackheath Hosp
Goldsmiths University of London
Northbrook CE School
Brooklands Primary School
Wingfield Primary School
Huntsman Sports Club
The Blackheath Clinic
Sports Ground
Riverston School
Old Colfeian Sports Club
Colfe's Prep School
Lee Station
Hither Green Stn
Lee Manor Primary School
Complementary Health Cen
St Winifreds RC Infant School
St Winifreds Catholic Junior Sch
Chiltonian Industrial Est
Woodlands Medical Centre
Ladywell Leisure Centre
Lewisham Park
Mountsfield Park
Holy Cross RC Primary School
Sandhurst Primary School
Baring Primary School
Torridon Primary School
Hither Green Cemetery
Morden College Homes
Manor Brook Medical Centre
Blackheath Preparatory School
Surgery
Works
Greenwich
Lewisham

134
114
133
153
A
B
C
D
E
1
2
3
4
5
6
7
SE3
SE12
Kidbrooke
ELTHAM
Mottingham
Kidbrooke Station
Eltham Station
Mottingham Station
A2
A20
A205
A208
A210
A2213
A207
Rochester Way
Kidbrooke Park Road
Sidcup Road
Westhorne Avenue
Eltham Road
Eltham Hill
Well Hall Road
Court Road
Broad Walk
Kidbrooke Park Primary School
Kidbrooke School
Morden College Homes
Manor Brook Medical Centre
Long Lane AFC
Thomas Tallis School
Sports Ground
Superstore
Wingfield Primary School
Huntsman Sports Club
Cemetery
St Thomas More RC Primary School
University of Greenwich Sports Ground
The Pleasaunce
Odeon
Gordon Primary School
Meadowside Leisure Centre
Sutcliffe Park
Sutcliffe Park Athletics Track
Riverston School
Old Colfeian Sports Club
Colfe's Prep School
Colfe's Senior School
Civil Service Sports Ground
Old Brockleians Sports Ground
Leathersellers Sports Ground
Eltham Green School
Moatbridge School
Eltham Hill Tech College
Eltham Health Clinic
Eltham Pools
Bingo Hall
Police Station
Council Building
The Bob Hope Theatre
Eltham Bus Station
Eltham Palace
Royal Blackheath Golf Club
Middle Park Primary School
Horn Park Primary School
Eltham College Junior School
Eltham College Senior School
Eric Liddell Sports Centre
Greenwich
Bromley
Lewisham
Green Chain Walk
1 grid square represents 500 metres

Eltham 135
Shooters Hill
115
Golf Club
Golf Course
Primary School
Eltham Common
Memorial Hospital
Kenilworth Gardens
Jack Wood
Oxleas Wood
Eastcote Primary School
DOVER ROAD
A207
BELLEGROVE
Sandringham Drive
Falconwood Avenue
Welling Way
Rochester Way
Crookston Road
Dairsie Road
Deansfield Primary School
Dumbreck
Elibank Road
Falconwood Station
Harris Academy Falconwood
Westwood Primary School
Falconwood
Northumberland Av
Eltham Park
Eltham Park Gdns
A2
ROCHESTER WAY RELIEF ROAD
EAST ROCHESTER WAY
Eltham Crematorium
Cemetery
136
Welling Medical Centre
Colepits Wood Rd
Glenlyon Road
Glenshiel Road
Primary School
Golf Course
Green Chain Walk
Crown Woods School
Eltham Warren Golf Club
Ridgeway West
Orchard Rise
Medical Centre
Reservoir
BEXLEY ROAD
A210
Fire Station
Eltham Health & Fitness Centre
University of Greenwich (Mansion Site)
Avery Hill Park
Avery Hill
AVERY HILL ROAD
Butterfly Sports Club
Trinity Court
St Thomas More RC School
Visage School of Hair & Beauty
FOOTSCRAY ROAD
Alderwood Primary School
Our Lady of the Rosary RC School
Berwick Crs
Surgery
Charlton RFC
University of Greenwich (Southwood Site)
Norfolk Crescent
SE9
Sports Ground
University of Greenwich Sports Ground
B2214
HALFWAY STREET
Golf Course
Starbuck Cl
GREEN LANE
B263
A211
Wyborne Primary School
Sparrows Lane
Avery Hill Rd
Blanmerle Road
Hainault Street
New Eltham Stn
New Eltham
Green Lane Business Park
St Mary's Preparatory School
154
Dulverton Primary School
Brooklands Avenue
Pinewood Av
Old Farm Avenue

136
116
135
155
A
B
C
D
E
1
2
3
4
5
6
7
DA16
DA15
Welling
BEXLEY
Blackfen
Cemetery
East Wickham Primary School
St Michaels CE Primary School
Welling School
Wickham Street
Upper Wickham Lane
Normanhurst Avenue
Swanley Road
Farnham Road
Elsa Road
Balliol Road
Somerhill Road
Lynmere Rd
Northdown Road
Holmesdale Road
Fairlawn Avenue
Barrington Rd
Barrington Primary School
Brampton Primary School
Victoria Business Centre
Graves Yard Industrial Estate
Health & Welfare Clinic
Welling Stn
William Foster Lane
Bellegrove Road
Welling High Street
Park View Road
Crook Log
Westbrooke School
Crook Log Sports Centre
Fosters Prim Sch
Palmeira Road
Marlborough Road
Hook Lane Primary School
Danson Mead
Welling United FC
Splashworld Swimming Centre
Crook Log Primary School
Danson Park
Danson House
Danson Watersports Centre
Danson Road
Danson Primary School
Bexley Grammar School
Little Danson Welfare Clinic
Welling Medical Centre
Rochester Way
East Rochester Way
Ingleton Avenue
Sutherland Avenue
Blackfen Road
Superstore
Medical Centre
Westerham Drive
Works
Blendon Road
Woodside Lane
Blackfen School for Girls
Sherwood Park Primary School
Sherwood Park Avenue
Days Lane Primary School
Our Lady of the Rosary RC School
Health & Welfare Clinic
Penhill Road
Harcourt Avenue
Burnt Oak Lane
Rowley Avenue
Golf Course
Hurstmere School
Rose Bruford College
Lamorbey Park
Chatsworth Infant School
Holy Trinity Lamorbey CE Prim Sch
Burnt Oak Jun Sch
Marlborough School
Hurst Primary School
Albany Park Station
Sidcup Golf Club
Station Road
Hurst Road
Longmead Drive
Penhill Road
Carisbrooke Avenue
Oakley Park
Oaklands Avenue
Harborough Av
Braundton Av
Days Lane
A2
A210
A221
A222
B2214
1 grid square represents 500 metres

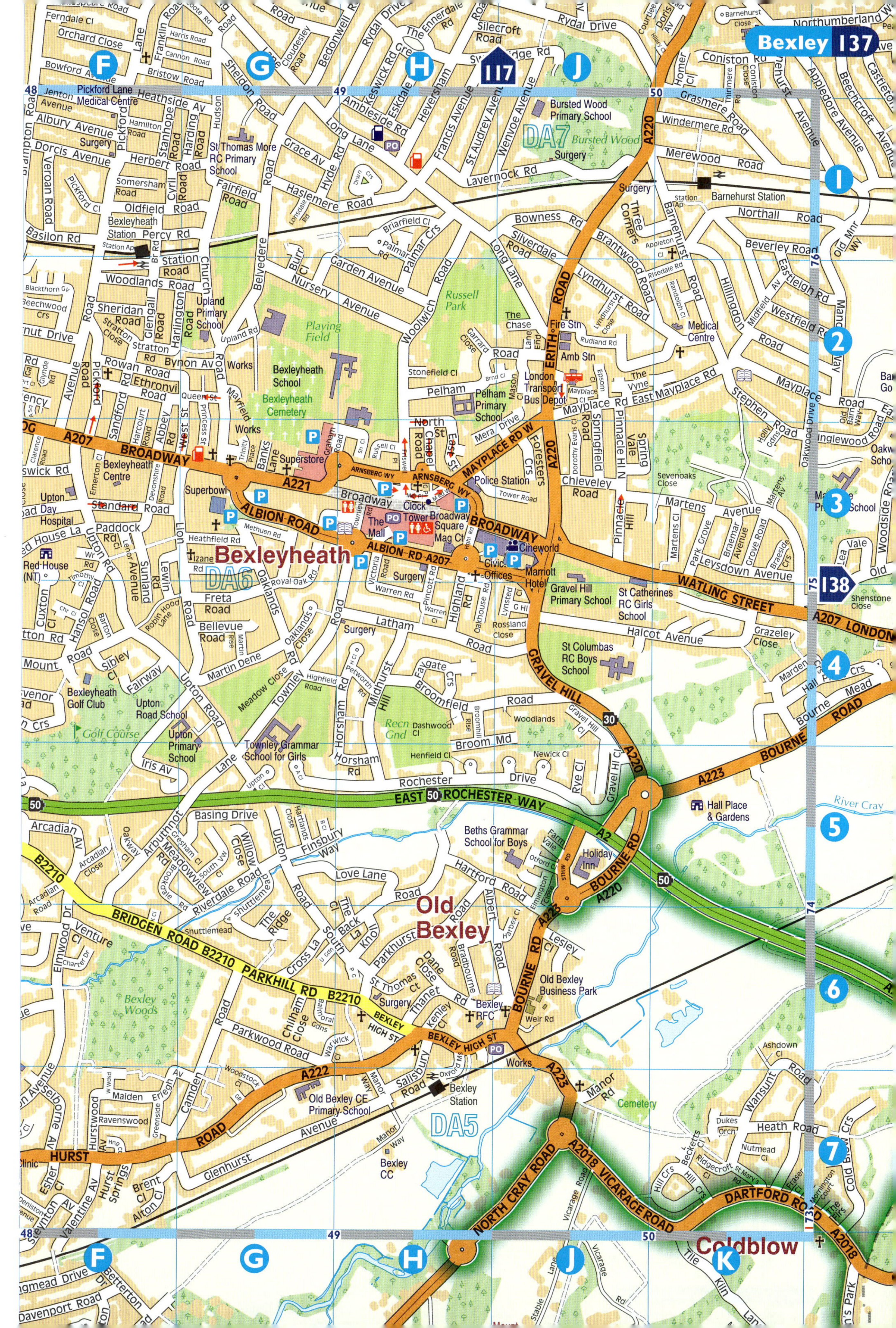
117
138
F
G
H
J
K
1
2
3
4
5
6
7
48
49
50
Bexleyheath
Old Bexley
Coldblow
DA5
DA6
DA7
BROADWAY
A207
A221
A220
A223
A222
A2
A2018
B2210
EAST ROCHESTER WAY
WATLING STREET
A207 LONDON
ALBION ROAD
ALBION RD A207
BRIDGEN ROAD B2210
PARKHILL RD B2210
BEXLEY HIGH ST
BOURNE RD
BOURNE ROAD
GRAVEL HILL
ERITH ROAD
MAYPLACE RD W
NORTH CRAY ROAD
A2018 VICARAGE ROAD
DARTFORD ROAD
HURST ROAD
Pickford Lane Medical Centre
St Thomas More RC Primary School
Bursted Wood Primary School
Bursted Wood
Barnehurst Station
Bexleyheath Station
Upland Primary School
Playing Field
Bexleyheath School
Bexleyheath Cemetery
Russell Park
Pelham Primary School
London Transport Bus Depot
Fire Stn
Amb Stn
Medical Centre
Superstore
Superbowl
Bexleyheath Centre
Upton Day Hospital
Red House (NT)
The Mall
Clock Tower
Broadway Square
Police Station
Cineworld
Civic Offices
Marriott Hotel
Gravel Hill Primary School
St Catherines RC Girls School
St Columbas RC Boys School
Bexleyheath Golf Club
Golf Course
Upton Road School
Upton Primary School
Townley Grammar School for Girls
Recn Gnd
Beths Grammar School for Boys
Holiday Inn
Hall Place & Gardens
River Cray
Bexley Woods
Old Bexley Business Park
Bexley RFC
Old Bexley CE Primary School
Bexley Station
Bexley CC
Cemetery
Surgery
Works
Sevenoaks Close
Shenstone Close

138
118
137
North End
Slade Green
Slade Green Station
Barnehurst
Barnehurst Station
Golf Course
Barnehurst Public Golf Club
Crayside Industrial Estate
Barnes Cray
Crayford
Crayford Station
Crayford Industrial Estate
Tower Retail Park
Acorn Industrial Park
Town Hall
Superstore
Crayford Commercial Centre
Crayford Leisure Centre & Greyhound Stadium
Bourne Road Industrial Park
River Cray
Bowmans
Maypole
Dartford Heath
Oldblow
Dartford Golf Club
Leyton Cross
Bracton Centre
Reynolds Health & Fitness
Normandy Primary School
Oakwood School
Mayplace Primary School
St Paulinus CE Primary School
St Josephs RC Primary School
Shenstone School
Barnes Cray Primary School
Geoffrey Whitworth Theatre
Medical Centre
Surgery
Works
Northend Road
A206
A2000
Perry Street
Thames Road
Crayford Way
B2186
Crayford High St
A207 London Road
Roman Way
Crayford Road A207
Dartford Road
A226
B2174
Princes Road
Shepherds Lane
A2018
A2
Rochester Way
Old Bexley Lane
Bourne Road
Oakfield Lane
Mayplace Road East
Iron Mill Lane
Station Road
Denton Road
Swan Lane
Heath Lane
Everley Avenue
Parkside Avenue
Holmsdale Grove
Northall Road
Whitehall Lane
Moat Lane
Lincoln Road
A B C D E
1 2 3 4 5 6 7
1 grid square represents 500 metres

119
Crayford Marshes
Kent County
Bexley
University Way
A206
Bob Dunn Way
Joyce Green Lane
Temple Hill
Swan Business Park
Millside Industrial Estate
Burnham Trading Estate
Burnham Road
Victoria Road
Riverside Industrial Estate
Victoria Industrial Park
Business Centre
Invicta Sports Club
Holy Trinity CE Prim Sch
Bus Garage
Industrial Estate
Works
Dartford Station
Central Road
Hythe St
Mill Pond Rd
Superstore
Civic Centre
Angel Centre
County Court
Orchard Theatre
Shopping Centre
Priory Shopping Cen
Sikh Temple
High St
Westgate Rd
West Hill
A226
Spital St
Council Building Magistrates Ct
Our Lady's Cath Prim Sch
Health Centre
School for Boys
Becket Sports Centre
Shepherds Lane
Miskin Road
Dartford Grammar Sch for Girls
Dartford Technology College
Dartford Adult Education Centre
Westgate Primary Sch
Instone Rd
Lowfield Street
Police Stn
Natural Health Centre
Lowfield Medical Centre
Dartford Mus & Lib
Fairfield Pool & Leisure Centre
Central Park
Central Park Arena
DARTFORD
Heath Lane
Olive Road
Laurel Cl
Links View
Laburnum Av
Superstore
A296
A225
Brooklands Lake
Council Building
New Town
Fulwich Road
Carrington Rd
Colney Road
St Martin's Road
Cem
Cemetery
East Hill
The Brent
Park Road
Livingstone Hospital
York Rd Junior Sch & Language Unit
Dene Road
Princes Park Stadium
Leigh Technology Academy
Grass Banks
Gateway Prim Sch
Pilgrims Way
A282
B260
St. Anselms RC Prim Sch
Temple Hill Prim Sch
Littlebrook Manor Way
Henderson Drive
Wodehouse Road
Marsh Street
Cemetery
Surgery
Knights Manor Way
Bow Arrow Lane
Hall Road
Trevithick Drive
Wellcome Av
Oakfield Primary School
University of Greenwich
Golf Course
Powder Mill
Walnut Tree Av
F
G
H
J
K
I
2
3
4
5
6
7
53
54
55
73
74
75
76

140
121
Bedfont Lakes Office Park
Fairholme Primary School
Bedfont Cemetery
Bedfont Road
Industrial Estate
Edward Pauling School
Bedfont Lakes Country Park
Lower Feltham
HM Young Offenders Institution
Feltham Hill Infant School
Feltham Hill Jun Sch
Feltham Cemetery
Bedfont Industrial Park
Ashford Industrial Estate
Shield Road
Chattern Hill
ASHFORD RD
B377
A244 CHERTSEY RD
HIGH STREET
HIGH ST
Superstore
Surgery
FELTHAM ROAD
Echelford Primary
Ashford CE Primary School
Spelthorne Infant School
Spelthorne Clnc
Felthamhill
Ashford Common
Sunbury Common
STAINES ROAD
WEST
STAINES RD W
STAINES ROAD EAST
Junction 1
M3
Spelthorne Sports Club
Windmill Trading Estate
Sunbury Business Centre
A244 CADBURY ROAD
WINDMILL ROAD
SUNBURY
Sunbury Stn
Sunbury Leisure Centre
Sunbury Manor School
St Pauls Catholic College
Springfield Primary School
Hounslow
Surrey County
Staines RFC
Summit Business Park
Travelodge
Gaflac Sports Ground Pavilion
Upper Halliford Station
Charlton
Works
1 grid square represents 500 metres

FELTHAM
Hanworth
TW13
TW16
Hanworth Park
HANWORTH ROAD
UXBRIDGE ROAD
HOUNSLOW ROAD
HAMPTON ROAD WEST
TWICKENHAM ROAD
GREAT CHERTSEY ROAD
HAMPTON RD E
COUNTRY WAY
STAINES ROAD
UPPER SUNBURY ROAD
EAST
A312
A314
A316
A308
A244
B3377
Feltham Community College
Feltham Superbowl
Cineworld
St Lawrence Business Cen
Feltham Airparcs Leisure Centre
Felthambrook Industrial Estate
Five Ways Business Cen
Hanworth Trading Est
Hampton Fm Industrial Est
Apex Retail Park
Oriel Primary School
Mount Medical Cen
Crematorium
Crane Park Island
Medical Centre
Superstore
Lindon Bennett School
Forge Lane Primary School
Kempton Park East Reservoir (disused)
Richmond upon Thames
Surrey County
Reservoir
Kempton Park Racecourse
Kempton Park Station
Lazards Sports Club
Richmond House School
Primary School
Shooting Star House (Childrens Hospice)
Infant School
The Hampton Medical Cen
Athelstan House Sch
Kingsway Business Park
Oldfield House Special School
Chennestone Community School
Hampton Comm College
Feltham 141
122
142
156

142
123
141
157
A
B
C
D
E
1
2
3
4
5
6
7
Twickenham Cemetery
Whitton Health Centre
Whitton Clinic
Whitton School
Whitton Sports & Fitness Centre
Richmond upon Thames
Hounslow
River Crane
GREAT CHERTSEY ROAD A316
HOSPITAL BR RD
STAINES ROAD
A305
B358
SIXTH CROSS ROAD
TWICKENHAM ROAD
Medical Centre
Amida Golf
Golf Course
HAMPTON RD E
A312
UXBRIDGE ROAD
Superstore
Waldegrave Girls School
Trafalgar Infant & Junior School
Archdeacon Cambridge's CE Prim Sch
Jack & Jill School
HAMPTON ROAD
A311
The Mall Sch
St James RC Primary School
Strawberry Hill Golf Club
Strawberry Hill
SOUTH ROAD
Garden Centre
Fulwell Golf Club
Fulwell Station
Stanley Infant School
Teddington Cemetery
WELLINGTON ROAD
Hampton Hill
A313
PARK ROAD
HAMPTON ROAD
STANLEY ROAD
B360
Hampton Community College
Hampton School
The Lady Eleanor Holles School
Richmond House School
Primary School
Shooting Star House (Childrens Hospice)
Jack & Jill School
Clarendon School
Longford Industrial Estate
Carlisle Infant School
St Clare Business Park
TEDDINGTON
Teddington Memorial Hospital
Teddington Clinic
National Physical Laboratory
HIGH STREET
TW12
Hampton Cem
Denmead School
The Hampton Medical Centre
Atholstan House Sch
Hampton Open Air Pool
Bartons Cottage
Bushy Park
Hampton
Twickenham Prep School
Hampton FC
Asquith Court School
Hampton Station
SUNBURY ROAD
THAMES ST
CHURCH STREET
King's Paddock
Surrey County
HAMPTON
1 grid square represents 500 metres

124
144
158
F
G
H
J
I
K
1
2
3
4
5
6
7
16
17
18
Ham
Hampton Wick
TW11
River Thames
Eel Pie Island
Ham Lands Nature Reserve
Teddington Lock
Trowlock Island
Bushy Park
Pheasantry Welcome Centre
Diana Fountain
Kingston upon Thames
Richmond upon Thames
Heath Road A305
Cross Deep A310
Strawberry Vale
Twickenham Rd
Manor Rd
Ferry Rd
Kingston Rd A310
Waldegrave Road A309
High Street A313
Broad St
Park Road A309
Queen's Road
Park Road B358
Sandy Lane
Church Grove
Upr Teddington Rd
High St
Horse Fair
Wood Street
Kingsgate Rd
Upr Ham Road A307
Petersham Road
Richmond Road
Ham Common
B352
Sandy Lane
Riverside Drive
Ham Street
Broom Road
Lower Ham Road
Thames Path
Mary Wallace Theatre
St James Independent School for Senior Boys
Grey Court School
Ham Health Clinic
St Richards with St Andrews CE Primary School
Meadlands Prim Sch
The Cassel Hospital
Dysart School
Ham & Petersham CC
St Georges Industrial Est
The Hawker Centre
Tiffin Girls School
Albany Park Canoe & Sailing Club
The Vine Clinic
Teddington School
Newland House School
The Waldegrave Clinic
Teddington Pool & Fitness Centre
Teddington Business Park
Teddington Station
St Mary & St Peters CE Prim Sch
Collis Primary School
Sacred Heart RC Primary School
Langdon Down Centre
Hampton Wick Infant School
St John the Baptist CE Junior Sch
Hampton Wick Stn
Kingston Stn
Bentalls Shopping Cen
The Rotunda
Council Bldg
Eden Walk Shopping Centre
Strathmore School
Deutsche Schule
Ham House Garden (NT)

144
125
143
159
TW10
KT2
Petersham
King Henry VIII Mound
Pembroke Lodge
Pen Ponds
Golf Course
The Richmond Golf Club
Richmond Park
Queen's Road
Sudbrook Gardens
Sudbrook Lane
Petersham Road
B352
Ham Gate Avenue
Ham Common
Church Road
Parkgate House
Isabella Plantation
Upr Ham Road
A307
Richmond Road
Latchmere Cl
Ham Ridings
Thatched House Lodge
Ladderstile Ride
Richmond upon Thames
Kingston upon Thames
Kingston Hill
Coombe Ridings
Coombe Pk
Warren Road
Canbury Sch
Tudor Drive
Cardinal Avenue
Tiffin Girls School
Latchmere Primary School
St Agatha's RC Primary School
The Vine Clinic
Kingston Gate
Queen's Road
Liverpool Road
George Road
Coombe Wood Golf Club
Holy Cross Preparatory School
Park Hill School
Kingston Hosp
A308
Richmond Road Medical Centre
Richmond Park Road
Acre Road Hlth Clinic
Superstore
St Lukes CE Prim Sch
Kingsgate Bus Cen
Canbury 2000 Bus Pk
Canbury Medical Cen
Wood Street
A308 Cromwell Rd
Kingston Stn
Bus Stn
Odeon
Megabowl
Travelodge
Telephone Exchange
Norbiton Station
Coombe Road
Coombe Lane
Birkenhead Avenue
Old London Rd
A238
Manorgate Medical Cen
Bentalls Shopping Cen
Grammar School
Norbiton
1 grid square represents 500 metres

The Royal Ballet School (White Lodge)
Richmond Park National Nature Reserve
Golf Course
Primary School
Dilton Gdns
Bessborough
Putney Vale Crematorium
Putney Vale Cemetery
Superstore
ROEHAMPTON VALE A3
Kingston University
London Cornish RFC
Friars Av
Stag Lane
Frensham Dr
Stroud Crescent
Putney Vale
Hall School Wimbledon Junior Dept
London Scottish Golf Club
Windmill
Wandsworth
Merton
Wimbledon Common
Windmill Road
KINGSTON VALE
A308
Robinwood Place
Woodview Cl
Cedar Cl
Derwent Avenue
Robin Hood Lane
Robin Hood Way
Vale Crs
Grasmere Avenue
Ullswater Crs
Windermere Rd
Robin Hood Primary School
Kingston University
Bowness Crs
Bowness Crescent
Rydal Gdns
Keswick Avenue
Coombe Park
ROBIN HOOD WAY
Robin Hood Rd
Kingston upon Thames
Merton
Robin Hood Rd
Windmill Rd
Sunset Road
Wimbledon Common Golf Club
North Vw
West Pl
Camp View
Camp Road
Caesar's Camp
Royal Wimbledon Golf Club
Helston Court Business Centre
Eversley Park
Kingston Vale
Warren Farm
Barham Road
Cannizaro House Hotel
Crooked Billet
Warren House
Wool Road
Dunstall Road
McKay Rd
(KINGSTON BY-PASS)
The Leigh
Henley Drive
Greenwood Pk
Coombe
Warren Cutting
Coombe Hill Golf Club
Golf Club Drive
Warren Rd
Edgecombe Cl
Coombe End
Kingston University
Coombe Hill
Beverley La
Coombe Hill Gld
Warbank La
Dewey Cl
Wimbledon RFC
Ellerton Road
Almer Road
Drax Av
Rowans School
Wolsey Cl
Grange Rd
Thurstan Rd
Rokeby Pl
Ernie Road
Copse Hill
Surgery
Wolfson Medical Centre
Atkinson Morley Hospital
Prospect Pl
Lindisfarne Rd
Copse Hill
Preston Road
Hood Road
Barham Road
Melville Av
Ballard Cl
A238
COOMBE LANE WEST
Fitzgeorge Av
B283
Oakcombe Close
Coombe House Chase
Wonford Close
New Victoria Hospital
BEVERLEY WAY
Hawkins Clinic
ROBIN HOOD WAY
COOMBE LANE
Holland Avenue
Copse Hill Av
Burdett Av
St Matthews CE Primary School
Cottenham Park Road
Cottenham Park
Melbury Gardens
Oakwood Road
Laurel Road
Cambridge Close
Cambridge Road
Panmuir Road
DURHAM ROAD
COTTENHAM PK RD
B281
Primary School
Coombe Hill J&I School
Warren Rise
Neville Av
The Fairway
Burghley Av
The Chesters
The Moat
Soames Walk
Cromford Way
Woodlands
Matlock
Buxton Dr
Darley Dr
Coombe Girls School
Badgers Walk
Bakewell Way
Langley Grove
TRAPS LANE
Beverley Wy (Kingston By-pass)
BEVERLEY WAY
Westcoombe Avenue
Coombe Gardens
A238
Richmond Road
Parkfields Av
Spencer Road
Amity Grove
Lambton Road
Kenwyn Road
Rosevine Road
SW20
Health Centre
Surgery
Raynes Park Station
Camberley Avenue
Somerset Av
Ely Close
Perth Close
Malden
F G H J K
126 160 146
1 2 3 4 5 6 7
21 22 23
70 71 72 73

146
127
145
161
Southfields
WIMBLEDON
SW19
Crooked Billet
Wimbledon Park
Wimbledon Park Athletics Track
Boating Lake
Wimbledon Park Golf Club
Wimbledon Park Station
The All England Lawn Tennis & Croquet Club
Wimbledon Lawn Tennis Museum
Golf Course
London Scottish Golf Club
Windmill
Windmill Road
Apostolic Nunciature
Embassy of The Holy See
Parkside Hospital
Buddhapadipa Temple
Ricards Lodge High School
Wimbledon Common
Royal Wimbledon Golf Club
Helston Court Business Centre
The Causeway
Cannizaro House Hotel
Kings College School
The Norwegian School
Wimbledon Com Pre-Prep Sch
Donhead (Wimbledon Coll Prep School)
Ursuline Preparatory School
Ursuline High School
Blossom House School
Hall School Wimbledon
Wimbledon High School
Telephone Exchange
The Study Preparatory School
The Foot Clinic
Wimbledon Station
Centre Court Shopping Centre
Police Station
Wimbledon Magistrates Court
Wimbledon Theatre
Odeon Cinema
Dundonald Road Stn
Railway Engineering Works
Squash & Badminton Club
Sorting Office
Dundonald Prim Sch
Wimbledon School of Art
Wimbledon Chase Primary School
Wimbledon Chase Station
Merton Park
Wimbledon House School
Merton Park Primary School
Theatre of the Dispossessed
Linden Lodge School
Albemarle Primary Sch
Southdean Gardens
Synagogue
Queensmere Road
PARKSIDE
A219
B281
B235
A218
A238
CANNIZARO RD
W SIDE COMMON
WOODHAYES RD
HIGH ST
WIMBLEDON HILL ROAD
THE BROADWAY
HARTFIELD RD
ALEXANDRA RD
LEOPOLD RD
WORPLE ROAD
KINGSTON ROAD
MERTON ROAD
DURNSFORD ROAD
COPSE HILL
COTTENHAM PK RD
London Tramlink
1 grid square represents 500 metres

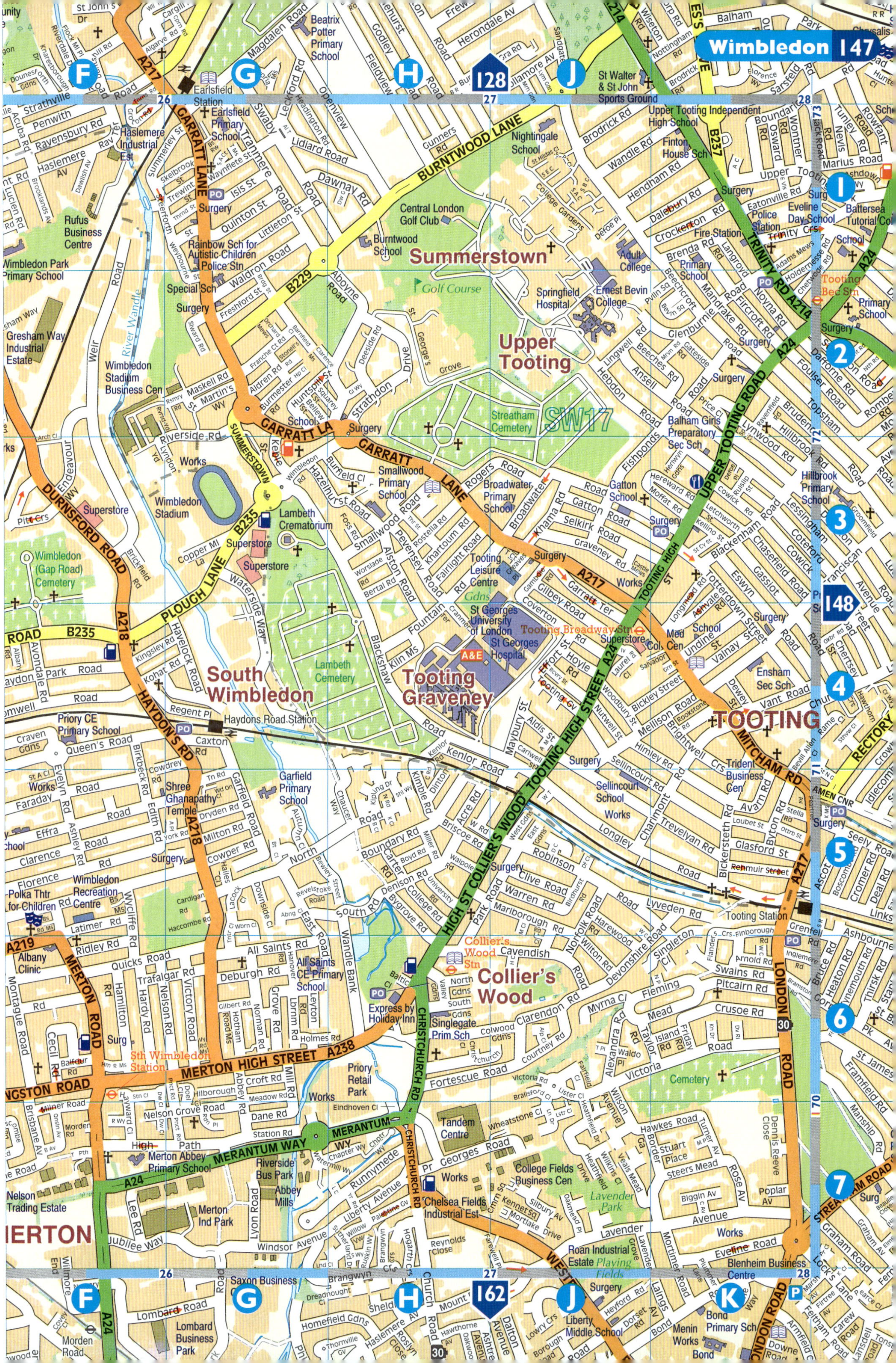

Summerstown
Upper Tooting
SW17
South Wimbledon
Tooting Graveney
TOOTING
Collier's Wood
MERTON
Earlsfield Station
Earlsfield Primary School
Beatrix Potter Primary School
Haslemere Industrial Est
Rufus Business Centre
Wimbledon Park Primary School
Gresham Way Industrial Estate
Wimbledon Stadium Business Cen
Wimbledon Stadium
Wimbledon (Gap Road) Cemetery
Central London Golf Club
Burntwood School
Golf Course
Nightingale School
Springfield Hospital
Ernest Bevin College
Adult College
Streatham Cemetery
Lambeth Crematorium
Lambeth Cemetery
Smallwood Primary School
Broadwater Primary School
Tooting Leisure Centre
St Georges University of London
St Georges Hospital
A&E
Tooting Broadway Stn
Tooting Bec Stn
Tooting Station
Haydons Road Station
Collier's Wood Stn
Sth Wimbledon Station
Balham Girls Preparatory Sec Sch
Hillbrook Primary School
Ensham Sec Sch
Trident Business Cen
Sellincourt School
Garfield Primary School
Priory CE Primary School
Shree Ghanapathy Temple
Wimbledon Recreation Centre
Polka Thtr for Children
Albany Clinic
All Saints CE Primary School
Priory Retail Park
Express by Holiday Inn
Singlegate Prim Sch
Tandem Centre
College Fields Business Cen
Chelsea Fields Industrial Est
Merton Abbey Primary School
Riverside Bus Park
Abbey Mills
Merton Ind Park
Nelson Trading Estate
Lombard Business Park
Saxon Business
Roan Industrial Estate
Playing Fields
Lavender Park
Cemetery
Liberty Middle School
Bond Primary Sch
Blenheim Business Centre
Upper Tooting Independent High School
Finton House Sch
Fire Station
Police Station
Eveline Day School
Battersea Tutorial Coll
St Walter & St John Sports Ground
Rainbow Sch for Autistic Children
Police Stn
Special Sch
BURNTWOOD LANE
GARRATT LANE
GARRATT LA
DURNSFORD ROAD
PLOUGH LANE
HAYDON'S RD
MERTON ROAD
MERTON HIGH STREET
MERANTUM WAY
CHRISTCHURCH RD
HIGH ST COLLIER'S WOOD
TOOTING HIGH STREET
UPPER TOOTING ROAD
TRINITY RD
MITCHAM RD
LONDON ROAD
STREATHAM ROAD
KINGSTON ROAD
AMEN CNR
A217
A218
A219
A24
A238
A214
B229
B235
B237
128
148
162
F
G
H
J
K
1
2
3
4
5
6
7
26
27
28

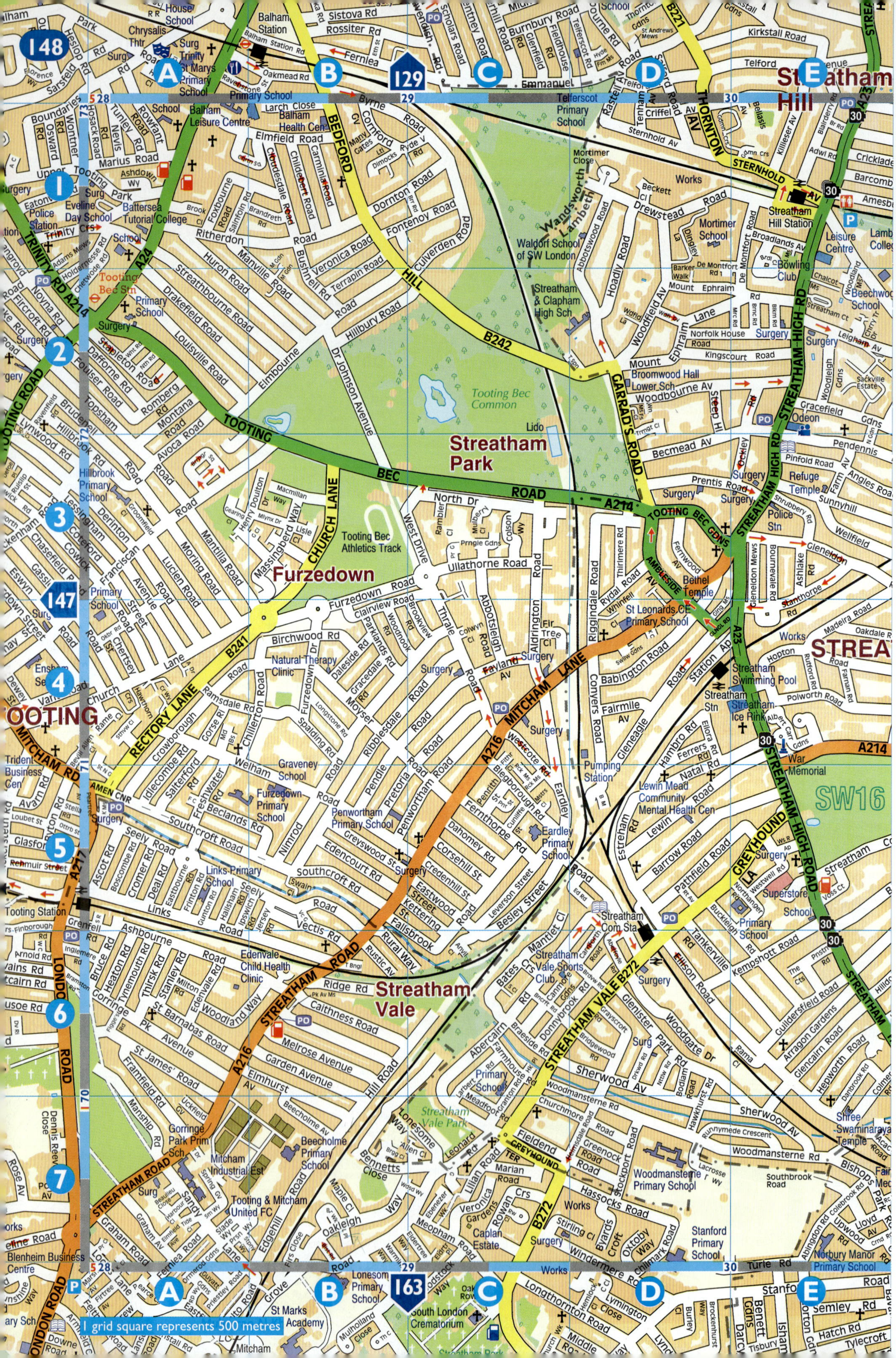
148
129
147
163
Balham Station
Streatham Hill
Streatham Hill Station
Tooting Bec Common
Streatham Park
Furzedown
Tooting Bec Athletics Track
TOOTING
STREATHAM
Streatham Stn
Streatham Com Sta
Streatham Vale
Streatham Vale Park
SW16
Tooting Station
TOOTING BEC ROAD
A214
CHURCH LANE
RECTORY LANE
B241
MITCHAM LANE
A216
STREATHAM ROAD
STREATHAM VALE B272
STREATHAM HIGH ROAD
A23
BEDFORD HILL
B242
GARRAD'S ROAD
TRINITY RD A214
TOOTING BEC GDNS
GREYHOUND LA
Mitcham Industrial Est
Tooting & Mitcham United FC
Streatham Swimming Pool
Streatham Ice Rink
South London Crematorium
Lido
Balham Leisure Centre
Wandsworth
Lambeth
1 grid square represents 500 metres

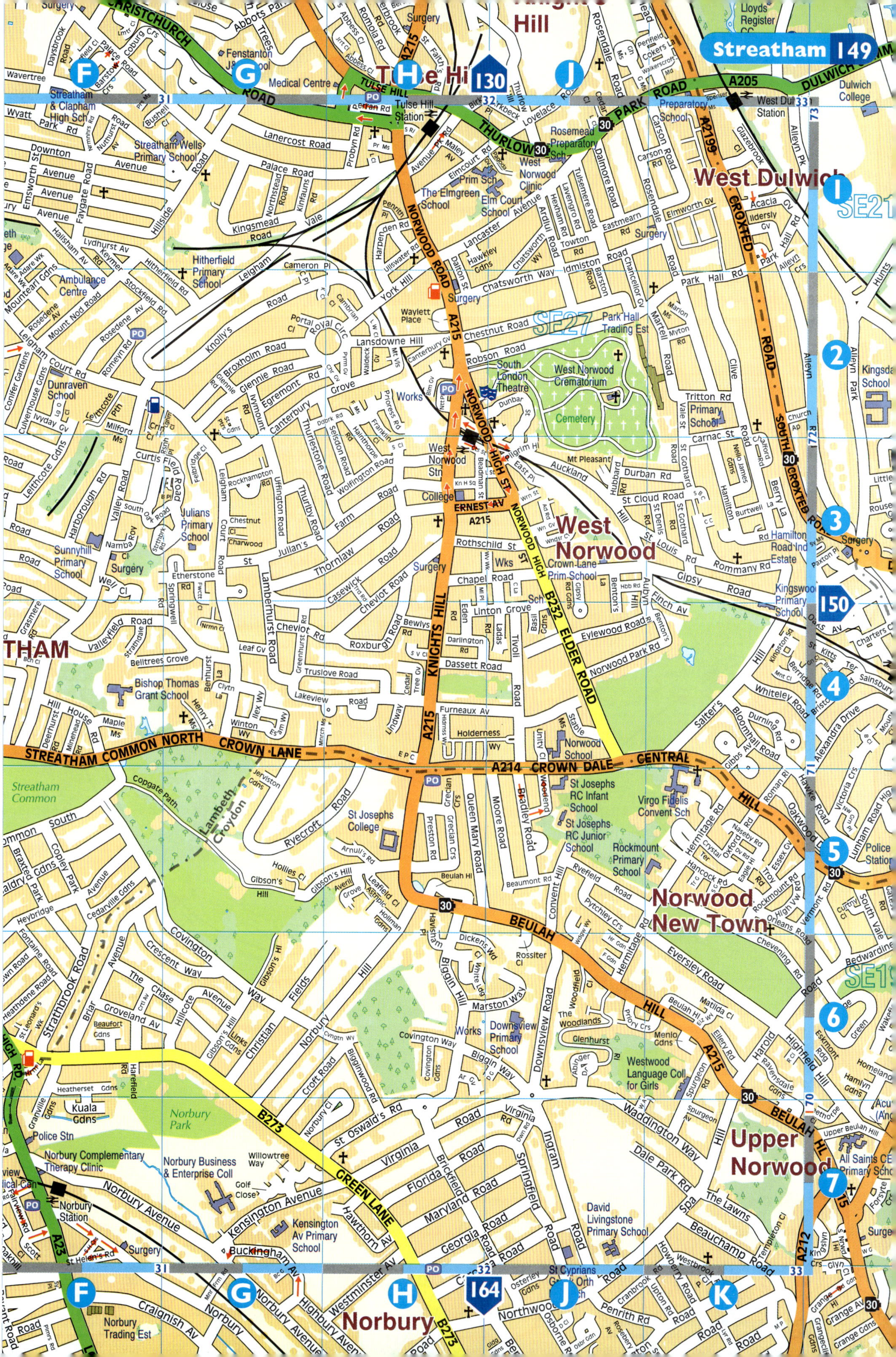

Tulse Hill
130
West Dulwich Station
Dulwich College
Tulse Hill Station
West Dulwich
SE21
SE27
West Norwood
West Norwood Crematorium
Cemetery
South London Theatre
Norwood Road
Norwood High St
Knights Hill
Elder Road
Crown Dale
Crown Lane
Streatham Common North
Streatham Common
Beulah Hill
Norwood New Town
Upper Norwood
Norbury
Norbury Station
Norbury Park
Green Lane
Croxted Road
South Croxted Road
Park Road
Thurlow Park Road
Christchurch Road
Leigham Court Road
Gipsy Road
Central Hill
Streatham & Clapham High Sch
Streatham Wells Primary School
Hitherfield Primary School
Ambulance Centre
Dunraven School
Julians Primary School
Sunnyhill Primary School
Bishop Thomas Grant School
St Josephs College
St Josephs RC Infant School
St Josephs RC Junior School
Virgo Fidelis Convent Sch
Rockmount Primary School
Kingswood Primary School
Crown Lane Prim School
Tritton Rd Primary School
Rosemead Preparatory Sch
Elm Court School
The Elmgreen School
West Norwood Clinic
Downsview Primary School
Westwood Language Coll for Girls
David Livingstone Primary School
Kensington Av Primary School
Norbury Complementary Therapy Clinic
Norbury Business & Enterprise Coll
Norbury Trading Est
Police Stn
Police Station
Park Hall Trading Est
Hamilton Road Ind Estate
Norwood School
All Saints CE Primary Sch
SE19
150
164
Lloyds Register
A205
A215
A214
A2199
A212
A23
B232
B273
31
32
33
F
G
H
J
K
1
2
3
4
5
6
7

150
131
149
165
A
B
C
D
E
1
2
3
4
5
6
7
33
34
35
70
71
72
73
30
A205
DULWICH COMMON
Dulwich College
West Dulwich Station
Lloyds Register CC
Marlborough CC
LORDSHIP LANE A205
The Horniman Museum & Gardens
LONDON ROAD
Forest Hill Station
West Dulwich
SE21
Dulwich
Golf Course
Dulwich College Track
Dulwich & Sydenham Hill Golf Club
Grange Lane
Tollgate
Hunts Slip Road
College Road
Croxted Road
South Croxted Road
Kingsdale School
Sydenham Hill Station
Langbourne Primary School
Peckarmans Wood
Crescent Wood Road
Sydenham Hill
Wells Park
Upper Sydenham
Primary School
Forest Hill Pools
Holy Trinity CE Prim Sch
Sydenham Girls Sch
Dartmouth Road
Police Station
Willow Business Park
St Bartholomews CE Primary School
Kirkdale A2216
Infant School
Surgery
Dulwich Wood Park
Gipsy Hill Station
Westwood Hill
Sydenham High Jun Sch
Sydenham High Senior School
Crystal Palace Park Road
Sydenham Station
SE26
Crystal Palace Park
Crystal Palace
National Sports Centre
Crystal Palace Museum
Crystal Palace Parade
A212
A2199
College Rd
Westow Hill
A214
Anerley Hill
Crystal Palace Station
Crystal Palace Station Road
Penge West Station
Penge East Station
Police Station
Shopping Centre
SE19
Church Road
Penge
Primary School
High St
Oakfield Road Industrial Est
Anerley Road
Anerley Stn
Anerley School
James Dixon Primary School
Harris City Academy Crystal Palace
Upper Norwood
Beulah Hill
All Saints CE Primary School
Acumen (Anglo School)
Franklin Industrial Est
Elmers End Rd
Croydon Road
Anerley
SE20
Cypress Infant School
1 grid square represents 500 metres

Penge 151
132
152
166
Forest Hill
Lower Sydenham
Sydenham
Bell Green
Bellingham
New Beckenham
Stanstead Road
Waldram Pk Rd
Perry Vale
Perry Hill
Perry Rise
Sydenham Road
Southend Lane
Stanton Wy
Bromley Road
Beckenham Hill Road
Southend Road
Beckenham Road
Parish Lane
Green Lane
Copers Cope Road
Manor Road
Bromley Road
High St
Worsley Bridge Road
Kent House Lane
Kent House Road
Lennard Road
Thesiger Road
Bridge Road
Brackley Road
Westgate Road
Albemarle Road
The Avenue
Foxgrove Road
Randlesdown Rd
Daneswood Av
Callander Road
Daneby Road
Arran Road
Newquay Road
Vancouver Road
Kilmorie Primary School
Catford Cyphers CC
Springfield Christian School
Greenvale School
Our Lady & St Philip Neri Inf Sch
Forest Hill School
London Living Theatre
Brent Knoll School
Primary School
The Vale Medical Centre
Superstore
Bellingham Trading Est
Bromley Road Retail Park
Catford Trading Estate
Catford & Bromley Synagogue
Catford Synagogue
Bellingham Stn
Council Building
Surgery
Elfrida Primary School
Police Station
South Lewisham Health Centre
Catford Wanderers Sports Club
London Ladies & Girls FC
Watergate School
St Augustines RC Primary School
Beckenham Hill Stn
Sedgehill School
Sydenham High School Sports Ground
Natwest Sports Club
Cuaco Sports Ground
Beckenham Place Park
Golf Course
Beckenham Place Park Golf Course
Worsley Bridge Junior School
Beckenham CC
The Bridge Leisure Centre
Lower Sydenham Stn
Bromsleigh Business Park
Lower Sydenham Industrial Estate
Abbey Trading Estate
Kangley Bus Cen
Orchard Bus Cen
Laker Ind Est
Gardener Industrial Estate
Gateway Business Centre
Metro Business Centre
Beckenham Business Centre
HSBC Sports Club
New Beckenham Station
Cator Park School for Girls
Alexandra Junior School
Alexandra Infant School
Royston Primary School
Kent House Station
Beckenham Road
Beckenham Leisure Centre
Clock House Station
Beckenham Junction Station
Christian Meeting Hall
Telephone Exchange
Infant School
Odeon Cinema
Fire Station
Pascals Coll
Our Lady & St Philip Neri RC Prim Sch
Green Chain Walk
River Pool
A212
A2218
A21
A2015
A213
A234
A222
B227
B230
F
G
H
J
K
1
2
3
4
5
6
7
36
37
38
70
71
72
73

CATFORD
SE6
Southend
Downham
Plaistow
Bromley Park
152
133
151
167
A
B
C
D
E
1
2
3
4
5
6
7
538
539
540
70
71
72
73
BROMLEY ROAD
BROMLEY HILL
LONDON ROAD
BECKENHAM HILL ROAD
BECKENHAM LANE
A21
A2015
A222
B230
Hither Green Cemetery
Lewisham Crematorium
Cemetery
Catford High School
Torridon Primary School
Forster Park Primary School
Pendragon School
Bedivere Primary School
New Woodlands School
Downderry Primary School
Bonus Pastor Catholic Coll
Downham Health Centre
Good Shepherd RC Primary School
Haberdashers Askes Knights Acad
Launcelot Primary School
Rangefield Primary School
Burnt Ash Prim Sch
Catford Wanderers Sports Club
Police Station
South Lewisham Health Centre
St John the Baptist CE Prim Sch
Beckenham Hill Stn
Beckenham Place Park Golf Course
Beckenham Place Park
Golf Course
Ashgrove Trading Estate
Best Western Bromley Court Hotel
Parish CE Primary School
London Lane Clinic
Bromley Cemetery
St Marys RC Primary School
Ravensbourne Station
Ravensbourne River
Sloane Hospital
Council Building
Bromley College
Valley Primary School
Recreation Playing Fields
Bishop Challoner School
St Christophers School
Shortlands Stn
Odeon Cin
HIGH STREET
TWEEDY ROAD
The Glades
Baring Road Medical Centre
Bromley Road Retail Park
Bellingham Trading Est
Catford Synagogue
Catford & Bromley Synagogue
Green Chain Walk
Whitefoot Lane
Business Centre
Surgery
North Clinic
Bromley Co Court
Mag Court
Fire Stn
1 grid square represents 500 metres

Plaistow 153
134
154
168
Mottingham
Grove Park
Elmstead
Sundridge
BROMLEY
Widmore
Eltham College Junior School
Eltham College Senior School
Eric Liddell Sports Centre
London Guildhall University Sports Ground
City of London School Sports Ground
Central YMCA
Coldharbour Leisure Centre
Mottingham Primary School
Mottingham Community Hlth Clinic
Grove Park Cemetery
Castlecombe Primary School
Granby Sports Club
Elmstead Wood
Ravensbourne College of Design & Communication
Babington House School
Elmstead Woods Station
Sundridge Park Golf Club
Golf Course
Sundridge Park
Sundridge Park Station
St Josephs Catholic Primary School
Holy Trinity College
Scotts Park Primary Sch
Breaside Prep Sch
Ripley Arts Centre
Bullers Wood School
Wood Lodge Gardens
Bromley Cricket Ground, Hockey Club & Tennis Courts
Chislehurst Station
BR1
CHINBROOK ROAD
GROVE PARK ROAD
B226
COURT ROAD
A208
MOTTINGHAM ROAD
SIDCUP ROAD
BURNT ASH LANE
A2212
WIDMORE RD
B264
Green Chain Walk

154
135
153
169
A
B
C
D
E
1
2
3
4
5
6
7
New Eltham
Longlands
Foxbury
Chislehurst West
CHISLEHURST
BR7
SIDCUP ROAD
A20 SIDCUP ROAD
SIDCUP BY-PASS
WHITE HORSE HILL
A208 RED HILL
CHISLEHURST HIGH ST
GREEN LANE
B263
PRINCE IMPERIAL RD
BROMLEY ROAD
A222
BROMLEY LANE
WATT'S LANE
MANOR PARK ROAD
OLD HILL B264
SUMMER HILL
CENTRE COMMON ROAD
ROYAL PARADE
Kemnal Road
Coldharbour Leisure Centre
Greenacres Primary School
Coldharbour Sports Ground
Green Lane Business Park
St Olaves Preparatory School
FIVEWAYS CORNER
Dulverton Primary School
Montbelle Prim Sch
Edgebury Primary School
Kemnal Manor
Ravensbourne College of Design & Communication
The Willows Clinic
Redhill Prim Sch
Chislehurst Natural Health Centre
Mead Road Infant School
Old Elthamians Sports Club
Beaverwood School for Girls
St Barts Hospital Sports Ground
Chislehurst Cemetery
Farrington & Stratford House School
Chislehurst Common
Golf Course
Chislehurst Golf Club
St. Nicholas School
Coopers Technology College
Marjorie McClure School
Chislehurst Caves
St Peter's RC Prim School
Chislehurst
1 grid square represents 500 metres

DA15
DA14
SIDCUP
Foots Cray
Lamorbey Park
Rose Bruford College
Hurstmere School
136
Burnt Oak Jun Sch
Holy Trinity Lamorbey CE Prim Sch
Sidcup Golf Club
Chislehurst & Sidcup Grammar Sch
Lamorbey Swimming Centre
Sidcup Station
Albany Park Station
Sidcup Cemetery
Surgery
Health & Fitness Centre
Birkbeck Primary School
West Lodge Preparatory School
Benedict Ho Prep Sch
Albany Clinic
Bird College
Health Cen
Cleeve Park School
Royal Park Primary Sch
Sidcup Sports Club
Medical Centre
Rectory Business Centre
Merton Court Preparatory School
David Lloyd Tennis Centre
St Luke's Catholic Sixth Form College
Middlesex Hospital Sports Ground
Frognal Corner
Queen Marys Hospital
A&E
Orchard Primary School
St Peter Chanel RC Primary School
Harenc School
Bedensfield Clinic
Works
Ruxley Corner Industrial Estate
Superstore
Kemnal Technology College
Midfield Primary School
The Meadow Special School
Scadbury Park
Bromley Ski Centre
Golf Course
Crayfields Business Park
Grays Farm Primary School
Ruxley Park Golf Centre
Cray Valley Golf Club
Riverside School
Crayfield Industrial Park
St Pauls Cray Health Clinic
Scadbury Gardens
River Cray
Maple Leaf Dr
Burnt Oak Lane
Old Farm Avenue
HURST ROAD
A222
B2214
STATION ROAD
Canterbury Avenue
Longmead Drive
Faraday Avenue
Melville Road
Jubilee Way
Longlands Road
Manor Road
Crescent Road
Sandhurst Rd
Victoria Road
Granville Road
HIGH STREET
ELM ROAD
THE GREEN
A2001
CHISLEHURST RD
Upperton Rd
Felton Lea
The Park
A20
A211
SIDCUP HILL
Birchwood Av
Lansdown Rd
Selborne Road
Rectory Lane
Knoll Road
Frognal Avenue
Leas Green
SIDCUP BY-PASS ROAD
Watery Lane
A223
EDGINGTON WAY
FOOTS CRAY HIGH ST
MAIDSTONE ROAD
CRAY ROAD
A224
Powerscroft Road
Sandy Lane
Lullingstone Crescent
Valley Road
Midfield Way
Grays Farm Road
Walsingham Road
Horsell Road
St Paul's Wood Hill
Beddington Road
Chorleywood Crescent
Broom Avenue
Dawson Avenue
Tilbury Close
SEVENOAKS
Main Road
Bexley Lane
Kimberley Drive
Maylands Dr
Burnham Road
Pembury Crs
St Andrews Road
Harvill Rd
Palm Av
Mount Culver Av
Whitney Walk
F
G
H
J
I
K
1
2
3
4
5
6
7
46
47
48
50
30
70
71
72
73

156
141
A
B
C
D
E
TW16
1
2
3
4
5
6
7
Lower Sunbury
WALTON-ON-THAMES
Field Common
River Thames
Thames Path
Sunbury Lock
Molesey Reservoirs
Bessborough Reservoir
Knight Reservoir
Queen Elizabeth II Reservoir
Sand & Gravel Works
HURST ROAD
A3050
WALTON ROAD
B369
TERRACE ROAD
STAINES ROAD EAST
A308
UPPER SUNBURY
Lower Hampton Road
Manor Lane
The Avenue
French Street
Darby Crs
Harfield Road
Bramwell Close
Kenton Avenue
Chennestone Community School
Beauclerc Infant School
Sunbury Court
Walton Casuals FC
Elmbridge Leisure Centre
Waterside Drive
Dunsmore Road
Cambridge Road
Sunbury Lane
Grovelands School
Sandy Lane
Walton Business Centre
Cottimore Lane
Cottimore Avenue
Vanbrugh Drive
Shaw Drive
Swansmere School
Ambleside Junior School
Ambleside Avenue
King George Avenue
Rydens Road
Holly Avenue
Molesey Road
Fieldcommon Lane
Weston Avenue
Molesey Avenue
John Nightingale School
Central Avenue
Monks Avenue
Pool Road
Esher RFC
North Weylands Industrial Est
Walton Swimming Pool
Screen Cinema
Health Centre
Works
1 grid square represents 500 metres

Hurst Park
East Molesey
KT8
Island Barn Reservoir
Weston Green
Richmond upon Thames
Surrey County
HAMPTON COURT ROAD
A308
HURST ROAD
A3050
WALTON ROAD
B369
ESHER ROAD
B3379
EMBER LANE
HAMPTON COURT WAY
A309
B364
EMBERCOURT ROAD
PORTSMOUTH ROAD
THAMES ST
CHURCH STREET
A311
HIGH STREET
BRIDGE RD
CREEK RD
Tagg's Island
Ash Island
East Molesey CC
Molesey Lock
The Carlton Mitre Hotel
Hampton Court House School
Hampton Court Station
Vine Medical Centre
St Lawrence Junior School
Molesey Cemetery
Council Building
Hurst Park Primary School
Chandlers Field Primary School
Molesey Hospital
Glenlyn Medical Cen
The Teddington Theatre Club
The Orchard School
Grist Memorial Sports Club
Old Tiffinians Sports Ground
Imber Court Trading Estate
Metropolitan Police FC
St Pauls RC Primary School
Esher College
Emberhurst School
Ember Sports Club
Weston Green School
Thames Ditton Station
River Mole Business Park
Sandown Industrial Park
Esher Station
River Ember
River Mole
Golf Course
Works
142
158
170

158
143
157
171
A
B
C
D
E
1
2
3
4
5
6
7
Bushy Park
Centre
Hampton Wick
Hampton Wick Stn
Surgery
PARK ROAD
CHURCH GROVE
HIGH ST
Diana Fountain
Hampton Court House School
Chestnut Avenue
Liongate Hotel
HAMPTON COURT ROAD
A308
HORSE FAIR
Old Br St
Home Park Terrace
Rose of Kingston (Kingston Theatre)
Guildhall
Pol Stn
KINGSTON UPON THAMES
HIGH STREET
Kingston Hall Rd
The Carlton Mitre Hotel
Hampton Court Palace
Stud House
Hampton Court Station
River Thames
Thames Path
HAMPTON COURT WAY
Hampton Court Park
Golf Course
Hampton Court Palace Golf Club
PORTSMOUTH ROAD
A307
Anglesea Road
Palace Road
Uxbridge Rd
Synagogue
Catherine Road
Grove Road
Cadogan Road
St Leonard's Rd
Cleaveland Road
Westfield Road
The Mall
SS Andrew & Marks C Jun Sch
Riverside Close
TAVR Centre
SURBITON ROAD
B3365
Woodbines Av
Milner Road
Richmond upon Thames
Kingston upon Thames
Grist Memorial Sports Club
Works
Summer Road
Queen's Road
Alexandra Rd
Riverbank
Riversdale Rd
Speer Road
Aragon Avenue
Wolsey Av
Warwick Rd
Thames Ditton Island
Ennismore Gardens
Thistledene
A309
Thames Ditton Infant School
Church Walk
Council Building
High St
Ashley Rd
Boyle Farm Road
Fitzgerald
Queen's Drive
Ferry Road
Cholmley Road
Seething Wells
Surrey County
Ferry
Simpson Way
Hastings Dr
Akerman Road
BRIGHTON ROAD
A243
VICTORIA ROAD
Surbiton Business Centre
Victoria Avenue
UPPER
B364
EMBERCOURT ROAD
STATION ROAD
WATTS ROAD
St Pauls RC Primary School
Thames Ditton Station
Basingfield Rd
Thames Ditton Junior School
KT7
Giggshill
GIGGS HILL RD
Giggs Hill Rd
Thames Ditton
St Leonard's Road
Portsmouth Avenue
Ditton Close
Southbank
Vaughan Rd
Houston Rd
Windmill Lane
Kingston Liberal Synagogue
Works
Balaclava Road
Lovelace Gardens
Beechwood Cl
Woodlands Road
Westville Rd
Southville Road
Rushett Rd
Ewell Road
Effingham Road
Thorkhill Road
Angel Road
Scott Farm Cl
Long Ditton St Marys CE Jun Sch
Long Ditton County Inf Sch
King's Road
SURBITON
Ditton Grange Drive
Ditton Gra Cl
Saffron Way
Oaks Way
Raphael Drive
Savile Cl
Hayward Rd
Surgery
Longmead Rd
Weston Green
Weston Green School
Newlands Avenue
Weston Avenue
Thames Ditton Weston Green Road
Long Ditton
Rectory Lane
Church Road
Sugden Road
Mayfield Close
Lynwood Road
Macaulay Avenue
Greenwood Road
Hinchley Wood School & Sixth Form Centre
Hinchley Wood
Bankside Drive
Long Ditton Cemetery
Garden Centre
Woodstock
Meadow
Church Meadow
Shrewsbury House School
Herne
Wentworth Close
PORTSMOUTH ROAD
1 grid square represents 500 metres

Norbiton
Berrylands
Tolworth
Old Malden
KT1
KT5
KT6
Kingston Cemetery
Kingston Crematorium
Surbiton Cemetery
Hogsmill River
Berrylands Station
Surbiton Station
Norbiton Station
Kingsmeadow Athletics Centre
Kingstonian FC
Kingston University
Fairfield Trade Park
Refuse Disposal Centre
Tiffin Sch & Sports Cen
St Josephs RC Primary School
Christ Church CE Primary School
Grand Avenue Primary School
St Matthews CE Primary School
Dysart School
The Hollyfield School
Our Lady Immaculate RC Prim Sch
Tolworth CP School
Knollmead Primary School
LSE Sports Club
Leigh Close Industrial Est
Roselands Clinic
The Mount Infant School
Cambridge Road
Kingston Rd
Ewell Road
Surbiton Hill Road
Penrhyn Road
Claremont Rd
St Mark's Hill
Upper Brighton Road
Brighton Road
Kingsdowne Road
Ditton Road
Tolworth Broadway
Warren Dr Nth
Tolworth Ri N (Kingston By-Pass)
Fairfield North
Old London Rd
A308 Cromwell Rd
A238
A2043
A240
A243
A3
B3363
B3370
144
160
172
F
G
H
J
K
18
19
20

160
145
159
173
A
B
C
D
E
1
2
3
4
5
6
7
SW20
KT3
KT4
New Malden
Motspur Park
Old Malden
Coombe Lane
Cromford Way
Buxton Drive
Coombe Girls School
Coombe Hill J&I School
Traps Lane B283
Coombe Road
High Street
Malden Road
A2043
Kingston Road
Burlington Road
Beverley Way
(Kingston By-Pass)
Malden Way
A3
A238
Bushey Road
West Barnes Lane
B282
Central Road
Church Road
Malden Golf Club
Raynes Park Sports Ground
Raynes Park High School
Superstore
Sacred Heart RC Primary School
Rainbow Industrial Estate
The Groves Medical Cen
Christ Church Malden CE Prim Sch
New Malden Stn
Murky Puddle Theatre
The Malden Centre
Burlington Inf Sch
Shannon Corner Retail Park
Leigh Close Industrial Estate
Roselands Clinic
Health Clinic
The Holy Cross Catholic Girls Sch
Aston Clinic
The Study School
Beverley School
Motspur Park Station
University of London Athletics Ground
LSE Sports Club
Malden Manor Prim School
Malden Manor Station
Malden Parochial Primary School
Manor Drive Health Centre
Worcester Park Station
BackCare Clnc
Green Lane Primary School
Merton
Sutton
Cuddington Cemetery
Surgery
Works
Bodnant Gardens
Cambridge Avenue
Rosebery Av
Orchard Av
Howard Road
Kings Avenue
Coombe Gardens
Blagdon Road
Cavendish Road
Cromwell Avenue
Thetford Road
Nelson Road
Lynton Road
Selwyn Road
Eton Avenue
Albemarle Gardens
Sandal Road
Rodney Road
Presburg Road
Motspur Park
Portland Avenue
Hollington Crescent
Ancaster Crescent
Bargate Close
Kingshill Avenue
Risborough Drive
Pembury Avenue
Caverleigh Way
Burford Road
Broadmead Avenue
Mayfair Avenue
Manor Drive
Manor Drive North
Sheephouse Way
Knightwood Crescent
Bramshaw Rise
Amberwood Rise
Minstead Way
Lawrence Avenue
Glebe Gardens
Leyfield
Cleveland Road
Dene Cl
St Michaels Close
Woodlands Avenue
1 grid square represents 500 metres

MERTON
Merton Park
Bushey Mead
Raynes Park
Cannon Hill
West Barnes
Morden Park
Morden
SM4
KINGSTON ROAD
A238
BUSHEY ROAD
A298
WORPLE ROAD
GRAND DRIVE
B279
B286
MARTIN WAY
CROWN LANE
LONDON ROAD
A24
A239
CENTRAL
GREEN LANE
EPSOM ROAD
TUDOR DRIVE
SUTTON COMMON ROAD
STONECOT HILL
Raynes Park Station
Wimbledon Chase Stn
South Merton Station
Morden Station
Morden South Station
St Helier Station
Nelson Hospital
Wimbledon Chase Primary School
Merton Park Primary School
Rutlish School
Merton Adult College
Poplar Primary School
Hillcross Primary School
Raynes Park Vale FC
St John Fisher RC Primary School
North East Surrey Crematorium
Morden Cemetery
Hatfield Primary School
Wyevale Garden Centre
Morden Park Pool
Travelodge
Morden First School
St Anne's Special School
Abbotsbury Primary School
Aragon Primary School
The Garth Road Industrial Cen
Beverley Trading Est
Dorchester Primary Sch
St Anthony's Hospital
Brookfield Primary School
St Raphaels Hospice
Kimpton Industrial Estate
Glenthorne High Specialist Arts
Innkeeper's Lodge
Abbey Prim Sch
Police Stn
Churchill College
Surgery
Works
146
162
174
Sutton Cemetery

162
147
161
175
MERTON
Morden
St Helier
Rosehill
A
B
C
D
E
1
2
3
4
5
6
7
A24
A239
A297
A217
A236
B278
B2230
MORDEN ROAD
MORDEN HALL ROAD
MORDEN ROAD
CENTRAL ROAD
ST HELIER AVENUE
BISHOPSFORD ROAD
REIGATE AVENUE
WESTERN ROAD
LONDON ROAD
GREEN LANE
CRANMER ROAD
CRICKET GREEN
WRYTHE
Morden Hall Park
Morden Hall Park (NT)
Morden Hall Medical Centre
Morden Station
Morden South Station
St Helier Station
Phipps Bridge
Belgrave Walk
Mitcham
Mitcham CC
Saxon Business Centre
Lombard Business Park
Merton Ind Park
Nelson Trading Estate
Bus Park
Abbey Mills
Chelsea Fields Industrial Est
Haslemere Primary School
Benedict Primary School
Liberty Middle School
Bond Primary Sch
Bond First School
Melrose Special School
Cricket Green Sch
Vestry Hall
Boundary Bus Park
Boundary Bus Park
London Tramlink
River Wandle
Central Medical Centre
St Anne's Special School
Abbotsbury Primary School
Phoenix College
Garth Primary School
Watermeads High School
Malmesbury Primary School
Green Wrythe Primary School
Tweeddale Primary School
Sutton Arena
Wandle Valley School
Abbey Prim Sch
Glenthorne High Spec Arts
Innkeeper's Lodge
St Helier Hospital
Queen Mary's Hospital for Children
Carshalton High School for Boys
Greenshaw High School
Capital Bus Cen
Connaught Business Centre
Abbey Industrial Est
Eagle Trading Estate
Grace Business
Cranmer Prim Sch
SS Peter & Paul RC Prim Sch
Mill Green Business
Wandle Trading Est
Blenheim Business Centre
Lavender Park
Police Stn
1 grid square represents 500 metres

Mitcham
Mitcham Common
Beddington Corner
Hackbridge
Beddington
CR4
Golf Course
Mitcham Golf Club
Mitcham Junction Station
Mitcham Eastfields Station
Hackbridge Station
London Tramlink
Streatham Park Cemetery
South London Crematorium
Croydon Crematorium
Croydon Cemetery
Lonesome Primary School
St Marks CE Academy
Mitcham Vale High School
Harris Academy Merton School
William Morris Primary School
Garden Primary School
Sherwood School
Stanford Primary School
Norbury Manor Primary School
Woodmansterne Primary School
Gonville Primary School
The Archbishop Lanfranc School
Hackbridge Primary School
Culvers House Primary Sch
St Thomas of Canterbury
Tooting & Mitcham United FC
Windmill Trading Estate
Brookmead Industrial Est
Therapia Trading Estate
Lamont Business Cen
Stirling Way Industrial Ests
Pioneers Ind Park
Beddington Trading Est
Thornton Road Industrial Est
Felnex Trading Estate
Vue Cinema
Beddington Lane
Merton
Sutton
CROYDON ROAD
A236
MITCHAM RD
MANOR ROAD
ROWAN ROAD
B272
WINDMILL ROAD
BEDDINGTON LANE
CARSHALTON ROAD
LONDON ROAD
A237
COMMONSIDE WEST
A239
Commonside East
Mile Road
Coomber Way
Therapia Lane
Westcombe Avenue
Northborough Road
Streatham Road
148
164
176
F
G
H
J
K
1
2
3
4
5
6
7
28
29
30

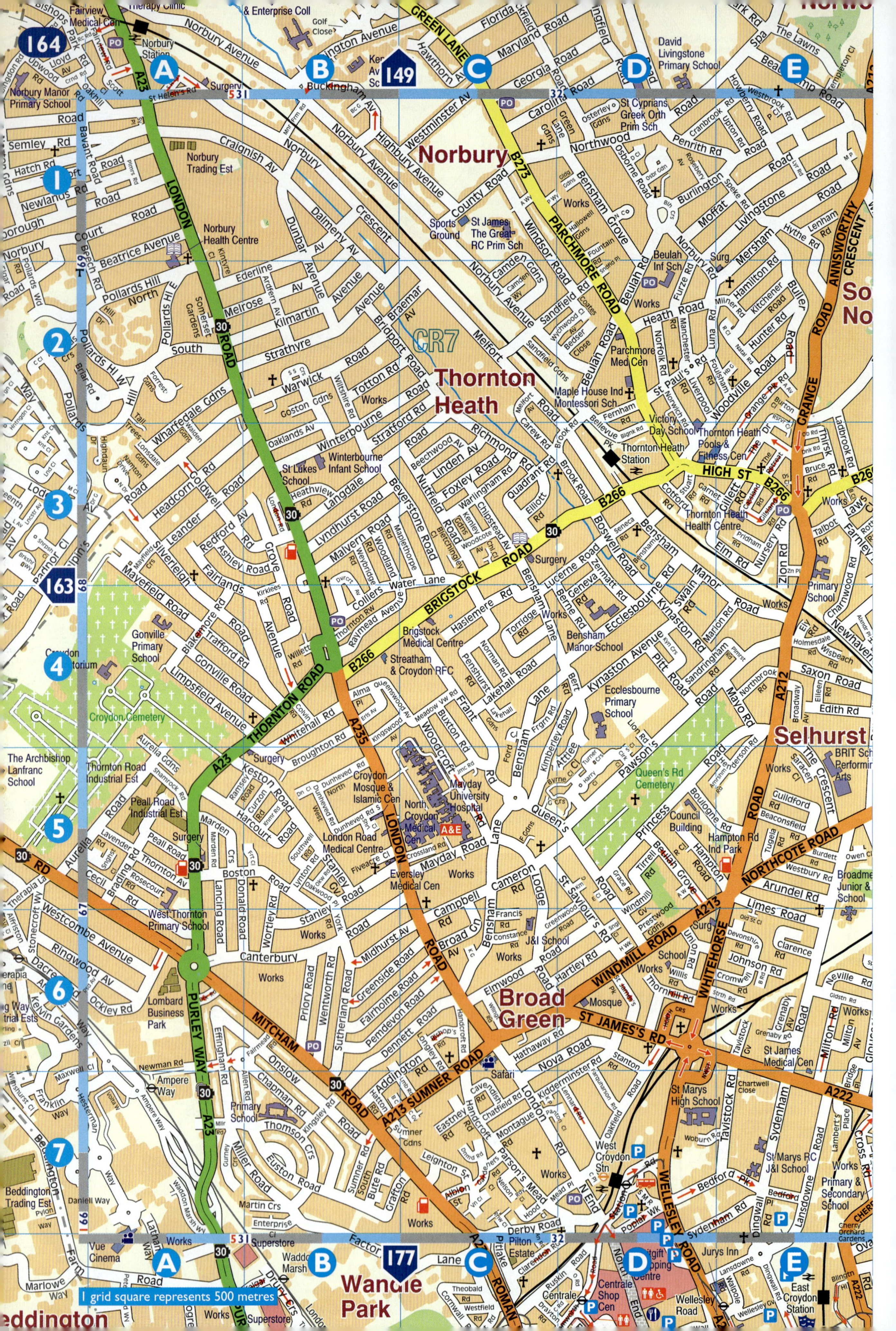
164
149
163
177
A
B
C
D
E
1
2
3
4
5
6
7
Norbury
Thornton Heath
CR7
Broad Green
Selhurst
Wandle Park
Beddington
Norbury Station
Thornton Heath Station
West Croydon Stn
East Croydon Station
Norbury Trading Est
Norbury Health Centre
Norbury Manor Primary School
David Livingstone Primary School
St Cyprians Greek Orth Prim Sch
St James The Great RC Prim Sch
Sports Ground
Parchmore Med Cen
Maple House Ind Montessori Sch
Victory Day School
Thornton Heath Pools & Fitness Cen
Thornton Heath Health Centre
Winterbourne Infant School
St Lukes School
Brigstock Medical Centre
Streatham & Croydon RFC
Bensham Manor School
Ecclesbourne Primary School
Gonville Primary School
Croydon Cemetery
Queen's Rd Cemetery
The Archbishop Lanfranc School
Thornton Road Industrial Est
Peall Road Industrial Est
Croydon Mosque & Islamic Cen
Mayday University Hospital
North Croydon Medical Cen
A&E
London Road Medical Centre
Eversley Medical Cen
West Thornton Primary School
Lombard Business Park
Council Building
Hampton Rd Ind Park
BRIT School Performing Arts
Broadmead Junior & Infant School
St Marys High School
St Marys RC J&I School
St James Medical Cen
Primary & Secondary School
Beddington Trading Est
Vue Cinema
Waddon Marsh
Superstore
Centrale Shop Cen
Whitgift Shopping Centre
Jurys Inn
LONDON ROAD
THORNTON ROAD
PURLEY WAY
MITCHAM ROAD
BRIGSTOCK ROAD
HIGH ST
PARCHMORE ROAD
GREEN LANE
WHITEHORSE ROAD
NORTHCOTE ROAD
WINDMILL ROAD
ST JAMES'S RD
SUMNER ROAD
WELLESLEY ROAD
ANNSWORTHY CRESCENT
GRANGE ROAD
A23
A235
A213
A212
A222
B266
B273
1 grid square represents 500 metres

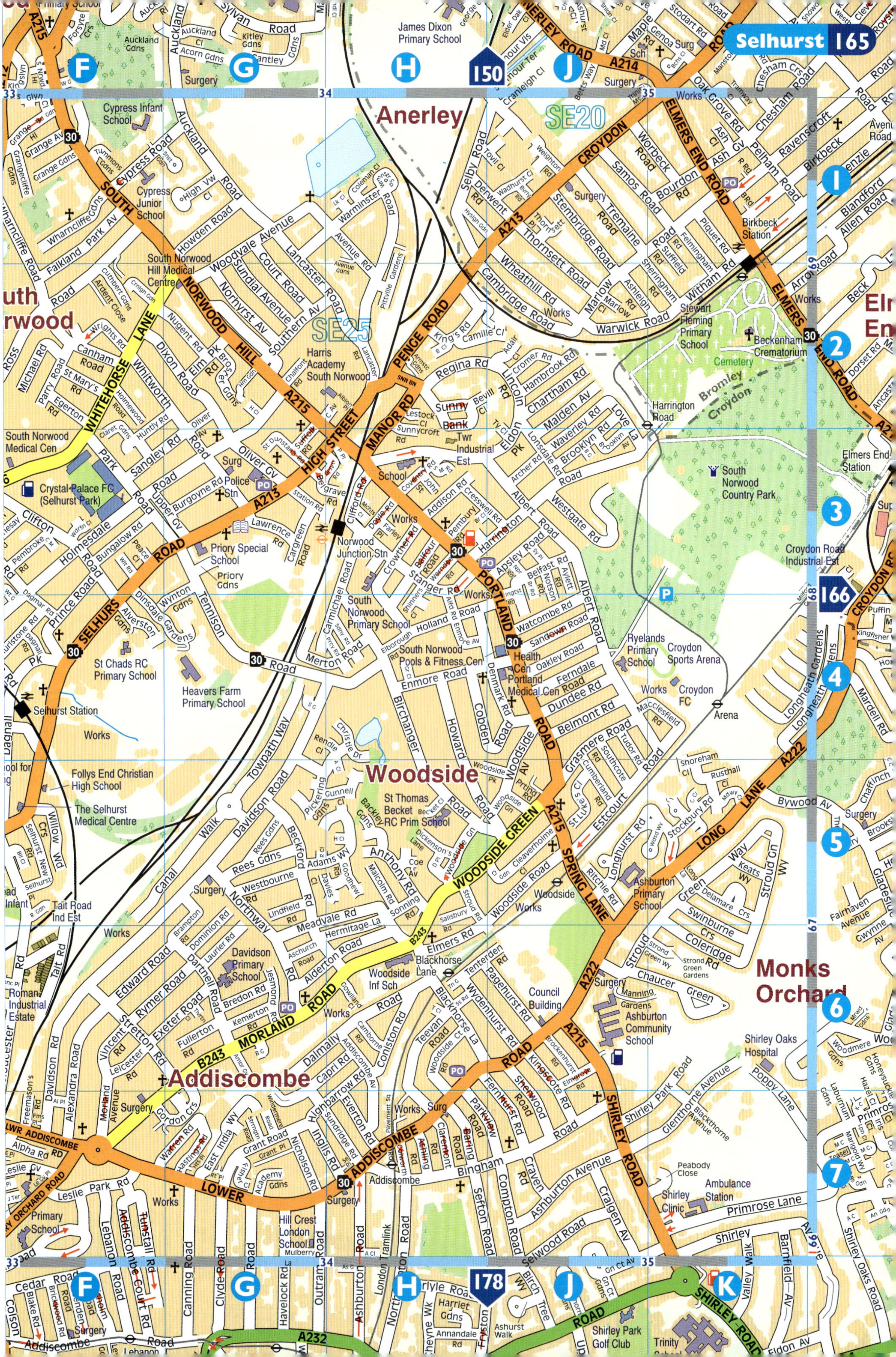

Anerley
SE20
SE25
Woodside
Addiscombe
Monks Orchard
South Norwood
Elmers End
James Dixon Primary School
Cypress Infant School
Cypress Junior School
South Norwood Hill Medical Centre
Harris Academy South Norwood
Crystal Palace FC (Selhurst Park)
South Norwood Medical Cen
Priory Special School
Priory Gdns
Norwood Junction Stn
South Norwood Primary School
South Norwood Pools & Fitness Cen
Health Cen
Portland Medical Cen
St Chads RC Primary School
Heavers Farm Primary School
Selhurst Station
Follys End Christian High School
The Selhurst Medical Centre
Tait Road Ind Est
St Thomas Becket RC Prim School
Woodside Inf Sch
Blackhorse Lane
Davidson Primary School
Council Building
Ashburton Primary School
Ashburton Community School
Shirley Oaks Hospital
Stewart Fleming Primary School
Beckenham Crematorium
Cemetery
Birkbeck Station
Harrington Road
South Norwood Country Park
Elmers End Station
Croydon Road Industrial Est
Ryelands Primary School
Croydon Sports Arena
Croydon FC
Arena
Peabody Close
Ambulance Station
Shirley Clinic
Hill Crest London School
Shirley Park Golf Club
Bromley
Croydon
SOUTH NORWOOD HILL
HIGH STREET
PENGE ROAD
MANOR RD
CROYDON ROAD
ELMERS END ROAD
WHITEHORSE LANE
SELHURST ROAD
PORTLAND ROAD
WOODSIDE GREEN
SPRING LANE
LONG LANE
MORLAND ROAD
LOWER ADDISCOMBE ROAD
ADDISCOMBE ROAD
SHIRLEY ROAD
A213
A214
A215
A222
A232
B243
150
166
178
F G H J K
1 2 3 4 5 6 7
33 34 35

166
151
179
165
30
A
B
C
D
E
1
2
3
4
5
6
7
536
37
69
68
67
BECKENHAM
Elmers End
Eden Park
Upper Elmers End
Monks Orchard
BR3
Beckenham Road
Clock House Station
Birkbeck Station
Elmers End Station
Eden Park Station
Beckenham Hospital
Recreation Ground
Kelsey Park
Elgood Playing Fields
Kelsey Park Sports College
Ralph Perring Court
Churchfields Primary Sch
Marion Vian Primary School
School of Art
Monks Orchard Primary School
Beckenham RFC
Beckenham Town FC
Bethlem Royal Hospital
Shirley Oaks Hospital
Edenham High School
Orchard Way Primary School
Beckmead School
Unicorn Primary School
Langley Park School for Boys
Langley Girls Sch
Oak Lodge JMI School
St Davids College
Innkeeper's Lodge
Croydon Road Industrial Est
Superstore
Works
Surgery
Odeon Cinema
Burnhill Bus Cen
Telephone Exchange
Meeting Hall
Theatre Cen
Fire Station
South Norwood Country Park
Medical Centres
ELMERS END ROAD
CROYDON ROAD
UPPER ELMERS END ROAD
WICKHAM ROAD
SOUTH EDEN PARK ROAD
LINKS WAY
MANOR ROAD
HIGH ST
BROMLEY ROAD
RECTORY ROAD
WICKHAM ROAD B230
A222
A214
A232
B230
Whitmore Road
Bramerton Road
Groveland Road
Gordon Rd
Derrick Road
Eden Park Avenue
Crossways Rd
Stone Park Av
Kelsey Way
Uplands
Manor Way
Village Way
Abbots Way
Lloyds Way
Aviemore Way
Aylesford Avenue
Bywood Av
Greenview Av
Tower View
Woodmere
Primrose Lane
Firsby Avenue
Pine Avenue
Hawksbrook Lane
Hawkhurst Way
Farm Drive
Ash Road
Oak Gdns
1 grid square represents 500 metres

Shortlands
Park Langley
West Wickham
Hayes
Beckenham Lane
Bromley Road
Bromley Rd
Albemarle Road
Westmoreland Road
Hayes Lane
Hayes Road B2212
Hayes Street
Pickhurst Lane
Kent Way
Masons Hl
Westmoreland Road B228
B251
A222
A21
A214
B265
Station Road
Glebe Way
Sloane Hospital
St Christophers School
Bishop Challoner School
Clare House Primary School
Valley Primary School
Playing Fields
Martin's Hill Recreation Ground
Bowling Green
Queens Mead
Shortlands Station
Pumping Station
Bromley College
Bromley Co Court
Odeon Cin
Tel Exchange
Churchill Theatre
The Glades Shopping Centre
The Pavilion Leisure Cen
Indoor Market
Bromley South Station
Superstore
Highfield Junior School
Highfield Infant School
Kingswood Avenue
Langley Park Golf Club
Golf Course
Pickhurst Junior School
Pickhurst Infant School
West Wickham Station
West Wickham Swimming Baths
Old Wilsonians Sports Club
Hawes Down Primary School
Glebe School
Hayes Station
Hayes School
The Ravensbourne School
Surgery
152
168
180
38
39
40
69
68
67
66
F
G
H
J
K
2
3
4
5
6
7

168
153
167
181
A
B
C
D
E
1
2
3
4
5
6
7
541
42
BROMLEY
Widmore
Bickley
Bromley Common
Hayes
South
BR2
WIDMORE RD
CHISLEHURST ROAD
B264
BICKLEY ROAD
A222
BICKLEY PARK ROAD
PAGE HEATH LANE
B265
KENTISH WAY
A21
MASONS HILL
HOMESDALE ROAD
HAYES LANE
BROMLEY COMMON
HASTINGS ROAD
HAYES STREET
HAYES LANE
B2212
HIGH STREET
TWEEDY ROAD
Bromley North Station
Bromley South Station
Bickley Station
Bromley Civic Centre
The Pavilion Leisure Cen
Widmore Centre
Playing Field
St Georges CE Primary School
Bickley Park CC
Bickley Park Pre Prep School
Bickley Park Prep School
Waldo Industrial Est
Chartwell Business Centre
Raglan Primary School
The Ravensbourne School
Old Bromlians CC
Bromley FC
Norman Park
Norman Park Athletics Track
Bromley College of FE & HE
Bromley Common
Oakley House
Bromley Golf Club
Bishop Justus CE (Secondary) School
Princes Plain Primary School
Hayes Primary School
Forge Clinic
Bickerly School of Dance
Cemetery
Golf Course
Newton Terrace
Hayes School
Tennis Club
Surgery
Works
Superstore
Indoor Market
Queens Gardens
Rec Gnd
Plaistow Lane
Harwood Avenue
Rochester Avenue
Murray Avenue
Forde Avenue
Bishops Avenue
Wanstead Road
Nightingale Lane
Canon Road
Liddon Road
Palace View
The Chase
Siward Road
Godwin Road
Langdon Rd
Glanville Road
Gundulph Road
Waldo Road
The Avenue
Southlands Grove
Rushmore
Oldfield Road
Tangleberry Close
Park Hill
Blenheim Road
Claremont Road
Burford Road
Waldegrave Road
Mayfield Road
Woodside Rd
Southborough Lane
Austin Av
Sunray Avenue
Green Way
Mons Wy
Narrow Way
Mosul Way
Magpie Hall Lane
Turpington Lane
Crown Lane
Rookery Lane
Victoria Road
Albert Road
Balfour Road
Herbert Road
Brooklyn Road
Whitehall Road
Chatterton Rd
Cowper Road
Southlands Road
Jaffray Road
Elliott Road
Bourne Road
Haywood Road
Havelock Rd
Sandford Road
Cromwell Ave
Wendover Road
Woldham Rd
Hawthorne Road
St Georges Road
St Matthews Drive
Woodlands
Hartley Close
Denbridge Road
Wells Road
The Spinneys
Pines Road
Bird-in-Hand Lane
Widmore Lodge Road
Tylney Road
Shawfield Park
Farm Close
Simone Close
Letchworth Drive
Fair Acres
Wolfe Close
Dartmouth Road
Southbourne
Cherry Walk
Hambro Av
Everard Avenue
George Lane
Hayes Wood Avenue
Glebe House Drive
Forge Close
The Knoll
Burwood Avenue
Church Lane
Prince's Plain
Lower Gravel Road
Jackson Road
Bradford Close
Trinity Close
Brewery Road
Lennard Road
Knowle Road
Cross Road
Fairway
Homemead Road
Holbrook Way
Parkfield Way
Cloisters Avenue
Brookmead
Springfield Gardens
Highfield Road
Sunningdale Rd
Salisbury Road
Union Road
Tredwell Close
Clarence Road
Falcon Av
Readon Road
I grid square represents 500 metres

Petts Wood
Chislehurst Station
Petts Wood Station
Orpington Station
Chislehurst Caves
Hawkwood Farm
Tongs Farm
Jubilee Country Park
Bromley High School GDST
St James RC Primary School
Southborough Primary School
St Peter & Paul RC Primary School
Marjorie McClure School
Coopers Technology College
Southborough
Broom Hill
Crofton
SUMMER HILL
BROMLEY
OLD HILL
ST PAUL'S CRAY ROAD A208
ORPINGTON ROAD
CHISLEHURST ROAD
A232
Station Approach
Gosshill Road
Botany Bay Lane
Hazelmere Road
Birchwood Road
Wood Ride
Kingsway
Petts Wood Road
Greencourt Road
Princes Avenue
The Chenies
West Way
Queensway
Towncourt Crescent
Crossway
Woodland Way
Great Thrift
Little Thrift
Silverdale Road
Manor Way
Southborough Lane
Franks Wood Avenue
Lakeswood Road
Crest View Drive
Oxhawth Crescent
Chesham Avenue
Woodhurst Avenue
Nightingale Road
Shepperton Road
Tudor Way
Priory Avenue
St Georges Road
St Johns Road
Beaumont Road
Fairfield Road
The Covert
Crofton Lane
Lynwood Grove
Derwent Drive
Broadcroft Road
Greenfield Gardens
Sparrow Drive
St Thomas Drive
Crofton Lane
Lansdowne Avenue
Drayton Avenue
Gumping Road
Allington Road
Andover Road
Oregon Square
Hollingworth Road
Rolleston Avenue
Prescott Avenue
Faringdon Avenue
Lovelace Avenue
Oxhawth Crescent
Thornet Wood Road
Stoneleigh Road
Golf Rd
Otford Cl
Barfield
Blackbrook Lane
Northumberland Gardens
Whitebeam Avenue
Larch Way
Almond Way
London Loop
Fairbank Av
Jasmine Close
Birch Mead
Hazel Grove
Wood Way
Cricket Ground Road
Onslow Crescent
Nortands Crescent
Sheridan Crescent
Lindenfield
Longmead
Walsingham Park
Manor Place
Riverwood Lane
Cookham Dene Close
St Paul's Wood Hill
Bridgewater Close
The Drive
Leesons Hill
Kenley Close
Berens Way
Kevington Drive
Marlings Park Av
Marlings Close
Scotsdale Close
Sefton Road
Sherborne
Poverest
Ladywood Avenue
Grosvenor Road
Sutherland Avenue
Bicknor Road
Irvine Way
Mayfield
Westholme
Eastcote
Bancroft Gardens
Hillview Cresc
Elm Grove
Hill View Road
Oakhill Rd
Yeovil Cl
York Rise
Cathcart Drive
Wyndham Close
Bramley Close
Romany Rise
Abbots Close
Monks Way

157
River Mole
River Mole Business Park
Sandown Industrial Park
Farm Road
Works
Sherriff Cl
Joseph
Locke Wy
Mill Road
Arran Way
Douglas
Blair Av
Road
Cranbrook Drive
Canleigh Road
The Woodlands
Woodend
Road
Station Road
Hampton Court
Weston Green Road
Weston Green
Newlands Avenue
Orchard Gate
Alma Road
Golf Course
Works
Esher Station
Thames Ditton & Esher Golf Club
Lower Green
Portsmouth Road
Couchmore Avenue
Montgomery Avenue
Westmont Rd
Hillmont
Kingston
Lower Green
Wynfrit Pl
The Furlongs
Er Cn Dr
Th Gllps
More Lane
Surgery
Esher CE High School
Vincent Close
Sandown Park Racecourse
Sandown Grandstand & Exhibition Centre
Sandown Sports Club & Dry Ski Slope
Littleworth Common
Heathside Close
Heathside
Medina Av
Harefield
Littleworth Road
Pelhams Walk
Wayneflete Tower Avenue
Pelhams
Winchester Cl
Electrical Trades Union College
Esher Pl Av
Esher Gn
Latton Close
Odeon
Warren Cl
Hillbrow Rd
Carrick Ga
Sandown Road
Ashburnham Park
Littleworth Common Road
Penates
Lrth Pl
Littleworth La
Civic Centre
PO
Willowmere
New Road
Martineau Close
Littlemead
Littleworth Road
Oaken Lane
Manor
Riverside Dr
Lammas Lane
A244
Hunting Cl
Clive Rd
Wolsey Road
High St
Church St
Esher Gn
ESHER
A244 Claremont Lane
Drake's Cl
Clive Rd
Dawes Ct
Belvedere Close
Grantley Pl
Simmons Ga
Broom Cl
Cranford Rl
Esher
Sandown Av
Broomfields
Park
Acorns Wy
Littleworth Av
Moore Place Golf Club
Pelhams Close
Golf Course
Esher Cl
Fir Tree Cl
Lynne Wk
Heatherset Cl
Rythe Road
Cavendish Drive
Wynd Gdns
West End Lane
Nightingale
Brisson Cl
Clare Hl (No2)
Clare Hill
Charlotte Ct
Milbourne La
Surgery
Milbourne Lodge Junior School
Raleigh Dr
Loseberry Rd
Station Rd
Aston Road
Simmil Rd
Hare Lane
The Avenue
Judge Walk
Meadow Rd
Oaken La
Park Close
The Mount
Milbourne La
Esher Church Prim Sch
Arbrook La
PH
KT10
Neville
Sports Club
Hawkshill Way
Hawkshill Cl
Courtlands Avenue
Old Chestnut Av
Pk Road
Portsmouth Road
Haymeads Dr
Orchard Way
Orchard Way
Brendon Dr
Arbrook Lane
Milbourne Lodge School
Claygate Station
The Pde
Torrington Rd
Albany Crs
Athlone
Hare Lane
Foley Ms
Fawcus Cl
Claremont Av
Claremont Pk Rd
Claremont Fan Court School
Claremont Drive
Home Farm Cl
Copsem Dr
Lakeside Dr
Copsem Wy
High Garth
Milbrook
Loseberry Farm
Gordon Road
Claremont Rd
Kings Ms
Foley
Claremont Park
Stony Hill
A307
Claremont Landscape Garden (NT)
Copsem La
Arbrook Common
Beaconsfield
Beaconsfield Gdns
Claygate Ldg Cl
Ou Anne Dr
Albany Cl
Meadway
Copsem Lane
A244
Blackhills
Arbrook Farm
Birchwood
Lane
Vale
Black Pond
Esher Common
1 grid square represents 500 metres

Esher 171
Weston Green
Long Ditton
158
SURBITON
Hinchley Wood
Hinchley Wood Stn
Hinchley Wood School & Sixth Form Centre
Hinchley Wood Primary Sch
Long Ditton Cemetery
Garden Centre
KINGSTON BY-PASS
A309
HOOK U/P
The Waffrons
Surbiton Golf Club
Golf Course
Woodstock Lane South
Woodstock Lane North
Surrey County
Kingston upon Thames
A3
Telegraph Lane
Claygate
Barwell
Barwell Court Farm
Lovelace Primary School
St Philips School
Chessington South Stn
Chessington Community College & Sports Cen
Chessington Golf Club
Chessington CC
Barwell Business Park
Holiday Inn
Chessington World of Adventures
LEATHERHEAD ROAD
A243
HOOK ROAD
172
Hook
Chessi
KT9
Rowan Preparatory School
Claygate Primary School
Park Farm
F G H J K
16 17 18
1 2 3 4 5 6 7
63 64 65 66

172
159
171
KT6
KT9
KT19
A
B
C
D
E
1
2
3
4
5
6
7
518
19
20
66
65
64
63
Hook
Chessington
KINGSTON BY-PASS
HOOK U/P
(KINGSTON BY-PASS) A3
TOLWORTH U/P (KINGSTON BY-PASS)
TOLWORTH BROADWAY
EWELL RD
WARREN DR NTH
HOOK ROAD
A243
RUXLEY LANE
B284
CHESSINGTON ROAD
Tolworth Station
Chessington North Stn
Chessington South Stn
Tolworth CP Schoo
Southborough Sch
Red Lion Business Park
Tolworth Girls School
Tolworth Recreation Centre
Charrington Bowl
Travelodge
Knollmead Primary School
Kingston Bus Cen
Hook Rise South Industrial Park
Corinthian Casuals FC
St Pauls CE Prim Sch
Gosbury Hill Health Cen
Moor Lane Junior School
St Marys CE Primary School
St Philips School
Chessington Golf Club
Golf Course
Barwell Business Park
Horton Country Park
Epsom & Ewell High School
Horton Park Golf & Country Club
Danetree School
Cemetery
St Ebba's Hospital
Horton Park Farm
Park Farm
Thames Down Link
Kingston upon Thames
Surrey County
Hook Rise South
Hook Rise North
Cox Lane
Moor Lane
Bridge Road
Jubilee Way
Horton Lane
1 grid square represents 500 metres

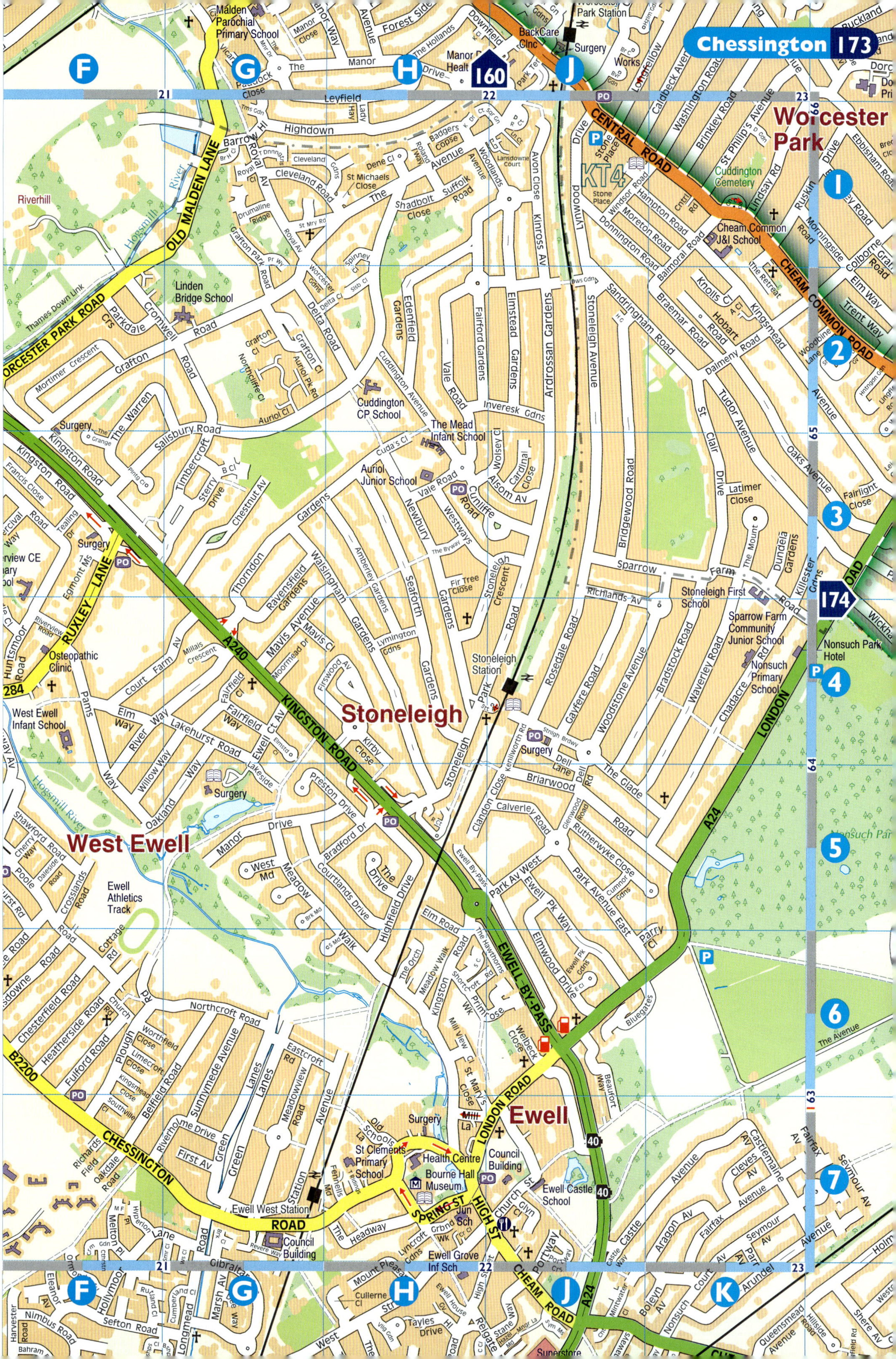
Worcester Park
Stoneleigh
West Ewell
Ewell
KT4
160
174
Malden Parochial Primary School
Manor Heath
BackCare Clnc
Surgery
Works
Leyfield
Highdown
OLD MALDEN LANE
WORCESTER PARK ROAD
CENTRAL ROAD
CHEAM COMMON ROAD
Cuddington Cemetery
Cheam Common J&I School
Riverhill
Hogsmill River
Linden Bridge School
Thames Down Link
Cuddington CP School
The Mead Infant School
Auriol Junior School
Cuddington Avenue
Edenfield Gardens
Fairford Gardens
Elmstead Gardens
Ardrossan Gardens
Stoneleigh Avenue
Sandringham Road
Inveresk Gdns
Vale Road
Kinross Av
Avon Close
Salisbury Road
Kingston Road
RUXLEY LANE
A240
KINGSTON ROAD
Osteopathic Clinic
West Ewell Infant School
Sparrow Farm
Stoneleigh First School
Sparrow Farm Community Junior School
Nonsuch Park Hotel
Nonsuch Primary School
Stoneleigh Station
Bridgewood Road
Woodstone Avenue
Gaynesford Road
Rosedale Road
Bradstock Road
Waverley Road
Chadacre Rd
LONDON ROAD
A24
Nonsuch Park
Latimer Close
Tudor Avenue
Oaks Avenue
Fairlight Close
Ewell Athletics Track
Preston Drive
Bradford Dr
Courtlands Drive
Highfield Drive
Briarwood Road
Calverley Road
Rutherwyke Close
Park Avenue East
EWELL-BY-PASS
Elmwood Drive
Northcroft Road
Sunnymede Avenue
Chesterfield Road
Heatherside Road
Fulford Road
B2200
CHESSINGTON ROAD
Ewell West Station
Council Building
St Clements Primary School
Health Centre
Bourne Hall Museum
SPRING ST
HIGH ST
Ewell Castle School
Ewell Grove Inf Sch
CHEAM ROAD
Sefton Road
Nimbus Road
Gibraltar
Cullerne Cl
Tayles Drive
Aragon Av
Castlemaine Av
Seymour Av
Arundel
The Avenue
Sunestone
21
22
23
63
64
65
66
F
G
H
J
K
1
2
3
4
5
6
7

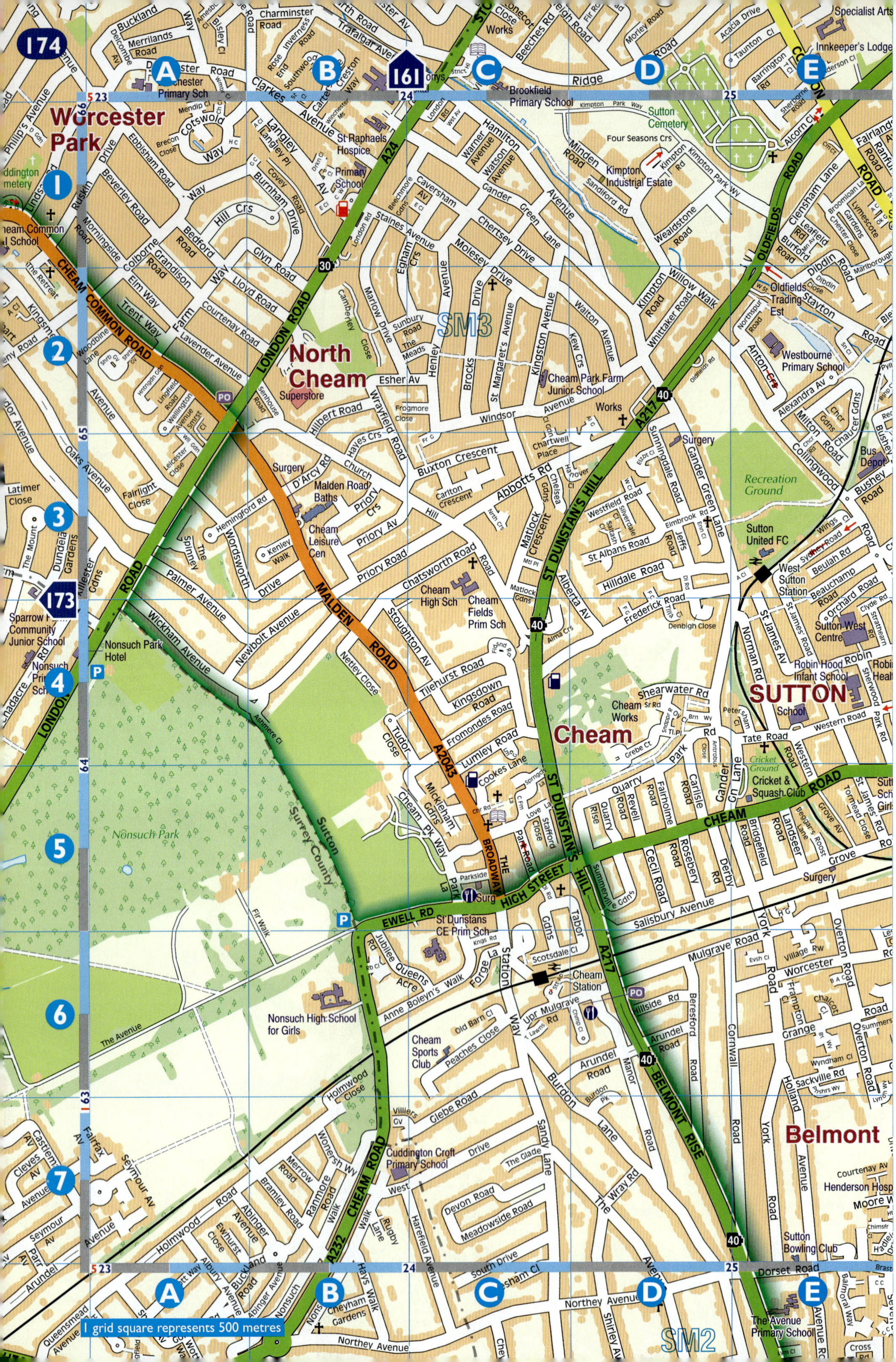
174
161
173
Worcester Park
North Cheam
Cheam
SUTTON
Belmont
SM3
SM2
Nonsuch Park
Recreation Ground
Buckland Way
Merrilands Road
Charminster Road
Trafalgar Avenue
Clarkes Avenue
Cotswold Way
Ruskin Drive
Ebbisham Road
Beverley Road
Morningside Road
Colborne Way
Grandison Road
Bedford Road
Elm Way
Trent Way
Burnham Drive
Glyn Road
Lloyd Road
Courtenay Road
Lavender Avenue
Hill Crs
Covey Road
London Road
A24
Cheam Common Road
Cheam Common Jl School
Worcester Park Cemetery
Kingsmead Avenue
St Raphaels Hospice
Primary School
Staines Avenue
Caversham Avenue
Chertsey Drive
Molesey Drive
Gander Green Lane
Hamilton Avenue
Watson Avenue
Warner Avenue
Marlow Drive
Egham Crs
Sunbury Road
The Meads
Henley Avenue
Brocks Drive
St Margaret's Avenue
Kingston Avenue
Kew Crs
Walton Avenue
Minden Road
Kimpton Industrial Estate
Kimpton Road
Kimpton Park Way
Four Seasons Crs
Sutton Cemetery
Brookfield Primary School
Works
Ridge Road
Morley Road
Acacia Drive
Taunton Cl
Barrington Rd
Specialist Arts
Innkeeper's Lodge
Oldfields Road
Clensham Lane
Oldfields Trading Est
Westbourne Primary School
Stayton Road
Willow Walk
Whittaker Road
Kimpton Road
Wealdstone Road
Cheam Park Farm Junior School
Windsor Avenue
Esher Av
Superstore
Hilbert Road
Wrayfield Road
Frogmore Close
Buxton Crescent
Carlton Crescent
Abbotts Rd
Chartwell Place
Matlock Crescent
Chelsea Gdns
St Dunstan's Hill
A217
Sunningdale Road
Gander Green Lane
Collingwood Road
Bushey Road
Bus Depot
Sutton United FC
West Sutton Station
Sydney Road
Beulah Rd
Surgery
Westfield Road
St Albans Road
Hilldale Road
Frederick Road
Denbigh Close
Jeffs Road
Elmbrook Rd
Oaks Avenue
Fairlight Close
Latimer Close
The Mount
Dundela Gardens
Sparrow Farm Community Junior School
Nonsuch Park Hotel
Malden Road
A2043
Malden Road Baths
Cheam Leisure Cen
Church Hill
Priory Crs
Priory Av
Priory Road
Chatsworth Road
Cheam High Sch
Cheam Fields Prim Sch
Hemingford Rd
Wordsworth Drive
Kenley Walk
The Spinney
Palmer Avenue
Wickham Avenue
Newbolt Avenue
Netley Close
Stoughton Av
Tilehurst Road
Kingsdown Road
Fromondes Road
Lumley Road
Tudor Close
Cookes Lane
Mickleham Gdns
Cheam Pk Way
The Broadway
Shearwater Rd
Cheam Works
Tate Road
Western Road
Cricket Ground
Cricket & Squash Club
Cheam Road
Quarry Rise
Quarry Park Road
Carlisle Road
Gander Green Lane
Fairholme Road
Revell Road
Cecil Road
Rosebery Road
Derby Rd
Bridgefield Road
Landseer Road
Grove Road
Salisbury Avenue
Surgery
High Street
Ewell Rd
St Dunstans CE Prim Sch
Park Lane
Surrey County
Sutton
Fir Walk
Nonsuch High School for Girls
The Avenue
Jubilee Queens Acre
Anne Boleyn's Walk
Forge La
Station Way
Cheam Station
Scotsdale Cl
Tabor Gdns
Mulgrave Road
Upr Mulgrave Rd
Old Barn Cl
Peaches Close
Cheam Sports Club
Hillside Rd
Beresford Road
Arundel Road
Cornwall Road
Belmont Rise
Burdon Lane
Manor Road
Worcester Road
Frampton Rd
Grange Road
Overton Road
Sackville Rd
Holland Avenue
York Road
Holmwood Close
Glebe Road
Villiers
Cuddington Croft Primary School
West Drive
Sandy Lane
The Glade
Devon Road
Meadowside Road
Harefield Avenue
Rugby Lane
Hays Walk
Cheam Road
A232
Wonersh Way
Merrow Road
Bramley Road
Ranmore Road
Abinger Avenue
Ewhurst Close
Holmwood Road
Buckland Road
Albury Avenue
Seymour Av
Fairfax Av
Castleton Av
Cleves Avenue
Arundel
Nonsuch
Cheyham Gardens
Northey Avenue
South Drive
The Wray Rd
Dorset Road
Sutton Bowling Club
Courtenay Av
Henderson Hosp
The Avenue Primary School
Balmoral Way
Shirley Av
Cross Rd
1 grid square represents 500 metres

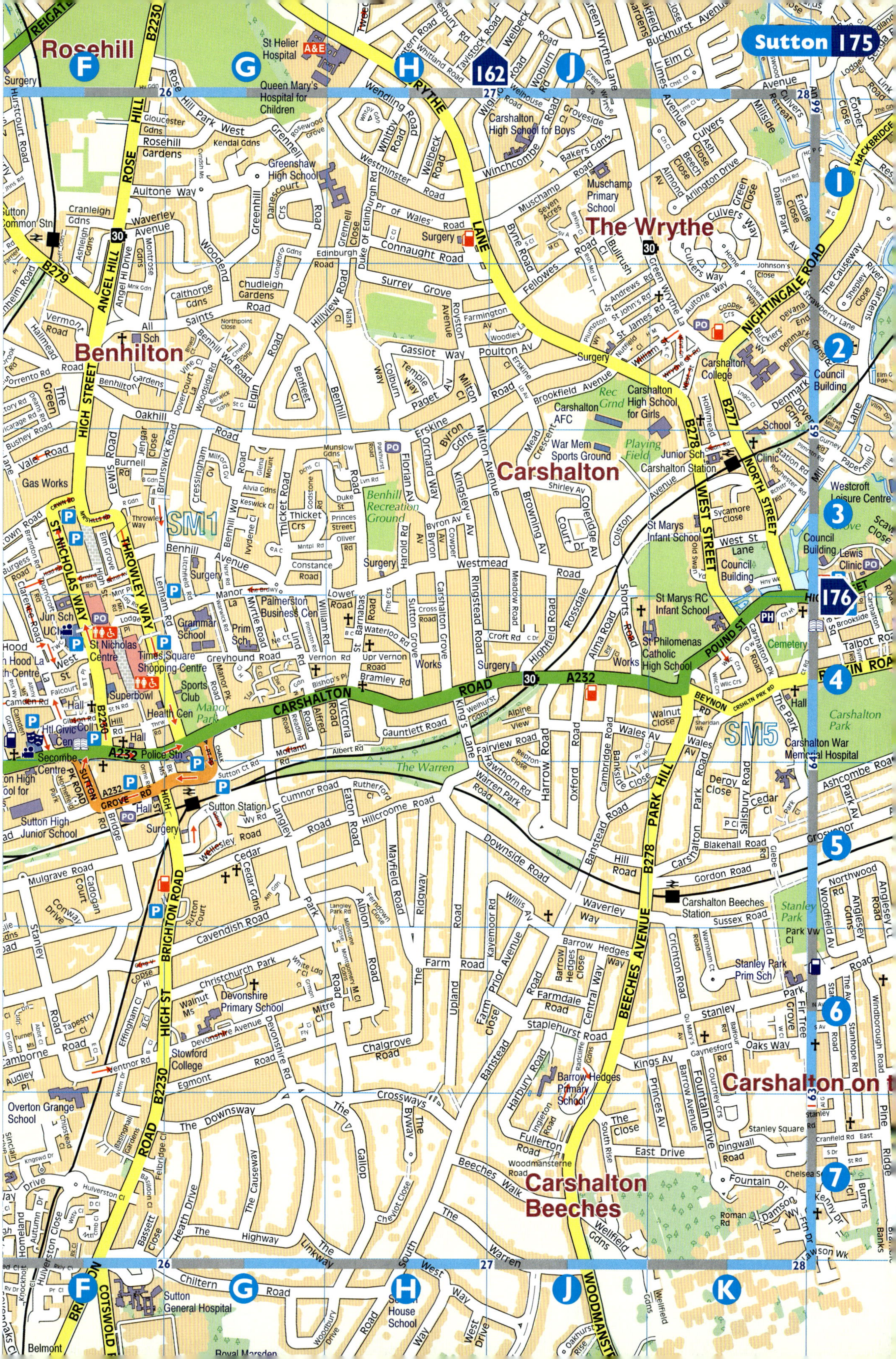
Rosehill
Benhilton
The Wrythe
Carshalton
Carshalton Beeches
Carshalton on t
SM1
SM5
St Helier Hospital
Queen Mary's Hospital for Children
Carshalton High School for Boys
Greenshaw High School
Muschamp Primary School
Carshalton College
Carshalton High School for Girls
Carshalton AFC
War Mem Sports Ground
Benhill Recreation Ground
St Nicholas Centre
Times Square Shopping Centre
Sutton Station
Carshalton Station
Carshalton Beeches Station
Carshalton War Memorial Hospital
Westcroft Leisure Centre
St Philomenas Catholic High School
St Marys Infant School
St Marys RC Infant School
Devonshire Primary School
Stowford College
Overton Grange School
Barrow Hedges Primary School
Stanley Park Prim Sch
Sutton High Junior School
Sutton General Hospital
Seaton House School
Carshalton Park
Stanley Park
The Warren
CARSHALTON ROAD
A232
B278
B277
B2230
BEECHES AVENUE
PARK HILL
NIGHTINGALE ROAD
WRYTHE LANE
BRIGHTON ROAD
HIGH STREET
ANGEL HILL
ROSE HILL
ST NICHOLAS WAY
THROWLEY WAY
WOODMANSTERNE
162
176
F
G
H
J
K
1
2
3
4
5
6
7
26
27
28

176
163
175
Hackbridge
Beddington
Bandonhill
Wallington
South Beddington
Carshalton on the Hill
Woodcote Green
Beddington Park
Carshalton Park
Stanley Park
Bandon Hill Cemetery
SM5
SM6
A237
A232
B271
B272
CROYDON ROAD
MANOR ROAD
WOODCOTE ROAD
LONDON ROAD
ACRE LANE
HIGH STREET
RUSKIN ROAD
PARK LANE
BOUNDARY ROAD
STANLEY PARK RD
STAFFORD ROAD
FORESTERS DRIVE
SANDY LANE S
PLOUGH LANE
BEDDINGTON LANE
HILLIER'S LA
HACKBRIDGE ROAD
NIGHTINGALE ROAD
Hackbridge Station
Wallington Station
Felnex Trading Estate
Edes Business Park
Carew Manor School
Beddington Park Primary School
Wallington Grammar School
Holy Trinity CE Junior School
Beddington Infants School
Sherwood Park School
Westcroft Leisure Centre
Carshalton War Memorial Hospital
Wallington High School for Girls
Stanley Park High School
Foresters Primary School
Roundshaw J&I School
Wilson's School
Purley Sports Club
1 grid square represents 500 metres

Wandle Park
Waddon
CROYDON
South Croydon
Roundshaw
PURLEY WAY
ROMAN WAY
OLD TOWN
WELLESLEY ROAD
PARK LA
BARCLAY RD
FAIRFIELD RD
ADDISCOMBE
DUPPAS HILL ROAD
THE CROYDON FLYOVER A232
LWR COOMBE ST
COOMBE ROAD
SOUTHBRIDGE ROAD
ST PETER'S RD B274
DENNING AVENUE
B275
WARHAM ROAD
CROHAM RD
SELSDON ROAD
BRIGHTON ROAD
SANDERSTEAD ROAD
A235
A212
A236
A23
A232
Whitgift Shopping Centre
Centrale Shop Cen
East Croydon Station
West Croydon Stn
Waddon Station
South Croydon Station
Sanderstead Station
Purley Oaks Stn
Whitgift School
Haling Manor High School
Croydon Airport Industrial Estate
Wyevale Garden Centre
Colonnades Leisure Park
Aerodrome Hotel
Mill Lane Trading Est
Croydon Coll
Fairfield Halls
Town Hall
Clocktower
Old Palace School
St Andrews CE VA HighSchool
Duppas Junior School
Croydon Bowling Club
Capital Business Centre
Two Bridges Business Park
Purley Oaks Primary School
Regina Coeli RC Primary School
St Giles School
164
178
F
G
H
I
J
K
31
32
33

Shirley
Upper Shirley
Addiscombe
Shirley Park Golf Club
Trinity School
Shirley Windmill
Golf Course
Addington Hills
Lloyd Park
Croham Hurst
Croham Hurst Golf Club
Royal Russell Preparatory Sch
Archbishop Tenisons CE School
Addiscombe CC
Park Hill Junior Sch
Occupational Health Centre
South Croydon Station
South Croydon Sports Club
St Peters Primary School
Capital Business Centre
Two Bridges Business Park
Sanderstead Station
Ridgeway Primary School
Selsdon Primary School
Heathfield
East Croydon Station
The Law Courts
Ambulance Station
Shirley Clinic
Peabody Close
Primrose Lane
Water Tower
Follys End Christian Sch
Addiscombe Road
Coombe Road
Coombe Lane
Upper Selsdon Road
Croham Valley Road
Ballards Way
Ballards Farm Road
Shirley Road
Fairfield Rd
Chepstow Road
Park Hill Road
Oaks Road
Sunken Rd
Vanguard Way
London Loop
London Tramlink
A232
A212
A222
B243
B275
A2022
CR0
165
177
178
1 grid square represents 500 metres

Spring Park
Addington
Forestdale
166
180
A232
A2022
A212
KENT GATE WAY
GRAVEL HILL
SELSDON PARK ROAD
WICKHAM ROAD
HIGH STREET
Shirley Church Road
Addington Golf Club
Golf Course
Addington Palace
Addington Palace Golf Club
Addington Village
Addington Court Golf Club
Spring Park Primary School
Benson Primary School
Coloma Convent Girls School
Shirley High School
St Johns CE Prim Sch
Gilbert Scott Primary School
Monks Hill Sports Centre
Selsdon High Sch
John Ruskin College
Forestdale Primary Sch
Applegarth Primary School
Good Shepherd RC Primary School
Castle Hill Primary School
Little Davids School
Timebridge Youth & Community Centre
Medical Centres
Medical Centre
Surgery
Police Stn
London Tramlink
Fieldway
King Henry's Drive
New Addington
Gravel Hill
Bishops Walk
Ash Road
Bushey Road
Links View Road
Oaklands Avenue
Highfield Drive
Bridle Road
Bridle Way
Spout Hill
Featherbed Lane
Falconwood Road
Lodge Lane
Bardolph Av
Linton Glade
F
G
H
J
K
I
2
3
4
5
6
7
36
37
38
63
64
65
66

180
179
167
A
B
C
D
E
1
2
3
4
5
6
7
38
39
40
166
165
164
163
HIGH STREET
PICKHURST LANE
GLEBE WAY
A232
A214
STATION ROAD
ADDINGTON ROAD
A2022
BR4
Wickham Swimming Baths
Sports Club
Surgery
Hayes Station
Down School
Hawes Down Clnc
Wickham Theatre
Old Beckenhamian RFC
Coney Hill School
Metropolitan Police Hayes Sports Club
Nash College of Further Education
Hayes Grove Priory Hospital
Spring Park
Shirley Wanderers RFC
Coney Hall
Rouse Farm
Bromley
Croydon
Castle Hill Primary School
Medical Centre
Good Shepherd RC Primary School
Wolsey Junior School
New Addington
Vulcan Business Centre
Addington Business Centre
Layhams Farm
King Henry's Drive
Works
Links Road
The Mead
Croft Av
Hayes Road
Keswick Road
Windermere Road
Addington Road
Coney Hill Rd
Tiepigs Lane
Hurstdene Av
Ridgeway
Warren Road
Holland Way
Westland Dr
Abbotsbury Rd
Lennard Av
Dukes Wy
Sherwood Way
Park Av
Southcroft Av
Wickham Court Rd
Rose Walk
Wickham Crs
Silver Lane
Corkscrew Hill
Stambourne Wy
Boleyn Gdns
Highfield Drive
Oaklands Avenue
The Avenue
Woodland Way
Wood Lodge Lane
Tudor Gdns
Courtfield Rise
Bencurtis Pk
Croydon Rd
South Walk
Church Drive
Kingsway
Princes Way
Farm Close
Harvest Bank Road
Robins Grove
Hartfield Crescent
Lawrence Road
Gates
Layhams Road
Sylvan Way
Hawthorn Dr
Chestnut Avenue
Birch Tree Avenue
Lime Tree Walk
Cherry Tree Wk
Monarch Cl
Queensway
Prestons Road
North Pole Lane
Nash Lane
North Walk
Field Way
Foxcombe
The Lindens
Oakbank
Eddinton Close
Dunley Drive
Merrow Wy
Pirbright Crs
Claygate Crs
Alford Gn
Brockham Crs
Mickleham Wy
Netley Close
Frimley Close
Thursley Crs
Headley Drive
Dunsfold Way
Horsley Dr
Frensham Dr
Frimley Crs
Avenue
Goldcrest Way
Kestrel Way
Castle Hill Av
Tilford Av
King Henry's Drive
Wolsey Crescent
Aldrich Crescent
Shaxton Crescent
Grenville Road
Rothwell Road
Queen Elizabeth's Drive
Rowdown Crs
Vulcan Way
Montacute Road
Gascoigne Road
Stowe Av
Godric Crs
N Downs Crs
Surgery
1 grid square represents 500 metres

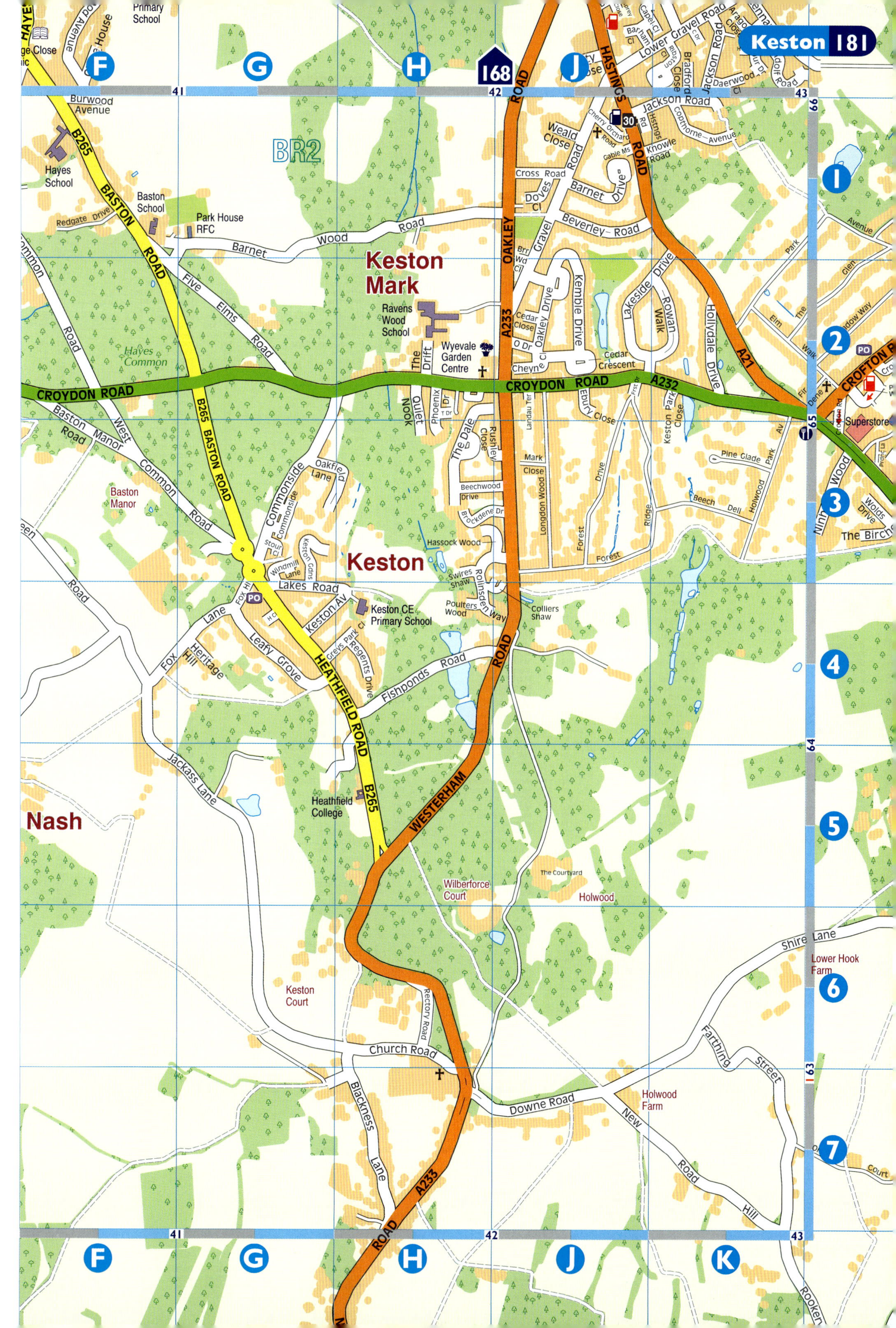
Primary School
Hayes School
Burwood Avenue
Baston School
Park House RFC
Redgate Drive
BR2
Barnet Wood Road
Keston Mark
Ravens Wood School
Wyevale Garden Centre
The Drift
Quiet Nook
Phoenix Dr
OAKLEY ROAD
A233
Cross Road
Doves Cl
Gravel
Beverley Road
Barnet Drive
Weald Close
Jackson Road
Lower Gravel Road
Bradford Close
HASTINGS ROAD
Cherry Orchard Road
Knowle Road
Cable Ms
Cedar Close
Oakley Drive
Kemble Drive
Cheyne Cl
Cedar Crescent
Lakeside Drive
Rowan Walk
Hollydale Drive
A21
Hayes Common
CROYDON ROAD
A232
BASTON ROAD
B265
Five Elms Road
Common Road
Baston Manor Road
West Common Road
Baston Manor
The Dale
Rushley Close
Landau Ter
Mark Close
Ebury Close
Keston Park Close
Pine Glade
Park Av
Beech Dell
Holwood
Beechwood Drive
Brockdene Dr
Longdon Wood
Forest Drive
Ridge
Commonside
Oakfield Lane
Hassock Wood
Keston
Stour Cl
Windmill Lane
Keston Gdns
Lakes Road
Swires Shaw
Rollinsden Way
Poulters Wood
Colliers Shaw
Keston Av
Keston CE Primary School
Fox Hill
Fox Lane
Heritage Hill
Leafy Grove
Greys Park Cl
Regents Drive
Fishponds Road
HEATHFIELD ROAD
WESTERHAM ROAD
Jackass Lane
Nash
Heathfield College
Wilberforce Court
The Courtyard
Holwood
Keston Court
Rectory Road
Church Road
Blackness Lane
Downe Road
Holwood Farm
New Road Hill
Farthing Street
Shire Lane
Lower Hook Farm
Superstore
CROFTON
The Birches
Avenue
Ninhams Wood
Wolds Drive
A233
ROAD
Rookery
Court
168
30
F G H J K
41 42 43
1 2 3 4 5 6 7
66 65 64 63

Abbey Wood 116 C3
Acton 86 E7
Acton Green 106 A3
Addington 179 J5
Addiscombe 165 G6
Aldborough Hatch 60 E3
Aldersbrook 59 G7
Alperton 68 A7
Anerley 165 H1
Arkley 25 K4
Ashford Common 140 B5
Avery Hill 135 H5
Balham 128 E6
Bandonhill 176 D4
Barking 78 D6
Barkingside 60 B2
Barnehurst 138 A2
Barnes 106 E7
Barnes Cray 138 E3
Barnet 26 D5
Barnet Gate 25 G5
Barnsbury 5 L1
Barwell 171 J6
Battersea 108 E6
Bayswater 8 E6
Beckenham 166 D1
Beckton 95 K5
Becontree 79 K4
Beddington 176 E1
Beddington Corner 163 F6
Bedford Park 106 C2
Belgravia 16 A5
Bell Green 151 H2
Bellingham 151 J3
Belmont 49 G1
Belmont 174 E7
Belvedere 117 J4
Benhilton 175 F2
Berrylands 159 G5
Bethnal Green 92 D2
Bexley 136 D3
Bexleyheath 137 G3
Bickley 168 D1
Blackfen 136 A5
Blackheath 133 J1
Blackheath Park 133 K3
Blackwall 94 B6
Bloomsbury 11 H2
Borehamwood 24 A2
The Borough 18 F2
Bow 93 J1
Bow Common 93 J4
Bowes Park 40 E5
Bowmans 138 C6
Brentford 104 E5
Brentford End 104 C5
Brimsdown 31 G1
Brixton 130 B3
Broad Green 164 C6
Brockley 132 C4
Bromley 93 K2
Bromley 168 A1
Bromley Common 168 C5
Bromley Park 152 C7
Brompton 15 J4
Brondesbury 70 C5
Brondesbury Park 70 B7
Brook Green 107 F2
Brunswick Park 40 A2
Buckhurst Hill 45 G2
Burnt Oak 37 F6
Bushey 22 C6
Bushey Heath 22 E6
Bushey Mead 161 G2
Bush Hill Park 30 A5
Caldecote Hill 23 F6
Camberwell 111 G7
Camden Town 4 B2
Canary Wharf 93 J7
Canning Town 95 F4
Cannon Hill 161 G3
Canonbury 6 E1
Canons Park 36 A6
Carpenders Park 33 K1
Carshalton 175 J3
Carshalton Beeches 175 J7
Carshalton on the Hill 175 K6
Castle Green 79 J7
Catford 133 F7
Chadwell Heath 61 K4
Charlton 114 C4
Cheam 174 C4
Chelsea 15 H8
Chessington 172 A5
Child's Hill 70 C1
China Town 11 H6
Chingford Hatch 44 C3
Chipping Barnet 26 C4
Chislehurst 154 C6
Chislehurst West 154 A5
Chiswick 106 C3
Church End 52 E1
Church End 69 H6
City of London 12 D6
Clapham 129 G1
Clapham Park 129 J5
Clapton Park 75 H3
Claremont Park 170 A6
Claygate 171 F5
Clayhall 59 K1
Clerkenwell 6 A9
Cockfosters 27 J4
Coldharbour 118 D3
Cole Park 124 B5
Colindale 51 G2
College Park 87 J2
Collier's Wood 147 H6
Colney Hatch 39 K5
Coney Hall 180 C3
Coombe 145 G6
Copse Hill 145 J6
Cottenham Park 145 K7
Cranbrook 60 A6
Cranford 101 K6
Cranley Gardens 54 A3
Crayford 138 D4
Creekmouth 96 E4
Cricklewood 70 B3
Crooked Billet 145 K5
Crouch End 54 C5
Croydon 177 K2
Crystal Palace 150 C5
Cubitt Town 113 F3
Custom House 95 J6
Dagenham 80 D6
Dartford 139 F6
Dartmouth Park 72 A1
Deacons Hill 24 C5
De Beauvoir Town 7 J3
Deptford 112 C5
Dollis Hill 69 K2
Dormer's Wells 84 B6
Downham 152 B4
Ducks Island 26 B6
Dudden Hill 69 J4
Dulwich 150 B1
Dulwich Village 131 F6
Ealing 85 J6
Earl's Court 14 A6
Earlsfield 128 B7
East Acton 87 H6
East Barnet 27 H6
East Bedfont 120 E6
Eastbury 32 D3
Eastcote 47 F6
Eastcote Village 47 F4
East Dulwich 131 H4
East Finchley 53 H2
East Ham 95 J1
East Molesey 157 H4
East Sheen 126 A4
East Wickham 116 B7
Eden Park 166 C3
Edgware 36 D3
Edmonton 42 A3
Elmers End 166 A2
Elm Park 81 K4
Elmstead 153 J4
Elstree 24 A5
Eltham 134 D5
Enfield 29 J3
Enfield Highway 30 E1
Enfield Town 29 K2
Erith 118 C4
Esher 170 C3
Ewell 173 J7
Fair Cross 79 F4
Falconwood 135 K3
Feltham 141 F1
Felthamhill 140 C5
Field Common 156 E6
Finchley 38 E7
Finsbury 6 A7
Finsbury Park 72 E1
Foots Cray 155 H5
Forestdale 179 G7
Forest Gate 76 E4
Forest Hill 132 A7
Fortis Green 53 K5
Foxbury 154 D4
Friday Hill 44 B2
Friern Barnet 39 J3
Fulham 107 G6
Furzedown 148 B3
Gants Hill 59 K5
Gidea Park 63 H1
Giggshill 158 B6
Globe Town 93 F2
Golders Green 52 C5
Goodmayes 79 H1
Gospel Oak 72 A4
Grange Park 29 G4
Greenford 84 D3
Greenhill 49 F4
Greenwich 113 G4
Grove Park 106 A7
Grove Park 153 G2
Hackbridge 176 B1
Hackney 74 E5
Hackney Wick 75 J5
Hadley 26 D2
Haggerston 7 M5
Hale End 44 B5
Ham 143 K2
Hammersmith 106 E3
Hampstead 71 H3
Hampstead Garden Suburb 53 F4
Hampton 142 B7
Hampton Hill 142 C3
Hampton Wick 143 H7
Hanwell 84 D7
Hanworth 141 H2
Harlesden 87 G1
Harlington 101 F5
Harringay 55 G4
Harrow 48 D5
Harrow on the Hill 48 E7
Harrow Weald 34 E6
Hatch End 33 J6
Hatton 121 H3
Hayes 82 A4
Hayes 168 A6
Hayes End 82 B3
Hayes Town 83 G7
Headstone 48 B3
Heath Park 63 K5
Hendon 51 K4
Herne Hill 130 D5
Heston 102 E6
Higham Hill 57 G1
Highams Park 43 K6
High Barnet 26 A2
Highbury 73 H4
Highgate 53 K6
Highwood Hill 37 H1
Hinchley Wood 171 F2
Hither Green 133 H5
Holborn 11 L3
Holders Hill 38 B7
Holywell 20 C5
Homerton 75 F5
Honor Oak 132 A5
Honor Oak Park 132 B5
Hook 172 A4
Hornsey 54 E3
Hornsey Vale 55 F4
Hounslow 123 F1
Hounslow West 122 C2
Hoxton 7 J6
Hurst Park 157 H1
The Hyde 51 H4
Ilford 78 B2
Isle of Dogs 113 F3
Isleworth 124 C2
Islington 6 A3
Kennington 109 K5
Kensal Green 88 A1
Kensal Rise 88 B1
Kensal Town 88 C3
Kensington 14 C4
Kentish Town 72 C5
Kenton 49 J4
Keston 181 H3
Keston Mark 181 H2
Kew 105 G6
Kidbrooke 134 B1
Kilburn 70 C7
Kingsbury 50 D5
Kingsland 7 J1
Kingston upon Thames 158 D2
Kingston Vale 145 F4
Knightsbridge 15 K1
Knight's Hill 130 D7
Ladywell 132 D3
Lambeth 18 A3
Lampton 103 G7
Lea Bridge 75 F2
Lee 133 J5
Lessness Heath 117 J5
Lewisham 133 F3
Leyton 76 B2
Leytonstone 58 D7
Limehouse 93 G6
Lisson Grove 9 M2
Little Heath 61 J3
Little Ilford 78 A4
Little Stanmore 36 B7
Long Ditton 158 C7
Longlands 154 C2
Lower Clapton 74 E3
Lower Edmonton 42 A1
Lower Feltham 140 C2
Lower Green 170 B1
Lower Holloway 73 F4
Lower Place 86 E1
Lower Sydenham 151 F3
Loxford 78 C4
Maida Vale 2 C7
Maitland Park 71 K5
Manor Park 77 J3
Marks Gate 62 A1
Marylebone 10 A3
Mayfair 10 C7
Maypole 138 B7
Merry Hill 22 B7
Merton 146 E7
Merton Park 161 J1
Mile End 93 G3
Mill Hill 37 J4
Mill Meads 94 B1
Millwall 112 E2
Mitcham 163 F2
Monken Hadley 26 C1
Monks Orchard 165 K6
Moor Park 32 A3
Morden 161 K3
Morden Park 161 H5
Mortlake 125 K1
Motspur Park 160 D5
Mottingham 153 G1
Muswell Hill 54 A1
Nash 181 F5
Neasden 69 F3
New Addington 180 B6
New Barnet 27 F4
New Beckenham 151 G5
Newbury Park 60 D5
New Charlton 114 C3
New Cross 132 B1
New Cross Gate 112 B7
New Eltham 154 B1
Newington 18 B4
New Malden 160 C2
New Southgate 40 C3
New Town 139 J5
Noel Park 55 H1
Norbiton 159 G1
Norbury 164 C1
North Acton 86 E3
North Cheam 174 B2
North End 53 G7
North End 118 C7
North Feltham 122 A4
North Finchley 39 G5
North Harrow 47 K5
North Hyde 102 D3
North Kensington 88 B4
Northolt 66 A6
North Sheen 125 J1
Northumberland Heath 117 K6
North Wembley 49 H7
Northwood 32 A7
Northwood Hills 46 B1
North Woolwich 114 D1
Norwood Green 103 F3
Norwood New Town 149 K5
Notting Hill 88 C6
Nunhead 131 K3
Oakleigh Park 39 H1
Oakwood 28 D5
Old Bexley 137 H6
Old Ford 75 G7
Old Malden 160 A6
Old Oak Common 87 H3
Osidge 40 C1
Osterley 103 H6
Oxhey 21 H5
Paddington 9 G3
Palmers Green 40 E2
Park Langley 167 F5
Park Royal 86 C2
Parsons Green 127 K1
Peckham 131 J1
Penge 150 E6
Pentonville 5 M5
Perivale 67 J7
Petersham 125 F7
Petts Wood 169 J3
Pimlico 16 E7
Pinner 47 H3
Pinner Green 47 G1
Pinnerwood Park 33 G6
Plaistow 94 D2
Plaistow 152 E5
Plashet 77 H5
Plumstead 115 H4
Plumstead Common 116 A5
Ponders End 30 E4
Poplar 93 J6
Preston 49 K7
Primrose Hill 4 B4
Purfleet 119 K4
Putney 127 G4
Putney Heath 127 F6
Putney Vale 145 J2
Queensbury 50 A2
Queen's Park 88 C1
Rainham 99 K2
Rayners Lane 47 K7
Raynes Park 161 F2
Redbridge 59 G4
Regent's Park 4 D6
Richmond 125 F4
Richmond Hill 125 F5
Roehampton 126 C4
Romford 62 E4
The Rookery 20 E6
Rosehill 162 A7
Rotherhithe 112 A2
Roundshaw 177 F5
Rowley Green 25 H3
Roxeth 66 C1
Ruislip 46 C5
Ruislip Common 46 A3
Ruislip Gardens 64 C2
Ruislip Manor 64 E1
Rush Green 63 F6
St George in the East 92 C6
St Giles 11 H4
St Helier 162 B7
St James's 11 G9
St Johns 132 D1
St John's Wood 2 F4
St Luke's 6 F9
St Margarets 124 D5
St Pancras 5 K8
Sands End 108 B7
Seething Wells 158 C5
Selhurst 164 E4
Seven Kings 60 E7
Shacklewell 74 C3
Shadwell 92 E6
Shepherd's Bush 87 K7
Shirley 178 E1
Shooters Hill 115 H7
Shoreditch 7 H8
Shortlands 167 H2
Sidcup 155 H3
Silvertown 114 B1
Sipson 100 C4
Slade Green 138 D1
Soho 11 G5
Somers Town 5 G6
Southall 102 C1
South Beddington 176 D5
Southborough 168 E5
South Bromley 94 B5
South Croydon 177 H5
Southend 152 A3
Southfields 127 K7
Southgate 28 E7
South Hackney 74 E7
South Hampstead 2 F1
South Harrow 66 B2
South Hornchurch 81 F7
South Kensington 14 E6
South Lambeth 109 K6
South Norwood 164 E2
South Oxhey 33 F2
South Ruislip 65 H3
South Tottenham 56 A4
South Wimbledon 147 G4
South Woodford 58 E1
Spitalfields 13 L2
Spring Grove 103 J7
Spring Park 179 J1
Stamford Hill 56 B6
Stanmore 35 H4
Stanwell 120 A5
Stepney 92 E4
Stockwell 129 K2
Stoke Newington 74 B1
Stoneleigh 173 H4
Strand 11 J6
Stratford 76 A6
Stratford Marsh 75 K7
Stratford New Town 76 A5
Strawberry Hill 142 D2
Streatham 148 E4
Streatham Hill 129 K7
Streatham Park 148 C3
Streatham Vale 148 B6
Stroud Green 55 G5
Sudbury 67 F4
Summerstown 147 H1
Sunbury 140 C7
Sunbury Common 140 D6
Sundridge 153 G5
Surbiton 158 D7
Sutton 174 E4
Swiss Cottage 3 H3
Sydenham 151 F4
Teddington 142 D5
Temple Hill 139 G3
Temple Mills 75 K4
Thames Ditton 158 B6
Thamesmead 97 G6
Thornton Heath 164 C2
Tokyngton 68 D5
Tolworth 159 H7
Tooting 147 K4
Tooting Graveney 147 H4
Tottenham 56 A1
Tottenham Hale 56 B2
Totteridge 26 D7
Totteridge Green 26 A7
Tufnell Park 72 C3
Tulse Hill 130 C7
Twickenham 123 K7
Underhill 26 E5
Upper Clapton 56 C7
Upper Edmonton 42 C3
Upper Elmers End 166 C4
Upper Holloway 54 C7
Upper Norwood 149 K7
Upper Shirley 178 E3
Upper Sydenham 150 C3
Upper Tooting 147 J2
Upper Walthamstow 58 A3
Upton 77 F6
Upton Park 77 G7
Vale of Health 71 H2
Vauxhall 17 K8
Waddon 176 E1
Walham Green 107 K7
Wallend 78 A7
Wallington 176 A4
Walthamstow 57 H3
Walworth 18 F8
Wandle Park 177 G1
Wandsworth 127 K3
Wanstead 59 F6
Wapping 92 D7
Watford 20 D2
Watford Heath 21 J6
Wealdstone 49 G2
Welling 136 C2
Welsh Harp 51 F7
Wembley 68 A3
Wembley Park 68 C2
West Acton 86 C5
West Barnes 161 F4
West Bedfont 120 C6
West Brompton 14 C9
West Drayton 100 A2
West Dulwich 149 K1
West Ealing 85 G7
West Ewell 173 F5
West Green 55 J2
West Hampstead 70 E4
West Harrow 48 C6
West Heath 71 F1
West Heath 116 E5
West Hendon 51 J6
West Hill 127 H6
West Kensington 107 G4
West Kilburn 88 C2
Westminster 16 F4
West Molesey 156 E3
West Norwood 149 J3
Weston Green 157 K7
West Ruislip 46 A7
West Watford 20 E4
West Wickham 167 G7
Whetstone 39 F1
Whitechapel 13 M6
Whitton 123 H5
Widmore 168 C1
Willesden 69 J5
Willesden Green 69 K6
Wimbledon 146 C4
Winchmore Hill 29 H7
Wood End 82 C5
Wood End Green 82 C4
Woodford 45 F5
Woodford Bridge 45 K6
Woodford Green 44 E6
Woodford Wells 45 F2
Wood Green 41 G7
Woodlands 123 J2
Woodside 165 H5
Woodside Park 38 E3
Woolwich 115 F2
Worcester Park 173 K1
World's End 29 G3
The Wrythe 175 J1
Yeading 83 G3

USING THE STREET INDEX

Street names are listed alphabetically. Each street name is followed by its postal town or area locality, the Postcode District, the page number, and the reference to the square in which the name is found.

Standard index entries are shown as follows:

1 Av *WOOL/PLUM* SE18 **115** G2

Street names and selected addresses not shown on the map due to scale restrictions are shown in the index with an asterisk:

Abbeville Ms *CLAP* SW4 * **129** J4

Entries in red indicate streets located within the London Congestion Zone. Refer to the map pages for the location of the Zone boundary.

GENERAL ABBREVIATIONS

ACC	ACCESS	ASS	ASSOCIATION	BND	BEND	BTM	BOTTOM	CATH	CATHEDRAL
ALY	ALLEY	AV	AVENUE	BNK	BANK	BUS	BUSINESS	CEM	CEMETERY
AP	APPROACH	BCH	BEACH	BR	BRIDGE	BVD	BOULEVARD	CEN	CENTRE
AR	ARCADE	BLDS	BUILDINGS	BRK	BROOK	BY	BYPASS	CFT	CROFT

CH CHURCH
CHA CHASE
CHYD CHURCHYARD
CIR CIRCLE
CIRC CIRCUS
CL CLOSE
CLFS CLIFFS
CMP CAMP
CNR CORNER
CO COUNTY
COLL COLLEGE
COM COMMON
COMM COMMISSION
CON CONVENT
COT COTTAGE
COTS COTTAGES
CP CAPE
CPS COPSE
CR CREEK
CREM CREMATORIUM
CRS CRESCENT
CSWY CAUSEWAY
CT COURT
CTRL CENTRAL
CTS COURTS
CTYD COURTYARD
CUTT CUTTINGS
CV COVE
CYN CANYON
DEPT DEPARTMENT
DL DALE
DM DAM
DR DRIVE
DRO DROVE
DRY DRIVEWAY
DWGS DWELLINGS
E EAST
EMB EMBANKMENT
EMBY EMBASSY
ESP ESPLANADE
EST ESTATE
EX EXCHANGE
EXPY EXPRESSWAY
EXT EXTENSION
F/O FLYOVER
FC FOOTBALL CLUB
FK FORK
FLD FIELD
FLDS FIELDS
FLS FALLS
FM FARM
FT FORT
FTS FLATS
FWY FREEWAY
FY FERRY
GA GATE
GAL GALLERY
GDN GARDEN
GDNS GARDENS
GLD GLADE
GLN GLEN
GN GREEN
GND GROUND
GRA GRANGE
GRG GARAGE
GT GREAT
GTWY GATEWAY
GV GROVE
HGR HIGHER
HL HILL
HLS HILLS
HO HOUSE
HOL HOLLOW
HOSP HOSPITAL
HRB HARBOUR
HTH HEATH
HTS HEIGHTS
HVN HAVEN
HWY HIGHWAY
IMP IMPERIAL
IN INLET
IND EST INDUSTRIAL ESTATE
INF INFIRMARY
INFO INFORMATION
INT INTERCHANGE
IS ISLAND
JCT JUNCTION
JTY JETTY
KG KING
KNL KNOLL
L LAKE
LA LANE
LDG LODGE
LGT LIGHT
LK LOCK
LKS LAKES
LNDG LANDING
LTL LITTLE
LWR LOWER
MAG MAGISTRATE
MAN MANSIONS
MD MEAD
MDW MEADOWS
MEM MEMORIAL
MI MILL
MKT MARKET
MKTS MARKETS
ML MALL
MNR MANOR
MS MEWS
MSN MISSION
MT MOUNT
MTN MOUNTAIN
MTS MOUNTAINS
MUS MUSEUM
MWY MOTORWAY
N NORTH
NE NORTH EAST
NW NORTH WEST
O/P OVERPASS
OFF OFFICE
ORCH ORCHARD
OV OVAL
PAL PALACE
PAS PASSAGE
PAV PAVILION
PDE PARADE
PH PUBLIC HOUSE
PK PARK
PKWY PARKWAY
PL PLACE
PLN PLAIN
PLNS PLAINS
PLZ PLAZA
POL POLICE STATION
PR PRINCE
PREC PRECINCT
PREP PREPARATORY
PRIM PRIMARY
PROM PROMENADE
PRS PRINCESS
PRT PORT
PT POINT
PTH PATH
PZ PIAZZA
QD QUADRANT
QU QUEEN
QY QUAY
R RIVER
RBT ROUNDABOUT
RD ROAD
RDG RIDGE
REP REPUBLIC
RES RESERVOIR
RFC RUGBY FOOTBALL CLUB
RI RISE
RP RAMP
RW ROW
S SOUTH
SCH SCHOOL
SE SOUTH EAST
SER SERVICE AREA
SH SHORE
SHOP SHOPPING
SKWY SKYWAY
SMT SUMMIT
SOC SOCIETY
SP SPUR
SPR SPRING
SQ SQUARE
ST STREET
STN STATION
STR STREAM
STRD STRAND
SW SOUTH WEST
TDG TRADING
TER TERRACE
THWY THROUGHWAY
TNL TUNNEL
TOLL TOLLWAY
TPK TURNPIKE
TR TRACK
TRL TRAIL
TWR TOWER
U/P UNDERPASS
UNI UNIVERSITY
UPR UPPER
V VALE
VA VALLEY
VIAD VIADUCT
VIL VILLA
VIS VISTA
VLG VILLAGE
VLS VILLAS
VW VIEW
W WEST
WD WOOD
WHF WHARF
WK WALK
WKS WALKS
WLS WELLS
WY WAY
YD YARD
YHA YOUTH HOSTEL

POSTCODE TOWNS AND AREA ABBREVIATIONS

ABYW Abbey Wood
ACT Acton
ALP/SUD Alperton/Sudbury
ARCH Archway
ASHF Ashford (Surrey)
BAL Balham
BANK Bank
BAR Barnet
BARB Barbican
BARK Barking
BARK/HLT Barkingside/Hainault
BARN Barnes
BAY/PAD Bayswater/Paddington
BCTR Becontree
BECK Beckenham
BELMT Belmont
BELV Belvedere
BERM/RHTH Bermondsey/Rotherhithe
BETH Bethnal Green
BFN/LL Blackfen/Longlands
BGVA Belgravia
BKHH Buckhurst Hill
BKHTH/KID Blackheath/Kidbrooke
BLKFR Blackfriars
BMLY Bromley
BMSBY Bloomsbury
BORE Borehamwood
BOW Bow
BROCKY Brockley
BRXN/ST Brixton north/Stockwell
BRXS/STRHM Brixton south/Streatham Hill
BRYLDS Berrylands
BTFD Brentford
BTSEA Battersea
BUSH Bushey
BXLY Bexley
BXLYHN Bexleyheath north
BXLYHS Bexleyheath south
CAMTN Camden Town
CAN/RD Canning Town/Royal Docks
CANST Cannon Street station
CAR Carshalton
CAT Catford
CAVSQ/HST Cavendish Square/Harley Street
CDALE/KGS Colindale/Kingsbury
CEND/HSY/T Crouch End/Hornsey/Turnpike Lane
CHARL Charlton
CHCR Charing Cross
CHDH Chadwell Heath
CHEAM Cheam
CHEL Chelsea
CHIG Chigwell
CHING Chingford
CHSGTN Chessington
CHST Chislehurst
CHSWK Chiswick
CITYW City of London west
CLAP Clapham
CLAY Clayhall
CLKNW Clerkenwell
CLPT Clapton
CMBW Camberwell
CONDST Conduit Street
COVGDN Covent Garden
CRICK Cricklewood
CROY/NA Croydon/New Addington
CRW Collier Row
DAGE Dagenham east
DAGW Dagenham west
DART Dartford
DEN/HRF Denham/Harefield
DEPT Deptford
DUL Dulwich
E/WMO/HCT East & West Molesey/Hampton Court
EA Ealing
EBAR East Barnet
EBED/NFELT East Bedfont/North Feltham
ECT Earl's Court
ED Edmonton
EDGW Edgware
EDUL East Dulwich
EFNCH East Finchley
EHAM East Ham
ELTH/MOT Eltham/Mottingham
EMB Embankment
EMPK Emerson Park
EN Enfield
ENC/FH Enfield Chase/Forty Hill
ERITH Erith
ERITHM Erith Marshes
ESH/CLAY Esher/Claygate
EW Ewell
FARR Farringdon
FBAR/BDGN Friern Barnet/Bounds Green
FELT Feltham
FENCHST Fenchurch Street
FITZ Fitzrovia
FLST/FETLN Fleet Street/Fetter Lane
FNCH Finchley
FSBYE Finsbury east
FSBYPK Finsbury Park
FSBYW Finsbury west
FSTGT Forest Gate
FSTH Forest Hill
FUL/PGN Fulham/Parsons Green
GDMY/SEVK Goodmayes/Seven Kings
GFD/PVL Greenford/Perivale
GINN Gray's Inn
GLDGN Golders Green
GNTH/NBYPK Gants Hill/Newbury Park
GNWCH Greenwich
GPK Gidea Park
GSTN Garston
GTPST Great Portland Street
GWRST Gower Street
HACK Hackney
HAMP Hampstead
HAYES Hayes
HBRY Highbury
HCH Hornchurch
HCIRC Holborn Circus
HDN Hendon
HDTCH Houndsditch
HEST Heston
HGDN/ICK Hillingdon/Ickenham
HGT Highgate
HHOL High Holborn
HMSMTH Hammersmith
HNHL Herne Hill
HNWL Hanwell
HOL/ALD Holborn/Aldwych
HOLWY Holloway
HOM Homerton
HOR/WEW Horton/West Ewell
HPTN Hampton
HRW Harrow
HSLW Hounslow
HSLWW Hounslow west
HTHAIR Heathrow Airport
HYS/HAR Hayes/Harlington
IL Ilford
IS Islington
ISLW Isleworth
KENS Kensington
KIL/WHAMP Kilburn/West Hampstead
KTBR Knightsbridge
KTN/HRWW/WS Kenton/Harrow Weald/Wealdstone
KTTN Kentish Town
KUT/HW Kingston upon Thames/Hampton Wick
KUTN/CMB Kingston upon Thames north/Coombe
LBTH Lambeth
LEE/GVPK Lee/Grove Park
LEW Lewisham
LEY Leyton
LINN Lincoln's Inn
LOTH Lothbury
LSQ/SEVD Leicester Square/Seven Dials
LVPST Liverpool Street
MANHO Mansion House
MBLAR Marble Arch
MHST Marylebone High Street
MLHL Mill Hill
MNPK Manor Park
MON Monument
MORT/ESHN Mortlake/East Sheen
MRDN Morden
MTCM Mitcham
MUSWH Muswell Hill
MV/WKIL Maida Vale/West Kilburn
MYFR/PICC Mayfair/Piccadilly
MYFR/PKLN Mayfair/Park Lane
NFNCH/WDSPK North Finchley/Woodside Park
NKENS North Kensington
NOXST/BSQ New Oxford Street/Bloomsbury Square
NRWD Norwood
NTGHL Notting Hill
NTHLT Northolt
NTHWD Northwood
NWCR New Cross
NWDGN Norwood Green
NWMAL New Malden
OBST Old Broad Street
ORP Orpington
OXHEY Oxhey
OXSTW Oxford Street west
PECK Peckham
PEND Ponders End
PGE/AN Penge/Anerley
PIM Pimlico
PIN Pinner
PLMGR Palmers Green
PLSTW Plaistow
POP/IOD Poplar/Isle of Dogs
PUR Purfleet
PUR/KEN Purley/Kenley
PUT/ROE Putney/Roehampton
RAIN Rainham (Gt Lon)
RCH/KEW Richmond/Kew
RCHPK/HAM Richmond Park/Ham
RDART Rural Dartford
REDBR Redbridge
REGST Regent Street
RKW/CH/CXG Rickmansworth/Chorleywood/Croxley Green
ROM Romford
ROMW/RG Romford west/Rush Green
RSLP Ruislip
RSQ Russell Square
RYLN/HDSTN Rayners Lane/Headstone
RYNPK Raynes Park
SAND/SEL Sanderstead/Selsdon
SCUP Sidcup
SDTCH Shoreditch
SEVS/STOTM Seven Sisters/South Tottenham
SHB Shepherd's Bush
SHPTN Shepperton
SKENS South Kensington
SNWD South Norwood
SOCK/AV South Ockendon/Aveley
SOHO/CST Soho/Carnaby Street
SOHO/SHAV Soho/Shaftesbury Avenue
SRTFD Stratford
STAN Stanmore
STBT St Bart's
STHGT/OAK Southgate/Oakwood
STHL Southall
STHWK Southwark
STJS St James's
STJSPK St James's Park
STJWD St John's Wood
STKPK Stockley Park
STLK St Luke's
STMC/STPC St Mary Cray/St Paul's Cray
STNW/STAM Stoke Newington/Stamford Hill
STP St Paul's
STPAN St Pancras
STRHM/NOR Streatham/Norbury
STWL/WRAY Stanwell/Wraysbury
SUN Sunbury
SURB Surbiton
SUT Sutton
SWFD South Woodford
SYD Sydenham
TEDD Teddington
THDIT Thames Ditton
THHTH Thornton Heath
THMD Thamesmead
TOOT Tooting
TOTM Tottenham
TPL/STR Temple/Strand
TRDG/WHET Totteridge/Whetstone
TWK Twickenham
TWRH Tower Hill
UED Upper Edmonton
UX/CGN Uxbridge/Colham Green
VX/NE Vauxhall/Nine Elms
WALTH Walthamstow
WALW Walworth
WAN Wanstead
WAND/EARL Wandsworth/Earlsfield
WAP Wapping
WAT Watford
WATN Watford north
WATW Watford west
WBLY Wembley
WBPTN West Brompton
WCHMH Winchmore Hill
WCHPL Whitechapel
WDGN Wood Green
WDR/YW West Drayton/Yiewsley
WEA West Ealing
WELL Welling
WEST Westminster
WESTW Westminster west
WFD Woodford
WHALL Whitehall
WHTN Whitton
WIM/MER Wimbledon/Merton
WKENS West Kensington
WLGTN Wallington
WLSDN Willesden
WNWD West Norwood
WOOL/PLUM Woolwich/Plumstead
WOT/HER Walton-on-Thames/Hersham
WPK Worcester Park
WWKM West Wickham
YEAD Yeading

Index - streets

1

1 Av *WOOL/PLUM* SE18 **115** G2

A

Aaron Hill Rd *EHAM* E6 **96** A4
Abberley Ms *BTSEA* SW11 **129** G2
Abbess Cl *BRXS/STRHM* SW2 **130** C7
Abbeville Ms *CLAP* SW4 * **129** J4
Abbeville Rd *CEND/HSY/T* N8 **54** D3
CLAP SW4 **129** H5
Abbey Av *ALP/SUD* HA0 **86** A1
Abbey Cl *HYS/HAR* UB3 **83** F7
NTHLT UB5 **83** K2
PIN HA5 **47** F2
ROM RM1 **63** H5
Abbey Crs *BELV* DA17 **117** H3
Abbeydale Rd *ALP/SUD* HA0 **68** B7
Abbey Dr *TOOT* SW17 **148** A4
Abbeyfield Cl *MTCM* CR4 **162** D1
Abbeyfield Est
BERM/RHTH SE16 **111** K3
Abbeyfield Rd
BERM/RHTH SE16 **111** K3
Abbeyfields Cl *WLSDN* NW10 **86** C2
Abbey Gdns *CHST* BR7 **154** A7
HMSMTH W6 **107** H5
STHWK SE1 **111** H3
STJWD NW8 **2** E6
Abbey Gv *ABYW* SE2 **116** C3
Abbeyhill Rd *BFN/LL* DA15 **136** D7
Abbey La *BECK* BR3 **151** J6
SRTFD E15 **94** A1
Abbey Ms *ISLW* TW7 **104** C7
WALTH E17 **57** J4
Abbey Mt *BELV* DA17 **117** G4
Abbey Orchard St *WEST* SW1P **17** H3
Abbey Pk *BECK* BR3 **151** J6
Abbey Pl *DART* DA1 * **139** G4
Abbey Rd *BARK* IG11 **78** B7
BELV DA17 **116** E3
CROY/NA CR0 **177** H2
EN EN1 **30** A4
GNTH/NBYPK IG2 **60** D4
KIL/WHAMP NW6 **2** C3
SRTFD E15 **94** B1
STJWD NW8 **2** E4
WIM/MER SW19 **147** G6
WLSDN NW10 **86** D1
Abbey St *PLSTW* E13 **94** E3
STHWK SE1 **19** L3
Abbey Vw *MLHL* NW7 **37** H2
Abbey Wk *E/WMO/HCT* KT8 **157** G2
Abbey Wood Rd *ABYW* SE2 **116** C3
Abbot Cl *RSLP* HA4 **65** H2
Abbotsbury Cl *SRTFD* E15 **94** A1
WKENS W14 **107** H1
Abbotsbury Gdns *PIN* HA5 **47** G5
Abbotsbury Ms *PECK* SE15 **131** K2
Abbotsbury Rd *MRDN* SM4 **162** A3
WKENS W14 **107** H1
WWKM BR4 **180** D1
Abbots Cl *STMC/STPC* BR5 **169** H7
Abbots Dr *RYLN/HDSTN* HA2 **66** A1
Abbotsford Av
SEVS/STOTM N15 **55** J3
Abbotsford Gdns *WFD* IG8 **44** E6
Abbotsford Rd
GDMY/SEVK IG3 **79** G1
Abbots Gdns *EFNCH* N2 **53** H3
Abbots Gn *CROY/NA* CR0 **179** F5
Abbotshade Rd
BERM/RHTH SE16 * **93** F7
Abbotshall Av
STHGT/OAK N14 **40** C2
Abbotshall Rd *CAT* SE6 **133** G7
Abbotsleigh Cl *BELMT* SM2 **175** F6
Abbotsleigh Rd
STRHM/NOR SW16 **148** C3
Abbots Mnr *PIM* SW1V **16** C7
Abbots Manor Est *PIM* SW1V **16** C7
Abbotsmede Cl *TWK* TW1 **143** F1
Abbots Pk *BRXS/STRHM* SW2 **130** B7
Abbot's Pl *KIL/WHAMP* NW6 **2** C3
Abbots Rd *EDGW* HA8 **37** F6
EHAM E6 **77** H7
Abbots Ter *CEND/HSY/T* N8 **54** E5
Abbotstone Rd
PUT/ROE SW15 **127** F2
Abbot St *HACK* E8 **74** B5
Abbots Wk *KENS* W8 * **14** C4
Abbots Wy *BECK* BR3 **166** B4
Abbotswell Rd *BROCKY* SE4 **132** C4
Abbotswood Cl *BELV* DA17 **117** F2
Abbotswood Gdns *CLAY* IG5 **59** K2
Abbotswood Rd *EDUL* SE22 **131** F3
STRHM/NOR SW16 **148** D2
Abbotswood Wy
HYS/HAR UB3 **83** F7
Abbott Av *RYNPK* SW20 **161** G1
Abbott Cl *HPTN* TW12 **141** J5
NTHLT UB5 **65** K5
Abbott Rd *POP/IOD* E14 **94** A4
Abbotts Cl *IS* N1 * **6** E1
ROMW/RG RM7 **62** D2
THMD SE28 **97** J6
Abbotts Crs *CHING* E4 **44** B3
ENC/FH EN2 **29** H1
Abbotts Dr *ALP/SUD* HA0 **67** H1
Abbotts Md
RCHPK/HAM TW10 * **143** J3
Abbotts Park Rd *LEY* E10 **58** A6
Abbotts Rd *BAR* EN5 **27** F3
CHEAM SM3 **174** C3
MTCM CR4 **163** H3
STHL UB1 **83** J7
Abbott's Wk *BXLYHN* DA7 **116** E6
Abchurch La *MANHO* EC4N **13** H6
Abdale Rd *SHB* W12 **87** K7
Aberavon Rd *BOW* E3 **93** G2
Abercairn Rd
STRHM/NOR SW16 **148** C6
Aberconway Rd *MRDN* SM4 **162** A2
Abercorn Cl *MLHL* NW7 **38** C6
STJWD NW8 **2** E6
Abercorn Crs
RYLN/HDSTN HA2 **48** B7
Abercorn Dell *BUSH* WD23 **34** C1
Abercorn Gdns *CHDH* RM6 **61** H5
KTN/HRWW/WS HA3 **49** K6

184 Abe - Ale

Street	Area/Postcode	Page	Grid
Abercorn Gv	RSLP HA4	46	B3
Abercorn Ms	RCHPK/HAM TW10	125	G4
Abercorn Pl	STJWD NW8	2	E7
Abercorn Rd	MLHL NW7	38	C6
	STAN HA7	35	J6
Abercorn Wk	STJWD NW8	2	E7
Abercrombie St	BTSEA SW11	128	C1
Aberdare Cl	WWKM BR4	180	A1
Aberdare Gdns	KIL/WHAMP NW6	2	B1
	MLHL NW7	38	B6
Aberdare Rd	PEND EN3	30	E2
Aberdeen Cots	STAN HA7 *	35	J6
Aberdeen La	HBRY N5	73	H4
Aberdeen Pde	UED N18	42	D4
Aberdeen Pk	HBRY N5	73	H4
Aberdeen Pl	BAY/PAD W2	9	G1
Aberdeen Rd	CROY/NA CR0	177	J3
	HBRY N5	73	J3
	KTN/HRWW/WS HA3	49	F1
	UED N18	42	D4
	WLSDN NW10	69	H4
Aberdeen Ter	BKHTH/KID SE3	133	F1
Aberdour Rd	GDMY/SEVK IG3	79	H2
Aberdour St	STHWK SE1	19	H6
Aberfeldy St	POP/IOD E14	94	B4
Aberford Gdns	WOOL/PLUM SE18	114	D7
Aberford Rd	BORE WD6	24	C1
Aberfoyle Rd	STRHM/NOR SW16	148	E6
Abergeldie Rd	LEE/GVPK SE12	134	A5
Abernethy Rd	LEW SE13	133	H3
Abersham Rd	HACK E8	74	B4
Abery St	WOOL/PLUM SE18	115	K3
Abingdon Cl	WIM/MER SW19	147	G5
	WPK KT4	173	K2
Abingdon Rd	FNCH N3	53	F2
	KENS W8	14	B4
	STRHM/NOR SW16	148	E7
Abingdon St	WEST SW1P	17	J2
Abingdon Vls	KENS W8	14	A4
Abinger Av	BELMT SM2	174	A7
Abinger Cl	BMLY BR1	168	E3
	CROY/NA CR0	180	A5
	GDMY/SEVK IG3	79	G4
	WLGTN SM6	176	E4
Abinger Dr	NRWD SE19	149	J6
Abinger Gdns	ISLW TW7	123	K2
Abinger Gv	DEPT SE8	112	C5
Abinger Ms	MV/WKIL W9	2	A7
Abinger Rd	CHSWK W4	106	C1
Ablett St	BERM/RHTH SE16	111	K4
Abney Park Ter	STNW/STAM N16	74	B1
Aboyne Dr	RYNPK SW20	160	D1
Aboyne Rd	TOOT SW17	147	G2
	WLSDN NW10	69	G2
Abraham Cl	OXHEY WD19	33	F3
Abridge Wy	BARK IG11	97	K1
Abyssinia Cl	BTSEA SW11	128	D3
Abyssinia Rd	BTSEA SW11 *	128	D3
Acacia Av	BTFD TW8	104	C6
	HCH RM12	81	H1
	HYS/HAR UB3	82	D5
	RSLP HA4	46	E7
	TOTM N17	41	J6
	WBLY HA9	68	A4
Acacia Cl	DEPT SE8	112	B3
	STAN HA7	34	E5
	STMC/STPC BR5	169	J5
Acacia Gdns	STJWD NW8	3	H5
	WWKM BR4	180	A1
Acacia Gv	DUL SE21	149	K1
	NWMAL KT3	160	B2
Acacia Ms	WDR/YW UB7	100	A5
Acacia Pl	STJWD NW8	3	H5
Acacia Rd	ACT W3	86	E6
	BECK BR3	166	C2
	HPTN TW12	142	A5
	MTCM CR4	163	F1
	STJWD NW8	3	H5
	STRHM/NOR SW16	148	E7
	WALTH E17	57	G5
	WAN E11	76	C2
	WDGN N22	41	G7
The Acacias	EBAR EN4 *	27	H4
Acacia Wy	BFN/LL DA15	136	A7
Academia Wy	TOTM N17	42	A4
Academy Fields Rd	GPK RM2	63	K4
Academy Gdns	CROY/NA CR0	165	G7
	NTHLT UB5	83	H1
Academy Pl	ISLW TW7	103	K6
	WOOL/PLUM SE18	114	C7
Acanthus Dr	STHWK SE1	111	H4
Acanthus Rd	BTSEA SW11	129	F2
Accommodation Rd	GLDGN NW11	52	D6
Ace Av	CHSGTN KT9	172	A6
Acer Av	YEAD UB4	83	J3
Acfold Rd	FUL/PGN SW6	108	A7
Achilles Cl	STHWK SE1	111	H4
Achilles Rd	KIL/WHAMP NW6	70	E4
Achilles St	NWCR SE14	112	B6
Acklam Rd	NKENS W10	88	D4
Acklington Dr	CDALE/KGS NW9	37	G2
Ackmar Rd	FUL/PGN SW6	107	K7
Ackroyd Dr	BOW E3	93	H4
Ackroyd Rd	FSTH SE23	132	B6
Acland Cr	WOOL/PLUM SE18	115	J6
Acland Rd	CRICK NW2	69	K5
Acock Gv	NTHLT UB5	66	B3
Acol Crs	RSLP HA4	65	F4
Acol Rd	KIL/WHAMP NW6	2	B1
Acorn Cl	CHING E4	43	K4
	CHST BR7	154	C4
	HPTN TW12	142	B5
	STAN HA7	35	H6
Acorn Gdns	ACT W3	87	F4
	NRWD SE19	150	B7
Acorn Gv	HYS/HAR UB3	101	K6
	RSLP HA4	64	E3
Acorn Pde	PECK SE15 *	111	J6
Acorns Wy	ESH/CLAY KT10	170	C4
Acorn Wy	BECK BR3	167	F4
	FSTH SE23	151	F2
Acre La	BRXS/STRHM SW2	130	A6
	CAR SM5	176	A3
Acre Rd	DAGE RM10	80	D6
	WIM/MER SW19	147	H5
Acre Wy	NTHWD HA6	32	D7
Acris St	WAND/EARL SW18	128	B5
Acton Cl	ED N9	42	C1
Acton Hill Ms	ACT W3 *	86	D7
Acton La	CHSWK W4	105	K2
	CHSWK W4	7	L3
Acton St	FSBYW WC1X	5	L8
Acuba Rd	WAND/EARL SW18	147	G1
Acworth Cl	ED N9	30	E6
Acworth Pl	DART DA1 *	139	F5
Ada Cl	FBAR/BDGN N11	39	K2
Ada Gdns	POP/IOD E14	94	B5
	SRTFD E15	76	D7
Adair Cl	SNWD SE25	165	J2
Adair Rd	NKENS W10	88	C3
Adam Cl	CAT SE6	151	H3
	FSTH SE23	150	E1
Adam & Eve Ms	KENS W8	14	B3
Adam Rd	CHING E4	43	H5
Adams Cl	BRYLDS KT5	159	G5
	FNCH N3	38	E6
	WBLY HA9	68	D1
Adams Ct	OBST EC2N	13	H4
Adams Ms	TOOT SW17	147	K1
	WDGN N22	41	F6
	HAMP NW3	71	H4
Adamson Rd	CAN/RD E16	94	E5
Adamson Wy	BECK BR3	167	F4
Adamsrill Cl	EN EN1	29	K5
Adamsrill Rd	SYD SE26	151	F3
Adams Rd	BECK BR3	166	B3
	TOTM N17	55	K1
Adam's Rw	MYFR/PKLN W1K	10	B7
Adam St	CHCR WC2N	11	K7
Adams Wk	KUT/HW KT1	159	F4
Adam Wk	FUL/PGN SW6	107	F6
Ada Pl	BETH E2	74	C7
Adare Wk	STRHM/NOR SW16	148	E1
Ada Rd	ALP/SUD HA0 *	67	J2
Ada St	HACK E8	74	D7
Adderley Gdns	ELTH/MOT SE9	154	A2
Adderley Gv	BTSEA SW11	129	F4
Adderley Rd	KTN/HRWW/WS HA3	35	F7
Adderley St	POP/IOD E14	94	A5
Addington Dr	NFNCH/WDSPK N12	39	J5
Addington Rd	CAN/RD E16	94	C3
	CROY/NA CR0	164	B7
	FSBYPK N4	55	G6
	WWKM BR4	180	A3
Addington Sq	CMBW SE5	110	D6
Addington St	STHWK SE1	17	M2
Addington Village Rd	CROY/NA CR0	179	H6
Addis Cl	EN EN1	30	E1
Addiscombe Cl	KTN/HRWW/WS HA3	49	J4
Addiscombe Court Rd	CROY/NA CR0	165	F7
Addiscombe Gv	CROY/NA CR0	177	K1
Addiscombe Rd	CROY/NA CR0	177	K1
	WATW WD18	21	F3
Addison Av	HSLW TW3	103	H7
	NTGHL W11	88	C7
	STHGT/OAK N14	28	B5
Addison Bridge Pl	WKENS W14	107	J3
Addison Cl	NTHWD HA6	32	E7
	STMC/STPC BR5	169	J5
Addison Crs	WKENS W14	107	H2
Addison Dr	LEE/GVPK SE12	134	A4
Addison Gdns	BRYLDS KT5	159	G3
	WKENS W14	107	G2
Addison Gv	CHSWK W4	106	B2
Addison Pl	NTGHL W11	88	C7
	SNWD SE25	165	H3
	TEDD TW11	143	H5
	WALTH E17	57	K4
	WAN E11	58	F5
Addison's Cl	CROY/NA CR0	179	H1
Addison Ter	CHSWK W4 *	105	K3
Addison Wy	GLDGN NW11	52	D2
	HYS/HAR UB3	82	E5
	NTHWD HA6	32	D7
Addle Hl	BLKFR EC4V	12	D6
Addle St	CITYW EC2V	12	F4
Adecroft Wy	E/WMO/HCT KT8	157	J3
Adela Av	NWMAL KT3	160	E4
Adelaide Av	BROCKY SE4	132	C3
Adelaide Cl	STAN HA7	35	G3
	EN EN1	30	A1
Adelaide Cots	HNWL W7	104	A1
Adelaide Gdns	CHDH RM6	62	A4
Adelaide Gv	SHB W12	87	J7
Adelaide Ms	CHST BR7	154	B4
	HAMP NW3	3	J1
	HEST TW5	102	D7
	IL IG1	78	A2
	LEY E10	76	A2
	NWDGN UB2	102	D3
	PUT/ROE SW15	127	K4
	RCH/KEW TW9	125	G3
	STJWD NW8	3	G2
	SURB KT6	159	F4
	TEDD TW11	143	F5
	WEA W13	104	B1
Adelaide St	CHCR WC2N	11	J7
	BTFD TW8 *	104	F4
Adela St	NKENS W10	88	C3
Adelina Gv	WCHPL E1	92	E4
Adelina Ms	BAL SW12	129	J7
Adeline Pl	RSQ WC1B	11	H3
Adeliza Rd	BARK IG11	78	C6
Adelphi Crs	HCH RM12	81	G2
Adelphi Rd	EPSOM KT17 *	82	C2
Adelphi Ter	CHCR WC2N	11	K7
Adelphi Wy	YEAD UB4	82	D4
Adeney Cl	HMSMTH W6	107	G5
Aden Gv	STNW/STAM N16	73	K3
Adenmore Rd	CAT SE6	132	D6
Aden Rd	IL IG1	60	A7
	PEND EN3	31	G3
Adhara Rd	NTHWD HA6	32	D4
Adie Rd	HMSMTH W6	107	F3
Adine Rd	PLSTW E13	95	F3
Adler St	WCHPL E1	92	C5
Adley St	CLPT E5	75	G4
Adlington Cl	UED N18	41	K4
Admaston Rd	WOOL/PLUM SE18	115	H6
Admiral Ms	NKENS W10	88	B3
Admiral Pl	BERM/RHTH SE16	93	F7
Admirals Cl	WALTH E17	58	F5
Admiral Seymour Rd	ELTH/MOT SE9	134	E3
Admiral's Ga	GNWCH SE10	112	E7
Admiral St	DEPT SE8	112	D7
Admiral's Wk	HAMP NW3	71	G2
Admirals Wy	POP/IOD E14	112	D1
Admiralty Cl	DEPT SE8	112	D7
Admiralty Rd	TEDD TW11	143	F5
Admiralty Wy	TEDD TW11 *	143	F5
Admiral Wk	MV/WKIL W9	2	B7
Adnams Wk	RAIN RM13	81	J4
Adolf St	CAT SE6	151	K4
Adolphus Rd	FSBYPK N4	73	H1
Adolphus St	DEPT SE8	112	C6
Adomar Rd	BCTR RM8	79	K2
Adpar St	BAY/PAD W2	9	G2
Adrian Cl	BAR EN5	26	B5
Adrienne Av	STHL UB1	83	K3
Advance Rd	WNWD SE27	149	J3
Advent Wy	UED N18	43	H4
Adys Lawn	CRICK NW2	69	K5
Ady's Rd	PECK SE15	131	G2
Aerodrome Rd	CDALE/KGS NW9	51	H2
Aerodrome Wy	HEST TW5	102	B5
Aeroville	CDALE/KGS NW9	51	G1
Affleck St	IS N1	5	M6
Afghan Rd	BTSEA SW11	128	D1
Aftab Ter	WCHPL E1 *	92	D3
Agamemnon Rd	KIL/WHAMP NW6	70	D4
Agar Cl	SURB KT6	172	B1
Agar Gv	CAMTN NW1	5	H1
Agar Pl	CAMTN NW1 *	4	F1
Agar St	CHCR WC2N	11	J7
Agate Cl	CAN/RD E16	95	H5
Agate Rd	HMSMTH W6	107	F2
Agaton Rd	ELTH/MOT SE9	154	C2
Agave Rd	CRICK NW2	70	A3
Agdon St	FSBYE EC1V	6	C9
Agincourt Rd	HAMP NW3	71	K3
Agnes Cl	EHAM E6	96	A6
Agnes Ct	IL IG1 *	78	A3
Agnesfield Cl	NFNCH/WDSPK N12	39	J5
Agnes Gdns	BCTR RM8	79	K3
Agnes Rd	ACT W3	106	C1
Agnes Riley Gdns	CLAP SW4 *	129	H6
Agnes St	POP/IOD E14	93	H5
Agnew Rd	FSTH SE23	132	B6
Agricola Pl	EN EN1	30	B5
Aidan Cl	BCTR RM8	80	A3
Ailsa Av	TWK TW1	124	B4
Ailsa Rd	TWK TW1	124	C4
Ailsa St	POP/IOD E14	94	A4
Ainger Ms	HAMP NW3 *	3	M2
Ainger Rd	HAMP NW3	3	L1
Ainsdale Cl	ORP BR6	169	J7
Ainsdale Crs	PIN HA5	48	A2
Ainsdale Dr	STHWK SE1	111	H4
Ainsdale Rd	EA W5	85	K3
	OXHEY WD19	33	G4
Ainsley Av	ROMW/RG RM7	62	E5
Ainsley Cl	ED N9	30	A7
Ainsley St	BETH E2	92	D2
Ainslie Wood Crs	CHING E4	43	K4
Ainslie Wood Gdns	CHING E4	43	K3
Ainslie Wood Rd	CHING E4	43	J4
Ainsty St	BERM/RHTH SE16 *	111	K1
Ainsworth Cl	CMBW SE5 *	131	F1
	CRICK NW2	69	J2
	HOM E9	74	E6
Ainsworth Rd	CROY/NA CR0	164	B7
Ainsworth Wy	STJWD NW8	2	F1
Aintree Av	EHAM E6	77	J7
Aintree Crs	BARK/HLT IG6	60	C1
Aintree Rd	GFD/PVL UB6	85	H1
Aintree Rd	FUL/PGN SW6	107	H6
Airco Cl	CDALE/KGS NW9	50	E2
Airdrie Cl	IS N1	5	L2
	YEAD UB4	83	J4
Airedale Av	CHSWK W4	106	C4
Airedale Av South	CHSWK W4	106	C4
Airedale Rd	BAL SW12	128	E6
	EA W5	104	D2
Airfield Wy	HCH RM12	81	K5
Airlie Gdns	IL IG1	60	B7
	KENS W8	8	C8
Air St	REGST W1B	10	F7
Airthrie Rd	GDMY/SEVK IG3	61	H7
Aisgill Av	WKENS W14	107	J4
Aisher Rd	THMD SE28	97	J6
Aislibie Rd	LEE/GVPK SE12	133	H3
Aiten Pl	HMSMTH W6 *	106	D3
Aitken Cl	HACK E8	74	C7
	MTCM CR4	162	E7
Aitken Rd	BAR EN5	26	A4
	CAT SE6	151	K1
Aitman Dr	BTFD TW8 *	105	G4
Ajax Av	CDALE/KGS NW9	51	G2
Ajax Rd	KIL/WHAMP NW6	70	D3
Akabusi Cl	CROY/NA CR0	165	H6
Akehurst St	PUT/ROE SW15	126	D5
Akenside Rd	HAMP NW3	71	H4
Akerman Rd	BRXN/ST SW9	110	C7
	SURB KT6	158	D5
Alabama St	WOOL/PLUM SE18	115	J6
Alacross Rd	EA W5	104	D1
Alandale Dr	PIN HA5	33	F7
Alander Ms	WALTH E17	57	K3
Alan Dr	BAR EN5	26	C5
Alan Gdns	ROMW/RG RM7	62	C6
Alan Hocken Wy	SRTFD E15	94	C1
Alan Rd	WIM/MER SW19	146	C4
Alaska St	STHWK SE1	12	A9
Alba Cl	YEAD UB4	83	H3
Alba Cots	LEW SE13 *	132	C5
Alba Gdns	GLDGN NW11	52	C5
Alban Hw	BUSH WD23	22	D5
Albany Cl	BXLY DA5	136	D6
	ESH/CLAY KT10	170	C5
	MORT/ESHN SW14	125	J3
	SEVS/STOTM N15	55	J3
Albany Cots	HNWL W7 *	85	F7
Albany Crs	EDGW HA8	36	C6
	ESH/CLAY KT10	170	D5
Albany Ms	BMLY BR1	152	E6
	CMBW SE5	110	D5
	IS N1	6	A2
	KUTN/CMB KT2 *	143	K5
	SUT SM1	175	F4
Albany Pde	BTFD TW8 *	105	F5
Albany Park Rd	KUTN/CMB KT2	143	K5
Albany Pl	BTFD TW8	105	F5
	BRYN N7 *	73	G3
Albany Rd	BELV DA17	117	G4
	BXLY DA5	136	D6
	CHDH RM6	61	K5
	CHST BR7	154	G5
	CMBW SE5	19	J9
	EA W5	85	J6
	ESH/CLAY KT10	170	C6
	HCH RM12	81	H3
	HSLW TW3	123	F3
	HYS/HAR UB3	82	C5
	LEY E10	57	J6
	MNPK E12	77	G2
	NWMAL KT3	160	A3
	RCHPK/HAM TW10 *	125	F3
	ROM RM1	63	H5
	RYLN/HDSTN HA2	48	C2
	SEVS/STOTM N15	56	A4
	SNWD SE25	165	J4
	SUT SM1	175	F3
	SWFD E18	59	F2
	TEDD TW11	143	F5
	TWK TW1	124	C7
	WALTH E17	57	H5
	WDGN N22	40	D7
Albert Rd North	WAT WD17	21	F2
Albert Rd South	WAT WD17	21	F2
Albert Sq	SRTFD E15	76	D4
	VX/NE SW8	110	A6
Albert St	CAMTN NW1	4	E3
	VX/NE SW8	110	A6
Albert Terrace Ms	CAMTN NW1 *	4	B3
Albert Wy	PECK SE15	111	J6
Albion Av	MUSWH N10	40	A7
	VX/NE SW8	129	J1
Albion Cl	BAY/PAD W2	9	K6
	ROMW/RG RM7	63	F6
Albion Dr	BAR EN5	7 *	M2
Albion Est	BERM/RHTH SE16 *	111	M2
Albion Ga	BAY/PAD W2	9	K6
Albion Gv	STNW/STAM N16	74	A3
Albion Ms	BAY/PAD W2	9	K6
	HMSMTH W6 *	106	D3
	IS N1	6	A3
Albion Pde	FARR EC1M	12	C2
	STNW/STAM N16 *	73	K2
Albion Pk	LEW SE13	132	D4
Albion Riverside	BTSEA SW11	108	D6
Albion Rd	BELMT SM2	175	G6
	BXLYHS DA6	137	G3
	HSLW TW3	123	F3
	HYS/HAR UB3	82	C5
	KUTN/CMB KT2	144	C7
	STNW/STAM N16	73	K3
	TOTM N17	56	B2
	WALTH E17	58	A2
	WHTN TW2	123	K7
Albion Sq	HACK E8	7	M1
Albion St	BAY/PAD W2	9	K5
	BERM/RHTH SE16	111	K1
	CROY/NA CR0	164	C7
Albion Ter	CHING E4	31	K6
	HACK E8	7	M1
Albion Villas Rd	SYD SE26	150	E2
Albion Wk	IS N1	5	K5
Albion Wy	LEW SE13	133	F3
	STBT EC1A	12	E3
Albion Yd	IS N1	5	K5
Albrighton Rd	EDUL SE22	131	F1
Albury Av	BELMT SM2	174	A5
	ISLW TW7	104	A7
Albury Cl	HOR/WEW KT19	172	D4
Albury Dr	PIN HA5	33	G7
Albury Ms	MNPK E12	59	G7
Albury St	DEPT SE8	112	D5
Albyfield	BMLY BR1	168	E2
Albyn Rd	DEPT SE8	112	D7
Alcester Crs	CLPT E5	74	F1
Alcock Cl	WLGTN SM6	176	D6
Alcock Rd	HEST TW5	102	C6
Alconbury Rd	CLPT E5	74	C1
Alcorn Cl	CHEAM SM3	174	E1
Alcott Cl	HNWL W7	85	F4
Aldborough Rd	DAGE RM10	80	E5
Aldborough Rd North	GNTH/NBYPK IG2	61	F4
Aldborough Rd South	GDMY/SEVK IG3	60	E7
Aldbourne Rd	SHB W12	87	H7
Aldbridge St	WALW SE17	19	K7
Aldburgh Ms	MHST W1U	10	B4
Aldbury Av	WBLY HA9	68	D6
Aldbury Ms	ED N9	29	K6
Aldebert Ter	VX/NE SW8	110	A6
Aldeburgh Cl	WFD IG8	44	E3
Aldeburgh St	SRTFD E15	94	D2
Aldenham Rd	BORE WD6	23	F1
	BUSH WD23	21	J4
	OXHEY WD19	21	H5
Aldenham St	CAMTN NW1	4	F6
Alden Md	PIN HA5 *	34	A6
Aldensley Rd	HMSMTH W6	106	E2
Alderbrook Rd	BAL SW12	129	G6
Alderbury Rd	BARN SW13	106	D5
Alder Cl	PECK SE15	111	G5
Alder Gv	CRICK NW2	69	J1
Alderholt Wy	PECK SE15 *	111	F6
Alderman Av	BARK IG11	97	G2
Aldermanbury	CITYW EC2V *	12	F4
Aldermanbury Sq	CITYW EC2V	12	F3
Alderman Judge Ml	KUT/HW KT1 *	159	F1
Alderman's Hl	PLMGR N13	40	E3
Alderman's Wk	BMLY BR1	152	E7
Aldermoor Rd	CAT SE6	151	H2
Alderney Av	HEST TW5	103	F6
Alderney Gdns	NTHLT UB5	65	K6
Alderney Ms	STHWK SE1	19	G3
Alderney Rd	ERITH DA8	118	D6
	WCHPL E1	93	F3
Alderney St	PIM SW1V	16	C6
Alder Rd	MORT/ESHN SW14	126	A2
	SCUP DA14	155	G2
Alders Av	WFD IG8	44	C5
Aldersbrook Av	EN EN1	30	A1
Aldersbrook Dr	KUTN/CMB KT2	144	B5
Aldersbrook La	MNPK E12	77	H2
Aldersbrook Rd	MNPK E12	77	J2
Alders Cl	EA W5	104	E2
	EDGW HA8	36	E4
	WAN E11	77	F1
Aldersey Gdns	BARK IG11	78	D5
Aldersford Cl	BROCKY SE4	132	A3
Aldersgate St	CITYW EC2V	12	E4
Aldersgrove	E/WMO/HCT KT8 *	157	J4
Aldersgrove Av	ELTH/MOT SE9	153	G2
Aldershot Rd	KIL/WHAMP NW6	70	D7
Aldershot Ter	WOOL/PLUM SE18 *	115	F6
Aldersmead Av	CROY/NA CR0	166	A5
Aldersmead Rd	BECK BR3	151	G6
Alderson Pl	NWDGN UB2	84	C7
Alderson St	NKENS W10	88	C3
Alders Rd	EDGW HA8	36	E4
The Alders	FELT TW13	141	J4
	HEST TW5	102	E5
	STRHM/NOR SW16 *	148	C3
	WCHMH N21	29	G5
	WWKM BR4	166	A7
Alderton Cl	WLSDN NW10	69	F2
Alderton Crs	HDN NW4	51	K4
Alderton Rd	CROY/NA CR0	165	G6
	HNHL SE24	130	D2
Alderton Wy	HDN NW4	51	K4
Alderville Rd	FUL/PGN SW6	127	J1
Alderwick Dr	HSLW TW3	123	J2
Alderwood Rd	ELTH/MOT SE9	135	K5
Aldford St	MYFR/PKLN W1K	10	A8
Aldgate	FENCHST EC3M	13	K5
Aldgate Barrs	WCHPL E1 *	13	M4
Aldgate High St	TWRH EC3N	13	L5
Aldine Pl	SHB W12 *	107	F1
Aldingham Gdns	HCH RM12	81	J1
Aldington Cl	CHDH RM6	61	J6
Aldington Rd	CHARL SE7	114	A2
Aldis Ms	TOOT SW17	147	J4
Aldis St	TOOT SW17	147	J4
Aldred Rd	KIL/WHAMP NW6	70	E4
Aldrich Crs	CROY/NA CR0	180	A7
Aldriche Wy	CHING E4	44	A5
Aldrich Gdns	CHEAM SM3	174	D1
Aldrich Ter	WAND/EARL SW18	147	G1
Aldridge Av	EDGW HA8	36	D2
	RSLP HA4	65	H1
	STAN HA7	36	A7
Aldridge Ri	NWMAL KT3	160	B6
Aldridge Road Vls	NTGHL W11	88	D4
Aldridge Wk	STHGT/OAK N14	28	E6
Aldrington Rd	STRHM/NOR SW16	148	C4
Aldsworth Cl	MV/WKIL W9	2	B8
Aldwick Cl	ELTH/MOT SE9	154	D2
Aldwick Rd	CROY/NA CR0	177	F2
Aldworth Gv	LEW SE13	133	F5
Aldworth Rd	SRTFD E15	76	C6
Aldwych	HOL/ALD WC2B	11	L5
Aldwych Av	BARK/HLT IG6	60	C3
Aldwych Cl	HCH RM12	81	J2
Alers Rd	BXLYHS DA6	136	E4
Alesia Cl	WDGN N22	40	E6
Alestan Beck Rd	CAN/RD E16	95	H5
Alexa Ct	KENS W8	14	C5
Alexander Av	WLSDN NW10	69	K6
Alexander Cl	BFN/LL DA15	135	K5
	EBAR EN4	27	H4
	HAYES BR2	181	J5
	NWDGN UB2	103	H2
	WHTN TW2	142	E2
Alexander Evans Ms	FSTH SE23 *	151	F1
Alexander Ms	BAY/PAD W2	8	C4
Alexander Pl	SKENS SW7	15	J5
Alexander Rd	ARCH N19	72	D2
	BXLYHN DA7	136	E1
	CHST BR7	154	B5
Alexander Sq	CHEL SW3	15	J5
Alexander St	BAY/PAD W2	8	B4
Alexander Ter	ABYW SE2 *	116	C4
Alexandra Av	BTSEA SW11 *	109	F7

Ale - App 185

Column 1

- RYLN/HDSTN HA2 ... 47 K3
- STHL UB1 ... 83 K6
- SUT SM1 ... 174 C2
- WDGN N22 ... 40 D7
- Alexandra Cots *NWCR SE14* ... 112 C7
- Alexandra Crs *BMLY BR1* ... 152 D5
- Alexandra Dr *BRYLDS KT5* ... 159 H6
- *NRWD SE19* ... 150 A4
- Alexandra Gdns *CAR SM5* ... 176 A3
- *HSLW TW3* ... 123 G1
- *MUSWH N10* ... 54 B1
- **Alexandra Ga** *SKENS SW7* ... **15** G7
- *NFNCH/WDSPK N12* ... 39 F4
- Alexandra Ms *EFNCH N2* ... 53 K2
- *WAT WD17* ... 20 E1
- Alexandra Palace Wy
- *CEND/HSY/T N8* ... 54 C3
- Alexandra Pde
- *RYLN/HDSTN HA2 *...66 B3
- Alexandra Park Rd
- *MUSWH N10* ... 54 B1
- Alexandra Pl *SNWD SE25* ... 164 B1
- *STJWD NW8* ... 2 A4
- Alexandra Rd *ASHF TW15* ... 140 B6
- *BTFD TW8 *... 104 E5
- *CEND/HSY/T N8* ... 55 G2
- *CHDH RM6* ... 61 K5
- *CHSWK W4* ... 106 A1
- *CROY/NA CR0* ... 165 F7
- *ED N9* ... 30 D6
- *EHAM E6* ... 96 A2
- *ERITH DA8* ... 118 C5
- *HDN NW4* ... 52 B3
- *HSLW TW3* ... 123 G1
- *KUTN/CMB KT2* ... 144 C6
- *LEY E10* ... 76 A2
- *MORT/ESHN SW14* ... 126 A2
- *MTCM CR4* ... 147 F6
- *MUSWH N10* ... 40 B7
- *PEND EN3* ... 31 F3
- *PGE/AN SE20* ... 151 F5
- *RAIN RM13* ... 81 H7
- *RCH/KEW TW9* ... 125 F1
- *ROM RM1* ... 63 H5
- *SEVS/STOTM N15* ... 55 K4
- *STJWD NW8* ... 2 A3
- *SWFD E18* ... 59 F2
- *THDIT KT7* ... 158 A4
- *TWK TW1* ... 124 D5
- *WALTH E17* ... 57 H5
- *WAT WD17* ... 20 E1
- *WIM/MER SW19* ... 146 E6
- Alexandra Sq *MRDN SM4* ... 161 K4
- Alexandra St *CAN/RD E16* ... 94 E4
- *NWCR SE14* ... 112 B6
- Alexandria Rd *WEA W13* ... 85 G6
- Alexis St *BERM/RHTH SE16* ... 111 H3
- Alfearn Rd *CLPT E5* ... 74 E3
- Alford Gn *CROY/NA CR0* ... 180 A5
- Alford Pl *IS N1 *... 6 F6
- Alford Rd *ERITH DA8* ... 117 K3
- Alfoxton Av *SEVS/STOTM N15* ... 55 H3
- Alfreda St *BTSEA SW11* ... 109 G7
- Alfred Cl *CHSWK W4* ... 106 A3
- *STHL UB1* ... 83 J6
- **Alfred Ms** *GWRST WC1E * ... **11** G2
- **Alfred Pl** *GWRST WC1E *... **11** G2
- Alfred Rd *ACT W3* ... 86 E7
- *BAY/PAD W2* ... 8 B2
- *BELV DA17* ... 117 G4
- *BKHH IG9* ... 45 H1
- *FELT TW13* ... 122 B2
- *KUT/HW KT1* ... 159 F2
- *SNWD SE25* ... 165 H4
- *SRTFD E15* ... 76 D4
- *SUT SM1* ... 175 G4
- Alfred's Gdns *BARK IG11* ... 96 E1
- Alfred St *BOW E3* ... 93 H2
- Alfred's Way (East Ham & Barking By-Pass)
- *BARK IG11* ... 96 D1
- Alfred Vis *WALTH E17 * ... 58 A3
- Alfreton Cl *WIM/MER SW19* ... 146 B2
- Alfriston Av *BRYLDS KT5* ... 159 G5
- Alfriston Av *CROY/NA CR0* ... 163 K6
- *RYLN/HDSTN HA2* ... 48 A5
- Alfriston Rd *BRYLDS KT5* ... 159 G5
- Alfriston St *BTSEA SW11* ... 128 E4
- Algar Cl *ISLW TW7* ... 124 B2
- *STAN HA7* ... 35 F3
- Algar Rd *ISLW TW7* ... 124 B2
- Algarve Rd *WAND/EARL SW18* ... 128 A7
- Algernon Rd *HDN NW4* ... 51 J5
- *KIL/WHAMP NW6* ... 2 A1
- *LEW SE13* ... 132 E2
- Algiers Rd *LEW SE13* ... 132 D3
- Alguin Cl *STAN HA7 * ... 35 J5
- Alibon Gdns *DAGE RM10* ... 80 C4
- Alibon Rd *DAGE RM10* ... 80 C4
- **Alice La** *BOW E3* ... 75 H7
- **Alice St** *STHWK SE1* ... **19** J4
- Alice Thompson Cl
- *LEE/GVPK SE12* ... 153 G1
- Alice Walker Cl *HNHL SE24 *... 130 C3
- Alice Wy *HSLW TW3* ... 123 G3
- Alicia Av *KTN/HRWW/WS HA3* ... 49 H3
- Alicia Cl *KTN/HRWW/WS HA3* ... 49 J3
- Alicia Gdns
- *KTN/HRWW/WS HA3* ... 49 H3
- Alie St *WCHPL E1* ... 13 M5
- Alington Crs *CDALE/KGS NW9* ... 50 D7
- Alington Gv *WLGTN SM6* ... 176 C7
- Alison Cl *CROY/NA CR0* ... 166 A7
- *EHAM E6* ... 96 A5
- Aliwal Ms *BTSEA SW11 *... 128 D3
- Aliwal Rd *BTSEA SW11* ... 128 D3
- Alkerden Rd *CHSWK W4* ... 106 B4
- Alkham Rd *STNW/STAM N16* ... 74 B1
- Allan Barclay Cl
- *SEVS/STOTM N15* ... 56 B5
- Allan Cl *NWMAL KT3* ... 160 A4
- Allandale Av *FNCH N3* ... 52 C2
- Allandale Rd *EMPK RM11* ... 63 K5
- Allan Wy *ACT W3* ... 86 D4
- Allard Crs *BUSH WD23* ... 34 C1
- Allardyce St *CLAP SW4* ... 130 A3
- Allbrook Cl *TEDD TW11* ... 142 E4
- Allcot Av *EBED/NFELT TW14* ... 121 J7
- Allcroft Rd *KTTN NW5* ... 72 A5
- Allder Wy *SAND/SEL CR2* ... 177 H6
- Allenby Cl *SAND/SEL CR2 *... 177 J7
- Allenby Rd *GFD/PVL UB6* ... 84 A2
- Allenby Rd *FSTH SE23* ... 151 G2
- *STHL UB1* ... 84 A5
- *WOOL/PLUM SE18* ... 115 H7
- Allen Cl *MTCM CR4* ... 148 B1
- *SUN TW16* ... 141 F7
- Allendale Av *STHL UB1* ... 84 A5
- Allendale Cl *CMBW SE5* ... 130 E1
- *SYD SE26* ... 151 F4
- Allendale Rd *GFD/PVL UB6* ... 67 H5

Column 2

- Allen Edwards Dr *VX/NE SW8* ... 109 K7
- Allen Rd *BECK BR3* ... 166 A1
- *BOW E3* ... 93 H1
- *CROY/NA CR0* ... 164 A6
- *STNW/STAM N16* ... 74 A3
- *SUN TW16* ... 141 F7
- Allensbury Pl *CAMTN NW1* ... 5 H2
- Allens Rd *PEND EN3* ... 30 E5
- **Allen St** *KENS W8* ... **14** B3
- Allenswood Rd
- *ELTH/MOT SE9* ... 134 D2
- Allerford Ct *HRW HA1* ... 48 B4
- Allerford Rd *CAT SE6* ... 151 K3
- Allerton Rd *STNW/STAM N16* ... 73 J1
- Allerton St *IS N1 *... 7 H6
- Allestree Rd *FUL/PGN SW6* ... 107 H6
- Alleyn Crs *DUL SE21* ... 149 K1
- Alleyndale Rd *BCTR RM8* ... 79 J1
- Alleyn Pk *DUL SE21* ... 149 K2
- *NWDGN UB2* ... 102 E3
- Alleyn Rd *DUL SE21* ... 149 K2
- Allfarthing La
- *WAND/EARL SW18* ... 128 B5
- Allgood Cl *MRDN SM4* ... 161 G5
- Allgood St *BETH E2* ... 7 M6
- **Allhallows La** *CANST EC4R* ... **13** G7
- All Hallows Rd *EHAM E6* ... 95 J5
- *TOTM N17* ... 42 A1
- Alliance Cl *ALP/SUD HA0* ... 67 K3
- *HSLWW TW4* ... 122 E4
- Alliance Rd *ACT W3* ... 86 D3
- *PLSTW E13* ... 95 G4
- *WOOL/PLUM SE18* ... 116 B5
- Allied Wy *ACT W3 *... 106 A1
- Allingham Cl *HNWL W7* ... 85 F6
- Allingham Ct *HDN NW4* ... 52 A3
- Allington Cl *GFD/PVL UB6* ... 66 C7
- *WIM/MER SW19* ... 146 B4
- Allington Ct *HDN NW4* ... 51 K6
- *NKENS W10* ... 88 C2
- *ORP BR6* ... 169 K7
- *RYLN/HDSTN HA2* ... 48 B1
- Allington Rd *BCVA SW1W* ... 16 D4
- *HDN NW4* ... 51 K5
- Allison Cl *GNWCH SE10* ... 113 F7
- Allison Gv *DUL SE21* ... 131 F7
- Allison Rd *ACT W3* ... 86 D5
- *CEND/HSY/T N8* ... 55 G4
- Allitsen Rd *STJWD NW8* ... 3 K6
- Allnutt Wy *CLAP SW4* ... 129 J4
- Alloa Rd *DEPT SE8* ... 112 A5
- *GDMY/SEVK IG3* ... 79 H1
- Allonby Gdns *WBLY HA9* ... 49 J7
- Alloway Rd *BOW E3* ... 93 G2
- Allport Ms *WCHPL E1 *... 92 E3
- All Saints' Cl *ED N9* ... 42 B1
- All Saints Dr *BKHTH/KID SE3* ... 133 J1
- All Saints Ms *KTN/HRWW/WS HA3* ... 34 E5
- All Saints Pas
- *WAND/EARL SW18 *... 127 K4
- All Saints Rd *SUT SM1* ... 175 F2
- *WIM/MER SW19* ... 147 G6
- All Saints St *ACT W3* ... 105 K2
- **NTGHL W11** ... **88** D4
- All Saints St *IS N1* ... 5 L5
- Allsop Pl *CAMTN NW1* ... 9 M1
- All Souls Av *WLSDN NW10* ... 87 K1
- **All Souls' Pl** *REGST W1B* ... **10** D3
- Allum Gv *OXHEY WD19* ... 33 H3
- Allum La *BORE WD6* ... 24 A4
- Allum Wy *TRDG/WHET N20* ... 27 G2
- Allwood Cl *SYD SE26* ... 151 F3
- Alma Av *CHING E4* ... 44 A6
- Almack Rd *CLPT E5* ... 74 E3
- Alma Cl *MUSWH N10* ... 40 B7
- Alma Cr *RYLN/HDSTN HA2 *... 66 D1
- Alma Crs *SUT SM1* ... 174 C4
- Alma Gv *STHWK SE1* ... 19 M6
- Alma Pl *NRWD SE19* ... 150 B6
- *THHTH CR7* ... 164 B4
- *WLSDN NW10* ... 87 K2
- Alma Rd *BFN/LL DA15* ... 155 J2
- *CAR SM5* ... 175 J4
- *ESH/CLAY KT10* ... 157 K7
- *MUSWH N10* ... 40 A6
- *PEND EN3* ... 31 J2
- *STHL UB1* ... 83 J6
- *WAND/EARL SW18* ... 128 B5
- Alma Rw
- *KTN/HRWW/WS HA3 *... 34 D7
- Alma Sq *STJWD NW8* ... 2 F7
- Alma St *KTTN NW5* ... 72 B5
- *SRTFD E15* ... 76 B5
- Alma Ter *BOW E3* ... 75 H7
- **KENS W8** ... **14** B4
- *WAND/EARL SW18* ... 128 C6
- Almeida St *IS N1* ... 6 C3
- Almeric Rd *BTSEA SW11* ... 128 E3
- Almer Rd *RYNPK SW20* ... 145 J6
- Almington St *FSBYPK N4* ... 55 K1
- Almond Av *CAR SM5* ... 175 K1
- *EA W5* ... 105 F2
- *WDR/YW UB7* ... 100 D2
- Almond Cl *FELT TW13* ... 121 K7
- *HAYES BR2* ... 169 F6
- *HYS/HAR UB3* ... 82 C6
- *PECK SE15* ... 131 H1
- *RSLP HA4* ... 65 F4
- Almond Rd *BTFD TW8* ... 104 E4
- Almond Rd *BERM/RHTH SE16* ... 111 J3
- *TOTM N17* ... 42 D6
- Almonds Av *BKHH IG9* ... 44 E2
- Almond Wy *BORE WD6* ... 24 D3
- *HAYES BR2* ... 169 F6
- *MTCM CR4* ... 163 H5
- *RYLN/HDSTN HA2* ... 48 B1
- Almorah Rd *HEST TW5* ... 102 C7
- *IS N1* ... 7 G2
- Almshouse La *CHSGTN KT9* ... 171 J7
- Alnwick Gv *MRDN SM4* ... 162 A3
- Alnwick Rd *CAN/RD E16* ... 95 G5
- *LEE/GVPK SE12* ... 134 A6
- Alperton La *ALP/SUD HA0* ... 85 K2
- Alperton St *NKENS W10* ... 88 C3
- Alphabet Gdns *CAR SM5* ... 162 C5
- Alphabet Sq *BOW E3* ... 93 K4
- Alpha Cl *CAMTN NW1* ... 9 K8
- Alpha Est *HYS/HAR UB3 *... 101 H1
- Alpha Gv *POP/IOD E14* ... 112 D1
- **Alpha Pl** *CHEL SW3* ... **15** K9
- *KIL/WHAMP NW6* ... 2 B5
- *MRDN SM4 *... 161 G5
- Alpha Rd *BRYLDS KT5* ... 159 G5
- *CHING E4* ... 43 J2
- *CROY/NA CR0* ... 178 A1
- *NWCR SE14* ... 112 C7
- *PEND EN3* ... 31 G3
- *TEDD TW11* ... 142 D4
- *UED N18* ... 42 C5
- Alpha St *PECK SE15* ... 131 H1
- Alpine Av *BRYLDS KT5* ... 172 E1
- Alpine Cl *CROY/NA CR0* ... 178 A2
- Alpine Copse *BMLY BR1* ... 169 F1
- Alpine Gv *HOM E9* ... 74 E6

Column 3

- Alpine Rd *BERM/RHTH SE16* ... 111 K3
- *LEY E10* ... 75 K1
- Alpine Vw *CAR SM5* ... 175 J4
- Alpine Wk *BUSH WD23* ... 34 E1
- *WLSDN NW10* ... 69 H5
- Alric Av *NWMAL KT3* ... 160 B2
- *WLSDN NW10* ... 69 H6
- Alroy Rd *FSBYPK N4* ... 55 G6
- Alsace Rd *WALW SE17* ... 19 J7
- Alscot Cl *STHWK SE1* ... 19 M4
- Alscot Wy *STHWK SE1* ... 19 L5
- Alsike Rd *ERITH DA8* ... 116 E2
- Alsom Av *WPK KT4* ... 173 K3
- Alston Cl *SURB KT6* ... 158 C6
- Alston Rd *BAR EN5* ... 26 C2
- *TOOT SW17* ... 147 H3
- *UED N18* ... 42 D4
- Altair Cl *TOTM N17* ... 42 B5
- Altair Wy *NTHWD HA6* ... 32 D4
- Altash Wy *ELTH/MOT SE9* ... 153 K1
- Altenburg Av *WEA W13* ... 104 C2
- Altenburg Gdns *BTSEA SW11* ... 128 E3
- Alt Gv *WIM/MER SW19* ... 146 D6
- Altham Ct *KTN/HRWW/WS HA3 *... 34 D7
- Altham Gdns *OXHEY WD19* ... 33 H3
- Altham Rd *PIN HA5* ... 33 J5
- Althea St *FUL/PGN SW6* ... 128 A1
- Althorne Gdns *SWFD E18* ... 58 D3
- Althorne Wy *DAGE RM10* ... 80 C1
- Althorp Cl *BAR EN5* ... 25 J6
- Althorpe Rd *HRW HA1* ... 48 C4
- Althorp Rd *TOOT SW17* ... 128 E7
- Altmore Av *EHAM E6* ... 77 K6
- Alton Av *STAN HA7* ... 35 F6
- Alton Cl *BXLY DA5* ... 137 F7
- *ISLW TW7* ... 124 A1
- Alton Gdns *BECK BR3* ... 151 J6
- *WHTN TW2* ... 123 J6
- Alton Rd *CROY/NA CR0* ... 177 G2
- *PUT/ROE SW15* ... 126 D7
- *RCH/KEW TW9* ... 125 F3
- *TOTM N17* ... 55 K2
- Alton St *POP/IOD E14* ... 93 K4
- Altyre Cl *BECK BR3* ... 166 C4
- Altyre Rd *CROY/NA CR0* ... 177 K1
- Altyre Wy *BECK BR3* ... 166 C4
- Alvanley Gdns
- *KIL/WHAMP NW6* ... 71 F4
- Alva Wy *OXHEY WD19* ... 33 H1
- Alverstone Av *EBAR EN4* ... 27 H6
- *WAND/EARL SW18* ... 146 A1
- Alverstone Gdns
- *ELTH/MOT SE9* ... 135 G7
- Alverstone Rd *CRICK NW2* ... 70 A6
- *MNPK E12* ... 78 A3
- *NWMAL KT3* ... 160 C3
- *WBLY HA9* ... 50 B7
- Alverston Gdns *SNWD SE25* ... 165 F4
- Alverton St *DEPT SE8* ... 112 C4
- Alveston Av *KTN/HRWW/WS HA3* ... 49 H2
- Alveston Sq *SWFD E18 *... 58 E1
- Alvey St *WALW SE17* ... 19 J7
- Alvia Gdns *SUT SM1* ... 175 G3
- Alvington Crs *HACK E8* ... 74 B4
- Alway Av *HOR/WEW KT19* ... 172 E4
- Alwin Pl *WATW WD18* ... 20 C3
- Alwold Crs *LEE/GVPK SE12* ... 134 B5
- Alwyn Av *CHSWK W4* ... 106 A4
- Alwyn Cl *BORE WD6* ... 24 D3
- *CROY/NA CR0* ... 179 K6
- Alwyne La *IS N1* ... 6 E1
- Alwyne Pl *IS N1* ... 6 E1
- Alwyne Rd *HNWL W7* ... 84 E6
- *IS N1* ... 6 E1
- *WIM/MER SW19* ... 146 D5
- Alwyne Sq *IS N1* ... 73 F5
- Alwyne Vls *IS N1* ... 6 D1
- Alwyn Gdns *ACT W3* ... 86 D5
- *HDN NW4* ... 51 J3
- Alyn Bank *CEND/HSY/T N8 *... 54 D5
- Alyth Gdns *GLDGN NW11* ... 52 D5
- Amalgamated Dr *BTFD TW8* ... 104 B5
- Amanda Ms *ROMW/RG RM7* ... 62 E4
- Amar Ct *WOOL/PLUM SE18* ... 116 A3
- Amardeep Ct
- *WOOL/PLUM SE18* ... 116 A4
- Amazon Cl *HSLW TW3* ... 122 F1
- Ambassador Cl *HSLW TW3* ... 122 D1
- Ambassador Gdns *EHAM E6* ... 95 K5
- Ambassador Sq *POP/IOD E14* ... 112 E3
- Amber Av *FNCH N3* ... 52 E7
- Amberden Av *FNCH N3* ... 52 E7
- Ambergate St *WALW SE17* ... 18 D7
- Amber Gv *CRICK NW2 *... 52 B7
- Amberley Cl *PIN HA5* ... 47 K2
- Amberley Ct *SCUP DA14* ... 155 J4
- Amberley Gdns
- *HOR/WEW KT19* ... 173 H3
- Amberley Gv *CROY/NA CR0* ... 165 G6
- *SYD SE26* ... 150 D4
- Amberley Rd *ABYW SE2* ... 116 E5
- *BKHH IG9* ... 30 E7
- *LEY E10* ... 57 J6
- *MV/WKIL W9* ... 8 B2
- *PLMGR N13* ... 41 F1
- Amberley Wy *HSLWW TW4 *... 122 B4
- *MRDN SM4* ... 161 J6
- *ROMW/RG RM7* ... 62 D3
- Amberside *SRTFD E15 *... 76 B7
- Amberwood Cl *WLGTN SM6* ... 176 E5
- Amberwood Ri *NWMAL KT3* ... 160 B5
- Amberwood Cl *LEE/GVPK SE12 *... 153 F2
- Amblecote Meadow
- *LEE/GVPK SE12* ... 153 F2
- Amblecote Mdw
- *LEE/GVPK SE12 *... 153 F2
- Amblecote Rd *LEE/GVPK SE12 *... 153 F2
- Ambler Rd *FSBYPK N4* ... 73 H2
- Ambleside *BMLY BR1* ... 151 G6
- *HCH RM12* ... 81 K4
- *STRHM/NOR SW16* ... 148 D3
- *WOT/HER KT12 *... 156 E2
- Ambleside Av *BECK BR3* ... 166 B4
- *HCH RM12* ... 81 J4
- *STRHM/NOR SW16* ... 148 D3
- *WOT/HER KT12* ... 156 B1
- Ambleside Cl *HOM E9* ... 74 E4
- *LEY E10* ... 57 K6
- *SEVS/STOTM N15* ... 56 B2
- Ambleside Crs *PEND EN3* ... 31 F3
- Ambleside Dr
- *EBED/NFELT TW14* ... 121 J6
- Ambleside Gdns *BELMT SM2* ... 175 G5
- *REDBR IG4* ... 59 J3
- *WBLY HA9* ... 49 K1
- Ambleside Rd *WLSDN NW10* ... 69 H6
- Ambrey Wy *WLGTN SM6* ... 176 D7
- Ambrook Rd *BELV DA17* ... 117 H2
- Ambrosden Av *WEST SW1P* ... **16** F4
- Ambrose Av *GLDGN NW11* ... 52 C6
- Ambrose St *BERM/RHTH SE16* ... 111 J3
- Ambulance Rd *WAN E11* ... 58 B4
- Amelia Cl *ACT W3* ... 86 D7
- Amelia St *WALW SE17* ... 18 E6

Column 4

- **Amen Cnr** *STP EC4M* ... **12** D5
- *TOOT SW17* ... 148 A5
- **Amen Ct** *STP EC4M* ... **12** D5
- Amenity Wy *MRDN SM4* ... 161 F6
- **America Sq** *TWRH EC3N* ... **13** L6
- **America Sq** *STHWK SE1* ... **12** C9
- Amerland Rd *PUT/ROE SW15* ... 127 J3
- Amersham Av *UED N18* ... 41 K5
- Amersham Gv *NWCR SE14* ... 112 C6
- Amersham Rd *CROY/NA CR0* ... 164 D5
- *NWCR SE14* ... 112 C7
- Amersham V *NWCR SE14* ... 112 C6
- Amery Gdns *WLSDN NW10* ... 69 K7
- Amery Rd *HRW HA1* ... 67 G1
- Amesbury Av
- *BRXS/STRHM SW2* ... 148 E2
- Amesbury Cl *WPK KT4* ... 161 F7
- Amesbury Dr *CHING E4* ... 31 K5
- Amesbury Rd *BMLY BR1* ... 168 C2
- *DAGW RM9* ... 79 K6
- *FELT TW13* ... 141 H1
- Ames Cots *POP/IOD E14 *... 93 G4
- Amethyst Rd *SRTFD E15* ... 76 B3
- Amherst Av *WEA W13* ... 85 J5
- Amherst Gdns *WEA W13 *... 85 J5
- Amherst Rd *WEA W13* ... 85 J5
- Amhurst Gdns *ISLW TW7* ... 104 A7
- Amhurst Pde
- *STNW/STAM N16 *... 56 B6
- Amhurst Pk *STNW/STAM N16* ... 74 A6
- Amhurst Rd *STNW/STAM N16* ... 74 B4
- Amhurst Ter *HACK E8* ... 74 C3
- Amidas Gdns *BCTR RM8* ... 79 H3
- Amiel St *WCHPL E1* ... 92 E3
- Amies St *BTSEA SW11* ... 128 E2
- Amina Wy *BERM/RHTH SE16* ... 111 H2
- Amis Av *HOR/WEW KT19* ... 172 C5
- Amity Gv *RYNPK SW20* ... 146 A7
- Amity Rd *SRTFD E15* ... 76 D6
- Ammanford Gn
- *CDALE/KGS NW9* ... 51 G5
- Amner Rd *BTSEA SW11* ... 129 F5
- Amor Rd *HMSMTH W6* ... 107 F2
- Amott Rd *PECK SE15* ... 131 H2
- Ampere Wy *CROY/NA CR0* ... 163 K6
- Ampleforth Rd *ABYW SE2* ... 116 C1
- Ampthill Est *CAMTN NW1 *... 4 E6
- Ampthill Sq *CAMTN NW1* ... 4 F6
- **Ampton Pl** *FSBYW WC1X* ... **5** L8
- Amroth Cl *FSTH SE23* ... 131 J7
- Amroth Gn *CDALE/KGS NW9* ... 51 G5
- Amsterdam Rd *POP/IOD E14* ... 113 F2
- Amwell Cl *ENC/FH EN2* ... 29 K4
- **Amwell St** *CLKNW EC1R* ... **6** A7
- Amyand Cots *TWK TW1 *... 124 C5
- Amyand Park Gdns *TWK TW1* ... 124 C6
- Amyand Park Rd *TWK TW1* ... 124 C6
- Amy Cl *WLGTN SM6* ... 176 E6
- Amyruth Rd *BROCKY SE4* ... 132 D4
- Amy Warne Cl *EHAM E6* ... 95 J3
- Anatola Rd *ARCH N19* ... 72 B1
- Ancaster Crs *NWMAL KT3* ... 160 D5
- Ancaster Ms *BECK BR3* ... 166 A2
- Ancaster Rd *BECK BR3* ... 166 A2
- Ancaster St *WOOL/PLUM SE18* ... 115 K6
- Anchorage Cl *WIM/MER SW19* ... 146 E4
- Anchor & Hope La *CHARL SE7 *... 114 A3
- Anchor Cl *BARK IG11* ... 97 H2
- Anchor Dr *RAIN RM13* ... 99 K2
- Anchor Ms *MNPK E12* ... 77 H2
- Anchor Rd *BERM/RHTH SE16* ... 111 J3
- Anchor Ter *WCHPL E1 *... 92 E3
- Ancill Cl *HMSMTH W6* ... 107 G5
- Ancona Rd *WLSDN NW10* ... 87 J1
- *WOOL/PLUM SE18* ... 115 J4
- Andace Park Gdns
- *BMLY BR1 *... 153 F7
- Andalus Rd *BRXN/ST SW9* ... 129 K3
- Ander Cl *ALP/SUD HA0* ... 67 K3
- Anderson Cl *ACT W3* ... 86 E5
- *CHEAM SM3* ... 161 K7
- *WCHMH N21* ... 29 F4
- Anderson Dr *ASHF TW15* ... 140 A3
- Anderson Ms *HOM E9* ... 75 F7
- *WFD IG8* ... 59 H2
- Anderson's Pl *HSLW TW3* ... 123 G3
- Anderson Sq *IS N1* ... 6 C4
- **Anderson St** *CHEL SW3* ... **15** L7
- Anderson Wy *BELV DA17* ... 117 J1
- Andover Av *CAN/RD E16* ... 95 H5
- Andover Cl *EBED/NFELT TW14* ... 121 J7
- *GFD/PVL UB6* ... 84 B3
- Andover Pl *KIL/WHAMP NW6 *... 2 C6
- Andover Rd *HOLWY N7* ... 73 F1
- *ORP BR6* ... 169 K7
- *WHTN TW2* ... 123 J7
- Andover Ter *HMSMTH W6 *... 106 E3
- Andre St *HACK E8* ... 74 C4
- **Andrew Borde St**
- *LSQ/SEVD WC2H *... **11** H4
- Andrewes Gdns *EHAM E6* ... 95 J5
- Andrew Pl *VX/NE SW8* ... 109 J7
- Andrews Cl *BKHH IG9* ... 45 G1
- *HRW HA1* ... 48 D6
- *WPK KT4* ... 174 B1
- Andrews Pl *BETH E2* ... 74 E1
- Andrew St *POP/IOD E14* ... 94 A5
- Andrews Wk *WALW SE17* ... 110 C5
- Andwell Cl *ABYW SE2* ... 116 C1
- Anerley Gv *NRWD SE19* ... 150 B6
- Anerley Hl *NRWD SE19* ... 150 C5
- Anerley Pk *PGE/AN SE20* ... 150 D6
- Anerley Park Rd *PGE/AN SE20* ... 150 D6
- Anerley Rd *PGE/AN SE20* ... 150 C7
- Anerley Station Rd
- *PGE/AN SE20* ... 150 D7
- Anerley V *NRWD SE19* ... 150 D6
- Anfield Cl *BAL SW12* ... 129 H6
- Angela Carter Ct
- *BRXN/ST SW9* ... 130 M3
- Angel Aly *WCHPL E1* ... 92 C5
- Angel Cl *HPTN TW12* ... 142 A5
- *UED N18* ... 42 B3
- **Angel Ct** *LOTH EC2R* ... **13** H4
- Angel Corner Pde *UED N18 *... 42 C4
- Angelfield *HSLW TW3* ... 123 G4
- Angel Hl *SUT SM1* ... 175 F2
- Angel Hill Dr *SUT SM1* ... 175 F2
- Angel La *HYS/HAR UB3* ... 82 B4
- Angelica Dr *EHAM E6* ... 96 A4
- Angel Pas *CANST EC4R* ... 13 G7
- Angell Park Gdns
- *BRXN/ST SW9* ... 130 B2
- Angell Rd *BRXN/ST SW9* ... 130 C2
- Angell Town Est
- *BRXN/ST SW9* ... 130 B1
- Angel Ms *FSBYPK N4 **UED N18* ... 126 E6
- *WCHPL E1* ... 92 C6
- **Angel Pas** *CANST EC4R* ... **13** G7
- Angel Rd *HRW HA1* ... 48 E5
- *THDIT KT7* ... 158 B7

Column 5

- Angel Road (North Circular)
- *UED N18* ... 42 C4
- Angel Sq *FSBYE EC1V *... 6 C7
- **Angel St** *STBT EC1A* ... **12** E4
- Angel Wk *HMSMTH W6* ... 107 F3
- Angel Wy *ROM RM1* ... 63 G4
- Angerstein La *BKHTH/KID SE3* ... 113 J6
- Anglers La *KTTN NW5* ... 72 B5
- Anglers Reach *SURB KT6 *... 158 E4
- Anglesea Ms
- *WOOL/PLUM SE18 *... 115 G3
- Anglesea Rd *KUT/HW KT1* ... 158 E3
- *WOOL/PLUM SE18* ... 115 G3
- Anglesey Court Rd *CAR SM5* ... 176 A5
- Anglesey Dr *RAIN RM13* ... 99 J3
- Anglesey Gdns *CAR SM5* ... 176 A5
- Anglesey Rd *OXHEY WD19* ... 33 G4
- *PEND EN3* ... 30 D3
- Anglesmede Crs *PIN HA5* ... 48 A3
- Anglesmede Wy *PIN HA5* ... 47 K2
- Angles Rd *STRHM/NOR SW16* ... 148 E3
- Anglia Cl *TOTM N17* ... 42 D6
- Anglian Rd *WAN E11* ... 76 B2
- Anglo Rd *BOW E3* ... 93 H1
- Angus Cl *CHSGTN KT9* ... 172 C4
- Angus Dr *RSLP HA4* ... 65 G3
- Angus Gdns *CDALE/KGS NW9* ... 37 F7
- Angus Rd *PLSTW E13* ... 95 G2
- Angus St *NWCR SE14* ... 112 B6
- Anhalt Rd *BTSEA SW11* ... 108 D6
- Ankerdine Crs
- *WOOL/PLUM SE18* ... 115 G7
- Anlaby Rd *TEDD TW11* ... 142 E4
- Anley Rd *HMSMTH W6* ... 107 G1
- Anmersh Gv *STAN HA7* ... 35 K7
- Annabel Cl *POP/IOD E14* ... 93 K5
- Anna Cl *HACK E8* ... 7 M3
- Annandale Gv
- *HCDN/ICK UB10* ... 64 A2
- Annandale Rd *BFN/LL DA15* ... 135 K6
- *CHSWK W4* ... 106 B5
- *CROY/NA CR0* ... 178 C1
- *GNWCH SE10* ... 113 J4
- Anna Neagle Cl *FSTGT E7 *... 76 E3
- Anne Case Ms *NWMAL KT3 *... 160 A2
- Anne Compton Ms
- *LEE/GVPK SE12* ... 133 J6
- Annesley Av *CDALE/KGS NW9* ... 51 F2
- Annesley Cl *WLSDN NW10* ... 69 G2
- Annesley Dr *CROY/NA CR0* ... 179 H2
- Annesley Rd *BKHTH/KID SE3* ... 114 A7
- Annesmere Gdns
- *BKHTH/KID SE3* ... 134 C2
- Anne St *PLSTW E13* ... 94 E3
- Annette Cl
- *KTN/HRWW/WS HA3* ... 48 E1
- Annette Rd *HOLWY N7* ... 73 F3
- Annie Besant Cl *BOW E3 *... 75 H7
- Anning St *WCHPL E1* ... 7 K9
- Annington Rd *EFNCH N2* ... 53 K2
- Annis Rd *HOM E9* ... 75 G5
- **Ann La** *WBPTN SW10* ... **108** C6
- Ann Moss Wy
- *BERM/RHTH SE16* ... 111 K2
- **Ann's Cl** *KTBR SW1X* ... **15** L2
- Ann St *WOOL/PLUM SE18* ... 115 J4
- Annsworthy Av *THHTH CR7* ... 164 E2
- Annsworthy Crs *SNWD SE25* ... 164 E1
- Ansar Gdns *WALTH E17* ... 57 G4
- Ansdell Rd *PECK SE15* ... 131 K1
- **Ansdell St** *KENS W8* ... **14** D3
- **Ansdell Ter** *KENS W8* ... **14** D3
- Ansell Gv *CAR SM5* ... 162 E7
- Ansell Rd *TOOT SW17* ... 147 J2
- Anselm Cl *CROY/NA CR0* ... 178 A2
- Anselm Rd *FUL/PGN SW6* ... 107 K5
- *PIN HA5* ... 33 K6
- Ansford Rd *BMLY BR1* ... 152 A4
- **Ansleigh Pl** *NTGHL W11* ... **88** B6
- Anson Cl *ROMW/RG RM7* ... 62 C3
- Anson Rd *ARCH N19* ... 72 C3
- *CRICK NW2* ... 69 K4
- Anson Wk *NTHWD HA6* ... 32 A3
- Anstead Dr *RAIN RM13* ... 99 J1
- Anstey Rd *PECK SE15* ... 131 H2
- Anstice Cl *CHSWK W4* ... 106 A6
- Anstridge Rd *ELTH/MOT SE9* ... 135 J5
- Antelope Rd
- *WOOL/PLUM SE18* ... 114 E2
- Anthony Cl *MLHL NW7* ... 37 G4
- *OXHEY WD19* ... 21 H7
- Anthony Rd *BORE WD6* ... 24 C1
- *GFD/PVL UB6* ... 84 E1
- *SNWD SE25* ... 165 H5
- *WELL DA16* ... 116 B7
- Anthony's Cl *WAP E1W* ... 92 C7
- Anthony St *WCHPL E1* ... 92 D5
- Antiqua Ms *NTHWD HA6* ... 32 M6
- Antill Rd *BOW E3* ... 93 G2
- *SEVS/STOTM N15* ... 56 C3
- Antill Ter *WCHPL E1* ... 93 F5
- Antlers HI *CHING E4* ... 31 K4
- Antoneys Cl *PIN HA5* ... 47 H1
- Anton Pl *WBLY HA9* ... 68 D2
- Anton St *HACK E8* ... 74 C4
- Antrim Gv *HAMP NW3* ... 71 K5
- Antrobus Cl *SUT SM1* ... 174 D4
- Antrobus Rd *CHSWK W4* ... 105 K3
- Anvil Cl *STRHM/NOR SW16* ... 148 C6
- Anworth Rd *WFD IG8* ... 45 F5
- Aostle Wy *THHTH CR7* ... 164 C1
- Apeldoorn Dr *WLGTN SM6* ... 176 E7
- Aperfield Rd *ERITH DA8* ... 118 C5
- Apex Cl *BECK BR3* ... 151 K7
- Apex Pde *MLHL NW7 *... 37 F3
- Aplin Wy *ISLW TW7* ... 103 J7
- Apollo Av *BMLY BR1* ... 153 F7
- *NTHWD HA6* ... 32 M6
- Apollo Cl *HCH RM12* ... 81 K1
- Apollo Pl *WAN E11* ... 76 C2
- **WBPTN SW10** ... **108** C6
- Apollo Wy *ERITH DA8* ... 118 A3
- *THMD SE28* ... 115 J2
- **Apothecary St** *BLKFR EC4V * ... **12** C5
- Appach Rd *BRXS/STRHM SW2* ... 130 B4
- Apple Blossom Ct
- *VX/NE SW8 *... 109 J6
- Appleby Cl *CHING E4* ... 44 A5
- *SEVS/STOTM N15* ... 55 K4
- *STMC/STPC BR5* ... 169 K6
- *UX/CGN UB8* ... 82 A5
- *WHTN TW2* ... 142 D1
- Appleby Gdns
- *EBED/NFELT TW14 *... 121 J7
- Appleby Rd *CAN/RD E16* ... 94 E5
- *HACK E8* ... 74 C6
- Appleby St *BETH E2* ... 7 L5
- Appledore Av *BXLYHN DA7* ... 117 J7

RSLP HA4 65 F2
Appledore Cl EDGW HA8 36 C7
HAYES BR2 167 J4
TOOT SW17 147 K1
Appledore Crs SCUP DA14 154 E2
Appledore Wy MLHL NW7 38 B6
Appleford Rd NKENS W10 88 C3
Apple Garth BTFD TW8 104 E3
Applegarth CROY/NA CR0 179 K6
ESH/CLAY KT10 171 F4
Applegarth Dr
GNTH/NBYPK IG2 61 F3
Applegarth Rd THMD SE28 97 H7
WKENS W14 * 107 G2
Apple Gv CHSGTN KT9 172 A3
EN EN1 30 A2
Apple Ldg ALP/SUD HA0 * 67 J2
Apple Market KUT/HW KT1 158 E1
Apple Rd WAN E11 76 C2
Appleton Gdns NWMAL KT3 160 D5
Appleton Rd ELTH/MOT SE9 134 D2
Appletree Cl PGE/AN SE20 150 D7
Appletree Gdns EBAR EN4 27 J3
Apple Tree Yd STJS SW1Y 10 F8
Applewood Cl CRICK NW2 69 K2
TRDG/WHET N20 27 J7
Applewood Dr PLSTW E13 95 F3
Appold St SDTCH EC2A 13 J2
Apprentice Gdns NTHLT UB5 83 K2
Apprentice Wy CLPT E5 74 D3
Approach La MLHL NW7 38 C4
Approach Rd ASHF TW15 140 A5
BETH E2 92 E1
E/WMO/HCT KT8 157 F4
EBAR EN4 27 G3
RYNPK SW20 161 F1
The Approach ACT W3 87 F5
EN EN1 30 D1
HDN NW4 52 B4
Aprey Gdns HDN NW4 52 A3
April Cl FELT TW13 140 E2
HNWL W7 84 E6
April Gln FSTH SE23 151 F2
April St HACK E8 74 B3
Apsley Cl HRW HA1 48 C4
Apsley Rd NWMAL KT3 159 K2
SNWD SE25 165 J3
Apsley Wy CRICK NW2 69 J1
MYFR/PICC W1J * 10 C9
Aquarius TWK TW1 * 124 C7
Aquarius Wy NTHWD HA6 32 E4
Aquila St STJWD NW8 3 H5
Aquinas St STHWK SE1 12 B9
Arabella Dr PUT/ROE SW15 126 B3
Arabin Rd BROCKY SE4 132 B3
Aragon Av EW KT17 173 K7
THDIT KT7 158 A4
Aragon Cl HAYES BR2 168 E7
SUN TW16 140 D6
Aragon Dr RSLP HA4 47 H7
Aragon Pl MRDN SM4 161 G6
Aragon Rd KUTN/CMB KT2 144 A4
MRDN SM4 161 G6
Arandora Crs CHDH RM6 61 H6
Arbery Rd BOW E3 93 G2
Arbor Cl BECK BR3 166 E1
Arborfield Cl
BRXS/STRHM SW2 130 A7
Arbor Rd CHING E4 44 B2
Arbour Rd PEND EN3 31 F3
Arbour Sq WCHPL E1 93 F5
Arbour Wy HCH RM12 81 K4
Arbroath Gn OXHEY WD19 32 E2
Arbroath Rd ELTH/MOT SE9 134 D2
Arbrook La ESH/CLAY KT10 170 D5
Arbuthnot La BXLY DA5 137 F5
Arbuthnot Rd NWCR SE14 132 A1
Arbutus St HACK E8 7 K3
Arcade Chambers
ELTH/MOT SE9 * 135 F5
Arcade Pde CHSGTN KT9 * 172 A3
The Arcade ELTH/MOT SE9 * 135 F5
LVPST EC2M * 13 J3
WALTH E17 * 57 J3
Arcadia Av FNCH N3 38 E7
Arcadia Cl CAR SM5 176 A3
Arcadian Av BXLY DA5 137 F5
Arcadian Cl BXLY DA5 137 F5
Arcadian Gdns WDGN N22 41 G6
Arcadian Pl WAND/EARL SW18 127 H6
Arcadian Rd BXLY DA5 137 F6
Arcadia St POP/IOD E14 93 J5
Archangel St
BERM/RHTH SE16 112 A1
Archbishop's Pl
BRXS/STRHM SW2 130 A5
Archdale Pl NWMAL KT3 159 J2
Archdale Rd EDUL SE22 131 G4
Archel Rd WKENS W14 107 J5
Archer Cl BAR EN5 26 D5
KUTN/CMB KT2 144 A6
Archer Ct FELT TW13 121 K7
Archer Ms HPTN TW12 142 C5
Archer Rd SNWD SE25 165 J3
Archers Dr PEND EN3 30 E1
Archer Sq NWCR SE14 112 B5
Archer St SOHO/SHAV W1D 11 G6
Archery Cl BAY/PAD W2 9 K5
KTN/HRWW/WS HA3 49 F2
Archery Rd ELTH/MOT SE9 134 E4
The Arches CHCR WC2N * 11 K8
RYLN/HDSTN HA2 66 B1
Archibald Rd HOLWY N7 72 D3
Archibold St BOW E3 93 J2
Archie Cl WDR/YW UB7 100 D1
Arch St STHWK SE1 18 E4
Archway Cl ARCH N19 * 72 C1
NKENS W10 88 B4
WIM/MER SW19 147 F3
WLGTN SM6 * 176 E2
Archway Rd ARCH N19 54 C7
HGT N6 53 K4
Archway St BARN SW13 126 B2
Arcola St HACK E8 74 B4
Arcon Dr NTHLT UB5 83 J3
Arctic St KTTN NW5 72 B4
Arcus Rd BMLY BR1 152 C5
Ardbeg Rd HNHL SE24 130 E5
Arden Cl BUSH WD23 23 F6
HRW HA1 66 D2
THMD SE28 97 K5
WHTN TW2 122 E6
Arden Court Gdns EFNCH N2 53 H5
Arden Crs DAGW RM9 79 K6
POP/IOD E14 112 D3
Arden Est IS N1 7 J6
Arden Mhor PIN HA5 47 F3
Arden Rd FNCH N3 52 C2
WEA W13 85 J6
Ardent Cl SNWD SE25 165 F2
Ardfern Av STRHM/NOR SW16 164 B2
Ardfillan Rd CAT SE6 133 G7
Ardgowan Rd CAT SE6 133 H6
Ardilaun Rd HBRY N5 73 J3
Ardingly Cl CROY/NA CR0 179 F2
Ardleigh Gdns CHEAM SM3 161 K7
Ardleigh Rd IS N1 73 K5
WALTH E17 43 H7
Ardleigh Ter WALTH E17 43 H7
Ardley Cl CAT SE6 151 G2
WLSDN NW10 69 G2
Ardlui Rd WNWD SE27 149 J1
Ardmay Gdns SURB KT6 * 159 F4
Ardmere Rd LEW SE13 133 G5
Ardoch Rd CAT SE6 152 B1
Ardra Rd ED N9 43 F2
Ardrossan Gdns WPK KT4 173 J2
Ardross Av NTHWD HA6 32 C4
Ardshiel Cl PUT/ROE SW15 127 G2
Ardwell Av BARK/HLT IG6 60 C4
Ardwell Rd BRXS/STRHM SW2 148 E1
Ardwick Rd CRICK NW2 70 E3
Arena Est FSBYPK N4 * 55 H5
The Arena STKPK UB11 * 82 A7
Argall Av LEY E10 57 F6
Argall Wy LEY E10 57 F7
Argenta Wy WLSDN NW10 68 D6
Argent Ct SURB KT6 172 C2
Argon Ms FUL/PGN SW6 107 K6
Argon Rd UED N18 42 E4
Argosy La STWL/WRAY TW19 120 A6
Argus Wy NTHLT UB5 83 J2
Argyle Av HSLW TW3 123 F5
Argyle Cl WEA W13 85 G3
Argyle Cnr WEA W13 * 85 H6
Argyle Ct WATW WD18 * 20 D3
Argyle Pl HMSMTH W6 106 E3
Argyle Rd BAR EN5 26 A3
CAN/RD E16 95 F5
GFD/PVL UB6 85 F2
HSLW TW3 123 G4
IL IG1 78 A1
NFNCH/WDSPK N12 38 E4
RYLN/HDSTN HA2 48 B5
SRTFD E15 76 C3
TOTM N17 42 C7
UED N18 42 C3
WCHPL E1 93 F3
WEA W13 85 G5
Argyle Sq STPAN WC1H 5 K7
Argyle St CAMTN NW1 5 J7
Argyle Wk STPAN WC1H * 5 J8
Argyle Wy BERM/RHTH SE16 111 H4
Argyll Av STHL UB1 84 B7
Argyll Cl BRXN/ST SW9 130 A2
Argyll Gdns EDGW HA8 50 D1
Argyll Rd KENS W8 14 A2
WOOL/PLUM SE18 115 H2
Argyll St SOHO/SHAV W1D 10 E5
Arhchie St STHWK SE1 19 K2
Arica Rd BROCKY SE4 132 B3
Ariel Rd KIL/WHAMP NW6 70 E5
Ariel Wy HSLWW TW4 122 A2
SHB W12 88 A7
Aristotle Rd CLAP SW4 129 J2
Arkell Gv NRWD SE19 149 H6
Arkindale Rd CAT SE6 152 A2
Arkley Crs WALTH E17 57 H4
Arkley Dr BAR EN5 25 J3
Arkley La BAR EN5 25 J2
Arkley Rd WALTH E17 57 H4
Arkley Vw BAR EN5 25 K3
Arklow Rd NWCR SE14 112 C5
Arkwright Rd HAMP NW3 71 G4
Arlesford Rd BRXN/ST SW9 129 K2
Arlingford Rd
BRXS/STRHM SW2 130 B5
Arlington NFNCH/WDSPK N12 38 E2
Arlington Av IS N1 6 F4
Arlington Cl BFN/LL DA15 135 K6
LEW SE13 133 G4
SUT SM1 174 E1
TWK TW1 * 124 D5
Arlington Ct HYS/HAR UB3 101 G4
Arlington Dr CAR SM5 175 K1
RSLP HA4 46 B5
Arlington Gdns CHSWK W4 105 K4
IL IG1 59 K6
Arlington Pde
BRXS/STRHM SW2 * 130 A3
Arlington Rd CAMTN NW1 4 C3
STHGT/OAK N14 40 B1
SURB KT6 158 E5
TEDD TW11 143 F3
WEA W13 85 H5
WFD IG8 44 E7
Arlington Sq IS N1 6 F4
Arlington St MYFR/PICC W1J 10 E8
Arlington Wy CLKNW EC1R 6 B7
Arliss Wy NTHLT UB5 65 G7
Arlow Rd WCHMH N21 29 G7
Armadale Cl TOTM N17 56 D3
Armadale Rd
EBED/NFELT TW14 121 K4
FUL/PGN SW6 107 K6
Armada St DEPT SE8 112 D5
Armada Wy CAN/RD E16 96 B6
Armagh Rd BOW E3 75 H7
Armfield Cl E/WMO/HCT KT8 156 E4
Armfield Crs MTCM CR4 162 E1
Arminger Rd SHB W12 87 K7
Armistice Gdns SNWD SE25 165 H2
Armitage Rd GLDGN NW11 52 C7
GNWCH SE10 113 J3
Armour Cl HOLWY N7 73 F5
Armoury Rd DEPT SE8 132 E1
Armoury Wy
WAND/EARL SW18 127 K4
Armstead Wk DAGE RM10 80 C6
Armstrong Av WFD IG8 44 C5
Armstrong Cl BCTR RM8 61 K6
BMLY BR1 168 D2
BORE WD6 24 E2
EHAM E6 95 K5
RSLP HA4 46 E5
Armstrong Crs EBAR EN4 27 H2
Armstrong Rd ACT W3 87 H7
FELT TW13 141 J4
WLSDN NW10 69 G6
WOOL/PLUM SE18 115 H2
Armstrong Wy NWDGN UB2 103 G1
Armytage Rd HEST TW5 102 C6
Arnal Crs WAND/EARL SW18 127 H6
Arncliffe Cl FBAR/BDGN N11 40 A5
Arne St LSQ/SEVD WC2H 11 K5
Arnett Sq CHING E4 43 H5
Arne Wk LEW SE13 133 J3
Arneways Av CHDH RM6 61 K3
Arneway St WEST SW1P 17 H4
Arnewood Cl PUT/ROE SW15 126 D7
Arney's La MTCM CR4 163 F5
Arngask Rd CAT SE6 133 G6
Arnheim Pl POP/IOD E14 112 D2
Arnison Rd E/WMO/HCT KT8 157 J3
Arnold Circ BETH E2 7 L8
Arnold Cl KTN/HRWW/WS HA3 50 B6
Arnold Crs ISLW TW7 123 J4
Arnold Dr CHSGTN KT9 171 K5
Arnold Est STHWK SE1 19 M2
Arnold Gdns PLMGR N13 41 H4
Arnold Rd BOW E3 93 J2
DAGW RM9 80 B6
NTHLT UB5 65 J5
SEVS/STOTM N15 56 B2
TOOT SW17 147 K6
Arnold Ter STAN HA7 * 35 F4
Arnos Gv STHGT/OAK N14 40 D3
Arnos Rd FBAR/BDGN N11 40 C4
Arnott Cl CHSWK W4 106 A3
THMD SE28 97 J7
Arnould Av CMBW SE5 130 E3
Arnside Gdns WBLY HA9 49 K7
Arnside St WALW SE17 18 F9
Arnulf St CAT SE6 151 K3
Arnull's Rd STRHM/NOR SW16 149 H5
Arodene Rd
BRXS/STRHM SW2 130 A5
Arosa Rd TWK TW1 124 E5
Arragon Gdns
STRHM/NOR SW16 148 E6
WWKM BR4 179 K2
Arragon Rd EHAM E6 77 H7
TWK TW1 124 B6
WAND/EARL SW18 127 K7
Arran Cl ERITH DA8 118 A5
WLGTN SM6 176 C3
Arran Dr MNPK E12 59 H7
STAN HA7 35 J3
Arran Gn OXHEY WD19 * 33 H3
Arran Ms EA W5 86 B7
Arranmore Ct BUSH WD23 * 21 J3
Arran Rd CAT SE6 151 K1
Arran Wk IS N1 6 E1
Arran Wy ESH/CLAY KT10 170 B1
Arras Av MRDN SM4 162 B4
Arrol Rd BECK BR3 165 K2
Arrow Rd BOW E3 93 K2
Arsenal Rd ELTH/MOT SE9 134 E1
Arsenal Wy CAN/RD E16 115 F1
WOOL/PLUM SE18 115 H3
Artemis Pl WAND/EARL SW18 127 J6
Arterberry Rd RYNPK SW20 146 A6
Artesian Cl ROM RM1 63 H5
WLSDN NW10 69 F6
Artesian Gv BAR EN5 27 G3
Artesian Houses
BAY/PAD W2 * 8 A5
Artesian Rd BAY/PAD W2 8 A5
Arthingworth St SRTFD E15 76 C7
Arthurdon Rd BROCKY SE4 132 D4
Arthur Gv WOOL/PLUM SE18 115 H3
Arthur Rd CHDH RM6 61 J6
ED N9 42 B1
EHAM E6 95 K1
HOLWY N7 73 F3
KUTN/CMB KT2 144 C6
NWMAL KT3 160 E4
WIM/MER SW19 146 D3
Arthur St BUSH WD23 21 H2
CANST EC4R 13 H7
ERITH DA8 118 C6
Artichoke Hl WAP E1W 92 D6
Artichoke Pl CMBW SE5 * 110 E7
Artillery Cl GNTH/NBYPK IG2 60 C5
Artillery La LVPST EC2M 13 K3
SHB W12 87 J5
Artillery Pas WCHPL E1 * 13 K3
Artillery Pl WOOL/PLUM SE18 114 E4
Artillery Rw WEST SW1P 17 G4
Artisan Cl EHAM E6 96 B6
Artizan St WCHPL E1 13 K4
Artwell Cl LEY E10 57 K5
Arundel Av MRDN SM4 161 J3
Arundel Cl BTSEA SW11 128 D4
BXLY DA5 137 G5
CROY/NA CR0 * 177 H2
HPTN TW12 142 B4
SRTFD E15 76 C3
Arundel Dr BORE WD6 24 E3
RYLN/HDSTN HA2 65 K3
WFD IG8 44 E6
Arundel Gdns EDGW HA8 37 F6
GDMY/SEVK IG3 79 G1
NTGHL W11 88 D6
WCHMH N21 29 G7
Arundel Gv IS N1 74 A4
Arundel Pl HOLWY N7 73 G5
Arundel Rd BELMT SM2 174 D6
CROY/NA CR0 164 E5
EBAR EN4 27 J2
HSLWW TW4 122 B2
KUT/HW KT1 159 J1
Arundel Sq HOLWY N7 73 G5
Arundel St TPL/STR WC2R 11 M6
Arundel Ter BARN SW13 106 E5
Arungford Ms
BRXS/STRHM SW2 130 B4
Arvon Rd HBRY N5 73 G4
Asbaston Ter IL IG1 78 C4
Ascalon St VX/NE SW8 109 H6
Ascham Dr CHING E4 43 K6
Ascham End WALTH E17 43 G7
Ascham St KTTN NW5 72 C4
Aschurch Rd CROY/NA CR0 165 G6
Ascot Cl BORE WD6 24 C4
NTHLT UB5 66 A4
Ascot Gdns STHL UB1 83 K4
Ascot Ms WLGTN SM6 176 C7
Ascot Pde CLAP SW4 * 129 K3
Ascot Rd EBED/NFELT TW14 120 D7
EHAM E6 95 K2
SEVS/STOTM N15 55 K4
TOOT SW17 148 A5
UED N18 42 C3
WATW WD18 20 C4
Ascott Av EA W5 105 F1
Ascott Ct PIN HA5 * 46 E3
Ashanti Ms HACK E8 * 74 D5
Ashborurne Sq NTHWD HA6 32 C5
Ashbourne Av GLDGN NW11 52 D4
RYLN/HDSTN HA2 * 66 D1
SWFD E18 59 F3
TRDG/WHET N20 39 K1
Ashbourne Cl EA W5 86 B4
NFNCH/WDSPK N12 39 F3
Ashbourne Gv CHSWK W4 106 B4
EDUL SE22 131 G4
MLHL NW7 37 F4
Ashbourne Pde EA W5 * 86 B3
GLDGN NW11 * 52 D3
Ashbourne Rd EA W5 86 B3
MTCM CR4 148 A5
Ashbourne Ter
WIM/MER SW19 146 E6
Ashbourne Wy GLDGN NW11 52 D4
Ashbridge Rd WAN E11 58 C6
Ashbridge St STJWD NW8 9 J1
Ashbrook EDGW HA8 * 36 B5
Ashbrook Rd ARCH N19 72 D1
DAGE RM10 80 D2
Ashburn Gdns SKENS SW7 14 E5
Ashburnham Av HRW HA1 49 F6
Ashburnham Cl EFNCH N2 53 H2
OXHEY WD19 * 32 E2
Ashburnham Dr OXHEY WD19 32 E2
Ashburnham Gdns HRW HA1 49 F5
Ashburnham Gv GNWCH SE10 112 E6
Ashburnham Pk
ESH/CLAY KT10 170 C3
Ashburnham Pl GNWCH SE10 112 E6
Ashburnham Retreat
GNWCH SE10 112 E6
Ashburnham Rd BELV DA17 117 K3
RCHPK/HAM TW10 143 H2
WBPTN SW10 * 108 B6
WLSDN NW10 88 A2
Ashburn Pl SKENS SW7 14 E5
Ashburton Av CROY/NA CR0 165 J7
GDMY/SEVK IG3 79 F3
Ashburton Cl CROY/NA CR0 165 H7
Ashburton Gdns
CROY/NA CR0 178 C1
Ashburton Rd CAN/RD E16 94 E5
CROY/NA CR0 178 C1
RSLP HA4 64 E1
Ashbury Gdns CHDH RM6 61 K4
Ashbury Pl WIM/MER SW19 147 G5
Ashbury Rd BTSEA SW11 128 E2
Ashby Av CHSGTN KT9 172 C5
Ashby Gv IS N1 6 F1
Ashby Ms BROCKY SE4 132 C2
Ashby Rd BROCKY SE4 132 C1
SEVS/STOTM N15 56 C4
Ashby St FSBYE EC1V 6 D8
Ashby Wk CROY/NA CR0 164 D5
Ashby Wy WDR/YW UB7 100 D6
Ashchurch Gv SHB W12 106 D1
Ashchurch Park Vls SHB W12 106 D2
Ashchurch Ter SHB W12 106 C2
Ash Cl CAR SM5 175 K1
EDGW HA8 36 E3
NWMAL KT3 160 A1
PGE/AN SE20 165 K1
SCUP DA14 155 H2
STAN HA7 35 G5
STMC/STPC BR5 169 J4
Ashcombe Av SURB KT6 158 E6
Ashcombe Gdns EDGW HA8 36 C3
Ashcombe Pk CRICK NW2 69 G2
Ashcombe Rd CAR SM5 176 A5
WIM/MER SW19 146 E4
Ashcombe Sq NWMAL KT3 159 K2
Ashcombe St FUL/PGN SW6 * 128 A1
Ash Ct HOR/WEW KT19 172 E3
Ashcroft PIN HA5 34 A5
Ashcroft Av BFN/LL DA15 136 B5
Ashcroft Crs BFN/LL DA15 136 B5
Ashcroft Rd BOW E3 93 G2
CHSGTN KT9 172 B2
Ashdale Cl WHTN TW2 123 G6
Ashdale Gv STAN HA7 35 F5
Ashdale Rd LEE/GVPK SE12 134 A7
Ashdene PIN HA5 47 G2
Ashdene Cl ASHF TW15 * 140 A6
Ashdon Cl WFD IG8 45 F5
Ashdon Rd BUSH WD23 21 H2
Ashdown WEA W13 * 85 H4
Ashdown Cl BECK BR3 166 E1
BXLY DA5 137 K6
Ashdown Crs KTTN NW5 * 72 A4
Ashdown Dr BORE WD6 24 B1
Ashdown Pl THDIT KT7 158 B5
Ashdown Rd KUT/HW KT1 159 F1
PEND EN3 30 E2
WLSDN NW10 69 G7
Ashdown Wy TOOT SW17 148 A1
Ashen EHAM E6 96 A5
Ashenden Rd CLPT E5 75 G4
Ashen Gv WIM/MER SW19 146 E2
Ashen V SAND/SEL CR2 179 F7
Asher Loftus Wy
FBAR/BDGN N11 39 K5
Asher Wy WAP E1W 92 D6
Ashfield Av BUSH WD23 22 B5
FELT TW13 122 A7
Ashfield Cl BECK BR3 151 J6
RCHPK/HAM TW10 125 F7
Ashfield Ct EA W5 * 86 A6
Ashfield La CHST BR7 154 C5
Ashfield Rd ACT W3 87 H7
FSBYPK N4 55 J5
STHGT/OAK N14 40 C2
Ashfield St WCHPL E1 92 D4
Ashfield Yd WCHPL E1 * 92 E4
Ashford Av CEND/HSY/T N8 54 E3
YEAD UB4 83 H5
Ashford Cl WALTH E17 57 H5
Ashford Crs PEND EN3 30 E1
Ashford Gn OXHEY WD19 33 H4
Ashford Ms TOTM N17 42 C7
Ashford Rd ASHF TW15 140 A6
CRICK NW2 70 B3
EHAM E6 77 K5
FELT TW13 140 B3
SWFD E18 59 F1
Ashford St IS N1 7 J7
Ash Gv ALP/SUD HA0 67 G3
CRICK NW2 70 B3
EA W5 105 F1
EBED/NFELT TW14 121 H7
EN EN1 30 A6
HACK E8 74 D7
HEST TW5 102 C7
HYS/HAR UB3 82 B6
MUSWH N10 54 B3
PGE/AN SE20 165 K1
PLMGR N13 41 J2
STHL UB1 84 A4
WWKM BR4 167 F7
Ashgrove Rd ASHF TW15 140 A4
BMLY BR1 152 B5
GDMY/SEVK IG3 61 F7
Ash Hill Cl BUSH WD23 22 B7
Ash Hill Dr PIN HA5 47 G2
Ashingdon Cl CHING E4 44 A3
Ashington Rd FUL/PGN SW6 * 127 J1
Ashlake Rd STRHM/NOR SW16 148 E3
Ashland Pl MHST W1U 10 A2
Ashlar Pl WOOL/PLUM SE18 115 G3
Ashleigh Gdns SUT SM1 175 F1
Ashleigh Rd
MORT/ESHN SW14 126 B2
PGE/AN SE20 165 J2
Ashley Av BARK/HLT IG6 60 B1
MRDN SM4 161 K4
Ashley Cl HDN NW4 52 A1
PIN HA5 47 F1
Ashley Crs BTSEA SW11 129 F2
WDGN N22 55 G1
Ashley Dr BORE WD6 24 E4
ISLW TW7 103 K5
WHTN TW2 123 G7
Ashley Gdns PLMGR N13 41 J3
RCHPK/HAM TW10 143 K2
WBLY HA9 68 A1
Ashley La CROY/NA CR0 177 H3
HDN NW4 52 A1
Ashley Pl WESTW SW1E 16 E4
Ashley Rd ARCH N19 54 E7
CHING E4 43 J4
FSTGT E7 77 G6
HPTN TW12 142 A7
PEND EN3 30 E1
RCH/KEW TW9 125 F2
THDIT KT7 158 A5
THHTH CR7 164 A3
TOTM N17 56 C2
WIM/MER SW19 147 F5
Ashleys Aly SEVS/STOTM N15 55 J3
Ashling Rd CROY/NA CR0 165 H7
Ashlin Rd SRTFD E15 76 B3
Ashlone Rd PUT/ROE SW15 127 F2
Ashlyn Cl BUSH WD23 21 J3
Ashlyns Wy CHSGTN KT9 171 K5
Ashmead STHGT/OAK N14 28 C4
Ashmead Ga BMLY BR1 153 G7
Ashmead Ms DEPT SE8 132 D1
Ashmead Rd DEPT SE8 132 D1
EBED/NFELT TW14 121 K7
Ashmere Av BECK BR3 167 G1
Ashmere Cl CHEAM SM3 174 B4
Ashmere Gv
BRXS/STRHM SW2 129 K3
Ash Ms KTTN NW5 * 72 C4
Ashmill St STJWD NW8 9 J2
Ashmole St VX/NE SW8 110 A5
Ashmore Cl PECK SE15 111 G6
Ashmore Gv WELL DA16 135 J2
Ashmore Rd MV/WKIL W9 88 D2
Ashmount Rd ARCH N19 54 C6
SEVS/STOTM N15 56 B4
Ashmount Ter EA W5 * 104 E3
Ashmour Gdns ROM RM1 63 F1
Ashneal Gdns HRW HA1 66 D2
Ashness Gdns GFD/PVL UB6 67 H5
Ashness Rd BTSEA SW11 128 E4
Ashridge Cl
KTN/HRWW/WS HA3 49 J5
Ashridge Crs
WOOL/PLUM SE18 115 H6
Ashridge Dr OXHEY WD19 33 G4
Ashridge Gdns PIN HA5 47 J3
PLMGR N13 40 E4
Ashridge Wy MRDN SM4 161 J3
SUN TW16 140 E5
Ash Rd CHEAM SM3 161 H7
CROY/NA CR0 179 J1
SRTFD E15 76 C4
Ash Rw HAYES BR2 169 F5
Ashtead Rd STNW/STAM N16 56 C6
Ashton Cl SUT SM1 174 E3
Ashton Gdns CHDH RM6 62 A5
HSLWW TW4 122 E3
Ashton Rd SRTFD E15 76 B4
Ashton St POP/IOD E14 94 A6
Ashtree Av MTCM CR4 162 C1
Ash Tree Cl CROY/NA CR0 166 B5
SURB KT6 159 F7
Ash Tree Dell CDALE/KGS NW9 50 E4
Ash Tree Wy CROY/NA CR0 166 B4
Ashurst Cl DART DA1 138 C2
NTHWD HA6 32 C6
PGE/AN SE20 150 D7
Ashurst Dr GNTH/NBYPK IG2 60 B5
Ashurst Gdns
BRXS/STRHM SW2 * 130 B7
Ashurst Rd EBAR EN4 27 K4
NFNCH/WDSPK N12 39 J4
Ashurst Wk CROY/NA CR0 178 D1
Ashvale Rd TOOT SW17 147 K4
Ashville Rd WAN E11 76 B1
Ash Wk ALP/SUD HA0 67 J3
Ashwell Cl EHAM E6 95 K5
Ashwin St HACK E8 74 B5
Ashwood Av RAIN RM13 99 K2
Ashwood Gdns CROY/NA CR0 179 K5
HYS/HAR UB3 101 J3
Ashwood Rd CHING E4 44 B2
Ashworth Cl CMBW SE5 130 E1
Ashworth Rd MV/WKIL W9 2 D7
Askern Cl BXLYHS DA6 136 E3
Aske St IS N1 7 J7
Askew Crs SHB W12 106 C1
Askew Rd NTHWD HA6 32 B1
SHB W12 106 C1
Askew Vls PLMGR N13 * 41 H2
Askham Rd SHB W12 87 J7
Askill Dr PUT/ROE SW15 127 H4
Askwith Rd RAIN RM13 99 F1
Asland Rd SRTFD E15 76 B7
Aslett St WAND/EARL SW18 128 A6
Asmara Rd CRICK NW2 70 C4
Asmuns Hl GLDGN NW11 52 E4
Asmuns Pl GLDGN NW11 52 D4
Asolando Dr WALW SE17 18 F7
Aspen Cl EA W5 105 G1
Aspen Copse BMLY BR1 168 E1
Aspen Ct HACK E8 * 74 C5
Aspen Dr ALP/SUD HA0 67 G2
Aspen Gdns ASHF TW15 140 A4
MTCM CR4 163 F4
Aspen Gn ERITHM DA18 117 G2
Aspen Gv PIN HA5 46 D2
Aspen La NTHLT UB5 83 J2
Aspenlea Rd HMSMTH W6 107 G5
Aspen Wy FELT TW13 141 F2
POP/IOD E14 94 A6
Aspern Gv HAMP NW3 71 J4
Aspinall Rd BROCKY SE4 132 A2
Aspinden Rd
BERM/RHTH SE16 111 J3
Aspley Rd WAND/EARL SW18 128 A4
Asplins Rd TOTM N17 42 C7
Asplins Vls TOTM N17 * 42 C7
Asprey Ms BECK BR3 166 C4
Asquith Cl BCTR RM8 61 J7
Assam St WCHPL E1 92 C5
Assata Ms IS N1 73 H5
Assembly Pas WCHPL E1 92 E4
Assembly Wk CAR SM5 162 D6
Ass House La
KTN/HRWW/WS HA3 34 B3
Astall Cl KTN/HRWW/WS HA3 34 D7
Astbury Rd PECK SE15 111 K7
Astell St CHEL SW3 15 K7
Asteys Rw IS N1 6 C1
Astle St BTSEA SW11 129 F1
Astley Av CRICK NW2 70 A4
Aston Av KTN/HRWW/WS HA3 49 J6
Aston Cl BUSH WD23 22 C5
SCUP DA14 155 G2
WATN WD24 21 G1
Aston Gn HSLWW TW4 122 B1
Astonplace
STRHM/NOR SW16 149 H5

Bank Ms SUT SM1 175 G5
Banksia Rd UED N18 42 E4
Bankside SAND/SEL CR2 178 B5
STHL UB1 83 H7
STHWK SE1 12 E7
Bankside Av LEW SE13 133 F2
NTHLT UB5 82 E1
Bankside Cl CAR SM5 175 J4
ISLW TW7 124 A3
Bankside Dr THDIT KT7 171 H1
Bankside Rd IL IG1 78 C4
Banks Rd BORE WD6 24 E1
Banks Wy MNPK E12 78 A3
Banksyard HEST TW5 102 E5
The Bank HGT N6 54 B7
Bankton Rd
BRXS/STRHM SW2 130 B3
Bankwell Rd LEW SE13 133 H3
Banner St STLK EC1Y 12 F1
Banning St GNWCH SE10 113 H4
Bannister Cl
BRXS/STRHM SW2 130 B7
GFD/PVL UB6 66 D4
Bannockburn Rd
WOOL/PLUM SE18 115 K3
Bannow Cl HOR/WEW KT19 173 G3
Banstead Ct SHB W12 87 H6
Banstead Gdns ED N9 41 K2
Banstead Rd CAR SM5 175 H6
Banstead St PECK SE15 131 K2
Banstead Wy WLGTN SM6 176 E4
Banstock Rd EDGW HA8 36 D5
Banting Dr WCHMH N21 29 F4
Banton Cl EN EN1 30 D1
Bantry St CMBW SE5 110 E6
Banwell Rd BXLY DA5 136 E5
Banyard Rd BERM/RHTH SE16 111 J2
Baptist Gdns KTTN NW5 72 A5
Barandon Wk NTGHL W11 * 88 B6
Barbara Castle Cl
FUL/PGN SW6 107 J5
Barbara Hucklesbury Cl
WDGN N22 55 H1
Barbauld Rd STNW/STAM N16 74 A2
Barber Cl WCHMH N21 29 G6
Barbers Rd SRTFD E15 93 K1
Barbican Rd GFD/PVL UB6 84 B5
Barb Ms HMSMTH W6 107 F2
Barbon Aly LVPST EC2M 13 K4
Barbon Cl BMSBY WC1N 11 K2
Barbot Cl ED N9 42 C2
Barchard St
WAND/EARL SW18 128 A4
Barchester Cl HNWL W7 85 F7
Barchester Rd
KTN/HRWW/WS HA3 34 D7
Barchester St POP/IOD E14 93 K4
Barclay Cl FUL/PGN SW6 * 107 K6
WATW WD18 20 E5
Barclay Ov WFD IG8 44 E3
Barclay Rd CROY/NA CR0 177 K2
FUL/PGN SW6 107 K6
PLSTW E13 95 G3
UED N18 41 K5
WALTH E17 58 A4
WAN E11 58 D7
Barcombe Av
BRXS/STRHM SW2 148 E1
Barden St WOOL/PLUM SE18 115 K6
Bardfield Av CHDH RM6 61 K2
Bardney Rd MRDN SM4 162 A3
Bardolph Av CROY/NA CR0 179 H7
Bardolph Rd HOLWY N7 72 E3
RCH/KEW TW9 125 G3
Bard Rd NKENS W10 88 B6
Bardsey Pl WCHPL E1 92 E3
Bardsey Wk IS N1 * 73 J5
Bardsley Cl CROY/NA CR0 178 B2
Bardsley La GNWCH SE10 113 F5
Barfett St NKENS W10 88 D3
Barfield Av TRDG/WHET N20 39 K1
Barfield Rd BMLY BR1 169 F2
WAN E11 * 58 D7
Barford Cl HDN NW4 51 J1
Barford St IS N1 6 B4
Barforth Rd PECK SE15 131 J2
Barfreston Wy PGE/AN SE20 150 D7
Bargate Cl NWMAL KT3 160 D6
WOOL/PLUM SE18 116 A4
Barge House St STHWK SE1 12 B8
Barge La BOW E3 75 H7
Bargery Rd CAT SE6 132 E7
Barge Wk KUT/HW KT1 158 E1
Bargrove Cl PGE/AN SE20 150 C6
Bargrove Crs CAT SE6 151 H1
Barham Av BORE WD6 24 B2
Barham Cl ALP/SUD HA0 67 H5
CHST BR7 154 B4
HAYES BR2 168 D7
ROMW/RG RM7 62 D1
Barham Ct ALP/SUD HA0 67 J5
Barham Rd CHST BR7 154 B4
RYNPK SW20 145 J6
SAND/SEL CR2 177 J3
WIM/MER SW19 145 H5
Baring Rd CROY/NA CR0 165 H7
EBAR EN4 27 H2
LEE/GVPK SE12 153 F1
LEE/GVPK SE12 153 F3
Baring St IS N1 7 G4
Barker Cl NTHWD HA6 32 D6
NWMAL KT3 159 J3
RCH/KEW TW9 125 J1
Barker Dr CAMTN NW1 4 F2
Barker St WBPTN SW10 14 E9
Barker Wk STRHM/NOR SW16 148 D2
Barkham Rd TOTM N17 41 K6
Barking Rd EHAM E6 95 H1
POP/IOD E14 94 C5
Bark Pl BAY/PAD W2 8 C6
Barkston Gdns ECT SW5 14 C6
Barkwood Cl ROMW/RG RM7 62 E4
Barkworth Rd
BERM/RHTH SE16 111 J4
Barlborough St NWCR SE14 112 A6
Barlby Gdns NKENS W10 88 B3
Barlby Rd NKENS W10 88 A4
Barley Cl ALP/SUD HA0 67 K3
BUSH WD23 22 B4
Barleycorn Wy POP/IOD E14 93 H6
Barley La GDMY/SEVK IG3 61 G5
Barley Mow Pas CHSWK W4 106 A4
Barlow Cl WLGTN SM6 176 E5
Barlow Dr BKHTH/KID SE3 114 D7
WOOL/PLUM SE18 114 D7
Barlow Pl MYFR/PICC W1J 10 D7
Barlow Rd ACT W3 86 D7
HPTN TW12 142 A6
KIL/WHAMP NW6 70 D5
Barlow St WALW SE17 19 H5
Barlow Wy RAIN RM13 99 F5
Barlow Wy South RAIN RM13 99 F5
Barmeston Rd CAT SE6 151 K1
Barmor Cl RYLN/HDSTN HA2 48 B1
Barmouth Av GFD/PVL UB6 85 F1
Barmouth Rd CROY/NA CR0 179 F1
WAND/EARL SW18 128 B5
Barnabas Rd HOM E9 75 F5
Barnaby Cl RYLN/HDSTN HA2 66 C1
Barnaby Pl SKENS SW7 15 G6
Barnard Cl CHST BR7 154 D7
SUN TW16 141 F6
WLGTN SM6 176 D6
WOOL/PLUM SE18 115 F3
Barnard Gdns NWMAL KT3 160 D3
YEAD UB4 83 F3
Barnard Hl MUSWH N10 54 B1
Barnard Ms BTSEA SW11 128 D3
Barnardo Dr BARK/HLT IG6 60 C3
Barnardo Gdns WCHPL E1 * 93 F5
Barnardo St WCHPL E1 93 F5
Barnard Rd BTSEA SW11 128 D3
EN EN1 30 D1
MTCM CR4 163 F2
Barnards Pl SAND/SEL CR2 177 H7
Barnby St CAMTN NW1 4 F6
SRTFD E15 76 C7
Barn Cl KTTN NW5 * 72 D4
NTHLT UB5 83 G1
Barn Crs STAN HA7 35 J5
Barneby Cl WHTN TW2 123 K7
Barnehurst Av BXLYHN DA7 117 K7
Barnehurst Cl ERITH DA8 117 K7
Barnehurst Rd BXLYHN DA7 137 K1
Barnes Av BARN SW13 106 D6
NWDGN UB2 102 E3
Barnes Br CHSWK W4 126 B1
Barnes Cl MNPK E12 77 H3
Barnes End NWMAL KT3 160 D4
Barnes High St BARN SW13 126 C1
Barnes Rd IL IG1 78 C4
UED N18 42 E3
Barnes St POP/IOD E14 93 G5
Barnes Ter DEPT SE8 112 C4
Barnet By-Pass BORE WD6 25 G4
Barnet Dr HAYES BR2 181 J1
Barnet Gate La BAR EN5 25 H5
Barnet Gv BETH E2 92 C2
Barnet Hl BAR EN5 26 D3
Barnet La BORE WD6 24 B5
TRDG/WHET N20 26 D7
Barnet Rd BAR EN5 25 G5
Barnett Cl ERITH DA8 138 C1
Barnetts Ct
RYLN/HDSTN HA2 * 66 B2
Barnett St WCHPL E1 92 D5
Barnet Way (Barnet By-Pass)
MLHL NW7 25 F6
Barnet Wood Rd HAYES BR2 * 181 F2
HAYES BR2 181 G1
Barney Cl CHARL SE7 114 B4
Barn Fld HAMP NW3 * 71 K4
Barnfield NWMAL KT3 160 B5
Barnfield Av CROY/NA CR0 165 K7
KUTN/CMB KT2 143 K3
MTCM CR4 163 G3
Barnfield Cl FSBYPK N4 54 E6
TOOT SW17 147 G2
Barnfield Gdns
KUTN/CMB KT2 144 A4
WOOL/PLUM SE18 * 115 G5
Barnfield Pl POP/IOD E14 112 D3
Barnfield Rd BELV DA17 117 G5
EA W5 85 J3
EDGW HA8 36 E7
SAND/SEL CR2 178 A7
WOOL/PLUM SE18 115 G5
Barnfield Wood Cl BECK BR3 167 G5
Barnfield Wood Rd BECK BR3 167 G5
Barnham Dr THMD SE28 97 F7
Barnham Rd GFD/PVL UB6 84 C2
Barnham St STHWK SE1 19 K1
Barnhill PIN HA5 47 G4
Barn Hl WBLY HA9 68 D1
Barnhill La YEAD UB4 83 F2
Barnhill Rd WBLY HA9 68 E2
YEAD UB4 83 F3
Barnhurst Pth OXHEY WD19 33 G4
Barningham Wy
CDALE/KGS NW9 50 E5
Barnlea Cl FELT TW13 141 J1
Barnmead Gdns DAGW RM9 80 B4
Barnmead Rd BECK BR3 151 F7
DAGW RM9 80 B4
Barn Ri WBLY HA9 50 C7
Barnsbury Cl NWMAL KT3 159 K3
Barnsbury Crs BRYLDS KT5 159 K7
Barnsbury Est IS N1 5 M4
Barnsbury Gv HOLWY N7 5 M1
Barnsbury La BRYLDS KT5 172 D1
Barnsbury Pk IS N1 6 A1
Barnsbury Rd IS N1 6 A4
Barnsbury Sq IS N1 6 A1
Barnsbury St IS N1 6 A2
Barnsbury Ter IS N1 5 M2
Barnscroft RYNPK SW20 160 E2
Barnsdale Av POP/IOD E14 112 E3
Barnsdale Rd MV/WKIL W9 88 D3
Barnsley St WCHPL E1 92 D3
Barnstaple La LEW SE13 133 F3
Barnstaple Rd RSLP HA4 65 G2
Barnston Wk IS N1 * 6 E3
Barn St STNW/STAM N16 74 A1
Barn Wy WBLY HA9 50 C7
Barnwell Rd
BRXS/STRHM SW2 130 B4
Barnwood Cl MV/WKIL W9 8 C1
RSLP HA4 64 B1
Baron Cl FBAR/BDGN N11 40 A4
Baroness Rd BETH E2 7 M7
Baronet Gv TOTM N17 42 C7
Baronet Rd TOTM N17 42 C7
Baron Gdns BARK/HLT IG6 60 C2
Baron Gv MTCM CR4 162 D3
Baron Rd BCTR RM8 61 K7
Barons Cl IS N1 * 6 A5
Baron's Court Rd WKENS W14 107 H4
Baronsfield Rd TWK TW1 * 124 C5
Barons Ga EBAR EN4 27 J5
Barons Keep WKENS W14 * 107 H4
Barons Md HRW HA1 48 E3
Baronsmead Rd BARN SW13 106 D7
Baronsmede EA W5 105 G1
Baronsmere Ct BAR EN5 * 26 C3
Baronsmere Rd EFNCH N2 53 J3
Baron's Pl STHWK SE1 18 B2
The Barons TWK TW1 124 C5
Baron St IS N1 6 B6
Baron's Wk CROY/NA CR0 166 B5
Barque Ms DEPT SE8 112 D5
Barrack Rd HSLWW TW4 122 C3
Barra Hall Rd HYS/HAR UB3 82 C6
Barratt Av WDGN N22 55 F1
Barratt Wy
KTN/HRWW/WS HA3 48 D2
Barrenger Rd MUSWH N10 39 K7
Barrett Rd WALTH E17 58 A3
Barrett's Green Rd
WLSDN NW10 86 E1
Barrett's Gv STNW/STAM N16 74 A4
Barrett St MHST W1U 10 B5
Barrhill Rd BRXS/STRHM SW2 148 E1
Barriedale NWCR SE14 112 B7
Barrier Point Rd CAN/RD E16 95 G7
Barringer Sq TOOT SW17 148 A3
Barrington Cl CLAY IG5 45 K7
KTTN NW5 72 A4
Barrington Rd BRXN/ST SW9 130 C2
BXLYHN DA7 136 E1
CEND/HSY/T N8 54 D4
CHEAM SM3 161 K7
MNPK E12 78 A5
Barrington Vls
WOOL/PLUM SE18 115 F7
Barrington Wk NRWD SE19 * 150 A5
Barrow Av CAR SM5 175 K6
Barrow Cl WCHMH N21 41 H2
Barrowdene Cl PIN HA5 47 J1
Barrowell Gn WCHMH N21 41 H1
Barrowgate Rd CHSWK W4 105 K4
Barrow Hedges Cl CAR SM5 175 J6
Barrow Hedges Wy CAR SM5 175 J6
Barrow Hl WPK KT4 173 G1
Barrow Hill Cl WPK KT4 173 G1
Barrow Hill Est STJWD NW8 3 J6
Barrow Hill Rd STJWD NW8 3 J6
Barrow Point Av PIN HA5 47 J1
Barrow Point La PIN HA5 47 J1
Barrow Rd CROY/NA CR0 177 G4
STRHM/NOR SW16 148 D5
Barrs Rd WLSDN NW10 69 F6
Barry Av SEVS/STOTM N15 56 B5
Barry Pde EDUL SE22 * 131 H3
Barry Rd EDUL SE22 131 H5
EHAM E6 95 J5
WLSDN NW10 68 E6
Barset Rd PECK SE15 131 K2
Barsons Cl PGE/AN SE20 150 E6
Barston Rd WNWD SE27 149 J1
Barstow Crs
BRXS/STRHM SW2 130 A7
Barter St NOXST/BSQ WC1A 11 K3
Barth Ms WOOL/PLUM SE18 115 K3
Bartholomew Cl STBT EC1A 12 E3
WAND/EARL SW18 128 B3
Bartholomew La OBST EC2N 13 H4
Bartholomew Rd KTTN NW5 72 C5
Bartholomew Sq FSBYE EC1V 6 F9
Bartholomew St STHWK SE1 19 G4
Bartholomew Vls KTTN NW5 72 C5
Barth Rd WOOL/PLUM SE18 115 K3
Bartle Av EHAM E6 95 J1
Bartle Rd NTGHL W11 88 B5
Bartlett Cl POP/IOD E14 93 J5
Bartlett Ct FLST/FETLN EC4A * 12 B4
Bartlett St SAND/SEL CR2 177 K4
Barton Av ROMW/RG RM7 62 E7
Barton Cl EHAM E6 95 K5
HDN NW4 51 J4
HOM E9 74 E4
PECK SE15 131 J2
Barton Gn NWMAL KT3 160 A1
Barton Mdw BARK/HLT IG6 60 B3
Barton Rd HCH RM12 63 J7
WKENS W14 107 H4
The Bartons BORE WD6 23 K5
Barton St WEST SW1P 17 J4
Barton Wy BORE WD6 24 C1
Bartram Rd BROCKY SE4 132 B4
Bartrip St HOM E9 75 G5
Barts Cl BECK BR3 166 D4
Barwell Ct CHSGTN KT9 * 171 J6
Barwell La CHSGTN KT9 171 J6
Barwick Rd FSTGT E7 77 F3
Barwood Av WWKM BR4 166 E7
Bascome St
BRXS/STRHM SW2 130 B5
Basden Gv FELT TW13 142 A1
Basedale Rd DAGW RM9 79 H6
Baseing Cl EHAM E6 96 A6
Basevi Wy DEPT SE8 112 D5
Bashley Rd WLSDN NW10 87 F3
Basil Av EHAM E6 95 J2
Basildene Rd HSLWW TW4 122 C2
Basildon Cl BELMT SM2 175 F7
WATW WD18 20 A5
Basildon Rd ABYW SE2 116 B3
Basil Gdns CROY/NA CR0 166 A7
WNWD SE27 149 J4
Basil St CHEL SW3 15 L2
Basin Ap CAN/RD E16 96 B6
POP/IOD E14 93 G5
Basing Cl THDIT KT7 158 A6
Basing Ct PECK SE15 111 G7
Basingdon Wy CMBW SE5 130 E3
Basing Dr BXLY DA5 137 G5
Basingfield Rd THDIT KT7 158 A6
Basinghall Av CITYW EC2V 13 G4
Basinghall Gdns BELMT SM2 175 F7
Basinghall St CITYW EC2V 13 G4
Basing Hl GLDGN NW11 52 D7
WBLY HA9 68 B1
Basing Pl BETH E2 7 K7
Basing St NTGHL W11 88 D5
Basing Wy FNCH N3 52 E2
THDIT KT7 158 A6
Basire St IS N1 6 F3
Baskerville Gdns
WLSDN NW10 69 G3
Baskerville Rd
WAND/EARL SW18 128 D6
Basket Gdns ELTH/MOT SE9 134 D4
Baslow Cl
KTN/HRWW/WS HA3 34 D7
Baslow Wk CLPT E5 75 F3
Basnett Rd BTSEA SW11 * 129 F2
Bassano St EDUL SE22 131 G4
Bassant Rd WOOL/PLUM SE18 116 A5
Bassein Park Rd SHB W12 106 C1
Bassett Cl BELMT SM2 175 F7
Bassett Gdns ISLW TW7 103 H6
Bassett Rd NKENS W10 88 B5
Bassett St KTTN NW5 72 A5
Bassett Wy GFD/PVL UB6 84 B5
Bassingham Rd ALP/SUD HA0 67 K5
WAND/EARL SW18 128 B6
Basswood Cl PECK SE15 131 J2
Bastable Av BARK IG11 97 F1
Bastion Rd ABYW SE2 116 B4
Baston Manor Rd WWKM BR4 181 F2
Baston Rd HAYES BR2 181 F1
HAYES BR2 181 G3
Bastwick St FSBYE EC1V 6 D9
Basuto Rd FUL/PGN SW6 107 K7
Batavia Ms NWCR SE14 112 B6
Batavia Rd NWCR SE14 112 B6
SUN TW16 141 F7
Batchelor St IS N1 6 A5
Batchworth La NTHWD HA6 32 A4
Bateman Cl BARK IG11 78 C5
Bateman Rd CHING E4 43 J5
Bateman's Blds
SOHO/SHAV W1D 11 G5
Batemans Cnr CHSWK W4 * 106 A4
Bateman's Rw SDTCH EC2A 7 K9
Bateman St SOHO/SHAV W1D 11 G5
Bates Crs CROY/NA CR0 177 G4
STRHM/NOR SW16 148 C6
Bate St POP/IOD E14 93 H6
Bath Cl PECK SE15 111 J6
Bathgate Rd WIM/MER SW19 146 B2
Bath Gv BETH E2 92 C1
Bath House Rd CROY/NA CR0 163 K7
Bath Pas KUT/HW KT1 158 E1
Bath Pl BAR EN5 26 D2
SDTCH EC2A * 7 J8
Bath Rd CHSWK W4 106 B3
ED N9 42 D1
FSTGT E7 77 H5
HSLWW TW4 122 C1
WDR/YW UB7 100 A7
Baths Ap FUL/PGN SW6 * 107 J6
Bath St FSBYE EC1V 6 F8
Bath Ter STHWK SE1 18 E4
Bathurst Av WIM/MER SW19 147 F7
Bathurst Gdns WLSDN NW10 87 K1
Bathurst Ms BAY/PAD W2 9 H6
Bathurst Rd IL IG1 60 B7
Bathurst St BAY/PAD W2 9 H6
Bathway WOOL/PLUM SE18 115 F3
Batley Cl MTCM CR4 162 E6
Batley Pl STNW/STAM N16 74 B2
Batley Rd STNW/STAM N16 74 B2
Batman Cl SHB W12 87 K7
Batoum Gdns HMSMTH W6 107 F2
Batson St SHB W12 106 D1
Batsworth Rd MTCM CR4 162 C2
Batten Cl EHAM E6 95 K5
Batten Cots POP/IOD E14 * 93 G4
Batten St BTSEA SW11 128 D2
Battersby Rd CAT SE6 152 B1
Battersea Br WBPTN SW10 108 C6
Battersea Bridge Rd
BTSEA SW11 108 D6
Battersea Church Rd
BTSEA SW11 108 C7
Battersea High St
BTSEA SW11 128 C1
Battersea Park Rd
BTSEA SW11 109 F7
Battersea Ri BTSEA SW11 128 D4
Battersea Sq BTSEA SW11 * 108 D6
Battery Rd THMD SE28 97 F7
THMD SE28 115 K1
Battishill St IS N1 6 C2
Battle Bridge La STHWK SE1 13 J9
Battle Cl WIM/MER SW19 147 G5
Battledean Rd HBRY N5 73 H4
Battle Rd ERITH DA8 117 K3
Batty St WCHPL E1 92 C5
Baudwin Rd CAT SE6 152 C1
Baugh Rd SCUP DA14 155 J4
The Baulk WAND/EARL SW18 127 K6
Bavant Rd STRHM/NOR SW16 163 K1
Bavaria Rd ARCH N19 72 E1
Bavdene Ms HDN NW4 51 K3
Bavent Rd CMBW SE5 130 D1
Bawdale Rd EDUL SE22 131 G4
Bawdsey Av GNTH/NBYPK IG2 61 F3
Bawtree Rd NWCR SE14 112 B6
Bawtry Rd TRDG/WHET N20 39 K2
Baxendale TRDG/WHET N20 39 G1
Baxendale St BETH E2 92 C2
Baxter Cl NWDGN UB2 103 G2
Baxter Rd CAN/RD E16 95 G5
IL IG1 78 B4
IS N1 73 K5
UED N18 42 D3
Bay Ct EA W5 * 105 F2
Baycroft Cl PIN HA5 * 47 G2
Bayfield Rd ELTH/MOT SE9 134 C3
Bayford Ms HACK E8 * 74 D6
Bayford Rd WLSDN NW10 88 B2
Bayford St HACK E8 74 D6
Baygrove Ms KUT/HW KT1 143 J7
Bayham Pl CAMTN NW1 4 E4
Bayham Rd CHSWK W4 106 A2
MRDN SM4 162 A3
WEA W13 85 H6
Bayham St CAMTN NW1 4 E3
Bayhurst Dr NTHWD HA6 32 D5
Bayleaf Cl HPTN TW12 142 D4
Bayley St FITZ W1T 11 G3
Baylis Ms TWK TW1 124 B6
Baylis Rd STHWK SE1 18 A3
Bayliss Av THMD SE28 97 K6
Bayliss Cl ENC/FH EN2 28 E4
Bayne Cl EHAM E6 95 K5
Baynes Ms HAMP NW3 71 H5
Baynes St CAMTN NW1 4 F2
Baynham Cl BXLY DA5 137 G5
Bayonne Rd HMSMTH W6 107 H5
Bays Cl SYD SE26 150 E4
Bayshill Ri NTHLT UB5 66 B5
Bayston Rd STNW/STAM N16 74 B2
Bayswater Rd BAY/PAD W2 8 E7
Baythorne St BOW E3 93 H4
Baytree Cl BFN/LL DA15 136 A7
BMLY BR1 153 H7
Baytree Rd BRXS/STRHM SW2 130 A3
Bazalgette Cl NWMAL KT3 159 K4
Bazalgette Gdns NWMAL KT3 160 A4
Bazely St POP/IOD E14 94 A6
Bazile Rd WCHMH N21 29 G5
Beacham Cl CHARL SE7 114 C5
Beachborough Rd BMLY BR1 152 A3
Beachcroft Rd WAN E11 76 C2
Beach Gv FELT TW13 142 A2
Beachy Rd BOW E3 75 J6
Beacon Ga NWCR SE14 132 A2
Beacon Hl HOLWY N7 72 E4
Beacon Pl CROY/NA CR0 176 E2
Beacon Rd ERITH DA8 118 E6
HTHAIR TW6 120 D5
LEW SE13 133 G5
Beaconsfield Cl CHSWK W4 105 K4
Beaconsfield Cots
TRDG/WHET N20 * 38 E2
Beaconsfield Gdns
ESH/CLAY KT10 170 E6
Beaconsfield Rd BMLY BR1 168 C2
CAN/RD E16 94 D3
CHSWK W4 106 A2
CROY/NA CR0 164 E5
EA W5 104 D1
ED N9 42 C2
ELTH/MOT SE9 153 J2
ESH/CLAY KT10 170 E6
LEY E10 * 76 A2
NWMAL KT3 160 A1
SEVS/STOTM N15 56 A3
SURB KT6 159 G6
TRDG/WHET N20 39 K2
TWK TW1 124 C5
WALTH E17 57 H5
WALW SE17 19 H9
WLSDN NW10 69 H5
YEAD UB4 83 G7
Beaconsfield Terrace Rd
WKENS W14 107 H2
Beaconsfield Wk
FUL/PGN SW6 107 J7
Beacontree Av WALTH E17 44 B7
Beacontree Rd WAN E11 58 D6
Beadlow Cl CAR SM5 162 C5
Beadman Pl WNWD SE27 * 149 H3
Beadman St WNWD SE27 149 H3
Beadnell Rd FSTH SE23 132 A7
Beadon Rd HMSMTH W6 107 F3
Beaford Gv RYNPK SW20 161 H2
Beagle Cl FELT TW13 141 F3
Beak St REGST W1B 10 E6
Beal Cl WELL DA16 116 B7
Beale Cl PLMGR N13 41 H4
Beale Pl BOW E3 93 H1
Beale Rd BOW E3 75 H7
Beal Rd IL IG1 78 A1
Beam Av DAGE RM10 80 D7
Beames Rd WLSDN NW10 69 F7
Beaminster Gdns
BARK/HLT IG6 60 B2
Beamish Dr BUSH WD23 22 C7
Beamish Rd ED N9 30 C7
Beamway DAGE RM10 81 F6
Beanacre Cl HOM E9 75 H5
Bean Rd BXLYHS DA6 136 E3
Beanshaw ELTH/MOT SE9 154 A3
Beansland Gv CHDH RM6 62 A1
Bear Cl ROMW/RG RM7 62 D5
Beardell St NRWD SE19 150 B5
Beardow Gv
STHGT/OAK N14 * 28 C5
Beard Rd KUTN/CMB KT2 144 B4
Beardsfield PLSTW E13 76 E7
Beard's Hl HPTN TW12 142 A7
Beard's Hill Cl HPTN TW12 142 A7
Beardsley Wy ACT W3 106 A1
Beards Rd ASHF TW15 140 C5
Bearfield Rd KUTN/CMB KT2 144 A6
Bear Gdns STHWK SE1 12 E8
Bear La STHWK SE1 12 D8
Bear Rd FELT TW13 141 H3
Bearstead Ri BROCKY SE4 132 C4
Bearstead Ter BECK BR3 * 151 J7
Bear St LSQ/SEVD WC2H 11 H6
Beasant House WATN WD24 * 21 H1
Beatrice Av
STRHM/NOR SW16 164 A2
WBLY HA9 68 A4
Beatrice Cl PIN HA5 46 E3
PLSTW E13 94 E3
Beatrice Pl KENS W8 14 C4
Beatrice Rd ED N9 30 E6
FSBYPK N4 55 G6
RCHPK/HAM TW10 125 G4
STHL UB1 83 K7
STHWK SE1 111 H3
WALTH E17 57 J4
Beattie Cl EBED/NFELT TW14 121 J6
Beattock Ri MUSWH N10 54 B3
Beatty Rd STAN HA7 35 J5
STNW/STAM N16 74 A3
Beatty St CAMTN NW1 * 4 E5
Beattyville Gdns CLAY IG5 60 A2
Beauchamp Cl CHSWK W4 105 K2
Beauchamp Pl CHEL SW3 15 K4
Beauchamp Rd BTSEA SW11 128 D3
E/WMO/HCT KT8 157 G4
FSTGT E7 77 F6
NRWD SE19 149 K7
SUT SM1 174 E4
TWK TW1 124 B6
Beauchamp St HCIRC EC1N 12 A3
Beauchamp Ter BARN SW13 126 E2
Beauclerc Rd HMSMTH W6 106 E2
Beauclerk Cl FELT TW13 122 A7
Beaufort EHAM E6 96 A4
Beaufort Av
KTN/HRWW/WS HA3 49 G3
Beaufort Cl CHING E4 43 K5
EA W5 86 B4
PUT/ROE SW15 127 F7
ROMW/RG RM7 62 E3
Beaufort Ct
RCHPK/HAM TW10 143 J3
Beaufort Dr GLDGN NW11 52 E3
Beaufort Gdns CHEL SW3 15 K3
HDN NW4 52 A5
HEST TW5 102 D7
IL IG1 60 A7
STRHM/NOR SW16 149 F6
Beaufort Rd EA W5 86 B4
KUT/HW KT1 159 F3
RCHPK/HAM TW10 143 J3
RSLP HA4 * 64 B1
Beaufort St CHEL SW3 15 G9
Beaufort Wy EW KT17 173 J6
Beaufoy Rd TOTM N17 42 A6
Beaufoy Wk LBTH SE11 17 M6
Beaulieu Av CAN/RD E16 95 F7
SYD SE26 150 D3
Beaulieu Cl CDALE/KGS NW9 51 G3
CMBW SE5 130 E2
HSLWW TW4 122 E4
MTCM CR4 148 A7
OXHEY WD19 21 G7
TWK TW1 124 E5
Beaulieu Dr PIN HA5 47 H5
Beaulieu Gdns WCHMH N21 29 J6
Beaulieu Pl CHSWK W4 105 K2
Beaumaris Gn
CDALE/KGS NW9 * 51 G5
Beaumont Av ALP/SUD HA0 67 J4
RCH/KEW TW9 125 G2
RYLN/HDSTN HA2 48 B5
WKENS W14 107 J4
Beaumont Cl EFNCH N2 53 J3
KUTN/CMB KT2 144 C6
Beaumont Ct ALP/SUD HA0 67 J4
Beaumont Crs RAIN RM13 81 J5
WKENS W14 107 J4
Beaumont Dr ASHF TW15 140 B4
WPK KT4 160 E7
Beaumont Gdns HAMP NW3 70 E1
Beaumont Gv WCHPL E1 93 F3
Beaumont Ms MHST W1U * 10 B2
PIN HA5 * 47 J2
Beaumont Pl FITZ W1T 4 F9
ISLW TW7 124 A4
Beaumont Ri ARCH N19 54 D7
Beaumont Rd CHSWK W4 105 K2
LEY E10 57 K6
NRWD SE19 149 J5
PLSTW E13 95 F2
STMC/STPC BR5 169 J5

WIM/MER SW19 127 H6
Beaumont Sq WCHPL E1 93 F4
Beaumont St CAVSQ/HST W1G 10 B2
Beaumont Ter LEW SE13 * 133 H6
Beaumont Wk HAMP NW3 3 M1
Beauvais Ter NTHLT UB5 83 H2
Beauval Rd EDUL SE22 131 G5
Beaverbank Rd
ELTH/MOT SE9 135 J7
Beaver Cl HPTN TW12 142 B7
MRDN SM4 161 F6
PGE/AN SE20 * 150 C6
Beavers Crs HSLWW TW4 122 C3
Beavers La HSLWW TW4 122 B2
Beaverwood Rd CHST BR7 154 E4
Beavor La HMSMTH W6 106 D3
Bebbington Rd
WOOL/PLUM SE18 * 115 K3
Beccles Dr BARK IG11 79 F5
Beccles St POP/IOD E14 93 H5
Bec Cl RSLP HA4 65 H2
Beck Cl GNWCH SE10 112 E7
Beckenham Gdns ED N9 42 A2
Beckenham Gv HAYES BR2 167 G1
Beckenham Hill Rd BECK BR3 151 K5
Beckenham La HAYES BR2 167 H1
Beckenham Place Pk
BECK BR3 151 K6
Beckenham Rd PGE/AN SE20 151 F7
Becket Av EHAM E6 96 A2
Becket Cl SNWD SE25 165 H5
WIM/MER SW19 * 147 F7
Becket Fold HRW HA1 * 49 F4
Becket Rd UED N18 42 E3
Becket St STHWK SE1 19 G3
Beckett Cl BELV DA17 117 F2
STRHM/NOR SW16 148 D1
WLSDN NW10 69 F5
Becketts Cl BXLY DA5 137 K7
EBED/NFELT TW14 122 A5
Becketts Pl KUT/HW KT1 143 K7
Beckett Wk BECK BR3 151 G5
Beckford Cl WKENS W14 107 J3
Beckford Dr STMC/STPC BR5 169 J6
Beckford Pl WALW SE17 * 18 F8
Beckford Rd CROY/NA CR0 165 G5
Beck La BECK BR3 166 A2
Becklow Rd SHB W12 106 C1
Beck River Pk BECK BR3 151 H7
Beck Rd HACK E8 74 D7
MTCM CR4 162 E5
Becks Rd SCUP DA14 155 G2
Beckton Rd CAN/RD E16 94 D4
Beck Wy BECK BR3 166 C2
Beckway Rd
STRHM/NOR SW16 163 J1
Beckway St WALW SE17 19 H6
Beckwith Rd HNHL SE24 130 E5
Beclands Rd TOOT SW17 148 A5
Becmead Av
KTN/HRWW/WS HA3 49 H4
STRHM/NOR SW16 148 D3
Becondale Rd NRWD SE19 150 A4
Becontree Av BCTR RM8 79 H3
Bective Rd FSTGT E7 76 E3
PUT/ROE SW15 127 H3
Bedale St STHWK SE1 * 13 G9
Beddington Cross
CROY/NA CR0 163 J7
Beddington Farm Rd
CROY/NA CR0 163 K7
Beddington Gdns CAR SM5 176 A5
Beddington Gn
STMC/STPC BR5 155 F7
Beddington Gv WLGTN SM6 176 D4
Beddington La CROY/NA CR0 163 H5
Beddington Rd
GDMY/SEVK IG3 61 F6
STMC/STPC BR5 154 E7
Beddington Ter
CROY/NA CR0 * 164 A6
Bede Cl PIN HA5 33 H7
Bede Rd CHDH RM6 61 J5
Bedevere Rd ED N9 42 C2
Bedfont Cl EBED/NFELT TW14 121 F5
MTCM CR4 163 F1
Bedfont Green Cl
EBED/NFELT TW14 121 F7
Bedfont La EBED/NFELT TW14 121 H6
Bedfont Rd STWL/WRAY TW19 120 C5
Bedford Av BAR EN5 26 D4
RSQ WC1B 11 H3
YEAD UB4 83 F5
Bedfordbury CHCR WC2N 11 J6
Bedford Cl CHSWK W4 106 B5
MUSWH N10 40 A6
Bedford Cnr CHSWK W4 * 106 B3
Bedford Ct CHCR WC2N 11 J7
Bedford Gdns KENS W8 8 A9
Bedford Hl BAL SW12 148 B1
Bedford Ms CAT SE6 151 K1
Bedford Pk CROY/NA CR0 164 D7
Bedford Pl CROY/NA CR0 164 E7
RSQ WC1B 11 J2
Bedford Rd BFN/LL DA15 154 E2
CEND/HSY/T N8 54 D5
CHSWK W4 106 A2
CLAP SW4 129 K3
ED N9 30 D6
EFNCH N2 53 J2
EHAM E6 78 A7
HRW HA1 48 C5
IL IG1 78 B2
MLHL NW7 37 G1
NTHWD HA6 32 B3
RSLP HA4 64 D3
SEVS/STOTM N15 55 K3
SWFD E18 58 E1
WALTH E17 57 J1
WDGN N22 40 E7
WEA W13 85 H6
WHTN TW2 142 D2
WPK KT4 174 A1
Bedford Rw GINN WC1R 11 M2
Bedford Sq RSQ WC1B 11 H3
Bedford St COVGDN WC2E 11 J6
Bedford Vls KUT/HW KT1 * 159 G1
Bedford Wy STPAN WC1H 11 H1
Bedgebury Gdns
WIM/MER SW19 146 C1
Bedgebury Rd ELTH/MOT SE9 134 C3
Bedlam Ms LBTH SE11 17 M5
Bedlow Cl STJWD NW8 9 H1
Bedlow Wy CROY/NA CR0 177 F3
Bedonwell Rd BELV DA17 117 F5
BXLYHN DA7 117 H5
Bedser Cl LBTH SE11 17 M9
THHTH CR7 164 D2
Bedser Dr GFD/PVL UB6 66 D4
Bedster Gdns
E/WMO/HCT KT8 157 G1
Bedwardine Rd NRWD SE19 150 A6
Bedwell Gdns HYS/HAR UB3 101 H3
Bedwell Rd BELV DA17 117 H4
TOTM N17 42 A7
Beeby Rd CAN/RD E16 95 F4
Beech Av ACT W3 87 G7
BFN/LL DA15 136 B6
BKHH IG9 45 F1
BTFD TW8 104 C6
RSLP HA4 47 F7
TRDG/WHET N20 27 J7
Beech Cl ASHF TW15 140 B4
CAR SM5 175 K1
DEPT SE8 112 C5
ED N9 30 C5
HCH RM12 81 K2
PUT/ROE SW15 126 D6
SUN TW16 156 C1
WDR/YW UB7 100 D2
WIM/MER SW19 146 A5
Beech Copse BMLY BR1 168 E1
SAND/SEL CR2 178 A4
Beech Ct ELTH/MOT SE9 * 134 D5
Beechcroft CHST BR7 154 A6
Beechcroft Av BXLYHN DA7 118 A7
GLDGN NW11 52 D6
NWMAL KT3 144 E7
RKW/CH/CXG WD3 20 A5
RYLN/HDSTN HA2 48 A6
STHL UB1 83 K7
Beechcroft Cl HEST TW5 102 D6
STRHM/NOR SW16 149 F4
Beechcroft Gdns WBLY HA9 68 B2
Beechcroft Rd BUSH WD23 21 J4
CHSGTN KT9 172 B3
MORT/ESHN SW14 * 125 K2
SWFD E18 59 F1
TOOT SW17 147 K2
Beechdale WCHMH N21 41 F1
Beechdale Rd
BRXS/STRHM SW2 130 A5
Beech Dell HAYES BR2 181 K3
Beech Dr BORE WD6 24 B1
EFNCH N2 53 K2
Beechen Cliff Wy ISLW TW7 104 A7
Beechengrove PIN HA5 47 K2
Beechen Gv WAT WD17 21 F2
Beechen Pl FSTH SE23 150 E1
Beeches Av CAR SM5 175 J6
Beeches Cl PGE/AN SE20 150 E7
Beeches Rd CHEAM SM3 161 H7
TOOT SW17 147 J2
The Beeches HNWL W7 * 104 A1
WATW WD18 * 21 F2
Beeches Wk BELMT SM2 175 H7
Beechfield Cl BORE WD6 24 A1
Beechfield Gdns
ROMW/RG RM7 62 E6
Beechfield Rd BMLY BR1 168 B1
CAT SE6 132 C7
FSBYPK N4 55 J5
Beech Gdns DAGE RM10 80 D6
EA W5 105 F1
Beech Gv MTCM CR4 163 J3
NWMAL KT3 160 A2
Beech Hall Crs CHING E4 44 B6
Beech Hall Rd CHING E4 44 A6
Beechhill Rd ELTH/MOT SE9 135 F4
Beech House Rd
CROY/NA CR0 177 K2
Beech Lawns
NFNCH/WDSPK N12 * 39 H4
Beechmont Cl BMLY BR1 152 C4
Beechmore Gdns CHEAM SM3 174 B1
Beechmore Rd BTSEA SW11 108 E7
Beechmount Av HNWL W7 84 D4
Beecholme Av MTCM CR4 148 B7
Beecholme Est CLPT E5 * 74 E2
Beech Rd EBED/NFELT TW14 121 H6
FBAR/BDGN N11 40 E5
STRHM/NOR SW16 163 K1
Beechrow KUTN/CMB KT2 144 A3
Beech St ROMW/RG RM7 62 E3
Beech Street (Below)
BARB EC2Y 12 E2
Beech Tree Cl IS N1 6 A1
STAN HA7 35 J4
Beech Tree Pl SUT SM1 175 F4
Beechvale Cl
NFNCH/WDSPK N12 39 J4
Beech Wk DART DA1 138 D3
MLHL NW7 37 F4
Beechway BXLY DA5 136 E5
Beech Wy WHTN TW2 142 A2
WLSDN NW10 69 F6
Beechwood Av FNCH N3 52 D2
GFD/PVL UB6 84 B2
HYS/HAR UB3 82 B6
RCH/KEW TW9 105 H7
RSLP HA4 64 D1
RYLN/HDSTN HA2 66 B2
SUN TW16 140 E5
THHTH CR7 164 C3
Beechwood Cl EFNCH N2 * 53 K3
MLHL NW7 37 F4
SURB KT6 158 D6
Beechwood Crs BXLYHN DA7 136 E2
Beechwood Dr HAYES BR2 181 H3
WFD IG8 44 D4
Beechwood Gdns CLAY IG5 59 K4
RAIN RM13 99 K4
RYLN/HDSTN HA2 66 B2
Beechwood Gv ACT W3 87 G6
Beechwood Ms ED N9 42 C1
Beechwood Pk SWFD E18 58 E2
Beechwood Ri CHST BR7 154 B3
Beechwood Rd
CEND/HSY/T N8 54 D3
HACK E8 74 B5
SAND/SEL CR2 178 A7
Beechworth Cl HAMP NW3 71 F1
Beecroft La BROCKY SE4 132 B4
Beecroft Ms BROCKY SE4 132 B4
Beecroft Rd BROCKY SE4 132 B4
Beehive Cl BORE WD6 23 K5
HACK E8 7 L1
Beehive La REDBR IG4 59 K4
Beehive Pl BRXN/ST SW9 130 B2
Beeleigh Rd MRDN SM4 162 A3
Beeston Cl HACK E8 74 C4
OXHEY WD19 33 H3
Beeston Pl BGVA SW1W 16 D4
Beeston Rd EBAR EN4 27 H5
Beeston Wy
EBED/NFELT TW14 122 B5
Beethoven Rd BORE WD6 23 J6
Beethoven St NKENS W10 88 C2
Beeton Cl PIN HA5 34 A6
Begbie Rd BKHTH/KID SE3 114 B7
Beggars Bush La
WATW WD18 20 B4
Beggar's Roost La SUT SM1 174 E5
Begonia Cl EHAM E6 95 J4
Begonia Pl HPTN TW12 142 A5
Beira St BAL SW12 129 G6
Bekesbourne St
POP/IOD E14 * 93 G5
Belcroft Cl BMLY BR1 152 D6
Beldham Gdns
E/WMO/HCT KT8 157 G2
Belfairs Dr CHDH RM6 61 J6
Belfairs Gdn OXHEY WD19 33 H4
Belfairs Gn OXHEY WD19 33 H4
Belfast Rd SNWD SE25 165 J3
STNW/STAM N16 74 B1
Belfield Rd HOR/WEW KT19 173 F7
Belford Gv WOOL/PLUM SE18 115 F3
Belfort Rd PECK SE15 131 K1
Belfry Cl BERM/RHTH SE16 * 111 J4
Belfry Rd MNPK E12 77 H1
Belgrade Rd HPTN TW12 142 B7
STNW/STAM N16 74 A3
Belgrave Cl ACT W3 105 K1
MLHL NW7 37 F4
STHGT/OAK N14 28 C4
Belgrave Crs SUN TW16 141 F7
Belgrave Gdns STAN HA7 35 J4
STHGT/OAK N14 28 D4
STJWD NW8 2 D4
Belgrave Ms South
KTBR SW1X 16 B3
Belgrave Ms West KTBR SW1X 16 A3
Belgrave Pl KTBR SW1X 16 B4
Belgrave Rd BARN SW13 106 C6
HSLWW TW4 122 E2
IL IG1 59 K7
LEY E10 58 A7
MTCM CR4 162 C2
PIM SW1V 16 E6
PLSTW E13 95 G3
SNWD SE25 165 G3
SUN TW16 141 F7
WALTH E17 57 J5
WAN E11 58 E7
Belgrave Sq KTBR SW1X 16 A3
Belgrave St WCHPL E1 93 F4
Belgrave Wk MTCM CR4 162 C2
Belgravia Cl BAR EN5 26 D2
Belgravia Gdns BMLY BR1 152 C5
Belgravia Ms KUT/HW KT1 158 E3
Belgrove St CAMTN NW1 5 J7
Belinda Rd BRXN/ST SW9 130 C2
Belitha Vls IS N1 5 M1
Bellamaine Cl THMD SE28 116 A1
Bellamy Cl EDGW HA8 36 E2
POP/IOD E14 112 D1
WKENS W14 107 J4
Bellamy Dr STAN HA7 35 H7
Bellamy Rd CHING E4 43 K5
ENC/FH EN2 * 29 K1
Bellamy St BAL SW12 129 G6
Bel La FELT TW13 141 J2
Bellarmine Cl THMD SE28 97 F7
Bellasis Av BRXS/STRHM SW2 129 K7
Bell Av WDR/YW UB7 100 C2
Bell Cl PIN HA5 47 G2
Bellclose Rd WDR/YW UB7 100 B1
Bell Dr WAND/EARL SW18 127 H6
Bellefields Rd BRXN/ST SW9 130 A2
Bellegrove Cl WELL DA16 136 A1
Bellegrove Rd WELL DA16 135 K1
Bellenden Rd PECK SE15 131 G1
Belle Staines Pleasaunce
CHING E4 43 J1
Belleville Rd BTSEA SW11 128 D4
Belle Vue GFD/PVL UB6 66 D7
Belle Vue La BUSH WD23 22 D7
Bellevue Pk THHTH CR7 164 D2
Bellevue Pl WCHPL E1 * 92 E3
Bellevue Rd FBAR/BDGN N11 40 A3
KUT/HW KT1 159 F2
TOOT SW17 128 E6
WEA W13 85 H3
BARN SW13 126 D1
Belle Vue Rd HDN NW4 52 B3
WALTH E17 58 B1
Bellew St TOOT SW17 147 G2
Bell Farm Av DAGE RM10 80 E2
Bellfield CROY/NA CR0 179 G7
Bellfield Av
KTN/HRWW/WS HA3 34 D5
Bellfield Cl BKHTH/KID SE3 114 A6
Bell Gdns LEY E10 * 57 J7
Bellgate Ms KTTN NW5 72 B3
Bell Gn SYD SE26 151 H3
Bell Green La SYD SE26 151 H4
Bell House Rd ROMW/RG RM7 62 E7
Bellina Ms KTTN NW5 72 B3
Bellingham Gn CAT SE6 151 J2
Bellingham Rd CAT SE6 152 A2
Bell La CAN/RD E16 94 D7
HDN NW4 52 B3
TWK TW1 124 B7
WBLY HA9 * 67 K1
WCHPL E1 13 L3
Bell Meadow NRWD SE19 150 A3
Bello Cl HNHL SE24 130 C7
Bellot St GNWCH SE10 113 H4
Bell Pde HSLW TW3 * 123 G3
WWKM BR4 * 180 A1
Bellring Cl BELV DA17 117 H5
Bell Rd E/WMO/HCT KT8 157 J4
HSLW TW3 123 G2
Bells Hl BAR EN5 26 B3
Bell St BAY/PAD W2 9 J2
WOOL/PLUM SE18 114 D7
Belltrees Gv
STRHM/NOR SW16 149 F4
Bell Water Ga
WOOL/PLUM SE18 115 F2
Bell Wharf La CANST EC4R 12 F7
Bellwood Rd PECK SE15 132 A3
Bell Yd LINN WC2A 12 A5
Bell Yard Ms STHWK SE1 19 K2
Belmont Av ALP/SUD HA0 68 B7
EBAR EN4 27 K4
ED N9 30 C7
NWDGN UB2 102 D2
NWMAL KT3 160 D4
PLMGR N13 40 E4
WELL DA16 135 K1
Belmont Cir
KTN/HRWW/WS HA3 * 35 H7
Belmont Cl CHING E4 44 B4
CLAP SW4 129 H2
EBAR EN4 27 K3
TRDG/WHET N20 27 F7
WFD IG8 45 F3
Belmont Gv CHSWK W4 106 A3
LEW SE13 133 G2
Belmont Hl LEW SE13 133 F2
Belmont La CHST BR7 154 C4
STAN HA7 35 J6
Belmont Pde CHST BR7 * 154 B4
GLDGN NW11 * 52 D4
Belmont Pk LEW SE13 133 G3
Belmont Park Cl LEW SE13 133 H3
Belmont Park Rd LEY E10 57 K5
Belmont Ri BELMT SM2 174 D6
Belmont Rd BECK BR3 166 B1
BUSH WD23 21 J3
CHST BR7 154 B4
CLAP SW4 129 H2
IL IG1 78 C2
KTN/HRWW/WS HA3 49 F2
SEVS/STOTM N15 55 J3
SNWD SE25 165 J4
WHTN TW2 142 D1
WLGTN SM6 176 C4
Belmont St CAMTN NW1 4 B1
Belmont Ter CHSWK W4 106 A3
Belmor BORE WD6 24 C4
Belmore Av YEAD UB4 82 E5
Belmore La HOLWY N7 72 D4
Belmore St VX/NE SW8 109 J7
Beloe Cl PUT/ROE SW15 126 D3
Belsham St HOM E9 74 E5
Belsize Av HAMP NW3 71 H5
PLMGR N13 41 F5
WEA W13 104 C2
Belsize Court Gdns
HAMP NW3 71 H4
Belsize Crs HAMP NW3 71 H4
Belsize Gdns SUT SM1 175 F3
Belsize Gv HAMP NW3 71 J5
Belsize La HAMP NW3 71 H5
Belsize Ms HAMP NW3 * 71 H5
Belsize Pk HAMP NW3 71 H5
Belsize Park Gdns HAMP NW3 71 H5
Belsize Park Ms HAMP NW3 71 H5
Belsize Pl HAMP NW3 71 H4
Belsize Rd KIL/WHAMP NW6 2 C3
KTN/HRWW/WS HA3 34 D6
Belsize Sq HAMP NW3 71 H5
Belsize Ter HAMP NW3 71 H5
Belson Rd WOOL/PLUM SE18 114 E3
Beltane Dr WIM/MER SW19 146 B2
Belthorn Crs BAL SW12 129 H6
Belton Rd FSTGT E7 77 F6
SCUP DA14 155 G3
TOTM N17 56 A2
WAN E11 76 C3
WLSDN NW10 69 J5
Belton Wy BOW E3 93 J4
Beltran Rd FUL/PGN SW6 128 A1
Beltwood Rd BELV DA17 117 K3
Belvedere Av CLAY IG5 60 B1
WIM/MER SW19 146 C4
Belvedere Blds STHWK SE1 18 D2
Belvedere Cl ESH/CLAY KT10 170 B4
TEDD TW11 142 E4
Belvedere Ct BELV DA17 117 G2
OXHEY WD19 21 H5
Belvedere Dr WIM/MER SW19 146 C4
Belvedere Gdns
E/WMO/HCT KT8 156 E4
Belvedere Gv WIM/MER SW19 146 C4
Belvedere Ms PECK SE15 131 K2
Belvedere Pl
BRXS/STRHM SW2 130 A3
Belvedere Rd ABYW SE2 97 K7
HNWL W7 103 K2
LEY E10 57 G7
NRWD SE19 150 B6
STHWK SE1 17 L1
Belvedere Sq WIM/MER SW19 146 C4
Belvedere Strd
CDALE/KGS NW9 51 H1
The Belvedere WBPTN SW10 * 108 B7
Belvedere Wy
KTN/HRWW/WS HA3 50 A5
Belvoir Rd EDUL SE22 131 H6
Belvue Cl NTHLT UB5 66 A6
Belvue Rd NTHLT UB5 66 A6
Bembridge Cl
KIL/WHAMP NW6 70 C6
Bembridge Gdns RSLP HA4 64 B1
Bemerton Est IS N1 5 L3
Bemerton St IS N1 5 L3
Bemish Rd PUT/ROE SW15 127 G2
Bempton Dr RSLP HA4 65 F1
Bemsted Rd WALTH E17 57 H2
Benares Rd WOOL/PLUM SE18 116 A3
Benbow Rd HMSMTH W6 106 E2
Benbow St DEPT SE8 112 D5
Benbury Cl BMLY BR1 152 A4
Bench Fld SAND/SEL CR2 178 B5
The Bench
RCHPK/HAM TW10 * 143 J2
Bencroft Rd
STRHM/NOR SW16 148 C6
Bencurtis Pk WWKM BR4 180 B2
Bendall Ms CAMTN NW1 9 K2
Bendemeer Rd
PUT/ROE SW15 127 G2
Bendish Rd EHAM E6 77 J6
Bendmore Av ABYW SE2 116 B4
Bendon Va WAND/EARL SW18 128 A6
Bendysh Rd BUSH WD23 21 J2
Benedict Dr
EBED/NFELT TW14 121 G6
Benedict Rd BRXN/ST SW9 130 A2
MTCM CR4 162 C2
Benedict Wy EFNCH N2 * 53 G2
Benedict Whf MTCM CR4 162 D2
Benett Gdns
STRHM/NOR SW16 163 K1
Benfleet Cl SUT SM1 175 G2
Benfleet Wy FBAR/BDGN N11 40 A1
Bengal Rd IL IG1 78 B3
Bengarth Dr
KTN/HRWW/WS HA3 48 D1
Bengarth Rd NTHLT UB5 65 H7
Bengeworth Rd CMBW SE5 130 D2
HRW HA1 67 G1
Ben Hale Cl STAN HA7 35 G4
Benham Cl CHSGTN KT9 171 J5
Benham Gdns HSLWW TW4 122 E4
Benham Rd HNWL W7 84 E4
Benhill Av SUT SM1 175 F3
Benhill Rd CMBW SE5 110 E6
SUT SM1 175 H2
Benhill Wood Rd SUT SM1 175 G3
Benhilton Gdns SUT SM1 175 F2
Benhurst Av HCH RM12 81 K3
Benhurst La
STRHM/NOR SW16 149 G4
Benin St LEW SE13 133 G6
Benjafield Cl UED N18 42 D3
Benjamin Cl EMPK RM11 63 J5
HACK E8 74 C7
Benjamin Ms BAL SW12 129 H6
Benjamin St FARR EC1M 12 C2
Ben Jonson Rd WCHPL E1 93 G4
Benledi St POP/IOD E14 94 B5
Bennelong Cl SHB W12 87 K6
Bennerley Rd BTSEA SW11 128 D4
Bennet Cl KUT/HW KT1 143 J7
Bennet's Hl BLKFR EC4V 12 D6
Bennett Cl HSLWW TW4 122 E4
NTHWD HA6 32 D6
WELL DA16 136 B1
Bennett Gv LEW SE13 112 E7
Bennett Pk BKHTH/KID SE3 133 J2
Bennett Rd BRXN/ST SW9 130 B1
CHDH RM6 62 A5
PLSTW E13 95 G3
Bennetts Av CROY/NA CR0 179 G1
GFD/PVL UB6 66 F7
Bennett's Castle La BCTR RM8 79 J3
Bennetts Cl MTCM CR4 148 B7
TOTM N17 42 B5
Bennetts Copse CHST BR7 153 J5
Bennett St CHSWK W4 106 B5
WHALL SW1A 10 E8
Bennetts Wy CROY/NA CR0 179 G1
Benningholme Rd EDGW HA8 37 G5
Bennington Rd TOTM N17 42 A7
WFD IG8 * 44 C6
Benn St HOM E9 75 G5
Bensbury Cl PUT/ROE SW15 126 E6
Bensham Cl THHTH CR7 164 D3
Bensham Gv THHTH CR7 164 D1
Bensham La CROY/NA CR0 164 C6
Bensham Manor Rd
THHTH CR7 164 D3
Benskin Rd WATW WD18 20 E4
Bensley Cl FBAR/BDGN N11 39 K4
Ben Smith Wy
BERM/RHTH SE16 111 H2
Benson Av PLSTW E13 95 G1
Benson Cl HSLW TW3 123 F3
Benson Quay WAP E1W 92 E6
Benson Rd CROY/NA CR0 177 G2
FSTH SE23 131 K7
Benthal Rd STNW/STAM N16 74 B1
Bentham Rd HOM E9 75 F5
THMD SE28 97 H7
Ben Tillet Cl BARK IG11 79 G6
CAN/RD E16 * 95 K7
Bentinck Ms MHST W1U 10 B4
Bentinck St MHST W1U 10 B4
Bentley Cl WIM/MER SW19 146 E2
Bentley Dr CRICK NW2 70 D2
GNTH/NBYPK IG2 60 C5
Bentley Ms EN EN1 29 K5
Bentley Rd IS N1 74 A5
Bentley Wy STAN HA7 35 G4
WFD IG8 44 E2
Benton Rd IL IG1 60 D7
OXHEY WD19 33 H4
Benton's La WNWD SE27 149 J3
Benton's Ri WNWD SE27 149 K4
Bentry Cl BCTR RM8 80 A1
Bentry Rd BCTR RM8 80 A1
Bentworth Rd SHB W12 87 K5
Benwell Ct SUN TW16 * 140 E7
Benwell Rd HOLWY N7 73 G3
Benwick Cl BERM/RHTH SE16 111 J3
Benwood Ct SUT SM1 175 G2
Benworth St BOW E3 93 H2
Benyon Rd IS N1 7 H3
Benyon Whf IS N1 * 7 K3
Berberis Wk WDR/YW UB7 100 B3
Berber Pde WOOL/PLUM SE18 114 D7
Berber Rd BTSEA SW11 * 128 E4
Bercta Rd ELTH/MOT SE9 154 C1
Berengers Pl DAGW RM9 79 H5
Berenger Wk WBPTN SW10 * 108 C6
Berens Rd WLSDN NW10 88 B2
Beresford Av ALP/SUD HA0 68 C7
BRYLDS KT5 159 J7
HNWL W7 84 D4
TRDG/WHET N20 39 K1
TWK TW1 124 D5
Beresford Dr BMLY BR1 168 C2
WFD IG8 45 G3
Beresford Gdns CHDH RM6 62 A4
EN EN1 30 A3
HSLWW TW4 122 E4
Beresford Rd BELMT SM2 174 D6
CEND/HSY/T N8 55 G4
EFNCH N2 53 J2
HBRY N5 73 K4
HRW HA1 48 D4
KUTN/CMB KT2 144 B7
NWMAL KT3 159 K3
STHL UB1 83 H6
WALTH E17 43 K7
Beresford Sq
WOOL/PLUM SE18 115 G3
Beresford St
WOOL/PLUM SE18 115 G2
Beresford Ter HBRY N5 73 J4
Berestede Rd HMSMTH W6 106 C4
Bere St WAP E1W 93 F6
Berger Cl STMC/STPC BR5 169 J5
Berger Rd HOM E9 75 F5
Berghem Ms WKENS W14 107 G2
Bergholt Av REDBR IG4 59 J4
Bergholt Crs STNW/STAM N16 56 A6
Bergholt Ms CAMTN NW1 4 F2
Bering Sq POP/IOD E14 112 D4
Bering Wk CAN/RD E16 95 H5
Berisford Ms
WAND/EARL SW18 128 B5
Berkeley Av BXLYHN DA7 116 E7
CLAY IG5 60 A1
GFD/PVL UB6 66 E5
HSLWW TW4 101 K7
Berkeley Cl BORE WD6 24 C4
KUTN/CMB KT2 144 A6
RSLP HA4 64 D2
STMC/STPC BR5 169 K6
Berkeley Ct
RKW/CH/CXG WD3 * 20 B4
WLGTN SM6 176 C2
Berkeley Crs EBAR EN4 27 H4
Berkeley Dr E/WMO/HCT KT8 156 E2
Berkeley Gdns ESH/CLAY KT10 171 G6
KENS W8 8 B9
WCHMH N21 29 K6
Berkeley Ms MBLAR W1H 9 M4
SUN TW16 156 B2
Berkeley Pl WIM/MER SW19 146 B5
Berkeley Rd BARN SW13 106 D7
CDALE/KGS NW9 50 C3
CEND/HSY/T N8 54 D4
HGDN/ICK UB10 64 A6
MNPK E12 77 J4
Berkeley Sq MYFR/PICC W1J 10 D7
The Berkeleys SNWD SE25 * 165 H3
Berkeley St MYFR/PICC W1J 10 D7
Berkeley Waye HEST TW5 102 D6
Berkhampstead Rd
BELV DA17 117 H4
Berkhamsted Av WBLY HA9 68 B5
Berkley Cl WHTN TW2 * 142 E2
Berkley Gv CAMTN NW1 4 A2
Berkley Rd CAMTN NW1 3 M2
Berkshire Gdns PLMGR N13 41 G5
UED N18 42 D4
Berkshire Rd HOM E9 75 H5
Berkshire Wy MTCM CR4 163 K3

This page is a street index (gazetteer) listing street names, postal codes, page numbers, and grid references. Due to the density and repetitive nature of the content, a full verbatim transcription of every entry is provided below in reading order, column by column.

Ble – Bra

Column 1:

- Blenheim Gdns
 - BRXS/STRHM SW2 ... 130 A5
 - CRICK NW2 ... 70 A4
 - KUTN/CMB KT2 ... 144 C3
 - WBLY HA9 ... 68 A2
 - WLGTN SM6 ... 176 B5
- Blenheim Gv PECK SE15 ... 131 G1
- Blenheim Park Rd
 - SAND/SEL CR2 ... 177 J7
- Blenheim Pas STJWD NW8 * ... 2 B1
- Blenheim Pl TEDD TW11 ... 143 F4
- Blenheim Ri
 - SEVS/STOTM N15 * ... 56 B3
- Blenheim Rd BAR EN5 ... 26 B2
 - BFN/LL DA15 ... 136 C1
 - BMLY BR1 ... 168 B3
 - CHSWK W4 ... 106 A2
 - EHAM E6 ... 95 H1
 - NTHLT UB5 ... 66 B3
 - PGE/AN SE20 ... 150 E6
 - RYLN/HDSTN HA2 ... 48 B5
 - RYNPK SW20 ... 161 G1
 - STJWD NW8 ... 2 B1
 - SUT SM1 ... 174 E2
 - WALTH E17 ... 57 F2
 - WAN E11 ... 76 C3
- Blenheim St CONDST W1S ... 10 B5
- Blenheim Ter STJWD NW8 ... 2 B1
- Blenheim Wy ISLW TW7 ... 104 B5
- Blenkarne Rd BTSEA SW11 ... 128 E5
- Bleriot Rd HEST TW5 ... 102 A5
- Blessbury Rd EDGW HA8 ... 36 E7
- Blessington Cl LEW SE13 ... 133 G2
- Blessington Rd LEW SE13 ... 133 G3
- Bletchingley Cl THHTH CR7 ... 164 B3
- Bletchley St IS N1 ... 6 F6
- Bletchmore Cl HYS/HAR UB3 ... 101 G4
- Bletsoe Wk IS N1 ... 6 F4
- Blincoe Cl WIM/MER SW19 ... 146 B1
- Blissett St GNWCH SE10 ... 113 F7
- Bliss Ms NKENS W10 ... 88 C2
- Blisworth Cl YEAD UB4 ... 83 J3
- Blithbury Rd DAGW RM9 ... 79 H5
- Blithdale Rd ABYW SE2 ... 116 B3
- Blithfield St KENS W8 ... 14 C4
- Blockley Rd ALP/SUD HA0 ... 67 H1
- Bloemfontein Av SHB W12 ... 87 K7
- Bloemfontein Rd SHB W12 ... 87 K6
- Blomfield Rd MV/WKIL W9 ... 8 D3
- Blomfield St LVPST EC2M ... 13 H3
- Blomfield Vls BAY/PAD W2 ... 8 D3
- Blomville Rd BCTR RM8 ... 80 A3
- Blondel St BTSEA SW11 ... 129 F1
- Blondin Av EA W5 ... 104 D3
- Blondin St BOW E3 ... 93 J1
- Bloomfield Crs
 - GNTH/NBYPK IG2 ... 60 B5
- Bloomfield Pl
 - MYFR/PKLN W1K ... 10 D6
- Bloomfield Rd HAYES BR2 ... 168 E4
 - HGT N6 ... 54 A5
 - KUT/HW KT1 ... 159 F3
 - WOOL/PLUM SE18 ... 115 G4
- Bloomfield Ter BGVA SW1W ... 16 B7
- Bloom Gv WNWD SE27 ... 149 H2
- Bloomhall Rd NRWD SE19 ... 149 K4
- Bloom Park Rd FUL/PGN SW6 ... 107 J6
- Bloomsbury Cl EA W5 ... 86 B6
- Bloomsbury Pl
 - NOXST/BSQ WC1A ... 11 K3
- Bloomsbury Sq
 - NOXST/BSQ WC1A ... 11 K3
- Bloomsbury St GWRST WC1E ... 11 H2
- Bloomsbury Wy
 - NOXST/BSQ WC1A ... 11 J3
- Blore Cl VX/NE SW8 ... 109 J7
- Blossom Cl DAGW RM9 ... 80 B7
 - EA W5 ... 105 F1
 - SAND/SEL CR2 ... 178 B4
- Blossom St WCHPL E1 ... 13 K1
- Blossom Wy WDR/YW UB7 ... 100 D3
- Blossom Waye HEST TW5 ... 102 D5
- Blount St POP/IOD E14 ... 93 G5
- Bloxam Gdns ELTH/MOT SE9 ... 134 D4
- Bloxhall Rd LEY E10 ... 57 H7
- Bloxham Crs HPTN TW12 ... 141 E7
- Bloxworth Cl WLGTN SM6 ... 176 C2
- Blucher Rd CMBW SE5 ... 110 D6
- Blue Anchor La
 - BERM/RHTH SE16 ... 111 H3
- Blue Anchor Yd WCHPL E1 ... 92 C6
- Blue Ball Yd WHALL SW1A ... 10 F1
- Bluebell Av MNPK E12 ... 77 H4
- Bluebell Cl HOM E9 ... 74 E7
 - NTHLT UB5 ... 65 H3
 - ROMW/RG RM7 ... 81 G1
 - SYD SE26 ... 150 B3
 - WLGTN SM6 ... 163 G7
- Bluebell Wy IL IG1 ... 78 B5
- Blueberry Cl WFD IG8 ... 44 E5
- Bluebird La DAGE RM10 ... 80 C6
- Bluebird Wy THMD SE28 ... 115 J1
- Bluefield Cl HPTN TW12 ... 142 H1
- Bluegates EW KT17 ... 173 J6
- Bluehouse Rd CHING E4 ... 44 C2
- Blue Lion Pl STHWK SE1 ... 19 J3
- Blue Riband Est
 - CROY/NA CR0 ... 177 H1
- Blundell Cl HACK E8 ... 74 C3
- Blundell Rd EDGW HA8 ... 37 F7
- Blundell St HOLWY N7 ... 5 K1
- Blunden Cl BCTR RM8 ... 61 J7
- Blunt Rd SAND/SEL CR2 ... 177 K4
- Blunts Rd ELTH/MOT SE9 ... 135 F4
- Blunts Av WDR/YW UB7 ... 100 D6
- Blurton Rd CLPT E5 ... 75 F3
- Blyth Cl TWK TW1 ... 124 A4
- Blythe Cl CAT SE6 ... 132 C6
- Blythe Hl CAT SE6 ... 132 C6
 - STMC/STPC BR5 ... 155 F1
- Blythe Hill La CAT SE6 ... 132 C6
- Blythe Hill Pl FSTH SE23 * ... 132 B6
- Blythe Ms WKENS W14 * ... 107 G2
- Blythe Rd WKENS W14 ... 107 G2
- Blythe St BETH E2 * ... 92 D2
- Blythe Vale CAT SE6 ... 132 C7
- Blyth Rd BMLY BR1 ... 152 E7
 - HYS/HAR UB3 ... 101 H1
 - THMD SE28 ... 97 J6
 - WALTH E17 ... 57 H6
- Blyth's Whf POP/IOD E14 * ... 93 G6
- Blythswood Rd
 - GDMY/SEVK IG3 ... 61 G7
- Blythwood Rd FSBYPK N4 ... 54 E6
 - PIN HA5 ... 33 H7
- Boadicea St IS N1 ... 5 L4
- Boakes Cl CDALE/KGS NW9 ... 50 E3
- Boardman Av CHING E4 ... 31 K4
- Boardman Cl BAR EN5 ... 26 C4
- Boardwalk Pl POP/IOD E14 ... 94 A7

Column 2:

- Boathouse Wk PECK SE15 ... 111 G6
 - RCH/KEW TW9 ... 104 E7
- Boat Lifter Wy
 - BERM/RHTH SE16 ... 112 B3
- Boat Quay CAN/RD E16 ... 95 G6
- Bob Anker Cl PLSTW E13 ... 94 E2
- Bob Marley Wy HNHL SE24 ... 130 B3
- Bockhampton Rd
 - KUTN/CMB KT2 ... 144 B6
- Bocking St HACK E8 ... 74 D7
- Boddicott Cl WIM/MER SW19 ... 146 C1
- Boddington Gdns ACT W3 ... 105 H1
- Bodiam Cl EN EN1 ... 29 K1
- Bodiam Rd STRHM/NOR SW16 ... 148 D7
- Bodiam Wy WLSDN NW10 ... 86 B2
- Bodicea Ms HSLWW TW4 ... 122 E5
- Bodley Cl NWMAL KT3 ... 160 B4
- Bodley Rd NWMAL KT3 ... 160 B5
- Bodmin Cl RYLN/HDSTN HA2 ... 65 K2
- Bodmin Gv MRDN SM4 ... 162 B4
- Bodmin St WAND/EARL SW18 ... 127 K7
- Bodnant Gdns RYNPK SW20 ... 160 D2
- Bodney Rd CLPT E5 ... 74 D2
- Boeing Wy NWDGN UB2 ... 102 A2
- Bofors House CHARL SE7 * ... 114 D6
- Bognor Gdns OXHEY WD19 * ... 33 G4
- Bognor Rd WELL DA16 ... 116 E7
- Bohemia Pl HACK E8 ... 74 E5
- Bohn Rd WCHPL E1 ... 93 G4
- Bohun Gv EBAR EN4 ... 27 J5
- Boileau Rd BARN SW13 ... 106 D6
 - EA W5 ... 86 B5
- Boilerhouse DEPT SE8 ... 132 E1
- Boldero Pl STJWD NW8 * ... 9 J1
- Bolderwood Wy WWKM BR4 ... 179 K1
- Boldmere Rd PIN HA5 ... 47 G6
- Boleyn Av EW/EMO/HCT KT8 ... 156 E4
 - RSLP HA4 ... 65 H1
- Boleyn Gdns DAGE RM10 ... 80 E6
 - WWKM BR4 ... 179 K1
- Boleyn Rd EHAM E6 ... 95 H1
 - FSTGT E7 ... 76 E6
 - STNW/STAM N16 ... 74 A4
- Boleyn Wy BAR EN5 ... 27 G2
- Bolina Rd BERM/RHTH SE16 ... 111 K4
- Bolingbroke Gv BTSEA SW11 ... 128 E4
- Bolingbroke Rd WKENS W14 ... 107 G2
- Bolingbroke Wk
 - BTSEA SW11 * ... 108 C6
- Bolingbroke Wy
 - HYS/HAR UB3 ... 82 B7
- Bollo Bridge Rd ACT W3 ... 105 J2
- Bollo La ACT W3 ... 105 J2
- Bolney Ga SKENS SW7 ... 15 J2
- Bolney St VX/NE SW8 ... 110 A6
- Bolsover St GTPST W1W ... 10 D1
- Bolstead Rd MTCM CR4 ... 148 B7
- Bolster Gv WDGN N22 * ... 40 F7
- Bolt Ct FLST/FETLN EC4A ... 12 B5
- Boltmore Cl HDN NW4 ... 52 B2
- Bolton Cl CHSGTN KT9 ... 171 K5
- Bolton Crs CMBW SE5 ... 110 D6
- Bolton Dr MRDN SM4 ... 162 B6
- Bolton Gdns BMLY BR1 ... 152 D5
 - TEDD TW11 ... 143 G5
 - WLSDN NW10 ... 88 B1
- Bolton Gardens Ms
 - WBPTN SW5 ... 14 D7
- Bolton Pl IS N1 * ... 6 C1
- Bolton Rd CHSGTN KT9 ... 171 K5
 - CHSWK W4 ... 105 K6
 - HRW HA1 ... 48 C5
 - SRTFD E15 ... 76 D5
 - STJWD NW8 ... 3 G4
 - UED N18 ... 42 B4
 - WLSDN NW10 ... 69 G7
- Bolton's La HYS/HAR UB3 ... 101 F6
- Boltons Pl ECT SW5 ... 14 D7
- The Boltons ALP/SUD HA0 ... 67 F3
 - WBPTN SW10 ... 14 E7
 - WFD IG8 * ... 44 E2
- Bolton St MYFR/PICC W1J ... 10 D8
- Bombay St BERM/RHTH SE16 ... 111 J3
- Bomer Cl WDR/YW UB7 ... 100 D6
- Bomore Rd NTGHL W11 ... 88 B6
- Bonaparte Ms PIM SW1V ... 17 G7
- Bonar Pl CHST BR7 ... 153 J6
- Bonar Rd PECK SE15 ... 111 H6
- Bonchester Cl CHST BR7 ... 154 A6
- Bonchurch Cl BELMT SM2 ... 175 F6
- Bonchurch Rd NKENS W10 ... 88 C4
 - WEA W13 ... 85 H7
- Bondfield Av YEAD UB4 ... 82 E1
- Bond Gdns WLGTN SM6 ... 176 C3
- Bond Rd MTCM CR4 ... 162 F1
 - SURB KT6 ... 172 B1
- Bond St EA W5 ... 85 K6
 - SRTFD E15 ... 76 C4
- Bondway VX/NE SW8 ... 17 K9
- Boneta Rd WOOL/PLUM SE18 ... 114 E2
- Bonfield Rd LEW SE13 ... 133 F3
- Bonham Gdns BCTR RM8 ... 79 K1
- Bonham Rd BCTR RM8 ... 79 K1
 - BRXS/STRHM SW2 ... 130 A4
- Bonheur Rd CHSWK W4 ... 106 A1
- Bonhill St SDTCH EC2A ... 13 H1
- Boniface Gdns
 - KTN/HRWW/WS HA3 ... 34 B6
- Boniface Wk
 - KTN/HRWW/WS HA3 ... 34 B6
- Bonita Ms PECK SE15 ... 132 A2
- Bonner Hill Rd KUT/HW KT1 ... 159 F2
- Bonner Rd BETH E2 ... 92 E1
- Bonnersfield Cl HRW HA1 ... 49 E5
- Bonnersfield La HRW HA1 ... 49 F5
- Bonner St BETH E2 * ... 92 E1
- Bonneville Gdns CLAP SW4 ... 129 H5
- Bonnington Sq VX/NE SW8 * ... 17 L9
- Bonny St CAMTN NW1 ... 4 F2
- Bonser Rd TWK TW1 ... 143 F1
- Bonsor St CMBW SE5 ... 111 F6
- Bonville Gdns HDN NW4 ... 51 J3
- Bonville Rd BMLY BR1 ... 152 D4
- Booker Rd UED N18 ... 42 C4
- Boones Rd LEW SE13 ... 133 H3
- Boone St LEW SE13 ... 133 H3
- Boord St GNWCH SE10 ... 113 H2
- Boothby Rd ARCH N19 ... 72 D1
- Booth Cl HOM E9 * ... 74 D7
 - THMD SE28 ... 97 H7
- Booth La BLKFR EC4V ... 12 E6
 - CDALE/KGS NW9 ... 37 F7
 - CROY/NA CR0 * ... 177 H1
- Booth Rd EDGW HA8 * ... 36 C5
- Boot St FSBYE EC1V ... 7 J8
- Bordars Rd HNWL W7 ... 84 E4
- Bordars Wk HNWL W7 ... 84 E4
- Borden Av EN EN1 ... 29 K5
- Border Crs SYD SE26 ... 150 D4
- Border Ga CROY/NA CR0 ... 179 K3

Column 3:

- Border Ga MTCM CR4 ... 147 J7
- Border Rd SYD SE26 ... 150 D4
- Bordesley Rd MRDN SM4 ... 162 A3
- Bordon Wk PUT/ROE SW15 ... 126 D6
- Boreas Wk IS N1 ... 6 D6
- Boreham Av CAN/RD E16 ... 94 E5
- Boreham Cl WAN E11 ... 58 A7
- Boreham Rd WDGN N22 ... 41 J1
- Borgard House CHARL SE7 * ... 114 D6
- Borgard Rd WOOL/PLUM SE18 ... 114 E4
- Borland Rd PECK SE15 ... 131 K3
 - TEDD TW11 ... 143 H5
- Borneo St PUT/ROE SW15 ... 127 F2
- Borough High St STHWK SE1 ... 18 E2
- Borough Hl CROY/NA CR0 ... 177 H2
- Borough Rd ISLW TW7 ... 103 K7
 - KUTN/CMB KT2 ... 144 C7
 - MTCM CR4 ... 162 D1
 - STHWK SE1 ... 18 C3
- Borough Sq STHWK SE1 ... 18 E2
- Borrett Cl WALW SE17 ... 18 E8
- Borrodaile Rd
 - WAND/EARL SW18 ... 128 A5
- Borrowdale Av
 - KTN/HRWW/WS HA3 ... 49 G1
- Borrowdale Cl EFNCH N2 ... 53 J3
 - REDBR IG4 ... 59 J3
- Borthwick Ms WAN E11 * ... 76 C3
- Borthwick Rd
 - CDALE/KGS NW9 ... 51 H5
 - SRTFD E15 ... 76 C3
- Borthwick St DEPT SE8 ... 112 C4
- Borwick Av WALTH E17 ... 57 H2
- Bosbury Rd CAT SE6 ... 152 A2
- Boscastle Rd KTTN NW5 ... 72 B2
- Boscobel Cl BMLY BR1 ... 168 E1
- Boscobel Pl BGVA SW1W ... 16 B5
- Boscobel St BAY/PAD W2 ... 9 H2
- Boscombe Av LEY E10 ... 58 B6
- Boscombe Cl CLPT E5 ... 75 G4
- Boscombe Gdns STRHM/NOR SW16 ... 148 E5
- Boscombe Rd SHB W12 ... 106 D1
 - TOOT SW17 ... 148 A5
 - WIM/MER SW19 ... 146 E7
 - WPK KT4 ... 161 F7
- Boss Cl FNCH N3 ... 38 C7
- Bostall Hl ABYW SE2 ... 116 C4
- Bostall La ABYW SE2 ... 116 B4
- Bostall Manorway ABYW SE2 ... 116 C3
- Bostall Park Av BXLYHN DA7 ... 117 G6
- Boston Gdns BTFD TW8 ... 104 F7
 - CHSWK W4 ... 106 B5
- Boston Gv RSLP HA4 ... 46 A5
- Boston Manor Rd BTFD TW8 ... 104 C4
- Boston Pde HNWL W7 * ... 104 B3
- Boston Park Rd BTFD TW8 ... 104 D4
- Boston Rd CAMTN NW1 ... 12 E1
 - EDGW HA8 ... 36 E6
 - EHAM E6 ... 95 K2
 - HNWL W7 ... 84 F7
 - WALTH E17 ... 57 J5
- Bostonthorpe Rd HNWL W7 * ... 103 K1
- Boston V HNWL W7 ... 104 B3
- Boswell Ct BMSBY WC1N ... 11 K2
- Boswell Rd THHTH CR7 ... 164 D3
- Boswell St BMSBY WC1N ... 11 K2
- Bosworth Cl WALTH E17 ... 43 H7
- Bosworth Rd BAR EN5 ... 26 E2
 - DAGE RM10 ... 80 C3
 - FBAR/BDGN N11 ... 40 D5
 - NKENS W10 ... 88 C3
- Botany Bay La CHST BR7 ... 169 H7
- Botany Cl EBAR EN4 ... 27 J3
- Botany Ter PUR RM19 ... 119 K4
- Boteley Cl CHING E4 ... 44 B1
- Botham Cl EDGW HA8 ... 36 E6
- Botha Rd PLSTW E13 ... 95 F4
- Bothwell Rd CROY/NA CR0 ... 180 C7
- Bothwell St HMSMTH W6 ... 107 G5
- Botolph Aly MON EC3R ... 13 J7
- Botolph La MON EC3R ... 13 J7
- Botsford Rd RYNPK SW20 ... 161 H1
- Bott's Ms BAY/PAD W2 ... 8 B5
- Botwell Common Rd
 - HYS/HAR UB3 ... 82 B6
- Botwell Crs HYS/HAR UB3 ... 82 C5
- Botwell La HYS/HAR UB3 ... 82 C5
- Boucher Cl TEDD TW11 ... 143 F4
- Boughton Av HAYES BR2 ... 167 J7
- Boughton Rd THMD SE28 ... 115 K2
- Boulcott St WCHPL E1 ... 93 F5
- Boulevard Dr
 - CDALE/KGS NW9 ... 51 H1
- The Boulevard FUL/PGN SW6 ... 128 B1
 - WATW WD18 * ... 20 B4
- Boulogne Rd CROY/NA CR0 ... 164 D5
- Boulter Cl BMLY BR1 ... 169 F2
- Boulter Gdns RAIN RM13 ... 81 J1
- Boulton Rd BCTR RM8 ... 79 K1
- Boultwood Rd EHAM E6 ... 95 K5
- Boulevard WATW WD18 * ... 20 B4
- Bouncers La ED N9 ... 42 E1
- Boundaries Rd BAL SW12 ... 147 H1
 - FELT TW13 ... 122 C7
- Boundary Av WALTH E17 ... 57 H6
- Boundary Business Ct
 - MTCM CR4 ... 162 C2
- Boundary Cl GDMY/SEVK IG3 ... 78 E3
 - KUT/HW KT1 ... 159 H2
 - NWDGN UB2 ... 103 F3
- Boundary La CMBW SE5 ... 110 D5
 - PLSTW E13 ... 95 H3
- Boundary Ms STJWD NW8 * ... 2 F3
- Boundary Pass WCHPL E1 ... 7 L9
- Boundary Rd BARK IG11 ... 96 C1
 - BFN/LL DA15 ... 135 K4
 - CAR SM5 ... 175 K5
 - ED N9 ... 30 E5
 - EFNCH N2 ... 39 H1
 - PIN HA5 ... 47 H5
 - PLSTW E13 ... 77 G7
 - ROM RM1 ... 63 J5
 - STJWD NW8 ... 2 E2
 - WALTH E17 ... 57 H6
 - WIM/MER SW19 ... 147 H5
 - WLGTN SM6 ... 176 B5
- Boundary Rw STHWK SE1 ... 18 C1
- Boundary St BETH E2 ... 7 L8
- Boundfield Rd CAT SE6 ... 152 C2
- Bounds Green Rd
 - FBAR/BDGN N11 ... 40 D5
- Bourchier St SOHO/SHAV W1D ... 11 G6
- Bourdon Pl MYFR/PKLN W1K ... 10 D7
- Bourdon St MYFR/PKLN W1K ... 10 D7
- Bourke Cl CLAP SW4 ... 129 K6
 - WLSDN NW10 ... 69 G5
- Bourlet Cl GTPST W1W ... 10 E3

Column 4:

- Bourn Av EBAR EN4 ... 27 H4
 - SEVS/STOTM N15 ... 55 K3
- Bournbrook Rd
 - BKHTH/KID SE3 ... 134 C2
- Bourne Av HYS/HAR UB3 ... 101 F2
 - RSLP HA4 ... 65 G3
 - STHGT/OAK N14 ... 40 E1
- Bourne Cl ISLW TW7 ... 123 K3
 - THDIT KT7 ... 171 F1
- Bourne Ct RSLP HA4 ... 65 F3
- Bourne Dr MTCM CR4 ... 162 C1
- Bourne End Rd NTHWD HA6 ... 32 C2
- Bourne Est HCIRC EC1N * ... 12 A2
- Bourne Gdns CHING E4 ... 43 K3
- Bournehall Av BUSH WD23 ... 22 B4
- Bournehall La BUSH WD23 ... 22 B5
- Bournehall Rd BUSH WD23 ... 22 B5
- Bourne Hl PLMGR N13 ... 40 F2
- Bourne Hill Cl PLMGR N13 ... 41 F1
- Bournemead BUSH WD23 ... 22 A6
- Bournemead Av NTHLT UB5 ... 82 E1
- Bournemead Cl NTHLT UB5 ... 82 E1
- Bournemouth Cl PECK SE15 ... 131 H1
- Bournemouth Rd PECK SE15 ... 131 H1
 - WIM/MER SW19 ... 146 E7
- Bourne Pde BXLY DA5 * ... 137 H6
 - BXLY DA5 ... 137 J5
- Bourne Rd BUSH WD23 ... 22 B5
 - BXLY DA5 ... 137 J5
 - CEND/HSY/T N8 ... 55 E5
 - HAYES BR2 ... 168 D3
 - WAN E11 ... 76 D2
- Bourneside Crs
 - STHGT/OAK N14 ... 28 D7
- Bourneside Gdns CAT SE6 ... 152 A4
- Bourne St BGVA SW1W ... 16 A6
 - CROY/NA CR0 ... 177 H1
- Bourne Ter BAY/PAD W2 ... 8 D2
- The Bourne STHGT/OAK N14 ... 28 D7
- Bournevale Rd
 - STRHM/NOR SW16 ... 148 E3
- Bourne Vw GFD/PVL UB6 ... 67 F5
- Bourne Wy HOR/WEW KT19 ... 172 E3
 - SUT SM1 ... 174 D4
- Bournewood Rd
 - WOOL/PLUM SE18 ... 116 B6
- Bournville Rd CAT SE6 ... 132 D6
- Bournwell Cl EBAR EN4 ... 27 K1
- Bourton Cl HYS/HAR UB3 ... 82 E7
- Bousfield Rd NWCR SE14 ... 132 A1
- Boutflower Rd BTSEA SW11 ... 128 D3
- Boutique Hall LEW SE13 * ... 133 F3
- Bouverie Gdns
 - KTN/HRWW/WS HA3 ... 49 K6
 - Bouverie Ms STNW/STAM N16 ... 74 A1
- Bouverie Pl BAY/PAD W2 ... 9 H4
- Bouverie Rd HRW HA1 ... 48 C5
 - STNW/STAM N16 ... 74 A1
- Bouverie St EMB EC4V ... 12 B5
- Boveney Rd FSTH SE23 ... 132 A6
- Bovill Rd FSTH SE23 ... 132 A6
- Bovingdon Av WBLY HA9 ... 68 C5
- Bovingdon Cl ARCH N19 ... 72 C1
- Bovingdon Dr ARCH N19 ... 72 C1
- Bovingdon La
 - CDALE/KGS NW9 ... 37 G2
- Bovingdon Rd FUL/PGN SW6 ... 108 A7
- Bowater Cl BRXS/STRHM SW2 ... 129 K5
 - CDALE/KGS NW9 ... 51 F4
- Bowater Gdns SUN TW16 ... 141 F7
- Bowater Pl BKHTH/KID SE3 ... 114 A6
- Bowater Rd WBLY HA9 ... 68 D2
 - WOOL/PLUM SE18 ... 114 C2
- Bow Bridge Est BOW E3 ... 93 K2
- Bow Common La BOW E3 ... 93 H4
- Bowden Cl EBED/NFELT TW14 ... 121 G7
- Bowden St LBTH SE11 ... 18 B7
- Bowditch DEPT SE8 ... 112 C4
- Bowdon Rd WALTH E17 ... 57 J6
- Bowen Dr DUL SE21 ... 150 A2
- Bowen Rd HRW HA1 ... 48 C6
- Bowen St POP/IOD E14 ... 93 K5
- Bowens Wd CROY/NA CR0 * ... 179 J7
- Bower Av GNWCH SE10 ... 113 H7
- Bower Cl NTHLT UB5 ... 83 G1
- Bowerdean St FUL/PGN SW6 ... 108 A7
- Bowerman Av NWCR SE14 ... 112 B5
- Bowes Cl BFN/LL DA15 ... 136 C5
- Bowes Rd ACT W3 ... 87 G6
 - BCTR RM8 ... 79 J3
 - FBAR/BDGN N11 ... 40 D5
- Bowfell Rd HMSMTH W6 ... 107 F5
- Bowhill Cl BRXN/ST SW9 ... 110 B6
- Bowie Cl CLAP SW4 ... 129 J6
- Bowland Rd CLAP SW4 ... 129 J3
 - WFD IG8 ... 45 G5
- Bow La NFNCH/WDSPK N12 ... 39 G6
 - STP EC4M ... 12 F5
- Bowl Ct WCHPL E1 ... 13 K1
- Bowley Cl NRWD SE19 ... 150 B5
- Bowley La NRWD SE19 ... 150 B4
- Bowley Rd POP/IOD E14 ... 93 H6
- Bowling Green Cl
 - PUT/ROE SW15 ... 126 E6
- Bowling Green Ct WBLY HA9 ... 68 B1
- Bowling Green La
 - CLKNW EC1R ... 12 B1
- Bowling Green Pl
 - STHWK SE1 ... 19 G1
- Bowling Green Rw
 - WOOL/PLUM SE18 * ... 114 E3
- Bowling Green St LBTH SE11 ... 18 A9
- Bowling Green Wk IS N1 ... 7 J7
- Bow Locks BOW E3 * ... 94 A3
- Bowls Cl STAN HA7 ... 35 H4
- Bowman Av CAN/RD E16 ... 94 D6
- Bowman Ms
 - WAND/EARL SW18 ... 127 J7
- Bowmans Cl WEA W13 ... 85 H7
- Bowmans Lea FSTH SE23 ... 131 K6
- Bowman's Meadow
 - WLGTN SM6 ... 176 B2
- Bowmans Ms WCHPL E1 ... 92 C5
- Bowman's Pl HOLWY N7 ... 72 E2
- Bowmead ELTH/MOT SE9 ... 153 K2
- Bowmore Wk CAMTN NW1 ... 5 F1
- Bowness Cl HACK E8 * ... 74 B5
- Bowness Crs PUT/ROE SW15 ... 145 F4
- Bowness Dr HSLWW TW4 ... 122 D3
- Bowness Rd CAT SE6 ... 132 E6
- Bowness Wy HCH RM12 ... 81 K1
- Bowood Rd BTSEA SW11 ... 129 F4
 - PEND EN3 ... 31 F1
- Bow On OXHEY WD19 ... 33 F1
- Bow Rd BOW E3 ... 93 H2
- Bowrons Av ALP/SUD HA0 ... 67 K6
- Bowsley Ct FELT TW13 ... 140 F1
- Bow St COVGDN WC2E ... 11 K5
 - SRTFD E15 ... 76 C4
- Bowyer Cl EHAM E6 ... 95 K4

Column 5:

- Bowyer Pl CMBW SE5 ... 110 D6
- Bowyers Ct TWK TW1 ... 124 C3
- Bowyer St CMBW SE5 ... 110 D6
- Boxall Rd DUL SE21 ... 131 F5
- Boxelder Cl EDGW HA8 ... 36 E4
- Boxgrove Rd ABYW SE2 ... 116 C1
- Box La BARK IG11 ... 97 H1
- Boxley Rd MRDN SM4 ... 162 B4
- Boxley St CAN/RD E16 ... 95 F7
- Boxmoor Rd
 - KTN/HRWW/WS HA3 ... 49 H3
- Boxoll Rd DAGW RM9 ... 80 B3
- Boxtree La
 - KTN/HRWW/WS HA3 ... 34 C7
- Boxtree Rd
 - KTN/HRWW/WS HA3 ... 34 D4
- Boxwood Cl WDR/YW UB7 ... 100 C1
- Boxworth Cl
 - NFNCH/WDSPK N12 ... 39 H4
- Boxworth Gv IS N1 ... 5 M3
- Boyard Rd WOOL/PLUM SE18 ... 115 G4
- Boyce Wy PLSTW E13 ... 94 E3
- Boycroft Av CDALE/KGS NW9 ... 50 E5
- Boyd Av STHL UB1 ... 83 K7
- Boyd Cl KUTN/CMB KT2 ... 144 C6
- Boydell Ct STJWD NW8 ... 3 G1
- Boyd Rd WIM/MER SW19 ... 147 H5
- Boyd St WCHPL E1 ... 92 C5
- Boyfield St STHWK SE1 ... 18 D2
- Boyland Rd BMLY BR1 ... 152 D4
- Boyle Av STAN HA7 ... 35 G5
- Boyle Farm Rd THDIT KT7 ... 158 B5
- Boyne Av HDN NW4 ... 52 B3
- Boyne Rd DAGE RM10 ... 80 C2
 - LEW SE13 ... 133 G2
- Boyne Terrace Ms NTGHL W11 ... 88 D7
- Boyson Rd WALW SE17 * ... 18 F9
- Boyton Cl CEND/HSY/T N8 ... 54 E2
 - WCHPL E1 ... 93 F3
- Boyton Rd CEND/HSY/T N8 ... 54 E2
- Brabant Rd WDGN N22 ... 55 F1
- Brabazon Av WLGTN SM6 ... 176 E6
- Brabazon Rd HEST TW5 ... 102 B6
 - NTHLT UB5 ... 84 A1
- Brabazon St POP/IOD E14 ... 93 K5
- Brabourne Cl NRWD SE19 ... 150 A4
- Brabourne Crs BXLYHN DA7 ... 117 G5
- Brabourne Ri BECK BR3 ... 167 F4
- Brabourn Gv PECK SE15 ... 131 K1
- Bracewell Av GFD/PVL UB6 ... 67 F4
- Bracewell Rd NKENS W10 ... 88 A4
- Bracewood Gdns
 - CROY/NA CR0 ... 178 B2
- Bracey St FSBYPK N4 * ... 72 E1
- Bracken Av BAL SW12 ... 129 F5
 - CROY/NA CR0 ... 179 J2
- Brackenbridge Dr RSLP HA4 ... 65 H3
- Brackenbury Gdns
 - HMSMTH W6 ... 106 E2
- Brackenbury Rd EFNCH N2 ... 53 G2
 - HMSMTH W6 ... 106 E2
- Bracken Cl EHAM E6 ... 95 K4
 - SUN TW16 * ... 140 D5
 - WHTN TW2 ... 123 F6
- Brackendale WCHMH N21 ... 41 F1
- Brackendale Cl HSLW TW3 ... 103 G7
- Bracken End ISLW TW7 ... 123 J4
- Bracken Gdns BARN SW13 ... 126 D1
- Brackenhill RSLP HA4 ... 65 J3
- Bracken Hill Cl BMLY BR1 ... 152 C7
- Bracken Hill La BMLY BR1 ... 152 D7
- Brackenridge ROMW/RG RM7 ... 62 C5
- The Brackens EN EN1 ... 30 A6
- Brackenwood SUN TW16 ... 140 E7
- Brackley Av PECK SE15 ... 131 K2
- Brackley Cl WLGTN SM6 ... 176 E6
- Brackley Rd BECK BR3 ... 151 H6
 - CHSWK W4 ... 106 B4
- Brackley Sq WFD IG8 ... 45 H6
- Brackley St BARB EC2Y ... 12 F2
- Brackley Ter CHSWK W4 ... 106 B4
- Bracklyn St IS N1 ... 7 G5
- Bracknell Cl WDGN N22 ... 41 G7
- Bracknell Gdns HAMP NW3 ... 71 F4
- Bracknell Wy HAMP NW3 ... 71 F4
- Bracondale ESH/CLAY KT10 ... 170 C4
- Bracondale Rd ABYW SE2 ... 116 B3
- Bradbourne St FUL/PGN SW6 ... 127 K1
- Bradbury Cl NWDGN UB2 ... 102 E3
 - STNW/STAM N16 * ... 74 A1
- Bradbury Ms STNW/STAM N16 ... 74 A1
- Braddock Cl ISLW TW7 ... 124 A2
- Braddon Rd BAR EN5 ... 26 C1
 - RCH/KEW TW9 ... 125 G1
- Braddyll St GNWCH SE10 ... 113 H4
- Bradenham Av WALL DA17 ... 136 A1
- Bradenham Rd
 - KTN/HRWW/WS HA3 ... 49 H3
 - YEAD UB4 ... 82 C2
- Braden St MV/WKIL W9 * ... 8 C1
- Bradfield Dr BARK IG11 ... 79 G5
- Bradfield Rd RSLP HA4 ... 65 J4
 - CAN/RD E16 ... 94 E7
- Bradford Cl HAYES BR2 ... 168 E7
 - SYD SE26 ... 150 D3
 - TOTM N17 ... 42 B5
- Bradford Dr HOR/WEW KT19 ... 173 H5
- Bradford Rd ACT W3 ... 106 B1
 - IL IG1 ... 60 D7
- Bradgate Rd CAT SE6 ... 132 E5
- Brading Crs WAN E11 ... 77 F1
- Brading Rd BRXS/STRHM SW2 ... 130 A6
 - CROY/NA CR0 ... 164 A5
- Brading Ter SHB W12 ... 106 D2
- Bradiston Rd MV/WKIL W9 ... 88 D2
- Bradley Cl HOLWY N7 ... 5 K1
- Bradley Gdns WEA W13 ... 85 H5
- Bradley Rd NRWD SE19 ... 149 J5
 - WDGN N22 ... 55 F1
- Bradley's Cl IS N1 ... 5 L5
- Bradley Stone Rd EHAM E6 ... 95 K5
- Bradman Rw EDGW HA8 * ... 36 E6
- Bradmead VX/NE SW8 ... 109 G7
- Bradmore Park Rd
 - HMSMTH W6 ... 106 E2
- Bradshaw Cl WIM/MER SW19 ... 146 E5
- Bradshaw Cots
 - POP/IOD E14 * ... 93 G5
- Bradshaw Dr MLHL NW7 ... 38 B7
- Bradshaws Cl SNWD SE25 ... 165 H2
- Bradstock Rd EW KT17 ... 173 K4
 - HOM E9 ... 75 F5
- Brad St STHWK SE1 ... 12 B9
- Bradwell Av DAGE RM10 ... 80 C1
- Bradwell Cl HCH RM12 ... 81 K5
 - SWFD E18 ... 58 D3
- Bradwell Ms UED N18 ... 42 C3
- Bradwell Rd BKHH IG9 ... 45 K1
- Bradymead EHAM E6 ... 96 A5
- Brady St WCHPL E1 ... 92 D3
- Braemar Av ALP/SUD HA0 ... 67 K6
 - THHTH CR7 ... 164 B2

WDGN N22 40 E7
WIM/MER SW19 146 E1
WLSDN NW10 69 F2
Braemar Gdns BFN/LL DA15 154 D2
CDALE/KGS NW9 37 F7
WWKM BR4 167 F7
Braemar Rd BTFD TW8 104 E5
PLSTW E13 94 D3
SEVS/STOTM N15 56 A4
WPK KT4 173 K2
Braeside BECK BR3 151 J4
Braeside Av RYNPK SW20 146 C7
Braeside Cl PIN HA5 34 A6
Braeside Crs BXLYHN DA7 137 K3
Braeside Rd
STRHM/NOR SW16 148 C6
Braes St IS N1 6 D2
Braesyde Cl BELV DA17 117 G3
Brafferton Rd CROY/NA CR0 177 J3
Braganza St WALW SE17 18 C8
Bragg Cl BCTR RM8 79 H5
Bragg Rd TEDD TW11 142 E6
Braham St WCHPL E1 13 M5
Braid Av ACT W3 87 G5
Braid Cl FELT TW13 141 K1
Braidwood Rd CAT SE6 133 G7
Braidwood St STHWK SE1 13 J9
Brailsford Cl WIM/MER SW19 147 J6
Brailsford Rd
BRXS/STRHM SW2 130 B5
Brainton Av
EBED/NFELT TW14 122 A6
Braintree Av REDBR IG4 59 J4
Braintree Rd DAGE RM10 80 C2
RSLP HA4 65 F3
Braintree St BETH E2 * 92 E2
Braithwaite Av
ROMW/RG RM7 62 C6
Braithwaite Gdns STAN HA7 35 J7
Braithwaite Rd PEND EN3 31 H2
Bramalea Cl HGT N6 54 A5
Bramall Cl SRTFD E15 76 D4
Bramber Ct EA W5 105 F3
Bramber Rd
NFNCH/WDSPK N12 39 J4
WKENS W14 107 J5
Bramble Acres Cl BELMT SM2 174 E6
Bramble Banks CAR SM5 176 A7
Bramblebury Rd
WOOL/PLUM SE18 115 J4
Bramble Cl BECK BR3 167 F4
CROY/NA CR0 179 J3
SEVS/STOTM N15 56 C3
STAN HA7 35 K6
Bramble Cft ERITH DA8 117 K3
Brambledown Cl WWKM BR4 167 H5
Brambledown Rd CAR SM5 176 A6
SAND/SEL CR2 178 A6
Bramble Gdns SHB W12 87 H6
Bramble La HPTN TW12 141 K5
Brambles Cl ISLW TW7 104 C6
The Brambles SUT SM1 * 175 H1
WDR/YW UB7 100 A4
WIM/MER SW19 * 146 D4
Bramblewood Cl CAR SM5 162 D7
Brambling Cl BUSH WD23 21 J3
The Bramblings CHING E4 44 B3
Bramcote Av MTCM CR4 162 E3
Bramcote Gv
BERM/RHTH SE16 111 K4
Bramcote Rd PUT/ROE SW15 126 E3
Bramerton Rd BECK BR3 166 C2
Bramerton St CHEL SW3 15 J9
Bramfield Rd BTSEA SW11 128 D5
Bramford Rd
WAND/EARL SW18 128 B3
Bramham Ct NTHWD HA6 * 32 C4
Bramham Gdns CHSGTN KT9 * 171 K4
ECT SW5 14 C7
Bramhope La CHARL SE7 114 A5
Bramlands Cl BTSEA SW11 128 D2
Bramleas WATW WD18 20 D4
Bramley Cl HYS/HAR UB3 82 E6
MLHL NW7 37 G2
ORP BR6 169 G7
PIN HA5 46 D2
SAND/SEL CR2 177 H4
STHGT/OAK N14 28 B4
WALTH E17 57 G1
WFD IG8 45 G6
WHTN TW2 123 H5
Bramley Crs GNTH/NBYPK IG2 60 A5
VX/NE SW8 109 J6
Bramley Gdns OXHEY WD19 33 G5
Bramley Hl SAND/SEL CR2 177 J3
Bramley Hyrst
SAND/SEL CR2 * 177 J4
Bramley Ldg ALP/SUD HA0 67 K3
Bramley Pde STHGT/OAK N14 28 C3
Bramley Rd BELMT SM2 174 B7
EA W5 104 D2
NKENS W10 88 B6
STHGT/OAK N14 28 B4
SUT SM1 175 H4
Bramley Wy HSLWW TW4 122 E4
WWKM BR4 179 K1
Brampton Cl CLPT E5 74 D1
Brampton Gv HDN NW4 51 K3
KTN/HRWW/WS HA3 49 G3
WBLY HA9 50 C7
Brampton La HDN NW4 52 A3
Brampton Park Rd
WDGN N22 55 G2
Brampton Rd BXLYHN DA7 116 E5
BXLYHN DA7 116 E6
BXLYHN DA7 136 E2
CDALE/KGS NW9 50 C3
CROY/NA CR0 165 G6
EHAM E6 95 H3
OXHEY WD19 32 E2
SEVS/STOTM N15 55 J4
Bramshaw Gdns
OXHEY WD19 33 H4
Bramshaw Ri NWMAL KT3 160 B5
Bramshaw Rd HOM E9 75 F5
Bramshill Gdns KTTN NW5 72 B2
Bramshill Rd WLSDN NW10 87 G1
Bramshot Av CHARL SE7 114 A5
Bramshot Wy OXHEY WD19 32 E1
Bramston Rd MTCM CR4 147 K6
WLSDN NW10 87 J1
Bramwell Cl SUN TW16 156 C1
Bramwell Ms IS N1 5 M3
Brancaster Dr MLHL NW7 37 J6
Brancaster Rd
GNTH/NBYPK IG2 60 D5
STRHM/NOR SW16 148 E2
Brancepeth Gdns BKHH IG9 44 E1
Branch Hl HAMP NW3 71 G2
Branch Pl IS N1 7 H3
Branch Rd POP/IOD E14 93 G5
Branch St CMBW SE5 111 F6
Brancker Rd
KTN/HRWW/WS HA3 49 K2
Brand Cl FSBYPK N4 55 H7
Brandlehow Rd
PUT/ROE SW15 127 J3
Brandon Est WALW SE17 18 E9
Brandon Ms BARB EC2Y * 13 G2
Brandon Rd HOLWY N7 5 J1
NWDGN UB2 102 E4
SUT SM1 175 F3
WALTH E17 58 A3
Brandon St WALW SE17 18 F5
Brandram Ms LEW SE13 * 133 H3
Brandram Rd LEW SE13 133 H2
Brandreth Ct HRW HA1 * 49 F5
Brandreth Rd EHAM E6 95 K5
TOOT SW17 148 B1
The Brandries WLGTN SM6 176 D2
Brand St GNWCH SE10 113 F6
Brandville Gdns BARK/HLT IG6 60 B3
Brandville Rd WDR/YW UB7 100 B1
Brandy Wy BELMT SM2 174 E6
Brangbourne Rd BMLY BR1 152 A4
Brangton Rd LBTH SE11 17 M8
Brangwyn Crs
WIM/MER SW19 147 H7
Branksea St FUL/PGN SW6 107 H6
Branksome Av UED N18 42 B5
Branksome Cl TEDD TW11 142 D3
Branksome Rd
BRXS/STRHM SW2 129 K4
WIM/MER SW19 146 E7
Branksome Wy
KTN/HRWW/WS HA3 50 B5
NWMAL KT3 159 K1
Bransby Rd CHSGTN KT9 172 A6
Branscombe Gdns
WCHMH N21 29 G6
Branscombe St LEW SE13 132 E2
Bransdale Cl KIL/WHAMP NW6 2 B3
Bransgrove Rd EDGW HA8 36 B7
Branston Crs STMC/STPC BR5 169 J7
Branstone Rd RCH/KEW TW9 105 G7
Brants Wk HNWL W7 84 E3
Brantwood Av ERITH DA8 117 K6
ISLW TW7 124 B3
Brantwood Cl WALTH E17 * 57 K2
Brantwood Gdns ENC/FH EN2 28 E3
REDBR IG4 59 J4
Brantwood Rd HNHL SE24 130 D4
SAND/SEL CR2 177 J7
TOTM N17 42 C5
Brasenose Dr BARN SW13 107 F5
Brasher Cl GFD/PVL UB6 66 D4
Brassey Cl
EBED/NFELT TW14 * 121 K7
Brassey Rd KIL/WHAMP NW6 70 D5
Brassey Sq BTSEA SW11 129 F2
Brassie Av ACT W3 87 G5
Brasted Cl BXLYHS DA6 136 E4
SYD SE26 150 E3
Brasted Rd ERITH DA8 118 B6
Brathway Rd
WAND/EARL SW18 127 K6
Bratley St WCHPL E1 92 C3
Braund Av GFD/PVL UB6 84 B3
Braundton Av BFN/LL DA15 136 A7
Braunston Dr YEAD UB4 83 J3
Bravington Pl MV/WKIL W9 88 D3
Bravington Rd MV/WKIL W9 88 D2
Bravingtons Wk IS N1 5 K6
Braxfield Rd BROCKY SE4 132 B3
Braxted Pk STRHM/NOR SW16 149 F5
Brayard's Rd PECK SE15 131 J1
Braybourne Dr ISLW TW7 104 A6
Braybrooke Gdns NRWD SE19 150 A6
Braybrook St SHB W12 87 H4
Brayburne Av VX/NE SW8 129 H1
Braycourt Av WOT/HER KT12 156 B6
Bray Crs BERM/RHTH SE16 112 A1
Braydon Rd STNW/STAM N16 56 B7
Bray Dr CAN/RD E16 94 D6
Brayfield Ter IS N1 6 A2
Brayford Sq WCHPL E1 * 92 E5
Bray Pl CHEL SW3 15 L7
Bray Rd MLHL NW7 38 B5
Brayton Gdns ENC/FH EN2 28 D3
Braywood Rd ELTH/MOT SE9 135 J3
Brazier Crs NTHLT UB5 83 K3
Brazil Cl CROY/NA CR0 163 K6
Breach La DAGW RM9 98 C2
Bread St STP EC4M 12 F5
Breakspears Dr
STMC/STPC BR5 155 G7
Breakspears Ms BROCKY SE4 132 D1
Breakspears Rd BROCKY SE4 132 C2
Bream Cl TOTM N17 56 D3
Bream Gdns EHAM E6 96 A2
Breamore Cl PUT/ROE SW15 126 D7
Breamore Rd GDMY/SEVK IG3 79 F1
Bream's Blds LINN WC2A 12 A4
Bream St BOW E3 75 J6
Breamwater Gdns
RCHPK/HAM TW10 143 H2
Brearley Cl EDGW HA8 36 E6
Breasley Cl PUT/ROE SW15 126 E3
Breasy Pl HDN NW4 * 51 K3
Brechin Pl SKENS SW7 14 F7
Brecknock Rd ARCH N19 72 C3
Brecknock Road Est
ARCH N19 * 72 D4
Brecon Cl MTCM CR4 163 K3
WPK KT4 174 A1
Brecon Gn CDALE/KGS NW9 * 51 G5
Brecon Ms HOLWY N7 72 D4
KTTN NW5 72 D5
Brecon Rd HMSMTH W6 107 H5
PEND EN3 30 E3
Brede Cl EHAM E6 96 A2
Bredgar Rd ARCH N19 72 B1
Bredhurst Cl PGE/AN SE20 150 E5
Bredon Rd CROY/NA CR0 165 G6
Breer St FUL/PGN SW6 128 A2
Breezer's Hl WAP E1W * 92 C6
Bremans Rw
WAND/EARL SW18 147 G1
Brember Rd RYLN/HDSTN HA2 66 C1
Bremer Ms WALTH E17 57 K3
Bremner Rd SKENS SW7 14 F3
Brenchley Cl CHST BR7 154 A7
HAYES BR2 167 J4
Brenchley Gdns EDUL SE22 131 K5
Brenchley Rd STMC/STPC BR5 154 E7
Brenda Rd TOOT SW17 147 K1
Brende Gdns E/WMO/HCT KT8 157 G3
Brendon SCUP DA14 * 155 G3
Brendon Av WLSDN NW10 69 G3
Brendon Cl ESH/CLAY KT10 170 C5
HYS/HAR UB3 101 F6
Brendon Dr ESH/CLAY KT10 170 C5
Brendon Gdns
RYLN/HDSTN HA2 66 B3
Brendon Gv EFNCH N2 53 G1
Brendon Rd BCTR RM8 62 B7
ELTH/MOT SE9 154 D1
Brendon St MBLAR W1H 9 K4
Brendon Vls WCHMH N21 * 29 J7
Brendon Wy EN EN1 30 A6
Brenley Cl MTCM CR4 163 F2
Brenley Gdns ELTH/MOT SE9 134 C3
Brent Cl BXLY DA5 137 F7
Brentcot Cl WEA W13 85 H3
Brent Crs WLSDN NW10 86 B1
Brent Cross F/O HDN NW4 52 A5
Brentfield WLSDN NW10 68 D6
Brentfield Cl WLSDN NW10 69 F5
Brentfield Gdns CRICK NW2 * 52 B6
Brentfield Rd WLSDN NW10 69 F5
Brentford Cl YEAD UB4 83 H3
Brent Gn HDN NW4 52 A4
Brentham Wy EA W5 85 K3
Brenthouse Rd HACK E8 74 D6
Brenthurst Rd WLSDN NW10 69 H5
Brent Lea BTFD TW8 104 D6
Brentmead Cl HNWL W7 84 E6
Brentmead Gdns
WLSDN NW10 86 B1
Brenton St POP/IOD E14 93 G5
Brent Park Rd
CDALE/KGS NW9 51 J7
Brent Pl BAR EN5 26 D4
Brent River Park Wk
HNWL W7 84 D4
Brent Rd BTFD TW8 104 D5
CAN/RD E16 94 E5
NWDGN UB2 102 B2
SAND/SEL CR2 178 D7
WOOL/PLUM SE18 115 G6
Brentside BTFD TW8 104 D5
Brentside Cl WEA W13 85 F3
Brent St HDN NW4 52 A3
Brent Ter CRICK NW2 70 A1
The Brent DART DA1 139 K6
Brentvale Av ALP/SUD HA0 68 B7
STHL UB1 84 D7
Brent View Rd
CDALE/KGS NW9 51 J5
Brent Wy BTFD TW8 104 E6
FNCH N3 38 E5
WBLY HA9 68 D5
Brentwick Gdns BTFD TW8 105 F3
Brentwood Cl ELTH/MOT SE9 135 H7
Brentwood Rd ROM RM1 63 H5
Brereton Rd TOTM N17 42 B6
Bressay Dr MLHL NW7 37 J6
Bressenden Pl WESTW SW1E 16 D3
Bressey Gv SWFD E18 58 D1
Brett Cl NTHLT UB5 83 H2
STNW/STAM N16 74 A1
Brett Crs WLSDN NW10 69 F7
Brettell St WALW SE17 19 H8
Brettenham Av WALTH E17 43 J7
Brettenham Rd UED N18 42 C3
WALTH E17 57 J1
Brett Gdns DAGW RM9 80 A6
Brett Pas HACK E8 74 D4
Brett Rd BAR EN5 26 A4
HACK E8 74 D4
Brett Vls ACT W3 * 87 F4
Brewer St REGST W1B 10 F6
Brewery Cl ALP/SUD HA0 67 G4
Brewery Rd HAYES BR2 168 D7
WOOL/PLUM SE18 115 J4
Brewery Sq FSBYE EC1V 12 D1
STHWK SE1 13 L9
Brewhouse La WAP E1W 92 D7
Brewhouse Rd
WOOL/PLUM SE18 114 E3
Brewhouse St PUT/ROE SW15 127 H3
Brewhouse Wk
BERM/RHTH SE16 93 G7
Brewhouse Yd FSBYE EC1V 6 C9
Brewood Rd BCTR RM8 79 H5
Brewster Gdns NKENS W10 88 A4
Brewster Rd LEY E10 57 K7
Brian Cl HCH RM12 81 K3
Brian Rd CHDH RM6 61 J4
Briants Cl PIN HA5 33 J7
Briant St NWCR SE14 112 A7
Briar Av STRHM/NOR SW16 149 F6
Briar Bank CAR SM5 176 A7
Briarbank Rd WEA W13 85 G5
Briar Cl BKHH IG9 45 H1
EFNCH N2 53 G1
HPTN TW12 141 K4
ISLW TW7 124 A4
PLMGR N13 41 J2
Briar Crs NTHLT UB5 66 B5
Briardale Gdns HAMP NW3 70 E2
Briarfield Av EFNCH N2 53 F2
Briar Gdns HAYES BR2 167 J7
Briar La CAR SM5 176 A7
CROY/NA CR0 179 K3
Briar Rd CRICK NW2 70 A3
KTN/HRWW/WS HA3 49 J4
STRHM/NOR SW16 163 K2
WHTN TW2 123 K7
Briar Wk EDGW HA8 36 E6
NKENS W10 * 88 C3
PUT/ROE SW15 126 E3
Briar Wy WDR/YW UB7 100 D1
Briarwood Cl
CDALE/KGS NW9 * 50 E5
FELT TW13 140 C2
Briar Wood Cl HAYES BR2 181 J1
HAYES BR2 181 J2
Briarwood Ct WPK KT4 * 160 D7
Briarwood Dr NTHWD HA6 46 E1
Briarwood Rd CLAP SW4 129 J4
EW KT17 173 J5
Briary Cl EDGW HA8 50 D1
Briary Ct SCUP DA14 155 H4
Briary Gdns BMLY BR1 153 F4
Briary La ED N9 42 A2
Brickbarn Cl WBPTN SW10 * 108 B6
Brick Ct EMB EC4Y * 12 A5
Brickett Cl RSLP HA4 46 A4
Brick Farm Cl RCH/KEW TW9 105 J7
Brickfield Cl BTFD TW8 104 D6
Brickfield Cots
WOOL/PLUM SE18 116 A5
Brickfield La BAR EN5 25 H5
HYS/HAR UB3 101 G5
Brickfield Rd BOW E3 93 K3
THHTH CR7 149 H7
WIM/MER SW19 147 F3
Brickfields RYLN/HDSTN HA2 66 D1
Brickfields Wy WDR/YW UB7 100 C2
Brickfield Vls CAR SM5 * 175 J2
Brick Kiln Cl OXHEY WD19 21 J5
Brick La BETH E2 7 M8
EN EN1 30 D1
NTHLT UB5 83 K2
STAN HA7 35 K6
WCHPL E1 13 M1
Brick St MYFR/PKLN W1K 10 C9
Brickwall La RSLP HA4 46 C7
Brickwood Cl SYD SE26 150 D2
Brickwood Rd CROY/NA CR0 178 A1
Brideale Cl PECK SE15 111 G5
Bride Ct EMB EC4Y 12 C5
Bride La EMB EC4Y 12 C5
Bridel Ms FSBYE EC1V 6 C6
Bride St HOLWY N7 73 F5
Bridewain St STHWK SE1 19 L3
Bridewell Pl BLKFR EC4V 12 C5
WAP E1W 92 D7
Bridford Ms GTPST W1W 10 D2
Bridge Ap CAMTN NW1 4 A1
Bridge Av HMSMTH W6 107 F4
HNWL W7 84 D4
Bridge Cl EN EN1 30 D1
NKENS W10 88 B5
ROMW/RG RM7 63 G5
Bridge Dr PLMGR N13 41 F3
Bridge End WALTH E17 44 A7
Bridge End Cl KUTN/CMB KT2 144 C7
Bridgefield Rd SUT SM1 174 E5
Bridge Gdns ASHF TW15 140 A6
E/WMO/HCT KT8 157 J3
Bridge Ga WCHMH N21 29 J6
Bridge House Quay
POP/IOD E14 94 A7
Bridgeland Rd CAN/RD E16 94 E6
Bridgelands Cl BECK BR3 151 H6
Bridge La BTSEA SW11 108 D7
HDN NW4 52 B3
Bridgeman Rd IS N1 5 M2
TEDD TW11 143 G5
Bridgeman St STJWD NW8 3 J6
Bridge Mdw NWCR SE14 112 A5
Bridgen Rd BXLY DA5 137 F6
Bridge Pde
STRHM/NOR SW16 * 148 E4
WCHMH N21 * 29 J6
Bridge Pk WAND/EARL SW18 127 K4
Bridge Pl CROY/NA CR0 164 E7
PIM SW1V 16 D5
WAT WD17 21 H4
Bridgepoint Pl HGT N6 54 B7
Bridgeport Pl WAP E1W * 92 C7
Bridge Rd BECK BR3 151 H6
CHSGTN KT9 172 A4
E/WMO/HCT KT8 157 K3
ED N9 42 C2
EHAM E6 77 K6
ERITH DA8 118 C7
HSLW TW3 123 J2
LEY E10 58 B5
NWDGN UB2 102 E1
RAIN RM13 99 J3
SRTFD E15 76 B7
SUT SM1 175 F5
TWK TW1 124 C5
WALTH E17 57 H6
WBLY HA9 68 C2
WDGN N22 40 E7
WLGTN SM6 176 B4
WLSDN NW10 69 G5
Bridge Rw CROY/NA CR0 * 164 E7
Bridges Ct BTSEA SW11 128 C2
Bridges La CROY/NA CR0 176 E3
Bridges Rd STAN HA7 35 F4
Bridges Road Ms
WIM/MER SW19 147 F5
Bridge St CHSWK W4 106 A3
PIN HA5 47 H2
TWK TW1 124 E5
WHALL SW1A 17 J2
Bridge Ter LEW SE13 * 133 G3
SRTFD E15 76 B6
The Bridge EA W5 * 86 B7
KTN/HRWW/WS HA3 49 F2
Bridgetown Cl NRWD SE19 150 A4
Bridgeview HMSMTH W6 107 F4
Bridge Vls WIM/MER SW19 * 146 E4
Bridgewater Cl
STMC/STPC BR5 169 K1
Bridgewater Gdns EDGW HA8 50 B1
Bridgewater Rd ALP/SUD HA0 67 H5
Bridgewater Sq BARB EC2Y * 12 E2
Bridgewater St BARB EC2Y 12 E2
Bridgewater Wy BUSH WD23 22 B5
Bridgeway ALP/SUD HA0 68 A6
BARK IG11 79 F6
Bridge Wy GLDGN NW11 52 D4
WHTN TW2 123 H6
Bridgeway St CAMTN NW1 4 F6
Bridge Wharf Rd ISLW TW7 124 C2
Bridgewood Cl PGE/AN SE20 150 D6
Bridgewood Rd
STRHM/NOR SW16 148 D6
WPK KT4 173 J3
Bridgford St
WAND/EARL SW18 147 G2
Bridgman Rd CHSWK W4 105 K2
Bridgwater Rd RSLP HA4 64 E3
Bridle Cl HOR/WEW KT19 172 E3
KUT/HW KT1 158 E3
Bridle La SOHO/CST W1F 10 F6
TWK TW1 124 C5
Bridle Pth CROY/NA CR0 176 E2
WAT WD17 21 F1
The Bridle Pth WFD IG8 44 C6
Bridlepath Wy
EBED/NFELT TW14 121 H6
Bridle Rd CROY/NA CR0 179 J3
ESH/CLAY KT10 171 H5
PIN HA5 47 G5
Bridle Wy CROY/NA CR0 179 J4
The Bridle Wy WLGTN SM6 176 C3
Bridlington Rd ED N9 30 D6
OXHEY WD19 33 H2
Bridport Av ROMW/RG RM7 62 D5
Bridport Pl IS N1 7 H4
Bridport Rd GFD/PVL UB6 66 B7
THHTH CR7 164 B2
UED N18 42 A4
Bridstow Pl BAY/PAD W2 8 B4
Brief St BRXN/ST SW9 110 C7
Brierley CROY/NA CR0 179 K5
Brierley Av ED N9 30 E7
Brierley Cl SNWD SE25 165 H3
Brierley Rd BAL SW12 148 C1
WAN E11 76 B3
Brierly Gdns BETH E2 * 92 E1
Brigade Cl RYLN/HDSTN HA2 66 D1
Brigade St BKHTH/KID SE3 * 133 J1
Briggeford Cl CLPT E5 74 C1
Briggs Cl MTCM CR4 148 B7
Bright Cl BELV DA17 116 E3
Brightfield Rd LEE/GVPK SE12 133 H4
Brightling Rd BROCKY SE4 132 C5
Brightlingsea Pl POP/IOD E14 93 H6
Brightman Rd
WAND/EARL SW18 128 C7
Brighton Av WALTH E17 57 H4
Brighton Dr NTHLT UB5 * 66 A5
Brighton Rd BELMT SM2 175 G6
EFNCH N2 53 G1
EHAM E6 96 A2
SAND/SEL CR2 177 J7
STNW/STAM N16 74 A3
SURB KT6 158 D5
Brighton Ter BRXN/ST SW9 130 A3
Brights Av RAIN RM13 99 K3
Brightside Rd LEW SE13 133 G5
Bright St POP/IOD E14 93 K5
Brightwell Cl CROY/NA CR0 164 B7
Brightwell Crs TOOT SW17 147 K4
Brightwell Rd WATW WD18 20 E4
Brightwen Gv STAN HA7 35 G1
Brig Ms DEPT SE8 112 D5
Brigstock Rd BELV DA17 117 J3
THHTH CR7 164 C4
Brill Pl CAMTN NW1 5 H6
Brim Hl EFNCH N2 53 G3
Brimpsfield Cl ABYW SE2 116 C2
Brindle Ga BFN/LL DA15 135 K7
Brindley Cl ALP/SUD HA0 67 J7
Brindley St BROCKY SE4 112 C7
Brindley Wy BMLY BR1 152 E4
STHL UB1 84 B6
Brindwood Rd CHING E4 43 J2
Brinkburn Cl ABYW SE2 116 B3
EDGW HA8 50 D2
Brinkburn Gdns EDGW HA8 50 C2
Brinkley Rd WPK KT4 173 K1
Brinklow Crs
WOOL/PLUM SE18 115 G6
Brinkworth Rd CLAY IG5 59 J2
Brinkworth Wy HOM E9 75 H5
Brinsdale Rd HDN NW4 52 B2
Brinsley Rd
KTN/HRWW/WS HA3 48 D1
Brinsley St WCHPL E1 * 92 D5
Brinsworth Cl WHTN TW2 142 D1
Brinton Wk STHWK SE1 12 C9
Brion Pl POP/IOD E14 94 A4
Brisbane Av WIM/MER SW19 147 F7
Brisbane Rd IL IG1 60 C6
LEY E10 75 K1
Brisbane St CMBW SE5 110 E6
Briscoe Cl WAN E11 76 D1
Briscoe Rd WIM/MER SW19 147 H5
Briset Rd ELTH/MOT SE9 134 C2
Briset St FARR EC1M 12 C2
Briset Wy HOLWY N7 73 F1
Bristol Cl HSLWW TW4 123 F6
STWL/WRAY TW19 120 B5
WLGTN SM6 176 E7
Bristol Gdns MV/WKIL W9 8 D1
Bristol Ms MV/WKIL W9 8 D1
Bristol Park Rd WALTH E17 * 57 G3
Bristol Rd FSTGT E7 77 G5
GFD/PVL UB6 66 B7
MRDN SM4 162 B4
Briston Gv CEND/HSY/T N8 54 E5
Bristowe Cl BRXS/STRHM SW2 130 B5
Bristow Rd CROY/NA CR0 176 E3
HSLW TW3 123 G2
NRWD SE19 150 A4
Britannia Cl CLAP SW4 129 J3
NTHLT UB5 83 H2
Britannia Ga CAN/RD E16 94 E7
Britannia La WHTN TW2 123 H6
Britannia Rd BRYLDS KT5 159 G6
FUL/PGN SW6 108 A6
IL IG1 78 B2
NFNCH/WDSPK N12 39 G2
POP/IOD E14 112 D3
Britannia Rw IS N1 6 D3
Britannia St FSBYW WC1X 5 L7
Britannia Wk IS N1 7 G6
Britannia Wy FUL/PGN SW6 108 A6
STWL/WRAY TW19 120 A6
WLSDN NW10 86 D3
British Est BOW E3 93 H2
British Gv HMSMTH W6 106 C4
British Grove Pas
CHSWK W4 * 106 C4
British Legion Rd CHING E4 44 D1
British St BOW E3 93 H2
Brittage Rd WLSDN NW10 69 G6
Brittain Rd BCTR RM8 80 A2
Britten Cl BORE WD6 23 K5
GLDGN NW11 53 F7
Britten Dr STHL UB1 84 A5
Britten St CHEL SW3 15 J8
Brittidge Rd WLSDN NW10 * 69 G6
Britton Cl CAT SE6 133 G6
Britton St FARR EC1M 12 C1
Brixham Crs RSLP HA4 46 E7
Brixham Gdns
GDMY/SEVK IG3 78 E4
Brixham Rd WELL DA16 116 E7
Brixham St CAN/RD E16 95 K7
Brixton Hl BRXS/STRHM SW2 130 A5
Brixton Hill Pl
BRXS/STRHM SW2 129 K6
Brixton Ov BRXS/STRHM SW2 130 B3
Brixton Rd BRXN/ST SW9 130 B3
LBTH SE11 110 B5
Brixton Station Rd
BRXN/ST SW9 130 B2
Brixton Water La
BRXS/STRHM SW2 130 A4
Broadbent Cl HGT N6 54 B7
Broadbent St
MYFR/PKLN W1K * 10 C6
Broadberry Ct UED N18 42 D4
Broad Common Est
STNW/STAM N16 * 56 C7
Broadcoombe SAND/SEL CR2 179 F6
Broad Ct COVGDN WC2E * 11 K5
Broadcroft Av STAN HA7 49 K1
Broadcroft Rd
STMC/STPC BR5 169 J6
Broadeaves Cl SAND/SEL CR2 178 A4
Broadfield Cl CRICK NW2 70 A2
ROM RM1 63 H4
Broadfield Ct BUSH WD23 34 E1
Broadfield La CAMTN NW1 5 J2
Broadfield Pde EDGW HA8 * 36 D2
Broadfield Rd CAT SE6 133 H7
Broadfields E/WMO/HCT KT8 157 J5
RYLN/HDSTN HA2 48 B1
Broadfields Av EDGW HA8 36 D2
WCHMH N21 29 G6
Broadfields Hts EDGW HA8 36 D3
Broadfields La OXHEY WD19 21 F7
Broadfield Sq EN EN1 30 D2
Broadfields Wy WLSDN NW10 69 H4
Broadfield Wy BKHH IG9 45 G2
Broadgates Rd
WAND/EARL SW18 128 C7
Broad Green Av CROY/NA CR0 164 C6
Broadhead Strd
CDALE/KGS NW9 51 H1
Broadheath Dr CHST BR7 153 K4
Broadhinton Rd CLAP SW4 129 G2
Broadhurst Av EDGW HA8 36 D3

Street	Area	Postcode	Page	Grid
Bucknall Wy	BECK	BR3	166	E3
Bucknell Cl	BRXS/STRHM	SW2	130	A3
Buckner Rd	BRXS/STRHM	SW2	130	A3
Buckrell Cl	CHING	E4	44	B1
Bucks Av	OXHEY	WD19	21	J6
Buckstone Cl	FSTH	SE23	131	K5
Buckstone Rd	UED	N18	42	C5
Buck St	CAMTN	NW1	4	B1
Buckters Rents	BERM/RHTH	SE16	93	G7
Buckthorne Rd	BROCKY	SE4	132	B5
Budd Cl	NFNCH/WDSPK	N12	39	F3
Buddings Cir	WBLY	HA9	68	E2
Budge Cl	WALTH	E17	57	H4
Budge La	MTCM	CR4	162	E6
Budge Rw	MANHO	EC4N	13	G6
Budleigh Crs	WELL	DA16	116	D7
Budoch Dr	GDMY/SEVK	IG3	79	E1
Buer Rd	FUL/PGN	SW6	127	H1
Bugsby's Wy	GNWCH	SE10	113	J3
Bulganak Rd	THHTH	CR7	164	G3
Bulinca St	WEST	SW1P *	17	J6
Bullace Rw	CMBW	SE5	110	E7
Bullard Rd	TEDD	TW11	142	E5
Bullards Pl	BETH	E2	93	F2
Bullbanks Rd	BELV	DA17	117	K3
Bulleid Wy	BGVA	SW1W	16	D6
Bullen St	BTSEA	SW11	128	D1
Buller Cl	PECK	SE15	111	H6
Buller Rd	BARK	IG11	78	E6
	THHTH	CR7	164	E2
	TOTM	N17	56	C1
	WDGN	N22	55	G1
	WLSDN	NW10	88	B2
Bullers Wood Dr	CHST	BR7	153	J7
Bullescroft Rd	EDGW	HA8	36	C2
Bullhead Rd	BORE	WD6	24	E3
Bullivant St	POP/IOD	E14	94	A6
Bull La	CHST	BR7	154	D6
	DAGE	RM10	80	D2
	UED	N18	42	H4
Bull Rd	SRTFD	E15	94	D1
Bullrush Cl	CAR	SM5	175	J1
	CROY/NA	CR0	165	F5
Bulls Aly	MORT/ESHN	SW14 *	126	A2
Bull's Br	NWDGN	UB2	101	K2
Bulls Bridge Rd	NWDGN	UB2	102	A2
Bullsbrook Rd	YEAD	UB4	83	G5
Bull's Gdns	CHEL	SW3	15	K5
Bull Yd	PECK	SE15	111	H7
Bulmer Gdns	KTN/HRWW/WS	HA3	49	K6
Bulmer Ms	NTGHL	W11 *	8	A8
Bulstrode Av	HSLW	TW3	122	E2
Bulstrode Gdns	HSLW	TW3	123	F2
Bulstrode Pl	MHST	W1U	10	B4
Bulstrode St	MHST	W1U	10	B4
Bulwer Court Rd	WAN	E11	58	B7
Bulwer Rd	BAR	EN5	27	G3
	UED	N18	42	A3
	WAN	E11	58	B7
Bulwer St	SHB	W12	88	A7
Bunces La	WFD	IG8	44	E6
Bungalow Rd	SNWD	SE25	165	F3
The Bungalows	RYLN/HDSTN	HA2 *	65	K2
	STRHM/NOR	SW16	148	E6
Bunhill Rw	STLK	EC1Y	7	C9
Bunhouse Pl	BGVA	SW1W	16	A7
Bunkers Hl	GLDGN	NW11	53	F5
Bunker's Hl	BELV	DA17	117	H3
Bunning Wy	HOLWY	N7	5	K1
Bunn's La	MLHL	NW7	37	G5
Bunsen St	BOW	E3	93	G1
Buntingbridge Rd	BARK/HLT	IG2	60	D4
Bunting Cl	ED	N9	31	F7
	MTCM	CR4	162	E4
Bunton St	WOOL/PLUM	SE18	115	F2
Bunyan Rd	WALTH	E17	57	F2
Burbage Cl	HYS/HAR	UB3	82	B5
	STHWK	SE1	19	G4
Burbage Rd	HNHL	SE24	130	E6
Burberry Cl	NWMAL	KT3	160	B1
Burbridge Wy	TOTM	N17	56	C1
Burcham St	POP/IOD	E14	93	K5
Burcharbro Rd	ABYW	SE2	116	E6
Burchell Ct	BUSH	WD23 *	22	C6
Burchell Rd	LEY	E10	57	K7
	PECK	SE15	111	F6
Burcher Gale Gv	PECK	SE15	111	F6
Burcote Rd	WAND/EARL	SW18	128	C7
Burden Cl	BTFD	TW8	104	D4
Burdenshott Av	RCHPK/HAM	TW10	125	J3
Burden Wy	WAN	E11	77	F1
Burder Cl	IS	N1	74	A5
Burder Rd	IS	N1	74	A5
Burdett Av	RYNPK	SW20	145	J7
Burdett Cl	HNWL	W7 *	85	F7
	CROY/NA	CR0	164	E5
	POP/IOD	E14	93	H5
	RCH/KEW	TW9	125	G1
Burdetts Rd	DAGW	RM9	80	B7
Burdock Cl	CROY/NA	CR0	166	A7
Burdock Rd	TOTM	N17	56	C1
Burdon La	BELMT	SM2	174	C6
Burdon Pk	BELMT	SM2	174	D7
Burfield Cl	TOOT	SW17	147	G3
Burford Cl	BARK/HLT	IG6	60	E1
	BCTR	RM8	61	H7
Burford Gdns	PLMGR	N13	41	F2
Burford Rd	BMLY	BR1	168	D3
	BTFD	TW8	105	F4
	CAT	SE6	151	H1
	EHAM	E6	95	J2
	SRTFD	E15	76	B6
	SUT	SM1	161	K7
	WPK	KT4	160	D6
Burford Wk	FUL/PGN	SW6 *	108	A6
Burford Wy	CROY/NA	CR0	180	A5
Burgate Cl	DART	DA1	138	C2
Burges Gv	BARN	SW13	106	E6
Burges Rd	EHAM	E6	77	K6
Burgess Av	CDALE/KGS	NW9	51	F5
Burgess Cl	FELT	TW13	141	J3
Burgess Hl	CRICK	NW2	70	E3
Burgess Ms	WIM/MER	SW19	147	F5
Burgess Rd	SRTFD	E15	76	C3
	SUT	SM1	175	F3
Burgess St	POP/IOD	E14	93	J4
Burge St	STHWK	SE1	19	G4
Burghill Rd	SYD	SE26	151	F3
Burghley Av	BORE	WD6	24	E4
	NWMAL	KT3	145	F7
Burghley Hall Cl	WIM/MER	SW19 *	127	H7
Burghley Pl	MTCM	CR4	162	E4
Burghley Rd	CEND/HSY/T	N8	55	G2
	KTTN	NW5	72	B3
	SRTFD	E15 *	76	B5
	WIM/MER	SW19	146	B3
Burgh St	IS	N1	6	B1
Burgon St	BLKFR	EC4V	12	D5
Burgos Cl	CROY/NA	CR0	177	G5
Burgos Gv	GNWCH	SE10	112	D7
Burgoyne Rd	BRXN/ST	SW9	130	A2
	FSBYPK	N4	55	H5
	SNWD	SE25	165	G3
	SUN	TW16	140	D5
Burham Cl	PGE/AN	SE20	150	E6
Burhill Gv	PIN	HA5	47	J1
Burke Cl	PUT/ROE	SW15	126	A3
Burke St	CAN/RD	E16	94	D4
Burket Cl	NWDGN	UB2	102	E3
Burland Rd	BTSEA	SW11	128	E4
Burleigh Av	BFN/LL	DA15	136	A5
	WLGTN	SM6	176	A2
Burleigh Cl	ROMW/RG	RM7	62	D3
Burleigh Ct	BUSH	WD23 *	21	J3
Burleigh Gdns	ASHF	TW15	140	A4
	STHGT/OAK	N14	28	C7
Burleigh Pde	STHGT/OAK	N14 *	28	D7
Burleigh Pl	PUT/ROE	SW15	127	G4
Burleigh Rd	CHEAM	SM3	161	H7
	EN	EN1	30	B3
Burleigh St	COVGDN	WC2E	11	K5
Burleigh Wk	CAT	SE6	133	F7
Burleigh Wy	ENC/FH	EN2	29	K2
Burley Cl	CHING	E4	43	J4
	STRHM/NOR	SW16	163	J2
Burley Rd	CAN/RD	E16	95	F4
Burlington Ar	CONDST	W1S	10	E7
Burlington Av	RCH/KEW	TW9	105	H7
	ROMW/RG	RM7	62	D5
Burlington Cl	EBED/NFELT	TW14	121	G6
	EHAM	E6	95	J5
	MV/WKIL	W9	2	A9
	PIN	HA5	47	F2
Burlington Gdns	CHDH	RM6	62	A6
	CHSWK	W4	105	K4
	CONDST	W1S	10	E7
Burlington La	CHSWK	W4	105	K6
Burlington Ms	ACT	W3	86	E7
Burlington Pde	CRICK	NW2 *	70	B3
Burlington Pl	FUL/PGN	SW6	127	H1
	WFD	IG8	44	E2
Burlington Ri	EBAR	EN4	27	J7
Burlington Rd	CHSWK	W4	105	K4
	FUL/PGN	SW6	127	H1
	ISLW	TW7	103	J7
	MUSWH	N10	54	A2
	NWMAL	KT3	160	C3
	THHTH	CR7	164	D1
	TOTM	N17	42	C7
Burma Rd	STNW/STAM	N16	73	K3
Burma Ter	NRWD	SE19 *	150	A4
Burmester Rd	TOOT	SW17	147	G2
Burnaby Crs	CHSWK	W4	105	J5
Burnaby Gdns	CHSWK	W4	105	J5
Burnaby St	WBPTN	SW10	108	B6
Burnbrae Cl	NFNCH/WDSPK	N12	39	F5
Burnbury Rd	BAL	SW12	129	H7
Burn Cl	GSTN	WD25 *	22	D3
Burncroft Av	PEND	EN3	30	E1
Burndell Wy	YEAD	UB4	83	H4
Burnell Av	RCHPK/HAM	TW10	143	J4
	WELL	DA16	136	B1
Burnell Gdns	STAN	HA7	49	K1
Burnell Rd	SUT	SM1	175	F3
Burnell Wk	STHWK	SE1 *	19	M7
Burnels Av	EHAM	E6	96	A2
Burness Cl	HOLWY	N7	73	F5
Burne St	CAMTN	NW1	9	J2
Burnet Cl	HOM	E9	74	F4
Burnett Rd	ERITH	DA8	119	C5
Burney Av	BRYLDS	KT5	159	F4
Burney St	GNWCH	SE10	113	F6
Burnfoot Av	FUL/PGN	SW6	107	H7
Burnham Av	HGDN/ICK	UB10	64	A3
Burnham Cl	KTN/HRWW/WS	HA3	49	J3
	MLHL	NW7	37	H6
	STHWK	SE1	19	M6
Burnham Crs	WAN	E11	59	K1
Burnham Dr	WPK	KT4	174	B1
Burnham Gdns	CROY/NA	CR0	165	G6
	HSLWW	TW4	102	A7
	HYS/HAR	UB3	101	F3
Burnham Rd	BETH	E2	92	E2
	KUTN/CMB	KT2	144	C6
Burnham Ter	DART	DA1 *	139	J5
Burnham Wy	SYD	SE26	151	H4
	WEA	W13	104	B3
Burnhill Rd	BECK	BR3	166	D1
Burnley Cl	OXHEY	WD19	33	G4
Burnley Rd	BRXN/ST	SW9	130	A1
	WLSDN	NW10	69	H4
Burnsall St	CHEL	SW3	15	K7
Burns Av	BFN/LL	DA15	136	C5
	CHDH	RM6	61	J6
	EBED/NFELT	TW14	121	K5
	STHL	UB1	84	A6
Burns Cl	CAR	SM5	176	A7
	WALTH	E17	58	A3
	WELL	DA16	116	A7
	WIM/MER	SW19	147	H5
	YEAD	UB4	82	K4
Burnside	CHING	E4	44	B4
Burnside Cl	BAR	EN5	26	E2
	BERM/RHTH	SE16	93	F7
	TWK	TW1	124	B5
Burnside Crs	ALP/SUD	HA0	67	K7
Burnside Rd	BCTR	RM8	79	J1
Burns Rd	ALP/SUD	HA0	86	A1
	BTSEA	SW11	128	E1
	WEA	W13 *	104	C1
Burn's Rd	WLSDN	NW10	69	H7
Burns Wy	HEST	TW5	102	D1
Burnt Ash Hl	LEE/GVPK	SE12	134	J5
Burnt Ash La	BMLY	BR1	153	F5
Burnt Ash Rd	LEE/GVPK	SE12	133	K4
Burnthwaite Rd	FUL/PGN	SW6	107	J6
Burnt Oak Broadway	EDGW	HA8	36	D6
Burnt Oak Flds	EDGW	HA8	50	E1
Burnt Oak La	BFN/LL	DA15	136	B5
	ERITH	DA8	138	C1
Burntwood Cl	WAND/EARL	SW18	128	C7
Burntwood Grange Rd	WAND/EARL	SW18	128	C7
Burntwood La	TOOT	SW17	147	K2
Burntwood Vw	NRWD	SE19 *	150	B4
Buross St	WCHPL	E1	92	D5
Burpham Cl	YEAD	UB4	83	H4
Burrage Gv	WOOL/PLUM	SE18	115	H3
Burrage Pl	WOOL/PLUM	SE18	115	H3
Burrage Rd	WOOL/PLUM	SE18	115	H3
Burrard Rd	KIL/WHAMP	NW6	70	E4
	CAN/RD	E16	95	C7
Burrell Cl	CROY/NA	CR0	166	A5
	EDGW	HA8	36	C1
Burrell Rw	BECK	BR3	166	D1
Burrell St	STHWK	SE1	12	C8
Burrells Wharf Sq	POP/IOD	E14	112	E4
Burrels Whf Pl	POP/IOD	E14	112	E4
Burritt Rd	KUT/HW	KT1	159	H1
Burroughs Cots	POP/IOD	E14 *	93	H4
The Burroughs	HDN	NW4	51	K3
Burrow Rd	EDUL	SE22	131	F3
Burrows Ms	STHWK	SE1	18	C1
Burrows Rd	WLSDN	NW10	88	A2
Burr Rd	WAND/EARL	SW18	127	K7
Bursar St	STHWK	SE1 *	13	J9
Bursdon Cl	BFN/LL	DA15	155	G1
Bursland Rd	PEND	EN3	31	F3
Burslem St	WCHPL	E1	92	D5
Burstock Rd	PUT/ROE	SW15	127	H3
Burston Rd	PUT/ROE	SW15	127	G4
Burstow Rd	RYNPK	SW20	146	C7
Burtenshaw Rd	THDIT	KT7	158	B6
Burtley Cl	FSBYPK	N4	55	J7
Burton Av	WATW	WD18	20	E3
Burton Bank	IS	N1 *	7	J2
Burton Cl	CHSGTN	KT9	171	K6
	THHTH	CR7	164	E2
Burton Gdns	HEST	TW5	102	E7
Burton Gv	WALW	SE17	19	G8
Burtonhole Cl	MLHL	NW7	38	B3
Burtonhole La	MLHL	NW7	38	B3
Burton La	BRXN/ST	SW9 *	130	B1
Burton Ms	BGVA	SW1W	16	B6
Burton Pl	STPAN	WC1H	5	H9
Burton Rd	BRXN/ST	SW9	130	B1
	KIL/WHAMP	NW6	70	D6
	KUTN/CMB	KT2	144	A1
	LEE/GVPK	SE12	144	E2
	SRTFD	E15	76	D6
Burtons Ct	SRTFD	E15 *	76	B6
Burton's Rd	HPTN	TW12	142	B3
Burton St	STPAN	WC1H	5	H9
Burtwell La	WNWD	SE27	149	K3
Burwash Rd	WOOL/PLUM	SE18	115	J4
Burway Cl	SAND/SEL	CR2	178	A5
Burwell Av	GFD/PVL	UB6	66	E6
Burwell Cl	WCHPL	E1	92	D5
Burwell Rd	LEY	E10	57	G7
Burwell Wk	BOW	E3	93	J3
Burwood Av	HAYES	BR2	181	F1
	PIN	HA5	47	G4
Burwood Cl	SURB	KT6	159	H7
Burwood Crs	CHSM	SM3	99	F2
Burwood Dr	NWMAL	KT3	160	A1
Burwood Gdns	ACT	W3	86	D6
Burwood Pl	BAY/PAD	W2	9	K4
Bury Av	RSLP	HA4	46	C5
	YEAD	UB4	82	C1
Bury Cl	BERM/RHTH	SE16	93	F7
Bury Ct	HDTCH	EC3A	13	K4
Bury Pl	NOXST/BSQ	WC1A	11	J3
Bury Rd	DAGE	RM10	80	E4
	WDGN	N22	55	G1
Buryside Cl	GNTH/NBYPK	IG2	61	F1
Bury St	ED	N9	30	B6
	HDTCH	EC3A	13	K5
	RSLP	HA4	46	B5
	STJS	SW1Y	10	F8
Bury St West	ED	N9	30	A6
Bury Wk	CHEL	SW3	15	J6
Busby Pl	KTTN	NW5	72	D5
Bushbaby Cl	STHWK	SE1	19	J4
Bushberry Rd	HOM	E9	75	G5
Bush Cl	GNTH/NBYPK	IG2	60	D4
Bush Cots	WAND/EARL	SW18 *	127	K4
Bushell Cl	BRXS/STRHM	SW2	149	F1
Bushell Gn	BUSH	WD23	34	D1
Bushell Wy	CHST	BR7	154	A4
Bush Elms Rd	EMPKM	RM11	63	H5
Bushey Av	STMC/STPC	BR5	169	J6
Bushey Cl	WALTH	E17	58	A2
Bushey Down	BAL	SW12	148	G1
Bushey Hall Dr	BUSH	WD23	21	J3
Bushey Hall Pk	BUSH	WD23 *	21	J3
Bushey Hall Rd	BUSH	WD23	21	H4
Bushey Hill Rd	CMBW	SE5	111	G7
Bushey La	SUT	SM1	174	E3
Bushey Lees	BFN/LL	DA15 *	136	A5
Bushey Mill La	BUSH	WD23	21	K1
Bushey Rd	CROY/NA	CR0	179	J1
	HYS/HAR	UB3	101	J1
	PLSTW	E13	95	G1
	RYNPK	SW20	160	E1
	SEVS/STOTM	N15	56	A5
	SUT	SM1	174	E3
Bushey Wy	BECK	BR3	167	H5
Bushfield Cl	EDGW	HA8	36	D1
Bushfield Crs	EDGW	HA8	36	C2
Bush Gv	CDALE/KGS	NW9	50	E6
	STAN	HA7	35	K6
Bushgrove Rd	BCTR	RM8	79	K3
Bush Hl	WCHMH	N21	29	J6
Bush Hill Pde	ED	N9 *	29	K6
Bush Hill Rd	KTN/HRWW/WS	HA3	50	B5
	WCHMH	N21	29	K5
Bush House	WOOL/PLUM	SE18 *	114	D6
Bush La	CANST	EC4R	13	G6
Bushmead Cl	SEVS/STOTM	N15 *	56	B3
Bushmoor Crs	WOOL/PLUM	SE18	115	G6
Bushnell Rd	TOOT	SW17	148	B1
Bush Rd	BKHH	IG9	45	H3
	DEPT	SE8	112	A3
	HACK	E8	74	D7
	RCH/KEW	TW9	105	F5
	WAN	E11	76	D2
Bushway	BCTR	RM8	79	K3
Bushwood	WAN	E11	58	D7
Bushwood Dr	STHWK	SE1	19	M6
Bushwood Rd	RCH/KEW	TW9	105	H5
Bushy Park Gdns	HPTN	TW12	142	D5
Bushy Park Rd	TEDD	TW11	143	H6
Bushy Rd	TEDD	TW11	143	F5
Busk Ms	WAP	E1W *	93	F7
Butchers La	ELTH/MOT	SE9	135	F5
Butchers Rd	CAN/RD	E16	94	E5
Bute Av	RCHPK/HAM	TW10	144	A1
Bute Gdns	HMSMTH	W6	107	G3
	WLGTN	SM6	176	C4
Bute Gdns West	WLGTN	SM6	176	C4
Bute Ms	GLDGN	NW11	53	F4
Bute Rd	BARK/HLT	IG6	60	B4
	CROY/NA	CR0	164	B7
	WLGTN	SM6	176	C3
Bute St	SKENS	SW7	15	G5
Bute Wk	IS	N1 *	73	K5
Butler Av	HRW	HA1	48	D6
Butler Cl	EDGW	HA8	50	D1
	HRW	HA1	48	B5
	WLSDN	NW10	69	H6
Butler Pl	WESTW	SW1E	17	F3
Butler Rd	BARK/HLT	IG6	60	B4
	CROY/NA	CR0	164	B7
	WLGTN	SM6	176	C3
Butlers & Colonial Whf	STHWK	SE1	19	M1
Butlers Farm Cl	RCHPK/HAM	TW10	143	K3
Butler St	BETH	E2	92	E2
Buttercup Sq	STWL/WRAY	TW19	120	A7
Butterfield Cl	BERM/RHTH	SE16	111	H1
	TOTM	N17	41	J5
	TWK	TW1	124	A5
Butterfield House	CHARL	SE7 *	114	D6
Butterfield Ms	WOOL/PLUM	SE18	115	G5
Butterfields	WALTH	E17	58	A4
Butterfield Sq	EHAM	E6	95	K3
Butterfly La	BORE	WD6	23	H2
	ELTH/MOT	SE9	135	G5
Butter Hl	CAR	SM5	176	A2
Butteridges Cl	DAGW	RM9	80	B7
Buttermere Cl	EBED/NFELT	TW14	121	J7
	MRDN	SM4	161	G6
	SRTFD	E15	76	B3
	STHWK	SE1	19	L6
Buttermere Dr	PUT/ROE	SW15	127	H4
Buttermere Rd	STMC/STPC	BR5	169	K4
Butterwick	HMSMTH	W6	107	F3
Butterworth Gdns	WFD	IG8	44	E5
Buttery Ms	STHGT/OAK	N14	40	E2
Buttesland St	IS	N1	7	H7
Butterfield Cl	DAGE	RM10	80	D5
Buttmarsh Cl	WOOL/PLUM	SE18	115	G4
Buttsbury Rd	IL	IG1	78	C4
Butts Crs	FELT	TW13	142	A2
Buttsmead	NTHWD	HA6	32	A6
Butts Piece	NTHLT	UB5	83	F1
Butts Rd	BMLY	BR1	152	E4
The Butts	BTFD	TW8	104	E5
Buxhall Crs	HOM	E9	75	H5
Buxted Rd	EDUL	SE22	131	F3
	HACK	E8	7	L1
	NFNCH/WDSPK	N12	39	J4
Buxton Cl	WFD	IG8	45	H5
Buxton Crs	CHEAM	SM3	174	C3
Buxton Dr	NWMAL	KT3	160	A1
	WAN	E11	58	D3
Buxton Gdns	ACT	W3	86	D6
Buxton Ms	CLAP	SW4	129	J1
Buxton Pth	OXHEY	WD19 *	33	G2
Buxton Rd	ARCH	N19	54	D7
	CRICK	NW2	69	K5
	EHAM	E6	95	J2
	ERITH	DA8	118	A6
	GNTH/NBYPK	IG2	60	E5
	MORT/ESHN	SW14	106	B7
	SRTFD	E15	76	C4
	THHTH	CR7	164	C4
	WALTH	E17	57	G3
Buxton St	WCHPL	E1	13	M1
Byam Cl	FUL/PGN	SW6	128	B1
Byards Cft	STRHM/NOR	SW16 *	148	D7
Bychurch End	TEDD	TW11 *	143	F4
Bycroft Rd	PGE/AN	SE20	151	F6
Bycroft St	STHL	UB1	84	A5
Bycullah Av	ENC/FH	EN2	29	H2
Bycullah Rd	ENC/FH	EN2	29	H2
Byelands Cl	BERM/RHTH	SE16 *	93	F7
The Bye	ACT	W3	87	G5
Byewaters	WATW	WD18	20	A5
Bye Ways	WHTN	TW2	142	E2
The Byeways	BRYLDS	KT5	159	K6
The Bye Wy	KTN/HRWW/WS	HA3	34	E7
The Byeway	MORT/ESHN	SW14	125	K2
Byfeld Gdns	BARN	SW13	106	D7
Byfield Cl	BERM/RHTH	SE16	112	B1
Byfield Rd	ISLW	TW7	124	B2
Byford Cl	SRTFD	E15	76	C6
Bygrove	CROY/NA	CR0	179	K5
Bygrove St	POP/IOD	E14	93	K5
Byland Cl	ABYW	SE2	116	D2
	CAR	SM5	162	D7
	WCHMH	N21	29	F6
Byne Rd	SAND/SEL	CR2	177	K5
	SYD	SE26	150	E5
Bynes Rd	SAND/SEL	CR2	177	K6
Byng Pl	GWRST	WC1E	11	H1
Byng Rd	BAR	EN5	26	B2
Byng St	POP/IOD	E14	112	D1
Byre Rd	STHGT/OAK	N14	28	A5
Byrne Cl	CROY/NA	CR0	164	C5
Byron Av	BAL	SW12	129	G7
	BORE	WD6	24	C4
	CDALE/KGS	NW9	50	D3
	MNPK	E12	77	J5
	NWMAL	KT3	160	D4
	SUT	SM1	175	H3
	SWFD	E18	58	D3
Byron Av East	SUT	SM1	175	H3
Byron Cl	HACK	E8	7	M3
	HPTN	TW12	141	K3
	PGE/AN	SE20 *	165	J2
	SYD	SE26	151	H3
	THMD	SE28	97	K6
	WOT/HER	KT12	156	D7
Byron Ct	ENC/FH	EN2	29	H1
Byron Dr	EFNCH	N2	53	H5
Byron Gdns	SUT	SM1	175	H3
Byron Hill Rd	RYLN/HDSTN	HA2	48	C5
Byron Ms	HAMP	NW3	71	J4
	MV/WKIL	W9	2	B9
Byron Rd	ALP/SUD	HA0	67	J2
	CRICK	NW2	69	K1
	HRW	HA1	48	E5
	KTN/HRWW/WS	HA3	49	K7
	LEY	E10	57	K7
	MLHL	NW7	37	K4
	WALTH	E17	57	J2
Byron St	POP/IOD	E14	94	A5
Byron Ter	ED	N9 *	30	E6
Byron Wy	NTHLT	UB5	83	J2
	WDR/YW	UB7	100	C3
	YEAD	UB4	82	C3
Bysouth Cl	SEVS/STOTM	N15	55	K3
By The Wood	OXHEY	WD19	33	H1
Bythorn St	BRXN/ST	SW9	130	A2
Byton Rd	TOOT	SW17	147	K5
Byward Av	EBED/NFELT	TW14	122	B5
Byward St	MON	EC3R	13	K7
Bywater Pl	BERM/RHTH	SE16	93	H7
Bywater St	CHEL	SW3	15	L7
The Byway	BELMT	SM2	175	H7
	HOR/WEW	KT19	173	H3
Bywell Pl	GTPST	W1W *	10	E3
Bywood Av	CROY/NA	CR0	165	K5

C

Street	Area	Postcode	Page	Grid
Cabbell St	CAMTN	NW1	9	J3
Cabinet Wy	CHING	E4	43	H5
Cable Pl	GNWCH	SE10	113	F7
Cables Cl	ERITH	DA8	117	K2
Cable St	WCHPL	E1	92	C6
Cabot Sq	POP/IOD	E14	93	H7
Cabot Wy	EHAM	E6	77	H7
Cabul Rd	BTSEA	SW11	128	D1
Cactus Cl	CMBW	SE5	131	F1
Cadbury Cl	ISLW	TW7	104	B7
	SUN	TW16	140	C6
Cadbury Rd	SUN	TW16	140	C6
Cadbury Wy	BERM/RHTH	SE16	19	M4
Caddington Cl	EBAR	EN4	27	J4
Caddington Rd	CRICK	NW2	70	C2
Caddis Cl	STAN	HA7 *	35	F6
Cadell Cl	BETH	E2	7	M6
Cade Rd	GNWCH	SE10	113	G7
Cader Rd	WAND/EARL	SW18	128	B5
Cadet Dr	STHWK	SE1	19	M7
Cadet Pl	GNWCH	SE10	113	H4
Cadiz Rd	DAGE	RM10	80	E6
Cadiz St	WALW	SE17	18	F8
Cadman Cl	BRXN/ST	SW9	110	C6
Cadmer Cl	NWMAL	KT3	160	B3
Cadmus Cl	CLAP	SW4	129	J3
Cadogan Cl	HOM	E9 *	75	H6
	RYLN/HDSTN	HA2	66	B3
	TEDD	TW11	142	E4
Cadogan Ct	BELMT	SM2	175	F5
Cadogan Gdns	CHEL	SW3	15	M5
	FNCH	N3	39	F7
	SWFD	E18	59	F3
	WCHMN	N21	29	G4
Cadogan Ga	KTBR	SW1X	15	M5
Cadogan La	KTBR	SW1X	16	A3
Cadogan Pl	KTBR	SW1X	15	M3
Cadogan Rd	SURB	KT6	158	E4
	WOOL/PLUM	SE18	115	H2
Cadogan Sq	KTBR	SW1X	15	L2
Cadogan St	CHEL	SW3	15	L6
Cadogan Ter	HOM	E9	75	H5
Cadoxton Av	SEVS/STOTM	N15	56	B5
Cadwallon Rd	ELTH/MOT	SE9	154	B1
Caedmon Rd	HOLWY	N7	73	F3
Caerleon Cl	ESH/CLAY	KT10	171	H6
	SCUP	DA14	155	J4
Caernarvon Cl	MTCM	CR4	163	K3
Caesars Wk	MTCM	CR4	162	E4
Cahill St	STLK	EC1Y *	12	F1
Cahir St	POP/IOD	E14	112	E3
Cain's La	EBED/NFELT	TW14	121	G4
Caird St	NKENS	W10	88	D2
Cairn Av	EA	W5	85	K7
Cairndale Cl	BMLY	BR1	152	D6
Cairnfield Av	CRICK	NW2	69	G2
Cairngorm Cl	TEDD	TW11	143	G4
Cairns Av	WFD	IG8	45	K5
Cairns Rd	BTSEA	SW11	128	D4
Cairn Wy	STAN	HA7	35	F5
Cairo New Rd	CROY/NA	CR0	177	J1
Cairo Rd	WALTH	E17	57	J3
Caister Ms	BAL	SW12	129	G6
Caistor Park Rd	SRTFD	E15	76	D7
Caistor Rd	BAL	SW12	129	G6
Caithness Gdns	BFN/LL	DA15	136	A5
Caithness Rd	MTCM	CR4	148	B6
	WKENS	W14	107	G2
Calabria Rd	HBRY	N5	73	H5
Calais St	CMBW	SE5	110	C7
Calbourne Av	HCH	RM12	81	K4
Calbourne Rd	BAL	SW12	128	E6
Caldbeck Av	WPK	KT4	173	K1
Caldecote Gdns	BUSH	WD23	22	E5
Caldecote La	BUSH	WD23	23	F6
Caldecot Rd	CMBW	SE5	130	D1
Caldecott Wy	CLPT	E5	75	F2
Calder Av	GFD/PVL	UB6	85	F1
Calder Gdns	EDGW	HA8	50	C2
Calderon Rd	WAN	E11	76	A3
Calder Rd	MRDN	SM4	162	B4
Caldervale Rd	CLAP	SW4	129	J4
Calderwood St	WOOL/PLUM	SE18	115	F3
Caldew St	CMBW	SE5	110	E6
Caldicote Gn	CDALE/KGS	NW9 *	51	G5
Caldwell Rd	OXHEY	WD19	33	H3
Caldwell St	BRXN/ST	SW9	110	A6
Caldy Rd	BELV	DA17	117	J2
Caldy Wk	IS	N1 *	73	J5
Caledonian Cl	GDMY/SEVK	IG3 *	61	H7
Caledonian Rd	HOLWY	N7	73	F4
	IS	N1	5	L2
Caledonian Sq	CAMTN	NW1 *	72	D5
Caledonian Wharf Rd	POP/IOD	E14	113	G3
Caledonia Rd	STWL/WRAY	TW19	120	B7
Caledonia St	IS	N1	5	K6
Caledon Rd	EHAM	E6	77	K7
	WLGTN	SM6	176	A3
Calendar Ms	SURB	KT6	158	E5
Cale St	CHEL	SW3	15	J7
Calidore Cl	BRXS/STRHM	SW2	130	A5
California La	BUSH	WD23	22	D7
California Rd	NWMAL	KT3	159	K3
Callaby Ter	IS	N1 *	73	K5
Callaghan Cl	LEW	SE13	133	H3
Callaghan Cots	WCHPL	E1 *	92	E4
Callander Rd	CAT	SE6	151	K1
The Callanders	BUSH	WD23 *	22	E7
Callard Av	PLMGR	N13	41	H4
Callcott Rd	KIL/WHAMP	NW6	70	D6
Callcott St	KENS	W8	8	A8
Callendar Rd	SKENS	SW7	15	G3
Callingham Cl	POP/IOD	E14	93	H4
Callis Farm Cl	STWL/WRAY	TW19	120	B5

Callisons Pl GNWCH SE10 113 H4
Callis Rd WALTH E17 57 H5
Callow St CHEL SW3 15 G9
Calmington Rd CMBW SE5 19 K8
Calmont Rd BMLY BR1 152 B5
Calonne Rd WIM/MER SW19 146 B3
Calshot Rd HTHAIR TW6 120 E1
Calshot St IS N1 5 L5
Calshot Wy ENC/FH EN2 29 H2
HTHAIR TW6 120 D1
Calthorpe Gdns EDGW HA8 36 B4
SUT SM1 175 G2
Calthorpe St FSBYW WC1X 5 M9
Calton Av DUL SE21 131 F5
Calton Rd BAR EN5 27 G5
Calverley Cl BECK BR3 151 K5
Calverley Crs DAGE RM10 80 C1
Calverley Gv ARCH N19 54 D7
Calverley Rd EW KT17 173 J5
Calvert Av WCHPL E1 7 K8
Calvert Cl BELV DA17 117 H3
Calverton Rd EHAM E6 78 A7
Calvert Rd BAR EN5 26 B1
GNWCH SE10 113 J4
Calvert St CAMTN NW1 4 A3
Calvin St WCHPL E1 13 L1
Calydon Rd CHARL SE7 114 A4
Calypso Crs PECK SE15 111 F6
Calypso Wy BERM/RHTH SE16 112 C2
Camac Rd WHTN TW2 123 J7
Camarthen Gn
CDALE/KGS NW9 * 51 G5
Cambalt Rd PUT/ROE SW15 127 G4
Camberley Av EN EN1 30 A3
RYNPK SW20 160 E1
Camberley Cl CHEAM SM3 174 B2
Camberley Rd HTHAIR TW6 120 D2
Cambert Wy BKHTH/KID SE3 134 A3
Camberwell Church St
CMBW SE5 110 E7
Camberwell Glebe CMBW SE5 110 E7
Camberwell Gn CMBW SE5 110 E7
Camberwell Gv CMBW SE5 110 E7
Camberwell New Rd
CMBW SE5 110 C6
Camberwell Rd CMBW SE5 110 D5
Camberwell Station Rd
CMBW SE5 110 D7
Cambeys Rd DAGE RM10 80 E4
Camborne Av WEA W13 104 C1
Camborne Cl HTHAIR TW6 120 D2
Camborne Crs HTHAIR TW6 120 D2
Camborne Ms
WAND/EARL SW18 127 K6
Camborne Rd BELMT SM2 174 E6
CROY/NA CR0 165 H6
MRDN SM4 161 G5
SCUP DA14 155 J2
WAND/EARL SW18 127 K6
WELL DA16 135 K1
Camborne Wy HEST TW5 103 F7
HTHAIR TW6 120 D2
Cambourne Av ED N9 31 F6
Cambourne Ms NTGHL W11 88 C5
Cambray Rd BAL SW12 129 H7
Cambria Cl BFN/LL DA15 135 J7
HSLW TW3 123 F3
Cambria Ct EBED/NFELT TW14 122 A6
Cambria Gdns
STWL/WRAY TW19 120 B6
Cambrian Av
GNTH/NBYPK IG2 60 E4
Cambrian Cl WNWD SE27 149 H2
Cambrian Gn CDALE/KGS NW9 51 G4
Cambrian Rd LEY E10 57 J6
RCHPK/HAM TW10 125 G5
Cambria Rd CMBW SE5 130 D2
Cambria St FUL/PGN SW6 108 A6
Cambridge Av GFD/PVL UB6 67 F4
KIL/WHAMP NW6 2 B5
NWMAL KT3 160 B1
WELL DA16 136 A3
Cambridge Barracks Rd
WOOL/PLUM SE18 114 E3
Cambridge Circ
SOHO/SHAV W1D 11 H5
Cambridge Cl EBAR EN4 28 A7
HSLWW TW4 122 D3
RYNPK SW20 145 K7
WALTH E17 57 H5
WDGN N22 * 41 G7
WDR/YW UB7 100 A5
WLSDN NW10 68 E2
Cambridge Crs BETH E2 92 D1
TEDD TW11 * 143 G4
Cambridge Dr RSLP HA4 65 G1
Cambridge Gdns EN EN1 30 C1
KIL/WHAMP NW6 2 B5
KUT/HW KT1 159 H1
MUSWH N10 40 A7
NKENS W10 88 B5
TOTM N17 41 K6
WCHMH N21 29 K6
Cambridge Ga CAMTN NW1 4 C8
Cambridge Gate Ms
CAMTN NW1 4 D8
Cambridge Gn ELTH/MOT SE9 135 G7
Cambridge Gv HMSMTH W6 106 E3
PGE/AN SE20 * 150 D7
Cambridge Grove Rd
KUT/HW KT1 159 H1
Cambridge Heath Rd
BETH E2 92 D2
Cambridge Pde EN EN1 * 30 C1
Cambridge Pk TWK TW1 124 D6
Cambridge Park Rd WAN E11 58 D6
Cambridge Pas HOM E9 74 E6
Cambridge Pl KENS W8 * 14 D2
Cambridge Rd ASHF TW15 140 A6
BARK IG11 78 C6
BARN SW13 126 C1
BMLY BR1 152 E6
BTSEA SW11 108 E7
CAR SM5 175 J5
E/WMO/HCT KT8 156 E3
GDMY/SEVK IG3 60 E7
HNWL W7 104 A1
HPTN TW12 141 K6
HSLWW TW4 122 D3
KIL/WHAMP NW6 2 B6
KUT/HW KT1 159 H1
MTCM CR4 163 H2
NWMAL KT3 160 A3
PGE/AN SE20 165 H2
RCH/KEW TW9 105 H6
RYLN/HDSTN HA2 48 A4
RYNPK SW20 145 K7
SCUP DA14 154 E3
STHL UB1 * 83 K7
TEDD TW11 143 G3
TWK TW1 124 E5
WAN E11 58 E5
WATW WD18 * 21 G3
WOT/HER KT12 156 A5
Cambridge Rd North
CHSWK W4 105 J4
Cambridge Rd South
CHSWK W4 105 J4
Cambridge Rw
WOOL/PLUM SE18 115 G4
Cambridge Sq BAY/PAD W2 9 J4
Cambridge St PIM SW1V 16 D7
Cambridge Ter CAMTN NW1 4 C8
ED N9 * 30 B6
Cambridge Terrace Ms
CAMTN NW1 * 4 D8
Cambridge Yd HNWL W7 * 104 A1
Cambus Cl YEAD UB4 83 J4
Cambus Rd CAN/RD E16 94 E4
Camdale Rd
WOOL/PLUM SE18 116 A6
Camden Av FELT TW13 141 G1
YEAD UB4 83 G6
Camden Cl CHST BR7 154 C7
Camden Gdns CAMTN NW1 4 D2
SUT SM1 175 F4
THHTH CR7 164 C2
Camden Gv CHST BR7 154 B5
Camden High St CAMTN NW1 4 D2
Camden Hill Rd NRWD SE19 150 A5
Camdenhurst St POP/IOD E14 93 G5
Camden Lock Pl CAMTN NW1 4 C2
Camden Ms CAMTN NW1 5 G1
Camden Park Rd CAMTN NW1 72 D5
CHST BR7 153 K6
Camden Pas IS N1 6 C5
Camden Rd BXLY DA5 137 G7
CAMTN NW1 4 E2
SUT SM1 175 F4
WALTH E17 57 H5
WAN E11 59 F5
Camden Road (Permanent
Way) CAMTN NW1 * 5 G4
Camden Rw BKHTH/KID SE3 133 H1
PIN HA5 * 47 G2
Camden Sq CAMTN NW1 5 G1
Camden St CAMTN NW1 4 D2
Camden Ter CAMTN NW1 72 D5
Camden Wk IS N1 6 C4
Camden Wy CHST BR7 153 K6
THHTH CR7 164 C2
Camelford Wk NTGHL W11 * 88 C5
Camel Gv KUTN/CMB KT2 143 K4
Camellia Pl WHTN TW2 123 G6
Camellia St VX/NE SW8 109 K6
Camelot Cl THMD SE28 115 J1
WIM/MER SW19 146 D3
Camel Rd CAN/RD E16 95 H7
CAN/RD E16 95 J7
Camera Pl WBPTN SW10 108 C5
Cameron Cl TRDG/WHET N20 39 J1
UED N18 42 D3
Cameron Crs EDGW HA8 36 D7
Cameron Pl
STRHM/NOR SW16 149 G1
Cameron Rd CAT SE6 * 151 H1
CROY/NA CR0 164 C5
GDMY/SEVK IG3 60 E7
Cameron Sq MTCM CR4 147 J7
Cameron Ter LEE/GVPK SE12 * 153 F2
Camerton Cl HACK E8 74 B5
Camilla Cl SUN TW16 * 140 D5
Camilla Rd BERM/RHTH SE16 111 J3
Camille Cl SNWD SE25 165 H2
Camlan Rd BMLY BR1 152 D3
Camlet St BETH E2 7 L9
Camlet Wy EBAR EN4 26 E1
Camley St CAMTN NW1 5 G2
Camm Gdns KUT/HW KT1 * 159 G1
THDIT KT7 157 K6
Camomile Av MTCM CR4 147 K7
Camomile St OBST EC2N 13 J4
Camomile Rd ROMW/RG RM7 81 F1
Campana Rd FUL/PGN SW6 107 K7
Campbell Av BARK/HLT IG6 60 C3
Campbell Cl RSLP HA4 46 E5
STRHM/NOR SW16 * 148 D4
WHTN TW2 123 J7
WOOL/PLUM SE18 115 F7
Campbell Cots MTCM CR4 * 163 F1
Campbell Cft EDGW HA8 36 C4
Campbell Gordon Wy
CRICK NW2 69 K3
Campbell Rd BOW E3 93 J2
CROY/NA CR0 164 C6
EHAM E6 77 J7
HNWL W7 84 E6
SRTFD E15 76 C3
TOTM N17 42 B7
WALTH E17 57 H3
WHTN TW2 142 D1
Campbell Wk IS N1 * 5 K3
Campdale Rd HOLWY N7 72 D2
Campden Crs ALP/SUD HA0 67 H2
BCTR RM8 79 J3
Campden Gv KENS W8 14 B1
Campden Hl KENS W8 14 A1
Campden Hill Gdns KENS W8 8 A8
Campden Hill Pl NTGHL W11 * 88 D7
Campden Hill Rd KENS W8 14 A1
Campden Hill Sq KENS W8 88 D7
Campden House Cl KENS W8 14 A1
Campden House Ter
KENS W8 * 8 B9
Campden Rd SAND/SEL CR2 178 A4
Campden St KENS W8 8 A9
Campden Ter CHSWK W4 * 106 B4
Campden Wy BCTR RM8 79 H3
Campen Cl WIM/MER SW19 146 C1
Camperdown St WCHPL E1 13 M5
Campfield Rd ELTH/MOT SE9 134 C6
Campion Cl CROY/NA CR0 178 A3
EHAM E6 95 K6
KTN/HRWW/WS HA3 50 B5
ROMW/RG RM7 81 F1
Campion Ct ALP/SUD HA0 * 86 A1
Campion Gdns WFD IG8 44 E4
Campion Pl THMD SE28 97 H7
Campion Rd ISLW TW7 104 A7
LEY E10 57 K6
PUT/ROE SW15 127 F3
Campion Ter CRICK NW2 70 B2
Campion Wy EDGW HA8 36 E3
Camplin Rd
KTN/HRWW/WS HA3 50 A4
Camplin St NWCR SE14 112 A6
Camp Rd WIM/MER SW19 145 K4
Campsbourne Pde
CEND/HSY/T N8 * 54 E3
Campsbourne Rd
CEND/HSY/T N8 54 E2
The Campsbourne
CEND/HSY/T N8 54 E3
Campsey Gdns DAGW RM9 79 H6
Campsey Rd DAGW RM9 79 H6
Campshill Pl LEW SE13 133 F4
Campshill Rd LEW SE13 133 F4
Campus Rd WALTH E17 57 H5
Camp Vw WIM/MER SW19 145 K4
Cam Rd SRTFD E15 76 B7
Camrose Av EDGW HA8 50 B1
ERITH DA8 117 J5
ERITH DA8 * 117 K5
FELT TW13 141 F3
STAN HA7 50 A1
Camrose Cl CROY/NA CR0 166 B6
MRDN SM4 161 K3
Camrose St WOOL/PLUM SE18 116 B4
Canada Av UED N18 41 J5
Canada Crs ACT W3 86 E4
Canada Park Pde
EDGW HA8 * 36 D7
Canada Rd ACT W3 86 E4
Canada Sq POP/IOD E14 93 K7
Canada St BERM/RHTH SE16 112 A1
Canada Wy SHB W12 87 K6
Canadian Av CAT SE6 132 E7
Canal Ap DEPT SE8 112 B4
Canal Bvd KTTN NW5 72 D5
Canal Cl NKENS W10 88 B3
WCHPL E1 93 G3
Canal Gv PECK SE15 111 H5
Canal Pth BETH E2 7 L4
Canal St CMBW SE5 110 E5
Canal Wk CROY/NA CR0 165 F5
IS N1 7 H3
WLSDN NW10 * 68 E6
Canal Wy NKENS W10 88 B3
Canal Whf GFD/PVL UB6 * 67 G7
Canal Yd NWDGN UB2 * 102 A3
Canberra Cl DAGE RM10 81 F6
HDN NW4 51 J2
Canberra Crs DAGE RM10 81 F6
Canberra Dr NTHLT UB5 83 G2
Canberra Rd HTHAIR TW6 120 D2
ABYW SE2 116 E5
CHARL SE7 114 B5
EHAM E6 77 K7
HTHAIR TW6 120 D2
WEA W13 85 G7
Canbury Av KUTN/CMB KT2 144 B7
Canbury Ms SYD SE26 150 C2
Canbury Park Rd
KUTN/CMB KT2 144 A7
Cancell Rd BRXN/ST SW9 110 B7
Candahar Rd BTSEA SW11 128 D1
Candle Gv PECK SE15 131 J2
Candlelight Ct SRTFD E15 76 D5
Candler Ms TWK TW1 124 B6
Candler St SEVS/STOTM N15 * 55 K5
Candover Cl WDR/YW UB7 100 A6
Candover Rd HCH RM12 63 K7
Candover St GTPST W1W * 10 E3
Candy St BOW E3 75 H7
Caney Ms CRICK NW2 70 B1
Canfield Dr RSLP HA4 65 F4
Canfield Gdns
KIL/WHAMP NW6 2 D1
Canfield Pl KIL/WHAMP NW6 71 G5
Canfield Rd RAIN RM13 81 H7
WFD IG8 45 J6
Canford Av NTHLT UB5 65 J7
Canford Cl ENC/FH EN2 29 G1
Canford Gdns NWMAL KT3 160 B5
Canford Pl TEDD TW11 143 J5
Canford Rd CLAP SW4 129 F3
Canham Rd CHSWK W4 106 B1
SNWD SE25 165 F2
Canmore Gdns
STRHM/NOR SW16 148 C6
Cann Hall Rd WAN E11 76 D3
Canning Crs WDGN N22 41 F7
Canning Cross CMBW SE5 131 F1
Canning Pas KENS W8 * 14 E3
Canning Pl KENS W8 14 E3
Canning Place Ms KENS W8 * 14 E3
Canning Rd CROY/NA CR0 178 B1
HBRY N5 73 H2
KTN/HRWW/WS HA3 48 E2
SRTFD E15 94 C1
WALTH E17 57 H2
Cannington Rd DAGW RM9 79 J5
Cannizaro Rd WIM/MER SW19 146 A5
Cannonbury Av PIN HA5 47 H5
Cannon Cl HPTN TW12 142 B5
RYNPK SW20 161 F2
Cannon Dr POP/IOD E14 93 J6
Cannon Hl KIL/WHAMP NW6 71 F4
STHGT/OAK N14 40 D2
Cannon Hill La RYNPK SW20 161 G4
Cannon Hill Ms
STHGT/OAK N14 40 E2
Cannon La HAMP NW3 71 H2
PIN HA5 47 J6
Cannon Pl CHARL SE7 114 D4
HAMP NW3 71 G2
Cannon Rd STHGT/OAK N14 40 E2
WATW WD18 21 G4
Cannon St BLKFR EC4V 12 E5
Cannon Street Rd WCHPL E1 92 D5
Cannon Wy E/WMO/HCT KT8 157 F3
Canon Av CHDH RM6 61 J4
Canon Beck Rd
BERM/RHTH SE16 111 K1
Canonbie Rd FSTH SE23 131 K6
Canonbury Crs IS N1 6 F1
Canonbury Gv IS N1 6 E1
Canonbury La IS N1 6 C1
Canonbury Pk North IS N1 73 J5
Canonbury Pk South IS N1 73 J5
Canonbury Rd IS N1 6 D1
Canonbury Sq IS N1 6 D1
Canonbury St IS N1 6 E1
Canonbury Vls IS N1 6 D2
Canonbury Yd East IS N1 73 H5
Canon Mohan Cl
STHGT/OAK N14 28 A5
Canon Rd BMLY BR1 168 B2
Canon Rw WHALL SW1A 17 J2
Canons Cl EDGW HA8 36 B5
EFNCH N2 53 H6
Canons Cots EDGW HA8 * 36 B5
Canons Ct EDGW HA8 * 36 B5
Canons Dr EDGW HA8 36 B5
Canonsleigh Rd DAGW RM9 79 H6
Canon St IS N1 6 E4
Canon's Wk CROY/NA CR0 179 F2
Canopus Wy NTHWD HA6 32 E3
STWL/WRAY TW19 120 B6
Canrobert St BETH E2 92 D1
Cantelowes Rd CAMTN NW1 72 D5
Canterbury Av BFN/LL DA15 155 J1
IL IG1 59 J6
Canterbury Cl BECK BR3 151 K7
CMBW SE5 * 130 D1
EHAM E6 95 K5
GFD/PVL UB6 84 B4
NTHWD HA6 32 D5
Canterbury Crs BRXN/ST SW9 130 B2
Canterbury Gv WNWD SE27 149 G2
Canterbury Pl WALW SE17 18 D6
Canterbury Rd BORE WD6 24 C1
CROY/NA CR0 164 A6
FELT TW13 141 J1
KIL/WHAMP NW6 2 A6
LEY E10 58 A6
MRDN SM4 162 B5
RYLN/HDSTN HA2 48 B4
WAT WD17 * 21 F1
Canterbury Ter
KIL/WHAMP NW6 2 A5
Canterbury Wy
RKW/CH/CXG WD3 20 A2
Cantley Gdns
GNTH/NBYPK IG2 60 C5
NRWD SE19 150 B7
Cantley Rd HNWL W7 104 B2
Canton St POP/IOD E14 93 J5
Cantrell Rd BOW E3 93 J3
Cantwell Rd
WOOL/PLUM SE18 115 G6
Canvey St STHWK SE1 12 E8
Cape Cl BARK IG11 78 B6
Capel Av WLGTN SM6 177 F4
Capel Cl HAYES BR2 168 D7
TRDG/WHET N20 39 G2
Capel Crs STAN HA7 35 G1
Capel Gdns GDMY/SEVK IG3 79 F3
PIN HA5 47 K3
Capella Rd NTHWD HA6 32 D4
Capel Rd EBAR EN4 27 J5
FSTGT E7 77 F3
OXHEY WD19 21 H5
Capeners Cl KTBR SW1X 15 M2
Capern Rd WAND/EARL SW18 128 B7
Cape Rd TOTM N17 56 C2
Cape Yd WAP E1W 92 C7
Capital Interchange Wy
BTFD TW8 105 H4
Capitol Wy CDALE/KGS NW9 50 E2
Capland St STJWD NW8 3 H9
Caple Pde WLSDN NW10 * 87 H1
Caple Rd WLSDN NW10 87 H1
Caprea Cl YEAD UB4 83 H4
Capri Rd CROY/NA CR0 165 G6
Capstan Cl CHDH RM6 61 H5
Capstan Dr RAIN RM13 99 J4
Capstan Ride ENC/FH EN2 29 G1
Capstan Rd DEPT SE8 112 C3
Capstan Sq POP/IOD E14 113 F1
Capstan Wy
BERM/RHTH SE16 93 G7
Capstone Rd BMLY BR1 152 D3
Capthorne Av
RYLN/HDSTN HA2 47 J7
Capuchin Cl STAN HA7 35 H5
Capulet Ms CAN/RD E16 94 E7
Capworth St LEY E10 57 J7
Caractacus Cottage Vw
WATW WD18 20 E6
Caractacus Gn WATW WD18 20 D5
Caradoc Cl BAY/PAD W2 8 A4
Caradoc Evans Cl
FBAR/BDGN N11 * 40 B4
Caradoc St GNWCH SE10 113 H4
Caradon Ct WAN E11 58 C7
Caradon Wy
SEVS/STOTM N15 * 55 K3
Caravel Cl POP/IOD E14 112 D2
Caravel Ms DEPT SE8 112 D5
Caraway Cl PLSTW E13 95 F4
Caraway Pl WLGTN SM6 176 B2
Carberry Rd NRWD SE19 150 A5
Carbery Av ACT W3 105 G1
Carbis Rd POP/IOD E14 93 H5
Carburton St GTPST W1W 10 D2
Cardale St POP/IOD E14 113 F2
Carden Rd PECK SE15 131 J2
Cardiff Rd HNWL W7 104 B2
PEND EN3 30 D3
WATW WD18 21 F5
Cardiff St WOOL/PLUM SE18 115 K6
Cardigan Gdns
GDMY/SEVK IG3 79 G1
Cardigan Pl LEW SE13 * 133 G1
Cardigan Rd BARN SW13 126 D1
BOW E3 93 H1
RCHPK/HAM TW10 125 F5
WIM/MER SW19 147 G5
Cardigan St LBTH SE11 18 A7
Cardigan Wk IS N1 * 6 F1
Cardinal Av BORE WD6 24 D2
KUTN/CMB KT2 144 A4
MRDN SM4 161 H5
Cardinal Bourne St
STHWK SE1 * 19 H4
Cardinal Cl CHST BR7 154 D7
EDGW HA8 36 E6
MRDN SM4 161 H5
WPK KT4 173 J3
Cardinal Crs NWMAL KT3 159 K1
Cardinal Dr WOT/HER KT12 156 C7
Cardinal Hinsey Cl
WLSDN NW10 87 J1
Cardinal Pl PUT/ROE SW15 127 G3
Cardinal Rd FELT TW13 122 A7
RSLP HA4 47 H7
Cardinals Wk SUN TW16 140 C5
Cardinal's Wk HPTN TW12 142 C6
Cardinals Wy ARCH N19 54 D7
Cardinal Wy
KTN/HRWW/WS HA3 * 48 E2
Cardine Ms PECK SE15 111 J6
Cardington Sq HSLWW TW4 122 C3
Cardington St CAMTN NW1 4 F7
Cardozo Rd HOLWY N7 72 E4
Cardrew Av
NFNCH/WDSPK N12 39 H4
Cardross St HMSMTH W6 106 E2
Cardwell Rd HOLWY N7 * 72 E3
Cardwell Ter HOLWY N7 * 72 E3
Carew Cl HOLWY N7 73 F1
Carew Rd ASHF TW15 140 A5
MTCM CR4 163 F1
NTHWD HA6 32 C5
THHTH CR7 164 C2
TOTM N17 56 C1
WEA W13 104 D1
WLGTN SM6 176 C5
Carew St CMBW SE5 130 D1
Carew Wy OXHEY WD19 33 K2
Carey Gdns VX/NE SW8 109 H7
Carey La CITYW EC2V 12 E4
Carey Pl PIM SW1V 17 G6
Carey Rd DAGW RM9 80 A3
Carey St LINN WC2A 11 M5
Carey Wy WBLY HA9 68 D3
Carfax Pl CLAP SW4 129 J3
Carfax Rd HCH RM12 81 H3
HYS/HAR UB3 101 K4
The Carfax SYD SE26 * 150 E2
Carfree Cl IS N1 6 B1
Cargill Rd WAND/EARL SW18 128 B7
Cargreen Rd SNWD SE25 165 G3
Carholme Rd FSTH SE23 132 C7
Carisbrooke Av BXLY DA5 136 E7
Carisbrooke Cl HSLWW TW4 122 D7
STAN HA7 49 K1
Carisbrooke Ct NTHLT UB5 * 65 K7
Carisbrooke Gdns
PECK SE15 * 111 G6
Carisbrooke Rd HAYES BR2 168 B3
MTCM CR4 163 K3
WALTH E17 * 57 G3
Carker's La ARCH N19 54 D6
KTTN NW5 72 B4
Carleton Av WLGTN SM6 176 D7
Carleton Cl ESH/CLAY KT10 157 J7
Carleton Gdns ARCH N19 * 72 C4
Carleton Rd HOLWY N7 72 D3
Carleton Vls KTTN NW5 * 72 C4
Carlile Cl BOW E3 93 H1
Carlina Gdns WFD IG8 45 F4
Carlingford Rd HAMP NW3 71 H3
MRDN SM4 161 G5
SEVS/STOTM N15 55 H2
Carlisle Av ACT W3 87 G5
TWRH EC3N 13 K5
Carlisle Cl KUTN/CMB KT2 144 C7
PIN HA5 47 J6
Carlisle Gdns IL IG1 59 J5
KTN/HRWW/WS HA3 49 K6
Carlisle La STHWK SE1 17 M3
Carlisle Pl FBAR/BDGN N11 40 B3
WEST SW1P 16 E4
Carlisle Rd CDALE/KGS NW9 50 E2
FSBYPK N4 55 G7
HPTN TW12 142 B6
KIL/WHAMP NW6 70 C7
LEY E10 57 J7
ROM RM1 63 H4
SUT SM1 174 D5
Carlisle St SOHO/SHAV W1D 11 G5
Carlisle Wk HACK E8 74 B5
Carlisle Wy TOOT SW17 148 A4
Carlos Pl MYFR/PKLN W1K 10 B7
Carlow St CAMTN NW1 4 E5
Carlton Av EBED/NFELT TW14 122 B5
HYS/HAR UB3 101 H3
KTN/HRWW/WS HA3 49 H4
SAND/SEL CR2 177 K6
STHGT/OAK N14 28 D4
Carlton Av East WBLY HA9 67 K1
Carlton Av West
ALP/SUD HA0 67 H1
Carlton Cl BORE WD6 25 F3
CHSGTN KT9 171 K5
EDGW HA8 36 C4
HAMP NW3 70 E1
Carlton Crs CHEAM SM3 174 C3
Carlton Dene EW KT17 * 173 K4
Carlton Dr BARK/HLT IG6 60 D2
PUT/ROE SW15 127 G4
Carlton Gdns EA W5 85 J5
Carlton Ga MV/WKIL W9 8 B2
Carlton Gn SCUP DA14 * 155 F3
Carlton Gv PECK SE15 111 J7
Carlton Hl STJWD NW8 2 D5
Carlton House Ter STJS SW1Y 11 G9
Carlton Ms KIL/WHAMP NW6 * 70 E4
Carlton Pde WBLY HA9 * 50 A7
Carlton Park Av RYNPK SW20 161 F1
Carlton Rd CHSWK W4 106 A1
EA W5 85 J6
ERITH DA8 117 J5
ERITH DA8 117 K5
FBAR/BDGN N11 40 A4
FSBYPK N4 55 G6
GPK RM2 63 J4
MNPK E12 77 H3
MORT/ESHN SW14 125 K2
NWMAL KT3 160 B1
SAND/SEL CR2 177 K6
SCUP DA14 155 F4
SUN TW16 140 D6
WALTH E17 43 G7
WAN E11 58 D7
WELL DA16 136 C2
WOT/HER KT12 156 A6
Carlton Sq WCHPL E1 * 93 F3
Carlton St STJS SW1Y 11 G7
Carlton Ter SYD SE26 150 E3
UED N18 * 41 K3
WAN E11 * 59 F4
Carlton Tower Pl KTBR SW1X 15 M3
Carlton V KIL/WHAMP NW6 2 A7
Carlwell St TOOT SW17 147 J4
Carlyle Av BMLY BR1 168 C2
STHL UB1 83 K6
Carlyle Cl E/WMO/HCT KT8 157 G1
EFNCH N2 53 G5
WLSDN NW10 69 F7
Carlyle Ct WBPTN SW10 * 108 B7
Carlyle Gdns STHL UB1 83 K6
Carlyle Pl PUT/ROE SW15 127 G3
Carlyle Rd CROY/NA CR0 178 C1
EA W5 104 D3
MNPK E12 77 J3
THMD SE28 97 H6
Carlyle Sq CHEL SW3 15 H8
Carlyon Av RYLN/HDSTN HA2 65 K3
Carlyon Cl ALP/SUD HA0 68 A7
Carlyon Rd ALP/SUD HA0 86 A1
YEAD UB4 83 G4
Carlys Cl BECK BR3 166 A1
Carmalt Gdns PUT/ROE SW15 127 F3
Carmel Ct KENS W8 14 C1
Carmelite Rd
KTN/HRWW/WS HA3 34 C7
Carmelite St EMB EC4Y 12 B6
Carmel Wy RCH/KEW TW9 125 H1
Carmen St POP/IOD E14 93 K5
Carmichael Cl BTSEA SW11 * 128 C2
RSLP HA4 64 E3
Carmichael Ms
WAND/EARL SW18 128 C6
Carmichael Rd SNWD SE25 165 H4
Carminia Rd TOOT SW17 148 B1
Carnaby St SOHO/CST W1F 10 E5
Carnac St WNWD SE27 149 K3
Carnanton Rd WALTH E17 44 B7
Carnarvon Av EN EN1 30 B1
Carnarvon Dr HYS/HAR UB3 101 F2
Carnarvon Rd BAR EN5 26 C2
LEY E10 58 A5
SRTFD E15 76 D5
SWFD E18 44 D7
Carnation Cl ROMW/RG RM7 81 G1
Carnation St ABYW SE2 116 C4
Carnbrook Rd BKHTH/KID SE3 134 C2
Carnecke Gdns
ELTH/MOT SE9 134 D4
Carnegie Cl SURB KT6 172 B1
Carnegie Pl WIM/MER SW19 146 B2
Carnegie St IS N1 5 L4

Carnet Cl DART DA1 138 B6
Carnforth Cl HOR/WEW KT19 172 D5
Carnforth Gdns HCH RM12 81 J4
Carnforth Rd
STRHM/NOR SW16 148 D6
Carnoustie Dr IS N1 5 L2
Carnoustie Cl THMD SE28 97 K5
Carnwath Rd FUL/PGN SW6 127 K2
Carol Cl HDN NW4 52 B3
Carolina Cl SRTFD E15 76 C4
Carolina Rd THHTH CR7 164 C1
Caroline Cl BAY/PAD W2 8 D7
CROY/NA CR0 178 A3
ISLW TW7 103 J6
MUSWH N10 54 B1
STRHM/NOR SW16 149 F2
WDR/YW UB7 100 A1
Caroline Ct STAN HA7 * 35 G5
Caroline Gdns BETH E2 7 K7
PECK SE15 * 111 J6
Caroline Pl BAY/PAD W2 8 D6
BTSEA SW11 129 F1
HYS/HAR UB3 101 H6
OXHEY WD19 21 J5
Caroline Place Ms
BAY/PAD W2 * 8 D7
Caroline Rd WIM/MER SW19 146 D6
Caroline St WCHPL E1 93 F5
Caroline Ter BGVA SW1W 16 A6
Caroline Wk HMSMTH W6 107 H5
Carol St CAMTN NW1 4 E3
Carpenders Av OXHEY WD19 33 J2
Carpenter Cl EW KT17 173 H7
Carpenter Gdns WCHMH N21 41 H1
Carpenters Cl BAR EN5 27 F5
Carpenters Ms HOLWY N7 * 72 E4
Carpenter's Pl CLAP SW4 129 J3
Carpenters Rd SRTFD E15 76 A6
Carpenter St MYFR/PKLN W1K 10 C7
Carrara Ms HACK E8 74 C4
Carrara Whf FUL/PGN SW6 127 H2
Carr Cl STAN HA7 35 G5
Carre Ms CMBW SE5 110 C7
Carr Gv WOOL/PLUM SE18 114 D3
Carriage Dr East CHEL SW3 109 F5
Carriage Dr North
BTSEA SW11 108 E6
Carriage Dr South
BTSEA SW11 108 E7
Carriage Dr West BTSEA SW11 108 E6
Carriage Ms IL IG1 78 C1
Carrick Cl ISLW TW7 124 B2
Carrick Gdns TOTM N17 42 A6
Carrick Ga ESH/CLAY KT10 170 C2
Carrick Ms DEPT SE8 112 D5
Carrill Wy BELV DA17 116 E3
Carrington Av BORE WD6 24 D4
HSLW TW3 123 G4
Carrington Cl BAR EN5 25 J4
CROY/NA CR0 166 B6
Carrington Gdns FSTGT E7 76 E3
Carrington Pl
ESH/CLAY KT10 * 170 B3
Carrington Rd
RCHPK/HAM TW10 125 H3
Carrington Sq
KTN/HRWW/WS HA3 34 C6
Carrington St MYFR/PICC W1J 10 C9
Carrol Cl KTTN NW5 72 B3
Carroll Cl SRTFD E15 76 D4
Carronade Pl THMD SE28 115 H2
Carron Cl POP/IOD E14 93 K5
Carroun Rd VX/NE SW8 110 A6
Carroway La GFD/PVL UB6 84 D2
Carrow Rd DAGW RM9 79 H6
Carr Rd NTHLT UB5 66 B6
WALTH E17 57 J1
Carrs La WCHMH N21 29 K4
Carr St POP/IOD E14 93 G4
Carshalton Gv SUT SM1 175 H3
Carshalton Park Rd CAR SM5 175 K5
Carshalton Pl CAR SM5 176 A3
Carshalton Rd MTCM CR4 163 F4
SUT SM1 175 G4
Carslake Rd PUT/ROE SW15 127 F5
Carson Rd CAN/RD E16 94 E4
DUL SE21 149 J1
EBAR EN4 27 K3
Carstairs Rd CAT SE6 152 A2
Carston Cl LEE/GVPK SE12 133 J4
Carswell Cl REDBR IG4 59 H3
Carswell Rd CAT SE6 133 F6
Carter Cl CDALE/KGS NW9 51 F5
WLGTN SM6 176 D6
Carteret St STJSPK SW1H 17 G2
Carteret Wy DEPT SE8 112 B3
Carterhatch Rd PEND EN3 31 G1
Carter La BLKFR EC4V 12 D5
Carter Pl WALW SE17 18 F8
Carter Rd PLSTW E13 77 F7
WIM/MER SW19 147 H5
Carters Cl KTTN NW5 * 72 D5
WPK KT4 174 B1
Carters Hill Cl ELTH/MOT SE9 134 B7
Carter St WALW SE17 18 E9
Carters Yd
WAND/EARL SW18 * 127 K4
Carthew Rd HMSMTH W6 106 E2
Carthew Vls HMSMTH W6 106 E2
Carthusian St FARR EC1M 12 E2
Carting La TPL/STR WC2R 11 K7
Cartmel Cl TOTM N17 42 D6
Cartmel Ct NTHLT UB5 65 J5
Cartmel Gdns MRDN SM4 162 B4
Cartwright Gdns STPAN WC1H 5 H8
Cartwright St WCHPL E1 13 M6
Cartwright Wy BARN SW13 106 E6
Carver Cl CHSWK W4 105 K2
Carver Rd HNHL SE24 130 D5
Carville Crs BTFD TW8 105 F3
Cary Rd WAN E11 76 C3
Carysfort Rd CEND/HSY/T N8 54 D4
STNW/STAM N16 73 K2
Cascade Av MUSWH N10 54 C3
Cascade Rd BKHH IG9 45 H1
Casella Rd NWCR SE14 112 A6
Casewick Rd WNWD SE27 149 H4
Casey Cl STJWD NW8 3 J8
Casimir Rd CLPT E5 74 D2
Casino Av HNHL SE24 130 D4
Caspian St CMBW SE5 110 E6
Caspian Wk CAN/RD E16 95 H5
Cassandra Cl NTHLT UB5 66 D3
Casselden Rd WLSDN NW10 69 F6
Cassidy Rd FUL/PGN SW6 107 K6
Cassilda Rd ABYW SE2 116 B3
Cassilis Rd POP/IOD E14 112 D1
TWK TW1 124 C5
Cassiobridge Rd WATW WD18 20 C3
Cassiobridge Ter
RKW/CH/CXG WD3 * 20 B4
Cassiobury Av
EBED/NFELT TW14 121 J6
Cassiobury Dr WAT WD17 20 E2
Cassiobury Park Av
WATW WD18 20 C2
Cassiobury Rd WALTH E17 57 F4
Cassio Pl WATW WD18 20 C3
Cassio Rd WATW WD18 21 F3
Cassio Whf WATW WD18 * 20 B4
Cassland Rd HOM E9 75 F6
THHTH CR7 164 E3
Casslee Rd CAT SE6 132 C6
Casson St WCHPL E1 92 C4
Castellain Rd MV/WKIL W9 2 C9
Castellan Av GPK RM2 63 K2
Castellane Cl STAN HA7 35 F6
Castello Av PUT/ROE SW15 127 F4
Castelnau BARN SW13 106 E6
Casterton St HACK E8 74 D5
Castile Rd WOOL/PLUM SE18 115 F3
Castillon Rd CAT SE6 152 C1
Castlands Rd CAT SE6 151 H1
Castle Av CHING E4 44 B4
EW KT17 173 J7
RAIN RM13 81 G6
Castlebar Hl WEA W13 85 H4
Castlebar Ms EA W5 85 H4
Castlebar Pk EA W5 85 H4
Castlebar Rd WEA W13 85 J5
Castle Baynard St
BLKFR EC4V 12 D6
Castlebrook Cl LBTH SE11 18 C5
Castle Cl ACT W3 105 J1
BUSH WD23 22 B5
HAYES BR2 167 H2
SUN TW16 140 C6
WIM/MER SW19 146 B2
Castlecombe Dr
WIM/MER SW19 127 G6
Castlecombe Rd
ELTH/MOT SE9 153 J4
Castle Ct BANK EC3V * 13 H5
SYD SE26 151 G3
Castledine Rd PGE/AN SE20 150 D6
Castle Dr REDBR IG4 59 J5
Castleford Av ELTH/MOT SE9 135 G7
Castleford Cl TOTM N17 42 B5
Castlegate RCH/KEW TW9 125 G2
Castlehaven Rd CAMTN NW1 4 C2
Castle Hill Av CROY/NA CR0 179 K7
Castle Hill Pde WEA W13 * 85 H6
Castle La WESTW SW1E 16 E3
Castleleigh Ct ENC/FH EN2 29 K4
Castlemaine Av EW KT17 173 K7
SAND/SEL CR2 178 B4
Castlemaine St WCHPL E1 92 D4
Castle Md CMBW SE5 * 110 D6
Castle Ms CAMTN NW1 72 B5
NFNCH/WDSPK N12 39 G4
TOOT SW17 147 J3
Castle Pde EW KT17 * 173 J6
Castle Pl CAMTN NW1 72 B5
Castlereagh St MBLAR W1H 9 L4
Castle Rd CAMTN NW1 72 B5
DAGW RM9 79 H7
ISLW TW7 124 A1
NFNCH/WDSPK N12 39 G4
NTHLT UB5 66 B5
NWDGN UB2 * 102 E2
Castle Rw CHSWK W4 * 106 A4
Castle St EHAM E6 95 G1
KUT/HW KT1 * 159 F1
Castleton Av BXLYHN DA7 118 A7
WBLY HA9 68 A3
Castleton Cl CROY/NA CR0 166 B5
Castleton Gdns WBLY HA9 68 A2
Castleton Rd ELTH/MOT SE9 153 H3
GDMY/SEVK IG3 61 H7
MTCM CR4 163 J3
RSLP HA4 47 H7
WALTH E17 58 B1
Castletown Rd WKENS W14 107 H4
Castleview Cl FSBYPK N4 55 J7
Castleview Gdns IL IG1 59 J5
Castle Vls CRICK NW2 * 69 J5
Castle Wk SUN TW16 * 156 B2
Castle Wy FELT TW13 141 G3
WIM/MER SW19 146 B2
Castlewood Dr ELTH/MOT SE9 134 E1
Castlewood Rd EBAR EN4 27 H2
STNW/STAM N16 56 C5
Castle Yd HGT N6 * 54 A6
RCH/KEW TW9 124 E4
STHWK SE1 * 12 D8
Castor La POP/IOD E14 93 K6
Catalina Rd HTHAIR TW6 120 E2
Catalpa Ct LEW SE13 133 G5
Caterham Av CLAY IG5 60 A1
Caterham Rd LEW SE13 133 F2
Catesby St WALW SE17 19 H6
Catford Broadway CAT SE6 132 E6
Catford Hl CAT SE6 132 C7
Catford Island CAT SE6 * 132 E6
Catford Rd CAT SE6 132 D7
Cathall Rd WAN E11 76 C2
Cathay St BERM/RHTH SE16 111 J1
Cathcart Hl ARCH N19 72 C2
Cathcart Rd WBPTN SW10 14 D9
Cathcart St KTTN NW5 72 B5
Cathedral St STHWK SE1 13 G8
Catherall Rd HBRY N5 73 J2
Catherine Ct STHGT/OAK N14 28 C4
Catherine Dr RCH/KEW TW9 125 F3
SUN TW16 140 D6
Catherine Gdns HSLW TW3 123 J3
Catherine Griffiths Ct
CLKNW EC1R 6 B9
Catherine Gv GNWCH SE10 112 E7
Catherine Pl HRW HA1 49 F4
WESTW SW1E 16 E3
Catherine Rd GPK RM2 63 K4
SURB KT6 158 E4
Catherines Cl WDR/YW UB7 * 100 A1
Catherine St HOL/ALD WC2B * 11 L6
Catherine Vls RYNPK SW20 * 145 K6
Catherine Wheel Aly
LVPST EC2M 13 K3
Catherine Wheel Rd
BTFD TW8 104 E6
Catherine Wheel Yd
WHALL SW1A 10 E9
Cat Hl EBAR EN4 27 J5
Cathles Rd BAL SW12 129 G5
Cathnor Rd SHB W12 106 E1
Catling Cl FSTH SE23 150 E2
Catlin's La PIN HA5 47 F2
Catlin St BERM/RHTH SE16 111 H4
Cator La BECK BR3 166 C1
Cato Rd CLAP SW4 129 J2
Cator Rd CAR SM5 175 K4
SYD SE26 151 F5
Cator St PECK SE15 111 G5
Cato St MBLAR W1H 9 K3
Catsey La BUSH WD23 22 C6
Catsey Wd BUSH WD23 22 C6
Catterick Cl FBAR/BDGN N11 40 A5
Cattistock Rd ELTH/MOT SE9 153 J4
Cattley Cl BAR EN5 26 C3
Catton St RSQ WC1B 11 L3
Caudwell Ter
WAND/EARL SW18 * 128 C5
Caulfield Rd EHAM E6 77 K6
PECK SE15 131 J1
Causeway EBED/NFELT TW14 122 A3
The Causeway BELMT SM2 175 G7
CAR SM5 176 A2
CHSGTN KT9 172 A3
EFNCH N2 53 H3
ESH/CLAY KT10 171 F6
TEDD TW11 143 F5
WAND/EARL SW18 128 A3
WIM/MER SW19 146 A4
Causeyware Rd ED N9 30 D6
Causton Cots POP/IOD E14 * 93 G4
Causton Rd HGT N6 * 54 B6
Causton Sq DAGE RM10 80 C6
Causton St WEST SW1P 17 H6
Cautley Av CLAP SW4 129 H4
Cavalier Cl CHDH RM6 61 J3
Cavalier Gdns HYS/HAR UB3 82 B5
Cavalry Crs HSLWW TW4 122 C3
Cavalry Gdns PUT/ROE SW15 127 H4
Cavan Pl PIN HA5 * 33 K7
Cavaye Pl WBPTN SW10 14 F8
Cavell Crs DART DA1 139 K3
Cavell Dr ENC/FH EN2 29 G1
Cavell Rd TOTM N17 41 K6
Cavell St WCHPL E1 92 D4
Cavendish Av BFN/LL DA15 136 B6
ERITH DA8 117 K5
FNCH N3 52 E1
HCH RM12 81 K5
HRW HA1 66 D3
NWMAL KT3 160 E4
RSLP HA4 65 F4
STJWD NW8 3 H6
WEA W13 85 G4
WELL DA16 136 A2
WFD IG8 45 F6
Cavendish Cl
KIL/WHAMP NW6 70 D5
STJWD NW8 3 H7
SUN TW16 140 D5
UED N18 * 42 D4
YEAD UB4 82 C4
Cavendish Ct
RKW/CH/CXG WD3 * 20 B4
SUN TW16 140 D5
Cavendish Crs BORE WD6 24 C3
HCH RM12 81 K5
Cavendish Dr EDGW HA8 36 B5
ESH/CLAY KT10 170 E4
WAN E11 58 B7
Cavendish Gdns BARK IG11 79 F4
CHDH RM6 62 A4
CLAP SW4 * 129 H5
IL IG1 60 A7
Cavendish Ms SUT SM1 175 G1
Cavendish Ms North
GTPST W1W 10 D2
Cavendish Ms South
GTPST W1W * 10 D3
Cavendish Pde CLAP SW4 * 129 H3
HSLWW TW4 * 122 D1
Cavendish Pl BMLY BR1 168 E2
CAVSQ/HST W1G 10 D4
CRICK NW2 70 B5
Cavendish Rd BAL SW12 129 H7
BAR EN5 26 A2
BELMT SM2 175 G6
CHING E4 44 A5
CHSWK W4 105 K7
CLAP SW4 129 G5
CROY/NA CR0 164 C7
FSBYPK N4 55 H5
KIL/WHAMP NW6 70 C6
NWMAL KT3 160 C4
SUN TW16 140 D5
UED N18 42 D4
WIM/MER SW19 147 J6
Cavendish Sq
CAVSQ/HST W1G 10 D4
Cavendish St IS N1 7 G6
Cavendish Ter BOW E3 * 93 H2
FELT TW13 * 140 E1
Cavendish Wy WWKM BR4 166 E7
Cavenham Gdns IL IG1 78 D2
Caverleigh Wy WPK KT4 160 D7
Caverley Gdns
KTN/HRWW/WS HA3 49 K6
Cave Rd PLSTW E13 95 F1
RCHPK/HAM TW10 143 J3
Caversham Av CHEAM SM3 174 C1
PLMGR N13 41 G2
Caversham Rd KTTN NW5 * 72 C5
KUT/HW KT1 159 G1
SEVS/STOTM N15 55 J3
Caversham St CHEL SW3 15 L9
Caverswall St SHB W12 88 A5
Cawdor Crs HNWL W7 104 B3
Cawnpore St NRWD SE19 150 A4
Caxton Gv BOW E3 93 J2
Caxton Ms BTFD TW8 104 D5
Caxton Rd NWDGN UB2 102 C2
SHB W12 88 B7
WDGN N22 55 F1
WIM/MER SW19 147 G4
The Caxtons BRXN/ST SW9 * 110 C6
Caxton St STJSPK SW1H 16 F3
Caxton St North CAN/RD E16 94 D5
Caxton Wy ROM RM1 63 G3
WATW WD18 20 B6
Cayenne Ct STHWK SE1 13 L9
Caygill Cl HAYES BR2 167 J3
Cayley Rd NWDGN UB2 103 G2
Cayton Rd GFD/PVL UB6 84 E1
Cayton St FSBYE EC1V 7 G8
Cazenove Rd
STNW/STAM N16 74 B1
WALTH E17 43 J7
Cecil Av BARK IG11 78 D6
EN EN1 30 B3
WBLY HA9 68 B4
Cecil Cl ASHF TW15 140 A5
CHSGTN KT9 171 K3
EA W5 * 85 K4
Cecil Ct BAR EN5 26 B2
LSQ/SEVD WC2H 11 H7
Cecile Pk CEND/HSY/T N8 54 E5
Cecilia Cl EFNCH N2 53 G2
Cecilia Rd HACK E8 74 B4
Cecil Manning Cl
GFD/PVL UB6 67 G7
Cecil Pk PIN HA5 47 J3
Cecil Pl MTCM CR4 162 E4
Cecil Rd ACT W3 86 E4
ASHF TW15 140 A6
CDALE/KGS NW9 51 F2
CHDH RM6 61 K6
CROY/NA CR0 163 K5
ENC/FH EN2 29 K3
HSLW TW3 123 H2
IL IG1 78 B3
KTN/HRWW/WS HA3 48 E2
MUSWH N10 54 B1
PLSTW E13 76 E7
STHGT/OAK N14 28 B7
SUT SM1 174 D5
WALTH E17 43 J7
WAN E11 76 C1
WIM/MER SW19 147 F6
WLSDN NW10 69 G7
Cedar Av BFN/LL DA15 136 B6
CHDH RM6 62 A4
EBAR EN4 27 J6
HYS/HAR UB3 82 E5
PEND EN3 30 E1
RSLP HA4 65 G4
WHTN TW2 123 G5
Cedar Cl BKHH IG9 45 H1
BOW E3 75 H7
CAR SM5 175 K5
DUL SE21 130 D7
HAYES BR2 181 J2
IL IG1 78 D4
KUTN/CMB KT2 145 F3
ROMW/RG RM7 62 E3
Cedar Copse BMLY BR1 168 E1
Cedar Ct CHARL SE7 * 114 B5
ELTH/MOT SE9 * 134 D5
WIM/MER SW19 146 B2
Cedar Crs HAYES BR2 181 J2
Cedarcroft Rd CHSGTN KT9 172 B3
Cedar Dr EFNCH N2 53 J3
GLDGN NW11 52 E3
PIN HA5 34 A5
Cedar Gdns BELMT SM2 175 G5
Cedar Gv BXLY DA5 136 E5
EA W5 104 E2
STHL UB1 84 A4
Cedar Hts RCHPK/HAM TW10 125 F7
Cedarhurst BMLY BR1 * 152 C6
Cedarhurst Dr ELTH/MOT SE9 134 B4
Cedar Lawn Av BAR EN5 26 C4
Cedar Mt ELTH/MOT SE9 134 C7
Cedarne Rd FUL/PGN SW6 107 K6
Cedar Park Gdns CHDH RM6 61 K6
WIM/MER SW19 145 K4
Cedar Pl CHARL SE7 114 B4
Cedar Ri STHGT/OAK N14 28 A6
Cedar Rd BELMT SM2 175 G5
BMLY BR1 168 B1
CRICK NW2 70 A3
CROY/NA CR0 178 A1
E/WMO/HCT KT8 157 K3
EBED/NFELT TW14 121 G7
ERITH DA8 118 D7
HSLWW TW4 122 B1
OXHEY WD19 21 G5
ROMW/RG RM7 62 E3
TEDD TW11 143 G4
TOTM N17 42 B7
Cedars Av MTCM CR4 163 F3
WALTH E17 57 J4
Cedars Cl BORE WD6 24 D3
HDN NW4 52 B2
LEW SE13 133 G2
Cedars Cots PUT/ROE SW15 * 126 D5
Cedars Ct ED N9 42 A1
Cedars Ms CLAP SW4 * 129 G3
Cedars Rd BARN SW13 126 C1
BECK BR3 166 B1
CHSWK W4 105 K5
CLAP SW4 129 G2
CROY/NA CR0 176 E2
ED N9 42 C1
KUT/HW KT1 143 J7
MRDN SM4 161 K3
SRTFD E15 76 C5
WCHMH N21 41 H1
The Cedars HOM E9 * 75 F6
SRTFD E15 * 76 D7
TEDD TW11 143 F5
Cedar Ter RCH/KEW TW9 125 F3
Cedar Tree Gv WNWD SE27 149 H4
Cedarville Gdns
STRHM/NOR SW16 149 F5
Cedar Wk ESH/CLAY KT10 171 F5
Cedar Wy CAMTN NW1 5 G2
SUN TW16 140 C6
Cedric Av ROM RM1 63 G2
Cedric Rd ELTH/MOT SE9 154 C2
Celadon Cl PEND EN3 31 G2
Celandine Cl POP/IOD E14 93 J4
Celandine Dr HACK E8 7 L1
THMD SE28 97 H7
Celandine Gv STHGT/OAK N14 28 C4
Celandine Wy SRTFD E15 94 C2
Celbridge Ms BAY/PAD W2 8 D4
Celestial Gdns LEW SE13 133 G3
Celia Rd ARCH N19 72 C3
Celtic Av HAYES BR2 167 H2
Celtic St POP/IOD E14 93 K4
Cemetery La CHARL SE7 114 D5
Cemetery Rd ABYW SE2 116 C5
FSTGT E7 76 D4
TOTM N17 42 A6
Cenacle Cl HAMP NW3 70 E2
Centaur Ct BTFD TW8 * 105 F4
Centaur St STHWK SE1 17 M3
Centenary Rd PEND EN3 31 H3
Centenary Wk MNPK E12 77 H2
WAN E11 58 C3
WFD IG8 44 C6
Centennial Av BORE WD6 23 H6
Centennial Pk BORE WD6 * 23 J6
Central Av E/WMO/HCT KT8 156 E4
ED N9 42 A2
EFNCH N2 53 H1
EN EN1 30 C1
HSLW TW3 123 H3
HYS/HAR UB3 101 J1
PIN HA5 47 K5
WAN E11 76 B1
WELL DA16 136 B1
WLGTN SM6 176 E4
Central Blds EA W5 * 85 K6
Central Circ HDN NW4 51 K4
Central Hall Blds ARCH N19 * 72 C1
Central Hl NRWD SE19 149 J4
Central Pde ACT W3 * 105 H1
BFN/LL DA15 * 155 G2
E/WMO/HCT KT8 * 156 E3
GFD/PVL UB6 * 85 G2
HRW HA1 49 F4
PEND EN3 * 30 E1
PGE/AN SE20 * 151 F6
STRHM/NOR SW16 * 148 E3
SURB KT6 * 159 F5
WALTH E17 * 57 J3
Central Park Av DAGE RM10 80 D2
Central Park Est
HSLWW TW4 * 122 C3
Central Park Rd EHAM E6 95 H1
Central Pl SNWD SE25 * 165 H3
Central Rd ALP/SUD HA0 67 H4
DART DA1 139 H3
MRDN SM4 162 A4
WPK KT4 173 J1
Central Sq E/WMO/HCT KT8 156 E3
GLDGN NW11 52 E5
Central St FSBYE EC1V 6 E7
Central Ter BECK BR3 * 166 A2
Central Wy CAR SM5 175 J6
EBED/NFELT TW14 122 A4
NTHWD HA6 32 C6
THMD SE28 97 G6
WLSDN NW10 86 E2
Centre Av ACT W3 87 F7
Centre Common Rd CHST BR7 154 C6
Centre Rd DAGE RM10 98 D1
WAN E11 76 E1
Centre St BETH E2 92 D1
Centre Wy ED N9 42 E1
Centric Cl CAMTN NW1 * 4 C3
Centurian Sq
WOOL/PLUM SE18 114 D7
Centurian Wy ERITHM DA18 117 G2
Centurion Cl HOLWY N7 5 L1
Centurion Ct WLGTN SM6 * 176 B1
Centurion La BOW E3 93 H1
Centurion Sq CHARL SE7 * 114 D6
Century Cl HDN NW4 52 B4
Century Ct WATW WD18 * 20 A6
Century Ms CLPT E5 * 74 E3
Century Pk WAT WD17 * 21 G4
Century Rd WALTH E17 57 G2
Cephas Av WCHPL E1 92 E3
Cephas St WCHPL E1 92 E3
Ceres Rd WOOL/PLUM SE18 116 A3
Cerise Rd PECK SE15 111 H7
Cerne Cl YEAD UB4 83 G6
Cerne Rd MRDN SM4 162 B5
Cerney Ms BAY/PAD W2 9 G6
Cervantes Ct BAY/PAD W2 8 D5
NTHWD HA6 32 D6
Ceylon Rd WKENS W14 107 G2
Chabot Dr PECK SE15 131 J2
Chadacre Av CLAY IG5 59 K2
Chadacre Rd EW KT17 173 K4
Chadbourn St POP/IOD E14 93 K4
Chad Crs ED N9 42 E2
Chadd Dr BMLY BR1 168 D2
Chadville Gdns CHDH RM6 61 K4
Chadway BCTR RM8 79 J1
Chadwell Av CHDH RM6 61 H6
Chadwell Heath La
CHDH RM6 61 H3
Chadwell La CEND/HSY/T N8 55 F2
Chadwell St CLKNW EC1R 6 B7
Chadwick Av CHING E4 44 B3
WCHMH N21 * 29 F4
WIM/MER SW19 146 E5
Chadwick Cl PUT/ROE SW15 126 C6
TEDD TW11 143 G5
Chadwick Pl SURB KT6 158 D5
Chadwick Rd IL IG1 78 B2
PECK SE15 131 G1
WAN E11 58 C6
WLSDN NW10 69 H7
Chadwick St WEST SW1P 17 G4
Chadwick Wy THMD SE28 97 K6
Chadwin Rd PLSTW E13 95 F4
Chadworth Wy
ESH/CLAY KT10 170 D4
Chaffinch Av CROY/NA CR0 166 A5
Chaffinch Cl CROY/NA CR0 166 A4
ED N9 31 F7
SURB KT6 172 C2
Chaffinch La WATW WD18 20 D6
Chaffinch Rd BECK BR3 151 G7
Chafford Wy CHDH RM6 61 J3
Chagford St CAMTN NW1 9 L1
Chailey Av EN EN1 30 B1
Chailey Cl HEST TW5 102 C7
Chailey St CLPT E5 74 E2
Chalbury Wk IS N1 5 M5
Chalcombe Rd ABYW SE2 116 C2
Chalcot Cl BELMT SM2 174 E6
Chalcot Crs CAMTN NW1 3 M3
Chalcot Gdns HAMP NW3 71 K5
Chalcot Ms STRHM/NOR SW16 148 E2
Chalcot Rd CAMTN NW1 4 A3
Chalcot Sq CAMTN NW1 4 A2
Chalcott Gdns SURB KT6 * 158 D7
Chalcroft Rd LEW SE13 133 H4
Chaldon Rd FUL/PGN SW6 107 H6
Chale Rd BRXS/STRHM SW2 129 K5
Chalet Cl ASHF TW15 140 B5
Chalet Est MLHL NW7 * 37 J3
Chalfont Av WBLY HA9 68 D5
Chalfont Gn ED N9 42 A2
Chalfont Ms
WAND/EARL SW18 127 J7
Chalfont Rd ED N9 42 A2
HYS/HAR UB3 101 K1
SNWD SE25 165 G2
Chalfont Wk PIN HA5 * 47 G1
Chalfont Wy WEA W13 104 C2
Chalford Cl E/WMO/HCT KT8 157 F3
Chalforde Gdns GPK RM2 63 K3
Chalford Rd DUL SE21 149 K3
Chalford Wk WFD IG8 45 H7
Chalgrove Av MRDN SM4 161 K4
Chalgrove Crs CLAY IG5 59 J1
Chalgrove Gdns FNCH N3 52 C2
Chalgrove Rd BELMT SM2 175 H6
HACK E8 74 E5
TOTM N17 42 D7
Chalice Cl WLGTN SM6 176 D5
Chalkenden Cl PGE/AN SE20 150 D6
Chalk Farm Pde HAMP NW3 * 4 A1
Chalk Farm Rd CAMTN NW1 4 A1
Chalk Hl OXHEY WD19 21 J5
Chalk Hill Rd HMSMTH W6 107 G3
Chalkhill Rd WBLY HA9 68 C2
Chalklands WBLY HA9 68 E2
Chalk La EBAR EN4 27 K2
Chalkley Cl MTCM CR4 162 E1
Chalkmill Dr EN EN1 30 D2
Chalk Pit Rd SUT SM1 175 G4
Chalk Rd PLSTW E13 95 F4
Chalkstone Cl WELL DA16 116 B7
Chalkwell Park Av EN EN1 30 A3
Chalky La CHSGTN KT9 171 K7
Challenge Cl WLSDN NW10 69 G7
Challenge Rd ASHF TW15 140 A2
Challice Wy BRXS/STRHM SW2 130 A7
Challin St PGE/AN SE20 150 E7
Challis Rd BTFD TW8 104 E4
Challoner Cl EFNCH N2 53 H1
Challoner Crs WKENS W14 107 J4
Challoners Cl
E/WMO/HCT KT8 157 J3

HOR/WEW KT19 173 F6
LEY E10 58 A6
Chesterfield St
MYFR/PICC W1J 10 C8
Chesterfield Wy
HYS/HAR UB3 * 101 K1
PECK SE15 111 K6
Chesterford Gdns HAMP NW3 71 F3
Chesterford Rd MNPK E12 77 K4
Chester Gdns MRDN SM4 162 B4
PEND EN3 30 D5
WEA W13 * 85 H5
Chester Ga CAMTN NW1 4 C8
Chester Ms KTBR SW1X 16 C3
Chester Pl CAMTN NW1 4 C7
NTHWD HA6 * 32 C6
Chester Rd ARCH N19 72 B1
BFN/LL DA15 135 K4
BORE WD6 24 E2
CAMTN NW1 4 B8
CAN/RD E16 94 C3
ED N9 30 D7
FSTGT E7 77 H6
GDMY/SEVK IG3 61 F7
HSLWW TW4 122 A2
HTHAIR TW6 120 D2
NTHWD HA6 32 D6
TOTM N17 55 K2
WALTH E17 57 F4
WAN E11 59 F5
WATW WD18 20 E4
WIM/MER SW19 146 A5
Chester Rw BGVA SW1W 16 A6
Chester Sq BGVA SW1W 16 B5
Chester Square Ms
BGVA SW1W * 16 C4
The Chesters NWMAL KT3 145 G7
Chester St BETH E2 92 C3
KTBR SW1X 16 B3
Chester Ter CAMTN NW1 4 C7
Chesterton Cl GFD/PVL UB6 84 B1
WAND/EARL SW18 127 K4
Chesterton Ct EA W5 * 85 K5
Chesterton Dr
STWL/WRAY TW19 120 C7
Chesterton Rd NKENS W10 88 B4
PLSTW E13 94 E2
Chesterton Sq KENS W8 107 J3
Chesterton Ter KUT/HW KT1 159 H1
PLSTW E13 94 E2
Chester Wy LBTH SE11 18 B6
Chesthunte Rd TOTM N17 41 J7
Chestnut Aly FUL/PGN SW6 * 107 J5
Chestnut Av ALP/SUD HA0 67 H4
BKHH IG9 45 H2
BTFD TW8 104 E4
CEND/HSY/T N8 54 E4
E/WMO/HCT KT8 158 A2
EDGW HA8 36 A5
ESH/CLAY KT10 157 J6
FSTGT E7 77 F3
HCH RM12 81 H1
HOR/WEW KT19 173 G3
HPTN TW12 142 A6
MORT/ESHN SW14 126 A2
NTHWD HA6 46 D1
WWKM BR4 180 C4
Chestnut Av South
WALTH E17 58 A3
Chestnut Cl BFN/LL DA15 155 G1
BKHH IG9 45 H2
CAR SM5 162 E7
CAT SE6 152 A3
HYS/HAR UB3 82 C6
HYS/HAR UB3 100 E6
NWCR SE14 112 C7
STHGT/OAK N14 28 C4
STNW/STAM N16 73 K1
STRHM/NOR SW16 149 G3
SUN TW16 140 D5
Chestnut Cots
TRDG/WHET N20 * 26 C7
Chestnut Dr BXLYHN DA7 136 E2
KTN/HRWW/WS HA3 35 F6
PIN HA5 47 H5
WAN E11 58 E5
Chestnut Gln HCH RM12 81 H1
Chestnut Gv ALP/SUD HA0 67 H4
BAL SW12 129 F6
EA W5 104 E2
EBAR EN4 27 K4
ISLW TW7 124 B3
MTCM CR4 163 J4
NWMAL KT3 160 A2
SAND/SEL CR2 178 D6
Chestnut La TRDG/WHET N20 26 C7
Chestnut Ms WFD IG8 44 E4
Chestnut Pl SYD SE26 150 B3
Chestnut Ri BUSH WD23 22 B6
WOOL/PLUM SE18 115 K4
Chestnut Rd KUTN/CMB KT2 144 A6
RYNPK SW20 161 G1
WHTN TW2 142 E1
WNWD SE27 149 H2
The Chestnuts BECK BR3 * 166 A2
PIN HA5 * 33 K6
Chestnut Ter SUT SM1 * 175 F3
Chestnut Wy FELT TW13 141 F2
Cheston Av CROY/NA CR0 166 B7
Chesworth Cl ERITH DA8 118 B7
Chettle Cl STHWK SE1 19 G3
Chetwode Rd TOOT SW17 147 K2
Chetwynd Av EBAR EN4 27 K7
Chetwynd Rd KTTN NW5 72 B3
Chetwynd Vls KTTN NW5 * 72 B3
Chevalier Cl STAN HA7 35 K2
Cheval Pl SKENS SW7 15 K3
Cheval St POP/IOD E14 112 D2
Cheveney Wk HAYES BR2 167 K2
Chevening Rd GNWCH SE10 113 J4
KIL/WHAMP NW6 88 B1
NRWD SE19 149 K6
The Chevenings SCUP DA14 155 H2
Cheverton Rd ARCH N19 54 D7
Chevet St HOM E9 75 G4
Chevington CRICK NW2 * 70 D5
Cheviot Cl BELMT SM2 175 H7
BUSH WD23 22 C5
ENC/FH EN2 29 K1
HYS/HAR UB3 101 G6
Cheviot Gdns CRICK NW2 70 B1
Cheviot Rd EMPK RM11 63 J6
WNWD SE27 149 G4
Cheviot Wy GNTH/NBYPK IG2 60 E4
Chevron Cl CAN/RD E16 94 E5
Chevy Rd NWDGN UB2 103 H1
Chewton Rd WALTH E17 57 G3
Cheyne Av SWFD E18 58 D2
WHTN TW2 122 E7
Cheyne Cl HAYES BR2 181 J2
Cheyne Ct BUSH WD23 * 21 J3
Cheyne Gdns CHEL SW3 15 K9
Cheyne Hl BRYLDS KT5 159 G3
Cheyne Park Dr WWKM BR4 180 A2
Cheyne Pth HNWL W7 85 F4
Cheyne Pl CHEL SW3 15 L9
Cheyne Rd ASHF TW15 140 B5
Cheyne Rw CHEL SW3 108 D5
Cheyne Wk CHEL SW3 108 D5
CROY/NA CR0 178 C1
HDN NW4 52 A5
WBPTN SW10 108 C6
WCHMH N21 29 G4
Cheyneys Av EDGW HA8 35 K5
Chichele Gdns CROY/NA CR0 178 A3
Chichele Rd CRICK NW2 70 B4
Chicheley Rd
KTN/HRWW/WS HA3 34 C6
Chicheley St STHWK SE1 17 M1
Chichester Av RSLP HA4 64 B1
Chichester Cl BKHTH/KID SE3 114 B6
EHAM E6 95 J5
HPTN TW12 141 K5
Chichester Ct EW KT17 * 173 H7
STAN HA7 50 A2
Chichester Gdns IL IG1 59 J6
Chichester Rd BAY/PAD W2 8 D2
CROY/NA CR0 178 A2
ED N9 30 B7
KIL/WHAMP NW6 2 A6
WAN E11 76 C2
Chichester St PIM SW1V 16 F8
Chichester Wy
EBED/NFELT TW14 122 B6
POP/IOD E14 113 G3
Chicksand St WCHPL E1 13 M3
Chiddingfold
NFNCH/WDSPK N12 38 E2
Chiddingstone St
FUL/PGN SW6 127 K1
Chieftan Dr PUR RM19 119 K3
Chignell Pl WEA W13 85 G7
Chigwell Hl WAP E1W 92 D6
Chigwell Rd SWFD E18 59 F2
WFD IG8 45 K5
Chilcott Cl ALP/SUD HA0 67 J3
Childebert Rd TOOT SW17 148 B1
Childeric Rd NWCR SE14 112 B6
Childerley St FUL/PGN SW6 107 H7
Childers St DEPT SE8 112 B5
The Childers WFD IG8 45 K4
Child La GNWCH SE10 113 J2
Childs Ct HYS/HAR UB3 82 E6
Childs La NRWD SE19 * 150 A5
Child's Ms ECT SW5 * 14 C6
Child's Pl ECT SW5 14 B6
Child's St ECT SW5 14 B5
Child's Wk ECT SW5 * 14 B5
Childs Wy GLDGN NW11 52 D4
Chilham Cl BXLY DA5 137 G6
GFD/PVL UB6 85 G1
Chilham Rd ELTH/MOT SE9 153 J3
Chillerton Rd TOOT SW17 148 A4
Chillington Dr BTSEA SW11 128 B3
Chillingworth Gdns
TWK TW1 * 143 F1
Chillingworth Rd HOLWY N7 73 F4
Chilmark Gdns NWMAL KT3 160 C5
Chilmark Rd
STRHM/NOR SW16 163 J1
Chiltern Av BUSH WD23 22 C5
WHTN TW2 123 F7
Chiltern Cl BORE WD6 24 B1
BUSH WD23 22 B5
BXLYHN DA7 118 B7
CROY/NA CR0 178 A2
WATW WD18 20 D3
WPK KT4 174 A1
Chiltern Dene ENC/FH EN2 29 F3
Chiltern Dr BRYLDS KT5 159 J5
Chiltern Gdns CRICK NW2 70 B2
HAYES BR2 167 J3
Chiltern Pl CLPT E5 74 D1
Chiltern Rd BOW E3 93 J3
GNTH/NBYPK IG2 60 E3
PIN HA5 47 G4
The Chilterns BELMT SM2 * 175 F7
Chiltern St MHST W1U 9 M2
Chiltern Wy WFD IG8 44 E2
Chilthorne Cl CAT SE6 132 C6
Chilton Av EA W5 104 E3
Chilton Gv DEPT SE8 112 A3
Chilton Rd EDGW HA8 36 C5
RCH/KEW TW9 125 H2
Chilton St BETH E2 7 M9
Chilvers Cl WHTN TW2 142 E1
Chilver St GNWCH SE10 113 J4
Chilwell Gdns OXHEY WD19 33 G3
Chilworth Gdns SUT SM1 175 G2
Chilworth Ms BAY/PAD W2 8 F5
Chilworth St BAY/PAD W2 8 F5
Chimes Av PLMGR N13 41 G3
China Hall Ms
BERM/RHTH SE16 111 K2
China Ms BRXS/STRHM SW2 130 A6
Chinbrook Crs LEE/GVPK SE12 153 F2
Chinbrook Rd LEE/GVPK SE12 153 F2
Chinchilla Dr HSLWW TW4 122 B1
The Chine ALP/SUD HA0 67 H4
MUSWH N10 54 B3
WCHMH N21 29 H5
Chingdale Rd CHING E4 44 C2
Chingford Av CHING E4 43 J2
Chingford La WFD IG8 44 C3
Chingford Mount Rd
CHING E4 43 J4
Chingford Rd CHING E4 43 J5
Chingley Cl BMLY BR1 152 C5
Ching Wy CHING E4 43 H5
Chinnor Crs GFD/PVL UB6 84 C1
Chipka St POP/IOD E14 113 F1
Chipley St NWCR SE14 112 B5
Chippendale St CLPT E5 75 F2
Chippenham Cl PIN HA5 * 46 D3
Chippenham Ms MV/WKIL W9 8 A1
Chippenham Rd MV/WKIL W9 2 A9
Chipping Cl BAR EN5 26 C2
Chipstead Av THHTH CR7 164 C3
Chipstead Cl BELMT SM2 175 F7
NRWD SE19 150 B6
Chipstead Gdns CRICK NW2 69 K1
Chipstead St FUL/PGN SW6 107 K7
Chirk Cl YEAD UB4 83 J3
Chisenhale Rd BOW E3 93 G1
Chisholm Rd CROY/NA CR0 178 A1
RCHPK/HAM TW10 125 G5
Chislehurst Av
NFNCH/WDSPK N12 39 G6
Chislehurst High St CHST BR7 154 B5
Chislehurst Rd BMLY BR1 168 D1
RCHPK/HAM TW10 125 F5
SCUP DA14 155 G4
STMC/STPC BR5 169 K3
Chislet Cl BECK BR3 151 J6
Chisley Rd SEVS/STOTM N15 56 A5
Chiswell Sq BKHTH/KID SE3 134 A1
Chiswell St CMBW SE5 * 110 E6
STLK EC1Y 13 G2
Chiswick Br CHSWK W4 125 K1
Chiswick Cl CROY/NA CR0 177 F2
Chiswick Common Rd
CHSWK W4 106 A3
Chiswick High Rd CHSWK W4 105 H4
Chiswick House Grounds
CHSWK W4 * 106 A5
Chiswick La CHSWK W4 106 B4
Chiswick La South CHSWK W4 106 C5
Chiswick Ml CHSWK W4 106 C5
Chiswick Pk CHSWK W4 * 105 K2
Chiswick Pier CHSWK W4 * 106 C6
Chiswick Quay CHSWK W4 105 K7
Chiswick Rd CHSWK W4 105 K3
ED N9 42 C1
Chiswick Sq CHSWK W4 106 B5
Chiswick Staithe CHSWK W4 105 K7
Chiswick Village CHSWK W4 105 H5
Chiswick Whf CHSWK W4 106 C5
Chitterfield Ga WDR/YW UB7 100 D6
Chitty's La BCTR RM8 79 K1
Chitty St FITZ W1T 10 F2
Chivalry Rd BTSEA SW11 128 D4
Chivenor Gv KUTN/CMB KT2 143 K4
Chivers Rd CHING E4 43 K2
Choats Manor Wy DAGW RM9 98 B2
Choats Rd BARK IG11 97 J1
Chobham Gdns
WIM/MER SW19 146 B1
Chobham Rd SRTFD E15 76 B4
Cholmeley Cl HGT N6 * 54 B6
Cholmeley Crs HGT N6 54 B6
Cholmeley Pk HGT N6 54 B7
Cholmley Gdns
KIL/WHAMP NW6 70 E4
Cholmley Rd THDIT KT7 158 C5
Cholmley Ter THDIT KT7 * 158 C6
Cholmley Vls THDIT KT7 * 158 C6
Cholmondeley Av
WLSDN NW10 87 J1
Chopwell Cl SRTFD E15 * 76 B6
Choumert Gv PECK SE15 131 H1
Choumert Ms PECK SE15 131 H1
Choumert Rd PECK SE15 131 G2
Chow Sq HACK E8 74 B4
Chrislaine Cl
STWL/WRAY TW19 120 A5
Chrisp St POP/IOD E14 93 K4
Christabel Cl ISLW TW7 123 K2
Christ Church Av ERITH DA8 118 A5
Christchurch Av ALP/SUD HA0 68 A5
KIL/WHAMP NW6 70 B7
KTN/HRWW/WS HA3 49 F3
NFNCH/WDSPK N12 39 G5
RAIN RM13 99 H1
TEDD TW11 143 G4
Christchurch Cl ENC/FH EN2 29 J1
NFNCH/WDSPK N12 * 39 H6
WIM/MER SW19 147 H6
Christchurch Gdns
KTN/HRWW/WS HA3 49 G3
Christchurch Hl HAMP NW3 71 H2
Christ Church La BAR EN5 26 C1
Christchurch Ldg EBAR EN4 * 27 K3
Christchurch Pk BELMT SM2 175 G6
Christ Church Rd BRYLDS KT5 159 G6
CEND/HSY/T N8 54 E5
BECK BR3 * 166 D1
Christchurch Rd BFN/LL DA15 155 F3
BRXS/STRHM SW2 130 A7
IL IG1 60 B7
MORT/ESHN SW14 125 J4
WIM/MER SW19 147 H6
Christchurch Sq HOM E9 74 E7
Christchurch St CHEL SW3 15 L9
Christchurch Ter CHEL SW3 * 15 L9
Christchurch Wy
GNWCH SE10 113 H4
Christian Flds
STRHM/NOR SW16 149 G6
Christian St WCHPL E1 92 C5
Christie Ct WATW WD18 20 E4
Christie Dr CROY/NA CR0 165 H4
Christie Rd HOM E9 75 G5
Christina Sq FSBYPK N4 55 H7
Christina St SDTCH EC2A 7 J9
Christine Worsley Cl
WCHMH N21 29 H7
Christopher Av HNWL W7 104 B2
Christopher Cl
BERM/RHTH SE16 112 A1
BFN/LL DA15 136 A4
Christopher Gdns DAGW RM9 79 K4
Christopher Pl CAMTN NW1 * 5 H7
Christopher Rd NWDGN UB2 102 A3
Christophers Ms NTGHL W11 * 88 C7
Christopher St SDTCH EC2A 13 H1
Christy Ter WFD IG8 45 J6
Chryssell Rd BRXN/ST SW9 110 B6
Chubworthy St NWCR SE14 112 B5
Chudleigh Crs GDMY/SEVK IG3 78 E3
Chudleigh Gdns SUT SM1 175 G2
Chudleigh Rd BROCKY SE4 132 C4
KIL/WHAMP NW6 70 A6
WHTN TW2 123 K5
Chudleigh St WCHPL E1 93 F5
Chudleigh Wy RSLP HA4 46 E7
Chulsa Rd SYD SE26 150 D4
Chumleigh St CMBW SE5 19 J9
Chumleigh Wk BRYLDS KT5 159 G3
Church Ap DUL SE21 149 K2
Church Av BECK BR3 151 J7
CAMTN NW1 72 B5
CHING E4 44 B5
MNPK E12 77 H1
MORT/ESHN SW14 126 A3
NTHLT UB5 65 K6
NWDGN UB2 102 D2
PIN HA5 47 J5
RSLP HA4 46 B7
SCUP DA14 155 G4
Churchbury Cl EN EN1 30 A1
Churchbury La EN EN1 30 A2
Churchbury Rd
ELTH/MOT SE9 134 C6
EN EN1 30 A1
Church Cl EDGW HA8 36 E4
HSLW TW3 122 E1
HYS/HAR UB3 82 B4
NTHWD HA6 32 D6
TRDG/WHET N20 39 J2
WDR/YW UB7 100 B2
Church Crs FNCH N3 38 D7
HOM E9 75 F6
MUSWH N10 54 B3
TRDG/WHET N20 39 J2
Churchcroft Cl BAL SW12 * 129 F6
Churchdown BMLY BR1 152 C3
Church Dr CDALE/KGS NW9 51 F7
RYLN/HDSTN HA2 48 A5
WWKM BR4 180 C2
Church Elm La DAGE RM10 80 C5
Church End HDN NW4 51 K2
WALTH E17 * 57 K3
Church Farm EBAR EN4 * 27 K6
Church Farm La CHEAM SM3 174 C5
Churchfield Av
NFNCH/WDSPK N12 39 G5
Churchfield Cl HYS/HAR UB3 82 D6
RYLN/HDSTN HA2 48 C3
Churchfield Rd ACT W3 86 E7
HNWL W7 103 K1
WEA W13 85 H7
WELL DA16 136 B2
Churchfields E/WMO/HCT KT8 157 F2
GNWCH SE10 113 F5
SWFD E18 44 E7
Churchfields Av FELT TW13 141 K2
Churchfields Rd BECK BR3 166 A1
Churchfield Wy
NFNCH/WDSPK N12 39 G5
Church Gdns ALP/SUD HA0 67 G3
EA W5 104 E1
Church Garth ARCH N19 * 72 D1
Church Ga FUL/PGN SW6 127 H2
Church Gn BRXN/ST SW9 * 130 B1
HYS/HAR UB3 82 D5
Church Gv KUT/HW KT1 143 J7
LEW SE13 132 E3
Church Hl CAR SM5 175 K4
HRW HA1 48 E7
WALTH E17 57 J3
WCHMH N21 29 F6
WIM/MER SW19 146 D4
WOOL/PLUM SE18 114 E2
Church Hill Rd CHEAM SM3 174 B3
EBAR EN4 27 J5
SURB KT6 159 F4
WALTH E17 57 K3
Church Hollow PUR RM19 119 K4
Church Hyde
WOOL/PLUM SE18 115 K5
Churchill Av
KTN/HRWW/WS HA3 49 H5
Churchill Cl EBED/NFELT TW14 121 J7
Churchill Gdns ACT W3 86 C5
PIM SW1V 16 E8
Churchill Gardens Rd
PIM SW1V 16 D8
Churchill Ms WFD IG8 44 D5
Churchill Pl POP/IOD E14 93 K7
Churchill Rd CAN/RD E16 95 G5
CRICK NW2 69 K5
EDGW HA8 36 B5
KTTN NW5 72 B3
SAND/SEL CR2 177 J7
Churchill Ter CHING E4 43 J3
Churchill Wk HOM E9 74 E4
Churchill Wy BMLY BR1 167 K1
SUN TW16 140 E4
Churchlands Wy WPK KT4 174 B1
Church La CDALE/KGS NW9 50 E7
CEND/HSY/T N8 55 F3
CHSGTN KT9 172 B5
CHST BR7 154 C7
DAGE RM10 80 D5
EA W5 104 D1
ED N9 42 C1
EFNCH N2 53 H2
ENC/FH EN2 29 K2
HAYES BR2 168 D7
KTN/HRWW/WS HA3 35 F7
PIN HA5 47 J2
PUR RM19 * 119 K4
ROM RM1 63 G3
TEDD TW11 143 F4
THDIT KT7 158 A5
TOOT SW17 147 K4
TOTM N17 42 A7
TWK TW1 124 B7
WALTH E17 57 K3
WAN E11 58 C7
WIM/MER SW19 146 E7
WLGTN SM6 176 D2
Churchley Rd SYD SE26 150 D3
Church Manor Wy ABYW SE2 116 B2
Church Md CMBW SE5 * 110 D6
Churchmead Cl EBAR EN4 27 J5
Church Meadow SURB KT6 171 J1
Churchmead Rd
WLSDN NW10 69 J5
Churchmore Rd
STRHM/NOR SW16 148 C7
Church Mt EFNCH N2 53 H4
Church Paddock Ct
WLGTN SM6 176 D2
Church Pas BAR EN5 * 26 D2
Church Pth CHSWK W4 105 K2
MTCM CR4 162 D2
NFNCH/WDSPK N12 * 39 G4
RYNPK SW20 161 J1
WAN E11 58 E4
Church Pl EA W5 104 E1
MTCM CR4 162 D2
Church Ri CHSGTN KT9 172 B5
FSTH SE23 132 A7
Church Rd ACT W3 105 K1
BARK IG11 78 C5
BARN SW13 126 D1
CHEAM SM3 174 C5
CROY/NA CR0 177 J2
E/WMO/HCT KT8 157 J2
ERITH DA8 117 K4
ESH/CLAY KT10 171 F5
FELT TW13 141 G4
GNTH/NBYPK IG2 60 E5
HAYES BR2 167 H2
HAYES BR2 181 H6
HAYES BR2 167 K1
HDN NW4 51 K3
HEST TW5 103 F6
HGT N6 54 A5
HNWL W7 84 E6
HOR/WEW KT19 173 F6
HYS/HAR UB3 82 D7
IS N1 73 J5
ISLW TW7 103 J7
KUT/HW KT1 159 G1
LEY E10 57 J7
LEY E10 75 K1
MNPK E12 77 J4
MTCM CR4 162 D2
NRWD SE19 150 A6
NTHLT UB5 83 H1
NTHWD HA6 32 D6
NWDGN UB2 102 E2
PEND EN3 30 E5
RCHPK/HAM TW10 125 F4
RCHPK/HAM TW10 144 B4
SCUP DA14 155 G3
STAN HA7 35 H4
SURB KT6 158 D7
TEDD TW11 142 E3
TOTM N17 42 A7
WALTH E17 57 G1
WDR/YW UB7 100 A1
WELL DA16 136 C1
WIM/MER SW19 162 C1
WLGTN SM6 176 C2
WLSDN NW10 69 G5
WPK KT4 160 B7
Church Rw CHST BR7 154 C6
FUL/PGN SW6 * 108 A6
HAMP NW3 71 G3
WAND/EARL SW18 128 A4
Church Row Ms CHST BR7 154 C6
Church St BAY/PAD W2 9 H2
CHSWK W4 106 B5
CROY/NA CR0 177 H2
DAGE RM10 80 D6
ED N9 29 K6
ENC/FH EN2 29 J2
ESH/CLAY KT10 170 B3
EW KT17 173 J7
HPTN TW12 142 C7
HSLW TW3 123 H4
ISLW TW7 124 C2
KUT/HW KT1 158 E1
SRTFD E15 76 C7
TWK TW1 124 B7
WATW WD18 * 21 G3
Church Street Est
STJWD NW8 9 H1
Church St North SRTFD E15 76 C7
Church Ter BKHTH/KID SE3 133 H2
FUL/PGN SW6 * 128 A1
HDN NW4 51 K2
RCHPK/HAM TW10 124 E4
Church V EFNCH N2 53 K2
FSTH SE23 150 E1
Church Vw FSTH SE23 151 F1
Churchview Rd WHTN TW2 123 J7
Church Wk BTFD TW8 104 D5
BUSH WD23 22 A5
CDALE/KGS NW9 69 F1
CRICK NW2 70 D2
HYS/HAR UB3 82 C5
RYNPK SW20 161 F2
STNW/STAM N16 73 K3
STRHM/NOR SW16 163 H1
THDIT KT7 158 A5
Churchway CAMTN NW1 5 H7
Church Wy EBAR EN4 27 K3
TRDG/WHET N20 39 J2
Churchyard Rw LBTH SE11 18 D5
Churston Av PLSTW E13 77 F7
Churston Cl
BRXS/STRHM SW2 * 130 C7
Churston Dr MRDN SM4 161 G4
Churston Gdns
FBAR/BDGN N11 40 C5
Churton Pl CHSWK W4 * 105 J5
PIM SW1V 16 F6
Churton St PIM SW1V 16 F6
Chyngton Cl BFN/LL DA15 155 F2
Cibber Rd FSTH SE23 151 F1
Cicada Rd WAND/EARL SW18 128 B5
Cicely Rd PECK SE15 111 H7
Cinderford Wy BMLY BR1 152 C3
Cinema Pde EDGW HA8 * 36 C5
Cinnamon Cl CROY/NA CR0 * 163 K6
PECK SE15 111 G6
Cinnamon St WAP E1W 92 D7
Cintra Pk NRWD SE19 150 B6
Circle Gdns WIM/MER SW19 161 K2
The Circle CRICK NW2 69 G2
MLHL NW7 37 F5
The Circuits PIN HA5 47 G3
Circular Rd TOTM N17 56 B2
Circular Wy WOOL/PLUM SE18 114 E5
Circus Ms MBLAR W1H * 9 L2
Circus Pl LVPST EC2M * 13 H3
Circus Rd STJWD NW8 3 G7
Circus St GNWCH SE10 113 F6
Cirencester St BAY/PAD W2 8 C2
Cissbury Ring North
NFNCH/WDSPK N12 38 D4
Cissbury Ring South
NFNCH/WDSPK N12 38 D4
Cissbury Rd SEVS/STOTM N15 55 K4
Citadel Pl LBTH SE11 17 L7
Citizen Rd HOLWY N7 73 G2
Citron Ter PECK SE15 * 131 J2
City Barracks SHB W12 * 88 A7
City Garden Rw IS N1 6 D6
City Rd FSBYE EC1V 6 C6
STLK EC1Y 13 H1
City Wk STHWK SE1 19 J3
Civic Wy BARK/HLT IG6 60 C3
RSLP HA4 65 H4
Clabon Ms KTBR SW1X 15 L4
Clack St BERM/RHTH SE16 111 K1
Clacton Rd TOTM N17 * 56 B1
WALTH E17 57 G5
Claire Ct NFNCH/WDSPK N12 39 G2
Claire Gdns STAN HA7 35 J4
Claire Pl POP/IOD E14 112 D2
Clairvale Rd HEST TW5 102 C7
Clairview Rd
STRHM/NOR SW16 148 B4
Clairville Gdns HNWL W7 84 E7
Clamp Hl STAN HA7 34 E4
Clancarty Rd FUL/PGN SW6 127 K1
Clandon Cl ACT W3 105 J1
EW KT17 173 H5
Clandon Gdns FNCH N3 52 E2
Clandon Rd GDMY/SEVK IG3 78 E1
Clandon St DEPT SE8 132 D1
Clandon Ter RYNPK SW20 * 161 G1
Clanricarde Gdns
BAY/PAD W2 8 B7
Clapgate Rd BUSH WD23 22 B5
Clapham Common North Side
CLAP SW4 129 F3
Clapham Common South Side
CLAP SW4 129 G4
Clapham Common West Side
BTSEA SW11 128 E3
Clapham Court Ter
CLAP SW4 * 129 K4
Clapham Crs CLAP SW4 129 J3
Clapham High St CLAP SW4 129 J3
Clapham Manor St CLAP SW4 129 H2
Clapham Park Est CLAP SW4 * 129 J6
Clapham Park Rd CLAP SW4 129 H3
Clapham Park Ter
BRXS/STRHM SW2 * 129 K4
Clapham Rd BRXN/ST SW9 129 K1
Claps Gate La EHAM E6 96 B3
Clapton Common CLPT E5 56 C6
Clapton Pas CLPT E5 74 E4
Clapton Sq CLPT E5 74 D4
Clapton Ter CLPT E5 56 C6
Clapton Wy CLPT E5 74 C3
Clara Pl WOOL/PLUM SE18 115 F3
Clare Cl BORE WD6 24 B5
EFNCH N2 53 G2

Coldharbour Wy
CROY/NA CR0 177 G4
Coldstream Gdns
WAND/EARL SW18 127 J5
Colebeck Ms IS N1 73 H5
Colebert Av WCHPL E1 92 E3
Colebrook Cl MLHL NW7 38 B6
Colebrooke Av WEA W13 85 H5
Colebrooke Dr WAN E11 59 F6
Colebrooke Pl IS N1 6 D4
Colebrooke Rw IS N1 5 K3
IS N1 6 C6
Colebrook Ri HAYES BR2 167 H1
Colebrook Rd
STRHM/NOR SW16 148 E7
Colebrook Wy
FBAR/BDGN N11 40 B4
Coleby Pth CMBW SE5 * 110 E6
Cole Cl THMD SE28 97 H7
Coledale Dr STAN HA7 35 J7
Coleford Rd
WAND/EARL SW18 128 B4
Cole Gdns HEST TW5 101 K6
Colegrave Rd SRTFD E15 76 B4
Colegrove Rd PECK SE15 111 G5
Coleherne Ms WBPTN SW10 14 C8
Coleherne Rd WBPTN SW10 14 C8
Colehill Gdns FUL/PGN SW6 * 107 H7
Colehill La FUL/PGN SW6 107 H7
Coleman Cl SNWD SE25 165 H1
Coleman Flds IS N1 6 F3
Coleman Rd BELV DA17 117 H2
CMBW SE5 111 F6
Colemans Heath
ELTH/MOT SE9 154 A2
Coleman St CITYW EC2V 13 G4
Colenso Dr MLHL NW7 37 J6
Colenso Rd CLPT E5 74 E3
GNTH/NBYPK IG2 60 E7
Cole Park Gdns TWK TW1 124 B5
Cole Park Rd TWK TW1 124 B6
Colepits Wood Rd
ELTH/MOT SE9 135 J4
Coleraine Rd BKHTH/KID SE3 113 J5
CEND/HSY/T N8 55 G2
Coleridge Av MNPK E12 77 J5
SUT SM1 175 J3
Coleridge Cl VX/NE SW8 129 G1
Coleridge Gdns
KIL/WHAMP NW6 2 E2
WBPTN SW10 108 B6
Coleridge Rd CEND/HSY/T N8 54 D5
CROY/NA CR0 165 K6
DART DA1 139 K3
FSBYPK N4 73 G1
NFNCH/WDSPK N12 39 G4
WALTH E17 57 H3
Coleridge Sq WEA W13 85 G5
Coleridge Wk GLDGN NW11 52 E3
Coleridge Wy BORE WD6 24 C3
WDR/YW UB7 100 B3
YEAD UB4 82 E5
Cole Rd TWK TW1 124 B5
Colesburg Rd BECK BR3 166 C2
Coles Crs RYLN/HDSTN HA2 66 B1
Coles Gn BUSH WD23 22 C7
Coles Green Rd CRICK NW2 51 J7
Coleshill Rd TEDD TW11 142 E5
Colestown St BTSEA SW11 128 D1
Cole St STHWK SE1 18 F2
Colet Cl PLMGR N13 41 H5
Colet Gdns WKENS W14 107 G4
Coley St FSBYW WC1X 11 M1
Colfe & Hatcliffe Glebe
LEW SE13 * 132 E4
Colfe Rd FSTH SE23 132 B7
Colina Ms SEVS/STOTM N15 55 H3
Colina Rd CEND/HSY/T N8 55 H4
Colin Cl CDALE/KGS NW9 51 G3
CROY/NA CR0 179 H2
WWKM BR4 180 D2
Colin Crs CDALE/KGS NW9 51 H4
Colindale Av CDALE/KGS NW9 51 F2
Colindeep Gdns HDN NW4 51 J4
Colindeep La CDALE/KGS NW9 51 H3
Colin Dr CDALE/KGS NW9 51 H4
Colinette Rd PUT/ROE SW15 127 F3
Colin Gdns CDALE/KGS NW9 51 H4
Colin Park Rd
CDALE/KGS NW9 51 G2
Colinton Rd GDMY/SEVK IG3 79 H1
Coliston Rd WAND/EARL SW18 127 K6
Collamore Av
WAND/EARL SW18 128 D7
Collapit Cl HRW HA1 48 B5
Collard Pl CAMTN NW1 4 C1
College Ap GNWCH SE10 113 F5
College Av
KTN/HRWW/WS HA3 34 E7
College Cl
KTN/HRWW/WS HA3 34 E6
UED N18 42 B4
WHTN TW2 123 J7
College Ct EA W5 * 86 A6
College Crs HAMP NW3 71 G5
College Cross IS N1 6 B1
College Dr RSLP HA4 46 E6
THDIT KT7 157 K6
College East WCHPL E1 * 13 M3
College Gdns CHING E4 31 K6
NWMAL KT3 160 C4
REDBR IG4 59 J4
TOOT SW17 147 J1
UED N18 * 42 B4
College Gn NRWD SE19 150 A6
College Gv CAMTN NW1 5 G4
College Hl CANST EC4R * 12 F6
College Hill Rd
KTN/HRWW/WS HA3 34 E6
College La KTTN NW5 72 B3
College Ms IS N1 6 B2
WEST SW1P 17 J3
College Pde
KIL/WHAMP NW6 * 70 C7
College Park Cl LEW SE13 133 F3
College Pl CAMTN NW1 4 F3
WALTH E17 58 C3
WBPTN SW10 * 108 B6
College Rd BMLY BR1 152 E7
CROY/NA CR0 177 K1
DUL SE21 131 F7
ENC/FH EN2 29 K1
HRW HA1 48 E5
ISLW TW7 104 A7
KTN/HRWW/WS HA3 34 E7
NRWD SE19 150 B4
TOTM N17 42 B5
WALTH E17 58 A4
WBLY HA9 49 K7
WCHMH N21 41 G1
WEA W13 85 H5
WIM/MER SW19 147 H5
WLSDN NW10 88 A1
College St CANST EC4R * 12 F6
College Ter FNCH N3 38 D7
College Vw ELTH/MOT SE9 134 C7
College Wy HYS/HAR UB3 82 E6
NTHWD HA6 32 B5
College Yd KIL/WHAMP NW6 * 70 C7
KTTN NW5 72 B3
Collent St HOM E9 74 E5
Colless Rd SEVS/STOTM N15 56 B4
Collett Rd BERM/RHTH SE16 111 H2
Collett Wy NWDGN UB2 103 G1
Collier Cl EHAM E6 96 B6
HOR/WEW KT19 172 C5
Collier Dr EDGW HA8 50 C1
Colliers Shaw HAYES BR2 181 J4
Collier St IS N1 5 L6
Colliers Water La THHTH CR7 164 B4
Collindale Av BFN/LL DA15 136 B7
CDALE/KGS NW9 51 G2
ERITH DA8 117 J5
Collingbourne Rd SHB W12 87 K7
Collingham Gdns ECT SW5 14 D6
Collingham Pl ECT SW5 14 C6
Collingham Rd ECT SW5 14 D5
Collings Cl WDGN N22 41 F5
Collington St GNWCH SE10 * 113 G4
Collingtree Rd SYD SE26 150 E3
Collingwood Av BRYLDS KT5 159 K7
MUSWH N10 54 A2
Colling Wood Cl PGE/AN SE20 150 D7
Collingwood Cl WHTN TW2 123 F6
Collingwood Rd MTCM CR4 162 D1
RAIN RM13 99 H1
SEVS/STOTM N15 56 A3
SUT SM1 174 E3
Collingwood St WCHPL E1 92 D3
Collins Av STAN HA7 50 A1
Collins Dr RSLP HA4 65 G1
Collinson St STHWK SE1 18 E2
Collinson Wk STHWK SE1 18 E2
Collins Rd HBRY N5 73 J3
Collins Sq BKHTH/KID SE3 * 133 J2
Collins St BKHTH/KID SE3 133 H1
Collinwood Av PEND EN3 30 E2
Collinwood Gdns
GNTH/NBYPK IG2 59 K4
Collyer Av CROY/NA CR0 176 E3
Collyer Pl PECK SE15 111 H7
Collyer Rd CROY/NA CR0 176 E3
Colman Pde EN EN1 * 30 A2
Colman Rd CAN/RD E16 95 G4
Colmar Cl WCHPL E1 93 F3
Colmer Pl
KTN/HRWW/WS HA3 34 D6
Colmer Rd STRHM/NOR SW16 148 E6
Colmore Ms PECK SE15 111 J7
Colmore Rd PEND EN3 30 E3
Colnbrook St STHWK SE1 18 C4
Colne Av OXHEY WD19 21 F5
Colne Ct HOR/WEW KT19 172 E3
Colne Ldg BUSH WD23 * 21 H3
Colne Rd CLPT E5 75 F3
WCHMH N21 29 K6
WHTN TW2 123 K7
Colne St PLSTW E13 94 E2
Colney Hatch La
FBAR/BDGN N11 39 K5
Cologne Rd BTSEA SW11 128 C3
Colombo Rd IL IG1 60 C7
Colombo St STHWK SE1 12 C9
Colomb St GNWCH SE10 113 H4
Colonels Wk ENC/FH EN2 29 H1
Colonial Av WHTN TW2 123 H5
Colonial Dr CHSWK W4 105 K3
Colonial Rd EBED/NFELT TW14 121 H6
Colonnade BMSBY WC1N 11 J1
The Colonnade DEPT SE8 * 112 C3
Colosseum Ter CAMTN NW1 4 D9
Colson Rd CROY/NA CR0 177 K1
Colson Wy STRHM/NOR SW16 148 C3
Colsterworth Rd
SEVS/STOTM N15 56 B3
Colston Av CAR SM5 175 J3
Colston Rd FSTGT E7 77 H5
MORT/ESHN SW14 125 K3
Colthurst Crs FSBYPK N4 73 H1
Colthurst Dr ED N9 42 D2
Coltness Crs ABYW SE2 116 C4
Colton Gdns TOTM N17 55 J2
Colton Rd HRW HA1 48 E4
Colts Yd WAN E11 * 58 D7
Columbas Dr HAMP NW3 71 H1
Columbia Av EDGW HA8 36 D7
RSLP HA4 47 F7
WPK KT4 160 C6
Columbia Rd BETH E2 7 L7
PLSTW E13 * 94 D3
Columbia Whf PEND EN3 * 31 G4
Columbine Av EHAM E6 95 J4
SAND/SEL CR2 177 H6
Columbine Wy LEW SE13 * 133 F1
Columbus Gdns NTHWD HA6 32 E7
Colvestone Crs HACK E8 74 B4
Colville Est IS N1 7 H4
Colville Gdns NTGHL W11 88 D5
Colville Houses NTGHL W11 88 D5
Colville Ms NTGHL W11 88 D5
Colville Pl FITZ W1T 10 F3
Colville Rd ACT W3 105 J2
ED N9 30 D7
NTGHL W11 88 D5
WALTH E17 57 G1
WAN E11 76 A2
Colville Sq NTGHL W11 * 88 D5
Colville Square Ms
NTGHL W11 * 88 D5
Colville Ter NTGHL W11 88 D5
Colvin Cl SYD SE26 150 E4
Colvin Gdns CHING E4 44 A2
SWFD E18 59 F3
Colvin Rd EHAM E6 77 J6
THHTH CR7 164 B4
Colwall Gdns WFD IG8 44 E4
Colwell Rd EDUL SE22 131 G4
Colwick Cl HGT N6 54 D6
Colwith Rd HMSMTH W6 107 F5
Colwood Gdns
WIM/MER SW19 147 H6
Colworth Gv WALW SE17 18 F6
Colworth Rd CROY/NA CR0 165 H7
WAN E11 58 C5
Colwyn Av GFD/PVL UB6 85 F1
Colwyn Cl STRHM/NOR SW16 148 C4
Colwyn Crs HSLW TW3 103 H7
Colwyn Gn CDALE/KGS NW9 * 51 G5
Colwyn Rd CRICK NW2 69 K2
Colyer Cl ELTH/MOT SE9 154 B1
Colyers Cl ERITH DA8 118 A7
Colyton Cl ALP/SUD HA0 67 J5
WELL DA16 116 E7
Colyton La STRHM/NOR SW16 149 G4
Colyton Rd EDUL SE22 131 J4
Colyton Wy UED N18 42 C4
Combe Av BKHTH/KID SE3 113 J6
Combemartin Rd
WAND/EARL SW18 127 H6
Comber Cl CRICK NW2 69 J1
Comber Gv CMBW SE5 110 D6
Combermere Rd
BRXN/ST SW9 130 A2
MRDN SM4 162 A5
Combe Rd WATW WD18 20 D5
Comberton Rd CLPT E5 74 D1
Combeside WOOL/PLUM SE18 116 A6
Combes Rd DAGW RM9 80 B6
Combwell Crs ABYW SE2 116 B2
Comely Bank Rd WALTH E17 58 A4
Comeragh Ms WKENS W14 107 H4
Comeragh Rd WKENS W14 107 H4
Comerford Rd BROCKY SE4 132 B3
Comet Cl MNPK E12 77 H3
PUR RM19 119 K3
Comet Pl DEPT SE8 112 D6
Comet Rd STWL/WRAY TW19 120 A6
Comet St DEPT SE8 112 D6
Comfort St PECK SE15 111 F6
Commerce Rd BTFD TW8 104 D5
WDGN N22 41 F7
Commerce Wy CROY/NA CR0 177 F2
Commercial Rd POP/IOD E14 93 G5
UED N18 42 A4
Commercial St WCHPL E1 13 L1
Commercial Wy CMBW SE5 111 G7
WLSDN NW10 86 D1
Commerell Pl GNWCH SE10 113 J4
Commerell St GNWCH SE10 113 H4
Commodore Pde
STRHM/NOR SW16 * 149 F6
Commodore St WCHPL E1 93 F4
Commondale PUT/ROE SW15 127 F1
Common La ESH/CLAY KT10 171 G6
Common Rd BARN SW13 126 D2
ESH/CLAY KT10 171 G5
STAN HA7 34 D2
Commonside HAYES BR2 181 G3
Commonside East MTCM CR4 163 J4
Commonside West
MTCM CR4 163 F2
The Common EA W5 86 A7
NWDGN UB2 102 C3
SRTFD E15 76 D5
STAN HA7 35 F1
Commonwealth Av
HYS/HAR UB3 82 B5
SHB W12 87 K6
Commonwealth Rd
TOTM N17 42 C6
Commonwealth Wy
ABYW SE2 116 C4
Community Cl HEST TW5 102 A7
Community Rd GFD/PVL UB6 66 C7
SRTFD E15 76 B4
Como Rd FSTH SE23 151 G1
Como St ROMW/RG RM7 63 F4
Compass Cl ASHF TW15 140 A6
EDGW HA8 36 B3
Compass Hl
RCHPK/HAM TW10 124 E5
Compayne Gdns
KIL/WHAMP NW6 2 C1
Compton Av ALP/SUD HA0 67 H3
EHAM E6 95 H1
GPK RM2 63 K2
HGT N6 53 J6
IS N1 73 H5
Compton Cl CAMTN NW1 4 D8
EDGW HA8 36 E6
ESH/CLAY KT10 170 D5
GLDGN NW11 70 B2
PECK SE15 111 H6
WEA W13 85 G5
Compton Crs CHSGTN KT9 172 A5
CHSWK W4 105 K5
NTHLT UB5 65 H7
TOTM N17 41 J6
Compton Pas FSBYE EC1V 6 D9
Compton Pl ERITH DA8 118 C5
OXHEY WD19 33 J3
STPAN WC1H 5 J9
Compton Ri PIN HA5 47 J4
Compton Rd CROY/NA CR0 165 J7
HYS/HAR UB3 82 C6
IS N1 73 H5
WCHMH N21 29 H7
WIM/MER SW19 146 D5
WLSDN NW10 88 B2
Compton St FSBYE EC1V 6 C9
Compton Ter IS N1 73 H5
WCHMH N21 * 29 G7
Comus Pl WALW SE17 19 J6
Comyn Rd BTSEA SW11 128 D3
Comyns Cl CAN/RD E16 94 D4
Comyns Rd DAGW RM9 80 C6
The Comyns BUSH WD23 22 C7
Conant Ms WCHPL E1 92 C6
Concanon Rd CLAP SW4 130 A3
Concert Hall Ap STHWK SE1 11 M9
Concord Cl NTHLT UB5 83 H2
Concorde Cl HSLW TW3 123 G1
Concorde Dr EHAM E6 95 K4
Concorde Wy
BERM/RHTH SE16 112 A3
Concord Rd ACT W3 86 D3
PEND EN3 30 E4
Concord Wy
BERM/RHTH SE16 * 112 A3
Condell Rd VX/NE SW8 109 H7
Conder St POP/IOD E14 93 G5
Condover Crs
WOOL/PLUM SE18 115 G6
Condray Pl BTSEA SW11 108 D6
Conduit Ct COVGDN WC2E * 11 J6
Conduit La SAND/SEL CR2 178 C4
UED N18 42 E4
Conduit Ms BAY/PAD W2 9 G5
Conduit Pl BAY/PAD W2 9 G5
Conduit Rd WOOL/PLUM SE18 115 G4
Conduit St CONDST W1S 10 D6
Conduit Wy WLSDN NW10 68 E6
Conewood St HBRY N5 73 H2
Coney Burrows CHING E4 44 C1
Coney Hall Pde WWKM BR4 * 180 C2
Coney Hill Rd WWKM BR4 180 C1
Coney Wy VX/NE SW8 110 A5
Conference Cl CHING E4 44 A1
Congleton Gv
WOOL/PLUM SE18 115 H4
Congo Dr ED N9 42 E2
Congo Rd WOOL/PLUM SE18 115 J4
Congreve Rd ELTH/MOT SE9 134 E2
Congreve St WALW SE17 19 J6
Conical Cnr ENC/FH EN2 29 J1
Conifer Gdns EN EN1 29 K5
STRHM/NOR SW16 149 F2
SUT SM1 175 F1
Conifers Cl TEDD TW11 143 H6
Conifer Wy ALP/SUD HA0 67 J2
HYS/HAR UB3 82 E6
Coniger Rd FUL/PGN SW6 127 K1
Coningham Ms SHB W12 87 J7
Coningham Rd SHB W12 106 E1
Coningsby Av
CDALE/KGS NW9 51 G1
Coningsby Cots EA W5 104 E1
Coningsby Gdns CHING E4 43 K5
Coningsby Rd EA W5 104 D1
FSBYPK N4 55 H6
SAND/SEL CR2 177 J7
Conington Rd LEW SE13 132 E1
Conisbee Ct STHGT/OAK N14 28 C4
Conisborough Crs CAT SE6 152 A2
Coniscliffe Cl CHST BR7 154 A7
Coniscliffe Rd PLMGR N13 41 J2
Coniston Av BARK IG11 78 E6
GFD/PVL UB6 85 H2
WELL DA16 135 K2
Coniston Cl BARN SW13 106 C6
BXLYHN DA7 117 K7
CHSWK W4 105 K7
MRDN SM4 161 G5
Coniston Ct BAY/PAD W2 * 9 K5
Conistone Wy HOLWY N7 5 K1
Coniston Gdns BELMT SM2 * 175 H5
CDALE/KGS NW9 51 F4
ED N9 30 E7
PIN HA5 46 E3
REDBR IG4 59 J3
WBLY HA9 49 J7
Coniston Rd BMLY BR1 152 C5
BXLYHN DA7 117 K7
CROY/NA CR0 165 H6
MUSWH N10 54 B1
TOTM N17 42 C5
WHTN TW2 123 G5
Coniston Wk HOM E9 74 E4
Coniston Wy CHSGTN KT9 172 A2
HCH RM12 81 J4
Conlan St NKENS W10 88 C3
Conley Rd WLSDN NW10 69 G5
Conley St GNWCH SE10 * 113 H4
Connaught Av EBAR EN4 27 K7
EN EN1 30 A1
HSLWW TW4 122 D4
MORT/ESHN SW14 125 K2
Connaught Br CAN/RD E16 95 H6
CAN/RD E16 95 H7
Connaught Cl BAY/PAD W2 9 J5
EN EN1 30 A1
LEY E10 75 G1
SUT SM1 175 H1
UX/CGN UB8 * 82 A4
Connaught Dr GLDGN NW11 52 E3
Connaught Gdns MRDN SM4 162 B4
MUSWH N10 54 B4
PLMGR N13 41 H3
Connaught La IL IG1 78 C1
Connaught Ms
FUL/PGN SW6 * 107 H7
HAMP NW3 * 71 J4
WOOL/PLUM SE18 115 F4
Connaught Rd BAR EN5 26 B5
CAN/RD E16 95 H7
FSBYPK N4 55 G6
IL IG1 78 D1
KTN/HRWW/WS HA3 35 F7
NWMAL KT3 160 B3
RCHPK/HAM TW10 * 125 G4
SUT SM1 175 H1
TEDD TW11 142 D4
WALTH E17 * 57 J4
WAN E11 58 B7
WEA W13 85 H6
WLSDN NW10 87 G1
WOOL/PLUM SE18 115 F4
Connaught Sq BAY/PAD W2 9 K5
Connaught St BAY/PAD W2 9 K5
Connaught Wy PLMGR N13 41 H3
Connect La BARK/HLT IG6 60 C1
Connell Crs EA W5 86 B3
Connemara Cl BORE WD6 * 24 E5
Connington Crs CHING E4 44 B2
Connor Cl WAN E11 58 C7
Connor Rd DAGW RM9 80 B3
Connor St HOM E9 * 75 F7
Conolly Rd HNWL W7 84 E7
Conrad Dr WPK KT4 161 F7
Conroy Ct SCUP DA14 155 G3
Consfield Av NWMAL KT3 160 D3
Consort Cl FBAR/BDGN N11 39 K4
Consort Ms ISLW TW7 123 J5
Consort Rd PECK SE15 111 J7
Cons St STHWK SE1 * 18 B1
Constable Av CAN/RD E16 95 F7
Constable Cl GLDGN NW11 53 F5
YEAD UB4 82 A1
Constable Crs
SEVS/STOTM N15 56 C4
Constable Gdns EDGW HA8 36 C7
ISLW TW7 123 J4
Constable Ms BCTR RM8 79 H4
Constable Wk DUL SE21 150 A2
Constance Crs HAYES BR2 167 J7
Constance Rd CROY/NA CR0 164 C6
EN EN1 30 A5
SUT SM1 175 G3
WHTN TW2 123 G6
Constance St CAN/RD E16 95 J7
Constantine Rd HAMP NW3 71 J4
Constitution Hl
MYFR/PICC W1J 16 C1
Constitution Ri
WOOL/PLUM SE18 115 F7
Consul Av DAGW RM9 98 E3
RAIN RM13 99 F2
Content St WALW SE17 18 F6
Control Tower Rd
HTHAIR TW6 120 D2
Convent Cl BECK BR3 152 A6
Convent Gdns EA W5 104 D3
NTGHL W11 88 D5
Convent Hl NRWD SE19 149 J5
Convent Wy NWDGN UB2 102 B3
Conway Cl RAIN RM13 81 J6
STAN HA7 35 G5
Conway Crs CHDH RM6 61 J6
GFD/PVL UB6 84 E1
Conway Dr ASHF TW15 140 A5
BELMT SM2 175 F5
HYS/HAR UB3 101 F2
Conway Gdns MTCM CR4 163 J3
WBLY HA9 49 J6
Conway Gv ACT W3 87 F4
Conway Ms FITZ W1T 10 E2
Conway Rd CRICK NW2 70 A1
FELT TW13 141 H4
HSLWW TW4 122 E6
RYNPK SW20 146 A7
SEVS/STOTM N15 55 J4
STHGT/OAK N14 40 E2
WOOL/PLUM SE18 115 J3
Conway St FITZ W1T 10 E1
Conybeare HAMP NW3 3 K1
Conyers Rd
STRHM/NOR SW16 148 D4
Conyer St BOW E3 * 93 G1
Cooden Cl BMLY BR1 153 F6
Cookes Cl WAN E11 76 D1
Cookes La CHEAM SM3 174 C5
Cookham Cl NWDGN UB2 103 G2
Cookham Dene Cl CHST BR7 154 D7
Cookhill Rd ABYW SE2 116 C1
Cooks Ferry Rbt UED N18 43 G4
Cooks Md BUSH WD23 22 B5
Cook's Rd SRTFD E15 93 K1
WALW SE17 18 C9
Coolfin Rd CAN/RD E16 94 E5
Coolgardie Av CHING E4 44 B4
Coolgardie Rd ASHF TW15 140 A4
Coolhurst Rd HGT N6 54 D5
Cool Oak Br CDALE/KGS NW9 51 H6
Cool Oak La CDALE/KGS NW9 51 H6
Coomassie Rd MV/WKIL W9 88 D3
Coombe Av CROY/NA CR0 178 A3
Coombe Bank KUTN/CMB KT2 145 G7
Coombe Cl EDGW HA8 50 B1
HSLW TW3 123 F3
Coombe Cnr WCHMH N21 29 H7
Coombe Crs HPTN TW12 141 J6
Coombe Dr RSLP HA4 47 F7
Coombe End KUTN/CMB KT2 145 F6
Coombefield Cl NWMAL KT3 160 B4
Coombe Gdns NWMAL KT3 160 C3
Coombe Hill Gld
KUTN/CMB KT2 145 G6
Coombe Hill Rd
KUTN/CMB KT2 145 G6
Coombe House Cha
NWMAL KT3 145 F7
Coombehurst Cl EBAR EN4 27 K1
Coombe La CROY/NA CR0 178 C5
RYNPK SW20 145 H7
Coombe La West
KUTN/CMB KT2 144 E7
Coombe Lea BMLY BR1 168 D2
Coombe Ldg CHARL SE7 114 B5
Coombe Neville
KUTN/CMB KT2 144 E6
Coombe Pk KUTN/CMB KT2 144 E4
Coombe Ridings
KUTN/CMB KT2 144 E4
Coombe Ri KUTN/CMB KT2 144 E7
Coombe Rd BUSH WD23 22 C6
CHSWK W4 106 B4
CROY/NA CR0 177 J3
HPTN TW12 141 K5
KUTN/CMB KT2 144 C7
SAND/SEL CR2 178 A3
SYD SE26 150 D3
WDGN N22 55 G1
WEA W13 104 C2
WLSDN NW10 69 F2
Coomber Wy CROY/NA CR0 163 J6
Coombe Vls
WAND/EARL SW18 * 127 K6
Coombewood Dr CHDH RM6 62 B5
Coombe Wood Rd
KUTN/CMB KT2 144 E4
Coombs St IS N1 6 D6
Coomer Ms FUL/PGN SW6 * 107 J5
Coomer Pl FUL/PGN SW6 107 J5
Cooms Wk EDGW HA8 36 D7
Cooperage Cl TOTM N17 42 B5
Cooper Av WALTH E17 43 F7
Cooper Cl STHWK SE1 18 B2
Cooper Crs CAR SM5 175 K2
Cooperdale Cl WFD IG8 45 G6
Cooper Rd CROY/NA CR0 177 G3
HDN NW4 52 B5
WLSDN NW10 69 H4
Coopersale Cl WFD IG8 45 G6
Coopersale Rd HOM E9 75 F4
Coopers Cl DAGE RM10 80 D5
WCHPL E1 92 E3
Coopers La CAMTN NW1 5 H5
LEE/GVPK SE12 153 F1
Cooper's La LEY E10 57 K7
Coopers Ms BECK BR3 166 D1
Cooper's Rd STHWK SE1 19 M8
Cooper's Rw TWRH EC3N 13 L6
Cooper St CAN/RD E16 94 D4
Coopers Yd IS N1 6 C2
Cooper's Yd NRWD SE19 150 A5
Coote Rd BCTR RM8 80 B2
Copeland Rd PECK SE15 131 H1
WALTH E17 57 K4
Copeman Cl SYD SE26 150 E4
Copenhagen Gdns CHEL SW3 15 H7
CHSWK W4 106 A1
Copenhagen Pl POP/IOD E14 93 H5
Copenhagen St IS N1 5 K4
Cope Pl KENS W8 14 A4
Copers Cope Rd BECK BR3 151 H6
Cope St BERM/RHTH SE16 112 A3
Copford Wk IS N1 * 6 E3
Copgate Pth
STRHM/NOR SW16 149 F5
Copland Av ALP/SUD HA0 67 K4
Copland Cl ALP/SUD HA0 67 J4
Copland Ms ALP/SUD HA0 68 A5
Copland Rd ALP/SUD HA0 68 A5
Copleston Rd PECK SE15 131 G2
Copley Cl HNWL W7 85 F5
WALW SE17 110 C5
Copley Dene BMLY BR1 153 H7
Copley Pk STRHM/NOR SW16 149 F5
Copley Rd STAN HA7 35 J4
Coppard Gdns CHSGTN KT9 171 J5
Coppelia Rd BKHTH/KID SE3 133 J3
Coppen Rd BCTR RM8 62 B6
Copperas St DEPT SE8 112 E5
Copper Cl NRWD SE19 150 B6
TOTM N17 42 D6
Copperdale Rd HYS/HAR UB3 101 K1
Copperfield Dr
SEVS/STOTM N15 56 B3
Copperfield Rd BOW E3 93 G3
THMD SE28 97 J5
Copperfields SUN TW16 * 140 D5
Copperfield St STHWK SE1 18 D1
Copperfield Wy CHST BR7 154 C5
PIN HA5 47 K3
Coppergate Cl BMLY BR1 153 F7
Coppermead Cl CRICK NW2 70 A2
Copper Mill Dr ISLW TW7 124 A1
Copper Mill La TOOT SW17 147 G3
Coppermill La WALTH E17 56 E5
Copper Rw STHWK SE1 13 L9
Coppetts Cl
NFNCH/WDSPK N12 39 K6
Coppetts Rd MUSWH N10 39 K7
Coppice Cl BECK BR3 166 E3
RSLP HA4 * 46 A5

RYNPK SW20 161 F2
STAN HA7 35 F5
Coppice Dr PUT/ROE SW15 126 D5
The Coppice BAR EN5 * 27 F5
ENC/FH EN2 29 H3
OXHEY WD19 21 G5
Coppice Wk TRDG/WHET N20 38 E2
Coppice Wy SWFD E18 58 D3
Coppies Gv FBAR/BDGN N11 40 B3
Copping Cl CROY/NA CR0 178 A3
The Coppins CROY/NA CR0 179 K5
KTN/HRWW/WS HA3 34 E5
Coppock Cl BTSEA SW11 128 D1
Coppsfield E/WMO/HCT KT8 157 F2
Copse Av WWKM BR4 179 K2
Copse Cl CHARL SE7 114 A5
NTHWD HA6 32 A7
WDR/YW UB7 100 A2
Copse Gld SURB KT6 158 E7
Copse Hl BELMT SM2 175 F6
RYNPK SW20 145 J7
WIM/MER SW19 146 A5
Copsem Dr ESH/CLAY KT10 170 B5
Copsem La ESH/CLAY KT10 170 B5
Copsem Wy ESH/CLAY KT10 170 C5
The Copse BUSH WD23 21 H2
EFNCH N2 * 53 K2
Copse Vw SAND/SEL CR2 179 F6
Copsewood Cl BFN/LL DA15 135 K5
Copse Wood Wy NTHWD HA6 32 A7
Coptefield Dr BELV DA17 116 E2
Copthall Av LOTH EC2R 13 H4
Copthall Dr MLHL NW7 37 J6
Copthall Gdns MLHL NW7 37 J6
TWK TW1 124 A7
Copthorne Av BAL SW12 129 J6
HAYES BR2 181 K1
Copthorne Ms HYS/HAR UB3 101 H3
Coptic St NOXST/BSQ WC1A 11 J3
Copton Cl BOW E3 93 J4
Copwood Cl
NFNCH/WDSPK N12 39 H3
Coral Cl CHDH RM6 61 J2
Coraline Cl STHL UB1 83 K2
Coral Rw BTSEA SW11 128 B2
Coral St STHWK SE1 18 B2
Coram St STPAN WC1H 11 J1
Coran Cl ED N9 31 F6
Corban Rd HSLW TW3 123 F2
Corbet Cl WLGTN SM6 163 F7
Corbet Pl WCHPL E1 13 L2
Corbett Gv FBAR/BDGN N11 40 E6
Corbett Rd WALTH E17 58 B1
WAN E11 59 G5
Corbett's La
BERM/RHTH SE16 111 K3
Corbicum WAN E11 58 C6
Corbiere Ct WIM/MER SW19 146 B5
Corbin's La RYLN/HDSTN HA2 66 B2
Corbridge Crs BETH E2 92 D1
Corbridge Ms ROM RM1 63 H4
Corby Crs ENC/FH EN2 28 E3
Corbylands Rd BFN/LL DA15 135 K6
Corbyn St FSBYPK N4 54 E7
Corby Rd WLSDN NW10 86 E1
Cordelia Cl HNHL SE24 130 C3
Cordelia Gdns
STWL/WRAY TW19 120 B6
Cordelia Rd STWL/WRAY TW19 120 B6
Cordelia St POP/IOD E14 93 K5
Cordingley Rd RSLP HA4 46 B7
Cording St POP/IOD E14 93 K4
Cordwell Rd LEW SE13 133 G4
Corelli Rd BKHTH/KID SE3 114 D7
Corfe Av RYLN/HDSTN HA2 66 A3
Corfe Cl BORE WD6 25 F2
HSLWW TW4 122 D7
YEAD UB4 83 G5
Corfield Rd WCHMH N21 29 F4
Corfield St BETH E2 92 D3
Corfton Rd EA W5 86 A5
Coriander Av POP/IOD E14 94 B5
Cories Cl BCTR RM8 79 K1
Corinium Cl WBLY HA9 68 B3
Corinne Rd ARCH N19 72 C3
Corkran Rd SURB KT6 158 E6
Cork St Ms CONDST W1S 10 E7
Corkscrew Hl WWKM BR4 180 A1
Cork Sq WAP E1W 92 C7
Cork St CONDST W1S 10 E7
Cork Tree Wy CHING E4 43 G4
Corlett St CAMTN NW1 9 J2
Cormont Rd CMBW SE5 110 C7
Cormorant Cl WALTH E17 43 F7
Cormorant Rd FSTGT E7 76 D4
Cornbury Rd EDGW HA8 35 K6
Cornelia Dr YEAD UB4 83 G4
Cornelia St HOLWY N7 73 F5
Corner Fielde
BRXS/STRHM SW2 * 130 A7
Corner Md CDALE/KGS NW9 37 H6
Cornerside ASHF TW15 140 A6
The Corner EA W5 * 86 A7
Corney Reach Wy CHSWK W4 106 B6
Corney Rd CHSWK W4 106 B5
Cornfield Rd BUSH WD23 22 B3
Cornflower La CROY/NA CR0 166 A7
Cornflower Ter EDUL SE22 131 J5
Cornford Gv BAL SW12 148 B1
Cornhill BANK EC3V 13 H5
Cornish Ct ED N9 30 D6
Cornish Gv PGE/AN SE20 150 D7
Cornmill La LEW SE13 132 E2
Cornmow Dr WLSDN NW10 69 H4
Cornshaw Rd BCTR RM8 61 K7
Cornthwaite Rd CLPT E5 74 E2
Cornwall Av BETH E2 92 E2
ESH/CLAY KT10 171 F6
FNCH N3 38 E6
STHL UB1 83 K4
WDGN N22 40 E7
WELL DA16 135 K2
Cornwall Cl BARK IG11 79 F5
Cornwall Crs NTGHL W11 88 C6
Cornwall Dr STMC/STPC BR5 155 J6
Cornwall Gdns SKENS SW7 14 E4
SNWD SE25 * 165 G3
WLSDN NW10 69 K5
Cornwall Gardens Wk
SKENS SW7 14 D4
Cornwall Gv CHSWK W4 106 B4
Cornwallis Av ED N9 42 D1
ELTH/MOT SE9 154 D1
Cornwallis Cl ERITH DA8 118 C5
Cornwallis Gv ED N9 42 D1
Cornwallis Rd ARCH N19 72 E1
DAGW RM9 80 A3
ED N9 42 D1
WALTH E17 57 F3
WOOL/PLUM SE18 115 H3
Cornwallis Sq ARCH N19 72 E1
Cornwallis Wk
ELTH/MOT SE9 134 E2
Cornwall Ms South
SKENS SW7 14 E4
Cornwall Ms West
SKENS SW7 * 14 D4
Cornwall Rd BELMT SM2 174 D6
CROY/NA CR0 177 H1
FSBYPK N4 55 G6
HRW HA1 48 C5
PIN HA5 33 K6
RSLP HA4 64 D1
SEVS/STOTM N15 55 K4
STHWK SE1 12 A8
TWK TW1 124 B6
UED N18 42 C4
Cornwall St WCHPL E1 92 D6
Cornwall Ter CAMTN NW1 9 M1
Cornwall Terrace Ms
CAMTN NW1 9 M1
Corn Wy WAN E11 76 B2
Cornwood Cl EFNCH N2 53 H4
Cornwood Dr WCHPL E1 92 E5
Cornworthy Rd BCTR RM8 79 J4
Coronation Cl BARK/HLT IG6 60 C3
BXLY DA5 136 E5
Coronation Dr HCH RM12 81 K4
Coronation Rd HYS/HAR UB3 101 J3
PLSTW E13 95 G2
WLSDN NW10 86 D3
Coronation Vls
WLSDN NW10 * 86 D3
Coronet Pde ALP/SUD HA0 * 68 A5
Coronet St IS N1 7 J8
Corporation Av HSLWW TW4 122 D3
Corporation Rw CLKNW EC1R 6 B9
Corporation St HOLWY N7 72 E4
SRTFD E15 94 C1
Corrance Rd
BRXS/STRHM SW2 129 K3
Corri Av STHGT/OAK N14 40 D3
Corrib Dr SUT SM1 175 J4
Corrigan Cl HDN NW4 52 A2
Corringham Rd GLDGN NW11 52 E6
WBLY HA9 68 C1
Corringway EA W5 86 B4
GLDGN NW11 53 F6
Corris Gn CDALE/KGS NW9 * 51 G5
Corry Dr BRXN/ST SW9 130 C3
Corsair Cl STWL/WRAY TW19 120 A6
Corsair Rd STWL/WRAY TW19 120 B6
Corscombe Cl KUTN/CMB KT2 144 E4
Corsehill St STRHM/NOR SW16 148 C5
Corsellis Sq TWK TW1 124 C3
Corsham St IS N1 7 H8
Corsica St HBRY N5 73 H5
Cortayne Rd FUL/PGN SW6 * 127 J1
Cortina Dr DAGW RM9 98 E2
Cortis Rd PUT/ROE SW15 126 E5
Cortis Ter PUT/ROE SW15 126 E4
Corunna Rd VX/NE SW8 109 H7
Corunna Ter VX/NE SW8 109 H7
Corwell Gdns UX/CGN UB8 82 A5
Corwell La UX/CGN UB8 82 A5
Coryton Pth MV/WKIL W9 88 D3
Cosbycote Av HNHL SE24 130 D4
Cosdach Av WLGTN SM6 176 D6
Cosedge Crs CROY/NA CR0 177 G4
Cosgrove Cl WCHMH N21 41 J1
YEAD UB4 83 H3
Cosmo Pl RSQ WC1B 11 K2
Cosmur Cl SHB W12 106 C2
Cossall Wk PECK SE15 111 J7
Cossar Ms BRXS/STRHM SW2 130 B5
Cosser St STHWK SE1 18 A3
Costa St PECK SE15 131 H1
Costons Av GFD/PVL UB6 84 D2
Costons La GFD/PVL UB6 84 D2
Cosway St CAMTN NW1 9 K2
Cotall St POP/IOD E14 93 J5
Coteford Cl PIN HA5 46 E4
Coteford St TOOT SW17 147 K3
Cotelands CROY/NA CR0 178 A2
Cotesbach Rd CLPT E5 74 E2
Cotesmore Gdns BCTR RM8 79 J3
Cotford Rd THHTH CR7 164 D3
Cotham St WALW SE17 18 F6
Cotherstone HOR/WEW KT19 173 F7
Cotherstone Rd
BRXS/STRHM SW2 130 A7
Cotleigh Av BXLY DA5 155 K1
Cotleigh Rd KIL/WHAMP NW6 2 A1
ROMW/RG RM7 63 F5
Cotman Cl GLDGN NW11 53 G5
Cotman Ms BCTR RM8 79 H4
Cotmans Cl HYS/HAR UB3 82 E7
Coton Rd WELL DA16 136 B2
Cotsford Av NWMAL KT3 159 K4
Cotswold Av BUSH WD23 22 C5
Cotswold Cl BXLYHN DA7 118 B7
ESH/CLAY KT10 171 F1
KUTN/CMB KT2 144 E5
Cotswold Gdns CRICK NW2 70 B1
EHAM E6 95 H2
GNTH/NBYPK IG2 60 D6
Cotswold Ga CRICK NW2 52 C7
Cotswold Gn ENC/FH EN2 29 F3
Cotswold Ms BTSEA SW11 108 C7
Cotswold Rd HPTN TW12 142 A5
Cotswold St WNWD SE27 149 H3
Cotswold Wy ENC/FH EN2 29 F2
WPK KT4 174 A1
Cottage Av HAYES BR2 168 D7
Cottage Cl RSLP HA4 46 B7
RYLN/HDSTN HA2 66 D1
WAT WD17 20 D1
Cottage Field Cl SCUP DA14 136 D7
Cottage Gn CMBW SE5 110 E6
Cottage Gv BRXN/ST SW9 129 K2
SURB KT6 158 E5
Cottage Pl CHEL SW3 15 J3
Cottage Rd HOLWY N7 73 F4
HOR/WEW KT19 173 F6
The Cottages EDGW HA8 * 36 D6
Cottage St POP/IOD E14 93 K6
Cottenham Dr
CDALE/KGS NW9 51 H2
RYNPK SW20 145 K6
Cottenham Park Rd
RYNPK SW20 145 J7
Cottenham Pl RYNPK SW20 145 K6
Cottenham Rd WALTH E17 57 H3
Cotterill Rd SURB KT6 172 B1
Cottesbrook St NWCR SE14 112 B6
Cottesloe Ms STHWK SE1 18 B3
Cottesmore Av CLAY IG5 59 K1
Cottesmore Gdns KENS W8 14 D3
Cottimore Av WOT/HER KT12 156 A7
Cottimore Crs WOT/HER KT12 156 A6
Cottimore La WOT/HER KT12 156 A6
Cottimore Ter WOT/HER KT12 156 A6
Cottingham Cha RSLP HA4 64 E2
Cottingham Rd PGE/AN SE20 151 F6
VX/NE SW8 110 A6
Cottington Rd FELT TW13 141 H2
Cottington St LBTH SE11 18 B7
Cotton Av ACT W3 87 F5
Cotton Cl DAGW RM9 79 J6
WAN E11 76 C1
Cotton Gardens Est
LBTH SE11 18 C6
Cottongrass Cl CROY/NA CR0 166 A7
Cottonham Cl
NFNCH/WDSPK N12 39 H4
Cotton Hl BMLY BR1 152 B3
Cotton Rw BTSEA SW11 128 C2
Cottons Ap ROMW/RG RM7 63 F4
Cotton's Gdns BETH E2 7 K7
Cotton St POP/IOD E14 94 A6
Couchmore Av CLAY IG5 59 K1
ESH/CLAY KT10 170 E1
Coulgate St BROCKY SE4 132 B2
Coulson Cl BCTR RM8 61 J7
Coulson St CHEL SW3 15 L7
Coulter Cl YEAD UB4 83 J3
Coulter Rd HMSMTH W6 106 E2
Councillor St CMBW SE5 110 D6
Counter St STHWK SE1 13 J8
Countess Rd KTTN NW5 72 C4
Countisbury Av EN EN1 30 B6
Country Wy FELT TW13 141 G4
County Ga BAR EN5 27 F5
ELTH/MOT SE9 154 C2
County Gv CMBW SE5 110 D7
County Pde BTFD TW8 * 104 E6
County Rd EHAM E6 96 B4
THHTH CR7 164 C1
County St STHWK SE1 18 F4
Coupland Pl
WOOL/PLUM SE18 115 H4
Courcy Rd CEND/HSY/T N8 55 G2
Courier Rd DAGW RM9 98 E3
Courland Gv VX/NE SW8 109 J7
Courland St VX/NE SW8 109 J7
The Course ELTH/MOT SE9 154 A2
Courtauld Rd ARCH N19 54 D7
Courtaulds Cl THMD SE28 97 G7
Court Av BELV DA17 117 G4
Court Cl KTN/HRWW/WS HA3 49 K2
STJWD NW8 * 3 G2
WHTN TW2 142 B2
WLGTN SM6 176 D6
Court Close Av WHTN TW2 142 B2
Court Crs CHSGTN KT9 171 K5
Court Downs Rd BECK BR3 166 E1
Court Dr CROY/NA CR0 177 F3
STAN HA7 36 A3
SUT SM1 175 J3
Courtenay Av BELMT SM2 174 E7
HGT N6 53 J6
KTN/HRWW/WS HA3 34 B6
Courtenay Dr BECK BR3 167 G1
Courtenay Ms WALTH E17 57 G4
Courtenay Pl WALTH E17 57 G4
Courtenay Rd PGE/AN SE20 151 F6
WALTH E17 57 F4
WAN E11 * 76 D2
WBLY HA9 * 67 K2
WPK KT4 174 A2
Courtenay Sq LBTH SE11 18 A8
Courtenay St LBTH SE11 17 M7
Courten Ms STAN HA7 35 J6
Court Farm Av
HOR/WEW KT19 173 F4
Court Farm Rd ELTH/MOT SE9 153 H1
NTHLT UB5 66 A6
Courtfield Av HRW HA1 * 49 F4
Courtfield Crs HRW HA1 49 F4
Courtfield Gdns ECT SW5 14 D6
RSLP HA4 64 D1
WEA W13 85 G5
Courtfield Ms ECT SW5 14 D6
Courtfield Ri WWKM BR4 180 B2
Courtfield Rd SKENS SW7 14 E5
Court Gdns HOLWY N7 73 G5
Courtgate Cl MLHL NW7 37 H5
Courthill Rd LEW SE13 133 F3
Courthope Rd GFD/PVL UB6 84 D1
HAMP NW3 71 K3
WIM/MER SW19 146 C4
Courthope Vls
WIM/MER SW19 146 C6
Courthouse La
STNW/STAM N16 74 B3
Court House Rd FNCH N3 39 F5
Courtland Av CHING E4 44 D1
IL IG1 77 K1
MLHL NW7 37 F2
STRHM/NOR SW16 149 F6
Courtland Gv THMD SE28 97 K6
Courtland Rd EHAM E6 77 J7
Courtlands CHST BR7 154 B6
RCHPK/HAM TW10 125 H4
Courtlands Av HAYES BR2 167 H7
HPTN TW12 141 K5
LEE/GVPK SE12 134 A4
RCH/KEW TW9 125 J1
Courtlands Cl RSLP HA4 46 D6
Courtlands Dr
HOR/WEW KT19 173 G5
Courtlands Rd BRYLDS KT5 159 H6
Court La DUL SE21 131 G6
Court Lane Gdns DUL SE21 131 F6
Courtleigh Gdns GLDGN NW11 52 C3
Courtman Rd TOTM N17 41 J6
Court Md NTHLT UB5 83 K2
Courtmead Cl HNHL SE24 130 D5
Courtnell St BAY/PAD W2 8 A4
Courtney Cl NRWD SE19 150 A5
Courtney Crs CAR SM5 175 K6
Courtney Pl CROY/NA CR0 177 G2
Courtney Rd CROY/NA CR0 177 G2
HOLWY N7 73 G4
HTHAIR TW6 120 D2
WBLY HA9 67 K2
WIM/MER SW19 147 J6
Courtney Wy HTHAIR TW6 120 D2
Courtrai Rd FSTH SE23 132 B5
Court Rd ELTH/MOT SE9 153 J1
NWDGN UB2 102 E3
SNWD SE25 165 G1
Courtside HGT N6 54 D5
SYD SE26 * 150 E2
The Courts
STRHM/NOR SW16 148 E6
Courtstreet BMLY BR1 167 K1
Court St WCHPL E1 92 D4
The Court MUSWH N10 * 54 C3
RSLP HA4 65 J3
Court Vw HGT N6 * 72 B1
Court Wy ACT W3 86 E4
BARK/HLT IG6 60 C2
CDALE/KGS NW9 51 G3
WHTN TW2 124 A6
The Courtway OXHEY WD19 33 J1
Court Yd ELTH/MOT SE9 134 D5
Courtyard Ms RAIN RM13 81 H7
STMC/STPC BR5 155 G6
The Courtyards
WATW WD18 * 20 B6
The Courtyard IS N1 5 M1
Cousin La CANST EC4R 13 G6
Couthurst Rd BKHTH/KID SE3 114 A5
BKHTH/KID SE3 114 A6
Coutts Av CHSGTN KT9 172 A4
Coutts Crs KTTN NW5 * 72 A2
Couzins Wk DART DA1 139 J1
Coval Gdns MORT/ESHN SW14 125 J3
Coval La MORT/ESHN SW14 125 J3
Coval Rd MORT/ESHN SW14 125 K3
Covelees Wall EHAM E6 96 A5
Covent Gdn COVGDN WC2E 11 K6
Covent Garden Piazza
COVGDN WC2E 11 K6
Coventry Cl EHAM E6 95 K5
KIL/WHAMP NW6 2 B5
Coventry Cross Est BOW E3 94 A3
Coventry Rd IL IG1 60 B7
SNWD SE25 165 H3
WCHPL E1 92 D3
Coventry St SOHO/SHAV W1D 11 G7
Coverack Cl CROY/NA CR0 166 B6
STHGT/OAK N14 28 C5
Coverdale Gdns CROY/NA CR0 178 B2
Coverdale Rd CRICK NW2 70 C6
FBAR/BDGN N11 40 A5
SHB W12 87 K7
The Coverdales BARK IG11 96 D1
Coverley Cl WCHPL E1 * 92 C4
Coverton Rd TOOT SW17 147 J3
Coverts Rd ESH/CLAY KT10 171 F6
The Covert NRWD SE19 * 150 B6
NTHWD HA6 32 A6
ORP BR6 169 K5
Covert Wy EBAR EN4 27 G1
Covey Cl WIM/MER SW19 162 A1
Covey Rd WPK KT4 174 B1
Covington Gdns
STRHM/NOR SW16 149 H6
Covington Wy
STRHM/NOR SW16 149 G6
Cowbridge La BARK IG11 78 B6
Cowbridge Rd
KTN/HRWW/WS HA3 50 B3
Cowcross St FARR EC1M 12 C2
Cowdenbeath Pth IS N1 5 L3
Cowden St CAT SE6 151 J3
Cowdray Rd HGDN/ICK UB10 64 A7
Cowdray Wy HCH RM12 81 J3
Cowdrey Cl EN EN1 30 A1
Cowdrey Rd WIM/MER SW19 147 F5
Cowen Av HRW HA1 66 D1
Cowgate Rd GFD/PVL UB6 84 D2
Cowick Rd TOOT SW17 147 K3
Cowings Md NTHLT UB5 65 J6
Cowland Av PEND EN3 30 E3
Cow La BUSH WD23 * 22 A5
Cow Leaze EHAM E6 96 A5
Cowleaze Rd KUTN/CMB KT2 144 A7
Cowley Cl SAND/SEL CR2 178 E7
Cowley Ct WAN E11 * 76 C2
Cowley La WAN E11 * 76 C2
Cowley Pl HDN NW4 52 A4
Cowley Rd ACT W3 87 H7
BRXN/ST SW9 110 B7
IL IG1 59 K6
MORT/ESHN SW14 126 B2
WAN E11 59 F4
Cowley St WEST SW1P 17 J4
Cowling Cl NTGHL W11 88 C6
Cowper Av EHAM E6 77 J6
SUT SM1 175 H3
Cowper Cl HAYES BR2 168 C3
WELL DA16 136 B4
Cowper Gdns STHGT/OAK N14 28 B5
WLGTN SM6 176 C5
Cowper Rd ACT W3 87 F7
BELV DA17 117 G3
HAYES BR2 168 C3
HNWL W7 85 F6
KUTN/CMB KT2 144 B4
RAIN RM13 99 J3
STHGT/OAK N14 28 B7
STNW/STAM N16 74 A3
UED N18 42 C4
WIM/MER SW19 147 G5
Cowper St STLK EC1Y 7 H9
Cowper Ter NKENS W10 * 88 B4
Cowslip Rd SWFD E18 59 F1
Cowthorpe Rd VX/NE SW8 109 J7
Coxe Pl KTN/HRWW/WS HA3 49 G3
Cox La CHSGTN KT9 172 A3
Coxmount Rd CHARL SE7 114 C4
Coxson Wy STHWK SE1 19 L2
Coxwell Rd NRWD SE19 150 A6
WOOL/PLUM SE18 115 J4
Crab Hl BECK BR3 152 B6
Crabtree Av ALP/SUD HA0 86 A1
CHDH RM6 61 K3
Crabtree Cl BETH E2 7 L6
BUSH WD23 22 B4
Crabtree La FUL/PGN SW6 107 G6
Crabtree Manorway North
BELV DA17 117 K1
Crabtree Manorway South
BELV DA17 117 K2
Craddock Rd EN EN1 30 B2
Craddock St KTTN NW5 * 72 A5
Cradley Rd ELTH/MOT SE9 135 J7
Cragie Lea MUSWH N10 * 54 B1
Craigdale Rd EMPK RM11 63 H5
Craigen Av CROY/NA CR0 165 J7
Craigen Gdns IL IG1 78 E3
Craigerne Rd BKHTH/KID SE3 114 A6
Craig Gdns SWFD E18 58 D1
Craigholm WOOL/PLUM SE18 135 F1
Craigmuir Pk ALP/SUD HA0 68 B7
Craignair Rd
BRXS/STRHM SW2 130 A6
Craignish Av
STRHM/NOR SW16 164 A1
Craig Park Rd UED N18 42 D3
Craig Rd RCHPK/HAM TW10 143 J3
Craig's Ct WHALL SW1A 11 J8
Craigton Rd ELTH/MOT SE9 134 E3
Craigweil Cl STAN HA7 35 K4
Craigweil Dr STAN HA7 35 K4
Craigwell Av FELT TW13 140 E2
Crail Rw WALW SE17 19 H6
Crakers Md WATW WD18 * 21 F2
Cramer St MHST W1U 10 B3
Crammond Cl HMSMTH W6 107 H5
Cramond Ct
EBED/NFELT TW14 121 G7
Crampton Rd PGE/AN SE20 150 E5
Crampton St WALW SE17 18 E7
Cranberry Cl NTHLT UB5 83 H1
Cranberry La CAN/RD E16 94 C3
Cranborne Av NWDGN UB2 103 F3
SURB KT6 172 C2
Cranborne Rd BARK IG11 78 D7
Cranborne Waye YEAD UB4 83 F5
Cranbourne Av WAN E11 59 F3
Cranbourne Cl
STRHM/NOR SW16 163 K2
Cranbourne Dr PIN HA5 47 H4
Cranbourne Gdns
BARK/HLT IG6 60 C2
GLDGN NW11 52 C4
Cranbourne Rd MNPK E12 77 J4
MUSWH N10 54 B1
NTHWD HA6 46 D2
SRTFD E15 76 A3
Cranbourn St
LSQ/SEVD WC2H 11 H6
Cranbrook Dr ESH/CLAY KT10 157 H7
GPK RM2 63 K3
WHTN TW2 123 G7
Cranbrook La
FBAR/BDGN N11 40 B3
Cranbrook Ms WALTH E17 57 H4
Cranbrook Pk WDGN N22 41 G7
Cranbrook Ri IL IG1 59 K5
Cranbrook Rd CHSWK W4 106 B4
DEPT SE8 112 D7
EBAR EN4 27 H5
GNTH/NBYPK IG2 60 A5
HSLWW TW4 122 E3
IL IG1 78 A1
THHTH CR7 164 D1
WIM/MER SW19 146 C6
Cranbrook St BETH E2 93 F1
Cranbury Rd FUL/PGN SW6 128 A1
Crane Av ACT W3 86 E6
ISLW TW7 124 B4
Cranebank Ms TWK TW1 * 124 C4
Cranebrook WHTN TW2 142 C1
Crane Cl DAGE RM10 80 C5
Crane Ct FLST/FETLN EC4A 12 B5
MORT/ESHN SW14 * 125 K3
Craneford Cl WHTN TW2 124 A6
Craneford Wy WHTN TW2 123 K6
Crane Gdns HYS/HAR UB3 101 J3
Crane Gv HOLWY N7 73 G5
Crane Lodge Rd HEST TW5 102 A5
Crane Md BERM/RHTH SE16 112 A3
Crane Park Rd WHTN TW2 142 B1
Crane Rd STWL/WRAY TW19 120 D5
WHTN TW2 123 K7
Cranesbill Cl CDALE/KGS NW9 51 F2
STRHM/NOR SW16 163 J1
Cranes Dr BRYLDS KT5 159 F3
Cranes Pk BRYLDS KT5 159 F3
Cranes Park Av BRYLDS KT5 159 F3
Cranes Park Crs BRYLDS KT5 159 G3
Crane St PECK SE15 111 G7
Craneswater HYS/HAR UB3 101 J6
Craneswater Pk NWDGN UB2 102 E4
Cranes Wy BORE WD6 24 E4
Crane Wy WHTN TW2 123 H6
Cranfield Dr CDALE/KGS NW9 37 G7
Cranfield Rd BROCKY SE4 132 C2
Cranfield Rd East CAR SM5 176 A7
Cranfield Rd West CAR SM5 * 175 K7
Cranford Av PLMGR N13 40 E4
STWL/WRAY TW19 120 B6
Cranford Cl RYNPK SW20 145 K6
STWL/WRAY TW19 120 B6
Cranford Cots WAP E1W * 93 F6
Cranford Dr HYS/HAR UB3 101 J3
Cranford La HTHAIR TW6 121 J2
Cranford Ms HAYES BR2 168 D4
Cranford Park Rd
HYS/HAR UB3 101 J3
Cranford Ri ESH/CLAY KT10 170 C4
Cranford St WAP E1W 93 F6
Cranford Wy CEND/HSY/T N8 55 F4
Cranham Rd EMPK RM11 63 K5
Cranhurst Rd CRICK NW2 70 A4
Cranleigh Cl BXLY DA5 * 137 J5
PGE/AN SE20 165 J1
Cranleigh Gdns BARK IG11 78 D6
KTN/HRWW/WS HA3 50 A4
KUTN/CMB KT2 144 B5
SNWD SE25 165 F2
STHL UB1 83 K5
SUT SM1 175 F1
WCHMH N21 29 G4
Cranleigh Ms BTSEA SW11 128 D1
Cranleigh Rd ESH/CLAY KT10 157 H7
FELT TW13 140 D3
SEVS/STOTM N15 55 J4
WIM/MER SW19 161 K2
Cranleigh St CAMTN NW1 4 F6
Cranley Dr GNTH/NBYPK IG2 60 C6
RSLP HA4 64 D1
Cranley Gdns MUSWH N10 54 B3
PLMGR N13 41 F2
SKENS SW7 14 F7
WLGTN SM6 176 C6
Cranley Ms SKENS SW7 14 F7
Cranley Pl SKENS SW7 15 G6
Cranley Rd GNTH/NBYPK IG2 60 C5
PLSTW E13 95 F4
Cranley Ter HDN NW4 * 52 B1
Cranmer Av WEA W13 104 C2
Cranmer Cl MRDN SM4 161 G5
RSLP HA4 47 H7
STAN HA7 35 J6
Cranmer Ct HPTN TW12 142 B4
KUTN/CMB KT2 143 K3
Cranmer Farm Cl MTCM CR4 162 E3
Cranmer Gdns DAGE RM10 80 E3
Cranmer Rd BRXN/ST SW9 110 B6
CROY/NA CR0 177 H2
EDGW HA8 36 D2
FSTGT E7 77 F3
HPTN TW12 142 B4
HYS/HAR UB3 82 B5
KUTN/CMB KT2 144 A4
MTCM CR4 162 E3
Cranmer Ter TOOT SW17 147 H4
Cranmore Av ISLW TW7 103 H6
Cranmore Rd BMLY BR1 152 C2
CHST BR7 153 K4
Cranmore Wy MUSWH N10 54 C3
Cranston Cl HGDN/ICK UB10 64 B1
HSLW TW3 122 D1
Cranston Est IS N1 7 H5
Cranston Gdns CHING E4 43 K5
Cranston Rd FSTH SE23 132 B7
Cranswick Rd
BERM/RHTH SE16 111 J4
Crantock Rd CAT SE6 152 A1
Cranwell Cl BOW E3 93 K3
Cranwich Av WCHMH N21 29 K6
Cranwich Rd STNW/STAM N16 56 A6
Cranwood St FSBYE EC1V 7 H8
Cranworth Gdns
BRXN/ST SW9 110 B7
Craster Rd BRXS/STRHM SW2 130 A6
Crathie Rd LEE/GVPK SE12 134 A5
Cravan Av FELT TW13 140 E1
Craven Av EA W5 85 J6

STHL UB1 83 K4
Craven Cl STNW/STAM N16 * 56 C6
YEAD UB4 82 E5
Craven Gdns BARK IG11 96 E1
BARK/HLT IG6 60 D1
WIM/MER SW19 147 F4
Craven Hl BAY/PAD W2 8 F6
Craven Hill Gdns BAY/PAD W2 8 E6
Craven Hill Ms BAY/PAD W2 8 F6
Craven Ms BTSEA SW11 129 F2
Craven Pk WLSDN NW10 69 F6
Craven Park Ms WLSDN NW10 69 G6
Craven Park Rd
SEVS/STOTM N15 56 B5
WLSDN NW10 69 G7
Craven Pas CHCR WC2N 11 J8
Craven Rd BAY/PAD W2 8 F6
CROY/NA CR0 165 J7
KUTN/CMB KT2 144 B7
WEA W13 85 J6
WLSDN NW10 69 F7
Craven St CHCR WC2N 11 J8
Craven Ter BAY/PAD W2 8 F6
Craven Wk CLPT E5 56 C6
Crawford Av ALP/SUD HA0 67 K4
Crawford Cl ISLW TW7 123 K1
Crawford Gdns NTHLT UB5 83 K2
PLMGR N13 41 H2
Crawford Ms MBLAR W1H * 9 L3
Crawford Pas CLKNW EC1R 12 A1
Crawford Pl MBLAR W1H 9 K4
Crawford Rd CMBW SE5 130 D1
Crawford St MBLAR W1H 9 L3
WLSDN NW10 69 F6
Crawley Rd EN EN1 30 A6
LEY E10 57 K7
WDGN N22 55 J1
Crawthew Gv EDUL SE22 131 G3
Craybrooke Rd SCUP DA14 155 H3
Craybury End ELTH/MOT SE9 154 C1
Crayford Rd HOLWY N7 72 E3
Crayke Hl CHSGTN KT9 172 A6
Crayleigh Ter SCUP DA14 * 155 J5
Crayonne Cl SUN TW16 140 C7
Cray Rd BELV DA17 117 H5
SCUP DA14 155 J5
Crealock Gv WFD IG8 44 D4
Crealock St WAND/EARL SW18 128 A5
Creasey Cl EMPK RM11 81 K1
Crebor St EDUL SE22 131 H5
Credenhall Dr HAYES BR2 168 E7
Credenhill St
STRHM/NOR SW16 148 C5
Crediton Hl KIL/WHAMP NW6 71 F4
Crediton Rd WLSDN NW10 70 B7
Crediton Wy ESH/CLAY KT10 171 G4
Credon Rd BERM/RHTH SE16 111 J4
PLSTW E13 95 G1
Creechurch La HDTCH EC3A 13 K4
Creechurch Pl HDTCH EC3A * 13 K5
Creed La BLKFR EC4V 12 D5
Creek Cots E/WMO/HCT KT8 * 157 K3
Creek Rd BARK IG11 97 F2
DEPT SE8 112 D5
E/WMO/HCT KT8 157 K3
Creekside DEPT SE8 112 E6
RAIN RM13 99 H3
Creek Wy RAIN RM13 99 G5
Creeland Gv CAT SE6 132 C7
Crefeld Cl HMSMTH W6 107 G5
Creffield Rd EA W5 86 C6
Creighton Av EFNCH N2 53 K1
EHAM E6 95 H1
Creighton Cl SHB W12 87 K6
Creighton Rd EA W5 104 E2
KIL/WHAMP NW6 88 B1
TOTM N17 42 A6
Creigton Av EFNCH N2 53 J2
Cremer St BETH E2 7 L6
Cremorne Est WBPTN SW10 * 108 C5
Cremorne Gdns
HOR/WEW KT19 173 F7
Cremorne Rd WBPTN SW10 108 B6
Crescent TWRH EC3N 13 L6
Crescent Ar GNWCH SE10 113 F5
Crescent Av HCH RM12 81 H1
Crescent Dr STMC/STPC BR5 169 H5
Crescent Gdns RSLP HA4 47 F6
WIM/MER SW19 146 E2
Crescent Gv CLAP SW4 129 H3
MTCM CR4 162 D3
Crescent La CLAP SW4 129 J4
Crescent Pl CHEL SW3 15 J5
Crescent Ri EBAR EN4 27 J4
FNCH N3 * 38 D7
WDGN N22 40 D7
Crescent Rd BECK BR3 166 E1
BFN/LL DA15 155 F2
BMLY BR1 152 E6
CEND/HSY/T N8 54 D5
DAGE RM10 80 D2
EBAR EN4 27 H3
ED N9 30 C7
EHAM E6 77 G7
ENC/FH EN2 29 H3
FBAR/BDGN N11 39 K3
FNCH N3 38 D7
KUTN/CMB KT2 144 C6
LEY E10 75 K1
PLSTW E13 76 E7
RYNPK SW20 146 B7
SEVS/STOTM N15 * 55 H2
SWFD E18 59 G1
WDGN N22 40 D7
WOOL/PLUM SE18 115 G4
Crescent Rw STLK EC1Y 12 E1
Crescent St IS N1 5 M1
The Crescent ACT W3 87 G5
ALP/SUD HA0 67 H1
BAR EN5 27 F2
BARN SW13 126 C1
BECK BR3 151 J7
BXLY DA5 136 D6
CRICK NW2 69 K2
CROY/NA CR0 164 E5
E/WMO/HCT KT8 156 E3
FBAR/BDGN N11 39 K3
GNTH/NBYPK IG2 60 A5
HYS/HAR UB3 101 F6
NWMAL KT3 159 K1
RYLN/HDSTN HA2 48 C7
SCUP DA14 155 F3
STHL UB1 102 D1
SURB KT6 159 F4
SUT SM1 175 H4
WALTH E17 57 G4
WATW WD18 21 G3
WIM/MER SW19 146 E2
WWKM BR4 167 H5
Crescent Wy BROCKY SE4 132 D2
STRHM/NOR SW16 149 F6
Crescentway
NFNCH/WDSPK N12 39 J5
Crescent Wood Rd SYD SE26 150 C2
Cresford Rd FUL/PGN SW6 108 A7
Crespigny Rd HDN NW4 51 K5
Cressage Cl STHL UB1 84 A3
Cresset Rd HOM E9 74 E5
Cresset St CLAP SW4 129 J2
Cressfield Cl KTTN NW5 72 A4
Cressida Rd ARCH N19 54 C7
Cressingham Gv SUT SM1 175 G3
Cressingham Rd EDGW HA8 37 F5
LEW SE13 133 F2
Cressington Cl
STNW/STAM N16 74 A4
Cresswell Gdns ECT SW5 * 14 E7
Cresswell Pk BKHTH/KID SE3 133 J2
Cresswell Pl WBPTN SW10 14 E7
Cresswell Rd FELT TW13 141 J2
SNWD SE25 165 H3
TWK TW1 124 E5
Cresswell Wy WCHMH N21 29 G6
Cressy Ct HMSMTH W6 106 E2
WCHPL E1 92 E4
Cressy Houses WCHPL E1 * 92 E4
Cressy Pl WCHPL E1 92 E4
Cressy Rd HAMP NW3 71 K3
Cressys Cnr HSLW TW3 * 123 G2
Crestbrook Av PLMGR N13 41 H2
Crestbrook Pl PLMGR N13 * 41 G2
Crestfield St CAMTN NW1 5 K7
Crest Gdns RSLP HA4 65 G2
Creston Wy WPK KT4 161 G7
Crest Rd CRICK NW2 69 J1
HAYES BR2 167 J6
SAND/SEL CR2 178 D6
The Crest BRYLDS KT5 159 H4
HDN NW4 52 A4
HOLWY N7 * 72 D4
PLMGR N13 41 G3
Crest Vw PIN HA5 47 H3
Crest View Dr
STMC/STPC BR5 169 G4
Crestway PUT/ROE SW15 126 D5
Crestwood Wy HSLWW TW4 122 E4
Creswell Dr BECK BR3 166 E4
Creswick Rd ACT W3 86 D6
Creswick Wk GLDGN NW11 52 D3
Creukhorne Rd
WLSDN NW10 * 69 G6
Crewdson Rd BRXN/ST SW9 110 A6
Crewe Pl WLSDN NW10 87 H2
Crews St POP/IOD E14 112 D3
Crewys Rd CRICK NW2 70 D1
PECK SE15 131 J1
Crichton Av WLGTN SM6 176 D4
Crichton Rd CAR SM5 175 K6
Crichton St VX/NE SW8 * 129 H1
Cricketers Arms Rd
ENC/FH EN2 * 29 J1
Cricketers Cl CHSGTN KT9 171 K4
ERITH DA8 118 B4
STHGT/OAK N14 28 C6
Cricketers Ms
WAND/EARL SW18 128 A4
Cricketers Wk SYD SE26 150 E4
Cricketfield Rd CLPT E5 74 D3
Cricket Gn MTCM CR4 162 E2
Cricket Ground Rd CHST BR7 154 B7
Cricket La BECK BR3 151 G5
Cricket Rw EFNCH N2 * 53 H2
Cricklade Av
BRXS/STRHM SW2 148 E1
Cricklewood Broadway
CRICK NW2 70 B3
Cricklewood La CRICK NW2 70 C3
Cridland St SRTFD E15 76 D7
Crieff Ct TEDD TW11 143 J6
Crieff Rd WAND/EARL SW18 128 B5
Criffel Av BRXS/STRHM SW2 148 D1
Crimscott St STHWK SE1 19 K4
Crimsworth Rd VX/NE SW8 109 J6
Crinan St IS N1 5 K5
Cringle St VX/NE SW8 109 H6
Cripplegate St BARB EC2Y * 12 E2
Crispen Rd FELT TW13 141 J3
Crispian Cl WLSDN NW10 69 G3
Crispin Crs CROY/NA CR0 176 D1
Crispin Rd EDGW HA8 36 E5
Crispin St WCHPL E1 13 L3
Crisp Rd HMSMTH W6 107 F4
Cristowe Rd FUL/PGN SW6 * 127 J1
Criterion Ms ARCH N19 72 D1
Crockerton Rd TOOT SW17 147 K1
Crockham Wy ELTH/MOT SE9 154 A3
Crocus Cl CROY/NA CR0 166 A7
Crocus Fld BAR EN5 26 D5
Croft Av WWKM BR4 167 F7
Croft Cl ABYW SE2 117 G4
CHST BR7 153 K4
HYS/HAR UB3 101 F6
MLHL NW7 37 G2
Croft Ct BORE WD6 25 F2
RSLP HA4 * 46 D7
SUT SM1 * 175 H1
Croftdown Rd KTTN NW5 72 A2
Crofters Cl ISLW TW7 123 J4
Crofters Ct DEPT SE8 112 B3
Crofters Md CROY/NA CR0 179 H7
Crofters Rd NTHWD HA6 32 C3
Crofters Wy CAMTN NW1 5 G3
Croft Gdns HNWL W7 104 B1
RSLP HA4 46 C7
Croft Lodge Cl WFD IG8 45 F5
Croft Ms NFNCH/WDSPK N12 39 G2
Crofton Av BXLY DA5 136 E6
CHSWK W4 105 K6
Crofton Gate Wy BROCKY SE4 132 B4
Crofton Gv CHING E4 44 B3
Crofton La ORP BR6 169 K6
STMC/STPC BR5 169 J7
Crofton Park Rd BROCKY SE4 132 C5
Crofton Rd CMBW SE5 111 F7
PLSTW E13 95 F3
Crofton Ter RCH/KEW TW9 125 G3
Crofton Wy BAR EN5 * 27 F5
ENC/FH EN2 29 G1
Croft Rd BMLY BR1 152 E5
STRHM/NOR SW16 149 G6
SUT SM1 175 H4
WIM/MER SW19 147 G6
Crofts Rd HRW HA1 49 G5
Croft St DEPT SE8 112 B3
WCHPL E1 92 C6
The Croft ALP/SUD HA0 67 J4
BAR EN5 26 C3
CHING E4 44 C1
EA W5 86 A4
HEST TW5 102 D6
PIN HA5 47 K6
RSLP HA4 65 G3
WLSDN NW10 87 H1
Croft Wy BFN/LL DA15 154 E2
RCHPK/HAM TW10 143 H2
Crogsland Rd CAMTN NW1 4 A1
Croham Cl SAND/SEL CR2 178 A6
Croham Manor Rd
SAND/SEL CR2 178 A6
Croham Mt SAND/SEL CR2 178 A6
Croham Park Av
SAND/SEL CR2 178 B4
Croham Rd SAND/SEL CR2 177 K4
Croham Valley Rd
SAND/SEL CR2 178 C5
Croindene Rd
STRHM/NOR SW16 148 E7
Cromartie Rd ARCH N19 54 D6
Cromarty Rd EDGW HA8 36 D1
Cromarty Vls BAY/PAD W2 * 8 E6
Crombie Cl REDBR IG4 59 K4
Crombie Ms BTSEA SW11 * 128 D1
Crombie Rd BFN/LL DA15 135 J7
Cromer Cl UX/CGN UB8 82 A5
Cromer Hyde MRDN SM4 * 162 A4
Crome Rd WLSDN NW10 69 G5
Cromer Rd BAR EN5 27 G3
CHDH RM6 62 A5
HTHAIR TW6 120 D2
LEY E10 58 B6
SNWD SE25 165 J2
TOOT SW17 148 A5
TOTM N17 56 C1
Cromer Rd West HTHAIR TW6 120 D2
Cromer St STPAN WC1H 5 K8
Cromer Ter HACK E8 74 C4
Cromer Villas Rd
WAND/EARL SW18 127 J5
Cromford Rd PUT/ROE SW15 127 J4
Cromford Wy NWMAL KT3 145 F7
Cromlix Cl CHST BR7 169 G1
Crompton St BAY/PAD W2 9 G1
Cromwell Av HAYES BR2 168 A2
HGT N6 54 B7
HMSMTH W6 106 E4
NWMAL KT3 160 C4
Cromwell Cl CHSWK W4 * 105 J4
EFNCH N2 53 H3
HAYES BR2 168 A3
WOT/HER KT12 156 A7
Cromwell Ct ALP/SUD HA0 86 A1
PEND EN3 31 F4
Cromwell Crs ECT SW5 14 A5
Cromwell Gdns SKENS SW7 15 H5
Cromwell Gv HMSMTH W6 107 F2
Cromwell Ms SKENS SW7 * 15 G5
Cromwell Pde ALP/SUD HA0 * 86 A1
Cromwell Pl ACT W3 86 E7
HGT N6 * 54 B7
MORT/ESHN SW14 125 K2
SKENS SW7 15 H5
Cromwell Rd ALP/SUD HA0 85 K1
BECK BR3 166 B1
BRXN/ST SW9 110 C7
CROY/NA CR0 164 E6
ECT SW5 14 B5
FELT TW13 122 A7
FNCH N3 53 G1
FSTGT E7 77 G6
HSLW TW3 123 F3
HYS/HAR UB3 82 B5
KUTN/CMB KT2 144 A7
MUSWH N10 40 A6
SKENS SW7 14 D5
TEDD TW11 143 G5
WALTH E17 58 A4
WIM/MER SW19 146 E4
WPK KT4 173 F2
Cromwell St HSLW TW3 123 F3
Cromwell Ter HSLW TW3 * 123 F3
Crondace Rd FUL/PGN SW6 107 K7
Crondall St IS N1 7 H6
Cronin St PECK SE15 111 G6
Crooked Billet Rbt CHING E4 43 K6
Crooked Usage FNCH N3 52 C2
Crooke Rd DEPT SE8 112 B4
Crookham Rd FUL/PGN SW6 107 J7
Crook Log BXLYHS DA6 136 E2
Crookston Rd ELTH/MOT SE9 135 F2
Croombs Rd CAN/RD E16 95 G4
Croom's Hl GNWCH SE10 113 G6
Croom's Hill Gv GNWCH SE10 113 F6
Cropley St IS N1 7 G5
Croppath Rd DAGE RM10 80 C3
Cropthorne Ct MV/WKIL W9 2 F8
Crosby Cl FELT TW13 141 J3
Crosby Rd DAGE RM10 98 D1
FSTGT E7 76 E5
Crosby Rw STHWK SE1 19 G2
Crosby Sq HDTCH EC3A 13 J5
Crosby Wk HACK E8 74 B5
Crosier Cl BKHTH/KID SE3 114 D7
Crosier Rd HGDN/ICK UB10 64 A3
Crosier Wy RSLP HA4 64 C2
Crosland Pl BTSEA SW11 129 F2
Crossbrook Rd
BKHTH/KID SE3 134 D1
Cross Deep TWK TW1 143 F2
Cross Deep Gdns TWK TW1 143 F1
Crossfield Est DEPT SE8 112 D6
Crossfield Rd HAMP NW3 71 H5
TOTM N17 55 J2
Crossfield St DEPT SE8 112 D6
Crossford St BRXN/ST SW9 130 A1
Crossgate EDGW HA8 36 C2
GFD/PVL UB6 67 H5
Cross Keys Cl ED N9 42 C1
MHST W1U 10 B3
Cross Lances Rd HSLW TW3 123 G3
Crossland Rd THHTH CR7 164 C5
Crosslands Av EA W5 86 B7
NWDGN UB2 102 E4
Crosslands Pde NWDGN UB2 * 103 F4
Crosslands Rd
HOR/WEW KT19 173 F5
Cross La BXLY DA5 137 G6
CEND/HSY/T N8 55 F3
MON EC3R 13 J7
Crosslet St WALW SE17 19 H5
Crosslet V GNWCH SE10 112 E7
Crossley St HOLWY N7 73 G5
Crossmead ELTH/MOT SE9 134 E7
OXHEY WD19 21 F5
Crossmead Av GFD/PVL UB6 84 A2
Crossness Rd BARK IG11 97 F2
Cross Rd CHDH RM6 61 J6
CMBW SE5 131 F1
CROY/NA CR0 164 E7
EN EN1 30 A3
FBAR/BDGN N11 40 B4
FELT TW13 141 J3
HAYES BR2 181 J1
HRW HA1 48 D3
KTN/HRWW/WS HA3 49 G1
KUTN/CMB KT2 144 B6
OXHEY WD19 21 J5
ROMW/RG RM7 62 C2
RYLN/HDSTN HA2 66 A2
SCUP DA14 155 H3
SUT SM1 175 H4
WDGN N22 41 G5
WFD IG8 45 K5
WIM/MER SW19 146 E6
Cross St BARN SW13 126 B1
HPTN TW12 142 C4
IS N1 6 D3
UED N18 42 C4
WAT WD17 21 G2
Crossthwaite Av HNHL SE24 130 E3
Crosswall TWRH EC3N 13 L6
Cross Wy HYS/HAR UB3 101 K1
Crossway BCTR RM8 79 J2
CDALE/KGS NW9 51 H3
EN EN1 30 A6
NFNCH/WDSPK N12 39 H5
NWMAL KT3 161 F3
PIN HA5 47 F1
RSLP HA4 65 G3
STMC/STPC BR5 169 J3
STNW/STAM N16 74 A4
THMD SE28 97 J5
WEA W13 85 F3
Crossway Pde WDGN N22 * 41 H6
Crossways BELMT SM2 175 H7
GPK RM2 63 K2
SAND/SEL CR2 179 G6
SUN TW16 140 D7
Crossways Rd BECK BR3 166 D3
MTCM CR4 163 G2
Crossways Ter CLPT E5 * 74 E3
The Crossways BRYLDS KT5 * 159 J7
HEST TW5 102 E6
WBLY HA9 68 C1
The Crossway ELTH/MOT SE9 153 H1
The Cross Wy
KTN/HRWW/WS HA3 48 E1
The Crossway WDGN N22 41 H6
Croston St HACK E8 74 C7
Crosts La WDGN N22 41 G6
Crothall Cl PLMGR N13 41 F2
Crouch Av BARK IG11 97 H1
Crouch Cl BECK BR3 151 J5
Crouch Cft ELTH/MOT SE9 154 A2
Crouch End Hl
CEND/HSY/T N8 54 D6
Crouch Hall Rd
CEND/HSY/T N8 54 D5
Crouch Hl CEND/HSY/T N8 54 E6
Crouchmans Cl SYD SE26 150 B2
Crouch Rd WLSDN NW10 69 F6
Crowborough Pth
OXHEY WD19 33 H3
Crowborough Rd TOOT SW17 148 A4
Crowden Wy THMD SE28 97 J6
Crowder Cl
NFNCH/WDSPK N12 39 G6
Crowder St WCHPL E1 92 D6
Crowfoot Cl HOM E9 75 H4
THMD SE28 96 E7
Crowhurst Cl BRXN/ST SW9 130 B1
Crowland Av HYS/HAR UB3 101 H3
Crowland Gdns
STHGT/OAK N14 28 E6
Crowland Rd
SEVS/STOTM N15 56 B4
THHTH CR7 * 164 E3
Crowlands Av ROMW/RG RM7 62 D5
Crowland Ter IS N1 7 G1
Crowland Wk MRDN SM4 162 A5
Crow La ROMW/RG RM7 62 B6
Crowley Crs CROY/NA CR0 177 G4
Crowline Wk IS N1 * 73 J5
Crowmarsh Gdns FSTH SE23 131 K6
Crown Ar KUT/HW KT1 * 158 E1
Crownbourne Ct SUT SM1 * 175 F3
Crown Cl BOW E3 75 J7
HYS/HAR UB3 101 J1
KIL/WHAMP NW6 71 F5
MLHL NW7 37 H1
WOT/HER KT12 156 B6
Crown Ct HOL/ALD WC2B 11 K5
Crown Dl NRWD SE19 149 J5
Crowndale Rd CAMTN NW1 4 F5
Crownfield Av
GNTH/NBYPK IG2 60 E4
Crownfield Rd SRTFD E15 76 B4
Crown Green Ms WBLY HA9 68 A1
Crown Hl CROY/NA CR0 * 177 J1
Crownhill Rd WFD IG8 45 J6
WLSDN NW10 69 H7
Crown La CHST BR7 154 C7
HAYES BR2 168 C4
MRDN SM4 161 K2
STHGT/OAK N14 28 C7
STRHM/NOR SW16 149 G4
Crown Lane Gdns
STRHM/NOR SW16 * 149 G4
Crown Lane Sp HAYES BR2 168 C5
Crownmead Wy
ROMW/RG RM7 62 D3
Crown Office Rw EMB EC4Y 12 A6
Crown Pde MRDN SM4 * 162 A3
STHGT/OAK N14 * 28 C7
Crown Pas STJS SW1Y 10 F9
Crown Pl KTTN NW5 72 B5
SDTCH EC2A 13 J1
Crown Rd BARK/HLT IG6 60 D3
EN EN1 30 C2
KUTN/CMB KT2 144 E7
MRDN SM4 161 K3
MUSWH N10 40 A6
RSLP HA4 65 H4
SUT SM1 174 E3
TWK TW1 124 C5
Crownstone Rd
BRXS/STRHM SW2 130 B4
Crown St ACT W3 86 D7
CMBW SE5 110 D6
DAGE RM10 80 E5
RYLN/HDSTN HA2 48 D7
Crown Ter CRICK NW2 * 70 B3
RCH/KEW TW9 125 G3
STHGT/OAK N14 * 28 D7
Crowntree Cl ISLW TW7 104 A5
Crown Vls ACT W3 * 105 K1
Crown Wk WBLY HA9 68 B2
Crown Woods La
WOOL/PLUM SE18 135 G1
Crown Woods Wy
ELTH/MOT SE9 135 J4
Crown Yd HSLW TW3 123 H2
Crowshott Av STAN HA7 35 J7
Crows Rd BARK IG11 78 B5
BOW E3 94 B2
Crowther Av BTFD TW8 105 F4
Crowther Cl FUL/PGN SW6 107 J5
Crowther Rd SNWD SE25 165 H3
Crowthorne Cl
WAND/EARL SW18 127 J6
Crowthorne Rd NKENS W10 88 B5
Croxdale Rd BORE WD6 24 B1
Croxden Cl EDGW HA8 50 C2
Croxden Wk MRDN SM4 162 B5
Croxford Gdns WDGN N22 41 H6
Croxford Wy ROMW/RG RM7 63 F7
Croxley Gn STMC/STPC BR5 155 H7
Croxley Rd MV/WKIL W9 88 D2
Croxley Vw WATW WD18 20 C5
Croxted Cl DUL SE21 130 D6
Croxted Ms HNHL SE24 130 D5
Croxted Rd DUL SE21 130 D6
Croyde Av GFD/PVL UB6 84 C2
HYS/HAR UB3 101 H3
Croyde Cl BFN/LL DA15 135 J6
The Croydon F/O
CROY/NA CR0 177 H3
Croydon Gv CROY/NA CR0 164 C7
Croydon Rd BECK BR3 166 A4
CROY/NA CR0 176 E3
HAYES BR2 181 J2
MTCM CR4 163 G4
PGE/AN SE20 165 J1
PLSTW E13 94 D3
WLGTN SM6 176 B3
WWKM BR4 180 C2
WWKM BR4 181 F2
Croyland Rd ED N9 30 C7
Croylands Dr SURB KT6 159 F6
Crozier Ter HOM E9 75 F4
Crucible Cl CHDH RM6 61 H5
Crucifix La STHWK SE1 19 J1
Cruden St IS N1 6 D4
Cruickshank St FSBYW WC1X 6 A7
Cruikshank Rd SRTFD E15 76 C3
Crummock Gdns
CDALE/KGS NW9 51 G4
Crundale Av CDALE/KGS NW9 50 C4
Crunden Rd SAND/SEL CR2 177 K6
Crusader Gdns CROY/NA CR0 178 A2
Crusader Wy WATW WD18 20 D5
Crusoe Ms STNW/STAM N16 73 K1
Crusoe Rd MTCM CR4 147 K6
Crutched Friars TWRH EC3N 13 K6
Crutchfield La WOT/HER KT12 156 A7
Crutchley Rd CAT SE6 152 C1
Crystal Palace NRWD SE19 * 150 C6
Crystal Palace Pde
NRWD SE19 150 B5
Crystal Palace Park Rd
SYD SE26 150 C4
Crystal Palace Rd EDUL SE22 131 G5
Crystal Palace Station Rd
NRWD SE19 150 C5
Crystal Ter NRWD SE19 149 K5
Crystal Wy BCTR RM8 61 J7
HRW HA1 49 F4
Cuba Dr PEND EN3 30 E1
Cuba St POP/IOD E14 112 D1
Cubitt Sq NWDGN UB2 * 84 C7
Cubitt St FSBYW WC1X 5 M8
Cubitt Ter CLAP SW4 129 H2
Cuckoo Av HNWL W7 84 E3
Cuckoo Dene HNWL W7 84 D4
Cuckoo Hall La ED N9 30 E6
Cuckoo Hl PIN HA5 47 G2
Cuckoo Hill Dr PIN HA5 47 G2
Cuckoo Hill Rd PIN HA5 47 H3
Cuckoo La HNWL W7 84 E6
Cuda's Cl HOR/WEW KT19 173 H3
Cuddington Av WPK KT4 173 H2
Cudham St CAT SE6 132 E6
Cudworth St WCHPL E1 92 D3
Cuff Crs ELTH/MOT SE9 134 C6
Culford Gdns CHEL SW3 15 M6
Culford Gv IS N1 74 A5
Culford Ms IS N1 73 K5
Culford Rd IS N1 7 J1
Culgaith Gdns ENC/FH EN2 28 E3
Cullera Cl NTHWD HA6 32 D5
Culling Rd BERM/RHTH SE16 111 K2
Cullington Cl
KTN/HRWW/WS HA3 49 G3
Cullingworth Rd
WLSDN NW10 69 K4
Culloden Cl BERM/RHTH SE16 111 H4
Culloden Rd ENC/FH EN2 29 H1
Culloden St POP/IOD E14 94 A5
Cullum St FENCHST EC3M 13 J6
Culmington Pde WEA W13 * 85 J6
Culmington Rd SAND/SEL CR2 177 J6
WEA W13 85 J7
Culmore Rd PECK SE15 111 J6
Culmstock Rd BTSEA SW11 129 F4
Culpepper Cl UED N18 42 D4
Culross Cl SEVS/STOTM N15 55 J3
Culross St MYFR/PKLN W1K 10 A7
Culsac Rd SURB KT6 172 A1
Culverden Rd BAL SW12 148 C2
OXHEY WD19 33 F2
Culver Gv STAN HA7 49 J1
Culverhouse Gdns
STRHM/NOR SW16 149 F3
Culverlands Cl STAN HA7 35 H3
Culverley Rd CAT SE6 132 E7
Culvers Av CAR SM5 175 K1
Culvers Retreat CAR SM5 162 E7
Culverstone Cl HAYES BR2 167 J5
Culvers Wy CAR SM5 175 K1
Culvert Pl BTSEA SW11 129 F1
Culvert Rd BTSEA SW11 128 E1
SEVS/STOTM N15 56 A4
Culworth St STJWD NW8 3 J6
Cumberland Av WELL DA16 135 K2
WLSDN NW10 86 D2
Cumberland Cl HACK E8 74 B5
RYNPK SW20 146 B6
TWK TW1 124 C5
Cumberland Crs WKENS W14 107 H3
Cumberland Dr
ESH/CLAY KT10 171 G1
Cumberland Gdns
FSBYW WC1X 5 M7
HDN NW4 * 52 B1
Cumberland Ga BAY/PAD W2 9 L6
CAMTN NW1 4 C7
Cumberland House
KUTN/CMB KT2 144 D6
Cumberland Market
CAMTN NW1 4 D7
Cumberland Ms LBTH SE11 18 B8
Cumberland Pk ACT W3 86 E6
Cumberland Pl CAMTN NW1 4 C7
CAT SE6 133 J7
Cumberland Rd ACT W3 86 E6
BARN SW13 106 C7
ED N9 30 E7
HAYES BR2 167 H3
HNWL W7 104 A1
HRW HA1 48 B4
MNPK E12 77 H3
PLSTW E13 95 F4
RCH/KEW TW9 105 H7
SNWD SE25 165 J5
STAN HA7 50 B2
WALTH E17 57 G1

WDGN N22 55 F1
Cumberland St PIM SW1V 16 D7
Cumberland Ter CAMTN NW1 4 C6
PGE/AN SE20 * 150 D6
Cumberland Terrace Ms
CAMTN NW1 4 C6
Cumberlow Av SNWD SE25 165 H2
Cumbernauld Gdns
SUN TW16 140 D4
Cumberton Rd TOTM N17 41 K7
Cumbrae Gdns SURB KT6 171 K1
Cumbrian Av BXLYHN DA7 138 B1
Cumbrian Gdns CRICK NW2 70 B1
Cumming St IS N1 5 M6
Cumnor Cl BRXN/ST SW9 * 130 A1
Cumnor Gdns EW KT17 173 J5
Cumnor Rd BELMT SM2 175 G5
Cunard Crs WCHMH N21 29 K5
Cunard Rd WLSDN NW10 87 F2
Cundy Rd CAN/RD E16 95 G5
Cundy St BGVA SW1W 16 B6
Cunliffe Rd HOR/WEW KT19 173 H3
Cunliffe St STRHM/NOR SW16 148 C5
Cunningham Cl CHDH RM6 61 J4
WWKM BR4 179 K1
Cunningham Pk HRW HA1 48 D4
Cunningham Pl STJWD NW8 3 G9
Cunningham Rd
SEVS/STOTM N15 * 56 C3
Cunnington St CHSWK W4 105 K2
Cupar Rd BTSEA SW11 109 F7
Cupola Cl BMLY BR1 153 F4
Cureton St WEST SW1P 17 H7
Curlew Cl THMD SE28 97 K6
Curlew St STHWK SE1 19 L1
Curlew Wy YEAD UB4 83 H4
Curness St LEW SE13 133 F3
Curnick's La WNWD SE27 149 J3
Curran Av BFN/LL DA15 136 A4
WLGTN SM6 176 A2
Currey Rd NTHLT UB5 66 C5
Curricle St ACT W3 87 G7
Currie Hill Cl WIM/MER SW19 146 D3
Curry Ri MLHL NW7 38 B5
Cursitor St FLST/FETLN EC4A 12 A4
Curtain Pl SDTCH EC2A 7 K8
Curtain Rd SDTCH EC2A 13 J1
Curthwaite Gdns ENC/FH EN2 28 D3
Curtis Dr ACT W3 87 F5
Curtis Field Rd
STRHM/NOR SW16 149 F3
Curtis La ALP/SUD HA0 68 A5
Curtis Rd HOR/WEW KT19 172 E3
HSLWW TW4 122 E6
Curtis St STHWK SE1 19 L5
Curtis Wy STHWK SE1 19 L5
The Curve SHB W12 87 J6
Curwen Av FSTGT E7 77 F3
Curwen Rd SHB W12 106 D1
Curzon Av PEND EN3 31 F4
STAN HA7 35 G7
Curzon Crs BARK IG11 97 F2
WLSDN NW10 69 G6
Curzon Pl PIN HA5 47 G4
Curzon Rd EA W5 85 H3
MUSWH N10 54 B1
THHTH CR7 164 B5
Curzon St MYFR/PKLN W1K 10 B9
Cusack Cl TWK TW1 * 143 F3
Custom House Reach
BERM/RHTH SE16 * 112 C2
Cutcombe Rd CMBW SE5 130 D1
Cuthberga Cl BARK IG11 78 C6
Cuthbert Gdns SNWD SE25 165 F2
Cuthbert Rd CROY/NA CR0 177 H1
UED N18 42 C4
WALTH E17 58 A2
Cuthbert St BAY/PAD W2 9 G1
Cutlers Gardens Ar
LVPST EC2M 13 K4
Cutler St HDTCH EC3A 13 K4
The Cut STHWK SE1 18 B1
Cyclamen Cl HPTN TW12 142 A5
Cyclamen Wy HOR/WEW KT19 172 E4
Cygnet Av EBED/NFELT TW14 122 B6
Cygnet Cl NTHWD HA6 32 A6
WLSDN NW10 69 F4
The Cygnets FELT TW13 141 J3
Cygnet St WCHPL E1 7 M9
Cygnet Wy YEAD UB4 83 H4
Cymbeline Ct HRW HA1 * 49 F5
Cynthia St IS N1 5 M6
Cypress Av WHTN TW2 123 H6
Cypress Cl CLPT E5 74 C1
Cypress Gdns BROCKY SE4 132 B4
Cypress Pl FITZ W1T 10 F1
Cypress Rd
KTN/HRWW/WS HA3 48 D1
SNWD SE25 165 F1
Cypress Tree Cl BFN/LL DA15 136 A7
Cyprus Av FNCH N3 52 C1
Cyprus Cl FSBYPK N4 55 G6
Cyprus Gdns FNCH N3 52 C1
Cyprus Pl BETH E2 92 E1
EHAM E6 96 A6
Cyprus Rd ED N9 42 B1
FNCH N3 52 D1
Cyprus St BETH E2 92 E1
Cyrena Rd EDUL SE22 131 G5
Cyrus St FSBYE EC1V 6 D9
Czar St DEPT SE8 112 D5

D

Dabbling Cl ERITH DA8 * 118 E6
Dabbs Hill La NTHLT UB5 65 K4
D'Abernon Cl ESH/CLAY KT10 170 A3
Dabin Crs GNWCH SE10 113 F7
Dacca St DEPT SE8 112 C5
Dace Rd BOW E3 75 J7
Dacre Av CLAY IG5 60 A1
Dacre Cl GFD/PVL UB6 84 B1
Dacre Gdns BORE WD6 25 F4
LEW SE13 133 H3
Dacre Pk LEW SE13 133 H2
Dacre Pl LEW SE13 133 H2
Dacre Rd CROY/NA CR0 163 K6
PLSTW E13 77 F7
WAN E11 58 D7
Dacres Est FSTH SE23 * 151 F2
Dacres Rd FSTH SE23 151 F2
Dacre St STJSPK SW1H 17 G3
Dade Wy NWDGN UB2 102 E4
Daerwood Cl HAYES BR2 168 E7
Daffodil Cl CROY/NA CR0 166 A7
HPTN TW12 142 A5
Daffodil Gdns IL IG1 78 B4
Daffodil St SHB W12 87 H6
Dafforne Rd TOOT SW17 147 K2
Dagenham Av DAGW RM9 80 A6
Dagenham Rd DAGE RM10 80 E3
LEY E10 57 H7
Dagger La BORE WD6 23 G5
Dagmar Av WBLY HA9 68 B3
Dagmar Gdns WLSDN NW10 88 B1
Dagmar Ms NWDGN UB2 102 D2
Dagmar Pas IS N1 6 C3
Dagmar Rd CMBW SE5 111 F7
DAGE RM10 80 E6
FSBYPK N4 55 G6
KUTN/CMB KT2 144 B7
NWDGN UB2 102 D2
SEVS/STOTM N15 55 K3
SNWD SE25 165 F3
WDGN N22 40 D7
Dagmar Ter IS N1 6 D3
Dagnall Pk SNWD SE25 165 F4
Dagnall Rd SNWD SE25 165 F4
Dagnall St BTSEA SW11 128 E1
Dagnan Rd BAL SW12 129 G6
Dahlia Gdns IL IG1 78 B5
MTCM CR4 163 J3
Dahlia Rd ABYW SE2 116 C4
Dahomey Rd
STRHM/NOR SW16 148 C5
Daimler Wy WLGTN SM6 176 E6
Daines Cl MNPK E12 77 K2
Dainford Cl BMLY BR1 152 B4
Daintry Cl
KTN/HRWW/WS HA3 49 G3
Dairsie Rd ELTH/MOT SE9 135 F2
Dairy Cl BMLY BR1 * 153 F6
THHTH CR7 164 D1
WLSDN NW10 69 J7
Dairy La WOOL/PLUM SE18 114 E3
Dairyman Cl CRICK NW2 70 B2
Daisy Cl CROY/NA CR0 166 A7
Daisy La FUL/PGN SW6 127 K2
Daisy Rd SWFD E18 59 F1
Dakin Pl WCHPL E1 93 G4
Dakota Cl WLGTN SM6 177 F6
Dalberg Rd BRXS/STRHM SW2 130 B4
Dalberg Wy ABYW SE2 116 E2
Dalby Rd WAND/EARL SW18 128 B3
Dalbys Crs TOTM N17 42 A5
Dalby St KTTN NW5 72 B5
Dalcross Rd HSLWW TW4 122 D1
Dale Av EDGW HA8 36 B7
HSLWW TW4 122 D2
Dalebury Rd TOOT SW17 147 K1
Dale Cl BAR EN5 27 F5
PIN HA5 33 F7
Dale Dr YEAD UB4 82 D3
Dale Gdns WFD IG8 45 F3
Dale Green Rd
FBAR/BDGN N11 40 B2
Dale Gv NFNCH/WDSPK N12 39 G4
Daleham Gdns HAMP NW3 71 H4
Daleham Ms HAMP NW3 * 71 H5
Dalemain Ms CAN/RD E16 94 E7
Dale Park Av CAR SM5 175 K1
Dale Park Rd NRWD SE19 149 J7
Dale Rd KTTN NW5 72 A4
STHL UB1 84 B6
SUN TW16 * 140 D6
SUT SM1 174 D3
WALW SE17 110 C5
Dale Rw NTGHL W11 88 C5
Daleside Rd HOR/WEW KT19 173 F5
STRHM/NOR SW16 148 B4
Dales Pth BORE WD6 * 25 F4
Dales Rd BORE WD6 25 F4
Dale St CHSWK W4 106 B4
The Dale HAYES BR2 181 H3
Dale Vw BAR EN5 * 26 D2
ERITH DA8 138 D1
Dale View Av CHING E4 44 A1
Dale View Crs CHING E4 44 A2
Dale View Gdns CHING E4 44 B2
Daleview Rd
SEVS/STOTM N15 56 A5
Dalewood Gdns WPK KT4 173 K1
Dale Wood Rd ORP BR6 169 K6
Daley St HOM E9 75 F5
Daley Thompson Wy
VX/NE SW8 129 G1
Dalgarno Gdns NKENS W10 88 A4
Dalgarno Wy NKENS W10 88 A3
Dalkeith Gv STAN HA7 35 K4
Dalkeith Rd DUL SE21 130 D7
IL IG1 78 C2
Dallas Rd CHEAM SM3 174 C5
EA W5 86 B4
HDN NW4 51 J6
SYD SE26 150 D3
Dallas Ter HYS/HAR UB3 101 J2
Dallega Cl HYS/HAR UB3 82 A6
Dallinger Rd LEE/GVPK SE12 133 J5
Dalling Rd HMSMTH W6 106 E3
Dallington Sq FSBYE EC1V * 6 D9
Dallington St FSBYE EC1V 6 D9
Dallin Rd BXLYHS DA6 136 E3
WOOL/PLUM SE18 115 G6
Dalmain Rd FSTH SE23 132 A7
Dalmally Rd CROY/NA CR0 165 G6
Dalmeny Av HOLWY N7 72 D3
STRHM/NOR SW16 164 B1
Dalmeny Cl ALP/SUD HA0 67 J5
Dalmeny Crs HSLW TW3 123 J3
Dalmeny Rd BAR EN5 27 G5
CAR SM5 176 A6
HOLWY N7 72 D3
WPK KT4 173 K2
Dalmeyer Rd WLSDN NW10 69 H5
Dalmore Av ESH/CLAY KT10 171 F5
Dalmore Rd DUL SE21 149 J1
Dalrymple Cl STHGT/OAK N14 28 D5
Dalrymple Rd BROCKY SE4 132 B3
Dalston Gdns STAN HA7 36 A7
Dalston La HACK E8 74 B5
Dalton Av MTCM CR4 162 D1
Dalton Cl YEAD UB4 82 B3
Dalton St WNWD SE27 149 H1
Dalton Wy WAT WD17 21 H4
Dalwood St CMBW SE5 111 F7
Dalyell Rd BRXN/ST SW9 130 A2
Damask Crs CAN/RD E16 94 C3
Damer Ter WBPTN SW10 108 B6
Dames Rd FSTGT E7 76 E3
Dame St IS N1 6 E5
Damien St WCHPL E1 92 D4
Damon Cl SCUP DA14 155 H2
Damsel Ct BERM/RHTH SE16 * 111 H1
Damson Dr HYS/HAR UB3 82 E6
Damson Wy CAR SM5 175 K7
Damsonwood Rd
NWDGN UB2 103 F2
Danbrook Rd
STRHM/NOR SW16 148 E7
Danbury Cl CHDH RM6 61 K2
Danbury Ms WLGTN SM6 176 B3
Danbury Rd RAIN RM13 81 H7
Danbury St IS N1 6 D5
Danbury Wy WFD IG8 45 G5
Danby St PECK SE15 131 G2
Dancer Rd FUL/PGN SW6 107 J7
RCH/KEW TW9 125 H2
Dandelion Cl ROMW/RG RM7 81 G1
Dando Crs BKHTH/KID SE3 134 A2
Dandridge Cl GNWCH SE10 113 J4
Danebury CROY/NA CR0 179 K5
Danebury Av PUT/ROE SW15 126 C6
Daneby Rd CAT SE6 152 A2
Dane Cl BXLY DA5 137 H6
Danecourt Gdns
CROY/NA CR0 178 B2
Danecroft Rd HNHL SE24 130 D4
Danehurst Gdns REDBR IG4 59 J4
Danehurst St FUL/PGN SW6 107 H7
Daneland EBAR EN4 27 K5
Danemead Gv NTHLT UB5 66 B4
Danemere St PUT/ROE SW15 127 F2
Dane Pl BOW E3 93 G1
Dane Rd ASHF TW15 140 A5
IL IG1 78 C4
STHL UB1 83 J6
UED N18 42 E3
WEA W13 85 J6
WIM/MER SW19 147 G7
Danesbury Rd FELT TW13 122 A7
Danescourt Crs SUT SM1 175 G1
Danescroft Av HDN NW4 * 52 B4
Danescroft Gdns HDN NW4 52 B4
Danesdale Rd HOM E9 75 G5
Danes Ga HRW HA1 48 E2
Danes Rd ROMW/RG RM7 62 E6
Dane St GINN WC1R 11 L3
Daneswood Av CAT SE6 152 A2
Danethorpe Rd ALP/SUD HA0 67 K5
Danetree Cl HOR/WEW KT19 172 E6
Danetree Rd HOR/WEW KT19 172 E6
Danette Gdns DAGE RM10 80 B1
Daneville Rd CMBW SE5 110 E7
Dangan Rd WAN E11 58 E5
Daniel Bolt Cl POP/IOD E14 93 K4
Daniel Cl HSLWW TW4 122 E6
TOOT SW17 147 J5
UED N18 42 E3
Daniel Gdns PECK SE15 111 G6
Daniell Wy CROY/NA CR0 163 K7
Daniel Pl HDN NW4 51 K5
Daniel Rd EA W5 86 B6
Daniel's Rd PECK SE15 131 K2
Dan Leno Wk FUL/PGN SW6 * 108 A6
Dansey Pl SOHO/SHAV W1D 11 G6
Dansington Rd WELL DA16 136 B3
Danson Crs WELL DA16 136 C2
Danson La WELL DA16 136 C3
Danson Md WELL DA16 136 D2
Danson Rd BXLYHS DA6 136 E4
Danson U/P BFN/LL DA15 136 D5
Dante Rd LBTH SE11 18 C5
Danube Cl ED N9 42 E2
Danube St CHEL SW3 15 K7
Danvers Rd CEND/HSY/T N8 54 D3
Danvers St CHEL SW3 108 C5
Daphne Gdns CHING E4 44 A2
Daphne St WAND/EARL SW18 128 B5
Daplyn St WCHPL E1 92 C4
D'Arblay St SOHO/CST W1F 10 F5
Darby Crs SUN TW16 156 B1
Darby Gdns SUN TW16 156 B1
Darcy Av WLGTN SM6 176 C3
Darcy Cl TRDG/WHET N20 39 H1
D'Arcy Dr
KTN/HRWW/WS HA3 49 K3
D'Arcy Gdns DAGW RM9 80 B7
KTN/HRWW/WS HA3 50 A3
Darcy Rd ISLW TW7 104 B7
STRHM/NOR SW16 163 K1
D'Arcy Rd CHEAM SM3 174 B3
Darell Rd RCH/KEW TW9 125 H2
Darenth Rd STNW/STAM N16 56 B6
WELL DA16 116 B7
Darent Valley Pth DART DA1 139 H6
ERITH DA8 117 G7
Darfield Rd BROCKY SE4 132 C4
Darfield Wy NKENS W10 88 B6
Darfur St PUT/ROE SW15 127 G2
Dargate Cl NRWD SE19 150 B6
Darien Rd BTSEA SW11 128 C2
Darlands Dr BAR EN5 26 B4
Darlan Rd FUL/PGN SW6 107 J6
Darlaston Rd WIM/MER SW19 146 B6
Darley Cl CROY/NA CR0 166 A5
Darley Dr NWMAL KT3 160 A1
Darley Gdns MRDN SM4 162 A5
Darley Rd BTSEA SW11 128 E5
ED N9 30 B7
Darling Rd BROCKY SE4 132 D2
Darling Rw WCHPL E1 92 D3
Darlington Rd WNWD SE27 149 H4
Darmaine Cl SAND/SEL CR2 177 J6
Darndale Cl WALTH E17 57 H1
Darnley Rd HACK E8 74 D5
WFD IG8 44 E7
Darnley Ter NTGHL W11 88 B7
Darrell Rd EDUL SE22 131 H4
Darren Cl FSBYPK N4 55 F6
Darris Cl YEAD UB4 83 J3
Darsley Dr VX/NE SW8 109 J7
Dartford Av ED N9 30 E5
Dartford Gdns CHDH RM6 61 H4
Dartford Rd BXLY DA5 137 K7
Dartford St WALW SE17 18 F9
Dartmoor Wk POP/IOD E14 * 112 D3
Dartmouth Cl NTGHL W11 88 D5
Dartmouth Gv GNWCH SE10 113 F7
Dartmouth Hl GNWCH SE10 113 F7
Dartmouth Park Av
KTTN NW5 72 B2
Dartmouth Park Hl
KTTN NW5 72 B2
Dartmouth Park Rd
KTTN NW5 72 B2
Dartmouth Pl CHSWK W4 106 B5
FSTH SE23 150 E1
Dartmouth Rd CRICK NW2 70 B5
HDN NW4 51 J5
RSLP HA4 64 E2
SYD SE26 150 D2
Dartmouth Rw GNWCH SE10 133 F1
Dartmouth St STJSPK SW1H 17 G2
Dartmouth Ter GNWCH SE10 113 G7
Dartnell Rd CROY/NA CR0 165 G6
Dartrey Wk WBPTN SW10 * 108 B6
Dart St NKENS W10 88 D2
Darville Rd STNW/STAM N16 74 B2
Darwell Cl EHAM E6 96 A1
Darwin Cl FBAR/BDGN N11 40 B2
Darwin Dr STHL UB1 84 B5
Darwin Gdns OXHEY WD19 33 G4
Darwin Rd EA W5 104 D4
WDGN N22 41 H7
WELL DA16 136 A2
Darwin St WALW SE17 19 H5
Darygton Dr GFD/PVL UB6 84 D1
Dashwood Rd
CEND/HSY/T N8 55 F5
Dassett Rd WNWD SE27 149 H4
Datchelor Pl CMBW SE5 * 110 E7
Datchet Rd CAT SE6 151 H2
Date St WALW SE17 19 G8
Daubeney Gdns TOTM N17 41 J6
Daubeney Rd CLPT E5 75 G3
TOTM N17 41 J6
Dault Rd WAND/EARL SW18 128 B5
Davema Cl CHST BR7 154 A7
Davenant Rd ARCH N19 72 D1
Davenant St WCHPL E1 92 C4
Davenham Av NTHWD HA6 32 D3
Davenport Cl TEDD TW11 * 143 G5
Davenport Rd CAT SE6 132 E5
SCUP DA14 155 K1
Daventer Dr STAN HA7 35 F6
Daventry Av WALTH E17 57 J5
Daventry St CAMTN NW1 9 J2
Davern Cl GNWCH SE10 113 J3
David's Rd FSTH SE23 131 K7
David St SRTFD E15 76 B5
David Twigg Cl
KUTN/CMB KT2 144 A7
Davies Cl CROY/NA CR0 165 G5
Davies La WAN E11 76 C1
Davies Ms MYFR/PKLN W1K 10 C6
Davies St MYFR/PKLN W1K 10 C6
Davies Wk ISLW TW7 103 J7
Davington Gdns BCTR RM8 79 H4
Davington Rd BCTR RM8 79 H5
Davinia Cl WFD IG8 45 K5
Davis Rd ACT W3 87 H7
CHSGTN KT9 172 C3
Davis St PLSTW E13 95 F1
Davisville Rd SHB W12 106 D1
Dawes Av ISLW TW7 124 B4
Dawes Ct ESH/CLAY KT10 170 B3
Dawes Rd FUL/PGN SW6 107 J6
Dawes St WALW SE17 19 H7
Dawley Pde HYS/HAR UB3 * 82 A6
Dawley Rd HYS/HAR UB3 101 G1
Dawlish Av GFD/PVL UB6 85 G1
PLMGR N13 40 E3
WAND/EARL SW18 147 F1
Dawlish Dr GDMY/SEVK IG3 79 F3
PIN HA5 47 J4
RSLP HA4 64 E1
Dawlish Rd CRICK NW2 70 B5
LEY E10 76 A1
TOTM N17 56 C2
Dawnay Gdns
WAND/EARL SW18 147 H1
Dawnay Rd WAND/EARL SW18 147 G1
Dawn Cl HSLWW TW4 122 D2
Dawn Crs SRTFD E15 76 B7
Dawpool Rd CRICK NW2 69 H1
Daws La MLHL NW7 37 H4
Dawson Av BARK IG11 79 F6
Dawson Cl HYS/HAR UB3 82 B4
WOOL/PLUM SE18 115 H3
Dawson Dr RAIN RM13 81 K6
Dawson Gdns BARK IG11 79 F6
Dawson Pl BAY/PAD W2 8 A6
Dawson Rd CRICK NW2 70 A4
KUT/HW KT1 159 G2
Dawson St BETH E2 7 M6
Dawson Ter ED N9 * 30 E6
Daybrook Rd WIM/MER SW19 162 B1
Daylesford Av PUT/ROE SW15 126 D3
Daymer Gdns PIN HA5 47 G3
Daysbrook Rd
BRXS/STRHM SW2 130 A7
Days La BFN/LL DA15 135 K6
BFN/LL DA15 136 A5
Dayton Dr ERITH DA8 119 G5
Dayton Gv PECK SE15 111 K7
Deacon Cl PUR/KEN CR8 176 E7
The Deacon Est CHING E4 * 43 H5
Deacon Ms IS N1 7 H2
Deacon Rd CRICK NW2 69 J5
KUTN/CMB KT2 144 B7
Deacons Cl BORE WD6 24 C3
PIN HA5 47 F1
Deacons Hts BORE WD6 24 C5
Deacons Hl OXHEY WD19 21 G5
Deacon's Hill Rd BORE WD6 24 B4
Deacons Ri EFNCH N2 53 H4
Deacons Ter IS N1 * 73 J5
Deacons Wk HPTN TW12 142 A3
Deacon Wy WALW SE17 18 E5
WFD IG8 45 K6
Deakin Cl WATW WD18 20 C6
Deal Porters Wy
BERM/RHTH SE16 111 K2
Deal Rd TOOT SW17 148 A5
Deals Gtwy LEW SE13 112 E7
Deal St WCHPL E1 92 C4
Dealtry Rd PUT/ROE SW15 127 F3
Deal Wk BRXN/ST SW9 110 B6
Dean Bradley St WEST SW1P 17 J4
Dean Cl BERM/RHTH SE16 93 F7
HOM E9 74 E4
Dean Ct ALP/SUD HA0 67 H2
Deancross St WCHPL E1 92 E5
Dean Dr STAN HA7 50 A1
Deane Av RSLP HA4 65 F4
Deane Ct NTHWD HA6 * 32 C7
Deane Croft Rd PIN HA5 47 G5
Deanery Cl EFNCH N2 53 J3
Deanery Ms
MYFR/PKLN W1K * 10 B8
Deanery Rd SRTFD E15 76 C5
Deanery St MYFR/PKLN W1K 10 B8
Dean Farrar St STJSPK SW1H 17 H3
Deanfield Gdns
CROY/NA CR0 * 177 K3
Dean Gdns WALTH E17 58 B3
Deanhill Ct
MORT/ESHN SW14 * 125 J3
Deanhill Rd
MORT/ESHN SW14 125 J3
Dean Rd CRICK NW2 70 A5
CROY/NA CR0 177 K3
HPTN TW12 142 A4
HSLW TW3 123 G4
THMD SE28 97 G6
Dean Ryle St WEST SW1P 17 J5
Deansbrook Cl EDGW HA8 36 E6
Deansbrook Rd EDGW HA8 36 D6
Dean's Blds WALW SE17 19 H6
Deans Cl CHSWK W4 105 J5
CROY/NA CR0 178 B2
EDGW HA8 36 E5
Dean's Ct STP EC4M 12 D5
Deanscroft Av
CDALE/KGS NW9 68 E1
Deans Dr PLMGR N13 41 H5
Dean's Dr EDGW HA8 37 F4
Deans Gate Cl FSTH SE23 151 F2
Dean's La EDGW HA8 36 E5
Dean's Ms CAVSQ/HST W1G * 10 D4
Deans Rd SUT SM1 175 F2
Dean's Rd HNWL W7 104 A1
Dean Stanley St WEST SW1P 17 J4
Dean St FSTGT E7 76 E4
SOHO/SHAV W1D 11 G4
Deans Wy EDGW HA8 36 E4
Deansway ED N9 42 A2
EFNCH N2 53 H3
Deans Yd WEST SW1P 17 H3
Dean Trench St WEST SW1P 17 J4
Dean Wy NWDGN UB2 103 G1
Dearne Cl STAN HA7 35 G4
De'Arn Gdns MTCM CR4 162 D2
Dearsley Rd EN EN1 30 C2
Deason St SRTFD E15 * 76 A7
De Barowe Ms HBRY N5 73 H3
Debden Cl CDALE/KGS NW9 37 G7
KUTN/CMB KT2 143 K4
WFD IG8 45 H6
De Beauvoir Crs IS N1 7 J3
De Beauvoir Est IS N1 7 J3
De Beauvoir Rd IS N1 7 J1
De Beauvoir Sq IS N1 7 K2
Debnams Rd
BERM/RHTH SE16 111 K3
De Bohun Av STHGT/OAK N14 28 B5
Deborah Cl ISLW TW7 103 K7
Deborah Crs RSLP HA4 46 B6
De Broome Rd FELT TW13 122 B7
Deburgh Rd WIM/MER SW19 147 G6
Decima St STHWK SE1 19 J3
Decimus Cl THHTH CR7 164 E3
Deck Cl BERM/RHTH SE16 93 F7
Decoy Av GLDGN NW11 52 C4
De Crespigny Pk CMBW SE5 130 E1
Deeley Rd VX/NE SW8 109 J7
Deena Cl ACT W3 86 B5
Deepdale WIM/MER SW19 146 B3
Deepdale Av HAYES BR2 167 J3
Deepdale Cl FBAR/BDGN N11 40 A5
Deepdene Av CROY/NA CR0 178 B2
Deepdene Cl WAN E11 58 E3
Deepdene Ct WCHMH N21 29 H5
Deepdene Gdns
BRXS/STRHM SW2 130 A6
Deepdene Rd HNHL SE24 130 D3
WELL DA16 136 B2
Deepwell Cl ISLW TW7 104 B7
Deepwood La GFD/PVL UB6 84 D2
Deerbrook Rd HNHL SE24 130 C7
Deerdale Rd HNHL SE24 130 D3
Deere Av RAIN RM13 81 J5
Deerfield Cl CDALE/KGS NW9 51 H4
Deerhurst Cl FELT TW13 140 E3
Deerhurst Crs HPTN TW12 142 C4
Deerhurst Rd
KIL/WHAMP NW6 70 B6
STRHM/NOR SW16 149 F4
Deerings Dr PIN HA5 46 E4
Deerleap Gv CHING E4 31 K4
Dee Rd RCH/KEW TW9 125 G3
Deer Park Cl KUTN/CMB KT2 144 D6
Deer Park Gdns MTCM CR4 * 162 C3
Deer Park Rd WIM/MER SW19 162 A1
Deer Park Wy WWKM BR4 180 D1
Deeside Rd TOOT SW17 147 H2
Dee St POP/IOD E14 94 A5
Defence Cl THMD SE28 96 E7
Defiant Wy WLGTN SM6 176 E6
Defoe Av RCH/KEW TW9 105 H6
Defoe Cl TOOT SW17 147 J5
Defoe Pl TOOT SW17 147 J1
Defoe Rd BERM/RHTH SE16 112 C1
STNW/STAM N16 74 A1
De Frene Rd SYD SE26 151 F3
Degema Rd CHST BR7 154 B4
Dehar Crs CDALE/KGS NW9 51 H6
De Haviland Dr
WOOL/PLUM SE18 115 G4
Dehavilland Cl NTHLT UB5 83 H2
De Havilland Ct IL IG1 60 D7
De Havilland Rd EDGW HA8 50 D1
HEST TW5 102 B6
De Havilland Wy
STWL/WRAY TW19 120 A5
Dekker Rd DUL SE21 131 F5
Delacourt Rd BKHTH/KID SE3 114 A6
Delafield Rd CHARL SE7 114 A4
Delaford Rd
BERM/RHTH SE16 111 J4
Delaford St FUL/PGN SW6 107 H6
Delamare Crs CROY/NA CR0 165 K5
Delamere Gdns MLHL NW7 37 F4
Delamere Rd EA W5 86 A7
RYNPK SW20 146 B7
YEAD UB4 83 H6
Delamere St BAY/PAD W2 8 E3
Delamere Ter BAY/PAD W2 8 D2
Delancey Pas CAMTN NW1 4 D4
Delancey St CAMTN NW1 4 D4
De Laune St WALW SE17 18 C8
Delaware Rd MV/WKIL W9 2 C9
Delawyk Crs HNHL SE24 130 E5
Delcombe Av WPK KT4 161 F7
Delhi Rd EN EN1 30 B6
Delhi St IS N1 5 K4
Delia St WAND/EARL SW18 128 A6
Delisle Rd THMD SE28 96 E7
THMD SE28 115 K1
Delius Cl BORE WD6 23 J5
Delius Gv SRTFD E15 94 A1
Della Pth CLPT E5 74 C2
Dellbow Rd
EBED/NFELT TW14 122 A4
Dell Cl SRTFD E15 76 B7
WFD IG8 45 F2
WLGTN SM6 176 C3
Dell Farm Rd RSLP HA4 46 B4
Dellfield Cl BECK BR3 152 A7
WAT WD17 20 E1
Dell La EW KT17 173 J4
Dellors Cl BAR EN5 26 B4
Dellow Cl GNTH/NBYPK IG2 60 D6
Dellow St WCHPL E1 92 D6
Dell Rd EW KT17 173 J5
WDR/YW UB7 100 C2
Dells Cl CHING E4 31 K6
TEDD TW11 143 F5
Dell's Ms PIM SW1V * 16 F6
The Dell ABYW SE2 116 B4

ALP/SUD HA0 67 H4
BECK BR3 * 151 J6
BTFD TW8 104 D5
EBED/NFELT TW14 122 A6
NRWD SE19 150 B7
NTHWD HA6 32 C1
PIN HA5 47 H1
WFD IG8 45 F2
Dell Wk NWMAL KT3 160 B1
Dell Wy WEA W13 85 J5
Dellwood Gdns CLAY IG5 60 A2
Delme Crs BKHTH/KID SE3 134 A1
Delmey Cl CROY/NA CR0 178 B2
Deloraine St DEPT SE8 112 D7
Delorme St HMSMTH W6 107 G5
Delta Cl WPK KT4 173 G2
Delta Est BETH E2 * 92 C2
Delta Gain OXHEY WD19 33 H1
Delta Gv NTHLT UB5 83 H2
Delta Rd WPK KT4 173 G2
Delta St BETH E2 * 92 C2
De Luci Rd ERITH DA8 117 K4
De Lucy St ABYW SE2 116 C3
Delvers Md DAGE RM10 80 E3
Delverton Rd WALW SE17 18 D7
Delvino Rd FUL/PGN SW6 107 K7
Demesne Rd WLGTN SM6 176 D3
Demeta Cl WBLY HA9 68 E2
De Montfort Pde
STRHM/NOR SW16 * 148 E2
De Montfort Rd
STRHM/NOR SW16 148 D1
De Morgan Rd FUL/PGN SW6 128 A2
Dempster Cl SURB KT6 158 D6
Dempster Rd
WAND/EARL SW18 128 B4
Denbar Pde ROMW/RG RM7 62 E3
Denberry Dr SCUP DA14 155 H2
Denbigh Cl CHST BR7 153 K5
NTGHL W11 88 D6
STHL UB1 83 K5
SUT SM1 174 D4
Denbigh Dr HYS/HAR UB3 101 F1
Denbigh Gdns
RCHPK/HAM TW10 125 G4
Denbigh Pl PIM SW1V 16 E7
Denbigh Rd EHAM E6 95 H2
HSLW TW3 123 G1
NTGHL W11 88 D6
STHL UB1 83 K5
WEA W13 85 H6
Denbigh St PIM SW1V 16 E6
Denbigh Ter NTGHL W11 88 D6
Denbridge Rd BMLY BR1 168 E1
Den Cl BECK BR3 167 G3
Dendy St BAL SW12 129 F7
Dene Av BFN/LL DA15 136 C6
HSLW TW3 122 E2
Dene Cl BROCKY SE4 132 B2
HAYES BR2 167 J7
WPK KT4 173 H1
Dene Gdns STAN HA7 35 J4
THDIT KT7 171 G1
Denehurst Gdns ACT W3 86 D7
HDN NW4 52 A5
RCHPK/HAM TW10 125 H3
WFD IG8 45 F3
WHTN TW2 123 J6
Dene Rd NTHWD HA6 32 A5
TRDG/WHET N20 27 K7
The Dene CROY/NA CR0 179 F3
E/WMO/HCT KT8 156 E4
WBLY HA9 68 A3
WEA W13 85 H4
Denewood BAR EN5 27 G4
Denewood Rd HGT N6 53 J5
Dengie Wk IS N1 6 E3
Denham Cl WELL DA16 136 D2
Denham Crs MTCM CR4 162 E3
Denham Dr GNTH/NBYPK IG2 60 C5
Denham Rd
EBED/NFELT TW14 122 B6
TRDG/WHET N20 39 K1
Denham Wy BARK IG11 78 E7
Denholme Rd MV/WKIL W9 88 D2
Denholme Wk RAIN RM13 81 H5
Denison Cl EFNCH N2 53 G2
Denison Rd EA W5 85 J3
FELT TW13 140 D3
WIM/MER SW19 147 H5
Deniston Av BXLY DA5 136 E7
Denleigh Gdns THDIT KT7 * 157 K5
WCHMH N21 29 G6
Denman Dr ESH/CLAY KT10 171 G4
GLDGN NW11 52 E4
Denman Dr North
GLDGN NW11 52 E4
Denman Dr South
GLDGN NW11 52 E4
Denman Rd PECK SE15 111 G7
Denman St SOHO/SHAV W1D 10 F7
Denmark Av WIM/MER SW19 146 C6
Denmark Ct MRDN SM4 161 K4
Denmark Gdns CAR SM5 175 K2
Denmark Gv IS N1 6 A5
Denmark Hl HNHL SE24 130 E3
Denmark Hill Dr
CDALE/KGS NW9 51 J2
Denmark Rd BMLY BR1 153 F7
CAR SM5 175 K2
CEND/HSY/T N8 55 F3
CMBW SE5 110 D7
KIL/WHAMP NW6 88 D1
KUT/HW KT1 159 F2
SNWD SE25 165 J4
WEA W13 85 H6
WHTN TW2 142 D2
WIM/MER SW19 146 B5
Denmark St LSQ/SEVD WC2H 11 H5
PLSTW E13 95 F4
TOTM N17 42 D7
WAN E11 76 C2
WAT WD17 21 F1
Denmark Ter EFNCH N2 * 53 K2
Denmead Rd CROY/NA CR0 164 C7
Dennan Rd SURB KT6 159 G7
Denner Rd CHING E4 43 J1
Denne Ter HACK E8 7 M4
Dennett Rd CROY/NA CR0 164 B6
Dennett's Gv NWCR SE14 132 A1
Dennett's Rd NWCR SE14 111 K7
Denning Av CROY/NA CR0 177 G4
Denning Cl HPTN TW12 141 K5
STJWD NW8 2 F7
Denning Ms BAL SW12 129 F5
Denning Rd HAMP NW3 71 H3
Dennington Park Rd
KIL/WHAMP NW6 70 E5
The Denningtons WPK KT4 173 G1
Dennis Av WBLY HA9 68 B4
Dennis Cl ASHF TW15 140 B6
Dennis Gdns STAN HA7 35 J4
Dennis La STAN HA7 35 H3
Dennis Pde STHGT/OAK N14 * 28 D7
Dennis Park Crs RYNPK SW20 146 C7
Dennis Reeve Cl MTCM CR4 147 K7
Dennis Rd E/WMO/HCT KT8 157 H3
Dennis Wy CLAP SW4 129 J2
Denny Crs LBTH SE11 18 B7
Denny Gdns DAGW RM9 79 H6
Denny Rd ED N9 30 D7
Denny St LBTH SE11 18 B7
Den Rd HAYES BR2 167 G2
Densham Rd SRTFD E15 76 C7
Densole Cl BECK BR3 * 151 G7
Densworth Gv ED N9 42 E1
Denton Cl BAR EN5 26 A4
Denton Rd CEND/HSY/T N8 55 F4
TWK TW1 124 E5
UED N18 42 A3
WELL DA16 116 D6
Denton St WAND/EARL SW18 128 A5
Denton Wy CLPT E5 75 F2
Dents Rd BTSEA SW11 128 E5
Denvale Trade Pk MTCM CR4 162 C3
Denver Cl ORP BR6 169 K5
Denver Rd STNW/STAM N16 56 A6
Denyer St CHEL SW3 15 K5
Denzil Rd WLSDN NW10 69 H4
Deodar Rd PUT/ROE SW15 127 H3
Deodora Cl TRDG/WHET N20 39 J2
Depot Ap CRICK NW2 70 B3
Depot Rd HSLW TW3 123 J2
Depot St CMBW SE5 110 E5
Deptford Br DEPT SE8 112 D7
Deptford Broadway
NWCR SE14 112 D7
Deptford Church St DEPT SE8 112 D5
Deptford Gn DEPT SE8 112 D5
Deptford High St DEPT SE8 112 D5
Deptford Whf DEPT SE8 112 C3
De Quincey Ms CAN/RD E16 94 E7
De Quincey Rd TOTM N17 41 K7
Derby Av KTN/HRWW/WS HA3 34 D7
NFNCH/WDSPK N12 39 G4
ROMW/RG RM7 62 D5
Derby Ga WHALL SW1A 17 J1
Derby Hl FSTH SE23 150 E1
Derby Hill Crs FSTH SE23 150 E1
Derby Rd BRYLDS KT5 159 H7
CROY/NA CR0 177 H1
FSTGT E7 77 H6
GFD/PVL UB6 66 B7
HOM E9 75 F7
HSLW TW3 123 G3
MORT/ESHN SW14 125 J3
PEND EN3 30 D4
SUT SM1 174 D5
SWFD E18 44 D7
UED N18 42 E4
WAT WD17 21 G3
WIM/MER SW19 146 E6
Derbyshire St BETH E2 92 D2
Derby St MYFR/PICC W1J 10 B9
Dereham Pl SDTCH EC2A 7 K9
Dereham Rd BARK IG11 79 F5
Derek Av HOR/WEW KT19 172 C5
WBLY HA9 68 D6
WLGTN SM6 176 B3
Derek Cl HOR/WEW KT19 172 D4
Derek Walcott Cl HNHL SE24 * 130 C4
Deri Av RAIN RM13 99 K3
Dericote St HACK E8 74 C7
Deri Dene Cl
STWL/WRAY TW19 * 120 B5
Derifall Cl EHAM E6 95 K4
Dering Pl CROY/NA CR0 177 J3
Dering Rd CROY/NA CR0 177 J3
Dering St OXSTW W1C 10 C5
Derinton Rd TOOT SW17 148 A3
Derley Rd NWDGN UB2 102 B2
Dermody Gdns LEW SE13 * 133 G4
Dermody Rd LEW SE13 133 G4
Deronda Rd HNHL SE24 130 C7
Deroy Cl CAR SM5 175 K5
Derrick Gdns CHARL SE7 114 B2
Derrick Rd BECK BR3 166 C2
Derry Rd CROY/NA CR0 176 E2
Derry St KENS W8 14 C2
Dersingham Av MNPK E12 77 K3
Dersingham Rd CRICK NW2 70 C2
Derwent Av CDALE/KGS NW9 51 G4
EBAR EN4 27 K7
MLHL NW7 37 F4
PIN HA5 33 J5
PUT/ROE SW15 145 G3
UED N18 41 K4
Derwent Cl EBED/NFELT TW14 121 J7
ESH/CLAY KT10 170 E5
Derwent Crs
NFNCH/WDSPK N12 39 G2
STAN HA7 49 J1
Derwent Dr STMC/STPC BR5 169 J6
YEAD UB4 82 C4
Derwent Gdns REDBR IG4 59 J3
WBLY HA9 49 J6
Derwent Gv EDUL SE22 131 G3
Derwent Ri CDALE/KGS NW9 51 G5
Derwent Rd EA W5 104 D2
PGE/AN SE20 165 H1
PLMGR N13 41 F3
RYNPK SW20 161 G5
STHL UB1 83 K5
WHTN TW2 123 G5
Derwent St GNWCH SE10 113 H4
Derwentwater Rd ACT W3 86 E7
Derwent Wy HCH RM12 81 K4
Derwent Yd EA W5 * 104 D2
De Salis Rd HGDN/ICK UB10 82 A3
Desenfans Rd DUL SE21 131 F5
Desford Rd CAN/RD E16 94 C3
Desmond St NWCR SE14 112 B5
Desmond Tutu Dr FSTH SE23 132 B7
Despard Rd ARCH N19 54 C7
Desvignes Dr LEW SE13 133 G5
Detling Rd BMLY BR1 152 E4
ERITH DA8 118 A6
Detmold Rd CLPT E5 74 D1
Devalls Cl EHAM E6 96 A6
Devana End CAR SM5 175 K2
Devas Rd RYNPK SW20 146 A7
Devas St BOW E3 93 K3
Devenay Rd SRTFD E15 76 D6
Devenish Rd ABYW SE2 116 B1
Deveraux Cl BECK BR3 167 F4
De Vere Cl WLGTN SM6 176 E6
De Vere Gdns IL IG1 59 K7
KENS W8 14 E2
Deverell St STHWK SE1 19 G4
De Vere Ms KENS W8 14 E3
Devereux Ct TPL/STR WC2R 12 A6
Devereux La BARN SW13 106 E6
Devereux Rd BTSEA SW11 128 E5
De Vere Wk WAT WD17 20 C1
Devey Cl KUTN/CMB KT2 145 H6
Devizes St IS N1 * 7 H4
Devon Av WHTN TW2 123 H7
Devon Cl BKHH IG9 45 F1
GFD/PVL UB6 67 J7
TOTM N17 56 B2
Devoncroft Gdns TWK TW1 124 B6
Devon Gdns FSBYPK N4 55 H5
Devonhurst Pl CHSWK W4 * 106 A4
Devonia Gdns UED N18 41 J5
Devonia Rd IS N1 6 D5
Devon Man
KTN/HRWW/WS HA3 * 49 J4
Devonport Gdns IL IG1 59 K5
Devonport Ms SHB W12 * 87 K7
Devonport Rd SHB W12 106 E1
Devonport St WCHPL E1 92 E5
Devon Ri EFNCH N2 53 H3
Devon Rd BARK IG11 78 E7
BELMT SM2 174 C7
Devons Est BOW E3 93 K2
Devonshire Av BELMT SM2 175 G6
Devonshire Cl
CAVSQ/HST W1G 10 C2
SRTFD E15 76 C3
Devonshire Ct FELT TW13 * 141 F1
Devonshire Crs MLHL NW7 38 B6
Devonshire Dr GNWCH SE10 112 E7
SURB KT6 158 E7
Devonshire Gdns CHSWK W4 105 K6
TOTM N17 41 J5
WCHMH N21 29 J6
Devonshire Gv PECK SE15 111 J5
Devonshire Hill La TOTM N17 41 J5
Devonshire Ms CHSWK W4 106 B4
Devonshire Ms South
CAVSQ/HST W1G 10 C2
Devonshire Ms West
CAVSQ/HST W1G 10 B1
Devonshire Pl
CAVSQ/HST W1G 10 B1
CRICK NW2 70 E2
KENS W8 * 14 C4
Devonshire Place Ms
CAVSQ/HST W1G 10 B1
Devonshire Rd BELMT SM2 175 G6
CAN/RD E16 95 F5
CAR SM5 176 A3
CHSWK W4 106 B4
CROY/NA CR0 164 E6
EA W5 104 D2
ED N9 30 E7
ELTH/MOT SE9 153 J1
FELT TW13 141 J2
FSTH SE23 132 A6
GNTH/NBYPK IG2 60 D6
HRW HA1 48 D5
MLHL NW7 38 B6
PIN HA5 47 G5
PLMGR N13 41 F3
STHL UB1 84 A4
TOTM N17 41 J5
WALTH E17 57 J5
WIM/MER SW19 147 J6
Devonshire Rw LVPST EC2M 13 K3
Devonshire Row Ms
GTPST W1W 10 D1
Devonshire Sq HAYES BR2 168 A3
LVPST EC2M 13 K4
Devonshire St
CAVSQ/HST W1G 10 B2
CHSWK W4 106 B4
Devonshire Ter BAY/PAD W2 8 F5
EDUL SE22 * 131 H3
Devonshire Wy CROY/NA CR0 179 H1
YEAD UB4 83 F5
Devons Rd BOW E3 93 J4
Devon St PECK SE15 111 J5
Devon Wy CHSGTN KT9 171 J3
HOR/WEW KT19 172 D4
Devon Waye HEST TW5 102 E6
De Walden St
CAVSQ/HST W1G 10 B3
Dewar St PECK SE15 131 H2
Dewberry Gdns EHAM E6 95 J4
Dewberry St POP/IOD E14 94 A5
Dewey La BRXS/STRHM SW2 130 B5
Dewey Rd DAGE RM10 80 E5
IS N1 6 A5
Dewey St TOOT SW17 147 K4
Dewhurst Rd HMSMTH W6 107 G2
Dewsbury Cl PIN HA5 47 J5
Dewsbury Gdns WPK KT4 173 J2
Dewsbury Rd WLSDN NW10 69 J4
Dexter Rd BAR EN5 26 B5
Deyncourt Rd TOTM N17 41 J7
Deynecourt Gdns WAN E11 59 G3
D'Eynsford Rd CMBW SE5 110 E7
Diadem Ct SOHO/CST W1F 11 G4
Diamedes Av
STWL/WRAY TW19 120 A6
Diameter Rd STMC/STPC BR5 169 G6
Diamond Cl BCTR RM8 61 J7
Diamond Rd RSLP HA4 65 H3
Diamond St CMBW SE5 111 F6
WLSDN NW10 69 F6
Diamond Ter GNWCH SE10 113 F7
Diana Cl DEPT SE8 112 C5
SWFD E18 45 F7
Diana Gdns SURB KT6 172 B1
Diana Rd WALTH E17 57 H2
Dianne Wy EBAR EN4 27 J3
Dianthus Cl ABYW SE2 * 116 C4
Diban Av HCH RM12 81 K3
Dibden St IS N1 6 E3
Dibdin Cl SUT SM1 174 E2
Dibdin Rd SUT SM1 174 E2
Dicey Av CRICK NW2 70 A4
Dickens Av DART DA1 139 K3
FNCH N3 39 G7
Dickens Cl HYS/HAR UB3 101 H3
RCHPK/HAM TW10 144 A1
Dickens Dr CHST BR7 154 C5
Dickens Est
BERM/RHTH SE16 * 111 H2
Dickens La UED N18 42 A4
Dickens Ms FARR EC1M 12 C1
Dickenson Cl ED N9 30 C7
Dickenson Rd
CEND/HSY/T N8 54 E6
FELT TW13 141 G4
Dickenson's La SNWD SE25 165 H5
Dickenson's Pl SNWD SE25 165 H5
Dickens Rd EHAM E6 95 H1
Dickens Sq STHWK SE1 18 F3
Dickens St VX/NE SW8 129 G1
Dickens Wy ROM RM1 63 G3
Dickens Wood Cl
NRWD SE19 149 H6
Dickerage La NWMAL KT3 159 K2
Dickerage Rd KUT/HW KT1 144 E7
NWMAL KT3 159 K1
Dickson Fold PIN HA5 47 H3
Dickson House CHARL SE7 * 114 D6
Dickson Rd ELTH/MOT SE9 134 D2
Dick Turpin Wy
EBED/NFELT TW14 121 J3
Didsbury Cl EHAM E6 77 K7
Digby Crs FSBYPK N4 73 J1
Digby Gdns DAGE RM10 80 C7
Digby Pl CROY/NA CR0 178 B2
Digby Rd BARK IG11 79 F6
HOM E9 75 F5
Digby St BETH E2 92 E2
Diggon St WCHPL E1 93 F4
Dighton Rd WAND/EARL SW18 128 B4
Dignum St IS N1 * 6 A5
Digswell St HOLWY N7 * 73 G5
Dilhorne Cl LEE/GVPK SE12 153 F2
Dilke St CHEL SW3 15 M9
Dillwyn Cl SYD SE26 151 G3
Dilston Cl NTHLT UB5 83 G2
Dilton Gdns PUT/ROE SW15 126 D7
Dimes Pl HMSMTH W6 106 E3
Dimmock Dr GFD/PVL UB6 66 D4
Dimond Cl FSTGT E7 76 E3
Dimsdale Dr CDALE/KGS NW9 50 E7
EN EN1 30 C6
Dimsdale Wk PLSTW E13 76 E7
Dimson Crs BOW E3 93 J3
Dingle Cl BAR EN5 25 H5
Dingle Gdns POP/IOD E14 * 93 J6
Dingley La STRHM/NOR SW16 148 D1
Dingley Pl FSBYE EC1V 6 F8
Dingley Rd FSBYE EC1V 6 E8
Dingwall Av CROY/NA CR0 177 J1
Dingwall Gdns GLDGN NW11 52 E5
Dingwall Rd CAR SM5 175 K7
CROY/NA CR0 177 K1
WAND/EARL SW18 128 B6
Dinmont St BETH E2 92 D1
Dinsdale Gdns BAR EN5 27 F4
SNWD SE25 165 F4
Dinsdale Rd BKHTH/KID SE3 113 J5
Dinsmore Rd BAL SW12 129 G6
Dinton Rd KUTN/CMB KT2 144 B6
WIM/MER SW19 147 H5
Diploma Av EFNCH N2 53 J3
Dirleton Rd SRTFD E15 76 D7
Disbrowe Rd HMSMTH W6 107 H5
Discovery Wk WAP E1W 92 D6
Dishforth La CDALE/KGS NW9 37 G7
Disney Pl STHWK SE1 18 F1
Disney St STHWK SE1 18 F1
Disraeli Cl THMD SE28 97 H7
Disraeli Rd EA W5 85 K7
FSTGT E7 76 E5
PUT/ROE SW15 127 H3
WLSDN NW10 86 E1
Diss St BETH E2 7 L7
Distaff La BLKFR EC4V 12 E6
Distillery La HMSMTH W6 107 F4
Distillery Rd HMSMTH W6 107 F4
Distin St LBTH SE11 18 A6
District Rd ALP/SUD HA0 67 H4
Ditchburn St POP/IOD E14 94 A6
Ditchfield Rd YEAD UB4 83 J3
Dittisham Rd ELTH/MOT SE9 153 J3
Ditton Cl THDIT KT7 158 B6
Dittoncroft Cl CROY/NA CR0 178 A3
Ditton Grange Cl SURB KT6 158 E7
Ditton Grange Dr SURB KT6 158 E7
Ditton Hl SURB KT6 158 D7
Ditton Hill Rd SURB KT6 158 D7
Ditton Lawn THDIT KT7 158 B7
Ditton Pl PGE/AN SE20 * 150 D7
Ditton Reach THDIT KT7 158 C5
Ditton Rd BXLYHS DA6 136 E4
NWDGN UB2 102 E4
SURB KT6 159 F7
Dixey Cots EFNCH N2 * 53 J4
Dixon Cl EHAM E6 95 K5
Dixon Pl WWKM BR4 166 E7
Dixon Rd NWCR SE14 112 B7
SNWD SE25 165 F2
Dixon Wy WLSDN NW10 69 G6
Dobbin Cl
KTN/HRWW/WS HA3 49 G1
Dobell Rd ELTH/MOT SE9 134 E4
Dobree Av WLSDN NW10 69 K6
Dobson Cl KIL/WHAMP NW6 3 G2
Dockers Tanner Rd
POP/IOD E14 112 D3
Dockhead STHWK SE1 19 M2
Dock Hill Av BERM/RHTH SE16 112 A1
Dockland St CAN/RD E16 96 A7
CAN/RD E16 115 F1
Dockley Rd BERM/RHTH SE16 111 H2
Dock Rd BTFD TW8 * 104 E6
CAN/RD E16 94 D6
Dockside Rd CAN/RD E16 95 H6
Dock St WCHPL E1 92 C6
Dockwell Cl
EBED/NFELT TW14 121 K3
Doctors Cl SYD SE26 150 E4
Docwra's Blds IS N1 74 A5
Dodbrooke Rd WNWD SE27 149 G2
Doddington Gv WALW SE17 18 C9
Doddington Pl WALW SE17 18 C9
Dodsley Pl ED N9 42 E2
Dodson St STHWK SE1 18 B2
Dod St POP/IOD E14 93 J5
Doebury Wk
WOOL/PLUM SE18 116 B5
Doel Cl WIM/MER SW19 147 G6
Doggett Rd CAT SE6 132 D6
Doggetts Ct EBAR EN4 27 J4
Doghurst Av WDR/YW UB7 100 E6
Doghurst Dr WDR/YW UB7 100 E6
Dog Kennel Hl CMBW SE5 131 F2
Dog La WLSDN NW10 69 G3
Dog Rose Ramble YEAD UB4 64 E7
Dog Rose Ramble & Hillingdon
Trail YEAD UB4 82 D1
Doherty Rd PLSTW E13 94 E3
Dolben Ct DEPT SE8 * 112 C3
Dolben St STHWK SE1 * 12 D9
Dolby Rd FUL/PGN SW6 127 J1
Dolland St LBTH SE11 17 M8
Dollary Pde KUT/HW KT1 * 159 J2
Dollis Av FNCH N3 38 D7
Dollis Crs RSLP HA4 47 G7
Dollis Hill Av CRICK NW2 69 K2
Dollis Hill Est CRICK NW2 * 69 J2
Dollis Hill La CRICK NW2 69 H3
Dollis Pk FNCH N3 38 D7
Dollis Rd MLHL NW7 38 C7
Dollis Valley Dr BAR EN5 26 D4
Dollis Valley Green Wk
FNCH N3 52 C3
TRDG/WHET N20 39 F2
Dollis Valley Wy EBAR EN4 27 H3
Dolman Cl FNCH N3 53 G1
Dolman Rd CHSWK W4 106 A3
Dolman St CLAP SW4 130 A3
Dolphin Ap ROM RM1 63 H3
Dolphin Cl BERM/RHTH SE16 112 A1
SURB KT6 158 E5
THMD SE28 97 J5
Dolphin Est SUN TW16 * 140 C7
Dolphin La POP/IOD E14 93 K6
Dolphin Rd NTHLT UB5 83 K1
SUN TW16 140 C7
Dolphin Rd North SUN TW16 140 B7
Dolphin Rd South SUN TW16 140 B7
Dolphin Rd West SUN TW16 140 C7
Dolphin Sq CHSWK W4 * 106 B6
PIM SW1V 16 F8
Dolphin St KUT/HW KT1 159 F1
Dombey St BMSBY WC1N 11 L2
Dome Blds RCH/KEW TW9 * 124 E4
Dome Hill Pk SYD SE26 150 B3
Domett Cl CMBW SE5 130 E3
Domingo St FSBYE EC1V 6 E9
Dominica Cl PLSTW E13 95 H2
Dominion Cl HSLW TW3 123 J1
Dominion Pde HRW HA1 * 49 F4
Dominion Rd CROY/NA CR0 165 G6
NWDGN UB2 102 D2
Dominion St LVPST EC2M 13 H2
Dominion Wy RAIN RM13 99 J2
Domonic Dr ELTH/MOT SE9 154 B2
Domville Cl TRDG/WHET N20 39 H1
Donald Dr CHDH RM6 61 J4
Donald Rd CROY/NA CR0 164 A5
PLSTW E13 77 F7
Donaldson Rd
KIL/WHAMP NW6 70 D7
WOOL/PLUM SE18 115 F7
Donald Woods Gdns
BRYLDS KT5 172 D1
Doncaster Dr NTHLT UB5 65 K4
Doncaster Gdns FSBYPK N4 * 55 J5
NTHLT UB5 65 K4
Doncaster Gn OXHEY WD19 33 G4
Doncaster Rd ED N9 30 D6
Donegal St IS N1 5 M6
Doneraile St FUL/PGN SW6 127 G1
Dongola Rd PLSTW E13 95 F2
TOTM N17 56 A2
WCHPL E1 93 G4
Dongola Rd West PLSTW E13 95 F2
Donington Av BARK/HLT IG6 60 C4
Donkey Aly EDUL SE22 131 H6
Donkey La EN EN1 30 C1
Donnefield Av EDGW HA8 36 A5
Donne Pl CHEL SW3 15 K5
MTCM CR4 163 G3
Donne Rd BCTR RM8 79 J1
Donnington Rd
KTN/HRWW/WS HA3 49 K5
WLSDN NW10 69 K7
WPK KT4 173 J1
Donnybrook Rd
STRHM/NOR SW16 148 C6
Donoghue Cots
POP/IOD E14 * 93 G4
Donovan Av MUSWH N10 54 B1
Donovan Pl WCHMH N21 29 F4
Don Phelan Cl CMBW SE5 110 E7
Doone Cl TEDD TW11 143 G5
Doon St STHWK SE1 12 A8
Doral Wy CAR SM5 175 K4
Dorando Cl SHB W12 * 87 K6
Doran Gv WOOL/PLUM SE18 115 K6
Dora Rd WIM/MER SW19 146 E4
Dora St POP/IOD E14 93 H5
Dora Wy BRXN/ST SW9 130 B1
Dorchester Av BXLY DA5 136 E7
PLMGR N13 41 J3
RYLN/HDSTN HA2 48 C5
Dorchester Cl ESH/CLAY KT10 171 F1
NTHLT UB5 66 B4
STMC/STPC BR5 155 H6
Dorchester Ct CRICK NW2 70 A2
HNHL SE24 130 D4
RKW/CH/CXG WD3 * 20 A4
STHGT/OAK N14 28 B6
Dorchester Dr
EBED/NFELT TW14 121 H5
HNHL SE24 130 D4
Dorchester Gdns CHING E4 43 J3
GLDGN NW11 * 52 E3
Dorchester Gv CHSWK W4 106 B5
Dorchester Ms TWK TW1 124 D5
Dorchester Pde
STRHM/NOR SW16 * 148 E1
Dorchester Rd MRDN SM4 162 A6
NTHLT UB5 66 B4
WPK KT4 161 F7
Dorchester Ter HDN NW4 * 52 B1
Dorchester Wy
KTN/HRWW/WS HA3 50 B4
Dorchester Waye YEAD UB4 83 F5
Dordrecht Rd ACT W3 87 G7
Dore Av MNPK E12 78 A4
Doreen Av CDALE/KGS NW9 51 F7
Dore Gdns MRDN SM4 162 A6
Dorell Cl STHL UB1 83 K4
Dorian Rd HCH RM12 63 J7
Doria Rd FUL/PGN SW6 127 J1
Doric Wy CAMTN NW1 5 G7
Dorie Ms NFNCH/WDSPK N12 39 F3
Dorien Rd RYNPK SW20 161 G1
Doris Ashby Cl GFD/PVL UB6 67 G7
Doris Rd ASHF TW15 140 B5
FSTGT E7 76 E6
Dorking Cl DEPT SE8 112 C5
WPK KT4 174 B1
Dorlcote Rd
WAND/EARL SW18 128 C6
Dorman Pl ED N9 42 C1
Dormans Cl NTHWD HA6 32 B6
Dorman Wy STJWD NW8 3 G3
Dormay St WAND/EARL SW18 128 A4
Dormer Cl BAR EN5 26 B4
SRTFD E15 76 D5
Dormer's Av STHL UB1 84 A5
Dormers Ri STHL UB1 84 B6
Dormer's Wells La STHL UB1 84 A5
Dormywood RSLP HA4 46 D4
Dornberg Rd
BKHTH/KID SE3 * 114 A6
Dorncliffe Rd FUL/PGN SW6 127 H1
Dorney Wy HSLWW TW4 122 D4
Dornfell St KIL/WHAMP NW6 70 D4
Dornton Rd BAL SW12 148 B1
SAND/SEL CR2 178 A4
Dorothy Av ALP/SUD HA0 68 A6
Dorothy Gdns BCTR RM8 79 H3
Dorothy Rd BTSEA SW11 128 E2
Dorrell Pl BRXN/ST SW9 130 B2
Dorrington St HCIRC EC1N 12 A2
Dorrington Wy BECK BR3 167 F4
Dorrit Ms UED N18 42 B3
Dorrit St STHWK SE1 * 18 F1
Dorrit Wy CHST BR7 154 C5
Dorrofield Cl
RKW/CH/CXG WD3 20 A4
Dors Cl CDALE/KGS NW9 51 F7
Dorset Av NWDGN UB2 103 F3

ROM RM1 63 F2
WELL DA16 136 A3
YEAD UB4 82 C2
Dorset Blds EMB EC4Y * 12 C5
Dorset Cl CAMTN NW1 9 L2
YEAD UB4 * 82 C2
Dorset Dr EDGW HA8 36 B5
Dorset Gdns MTCM CR4 164 A3
Dorset Ms FNCH N3 38 E7
KTBR SW1X 16 C3
Dorset Pl SRTFD E15 76 B5
Dorset Ri EMB EC4Y 12 C5
Dorset Rd BECK BR3 166 A2
EA W5 104 D2
ELTH/MOT SE9 153 J1
FSTGT E7 77 G6
HRW HA1 48 C5
MTCM CR4 162 D1
SEVS/STOTM N15 55 K3
VX/NE SW8 110 A6
WDGN N22 40 E7
WIM/MER SW19 146 E7
Dorset Sq CAMTN NW1 9 L1
Dorset St MHST W1U 9 M3
Dorset Wy WHTN TW2 123 H7
Dorset Waye HEST TW5 102 E6
Dorton Cl PECK SE15 111 F6
Dorville Crs HMSMTH W6 106 E2
Dothill Rd WOOL/PLUM SE18 115 J6
Douai Gv HPTN TW12 142 C7
Doughty Ms BMSBY WC1N 11 L1
Doughty St BMSBY WC1N 5 L9
Douglas Av ALP/SUD HA0 68 A6
NWMAL KT3 160 E3
WALTH E17 43 J7
Douglas Cl STAN HA7 35 G4
WLGTN SM6 176 E5
Douglas Crs YEAD UB4 83 G3
Douglas Dr CROY/NA CR0 179 J2
Douglas Est IS N1 * 73 J5
Douglas Ms CRICK NW2 70 C2
Douglas Pth POP/IOD E14 113 F4
Douglas Pl POP/IOD E14 * 113 F4
Douglas Rd CAN/RD E16 94 E4
ESH/CLAY KT10 170 B1
GDMY/SEVK IG3 61 G6
HSLW TW3 123 G2
IS N1 6 E1
KIL/WHAMP NW6 70 D7
KUT/HW KT1 159 J1
ROM RM1 63 H5
STWL/WRAY TW19 120 A5
SURB KT6 172 B1
WDGN N22 41 G7
WELL DA16 116 C7
Douglas Rd North IS N1 73 J5
Douglas Rd South IS N1 * 73 J5
Douglas St WEST SW1P 17 G6
Douglas Ter WALTH E17 43 H7
Douglas Vls KUT/HW KT1 * 159 G1
Douglas Wy NWCR SE14 112 C6
Doulton Ms KIL/WHAMP NW6 71 F5
Dounesforth Gdns
WAND/EARL SW18 128 A7
Douro Pl KENS W8 14 D3
Douro St BOW E3 93 J1
Douthwaite Sq WAP E1W 92 C7
Dove Ap EHAM E6 95 J4
Dove Cl MLHL NW7 37 J6
NTHLT UB5 83 H3
WLGTN SM6 177 F6
Dovecot Cl PIN HA5 47 G4
Dove Ct LOTH EC2R * 13 G5
Dovedale Av CLAY IG5 60 A1
KTN/HRWW/WS HA3 49 J5
Dovedale Cl WELL DA16 116 B7
Dovedale Ri MTCM CR4 147 K6
Dovedale Rd EDUL SE22 131 J4
Dovedon Cl STHGT/OAK N14 40 E1
Dove House Gdns CHING E4 43 J1
Dovehouse Md BARK IG11 96 D1
Dovehouse St CHEL SW3 15 J8
Dove Ms ECT SW5 14 E6
Dove Pk PIN HA5 33 K6
Dove Pl ESH/CLAY KT10 171 G7
Dover Cl CRICK NW2 70 B1
CRW RM5 62 E1
Dovercourt Av THHTH CR7 164 B3
Dovercourt Est IS N1 73 K5
Dovercourt Gdns STAN HA7 36 A4
Dovercourt La SUT SM1 175 G2
Dovercourt Rd DUL SE21 131 F5
Doverfield Rd
BRXS/STRHM SW2 129 K5
Dover Gdns CAR SM5 175 K2
Dover House Rd
PUT/ROE SW15 126 D3
Doveridge Gdns PLMGR N13 41 H3
Dove Rd IS N1 73 K5
Dove Rw BETH E2 92 C1
Dover Park Dr PUT/ROE SW15 126 E5
Dover Patrol BKHTH/KID SE3 134 A1
Dover Rd ED N9 42 E1
MNPK E12 77 G1
NRWD SE19 149 K5
WOOL/PLUM SE18 135 G1
Dover St CONDST W1S 10 D7
Dover Ter RCH/KEW TW9 * 125 H1
Dover Wy RKW/CH/CXG WD3 20 A3
Dover Yd MYFR/PICC W1J 10 D8
Doves Cl HAYES BR2 181 J1
Doves Yd IS N1 6 A4
Doveton Rd SAND/SEL CR2 177 K4
Doveton St WCHPL E1 92 E3
Dowanhill Rd CAT SE6 133 G7
Dowd Cl FBAR/BDGN N11 40 A1
Dowdeswell Cl
PUT/ROE SW15 126 B3
Dowding Cl HCH RM12 81 K6
Dowding Pl STAN HA7 35 G5
Dowdney Cl KTTN NW5 72 C4
Dower Av WLGTN SM6 176 B7
Dowgate Hl CANST EC4R 13 G6
Dowland St NKENS W10 88 C2
Dowlas St CMBW SE5 111 F6
Dowman Cl WIM/MER SW19 147 F6
Downage HDN NW4 52 A2
Downalong BUSH WD23 22 D7
Downbank Av BXLYHN DA7 118 A7
Down Barns Rd RSLP HA4 65 H3
Down Cl NTHLT UB5 83 F2
Downderry Rd BMLY BR1 152 B2
Downe Cl WELL DA16 116 D6
Downend WOOL/PLUM SE18 115 G6
Downe Rd HAYES BR2 181 J7
MTCM CR4 162 E1
Downer's Cots CLAP SW4 129 H3
Downes Cl TWK TW1 124 C5
Downes Ct WCHMH N21 29 G7
Downfield WPK KT4 160 C7
Downfield Cl MV/WKIL W9 8 C1
Down Hall Rd KUT/HW KT1 143 K7
Downham La BMLY BR1 152 B4
Downham Rd IS N1 7 G2
Downham Wy BMLY BR1 152 C4
Downhills Av TOTM N17 55 K2
Downhills Park Rd TOTM N17 55 J2
Downhills Wy TOTM N17 55 J1
Downhurst Av MLHL NW7 37 F4
Downing Cl RYLN/HDSTN HA2 48 C2
Downing Dr GFD/PVL UB6 66 E7
Downing Rd DAGW RM9 80 B7
Downings EHAM E6 96 A5
Downing St WHALL SW1A 17 J1
Downland Cl TRDG/WHET N20 27 G7
Downleys Cl ELTH/MOT SE9 153 J1
Downman Rd ELTH/MOT SE9 134 D2
Down Pl HMSMTH W6 106 E3
Down Rd TEDD TW11 143 H5
Downs Av CHST BR7 153 K4
PIN HA5 47 K5
Downs Bridge Rd BECK BR3 152 B7
Downs Court Pde HACK E8 * 74 D4
Downsell Rd SRTFD E15 76 B3
Downsfield Rd WALTH E17 57 G5
Downshall Av GDMY/SEVK IG3 60 E5
Downs Hl BECK BR3 152 B7
Downshire Hl HAMP NW3 71 H3
Downside BECK BR3 * 151 J7
SUN TW16 140 E7
TWK TW1 143 F2
Downside Cl WIM/MER SW19 147 G5
Downside Crs HAMP NW3 71 J4
WEA W13 85 G3
Downside Rd BELMT SM2 175 H5
Downs La CLPT E5 74 D3
Downs Park Rd HACK E8 74 C4
Downs Rd BECK BR3 166 E1
CLPT E5 74 C3
EN EN1 30 A3
THHTH CR7 149 J7
The Downs RYNPK SW20 146 B6
Down St E/WMO/HCT KT8 157 F4
MYFR/PICC W1J 10 C9
Downs Vw ISLW TW7 104 A7
Downsview Gdns NRWD SE19 149 J6
Downsview Rd NRWD SE19 149 J6
The Downsway BELMT SM2 175 G7
Downton Av
BRXS/STRHM SW2 149 F1
Downtown Rd
BERM/RHTH SE16 112 B1
Downway
NFNCH/WDSPK N12 39 J6
Down Wy NTHLT UB5 83 F2
Dowrey St IS N1 * 6 A3
Dowsett Rd TOTM N17 56 C1
Dowson Cl CMBW SE5 * 130 E3
Doyce St STHWK SE1 * 18 E1
Doyle Cl ERITH DA8 118 B7
Doyle Gdns WLSDN NW10 69 K7
Doyle Rd SNWD SE25 165 H3
D'Oyley St BGVA SW1W 16 A5
Doynton St ARCH N19 * 72 B1
Draco Ga PUT/ROE SW15 * 127 F2
Draco St WALW SE17 18 E9
Dragonfly Cl PLSTW E13 95 F2
Dragon Rd LBTH SE11 17 M6
PECK SE15 111 F5
Dragoon Rd DEPT SE8 112 C4
Dragor Rd WLSDN NW10 86 E2
Drake Cl BERM/RHTH SE16 112 A1
Drake Crs THMD SE28 97 J5
Drakefell Rd NWCR SE14 132 A1
Drakefield Rd TOOT SW17 148 A2
Drake Ms HAYES BR2 168 B3
HCH RM12 81 J6
Drake Rd BROCKY SE4 132 D2
CHSGTN KT9 172 C4
MTCM CR4 163 F5
RYLN/HDSTN HA2 65 K1
Drake's Cl ESH/CLAY KT10 170 A4
Drakes Ctyd KIL/WHAMP NW6 70 D6
Drake St FSBYW WC1X 11 L3
Drakewood Rd
STRHM/NOR SW16 148 D6
Draper Cl BELV DA17 117 G3
ISLW TW7 123 J1
Draper Est STHWK SE1 18 D5
Draper Pl IS N1 6 D3
Drapers Rd ENC/FH EN2 29 H1
SRTFD E15 76 A3
TOTM N17 56 B2
Drappers Wy
BERM/RHTH SE16 111 H3
Draven Cl HAYES BR2 167 J6
Drawell Cl WOOL/PLUM SE18 115 K4
Drax Av RYNPK SW20 145 J6
Draxmont WIM/MER SW19 146 C5
Draycot Rd SURB KT6 159 H7
WAN E11 59 F5
Draycott Av CHEL SW3 15 K6
KTN/HRWW/WS HA3 49 H5
Draycott Cl CMBW SE5 110 E6
CRICK NW2 70 B2
KTN/HRWW/WS HA3 49 H5
Draycott Pl CHEL SW3 15 L6
Draycott Ter CHEL SW3 15 L5
Dray Ct ALP/SUD HA0 * 67 J5
Drayford Cl MV/WKIL W9 * 88 D3
Dray Gdns BRXS/STRHM SW2 130 A4
Draymans Ms PECK SE15 131 G1
Draymans Wy ISLW TW7 124 A2
Drayson Ms KENS W8 14 B2
Drayton Av ORP BR6 169 G7
WEA W13 85 G6
Drayton Bridge Rd HNWL W7 85 F6
Drayton Cl HSLWW TW4 122 E4
IL IG1 60 D7
Drayton Ct WDR/YW UB7 * 100 C3
Drayton Court Chambers
WEA W13 * 85 H6
Drayton Gdns WBPTN SW10 14 F7
WCHMH N21 29 H6
WDR/YW UB7 100 A1
WEA W13 85 G6
Drayton Gn WEA W13 85 G6
Drayton Green Rd WEA W13 85 H6
Drayton Gv WEA W13 85 G6
Drayton Pk HBRY N5 73 G4
Drayton Park Ms HOLWY N7 * 73 G4
Drayton Rd BORE WD6 24 C3
CROY/NA CR0 177 H1
TOTM N17 56 A1
WAN E11 58 B7
WEA W13 85 G5
WLSDN NW10 69 H7
Dreadnought Cl
WIM/MER SW19 162 B1
Dreadnought St GNWCH SE10 113 H2
Drenon Sq HYS/HAR UB3 82 D6
Dresden Cl KIL/WHAMP NW6 71 F5
Dresden Rd ARCH N19 54 C7
Dressington Av BROCKY SE4 132 D5
Drew Av MLHL NW7 38 C5
Drewery Ct BKHTH/KID SE3 * 133 H2
Drew Gdns GFD/PVL UB6 67 F5
Drew Rd CAN/RD E16 95 J7
Drews Cots
STRHM/NOR SW16 * 148 D1
Drewstead Rd
STRHM/NOR SW16 148 D1
Driffield Rd BOW E3 93 G1
The Drift HAYES BR2 181 H2
The Driftway MTCM CR4 148 A7
Drinkwater Rd
RYLN/HDSTN HA2 66 B1
Drive Ct EDGW HA8 * 36 C4
The Drive ACT W3 86 E5
ASHF TW15 140 B6
BAR EN5 27 G5
BARK IG11 79 F6
BECK BR3 166 D1
BXLY DA5 136 D5
CHST BR7 155 F6
EBED/NFELT TW14 122 A6
EDGW HA8 36 C4
ESH/CLAY KT10 157 H7
FBAR/BDGN N11 40 C5
FNCH N3 38 E6
GLDGN NW11 52 C6
HGT N6 53 K4
HOLWY N7 73 F5
HOR/WEW KT19 173 H5
HSLW TW3 123 J1
IL IG1 59 J5
KUTN/CMB KT2 144 E6
MRDN SM4 162 B4
NTHWD HA6 32 C7
RYLN/HDSTN HA2 48 A6
RYNPK SW20 146 A6
SCUP DA14 155 H2
SURB KT6 159 F6
SWFD E18 58 E2
THHTH CR7 164 E3
WALTH E17 57 K2
WBLY HA9 68 E1
WWKM BR4 167 G6
Dr Johnson Av TOOT SW17 148 B2
Droitwich Cl SYD SE26 150 C2
Dromey Gdns
KTN/HRWW/WS HA3 35 F6
Dromore Rd PUT/ROE SW15 127 H5
Dronfield Gdns BCTR RM8 79 J4
Droop St NKENS W10 88 C3
Drovers Pl PECK SE15 111 J6
Drovers Rd SAND/SEL CR2 177 K4
Drovers Wy HOLWY N7 72 E5
Druce Rd DUL SE21 131 F5
Druid St STHWK SE1 19 K1
Druids Wy HAYES BR2 167 G3
Drumaline Rdg WPK KT4 173 G1
Drummond Av
ROMW/RG RM7 63 F3
Drummond Cl ERITH DA8 118 B7
Drummond Crs CAMTN NW1 5 G7
Drummond Dr STAN HA7 35 F6
Drummond Ga PIM SW1V 17 H7
Drummond Rd
BERM/RHTH SE16 111 J2
CROY/NA CR0 177 J1
ROMW/RG RM7 62 E3
WAN E11 59 F5
Drummonds Pl
RCH/KEW TW9 125 F3
Drummond St CAMTN NW1 4 E9
Drum St WCHPL E1 13 M4
Drury Crs CROY/NA CR0 177 G1
Drury La HOL/ALD WC2B 11 J4
Drury Rd HRW HA1 48 C6
Drury Wy WLSDN NW10 69 F4
Dryad St PUT/ROE SW15 127 G2
Dryburgh Gdns
CDALE/KGS NW9 50 C2
Dryburgh Rd PUT/ROE SW15 126 E2
Dryden Av HNWL W7 85 F5
Dryden Cl CLAP SW4 129 J4
Dryden Rd EN EN1 30 A5
KTN/HRWW/WS HA3 35 F7
WELL DA16 116 A7
WIM/MER SW19 147 G5
Dryden St COVGDN WC2E 11 K5
Dryfield Cl WLSDN NW10 68 E5
Dryfield Rd EDGW HA8 36 E5
Dryhill Rd BELV DA17 117 G5
Drylands Rd CEND/HSY/T N8 54 E5
Drysdale Av CHING E4 31 K5
Drysdale Cl NTHWD HA6 32 C6
Drysdale Dwellings HACK E8 * 74 B4
Drysdale Pl IS N1 7 K7
Drysdale St IS N1 7 K8
Dublin Av HACK E8 74 C7
Du Burstow Ter HNWL W7 103 K1
Ducal St BETH E2 7 M8
Du Cane Cl SHB W12 * 88 A5
Du Cane Rd SHB W12 87 J5
Duchess Cl FBAR/BDGN N11 40 B4
SUT SM1 175 G3
Duchess Gv BKHH IG9 * 45 F1
Duchess Ms CAVSQ/HST W1G 10 D3
Duchess of Bedford's Wk
KENS W8 107 J1
Duchess St REGST W1B 10 D3
Duchy St STHWK SE1 12 B8
Ducie St CLAP SW4 129 K3
Duckett Rd FSBYPK N4 55 H5
Duckett St WCHPL E1 93 F4
Ducking Stool Ct ROM RM1 63 G3
Duck La SOHO/CST W1F 11 G5
Duck Lees La PEND EN3 31 G3
Du Cros Dr STAN HA7 35 K5
Du Cros Rd ACT W3 87 G7
Dudden Hill La WLSDN NW10 69 H3
Dudden Hill Pde
WLSDN NW10 * 69 H3
Duddington Cl ELTH/MOT SE9 153 H3
Dudley Av
KTN/HRWW/WS HA3 49 J2
Dudley Dr MRDN SM4 161 H7
RSLP HA4 65 F4
Dudley Gdns
RYLN/HDSTN HA2 48 D7
WEA W13 104 C1
Dudley Pl HYS/HAR UB3 101 G3
Dudley Rd EBED/NFELT TW14 121 G7
FNCH N3 53 F1
IL IG1 78 B3
KIL/WHAMP NW6 88 C1
KUT/HW KT1 159 G2
NWDGN UB2 102 C1
RCH/KEW TW9 125 G1
RYLN/HDSTN HA2 66 C1
WALTH E17 57 J1
WIM/MER SW19 146 E5
Dudley St BAY/PAD W2 * 9 G3
Dudlington Rd CLPT E5 74 E1
Dudmaston Ms CHEL SW3 15 H7
Dudrich Cl
NFNCH/WDSPK N12 39 K5
Dudrich Ms EDUL SE22 131 G4
Dudset La HEST TW5 101 K7
Dufferin Av STLK EC1Y 13 G1
Dufferin St STLK EC1Y 12 F1
Duffield Cl HRW HA1 49 F4
Duffield Dr SEVS/STOTM N15 56 B3
Duff St POP/IOD E14 93 K5
Dufour's Pl SOHO/CST W1F 10 F5
Dugard Wy LBTH SE11 18 C5
Duggan Dr CHST BR7 153 J5
Dugolly Av WBLY HA9 68 D2
Duke Humphrey Rd
BKHTH/KID SE3 113 H7
Duke of Cambridge Cl
WHTN TW2 123 J5
Duke of Edinburgh Rd
SUT SM1 175 H2
The Duke of Wellington Av
WOOL/PLUM SE18 115 G2
Duke of Wellington Pl
KTBR SW1X 16 B2
Duke of York Sq CHEL SW3 15 M7
Duke of York St STJS SW1Y 10 F8
Duke Rd BARK/HLT IG6 60 D3
CHSWK W4 106 A4
Dukes Av EDGW HA8 36 B5
FNCH N3 39 F7
HRW HA1 48 E3
HSLWW TW4 122 D3
MUSWH N10 54 C2
NTHLT UB5 65 J6
NWMAL KT3 160 B2
PIN HA5 47 K5
RCHPK/HAM TW10 143 J3
Duke's Av CHSWK W4 106 A4
Dukes Cl ASHF TW15 140 A3
HPTN TW12 141 K4
Dukes Ga CHSWK W4 * 105 K3
Dukes Green Av
EBED/NFELT TW14 121 K4
Dukes La KENS W8 14 C1
Dukes Ms MUSWH N10 54 B2
Duke's Ms MHST W1U 10 B4
Dukes Orch BXLY DA5 137 K7
Duke's Pl HDTCH EC3A 13 L5
Dukes Point HGT N6 54 B7
Dukes Rd ACT W3 86 C3
EHAM E6 78 A7
Duke's Rd CAMTN NW1 5 H8
Dukesthorpe Rd SYD SE26 151 F3
Duke St MHST W1U 10 B4
RCH/KEW TW9 124 E3
SUT SM1 175 H3
WAT WD17 21 G2
Duke Street Hl STHWK SE1 13 H8
Duke Street St James's
MYFR/PICC W1J 10 F8
Dukes Wy WBLY HA9 68 A4
WWKM BR4 180 C2
Duke's Yd MYFR/PKLN W1K 10 B6
Dulas St FSBYPK N4 55 F7
Dulford St NTGHL W11 88 C6
Dulka Rd BTSEA SW11 128 E4
Dulverton Rd ELTH/MOT SE9 154 C1
RSLP HA4 64 E1
Dulwich Common DUL SE21 130 E7
The Dulwich Oaks DUL SE21 * 150 B2
Dulwich Rd HNHL SE24 130 B4
Dulwich Village DUL SE21 130 E5
Dulwich Wood Av NRWD SE19 150 A4
Dulwich Wood Pk
NRWD SE19 150 A3
Dumbarton Rd
BRXS/STRHM SW2 129 K5
Dumbleton Cl KUT/HW KT1 144 D7
Dumbreck Rd ELTH/MOT SE9 135 F3
Dumfries Cl OXHEY WD19 32 E2
Dumont Rd STNW/STAM N16 74 A2
Dumpton Pl CAMTN NW1 4 A2
Dunbar Av BECK BR3 166 B3
DAGE RM10 80 C2
STRHM/NOR SW16 164 B1
Dunbar Cl YEAD UB4 82 E4
Dunbar Gdns DAGE RM10 80 C4
Dunbar Rd FSTGT E7 76 E5
NWMAL KT3 159 K3
WDGN N22 41 G7
Dunbar St WNWD SE27 149 J2
Dunblane Rd ELTH/MOT SE9 134 D2
Dunboyne Rd HAMP NW3 71 K4
Dunbridge St BETH E2 92 C3
Duncan Cl BAR EN5 27 G3
Duncan Gv ACT W3 87 G5
Duncannon St CHCR WC2N 11 J7
Duncan Rd HACK E8 74 D7
RCH/KEW TW9 125 F3
Duncan St IS N1 6 C5
Duncan Ter IS N1 6 C6
Duncan Wy BUSH WD23 21 K1
Dunch St WCHPL E1 92 D5
Duncombe Hl FSTH SE23 132 B6
Duncombe Rd ARCH N19 54 D7
Duncrievie Rd LEW SE13 133 G5
Duncroft WOOL/PLUM SE18 115 K6
Dundalk Rd BROCKY SE4 132 B2
Dundas Gdns
E/WMO/HCT KT8 157 G2
Dundas Rd PECK SE15 131 K1
Dundee Rd PLSTW E13 95 F1
SNWD SE25 165 J4
Dundee St WAP E1W 92 D7
Dundee Wy PEND EN3 31 G2
Dundee Whf POP/IOD E14 93 H6
Dundela Gdns WPK KT4 173 K3
Dundonald Cl EHAM E6 95 J5
Dundonald Rd
WIM/MER SW19 146 D6
WLSDN NW10 70 B7
Dunedin Rd IL IG1 60 C7
LEY E10 75 K2
RAIN RM13 99 H2
Dunedin Wy YEAD UB4 83 G3
Dunelm St WCHPL E1 93 F5
Dunfield Rd CAT SE6 151 K4
Dunford Rd HOLWY N7 73 F3
Dungarvan Av PUT/ROE SW15 126 D3
Dunheved Cl THHTH CR7 164 B5
Dunheved Rd North
THHTH CR7 164 B5
Dunheved Rd South
THHTH CR7 164 B5
Dunheved Rd West
THHTH CR7 164 B5
Dunholme Gn ED N9 42 B2
Dunholme La ED N9 42 B2
Dunholme Rd ED N9 42 B2
Dunkeld Rd BCTR RM8 79 H1
SNWD SE25 164 E3
Dunkery Rd ELTH/MOT SE9 153 H3
Dunkin Rd DART DA1 139 K3
Dunkirk St WNWD SE27 * 149 J3
Dunlace Rd CLPT E5 74 E4
Dunleary Cl HSLWW TW4 122 E6
Dunley Dr CROY/NA CR0 180 A5
Dunloe Av TOTM N17 55 K2
Dunloe St BETH E2 7 L6
Dunlop Pl BERM/RHTH SE16 19 M4
Dunmore Rd
KIL/WHAMP NW6 70 C7
RYNPK SW20 146 A7
Dunmow Cl CHDH RM6 61 J4
FELT TW13 * 141 J3
Dunmow Dr RAIN RM13 81 H7
Dunmow Rd SRTFD E15 76 B3
Dunmow Wk IS N1 * 6 E3
Dunnage Crs
BERM/RHTH SE16 112 B3
Dunningford Cl HCH RM12 81 H4
Dunn Md CDALE/KGS NW9 37 H6
Dunnock Cl BORE WD6 24 C3
ED N9 31 F7
Dunnock Rd EHAM E6 95 J5
Dunn St HACK E8 74 B4
Dunollie Pl KTTN NW5 72 C4
Dunollie Rd KTTN NW5 72 C4
Dunoon Gdns FSTH SE23 * 132 A6
Dunoon Rd FSTH SE23 131 K6
Dunraven Dr ENC/FH EN2 29 G1
Dunraven Rd SHB W12 87 J7
Dunraven St MYFR/PKLN W1K 9 M6
Dunsany Rd HMSMTH W6 107 G2
Dunsbury Cl BELMT SM2 175 F7
Dunsfold Wy CROY/NA CR0 179 K6
Dunsford Wy PUT/ROE SW15 126 E6
Dunsmore OXHEY WD19 * 33 H1
Dunsmore Cl BUSH WD23 22 D5
YEAD UB4 83 H3
Dunsmore Rd WOT/HER KT12 156 A4
Dunsmore Wy BUSH WD23 22 C5
Dunsmure Rd
STNW/STAM N16 56 A7
Dunspring La CLAY IG5 60 B1
Dunstable Ms
CAVSQ/HST W1G 10 B2
Dunstable Rd
E/WMO/HCT KT8 156 E3
RCH/KEW TW9 125 F3
Dunstall Rd RYNPK SW20 145 K5
Dunstall Wy E/WMO/HCT KT8 157 G2
Dunstall Welling Est
WELL DA16 * 136 C1
Dunstan Cl EFNCH N2 * 53 G2
Dunstan Gld
STMC/STPC BR5 * 169 J5
Dunstan Houses WCHPL E1 * 92 E4
Dunstan Rd GLDGN NW11 52 D7
Dunstan's Gv EDUL SE22 131 J5
Dunstan's Rd EDUL SE22 131 H6
Dunster Av MRDN SM4 161 G7
Dunster Cl BAR EN5 26 B3
CRW RM5 62 E1
Dunster Ct BORE WD6 25 F2
MON EC3R 13 J6
Dunster Dr CDALE/KGS NW9 50 E7
Dunster Gdns
KIL/WHAMP NW6 70 D6
Dunsterville Wy STHWK SE1 19 H2
Dunster Wy RYLN/HDSTN HA2 65 J2
Dunston Rd BTSEA SW11 129 F1
HACK E8 7 L4
Dunston St HACK E8 7 K3
Dunton Cl SURB KT6 159 F7
Dunton Rd LEY E10 57 K6
ROM RM1 63 G3
STHWK SE1 19 L6
Duntshill Rd
WAND/EARL SW18 128 A7
Dunvegan Cl E/WMO/HCT KT8 157 G3
Dunvegan Rd ELTH/MOT SE9 134 E3
Dunworth Ms NTGHL W11 88 D5
Duplex Ride KTBR SW1X 15 M2
Dupont Rd RYNPK SW20 161 G1
Duppas Av CROY/NA CR0 177 H3
Duppas Hill Rd CROY/NA CR0 177 G3
Duppas Hill Ter CROY/NA CR0 177 H2
Duppas Rd CROY/NA CR0 177 G2
Dupree Rd CHARL SE7 114 A4
Dura Den Cl BECK BR3 151 K6
Durand Gdns BRXN/ST SW9 110 A7
Durand Wy WLSDN NW10 68 E6
Durants Park Av PEND EN3 31 F3
Durants Rd PEND EN3 30 E3
Durant St BETH E2 92 C1
Durban Gdns DAGE RM10 80 E6
Durban Rd BECK BR3 166 C1
GNTH/NBYPK IG2 60 E7
SRTFD E15 94 C2
TOTM N17 42 A5
WNWD SE27 149 J3
Durban Rd East WATW WD18 20 E3
Durban Rd West WATW WD18 20 E3
Durbin Rd CHSGTN KT9 172 A3
Durdans Rd STHL UB1 83 K5
Durell Gdns DAGW RM9 79 K4
Durell Rd DAGW RM9 79 K4
Durfey Pl CMBW SE5 110 E6
Durford Crs PUT/ROE SW15 126 D7
Durham Av HAYES BR2 167 J3
HEST TW5 102 E5
WFD IG8 45 H4
Durham Hl BMLY BR1 152 D3
Durham House St
CHCR WC2N * 11 K7
Durham Pl CHEL SW3 15 L8
Durham Ri WOOL/PLUM SE18 115 H4
Durham Rd BORE WD6 24 E2
CAN/RD E16 94 C3
DAGE RM10 80 E4
EA W5 104 E2
EBED/NFELT TW14 122 B6
ED N9 42 C1
EFNCH N2 53 J2
HOLWY N7 73 F1
HRW HA1 48 B4
MNPK E12 77 H3
RYNPK SW20 145 K7
SCUP DA14 155 H4
Durham Rw WCHPL E1 93 F4
Durham St LBTH SE11 17 L8
Durham Ter BAY/PAD W2 8 C4
PGE/AN SE20 * 150 D6
Durham Wharf Dr BTFD TW8 104 D6
Durham Yd BETH E2 * 92 D2
Durley Av PIN HA5 47 J5
Durley Rd STNW/STAM N16 56 A6
Durlston Rd CLPT E5 74 C1
KUTN/CMB KT2 144 A5
Durnford St SEVS/STOTM N15 56 A4
Durning Rd NRWD SE19 149 K4
Durnsford Av WIM/MER SW19 146 E1
Durnsford Rd WDGN N22 40 D6
WIM/MER SW19 146 E2
Durrants Dr
RKW/CH/CXG WD3 20 A2
Durrell Rd FUL/PGN SW6 107 H7
Durrington Av RYNPK SW20 146 A6

206 Dur - Eld

Street	Area	Page	Grid
Durrington Park Rd RYNPK SW20		146	A7
Durrington Rd CLPT E5		75	C3
Dursley Cl BKHTH/KID SE3		134	E2
Dursley Gdns BKHTH/KID SE3		134	E1
Dursley Rd BKHTH/KID SE3		134	E2
Durward St WCHPL E1		92	D4
Durweston Ms MHST W1U *		9	M2
Durweston St MBLAR W1H		9	L3
Dutch Barn Cl STWL/WRAY TW19		118	A7
Dutch Gdns KUTN/CMB KT2		144	D5
Dutch Yd WAND/EARL SW18 *		127	K4
Duthie St POP/IOD E14		94	A6
Dutton St GNWCH SE10		113	F1
Duxberry Cl HAYES BR2		168	D4
Duxford Cl HCH RM12		81	K5
Dwight Rd WATW WD18		20	B6
Dye House La BOW E3		75	J7
Dyer's Blds FLST/FETLN EC4A		12	A3
Dyers Hall Rd WAN E11		76	B1
Dyer's La PUT/ROE SW15		126	E2
Dykes Wy HAYES BR2		167	J2
Dylan Cl BORE WD6 *		23	K6
Dylan Rd BELV DA17		117	H2
HNHL SE24		130	C3
Dylways CMBW SE5		130	E3
Dymchurch Cl CLAY IG5		60	B1
Dymock St FUL/PGN SW6		128	A2
Dymoke Rd ROM RM1		63	H6
Dyneley Rd LEE/GVPK SE12		153	F3
Dyne Rd KIL/WHAMP NW6		70	D6
Dynevor Rd RCHPK/HAM TW10		125	F4
STNW/STAM N16		74	J2
Dynham Rd KIL/WHAMP NW6 *		2	E1
Dyott St RSQ WC1B		11	H3
Dysart Av KUTN/CMB KT2		143	J2
Dysarts SDTCH EC2A		13	H1
Dyson Ct ALP/SUD HA0		67	G3
Dyson Rd SRTFD E15		76	D5
WAN E11		58	C5
Dyson's Rd UED N18		42	D5

E

Street	Area	Page	Grid
Eade Rd FSBYPK N4		55	J6
Eagans Cl EFNCH N2 *		53	H2
Eagle Av CHDH RM6		61	A5
Eagle Cl BERM/RHTH SE16		111	J6
HCH RM12		81	K5
PEND EN3		30	E1
WLGTN SM6		176	B5
Eagle Ct FARR EC1M		12	C2
Eagle Dr CDALE/KGS NW9		51	G1
Eagle Hts NRWD SE19		149	K6
Eagle House Ms CLAP SW4		129	F4
Eagle La WAN E11		58	E3
Eagle Ms IS N1		74	A5
Eagle Pl SKENS SW7		14	F7
Eagle Rd ALP/SUD HA0		67	K6
HTHAIR TW6		121	J2
Eaglesfield Rd WOOL/PLUM SE18		115	G7
Eagle St HHOL WC1V		11	L3
Eagle Ter WFD IG8		45	F6
Eagle Wharf Rd IS N1		6	F5
Eagling Cl BOW E3		93	J2
Ealdham Sq ELTH/MOT SE9		134	B3
Ealing Gn EA W5		85	K7
Ealing Park Gdns EA W5		104	A1
Ealing Rd ALP/SUD HA0		86	A1
BOW E3		93	A2
EA W5		104	E3
NTHLT UB5		66	A6
Ealing Village EA W5		86	A5
Eamont St STJWD NW8		3	J5
Eardley Crs ECT SW5		14	C8
Eardley Rd BELV DA17		117	H4
STRHM/NOR SW16		148	C5
Earl Cl FBAR/BDGN N11		40	B4
Earldom Rd PUT/ROE SW15		127	F3
Earle Gdns KUTN/CMB KT2		144	A6
Earlham Gv FSTGT E7		76	E4
WDGN N22		41	F6
Earlham St LSO/SEVD WC2H		11	H5
Earl Ri WOOL/PLUM SE18		115	J4
Earl Rd MORT/ESHN SW14		125	K3
Earl's Court Gdns ECT SW5		14	C6
Earl's Court Rd KENS W8		14	B5
Earl's Court Sq ECT SW5		14	C7
Earls Crs HRW HA1		48	E3
Earlsferry Wy IS N1		5	K2
Earlsfield Rd WAND/EARL SW18		128	B7
Earlshall Rd ELTH/MOT SE9		134	E4
Earlsmead RYLN/HDSTN HA2		65	K3
Earlsmead Rd SEVS/STOTM N15		56	B4
WLSDN NW10		88	B2
Earls Ms WAND/EARL SW18		128	B6
Earls Ter KENS W8		107	K3
Earlsthorpe Ms BAL SW12		129	F5
Earlsthorpe Rd SYD SE26		151	F3
Earlstoke Est FSBYE EC1V		6	C7
Earlstoke St FSBYE EC1V		6	C7
Earlston Gv HOM E9		74	E7
Earl St SDTCH EC2A		13	J2
WAT WD17		21	G2
Earls Wk BCTR RM8		79	H3
KENS W8		14	A4
Earlswood Av THHTH CR7		164	B4
Earlswood Gdns CLAY IG5		60	B2
Earlswood St GNWCH SE10		113	H4
Early Ms CAMTN NW1		4	D3
Earnshaw St NOXST/BSQ WC1A		11	H4
Easby Rd WKENS W14		107	H3
Easby Crs MRDN SM4		162	A5
Easebourne Rd BCTR RM8		79	J4
Easedale Dr HCH RM12		81	K4
East Acton Ct ACT W3 *		87	H6
East Acton La ACT W3		87	G6
East Arbour St WCHPL E1		93	F5
East Av EHAM E6		95	J3
HYS/HAR UB3		101	J1
STHL UB1		83	K6
WALTH E17		57	K3
WLGTN SM6		177	G4
East Bank STNW/STAM N16		56	A6
Eastbank Rd HPTN TW12		142	C4
East Barnet Rd BAR EN5		27	G5
Eastbourne Av ACT W3		87	F5
Eastbourne Gdns MORT/ESHN SW14		125	K2
Eastbourne Ms BAY/PAD W2		8	F4
Eastbourne Rd BTFD TW8		104	D4
CHSWK W4		105	K5
EHAM E6		96	A2
FELT TW13		141	H1
SEVS/STOTM N15		56	A5
SRTFD E15		76	C7
TOOT SW17		148	A5
Eastbournia Av ED N9		42	D2
Eastbrook Av ED N9		30	E6
Eastbrook Cl DAGE RM10		80	E3
Eastbrook Rd BKHTH/KID SE3		114	A3
Eastbury Av BARK IG11		78	E7
NTHWD HA6		32	A4
Eastbury Ct OXHEY WD19 *		21	G6
Eastbury Gv CHSWK W4		106	B4
Eastbury Rd EHAM E6		96	A3
KUTN/CMB KT2		144	A6
NTHWD HA6		32	C5
OXHEY WD19		21	G6
ROMW/RG RM7		63	F5
STMC/STPC BR5		169	J5
Eastbury Sq BARK IG11		79	F7
Eastbury Ter WCHPL E1		93	F3
Eastcastle St GTPST W1W		10	E4
Eastcheap FENCHST EC3M		13	H6
East Churchfield Rd ACT W3		87	F7
Eastchurch Rd HTHAIR TW6		121	H1
East Cl EA W5		86	C5
EBAR EN4		28	A3
GFD/PVL UB6		84	C1
RAIN RM13		99	K3
Eastcombe Av CHARL SE7		114	A5
Eastcote Av E/WMO/HCT KT8		156	E4
GFD/PVL UB6		67	G4
RYLN/HDSTN HA2		66	A1
Eastcote La NTHLT UB5		65	K5
Eastcote La North NTHLT UB5		66	A6
Eastcote Rd RSLP HA4		46	C7
RYLN/HDSTN HA2		66	C2
WELL DA16		135	J1
Eastcote St BRXN/ST SW9		129	K1
Eastcote Vw PIN HA5		47	H3
Eastcote Ct ALP/SUD HA0		67	J4
Eastcott Cl CEN EN1		30	A4
Eastcote Rd HOR/WEW KT19		173	G6
East Cross Route HOM E9		75	H5
Eastdown Pk LEE/GVPK SE13		133	G3
East Dr CAR SM5		175	K7
NTHWD HA6		32	C1
East Duck Lees La PEND EN3		31	H4
East Dulwich Gv EDUL SE22		131	F4
East Dulwich Rd EDUL SE22		131	G3
East End Rd FNCH N3		52	E1
East End Wy PIN HA5		47	J2
East Entrance DAGE RM10		98	D1
Eastern Av CHDH RM6		61	H3
GNTH/NBYPK IG2		60	C5
PIN HA5		47	H5
WAN E11		59	G5
Eastern Av East ROM RM1		63	F2
Eastern Av West CHDH RM6		62	A3
Eastern Gtwy CAN/RD E16		95	G6
Eastern Perimeter Rd HTHAIR TW6		121	K3
Eastern Rd BROCKY SE4		132	D3
EFNCH N2		53	K2
PLSTW E13		95	F1
ROM RM1		63	G5
WALTH E17		58	A4
WDCN N22		40	E7
Easternville Gdns GNTH/NBYPK IG2		60	C5
Eastern Wy ERITHM DA18		117	H1
THMD SE28		97	K7
THMD SE28		116	A1
East Ferry Rd POP/IOD E14		112	E3
Eastfield Gdns DAGE RM10		80	C3
Eastfield Rd CEND/HSY/T N8		54	E4
DAGE RM10		80	D3
PEND EN3		31	F2
WALTH E17		57	J3
Eastfields PIN HA5		47	G4
Eastfields Av WAND/EARL SW18		127	K3
Eastfields Rd ACT W3		86	K5
MTCM CR4		163	F1
Eastfield St POP/IOD E14		93	G4
East Gdns TOOT SW17		147	J5
Eastgate Cl THMD SE28		97	K5
Eastglade NTHWD HA6		32	C4
Eastham Cl BAR EN5		26	C4
East Ham Manor Wy EHAM E6		96	A5
East Harding St FLST/FETLN EC4A		12	B4
East Heath Rd HAMP NW3		71	H2
East Hi WAND/EARL SW18		128	B4
WBLY HA9		68	C1
Eastholm GLDGN NW11		53	F3
East Holme ERITH DA8		118	A4
Eastholme HYS/HAR UB3		82	E7
East India Dock Rd POP/IOD E14		93	K5
East India Wy CROY/NA CR0		165	G7
Eastlake Rd CMBW SE5		130	C1
Eastlands Crs EDUL SE22		131	J2
East La ALP/SUD HA0		67	J2
BERM/RHTH SE16		111	H1
KUT/HW KT1		158	E2
Eastlea Ms CAN/RD E16		94	C3
Eastleigh Av RYLN/HDSTN HA2		66	A1
Eastleigh Cl BELMT SM2		175	F6
CRICK NW2		69	G2
Eastleigh Rd BXLYHN DA7		137	K1
WALTH E17		57	H1
Eastleigh Wy EBED/NFELT TW14		121	K7
Eastman Rd ACT W3		106	A1
East Md RSLP HA4		65	H2
Eastmead Av GFD/PVL UB6		84	B2
Eastmead Cl BMLY BR1		168	E1
Eastmearn Rd WNWD SE27		149	H3
Eastmont Rd ESH/CLAY KT10		171	F1
Eastmoor Pl CHARL SE7		114	C2
Eastmoor St CHARL SE7		114	C2
WOOL/PLUM SE18		114	C2
East Mount St WCHPL E1 *		92	D4
Eastney Rd CROY/NA CR0		164	C7
Eastney St GNWCH SE10		113	G4
Eastnor Rd ELTH/MOT SE9		135	H7
Easton Gdns BORE WD6		25	G3
Easton St FSBYW WC1X		6	A9
East Pk Cl CHDH RM6		61	K4
East Parkside GNWCH SE10		113	H1
East Pas FARR EC1M		12	D2
East Pl WNWD SE27		149	J3
East Pole Cots STHGT/OAK N14 *		28	D3
East Poultry Av FARR EC1M		12	C3
East Rp HTHAIR TW6		100	E7
East Rd CHDH RM6		61	K4

Street	Area	Page	Grid
IS N1		7	H7
KUTN/CMB KT2		144	A7
ROMW/RG RM7		63	F6
SRTFD E15		76	E7
WDR/YW UB7		100	C3
WELL DA16		136	C1
WIM/MER SW19		147	G5
East Rochester Wy BFN/LL DA15		135	K4
BFN/LL DA15		136	D1
BXLY DA1		137	H5
DART DA1		138	A6
East Rw NKENS W10		88	C3
WAN E11		58	E5
Eastry Av HAYES BR2		167	J3
East Sheen Av MORT/ESHN SW14		126	A3
East Side SHB W12 *		107	F1
Eastside Rd GLDGN NW11		52	D3
East Smithfield WAP E1W		13	M7
East St BARK IG11		78	C6
BMLY BR1		167	K1
BTFD TW8		104	D6
WALW SE17		18	F7
East Surrey Gv PECK SE15		111	G6
East Tenter St WCHPL E1		13	M5
East Ter BFN/LL DA15 *		135	K3
East Towers PIN HA5		47	H5
East V ACT W3 *		87	H7
East Vw BAR EN5		26	D1
CHING E4		44	A4
Eastview Av WOOL/PLUM SE18		115	K6
Eastville Av GLDGN NW11		52	D4
East Wk EBAR EN4		28	A7
HYS/HAR UB3		101	K1
East Wy CROY/NA CR0		179	G1
HAYES BR2		167	K7
RSLP HA4		46	E7
Eastway BOW E3		75	G7
MRDN SM4		161	G4
WAN E11		59	F4
WIM/MER SW6		176	B3
Eastway Crs RYLN/HDSTN HA2		66	B1
Eastwell Cl BECK BR3		151	G7
Eastwood Cl HOLWY N7		73	G4
SWFD E18		58	E1
TOTM N17 *		42	D6
Eastwood Dr RAIN RM13		99	K5
Eastwood Gdns GDMY/SEVK IG3		61	G6
Eastwood Rd GDMY/SEVK IG3		61	G6
MUSWH N10		54	A1
SWFD E18		58	E1
WDR/YW UB7		100	D1
Eastwood St STRHM/NOR SW16		148	C5
Eatington Rd LEY E10		58	B4
Eaton Cl BCVA SW1W		16	A5
STAN HA7		35	H3
Eaton Dr BRXN/ST SW9		130	C3
KUTN/CMB KT2		144	C6
Eaton Ga BCVA SW1W		16	A5
EDGW HA8		36	C4
NTHWD HA6		32	A7
Eaton La BCVA SW1W		16	D4
Eaton Ms North KTBR SW1X		16	A4
Eaton Ms South BCVA SW1W		16	B5
Eaton Ms West BCVA SW1W		16	B5
Eaton Park Rd PLMGR N13		41	G1
Eaton Pl KTBR SW1X		16	A4
Eaton Ri EA W5		85	J4
WAN E11		59	G4
Eaton Rd BELMT SM2		175	F5
EN EN1		30	A2
HDN NW4		52	A4
HSLW TW3		123	J3
SCUP DA14		155	K1
Eaton Rw BGVA SW1W		16	C4
Eatons Md CHING E4		43	J1
Eaton Sq BGVA SW1W		16	C4
Eaton Ter BCVA SW1W		16	A5
BOW E3		93	G2
Eaton Terrace Ms BGVA SW1W *		16	A5
Eatonville Rd TOOT SW17		147	K1
Eatonville Vls TOOT SW17		147	K1
Ebbisham Dr VX/NE SW8		17	L9
Ebbisham Rd WPK KT4		174	A1
Ebbsfleet Rd CRICK NW2		70	C4
Ebdon Wy BKHTH/KID SE3		134	A2
Ebenezer Cl IS N1		7	G7
Ebenezer Ms STRHM/NOR SW16		148	C7
Ebley Cl PECK SE15		111	G6
Ebner St WAND/EARL SW18		128	A4
Ebor St BETH E2		7	L9
Ebrington Rd KTN/HRWW/WS HA3		49	K5
Ebsworth St FSTH SE23		132	A6
Eburne Rd HOLWY N7		72	E2
Ebury Br BGVA SW1W		16	C7
Ebury Bridge Rd BGVA SW1W		16	B8
Ebury Cl HAYES BR2		181	J2
NTHWD HA6		32	A5
Ebury Ms BGVA SW1W		16	B5
Ebury Ms East BGVA SW1W		16	C5
Ebury Sq BGVA SW1W		16	B6
Ebury St BGVA SW1W		16	B6
Ecclesbourne Cl PLMGR N13		41	G4
Ecclesbourne Gdns PLMGR N13		41	G4
Ecclesbourne Rd IS N1		6	F1
THHTH CR7		164	D4
Eccles Rd BTSEA SW11		128	E3
Eccleston Cl EBAR EN4		27	K3
ORP BR6 *		169	J7
Eccleston Crs CHDH RM6		61	G6
Eccleston Ms WBLY HA9		68	A2
Eccleston Pl BGVA SW1W		16	C5
Eccleston Ms KTBR SW1X *		16	B4
Eccleston Rd WEA W13		85	G6
Eccleston Sq PIM SW1V		16	D6
Eccleston Square Ms PIM SW1V		16	D6
Eccleston St BGVA SW1W		16	B4
Echo Hts CHING E4 *		31	K7
Eckford St IS N1		6	A5
Eckstein Rd BTSEA SW11		128	D3
Eclipse Rd PLSTW E13		95	F4
Ector Rd CAT SE6		152	C1
Edans Ct SHB W12		106	C1
Edbrooke Rd MV/WKIL W9		8	A1
Eddinton Cl CROY/NA CR0		180	A6
Eddiscombe Rd FUL/PGN SW6		127	J1
Eddy Cl ROMW/RG RM7		62	D5
Eddystone Rd BROCKY SE4		132	B4
Edenbridge Cl BERM/RHTH SE16 *		111	J4
Edenbridge Rd EN EN1		30	B6
HOM E9		75	F6

Street	Area	Page	Grid
Eden Cl ALP/SUD HA0		67	K7
HAMP NW3		70	E1
KENS W8		14	B3
Edencourt Rd STRHM/NOR SW16		148	B5
Edendale Rd BXLYHN DA7		118	A7
Edenfield Gdns WPK KT4		173	H2
Eden Gv HOLWY N7		73	F4
WLSDN NW10		69	K5
Edenham Wy NKENS W10		88	D3
Edenhurst Av FUL/PGN SW6		127	J2
Eden Pde BECK BR3 *		166	B3
Eden Park Av BECK BR3		166	B3
Eden Rd BECK BR3		166	B3
BXLY DA5		137	G7
CROY/NA CR0		177	K3
WALTH E17		57	K4
WNWD SE27		149	H4
Edensor Gdns CHSWK W4		106	B6
Edensor Rd CHSWK W4		106	B6
Eden St KUT/HW KT1		158	E1
Edenvale Rd MTCM CR4		148	A6
Edenvale St FUL/PGN SW6		128	A1
Eden Wk KUT/HW KT1 *		159	F1
WIM/MER SW19 *		166	B3
BOW E3		75	H7
Ederline Av STRHM/NOR SW16		164	A2
Edgar Kail Wy CMBW SE5		131	F2
Edgarley Ter FUL/PGN SW6 *		107	H7
Edgar Rd BOW E3		93	K2
HSLW TW4		122	E5
Edgar Vw ACT W3 *		87	K7
Edgar Wallace Cl PECK SE15		111	F6
Edgeborough Wy BMLY BR1		153	G7
Edgebury CHST BR7		154	B3
Edgecoombe SAND/SEL CR2		179	F7
Edgecote Cl ACT W3		86	E7
Edgefield Av BARK IG11		79	F6
Edge Hill WIM/MER SW19		146	B6
WOOL/PLUM SE18		115	G5
Edge Hill Av FNCH N3		52	E3
Edge Hill Ct SCUP DA14 *		156	B2
Edgehill Gdns DAGE RM10		80	C3
Edgehill Rd CHST BR7		154	C2
MTCM CR4		148	B7
WEA W13		85	H5
Edgeley La CLAP SW4		129	J2
Edgeley Rd CLAP SW4		129	H2
Edgel St WAND/EARL SW18		128	A3
Edge Point Cl WNWD SE27		149	H4
Edge St KENS W8		8	B8
Edgeworth Av HDN NW4		51	J4
Edgeworth Crs HDN NW4		51	J4
Edgeworth Rd EBAR EN4		27	J3
ELTH/MOT SE9		134	B3
Edgington Rd STRHM/NOR SW16		148	D5
Edgington Wy SCUP DA14		155	J6
Edgware Bury La EDGW HA8		24	B7
Edgware Rd BAY/PAD W2		8	K3
CDALE/KGS NW9		37	F7
CRICK NW2		70	A1
Edgware Road High St EDGW HA8		36	C5
Edgware Road The Hyde CDALE/KGS NW9		51	J2
Edgware Road Wy CRICK NW2		69	H1
Edgware Way (Watford By-Pass) EDGW HA8		36	A1
Edinburgh Cl BETH E2		92	E1
KUT/HW KT1 *		159	J6
PIN HA5		47	J6
Edinburgh Ga KTBR SW1X		15	L1
Edinburgh Rd HNWL W7		104	A1
PLSTW E13		95	F1
SUT SM1		175	G1
UED N18 *		42	C4
WALTH E17		57	J4
Edington Rd ABYW SE2		116	C2
PEND EN3		30	E1
Edison Cl HCH RM12		63	H7
WALTH E17 *		57	J4
Edison Dr STHL UB1		84	B5
WBLY HA9		68	A1
Edison Gv WOOL/PLUM SE18		116	A6
Edison Rd CEND/HSY/T N8		54	D5
HAYES BR2		167	K1
WELL DA16		116	A7
Edis St CAMTN NW1		4	A3
Edith Cavell Wy WOOL/PLUM SE18		114	D7
Edith Gdns BRYLDS KT5		159	H6
Edith Gv WBPTN SW10		108	B5
Edith Ms ST BRXN/ST SW9		129	K2
Edith Nesbit Wk ELTH/MOT SE9		134	D4
Edith Neville Cots CAMTN NW1 *		5	G7
Edith Rd CHDH RM6		61	K6
EHAM E6		77	H6
FBAR/BDGN N11		40	D6
SNWD SE25		164	E4
SRTFD E15		76	B4
WIM/MER SW19		147	F5
WKENS W14		107	H4
Edith Rw FUL/PGN SW6		108	A7
Edith St BETH E2		7	M5
Edith Ter WBPTN SW10		108	B6
Edith Vls WKENS W14		107	J4
Edith Yd WBPTN SW10		108	C6
Edison Cl WALTH E17 *		57	J4
Edmansons Cl TOTM N17		56	A1
Edmeston Cl HOM E9		75	G5
Edmonds Ct E/WMO/HCT KT8		157	J2
Edmund Gv FELT TW13		141	K1
Edmund Halley Wy GNWCH SE10		113	H1
Edmund Hurst Dr EHAM E6		96	A4
Edmund Rd MTCM CR4		162	D3
RAIN RM13		99	G2
WELL DA16		136	B2
Edmunds Av STMC/STPC BR5		155	J7
Edmunds Cl YEAD UB4		83	F4
Edmunds Wk EFNCH N2		53	J3
Edna Rd RYNPK SW20		161	G1
Edna St BTSEA SW11		108	D7
Edrich Rw CAR SM5		176	A7
Edrick Rd EDGW HA8		36	E5
Edrick Wk EDGW HA8		36	E5
Edric Rd NWCR SE14		112	A6
Edridge Cl BUSH WD23		22	C5
Edridge Rd CROY/NA CR0		177	J2
Edulf Rd BORE WD6		24	D1
Edward Av CHING E4		43	K5
MRDN SM4		162	C4
Edward Cl CRICK NW2 *		70	B3
ED N9		30	B6
HPTN TW12		142	C4

Street	Area	Page	Grid
Edward Ct CAN/RD E16		94	E4
Edwardes Pl WKENS W14		107	J2
Edwardes Sq KENS W8		14	A4
Edward Gv EBAR EN4		27	H4
Edward Mann Cl East WCHPL E1 *		93	F5
Edward Mann Cl West WCHPL E1 *		93	F5
Edward Ms CAMTN NW1 *		4	D7
Edward Pl DEPT SE8		112	C5
Edward Rd BMLY BR1		153	F6
CHDH RM6		62	A5
CHST BR7		154	B4
CROY/NA CR0		165	F6
EBAR EN4		27	H4
EBED/NFELT TW14		121	G5
HPTN TW12		142	C4
NTHLT UB5		83	G1
PGE/AN SE20		151	F6
RYLN/HDSTN HA2		48	C2
WALTH E17		57	F3
Edwards Av RSLP HA4		65	G4
Edwards Cl WPK KT4		174	B1
Edwards Dr FBAR/BDGN N11		40	D6
Edward's La STNW/STAM N16		73	K1
Edwards Ms IS N1		6	B1
MHST W1U		10	A5
Edwards Pl FBAR/BDGN N11		40	D6
Edward Sq IS N1		5	L4
Edwards Rd BELV DA17		117	H3
Edward Sq CAN/RD E16		94	F3
NWCR SE14		112	B6
Edward Temme Av SRTFD E15		76	D6
Edward Tyler Rd LEE/GVPK SE12		153	F1
Edwina Gdns REDBR IG4		59	J4
Edwin Cl BXLYHN DA7		117	G5
Edwin Hall Pl LEW SE13		133	G5
Edwin Pl CROY/NA CR0		164	E7
Edwin Rd EDGW HA8		37	F5
WHTN TW2		123	K7
Edwin's Md HOM E9		75	G4
Edwin St CAN/RD E16		94	E4
WCHPL E1		92	E3
Edwin Ware Ct PIN HA5 *		47	G1
Edwyn Cl BAR EN5		26	A5
Effie Pl FUL/PGN SW6		107	K6
Effie Rd FUL/PGN SW6		107	K6
Effingham Cl BELMT SM2		175	F6
Effingham Rd CEND/HSY/T N8		55	G4
CROY/NA CR0		164	A6
LEE/GVPK SE12		133	H4
SURB KT6		158	C6
Effort St TOOT SW17		147	J4
Effra Pde BRXS/STRHM SW2		130	B4
Effra Rd BRXS/STRHM SW2		130	B4
WIM/MER SW19		147	F5
Egan Wy HYS/HAR UB3		82	C6
Egbert St CAMTN NW1		4	A3
Egerton Cl PIN HA5		46	E3
Egerton Crs CHEL SW3		15	K5
Egerton Dr GNWCH SE10		112	E7
Egerton Gdns CHEL SW3		15	J4
GDMY/SEVK IG3		79	F2
HDN NW4		51	K3
WEA W13		85	H5
WLSDN NW10 *		70	A7
Egerton Gardens Ms CHEL SW3		15	K4
Egerton Pl CHEL SW3 *		15	K4
Egerton Rd ALP/SUD HA0		68	B6
NWMAL KT3		160	C3
SNWD SE25		165	F2
STNW/STAM N16		56	B6
WHTN TW2		123	K6
Egerton Ter CHEL SW3		15	K4
Egerton Wy HYS/HAR UB3		100	E6
Egham Cl CHEAM SM3		174	C1
Egham Crs CHEAM SM3		174	B2
Egham Rd PLSTW E13		95	F4
Eglantine Rd WAND/EARL SW18		128	B4
Egleston Rd MRDN SM4		162	A5
Eglinton Hl WOOL/PLUM SE18		115	G6
Eglinton Rd WOOL/PLUM SE18		115	F5
Egliston Ms PUT/ROE SW15		127	F2
Egliston Rd PUT/ROE SW15		127	F2
Egion Ms CAMTN NW1		3	M2
Egmont Av SURB KT6		159	G7
Egmont Rd BELMT SM2		175	F6
NWMAL KT3		160	C3
SURB KT6		159	G7
WOT/HER KT12		156	A7
Egmont St NWCR SE14		112	A6
Egremont Rd WNWD SE27		149	G2
Egret Wy YEAD UB4		83	H5
Eider Cl SRTFD E15		76	D4
Eighteenth Rd MTCM CR4		163	K3
Eighth Av HYS/HAR UB3		82	E7
MNPK E12		77	K3
Eileen Rd SNWD SE25		164	E4
Eindhoven Cl CAR SM5		163	F7
Eisenhower Dr EHAM E6		95	J4
Elaine Av HTHAIR TW5		72	A4
Elam Cl CMBW SE5		130	C1
Elam St CMBW SE5		130	C1
Eland Rd BTSEA SW11		128	E2
CROY/NA CR0		177	H2
Elba Pl WALW SE17 *		18	F5
Elberon Av CROY/NA CR0		163	H5
Elbe St FUL/PGN SW6		128	B1
Elborough Rd SNWD SE25		165	H4
Elborough St WAND/EARL SW18		127	K7
Elbury Dr CAN/RD E16		94	E5
Elcho St BTSEA SW11		108	D6
Elcot Av PECK SE15		111	J6
Elder Av CEND/HSY/T N8		54	E4
Elderberry Rd EA W5		105	F1
Elder Cl BFN/LL DA15		136	A7
TRDG/WHET N20		39	F1
Elder Ct BUSH WD23		34	E1
Elderfield Pl TOOT SW17		148	B3
Elderfield Wk WAN E11		59	F4
Elderflower Wy SRTFD E15		76	C6
Elder Oak Cl PGE/AN SE20		150	D7
Elder Rd WNWD SE27		149	J4
Elderslie Cl BECK BR3		166	E5
Elderslie Rd ELTH/MOT SE9		135	F4
Elder St WCHPL E1		13	L2
Elderton Rd SYD SE26		151	G3
Eldertree Pl MTCM CR4		148	C7
Eldertree Wy MTCM CR4		148	B7
Elder Wk IS N1		6	D3
Eldon Av BORE WD6		24	C1

CROY/NA CR0 178 E1
HEST TW5 103 F6
Eldon Gv HAMP NW3 71 H4
Eldon Pde WDGN N22 * 41 H7
Eldon Pk SNWD SE25 165 J3
Eldon Rd ED N9 30 E7
KENS W8 14 D4
WALTH E17 57 H3
WDGN N22 41 H7
Eldon St LVPST EC2M 13 H3
Eldon Wy WLSDN NW10 86 D1
Eldridge Cl EBED/NFELT TW14 121 K7
Eleanora Ter SUT SM1 * 175 G4
Eleanor Cl BERM/RHTH SE16 112 A1
SEVS/STOTM N15 56 B2
Eleanor Crs MLHL NW7 38 B3
Eleanor Gdns BAR EN5 26 B4
Eleanor Gv BARN SW13 126 B2
Eleanor Rd FBAR/BDGN N11 40 E5
HACK E8 74 D5
SRTFD E15 76 D5
Eleanor St BOW E3 93 J2
Electra Av HTHAIR TW6 121 J2
Electric Av BRXN/ST SW9 130 B3
Electric La BRXN/ST SW9 * 130 B3
Electric Pde SURB KT6 158 E5
Elephant & Castle STHWK SE1 18 D5
Elephant La BERM/RHTH SE16 111 K1
Elephant Rd WALW SE17 18 E5
Elers Rd HYS/HAR UB3 101 F3
WEA W13 104 D1
Eley Rd UED N18 43 F4
Elfindale Rd HNHL SE24 130 D4
Elfin Gv TEDD TW11 143 F4
Elford Cl BKHTH/KID SE3 134 B3
Elfort Rd HBRY N5 73 G3
Elfrida Crs CAT SE6 151 J3
Elfrida Rd WATW WD18 21 G4
Elf Rw WAP E1W 92 E6
Elfwine Rd HNWL W7 84 E4
Elgar Av BRYLDS KT5 159 J7
EA W5 105 F1
STRHM/NOR SW16 163 K2
WLSDN NW10 69 F5
Elgar Cl BKHH IG9 45 H1
BORE WD6 23 J6
DEPT SE8 112 D6
PLSTW E13 95 G1
Elgar St BERM/RHTH SE16 112 B1
Elgin Av ASHF TW15 140 A5
KTN/HRWW/WS HA3 49 H1
MV/WKIL W9 8 A1
SHB W12 106 D1
Elgin Cl SHB W12 106 E1
Elgin Crs HTHAIR TW6 121 H1
NTGHL W11 88 C6
Elgin Dr NTHWD HA6 32 C6
Elgin Est MV/WKIL W9 8 A1
Elgin Ms NTGHL W11 88 C5
Elgin Ms North MV/WKIL W9 2 D7
Elgin Ms South MV/WKIL W9 2 D8
Elgin Rd CROY/NA CR0 178 B1
GDMY/SEVK IG3 60 E7
SUT SM1 175 G2
WDGN N22 54 C1
WLGTN SM6 176 C5
Elgood Av NTHWD HA6 32 E5
Elgood Cl NTGHL W11 88 C6
Elham Cl BMLY BR1 153 H6
Elia Ms IS N1 6 C6
Elias Pl VX/NE SW8 110 B5
Elia St IS N1 6 C6
Elibank Rd ELTH/MOT SE9 135 F3
Elim St STHWK SE1 19 J3
Elim Wy PLSTW E13 94 D2
Eliot Bank FSTH SE23 150 D1
Eliot Dr RYLN/HDSTN HA2 66 B1
Eliot Gdns PUT/ROE SW15 126 D3
Eliot Hl LEW SE13 133 F1
Eliot Ms STJWD NW8 2 E6
Eliot Pk LEW SE13 133 F1
Eliot Pl BKHTH/KID SE3 133 H1
Eliot Rd DAGW RM9 79 K3
Eliot V BKHTH/KID SE3 133 G1
Elizabethan Wy
STWL/WRAY TW19 120 A6
Elizabeth Av ENC/FH EN2 29 H2
IL IG1 78 D1
IS N1 6 F2
Elizabeth Barnes Ct
FUL/PGN SW6 * 128 A1
Elizabeth Br BGVA SW1W 16 C6
Elizabeth Cl BAR EN5 26 B2
MV/WKIL W9 * 8 F1
SUT SM1 174 D3
Elizabeth Clyde Cl
SEVS/STOTM N15 56 A3
Elizabeth Cots RCH/KEW TW9 105 G7
Elizabeth Fry Pl
WOOL/PLUM SE18 114 D7
Elizabeth Gdns ACT W3 87 H7
ISLW TW7 124 B3
STAN HA7 35 J5
SUN TW16 156 B2
Elizabeth Ms HAMP NW3 71 J5
Elizabeth Pl SEVS/STOTM N15 55 K3
Elizabeth Ride ED N9 30 D6
Elizabeth Rd EHAM E6 77 H7
RAIN RM13 99 K4
SEVS/STOTM N15 56 A4
Elizabeth Sq
BERM/RHTH SE16 93 G6
Elizabeth St BGVA SW1W 16 B5
Elizabeth Wy FELT TW13 141 G3
NRWD SE19 149 K6
Elkanette Ms
TRDG/WHET N20 39 G1
Elkington Rd PLSTW E13 95 F3
The Elkins ROM RM1 63 G1
Elkstone Rd NKENS W10 88 D4
Ellaline Rd HMSMTH W6 107 G5
Ella Ms HAMP NW3 71 K3
Ellanby Crs UED N18 42 D4
Elland Cl BAR EN5 27 H4
Elland Rd PECK SE15 131 K3
Ella Rd CEND/HSY/T N8 54 E6
Ellement Cl PIN HA5 47 H4
Ellenborough Pl
PUT/ROE SW15 126 D3
Ellenborough Rd SCUP DA14 155 K5
WDGN N22 41 J7
Ellenbridge Wy
SAND/SEL CR2 178 A7
Ellen Cl BMLY BR1 168 C2
Ellen Ct ED N9 42 E1
Ellen St WCHPL E1 * 92 C5
Ellen Webb Dr
KTN/HRWW/WS HA3 48 E2
Elleray Rd TEDD TW11 143 F5
Ellerby St FUL/PGN SW6 107 G7
Ellerdale Cl HAMP NW3 71 G4
Ellerdale Rd HAMP NW3 71 G4
Ellerdale St LEW SE13 132 E3
Ellerdine Rd HSLW TW3 123 H3
Ellerker Gdns
RCHPK/HAM TW10 125 F5
Ellerman Av WHTN TW2 122 E7
Ellerslie Rd SHB W12 87 K7
Ellerton Gdns DAGW RM9 79 J6
Ellerton Rd BARN SW13 * 106 D7
DAGW RM9 79 J6
RYNPK SW20 145 J6
SURB KT6 172 B1
WAND/EARL SW18 128 C7
Ellery Rd NRWD SE19 149 K6
Ellery St PECK SE15 131 J1
Ellesborough Cl OXHEY WD19 33 G4
Ellesmere Av BECK BR3 166 E1
MLHL NW7 37 F2
Ellesmere Cl RSLP HA4 46 A6
WAN E11 58 D4
Ellesmere Gdns REDBR IG4 59 J4
Ellesmere Gv BAR EN5 26 D4
Ellesmere Rd BOW E3 93 G1
GFD/PVL UB6 84 C3
TWK TW1 124 D5
WLSDN NW10 69 J4
Ellesmere St POP/IOD E14 93 K5
Ellingfort Rd HACK E8 74 D6
Ellingham Rd CHSGTN KT9 171 K5
SHB W12 106 D1
SRTFD E15 76 B3
Ellington Rd FELT TW13 140 D3
HSLW TW3 123 G1
MUSWH N10 54 B3
Ellington St HOLWY N7 73 G5
Elliot Cl SRTFD E15 76 C6
WBLY HA9 68 B2
WFD IG8 45 H5
Elliot Rd HDN NW4 51 K5
Elliott Av RSLP HA4 65 F1
Elliott Rd BRXN/ST SW9 110 C6
CHSWK W4 106 B3
HAYES BR2 168 C3
STAN HA7 35 G5
THHTH CR7 164 C3
Elliott's Pl IS N1 6 D4
Elliott Sq HAMP NW3 3 K2
Elliott's Rw LBTH SE11 18 D5
Ellis Av RAIN RM13 99 J4
Ellis Cl EDGW HA8 37 G5
ELTH/MOT SE9 154 C1
WLSDN NW10 70 A5
Elliscombe Mt CHARL SE7 * 114 B5
Elliscombe Rd CHARL SE7 114 B4
Ellisfield Dr PUT/ROE SW15 126 C6
Ellison Gdns NWDGN UB2 102 E3
Ellison Rd BARN SW13 126 C1
BFN/LL DA15 135 J7
STRHM/NOR SW16 148 D6
Ellis Rd MTCM CR4 162 E5
NWDGN UB2 84 C7
Ellis St KTBR SW1X 15 M5
Ellora Rd STRHM/NOR SW16 148 D4
Ellsworth St BETH E2 * 92 D2
Elmar Rd SEVS/STOTM N15 55 K3
Elm Av EA W5 86 A7
OXHEY WD19 21 J6
RSLP HA4 46 E7
Elmbank STHGT/OAK N14 28 E6
Elmbank Av BAR EN5 26 A3
Elmbank Dr BMLY BR1 168 C1
Elm Bank Gdns BARN SW13 126 B1
Elmbank Wy HNWL W7 84 D4
Elmbourne Dr BELV DA17 117 J3
Elmbourne Rd TOOT SW17 148 B2
Elmbridge Av BRYLDS KT5 159 K5
Elmbridge Cl RSLP HA4 46 E5
Elmbridge Dr RSLP HA4 46 E5
Elmbridge Wk HACK E8 * 74 C6
Elmbrook Cl SUN TW16 141 F7
Elmbrook Gdns
ELTH/MOT SE9 134 D3
Elmbrook Rd SUT SM1 174 D3
Elm Cl BKHH IG9 45 H1
BRYLDS KT5 159 K6
CAR SM5 162 E7
HDN NW4 52 B4
HYS/HAR UB3 82 E5
RYLN/HDSTN HA2 48 B5
RYNPK SW20 161 F3
SAND/SEL CR2 177 K5
STWL/WRAY TW19 120 A7
WAN E11 59 F5
WHTN TW2 142 B1
Elm Cots MTCM CR4 * 162 E1
Elm Ct WAT WD17 * 21 F2
Elmcourt Rd WNWD SE27 149 H1
Elm Crs EA W5 105 F1
KUTN/CMB KT2 144 A7
Elmcroft CEND/HSY/T N8 55 F4
Elmcroft Av BFN/LL DA15 136 A6
ED N9 30 D5
GLDGN NW11 52 D6
WAN E11 59 F4
Elmcroft Cl CHSGTN KT9 * 172 A2
EA W5 85 K5
EBED/NFELT TW14 121 J5
Elmcroft Crs GLDGN NW11 52 B6
RYLN/HDSTN HA2 48 A2
Elmcroft Dr CHSGTN KT9 172 A2
Elmcroft Gdns
CDALE/KGS NW9 50 C4
Elmcroft St CLPT E5 74 E3
Elmdale Rd PLMGR N13 41 F4
Elmdene BRYLDS KT5 159 K7
Elmdene Cl BECK BR3 166 C4
Elmdene Rd
WOOL/PLUM SE18 115 G4
Elmdon Rd HSLWW TW4 122 C1
HTHAIR TW6 121 J2
Elm Dr RYLN/HDSTN HA2 48 B5
SUN TW16 156 B1
Elmer Cl ENC/FH EN2 29 F2
RAIN RM13 81 J6
Elmer Gdns EDGW HA8 36 D6
ISLW TW7 123 J2
RAIN RM13 81 J6
Elmer Rd CAT SE6 133 F6
Elmer's Dr TEDD TW11 143 H5
Elmers End Rd BECK BR3 165 K2
Elmerside Rd BECK BR3 166 B3
Elmers Rd SNWD SE25 165 H6
Elmfield Av CEND/HSY/T N8 54 E4
MTCM CR4 148 A7
TEDD TW11 143 F4
Elmfield Cl HRW HA1 66 E1
Elmfield Pk BMLY BR1 167 K2
Elmfield Rd BMLY BR1 167 K2
CHING E4 44 A1
EFNCH N2 53 H2
NWDGN UB2 102 D2
TOOT SW17 148 B1
WALTH E17 57 F5
Elmfield Wy MV/WKIL W9 8 A2
SAND/SEL CR2 178 B7
Elm Friars Wk CAMTN NW1 5 H2
Elm Gdns EFNCH N2 53 G2
ESH/CLAY KT10 171 F5
MTCM CR4 163 J3
Elmgate Av FELT TW13 141 F2
Elmgate Gdns EDGW HA8 36 E4
Elm Gn ACT W3 87 G5
Elmgreen Cl SRTFD E15 76 C7
Elm Gv CEND/HSY/T N8 54 E5
CRICK NW2 70 B3
ERITH DA8 118 A6
KUTN/CMB KT2 144 A7
PECK SE15 131 H1
RYLN/HDSTN HA2 48 A6
SUT SM1 175 F3
WIM/MER SW19 146 C6
Elmgrove Crs HRW HA1 49 F4
Elmgrove Gdns HRW HA1 49 G4
Elm Grove Pde CAR SM5 176 A2
Elm Grove Rd EA W5 105 F1
BARN SW13 126 D1
Elmgrove Rd CROY/NA CR0 165 J6
HRW HA1 49 F4
Elm Hall Gdns WAN E11 59 F5
Elm Hatch PIN HA5 33 K6
Elmhurst BELV DA17 117 F5
Elmhurst Av EFNCH N2 53 H2
MTCM CR4 148 A6
Elmhurst Cl BUSH WD23 21 J3
Elmhurst Crs EFNCH N2 53 H2
Elmhurst Dr SWFD E18 58 E1
Elmhurst Rd ELTH/MOT SE9 153 J1
FSTGT E7 77 F6
TOTM N17 56 A1
Elmhurst St CLAP SW4 129 J2
Elmington Cl BXLY DA5 137 J6
Elmington Est CMBW SE5 110 D6
Elmington Rd CMBW SE5 110 E7
Elmira St LEW SE13 132 E2
Elm La CAT SE6 151 H1
Elmlee Cl CHST BR7 153 K5
Elmley St WOOL/PLUM SE18 115 J3
Elmore Cl ALP/SUD HA0 86 A1
Elmore Rd WAN E11 76 A2
Elmore St IS N1 7 C1
Elm Pde SCUP DA14 * 155 C3
Elm Pk BRXS/STRHM SW2 130 A5
STAN HA7 35 H4
Elm Park Av HCH RM12 81 J3
SEVS/STOTM N15 56 B4
Elm Park Gdns HDN NW4 52 B4
WBPTN SW10 15 G8
Elm Park La CHEL SW3 15 G9
Elm Park Rd CHEL SW3 15 G9
FNCH N3 38 D6
LEY E10 57 G7
PIN HA5 47 H2
SNWD SE25 165 G2
WCHMH N21 29 J6
Elm Pl SKENS SW7 15 G7
Elm Rd BAR EN5 26 D3
BECK BR3 166 C1
CHSGTN KT9 172 A3
EBED/NFELT TW14 121 G7
ERITH DA8 118 D7
ESH/CLAY KT10 171 F5
EW KT17 173 H5
FSTGT E7 76 D5
KUTN/CMB KT2 144 B6
MORT/ESHN SW14 125 K2
NWMAL KT3 160 A2
ROMW/RG RM7 62 D1
SCUP DA14 155 G3
THHTH CR7 164 D3
WALTH E17 58 A4
WBLY HA9 68 A4
WDGN N22 41 H7
WLGTN SM6 163 F7
Elm Rd West CHEAM SM3 161 J6
Elm Rw HAMP NW3 71 G2
Elms Av HDN NW4 52 A4
MUSWH N10 54 B2
Elmscott Gdns WCHMH N21 29 J5
Elmscott Rd BMLY BR1 152 C4
Elms Ct ALP/SUD HA0 67 F3
Elms Crs CLAP SW4 129 H5
Elmsdale Rd WALTH E17 57 H3
Elms Gdns ALP/SUD HA0 67 G3
DAGW RM9 80 B3
Elmshaw Rd PUT/ROE SW15 126 D4
Elmshurst Crs EFNCH N2 53 G3
Elmside CROY/NA CR0 179 K5
Elmside Rd WBLY HA9 68 C2
Elms La ALP/SUD HA0 67 G3
Elmsleigh Av
KTN/HRWW/WS HA3 49 H3
Elmsleigh Rd WHTN TW2 142 D1
Elmslie Cl WFD IG8 45 K5
Elms Ms BAY/PAD W2 9 G6
Elms Park Av ALP/SUD HA0 67 G3
Elms Rd CLAP SW4 129 H4
KTN/HRWW/WS HA3 34 E6
Elmstead Av CHST BR7 153 K4
WBLY HA9 50 A7
Elmstead Cl HOR/WEW KT19 173 G4
TRDG/WHET N20 38 E1
Elmstead Gdns WPK KT4 173 J2
Elmstead Gld CHST BR7 153 K5
Elmstead La CHST BR7 153 J6
CHST BR7 153 K4
Elmstead Rd ERITH DA8 118 B7
GDMY/SEVK IG3 78 E1
The Elms BARN SW13 126 C2
ESH/CLAY KT10 * 171 F6
NFNCH/WDSPK N12 * 39 J4
TOOT SW17 * 148 A2
WLGTN SM6 * 176 C3
Elmstone Rd FUL/PGN SW6 107 K7
Elm St FSBYW WC1X 11 M1
Elmsworth Av HSLW TW3 123 G1
Elm Ter CRICK NW2 70 E2
ELTH/MOT SE9 135 F5
KTN/HRWW/WS HA3 34 D6
Elmton Wy CLPT E5 74 C2
Elm Tree Av ESH/CLAY KT10 157 J6
Elm Tree Cl NTHLT UB5 83 K1
STJWD NW8 3 G7
Elm Tree Ct CHARL SE7 * 114 B5
Elm Tree Rd STJWD NW8 3 G7
Elmtree Rd TEDD TW11 142 E4
Elm Vls HNWL W7 * 84 E6
Elm Wk GPK RM2 63 J2
HAMP NW3 70 E1
ORP BR6 181 K2
RYNPK SW20 161 F3
Elm Wy FBAR/BDGN N11 40 A5
HOR/WEW KT19 173 F4
WLSDN NW10 69 G3
WPK KT4 174 A2
Elmwood Av BORE WD6 24 D3
FELT TW13 141 F2
KTN/HRWW/WS HA3 49 G4
PLMGR N13 40 E4
Elmwood Cl EW KT17 173 J6
WLGTN SM6 176 B1
Elmwood Crs
CDALE/KGS NW9 50 E3
Elmwood Dr BXLY DA5 137 F6
EW KT17 173 J6
Elmwood Gdns HNWL W7 84 E5
Elmwood Rd CHSWK W4 105 K5
CROY/NA CR0 164 C6
HNHL SE24 130 E4
MTCM CR4 162 E2
Elmworth Gv DUL SE21 149 K1
Elnathan Ms MV/WKIL W9 8 D1
Elphinstone Rd WALTH E17 57 H1
Elphinstone St HBRY N5 73 H3
Elrington Rd HACK E8 74 C5
WFD IG8 44 E4
Elruge Cl WDR/YW UB7 100 A2
Elsa Cots POP/IOD E14 * 93 G4
Elsa Rd WELL DA16 136 D1
Elsa St WCHPL E1 * 93 G4
Elsdale St HOM E9 74 E5
Elsden Ms BETH E2 * 92 E1
Elsden Rd TOTM N17 42 B7
Elsenham Rd MNPK E12 77 K4
Elsenham St
WAND/EARL SW18 127 J7
Elsham Rd WAN E11 76 C2
WKENS W14 107 H1
Elsham Ter WKENS W14 * 107 H1
Elsiedene Rd WCHMH N21 29 J6
Elsie Lane Ct BAY/PAD W2 8 B3
Elsiemaud Rd BROCKY SE4 132 C4
Elsie Rd EDUL SE22 131 G3
Elsinore Av
STWL/WRAY TW19 * 120 B6
Elsinore Gdns CRICK NW2 * 70 C2
Elsinore Rd FSTH SE23 132 B7
Elsinore Wy RCH/KEW TW9 125 J2
Elsley Rd BTSEA SW11 128 E2
Elspeth Rd ALP/SUD HA0 68 A4
BTSEA SW11 128 E3
Elsrick Av MRDN SM4 161 K4
Elstan Wy CROY/NA CR0 166 B6
Elsted St WALW SE17 19 H6
Elstow Cl ELTH/MOT SE9 134 E4
RSLP HA4 47 H6
Elstow Gdns DAGW RM9 80 A7
Elstow Rd DAGW RM9 80 A6
Elstree Cl HCH RM12 81 K6
Elstree Gdns BELV DA17 117 F3
ED N9 30 D7
IL IG1 78 C4
Elstree Ga BORE WD6 * 25 F1
Elstree Hl BMLY BR1 152 C6
Elstree Hl North BORE WD6 23 K4
Elstree Hl South BORE WD6 23 J6
Elstree Pk BORE WD6 * 25 F5
Elstree Rd BUSH WD23 22 D7
Elstree Wy BORE WD6 24 E1
Elswick Rd LEW SE13 132 E1
Elswick St FUL/PGN SW6 128 B1
Elsworth Cl
EBED/NFELT TW14 121 H7
Elsworthy THDIT KT7 157 K5
Elsworthy Ri HAMP NW3 3 K2
Elsworthy Rd HAMP NW3 3 J3
Elsworthy Ter HAMP NW3 3 K2
Elsynge Rd WAND/EARL SW18 128 C4
Eltham Gn ELTH/MOT SE9 134 B4
Eltham Green Rd
ELTH/MOT SE9 134 B3
Eltham High St
ELTH/MOT SE9 134 E5
Eltham Hl ELTH/MOT SE9 134 C4
Eltham Palace Rd
ELTH/MOT SE9 134 B5
Eltham Park Gdns
ELTH/MOT SE9 135 F3
Eltham Rd ELTH/MOT SE9 134 B4
Elthiron Rd FUL/PGN SW6 107 K7
Elthorne Av HNWL W7 104 A1
Elthorne Ct FELT TW13 122 B7
Elthorne Park Rd HNWL W7 104 A2
Elthorne Rd ARCH N19 72 D1
CDALE/KGS NW9 51 F6
Elthorne Wy CDALE/KGS NW9 51 F5
Elthruda Rd LEW SE13 133 G5
Eltisley Rd IL IG1 78 B3
Elton Av ALP/SUD HA0 67 H4
BAR EN5 26 D4
GFD/PVL UB6 67 F5
Elton Cl KUT/HW KT1 143 J6
Elton Pk WAT WD17 20 E1
Elton Pl STNW/STAM N16 74 A4
Elton Rd KUTN/CMB KT2 144 B7
Eltringham St
WAND/EARL SW18 128 B3
Elvaston Ms SKENS SW7 14 F4
Elvaston Pl SKENS SW7 14 E4
Elveden Pl WLSDN NW10 86 C1
Elveden Rd WLSDN NW10 86 C1
Elvedon Rd FELT TW13 140 D2
Elvendon Rd FBAR/BDGN N11 40 E5
Elver Gdns BETH E2 92 C2
Elverson Ms DEPT SE8 * 112 C6
Elverson Rd DEPT SE8 132 E1
Elverton St WEST SW1P 17 G5
Elvington Gn HAYES BR2 167 J4
Elvington La CDALE/KGS NW9 37 G7
Elvino Rd SYD SE26 151 F4
Elvis Rd CRICK NW2 70 A5
Elwill Wy BECK BR3 167 F3
Elwin St BETH E2 92 C2
Elwood St HBRY N5 73 H2
Ely Cl ERITH DA8 138 C1
NWMAL KT3 160 C1
Ely Cots VX/NE SW8 * 110 A6
Ely Gdns BORE WD6 25 F4
DAGE RM10 80 E2
Elyne Rd FSBYPK N4 55 G5
Ely Pl HCIRC EC1N 12 B3
Ely Rd CROY/NA CR0 164 E4
HSLWW TW4 122 B2
HTHAIR TW6 121 J1
LEY E10 58 A5
Elysan Pl SAND/SEL CR2 177 J6
Elysian Av STMC/STPC BR5 169 K5
Elysium Pl FUL/PGN SW6 127 J1
Elysium St FUL/PGN SW6 127 J1
Elystan Cl WLGTN SM6 176 C7
Elystan Pl CHEL SW3 15 K7
Elystan St CHEL SW3 15 J6
Elystan Wk IS N1 6 A4
Emanuel Av ACT W3 86 E5
Embankment PUT/ROE SW15 127 G2
Embankment Gdns CHEL SW3 15 M9
Embankment Pl CHCR WC2N 11 K8
The Embankment TWK TW1 124 B7
Embassy Ct SCUP DA14 155 H2
WLGTN SM6 * 176 B5
Emba St BERM/RHTH SE16 111 H1
Ember Cl STMC/STPC BR5 169 H6
Embercourt Rd THDIT KT7 157 K5
Ember Farm Av
E/WMO/HCT KT8 157 J5
Ember Farm Wy
E/WMO/HCT KT8 157 J4
Ember Gdns THDIT KT7 157 K6
Ember La ESH/CLAY KT10 157 J6
Emblem Ct EDUL SE22 131 H4
Embleton Rd LEW SE13 132 E3
OXHEY WD19 32 E2
Embry Cl STAN HA7 35 G3
Embry Dr STAN HA7 35 G5
Embry Wy STAN HA7 35 G4
Emden Cl WDR/YW UB7 100 D1
Emden St FUL/PGN SW6 108 A7
Emerald Cl CAN/RD E16 95 J5
Emerald Gdns BCTR RM8 62 B7
Emerald Sq NWDGN UB2 102 C2
Emerald St BMSBY WC1N 11 L2
Emerson Gdns
KTN/HRWW/WS HA3 50 B5
Emerson Rd IL IG1 60 A6
Emerson St STHWK SE1 12 E8
Emery Hill St WEST SW1P 16 F4
Emery St STHWK SE1 18 B3
Emes Rd ERITH DA8 117 K6
Emilia Cl PEND EN3 30 D4
Emily St CAN/RD E16 94 D5
Emlyn Rd SHB W12 106 B1
Emmanuel Rd BAL SW12 129 H7
NTHWD HA6 32 D6
Emma Rd PLSTW E13 94 D1
Emma St BETH E2 92 D1
Emma Ter RYNPK SW20 * 146 A6
Emmott Av BARK/HLT IG6 60 C4
Emmott Cl GLDGN NW11 53 G5
WCHPL E1 93 G3
Emperor's Ga SKENS SW7 14 E5
Empire Av UED N18 41 J5
Empire Pde UED N18 * 41 K5
WBLY HA9 * 68 C2
Empire Rd GFD/PVL UB6 67 H7
Empire Sq STHWK SE1 19 G2
Empire Wy WBLY HA9 68 B3
Empire Wharf Rd
POP/IOD E14 113 G3
Empress Av CHING E4 43 K6
IL IG1 78 A1
MNPK E12 77 G1
WFD IG8 44 D6
Empress Dr CHST BR7 154 B5
Empress Pde CHING E4 * 43 J6
Empress Pl FUL/PGN SW6 14 A8
Empress St WALW SE17 18 F9
Empson St BOW E3 93 K3
Emsworth Cl ED N9 30 E7
Emsworth Rd BARK/HLT IG6 60 B1
Emsworth St
BRXS/STRHM SW2 149 F1
Emu Rd VX/NE SW8 129 G1
Ena Rd STRHM/NOR SW16 163 K2
Enbrook St NKENS W10 88 C2
Enclave Ct FSBYE EC1V 6 D9
Endale Cl CAR SM5 175 K1
Endeavour Wy BARK IG11 97 G1
CROY/NA CR0 163 J6
WIM/MER SW19 147 F3
Endell St LSQ/SEVD WC2H 11 J4
Enderby St GNWCH SE10 113 H4
Enderley Rd
KTN/HRWW/WS HA3 34 D7
Endersby Rd BAR EN5 26 A4
Endersleigh Gdns HDN NW4 51 J3
Endlebury Rd CHING E4 44 A1
Endlesham Rd BAL SW12 129 F6
Endsleigh Gdns IL IG1 59 K7
STPAN WC1H 5 G9
SURB KT6 158 D5
Endsleigh Pl STPAN WC1H 5 H9
Endsleigh Rd NWDGN UB2 102 D3
WEA W13 85 G7
Endsleigh St STPAN WC1H 5 H9
Endway BRYLDS KT5 159 H6
Endwell Rd BROCKY SE4 132 B1
Endymion Rd
BRXS/STRHM SW2 130 A5
FSBYPK N4 55 H6
Energen Cl WLSDN NW10 69 G5
Enfield Rd ACT W3 105 J1
BTFD TW8 104 E4
ENC/FH EN2 28 D3
HTHAIR TW6 121 H1
IS N1 7 K2
Enford St CAMTN NW1 9 L2
Engadine Cl CROY/NA CR0 178 B2
Engadine St
WAND/EARL SW18 127 J7
Engate St LEW SE13 133 F3
Engel Pk MLHL NW7 38 A5
Engineer Cl WOOL/PLUM SE18 115 F5
Engineers Wy WBLY HA9 68 C3
England's La HAMP NW3 71 K5
England Wy NWMAL KT3 159 J3
Englefield Cl CROY/NA CR0 164 D5
ENC/FH EN2 29 G1
Englefield Rd IS N1 7 H1
Engleheart Dr
EBED/NFELT TW14 121 J5
Engleheart Rd CAT SE6 132 E6
Englewood Rd BAL SW12 129 G5
English St BOW E3 93 H3
Enid St BERM/RHTH SE16 19 M3
Enmore Av SNWD SE25 165 H4
Enmore Gdns
MORT/ESHN SW14 126 A4
Enmore Rd PUT/ROE SW15 127 F3
SNWD SE25 165 H4
STHL UB1 84 A3
Ennerdale Av HCH RM12 81 J4
STAN HA7 49 J2
Ennerdale Cl
EBED/NFELT TW14 121 J7
SUT SM1 174 D3
Ennerdale Dr CDALE/KGS NW9 51 G4
Ennerdale Gdns WBLY HA9 49 J7
Ennerdale Rd RCH/KEW TW9 125 G1
Ennersdale Rd LEW SE13 133 G4
Ennismore Av CHSWK W4 106 B3
GFD/PVL UB6 66 E5
Ennismore Gdns SKENS SW7 15 H3
THDIT KT7 157 K5
Ennismore Gardens Ms
SKENS SW7 15 H3
Ennismore Ms SKENS SW7 15 J2
Ennismore St SKENS SW7 15 J3
Ennis Rd FSBYPK N4 55 G7
WOOL/PLUM SE18 115 J5
Ensign Cl HTHAIR TW6 121 H1
STWL/WRAY TW19 120 A7
Ensign Dr PLMGR N13 41 J2
Ensign St WCHPL E1 92 C6
Ensign Wy STWL/WRAY TW19 120 A7
WLGTN SM6 176 E6

WALTH E17 57 K2
Falmouth Av CHING E4 44 B4
Falmouth Cl LEE/GVPK SE12 133 J4
WDGN N22 41 F6
Falmouth Gdns REDBR IG4 59 H3
Falmouth Rd STHWK SE1 18 F4
Falmouth St SRTFD E15 76 B4
Falstaff Ms HPTN TW12 142 D4
Fambridge Cl SYD SE26 151 H3
Fambridge Rd BCTR RM8 62 C7
Fane St WKENS W14 107 J5
Fann St FARR EC1M 12 E1
Fanshawe Av BARK IG11 78 C5
Fanshawe Crs DAGW RM9 80 A4
Fanshawe Rd
RCHPK/HAM TW10 143 J3
Fanshaw St IS N1 7 J7
Fantail Cl THMD SE28 97 J5
Fanthorpe St PUT/ROE SW15 127 F2
Faraday Av SCUP DA14 155 H1
Faraday Cl HOLWY N7 73 F5
WATW WD18 20 B5
Faraday Pl E/WMO/HCT KT8 157 F3
Faraday Rd ACT W3 86 E6
E/WMO/HCT KT8 157 F3
NKENS W10 88 C4
SRTFD E15 76 D5
STHL UB1 84 B6
WELL DA16 136 B2
WIM/MER SW19 147 F5
Faraday Wy
WOOL/PLUM SE18 114 C2
Fareham Rd
EBED/NFELT TW14 122 B6
Fareham St SOHO/CST W1F * 11 G4
Farewell Pl MTCM CR4 147 H7
Faringdon Av HAYES BR2 169 F6
Faringford Rd SRTFD E15 76 C6
Farjeon Rd BKHTH/KID SE3 114 C7
Farleigh Court Rd
CROY/NA CR0 177 F1
Farleigh Pl STNW/STAM N16 74 B3
Farleigh Rd STNW/STAM N16 74 B3
Farley Dr GDMY/SEVK IG3 60 E7
Farley Ms CAT SE6 133 F6
Farley Pl SNWD SE25 165 H3
Farley Rd CAT SE6 133 F6
SAND/SEL CR2 178 C6
Farlington Pl PUT/ROE SW15 126 E6
Farlow Rd PUT/ROE SW15 127 G2
Farlton Rd WAND/EARL SW18 128 A6
Farman Ter
KTN/HRWW/WS HA3 * 49 K3
Farm Av ALP/SUD HA0 67 J5
CRICK NW2 70 C2
RYLN/HDSTN HA2 48 A6
STRHM/NOR SW16 148 E3
Farmborough Cl HRW HA1 48 D6
Farm Cl BAR EN5 25 K4
BELMT SM2 175 H6
BKHH IG9 45 G2
DAGE RM10 80 E6
FUL/PGN SW6 * 107 K6
STHL UB1 84 B6
WWKM BR4 180 C2
Farm Cots E/WMO/HCT KT8 * 158 B3
Farmdale Rd CAR SM5 175 J6
Farm Dr CROY/NA CR0 179 H1
Farmer Rd LEY E10 57 K7
Farmers Rd CMBW SE5 110 C6
Farmer St KENS W8 8 A8
Farmfield Rd BMLY BR1 152 C4
Farmhouse Rd
STRHM/NOR SW16 148 C6
Farmilo Rd WALTH E17 57 J6
Farmington Av SUT SM1 175 H2
Farmlands PIN HA5 46 E3
The Farmlands NTHLT UB5 65 K5
Farmland Wk CHST BR7 154 B4
Farm La CROY/NA CR0 179 H1
FUL/PGN SW6 107 K5
STHGT/OAK N14 28 A5
Farmleigh STHGT/OAK N14 28 C6
Farm Pl KENS W8 8 A8
Farm Rd BELMT SM2 175 H6
EDGW HA8 36 E4
ESH/CLAY KT10 157 F7
HSLWW TW4 122 D7
MRDN SM4 162 A4
NTHWD HA6 32 A4
WCHMH N21 29 J7
WLSDN NW10 69 F7
Farmstead Rd CAT SE6 151 K3
KTN/HRWW/WS HA3 34 D7
Farm St MYFR/PICC W1J 10 C7
The Farm WIM/MER SW19 * 127 G6
Farm V BXLY DA5 137 J5
Farm Wk GLDGN NW11 52 D4
Farmway BCTR RM8 79 J3
Farm Wy BKHH IG9 45 G3
BUSH WD23 22 B3
HCH RM12 81 K3
NTHWD HA6 32 C3
WPK KT4 174 A2
Farnaby Rd BMLY BR1 152 C7
ELTH/MOT SE9 134 B3
Farnan Av WALTH E17 57 J1
Farnan Rd STRHM/NOR SW16 148 E4
Farnborough Av
SAND/SEL CR2 179 G6
WALTH E17 * 57 G2
Farnborough Cl WBLY HA9 68 D1
Farnborough Crs HAYES BR2 167 J7
SAND/SEL CR2 179 G7
Farnborough Wy PECK SE15 * 111 F6
Farncombe St
BERM/RHTH SE16 111 H1
Farndale Av PLMGR N13 41 H2
Farndale Crs GFD/PVL UB6 84 C2
Farnell Ms ECT SW5 14 C7
Farnell Pl ACT W3 86 D6
Farnell Rd ISLW TW7 123 J2
Farnham Cl TRDG/WHET N20 27 G6
Farnham Gdns RYNPK SW20 160 E1
Farnham Pl STHWK SE1 12 D9
Farnham Rd GDMY/SEVK IG3 61 F5
WELL DA16 136 D1
Farnham Royal LBTH SE11 17 M8
Farningham Rd TOTM N17 42 C6
Farnley Rd SNWD SE25 164 E3
Faro Cl BMLY BR1 169 F1
Faroe Rd WKENS W14 107 G2
Farquhar Rd NRWD SE19 150 B4
WIM/MER SW19 146 E2
Farquharson Rd
CROY/NA CR0 164 D6
Farraline Rd WATW WD18 21 F3
Farrance Rd CHDH RM6 62 A5
Farrance St POP/IOD E14 93 J5
Farrant Av WDGN N22 55 G1
Farr Av BARK IG11 97 G1
Farren Rd FSTH SE23 151 G1
Farrer Ms CEND/HSY/T N8 54 C3
Farrer Rd CEND/HSY/T N8 54 C3
KTN/HRWW/WS HA3 50 A4
Farrier Cl BMLY BR1 168 C2
Farrier Pl SUT SM1 175 F2
Farrier Rd NTHLT UB5 84 A1
Farrier St CAMTN NW1 4 D1
Farriers Wy BORE WD6 25 F5
Farrier Wk WBPTN SW10 14 E9
Farringdon La CLKNW EC1R 12 B1
Farringdon Rd CLKNW EC1R 6 A9
HCIRC EC1N 12 C3
Farringdon St
FLST/FETLN EC4A 12 C4
Farrington Pl CHST BR7 154 D6
Farrins Rents
BERM/RHTH SE16 93 G7
Farrow La NWCR SE14 111 K6
Farrow Pl BERM/RHTH SE16 112 B2
Farthingale Wk SRTFD E15 76 B6
Farthing Aly STHWK SE1 * 111 H1
Farthing Cl WATW WD18 21 G4
Farthing Flds WAP E1W 92 D7
Farthings Cl CHING E4 44 C2
PIN HA5 47 F5
The Farthings KUTN/CMB KT2 144 C7
Farthing St HAYES BR2 181 K6
Farwell Rd SCUP DA14 155 H3
Farwig La BMLY BR1 152 E7
Fashion St WCHPL E1 13 L3
Fashoda Rd HAYES BR2 168 C3
Fassett Rd HACK E8 74 C5
KUT/HW KT1 159 F3
Fassett Sq HACK E8 74 C5
Fauconberg Rd CHSWK W4 105 K5
Faulkner Cl BCTR RM8 61 K6
Faulkner St NWCR SE14 111 K7
Fauna Cl CHDH RM6 61 J5
STAN HA7 35 K2
Faunce St WALW SE17 18 C8
Favart Rd FUL/PGN SW6 107 K7
Faversham Av EN EN1 29 K5
Faversham Rd BECK BR3 166 C1
CAT SE6 132 C6
MRDN SM4 162 A5
Fawcett Cl BTSEA SW11 128 C1
STRHM/NOR SW16 149 G3
Fawcett Est CLPT E5 * 56 C7
Fawcett Rd CROY/NA CR0 177 H2
WLSDN NW10 69 H6
Fawcett St WBPTN SW10 14 E9
Fawcus Cl ESH/CLAY KT10 170 E5
Fawe Park Rd PUT/ROE SW15 127 J3
Fawe St POP/IOD E14 93 K4
Fawley Rd KIL/WHAMP NW6 71 F4
Fawnbrake Av HNHL SE24 130 C4
Fawn Rd PLSTW E13 95 G1
Fawns Manor Rd
EBED/NFELT TW14 121 G7
Fawood Av WLSDN NW10 69 F6
Faygate Rd BRXS/STRHM SW2 149 F1
Fayland Av STRHM/NOR SW16 148 C4
Fearnley Crs HPTN TW12 141 J4
Fearnley St WATW WD18 21 F3
Featherbed La SAND/SEL CR2 179 H6
Feathers Pl GNWCH SE10 113 G5
Featherstone Av FSTH SE23 150 D1
Featherstone Gdns
BORE WD6 25 F3
Featherstone Rd MLHL NW7 37 K5
NWDGN UB2 102 D2
Featherstone St STLK EC1Y 7 G9
Featherstone Ter
NWDGN UB2 102 D2
Featley Rd BRXN/ST SW9 130 C2
Federal Rd GFD/PVL UB6 85 J1
Fee Farm Rd ESH/CLAY KT10 171 F6
Feeny Cl WLSDN NW10 69 H3
Felbridge Av STAN HA7 35 G7
Felbridge Cl BELMT SM2 175 F7
STRHM/NOR SW16 149 G3
Felbrigge Rd GDMY/SEVK IG3 79 F1
Felday Rd LEW SE13 132 E5
Felden Cl PIN HA5 33 J6
Felden St FUL/PGN SW6 107 J7
Feldman Cl STNW/STAM N16 56 C7
Felgate Ms HMSMTH W6 106 E3
Felhampton Rd
ELTH/MOT SE9 154 B2
Felix Av CEND/HSY/T N8 54 E5
Felix Pl BRXS/STRHM SW2 130 B4
Felix Rd WEA W13 85 G6
Felixstowe Rd ABYW SE2 116 C2
ED N9 42 C2
SEVS/STOTM N15 56 B2
WLSDN NW10 87 K2
Felix St BETH E2 * 92 D1
Fellbrigg Rd EDUL SE22 131 G4
Fellbrigg St WCHPL E1 92 D3
Fellbrook RCHPK/HAM TW10 143 H2
Fellmongers Yd
CROY/NA CR0 177 J2
Fellowes Cl YEAD UB4 83 H3
Fellowes Rd CAR SM5 175 J2
Fellows Rd HAMP NW3 3 H1
Fell Pth BORE WD6 * 25 F4
Fell Rd CROY/NA CR0 177 J2
Felmersham Cl CLAP SW4 129 K3
Felmingham Rd PGE/AN SE20 165 K1
Felsberg Rd
BRXS/STRHM SW2 129 K5
Fels Cl DAGE RM10 80 D2
Fels Farm Av DAGE RM10 80 E2
Felsham Ms PUT/ROE SW15 127 G2
Felsham Rd PUT/ROE SW15 127 F2
Felspar Cl WOOL/PLUM SE18 116 A4
Felstead Rd HOM E9 75 J5
WAN E11 58 E6
Felstead St HOM E9 75 H5
Felsted Rd CAN/RD E16 95 H5
Feltham Av E/WMO/HCT KT8 157 K3
Felthambrook Wy FELT TW13 141 F2
Feltham Hill Rd ASHF TW15 140 A5
Feltham Rd MTCM CR4 162 E1
Felton Cl STMC/STPC BR5 169 G5
Felton Lea SCUP DA14 155 F4
Felton Rd BARK IG11 96 E1
WEA W13 104 D1
Felton St IS N1 7 H4
Fenchurch Av FENCHST EC3M 13 J5
Fenchurch Blds
FENCHST EC3M 13 K5
Fenchurch Pl
FENCHST EC3M * 13 K6
Fenchurch St FENCHST EC3M 13 J6
Fendall Rd HOR/WEW KT19 172 E4
Fendall St STHWK SE1 19 K3
Fendt Cl CAN/RD E16 94 D5
Fendyke Rd BELV DA17 116 E3
Fenelon Pl WKENS W14 107 J3
Fen Gv BFN/LL DA15 136 A5
Fenham Rd PECK SE15 111 H6
Fenman Ct TOTM N17 42 D7
Fenman Gdns GDMY/SEVK IG3 61 H7
Fenn Cl BMLY BR1 152 E5
Fennel Cl CAN/RD E16 94 C3
CROY/NA CR0 166 A7
Fennells Md HOR/WEW KT19 173 H7
Fennell St WOOL/PLUM SE18 115 F5
Fenner Cl BERM/RHTH SE16 111 J3
Fenner Sq BTSEA SW11 * 128 C2
Fenning St STHWK SE1 19 J1
Fenn St HOM E9 75 F4
Fenstanton Av
NFNCH/WDSPK N12 39 H4
Fen St CAN/RD E16 94 D6
Fentiman Rd VX/NE SW8 110 A5
Fentiman Wy
RYLN/HDSTN HA2 66 B1
Fenton Cl BRXN/ST SW9 * 130 A1
CHST BR7 153 K4
HACK E8 74 B5
Fenton Rd TOTM N17 41 J6
Fenton's Av PLSTW E13 95 F2
Fenton St WCHPL E1 92 D5
Fenwick Gv PECK SE15 131 H2
Fenwick Pl BRXN/ST SW9 129 K2
SAND/SEL CR2 177 H6
Fenwick Rd PECK SE15 131 H2
Ferdinand Pl CAMTN NW1 4 B1
Ferdinand St CAMTN NW1 4 B1
Ferguson Av BRYLDS KT5 159 G4
Ferguson Cl BECK BR3 167 F2
Ferguson Dr ACT W3 87 F5
Ferguson's Cl POP/IOD E14 112 D3
Fergus Rd HBRY N5 73 H4
Ferme Park Rd
CEND/HSY/T N8 54 E4
Fermor Rd FSTH SE23 132 B7
Fermoy Rd GFD/PVL UB6 84 B3
MV/WKIL W9 88 D3
Fern Av MTCM CR4 163 J3
Fernbank Av ALP/SUD HA0 67 F3
WOT/HER KT12 156 D6
Fernbank Ms BAL SW12 129 G5
Fernbrook Dr
RYLN/HDSTN HA2 48 B6
Fernbrook Rd LEW SE13 133 H5
Ferncliff Rd HACK E8 74 C4
Fern Cl IS N1 7 J5
Fern Ct NWCR SE14 132 A1
Ferncroft Av HAMP NW3 70 E2
NFNCH/WDSPK N12 39 J5
RSLP HA4 65 G1
Ferndale BMLY BR1 168 B1
Ferndale Av HSLWW TW4 122 D2
WALTH E17 58 B4
Ferndale Rd CLAP SW4 129 K3
CRW RM5 62 E1
FSTGT E7 77 F6
SEVS/STOTM N15 56 B5
SNWD SE25 165 J4
WAN E11 76 D1
Ferndale St EHAM E6 96 B6
Ferndale Ter HRW HA1 49 F3
Fern Dene WEA W13 85 H4
Ferndene Rd HNHL SE24 130 D3
Fernden Wy ROMW/RG RM7 62 D5
Ferndown NTHWD HA6 46 E1
Ferndown Av ORP BR6 169 J7
Ferndown Cl BELMT SM2 175 H5
PIN HA5 33 J6
Ferndown Rd ELTH/MOT SE9 134 C6
OXHEY WD19 33 G2
Ferney Meade Wy ISLW TW7 124 B1
Ferney Rd EBAR EN4 28 A6
Fern Gv EBED/NFELT TW14 122 A6
Fernhall Dr REDBR IG4 59 H4
Fernham Rd THHTH CR7 164 D2
Fernhead Rd MV/WKIL W9 88 D2
Fernhill Ct WALTH E17 58 B1
Fernhill Gdns KUTN/CMB KT2 143 K4
Fernhill St CAN/RD E16 95 K7
Fernholme Rd PECK SE15 132 A4
Fernhurst Gdns EDGW HA8 36 C5
Fernhurst Rd ASHF TW15 140 A3
CROY/NA CR0 165 H6
FUL/PGN SW6 107 H7
Fern La HEST TW5 102 E4
Fernlea Rd BAL SW12 129 G7
MTCM CR4 163 F1
Fernleigh Cl CROY/NA CR0 177 G3
MV/WKIL W9 88 D2
Fernleigh Ct
RYLN/HDSTN HA2 48 B1
WBLY HA9 50 A7
Fernleigh Rd WCHMH N21 41 G1
Fernley Cl PIN HA5 46 E3
Fernsbury St FSBYW WC1X 6 A8
Fernshaw Cl WBPTN SW10 * 108 B5
Fernshaw Rd WBPTN SW10 108 B5
Fernside GLDGN NW11 70 E1
THDIT KT7 158 C7
Fernside Av FELT TW13 141 F3
MLHL NW7 37 F2
Fernside Rd BAL SW12 128 E7
Ferns Rd SRTFD E15 76 C5
Fern St BOW E3 93 J3
Fernthorpe Rd
STRHM/NOR SW16 148 C5
Ferntower Rd HBRY N5 73 K4
Fern Wk BERM/RHTH SE16 111 H4
Fernways IL IG1 78 B2
Fernwood Av ALP/SUD HA0 67 J5
STRHM/NOR SW16 148 D3
Fernwood Cl BMLY BR1 168 B1
Fernwood Crs
TRDG/WHET N20 39 K2
Ferranti Cl WOOL/PLUM SE18 114 C2
Ferraro Cl HEST TW5 103 F5
Ferrers Av WDR/YW UB7 100 A1
WLGTN SM6 176 D3
Ferrers Rd STRHM/NOR SW16 148 D4
Ferrestone Rd
CEND/HSY/T N8 55 F3
Ferrey Ms BRXN/ST SW9 130 B1
Ferriby Cl IS N1 6 A1
Ferrier St WAND/EARL SW18 128 A3
Ferring Cl RYLN/HDSTN HA2 48 C7
Ferrings DUL SE21 150 A1
Ferris Av CROY/NA CR0 179 H2
Ferris Rd EDUL SE22 131 H3
Ferron Rd CLPT E5 * 74 D2
Ferro Rd RAIN RM13 99 J3
Ferryhills Cl OXHEY WD19 33 G2
Ferry La BARN SW13 106 C5
BTFD TW8 105 F5
RAIN RM13 99 G5
TOTM N17 56 D3
Ferrymead Av GFD/PVL UB6 84 A1
Ferrymead Dr GFD/PVL UB6 84 A2
Ferrymead Gdns
GFD/PVL UB6 84 C1
Ferrymoor RCHPK/HAM TW10 143 H2
Ferry Rd BARN SW13 106 D6
E/WMO/HCT KT8 157 F2
TEDD TW11 143 H4
THDIT KT7 158 C5
TWK TW1 124 C7
Ferry Sq BTFD TW8 105 F5
Ferry St POP/IOD E14 113 F4
Festing Rd PUT/ROE SW15 127 G2
Festival Cl BXLY DA5 136 E7
Festoon Wy CAN/RD E16 95 H6
Fetter La FLST/FETLN EC4A 12 B4
Ffinch St DEPT SE8 112 D6
Fidgeon Cl BMLY BR1 169 F2
Fidler Pl BUSH WD23 22 B5
Field Cl BKHH IG9 45 G2
BMLY BR1 168 B1
CHING E4 43 K5
CHSGTN KT9 171 J4
CRICK NW2 69 J1
E/WMO/HCT KT8 157 G4
HSLWW TW4 102 A7
HYS/HAR UB3 101 F6
RSLP HA4 46 A7
Fieldcommon La
WOT/HER KT12 156 D7
Field Cots EFNCH N2 * 53 K2
FUL/PGN SW6 * 127 J1
Field Ct GINN WC1R 11 M3
Field End BAR EN5 25 K3
RSLP HA4 65 H5
Fieldend TEDD TW11 143 F3
Field End Cl OXHEY WD19 21 J6
Field End Rd PIN HA5 47 F4
RSLP HA4 65 H2
Fieldend Rd
STRHM/NOR SW16 148 C7
Fielders Cl EN EN1 30 A3
RYLN/HDSTN HA2 48 C7
Fieldfare Rd THMD SE28 97 J6
Fieldgate St WCHPL E1 92 C4
Fieldhouse Cl SWFD E18 45 F7
Fieldhouse Rd BAL SW12 129 H7
Fielding Av WHTN TW2 142 C2
Fielding La HAYES BR2 168 B3
Fielding Rd CHSWK W4 106 A2
WKENS W14 107 G2
The Fieldings FSTH SE23 131 K7
Fielding St WALW SE17 18 E9
Fielding Ter EA W5 * 86 B6
Field La BTFD TW8 104 D6
TEDD TW11 143 G4
Field Md CDALE/KGS NW9 37 G6
Fieldpark Gdns CROY/NA CR0 166 B7
Field Pl NWMAL KT3 160 C5
Field Rd EBED/NFELT TW14 122 A5
FSTGT E7 76 E3
HMSMTH W6 107 H4
OXHEY WD19 21 J5
TOTM N17 55 K2
Fieldsend Rd CHEAM SM3 174 C4
Fields Est HACK E8 * 74 C6
Fieldside Cots
TRDG/WHET N20 * 26 D6
Fieldside Rd BMLY BR1 152 B4
Fields Park Crs CHDH RM6 61 K4
Field St FSBYW WC1X 5 L7
Field Vw FELT TW13 140 B3
Fieldview WAND/EARL SW18 128 C7
Field View Cl ROMW/RG RM7 62 C2
Fieldview Cots
STHGT/OAK N14 * 40 D1
Fieldway BCTR RM8 79 H3
Field Wy CROY/NA CR0 179 K5
GFD/PVL UB6 66 B7
RSLP HA4 46 A7
Fieldway STMC/STPC BR5 169 J5
Field Wy WLSDN NW10 68 E6
Fieldway Crs HBRY N5 73 G4
Fiennes Cl BCTR RM8 61 J7
Fiesta Dr RAIN RM13 98 E3
Fife Rd CAN/RD E16 94 E4
KUT/HW KT1 159 F1
MORT/ESHN SW14 125 K4
WDGN N22 41 H6
Fife Ter IS N1 5 M5
Fifield Pth FSTH SE23 151 F2
Fifth Av HYS/HAR UB3 82 D7
MNPK E12 77 K3
NKENS W10 88 C3
Fifth Cross Rd WHTN TW2 142 D1
Fifth Wy WBLY HA9 68 D3
Figge's Rd MTCM CR4 148 A6
Fig Tree Cl WLSDN NW10 69 G7
Filby Rd CHSGTN KT9 172 B5
Filey Av STNW/STAM N16 56 C7
Filey Cl BELMT SM2 175 G6
Filey Waye RSLP HA4 64 E1
Fillebrook Av EN EN1 30 A1
Fillebrook Rd WAN E11 58 B7
Filmer Chambers
FUL/PGN SW6 * 107 J7
Filmer Rd FUL/PGN SW6 107 J7
Filton Cl CDALE/KGS NW9 51 G1
Finborough Rd TOOT SW17 147 K6
WBPTN SW10 14 D9
Finchale Rd ABYW SE2 116 B2
Fincham Cl HGDN/ICK UB10 64 A2
Finch Av WNWD SE27 149 K3
Finch Cl BAR EN5 26 E4
Finch Dr EBED/NFELT TW14 122 C6
Finch Gdns CHING E4 43 J4
Finchingfield Av WFD IG8 45 G6
Finch La BANK EC3V 13 H5
BUSH WD23 22 A4
Finchley La HDN NW4 52 B3
Finchley Pk
NFNCH/WDSPK N12 39 G3
Finchley Pl STJWD NW8 3 G5
Finchley Rd GLDGN NW11 52 D4
HAMP NW3 70 E3
STJWD NW8 3 G4
Finchley Vls
NFNCH/WDSPK N12 * 39 H3
Finchley Wy FNCH N3 38 E5
Finch Ms PECK SE15 * 111 G7
Finchs Ct POP/IOD E14 93 K6
Finden Rd FSTGT E7 77 F4
Findhorn Av YEAD UB4 83 F4
Findhorn St POP/IOD E14 94 A5
Findon Cl RYLN/HDSTN HA2 * 66 B2
WAND/EARL SW18 127 K5
Findon Gdns RAIN RM13 99 J4
Findon Rd ED N9 30 D7
SHB W12 106 D1
Fingal St GNWCH SE10 113 J4
Finland Rd BROCKY SE4 132 B2
Finland St BERM/RHTH SE16 112 B2
Finlays Cl CHSGTN KT9 172 C4
Finlay St FUL/PGN SW6 107 G7
Finney La ISLW TW7 104 B7
Finnis St BETH E2 92 D2
Finnymore Rd DAGW RM9 80 A6
Finsbury Av LVPST EC2M * 13 H3
Finsbury Circ LVPST EC2M 13 H3
Finsbury Cots WDGN N22 40 E6
Finsbury Est CLKNW EC1R 6 B8
Finsbury Market SDTCH EC2A 13 J1
Finsbury Park Av FSBYPK N4 55 J5
Finsbury Park Rd FSBYPK N4 73 H1
Finsbury Pavement
LVPST EC2M 13 H2
Finsbury Rd WDGN N22 41 F6
Finsbury Sq SDTCH EC2A 13 H1
Finsbury St STLK EC1Y 13 G2
Finsbury Wy BXLY DA5 137 G5
Finsen Rd CMBW SE5 130 D3
Finstock Rd NKENS W10 88 B5
Finucane Gdns RAIN RM13 81 J5
Finucane Ri BUSH WD23 34 C1
Finway Ct WATW WD18 * 20 D4
Fiona Ct ENC/FH EN2 * 29 H2
Firbank Cl CAN/RD E16 95 H4
ENC/FH EN2 29 J3
Firbank Dr OXHEY WD19 21 J6
Firbank Rd PECK SE15 131 J1
Fircroft Gdns HRW HA1 66 E2
Fircroft Rd CHSGTN KT9 172 B3
TOOT SW17 147 K2
Firdene BRYLDS KT5 159 K7
Fir Dene ORP BR6 181 K2
Fire Bell Aly SURB KT6 159 F5
Firebell Ms SURB KT6 159 F5
Firecrest Dr HAMP NW3 71 F2
Firefly Cl WLGTN SM6 * 176 E6
Firefly Gdns EHAM E6 95 J3
Firemans Cots EFNCH N2 54 A2
Firethorn Cl EDGW HA8 36 E3
Fir Gv NWMAL KT3 160 C5
Fir Grove Rd BRXN/ST SW9 * 130 B1
Firhill Rd CAT SE6 151 J2
Firle Pl WAND/EARL SW18 128 B6
Fir Rd CHEAM SM3 161 J7
FELT TW13 141 H4
Firs Av FBAR/BDGN N11 40 A5
MORT/ESHN SW14 125 K3
MUSWH N10 54 A2
Firsby Av CROY/NA CR0 166 A7
Firsby Rd STNW/STAM N16 56 B7
Firs Cl ESH/CLAY KT10 170 E5
FSTH SE23 132 A6
MTCM CR4 163 G1
Firscroft PLMGR N13 41 J2
Firs Dr HEST TW5 102 A6
Firside Gv BFN/LL DA15 136 A7
Firs La PLMGR N13 41 J2
Firs Park Av WCHMH N21 29 K7
Firs Park Gdns WCHMH N21 29 K7
First Av ACT W3 87 H7
BXLYHN DA7 116 D6
CHDH RM6 61 J4
DAGE RM10 98 D1
E/WMO/HCT KT8 156 E3
EN EN1 30 B4
HDN NW4 52 A3
HOR/WEW KT19 173 G7
HYS/HAR UB3 82 D7
MNPK E12 77 J3
MORT/ESHN SW14 126 B1
NKENS W10 88 D3
PLSTW E13 94 E2
UED N18 42 E3
WALTH E17 57 K4
WBLY HA9 67 K1
WOT/HER KT12 156 A5
First Cl E/WMO/HCT KT8 157 H3
First Cross Rd WHTN TW2 142 E1
First Dr WLSDN NW10 68 E6
The Firs EA W5 85 K4
EBED/NFELT TW14 * 121 H5
EDGW HA8 * 37 F3
TRDG/WHET N20 27 H7
First St CHEL SW3 15 K5
Firstway RYNPK SW20 161 F1
First Wy WBLY HA9 68 D3
Firs Wk NTHWD HA6 32 B5
WFD IG8 44 E4
Firswood Av HOR/WEW KT19 173 G4
Firth Gdns FUL/PGN SW6 107 H7
Firtree Av MTCM CR4 163 F1
Fir Tree Av WDR/YW UB7 100 D2
Fir Tree Cl EA W5 86 A5
ESH/CLAY KT10 170 C4
HOR/WEW KT19 173 H3
ROM RM1 63 F2
STRHM/NOR SW16 148 C4
Fir Tree Ct BORE WD6 24 B3
Fir Tree Gdns CROY/NA CR0 179 J3
Fir Tree Gv CAR SM5 175 K6
Fir Tree Rd HSLWW TW4 122 D3
Fir Trees Cl BERM/RHTH SE16 93 G7
Fir Tree Wk EN EN1 30 A2
Fir Wk CHEAM SM3 174 B5
Fisher Cl CROY/NA CR0 165 G7
GFD/PVL UB6 84 A2
Fisherdene ESH/CLAY KT10 171 G6
Fisherman Cl
RCHPK/HAM TW10 143 J3
Fishermans Dr
BERM/RHTH SE16 112 A1
Fisher Rd
KTN/HRWW/WS HA3 49 F1
Fishers Cl BUSH WD23 21 J3
STRHM/NOR SW16 148 D2
Fishers Ct NWCR SE14 112 A7
Fisher's La CHSWK W4 106 A3
Fisher St CAN/RD E16 94 E4
RSQ WC1B 11 L3
Fisher's Wy BELV DA17 98 E7
Fisherton St STJWD NW8 9 G1
Fishguard Wy CAN/RD E16 96 B7
CAN/RD E16 115 G1
Fishponds Rd HAYES BR2 181 H4
TOOT SW17 147 J3
Fish Street Hl MON EC3R 13 H7
Fisk Cl SUN TW16 140 D5
Fisons Rd CAN/RD E16 94 E7
Fitzalan Rd ESH/CLAY KT10 170 E6
FNCH N3 52 C2
Fitzalan St LBTH SE11 17 M5
Fitzgeorge Av NWMAL KT3 145 F7
WKENS W14 107 H3
Fitzgerald Av
MORT/ESHN SW14 126 B2
Fitzgerald Rd
MORT/ESHN SW14 126 A2
THDIT KT7 158 B5
WAN E11 58 E4
Fitzhardinge St MBLAR W1H 10 A4
Fitzhugh Gv
WAND/EARL SW18 128 C5
Fitzjames Av CROY/NA CR0 178 C1
WKENS W14 107 H3
Fitzjohn Av BAR EN5 26 C4
Fitzjohn's Av HAMP NW3 71 H4
Fitzmaurice Pl
MYFR/PICC W1J * 10 D8
Fitzneal St SHB W12 87 H5
Fitzroy Cl HGT N6 53 K7
Fitzroy Crs CHSWK W4 * 106 A6

Fitzroy Gdns NRWD SE19 150 A6
Fitzroy Ms FITZ W1T 10 E1
Fitzroy Pk HGT N6 53 K7
Fitzroy Rd CAMTN NW1 4 A3
Fitzroy Sq FITZ W1T 10 E1
Fitzroy St FITZ W1T 10 E2
Fitzstephen Rd BCTR RM8 79 H4
Fitzwarren Gdns HGT N6 54 C7
Fitzwilliam Av RCH/KEW TW9 125 G1
Fitzwilliam Cl
TRDG/WHET N20 27 K7
Fitzwilliam Ms CAN/RD E16 94 E6
Fitzwilliam Rd CLAP SW4 129 H2
Fitz Wygram Cl HPTN TW12 142 C4
Five Acre CDALE/KGS NW9 51 H1
Fiveacre Cl CROY/NA CR0 164 B5
Five Elms Rd DAGW RM9 80 B2
HAYES BR2 181 G2
Five Fields Cl OXHEY WD19 33 K1
Fiveways Cnr ELTH/MOT SE9 154 B1
Five Ways Jct HDN NW4 37 J7
Fiveways Rd BRXN/ST SW9 130 B1
Fladbury Rd SEVS/STOTM N15 55 K5
Fladgate Rd WAN E11 58 C5
Flag Cl CROY/NA CR0 166 A7
Flag Wk PIN HA5 46 E5
Flambard Rd HRW HA1 49 G5
Flamborough Rd RSLP HA4 64 E2
Flamborough St
POP/IOD E14 93 G5
Flamborough Wk
POP/IOD E14 * 93 G5
Flamingo Wk HCH RM12 81 J6
Flamstead Gdns DAGW RM9 79 J6
Flamstead Rd DAGW RM9 79 J6
Flamsted Av WBLY HA9 68 C5
Flamsteed Rd CHARL SE7 114 D4
Flanchford Rd SHB W12 106 C2
Flanders Crs TOOT SW17 147 K6
Flanders Rd CHSWK W4 106 B3
EHAM E6 95 K1
Flanders Wy HOM E9 75 F5
Flank St WCHPL E1 92 C6
Flask Wk HAMP NW3 71 G3
Flather Cl STRHM/NOR SW16 148 C5
Flavell Ms GNWCH SE10 113 H4
Flaxen Cl CHING E4 43 K2
Flaxen Rd CHING E4 43 K2
Flaxley Rd MRDN SM4 162 A5
Flaxman Rd CMBW SE5 130 C1
Flaxman Ter STPAN WC1H 5 H8
Flaxton Rd WOOL/PLUM SE18 115 J7
Flecker Cl STAN HA7 35 F4
Fleece Dr ED N9 42 C3
Fleece Rd SURB KT6 158 D7
Fleece Wk HOLWY N7 * 72 E5
Fleeming Cl WALTH E17 57 H1
Fleeming Rd WALTH E17 57 H1
Fleet Cl E/WMO/HCT KT8 156 E4
RSLP HA4 46 A5
Fleet Pl FLST/FETLN EC4A 12 C4
Fleet Rd HAMP NW3 71 J4
Fleetside E/WMO/HCT KT8 156 E4
Fleet Sq FSBYW WC1X 5 L8
Fleet St EMB EC4Y 12 A5
Fleet Street Hl WCHPL E1 * 92 C3
Fleet Ter CAT SE6 * 133 F6
Fleetwood Cl CAN/RD E16 95 H4
CHSGTN KT9 171 K6
CROY/NA CR0 178 B2
Fleetwood Rd KUT/HW KT1 159 J2
WLSDN NW10 69 J4
Fleetwood Sq KUT/HW KT1 159 J2
Fleetwood St
STNW/STAM N16 74 A1
Fleetwood Wy OXHEY WD19 33 G3
Fleming Cl MV/WKIL W9 8 A1
Fleming Ct CROY/NA CR0 177 G4
Fleming Dr WCHMH N21 29 F4
Fleming Md MTCM CR4 147 J6
Fleming Rd STHL UB1 84 B5
WALW SE17 18 D9
Fleming Wk
CDALE/KGS NW9 * 51 G1
Fleming Wy ISLW TW7 124 A2
THMD SE28 97 K6
Flemming Av RSLP HA4 47 F7
Flempton Rd LEY E10 57 G7
Fletcher Cl EHAM E6 96 B6
Fletcher La LEY E10 58 A6
Fletcher Rd CHSWK W4 105 K2
Fletchers Cl HAYES BR2 168 A3
Fletcher St WCHPL E1 92 C6
Fletching Rd CHARL SE7 114 C5
CLPT E5 74 E2
Fletton Rd FBAR/BDGN N11 40 E6
Fleur De Lis St WCHPL E1 13 K1
Fleur Gates WIM/MER SW19 127 G6
Flexmere Rd TOTM N17 41 K7
Flight Ap CDALE/KGS NW9 * 37 H7
Flimwell Cl BMLY BR1 152 C4
Flint Cl SRTFD E15 76 D5
Flint Down Cl
STMC/STPC BR5 * 155 G7
Flintmill Crs BKHTH/KID SE3 134 D1
ELTH/MOT SE9 134 D2
Flinton St WALW SE17 19 K7
Flint St WALW SE17 19 H6
Flitcroft St LSQ/SEVD WC2H 11 H5
Floathaven Cl THMD SE28 97 G7
Flock Mill Pl
WAND/EARL SW18 128 A7
Flockton St BERM/RHTH SE16 111 H1
Flodden Rd CMBW SE5 110 D7
Flood La TWK TW1 * 124 B7
Flood St CHEL SW3 15 K8
Flood Wk CHEL SW3 15 K9
Flora Cl POP/IOD E14 93 K5
STAN HA7 35 K2
Flora Gdns CHDH RM6 61 J5
HMSMTH W6 106 E3
Floral Pl IS N1 73 K4
Floral St COVGDN WC2E 11 K6
Flora St BELV DA17 117 G4
Florence Av ENC/FH EN2 29 J2
MRDN SM4 162 B4
Florence Cl WOT/HER KT12 156 A6
Florence Ct WAN E11 59 F3
Florence Dr ENC/FH EN2 29 J2
Florence Elson Cl MNPK E12 78 A3
Florence Gdns CHSWK W4 105 K5
Florence Rd BECK BR3 166 A1
BMLY BR1 152 E7
CHSWK W4 106 A2
EA W5 86 A6
EHAM E6 77 G7
FELT TW13 122 A7
FSBYPK N4 55 F6
KUTN/CMB KT2 144 B6
NWCR SE14 112 C7
NWDGN UB2 102 C3
PLSTW E13 94 E1
SAND/SEL CR2 177 K7
WIM/MER SW19 147 F5
WOT/HER KT12 156 A6
Florence St CAN/RD E16 94 D3
HDN NW4 52 A3
IS N1 6 C2
Florence Ter NWCR SE14 112 C7
Florence Vls HGT N6 * 54 B6
Florence Wy BAL SW12 128 E7
Florey Sq WCHMH N21 29 F4
Florfield Rd HACK E8 74 D5
Florian Av SUT SM1 175 H3
Florian Rd PUT/ROE SW15 127 H3
Florida Cl BUSH WD23 34 D1
Florida Rd THHTH CR7 149 H7
Florida St BETH E2 92 C2
Florin Ct UED N18 42 A3
Floris Pl CLAP SW4 129 H2
Floriston Av HGDN/ICK UB10 64 A6
Floriston Cl STAN HA7 35 H7
Floriston Gdns STAN HA7 35 H7
Floss St PUT/ROE SW15 127 F1
Flower & Dean Wk WCHPL E1 13 M3
Flower La MLHL NW7 37 H4
Flower Ms GLDGN NW11 52 C5
Flowerpot Cl
SEVS/STOTM N15 56 B5
Flowers Cl CRICK NW2 69 J2
Flowers Ms ARCH N19 72 C1
Floyd Rd CHARL SE7 114 B4
Floyer Cl RCHPK/HAM TW10 125 G4
Fludyer St LEW SE13 133 H3
Foley Ms ESH/CLAY KT10 170 E5
Foley Rd ESH/CLAY KT10 170 E6
Foley St GTPST W1W 10 E3
Foley Wd ESH/CLAY KT10 171 F6
Folgate St WCHPL E1 13 K2
Foliot St SHB W12 87 H5
Folkestone Rd EHAM E6 96 A1
UED N18 42 C3
WALTH E17 57 K3
Folkingham La
CDALE/KGS NW9 37 F7
Folkington Cnr
NFNCH/WDSPK N12 38 D4
Follett St POP/IOD E14 94 A5
Folly La WALTH E17 43 G7
Folly Wall POP/IOD E14 113 F1
Fontaine Rd
STRHM/NOR SW16 149 F5
Fontarabia Rd BTSEA SW11 129 F3
Fontayne Av RAIN RM13 81 G6
ROM RM1 63 G1
Fontenoy Rd BAL SW12 148 B1
Fonteyne Gdns WFD IG8 59 H1
Fonthill Ms FSBYPK N4 73 F1
Fonthill Rd FSBYPK N4 73 F1
Font Hills EFNCH N2 53 G1
Fontley Wy PUT/ROE SW15 126 D6
Fontwell Cl
KTN/HRWW/WS HA3 34 E6
NTHLT UB5 66 A5
Fontwell Dr HAYES BR2 169 F4
The Footpath
PUT/ROE SW15 * 126 D4
Foots Cray High St
SCUP DA14 155 J5
Foots Cray La SCUP DA14 136 D7
Footscray Rd ELTH/MOT SE9 135 F5
ELTH/MOT SE9 135 G7
Forbes Cl CRICK NW2 69 J2
HCH RM12 63 K7
Forbes St WCHPL E1 92 C5
Forbes Wy RSLP HA4 65 F1
Forburg Rd STNW/STAM N16 56 C7
Ford Cl BUSH WD23 22 C3
HRW HA1 48 D6
RAIN RM13 81 H6
THHTH CR7 164 C5
Forde Av BMLY BR1 168 B2
Fordel Rd CAT SE6 133 G7
Ford End WFD IG8 45 F5
Fordham Cl WPK KT4 160 E7
Fordham Rd EBAR EN4 27 H2
Fordham St WCHPL E1 92 C5
Fordhook Av EA W5 86 B6
Fordingley Rd MV/WKIL W9 88 D2
Fordington Rd HGT N6 53 K3
Ford La RAIN RM13 81 H6
Fordmill Rd CAT SE6 151 J1
Ford Rd BOW E3 93 G1
DAGW RM9 80 B6
Ford's Gv WCHMH N21 29 J7
Fords Park Rd CAN/RD E16 94 E5
Ford Sq WCHPL E1 92 D4
Ford St BOW E3 93 G1
Fordwych Rd CRICK NW2 70 C4
Fordyce Rd LEW SE13 133 F5
Fordyke Rd BCTR RM8 80 A1
Foreland Ct HDN NW4 38 C7
Foreland St
WOOL/PLUM SE18 115 J3
Foreshore DEPT SE8 112 C4
Forest Ap WFD IG8 44 D6
Forest Cl CHST BR7 154 A7
KIL/WHAMP NW6 70 C6
WAN E11 58 D4
WFD IG8 45 F3
Forest Ct WAN E11 58 C3
Forestdale STHGT/OAK N14 40 D3
Forest Dr HAYES BR2 181 J2
MNPK E12 77 H2
SUN TW16 140 D6
WFD IG8 44 B6
Forest Dr East WAN E11 58 B6
Forest Dr West WAN E11 58 A6
Forest Edge BKHH IG9 45 G2
Forester Rd PECK SE15 131 J3
Foresters Cl WLGTN SM6 176 D6
Foresters Dr WALTH E17 58 B3
WLGTN SM6 176 D6
Forest Gdns TOTM N17 56 B1
Forest Ga CDALE/KGS NW9 51 G3
Forest Gld CHING E4 44 C4
WAN E11 58 C5
Forest Gv HACK E8 74 B5
Forest Hill Rd EDUL SE22 131 J5
Forestholme Cl FSTH SE23 150 E1
Forest La FSTGT E7 76 E4
Forest Mount Rd WFD IG8 44 B6
Fore St BARB EC2Y 13 G3
PIN HA5 46 D3
UED N18 42 C4
Forest Rdg BECK BR3 166 D2
HAYES BR2 181 J3
Forest Ri WALTH E17 58 B3
Forest Rd CHEAM SM3 161 K7
ED N9 30 D7
ERITH DA8 118 D7
FELT TW13 141 G1
FSTGT E7 76 E3
HACK E8 74 B5
RCH/KEW TW9 105 H6
ROMW/RG RM7 62 D2
TOTM N17 56 E3
WALTH E17 57 J2
WAN E11 58 A6
WFD IG8 44 E2
Forest Side FSTGT E7 77 F3
WPK KT4 160 C7
Forest St FSTGT E7 76 E4
The Forest WAN E11 58 C3
Forest Vw WAN E11 58 D6
Forest View Av LEY E10 58 B4
Forest View Rd MNPK E12 77 J3
WALTH E17 44 A7
Forest Wy BFN/LL DA15 135 J6
WFD IG8 45 F3
Forfar Rd BTSEA SW11 109 F7
WDGN N22 41 H7
Forge Cots EA W5 * 85 K7
Forge Dr ESH/CLAY KT10 171 G6
Forge La CHEAM SM3 174 C6
FELT TW13 141 J4
NTHWD HA6 32 C6
RCHPK/HAM TW10 125 F7
Forge Ms CROY/NA CR0 179 J4
Forge Pl CAMTN NW1 72 A5
Formby Av
KTN/HRWW/WS HA3 49 J2
Formosa St MV/WKIL W9 8 D1
Formunt Cl CAN/RD E16 94 D4
Forres Gdns GLDGN NW11 52 E5
Forrester Pth SYD SE26 150 E3
Forrest Gdns
STRHM/NOR SW16 164 A2
Forris Av HYS/HAR UB3 82 D7
Forset St MBLAR W1H 9 K4
Forstal Cl HAYES BR2 167 K2
Forster Cl CHING E4 44 B6
Forster Rd BECK BR3 166 B2
BRXS/STRHM SW2 129 K6
TOTM N17 56 B2
Forsters Cl CHDH RM6 62 B5
Forston St IS N1 6 F5
Forsyte Crs NRWD SE19 150 A7
Forsyth Gdns WALW SE17 18 D9
Forsythia Cl IL IG1 78 B4
Forsyth Pl EN EN1 30 A4
Forterie Gdns GDMY/SEVK IG3 79 G2
Fortescue Av WHTN TW2 142 C2
Fortescue Rd EDGW HA8 37 F7
WIM/MER SW19 147 H6
Fortess Gv KTTN NW5 72 C4
Fortess Rd KTTN NW5 72 B4
Fortess Wk KTTN NW5 72 B4
Forthbridge Rd BTSEA SW11 129 F3
Fortis Cl CAN/RD E16 95 G5
Fortis Gn EFNCH N2 53 K2
Fortis Green Av EFNCH N2 54 A2
Fortis Green Rd MUSWH N10 54 A2
Fortismere Av MUSWH N10 54 A2
Fortnam Rd ARCH N19 72 D1
Fortnums Acre STAN HA7 35 F5
Fort Rd NTHLT UB5 66 A6
STHWK SE1 19 M6
Fortrose Cl POP/IOD E14 94 B5
Fortrose Gdns
BRXS/STRHM SW2 129 K7
Fort St CAN/RD E16 95 F7
WCHPL E1 * 13 K3
Fortuna Cl HOLWY N7 * 73 F5
Fortune Av EDGW HA8 36 D7
Fortunegate Rd
WLSDN NW10 69 G7
Fortune Green Rd
KIL/WHAMP NW6 70 E4
Fortune La BORE WD6 23 K5
Fortune Pl STHWK SE1 19 M8
Fortunes Md NTHLT UB5 65 J5
Fortune St STLK EC1Y 12 F1
Fortune Wy WLSDN NW10 87 J2
Forty Acre La CAN/RD E16 94 E4
Forty Av WBLY HA9 68 B2
Forty Cl WBLY HA9 68 B2
Forty La WBLY HA9 68 D1
Forum Cl BOW E3 75 J7
Forum Magnum Sq
STHWK SE1 17 L1
Forumside EDGW HA8 36 C5
The Forum E/WMO/HCT KT8 157 G3
Forval Cl MTCM CR4 162 E4
Forward Dr
KTN/HRWW/WS HA3 49 F3
Foscote Ms MV/WKIL W9 8 B1
Foscote Rd HDN NW4 51 K5
Foskett Rd FUL/PGN SW6 127 J1
Foss Av CROY/NA CR0 177 G4
Fossdene Rd CHARL SE7 114 A4
Fossdyke Cl YEAD UB4 83 J4
Fosse Wy WEA W13 85 G4
Fossil Rd LEW SE13 132 D2
Fossington Rd BELV DA17 116 E3
Foss Rd TOOT SW17 147 H3
Fossway BCTR RM8 79 J1
Foster La CITYW EC2V 12 E4
Foster Rd ACT W3 87 G6
CHSWK W4 106 A4
PLSTW E13 94 E3
Fosters Cl CHST BR7 153 K4
SWFD E18 45 F7
Foster St HDN NW4 52 A3
Foster Wk HDN NW4 52 A3
Fothergill Cl PLSTW E13 76 E7
Fothergill Dr WCHMH N21 28 E4
Fotheringham Rd EN EN1 30 B3
Foubert's Pl SOHO/CST W1F 10 E5
Foulden Rd STNW/STAM N16 74 B3
Foulden Ter STNW/STAM N16 74 B3
Foulis Ter SKENS SW7 15 G6
Foulser Rd TOOT SW17 147 K2
Foulsham Rd THHTH CR7 164 D2
Foundation Pl
ELTH/MOT SE9 * 135 F4
Founder Cl EHAM E6 96 B5
Founders Cl NTHLT UB5 83 K2
Founders Gdns NRWD SE19 149 J6
Foundry Cl BERM/RHTH SE16 93 G7
Foundry Ms CAMTN NW1 4 F9
HSLW TW3 123 G3
Foundry Pl
WAND/EARL SW18 * 128 A6
Fountain Cl UX/CGN UB8 82 A4
Fountain Dr CAR SM5 175 K6
NRWD SE19 150 B3
Fountain Green Sq
BERM/RHTH SE16 111 H1
Fountain Ms HAMP NW3 71 K5
Fountain Pl BRXN/ST SW9 110 B7
Fountain Rd THHTH CR7 164 D1
TOOT SW17 147 H4
Fountains Av FELT TW13 141 K2
Fountains Cl FELT TW13 141 K1
Fountains Crs
STHGT/OAK N14 28 E6
Fountayne Rd
SEVS/STOTM N15 56 C3
STNW/STAM N16 74 C1
Fount St VX/NE SW8 109 J6
Fourland Wk EDGW HA8 36 E5
Fournier St WCHPL E1 13 L2
Four Seasons Cl BOW E3 93 J1
Four Seasons Crs CHEAM SM3 174 D1
Fourth Av HYS/HAR UB3 82 D7
MNPK E12 77 K3
NKENS W10 88 C3
ROMW/RG RM7 62 E7
Fourth Cross Rd WHTN TW2 142 D1
Fourth Wy WBLY HA9 68 D3
The Four Tubs BUSH WD23 22 D6
The Four Wents CHING E4 44 B1
Fowey Av REDBR IG4 59 H4
Fowey Cl WAP E1W 92 D7
Fowler Cl BTSEA SW11 128 C2
Fowler Rd FSTGT E7 76 E3
IS N1 6 D3
Fowler's Wk EA W5 85 K3
Fownes St BTSEA SW11 128 D2
Foxberry Rd BROCKY SE4 132 B3
Foxborough Gdns
BROCKY SE4 132 D5
Foxbourne Rd TOOT SW17 148 A1
Foxbury Av CHST BR7 154 D5
Foxbury Cl BMLY BR1 153 F5
Foxbury Rd BMLY BR1 153 F5
Fox Cl BORE WD6 23 K5
BUSH WD23 22 B4
CAN/RD E16 94 E4
WCHPL E1 92 E3
Foxcombe CROY/NA CR0 179 K5
Foxcroft Rd
WOOL/PLUM SE18 115 G7
Foxdell NTHWD HA6 32 B5
Foxdene Cl SWFD E18 59 F2
Foxearth Sp SAND/SEL CR2 178 E7
Foxes Dl HAYES BR2 167 G2
Foxfield Cl NTHWD HA6 32 D5
Foxglove Cl BFN/LL DA15 136 B5
ED N9 30 E7
STHL UB1 83 J6
STWL/WRAY TW19 120 A7
Foxglove Gdns WAN E11 59 G3
Foxglove La CHSGTN KT9 172 C3
Foxglove Pth THMD SE28 115 K1
Foxglove Rd ROMW/RG RM7 81 G1
Foxglove St ACT W3 87 H6
Foxglove Wy WLGTN SM6 163 F6
Foxgrove STHGT/OAK N14 40 E2
Fox Gv WOT/HER KT12 156 A6
Foxgrove Av BECK BR3 151 K6
Foxgrove Pth OXHEY WD19 33 H4
Foxgrove Rd BECK BR3 151 K6
Foxham Rd ARCH N19 72 D2
Fox Hl HAYES BR2 181 G4
NRWD SE19 150 B6
Fox Hill Gdns NRWD SE19 150 B6
Foxhole Rd ELTH/MOT SE9 134 D4
Fox Hollow Cl
WOOL/PLUM SE18 115 K4
Fox Hollow Dr BXLYHN DA7 136 E2
Foxholt Gdns WLSDN NW10 68 E6
Foxhome Cl CHST BR7 154 A5
Fox House Rd BELV DA17 117 J3
Fox & Knot St FARR EC1M * 12 D2
Foxlands Crs DAGE RM10 80 E4
Foxlands Rd DAGE RM10 80 E4
Fox La EA W5 86 A4
HAYES BR2 181 F4
PLMGR N13 41 F2
Foxlees ALP/SUD HA0 67 G3
Foxley Cl HACK E8 74 C4
Foxley Rd CMBW SE5 110 B6
THHTH CR7 164 C3
Foxleys OXHEY WD19 33 J2
Foxley Sq BRXN/ST SW9 * 110 C6
Foxmead Cl ENC/FH EN2 29 F2
Foxmore St BTSEA SW11 108 E7
Fox Rd CAN/RD E16 94 D4
Foxton Gv MTCM CR4 162 C1
Foxwarren ESH/CLAY KT10 171 F7
Foxwell St BROCKY SE4 132 B2
Foxwood Cl FELT TW13 141 F2
MLHL NW7 37 G3
Foxwood Green Cl EN EN1 30 A5
Foxwood Rd BKHTH/KID SE3 133 J3
Foyle Rd BKHTH/KID SE3 113 J5
TOTM N17 42 C7
Framfield Cl
NFNCH/WDSPK N12 38 E3
Framfield Rd HBRY N5 73 H4
HNWL W7 85 F5
MTCM CR4 148 A6
Framlingham Crs
ELTH/MOT SE9 153 J3
Frampton Cl BELMT SM2 174 E6
Frampton Park Rd HOM E9 74 E5
Frampton Rd HSLWW TW4 122 D4
Frampton St STJWD NW8 9 H1
Francemary Rd LEW SE13 132 D4
Frances Rd CHING E4 43 J5
Frances St WOOL/PLUM SE18 114 E3
Franche Court Rd TOOT SW17 147 G2
Francis Av FELT TW13 140 E2
IL IG1 78 D1
Francis Barber Cl
STRHM/NOR SW16 * 149 F3
Francis Bentley Ms CLAP SW4 129 H2
Franciscan Rd TOOT SW17 148 A3
Francis Chichester Wy
BTSEA SW11 * 109 F7
Francis Cl HOR/WEW KT19 173 F3
Francis Gv WIM/MER SW19 146 D6
Francis Ms LEE/GVPK SE12 * 133 J5
Francis Rd CROY/NA CR0 164 C6
EFNCH N2 * 53 K3
GFD/PVL UB6 85 J1
HRW HA1 49 G4
HSLWW TW4 122 C1
LEY E10 76 A1
PIN HA5 47 G4
WATW WD18 21 F3
WLGTN SM6 176 C5
Francis St SRTFD E15 76 C4
WEST SW1P 16 F5
Francis Ter ARCH N19 72 C2
Francis Wk IS N1 5 L3
Francklyn Gdns EDGW HA8 36 C2
Francombe Gdns ROM RM1 63 J5
Franconia Rd CLAP SW4 129 H4
Frank Burton Cl CHARL SE7 114 A4
Frank Dixon Cl DUL SE21 131 F6
Frank Dixon Wy DUL SE21 131 F7
Frankfurt Rd HNHL SE24 130 D4
Frankham St DEPT SE8 112 D6
Frankland Cl
BERM/RHTH SE16 111 J2
WFD IG8 45 G4
Frankland Rd CHING E4 43 J4
SKENS SW7 15 G4
Franklin Av WATW WD18 20 E5
Franklin Cl KUT/HW KT1 159 H2
LEW SE13 112 E7
TRDG/WHET N20 27 G6
WNWD SE27 149 H2
Franklin Crs MTCM CR4 163 H3
Franklin Pl GNWCH SE10 112 E7
Franklin Rd PGE/AN SE20 150 E6
WAT WD17 21 F1
Franklins Ms
RYLN/HDSTN HA2 66 C1
Franklin Sq WKENS W14 107 J4
Franklin's Rw CHEL SW3 15 M7
Franklin St BOW E3 93 K2
SEVS/STOTM N15 56 A5
Franklin Wy CROY/NA CR0 163 K7
Franklyn Rd WLSDN NW10 69 H6
WOT/HER KT12 156 A5
Franks Av NWMAL KT3 159 K3
Franks Wood Av
STMC/STPC BR5 169 G4
Franlaw Crs PLMGR N13 41 J3
Franmil Rd HCH RM12 63 H6
Fransfield Gv SYD SE26 150 D2
Franshams BUSH WD23 * 34 E1
Frant Cl PGE/AN SE20 150 E6
Frant Rd THHTH CR7 164 C4
Fraser Cl BXLY DA5 137 K7
EHAM E6 95 J5
Fraser Rd ED N9 42 D2
ERITH DA8 117 K4
GFD/PVL UB6 67 J7
WALTH E17 57 K4
Fraser St CHSWK W4 106 B4
Frating Crs WFD IG8 44 E5
Frays Av WDR/YW UB7 100 A1
Frays Cl WDR/YW UB7 100 A2
Frazer Av RSLP HA4 65 G4
Frazer Cl ROM RM1 63 H6
Frazier St STHWK SE1 18 A2
Frean St BERM/RHTH SE16 111 H2
Freda Corbett Cl PECK SE15 111 H6
Frederica St HOLWY N7 5 L1
Frederick Cl BAY/PAD W2 9 K6
SUT SM1 174 D3
Frederick Crs BRXN/ST SW9 110 C6
PEND EN3 30 E1
Frederick Gdns CROY/NA CR0 164 C5
SUT SM1 174 D4
Frederick Pl
WOOL/PLUM SE18 115 G4
Frederick Rd RAIN RM13 99 F1
SUT SM1 174 D4
WALW SE17 * 18 D8
Frederick's Pl LOTH EC2R * 13 G5
NFNCH/WDSPK N12 39 G3
Frederick Sq
BERM/RHTH SE16 93 G6
Frederick's Rw FSBYE EC1V 6 C7
Frederick St FSBYW WC1X 5 L8
Frederick Ter HACK E8 7 L3
Frederic Ms KTBR SW1X * 16 A2
Frederic St WALTH E17 57 G4
Fredora Av YEAD UB4 82 D3
Freeborne Gdns RAIN RM13 81 J5
Freedom Cl WALTH E17 57 F3
Freedom Rd TOTM N17 55 K1
Freedom St BTSEA SW11 128 E1
Freegrove Rd HOLWY N7 72 E4
Freeland Pk HDN NW4 52 C1
Freeland Rd EA W5 86 B6
Freelands Av SAND/SEL CR2 179 F7
Freelands Gv BMLY BR1 153 F7
Freelands Rd BMLY BR1 153 F7
Freeland Wy ERITH DA8 118 D7
Freeling St IS N1 * 5 L2
Freeman Cl NTHLT UB5 65 J6
Freeman Dr E/WMO/HCT KT8 156 E3
Freeman Rd MRDN SM4 162 C4
Freemans La HYS/HAR UB3 82 C6
Freemantle Av PEND EN3 31 F4
Freemantle St WALW SE17 19 J7
Freemasons Pl CROY/NA CR0 165 F7
Freemasons Rd CAN/RD E16 95 F4
Freemason's Rd
CROY/NA CR0 165 F7
Freethorpe Cl NRWD SE19 150 A7
Freightmaster Est
RAIN RM13 * 118 D3
Freke Rd BTSEA SW11 129 F2
Fremantle Rd BARK/HLT IG6 60 B1
BELV DA17 117 H3
Fremont St HOM E9 74 D7
French Pl SDTCH EC2A 7 K8
French St SUN TW16 156 B1
Frendsbury Rd BROCKY SE4 132 B3
Frensham Cl STHL UB1 83 K3
Frensham Dr CROY/NA CR0 180 A6
PUT/ROE SW15 145 J1
Frensham Rd ELTH/MOT SE9 154 D1
Frensham St PECK SE15 111 H5
Frere St BTSEA SW11 128 D1
Freshfield Av HACK E8 7 L1
Freshfield Cl LEW SE13 133 G3
Freshfield Dr
STHGT/OAK N14 28 B6
Freshfields CROY/NA CR0 166 C6
Freshford St TOOT SW17 147 G2
Fresh Mill La STHL UB1 84 A3
Freshwater Cl TOOT SW17 148 A5
Freshwater Rd BCTR RM8 61 K7
TOOT SW17 148 A5
Freshwell Av CHDH RM6 61 J3
Fresh Wharf Rd BARK IG11 78 B7
Freshwood Cl BECK BR3 151 K7
Freshwood Wy WLGTN SM6 176 C7
Freston Gdns EBAR EN4 28 A4
Freston Pk FNCH N3 52 D1
Freston Rd NKENS W10 88 B6
Frewin Rd WAND/EARL SW18 128 C7
Friar Ms WNWD SE27 149 H2
Friar Rd YEAD UB4 83 H3
Friars Av PUT/ROE SW15 145 H2
TRDG/WHET N20 39 J2
Friars Cl CHING E4 44 A2
IL IG1 60 D7
NTHLT UB5 83 G2
STHWK SE1 * 12 D8
Friars Gdns ACT W3 87 F5
Friars Gate Cl WFD IG8 44 E3
Friars La RCH/KEW TW9 124 E4
Friars Md POP/IOD E14 113 F2
Friars Ms ELTH/MOT SE9 135 F4
Friars Place La ACT W3 87 F6
Friar's Rd EHAM E6 77 H7
Friars Stile Rd
RCHPK/HAM TW10 125 F5
Friars Wk ABYW SE2 116 E4
STHGT/OAK N14 28 B7
Friars Wy ACT W3 87 F5
Friars Wd CROY/NA CR0 179 G7
Friary Cl NFNCH/WDSPK N12 39 J4
Friary Est PECK SE15 * 111 H6
Friary La WFD IG8 44 E3

This page is a street index (gazetteer) listing street names, area codes, postcodes, page numbers, and grid references in multi-column format. Due to the extremely dense tabular nature with thousands of entries, a faithful transcription would reproduce each entry row-by-row. Below is the content in reading order by column.

Column 1

- Friary Pk *NFNCH/WDSPK* N12 * ... 39 J3
- Friary Park Ct *ACT* W3 * ... 86 E5
- Friary Rd *ACT* W3 ... 86 E5
- *NFNCH/WDSPK* N12 ... 39 H3
- *PECK* SE15 ... 111 H6
- Friary Wy *NFNCH/WDSPK* N12... 39 J3
- Friday HI *CHING* E4 ... 44 C2
- Friday HI East *CHING* E4 ... 44 C2
- Friday HI West *CHING* E4 ... 44 C2
- Friday Rd *ERITH* DA8 ... 118 A4
- *MTCM* CR4 ... 147 K6
- **Friday St** *STP* EC4M ... 12 E6
- Frideswide PI *KTTN* NW5 ... 72 C4
- Friendly PI *LEW* SE13 ... 112 H1
- Friendly St *DEPT* SE8 ... 112 D7
- Friendly Street Ms *DEPT* SE8 ... 132 E1
- Friendship Wy *SRTFD* E15 * ... 76 A7
- Friends' Av *CROY/NA* CR0 ... 177 K2
- **Friend St** *FSBYE* EC1V ... 6 A4
- Friern Barnet La *TRDG/WHET* N20 ... 39 H2
- Friern Barnet Rd *FBAR/BDGN* N11 ... 40 A3
- Friern Mount Dr *TRDG/WHET* N20 ... 27 G6
- Friern Pk *NFNCH/WDSPK* N12 ... 39 H4
- Friern Rd *EDUL* SE22 ... 131 H5
- Friern Watch Av *NFNCH/WDSPK* N12 ... 39 H3
- Frigate Ms *DEPT* SE8 ... 112 D5
- Frimley Av *WLGTN* SM6 ... 176 F4
- Frimley CI *CROY/NA* CR0 ... 180 A6
- *WIM/MER* SW19 ... 146 C1
- Frimley Ct *SCUP* DA14 ... 155 J4
- Frimley Crs *CROY/NA* CR0 ... 180 A6
- Frimley Gdns *MTCM* CR4 ... 162 D2
- Frimley Rd *CHSGTN* KT9 ... 171 K4
- *GDMY/SEVK* IG3 ... 78 E2
- Frimley Wy *WCHPL* E1 * ... 93 F3
- Frinsted Rd *ERITH* DA8 ... 118 A6
- Frinton CI *OXHEY* WD19 ... 33 F1
- Frinton Dr *WFD* IG8 ... 44 B6
- Frinton Ms *GNTH/NBYPK* IG2 ... 60 C5
- Frinton Rd *EHAM* E6 ... 95 H2
- *SEVS/STOTM* N15 ... 56 A5
- *TOOT* SW17 ... 148 A5
- Friston St *FUL/PGN* SW6 ... 128 A1
- Fritham CI *NWMAL* KT3 ... 160 B5
- Frith Ct *MLHL* NW7 ... 38 C6
- Frith La *MLHL* NW7 ... 38 C5
- Frith Manor Farm Cotts *MLHL* NW7 * ... 38 C4
- Frith Rd *CROY/NA* CR0 ... 177 J1
- *WAN* E11 ... 76 D2
- **Frith St** *SOHO/SHAV* W1D * ... 11 G5
- Frithville Gdns *SHB* W12 ... 88 A7
- Frithwood Av *NTHWD* HA6 ... 32 D5
- Frizlands La *DAGE* RM10 ... 80 D2
- Frobisher CI *BUSH* WD23 ... 22 A5
- *PIN* HA5 ... 47 H6
- **Frobisher Crs** *BARB* EC2Y * ... 12 F2
- *STWL/WRAY* TW19 ... 120 B6
- Frobisher Gdns *LEY* E10 * ... 57 K5
- Frobisher Ms *ENC/FH* EN2 ... 29 K3
- Frobisher Rd *CEND/HSY/T* N8 ... 55 G3
- *EHAM* E6 ... 95 K5
- Frog La *RAIN* RM13 ... 99 F4
- Frogley Rd *EDUL* SE22 ... 131 G3
- Frogmore *WAND/EARL* SW18 ... 127 K4
- Frogmore Ct *YEAD* UB4 ... 82 D5
- Frogmore CI *CHEAM* SM3 ... 174 B2
- Frogmore Est *HBRY* N5 * ... 73 J3
- Frogmore Gdns *CHEAM* SM3 ... 174 C3
- *YEAD* UB4 ... 82 C3
- Frognal *HAMP* NW3 ... 71 G4
- Frognal Av *HRW* HA1 ... 49 F3
- *SCUP* DA14 ... 155 H3
- Frognal CI *HAMP* NW3 ... 71 G4
- Frognal Ct *HAMP* NW3 * ... 71 G5
- Frognal Gdns *HAMP* NW3 ... 71 G3
- Frognal La *HAMP* NW3 ... 71 F4
- Frognal Man *HAMP* NW3 * ... 71 G3
- Frognal Pde *HAMP* NW3 * ... 71 G5
- Frognal Pl *SCUP* DA14 ... 155 G5
- Frognal Ri *HAMP* NW3 ... 71 G2
- Frognal Wy *HAMP* NW3 ... 71 G3
- Froissart Rd *ELTH/MOT* SE9 ... 134 D4
- Frome Rd *SEVS/STOTM* N15 ... 55 H2
- **Frome St** *IS* N1 ... 6 D2
- Fromondes Rd *CHEAM* SM3 ... 174 C4
- Fromows Cnr *CHSWK* W4 * ... 105 K4
- Frostic Wk *WCHPL* E1 ... 13 M3
- Froude St *VX/NE* SW8 ... 129 G1
- Fruen Rd *EBED/NFELT* TW14 ... 121 J6
- Fryatt Rd *TOTM* N17 ... 41 K6
- Fryday Grove Ms *BAL* SW12 * ... 129 H6
- Fryent CI *KTN/HRWW/WS* HA3 ... 50 A6
- Fryent Crs *CDALE/KGS* NW9 ... 51 G5
- Fryent Flds *CDALE/KGS* NW9 ... 51 G5
- Fryent Gv *CDALE/KGS* NW9 ... 51 G5
- Fryent Wy *CDALE/KGS* NW9 ... 50 D5
- **Frying Pan Aly** *WCHPL* E1 * ... 13 L3
- Fry Rd *EHAM* E6 ... 77 H6
- *WLSDN* NW10 ... 69 H7
- Fryston Av *CROY/NA* CR0 ... 178 C1
- Fuchsia CI *ROMW/RG* RM7 ... 81 G1
- Fuchsia St *ABYW* SE2 ... 116 C4
- Fulbeck Dr *CDALE/KGS* NW9 ... 37 G7
- Fulbeck Rd *RYLN/HDSTN* HA2 ... 48 C1
- Fulbourne Rd *WALTH* E17 ... 44 A7
- Fulbourne St *WCHPL* E1 ... 92 D4
- Fulbrook Ms *ARCH* N19 ... 72 C3
- Fulbrook Rd *ARCH* N19 ... 72 C3
- Fulford Gv *OXHEY* WD19 ... 33 F1
- Fulford Rd *HOR/WEW* KT19 ... 173 F6
- *ELTH/BERM/RHTH* SE16 ... 111 J4
- Fulham Broadway *FUL/PGN* SW6 ... 107 K6
- Fulham CI *HGDN/ICK* UB10 ... 81 F3
- Fulham High St *FUL/PGN* SW6 ... 127 H1
- Fulham Palace Rd *FUL/PGN* SW6 ... 107 G6
- Fulham Park Gdns *FUL/PGN* SW6 ... 127 J1
- Fulham Park Rd *FUL/PGN* SW6 ... 127 J1
- **Fulham Rd** *CHEL* SW3 ... 15 J8
- *FUL/PGN* SW6 ... 127 H1
- *WBPTN* SW10 ... 14 F9
- Fullbrooks Av *WPK* KT4 ... 160 C7
- Fuller CI *BETH* E2 * ... 92 C3
- *BUSH* WD23 ... 22 D6
- Fullerian Crs *WATW* WD18 ... 20 D3
- Fuller Rd *BCTR* RM8 ... 79 J2
- Fullers Av *SURB* KT6 ... 172 B1
- Fuller's Rd *SWFD* E18 ... 44 D4
- Fuller St *HDN* NW4 ... 52 A3
- Fullers Wy North *SURB* KT6 ... 172 B3
- Fuller's Wd *CROY/NA* CR0 ... 179 J4
- Fullerton Rd *CAR* SM5 ... 175 J7
- *CROY/NA* CR0 ... 165 G6

Column 2

- *WAND/EARL* SW18 ... 128 B4
- **Fullwood PI** *GINN* WC1R * ... 11 M3
- Fullwood's Ms *IS* N1 ... 7 H3
- Fulmar Ct *BRYLDS* KT5 ... 159 G5
- Fulmar Rd *HCH* RM12 ... 81 J6
- Fulmead St *FUL/PGN* SW6 ... 108 A7
- Fulmer CI *HPTN* TW12 ... 141 J4
- Fulmer Rd *CAN/RD* E16 ... 95 H4
- Fulmer Wy *WEA* W13 ... 104 C2
- Fulready Rd *LEY* E10 ... 58 B5
- Fulstone CI *HSLW* TW4 ... 122 E3
- Fulthorp Rd *BKHTH/KID* SE3 ... 133 J1
- **Fulton Ms** *BAY/PAD* W2 * ... 8 C6
- Fulton Rd *WBLY* HA9 ... 68 C2
- Fulwell Park Av *WHTN* TW2 ... 142 C1
- Fulwell Rd *TEDD* TW11 ... 142 D3
- Fulwood Av *ALP/SUD* HA0 ... 86 B1
- Fulwood Gdns *TWK* TW1 ... 124 A5
- Fulwood Wk *WIM/MER* SW19 ... 127 H7
- Furber St *HMSMTH* W6 ... 106 E3
- Furham Fld *PIN* HA5 ... 34 A6
- Furley Rd *PECK* SE15 ... 111 H6
- Furlong CI *WLGTN* SM6 ... 163 G7
- Furlong Rd *HOLWY* N7 ... 73 G5
- The Furlongs *ESH/CLAY* KT10 ... 170 C1
- Furmage St *WAND/EARL* SW18 ... 128 A6
- Furneaux Av *WNWD* SE27 ... 149 H4
- Furner CI *DART* DA1 ... 138 C2
- Furness Rd *FUL/PGN* SW6 ... 128 A1
- *MRDN* SM4 ... 162 A5
- *RYLN/HDSTN* HA2 ... 48 B6
- *WLSDN* NW10 ... 87 J1
- Furness Wy *HCH* RM12 ... 81 J4
- **Furnival St** *FLST/FETLN* EC4A * ... 12 A4
- Furrow La *HOM* E9 ... 74 E4
- Fursby Av *FNCH* N3 ... 38 E5
- Further Acre *CDALE/KGS* NW9 ... 51 H1
- Furtherfield CI *CROY/NA* CR0 ... 164 B5
- Further Green Rd *CAT* SE6 ... 133 H6
- Furze CI *OXHEY* WD19 ... 33 G4
- Furzedown Dr *TOOT* SW17 ... 148 B4
- Furzedown Rd *TOOT* SW17 ... 148 B4
- Furze Farm CI *CHDH* RM6 ... 62 A1
- Furzefield CI *CHST* BR7 ... 154 B5
- Furzefield Rd *BKHTH/KID* SE3 ... 114 A5
- Furzeground Wy *STKPK* UB11 ... 82 A7
- Furzeham Rd *WDR/YW* UB7 ... 100 B1
- Furzehill Pde *BORE* WD6 * ... 24 E1
- Furzehill Rd *BORE* WD6 ... 24 D3
- Furze Rd *THHTH* CR7 ... 164 D2
- **Furze St** *BOW* E3 ... 93 J4
- Furzewood *SUN* TW16 ... 140 E7
- **Fye Foot La** *BLKFR* EC4V * ... 12 E6
- Fyfe Wy *BMLY* BR1 ... 167 K1
- Fyfield CI *HAYES* BR2 ... 167 G3
- Fyfield Rd *BRXN/ST* SW9 ... 130 B2
- *EN* EN1 ... 30 A2
- *RAIN* RM13 ... 81 H7
- *WALTH* E17 ... 58 B2
- **Fynes St** *WEST* SW1P ... 17 G5

G

- Gable CI *PIN* HA5 ... 34 A6
- Gable Ct *SYD* SE26 ... 150 D3
- Gable Ms *HAYES* BR2 ... 181 J1
- Gables Av *BORE* WD6 ... 24 B2
- Gables CI *CMBW* SE5 ... 111 F7
- The Gables *NRWD* SE19 * ... 150 A7
- *WBLY* HA9 ... 68 B2
- Gabriel CI *FELT* TW13 ... 141 J3
- Gabrielle Av *WBLY* HA9 ... 68 B2
- Gabriel St *FSTH* SE23 ... 132 A6
- **Gabriel's Whf** *STHWK* SE1 * ... 12 A8
- Gad CI *PLSTW* E13 ... 95 F2
- Gaddesden Av *WBLY* HA9 ... 68 B5
- Gade Av *WATW* WD18 ... 20 A3
- Gade Bank *RKW/CH/CXG* WD3 ... 20 B3
- Gade CI *HYS/HAR* UB3 ... 87 F7
- *WATW* WD18 ... 20 C3
- Gadesden Rd *HOR/WEW* KT19 ... 172 E5
- Gadsbury CI *CDALE/KGS* NW9 ... 51 H5
- Gadwall CI *CAN/RD* E16 ... 95 F5
- Gage Rd *CAN/RD* E16 ... 94 C4
- **Gage St** *BMSBY* WC1N * ... 11 K2
- Gainford St *IS* N1 ... 6 A1
- Gainsboro Gdns *GFD/PVL* UB6 ... 66 E4
- Gainsborough Av *MNPK* E12 ... 78 A4
- Gainsborough CI *BECK* BR3 ... 151 J6
- *ESH/CLAY* KT10 * ... 157 J6
- Gainsborough Ct *SHB* W12 ... 107 F1
- Gainsborough Gdns *EDGW* HA8 ... 50 B1
- *GLDGN* NW11 ... 52 D6
- *HAMP* NW3 ... 71 H2
- *HSLW* TW3 ... 123 J4
- Gainsborough Ms *DUL* SE21 ... 130 D7
- *SYD* SE26 * ... 150 D2
- Gainsborough Rd *BCTR* RM8 ... 79 H3
- *CHSWK* W4 ... 106 C3
- *NFNCH/WDSPK* N12 ... 39 F4
- *NWMAL* KT3 ... 160 A5
- *RAIN* RM13 ... 81 J7
- *RCH/KEW* TW9 ... 125 G2
- *SRTFD* E15 ... 94 C2
- *WAN* E11 ... 58 C6
- *WFD* IG8 ... 45 J5
- *YEAD* UB4 ... 82 D4
- Gainsborough Sq *BXLYHS* DA6 ... 136 E2
- Gainsborough St *HOM* E9 * ... 75 H5
- Gainsborough Ter *BELMT* SM2 * ... 174 D6
- Gainsford Rd *WALTH* E17 ... 57 H3
- Gairloch Rd *CMBW* SE5 ... 131 F1
- Gaisford St *KTTN* NW5 ... 72 C5
- Gaitskell Rd *ELTH/MOT* SE9 ... 135 H7
- **Gaitskell Wy** *STHWK* SE1 ... 18 E1
- Galahad Rd *ED* N9 ... 42 C1
- Galata Rd *BARN* SW13 ... 106 D6
- Galatea Sq *PECK* SE15 ... 131 J2
- Galbraith St *POP/IOD* E14 ... 113 F2
- Galdana Av *BAR* EN5 ... 27 G2
- Galeborough Av *WFD* IG8 ... 44 B7
- Gale CI *HPTN* TW12 ... 141 J5
- *MTCM* CR4 ... 162 C2
- Galena Rd *HMSMTH* W6 ... 106 E3
- Galesbury Rd *WAND/EARL* SW18 ... 128 B5
- Gales Gdns *BETH* E2 ... 92 D2
- **Gale St** *BOW* E3 ... 93 K4
- *DAGW* RM9 ... 79 K6
- Gales Wy *WFD* IG8 ... 45 J6
- Galgate CI *WIM/MER* SW19 ... 127 G7
- Gallants Farm Rd *EBAR* EN4 ... 27 J6
- Galleon CI *BERM/RHTH* SE16 ... 111 K1
- Galleons Dr *BARK* IG11 ... 97 K2
- The Galleries *IS* N1 * ... 6 C1
- Gallery Gdns *NTHLT* UB5 ... 83 H1

Column 3

- Gallery Rd *DUL* SE21 ... 130 E7
- Galley La *BAR* EN5 ... 25 K2
- Galleywall Rd *BERM/RHTH* SE16 ... 111 J3
- Galliard Rd *ED* N9 ... 30 C6
- Gallia Rd *HBRY* N5 ... 73 H4
- Gallions CI *BARK* IG11 ... 97 G2
- Gallions Rd *CHARL* SE7 ... 113 K4
- Gallions View Rd *THMD* SE28 * ... 115 K1
- Gallon CI *CHARL* SE7 ... 114 B3
- The Gallops *ESH/CLAY* KT10 ... 170 A2
- The Gallop *BELMT* SM2 ... 175 H7
- *SAND/SEL* CR2 ... 178 D6
- Gallosson Rd *WOOL/PLUM* SE18 ... 115 K3
- Galloway Pth *CROY/NA* CR0 ... 177 K3
- Galloway Rd *SHB* W12 ... 87 J7
- Gallus CI *WCHMH* N21 ... 29 F5
- Gallus Sq *BKHTH/KID* SE3 ... 134 A2
- Galpin's Rd *THHTH* CR7 ... 163 K3
- Galsworthy Av *CHDH* RM6 ... 61 H5
- *POP/IOD* E14 ... 93 G4
- Galsworthy CI *THMD* SE28 ... 97 J7
- Galsworthy Crs *BKHTH/KID* SE3 ... 114 B7
- Galsworthy Rd *CRICK* NW2 ... 70 C3
- *KUTN/CMB* KT2 ... 144 D7
- Galton St *NKENS* W10 ... 88 C3
- Galva CI *EBAR* EN4 ... 28 A3
- Galveston Rd *PUT/ROE* SW15 ... 127 J4
- Galway CI *BERM/RHTH* SE16 * ... 111 J4
- **Galway St** *FSBYE* EC1V ... 6 F8
- Gambetta St *VX/NE* SW8 ... 129 G1
- **Gambia St** *STHWK* SE1 ... 12 D9
- Gambole Rd *TOOT* SW17 ... 147 J3
- Games Rd *EBAR* EN4 ... 27 K2
- Gamlen Rd *PUT/ROE* SW15 ... 127 G3
- Gamuel CI *WALTH* E17 ... 57 J5
- Gander Green Crs *HPTN* TW12 ... 142 A7
- Gander Green La *CHEAM* SM3 ... 174 D5
- Gandhi CI *WALTH* E17 ... 57 J5
- Gandhi St *WATW* WD24 ... 21 H1
- Gandolfi St *CMBW* SE5 ... 111 F5
- **Ganton St** *REGST* W1B ... 10 E6
- Ganton Wk *OXHEY* WD19 * ... 33 J3
- Gantshills Crs *GNTH/NBYPK* IG2 ... 60 A4
- Gap Rd *WIM/MER* SW19 ... 146 E4
- Garage Rd *ACT* W3 ... 86 B5
- Garbrand Wk *EW* KT17 ... 173 H7
- **Garbutt PI** *MHST* W1U * ... 10 B2
- Garden Av *MTCM* CR4 ... 148 B6
- Garden City *EDGW* HA8 ... 36 C5
- Garden CI *ASHF* TW15 ... 140 A5
- *BAR* EN5 ... 26 A3
- *CHING* E4 ... 43 J4
- *HPTN* TW12 ... 141 J4
- *LEE/GVPK* SE12 ... 153 F2
- *NTHLT* UB5 ... 65 J7
- *PUT/ROE* SW15 ... 126 E6
- *RSLP* HA4 ... 64 C1
- *WAT* WD17 ... 20 D1
- *WLGTN* SM6 ... 176 E4
- Garden Ct *CHSWK* W4 ... 105 K4
- **EMB** EC4Y * ... 12 A6
- *CHING* E4 ... 43 J4
- *HPTN* TW12 ... 141 K4
- Gardeners Rd *CROY/NA* CR0 ... 164 C7
- Garden Flats *HMSMTH* W6 * ... 107 F2
- Gardenia Rd *BMLY* BR1 ... 169 F2
- *EN* EN1 ... 30 A5
- Gardenia Wy *WFD* IG8 ... 44 E5
- Garden La *BMLY* BR1 ... 153 F5
- *BRXS/STRHM* SW2 ... 130 A7
- Garden Lodge Ct *EFNCH* N2 * ... 53 H2
- Garden PI *HACK* E8 ... 7 L3
- Garden Rd *BMLY* BR1 ... 153 F5
- *PGE/AN* SE20 ... 150 E7
- *RCH/KEW* TW9 ... 125 H1
- *STJWD* NW8 ... 2 F7
- *WOT/HER* KT12 ... 156 A6
- **Garden Rw** *STHWK* SE1 ... 18 C4
- The Gardens *BECK* BR3 ... 167 F1
- *CEND/HSY/T* N8 * ... 54 E3
- *CLPT* E5 * ... 56 D5
- *EBED/NFELT* TW14 ... 121 G5
- *EDUL* SE22 ... 131 H3
- *ESH/CLAY* KT10 ... 170 A3
- *HRW* HA1 ... 48 D5
- *PIN* HA5 * ... 47 K5
- *WAT* WD17 ... 20 D1
- *WCHPL* E1 ... 93 F4
- Garden Studios *BAY/PAD* W2 * ... 8 B3
- **Garden Ter** *PIM* SW1V ... 17 G7
- Garden Vis *ESH/CLAY* KT10 * ... 171 F6
- Garden Wk *BECK* BR3 ... 151 H7
- *SDTCH* EC2A ... 7 J9
- Garden Wy *WLSDN* NW10 ... 68 E5
- Gardiner Av *CRICK* NW2 ... 70 A4
- Gardiner CI *BCTR* RM8 ... 79 K3
- *PEND* EN3 ... 31 F5
- Gardiner House *CHARL* SE7 * ... 114 D6
- Gardner CI *WAN* E11 ... 59 F5
- Gardner PI *EBED/NFELT* TW14 ... 122 A5
- Gardner Rd *PLSTW* E13 ... 95 F3
- Gardners La *BLKFR* EC4V ... 12 E6
- Gardnor Rd *HAMP* NW3 ... 71 H3
- **Gard St** *FSBYE* EC1V ... 6 D7
- Garendon Gdns *MRDN* SM4 ... 162 A6
- Garendon Rd *MRDN* SM4 ... 162 A6
- Gareth CI *WPK* KT4 ... 174 A1
- Gareth Dr *ED* N9 ... 42 C1
- Garfield Ms *BTSEA* SW11 * ... 129 G2
- Garfield Rd *BTSEA* SW11 ... 129 F2
- *PEND* EN3 ... 30 E3
- *PLSTW* E13 ... 94 D3
- *TWK* TW1 ... 124 C7
- *WIM/MER* SW19 ... 147 G5
- Garford CI *POP/IOD* E14 ... 93 J6
- Garganey Wk *THMD* SE28 ... 97 J6
- Garibaldi St *WOOL/PLUM* SE18 ... 115 K3
- Garland Dr *HSLW* TW3 ... 123 H1
- Garland Rd *STAN* HA7 ... 35 K7
- *WOOL/PLUM* SE18 ... 115 H6
- **Garlick HI** *BLKFR* EC4V ... 12 F6
- Garlies Rd *FSTH* SE23 ... 151 G2
- Garlinge Rd *CRICK* NW2 ... 70 D5
- Garman CI *UED* N18 ... 41 K4
- Garman Rd *TOTM* N17 ... 42 E6
- **Garnault Ms** *CLKNW* EC1R * ... 6 B8
- **Garnault PI** *CLKNW* EC1R ... 6 B8
- Garner CI *BCTR* RM8 ... 61 K7
- Garner Rd *WALTH* E17 ... 44 A7
- **Garner St** *BETH* E2 ... 92 C1
- Garnet Rd *THHTH* CR7 ... 164 D3
- *WLSDN* NW10 ... 69 G5
- Garnet St *WAP* E1W ... 92 E7
- Garnett CI *ELTH/MOT* SE9 ... 134 E2
- Garnett Rd *HAMP* NW3 ... 71 K4
- Garnham St *STNW/STAM* N16 ... 74 B1
- Garnies CI *PECK* SE15 ... 111 G6

Column 4

- Garrad's Rd *STRHM/NOR* SW16 ... 148 D2
- Garrard CI *CHST* BR7 ... 154 B4
- Garrard Wk *WLSDN* NW10 ... 69 G5
- Garratt CI *CROY/NA* CR0 ... 176 E3
- Garratt La *TOOT* SW17 ... 147 G2
- Garratt Rd *EDGW* HA8 ... 36 C6
- Garratt Ter *TOOT* SW17 ... 147 J3
- Garretts Rd *BUSH* WD23 ... 22 C5
- Garrett CI *ACT* W3 ... 87 F4
- **Garrett St** *STLK* EC1Y * ... 6 E9
- Garrick Av *GLDGN* NW11 ... 52 C5
- Garrick CI *EA* W5 ... 86 A3
- *RCH/KEW* TW9 ... 124 E4
- *WAND/EARL* SW18 ... 128 B3
- Garrick Crs *CROY/NA* CR0 ... 178 A1
- Garrick Dr *HDN* NW4 ... 52 A1
- *THMD* SE28 ... 115 J2
- Garrick Gdns *E/WMO/HCT* KT8 ... 157 F2
- Garrick Rd *CDALE/KGS* NW9 ... 51 H5
- *GFD/PVL* UB6 ... 84 B3
- *RCH/KEW* TW9 ... 125 H2
- **Garrick St** *COVGDN* WC2E * ... 11 J6
- Garrick Wy *HDN* NW4 ... 52 A3
- **Garrison CI** *HSLWW* TW4 ... 122 E4
- *WOOL/PLUM* SE18 ... 115 F6
- Garrison La *CHSGTN* KT9 ... 172 A6
- Garsdale Ter *WKENS* W14 * ... 107 J4
- Garside CI *HPTN* TW12 ... 142 B5
- *THMD* SE28 ... 115 J2
- Garsington Ms *BROCKY* SE4 ... 132 C2
- Garter Wy *BERM/RHTH* SE16 ... 112 A1
- Garth CI *KUTN/CMB* KT2 ... 144 B4
- *MRDN* SM4 ... 161 G6
- *RSLP* HA4 ... 47 H7
- Garthland Dr *BAR* EN5 ... 25 K4
- Garth Ms *EA* W5 * ... 86 A3
- Garthorne Rd *FSTH* SE23 ... 132 A6
- Garth Rd *CHSWK* W4 ... 106 A5
- *CRICK* NW2 ... 70 D1
- *KUTN/CMB* KT2 ... 144 B4
- *MRDN* SM4 ... 161 F5
- The Garth *KTN/HRWW/WS* HA3 ... 50 B5
- *KTN/HRWW/WS* HA3 ... 50 B5
- *NFNCH/WDSPK* N12 * ... 39 G4
- Garthway *NFNCH/WDSPK* N12 ... 39 H5
- Gartlet Rd *WAT* WD17 ... 21 F2
- Gartmoor Gdns *WIM/MER* SW19 ... 127 J7
- Gartmore Gdns *GDMY/SEVK* IG3 ... 61 G7
- Garton PI *WAND/EARL* SW18 ... 128 B5
- Gartons CI *PEND* EN3 ... 30 E4
- Gartons Wy *BTSEA* SW11 ... 128 B2
- Garvary Rd *CAN/RD* E16 ... 95 F5
- **Garway Rd** *BAY/PAD* W2 * ... 8 C5
- Gascoigne PI *BETH* E2 ... 7 L7
- Gascoigne Rd *BARK* IG11 ... 78 C7
- *CROY/NA* CR0 ... 180 A7
- Gascony Av *KIL/WHAMP* NW6 ... 2 A2
- Gascoyne Dr *DART* DA1 ... 138 C2
- Gascoyne Rd *HOM* E9 ... 75 F6
- Gaselee St *POP/IOD* E14 ... 94 A6
- Gasholder PI *LBTH* SE11 ... 17 M8
- Gaskarth Rd *BAL* SW12 ... 129 G5
- *EDGW* HA8 ... 36 E7
- Gaskell Rd *HGT* N6 ... 53 K5
- Gaskell St *CLAP* SW4 ... 129 K1
- Gaskin St *IS* N1 ... 6 C1
- **Gaspar CI** *ECT* SW5 * ... 14 E5
- **Gaspar Ms** *ECT* SW5 ... 14 D5
- Gassiot Rd *TOOT* SW17 ... 147 K3
- Gassiot Wy *SUT* SM1 ... 175 H2
- Gastein Rd *HMSMTH* W6 ... 107 G5
- Gaston Bell CI *RCH/KEW* TW9 ... 125 G2
- Gaston Rd *MTCM* CR4 ... 163 F2
- Gataker St *BERM/RHTH* SE16 ... 111 J2
- Gatcombe Ms *EA* W5 ... 86 B6
- Gatcombe Wy *EBAR* EN4 ... 27 K2
- Gate Cots *EDGW* HA8 * ... 36 C1
- Gate End *NTHWD* HA6 ... 32 E6
- Gateforth St *STJWD* NW8 ... 9 J1
- Gatehill Rd *NTHWD* HA6 ... 32 E6
- Gatehouse CI *KUTN/CMB* KT2 ... 144 E6
- **Gatehouse Sq** *STHWK* SE1 * ... 12 F8
- Gateley Rd *BRXN/ST* SW9 ... 130 A2
- **Gate Ms** *SKENS* SW7 ... 15 L2
- Gates Green Rd *WWKM* BR4 ... 180 E2
- Gateshead Rd *BORE* WD6 ... 24 B1
- Gateside Rd *TOOT* SW17 ... 147 K2
- Gatestone Rd *NRWD* SE19 ... 150 A5
- **Gate St** *LINN* WC2A * ... 11 L4
- Gateway *WALW* SE17 ... 18 F9
- Gateway Ar *IS* N1 * ... 6 C5
- Gateway Ms *HACK* E8 ... 74 B4
- Gateway Rd *LEY* E10 ... 75 K3
- Gateways Rd *FBAR/BDGN* N11 * ... 40 A5
- The Gateways *RCH/KEW* TW9 * ... 124 E3
- The Gateway *WATW* WD18 ... 20 D1
- Gatfield Gv *FELT* TW13 ... 142 A1
- Gathorne Rd *WDGN* N22 ... 55 G1
- Gathorne St *BETH* E2 ... 93 F1
- Gatley Av *HOR/WEW* KT19 ... 172 D4
- **Gatliff CI** *BGVA* SW1W ... 16 B8
- Gatling Rd *ABYW* SE2 ... 116 B4
- Gatonby St *PECK* SE15 ... 111 G7
- Gatton CI *BELMT* SM2 ... 175 F7
- Gatton Rd *TOOT* SW17 ... 147 J3
- Gatward CI *WCHMH* N21 ... 29 H5
- Gatward Gn *ED* N9 ... 30 A7
- Gatwick Rd *WAND/EARL* SW18 ... 127 J6
- Gauden CI *CLAP* SW4 ... 129 J2
- Gauden Rd *CLAP* SW4 ... 129 J1
- Gaumont Ap *WAT* WD17 ... 21 F2
- Gaumont Ter *SHB* W12 * ... 107 F1
- Gauntlet CI *NTHLT* UB5 ... 65 J6
- Gauntlett Ct *ALP/SUD* HA0 ... 67 G4
- Gauntlett Rd *SUT* SM1 ... 175 H4
- Gautrey Rd *PECK* SE15 ... 131 K1
- Gavel St *WALW* SE17 * ... 19 H5
- Gaverick Ms *POP/IOD* E14 ... 112 D3
- Gavestone Crs *LEE/GVPK* SE12 ... 134 A6
- Gavestone Rd *LEE/GVPK* SE12 ... 134 A6
- Gavina CI *MRDN* SM4 ... 162 D4
- Gawain Wk *ED* N9 * ... 42 C2
- Gawber St *BETH* E2 ... 92 E2
- Gawsworth CI *SRTFD* E15 ... 76 D4
- Gawthorne Av *MLHL* NW7 ... 38 C5
- Gay CI *CRICK* NW2 ... 69 K4
- Gaydon La *CDALE/KGS* NW9 ... 37 G7
- Gayfere Rd *CLAY* IG5 ... 59 J1
- *EW* KT17 ... 173 H4
- **Gayfere St** *WEST* SW1P ... 17 J4

Column 5

- Gayford Rd *SHB* W12 ... 106 C1
- Gay Gdns *DAGE* RM10 ... 80 E3
- Gayhurst Rd *HACK* E8 ... 74 C6
- Gaylor Rd *NTHLT* UB5 ... 65 K4
- Gaynesford Rd *CAR* SM5 ... 175 K7
- *FSTH* SE23 ... 151 F1
- Gaynes Hill Rd *WFD* IG8 ... 45 J5
- Gay Rd *SRTFD* E15 ... 94 B1
- Gaysham Av *GNTH/NBYPK* IG2 ... 60 A4
- Gay St *PUT/ROE* SW15 ... 127 G2
- Gayton Crs *HAMP* NW3 ... 71 H3
- Gayton Rd *HAMP* NW3 ... 71 H3
- *HRW* HA1 ... 49 F5
- Gayville Rd *BTSEA* SW11 ... 128 E5
- Gaywood CI *BRXS/STRHM* SW2 ... 130 A7
- Gaywood Rd *WALTH* E17 ... 57 J2
- **Gaywood St** *STHWK* SE1 ... 18 D4
- Gaza St *WALW* SE17 ... 18 C8
- Geariesville Gdns *BARK/HLT* IG6 ... 60 B3
- Gearing CI *TOOT* SW17 ... 148 B3
- Geary Rd *WLSDN* NW10 ... 69 J4
- Geary St *HOLWY* N7 ... 73 F4
- Geddes Rd *BUSH* WD23 * ... 22 C3
- Gedeney Rd *TOTM* N17 ... 41 J7
- Gedling PI *STHWK* SE1 ... 19 M3
- Geere Rd *SRTFD* E15 ... 76 D7
- **Gees Ct** *MHST* W1U ... 10 B5
- **Gee St** *FSBYE* EC1V ... 6 E9
- Geffrye Est *IS* N1 ... 7 K6
- **Geffrye St** *BETH* E2 ... 7 L5
- Geldart Rd *PECK* SE15 ... 111 J6
- Geldeston Rd *CLPT* E5 ... 74 C1
- Gellatly Rd *NWCR* SE14 ... 131 K1
- General Gordon PI *WOOL/PLUM* SE18 ... 115 G2
- General Wolfe Rd *GNWCH* SE10 ... 113 G7
- Genesis CI *STWL/WRAY* TW19 ... 120 C7
- Genesta Rd *WOOL/PLUM* SE18 ... 115 G5
- Geneva Dr *BRXN/ST* SW9 ... 130 B3
- Geneva Gdns *CHDH* RM6 ... 62 A4
- Geneva Rd *KUT/HW* KT1 ... 159 F3
- *THHTH* CR7 ... 164 D4
- Genever CI *CHING* E4 ... 43 J4
- Genista Rd *UED* N18 ... 42 E4
- Genoa Av *PUT/ROE* SW15 ... 127 F4
- Genoa Rd *PGE/AN* SE20 ... 150 E7
- Genotin Rd *EN* EN1 ... 30 A2
- Gentleman's Rw *ENC/FH* EN2 ... 29 J2
- Geoffrey CI *CMBW* SE5 ... 130 D1
- Geoffrey Gdns *EHAM* E6 ... 95 J1
- Geoffrey Rd *BROCKY* SE4 ... 132 C2
- George Beard Rd *DEPT* SE8 ... 112 C3
- George Crs *MUSWH* N10 ... 40 A6
- George Downing Est *STNW/STAM* N16 ... 74 B1
- George Gange Wy *KTN/HRWW/WS* HA3 ... 48 E2
- George Groves Rd *PGE/AN* SE20 ... 150 C7
- George La *HAYES* BR2 ... 168 A7
- *LEW* SE13 ... 133 F5
- *SWFD* E18 ... 58 E1
- George Lowe Ct *BAY/PAD* W2 * ... 8 C2
- George Mathers Rd *LBTH* SE11 * ... 18 C5
- George Ms *BRXN/ST* SW9 ... 130 B1
- *CAMTN* NW1 ... 4 E8
- George Rd *CHING* E4 ... 43 J5
- *KUTN/CMB* KT2 ... 144 C6
- *NWMAL* KT3 ... 160 C3
- George Rw *BERM/RHTH* SE16 ... 111 H1
- Georges Md *BORE* WD6 ... 24 B1
- George Sq *HOLWY* N7 ... 73 F5
- George St *BARK* IG11 ... 78 C6
- *CAN/RD* E16 ... 94 D5
- *CROY/NA* CR0 ... 177 J1
- *HNWL* W7 ... 84 E7
- *HSLW* TW3 ... 122 E1
- **MBLAR** W1H ... 9 L4
- *NWDGN* UB2 ... 102 D3
- *RCH/KEW* TW9 ... 124 E4
- *ROM* RM1 ... 63 G5
- *WATW* WD18 ... 21 G3
- Georgetown CI *NRWD* SE19 ... 150 A4
- Georgette PI *GNWCH* SE10 ... 113 F6
- George V Av *PIN* HA5 ... 47 K2
- Georgeville Gdns *BARK/HLT* IG6 ... 60 B3
- George V Wy *GFD/PVL* UB6 ... 67 H6
- George Wyver CI *WIM/MER* SW19 * ... 127 H6
- **George Yd** *BANK* EC3V ... 13 H5
- *MYFR/PKLN* W1K ... 10 B6
- Georgiana St *CAMTN* NW1 ... 4 E3
- Georgian CI *HAYES* BR2 ... 168 A7
- *STAN* HA7 ... 35 G6
- Georgian Ct *WBLY* HA9 ... 68 C5
- Georgian Wy *HRW* HA1 ... 66 D1
- Georgia Rd *NWMAL* KT3 ... 159 K3
- *THHTH* CR7 ... 149 J7
- Georgina Gdns *BETH* E2 * ... 7 M7
- Geraldine Rd *CHSWK* W4 ... 105 H5
- *WAND/EARL* SW18 ... 128 B4
- **Geraldine St** *LBTH* SE11 ... 18 C4
- Gerald Rd *BCTR* RM8 ... 80 B1
- **BGVA** SW1W ... 16 B5
- *CAN/RD* E16 ... 94 D3
- Gerard Av *HSLWW* TW4 ... 123 F6
- Gerard Gdns *RAIN* RM13 ... 99 G1
- Gerard Rd *BARN* SW13 ... 106 C7
- *HRW* HA1 ... 49 G5
- Gerards CI *BERM/RHTH* SE16 ... 111 K5
- Gerda Rd *ELTH/MOT* SE9 ... 154 B1
- Germander Wy *SRTFD* E15 ... 94 C2
- Gernon Rd *BOW* E3 ... 93 G1
- Geron Wy *CRICK* NW2 ... 70 A1
- Gerrard Gdns *PIN* HA5 ... 46 E4
- **Gerrard PI** *SOHO/SHAV* W1D * ... 11 H6
- Gerrard Rd *IS* N1 ... 6 C5
- Gerrards CI *STHGT/OAK* N14 ... 28 C4
- **Gerrard St** *SOHO/SHAV* W1D ... 11 H6
- Gerridge St *STHWK* SE1 ... 18 B3
- Gertrude Rd *BXLY* DA17 ... 117 H3
- **Gertrude St** *WBPTN* SW10 ... 108 B5
- Gervase CI *WBLY* HA9 ... 68 E2
- Gervase Rd *EDGW* HA8 ... 36 E7
- Gervase St *PECK* SE15 ... 111 J6
- Ghent St *CAT* SE6 ... 151 J1
- Ghent Wy *HACK* E8 ... 74 B5
- Giant Arches Rd *HNHL* SE24 ... 130 D6
- Giant Tree HI *BUSH* WD23 ... 34 D1
- Gibbfield CI *CHDH* RM6 ... 62 A2
- Gibbon Rd *ACT* W3 ... 87 G6
- *KUTN/CMB* KT2 ... 144 A7
- *PECK* SE15 ... 131 K1
- Gibbons Ms *GLDGN* NW11 ... 52 D4
- Gibbons Rd *WLSDN* NW10 ... 69 F5
- Gibbon Wk *PUT/ROE* SW15 * ... 126 D4

Gibbs Av NRWD SE19 149 K5
Gibbs Cl NRWD SE19 * 149 K4
Gibbs Couch OXHEY WD19 33 H2
Gibbs Gn EDGW HA8 36 E3
WKENS W14 * 107 J4
Gibbs Green Cl WKENS W14 107 J4
Gibbs Rd UED N18 42 E3
Gibbs Sq NRWD SE19 * 149 K4
Gibraltar Wk BETH E2 7 M8
Gibson Cl CHSGTN KT9 171 J4
ISLW TW7 123 J2
WCHMH N21 29 G5
WCHPL E1 92 E3
Gibson Gdns
STNW/STAM N16 * 74 B1
Gibson Rd BCTR RM8 61 J7
LBTH SE11 17 M6
SUT SM1 175 F4
Gibson's Hl STRHM/NOR SW16 149 G6
Gibson Sq IS N1 6 B3
Gibson St GNWCH SE10 113 H4
Gidea Av GPK RM2 63 J2
Gidea Cl GPK RM2 63 J2
Gideon Cl BELV DA17 117 J3
Gideon Ms EA W5 * 104 E1
Gideon Rd BTSEA SW11 129 F2
Giesbach Rd ARCH N19 72 C1
Giffard Rd UED N18 42 A4
Giffin St DEPT SE8 112 D6
Gifford Gdns HNWL W7 84 D4
Gifford Rd WLSDN NW10 69 G6
Gifford St IS N1 5 K2
Gift La SRTFD E15 76 C7
Giggs Hill Gdns THDIT KT7 158 B7
Giggs Hill Rd THDIT KT7 158 B6
Gilbert Cl WIM/MER SW19 * 147 F7
WOOL/PLUM SE18 114 E7
Gilbert Gv EDGW HA8 36 E7
Gilbert Pl NOXST/BSQ WC1A 11 J3
Gilbert Rd BELV DA17 117 H2
BMLY BR1 152 E6
LBTH SE11 18 B5
PIN HA5 47 H3
ROM RM1 63 H3
WIM/MER SW19 147 G6
Gilbert St HSLW TW3 123 H2
MYFR/PKLN W1K 10 B5
SRTFD E15 76 C3
Gilbert White Cl GFD/PVL UB6 67 G7
Gilbey Rd TOOT SW17 147 J3
Gilbeys Yd CAMTN NW1 4 B2
Gilbourne Rd
WOOL/PLUM SE18 116 A5
Gilda Av PEND EN3 31 G4
Gilda Crs STNW/STAM N16 56 C7
Gildea Cl PIN HA5 34 A6
Gildea St GTPST W1W 10 D3
Gilden Crs KTTN NW5 72 A4
Gildersome St
WOOL/PLUM SE18 115 F5
Gilders Rd CHSGTN KT9 172 B5
Giles Coppice NRWD SE19 150 B3
Gilkes Crs DUL SE21 131 F5
Gilkes Pl DUL SE21 131 F5
Gillam Wy RAIN RM13 81 J5
Gillan Gn BUSH WD23 34 C1
Gillards Ms WALTH E17 57 J3
Gillards Wy WALTH E17 57 J3
Gill Av CAN/RD E16 94 E5
Gill Cl WATW WD18 20 A5
Gillender St BOW E3 94 A3
Gillespie Rd HBRY N5 73 G2
Gillett Av EHAM E6 95 J1
Gillett Pl HACK E8 74 B4
Gillett Rd THHTH CR7 164 E3
Gillett St STNW/STAM N16 74 A4
Gillham Ter TOTM N17 42 C5
Gillian Park Rd CHEAM SM3 161 J7
Gillian St LEW SE13 132 E4
Gillian Ter BRYLDS KT5 * 159 G5
Gillies St KTTN NW5 72 A4
Gillingham Rd CRICK NW2 70 C2
Gillingham Rw PIM SW1V 16 E5
Gillingham St PIM SW1V 16 D6
Gillison Wk
BERM/RHTH SE16 * 111 H2
Gillman Dr SRTFD E15 76 C7
Gill St POP/IOD E14 93 H5
Gillum Cl EBAR EN4 27 K7
Gilmore Rd LEW SE13 133 G3
Gilpin Av MORT/ESHN SW14 126 A3
Gilpin Cl BAY/PAD W2 8 F3
MTCM CR4 162 D1
Gilpin Crs UED N18 42 B4
WHTN TW2 123 G6
Gilpin Rd CLPT E5 75 G3
Gilpin Wy HYS/HAR UB3 101 G6
Gilroy Cl RAIN RM13 81 H5
Gilsland Rd THHTH CR7 164 E3
Gilson Pl MUSWH N10 39 K6
Gilstead Rd FUL/PGN SW6 128 A1
Gilston Rd WBPTN SW10 14 F8
Gilton Rd CAT SE6 152 C2
Giltspur St STBT EC1A 12 D4
Gilwell Cl CHING E4 31 K3
Gippeswyck Cl PIN HA5 33 H7
Gipsy Hl NRWD SE19 150 A4
Gipsy La PUT/ROE SW15 126 D2
Gipsy Rd WELL DA16 116 E7
WNWD SE27 149 K3
Gipsy Road Gdns WNWD SE27 149 J3
Giralda Cl CAN/RD E16 95 H4
Giraud St POP/IOD E14 93 K5
Girdlers Rd WKENS W14 107 H2
Girdwood Rd
WAND/EARL SW18 127 H6
Girling Wy EBED/NFELT TW14 121 K2
Gironde Rd FUL/PGN SW6 107 J6
Girtin Rd BUSH WD23 22 B4
Girton Av CDALE/KGS NW9 50 C2
Girton Cl NTHLT UB5 66 C5
Girton Gdns CROY/NA CR0 179 J2
Girton Rd NTHLT UB5 66 C5
SYD SE26 151 F4
Girton Wy RKW/CH/CXG WD3 20 A4
Gisbourne Cl WLGTN SM6 176 D2
Gisburn Rd CEND/HSY/T N8 55 F3
Gissing Wk IS N1 6 B2
Gittens Cl BMLY BR1 152 D3
Glacier Wy ALP/SUD HA0 85 K1
Gladbeck Wy ENC/FH EN2 29 H3
Gladding Rd MNPK E12 77 H3
Glade Cl SURB KT6 * 171 K1
Glade Gdns CROY/NA CR0 166 B6
Glade La NWDGN UB2 103 G1
Gladeside CROY/NA CR0 166 A6
WCHMH N21 29 F6
Gladesmore Rd
SEVS/STOTM N15 56 B5
The Glade BELMT SM2 174 C7
BMLY BR1 168 C1
CHARL SE7 114 B6
CLAY IG5 45 K7
CROY/NA CR0 166 A4
ENC/FH EN2 29 G2
EW KT17 173 J5
HACK E8 * 74 B5
NFNCH/WDSPK N12 * 39 H3
SHB W12 106 E1
WCHMH N21 29 F5
WFD IG8 45 F2
WWKM BR4 179 K2
Gladiator St FSTH SE23 132 B5
Glading Ter STNW/STAM N16 74 B2
Gladioli Cl HPTN TW12 142 A5
Gladsdale Dr PIN HA5 46 E3
Gladsmuir Rd ARCH N19 54 C7
BAR EN5 26 C1
Gladstone Av
EBED/NFELT TW14 121 K5
MNPK E12 77 J6
WDGN N22 55 G1
WHTN TW2 123 J6
Gladstone Gdns HSLW TW3 103 H7
Gladstone Ms
KIL/WHAMP NW6 * 70 D6
PGE/AN SE20 150 E6
WDGN N22 55 G1
Gladstone Pde CRICK NW2 * 70 A2
Gladstone Park Gdns
CRICK NW2 69 K2
Gladstone Pl BAR EN5 * 26 B3
E/WMO/HCT KT8 * 157 K4
Gladstone Rd CHSWK W4 * 106 A2
CROY/NA CR0 164 E6
KUT/HW KT1 159 H2
NWDGN UB2 102 D1
SURB KT6 171 K1
WAT WD17 21 G2
WIM/MER SW19 146 E6
Gladstone St STHWK SE1 18 C3
Gladstone Ter VX/NE SW8 * 109 G7
WNWD SE27 * 149 J3
Gladstone Wy
KTN/HRWW/WS HA3 48 E2
Gladwell Rd BMLY BR1 152 E5
CEND/HSY/T N8 55 F5
Gladwyn Rd PUT/ROE SW15 127 G2
Gladys Rd KIL/WHAMP NW6 2 B1
Glaisher St DEPT SE8 112 D5
Glamis Crs HYS/HAR UB3 101 F2
Glamis Pl WAP E1W 92 E6
Glamis Rd WAP E1W 92 E6
Glamis Wy NTHLT UB5 66 C5
Glamorgan Cl MTCM CR4 163 K2
Glamorgan Rd KUT/HW KT1 143 J6
Glandford Wy CHDH RM6 61 H4
Glanfield Rd BECK BR3 166 C3
Glanleam Rd STAN HA7 35 K3
Glanville Ms STAN HA7 35 G4
Glanville Rd
BRXS/STRHM SW2 129 K4
HAYES BR2 168 A2
Glasbrook Av WHTN TW2 122 E7
Glasbrook Rd ELTH/MOT SE9 134 C6
Glaserton Rd
STNW/STAM N16 56 A6
Glasford St TOOT SW17 147 K5
Glasgow Rd PLSTW E13 95 F1
UED N18 42 D4
Glasgow Ter PIM SW1V 16 E8
Glaskin Ms HOM E9 75 G5
Glasse Cl WEA W13 85 G6
Glasshill St STHWK SE1 18 D1
Glasshouse Flds WAP E1W 93 F6
Glasshouse St REGST W1B 10 F7
Glasshouse Wk LBTH SE11 17 K7
Glasshouse Yd FARR EC1M 12 E1
Glasslyn Rd CEND/HSY/T N8 54 D4
Glassmill La HAYES BR2 167 J1
Glass St BETH E2 * 92 D3
Glass Yd WOOL/PLUM SE18 115 F2
Glastonbury Av WFD IG8 45 H6
Glastonbury Pl WCHPL E1 92 E5
Glastonbury Rd ED N9 30 C7
MRDN SM4 161 K5
Glastonbury St
KIL/WHAMP NW6 70 D4
Glaston Ct EA W5 * 85 K7
Glaucus St BOW E3 93 K4
Glazbury Rd WKENS W14 107 H3
Glazebrook Cl DUL SE21 149 K1
Glebe Av ENC/FH EN2 29 H2
HGDN/ICK UB10 64 A3
KTN/HRWW/WS HA3 50 A2
MTCM CR4 162 D1
RSLP HA4 65 F5
WFD IG8 44 E5
Glebe Cl CHSWK W4 * 106 B4
HGDN/ICK UB10 64 A3
Glebe Ct BKHTH/KID SE3 * 133 H2
EA W5 * 85 K7
STAN HA7 35 J4
Glebe Crs HDN NW4 52 A3
KTN/HRWW/WS HA3 50 A2
Glebe Gdns NWMAL KT3 160 B6
Glebe House Dr HAYES BR2 168 A7
Glebelands DART DA1 138 C3
E/WMO/HCT KT8 157 G4
ESH/CLAY KT10 171 F7
Glebelands Av
GNTH/NBYPK IG2 60 D6
SWFD E18 58 E1
Glebelands Cl CMBW SE5 131 F2
NFNCH/WDSPK N12 39 H7
Glebelands Rd
EBED/NFELT TW14 121 K6
Glebe La BAR EN5 25 J4
KTN/HRWW/WS HA3 50 A3
Glebe Pth MTCM CR4 162 E2
Glebe Pl CHEL SW3 15 J9
Glebe Rd BARN SW13 126 D1
BELMT SM2 174 C7
BMLY BR1 152 E7
CAR SM5 175 K5
CEND/HSY/T N8 55 F3
DAGE RM10 80 D5
FNCH N3 39 G7
HACK E8 7 L1
RAIN RM13 99 K2
STAN HA7 35 J4
WLSDN NW10 69 J5
Glebe Side TWK TW1 124 A5
Glebe Sq MTCM CR4 * 162 E2
Glebe St CHSWK W4 106 A4
The Glebe BKHTH/KID SE3 133 H2
CHST BR7 154 C7
STRHM/NOR SW16 * 148 D3
WDR/YW UB7 100 B3
WPK KT4 160 C7
Glebe Wy WWKM BR4 180 A1
ERITH DA8 118 B5
FELT TW13 142 A2
Glebeway WFD IG8 45 G4
Gledhow Gdns ECT SW5 14 E6
Gledstanes Rd WKENS W14 107 H4
Gledwood Av YEAD UB4 82 E4
Gledwood Crs YEAD UB4 82 D4
Gledwood Dr YEAD UB4 82 D4
Gledwood Gdns YEAD UB4 82 E4
Gleed Av BUSH WD23 34 D1
Glegg Pl PUT/ROE SW15 * 127 G3
Glenaffric Av POP/IOD E14 113 F3
Glen Albyn Rd
WIM/MER SW19 146 B1
Glenalla Rd RSLP HA4 46 D6
Glenalmond Rd
KTN/HRWW/WS HA3 50 A3
Glenalvon Wy
WOOL/PLUM SE18 114 D3
Glena Mt SUT SM1 175 G3
Glenarm Rd CLPT E5 74 E3
Glenavon Cl ESH/CLAY KT10 171 G5
Glenavon Rd SRTFD E15 76 C6
Glenbarr Cl ELTH/MOT SE9 135 G2
Glenbow Rd BMLY BR1 152 C5
Glenbrook North ENC/FH EN2 29 F3
Glenbrook Rd
KIL/WHAMP NW6 70 E4
Glenbrook South ENC/FH EN2 29 F3
Glenbuck Rd SURB KT6 158 E5
Glenburnie Rd TOOT SW17 147 K2
Glencairn Dr EA W5 85 H3
Glencairne Cl CAN/RD E16 95 H4
Glencairn Rd
STRHM/NOR SW16 148 E6
Glencoe Av GNTH/NBYPK IG2 60 E6
Glencoe Rd BUSH WD23 22 A5
DAGE RM10 80 C3
YEAD UB4 83 H3
Glencorse Gn OXHEY WD19 * 33 H3
Glen Crs WFD IG8 45 F5
Glendale Av CHDH RM6 61 J6
EDGW HA8 36 B3
WDGN N22 41 G6
Glendale Cl ELTH/MOT SE9 135 F2
Glendale Dr WIM/MER SW19 146 D4
Glendale Gdns WBLY HA9 49 K7
Glendale Ms BECK BR3 151 K7
Glendale Rd ERITH DA8 117 K3
Glendale Wy THMD SE28 97 J7
Glendall St BRXN/ST SW9 130 A2
Glendarvon St PUT/ROE SW15 127 G2
Glendevon Cl EDGW HA8 36 D2
Glendish Rd TOTM N17 42 C7
Glendor Gdns MLHL NW7 37 F3
Glendower Gdns
MORT/ESHN SW14 126 A2
Glendower Pl SKENS SW7 15 G5
Glendower Rd
MORT/ESHN SW14 126 A2
Glendown Rd ABYW SE2 116 B4
Glendun Rd ACT W3 87 G6
Gleneagle Ms
STRHM/NOR SW16 148 D4
Gleneagle Rd
STRHM/NOR SW16 148 D4
Gleneagles STAN HA7 35 H5
Gleneagles Cl
BERM/RHTH SE16 * 111 J4
ORP BR6 169 J7
OXHEY WD19 * 33 H4
Gleneldon Ms
STRHM/NOR SW16 148 E4
Gleneldon Rd
STRHM/NOR SW16 148 E3
Glenelg Rd BRXS/STRHM SW2 129 K4
Glenesk Rd ELTH/MOT SE9 135 F2
Glenfarg Rd CAT SE6 133 G7
Glenfield Crs RSLP HA4 46 B6
Glenfield Rd BAL SW12 129 H7
WEA W13 104 C1
Glenfinlas Wy CMBW SE5 110 C6
Glenforth St GNWCH SE10 113 J3
Glengall Br POP/IOD E14 112 E2
Glengall Gv POP/IOD E14 112 E2
Glengall Rd EDGW HA8 36 D2
KIL/WHAMP NW6 70 D7
PECK SE15 19 M9
WFD IG8 44 E5
Glengall Ter PECK SE15 19 M9
Glen Gdns CROY/NA CR0 177 G2
Glengarnock Av POP/IOD E14 113 F3
Glengarry Rd EDUL SE22 131 F3
Glenham Dr GNTH/NBYPK IG2 60 B4
Glenhaven Av BORE WD6 24 C2
Glenhead Cl ELTH/MOT SE9 135 G2
Glenhill Cl FNCH N3 52 E1
Glenhouse Rd ELTH/MOT SE9 135 F4
Glenhurst Av BXLY DA5 137 G7
KTTN NW5 72 A3
RSLP HA4 46 A6
Glenhurst Ri NRWD SE19 149 J6
Glenhurst Rd BTFD TW8 104 D5
NFNCH/WDSPK N12 39 H3
Glenilla Rd HAMP NW3 71 J5
Glenister Park Rd
STRHM/NOR SW16 148 D6
Glenister Rd GNWCH SE10 113 J4
Glenlea Rd ELTH/MOT SE9 135 F4
Glenloch Rd HAMP NW3 71 J5
PEND EN3 30 E1
Glenluce Rd BKHTH/KID SE3 134 A2
Glenlyon Rd ELTH/MOT SE9 135 F4
Glenmere Av MLHL NW7 37 J6
Glenmere Rw LEE/GVPK SE12 133 J5
Glenmill HPTN TW12 141 K4
Glenmore Lawns WEA W13 * 85 G5
Glenmore Pde ALP/SUD HA0 * 68 A7
Glenmore Rd HAMP NW3 71 J5
WELL DA16 116 A7
Glenmore Wy BARK IG11 97 G2
Glennie Rd WNWD SE27 149 G2
Glenny Rd BARK IG11 78 C5
Glenorchy Cl YEAD UB4 83 J4
Glenparke Rd FSTGT E7 77 F5
Glen Ri WFD IG8 45 F5
Glen Rd CHSGTN KT9 172 A2
PLSTW E13 95 G3
WALTH E17 57 H4
Glen Road End WLGTN SM6 176 B7
Glenrosa St FUL/PGN SW6 128 B1
Glenroy St SHB W12 88 A5
Glensdale Rd BROCKY SE4 132 C2
Glenshiel Rd ELTH/MOT SE9 135 F4
Glentanner Wy TOOT SW17 147 H2
Glentham Cots BARN SW13 * 106 D5
Glentham Gdns BARN SW13 106 E4
Glentham Rd BARN SW13 106 D5
The Glen BELMT SM2 * 175 G5
CROY/NA CR0 179 F2
ENC/FH EN2 29 H3
HAYES BR2 167 H1
NTHWD HA6 32 B6
NWDGN UB2 102 E4
ORP BR6 181 K2
PIN HA5 47 F4
WBLY HA9 67 K3
Glenthorne Av CROY/NA CR0 165 K7
Glenthorne Cl CHEAM SM3 161 K7
Glenthorne Gdns
BARK/HLT IG6 60 A2
CHEAM SM3 161 K7
Glenthorne Rd
FBAR/BDGN N11 39 K4
HMSMTH W6 106 E3
KUT/HW KT1 159 G3
WALTH E17 57 G4
Glenthorpe Rd MRDN SM4 161 G4
Glenton Rd LEW SE13 133 H3
Glentworth St CAMTN NW1 9 M1
Glenure Rd ELTH/MOT SE9 135 F4
Glenview ABYW SE2 116 E5
Glen View Rd BMLY BR1 168 C1
Glenville Gv DEPT SE8 112 C6
Glenville Ms
WAND/EARL SW18 128 A6
Glenville Rd KUTN/CMB KT2 144 C7
Glenwood Av
CDALE/KGS NW9 51 G7
RAIN RM13 99 J3
Glenwood Cl HRW HA1 49 F4
Glenwood Dr GPK RM2 63 J4
Glenwood Gdns
GNTH/NBYPK IG2 60 A4
Glenwood Gv
CDALE/KGS NW9 50 E7
Glenwood Rd CAT SE6 132 C7
EW KT17 173 J5
HSLW TW3 123 J2
MLHL NW7 37 G2
SEVS/STOTM N15 55 H4
Glenwood Rw NRWD SE19 * 150 B7
Glenwood Wy CROY/NA CR0 166 A5
Glenworth Av POP/IOD E14 113 G3
Gliddon Dr CLPT E5 74 D3
Gliddon Rd WKENS W14 107 H3
Glimpsing Gn ERITHM DA18 117 F2
Globe Pond Rd
BERM/RHTH SE16 93 G7
Globe Rd BETH E2 92 E2
EMPK RM11 63 J5
SRTFD E15 76 D4
WFD IG8 45 G5
Globe St STHWK SE1 19 G2
Globe Ter BETH E2 92 E2
Glossop Rd SAND/SEL CR2 177 K7
Gloster Rd NWMAL KT3 160 B3
Gloucester Av BFN/LL DA15 154 E1
CAMTN NW1 4 A2
WELL DA16 136 A4
Gloucester Circ GNWCH SE10 113 F6
Gloucester Cl THDIT KT7 * 158 B7
WLSDN NW10 69 F6
Gloucester Ct MTCM CR4 * 163 K4
RCH/KEW TW9 * 105 H6
Gloucester Crs CAMTN NW1 4 C3
Gloucester Dr FSBYPK N4 73 H1
GLDGN NW11 52 E3
Gloucester Gdns BAY/PAD W2 8 D4
EBAR EN4 28 A3
GLDGN NW11 52 D6
IL IG1 59 J6
SUT SM1 175 F1
Gloucester Ga CAMTN NW1 4 B5
Gloucester Gate Ms
CAMTN NW1 4 C5
Gloucester Gv EDGW HA8 37 F7
Gloucester Ms BAY/PAD W2 8 F5
LEY E10 57 J6
Gloucester Ms West
BAY/PAD W2 8 E5
Gloucester Pde
BFN/LL DA15 * 136 B4
HYS/HAR UB3 * 101 F2
Gloucester Pl CAMTN NW1 3 L9
MHST W1U 9 M3
Gloucester Place Ms
MHST W1U 9 M4
Gloucester Rd ACT W3 105 K1
BAR EN5 27 F4
BELV DA17 117 G4
CROY/NA CR0 164 E6
EA W5 104 D1
FELT TW13 122 B7
HPTN TW12 142 B6
HRW HA1 48 B4
HSLWW TW4 122 D3
KUT/HW KT1 159 H1
LEY E10 57 J6
MNPK E12 77 K2
RCH/KEW TW9 105 H6
ROM RM1 63 G5
SKENS SW7 14 E3
TEDD TW11 142 E4
TOTM N17 55 K1
UED N18 42 B4
WALTH E17 57 F1
WAN E11 59 F4
WHTN TW2 123 H7
Gloucester Sq BAY/PAD W2 9 H5
BETH E2 74 C7
Gloucester St PIM SW1V 16 E7
Gloucester Ter BAY/PAD W2 8 D4
STHGT/OAK N14 * 28 D7
Gloucester Wk KENS W8 14 B1
Gloucester Wy CLKNW EC1R 6 B8
Glover Dr UED N18 42 E5
Glover Rd PIN HA5 47 H5
Glycena Rd BTSEA SW11 128 E2
Glyn Av EBAR EN4 27 H3
Glyn Cl EW KT17 173 J7
SNWD SE25 165 F1
Glyn Ct STAN HA7 35 H5
Glynde Ms CHEL SW3 15 K4
Glynde Rd BXLYHN DA7 136 E2
Glynde St BROCKY SE4 132 C5
Glyndon Rd
WOOL/PLUM SE18 115 H3
Glyn Dr SCUP DA14 155 H3
Glynfield Rd WLSDN NW10 69 G6
Glynne Rd WDGN N22 55 G1
Glyn Rd CLPT E5 75 F3
PEND EN3 30 E3
WPK KT4 174 B1
Glyn St LBTH SE11 17 L8
Glynwood Ct FSTH SE23 150 E1
Goat Rd MTCM CR4 163 F6
Goat Whf BTFD TW8 105 F5
Godalming Av WLGTN SM6 176 E4
Godalming Rd POP/IOD E14 93 K4
Godbold Rd SRTFD E15 94 C3
Goddard Pl ARCH N19 72 C2
Goddard Rd BECK BR3 166 A3
Goddards Wy IL IG1 60 D7
Godfrey Av NTHLT UB5 65 J7
WHTN TW2 123 J6
Godfrey Hl WOOL/PLUM SE18 114 D3
Godfrey Rd WOOL/PLUM SE18 114 E3
Godfrey St CHEL SW3 15 K7
SRTFD E15 94 A1
Godfrey Wy HSLWW TW4 122 D6
Goding St LBTH SE11 17 K8
Godley Rd WAND/EARL SW18 128 C7
Godliman St BLKFR EC4V 12 D5
STP EC4M * 12 D5
Godman Rd PECK SE15 * 131 J1
Godolphin Cl PLMGR N13 41 H5
Godolphin Pl ACT W3 87 F6
Godolphin Rd SHB W12 106 E1
Godric Crs CROY/NA CR0 180 B7
Godson Rd CROY/NA CR0 177 G2
Godson St IS N1 6 A5
Godstone Rd SUT SM1 175 G3
TWK TW1 124 B5
Godwin Cl HOR/WEW KT19 172 E5
IS N1 6 F5
Godwin Rd FSTGT E7 77 F3
HAYES BR2 168 B2
Goffers Rd BKHTH/KID SE3 113 H7
Goffs Rd ASHF TW15 140 B5
Goidel Cl WLGTN SM6 176 D3
Golborne Gdns NKENS W10 * 88 C3
Golborne Ms NKENS W10 88 C4
Golborne Rd NKENS W10 88 C4
Golda Cl BAR EN5 26 B5
Goldbeaters Gv EDGW HA8 37 G5
Goldcliff Cl MRDN SM4 161 K6
Goldcrest Cl CAN/RD E16 95 H4
THMD SE28 97 J6
Goldcrest Ms EA W5 * 85 K4
Goldcrest Wy BUSH WD23 22 C7
CROY/NA CR0 180 B7
Golden Ct HSLW TW3 123 J1
Golden Crs HYS/HAR UB3 82 C7
Golden Cross Ms
NTGHL W11 * 88 D5
Golden Hind Pl DEPT SE8 * 112 C3
Golden Jubilee Br STHWK SE1 11 L8
Golden La STLK EC1Y 6 E9
Golden Lane Est STLK EC1Y 12 E1
Golden Mnr HNWL W7 84 E6
Golden Pde WALTH E17 * 58 A2
Golden Plover Cl CAN/RD E16 94 E5
Golden Sq SOHO/CST W1F 10 F6
Golden Yd HAMP NW3 71 G3
Golders Cl EDGW HA8 36 D4
Golders Gdns GLDGN NW11 52 C6
Golders Green Crs
GLDGN NW11 52 D6
Golders Green Rd
GLDGN NW11 52 C5
Golders Hl HAMP NW3 * 71 F1
Golderslea GLDGN NW11 * 52 E7
Golders Manor Dr
GLDGN NW11 52 B5
Golders Park Cl GLDGN NW11 52 E7
Golders Ri HDN NW4 52 B4
Golders Wy GLDGN NW11 52 D6
Goldfinch Rd THMD SE28 115 J2
Goldfinch Wy BORE WD6 24 C3
Goldhawk Ms SHB W12 106 E1
Goldhawk Rd HMSMTH W6 106 C3
Goldhaze Cl WFD IG8 45 G6
Gold Hl EDGW HA8 37 F5
Goldhurst Ter
KIL/WHAMP NW6 2 D2
Golding St WCHPL E1 92 C5
Goldington Crs CAMTN NW1 4 F5
Goldington St CAMTN NW1 5 G5
Gold La EDGW HA8 37 F5
Goldman Cl BETH E2 92 C3
Goldney Rd MV/WKIL W9 8 A1
Goldrill Dr FBAR/BDGN N11 40 A1
Goldsboro Rd VX/NE SW8 109 J7
Goldsborough Crs CHING E4 43 K1
Goldsdown Cl PEND EN3 31 G1
Goldsdown Rd PEND EN3 31 F1
Goldsmid St
WOOL/PLUM SE18 115 K4
Goldsmith Av ACT W3 87 F6
CDALE/KGS NW9 51 G4
MNPK E12 77 J5
ROMW/RG RM7 62 C6
Goldsmith Cl
RYLN/HDSTN HA2 48 A7
Goldsmith La
CDALE/KGS NW9 50 E3
Goldsmith Pl
KIL/WHAMP NW6 * 2 C4
Goldsmith Rd ACT W3 87 F7
FBAR/BDGN N11 39 K4
LEY E10 57 K7
PECK SE15 111 H7
WALTH E17 57 F1
Goldsmiths Cl ACT W3 * 87 F7
Goldsmith's Rw BETH E2 92 C1
Goldsmith St CITYW EC2V 12 F4
Goldsworthy Gdns
BERM/RHTH SE16 111 K3
Goldwell Rd THHTH CR7 164 A3
Goldwing Cl CAN/RD E16 94 E5
Golf Cl BUSH WD23 21 H2
STAN HA7 35 J6
THHTH CR7 149 G7
Golf Club Dr KUTN/CMB KT2 145 F6
Golfe Rd IL IG1 78 D2
Golf Rd BMLY BR1 169 F2
EA W5 * 86 B5
Golf Side WHTN TW2 142 D2
Golf Side Cl NWMAL KT3 160 B1
Golfside Cl TRDG/WHET N20 39 J2
Gollogly Ter CHARL SE7 114 B4
Gomer Gdns TEDD TW11 143 G5
Gomer Pl TEDD TW11 143 G5
Gomm Rd BERM/RHTH SE16 111 K2
Gomshall Av WLGTN SM6 176 E4
Gondar Gdns CRICK NW2 70 D4
Gonson St DEPT SE8 112 E5
Gonston Cl WIM/MER SW19 146 C1
Gonville Crs NTHLT UB5 66 B5
Gonville Rd THHTH CR7 164 A4
Gonville St FUL/PGN SW6 127 H2
Goodall Rd WAN E11 76 A2
Gooden Ct HRW HA1 66 E2
Goodenough Rd
WIM/MER SW19 146 D6
Goodey Rd BARK IG11 79 F6
Goodge Pl FITZ W1T 10 F3
Goodge St FITZ W1T 10 F3
Goodhall Cl STAN HA7 35 G5
Goodhall St WLSDN NW10 87 G2
Goodhart Wy WWKM BR4 167 H5
Goodhew Rd CROY/NA CR0 165 H5
Gooding Cl NWMAL KT3 159 K3
Goodinge Cl HOLWY N7 72 E4
Goodinge Rd HOLWY N7 72 E5
Goodison Cl BUSH WD23 22 C4
Goodman Ct ALP/SUD HA0 * 67 K3
Goodman Crs
BRXS/STRHM SW2 148 D1
CROY/NA CR0 164 C5
Goodman Rd LEY E10 58 A6
Goodmans Ct ALP/SUD HA0 67 K3
Goodman's Yd TWRH EC3N 13 L6

H

Haarlem Rd WKENS W14 107 G2
Haberdasher Pl IS N1 7 H7
Haberdasher St IS N1 7 H7
Habington Cl CMBW SE5 * 110 E6
Habitat Cl PECK SE15 131 J1
Haccombe Rd
WIM/MER SW19 147 G5
Hackbridge Park Gdns
CAR SM5 175 K1
Hackbridge Rd CAR SM5 176 A1
Hackford Rd BRXN/ST SW9 110 A7
Hackford Wk BRXN/ST SW9 110 A7
Hackforth Cl BAR EN5 25 K4
Hackington Crs BECK BR3 151 J5
Hackney Cl BORE WD6 25 F4
Hackney Gv HACK E8 * 74 D5
Hackney Rd BETH E2 7 L7
Hackney Wick HOM E9 75 H5
Hadar Cl TRDG/WHET N20 26 E7
Haddenham Ct
OXHEY WD19 * 33 H2
Hadden Rd THMD SE28 115 K2
Hadden Wy GFD/PVL UB6 66 D5
Haddington Rd BMLY BR1 152 B2
Haddon Cl BORE WD6 24 C1
EN EN1 30 C5
NWMAL KT3 160 C4
Haddon Gv BFN/LL DA15 136 B6
Haddon Rd SUT SM1 175 F3
Haddo St GNWCH SE10 112 E5
Hadfield Cl STHL UB1 83 K2
Hadfield Rd
STWL/WRAY TW19 120 A5
Hadleigh Cl RYNPK SW20 161 J1
WCHPL E1 92 E3
Hadleigh Dr BELMT SM2 174 E7
Hadleigh Rd ED N9 30 D6
Hadleigh St BETH E2 92 E3
Hadley Cl BORE WD6 24 B4
WCHMH N21 29 G5
Hadley Common BAR EN5 27 G1
Hadley Gdns CHSWK W4 106 A4
NWDGN UB2 102 E4
Hadley Gn BAR EN5 26 D2
Hadley Green Rd BAR EN5 26 D1
Hadley Gn West BAR EN5 26 C1
Hadley Gv BAR EN5 26 C1
Hadley Pde BAR EN5 * 26 C2
Hadley Rdg BAR EN5 26 D2
Hadley Rd BAR EN5 27 F2
BELV DA17 117 G3
MTCM CR4 163 J3
Hadley St KTTN NW5 72 B5
Hadley Wy WCHMH N21 29 G5
Hadley Wood Rd BAR EN5 26 E1
Hadlow Pl NRWD SE19 150 C6
Hadlow Rd SCUP DA14 155 G3
WELL DA16 116 D6
Hadrian Cl BOW E3 75 J7
STWL/WRAY TW19 120 B6
Hadrian Est BETH E2 * 92 C1
Hadrian's Ride EN EN1 30 B4
Hadrian St GNWCH SE10 113 H4
Hadrian Wy
STWL/WRAY TW19 120 A6
Hadyn Park Rd SHB W12 106 D1
Hafer Rd BTSEA SW11 128 E3
Hafton Rd CAT SE6 133 H7
Hagden La WATW WD18 20 D3
Haggard Rd TWK TW1 124 C6
Hagger Ct WALTH E17 * 58 B2
Haggerston Rd HACK E8 7 L3
Hague St BETH E2 92 C2
Ha-Ha Rd WOOL/PLUM SE18 114 E5
Haig Rd STAN HA7 35 J4
UX/CGN UB8 82 A4
Haig Rd East PLSTW E13 95 G2
Haig Rd West PLSTW E13 95 G2
Haigville Gdns BARK/HLT IG6 60 B3
Hailes Cl WIM/MER SW19 147 G5
Haileybury Av EN EN1 30 B5
Hailey Rd ERITHM DA18 117 H1
Hailsham Av
BRXS/STRHM SW2 149 F1
Hailsham Cl SURB KT6 158 E6
Hailsham Dr HRW HA1 48 D2
Hailsham Rd TOOT SW17 148 A5
Hailsham Ter UED N18 * 41 K4
Haimo Rd ELTH/MOT SE9 134 C4
Hainault Blds LEY E10 * 58 A7
Hainault Gore CHDH RM6 62 A4
Hainault Rd CHDH RM6 61 H2
CRW RM5 62 E2
WAN E11 58 A7
Hainault St ELTH/MOT SE9 135 G7
IL IG1 78 B1
Haines Wk MRDN SM4 162 A6
Hainford Cl PECK SE15 132 A3
Haining Cl CHSWK W4 105 H4
Hainthorpe Rd WNWD SE27 149 H2
Hainton Cl WCHPL E1 92 D5
Halberd Ms CLPT E5 74 D1
Halbutt St DAGW RM9 80 B3
Halcomb St IS N1 7 J4
Halcot Av BXLYHS DA6 137 J4
Halcrow St WCHPL E1 * 92 D4
Haldane Cl MUSWH N10 40 B6
Haldane Pl WAND/EARL SW18 128 A7
Haldane Rd EHAM E6 95 H2
FUL/PGN SW6 107 J6
STHL UB1 84 C6
THMD SE28 97 K6
Haldan Rd CHING E4 44 A5
Haldon Rd WAND/EARL SW18 127 J5
Hale Cl CHING E4 44 A2
EDGW HA8 36 E4
Hale Dr MLHL NW7 36 E5
Hale End Cl RSLP HA4 46 E5
Hale End Rd WALTH E17 58 B1
Halefield Rd TOTM N17 42 C7
Hale Gdns ACT W3 86 C7
TOTM N17 56 C2
Hale Grove Gdns MLHL NW7 37 F4
Hale House
WOOL/PLUM SE18 * 114 D6
Hale La EDGW HA8 36 E4
Hale Rd EHAM E6 95 J3
TOTM N17 56 C2
Halesowen Rd MRDN SM4 162 A6
Hales St DEPT SE8 112 D6
Hale St POP/IOD E14 93 K6
Halesworth Rd LEW SE13 132 E2
The Hale CHING E4 44 B6
TOTM N17 56 C2
Haley Rd HDN NW4 52 A5
Half Acre BTFD TW8 104 E5
Half Acre Ms BTFD TW8 104 E6
Half Acre Rd HNWL W7 84 E7
Half Moon Crs IS N1 5 M5
Half Moon La HNHL SE24 130 D5
Half Moon Pas WCHPL E1 13 M5
Half Moon St MYFR/PICC W1J 10 D8
Halford Cl EDGW HA8 50 D1
Halford Rd FUL/PGN SW6 107 K5
LEY E10 58 B4
RCHPK/HAM TW10 125 F4
Halfway Ct PUR RM19 119 K3
Halfway St BFN/LL DA15 135 K7
Haliburton Rd TWK TW1 124 B4
Haliday Wk IS N1 73 K5
Halifax Cl TEDD TW11 142 E5
Halifax Rd ENC/FH EN2 29 J1
GFD/PVL UB6 66 B7
Halifax St SYD SE26 150 D2
Halifield Dr BELV DA17 117 F2
Haling Gv SAND/SEL CR2 177 J6
Haling Park Gdns
SAND/SEL CR2 177 H5
Haling Park Rd SAND/SEL CR2 177 H5
Haling Rd SAND/SEL CR2 177 K5
Halkin Ar KTBR SW1X 16 A3
Halkin Ms KTBR SW1X * 16 A3
Halkin Pl KTBR SW1X 16 A3
Halkin St KTBR SW1X 16 B2
Hallam Cl CHST BR7 153 K4
WATN WD24 21 G1
Hallam Gdns PIN HA5 33 J6
Hallam Ms GTPST W1W 10 D2
Hallam Rd BARN SW13 126 E2
SEVS/STOTM N15 55 H3
Hallam St GTPST W1W 10 D2
Halland Wy NTHWD HA6 32 B5
Hall Cl EA W5 86 A4
Hall Ct TEDD TW11 143 F4
Hall Dr SYD SE26 150 E4
Halley Gdns LEW SE13 133 G3
Halley Rd FSTGT E7 77 G5
Halley St POP/IOD E14 93 G4
Hall Farm Cl STAN HA7 35 H3
Hall Farm Dr WHTN TW2 123 J6
Hallfield Est BAY/PAD W2 8 D5
Hall Gdns CHING E4 43 H3
Hall Ga STJWD NW8 2 F8
Halliday Sq NWDGN UB2 84 D7
Halliford St IS N1 6 F1
Halliwell Rd
BRXS/STRHM SW2 130 A5
Halliwick Court Pde
NFNCH/WDSPK N12 * 39 K4
Halliwick Rd MUSWH N10 40 A7
Hall La CHING E4 43 H3
HDN NW4 51 J1
HYS/HAR UB3 101 G6
Hallmead Rd SUT SM1 175 F2
Hall Oak Wk KIL/WHAMP NW6 70 D5
Hallowell Av CROY/NA CR0 176 E3
Hallowell Cl MTCM CR4 163 F2
Hallowell Gdns THHTH CR7 164 D1
Hallowell Rd NTHWD HA6 32 C6
Hallowes Crs OXHEY WD19 32 E2
Hallowfield Wy MTCM CR4 162 C2
Hallows Gv SUN TW16 140 D4
Hall Pl BAY/PAD W2 9 G1
Hall Rd CHDH RM6 61 J5
DART DA1 139 J3
EHAM E6 77 K7
GPK RM2 63 K2
ISLW TW7 123 J4
MV/WKIL W9 2 F8
SRTFD E15 76 B3
WLGTN SM6 176 B7
Hall St FSBYE EC1V 6 D7
NFNCH/WDSPK N12 39 G4
Hallsville Rd CAN/RD E16 94 D5
Hallswelle Pde GLDGN NW11 * 52 D4
Hallswelle Rd GLDGN NW11 52 D4
Hall Vw ELTH/MOT SE9 153 H1
Hallywell Crs EHAM E6 95 K4
Halons Rd ELTH/MOT SE9 135 F6
Halpin Pl WALW SE17 19 H6
Halsbrook Rd BKHTH/KID SE3 134 B2
Halsbury Cl STAN HA7 35 H4
Halsbury Rd SHB W12 87 K7
Halsbury Rd East NTHLT UB5 66 C3
Halsbury Rd West NTHLT UB5 66 B4
Halsend HYS/HAR UB3 * 83 F7
Halsey Rd WATW WD18 21 F2
Halsey St CHEL SW3 15 L5
Halsham Crs BARK IG11 79 F5
Halsmere Rd CMBW SE5 110 C7
Halstead Cl CROY/NA CR0 177 J2
Halstead Gdns WCHMH N21 29 K7
Halstead Rd EN EN1 30 A3
ERITH DA8 118 B7
WAN E11 59 F4
WCHMH N21 29 K7
Halston Cl BTSEA SW11 128 E5
Halstow Rd WLSDN NW10 88 B2
Halsway HYS/HAR UB3 82 E7
Halter Cl BORE WD6 25 F4
Halton Cl FBAR/BDGN N11 39 K5
Halton Cross St IS N1 * 6 D3
Halton Pl IS N1 * 6 E3
Halton Rd IS N1 6 D2
Halt Pde CDALE/KGS NW9 * 51 F3
Halt Robin Rd BELV DA17 117 H3
Hambalt Rd CLAP SW4 129 H4
Hamble Cl RSLP HA4 64 C1
Hambledon Ct EA W5 * 86 A6
Hambledon Gdns SNWD SE25 165 G2
Hambledon Pl DUL SE21 131 G7
Hambledon Rd
WAND/EARL SW18 127 J6
Hambledown Rd
BFN/LL DA15 * 135 J6
Hamble St FUL/PGN SW6 128 A2
Hambleton Cl WPK KT4 174 A1
Hambrook Rd SNWD SE25 165 J2
Hambro Rd
STRHM/NOR SW16 148 D5
Hambrough Rd STHL UB1 83 J7
Ham Common
RCHPK/HAM TW10 143 K2
Ham Croft Cl FELT TW13 140 E2
Hamden Crs DAGE RM10 80 D2
Hamel Cl KTN/HRWW/WS HA3 49 K3
Hameway EHAM E6 96 A3
Ham Farm Rd
RCHPK/HAM TW10 143 K3
Hamfrith Rd SRTFD E15 76 D5
Ham Gate Av
RCHPK/HAM TW10 144 A3
Hamilton Av BARK/HLT IG6 60 B3
CHEAM SM3 174 C1
ED N9 30 C6
ROM RM1 63 F1
SURB KT6 172 C1
Hamilton Cl BERM/RHTH SE16 112 B1
EBAR EN4 27 J3
FELT TW13 140 D4
STJWD NW8 3 G8
TEDD TW11 143 H5
TOTM N17 56 B2
Hamilton Ct EA W5 86 B6
Hamilton Crs HSLW TW3 123 G4
PLMGR N13 41 G3
RYLN/HDSTN HA2 65 K2
Hamilton Gdns STJWD NW8 2 F7
Hamilton Ms MYFR/PICC W1J 16 C1
Hamilton Pde FELT TW13 * 140 E3
Hamilton Pk HBRY N5 73 H3
Hamilton Pk West HBRY N5 73 H3
Hamilton Pl MYFR/PKLN W1K 10 B9
SUN TW16 141 F6
Hamilton Rd BTFD TW8 104 E5
CHSWK W4 106 B2
EA W5 86 A6
EBAR EN4 27 J3
ED N9 30 C6
EFNCH N2 53 G2
FELT TW13 140 D3
GLDGN NW11 52 B6
GPK RM2 63 K4
HRW HA1 48 E4
HYS/HAR UB3 83 F6
IL IG1 78 B3
OXHEY WD19 33 F2
SCUP DA14 155 G3
SRTFD E15 94 C2
STHL UB1 83 K7
THHTH CR7 164 E2
WALTH E17 57 G1
WHTN TW2 123 K7
WIM/MER SW19 147 F6
WLSDN NW10 69 J4
WNWD SE27 149 K3
Hamilton Road Ms
WIM/MER SW19 147 F6
Hamilton Sq
NFNCH/WDSPK N12 * 39 G5
Hamilton St DEPT SE8 112 D5
WATW WD18 21 G4
Hamilton Ter STJWD NW8 2 E6
Hamilton Wy FNCH N3 38 E5
PLMGR N13 41 H3
WLGTN SM6 176 D7
Hamlet Cl LEW SE13 133 H3
Hamlet Gdns HMSMTH W6 106 D3
Hamlet Rd NRWD SE19 150 B6
Hamlet Sq CRICK NW2 70 C2
Hamlets Wy BOW E3 93 H3
The Hamlet CMBW SE5 130 E2
Hamlet Wy STHWK SE1 19 H2
Hamlin Crs PIN HA5 47 G4
Hamlyn Cl EDGW HA8 36 A2
Hamlyn Gdns NRWD SE19 150 A6
Hammelton Rd BMLY BR1 152 E7
Hammers La MLHL NW7 37 J3
Hammersmith Br
HMSMTH W6 106 E4
Hammersmith Bridge Rd
BARN SW13 106 E4
Hammersmith Broadway
HMSMTH W6 107 F3
Hammersmith Emb
HMSMTH W6 * 107 F5
Hammersmith F/O
HMSMTH W6 107 F4
Hammersmith Gv
HMSMTH W6 107 F2
Hammersmith Rd
HMSMTH W6 107 G3
Hammersmith Ter
HMSMTH W6 * 106 D4
Hammet Cl YEAD UB4 83 H4
Hammett St TWRH EC3N 13 L6
Hammond Av MTCM CR4 163 G1
Hammond Cl BAR EN5 26 C4
GFD/PVL UB6 66 D4
HPTN TW12 142 A7
Hammond Rd EN EN1 30 D2
NWDGN UB2 102 D2
Hammonds Cl BCTR RM8 79 J2
Hammond St KTTN NW5 72 C5
Hamond Cl SAND/SEL CR2 177 H7
Hamonde Cl EDGW HA8 36 D1
Hamond Sq IS N1 7 J5
Ham Park Rd SRTFD E15 76 D6
Hampden Av BECK BR3 166 B1
Hampden Cl CAMTN NW1 5 H6
Hampden Gurney St
MBLAR W1H 9 L5
Hampden La TOTM N17 42 B7
Hampden Rd ARCH N19 72 D1
BECK BR3 166 B1
CEND/HSY/T N8 55 G3
KTN/HRWW/WS HA3 34 C7
KUT/HW KT1 159 H2
MUSWH N10 40 A6
TOTM N17 42 C7
Hampden Wy STHGT/OAK N14 40 B2
Hampermill La OXHEY WD19 20 E7
Hampshire Cl UED N18 42 D4
Hampshire Hog La
HMSMTH W6 * 106 E3
Hampshire Rd WDGN N22 41 F6
Hampshire St KTTN NW5 * 72 D5
Hampson Wy VX/NE SW8 110 A7
Hampstead Cl THMD SE28 97 H7
Hampstead Gdns
GLDGN NW11 52 E5
Hampstead Ga HAMP NW3 71 G4
Hampstead Gn HAMP NW3 71 J4
Hampstead Gv HAMP NW3 71 G3
Hampstead Hts EFNCH N2 53 G3
Hampstead Hill Gdns
HAMP NW3 71 J3
Hampstead La HGT N6 53 K6
Hampstead Rd CAMTN NW1 4 E8
Hampstead Sq HAMP NW3 71 G2
Hampstead Wy GLDGN NW11 52 E5
Hampton Cl BORE WD6 24 E4
FBAR/BDGN N11 40 A4
KIL/WHAMP NW6 2 A8
RYNPK SW20 * 146 A6
Hampton Ct IS N1 73 H5
Hampton Court Av
E/WMO/HCT KT8 157 J5
Hampton Court Crs
E/WMO/HCT KT8 * 157 J2
Hampton Court Est
THDIT KT7 * 157 K4
Hampton Court Rd
HPTN TW12 157 J1
Hampton Court Wy
ESH/CLAY KT10 170 E1
Hampton La FELT TW13 141 J3
Hampton Ri
KTN/HRWW/WS HA3 50 A5
Hampton Rd CHING E4 43 H4
CROY/NA CR0 164 D5
FSTGT E7 77 F4
IL IG1 78 C3
TEDD TW11 142 D4
WAN E11 58 B7
WPK KT4 173 J1
Hampton Rd East FELT TW13 141 K2
Hampton Rd West FELT TW13 141 J1
Hampton St WALW SE17 18 D6
Ham Ridings
RCHPK/HAM TW10 144 B4
Ham Shades Cl BFN/LL DA15 155 F2
Ham St RCHPK/HAM TW10 143 J1
The Ham BTFD TW8 104 D6
Ham Vw CROY/NA CR0 166 B5
Ham Yd SOHO/SHAV W1D * 11 G6
Hanameel St CAN/RD E16 94 E7
CAN/RD E16 95 F7
Hanbury Cl HDN NW4 52 A2
Hanbury Ct HRW HA1 * 49 F5
Hanbury Dr WAN E11 58 D6
WCHMH N21 29 F3
Hanbury Rd ACT W3 105 J1
TOTM N17 56 D1
Hanbury St WCHPL E1 13 M2
Hancock Rd BOW E3 94 A2
NRWD SE19 149 K5
Handa Wk IS N1 73 J5
Hand Ct HHOL WC1V 11 M3
Handcroft Rd CROY/NA CR0 164 C6
Handel Cl EDGW HA8 36 B5
Handel Pde EDGW HA8 * 36 C5
Handel Pl WLSDN NW10 69 F5
Handel St BMSBY WC1N 5 J9
Handel Wy EDGW HA8 36 C6
Handen Rd LEE/GVPK SE12 133 H4
Handforth Rd BRXN/ST SW9 110 B6
IL IG1 78 B2
Handley Gv CRICK NW2 70 B2
Handley Page Rd WLGTN SM6 177 F6
Handley Rd HOM E9 74 E6
Handowe Cl HDN NW4 51 J3
Handside Cl WPK KT4 161 G7
Handsworth Av CHING E4 44 B5
Handsworth Cl OXHEY WD19 32 E2
Handsworth Rd TOTM N17 55 K2
Handtrough Wy BARK IG11 96 B1
Hanford Cl WAND/EARL SW18 127 K7
Hangar Lane (North Circular
Road) EA W5 86 B4
Hangar Ruding OXHEY WD19 33 K2
Hanger Gn EA W5 86 C3
Hanger La EA W5 86 A1
Hanger Vale La EA W5 86 B4
Hanger View Wy ACT W3 86 C5
Hankey Pl STHWK SE1 19 H2
Hankins La MLHL NW7 37 G1
Hanley Gdns FSBYPK N4 55 F7
Hanley Pl BECK BR3 151 J6
Hanley Rd FSBYPK N4 54 E7
Hanmer Wk HOLWY N7 73 F1
Hannah Cl BECK BR3 166 E2
WLSDN NW10 68 E3
Hannah Mary Wy
STHWK SE1 * 111 H3
Hannay La ARCH N19 54 D6
Hannell Rd FUL/PGN SW6 107 H6
Hannen Rd WNWD SE27 * 149 H2
Hannibal Rd
STWL/WRAY TW19 120 B6
WCHPL E1 92 E4
Hannibal Wy CROY/NA CR0 177 F4
Hannington Rd CLAP SW4 129 G2
Hanno Cl WLGTN SM6 176 D6
Hanover Av CAN/RD E16 94 E7
FELT TW13 121 K7
Hanover Cir HYS/HAR UB3 82 A5
Hanover Cl CHEAM SM3 174 C3
RCH/KEW TW9 105 H6
Hanover Dr CHST BR7 154 C3
Hanover Gdns LBTH SE11 110 B5
Hanover Pk PECK SE15 111 H7
Hanover Pl COVGDN WC2E 11 K5
Hanover Rd SEVS/STOTM N15 56 B3
WIM/MER SW19 147 G6
WLSDN NW10 70 A6
Hanover Sq CONDST W1S 10 D5
Hanover Steps BAY/PAD W2 * 9 K5
Hanover St CONDST W1S 10 D5
CROY/NA CR0 177 H2
Hanover Ter CAMTN NW1 3 L8
Hanover Terrace Ms
CAMTN NW1 3 K8
Hanover Wy BXLYHS DA6 136 E2
Hanover Yd IS N1 * 6 D5
Hansard Ms WKENS W14 107 G1
Hans Crs KTBR SW1X 15 L3
Hanselin Cl STAN HA7 35 F4
Hansen Dr WCHMH N21 29 F4
Hanshaw Dr EDGW HA8 37 F7
Hansler Gv E/WMO/HCT KT8 157 J4
Hansler Rd EDUL SE22 131 G4
Hansom Ter BMLY BR1 * 153 F7
Hanson Cl BAL SW12 129 G6
BECK BR3 * 151 K5
MORT/ESHN SW14 125 K2
WDR/YW UB7 100 C2
Hanson Gdns STHL UB1 102 D1
Hanson St GTPST W1W 10 E2
Hans Pl KTBR SW1X 15 L3
Hans Rd CHEL SW3 15 L3
Hans St KTBR SW1X 15 M4
Hanway Pl FITZ W1T 11 G4
Hanway Rd HNWL W7 84 D5
Hanway St FITZ W1T 11 G4
Hanworth Rd FELT TW13 122 A7
HPTN TW12 141 K3
HSLW TW3 123 G2
HSLWW TW4 122 E6
SUN TW16 140 E6
Hanworth Ter HSLW TW3 123 G3
Hapgood Cl GFD/PVL UB6 66 D4
Harben Pde HAMP NW3 * 3 G1
Harben Rd KIL/WHAMP NW6 2 F1
Harberson Rd BAL SW12 129 G7
SRTFD E15 76 D7
Harberton Rd ARCH N19 54 C7
Harbet Rd BAY/PAD W2 9 H3
UED N18 43 F4
Harbex Cl BXLY DA5 137 J6
Harbinger Rd POP/IOD E14 112 E3
Harbledown Rd
FUL/PGN SW6 107 K7
Harbord Cl CMBW SE5 130 E1
Harbord St FUL/PGN SW6 107 G7
Harborne Cl OXHEY WD19 33 G4
Harborough Av BFN/LL DA15 135 K6
Harborough Rd
STRHM/NOR SW16 149 F3
Harbour Av WBPTN SW10 108 B7
Harbour Cl MTCM CR4 148 A7
Harbour Exchange Sq
POP/IOD E14 112 E1
Harbour Rd CMBW SE5 130 D2
Harbour Yd WBPTN SW10 * 108 B7
Harbridge Av PUT/ROE SW15 126 C6
Harbury Rd CAR SM5 175 J7
Harbut Rd BTSEA SW11 128 C3
Harcastle Cl YEAD UB4 83 J3
Harcombe Rd
STNW/STAM N16 74 A2
Harcourt Av BFN/LL DA15 136 D5
EDGW HA8 36 E2
MNPK E12 77 K3
WLGTN SM6 176 B3
Harcourt Blds EMB EC4Y * 12 A6
Harcourt Cl ISLW TW7 124 B2
Harcourt Fld WLGTN SM6 176 B3
Harcourt Ms GPK RM2 63 H4
Harcourt Rd BROCKY SE4 132 C3
BUSH WD23 22 C4
SRTFD E15 94 D1
THHTH CR7 164 A5
WDGN N22 40 D7
WIM/MER SW19 146 E6
WLGTN SM6 176 B3
Harcourt St MBLAR W1H 9 K3
Harcourt Ter WBPTN SW10 14 D8
Hardcastle Cl CROY/NA CR0 165 H5
Hardcourts Cl WWKM BR4 179 K3
Hardel Wk BRXS/STRHM SW2 130 B6
Hardens Manorway
WOOL/PLUM SE18 114 C2
Harders Rd PECK SE15 131 J1
Hardess St HNHL SE24 130 D2
Hardie Cl WLSDN NW10 69 F4
Hardie Rd DAGE RM10 80 E2
Harding Cl CROY/NA CR0 178 B2
KUTN/CMB KT2 144 B7
WALW SE17 18 E9
Hardinge Rd UED N18 42 A4
WLSDN NW10 70 A7
Hardinge St WCHPL E1 92 E5
WOOL/PLUM SE18 115 G2
Hardings La PGE/AN SE20 151 F5
Hardinge Crs
WOOL/PLUM SE18 115 H2
Hardman Rd CHARL SE7 114 A4
KUTN/CMB KT2 159 F1
Hardwick Cl STAN HA7 35 J4
Hardwicke Av HEST TW5 * 103 F7
Hardwicke Ms FSBYW WC1X * 5 M8
Hardwicke Rd CHSWK W4 105 K3
PLMGR N13 40 E4
RCHPK/HAM TW10 143 J3
Hardwicke St BARK IG11 78 C7
Hardwick Gn WEA W13 85 H4
Hardwick Pl
STRHM/NOR SW16 148 C6
Hardwick St CLKNW EC1R 6 B8
Hardwick's Wy
WAND/EARL SW18 127 K4
Hardwidge St STHWK SE1 19 J1
Hardy Av CAN/RD E16 94 E7
RSLP HA4 65 F4
Hardy Cl BAR EN5 26 C4
BERM/RHTH SE16 112 A1
PIN HA5 47 H6
Hardy Cots GNWCH SE10 * 113 G5
Hardy Gv DART DA1 139 K3
Hardy Pas WDGN N22 41 F7
Hardy Rd BKHTH/KID SE3 113 J5
CHING E4 43 H5
WIM/MER SW19 147 F6
Hardys Ms E/WMO/HCT KT8 157 K3
Harebell Dr EHAM E6 96 A4
Hare & Billet Rd
BKHTH/KID SE3 113 G7
Hare Ct EMB EC4Y * 12 A5
Harecourt Rd IS N1 73 J5
Haredale Rd HNHL SE24 130 D3
Haredon Cl FSTH SE23 131 K6
Harefield ESH/CLAY KT10 170 E2
Harefield Av BELMT SM2 174 C7
Harefield Ms BROCKY SE4 132 C2
Harefield Rd BROCKY SE4 132 C2
CEND/HSY/T N8 54 D4
SCUP DA14 155 K1
STRHM/NOR SW16 149 F6
Hare Hall La GPK RM2 63 K3
Hare La ESH/CLAY KT10 170 D5
Hare Marsh BETH E2 92 C3
Harepit Cl SAND/SEL CR2 177 H6
Hare Rw BETH E2 92 D1
Haresfield Rd DAGE RM10 80 C5
Hare St WOOL/PLUM SE18 115 F2
Hare Wk IS N1 7 K6
Harewood Av CAMTN NW1 9 K1
NTHLT UB5 65 J6
STJWD NW8 3 K9
Harewood Cl NTHLT UB5 65 K6
Harewood Dr CLAY IG5 59 K1
Harewood Pl CONDST W1S 10 D5
Harewood Rd ISLW TW7 104 A6
OXHEY WD19 33 F1
SAND/SEL CR2 178 A5
WIM/MER SW19 147 J5
Harewood Rw CAMTN NW1 9 K2
Harewood Ter NWDGN UB2 102 E3
Harfield Gdns CMBW SE5 * 131 F2
Harfield Rd SUN TW16 156 C1
Harford Cl CHING E4 31 K6
Harford Rd CHING E4 31 K6
Harford St WCHPL E1 93 G3
Harford Wk EFNCH N2 53 H3
Harglaze Ter
CDALE/KGS NW9 * 51 G2
Hargood Cl
KTN/HRWW/WS HA3 50 A5
Hargood Rd BKHTH/KID SE3 114 B7
Hargrave Pk ARCH N19 72 C1
Hargrave Pl KTTN NW5 72 D4
Hargrave Rd ARCH N19 72 C1
Hargwyne St BRXN/ST SW9 130 A2
Haringey Pk CEND/HSY/T N8 54 E5
Haringey Rd CEND/HSY/T N8 54 E3
Harington Ter UED N18 * 41 K3
Harkett Cl
KTN/HRWW/WS HA3 49 F1
Harland Av BFN/LL DA15 154 D2
CROY/NA CR0 178 B2
Harland Cl WIM/MER SW19 162 A2
Harlech Gdns HEST TW5 102 B5
PIN HA5 47 H6
Harlech Rd STHGT/OAK N14 40 E2
Harlequin Av BTFD TW8 104 B5
Harlequin Cl ISLW TW7 123 K4
YEAD UB4 83 H4
Harlequin Ct EA W5 * 85 J6
Harlequin Rd TEDD TW11 * 143 H6
The Harlequin WAT WD17 * 21 G3
Harlescott Rd PECK SE15 132 A3
Harlesden Gdns WLSDN NW10 69 H7
Harlesden Rd WLSDN NW10 87 J1
Harley Cl ALP/SUD HA0 * 67 K5
Harley Crs HRW HA1 48 D3
Harleyford BMLY BR1 153 G7
Harleyford Rd LBTH SE11 17 L9
Harleyford St LBTH SE11 110 B5
Harley Gdns WBPTN SW10 14 F8
Harley Gv BOW E3 93 H2

Harley Pl CAVSQ/HST W1G 10 C3
Harley Rd HAMP NW3 3 H2
HRW HA1 48 D3
WLSDN NW10 87 G1
Harley St CAVSQ/HST W1G 10 C1
Harley Vls WLSDN NW10 * 87 G1
Harlinger St
WOOL/PLUM SE18 114 D2
Harlington Cl HYS/HAR UB3 101 F6
Harlington Rd East
EBED/NFELT TW14 122 A6
Harlington Rd West
EBED/NFELT TW14 122 A5
Harlow Rd PLMGR N13 41 K2
RAIN RM13 81 H7
Harlyn Dr PIN HA5 47 F2
Harman Av WFD IG8 44 D6
Harman Cl CHING E4 44 B3
CRICK NW2 70 C2
STHWK SE1 * 111 H4
Harman Dr BFN/LL DA15 136 A5
CRICK NW2 70 C2
Harman Rd EN EN1 30 B4
Harmondsworth La
WDR/YW UB7 100 B5
Harmondsworth Rd
WDR/YW UB7 100 B2
Harmony Cl GLDGN NW11 52 C4
WLGTN SM6 176 E7
Harmony Pl STHWK SE1 19 M7
Harmony Wy BMLY BR1 167 K1
HDN NW4 52 A3
Harmood Gv CAMTN NW1 * 4 C1
Harmood St CAMTN NW1 4 C1
Harmsworth Ms STHWK SE1 18 B4
Harmsworth St WALW SE17 18 C8
Harmsworth Wy
TRDG/WHET N20 26 D7
Harness Rd THMD SE28 116 B1
Harold Av BELV DA17 117 G4
HYS/HAR UB3 101 J2
Harold Rd CEND/HSY/T N8 55 F4
CHING E4 44 A2
NRWD SE19 149 K6
PLSTW E13 77 F7
SEVS/STOTM N15 56 B4
SUT SM1 175 H3
SWFD E18 44 E7
WAN E11 58 C7
WLSDN NW10 87 F2
Haroldstone Rd WALTH E17 57 F4
Harpenden Rd MNPK E12 77 G1
WNWD SE27 149 H1
Harper Rd EHAM E6 95 K5
STHWK SE1 18 F3
Harpers Yd ISLW TW7 * 124 A1
Harp Island Cl WLSDN NW10 69 F1
Harp La MON EC3R 13 J7
Harpley Sq WCHPL E1 92 E3
Harpour Rd BARK IG11 78 C5
Harp Rd HNWL W7 85 F3
Harpsden St BTSEA SW11 109 F7
Harpur Ms BMSBY WC1N 11 L2
Harpur St BMSBY WC1N 11 L2
Harraden Rd BKHTH/KID SE3 114 B7
Harrier Cl HCH RM12 81 K5
Harrier Ms THMD SE28 115 J1
Harrier Rd CDALE/KGS NW9 51 G1
Harriers Cl EA W5 86 A6
Harrier Wy EHAM E6 95 K4
Harries Rd YEAD UB4 83 G3
Harriet Cl HACK E8 74 C7
Harriet Gdns CROY/NA CR0 178 C1
Harriet Ms WELL DA16 136 C1
Harriet St KTBR SW1X 15 M2
Harriet Tubman Cl
BRXS/STRHM SW2 130 B6
Harriet Wk KTBR SW1X 15 M2
Harriet Wy BUSH WD23 22 D6
Harringay Gdns
CEND/HSY/T N8 55 H3
Harringay Rd
SEVS/STOTM N15 55 H4
Harrington Cl CROY/NA CR0 176 E1
WLSDN NW10 69 F2
Harrington Ct NKENS W10 * 88 D2
Harrington Gdns SKENS SW7 14 D6
Harrington Hl CLPT E5 56 D7
Harrington Rd SKENS SW7 15 G5
SNWD SE25 165 H3
WAN E11 58 C7
Harrington Sq CAMTN NW1 4 E5
Harrington St CAMTN NW1 4 E6
Harrington Wy
WOOL/PLUM SE18 114 C2
Harriott Cl GNWCH SE10 113 J3
Harris Cl HSLW TW3 103 F7
Harrison Cl NTHWD HA6 32 A5
TRDG/WHET N20 27 J7
Harrison Dr BMLY BR1 169 G3
Harrison Rd DAGE RM10 80 D5
WLSDN NW10 69 F7
Harrison's Ri CROY/NA CR0 177 H2
Harrison St STPAN WC1H 5 K8
Harris Rd DAGW RM9 80 B4
Harris St CMBW SE5 110 E6
WALTH E17 57 H6
Harris Wy SUN TW16 140 C7
Harrods Gn EDGW HA8 36 C4
Harrogate Rd OXHEY WD19 33 G2
Harrold Rd BCTR RM8 79 H4
Harrow Av EN EN1 30 B5
Harroway Rd BTSEA SW11 128 C1
Harrowby St MBLAR W1H 9 K4
Harrow Cl CHSGTN KT9 171 K6
Harrowdene Cl ALP/SUD HA0 67 K3
Harrowdene Gdns
TEDD TW11 143 G6
Harrowdene Rd ALP/SUD HA0 67 K3
Harrow Dr ED N9 30 B7
Harrowes Meade EDGW HA8 36 C2
Harrow Fields Gdns HRW HA1 66 E2
Harrowgate Rd HOM E9 75 G5
Harrow Gn WAN E11 76 C2
Harrow La POP/IOD E14 94 A6
Harrow Manor Wy ABYW SE2 97 J7
Harrow Pk HRW HA1 66 E1
Harrow Pl WCHPL E1 13 K4
Harrow Rd ALP/SUD HA0 67 G3
CAR SM5 175 J5
EBED/NFELT TW14 120 D7
EHAM E6 77 J6
IL IG1 78 C3
MV/WKIL W9 8 A1
WAN E11 76 D2
WBLY HA9 68 C4
WLSDN NW10 87 K2
Harrow Road F/O
BAY/PAD W2 9 H3
Harrow St CAMTN NW1 * 9 K2
Harrow Vw HGDN/ICK UB10 82 A2
HRW HA1 48 D3
HYS/HAR UB3 82 E6
RYLN/HDSTN HA2 48 D2
Harrow View Rd EA W5 85 H3
Harrow Wy OXHEY WD19 33 J2
Harrow Weald Pk
KTN/HRWW/WS HA3 34 D5
Harry Cl THHTH CR7 164 D3
Hartcliff Ct HNWL W7 * 104 A1
Harte Rd HSLW TW3 122 E1
Hartfield Av BORE WD6 24 C3
NTHLT UB5 83 F1
Hartfield Cl BORE WD6 24 C4
Hartfield Crs WIM/MER SW19 146 D6
WWKM BR4 180 E2
Hartfield Gv PGE/AN SE20 150 D7
Hartfield Rd CHSGTN KT9 171 K4
WIM/MER SW19 146 D5
WWKM BR4 180 E3
Hartfield Ter BOW E3 93 J1
Hartford Av
KTN/HRWW/WS HA3 49 G2
Hartforde Rd BORE WD6 24 C1
Hartford Rd BXLY DA5 137 H5
HOR/WEW KT19 172 C5
Hart Gv EA W5 86 C7
STHL UB1 84 A5
Hartham Cl HOLWY N7 72 E4
ISLW TW7 104 B7
Hartham Rd HOLWY N7 72 E4
ISLW TW7 104 A7
TOTM N17 56 B1
Harting Rd ELTH/MOT SE9 153 J3
Hartington Cl HRW HA1 66 E3
Hartington Rd CAN/RD E16 95 F5
CHSWK W4 105 J6
NWDGN UB2 * 102 D2
TWK TW1 124 C6
VX/NE SW8 109 K7
WALTH E17 57 G5
WEA W13 85 H6
Hartismere Rd FUL/PGN SW6 107 J6
Hartlake Rd HOM E9 75 F5
Hartland Cl EDGW HA8 36 C1
WCHMH N21 29 J5
Hartland Dr EDGW HA8 36 C1
RSLP HA4 65 F2
Hartland Rd CAMTN NW1 4 C1
FBAR/BDGN N11 39 K4
HCH RM12 81 J1
HPTN TW12 142 B3
ISLW TW7 124 B2
KIL/WHAMP NW6 88 D1
MRDN SM4 161 K6
SRTFD E15 76 D6
Hartland Road Arches
CAMTN NW1 * 4 B1
Hartlands Cl BXLY DA5 137 G5
The Hartlands HEST TW5 102 A5
Hartland Wy CROY/NA CR0 179 G1
MRDN SM4 161 J6
Hartley Av EHAM E6 77 J7
MLHL NW7 37 H4
Hartley Cl BMLY BR1 168 E1
MLHL NW7 37 H4
Hartley Rd CROY/NA CR0 164 D6
WAN E11 58 D7
WELL DA16 116 D7
Hartley St BETH E2 92 E2
Hartmann Rd CAN/RD E16 95 H7
Hartnoll St HOLWY N7 73 F4
Harton Cl BMLY BR1 153 H7
Harton Rd ED N9 42 D1
Harton St DEPT SE8 112 D7
Hartsbourne Av BUSH WD23 34 C1
Hartsbourne Cl BUSH WD23 34 D1
Hartsbourne Rd BUSH WD23 34 D1
Harts Cl BUSH WD23 22 A1
Hartscroft CROY/NA CR0 179 G7
Harts Gv WFD IG8 44 E4
Hartshorn Gdns EHAM E6 96 A3
Harts La BARK IG11 78 B6
Hart's La NWCR SE14 112 B6
Hartslock Dr ABYW SE2 116 E1
Hartsmead Rd ELTH/MOT SE9 153 K1
Hartspring La BUSH WD23 22 A1
Hart Sq MRDN SM4 * 162 A4
Hart St MON EC3R 13 K6
Hartsway PEND EN3 30 D3
Hartswood Cl BUSH WD23 22 A1
Hartswood Gdns SHB W12 * 106 C2
Hartswood Gn BUSH WD23 34 D1
Hartswood Rd SHB W12 106 C1
Hartsworth Cl PLSTW E13 94 D1
Hartville Rd
WOOL/PLUM SE18 115 K3
Hartwell Cl BRXS/STRHM SW2 130 A7
Hartwell Dr CHING E4 44 A5
Hartwell St HACK E8 74 B5
Harvard Hl CHSWK W4 105 J4
Harvard Rd CHSWK W4 105 J4
ISLW TW7 103 K7
LEW SE13 133 F4
Harvel Crs ABYW SE2 116 E4
Harvest Bank Rd WWKM BR4 180 E2
Harvesters Cl ISLW TW7 123 J4
Harvest La THDIT KT7 158 B5
Harvest Rd BUSH WD23 22 D1
FELT TW13 140 E3
Harvey Dr HPTN TW12 142 B7
Harvey Gdns CHARL SE7 114 B4
Harvey Rd CEND/HSY/T N8 55 F4
CMBW SE5 110 E7
HSLWW TW4 122 E6
IL IG1 78 B4
NTHLT UB5 65 G6
WAN E11 58 C7
Harvey's La ROMW/RG RM7 81 F1
Harvey St IS N1 7 H4
Harvill Rd SCUP DA14 155 K4
Harvington Wk HACK E8 * 74 C6
Harvist Rd KIL/WHAMP NW6 88 C1
Harwell Cl RSLP HA4 46 B7
Harwood Av BMLY BR1 168 A1
MTCM CR4 162 D2
Harwood Cl ALP/SUD HA0 67 K3
NFNCH/WDSPK N12 39 J5
Harwood Ms FUL/PGN SW6 * 108 A6
Harwood Rd FUL/PGN SW6 107 K6
Harwoods Rd WATW WD18 20 E3
Harwood Ter FUL/PGN SW6 108 A7
Hascombe Ter CMBW SE5 * 130 E1
Haselbury Rd UED N18 42 A3
Haseley End FSTH SE23 * 131 K6
Haselrigge Rd CLAP SW4 129 J3
Haseltine Rd SYD SE26 151 H3
Haselwood Dr ENC/FH EN2 29 H3
Haskard Rd DAGW RM9 79 K3
Hasker St CHEL SW3 15 K5
Haslam Av CHEAM SM3 161 H7
Haslam Cl HGDN/ICK UB10 64 A1
IS N1 6 B1
Haslam St PECK SE15 111 G7
Haslemere Av EBAR EN4 27 K7
HDN NW4 52 B5
HEST TW5 122 B1
HNWL W7 104 B2
MTCM CR4 162 C1
WAND/EARL SW18 147 F1
Haslemere Cl HPTN TW12 141 K4
WLGTN SM6 176 E4
Haslemere Gdns FNCH N3 52 D2
Haslemere Heathrow Est
HSLWW TW4 * 122 A1
Haslemere Rd
CEND/HSY/T N8 54 E6
GDMY/SEVK IG3 79 F1
THHTH CR7 164 C4
WCHMH N21 41 H1
Hasler Cl THMD SE28 97 H6
Hasluck Gdns BAR EN5 27 G5
Hassard St BETH E2 7 M6
Hassendean Rd
BKHTH/KID SE3 114 A5
Hassett Rd HOM E9 75 F5
Hassocks Cl SYD SE26 150 D2
Hassocks Rd
STRHM/NOR SW16 148 D7
Hassock Wd HAYES BR2 181 H3
Hassop Rd CRICK NW2 70 B3
Hasted Rd CHARL SE7 114 C4
Hastings Av BARK/HLT IG6 60 C3
Hastings Cl ALP/SUD HA0 67 J3
BAR EN5 27 G3
PECK SE15 * 111 H6
Hastings Dr SURB KT6 158 D5
Hastings Pl CROY/NA CR0 165 G7
Hastings Rd CROY/NA CR0 165 G7
FBAR/BDGN N11 40 C4
GPK RM2 63 K4
HAYES BR2 168 D7
TOTM N17 * 55 K2
WEA W13 85 H6
Hastings St STPAN WC1H 5 J8
Hastings Ter
SEVS/STOTM N15 * 55 J4
Hastings Wy BUSH WD23 21 J3
Hastingwood St WOOL/PLUM SE18 115 H2
Hastoe Cl YEAD UB4 83 J3
Hatcham Park Ms NWCR SE14 112 A7
Hatcham Park Rd NWCR SE14 112 A7
Hatcham Rd PECK SE15 111 K5
Hatchard Rd ARCH N19 72 D1
Hatchcroft HDN NW4 51 K2
Hatchers Ms STHWK SE1 19 K2
Hatchett Rd
EBED/NFELT TW14 121 F7
Hatch Gv CHDH RM6 62 A3
Hatch La CHING E4 44 B3
WDR/YW UB7 100 A6
Hatch Pl KUTN/CMB KT2 144 B4
Hatch Rd STRHM/NOR SW16 163 K1
Hatchwoods WFD IG8 44 D3
Hatcliffe Cl BKHTH/KID SE3 133 J2
Hatcliffe St GNWCH SE10 113 J4
Hatfield Cl BARK/HLT IG6 60 B2
BELMT SM2 174 E7
MTCM CR4 * 162 C3
Hatfield Rd CHSWK W4 106 A1
HNWL W7 85 G7
SRTFD E15 76 C4
Hatfields STHWK SE1 12 B8
Hathaway Cl HAYES BR2 168 E7
RSLP HA4 64 D3
STAN HA7 35 G4
Hathaway Crs MNPK E12 77 K5
Hathaway Gdns CHDH RM6 61 K4
WEA W13 85 F4
Hathaway Rd CROY/NA CR0 164 C6
Hatherleigh Cl CHSGTN KT9 171 K4
MRDN SM4 161 K3
Hatherleigh Rd RSLP HA4 64 E1
Hatherley Crs BFN/LL DA15 155 G1
Hatherley Gdns
CEND/HSY/T N8 54 E5
EHAM E6 95 H2
Hatherley Gv BAY/PAD W2 8 C4
Hatherley Ms WALTH E17 57 J3
Hatherley Rd RCH/KEW TW9 105 G7
SCUP DA14 155 G2
WALTH E17 57 H3
Hatherley St WEST SW1P 16 F6
Hathern Gdns ELTH/MOT SE9 154 A3
Hatherop Rd HPTN TW12 141 K6
Hathorne Cl PECK SE15 131 J1
Hathorne Ter ARCH N19 * 54 D7
Hathway St PECK SE15 131 K1
Hatley Av BARK/HLT IG6 60 C3
Hatley Cl FBAR/BDGN N11 39 K4
Hatley Rd FSBYPK N4 73 F1
Hat & Mitre Ct FARR EC1M 12 D1
Hatteraick St
BERM/RHTH SE16 111 K1
Hattersfield Cl BELV DA17 117 G3
Hatters La WATW WD18 20 B5
Hatton Cl WOOL/PLUM SE18 115 J6
Hatton Cross Est
HTHAIR TW6 * 121 J3
Hatton Gdn HCIRC EC1N 12 B2
Hatton Gdns MTCM CR4 162 E4
Hatton Gn
EBED/NFELT TW14 121 K3
Hatton Gv WDR/YW UB7 * 100 A1
Hatton Pl HCIRC EC1N 12 B1
Hatton Rd CROY/NA CR0 164 B7
EBED/NFELT TW14 121 F6
HTHAIR TW6 121 J3
Hatton Rw STJWD NW8 * 9 H1
Hatton St STJWD NW8 9 H1
Hatton Wall HCIRC EC1N 12 A2
Haunch of Venison Yd
OXSTW W1C * 10 C5
Havana Cl ROM RM1 63 G4
Havana Rd WIM/MER SW19 146 E1
Havannah St POP/IOD E14 112 D1
Havant Rd WALTH E17 58 A2
Havelock Cl SHB W12 * 87 K6
Havelock Pl HRW HA1 48 E5
Havelock Rd BELV DA17 * 117 G3
CROY/NA CR0 178 B1
HAYES BR2 168 B3
KTN/HRWW/WS HA3 48 E2
NWDGN UB2 102 D2
TOTM N17 56 C1
WIM/MER SW19 147 G4
Havelock St IS N1 5 K3
Havelock Ter VX/NE SW8 109 G6
Havelock Wk FSTH SE23 131 K7
Haven Cl ELTH/MOT SE9 153 K2
ESH/CLAY KT10 170 E1
SCUP DA14 155 J5
WIM/MER SW19 146 B2
YEAD UB4 82 C4
Haven Ct BRYLDS KT5 * 159 G5
Haven Gn EA W5 85 K5
Havenhurst Ri ENC/FH EN2 29 G1
Haven La EA W5 86 A5
Havens Ms BOW E3 93 H4
Haven St CAMTN NW1 * 4 C2
Havenswood Ct
KUTN/CMB KT2 144 D5
The Haven RCH/KEW TW9 125 H2
SUN TW16 140 E6
Havenwood WBLY HA9 68 D2
Haverfield Est BTFD TW8 105 F5
Haverfield Gdns
RCH/KEW TW9 105 H6
Haverfield Rd BOW E3 93 G2
Haverford Wy EDGW HA8 36 B7
Havergal Vls
SEVS/STOTM N15 * 55 H3
Haverhill Rd BAL SW12 129 H7
Havering Dr ROM RM1 63 G3
Havering Gdns CHDH RM6 61 J4
Havering Rd ROM RM1 63 F1
Havering St WCHPL E1 93 F5
Havering Wy BARK IG11 97 H2
Haversham Cl TWK TW1 124 E6
Haversham Pl HGT N6 71 K1
Haverstock Hl HAMP NW3 71 J5
Haverstock Pl FSBYE EC1V 6 B6
Haverstock Rd KTTN NW5 72 A4
Haverstock St IS N1 6 D6
Havil St CMBW SE5 111 F7
Havisham Pl NRWD SE19 149 H5
Hawarden Gv HNHL SE24 130 D6
Hawarden Hl CRICK NW2 69 J2
Hawarden Rd WALTH E17 57 F3
Hawbridge Rd WAN E11 58 B7
Hawes Cl NTHWD HA6 32 D6
Hawes La WWKM BR4 167 F7
Hawes Rd BMLY BR1 153 F7
UED N18 42 D5
Hawes St IS N1 6 D2
Hawgood St BOW E3 93 J4
Hawkdene CHING E4 31 K5
Hawke Park Rd WDGN N22 55 H2
Hawke Pl BERM/RHTH SE16 * 112 A1
Hawke Rd NRWD SE19 149 K5
Hawker Pl WALTH E17 58 A1
Hawker Rd CROY/NA CR0 177 F5
Hawkesbury Rd
PUT/ROE SW15 126 E4
Hawkesfield Rd FSTH SE23 151 G1
Hawkesley Cl TWK TW1 143 G3
Hawkes Rd EBED/NFELT TW14 121 K6
MTCM CR4 147 J7
Hawkesworth Cl NTHWD HA6 32 C6
Hawkhurst Rd
STRHM/NOR SW16 148 D6
Hawkhurst Wy NWMAL KT3 160 A4
WWKM BR4 179 K1
Hawkins Cl BORE WD6 24 E1
EDGW HA8 37 F4
HRW HA1 48 D6
Hawkins Rd TEDD TW11 143 H5
WLSDN NW10 69 G6
Hawkins Ter CHARL SE7 114 D4
Hawkins Wy CAT SE6 151 J4
Hawkley Gdns WNWD SE27 149 H1
Hawkridge Cl CHDH RM6 61 J6
Hawksbrook La BECK BR3 166 E5
Hawkshaw Cl
BRXS/STRHM SW2 129 K6
Hawkshead Cl BMLY BR1 152 C6
Hawkshead Rd CHSWK W4 106 B2
WLSDN NW10 * 69 H6
Hawkshill Cl ESH/CLAY KT10 170 A5
Hawkshill Pl ESH/CLAY KT10 * 170 A5
Hawkslade Rd PECK SE15 132 A4
Hawksley Rd
STNW/STAM N16 73 K2
Hawks Ms GNWCH SE10 * 113 F6
Hawksmoor Cl EHAM E6 95 J5
WOOL/PLUM SE18 115 K4
Hawksmoor Ms WCHPL E1 92 D6
Hawksmoor St HMSMTH W6 107 G5
Hawksmouth CHING E4 31 K6
Hawks Rd KUT/HW KT1 159 G1
Hawkstone Est
BERM/RHTH SE16 111 K3
Hawkstone Rd
BERM/RHTH SE16 111 K3
Hawkwell Wk IS N1 * 6 F3
Hawkwood Crs CHING E4 31 K5
Hawkwood La CHST BR7 154 C7
Hawkwood Mt CLPT E5 56 D7
Hawlands Dr PIN HA5 47 J6
Hawley Cl HPTN TW12 141 K5
Hawley Crs CAMTN NW1 4 D2
Hawley Ms CAMTN NW1 4 C1
Hawley Rd CAMTN NW1 4 C1
UED N18 43 F4
Hawley St CAMTN NW1 4 C2
Hawstead Rd CAT SE6 132 E5
Hawthorn Av PLMGR N13 40 E4
RAIN RM13 99 K3
THHTH CR7 149 H7
Hawthorn Centre HRW HA1 49 F3
Hawthorn Cl HEST TW5 102 A6
HPTN TW12 142 A4
STMC/STPC BR5 169 J5
Hawthorn Ct ASHF TW15 140 A6
Hawthorn Crs TOOT SW17 148 A4
Hawthornden Cl
NFNCH/WDSPK N12 39 J5
Hawthorndene Cl HAYES BR2 180 D1
Hawthorn Dr
RYLN/HDSTN HA2 48 A5
WWKM BR4 180 C3
Hawthorne Av BOW E3 75 H7
CAR SM5 176 A6
KTN/HRWW/WS HA3 49 G5
MTCM CR4 162 C1
RSLP HA4 47 F5
Hawthorne Cl BMLY BR1 168 E2
IS N1 74 A5
Hawthorne Ct
STWL/WRAY TW19 * 120 A6
Hawthorne Crs WDR/YW UB7 100 C1
Hawthorne Gv
CDALE/KGS NW9 50 E6
Hawthorne Rd BMLY BR1 168 E2
UED N18 42 B5
WALTH E17 57 J2
Hawthorne Wy ED N9 42 B1
STWL/WRAY TW19 120 A6
Hawthorn Farm Av
NTHLT UB5 65 J7
Hawthorn Gdns EA W5 104 E2
Hawthorn Gv PGE/AN SE20 150 D7
Hawthorn Hatch BTFD TW8 104 C6
Hawthorn Ms MLHL NW7 38 C7
Hawthorn Pl ERITH DA8 117 K4
HYS/HAR UB3 * 82 D6
Hawthorn Rd BTFD TW8 104 C6
CEND/HSY/T N8 54 D2
FELT TW13 121 K7
SUT SM1 175 H4
WFD IG8 45 G3
WLGTN SM6 176 B6
WLSDN NW10 69 J6
Hawthorns WFD IG8 44 E2
The Hawthorns EW KT17 173 H5
Hawthorn Ter BFN/LL DA15 136 A5
Hawthorn Wk NKENS W10 88 C3
Hawtrey Av NTHLT UB5 83 H1
Hawtrey Dr RSLP HA4 46 E6
Hawtrey Rd HAMP NW3 3 J2
Haxted Rd BMLY BR1 153 F7
Hayburn Wy HCH RM12 63 H7
Hay Cl BORE WD6 24 E1
SRTFD E15 76 C6
Haycroft Gdns WLSDN NW10 69 J7
Haycroft Rd
BRXS/STRHM SW2 129 K4
SURB KT6 171 K1
Hay Currie St POP/IOD E14 93 K5
Hayday Rd CAN/RD E16 94 E3
Hayden Dell BUSH WD23 21 K5
Hayden's Pl NTGHL W11 88 D5
Hayden Wy CRW RM5 62 E1
Haydock Av NTHLT UB5 66 A5
Haydock Gn NTHLT UB5 66 A5
Haydon Cl CDALE/KGS NW9 50 E3
EN EN1 30 A5
Haydon Dell Farm
BUSH WD23 * 21 K6
Haydon Dr PIN HA5 46 E3
Haydon Park Rd
WIM/MER SW19 146 E4
Haydon Rd BCTR RM8 79 J1
OXHEY WD19 21 J5
Haydon's Rd WIM/MER SW19 147 F4
Haydon St TWRH EC3N 13 L6
Haydon Wk WCHPL E1 13 L5
Haydon Wy WAND/EARL SW18 128 B3
Hayes Cha WWKM BR4 167 G5
Hayes Cl CHEAM SM3 174 B3
GLDGN NW11 52 D4
Hayes Dr RAIN RM13 81 K6
Hayes End Dr YEAD UB4 82 B4
Hayes End Rd YEAD UB4 82 B3
Hayesford Park Dr
HAYES BR2 167 J4
Hayes Gv EDUL SE22 131 G2
Hayes Hl HAYES BR2 167 H7
Hayes Hill Rd HAYES BR2 167 J7
Hayes La BECK BR3 167 G2
HAYES BR2 168 A3
Hayes Mead Rd HAYES BR2 167 H7
Hayes Pl CAMTN NW1 9 K1
Hayes Rd NWDGN UB2 102 A3
Hayes St HAYES BR2 168 A7
Hayes Wy BECK BR3 167 F3
Hayes Wood Av HAYES BR2 168 A7
Hayfield Cl BUSH WD23 22 B3
Hayfield Pas WCHPL E1 92 E3
Haygarth Pl WIM/MER SW19 146 B4
Haygreen Cl KUTN/CMB KT2 144 D5
Hay Hl MYFR/PICC W1J 10 D7
Hayland Cl CDALE/KGS NW9 51 F3
Hay La CDALE/KGS NW9 51 F3
Hayles St LBTH SE11 18 C5
Haylett Gdns KUT/HW KT1 * 158 E3
Hayling Av FELT TW13 140 E2
Hayling Cl STNW/STAM N16 74 A4
Hayling Rd OXHEY WD19 32 D2
Hayman Crs YEAD UB4 82 B1
Haymarket STJS SW1Y 11 G7
Haymeads Dr ESH/CLAY KT10 170 C5
Haymer Gdns WPK KT4 173 J2
Haymerle Rd PECK SE15 111 H5
Haymill Cl GFD/PVL UB6 85 F2
Hayne Rd BECK BR3 151 H7
Haynes Cl BKHTH/KID SE3 133 H2
FBAR/BDGN N11 40 A2
TOTM N17 42 D6
Haynes Dr ED N9 42 D2
Haynes La NRWD SE19 150 A5
Haynes Rd ALP/SUD HA0 68 A6
Hayne St STBT EC1A 12 D2
Haynt Wk RYNPK SW20 161 H2
Hay's La STHWK SE1 13 J8
Haysleigh Gdns PGE/AN SE20 165 H1
Hay's Ms MYFR/PICC W1J 10 C7
Haysoms Cl ROM RM1 63 G3
Haystall Cl YEAD UB4 82 C1
Hay St BETH E2 74 C7
Hayter Rd BRXS/STRHM SW2 129 K4
Hayton Cl HACK E8 74 B5
Hayward Cl WIM/MER SW19 147 F6
Hayward Gdns
PUT/ROE SW15 127 F5
Hayward Rd THDIT KT7 158 A7
TRDG/WHET N20 39 G1
Haywards Cl CHDH RM6 61 J4
Hayward's Pl CLKNW EC1R * 12 C1
Haywood Cl PIN HA5 47 H1
Haywood Rd HAYES BR2 168 C3
Hazel Av WDR/YW UB7 100 D2
Hazelbank BRYLDS KT5 159 K7
Hazelbank Rd CAT SE6 152 B1
Hazelbourne Rd BAL SW12 129 G5
Hazelbury Cl WIM/MER SW19 161 K1
Hazelbury Gn ED N9 42 A2
Hazelbury La ED N9 42 A2
Hazel Cl BTFD TW8 * 104 C6
CDALE/KGS NW9 51 H1
CROY/NA CR0 166 A6
HCH RM12 81 K2
MTCM CR4 163 J3
PLMGR N13 41 K2
WHTN TW2 123 H6
Hazelcroft PIN HA5 34 A5
Hazeldean Rd WLSDN NW10 69 F6
Hazeldene Dr PIN HA5 47 G2
Hazeldene Gdns
HGDN/ICK UB10 64 A7
Hazeldene Rd GDMY/SEVK IG3 79 H1
WELL DA16 136 D1
Hazeldon Rd BROCKY SE4 132 B4
Hazel Dr ERITH DA8 118 D7
Hazeleigh Gdns WFD IG8 45 J4
Hazel Gdns EDGW HA8 36 D3
Hazelgreen Cl WCHMH N21 29 H7
Hazel Gv ALP/SUD HA0 68 A7
CHDH RM6 62 A2
EN EN1 * 30 C5
FELT TW13 121 K7
SYD SE26 151 F3
Hazelhurst BECK BR3 152 B7
Hazelhurst Rd TOOT SW17 147 G3
Hazellville Rd ARCH N19 54 D6
Hazel Md BAR EN5 25 K4
Hazelmere Cl
EBED/NFELT TW14 121 G5
NTHLT UB5 83 K1
Hazelmere Dr NTHLT UB5 83 K1
Hazelmere Gdns EMPK RM11 63 K4
Hazelmere Rd
KIL/WHAMP NW6 2 A4
NTHLT UB5 83 K1
STMC/STPC BR5 169 H3
Hazelmere Wk NTHLT UB5 83 K1

Hazel Rd SRTFD E15 * 76 C4
WLSDN NW10 87 K2
Hazel Rw
NFNCH/WDSPK N12 * 39 H4
Hazeltree La NTHLT UB5 83 J2
Hazel Wk HAYES BR2 169 F5
Hazel Wy CHING E4 43 H5
STHWK SE1 19 L5
Hazelwood Av MRDN SM4 162 A3
Hazelwood Cl CLPT E5 75 G2
EA W5 105 F1
RYLN/HDSTN HA2 48 B3
Hazelwood Ct SURB KT6 159 F5
Hazelwood Dr PIN HA5 47 F1
Hazelwood La PLMGR N13 41 G3
Hazelwood Rd EN EN1 30 B5
RKW/CH/CXG WD3 20 A5
WALTH E17 57 G4
Hazlebury Rd FUL/PGN SW6 128 A1
Hazledean Rd CROY/NA CR0 177 K1
Hazledene Rd CHSWK W4 105 K5
Hazlemere Gdns WPK KT4 160 D7
Hazlewell Rd PUT/ROE SW15 127 F4
Hazlewood Crs NKENS W10 88 C3
Hazlitt Cl FELT TW13 141 J3
Hazlitt Ms WKENS W14 * 107 H2
Hazlitt Rd WKENS W14 107 H2
Heacham Av HGDN/ICK UB10 64 A2
Headcorn Rd THHTH CR7 164 A3
TOTM N17 42 B6
Headfort Pl KTBR SW1X 16 B2
Headington Rd
WAND/EARL SW18 128 B7
Headlam Rd CLAP SW4 129 J5
Headlam St WCHPL E1 92 D3
Headley Ap GNTH/NBYPK IG2 60 A4
Headley Av WLGTN SM6 177 F4
Headley Cl CHSGTN KT9 172 C5
Headley Dr CROY/NA CR0 180 A6
GNTH/NBYPK IG2 60 B5
Heads Ms NTGHL W11 8 A5
Headstone Dr HRW HA1 48 D3
Headstone Gdns
RYLN/HDSTN HA2 48 C3
Headstone La
RYLN/HDSTN HA2 48 B1
Headstone Pde HRW HA1 * 48 D3
Headstone Rd HRW HA1 48 E4
Head St WCHPL E1 93 F5
Headway Cl
RCHPK/HAM TW10 143 J3
The Headway EW KT17 173 H7
Heald St NWCR SE14 112 C7
Healey Rd WATW WD18 20 D5
Healey St CAMTN NW1 * 72 B5
Hearne Rd CHSWK W4 105 H4
Hearn Ri NTHLT UB5 65 H7
Hearn Rd ROM RM1 63 H5
Hearn's Blds WALW SE17 19 H6
Hearnshaw St POP/IOD E14 93 G5
Hearn St SDTCH EC2A 13 K1
Hearnville Rd BAL SW12 129 F7
Heatham Pk WHTN TW2 124 A6
Heath Av BXLYHN DA7 116 E5
Heathbourne Rd BUSH WD23 34 E1
Heath Brow HAMP NW3 71 G2
Heath Cl EA W5 86 B3
GLDGN NW11 53 F6
GPK RM2 63 J2
HYS/HAR UB3 101 G6
SAND/SEL CR2 177 H5
Heathcote Av CLAY IG5 59 K1
Heathcote Gv CHING E4 44 A2
Heathcote Rd TWK TW1 124 C5
Heathcote St BMSBY WC1N 5 L9
Heathcroft EA W5 86 B3
Heathcroft Av SUN TW16 140 D6
Heathcroft Gdns WALTH E17 44 B7
Heathdale Av HSLWW TW4 122 D2
Heathdene Dr BELV DA17 117 J3
Heathdene Rd
STRHM/NOR SW16 149 F6
WLGTN SM6 176 B6
Heath Dr BELMT SM2 175 G7
HAMP NW3 71 F3
RYNPK SW20 161 F3
Heathedge SYD SE26 * 150 D1
Heather Av ROM RM1 63 F1
Heatherbank CHST BR7 169 F1
ELTH/MOT SE9 134 E1
Heather Cl EHAM E6 96 A5
HPTN TW12 141 K7
ISLW TW7 123 J4
LEW SE13 133 G5
VX/NE SW8 129 G2
Heatherdale Cl
KUTN/CMB KT2 144 C5
Heatherdene Cl MTCM CR4 162 C3
NFNCH/WDSPK N12 39 G7
Heather Dr ENC/FH EN2 29 H1
ROM RM1 63 F1
Heatherfold Wy PIN HA5 46 D2
Heather Gdns BELMT SM2 174 E5
GLDGN NW11 52 C5
ROM RM1 63 F1
Heather Gln ROM RM1 63 F1
Heatherlands SUN TW16 140 E5
Heatherlea Gv WPK KT4 161 F7
Heatherley Dr CLAY IG5 59 K2
Heather Park Dr
ALP/SUD HA0 68 C6
Heather Park Pde
ALP/SUD HA0 * 68 B6
Heather Pl ESH/CLAY KT10 170 B3
Heather Ri BUSH WD23 21 K1
Heather Rd CHING E4 43 H5
CRICK NW2 69 H1
Heatherset Cl ESH/CLAY KT10 170 C4
Heatherset Gdns
STRHM/NOR SW16 149 F6
Heatherside Rd
HOR/WEW KT19 173 F6
SCUP DA14 155 J2
The Heathers
STWL/WRAY TW19 120 C6
Heather Wk EDGW HA8 36 D4
NKENS W10 88 C3
Heather Wy SAND/SEL CR2 179 F7
STAN HA7 35 F5
Heatherwood Cl MNPK E12 77 F1
Heatherwood Dr YEAD UB4 82 B1
Heathfield CHING E4 44 A2
CHST BR7 154 C5
HRW HA1 * 49 F6
Heathfield Av
WAND/EARL SW18 128 C6
Heathfield Cl CAN/RD E16 95 H4
HAYES BR2 181 G4
OXHEY WD19 21 G6
Heathfield Dr MTCM CR4 147 J6
Heathfield Gdns CHSWK W4 105 K4
CROY/NA CR0 * 177 J3
GLDGN NW11 52 B5
WAND/EARL SW18 128 C5
Heathfield La CHST BR7 154 C5
Heathfield North WHTN TW2 123 K6
Heathfield Pk CRICK NW2 70 A5
Heathfield Park Dr
CHDH RM6 61 H4
Heathfield Ri RSLP HA4 46 A6
Heathfield Rd ACT W3 105 J1
BMLY BR1 152 D6
BUSH WD23 21 J3
HAYES BR2 181 G4
SAND/SEL CR2 177 K4
WAND/EARL SW18 128 B5
Heathfield South WHTN TW2 124 A6
Heathfield Sq
WAND/EARL SW18 128 C6
Heathfield Ter CHSWK W4 105 K4
WOOL/PLUM SE18 115 K5
Heathfield V SAND/SEL CR2 179 F7
Heath Gdns DART DA1 * 139 F7
TWK TW1 124 A7
Heathgate GLDGN NW11 53 F5
Heathgate Pl HAMP NW3 71 K3
Heath Gv PGE/AN SE20 150 E6
SUN TW16 140 D6
Heath Hurst Rd HAMP NW3 71 J3
Heathhurst Rd SAND/SEL CR2 178 A7
Heathland Rd
STNW/STAM N16 56 A7
Heathlands Cl TWK TW1 143 F1
Heathlands Ct HSLWW TW4 122 D4
Heathlands Wy HSLWW TW4 122 D4
Heath La BKHTH/KID SE3 133 G1
Heathlee Rd BKHTH/KID SE3 133 J3
Heathley End CHST BR7 154 C5
Heath Ldg BUSH WD23 * 22 D7
Heathman's Rd FUL/PGN SW6 107 J7
Heath Md WIM/MER SW19 146 B2
Heath Park Dr BMLY BR1 168 D2
Heath Park Rd GPK RM2 63 J4
Heath Ri PUT/ROE SW15 127 G5
Heath Rd BXLY DA5 137 K7
CHDH RM6 61 K6
HGDN/ICK UB10 82 A3
HRW HA1 48 C6
HSLW TW3 123 H3
OXHEY WD19 21 H6
THHTH CR7 164 D2
TWK TW1 124 A7
VX/NE SW8 129 G1
Heath's Cl EN EN1 29 K1
Heathside ESH/CLAY KT10 170 E2
HAMP NW3 71 H3
HSLWW TW4 122 E6
Heath Side STMC/STPC BR5 169 H7
Heathside Cl ESH/CLAY KT10 170 E2
GNTH/NBYPK IG2 60 D4
NTHWD HA6 32 B4
Heathside Rd NTHWD HA6 32 B3
Heathstan Rd SHB W12 87 J5
Heath St HAMP NW3 71 G3
The Heath HNWL W7 * 103 K1
Heath Vw EFNCH N2 53 G3
Heath View Cl EFNCH N2 53 G3
Heath View Dr ABYW SE2 116 E5
Heathview Gdns
PUT/ROE SW15 127 F6
Heathview Rd THHTH CR7 164 B3
Heath Vls WAND/EARL SW18 * 128 B7
WOOL/PLUM SE18 116 A4
Heathville Rd ARCH N19 54 E6
Heathwall St BTSEA SW11 128 E2
Heathway CROY/NA CR0 179 H2
DAGW RM9 80 B3
NWDGN UB2 * 102 C3
WFD IG8 45 G3
Heathwood Gdns CHARL SE7 114 D3
Heaton Cl CHING E4 44 A2
Heaton Rd MTCM CR4 148 A6
PECK SE15 131 J2
Heaven Tree Cl IS N1 73 J4
Heaver Rd BTSEA SW11 * 128 C2
Heavitree Cl
WOOL/PLUM SE18 115 J4
Heavitree Rd
WOOL/PLUM SE18 115 J4
Hebden Ter TOTM N17 42 A5
Hebdon Rd TOOT SW17 147 J2
Heber Rd CRICK NW2 70 B4
EDUL SE22 131 G5
Hebron Rd HMSMTH W6 106 E2
Hecham Cl WALTH E17 57 G1
Heckfield Pl FUL/PGN SW6 107 K6
Heckford Cl WATW WD18 20 A5
Heckford St WAP E1W 93 F6
Hector Cl ED N9 42 C1
Hector St WOOL/PLUM SE18 * 115 K3
Heddington Gv HOLWY N7 73 F4
Heddon Cl ISLW TW7 124 B3
Heddon Court Av EBAR EN4 27 K4
Heddon Court Pde
EBAR EN4 * 28 A4
Heddon Rd EBAR EN4 27 K4
Heddon St CONDST W1S 10 E7
Hedge La PLMGR N13 41 H2
Hedgeley REDBR IG4 59 K3
Hedgemans Rd DAGW RM9 79 K6
Hedgemans Wy DAGW RM9 80 A5
Hedgerley Gdns GFD/PVL UB6 84 C1
Hedgerow La BAR EN5 25 K4
Hedger's Gv HOM E9 * 75 G5
Hedger St LBTH SE11 18 C5
Hedgewood Gdns CLAY IG5 60 A3
Hedgley St LEE/GVPK SE12 133 J4
Hedingham Cl IS N1 6 E2
Hedingham Rd BCTR RM8 79 H4
Hedley Rd WHTN TW2 123 F6
Hedley Rw HBRY N5 73 K4
Heenan Cl BARK IG11 78 C5
Heene Rd ENC/FH EN2 29 K1
Heidegger Crs BARN SW13 106 E6
Heigham Rd EHAM E6 77 J6
Heighton Gdns CROY/NA CR0 177 H4
Heights Cl RYNPK SW20 145 K6
The Heights BECK BR3 * 152 A6
CHARL SE7 114 B4
NTHLT UB5 66 A4
Heiron St WALW SE17 110 C5
Helby Rd CLAP SW4 129 J5
Helder Gv LEE/GVPK SE12 133 J6
Helder St SAND/SEL CR2 177 K5
Heldmann Cl HSLW TW3 123 J3
Helena Pl HACK E8 74 D7
Helena Rd EA W5 85 K4
PLSTW E13 94 D1
WALTH E17 57 J4
WLSDN NW10 69 K4
Helena Sq BERM/RHTH SE16 93 G6
Helen Av EBED/NFELT TW14 122 A6
Helen Cl E/WMO/HCT KT8 157 G3
EFNCH N2 53 G2
Helenslea Av GLDGN NW11 52 D7
Helen's Pl BETH E2 92 E2
Helen St WOOL/PLUM SE18 * 115 G3
Helford Cl RSLP HA4 64 C1
Helgiford Gdns SUN TW16 140 C6
Helios Rd WLGTN SM6 163 F7
Helix Gdns BRXS/STRHM SW2 130 A5
Helix Rd BRXS/STRHM SW2 130 A5
Hellings St WAP E1W 92 C7
Helme Cl WIM/MER SW19 146 D4
Helmet Rw FSBYE EC1V 6 F9
Helmore Rd BARK IG11 79 F6
Helmsdale Cl YEAD UB4 * 83 J3
Helmsdale Rd
STRHM/NOR SW16 148 C7
Helmsley Pl HACK E8 74 D6
Helmsley St HACK E8 74 D7
Helperby Rd WLSDN NW10 69 G6
Helsinki Sq BERM/RHTH SE16 112 B2
Helston Cl PIN HA5 33 K6
Helvetia St CAT SE6 151 H1
Hemans St VX/NE SW8 109 J6
Hemery Rd GFD/PVL UB6 66 D4
Hemingford Cl
NFNCH/WDSPK N12 39 H4
Hemingford Rd CHEAM SM3 174 A3
IS N1 5 M3
Heming Rd EDGW HA8 36 D5
Hemington Av
FBAR/BDGN N11 39 K4
Hemlock Cl STRHM/NOR SW16 163 J1
Hemlock Rd SHB W12 87 H6
Hemmen La HYS/HAR UB3 82 D6
Hemming Cl HPTN TW12 142 A7
Hemmings Cl SCUP DA14 155 H1
Hemmingsmead
HOR/WEW KT19 172 E5
Hemming St WCHPL E1 92 C3
Hemmingway Cl KTTN NW5 72 A3
Hempstead Cl BKHH IG9 44 E1
Hempstead Rd WALTH E17 58 B2
WAT WD17 20 E1
Hemp Wk WALW SE17 19 H5
Hemsby Rd CHSGTN KT9 172 B5
Hemstal Rd KIL/WHAMP NW6 2 A1
Hemsted Rd ERITH DA8 118 B7
Hemswell Dr CDALE/KGS NW9 37 G7
Hemsworth St IS N1 7 J5
Henbury Wy OXHEY WD19 33 H2
Henchman St SHB W12 87 H5
Hendale Av HDN NW4 51 J2
Henderson Cl EMPK RM11 81 K1
WLSDN NW10 68 E5
Henderson Dr DART DA1 139 K3
STJWD NW8 3 G9
Henderson Rd CROY/NA CR0 164 E5
ED N9 30 D7
FSTGT E7 77 G5
WAND/EARL SW18 128 D6
YEAD UB4 82 E2
Hendham Rd TOOT SW17 147 J1
Hendon Av FNCH N3 38 C7
Hendon Gv HOR/WEW KT19 172 C7
Hendon Hall Ct HDN NW4 * 52 B2
Hendon La FNCH N3 52 C2
Hendon Park Rw
GLDGN NW11 * 52 D5
Hendon Rd ED N9 42 C1
Hendon Ter ASHF TW15 * 140 B5
Hendon Wy CRICK NW2 52 B6
STWL/WRAY TW19 120 A4
Hendon Wood La MLHL NW7 25 J7
Hendren Cl GFD/PVL UB6 66 D4
Hendre Rd STHWK SE1 19 K6
Hendrick Av BAL SW12 128 E5
Heneage La HDTCH EC3A 13 K5
Heneage St WCHPL E1 13 M2
Henfield Cl ARCH N19 54 C7
BXLY DA5 137 H5
Henfield Rd WIM/MER SW19 146 D7
Hengelo Gdns MTCM CR4 162 C3
Hengist Rd ERITH DA8 117 K6
LEE/GVPK SE12 134 A6
Hengist Wy HAYES BR2 167 G3
Hengrave Rd FSTH SE23 131 K6
Hengrove Ct BXLY DA5 137 F7
Henley Av CHEAM SM3 174 C2
Henley Cl BERM/RHTH SE16 * 111 K1
GFD/PVL UB6 * 84 C1
ISLW TW7 104 A7
Henley Dr KUTN/CMB KT2 145 H6
STHWK SE1 19 M5
Henley Gdns CHDH RM6 62 A4
PIN HA5 47 F2
Henley Rd CAN/RD E16 114 E1
IL IG1 78 C3
UED N18 42 A3
WLSDN NW10 70 A7
Henley St BTSEA SW11 129 F1
Henley Wy FELT TW13 141 H4
Hennel Cl FSTH SE23 150 E2
Hennessy Rd ED N9 42 E1
Henniker Gdns EHAM E6 95 H2
Henniker Ms CHEL SW3 15 G9
Henniker Rd SRTFD E15 76 B4
Henningham Rd TOTM N17 41 K7
Henning St BTSEA SW11 108 D7
Henrietta Cl DEPT SE8 112 D5
Henrietta Ms BMSBY WC1N 5 K9
Henrietta Pl CAVSQ/HST W1G 10 C4
Henrietta St COVGDN WC2E 11 K6
SRTFD E15 76 A4
Henriques St WCHPL E1 92 C5
Henry Addlington Cl
EHAM E6 96 B4
Henry Cooper Wy
ELTH/MOT SE9 153 H2
Henry Darlot Dr MLHL NW7 38 B4
Henry Dickens Ct NTGHL W11 88 B6
Henry Doulton Dr TOOT SW17 148 A3
Henry Jackson Rd
PUT/ROE SW15 127 G2
Henry Macaulay Av
KUTN/CMB KT2 143 K7
Henry Peters Dr TEDD TW11 142 E4
Henry Rd EBAR EN4 27 H4
EHAM E6 95 J1
FSBYPK N4 55 J7
Henry's Av WFD IG8 44 D4
Henryson Rd BROCKY SE4 132 D4
Henry St BMLY BR1 153 F7
Henry Tate Ms
STRHM/NOR SW16 149 G4
Hensby Ms OXHEY WD19 21 J5
Henshall St IS N1 73 K5
Henshawe Rd BCTR RM8 79 K2
Henshaw St WALW SE17 19 G5
Henslowe Rd EDUL SE22 131 H4
Henson Av CRICK NW2 70 A4
Henson Pl NTHLT UB5 65 G7
Henstridge Pl STJWD NW8 3 J5
Henty Cl BTSEA SW11 108 D6
Henty Wk PUT/ROE SW15 126 E4
Henville Rd BMLY BR1 153 F7
Henwick Rd ELTH/MOT SE9 134 C2
Henwood Side WFD IG8 45 K5
Hepburn Gdns HAYES BR2 167 J7
Hepple Cl ISLW TW7 124 C1
Hepscott Rd HOM E9 75 J5
Hepworth Gdns BARK IG11 79 G4
Hepworth Rd
STRHM/NOR SW16 148 E6
Herald Gdns WLGTN SM6 176 B2
Heralds Pl LBTH SE11 18 C5
Herald St BETH E2 92 D3
Herbal Hl CLKNW EC1R 12 B1
Herbert Crs KTBR SW1X 15 M3
Herbert Gdns CHDH RM6 61 K6
CHSWK W4 105 J5
WLSDN NW10 87 K1
Herbert Ms BRXS/STRHM SW2 130 B5
Herbert Pl ISLW TW7 123 J1
WOOL/PLUM SE18 115 G5
Herbert Rd CDALE/KGS NW9 51 J5
FBAR/BDGN N11 40 E6
GDMY/SEVK IG3 78 E1
HAYES BR2 168 C4
KUT/HW KT1 159 G2
MNPK E12 77 J3
SEVS/STOTM N15 56 B4
STHL UB1 83 K7
WALTH E17 57 H6
WIM/MER SW19 146 D6
WOOL/PLUM SE18 115 G6
Herbert St KTTN NW5 72 A5
PLSTW E13 94 E1
Herbrand St BMSBY WC1N 5 J9
Hercules Pl HOLWY N7 72 E2
Hercules Rd STHWK SE1 17 M4
Hercules St HOLWY N7 72 E2
Hereford Av EBAR EN4 27 K7
Hereford Gdns IL IG1 59 J6
PIN HA5 47 J4
WHTN TW2 * 123 H7
Hereford Ms BAY/PAD W2 8 B4
Hereford Pl NWCR SE14 * 112 C6
Hereford Retreat PECK SE15 111 H6
Hereford Rd ACT W3 86 E6
BAY/PAD W2 8 B5
BOW E3 93 H1
EA W5 104 D2
FELT TW13 122 B7
WAN E11 59 F4
Hereford Sq SKENS SW7 14 F6
Hereford St BETH E2 92 C3
Hereford Wy CHSGTN KT9 171 J4
Herent Dr CLAY IG5 59 K2
Heretage Cl BRXN/ST SW9 130 C2
Hereward Gdns PLMGR N13 41 G4
Hereward Rd TOOT SW17 147 J3
Herga Ct WAT WD17 20 E1
Herga Rd KTN/HRWW/WS HA3 49 F3
Heriot Av CHING E4 43 J1
Heriot Rd HDN NW4 52 A4
Heriots Cl STAN HA7 35 G3
Heritage Av CDALE/KGS NW9 51 H1
Heritage Cl SUN TW16 140 E7
Heritage Hl HAYES BR2 181 G4
Heritage Pl
WAND/EARL SW18 * 128 C5
Heritage Vw HRW HA1 67 F2
Herkomer Cl BUSH WD23 22 B5
Herkomer Rd BUSH WD23 22 A4
Herlwyn Av RSLP HA4 64 C2
Herlwyn Gdns TOOT SW17 147 K3
Herm Cl ISLW TW7 103 H6
Hermes Cl MV/WKIL W9 8 A1
Hermes Ct BRXS/STRHM SW2 130 A4
Hermes St IS N1 6 A6
Hermes Wy WLGTN SM6 176 D6
Hermiston Av
CEND/HSY/T N8 54 E4
Hermitage Cl ENC/FH EN2 29 H1
ESH/CLAY KT10 171 G5
RCHPK/HAM TW10 * 124 E4
SWFD E18 58 D3
Hermitage Cots STAN HA7 * 34 E4
Hermitage Gdns CRICK NW2 70 E2
NRWD SE19 149 J6
Hermitage La CRICK NW2 70 E2
CROY/NA CR0 165 G6
STRHM/NOR SW16 149 F6
UED N18 41 K4
Hermitage Rd FSBYPK N4 55 J6
NRWD SE19 149 J6
Hermitage Rw HACK E8 * 74 C4
Hermitage St BAY/PAD W2 9 G3
The Hermitage BARN SW13 * 106 C7
FELT TW13 * 140 D2
FSTH SE23 131 K7
KUT/HW KT1 * 158 E3
LEW SE13 * 133 F1
RCHPK/HAM TW10 125 F4
Hermitage Wk SWFD E18 58 D3
Hermitage Wall WAP E1W 92 C7
Hermitage Wy STAN HA7 35 G7
Hermit Pl KIL/WHAMP NW6 2 C4
Hermit Rd CAN/RD E16 94 D3
Hermit St FSBYE EC1V 6 C7
Hermon Gv HYS/HAR UB3 82 E7
Hermon Hl WAN E11 58 E3
Herndon Rd
WAND/EARL SW18 128 B4
Herne Cl HYS/HAR UB3 82 D5
WLSDN NW10 69 F4
Herne Ct BUSH WD23 * 22 C7
Herne Hl HNHL SE24 130 D4
Herne Hill Rd HNHL SE24 130 D2
Herne Ms UED N18 42 C3
Herne Pl HNHL SE24 130 C5
Herne Rd BUSH WD23 22 B5
SURB KT6 171 K1
Heron Cl WALTH E17 57 H1
WLSDN NW10 69 G5
Heron Ct HAYES BR2 168 B3
KUT/HW KT1 * 159 F2
Heron Crs SCUP DA14 154 E3
Herondale SAND/SEL CR2 179 F7
Herondale Av
WAND/EARL SW18 128 C7
Heron Dr FSBYPK N4 73 J1
Heron Flight Av HCH RM12 81 J6
Herongate Rd MNPK E12 77 G1
Heron Hl BELV DA17 117 G3
Heron Ms IL IG1 78 B1
Heron Pl BERM/RHTH SE16 93 G7
Heron Quays POP/IOD E14 93 J7
Heron Rd CROY/NA CR0 * 165 F7
HNHL SE24 130 D3
TWK TW1 124 B3
Heronsforde WEA W13 85 J5
Heronsgate EDGW HA8 36 C4
Herons Lea HGT N6 * 53 K5
Heronslea Dr STAN HA7 36 A4
Herons Pl ISLW TW7 124 C2
Herons Ri EBAR EN4 27 J3
Heron Wk NTHWD HA6 32 C3
Heron Wy EBED/NFELT TW14 121 K3
Herrick Rd HBRY N5 73 J2
Herrick St WEST SW1P 17 H6
Herries St NKENS W10 88 C1
Herringham Rd CHARL SE7 114 B2
Herrongate Cl EN EN1 30 A1
Hersant Cl WLSDN NW10 69 J7
Herschell Rd FSTH SE23 132 A6
Hersham Cl PUT/ROE SW15 126 D6
Hershell Ct
MORT/ESHN SW14 * 125 J3
Hertford Av
MORT/ESHN SW14 126 A4
Hertford Cl EBAR EN4 27 H2
Hertford Ct STAN HA7 * 35 K6
Hertford End Ct
NTHWD HA6 * 32 C4
Hertford Pl FITZ W1T 10 E1
Hertford Rd BARK IG11 78 A6
EBAR EN4 27 G2
ED N9 30 D7
EFNCH N2 53 J2
GNTH/NBYPK IG2 60 E5
IS N1 7 K3
PEND EN3 30 E2
Hertford Road High St
PEND EN3 30 E5
Hertford St MYFR/PICC W1J 10 C8
Hertford Wy MTCM CR4 163 K3
Hertslet Rd HOLWY N7 73 F2
Hertsmere Rd POP/IOD E14 93 J6
Hertswood Ct BAR EN5 * 26 C3
Hervey Cl FNCH N3 38 E7
Hervey Park Rd WALTH E17 57 G3
Hesa Rd HYS/HAR UB3 82 E5
Hesewall Cl CLAP SW4 129 H1
Hesketh Pl NTGHL W11 88 C6
Hesketh Rd FSTGT E7 76 E2
Heslop Rd BAL SW12 128 E7
Hesper Ms ECT SW5 14 C7
Hesperus Crs POP/IOD E14 112 E3
Hessel Rd WEA W13 104 B1
Hessel St WCHPL E1 92 D5
Hesselyn Dr RAIN RM13 81 K6
Hestercombe Av
FUL/PGN SW6 127 H1
Hesterman Wy CROY/NA CR0 163 K7
Hester Rd BTSEA SW11 108 D6
UED N18 42 C4
Hester Ter RCH/KEW TW9 125 H2
Heston Av HEST TW5 102 D6
Heston Grange La HEST TW5 102 E5
Heston Rd HEST TW5 103 F6
Heston St NWCR SE14 112 C7
Heswell Gn OXHEY WD19 * 32 E2
Hetherington Rd CLAP SW4 129 K3
Hetley Rd SHB W12 87 K7
Heton Gdns HDN NW4 51 J3
Hevelius Cl GNWCH SE10 113 J4
Hever Cft ELTH/MOT SE9 154 A3
Hever Gdns BMLY BR1 169 F1
Heverham Rd
WOOL/PLUM SE18 115 K3
Hevingham Dr CHDH RM6 61 J4
Hewens Rd HGDN/ICK UB10 82 A2
Hewer St NKENS W10 88 B4
Hewett Cl STAN HA7 35 H3
Hewett St SDTCH EC2A 13 K1
Hewish Rd UED N18 42 A3
Hewison St BOW E3 93 H1
Hewitt Av WDGN N22 55 H1
Hewitt Cl CROY/NA CR0 179 J2
Hewitt Rd CEND/HSY/T N8 55 G4
Hewlett Rd BOW E3 93 G1
The Hexagon HGT N6 53 K7
Hexal Rd CAT SE6 152 C2
Hexham Gdns ISLW TW7 104 B6
Hexham Rd BAR EN5 27 F3
MRDN SM4 162 A7
WNWD SE27 149 J1
Heybourne Rd TOTM N17 42 D6
Heybridge Av
STRHM/NOR SW16 149 F5
Heybridge Dr BARK/HLT IG6 60 D2
Heybridge Wy LEY E10 57 G6
Heyford Av RYNPK SW20 161 J2
VX/NE SW8 109 K6
Heyford Rd MTCM CR4 162 D1
Heyford Ter VX/NE SW8 109 K6
Heygate Est WALW SE17 18 F5
Heygate St WALW SE17 18 E6
Heynes Rd BCTR RM8 79 J3
Heysham Dr OXHEY WD19 33 G4
Heysham La HAMP NW3 71 F2
Heysham Rd
SEVS/STOTM N15 55 K5
Heythorp St
WAND/EARL SW18 146 D1
Heywood Av CDALE/KGS NW9 37 G7
Heyworth Rd CLPT E5 74 D3
SRTFD E15 76 D3
Hibbert Rd
KTN/HRWW/WS HA3 49 F1
WALTH E17 57 H6
Hibbert St BTSEA SW11 128 B2
Hibernia Gdns HSLW TW3 123 F4
Hibernia Rd HSLW TW3 123 F3
Hichisson Rd PECK SE15 131 K4
Hicken Rd BRXS/STRHM SW2 130 A4
Hickin Cl CHARL SE7 114 C3
Hickin St POP/IOD E14 113 F2
Hickling Rd IL IG1 78 B4
Hickman Av CHING E4 44 A5
Hickman Cl CAN/RD E16 95 H4
Hickman Rd CHDH RM6 61 J6
Hickory Cl ED N9 30 C6
Hicks Av GFD/PVL UB6 84 D2
Hicks Cl BTSEA SW11 128 D2
Hicks St DEPT SE8 112 B4
Hidcote Gdns RYNPK SW20 160 E2
Hide Pl WEST SW1P 17 G6
Hide Rd HRW HA1 48 D3
Higham Hill Rd WALTH E17 57 G2
Higham Ms NTHLT UB5 83 K3
Higham Pl WALTH E17 57 G2
Higham Rd TOTM N17 55 K2
WFD IG8 44 E5
Higham Station Av CHING E4 43 K5
The Highams WALTH E17 * 44 A7
Higham St WALTH E17 57 G1
Highbank Pl
WAND/EARL SW18 * 128 A7
Highbanks Cl WELL DA16 116 B6
Highbanks Rd PIN HA5 34 B5
Highbank Wy CEND/HSY/T N8 55 G5
Highbarrow Rd CROY/NA CR0 165 G7
High Beech SAND/SEL CR2 178 A6
Highbridge Rd BARK IG11 78 B7
Highbrook Rd BKHTH/KID SE3 134 C2
High Broom Crs WWKM BR4 166 E6
Highbury Av THHTH CR7 164 B1
Highbury Cl NWMAL KT3 159 K3
WWKM BR4 179 K1
Highbury Cnr IS N1 73 H5

218 Hig - Hol

Street	Area	Page	Grid
Highbury Crs	HBRY N5	73	G4
Highbury Est	HBRY N5	73	J4
Highbury Gdns	GDMY/SEVK IG3	78	E1
Highbury Gra	HBRY N5	73	H3
Highbury Gv	HBRY N5	73	H5
Highbury Hl	HBRY N5	73	H3
Highbury New Pk	HBRY N5	73	H5
Highbury Pk	HBRY N5	73	H3
Highbury Pl	HBRY N5	73	H5
Highbury Qd	HBRY N5	73	J2
Highbury Rd	WIM/MER SW19	146	C4
Highbury Station Pde	HBRY N5 *	73	H5
Highbury Station Rd	IS N1 *	73	H5
Highbury Ter	HBRY N5	73	H5
Highbury Terrace Ms	HBRY N5	73	H4
High Cedar Dr	RYNPK SW20	145	K6
Highclere Rd	NWMAL KT3	160	A2
Highclere St	SYD SE26	151	G3
Highcliffe Dr	PUT/ROE SW15	126	C5
Highcliffe Gdns	REDBR IG4	59	J4
Highcombe	CHARL SE7	114	A6
Highcombe Cl	ELTH/MOT SE9	134	C7
High Coombe Pl	KUTN/CMB KT2	145	F6
Highcroft	CDALE/KGS NW9	51	G4
Highcroft Av	ALP/SUD HA0	68	B6
Highcroft Gdns	GLDGN NW11	52	D5
Highcroft Rd	ARCH N19	54	E6
High Cross Rd	TOTM N17	56	C7
High Cross Wy	PUT/ROE SW15	126	D7
Highdaun Dr	STRHM/NOR SW16	164	A3
Highdown	WPK KT4	173	G1
Highdown Rd	PUT/ROE SW15	126	E5
High Dr	NWMAL KT3	144	E7
High Elms	WFD IG8	44	H4
High Elms Cl	NTHWD HA6	32	K5
Highfield	OXHEY WD19	33	K2
Highfield Av	CDALE/KGS NW9	50	E4
	ERITH DA8	117	J3
	ERITH DA8 *	117	K5
	GFD/PVL UB6	66	E4
	GLDGN NW11	52	B6
	PIN HA5	47	K4
	WBLY HA9	68	A2
Highfield Cl	CDALE/KGS NW9	50	E4
	LEW SE13	133	G6
	NTHWD HA6	32	C7
	SURB KT6	158	C7
	WDGN N22	41	G6
Highfield Ct	STHGT/OAK N14	28	C5
Highfield Crs	NTHWD HA6	32	C7
Highfield Dr	HAYES BR2	167	H2
	HOR/WEW KT19	173	H6
	WWKM BR4	179	K1
Highfield Gdns	GLDGN NW11	52	C5
Highfield Hl	NRWD SE19	149	H6
Highfield Rd	ACT W3	86	D4
	BMLY BR1	168	E3
	BRYLDS KT5	159	K6
	BUSH WD23	21	J4
	FELT TW13	121	K7
	GLDGN NW11	52	C5
	ISLW TW7	104	A7
	NTHWD HA6	32	C7
	SUT SM1	175	J4
	WCHPL E1	41	H1
	WFD IG8	45	J6
Highfields Gv	HGT N6	54	A1
High Foleys	ESH/CLAY KT10	171	H6
High Garth	ESH/CLAY KT10	170	C5
Highgate Av	HGT N6	54	A6
Highgate Cl	HGT N6	54	A6
Highgate Edge	EFNCH N2 *	53	J4
Highgate High St	HGT N6	54	A7
Highgate Hl	ARCH N19	54	B7
Highgate Rd	KTTN NW5	72	A2
Highgate Spinney	CEND/HSY/T N8 *	54	D5
Highgate Wk	FSTH SE23	150	E1
Highgate West Hl	HGT N6	54	A7
High Gv	BMLY BR1	153	G7
	WOOL/PLUM SE18	115	H6
Highgrove Cl	CHST BR7	153	J7
	FBAR/BDGN N11	40	A4
Highgrove Ms	CAR SM5	175	J2
Highgrove Rd	BCTR RM8	79	J4
Highgrove Wy	RYLN/HDSTN HA2	46	E5
High Hill Ferry	CLPT E5	56	D7
High Holborn	HHOL WC1V	11	K4
Highland Av	DAGE RM10	80	E2
	HNWL W7	84	E6
Highland Cots	WLGTN SM6 *	176	B3
Highland Cft	BECK BR3	151	K4
Highland Dr	BUSH WD23	22	B6
Highland Pk	FELT TW13	140	D3
Highland Rd	BMLY BR1	152	D7
	HAYES BR2	167	J1
	NRWD SE19	150	A5
	NTHWD HA6	46	E1
Highlands	OXHEY WD19	21	G7
	WCHMH N21	29	H4
Highlands Av	ACT W3	86	E6
	HSLW TW3	103	G7
Highlands Gdns	IL IG1	59	K7
Highlands Heath	PUT/ROE SW15	127	F6
Highlands Rd	BAR EN5	26	E6
The Highlands	BAR EN5	26	K1
	EDGW HA8	50	D1
Highland Ter	LEW SE13 *	132	E2
High La	HNWL W7	84	D5
Highlea Cl	CDALE/KGS NW9	37	G6
High Level Dr	SYD SE26	150	C3
Highlever Rd	NKENS W10	88	A4
High Limes	NRWD SE19 *	150	A5
High Md	HRW HA1	48	E5
Highmead	WOOL/PLUM SE18	116	A6
High Md	WWKM BR4	180	B1
Highmead Crs	ALP/SUD HA0	68	B6
High Meadow Cl	PIN HA5	47	K3
High Meadow Crs	CDALE/KGS NW9	51	F4
High Meads Rd	CAN/RD E16	95	H5
Highmore Rd	BKHTH/KID SE3	113	J6
High Mt	HDN NW4	51	J5
The High Pde	STRHM/NOR SW16 *	148	E2
High Park Rd	RCH/KEW TW9	105	H7
High Pth	WIM/MER SW19	147	F7
High Point	ELTH/MOT SE9	154	B2
High Rdg	MUSWH N10 *	40	B7
High Rd	BUSH WD23	22	D5
	CHDH RM6	61	K6
	EFNCH N2	53	H2
	FBAR/BDGN N11	40	A4
	FNCH N3	39	H7
	GDMY/SEVK IG3	61	G7
	IL IG1	78	B2

Street	Area	Page	Grid
	KTN/HRWW/WS HA3	34	E7
	LEY E10	57	K5
	NFNCH/WDSPK N12	39	G6
	SEVS/STOTM N15	56	B5
	TOTM N17	56	B7
	TRDG/WHET N20	27	F6
	WBLY HA9	68	A4
	WDGN N22	41	F6
	WLSDN NW10	69	G5
High Road Eastcote	PIN HA5	47	J4
High Road Leyton	LEY E10	75	K1
High Road Leytonstone	WAN E11	76	D2
High Road Woodford Gn	SWFD E18	44	E7
Highshore Rd	PECK SE15	131	G1
Highstead Crs	ERITH DA8	118	B7
Highstone Av	WAN E11	58	E5
High St	ACT W3	86	E7
	BAR EN5	26	C2
	BARK/HLT IG6	60	C1
	BECK BR3	151	J7
	BELMT SM2	175	G6
	BMLY BR1	167	K1
	BTFD TW8	104	E6
	BUSH WD23	22	B5
	CAR SM5	175	K4
	CEND/HSY/T N8	54	E3
	CHEAM SM3	174	C5
	CROY/NA CR0	177	J2
	DART DA1	139	H5
	HRW/HCT KT8	157	F4
	EA W5	85	K6
	EW/CLAY KT10	170	A5
	EW KT17	173	H7
	FBAR/BDGN N11	40	A4
	FELT TW13	140	A1
	HEST TW5	102	A5
	HPTN TW12	142	C6
	HRW HA1	48	E1
	HSLW TW3	123	G2
	HYS/HAR UB3	101	J2
	KTN/HRWW/WS HA3	48	E2
	KUT/HW KT1	143	J7
	MLHL NW7	37	K4
	NTHWD HA6	32	D7
	NWMAL KT3	160	B3
	OXHEY WD19	21	H2
	PGE/AN SE20	150	E6
	PIN HA5	47	J2
	PLSTW E13	94	E1
	ROM RM1	63	G4
	RSLP HA4	46	E7
	SCUP DA14	155	G3
	SNWD SE25	165	G3
	SRTFD E15	94	A1
	STHGT/OAK N14	28	D7
	STRHM/NOR SW16	149	F5
	STWL/WRAY TW19	120	A5
	SUT SM1	175	F5
	TEDD TW11	143	G4
	THDIT KT7	158	B5
	THHTH CR7	164	D3
	WALTH E17	57	H3
	WAN E11	59	F5
	WAT WD17	21	F2
	WBLY HA9	68	B3
	WDR/YW UB7	100	A5
	WHTN TW2	123	H6
	WIM/MER SW19	146	B4
	WKM BR4	166	E6
High Street Collier's Wd	WIM/MER SW19	147	H6
High Street Harlesden	WLSDN NW10	69	G7
High Street Harlington	HTHAIR TW6	101	G6
High Street Ms	WIM/MER SW19	146	C4
High St North	EHAM E6	77	J7
High St South	EHAM E6	95	K1
High Timber St	BLKFR EC4V	12	E6
High Tor Cl	BMLY BR1	153	F6
High Trees	BRXS/STRHM SW2	130	B7
	CROY/NA CR0	166	B7
	EBAR EN4	27	J4
High Vw	PIN HA5	47	G3
	WATW WD18	20	B5
Highview Av	EDGW HA8	36	E3
High View Cl	NRWD SE19	165	K1
Highview Gdns	EDGW HA8	36	E3
	FBAR/BDGN N11	40	C4
	FNCH N3	52	C2
High View Rd	NRWD SE19	149	K5
	SCUP DA14	155	H3
	SWFD E18	58	D1
Highview Rd	WEA W13	85	G5
Highview Ter	DART DA1 *	139	G4
The Highway	BELMT SM2	175	G7
	STAN HA7	35	F7
	WCHPL E1	92	C6
Highwood Av	NFNCH/WDSPK N12	39	G3
Highwood Cl	EDUL SE22	131	H7
Highwood Gdns	CLAY IG5	59	K4
Highwood Gv	MLHL NW7	37	G4
Highwood Hl	MLHL NW7	37	H1
Highwood Rd	ARCH N19	72	E2
High Worple	RYLN/HDSTN HA2	47	J6
Highworth Rd	FBAR/BDGN N11	40	D5
Highworth St	CAMTN NW1 *	9	K2
Hilary Av	MTCM CR4	163	F2
Hilary Cl	FUL/PGN SW6 *	108	A6
Hilary Rd	SHB W12	87	H6
Hilberry Ct	BUSH WD23 *	22	B6
Hilbert Rd	CHEAM SM3	174	B3
Hilborough Cl	WIM/MER SW19	147	G6
Hilborough Rd	HACK E8 *	7	M2
Hilda Lockert Wk	BRXN/ST SW9 *	130	C1
Hilda Rd	CAN/RD E16	94	C3
	EHAM E6	77	H7
Hilda Ter	BRXN/ST SW9 *	130	B1
Hildenborough Gdns	BMLY BR1	152	C5
Hilden Dr	ERITH DA8	118	E6
Hildenlea Pl	HAYES BR2	167	H1
Hildreth St	BAL SW12	129	G7
Hildyard Rd	FUL/PGN SW6	107	K5
Hiley Rd	WLSDN NW10	88	A2
Hilfield La	GSTN WD25	22	A1
Hilgrove Rd	KIL/WHAMP NW6	2	E1
Hiliary Gdns	STAN HA7	49	J1
Hillary Dr	ISLW TW7	124	B3
Hillary Ri	BAR EN5	26	E3
Hillary Rd	NWDGN UB2	103	F3
Hillbeck Cl	PECK SE15	111	K6
Hillbeck Wy	GFD/PVL UB6	66	D7
Hillborne Cl	HYS/HAR UB3	101	K4

Street	Area	Page	Grid
Hillborough Cl	WIM/MER SW19	147	G6
Hillbrook Rd	TOOT SW17	147	K2
Hill Brow	BMLY BR1	153	H7
Hillbrow	NWMAL KT3	160	C6
Hillbrow Rd	BMLY BR1	152	B7
	ESH/CLAY KT10	170	C6
Hillbury Av	KTN/HRWW/WS HA3	49	H5
Hillbury Rd	TOOT SW17	148	B2
Hill Cl	BAR EN5	26	A4
	CHST BR7	154	B4
	CRICK NW2	69	K2
	GLDGN NW11	52	E5
	HRW HA1	66	E2
	STAN HA7	35	H3
Hill Crest	BFN/LL DA15	136	B6
	HGT N6	54	A6
	HNHL SE24 *	130	E3
Hill Crest	SURB KT6 *	159	F6
Hillcrest	HGT N6	53	K7
Hillcrest Av	EDGW HA8	36	C5
	GLDGN NW11	52	C5
	PIN HA5	47	H3
Hillcrest Cl	BECK BR3	166	C6
	SYD SE26	150	C3
Hillcrest Gdns	ESH/CLAY KT10	171	F4
	HDN NW4	51	J2
Hillcrest Rd	ACT W3	86	B7
	BMLY BR1	152	E4
	DART DA1	138	B6
	EA W5	86	A4
	EMPK RM11	63	J6
	WALTH E17	58	B1
Hillcrest Vw	BECK BR3	166	C6
Hillcroft Av	PIN HA5	47	K5
Hillcroft Crs	EA W5	85	K5
	OXHEY WD19	21	F7
	RSLP HA4	65	H2
	WBLY HA9	68	B3
Hillcroft Rd	EHAM E6	96	B4
Hillcrome Rd	BELMT SM2	175	H5
Hillcross Av	MRDN SM4	161	H5
Hilldale Rd	SUT SM1	174	D4
Hilldown Rd	HAYES BR2	167	H7
	STRHM/NOR SW16	148	E6
Hill Dr	CDALE/KGS NW9	50	D7
	STRHM/NOR SW16	164	A4
Hilldrop Crs	HOLWY N7	72	D4
Hilldrop Est	HOLWY N7 *	72	D3
Hilldrop La	HOLWY N7	72	D4
Hilldrop Rd	BMLY BR1	152	E5
	HOLWY N7	72	D4
Hill End	WOOL/PLUM SE18	115	F7
Hillersdon Av	BARN SW13	126	D1
	EDGW HA8	36	B4
Hillery Cl	WALW SE17	19	H6
Hill Farm Rd	NKENS W10	88	A4
Hillfield Av	ALP/SUD HA0	68	A6
	CDALE/KGS NW9	51	G4
	CEND/HSY/T N8	55	F5
	MRDN SM4	162	D5
Hillfield Cl	RYLN/HDSTN HA2	48	C5
Hillfield La South	BUSH WD23	22	E5
Hillfield Ms	CEND/HSY/T N8	55	F3
Hillfield Pde	MRDN SM4 *	162	C5
Hillfield Pk	MUSWH N10	54	B2
	WCHMH N21	41	G1
Hillfield Park Ms	MUSWH N10	54	B3
Hill Field Rd	HPTN TW12	141	K6
Hillfield Rd	KIL/WHAMP NW6	70	D4
Hill Gardens Craven	BAY/PAD W2 *	8	E6
Hillgate Pl	BAL SW12	129	G6
	KENS W8	8	A8
Hillgate St	KENS W8	8	A8
Hill Gv	FELT TW13	141	K1
	ROM RM1	63	G2
Hill House Av	STAN HA7	35	F6
Hill House Cl	WCHMH N21	29	G6
Hill House Dr	HPTN TW12	142	A7
Hill House Rd	STRHM/NOR SW16	149	F4
Hilliard's Ct	WAP E1W *	92	E7
Hillier Cl	BAR EN5	27	F5
Hillier Gdns	CROY/NA CR0	177	G5
Hillier Pl	CHSGTN KT9	171	K5
Hilliers La	CROY/NA CR0	176	E2
Hillingdon Av	STWL/WRAY TW19	120	B7
Hillingdon Rd	BXLYHN DA7	137	K2
Hillingdon St	WALW SE17	110	D6
Hillingdon Trail	HGDN/ICK UB10	64	A5
	HYS/HAR UB3	101	K4
	RSLP HA4	46	K4
Hillman Cl	HCH RM12	63	K1
Hillman Dr	NKENS W10	88	A3
Hillman St	HACK E8	74	D5
Hillmarton Rd	HOLWY N7	72	E4
Hillmead Dr	BRXN/ST SW9	130	C3
Hillmont Rd	ESH/CLAY KT10	170	E3
Hillmore Gv	SYD SE26	151	F4
Hillreach	WOOL/PLUM SE18	114	E4
Hill Ri	ED N9	30	D5
	ESH/CLAY KT10	171	H1
	GFD/PVL UB6	66	C7
	GLDGN NW11	53	F3
	RCHPK/HAM TW10	124	E4
	RSLP HA4	46	E6
Hillrise Rd	ARCH N19	54	E6
Hill Rd	ALP/SUD HA0	67	H2
	CAR SM5	175	J5
	HRW HA1	49	F5
	MTCM CR4	148	B7
	MUSWH N10	54	A1
	NTHWD HA6	32	B5
	PIN HA5	47	H3
	STJWD NW8	2	E3
	STNW/STAM N16	55	K7
Hillsboro Rd	EDUL SE22	131	F4
Hillsborough Gn	OXHEY WD19 *	32	E2
Hillside	BAR EN5	27	H4
	CDALE/KGS NW9	51	F3
	ESH/CLAY KT10	170	D4
	WIM/MER SW19	146	B5
	WLSDN NW10	69	F7

Street	Area	Page	Grid
Hillside Av	BORE WD6	24	D3
	FBAR/BDGN N11	39	K6
	WBLY HA9	68	B3
	WFD IG8	45	H4
Hillside Cl	MRDN SM4	161	H3
	STJWD NW8	2	B2
Hillside Crs	NTHWD HA6	32	E6
	OXHEY WD19	21	H5
	RYLN/HDSTN HA2	66	C1
Hillside Dr	EDGW HA8	36	C5
Hillside Gdns	BAR EN5	26	C3
	BRXS/STRHM SW2	149	G1
	EDGW HA8	36	B3
	FBAR/BDGN N11	40	C5
	KTN/HRWW/WS HA3	50	A6
	NTHWD HA6	32	E6
	WALTH E17	58	B2
	WLGTN SM6	176	C6
Hillside Gv	MLHL NW7	37	J6
	STHGT/OAK N14	28	D6
Hillside Ri	NTHWD HA6	32	E6
Hillside Rd	KIL/WHAMP NW6	2	B1
	BRXS/STRHM SW2	149	G1
	BUSH WD23	21	J4
	CROY/NA CR0	177	H4
	EA W5	86	A4
	HAYES BR2	167	J2
	NTHWD HA6	32	D6
	SEVS/STOTM N15	56	A5
	STHL UB1	84	A3
	STMC/STPC BR5	169	K5
	SURB KT6	159	F4
	SUT SM1	174	D6
	TOOT SW17	148	B5
	WHTN TW2	123	K7
Hills La	NTHWD HA6	32	C7
Hills Ms	EA W5 *	86	A6
Hillsleigh Rd	KENS W8	88	E7
Hills Pl	SOHO/SHAV W1D	10	E5
Hill St	MYFR/PICC W1J	10	C8
	RCH/KEW TW9	124	E4
Hill Top	CHEAM SM3	161	J7
	GLDGN NW11	53	F3
Hilltop	WALTH E17 *	57	J1
Hilltop Av	WLSDN NW10	68	E6
Hilltop Cots	SYD SE26 *	150	E3
Hilltop Gdns	DART DA1	139	F5
	HDN NW4	51	K1
Hilltop Rd	KIL/WHAMP NW6	2	B1
Hill Top Vw	WFD IG8 *	45	K5
Hilltop Wy	STAN HA7	35	G2
Hillview	RYNPK SW20	145	K6
Hillview Av	KTN/HRWW/WS HA3	50	A4
	PIN HA5	33	K6
	WBLY HA9	68	B1
Hillview Crs	IL IG1	59	K5
	ORP BR6	169	K7
Hill View Dr	THMD SE28	96	E7
	WELL DA16	135	K1
Hill View Gdns	CDALE/KGS NW9	51	F4
Hillview Gdns	HDN NW4	52	B3
	RYLN/HDSTN HA2	48	A2
Hill View Rd	TWK TW1	124	B5
Hillview Rd	CHST BR7	154	A4
	ESH/CLAY KT10	171	G4
	MLHL NW7	38	B4
	PIN HA5	33	K6
	SUT SM1	175	G3
Hillway	CDALE/KGS NW9	51	G7
	HGT N6	72	A1
Hillworth	BECK BR3 *	166	E1
Hillworth Rd	BRXS/STRHM SW2	130	B6
Hillyard Rd	HNWL W7	84	E4
Hillyard St	BRXN/ST SW9	110	B7
Hillyfield	WALTH E17	57	G1
Hillyfield Cl	HOM E9	75	G4
Hilly Flds	BROCKY SE4	132	D3
Hilly Fields Crs	BROCKY SE4	132	D2
Hilsea St	CLPT E5	74	E3
Hilton Av	NFNCH/WDSPK N12	39	H4
Himalayan Wy	WATW WD18	20	D5
Himley Rd	TOOT SW17	147	J4
Hinchley Cl	ESH/CLAY KT10	171	F3
Hinchley Dr	ESH/CLAY KT10	171	F3
Hinchley Wy	ESH/CLAY KT10	171	G3
Hinckley Rd	PECK SE15	131	H4
Hind Ct	FLST/FETLN EC4A	12	B5
Hind Crs	ERITH DA8	117	K6
Hinde Ms	MHST W1U *	10	B4
Hindes Rd	HRW HA1	48	E4
Hinde St	MHST W1U	10	B4
Hind Gv	POP/IOD E14	93	J5
Hindhead Gdns	NTHLT UB5	65	J7
Hindhead Gn	OXHEY WD19	33	G4
Hindhead Wy	WLGTN SM6	176	E4
Hindmans Wy	DAGW RM9	98	B2
Hindmarsh Cl	WCHPL E1 *	92	C6
Hindsley's Pl	FSTH SE23	150	E1
Hinkler Rd	KTN/HRWW/WS HA3	49	K2
Hinksey Pth	ABYW SE2	116	E2
Hinstock Rd	WOOL/PLUM SE18	115	H6
Hinton Av	HSLWW TW4	122	C4
Hinton Cl	ELTH/MOT SE9	134	D7
Hinton Rd	BRXN/ST SW9	130	C2
	UED N18	42	A3
	WLGTN SM6	176	C5
Hippodrome Pl	NTGHL W11	88	C6
Hirst Crs	WBLY HA9	68	A2
Hitcham Rd	WALTH E17	57	H6
Hithe Gv	BERM/RHTH SE16	111	K2
Hitherbroom Rd	HYS/HAR UB3	82	E7
Hither Farm Rd	BKHTH/KID SE3	134	B2
Hitherfield Rd	BCTR RM8	80	A1
	STRHM/NOR SW16	149	H1
Hither Green La	LEW SE13	133	F5
Hitherwell Dr	KTN/HRWW/WS HA3	34	D6
Hitherwood Dr	NRWD SE19	150	B3
Hive Cl	BUSH WD23	34	D1
Hive Rd	BUSH WD23	34	D1
Hoadly Rd	STRHM/NOR SW16	148	D1
Hobart Cl	TRDG/WHET N20	39	J1
	YEAD UB4	83	H3
Hobart Dr	YEAD UB4	83	H3
Hobart Gdns	THHTH CR7	164	E2
Hobart La	YEAD UB4	83	H3
Hobart Pl	BGVA SW1W	16	C4
	RCHPK/HAM TW10	125	F6
Hobart Rd	BARK/HLT IG6	60	C1
	DAGW RM9	79	K3
	WPK KT4	173	K3
	YEAD UB4	83	H3
Hobbayne Rd	HNWL W7	84	D5
Hobbes Wk	PUT/ROE SW15	126	D4
Hobb Gn	EFNCH N2	53	G2
Hobbs Ms	GDMY/SEVK IG3	79	F1
Hobbs Pl	IS N1	7	M4
Hobbs Place Est	IS N1 *	7	M4

Street	Area	Page	Grid
Hobbs Rd	WNWD SE27	149	J3
Hobby St	PEND EN3	31	F4
Hobday St	POP/IOD E14	93	K5
Hoblands End	CHST BR7	154	E5
Hobsons Pl	WCHPL E1 *	92	C4
Hobury St	WBPTN SW10	108	B5
Hocker St	BETH E2 *	7	L8
Hockley Av	EHAM E6	95	J1
Hockley Dr	GPK RM2	63	K1
Hockley Ms	BARK IG11	96	E1
Hocroft Av	CRICK NW2	70	D2
Hocroft Rd	CRICK NW2	70	D3
Hocroft Wk	CRICK NW2	70	D2
Hodder Dr	GFD/PVL UB6	85	F1
Hoddesdon Rd	BELV DA17	117	H4
Hodes Rw	HAMP NW3	71	K4
Hodford Rd	GLDGN NW11	52	D7
Hodgkins Ms	STAN HA7	35	H4
Hodister Cl	CMBW SE5	110	D6
Hodnet Gv	BERM/RHTH SE16	111	K3
Hodson Pl	RYLN/HDSTN HA2	65	K3
Hoe St	WALTH E17	57	J4
The Hoe	OXHEY WD19	33	H1
Hoffmann Gdns	SAND/SEL CR2	178	C5
Hoffman St	IS N1 *	7	H7
Hofland Rd	WKENS W14	107	H2
Hogan Ms	BAY/PAD W2	9	G2
Hogarth Av	ASHF TW15	140	A5
Hogarth Cl	CAN/RD E16	95	H4
	EA W5	86	A4
Hogarth Crs	CROY/NA CR0	164	D6
	WIM/MER SW19	147	F6
Hogarth Gdns	HEST TW5	103	F6
Hogarth Hl	GLDGN NW11	52	D3
Hogarth Pl	ECT SW5 *	14	C6
Hogarth Rd	BCTR RM8	79	H4
	ECT SW5	14	C6
	EDGW HA8	50	C1
Hogarth Ter	CHSWK W4 *	106	B5
Hogarth Wy	HPTN TW12	142	C7
Hogg La	BORE WD6	23	G3
Hogshead Pas	WAP E1W *	92	D6
Hogsmill Wy	HOR/WEW KT19	172	E4
Holbeach Gdns	BFN/LL DA15	135	K5
Holbeach Rd	CAT SE6	132	E6
Holbeck Rw	PECK SE15	111	H6
Holbein Ga	NTHWD HA6	32	C5
Holbein Ms	BGVA SW1W	16	A7
Holbein Pl	BGVA SW1W	16	A6
Holberton Gdns	WLSDN NW10	87	K2
Holborn	HCIRC EC1N	12	A3
Holborn Circ	HCIRC EC1N	12	A3
Holborn Pl	HHOL WC1V *	11	L3
Holborn Rd	PLSTW E13	95	F4
Holborn Viad	STBT EC1A	12	C3
Holbrook Wy	MTCM CR4	162	E1
Holbrook La	CHST BR7	154	D6
Holbrook Rd	SRTFD E15	94	D1
Holbrook Wy	HAYES BR2	168	E5
Holburne Cl	BKHTH/KID SE3	114	B7
Holburne Gdns	BKHTH/KID SE3	114	C7
	BKHTH/KID SE3	114	B7
Holburn	GINN WC1R	12	A3
Holcombe Hl	MLHL NW7	37	J2
Holcombe Rd	IL IG1	60	A6
	TOTM N17	56	B2
Holcombe St	HMSMTH W6	106	E4
Holcote Cl	BELV DA17	117	F2
Holcroft Rd	HOM E9	74	E7
Holden Av	CDALE/KGS NW9	50	E7
	NFNCH/WDSPK N12	39	F5
Holdenby Rd	BROCKY SE4	132	B4
Holden Cl	BCTR RM8	79	H2
Holdenhurst Av	FNCH N3	52	E2
Holden Rd	NFNCH/WDSPK N12	39	F3
Holden St	BTSEA SW11	129	F1
Holdernesse Rd	ISLW TW7	104	A7
	TOOT SW17	147	K2
Holderness Wy	WNWD SE27	149	H4
Holders Hill Av	HDN NW4	52	B1
Holders Hill Crs	HDN NW4	52	B1
Holders Hill Dr	HDN NW4	52	B1
Holders Hill Gdns	HDN NW4	52	B1
Holders Hill Pde	MLHL NW7 *	52	B1
Holders Hill Rd	MLHL NW7	52	B1
Holford Ms	FSBYW WC1X *	5	L7
Holford Rd	HAMP NW3	71	G2
Holford St	FSBYW WC1X	5	L7
Holford Yd	FSBYW WC1X *	6	A6
Holgate Av	BTSEA SW11	128	C2
Holgate Rd	DAGE RM10	80	C4
Holgate St	CHARL SE7	114	C2
	WLSDN NW10	87	H4
Holland Av	BELMT SM2	174	D7
	RYNPK SW20	145	H7
Holland Cl	BAR EN5	27	H6
	HAYES BR2	180	D1
	ROMW/RG RM7	62	E4
	STAN HA7	35	H4
Holland Dr	FSTH SE23	151	G2
Holland Gdns	BTFD TW8	105	F5
	WKENS W14	107	H2
Holland Gv	BRXN/ST SW9	110	B6
Holland Pk	NTGHL W11	107	J1
Holland Park Av	GDMY/SEVK IG3	60	E6
	NTGHL W11	88	C7
Holland Park Gdns	WKENS W14	107	H1
Holland Park Rd	WKENS W14	107	J3
Holland Park Ter	NTGHL W11 *	88	C7
Holland Pas	IS N1 *	6	E3
Holland Pl	KENS W8	14	C1
Holland Rd	ALP/SUD HA0	67	K7
	EHAM E6	77	K7
	SNWD SE25	165	H4
	SRTFD E15	94	C2
	WKENS W14	107	G1
	WLSDN NW10	69	J7
The Hollands	WPK KT4	160	C7
Holland St	KENS W8	14	B2
	STHWK SE1	12	D8
Holland Villas Rd	WKENS W14	107	H1
Holland Wk	KENS W8	107	K1
	STAN HA7	35	G4
Holland Wy	HAYES BR2	180	D1
Hollar Rd	STNW/STAM N16	74	B2
Hollen St	SOHO/CST W1F	10	F5
Hollickwood Av	NFNCH/WDSPK N12	39	K5
Holliday Sq	BTSEA SW11 *	128	C2
Hollidge Wy	DAGE RM10	80	D6
Hollies Av	BFN/LL DA15	155	F1
Hollies Cl	STRHM/NOR SW16	149	G5

TWK TW1 143 F1
Hollies End MLHL NW7 37 K4
Hollies Rd EA W5 104 D3
The Hollies BAR EN5 * 25 J4
KTN/HRWW/WS HA3 49 G3
Hollies Wy BAL SW12 * 129 F6
Holligrave Rd BMLY BR1 152 E7
Hollingbourne Gdns
WEA W13 85 G4
Hollingbourne Rd HNHL SE24 130 D4
Hollingsworth Rd
CROY/NA CR0 178 D5
Hollington Crs NWMAL KT3 160 C5
Hollington Rd EHAM E6 95 K2
TOTM N17 56 C1
Hollingworth Cl
E/WMO/HCT KT8 156 E3
Hollingworth Rd
STMC/STPC BR5 169 G6
Hollman Gdns
STRHM/NOR SW16 149 H5
Holloway La WDR/YW UB7 100 C4
Holloway Rd ARCH N19 72 D1
EHAM E6 95 K2
HOLWY N7 73 F3
WAN E11 76 B2
Holloway St HSLW TW3 123 G2
The Hollow WFD IG8 44 D3
Holly Av STAN HA7 50 A1
WOT/HER KT12 156 C7
Holly Bank MUSWH N10 * 54 C3
Hollybank Cl HPTN TW12 142 A4
Hollybrake Cl CHST BR7 154 D6
Hollybush Cl
KTN/HRWW/WS HA3 34 E7
OXHEY WD19 21 G6
WAN E11 58 E4
Hollybush Gdns BETH E2 92 D2
Hollybush Hl WAN E11 58 D5
Holly Bush La HPTN TW12 141 K6
Hollybush Pl BETH E2 92 D2
Hollybush Rd KUTN/CMB KT2 144 A4
Hollybush St PLSTW E13 95 F2
Hollybush Ter NRWD SE19 * 150 A5
Holly Bush V HAMP NW3 * 71 G3
Holly Cl BECK BR3 167 F3
BKHH IG9 45 H2
FELT TW13 141 J4
WLGTN SM6 176 B6
WLSDN NW10 69 G6
Holly Crs BECK BR3 166 C4
WFD IG8 44 B6
Hollycroft Av HAMP NW3 70 E2
WBLY HA9 68 A1
Hollycroft Cl SAND/SEL CR2 178 A4
WDR/YW UB7 100 D5
Hollycroft Gdns WDR/YW UB7 100 D5
Hollydale Cl NTHLT UB5 66 B4
Hollydale Dr HAYES BR2 181 K2
Hollydale Rd PECK SE15 131 K1
Hollydown Wy WAN E11 76 B2
Holly Dr CHING E4 31 K6
Holly Farm Rd NWDGN UB2 102 D4
Hollyfield Av FBAR/BDGN N11 39 K4
Hollyfield Rd BRYLDS KT5 159 G6
Holly Gdns WDR/YW UB7 100 C1
Hollygrove BUSH WD23 22 D6
Holly Gv CDALE/KGS NW9 50 E6
PECK SE15 131 G1
PIN HA5 33 J7
Hollygrove Cl HSLW TW3 122 E3
Holly Hedge Ter LEW SE13 133 F4
Holly Hl HAMP NW3 71 G3
WCHMH N21 29 F5
Holly Hill Rd BELV DA17 117 J4
Holly Lodge Gdns HGT N6 72 A1
Hollymead CAR SM5 175 K2
Holly Ms WBPTN SW10 14 F8
Holly Mt HAMP NW3 * 71 G3
Hollymount Cl GNWCH SE10 113 F7
Holly Pk FNCH N3 52 D2
FSBYPK N4 54 E6
Holly Park Gdns FNCH N3 52 E2
Holly Park Rd
FBAR/BDGN N11 40 A4
HNWL W7 85 F7
Holly Rd CHSWK W4 * 106 A3
HPTN TW12 142 C5
HSLW TW3 123 G3
TWK TW1 124 B7
WAN E11 58 D6
Hollytree Cl WIM/MER SW19 127 G7
Hollytree Pde SCUP DA14 * 155 J4
Hollyview Cl HDN NW4 51 J5
Holly Vls HMSMTH W6 * 106 E2
Holly Wk HAMP NW3 71 G3
Holly Wy MTCM CR4 163 J3
Hollywood Gdns YEAD UB4 83 F5
Hollywood Ms WBPTN SW10 14 E9
Hollywood Rd CHING E4 43 G4
WBPTN SW10 14 E9
Hollywoods CROY/NA CR0 179 H7
Hollywood Wy WFD IG8 44 B6
Holman Ct EW KT17 * 173 J7
Holman Rd BTSEA SW11 128 C1
HOR/WEW KT19 172 E4
Holmbridge Gdns PEND EN3 31 F3
Holmbrook Dr HDN NW4 52 B4
Holmbury Cl BUSH WD23 34 E1
Holmbury Ct WIM/MER SW19 147 J6
Holmbury Gdns HYS/HAR UB3 82 D7
Holmbury Gv CROY/NA CR0 179 H6
Holmbury Mnr SCUP DA14 * 155 G3
Holmbury Pk BMLY BR1 153 J6
Holmbury Vw CLPT E5 56 D7
Holmbush Rd PUT/ROE SW15 127 H5
Holmcote Gdns HBRY N5 73 J4
Holmcroft Wy HAYES BR2 168 E4
Holmdale Cl BORE WD6 24 B1
Holmdale Gdns HDN NW4 52 B4
Holmdale Rd CHST BR7 154 C4
KIL/WHAMP NW6 70 E4
Holmdale Ter
SEVS/STOTM N15 56 A5
Holmdene Av HNHL SE24 130 D4
MLHL NW7 37 J5
RYLN/HDSTN HA2 48 B2
Holmdene Cl BECK BR3 167 F1
Holmdene Ct BMLY BR1 168 D2
Holmead Rd FUL/PGN SW6 108 A6
Holmebury Cl BUSH WD23 * 34 E1
Holme Ct ISLW TW7 124 B2
Holme Lacey Rd
LEE/GVPK SE12 133 J5
Holme Pk BORE WD6 24 B1
Holme Rd EHAM E6 77 J7
Holmes Av MLHL NW7 38 C4
WALTH E17 57 H2
Holmes Cl EDUL SE22 131 H3
Holmesdale Av
MORT/ESHN SW14 125 J2
Holmesdale Cl SNWD SE25 165 G2
Holmesdale Rd BXLYHN DA7 136 E1
CROY/NA CR0 164 E4
HGT N6 54 B6
RCH/KEW TW9 105 G7
SNWD SE25 165 F3
TEDD TW11 143 J6
Holmesley Rd FSTH SE23 132 B5
Holmes Rd KTTN NW5 72 B4
TWK TW1 143 F1
WIM/MER SW19 147 G6
Holmes Ter STHWK SE1 18 A1
Holme Wy STAN HA7 35 F5
Holmewood Gdns
BRXS/STRHM SW2 130 A6
Holmewood Rd
BRXS/STRHM SW2 129 K6
SNWD SE25 165 F2
Holmfield Av HDN NW4 52 B4
Holmhurst Rd BELV DA17 117 J4
Holmleigh Rd
STNW/STAM N16 56 A7
Holm Oak Cl PUT/ROE SW15 127 J5
Holm Oak Pk WATW WD18 * 20 E4
Holmshaw Cl SYD SE26 151 G3
Holmside Ri OXHEY WD19 33 F2
Holmside Rd BAL SW12 129 F5
Holmsley Cl NWMAL KT3 160 C5
Holmstall Av EDGW HA8 50 E1
Holmstall Pde EDGW HA8 * 50 E1
Holmwood Cl BELMT SM2 174 B7
NTHLT UB5 66 B5
RYLN/HDSTN HA2 48 C2
Holmwood Gdns FNCH N3 52 E1
WLGTN SM6 176 B5
Holmwood Gv MLHL NW7 37 F4
Holmwood Rd BELMT SM2 174 A7
CHSGTN KT9 172 A4
GDMY/SEVK IG3 78 E1
Holne Cha EFNCH N2 53 G5
MRDN SM4 161 K5
Holness Rd SRTFD E15 76 D5
Holroyd Rd ESH/CLAY KT10 171 F7
PUT/ROE SW15 127 F3
Holstein Wy ERITHM DA18 116 E2
Holstock Rd IL IG1 78 C1
Holsworth Cl
RYLN/HDSTN HA2 48 C4
Holsworthy Sq FSBYW WC1X 11 M1
Holsworthy Wy CHSGTN KT9 171 J4
Holt Cl BORE WD6 24 B3
MUSWH N10 54 A3
THMD SE28 97 H6
Holton St WCHPL E1 93 F3
Holt Rd ALP/SUD HA0 67 H2
CAN/RD E16 95 J7
The Holt MRDN SM4 * 161 K3
WLGTN SM6 176 C3
Holtwhite Av ENC/FH EN2 29 J1
Holwell Pl PIN HA5 47 J3
Holwood Park Av ORP BR6 181 K3
Holwood Pl CLAP SW4 129 J3
Holybourne Av
PUT/ROE SW15 126 D6
Holyhead Cl BOW E3 93 J2
Holyoake Ct
BERM/RHTH SE16 112 B1
Holyoake Wk EA W5 85 J3
EFNCH N2 53 G2
Holyoak Rd LBTH SE11 18 C5
Holyport Rd FUL/PGN SW6 107 F6
Holyrood Av
RYLN/HDSTN HA2 65 J3
Holyrood Gdns EDGW HA8 50 D1
Holyrood Ms CAN/RD E16 94 E7
Holyrood Rd BAR EN5 27 G5
Holyrood St STHWK SE1 13 J9
Holywell Cl
BERM/RHTH SE16 * 111 J4
STWL/WRAY TW19 120 B7
Holywell La SDTCH EC2A 7 K9
Holywell Rd WATW WD18 20 E4
Holywell Rw SDTCH EC2A 13 J1
Holywell Wy
STWL/WRAY TW19 120 B7
Home Cl CAR SM5 175 K1
NTHLT UB5 83 K2
Home Ct FELT TW13 * 121 K7
SURB KT6 * 158 E4
Homecroft Rd SYD SE26 150 E4
WDGN N22 41 H7
Home Farm Cl ESH/CLAY KT10 170 B5
THDIT KT7 158 A6
Homefarm Rd HNWL W7 84 E5
Homefield Av
GNTH/NBYPK IG2 60 E4
Homefield Cl WLSDN NW10 68 E5
YEAD UB4 83 H3
Homefield Gdns EFNCH N2 53 H2
WIM/MER SW19 162 B1
Homefield Ms BECK BR3 * 151 J7
Homefield Pk SUT SM1 175 F5
Homefield Rd ALP/SUD HA0 67 G3
BMLY BR1 153 G7
BUSH WD23 22 A4
CHSWK W4 106 C3
EDGW HA8 37 F5
WIM/MER SW19 146 C5
WOT/HER KT12 156 E6
Homefield St IS N1 * 7 J6
The Homefield MRDN SM4 * 161 K3
Home Gdns DAGE RM10 80 E2
Homeland Dr BELMT SM2 175 F7
Homelands Dr NRWD SE19 150 A6
Homeleigh Rd PECK SE15 132 A4
Home Md STAN HA7 35 J7
Homemead Rd CROY/NA CR0 163 H5
HAYES BR2 168 E4
Home Park Ct KUT/HW KT1 * 158 E3
Home Park Rd
WIM/MER SW19 146 D3
Home Park Ter KUT/HW KT1 158 E1
Home Park Wk KUT/HW KT1 158 E3
Homer Dr POP/IOD E14 112 D3
Home Rd BTSEA SW11 128 D1
Homer Rd CROY/NA CR0 166 A5
HOM E9 75 G5
Homer Rw CAMTN NW1 9 K3
Homersham Rd KUT/HW KT1 159 H1
Homer St MBLAR W1H 9 K3
Homerton Gv HOM E9 75 F4
Homerton High St HOM E9 75 F4
Homerton Rd HOM E9 75 H4
Homerton Rw HOM E9 74 E4
Homerton Ter HOM E9 74 E5
Homesdale Cl WAN E11 58 E4
Homesdale Rd HAYES BR2 168 B3
ORP BR6 169 K6
Homesfield GLDGN NW11 52 E4
Homestall Rd EDUL SE22 131 K4
Homestead Gdns
ESH/CLAY KT10 170 E4
Homestead Paddock
STHGT/OAK N14 28 B4
Homestead Pk CRICK NW2 69 H2
Homestead Rd BCTR RM8 80 B1
FUL/PGN SW6 107 J6
Homewaters Av SUN TW16 140 D7
Homewillow Cl WCHMH N21 29 H5
Homewood Cl HPTN TW12 141 K5
Homewood Crs CHST BR7 154 E5
Homewood Gdns
SNWD SE25 * 165 F4
Honduras St FSBYE EC1V 6 E9
Honeybourne Rd
KIL/WHAMP NW6 71 F4
Honeybourne Wy
STMC/STPC BR5 169 H7
Honeybrook Rd BAL SW12 129 H6
Honey Cl DAGE RM10 80 E5
Honeyman Cl CRICK NW2 70 B6
Honeypot Cl CDALE/KGS NW9 50 B3
Honeypot La CDALE/KGS NW9 50 B3
STAN HA7 35 K7
Honeysett Rd TOTM N17 56 B1
Honeysuckle Cl STHL UB1 83 J6
Honeysuckle Gdns
CROY/NA CR0 166 A6
Honeywell Rd BTSEA SW11 128 D5
Honeywood Rd ISLW TW7 * 124 B3
WLSDN NW10 87 H1
Honeywood Wk CAR SM5 175 K3
Honister Cl STAN HA7 35 H7
Honister Gdns STAN HA7 35 H6
Honister Pl STAN HA7 35 H7
Honiton Gdns MLHL NW7 38 B6
PECK SE15 * 131 K1
Honiton Rd KIL/WHAMP NW6 88 D1
ROMW/RG RM7 63 F5
WELL DA16 136 A1
Honley Rd CAT SE6 132 E6
Honnor Gdns ISLW TW7 123 J1
Honor Oak Pk FSTH SE23 131 K6
Honor Oak Ri FSTH SE23 131 K5
Honor Oak Rd FSTH SE23 131 K7
Hood Av MORT/ESHN SW14 125 K4
STHGT/OAK N14 28 B5
Hood Cl CROY/NA CR0 164 C7
Hoodcote Gdns WCHMH N21 29 H6
Hood Rd RAIN RM13 81 G7
RYNPK SW20 145 H6
Hooker's Rd WALTH E17 57 F2
Hook Farm Rd HAYES BR2 168 C4
Hooking Gn RYLN/HDSTN HA2 48 B4
Hook La WELL DA16 136 B2
Hook Ri North SURB KT6 172 B2
Hook Ri South CHSGTN KT9 172 B2
Hook Rd CHSGTN KT9 171 K4
HOR/WEW KT19 172 E6
SURB KT6 172 A1
Hooks Hall Dr DAGE RM10 80 E2
Hookstone Wy WFD IG8 45 H6
The Hook BAR EN5 27 H5
Hook Underpass (Kingston
By-Pass) SURB KT6 171 K2
Hook Wk EDGW HA8 36 E5
Hooper Rd CAN/RD E16 94 E5
Hoopers Ms BUSH WD23 22 B7
Hooper's Ms ACT W3 86 E7
Hooper St WCHPL E1 92 C6
Hoop La GLDGN NW11 52 D6
Hop Ct ALP/SUD HA0 * 67 J5
Hope Cl BTFD TW8 105 F4
CHDH RM6 61 K3
IS N1 73 J5
LEE/GVPK SE12 153 F2
SUT SM1 175 G4
Hopedale Rd CHARL SE7 114 A5
Hopefield Av
KIL/WHAMP NW6 88 C1
Hope Gdns ACT W3 105 J1
Hope La ELTH/MOT SE9 154 B2
Hope Pk BMLY BR1 152 D6
Hopes Cl HEST TW5 103 F5
Hope Sq LVPST EC2M 13 J3
Hope St BTSEA SW11 128 C2
Hopewell St CMBW SE5 110 E6
Hopewell Yd CMBW SE5 110 E6
Hop Gdns CHCR WC2N 11 J7
Hopgood St SHB W12 107 F1
Hopkins Cl MUSWH N10 40 A6
Hopkins Ms SRTFD E15 76 D7
Hopkinsons Pl CAMTN NW1 3 M3
Hopkins Rd LEY E10 57 K6
Hopkins St SOHO/CST W1F 10 F5
Hoppers Rd WCHMH N21 41 G1
Hoppett Rd CHING E4 44 C2
Hopping La IS N1 * 73 H5
Hoppingwood Av NWMAL KT3 160 B2
Hoppner Rd YEAD UB4 82 B1
Hop St GNWCH SE10 113 J3
Hopton Gdns NWMAL KT3 160 D5
Hopton Pde
STRHM/NOR SW16 * 148 E4
Hopton Rd STRHM/NOR SW16 148 E4
WOOL/PLUM SE18 115 G2
Hoptons Gdns STHWK SE1 * 12 D8
Hopton St STHWK SE1 12 D7
Hoptree Cl
NFNCH/WDSPK N12 * 39 F3
Hopwood Cl TOOT SW17 147 G2
Hopwood Rd WALW SE17 19 H9
Hopwood Wk HACK E8 * 74 C6
Horace Av ROMW/RG RM7 63 F7
Horace Rd BARK/HLT IG6 60 C2
FSTGT E7 77 F3
KUT/HW KT1 159 G2
Horatio Pl POP/IOD E14 113 F1
Horatio St BETH E2 7 M6
Horatius Wy CROY/NA CR0 177 F5
Horbury Crs NTGHL W11 8 A7
Horbury Ms NTGHL W11 88 D6
Horder Rd FUL/PGN SW6 107 H7
Hordle Prom East PECK SE15 111 G6
Hordle Prom North
PECK SE15 111 G6
Hordle Prom West PECK SE15 111 F6
Horley Rd ELTH/MOT SE9 153 J3
Hormead Rd MV/WKIL W9 88 D3
Hornbeam Cl IL IG1 78 D4
LBTH SE11 18 A5
MLHL NW7 37 H2
NTHLT UB5 65 K4
Hornbeam Crs BTFD TW8 104 C6
Hornbeam Gdns NWMAL KT3 160 D5
Hornbeam Gv CHING E4 44 C2
Hornbeam Rd BKHH IG9 45 H2
YEAD UB4 83 G4
Hornbeam Sq BOW E3 75 H7
Hornbeams Ri
FBAR/BDGN N11 40 A5
Hornbeam Wy HAYES BR2 169 F5
Hornbuckle Cl
RYLN/HDSTN HA2 66 D1
Hornby Cl HAMP NW3 3 H1
Hornchurch Cl KUTN/CMB KT2 143 K4
Hornchurch Rd HCH RM12 63 J7
Horndean Cl PUT/ROE SW15 126 D7
Horne House CHARL SE7 * 114 D6
Horner La MTCM CR4 162 C1
The Hornets WATW WD18 21 F3
Horne Wy PUT/ROE SW15 127 F1
Hornfair Rd CHARL SE7 114 C5
CHARL SE7 114 C6
Hornford Wy ROMW/RG RM7 63 G6
Horniman Dr FSTH SE23 131 J7
Horniman Gdns FSTH SE23 * 131 J7
Horning Cl ELTH/MOT SE9 153 J3
Horn La ACT W3 86 E7
WFD IG8 44 E5
Horn Park Cl LEE/GVPK SE12 134 A4
Horn Park La LEE/GVPK SE12 134 A4
Hornscroft Cl BARK IG11 78 E6
Horns End Pl PIN HA5 47 G3
Hornsey Chambers CLPT E5 * 74 D1
Hornsey La HGT N6 54 C6
Hornsey Lane Est ARCH N19 * 54 D6
Hornsey Lane Gdns HGT N6 54 C6
Hornsey Park Rd
CEND/HSY/T N8 55 F2
Hornsey Ri ARCH N19 54 D6
Hornsey Rise Gdns ARCH N19 54 D6
Hornsey Rd ARCH N19 54 E7
Hornsey St HOLWY N7 73 F4
Hornshay St PECK SE15 111 K5
Horns Rd BARK/HLT IG6 60 C4
Hornton Pl KENS W8 14 B2
Hornton St KENS W8 14 B1
Horsa Rd ERITH DA8 117 K6
LEE/GVPK SE12 134 B6
Horsebridges Cl DAGW RM9 80 A7
Horsecroft Rd EDGW HA8 37 F6
Horse Fair KUT/HW KT1 158 E1
Horseferry Pl GNWCH SE10 113 F5
Horseferry Rd POP/IOD E14 93 G6
WEST SW1P 17 G4
Horse Guards Av WHALL SW1A 11 J9
Horse Guards Rd
WHALL SW1A 11 H9
Horse Leaze EHAM E6 96 B5
Horsell Rd HBRY N5 73 G4
STMC/STPC BR5 155 G7
Horselydown La STHWK SE1 19 L1
Horsenden Av GFD/PVL UB6 66 E4
Horsenden Crs GFD/PVL UB6 67 F4
Horsenden La North
GFD/PVL UB6 66 E5
Horsenden La South
GFD/PVL UB6 67 G7
Horseshoe Cl CRICK NW2 69 K1
POP/IOD E14 113 F4
Horse Shoe Crs NTHLT UB5 84 A1
Horseshoe La ENC/FH EN2 29 J2
TRDG/WHET N20 26 B7
Horseshoe Ms
BRXS/STRHM SW2 129 K3
Horse Yd IS N1 6 D3
Horsfeld Gdns ELTH/MOT SE9 134 D4
Horsfeld Rd ELTH/MOT SE9 134 C4
Horsford Rd
BRXS/STRHM SW2 130 A4
Horsham Av
NFNCH/WDSPK N12 39 J4
Horsham Rd BXLYHS DA6 137 G5
EBED/NFELT TW14 121 F5
Horsley Dr CROY/NA CR0 180 A6
KUTN/CMB KT2 143 K4
Horsley Rd BMLY BR1 153 F7
CHING E4 44 A1
Horsley St WALW SE17 19 G9
Horsmans Pl DART DA1 * 139 H6
Horsman St CMBW SE5 110 D5
Horsmonden Cl ORP BR6 169 K6
Horsmonden Rd BROCKY SE4 132 C4
Hortensia Rd WBPTN SW10 108 B5
Horticultural Pl CHSWK W4 106 A4
Horton Av CRICK NW2 70 C3
Horton La HOR/WEW KT19 172 D7
Horton Rd HACK E8 74 D5
Horton St LEW SE13 132 E2
Horton Wy CROY/NA CR0 166 A4
Hortus Rd NWDGN UB2 102 E1
Hosack Rd TOOT SW17 147 K1
Hosier La STBT EC1A 12 C3
Hoskins Cl HYS/HAR UB3 101 J4
Hoskin's Cl CAN/RD E16 95 G5
Hoskins St GNWCH SE10 113 G4
Hospital Bridge Rd
WHTN TW2 123 F6
Hospital Rd HSLW TW3 123 F2
LEY E10 58 B5
Hospital Wy LEW SE13 133 G5
Hotham Cl E/WMO/HCT KT8 157 F2
Hotham Rd PUT/ROE SW15 127 F2
Hotham Road Ms
WIM/MER SW19 147 G6
Hotham St SRTFD E15 76 C7
Hothfield Pl
BERM/RHTH SE16 111 K2
Hotspur Rd NTHLT UB5 84 A1
Hotspur St LBTH SE11 18 A7
Houblon Rd
RCHPK/HAM TW10 125 F4
Houghton Cl HACK E8 * 74 B5
HPTN TW12 141 J5
Houghton Rd
SEVS/STOTM N15 56 B3
Houghton St LINN WC2A * 11 M5
Houlder Crs CROY/NA CR0 177 H4
Houndsden Rd WCHMH N21 29 F5
Houndsditch HDTCH EC3A 13 K4
Houndsfield Rd ED N9 30 D6
Hounslow Av HSLW TW3 123 G4
Hounslow Gdns HSLW TW3 123 G4
Hounslow Rd
EBED/NFELT TW14 122 A6
Houseman Wy CMBW SE5 110 E6
Houston Rd FSTH SE23 151 G1
SURB KT6 158 C5
Hove Av WALTH E17 57 H4
Hoveden Rd CRICK NW2 70 B4
Hove Gdns SUT SM1 162 A7
Hoveton Rd THMD SE28 97 J5
Howard Av BXLY DA5 136 D7
Howard Cl ACT W3 86 D5
BUSH WD23 22 E6
CRICK NW2 * 70 C3
FBAR/BDGN N11 40 A1
HPTN TW12 142 C6
SUN TW16 140 D5
Howard Dr BORE WD6 25 F3
Howard Rd BARK IG11 78 D7
BMLY BR1 152 E6
CRICK NW2 70 B3
EHAM E6 95 K1
IL IG1 78 B3
ISLW TW7 124 A2
NWMAL KT3 160 B2
PGE/AN SE20 150 E7
SEVS/STOTM N15 56 A5
SNWD SE25 165 H4
STHL UB1 84 B5
STNW/STAM N16 73 K3
SURB KT6 159 G5
WALTH E17 57 J2
WAN E11 76 C2
Howards Cl PIN HA5 * 47 F1
Howards Crest Cl BECK BR3 167 F1
Howard's La PUT/ROE SW15 127 F3
Howard's Rd PLSTW E13 94 E2
Howard St THDIT KT7 158 C6
Howards Yd
WAND/EARL SW18 128 A6
Howard Wk EFNCH N2 53 G3
Howard Wy BAR EN5 26 B4
Howarth Rd ABYW SE2 116 B4
Howberry Cl EDGW HA8 35 K5
Howberry Rd EDGW HA8 35 K5
THHTH CR7 149 K7
Howbury Rd PECK SE15 131 K2
Howcroft Crs FNCH N3 38 E6
Howcroft La GFD/PVL UB6 84 D2
Howden Cl THMD SE28 97 J6
Howden Rd SNWD SE25 165 G1
Howden St PECK SE15 131 H2
Howell Cl CHDH RM6 61 K4
Howell Wk STHWK SE1 18 D6
Howerd Wy
WOOL/PLUM SE18 114 D7
Howes Cl FNCH N3 52 E2
Howfield Pl TOTM N17 * 56 B2
Howgate Rd
MORT/ESHN SW14 126 A2
Howick Pl WESTW SW1E 16 F4
Howie St BTSEA SW11 108 D6
Howitt Cl HAMP NW3 71 J5
Howitt Rd HAMP NW3 71 J5
Howitts Cl ESH/CLAY KT10 170 A5
Howland Ct PIN HA5 * 34 A5
Howland Ms East FITZ W1T 10 F2
Howland St FITZ W1T 10 F2
Howland Wy
BERM/RHTH SE16 112 B1
Howletts La RSLP HA4 46 A5
Howletts Rd HNHL SE24 130 D5
Howley Pl BAY/PAD W2 8 F2
Howley Rd CROY/NA CR0 177 H2
Howsman Rd BARN SW13 106 D5
Howson Rd BROCKY SE4 132 B3
Howson Ter
RCHPK/HAM TW10 * 125 F5
How's St BETH E2 7 L5
Howton Pl BUSH WD23 22 D7
Hoxton Market IS N1 7 J8
Hoxton Sq IS N1 7 J8
Hoxton St IS N1 7 J4
Hoylake Gdns MTCM CR4 163 H2
OXHEY WD19 33 H3
RSLP HA4 47 F7
Hoylake Rd ACT W3 87 G5
Hoyland Cl PECK SE15 * 111 J6
Hoyle Rd TOOT SW17 147 J4
Hoy St CAN/RD E16 94 D5
Hubbard Dr CHSGTN KT9 171 J5
Hubbard Rd WNWD SE27 149 J3
Hubbard St SRTFD E15 76 C7
Hubert Cl WIM/MER SW19 * 147 G7
Hubert Gv BRXN/ST SW9 129 K2
Hubert Rd EHAM E6 95 H2
RAIN RM13 99 H2
Huddart St BOW E3 93 H4
Huddleston Cl BETH E2 * 92 E1
Huddlestone Rd CRICK NW2 69 K5
FSTGT E7 76 D3
Huddleston Rd HOLWY N7 72 C2
Hudson Cl SHB W12 * 87 K6
Hudson Pl WOOL/PLUM SE18 115 H4
Hudson Rd HYS/HAR UB3 101 G5
Huggin Hl BLKFR EC4V 12 F6
Huggins Pl BRXS/STRHM SW2 130 A7
Hughan Rd SRTFD E15 76 B4
Hugh Dalton Av
FUL/PGN SW6 107 J5
Hughenden Av
KTN/HRWW/WS HA3 49 H4
Hughenden Gdns NTHLT UB5 83 G2
Hughenden Rd WPK KT4 160 D6
Hughes Cl NFNCH/WDSPK N12 39 G4
Hughes Rd ASHF TW15 140 A6
HYS/HAR UB3 83 F6
Hughes Ter CAN/RD E16 * 94 D4
Hughes Wk CROY/NA CR0 164 D6
Hugh Gaitskell Cl
FUL/PGN SW6 * 107 J5
Hugh Ms PIM SW1V 16 D6
Hugh Pl WEST SW1P 17 G5
Hugh St PIM SW1V 16 D6
Hugo Cl WATW WD18 20 C3
Hugo Gdns RAIN RM13 81 H5
Hugon Rd FUL/PGN SW6 128 A2
Hugo Rd ARCH N19 72 C3
Huguenot Pl
WAND/EARL SW18 128 B4
WCHPL E1 13 M2
Huitt Sq BTSEA SW11 128 C2
Hullbridge Ms IS N1 7 G3
Hull Cl BERM/RHTH SE16 * 93 F7
Hull St FSBYE EC1V 6 E8
Hulme Pl STHWK SE1 18 F2
Hulse Av BARK IG11 78 E5
Hulverston Cl BELMT SM2 175 F7
Humber Dr NKENS W10 88 B3
Humber Rd CRICK NW2 69 K1
Humberstone Rd PLSTW E13 95 G2
Humbolt Rd HMSMTH W6 107 H5
Humes Av HNWL W7 104 A2
Hume Wy RSLP HA4 46 E5
Humphrey Cl CLAY IG5 * 45 K7
Humphrey St STHWK SE1 19 L7
Humphries Cl DAGW RM9 80 B3
Hundred Acre
CDALE/KGS NW9 51 H1
Hungerford Rd HOLWY N7 72 D5
Hungerford St WCHPL E1 * 92 D5
Hunsdon Cl DAGW RM9 80 A5
Hunsdon Rd NWCR SE14 112 A6
Hunslett St BETH E2 * 92 E1
Hunston Rd MRDN SM4 162 A7
Hunt Cl NTGHL W11 88 B7
Hunter Cl BAL SW12 129 F7
BORE WD6 24 E4
STHWK SE1 19 H4
WLGTN SM6 176 E6
Hunter Ct CMBW SE5 * 130 E3
Huntercrombe Gdns
OXHEY WD19 33 G4
Hunter Rd RYNPK SW20 146 A7
THHTH CR7 164 E2
Hunters Ct RCH/KEW TW9 124 E4
Hunters Gv HYS/HAR UB3 82 E7
KTN/HRWW/WS HA3 49 J3
Hunters Hall Rd DAGE RM10 80 C3
Hunters Hl RSLP HA4 65 G2
Hunters Meadow NRWD SE19 150 A3

Hunters Rd CHSGTN KT9 172 A2
IL IG1 78 B4
Hunters Sq DAGE RM10 80 C3
Hunter St BMSBY WC1N 5 K9
Hunters Wy CROY/NA CR0 178 A3
Hunting Cl ESH/CLAY KT10 170 A3
Huntingdon Cl MTCM CR4 163 K3
NTHLT UB5 66 A5
Huntingdon Gdns CHSWK W4 105 K6
WPK KT4 174 A2
Huntingdon Rd ED N9 30 E7
EFNCH N2 53 J2
Huntingdon St CAN/RD E16 94 D5
IS N1 5 M1
Huntingfield CROY/NA CR0 179 H6
Huntingfield Rd
PUT/ROE SW15 126 D5
Hunting Gate Cl ENC/FH EN2 29 G2
Hunting Gate Dr CHSGTN KT9 172 A6
Hunting Gate Ms WHTN TW2 * 123 K7
Huntings Rd DAGE RM10 80 C5
Huntland Cl RAIN RM13 99 K4
Huntley Cl STWL/WRAY TW19 120 B6
Huntley St GWRST WC1E 10 F1
Huntley Wy RYNPK SW20 * 160 D1
Huntly Dr FNCH N3 38 E5
Huntly Rd SNWD SE25 165 F2
Hunton St WCHPL E1 92 C4
Hunt Rd NWDGN UB2 103 F2
Hunt's La SRTFD E15 94 A1
Huntsman Cl FELT TW13 141 F3
Huntsman St WALW SE17 19 J6
Hunts Md PEND EN3 31 F2
Hunts Medde Cl CHST BR7 153 J6
Huntsmoor Rd
HOR/WEW KT19 173 F4
Huntspill St TOOT SW17 147 G2
Hunts Slip Rd DUL SE21 150 A1
Huntsworth Ms CAMTN NW1 3 L9
Hurdwick Pl CAMTN NW1 * 4 E5
Hurley Crs BERM/RHTH SE16 93 F7
Hurley Rd GFD/PVL UB6 84 B4
Hurlingham Gdns
FUL/PGN SW6 127 J2
Hurlingham Pk
FUL/PGN SW6 * 127 J2
Hurlingham Rd FUL/PGN SW6 127 J1
Hurlingham Sq
FUL/PGN SW6 * 127 K2
Hurlock St HBRY N5 73 H2
Hurlstone Rd SNWD SE25 164 E4
Hurn Court Rd HSLWW TW4 122 C1
Huron Rd TOOT SW17 148 A1
Hurren Cl BKHTH/KID SE3 133 H2
Hurricane House
WOOL/PLUM SE18 * 114 D6
Hurricane Rd WLGTN SM6 176 E6
Hurry Cl SRTFD E15 76 C6
Hurst Av CHING E4 43 J2
HCT N6 54 C5
Hurstbourne ESH/CLAY KT10 171 F5
Hurstbourne Gdns BARK IG11 78 D5
Hurstbourne Rd FSTH SE23 132 B7
Hurst Cl CHING E4 43 J2
CHSGTN KT9 172 C4
GLDGN NW11 53 F5
HAYES BR2 167 J7
NTHLT UB5 65 K5
Hurstcourt Rd SUT SM1 162 A7
Hurstdene Av HAYES BR2 167 J7
Hurstdene Gdns
SEVS/STOTM N15 56 A6
Hurstfield Crs YEAD UB4 82 C4
Hurstfield Rd
E/WMO/HCT KT8 157 F2
Hurst La ABYW SE2 116 E4
E/WMO/HCT KT8 157 H3
Hurstleigh Gdns CLAY IG5 45 K7
Hurst Pl DART DA1 * 139 F5
Hurst Ri BAR EN5 26 E2
Hurst Rd BFN/LL DA15 155 H1
BXLY DA5 137 F7
CROY/NA CR0 177 K4
E/WMO/HCT KT8 157 F2
ERITH DA8 117 K6
WALTH E17 57 K2
WCHMH N21 29 G7
WOT/HER KT12 156 C3
Hurst Springs BXLY DA5 137 F7
Hurst St HNHL SE24 130 C5
Hurst View Rd SAND/SEL CR2 178 A6
Hurst Wy SAND/SEL CR2 178 A5
Hurstway Rd NTGHL W11 * 88 B6
Hurstway Wk NTGHL W11 * 88 B6
Hurstwood Av BXLY DA5 137 F7
SWFD E18 59 F3
Hurstwood Dr BMLY BR1 168 E2
Hurstwood Rd GLDGN NW11 52 C3
Hurtwood Rd WOT/HER KT12 156 E6
Huson Cl HAMP NW3 3 J1
Hussain Cl HRW HA1 67 F3
Hussars Cl HSLWW TW4 122 D2
Hutching's St POP/IOD E14 112 D1
Hutchings Wk GLDGN NW11 53 F3
Hutchins Cl SRTFD E15 76 A6
Hutchinson Ter WBLY HA9 67 K2
Hutchins Rd THMD SE28 97 G6
Hutton Cl GFD/PVL UB6 66 D4
WFD IG8 45 F5
Hutton Gv
NFNCH/WDSPK N12 39 F4
Hutton La
KTN/HRWW/WS HA3 34 C6
Hutton Rw EDGW HA8 36 E6
Hutton St EMB EC4Y 12 B5
Hutton Wk
KTN/HRWW/WS HA3 34 C6
Huxbear St BROCKY SE4 132 C4
Huxley UED N18 * 41 K4
Huxley Cl NTHLT UB5 83 J1
Huxley Dr CHDH RM6 61 H6
Huxley Gdns WLSDN NW10 86 B2
Huxley Pde UED N18 * 41 K4
Huxley Pl PLMGR N13 41 H3
Huxley Rd LEY E10 76 A1
UED N18 41 K3
WELL DA16 136 A2
Huxley Sayze UED N18 * 41 K4
Huxley St NKENS W10 88 C2
Hyacinth Cl HPTN TW12 142 A5
IL IG1 78 B5
Hyacinth Rd PUT/ROE SW15 126 D7
Hyde Cl BAR EN5 26 D2
PLSTW E13 94 E1
Hyde Crs CDALE/KGS NW9 51 G4
Hyde Estate Rd
CDALE/KGS NW9 51 H4
Hyde Farm Ms BAL SW12 129 J7
Hydefield Cl WCHMH N21 29 K7
Hydefield Ct ED N9 42 A1
Hyde Gv DART DA1 139 J1
Hyde La BTSEA SW11 108 D7
Hyde Park Av WCHMH N21 41 J1
Hyde Park Cnr
MYFR/PICC W1J 16 B1
Hyde Park Crs BAY/PAD W2 9 J5
Hyde Park Gdns BAY/PAD W2 9 H6
WCHMH N21 29 J7
Hyde Park Gardens Ms
BAY/PAD W2 9 H6
Hyde Park Ga SKENS SW7 14 E2
Hyde Park Gate Ms
SKENS SW7 * 14 F2
Hyde Park Pl BAY/PAD W2 9 K6
Hyde Park Sq BAY/PAD W2 9 J5
Hyde Park Square Ms
BAY/PAD W2 9 J5
Hyde Park St BAY/PAD W2 9 J6
Hyderabad Wy SRTFD E15 76 C6
Hyde Rd IS N1 7 H4
RCHPK/HAM TW10 125 G4
WAT WD17 20 E2
Hydeside Gdns ED N9 42 B1
Hyde's Pl IS N1 6 C1
Hyde St DEPT SE8 112 D5
Hyde Ter ASHF TW15 140 C5
The Hyde CDALE/KGS NW9 51 G4
Hydethorpe Av ED N9 42 B1
Hydethorpe Rd BAL SW12 129 H7
Hyde V GNWCH SE10 113 F6
Hyde Wk MRDN SM4 161 K6
Hyde Wy ED N9 42 B1
HYS/HAR UB3 101 J3
Hyland Cl EMPK RM11 63 K6
Hylands Rd WALTH E17 58 B1
Hyland Wy EMPK RM11 63 K6
Hylton St WOOL/PLUM SE18 116 A3
Hyndewood FSTH SE23 * 151 F2
Hyndman St PECK SE15 111 J5
Hynton Rd BCTR RM8 79 J1
Hyperion Pl HOR/WEW KT19 173 F7
Hyrstdene SAND/SEL CR2 177 H3
Hyson Rd BERM/RHTH SE16 111 J4
Hythe Cl UED N18 42 C3
Hythe Rd THHTH CR7 164 E1
WLSDN NW10 87 H2
Hyver Hl BAR EN5 25 F5

I

Ibbotson Av CAN/RD E16 94 D5
Ibbott St WCHPL E1 92 E3
Iberian Av WLGTN SM6 176 D3
Ibis La CHSWK W4 105 K7
Ibis Wy YEAD UB4 83 H5
Ibscott Cl DAGE RM10 80 E5
Ibsley Gdns PUT/ROE SW15 126 D7
Ibsley Wy EBAR EN4 27 J4
Iceland Rd BOW E3 75 J7
Ickburgh Est CLPT E5 * 74 D1
Ickburgh Rd CLPT E5 74 D2
Ickenham Cl RSLP HA4 64 B1
Ickenham Rd RSLP HA4 46 B7
Ickleton Rd ELTH/MOT SE9 153 J3
Icknield Dr GNTH/NBYPK IG2 60 B4
Ickworth Park Rd WALTH E17 57 G3
Ida Rd SEVS/STOTM N15 55 K4
Ida St POP/IOD E14 94 A5
Iden Cl HAYES BR2 167 H2
Idlecombe Rd TOOT SW17 148 A5
Idmiston Rd SRTFD E15 76 D4
WNWD SE27 149 J2
WPK KT4 160 C6
Idmiston Sq WPK KT4 160 C6
Idol La MON EC3R 13 J7
Idonia St DEPT SE8 112 C6
Iffley Rd HMSMTH W6 106 E2
Ifield Rd WBPTN SW10 14 D9
Ilbert St NKENS W10 88 C2
Ilchester Gdns BAY/PAD W2 8 C6
Ilchester Pl WKENS W14 107 J2
Ilchester Rd BCTR RM8 79 H4
Ildersly Gv DUL SE21 149 K1
Ilderton Rd PECK SE15 111 K5
Ilex Cl SUN TW16 156 B1
Ilex Rd WLSDN NW10 69 H5
Ilex Wy STRHM/NOR SW16 149 G4
Ilford Hl MNPK E12 77 K3
Ilford La IL IG1 78 B3
Ilfracombe Gdns CHDH RM6 61 H6
Ilfracombe Rd BMLY BR1 152 D2
Iliffe St WALW SE17 18 D7
Iliffe Yd WALW SE17 18 D7
Ilkley Cl NRWD SE19 * 149 K5
Ilkley Ct FBAR/BDGN N11 40 A5
Ilkley Rd CAN/RD E16 95 G4
OXHEY WD19 33 H4
Illingworth Wy EN EN1 30 A4
Ilmington Rd
KTN/HRWW/WS HA3 49 K5
Ilminster Gdns BTSEA SW11 128 D3
Imber Cl STHGT/OAK N14 28 C6
Imber Cross THDIT KT7 * 158 A6
Imber Gv ESH/CLAY KT10 157 J6
Imber Park Rd ESH/CLAY KT10 157 J7
Imber St IS N1 7 G4
Imperial Av STNW/STAM N16 * 74 A3
Imperial Cl CRICK NW2 69 K4
RYLN/HDSTN HA2 48 A5
Imperial College Rd
SKENS SW7 15 G4
Imperial Crs FUL/PGN SW6 128 B1
Imperial Dr RYLN/HDSTN HA2 48 A6
Imperial Gdns MTCM CR4 163 G2
Imperial Ms EHAM E6 95 H1
Imperial Pl BORE WD6 * 24 D2
CHST BR7 154 A7
Imperial Rd
EBED/NFELT TW14 121 H6
FUL/PGN SW6 108 A7
WDGN N22 40 E6
Imperial Sq FUL/PGN SW6 108 A7
Imperial St BOW E3 94 A2
Imperial Wy CHST BR7 154 C2
CROY/NA CR0 177 F5
KTN/HRWW/WS HA3 50 A5
Imre Cl SHB W12 87 K7
Inca Dr ELTH/MOT SE9 135 G6
Inchmery Rd CAT SE6 151 K1
Inchwood CROY/NA CR0 179 K3
Independent Pl HACK E8 74 B4
Independents Rd
BKHTH/KID SE3 133 J2
Inderwick Rd CEND/HSY/T N8 55 F5
Indescon Ct POP/IOD E14 112 E1
India St TWRH EC3N 13 L5
India Wy SHB W12 87 K6
Indigo Ms POP/IOD E14 * 94 A6
STNW/STAM N16 73 K2
Indus Rd CHARL SE7 114 B6
Infant House
WOOL/PLUM SE18 * 114 D6
Ingal Rd PLSTW E13 94 E3
Ingate Pl VX/NE SW8 109 G7
Ingatestone Rd MNPK E12 59 G7
SNWD SE25 165 J4
WFD IG8 45 F6
Ingelow Rd VX/NE SW8 129 G1
Ingersoll Rd SHB W12 87 K7
Ingestre Pl SOHO/CST W1F 10 F5
Ingestre Rd FSTGT E7 76 E3
KTTN NW5 72 B3
Ingham Cl SAND/SEL CR2 179 F7
Ingham Rd KIL/WHAMP NW6 70 E3
SAND/SEL CR2 178 E7
Inglebert St CLKNW EC1R 6 A7
Ingleborough St
BRXN/ST SW9 130 B1
Ingleby Dr HRW HA1 66 D2
Ingleby Rd DAGE RM10 80 D5
HOLWY N7 72 E2
IL IG1 60 B7
Ingleby Wy CHST BR7 154 A4
WLGTN SM6 176 D7
Ingle Cl PIN HA5 47 K2
Ingledew Rd
WOOL/PLUM SE18 115 J4
Inglefield Sq WAP E1W * 92 D7
Inglehurst Gdns REDBR IG4 59 K4
Inglemere Rd FSTH SE23 151 F2
TOOT SW17 147 K6
Ingleside Cl BECK BR3 151 J6
Ingleside Gv BKHTH/KID SE3 113 J5
Inglethorpe St FUL/PGN SW6 107 G7
Ingleton Av WELL DA16 136 B4
Ingleton Rd CAR SM5 175 J7
UED N18 42 C5
Ingleton St BRXN/ST SW9 130 B1
Ingleway NFNCH/WDSPK N12 39 H5
Inglewood CROY/NA CR0 179 G7
Inglewood Cl POP/IOD E14 112 D3
Inglewood Copse BMLY BR1 168 D1
Inglewood Ms SURB KT6 159 H7
Inglewood Rd BXLYHN DA7 138 A3
KIL/WHAMP NW6 70 E4
Inglis Rd CROY/NA CR0 165 G7
EA W5 86 B6
Inglis St CMBW SE5 110 C7
Ingram Av GLDGN NW11 53 G6
Ingram Cl LBTH SE11 17 M5
STAN HA7 35 J4
Ingram Rd EFNCH N2 53 J3
THHTH CR7 149 J7
Ingram Wy GFD/PVL UB6 66 D7
Ingrave Rd ROM RM1 63 F3
Ingrave St BTSEA SW11 128 C2
Ingrebourne Rd RAIN RM13 99 K3
Ingress St CHSWK W4 106 B4
Inigo Jones Rd CHARL SE7 114 C6
Inkerman Rd KTTN NW5 72 B5
Inks Gn CHING E4 44 A4
Inkwell Cl NFNCH/WDSPK N12 39 G2
Inman Rd WAND/EARL SW18 128 B6
WLSDN NW10 69 G7
Inmans Rw WFD IG8 44 E3
Inner Cir CAMTN NW1 4 A8
Inner Park Rd
WIM/MER SW19 146 B1
Inner Ring East HTHAIR TW6 120 E2
Innes Cl RYNPK SW20 161 H1
Innes Gdns PUT/ROE SW15 126 E5
Innes St PECK SE15 111 F6
Innes Yd CROY/NA CR0 177 J2
Inniskilling Rd PLSTW E13 95 G1
Innovation Cl ALP/SUD HA0 68 A7
Inskip Cl LEY E10 75 K1
Inskip Rd BCTR RM8 61 K7
Institute Pl HACK E8 74 D4
Integer Gdns WAN E11 * 58 B6
International Av HEST TW5 102 B4
International Wy SUN TW16 140 C7
Inver Ct BAY/PAD W2 8 D5
Inveresk Gdns WPK KT4 173 H2
Inverforth Cl HAMP NW3 71 G1
Inverforth Rd
FBAR/BDGN N11 40 B4
Inverine Rd CHARL SE7 114 A4
Invermore Pl
WOOL/PLUM SE18 115 H3
Inverness Gdns KENS W8 8 C9
Inverness Ms BAY/PAD W2 8 D6
Inverness Pl BAY/PAD W2 8 D6
Inverness Rd HSLW TW3 122 E3
NWDGN UB2 102 D3
UED N18 42 D4
WPK KT4 161 G7
Inverness St CAMTN NW1 4 C3
Inverness Ter BAY/PAD W2 8 D7
WDGN N22 * 41 H7
Inverton Rd PECK SE15 132 A3
Invicta Cl CHST BR7 154 A4
EBED/NFELT TW14 121 J7
Invicta Gv NTHLT UB5 83 K2
Invicta Pde SCUP DA14 * 155 H3
Invicta Plaza STHWK SE1 12 C8
Inville Rd WALW SE17 19 H8
Inwood Av HSLW TW3 123 H2
Inwood Cl CROY/NA CR0 179 G1
Inwood Rd HSLW TW3 123 H3
Inworth St BTSEA SW11 128 D1
Inworth Wk IS N1 * 6 E3
Iona Cl CAT SE6 132 D6
MRDN SM4 162 A6
Ion Sq BETH E2 * 92 C1
Ipswich Rd TOOT SW17 148 A5
Ireland Cl EHAM E6 95 K4
Ireland Pl WDGN N22 40 E6
Irene Ms HNWL W7 * 85 F7
Irene Rd FUL/PGN SW6 107 K7
Ireton Cl MUSWH N10 40 A6
Ireton St BOW E3 93 J3
Iris Av BXLY DA5 137 F5
Iris Cl CROY/NA CR0 166 A7
EHAM E6 95 J4
SURB KT6 * 159 G6
Iris Crs BXLYHN DA7 117 G5
Iris Rd HOR/WEW KT19 172 D4
Iris Wy CHING E4 43 H5
Iron Bridge Cl NWDGN UB2 84 C7
WLSDN NW10 69 G4
Iron Bridge Rd South
WDR/YW UB7 100 D1
Iron Mill Pl
WAND/EARL SW18 * 128 A5
Iron Mill Rd WAND/EARL SW18 128 A5
Ironmonger La CITYW EC2V 13 G5
Ironmonger Rw FSBYE EC1V 6 F8
Ironmongers Pl POP/IOD E14 112 D3
Ironside Cl BERM/RHTH SE16 112 A1
Irvine Av KTN/HRWW/WS HA3 49 G2
Irvine Cl POP/IOD E14 93 K4
TRDG/WHET N20 39 J1
Irving Av NTHLT UB5 65 H7
Irving Gv BRXN/ST SW9 130 A1
Irving Ms IS N1 73 J5
Irving Rd WKENS W14 107 G2
Irving St LSQ/SEVD WC2H 11 H7
Irving Wy CDALE/KGS NW9 51 H4
Irwell Est BERM/RHTH SE16 * 111 K1
Irwin Av WOOL/PLUM SE18 115 K6
Irwin Gdns WLSDN NW10 69 K7
Isaac Wy STHWK SE1 18 F1
Isabella Cl STHGT/OAK N14 28 C6
Isabella Ct
RCHPK/HAM TW10 * 125 G5
Isabella Ms IS N1 * 74 A5
Isabella Pl KUTN/CMB KT2 144 B4
Isabella Rd HOM E9 * 74 E4
Isabella St STHWK SE1 12 C9
Isabel St BRXN/ST SW9 110 A7
Isambard Ms POP/IOD E14 113 F2
Isambard Pl
BERM/RHTH SE16 92 E7
Isham Rd STRHM/NOR SW16 163 K1
Isis Cl PUT/ROE SW15 127 F3
RSLP HA4 46 A5
Isis St WAND/EARL SW18 147 G1
Island Farm Av
E/WMO/HCT KT8 156 E4
Island Farm Rd
E/WMO/HCT KT8 156 E4
Island Rd BERM/RHTH SE16 112 A3
MTCM CR4 147 K6
Island Rw POP/IOD E14 93 H5
Isla Rd WOOL/PLUM SE18 115 H5
Islay Gdns HSLWW TW4 122 C4
Islay Wk IS N1 * 73 J5
Islay Whf POP/IOD E14 * 94 A4
Isledon Rd HOLWY N7 73 G2
Islehurst Cl CHST BR7 154 A7
Islington Gn IS N1 6 C4
Islington High St IS N1 6 C5
Islington Park Ms IS N1 6 C1
Islington Park St IS N1 6 B1
Islip Gdns EDGW HA8 37 F5
NTHLT UB5 65 J6
Islip Manor Rd NTHLT UB5 65 J6
Islip St KTTN NW5 72 C4
Ismailia Rd FSTGT E7 77 F6
Isom Cl PLSTW E13 95 F2
Issa Rd HSLW TW3 122 E3
Ivanhoe Dr
KTN/HRWW/WS HA3 49 H1
Ivanhoe Rd CMBW SE5 131 G2
HSLWW TW4 122 C2
Ivatt Pl WKENS W14 107 J4
Ivatt Wy SEVS/STOTM N15 55 H2
Iveagh Av WLSDN NW10 86 C1
Iveagh Cl HOM E9 75 F7
WLSDN NW10 86 C1
Ivedon Rd WELL DA16 136 D1
Ive Farm Cl LEY E10 75 J1
Ive Farm La LEY E10 75 J1
Iveley Rd CLAP SW4 129 H1
Ivere Dr BAR EN5 27 F5
Iverhurst Cl BXLYHS DA6 136 E4
Iverna Ct KENS W8 14 B3
Iverna Gdns
EBED/NFELT TW14 121 G4
KENS W8 14 B3
Iverson Rd KIL/WHAMP NW6 70 D5
Ivers Wy CROY/NA CR0 179 K6
Ives Gdns ROM RM1 63 H3
Ives Rd CAN/RD E16 94 C4
Ives St CHEL SW3 15 K5
Ivimey St BETH E2 * 92 C2
Ivinghoe Cl EN EN1 30 A1
Ivinghoe Rd BCTR RM8 79 H4
BUSH WD23 22 D5
Ivor Gv ELTH/MOT SE9 135 G7
Ivor Pl CAMTN NW1 9 L1
Ivor St CAMTN NW1 4 E2
Ivory Ct FELT TW13 121 K7
Ivybridge Cl TWK TW1 124 B5
Ivychurch Cl PGE/AN SE20 150 D6
Ivy Church La WALW SE17 * 19 L7
Ivy Cl PIN HA5 47 G6
RYLN/HDSTN HA2 65 K3
SUN TW16 156 B1
Ivy Ct BERM/RHTH SE16 * 111 H4
Ivy Crs CHSWK W4 105 K3
Ivydale Rd CAR SM5 175 K1
PECK SE15 132 A4
Ivyday Gv STRHM/NOR SW16 149 F2
Ivydene E/WMO/HCT KT8 156 E4
Ivydene Cl SUT SM1 175 G3
Ivy Gdns CEND/HSY/T N8 54 E5
MTCM CR4 163 J2
Ivyhouse Rd DAGW RM9 79 K5
Ivy La HSLWW TW4 122 E3
Ivymount Rd WNWD SE27 149 G2
Ivy Rd BROCKY SE4 132 C3
CAN/RD E16 94 E5
CRICK NW2 70 A3
HSLW TW3 123 G3
STHGT/OAK N14 28 C6
SURB KT6 * 172 C1
TOOT SW17 147 J4
WALTH E17 57 J5
Ivy St IS N1 7 J5
Ivy Wk DAGW RM9 80 A5
NTHWD HA6 * 32 C7
Ixworth Pl CHEL SW3 15 J6

J

Jacaranda Cl NWMAL KT3 160 B2
Jacaranda Gv HACK E8 7 M1
Jackass La HAYES BR2 181 F5
Jack Clow Rd SRTFD E15 94 C1
Jack Cornwell St MNPK E12 78 A3
Jack Dash Wy EHAM E6 95 J3
Jack Jones Wy DAGW RM9 80 B7
Jackman Ms WLSDN NW10 69 G2
Jackman St HACK E8 74 D7
Jackson Cl HOM E9 75 F6
Jackson Rd BARK IG11 78 D7
EBAR EN4 27 H5
HAYES BR2 181 J1
HOLWY N7 73 F3
Jackson's La HGT N6 54 A6
Jackson's Pl CROY/NA CR0 164 E7
Jackson St WOOL/PLUM SE18 115 F5
Jackson's Wy CROY/NA CR0 179 J2
Jackson Wy HOR/WEW KT19 172 C7
NWDGN UB2 103 G1
Jack Walker Ct HBRY N5 73 H3
Jacobs Cl DAGE RM10 80 D3
Jacob St STHWK SE1 19 M1
Jacob's Well Ms MHST W1U 10 B4
Jacqueline Cl NTHLT UB5 65 J7
Jacqueline Creft Ter HGT N6 * 54 A5
Jacqueline Vls WALTH E17 * 58 A4
Jade Cl BCTR RM8 61 J7
CAN/RD E16 95 H5
CRICK NW2 52 B6
Jade Ter KIL/WHAMP NW6 * 2 F1
Jaffe Rd IL IG1 60 C7
Jaffray Rd HAYES BR2 168 C3
Jaggard Wy BAL SW12 128 E6
Jago Cl WOOL/PLUM SE18 115 H5
Jago Wk CMBW SE5 110 E6
Jamaica Rd STHWK SE1 19 M2
THHTH CR7 164 C5
Jamaica St WCHPL E1 92 E4
James Av BCTR RM8 62 B7
CRICK NW2 70 A4
James Bedford Cl PIN HA5 47 G1
James Cl BUSH WD23 21 J4
GLDGN NW11 * 52 C5
GPK RM2 63 J4
PLSTW E13 94 E1
James Collins Cl MV/WKIL W9 88 D3
James Gdns TOTM N17 41 J6
James Joyce Wk
BRXN/ST SW9 130 C3
James La WAN E11 58 A6
Jameson St KENS W8 8 B8
James Pl TOTM N17 42 B6
James St BARK IG11 78 C6
COVGDN WC2E 11 K6
EN EN1 30 B4
HSLW TW3 123 J2
MHST W1U 10 B5
Jamestown Rd CAMTN NW1 4 C3
Jamestown Wy POP/IOD E14 94 B6
James Voller Wy WCHPL E1 92 E5
James Wy OXHEY WD19 33 H3
James Yd CHING E4 * 44 B5
Jamuna Cl POP/IOD E14 93 G4
Jane St WCHPL E1 92 D5
Janet St POP/IOD E14 112 D2
Janeway Pl BERM/RHTH SE16 111 J1
Janeway St BERM/RHTH SE16 111 H1
Janson Cl SRTFD E15 76 C4
WLSDN NW10 69 F2
Janson Rd SRTFD E15 76 C4
Jansons Rd SEVS/STOTM N15 56 A2
Japan Crs FSBYPK N4 55 F7
Japan Rd CHDH RM6 61 K5
Jardine Rd WAP E1W 93 F6
Jarrett Cl BRXS/STRHM SW2 130 C7
Jarrow Cl MRDN SM4 162 A4
Jarrow Rd BERM/RHTH SE16 111 K3
CHDH RM6 61 J5
TOTM N17 56 D3
Jarrow Wy HOM E9 75 H3
Jarvis Cl BAR EN5 26 B4
BARK IG11 78 D7
Jarvis Rd EDUL SE22 131 F3
SAND/SEL CR2 177 K5
Jasmin Cl NTHWD HA6 32 D7
Jasmine Cl IL IG1 78 B4
STHL UB1 83 J6
Jasmine Gdns CROY/NA CR0 179 K2
RYLN/HDSTN HA2 66 A1
Jasmine Gv PGE/AN SE20 150 D7
Jasmine Rd HOR/WEW KT19 172 D5
ROMW/RG RM7 81 G1
Jasmine Ter WDR/YW UB7 100 D1
Jasmin Rd HOR/WEW KT19 172 D4
Jason Wk ELTH/MOT SE9 154 A3
Jasper Rd CAN/RD E16 95 H5
NRWD SE19 150 B5
Javelin Wy NTHLT UB5 83 H2
Jay Gdns CHST BR7 153 K3
Jay Ms SKENS SW7 14 F2
Jean Batten Cl WLGTN SM6 177 F6
Jebb Av BRXS/STRHM SW2 129 K5
Jebb St BOW E3 93 J1
Jedburgh Rd PLSTW E13 95 G2
Jedburgh St BTSEA SW11 129 F3
Jeddo Ms SHB W12 106 C1
Jeddo Rd SHB W12 106 C1
Jefferson Cl GNTH/NBYPK IG2 60 B4
WEA W13 104 C2
Jeffrey's Pl CAMTN NW1 4 E1
Jeffreys Rd CLAP SW4 129 K1
PEND EN3 31 H3
Jeffrey's St CAMTN NW1 4 D1
Jeffs Cl HPTN TW12 * 142 B5
Jeffs Rd SUT SM1 174 D3
Jeger Av BETH E2 7 L4
Jeken Rd ELTH/MOT SE9 134 B3
Jelf Rd BRXS/STRHM SW2 130 B4
Jellicoe Gdns STAN HA7 35 F5
Jellicoe Rd TOTM N17 41 K6
WATW WD18 20 E5
Jemmett Cl KUTN/CMB KT2 144 D7
Jem Paterson Ct HRW HA1 * 66 E3
Jengar Cl SUT SM1 175 F3
Jenkins La BARK IG11 96 B1
Jenkins Rd PLSTW E13 95 F3
Jenner Av ACT W3 87 F4
Jenner Cl SCUP DA14 155 G3
Jenner Pl BARN SW13 106 E5
Jenner Rd STNW/STAM N16 74 B1
Jenner Wy HOR/WEW KT19 172 C7
Jennett Rd CROY/NA CR0 177 G2
Jennifer Rd BMLY BR1 152 D2
Jennings Cl SURB KT6 158 D6
Jennings Rd EDUL SE22 131 G5
Jennings Wy BAR EN5 26 A2
Jenningtree Rd ERITH DA8 118 E6
Jenningtree Wy BELV DA17 117 K1
Jenny Hammond Cl WAN E11 76 D2
Jenson Wy NRWD SE19 150 B6
Jephson Rd FSTGT E7 77 G6
Jephson St CMBW SE5 110 E7
Jephtha Rd WAND/EARL SW18 127 K5
Jeppo's La MTCM CR4 162 E3
Jerdan Pl FUL/PGN SW6 107 K6
Jeremiah St POP/IOD E14 93 K5
Jeremy's Gn UED N18 42 D3
Jermyn St STJS SW1Y 10 E8
Jerningham Av CLAY IG5 60 B1
Jerningham Rd NWCR SE14 132 B1
Jerome St WCHPL E1 13 L2
Jerrard St LEW SE13 132 E2
Jerrold St IS N1 * 7 K6
Jersey Av
KTN/HRWW/WS HA3 49 H1
Jersey Dr STMC/STPC BR5 169 J5
Jersey Rd CAN/RD E16 95 G4
HEST TW5 103 G6
HNWL W7 104 B1
HSLW TW3 103 G7
IL IG1 78 B3
ISLW TW7 103 H6
LEY E10 58 B7
RAIN RM13 81 J6
TOOT SW17 148 B6
Jersey St BETH E2 92 D2
Jersey Vls HNWL W7 * 103 K1
Jerusalem Pas CLKNW EC1R 12 C1
Jerviston Gdns
STRHM/NOR SW16 149 G5
Jervois House
WOOL/PLUM SE18 * 114 D6
Jesmond Av WBLY HA9 68 B5
Jesmond Cl MTCM CR4 163 G2

Jes - Kes 221

Street	Map Ref
Jesmond Dene *HAMP* NW3 *	71 G5
Jesmond Rd *CROY/NA* CR0	165 G1
Jesmond Wy *STAN* HA7	36 A4
Jessam Av *CLPT* E5	56 C7
Jessamine Rd *HNWL* W7	66 A7
Jesse Rd *LEY* E10	58 H1
Jessica Rd *WAND/EARL* SW18	128 B5
Jessop Av *NWDGN* UB2	102 E4
Jessop Rd *POP/IOD* E14 *	93 J3
Jessops Wy *CROY/NA* CR0	163 H5
Jessup Cl *WOOL/PLUM* SE18	115 H3
Jetstar Wy *NTHLT* UB5	83 J2
Jevington Wy *LEE/GVPK* SE12	134 B7
Jewel Rd *WALTH* E17	57 J3
Jewry St *TWRH* EC3N	13 L5
Jews Rw *WAND/EARL* SW18	128 B3
Jews Wk *SYD* SE26	150 D3
Jeymer Av *WLSDN* NW10	69 K4
Jeymer Dr *GFD/PVL* UB6	66 E7
Jeypore Rd *WAND/EARL* SW18	128 B6
Jillian Cl *HPTN* TW12	142 E7
Jim Bradley Cl	
WOOL/PLUM SE18	115 F3
Joan Crs *ELTH/MOT* SE9	134 C6
Joan Gdns *BCTR* RM8	80 A1
Joan Rd *BCTR* RM8	80 A1
Joan St *STHWK* SE1	12 C9
Jocelyn Rd *RCH/KEW* TW9	125 F2
Jocelyn St *PECK* SE15	111 H7
Jockey's Flds *FSBYW* WC1X	11 M2
Jodane St *DEPT* SE8	112 C3
Jodrell Cl *ISLW* TW7	104 B7
Jodrell Rd *BOW* E3	75 H7
Joel St *NTHWD* HA6	46 B1
Johanna St *STHWK* SE1 *	18 A3
John Adam St *CHCR* WC2N	11 K8
John Aird Ct *BAY/PAD* W2	8 F2
John Archer Wy	
WAND/EARL SW18	128 C5
John Ashby Cl	
BRXS/STRHM SW2	129 K5
John Austin Cl *KUTN/CMB* KT2 *	144 B7
John Bradshaw Rd	
STHGT/OAK N14	28 D7
John Burns Dr *BARK* IG11	78 E7
John Campbell Rd	
STNW/STAM N16	74 A4
John Carpenter St *EMB* EC4Y	12 B6
John Felton Rd	
BERM/RHTH SE16	111 H1
John Fisher St *WCHPL* E1	92 C6
John Goodchild Wy	
KUT/HW KT1	159 J2
John Harrison Wy	
BERM/RHTH SE16	112 A1
John Islip St *WEST* SW1P	17 H7
John Lamb Ct	
KTN/HRWW/WS HA3	34 E1
John Maurice Cl *WALW* SE17	19 G5
John McKenna Wk	
BERM/RHTH SE16	111 H2
John Parker Sq *BTSEA* SW11 *	128 C2
John Penn St *LEW* SE13	112 F7
John Perrin Pl	
KTN/HRWW/WS HA3	50 A6
John Prince's St	
CAVSQ/HST W1G	10 D4
John Rennie Wk *WAP* E1W *	92 D6
John Roll Wy	
BERM/RHTH SE16	111 H2
John Ruskin St *CMBW* SE5	110 C6
John's Av *HDN* NW4	52 A3
John's Cl *ASHF* TW15	140 A3
John Silkin La *DEPT* SE8	112 A4
Johns La *MRDN* SM4	162 B4
John's Ms *BMSBY* WC1N	11 M1
John Smith Av *FUL/PGN* SW6 *	107 J6
John Smith Ms *POP/IOD* E14 *	94 B6
Johnson Cl *HACK* E8	74 C7
Johnson Rd *CROY/NA* CR0	164 E6
HAYES BR2	168 C4
HEST TW5	102 B7
WLSDN NW10	69 F7
Johnson's Cl *CAR* SM5	175 K2
Johnson's Ct	
FLST/FETLN EC4A	12 B5
Johnsons Dr *HPTN* TW12	142 C7
Johnson's Pl *PIM* SW1V	16 F8
Johnson St *NWDGN* UB2	102 B2
WCHPL E1	92 E5
Johnsons Wy *WLSDN* NW10	86 D3
John Spencer Sq *IS* N1 *	73 H5
John's Pl *WCHPL* E1	92 D5
John's Ter *CROY/NA* CR0	164 E6
Johnston Cl *BRXN/ST* SW9	110 A7
Johnstone Rd *EHAM* E6 *	95 K2
Johnstone Ter *CRICK* NW2	70 B2
Johnston Rd *WFD* IG8	44 E4
John St *BMSBY* WC1N	11 M1
EN EN1	30 B4
HSLW TW3	122 D1
SNWD SE25	165 H3
SRTFD E15	76 D7
John Trundle Highwalk	
BARB EC2Y *	12 E2
John Watkin Cl	
HOR/WEW KT19	172 D7
John Wesley Cl *EHAM* E6 *	95 K2
John William Cl	
KUTN/CMB KT2 *	144 A7
John Williams Cl *NWCR* SE14	112 A5
John Wilson St	
WOOL/PLUM SE18	115 F3
John Woolley Cl *LEW* SE13 *	133 H3
Joiners Arms Yd *CMBW* SE5 *	110 E7
Joiner St *STHWK* SE1	13 H9
Jollys La *YEAD* UB4	83 H4
Jonathan St *LBTH* SE11	17 L7
Jones Rd *PLSTW* E13	95 F3
Jonson Cl *MTCM* CR4	163 G3
YEAD UB4	82 E4
Jordan Cl *RYLN/HDSTN* HA2	65 K2
Jordan Rd *GFD/PVL* UB6	67 H7
Jordans Cl *DAGE* RM10	80 D3
Jordans Ms *WHTN* TW2	142 E1
Joseph Av *ACT* W3	87 F5
Joseph Hardcastle Cl	
NWCR SE14	112 A6
Josephine Av	
BRXS/STRHM SW2	130 A4
Joseph Locke Wy	
ESH/CLAY KT10	170 A1
Joseph Powell Cl *BAL* SW12 *	129 H5
Joseph Ray Rd *WAN* E11	76 C1
Joseph St *BOW* E3	93 H4
Joseph Trotter Cl	
CLKNW EC1R	6 B8
Joshua Cl *MUSWH* N10	40 A4
SAND/SEL CR2	177 H6
Joshua St *POP/IOD* E14	94 A5
Joslings Cl *SHB* W12	87 H6
Joubert St *BTSEA* SW11	128 E1
Jowett St *PECK* SE15	111 G6

Street	Map Ref
Joyce Av *UED* N18	42 B4
Joyce Green La *DART* DA1	139 J3
Joydon Dr *CHDH* RM6	61 H5
Joyners Cl *DAGW* RM9	80 B3
Jubilee Av *BETH* E2	44 A5
ROMW/RG RM7	62 E4
WHTN TW2	123 H7
Jubilee Cl *CDALE/KGS* NW9	51 F5
KUT/HW KT1 *	143 J7
ROMW/RG RM7	62 D4
WLSDN NW10	69 H7
Jubilee Crs *ED* N9	30 C7
Jubilee Dr *RSLP* HA4	65 H3
Jubilee Gdns *STHL* UB1	84 A4
STHWK SE1 *	11 M9
Jubilee Pl *CHEL* SW3	15 K7
Jubilee Pde *CHEAM* SM3	174 B6
GFD/PVL UB6	67 H7
Jubilee St *WCHPL* E1	92 E5
Jubilee Ter *FUL/PGN* SW6 *	127 H1
The Jubilee *GNWCH* SE10 *	112 E6
Jubilee Vls *ESH/CLAY* KT10 *	157 K7
Jubilee Wy *CHSGTN* KT9	172 E3
EBED/NFELT TW14	121 J7
SCUP DA14	155 G2
WIM/MER SW19	147 F7
Judd St *STPAN* WC1H	5 J8
Jude St *CAN/RD* E16	94 D5
Judge Heath La *HYS/HAR* UB3	82 A5
Judges' Wk *HAMP* NW3	71 G2
Judge Wk *ESH/CLAY* KT10	170 E5
Juer St *BTSEA* SW11	108 D6
Jules Thorn Av *EN* EN1	30 C2
Julia Gdns *BARK* IG11	97 K1
Juliana Cl *EFNCH* N2	53 G2
Julian Av *ACT* W3	86 D6
Julian Cl *BAR* EN5	27 F2
Julian Hl *HRW* HA1	66 E1
Julian Pl *POP/IOD* E14	112 E4
Julian Tayler Pth *FSTH* SE23 *	150 F1
Julien Rd *EA* W5	104 D2
Juliette Rd *PLSTW* E13	94 E1
Juliette Wy *RAIN* RM15	119 J1
Julius Caesar Wy *STAN* HA7	35 J2
Julius Nyerere Cl *IS* N1	5 M4
Junction Ap *BTSEA* SW11	128 E2
LEW SE13	133 F2
Junction Ms *BAY/PAD* W2	9 J4
Junction Pl *BAY/PAD* W2 *	9 H4
Junction Rd *ARCH* N19	72 C3
ASHF TW15	140 A4
EA W5	104 D3
ED N9	30 C7
HRW HA1	48 D5
PLSTW E13	77 F7
ROM RM1	63 H3
SAND/SEL CR2	177 K5
TOTM N17	56 C2
Junction Rd East *CHDH* RM6	62 A6
Junction Rd West *CHDH* RM6	61 K6
Juniper Cl *BAR* EN5	26 A4
CHSGTN KT9	172 B5
WBLY HA9	68 B4
Juniper Crs *CAMTN* NW1	4 B2
Juniper Ct *CHDH* RM6	61 H5
KTN/HRWW/WS HA3 *	49 F1
NTHWD HA6 *	32 E7
Juniper Crs *CAMTN* NW1	4 B2
Juniper Dr *WAND/EARL* SW18	128 B3
Juniper Gdns *MTCM* CR4	148 C7
SUN TW16	140 D5
Juniper La *EHAM* E6	95 J4
Juniper Rd *IL* IG1	78 B3
Juniper St *WCHPL* E1	92 E6
Juniper Wy *HYS/HAR* UB3	82 B5
Juno Wy *NWCR* SE14	112 A5
Jupiter Wy *HOLWY* N7	73 F5
Jupp Rd *SRTFD* E15	76 B6
Jupp Rd West *SRTFD* E15	76 B7
Justice Wk *CHEL* SW3	108 C6
Justin Cl *BTFD* TW8	104 E6
Justin Rd *CHING* E4	43 H5
Jute La *PEND* EN3	31 G1
Jutland Cl *ARCH* N19	54 E7
Jutland Rd *CAT* SE6	133 F6
PLSTW E13	94 E3
Jutsums Av *ROMW/RG* RM7	62 D5
Jutsums La *ROMW/RG* RM7	62 D5
Juxon Cl *KTN/HRWW/WS* HA3	34 B7
Juxon St *LBTH* SE11	17 M5

K

Street	Map Ref
Kaduna Cl *PIN* HA5	47 F4
Kaine Pl *CROY/NA* CR0	166 C6
Kale Rd *ERITHM* DA18	116 E1
Kambala Rd *BTSEA* SW11	128 C1
Kangley Bridge Rd *SYD* SE26	151 H4
Kaplan Dr *WNWD* N21	29 F4
Kara Wy *CRICK* NW2	70 B3
Karen Cl *RAIN* RM13	99 G1
Karen Ct *BMLY* BR1	152 D7
ELTH/MOT SE9	134 B4
Karenza Ct *WBLY* HA9 *	49 J6
Karma Wy *RYLN/HDSTN* HA2	48 A7
Kashgar Rd *WOOL/PLUM* SE18	116 A4
Kashmir Rd *CHARL* SE7	114 C6
Kassala Rd *BTSEA* SW11	108 E7
Kates Cl *BAR* EN5	25 J4
Katharine St *CROY/NA* CR0	177 J2
Katherine Cl	
BERM/RHTH SE16	93 F7
Katherine Gdns	
ELTH/MOT SE9	134 C3
Katherine Rd *EHAM* E6	77 H6
Katherine Sq *NTGHL* W11 *	88 C7
Kathleen Av *ACT* W3	86 K4
ALP/SUD HA0	68 A6
Kathleen Rd *BTSEA* SW11	128 E2
Kayemoor Rd *BELMT* SM2	175 J6
Kay Rd *BRXN/ST* SW9	129 K1
Kays Ter *SWFD* E18 *	58 D1
Kay St *BETH* E2	92 C1
SRTFD E15	76 B6
WELL DA16	116 C7
Kean St *HOL/ALD* WC2B	11 L5
Keatley Gn *CHING* E4	43 H5
Keats Av *CAN/RD* E16	95 F7
Keats Cl *BORE* WD6	24 B1
PEND EN3	31 H4
STHWK SE1	19 L6
WAN E11	59 F4
WIM/MER SW19	147 H5
Keats Est *STNW/STAM* N16 *	74 B1
Keats Gv *HAMP* NW3	71 H3
Keats Pde *ED* N9	42 C1
Keats Rd *BELV* DA17	117 K2
WELL DA16	115 K7
Keats Wy *CROY/NA* CR0	165 K5
GFD/PVL UB6	84 B3
WDR/YW UB7	100 C3

Street	Map Ref
Keble Cl *NTHLT* UB5	66 C4
WPK KT4	160 C7
Keble Pl *BARN* SW13	106 E5
Keble St *TOOT* SW17	147 G3
Kedleston Wk *BETH* E2	92 D2
Keedonwood Rd *BMLY* BR1	152 C4
Keel Cl *BARK* IG11	97 J1
BERM/RHTH SE16	93 F7
Keeley Rd *CROY/NA* CR0	177 J1
Keeley St *HOL/ALD* WC2B	11 L5
Keeling Rd *ELTH/MOT* SE9	134 C4
Kendalmere Cl *MUSWH* N10	40 B7
Keemor Cl	
WOOL/PLUM SE18 *	115 F6
Keens Cl *STRHM/NOR* SW16	148 D4
Keen's Rd *CROY/NA* CR0	177 J3
Keen's Yd *IS* N1	73 H5
Keepers Ms *TEDD* TW11	143 J5
The Keep *KUTN/CMB* KT2	144 B5
Keesey St *WALW* SE17	19 G9
Keetons Rd	
BERM/RHTH SE16	111 J2
Keeton's Rd	
BERM/RHTH SE16	111 J2
Keevil Dr *WIM/MER* SW19	127 G6
Keighley Cl *HOLWY* N7	72 E3
Keightley Rd *ELTH/MOT* SE9	135 H7
Keildon Rd *BTSEA* SW11	128 E3
Keir Hardie Est *CLPT* E5 *	56 D7
Keir Hardie Wy *BARK* IG11	79 G6
YEAD UB4 *	82 E2
Keith Connor Cl *VX/NE* SW8	129 G2
Keith Gv *SHB* W12	106 D1
Keith Rd *BARK* IG11	96 D1
HYS/HAR UB3	101 H3
WALTH E17	43 H7
Kelbrook Rd *BKHTH/KID* SE3	134 B1
Kelburn Wy *RAIN* RM13	99 J3
Kelceda Cl *CRICK* NW2	69 J1
Kelf Gv *HYS/HAR* UB3	82 D5
Kelfield Gdns *NKENS* W10	88 A5
Kelfield Ms *NKENS* W10	88 B4
Kelland Cl *CEND/HSY/T* N8 *	54 D4
Kelland Rd *PLSTW* E13	94 E3
Kellaway Rd *BKHTH/KID* SE3	134 B1
Keller Crs *MNPK* E12	77 H3
Kellerton Rd *LEW* SE13	133 H4
Kellett Rd *BRXS/STRHM* SW2	130 B3
Kelling Gdns *CROY/NA* CR0	164 C6
Kellino St *TOOT* SW17	147 K3
Kellner Rd *THMD* SE28	116 A2
Kell St *STHWK* SE1	18 D3
Kelly Av *PECK* SE15	111 G6
Kelly Cl *BORE* WD6	25 F1
WLSDN NW10	69 F2
Kelly Ms *MV/WKIL* W9 *	88 D4
Kelly Rd *MLHL* NW7	38 D5
Kelly St *CAMTN* NW1	72 B5
Kelly Wy *CHDH* RM6	62 A4
Kelman Cl *CLAP* SW4	129 J1
Kelmore Gv *EDUL* SE22	131 H3
Kelmscott Cl *WALTH* E17	43 H7
Kelmscott Gdns *SHB* W12	106 D2
Kelmscott Rd *BTSEA* SW11	128 E4
Kelross Rd *HBRY* N5	73 H3
Kelsall Cl *BKHTH/KID* SE3	134 A1
Kelsall Ms *RCH/KEW* TW9	105 J7
Kelsey Cl *BECK* BR3	166 C2
Kelsey Park Av *BECK* BR3	166 E2
Kelsey Park Rd *BECK* BR3	166 D1
Kelsey Sq *BECK* BR3	166 D1
Kelsey St *BETH* E2	92 C3
Kelsey Wy *BECK* BR3	166 D2
Kelso Pl *KENS* W8	14 C3
Kelso Rd *CAR* SM5	162 B6
Kelston Rd *BARK/HLT* IG6	60 B1
Kelton Vls *KUT/HW* KT1 *	159 G1
Kelvedon Cl *KUTN/CMB* KT2	144 C5
Kelvedon Rd *FUL/PGN* SW6	107 J6
Kelvedon Wy *WFD* IG8	45 K5
Kelvin Av *WDGN* N22	41 G2
Kelvinbrook *E/WMO/HCT* KT8	157 G2
Kelvin Crs	
KTN/HRWW/WS HA3	34 E6
Kelvin Dr *TWK* TW1	124 C5
Kelvin Gdns *CROY/NA* CR0	163 K6
STHL UB1	84 A4
Kelvin Gv *CHSGTN* KT9	171 K7
SYD SE26	150 D2
Kelvington Cl *CROY/NA* CR0	166 B6
Kelvington Rd *PECK* SE15	132 A5
Kelvin Pde *ORP* BR6	169 K7
Kelvin Rd *HBRY* N5	73 H3
WELL DA16	136 B2
Kember St *IS* N1	5 L2
Kemble Dr *HAYES* BR2	181 J3
Kemble Rd *CROY/NA* CR0	177 H2
FSTH SE23	132 A7
TOTM N17	42 C7
Kemble St *HOL/ALD* WC2B	11 L5
Kemerton Rd *BECK* BR3	166 E1
CMBW SE5	130 D2
CROY/NA CR0	165 G6
Kemey's St *HOM* E9	75 G4
Kemnal Rd *CHST* BR7	154 D2
Kempe Rd *KIL/WHAMP* NW6	88 B1
Kemp Gdns *CROY/NA* CR0	164 D5
Kempis Wy *EDUL* SE22 *	131 F4
Kemplay Rd *HAMP* NW3	71 H3
Kemp Pl *BUSH* WD23	22 D6
Kemps Dr *NTHWD* HA6	32 D6
POP/IOD E14	93 J6
Kempsford Gdns *ECT* SW5	14 B8
Kempsford Rd *LBTH* SE11	18 B6
Kempshott Rd	
STRHM/NOR SW16	148 D6
Kempson Rd *FUL/PGN* SW6	107 K7
Kempthorne Rd *DEPT* SE8	112 B3
Kempton Av *NTHLT* UB5	66 A5
SUN TW16	141 F7
Kempton Cl *ERITH* DA8	117 K5
HGDN/ICK UB10	64 A3
Kempton Pk *SUN* TW16	141 F7
Kempton Rd *EHAM* E6	77 K7
HPTN TW12	141 K7
Kempton Wk *CROY/NA* CR0	166 B5
Kempt St	
WOOL/PLUM SE18	115 F5
Kemsing Cl *ERITH* DA17	117 K5
HAYES BR2	167 J2
THHTH CR7 *	164 D3
Kemsing Rd *GNWCH* SE10	113 K4
Kemsley *LEW* SE13	132 E4
Kenbury Gdns *CMBW* SE5	130 D1
Kenbury St *CMBW* SE5	130 D1
Kencot Wy *ERITHM* DA18	117 H1
Kendal Av *ACT* W3	86 B3

Street	Map Ref
WFD IG8	44 D7
YEAD UB4	82 C1
Kendal Ct *ACT* W3	86 C1
Kendal Cft *HCH* RM12	81 J4
Kendale Rd *BMLY* BR1	152 C4
Kendal Gdns *SUT* SM1	175 G2
UED N18	41 K3
Kendall Av *BECK* BR3	166 A1
SAND/SEL CR2	177 K7
Kendall Pl *MHST* W1U	10 A4
Kendall Rd *BECK* BR3	166 A1
ISLW TW7	124 B1
WOOL/PLUM SE18	114 E7
Kendalmere Cl *MUSWH* N10	40 B7
Kendal Pde *UED* N18	41 K3
Kendal Pl *PUT/ROE* SW15	127 K4
Kendal Rd *WLSDN* NW10	69 J3
Kendal Steps *BAY/PAD* W2 *	9 K5
Kendal St *BAY/PAD* W2	9 K5
Kender St *NWCR* SE14	111 K6
Kendoa Rd *CLAP* SW4	129 J3
Kendon Cl *WAN* E11	59 F4
Kendra Hall Rd *SAND/SEL* CR2	177 H6
Kendrey Gdns *WHTN* TW2	123 K5
Kendrick Ms *SKENS* SW7	15 H5
Kendrick Pl *SKENS* SW7 *	15 G5
Kenelm Cl *HRW* HA1	67 G1
Kenerne Dr *BAR* EN5	26 C4
Keniford Rd *BAL* SW12	129 G6
Kenilworth Av	
RYLN/HDSTN HA2	65 K3
WALTH E17	57 J1
WIM/MER SW19	146 E4
Kenilworth Dr *BORE* WD6	24 D1
Kenilworth Gdns	
GDMY/SEVK IG3	79 F1
OXHEY WD19	33 G4
STHL UB1	83 K4
WOOL/PLUM SE18	135 G1
YEAD UB4	82 D4
Kenilworth Rd *BOW* E3	93 G1
EA W5	86 A7
EDGW HA8	36 E1
EW KT17	173 H5
KIL/WHAMP NW6	70 D7
PGE/AN SE20	151 F7
STMC/STPC BR5	169 H5
Kenilworth Ter *BELMT* SM2 *	174 E7
Kenley Av *CDALE/KGS* NW9	37 F1
Kenley Cl *BXLY* DA5	137 H6
CHST BR7	169 K2
EBAR EN4	27 J3
Kenley Gdns *THHTH* CR7	164 C3
Kenley Rd *KUT/HW* KT1	159 J1
TWK TW1	124 B5
WIM/MER SW19	161 K2
Kenley Wk *CHEAM* SM3	174 B3
NTGHL W11 *	88 C7
Kenlor Rd *TOOT* SW17	147 H5
Kenmare Dr *MTCM* CR4	148 A6
TOTM N17	56 B1
Kenmare Gdns *PLMGR* N13	41 J3
Kenmare Rd *THHTH* CR7	164 B5
Kenmere Gdns *ALP/SUD* HA0	68 C7
Kenmere Rd *WELL* DA16	136 D1
Kenmont Gdns *WLSDN* NW10	87 K2
Kenmore Av	
KTN/HRWW/WS HA3	49 G4
Kenmore Crs *YEAD* UB4	82 D2
Kenmore Gdns *EDGW* HA8	50 D1
Kenmore Rd	
KTN/HRWW/WS HA3	49 K2
Kenmure Rd *HACK* E8	74 D4
Kenmure Yd *HACK* E8 *	74 D4
Kennacraig Cl *CAN/RD* E16	95 F7
Kennard Rd *FBAR/BDGN* N11	39 K4
SRTFD E15	76 B6
Kennard St *BTSEA* SW11	109 F7
CAN/RD E16	95 K7
Kennedy Av *PEND* EN3	30 E5
Kennedy Cl *MTCM* CR4	163 F1
PIN HA5	33 K5
PLSTW E13	94 E1
STMC/STPC BR5	169 J5
Kennedy Rd *BARK* IG11	78 E7
HNWL W7	84 E4
Kennedy Wk *WALW* SE17 *	19 H6
Kennet Cl *BTSEA* SW11	128 C3
Kennet Dr *YEAD* UB4	83 J4
Kenneth Av *IL* IG1	78 B3
Kenneth Crs *CRICK* NW2	69 K4
Kenneth Gdns *STAN* HA7	35 G5
Kenneth More Rd *IL* IG1 *	78 B2
Kenneth Rd *CHDH* RM6	62 K6
Kennet Rd *DART* DA1	138 D2
ISLW TW7	124 A2
MV/WKIL W9	88 D3
Kennet Sq *MTCM* CR4	147 J7
Kennet St *WAP* E1W	92 D7
Kennett Wharf La	
BLKFR EC4V	12 F6
Kenninghall Rd *CLPT* E5	74 D2
UED N18	42 E4
Kenning St *BERM/RHTH* SE16	111 H1
Kennings Wy *LBTH* SE11	18 B7
Kennington Gdns	
KUT/HW KT1	158 E2
Kennington La *LBTH* SE11	17 M7
Kennington Ov *LBTH* SE11	17 M9
Kennington Park Gdns	
LBTH SE11	18 C9
Kennington Park Pl	
LBTH SE11	18 B8
Kennington Park Rd	
LBTH SE11	18 B8
Kennington Rd *LBTH* SE11	18 A8
Kenny Dr *CAR* SM5	176 A7
Kenrick Pl *MHST* W1U	10 A2
Kensal Rd *NKENS* W10	88 C3
Kensal Whf *NKENS* W10 *	88 B3
Kensington Av *MNPK* E12	77 J5
THHTH CR7	149 G7
WATW WD18	20 D3
Kensington Church Ct	
KENS W8	14 C2
Kensington Church St	
KENS W8	8 B8
Kensington Church Wk	
KENS W8	14 C1
Kensington Cl	
FBAR/BDGN N11 *	40 A5
Kensington Ct *KENS* W8	14 D2
Kensington Court Gdns	
KENS W8 *	14 D3
Kensington Court Ms	
KENS W8 *	14 D3
Kensington Court Pl	
KENS W8	14 D3
Kensington Dr *WFD* IG8	59 H1
Kensington Gdns *IL* IG1	59 K7
Kensington Gardens Sq	
BAY/PAD W2	8 C5
Kensington Ga *KENS* W8	14 E3

Street	Map Ref
Kensington Hall Gdns	
WKENS W14 *	107 J4
Kensington High St *KENS* W8 *	14 B3
WKENS W14	107 H3
Kensington Ml *KENS* W8	8 B8
Kensington Palace *KENS* W8 *	8 E7
Kensington Palace Gdns	
KENS W8	8 C8
Kensington Park Gdns	
NTGHL W11	88 D6
Kensington Park Ms	
NTGHL W11	88 D5
Kensington Park Rd	
NTGHL W11	88 D5
Kensington Pl *KENS* W8	8 A9
Kensington Rd *KENS* W8	14 D2
NTHLT UB5	84 A1
ROMW/RG RM7	62 E5
SKENS SW7	14 F2
Kensington Sq *KENS* W8	14 C2
Kensington Ter	
SAND/SEL CR2	177 K6
Kensington Wy *BORE* WD6	25 F2
Kent Av *DAGW* RM9	98 C3
WEA W13	85 H4
WELL DA16	136 A4
Kent Cl *MTCM* CR4	163 K3
Kent Ct *CDALE/KGS* NW9	51 G1
Kent Dr *EBAR* EN4	28 A3
TEDD TW11	142 E4
Kentford Wy *NTHLT* UB5	65 J7
Kent Gdns *RSLP* HA4	47 F5
WEA W13	85 H4
Kent Gate Wy *CROY/NA* CR0	179 H5
Kent House La *BECK* BR3	151 F5
Kent House Rd *BECK* BR3	151 F6
Kentish Rd *BELV* DA17	117 H3
Kentish Town Rd *CAMTN* NW1	4 D2
Kentish Wy *BMLY* BR1	168 A1
Kentlea Rd *THMD* SE28	115 K1
Kentmere Rd	
WOOL/PLUM SE18	115 K3
Kenton Av *HRW* HA1	49 F6
STHL UB1	84 A6
SUN TW16	156 C1
Kenton Gdns	
KTN/HRWW/WS HA3	35 F6
Kenton La	
KTN/HRWW/WS HA3	34 E3
Kenton Park Av	
KTN/HRWW/WS HA3	49 K3
Kenton Park Cl	
KTN/HRWW/WS HA3	49 J3
Kenton Park Crs	
KTN/HRWW/WS HA3	49 K3
Kenton Park Pde	
KTN/HRWW/WS HA3	49 J4
Kenton Park Rd	
KTN/HRWW/WS HA3	49 J3
Kenton Rd *HOM* E9	75 F5
KTN/HRWW/WS HA3	49 G6
Kenton St *STPAN* WC1H	5 J9
Kenton Wy *YEAD* UB4	82 C2
Kent Pas *CAMTN* NW1	3 L9
Kent Rd *CHSWK* W4	105 K3
DAGE RM10	80 D4
E/WMO/HCT KT8	157 H3
KUT/HW KT1	158 E2
RCH/KEW TW9	105 H6
WCHMH N21	29 K7
WWKM BR4	166 E7
Kent St *BETH* E2	7 M5
PLSTW E13	95 F2
Kent Ter *CAMTN* NW1	3 K7
Kent View Gdns	
GDMY/SEVK IG3	78 E3
Kent Wy *SURB* KT6	172 A2
Kentwell Cl *BROCKY* SE4 *	132 B3
Kentwode Gn *BARN* SW13	106 D6
Kent Yd *SKENS* SW7	15 K2
Kenver Av	
NFNCH/WDSPK N12	39 H5
Kenward Rd *ELTH/MOT* SE9	134 B4
Kenway *CRW* RM5	62 E2
Ken Wy *WBLY* HA9	68 E1
Kenway Rd *ECT* SW5	14 C6
Kenwood Cl *HAMP* NW3	53 H7
WDR/YW UB7	100 D5
Kenwood Dr *BECK* BR3	167 F2
Kenwood Gdns *CLAY* IG5	60 A5
SWFD E18	59 F2
Kenwood Rd *ED* N9	42 C1
HGT N6	53 K5
Kenworthy Rd *HOM* E9	75 G4
Kenwyn Dr *CRICK* NW2	69 F2
Kenwyn Rd *CLAP* SW4	129 J3
RYNPK SW20	146 A7
Kenya Rd *CHARL* SE7	114 C6
Kenyngton Dr *SUN* TW16	140 E4
Kenyngton Pl	
KTN/HRWW/WS HA3	49 J4
Kenyon St *FUL/PGN* SW6	107 G7
Keogh Rd *SRTFD* E15	76 C5
Kepler Rd *CLAP* SW4	129 K3
Keppel Rd *DAGW* RM9	80 B3
EHAM E6	77 K6
Keppel St *GWRST* WC1E	11 H2
Kerbela St *BETH* E2	92 C3
Kerbey St *POP/IOD* E14	93 K5
Kerfield Crs *CMBW* SE5	110 E7
Kerfield Pl *CMBW* SE5	110 E7
Kerri Cl *EA* W5	85 H6
Kerrison Pl *EA* W5	85 K7
Kerrison Rd *BTSEA* SW11	128 D2
EA W5	85 K7
SRTFD E15	76 B7
Kerry Av *SOCK/AV* RM15	119 J5
STAN HA7	35 K3
Kerry Cl *CAN/RD* E16	95 F5
PLMGR N13	41 F1
Kerry Pth *NWCR* SE14	112 C5
Kerry Rd *NWCR* SE14	112 C5
Kersfield Rd *PUT/ROE* SW15	127 G5
Kershaw Cl *WAND/EARL* SW18	128 C5
Kershaw Rd *DAGE* RM10	80 C2
Kersley Ms *BTSEA* SW11	108 E7
Kersley Rd *STNW/STAM* N16	74 A1
Kersley St *BTSEA* SW11	128 E1
Kerstin Cl *HYS/HAR* UB3	82 D6
Kerswell Cl *SEVS/STOTM* N15	56 A4
Kerwick Cl *HOLWY* N7	5 K1
Keslake Rd *KIL/WHAMP* NW6	88 B1
Kessock Cl *TOTM* N17	56 D4
Kesters Rd *HAYES* BR2	181 K6
Keston Cl *UED* N18	116 C6
Keston Gdns *HAYES* BR2	181 G6
Keston Ms *WAT* WD17	21 F1
Keston Park Cl *HAYES* BR2	131 H2
THHTH CR7	164 A3
TOTM N17	55 D2

Street	District	Page	Grid
Kestrel Av	EHAM E6	95	J4
	HNHL SE24	130	C4
Kestrel Cl	CDALE/KGS NW9	51	G1
	HCH RM12	81	H4
	KUTN/CMB KT2	143	K3
	WLSDN NW10	69	H4
Kestrel Pl	NWCR SE14 *	112	B5
Kestrel Wy	CROY/NA CRO	180	B7
	HYS/HAR UB3	101	K1
Keswick Cl	PUT/ROE SW15	145	G4
	WIM/MER SW19	161	K1
Keswick Ct	REDBR IG4	59	J4
	RSLP HA4	46	B4
	WBLY HA9	68	A4
Keswick Ms	EA W5	86	A5
Keswick Rd	PUT/ROE SW15	127	H4
	WHTN TW2	123	H5
	WWKM BR4	180	D1
Kettering St	STRHM/NOR SW16	148	B5
Kett Gdns	BRXS/STRHM SW2	130	A4
Kettlebaston Rd	LEY E10	57	H7
Kettlewell Cl	FBAR/BDGN N11	40	A5
Kevelioc Cl	TOTM N17	41	J7
Kevin Cl	HSLWW TW4	122	C1
Kew Br	RCH/KEW TW9	105	H4
Kew Bridge Arches	CHSWK W4 *	105	H5
Kew Bridge Ct	BTFD TW8	105	H4
Kew Bridge Rd	BTFD TW8	105	J5
Kew Crs	CHEAM SM3	174	D2
Kewferry Rd	NTHWD HA6	32	A5
Kew Foot Rd	RCH/KEW TW9	125	F3
Kew Gardens Rd	RCH/KEW TW9	105	G6
Kew Gn	RCH/KEW TW9	105	G5
Kew Meadow Pth	RCH/KEW TW9	105	H7
Kew Riverside Pk	RCH/KEW TW9	105	J6
Kew Rd	RCH/KEW TW9	125	F3
Key Cl	WCHPL E1	92	D3
Keyes Rd	CRICK NW2	70	B4
Keymer Rd	BRXS/STRHM SW2	149	F1
Keynes Cl	EFNCH N2	53	K2
Keynsham Av	WFD IG8	44	C3
Keynsham Gdns	ELTH/MOT SE9	134	D5
Keynsham Rd	ELTH/MOT SE9	134	C5
	MRDN SM4	162	A7
Keysham Av	HEST TW5	101	K1
Keystone Crs	IS N1	5	K6
Keywood Dr	SUN TW16	140	F5
Keyworth Cl	CLPT E5	75	G3
Keyworth St	STHWK SE1	18	D3
Kezia St	DEPT SE8	112	B4
Khama Rd	TOOT SW17	147	J3
Khartoum Rd	IL IG1	78	B3
	PLSTW E13	95	F2
	TOOT SW17	147	H3
Khyber Rd	BTSEA SW11	128	D1
Kibworth St	VX/NE SW8	110	A6
Kidbrooke Gdns	BKHTH/KID SE3	133	K1
Kidbrooke Park Cl	BKHTH/KID SE3	114	A7
Kidbrooke Park Rd	BKHTH/KID SE3	114	A7
	LEE/GVPK SE12	134	A4
Kidbrooke Wy	BKHTH/KID SE3 *	134	A1
Kidderminster Pl	CROY/NA CRO	164	C7
Kidderminster Rd	CROY/NA CRO	164	C7
Kidderpore Av	HAMP NW3	70	E3
Kidderpore Gdns	HAMP NW3	70	E3
Kidd Pl	CHARL SE7	114	E4
Kiffen St	SDTCH EC2A *	7	H5
Kilberry Cl	ISLW TW7	103	J7
Kilberry Br	KIL/WHAMP NW6	2	B4
Kilburn High Rd	KIL/WHAMP NW6	2	B3
Kilburn La	NKENS W10	88	B2
Kilburn Park Rd	MV/WKIL W9	2	A6
Kilburn Pl	KIL/WHAMP NW6	2	A2
Kilburn Priory	KIL/WHAMP NW6	2	C4
Kilburn Sq	KIL/WHAMP NW6	2	A3
Kilburn V	KIL/WHAMP NW6	2	B4
Kildare Cl	RSLP HA4	47	G7
Kildare Gdns	BAY/PAD W2	8	B4
Kildare Rd	CAN/RD E16	94	E4
Kildare Ter	BAY/PAD W2	8	B4
Kildoran Rd	CLAP SW4	129	K6
Kildowan Rd	GDMY/SEVK IG3	61	J7
Kilgour Rd	FSTH SE23	132	B5
Kilkie St	FUL/PGN SW6	128	B1
Killarney Rd	WAND/EARL SW18	128	B5
Killburns Mill Cl	WLGTN SM6	176	B1
Killearn Rd	CAT SE6	133	G7
Killester Gdns	WPK KT4	173	K3
Killick St	IS N1	5	L5
Killieser Av	BRXS/STRHM SW2	148	E1
Killip Cl	CAN/RD E16	94	E5
Killowen Av	NTHLT UB5	66	C4
Killowen Rd	HOM E9	75	F5
Killyon Rd	VX/NE SW8	129	H1
Kilmaine Rd	FUL/PGN SW6	107	H6
Kilmarnock Gdns	BCTR RM8	79	J2
Kilmarnock Rd	OXHEY WD19	33	H3
Kilmarsh Rd	HMSMTH W6	107	F3
Kilmartin Av	STRHM/NOR SW16	164	B1
Kilmartin Rd	GDMY/SEVK IG3	79	G1
Kilmartin Wy	HCH RM12	81	K4
Kilmington Rd	BARN SW13	106	D5
Kilmorey Gdns	TWK TW1	124	C2
Kilmorey Rd	TWK TW1	124	C2
Kilmorie Rd	FSTH SE23	132	B7
Kiln Cl	HYS/HAR UB3	101	G5
Kilnside	ESH/CLAY KT10	171	G6
Kiln Ms	TOOT SW17	147	H4
Kiln Pl	KTTN NW5	72	A3
Kiln Wy	NTHWD HA6	32	C5
Kilpatrick Wy	YEAD UB4	83	J4
Kilravock St	NKENS W10	88	C2
Kilross Rd	EBED/NFELT TW14	121	G7
Kilsha Rd	WOT/HER KT12	156	A5
Kimbell Gdns	FUL/PGN SW6	107	H7
Kimbell Pl	BKHTH/KID SE3	134	C3
Kimberley Av	EHAM E6	95	J1
	GNTH/NBYPK IG2	60	D6
	PECK SE15	131	J1
	ROMW/RG RM7	62	D5
Kimberley Ct	KIL/WHAMP NW6 *	70	C6
Kimberley Dr	SCUP DA14	155	K1
Kimberley Gdns	EN EN1	30	B2
	FSBYPK N4	55	H4
Kimberley Rd	BECK BR3	166	A1
	BRXN/ST SW9	129	K1
	CAN/RD E16	94	D3
	CROY/NA CRO	164	C5
	KIL/WHAMP NW6	70	C1
	TOTM N17	56	D1
	WAN E11	76	B1
Kimber Rd	WAND/EARL SW18	128	A6
Kimble Cl	WATW WD18 *	20	C5
Kimble Crs	BUSH WD23	22	B6
Kimble Rd	WIM/MER SW19	147	H5
Kimbolton Cl	LEE/GVPK SE12	133	J5
Kimbolton Gn	BORE WD6	24	E3
Kimmeridge Av	ELTH/MOT SE9	153	K2
Kimmeridge Rd	ELTH/MOT SE9	153	K2
Kimpton Park Wy	CHEAM SM3	174	D1
Kimpton Rd	CHEAM SM3	174	D2
	CMBW SE5	110	E7
Kinburn St	BERM/RHTH SE16 *	112	A1
Kincaid Rd	PECK SE15	111	J6
Kincardine Gdns	MV/WKIL W9 *	8	A1
Kinch Gv	WBLY HA9	50	B6
Kinder Cl	THMD SE28	97	J6
Kinder St	WCHPL E1	92	D5
Kinfauns Rd	BRXS/STRHM SW2	149	G1
	GDMY/SEVK IG3	61	H7
Kingaby Gdns	RAIN RM13	81	J5
King Alfred Av	CAT SE6	151	J3
King and Queen Cl	ELTH/MOT SE9	153	J3
King Arthur Cl	PECK SE15	111	K6
King Charles I Island	WHALL SW1A	11	J8
King Charles St	BRYLDS KT5	159	G6
King Charles St	WHALL SW1A *	17	H1
King Charles Ter	WAP E1W *	92	D6
King Charles Wk	WIM/MER SW19 *	127	H7
Kingcup Cl	CROY/NA CRO	166	A7
King David La	WCHPL E1	92	E6
Kingdon Rd	KIL/WHAMP NW6	70	E5
King Edward Dr	CHSGTN KT9	172	A2
King Edward III Ms	BERM/RHTH SE16	111	J1
King Edward Rd	BAR EN5	26	E3
	LEY E10	58	A7
	OXHEY WD19	21	J5
	ROM RM1	63	H5
	WALTH E17	57	G2
King Edward's Gdns	ACT W3	86	B7
King Edward's Gv	TEDD TW11	143	H5
King Edwards Rd	ACT W3	86	C7
	BARK IG11	78	D7
	ED N9	30	D6
	HACK E8	74	B7
	PEND EN3	31	F3
King Edward St	STBT EC1A *	12	E4
King Edward Wk	STHWK SE1	18	B3
Kingfield Rd	EA W5	85	K3
Kingfield St	POP/IOD E14	113	F3
Kingfisher Cl	KTN/HRWW/WS HA3	35	F2
	STHGT/OAK N14 *	28	C7
	THMD SE28	97	J6
Kingfisher Dr	RCHPK/HAM TW10	143	J3
Kingfisher Ms	LEW SE13	132	E4
Kingfisher Pl	WDGN N22 *	55	F1
Kingfisher St	EHAM E6	95	J4
Kingfisher Wy	BECK BR3	166	A5
	WLSDN NW10	69	F4
King Gdns	CROY/NA CRO	177	H4
King Garth Ms	FSTH SE23 *	150	E1
King George Av	BUSH WD23	22	B5
	CAN/RD E16	95	H5
	GNTH/NBYPK IG2	60	D4
	WOT/HER KT12	156	C7
King George Cl	ROMW/RG RM7	62	E2
	SUN TW16 *	140	C4
King George Rd	WATW WD18 *	20	D4
King George Sq	RCHPK/HAM TW10	125	G6
King George St	GNWCH SE10	113	F6
King George VI Av	MTCM CR4	162	E3
Kingham Cl	NTGHL W11	107	J1
	WAND/EARL SW18	128	B6
King Harolds Wy	BXLYHN DA7	116	E6
King Henry Ms	HRW HA1 *	48	E6
King Henry's Dr	CROY/NA CRO	180	A7
King Henry's Reach	HMSMTH W6	107	F5
King Henry's Rd	HAMP NW3	3	J2
	KUT/HW KT1	159	J2
King Henry St	STNW/STAM N16	74	A4
King Henry's Wk	IS N1	74	A5
King Henry Ter	WAP E1W *	92	D6
Kinghorn St	STBT EC1A	12	E3
King James St	STHWK SE1	18	D2
King John Ct	SDTCH EC2A *	7	K9
King John St	WCHPL E1	93	F4
King John's Wk	ELTH/MOT SE9	134	D6
Kinglake Est	WALW SE17 *	19	J7
Kinglake St	WALW SE17	19	J8
Kinglet Cl	FSTGT E7	76	E5
King & Queen Cl	ELTH/MOT SE9 *	153	J3
King & Queen St	WALW SE17	18	F7
King & Queen Whf	BERM/RHTH SE16 *	93	F7
King's Arms Yd	LOTH EC2R *	13	G4
Kingsash Dr	YEAD UB4	83	J3
Kings Av	BAL SW12	129	J7
	BMLY BR1	152	D5
	CAR SM5	175	J7
	CHDH RM6	62	B5
	CLAP SW4	129	K5
	EA W5	85	K5
	MUSWH N10	54	A2
	NWMAL KT3	160	B3
	WFD IG8	45	F5
King's Av	GFD/PVL UB6	84	B5
	HSLW TW3	103	H7
	SUN TW16	140	D4
	WCHMH N21	29	H7
	WFD IG8	45	F5
King's Bench St	STHWK SE1	18	D1
King's Bench Wk	EMB EC4Y *	12	B6
Kingsbridge Av	ACT W3	105	G1
Kingsbridge Cl	POP/IOD E14	112	D2
Kingsbridge Crs	STHL UB1	83	K4
Kingsbridge Dr	MLHL NW7	38	D6
Kingsbridge Rd	BARK IG11	96	D1
	MRDN SM4	161	G6
	NKENS W10	88	A5
	NWDGN UB2	102	E3
	WOT/HER KT12	156	A6
Kingsbury Gn	CDALE/KGS NW9 *	50	E4
Kingsbury Rd	CDALE/KGS NW9	50	C4
	IS N1	74	A5
Kingsbury Ter	IS N1 *	74	A5
Kings Cha	E/WMO/HCT KT8	157	F2
Kingsclere Cl	PUT/ROE SW15	126	D6
Kingsclere Pde	NTHLT UB5 *	65	K6
Kingscliffe Gdns	WIM/MER SW19	127	J7
Kings Cl	HDN NW4	52	B3
	LEY E10	57	K6
	NTHWD HA6	32	D5
	THDIT KT7	158	B5
	WATW WD18	21	G3
	WOT/HER KT12	156	A7
Kings College Rd	RSLP HA4	46	D5
King's College Rd	HAMP NW3	3	H1
Kingscote Rd	CHSWK W4	106	A2
	CROY/NA CRO	165	J6
	NWMAL KT3	159	K3
Kingscote St	BLKFR EC4V	12	C6
Kingscourt Rd	STRHM/NOR SW16	148	D2
King's Crs	FSBYPK N4	73	J2
Kingscroft Rd	CRICK NW2	70	D5
King's Cross Br	IS N1 *	5	K7
King's Cross Rd	FSBYW WC1X	5	L7
Kingsdale Gdns	NTGHL W11	88	B7
Kingsdale Rd	PGE/AN SE20	151	F6
	WOOL/PLUM SE18	116	A5
Kingsdown Av	ACT W3	87	G6
	SAND/SEL CR2	177	J7
	WEA W13	104	C1
Kingsdown Cl	BERM/RHTH SE16 *	111	J4
	NKENS W10	88	B5
Kingsdowne Ct	EA W5 *	86	A6
Kingsdowne Rd	SURB KT6	159	F6
Kingsdown Rd	ARCH N19	72	D2
	CHEAM SM3	174	C4
	WAN E11	76	C2
Kings Dr	BRYLDS KT5	159	H6
	EDGW HA8	36	B3
	WBLY HA9	68	D1
King's Dr	THDIT KT7	158	C5
Kingsend	RSLP HA4	46	C7
Kingsend Ct	RSLP HA4 *	46	C7
Kings Farm	WALTH E17 *	43	K7
Kings Farm Av	RCHPK/HAM TW10	125	H3
Kingsfield Av	RYLN/HDSTN HA2	48	B4
Kingsfield Ct	OXHEY WD19	21	H5
Kingsfield Rd	HRW HA1 *	48	D6
	OXHEY WD19	21	H6
Kingsfield Ter	DART DA1 *	139	G5
Kingsford St	KTTN NW5	71	K4
Kingsford Wy	EHAM E6	95	K4
Kings Gdns	IL IG1	60	D7
	KIL/WHAMP NW6	2	A2
Kingsgate	WBLY HA9	68	E2
Kingsgate Av	FNCH N3	52	E2
Kingsgate Est	IS N1 *	74	A5
Kingsgate Pl	KIL/WHAMP NW6	2	A2
Kingsgate Rd	KIL/WHAMP NW6	2	A2
	KUT/HW KT1	144	A7
Kingsground	ELTH/MOT SE9	134	C6
King's Gv	ROM RM1	63	J4
	PECK SE15	111	J6
Kings Hall Ms	LEW SE13 *	133	F2
Kings Hall Rd	BECK BR3	151	F6
King's Head HI	CHING E4	31	K7
King's Hwy	WOOL/PLUM SE18 *	115	K5
Kingshill Av	KTN/HRWW/WS HA3	49	H3
	NTHLT UB5	83	F2
	WPK KT4	160	D6
	YEAD UB4	82	C3
Kingshill Cl	YEAD UB4	82	B2
Kingshill Ct	BAR EN5 *	26	C3
Kingshill Dr	KTN/HRWW/WS HA3	49	H1
Kingshold Rd	HOM E9	74	E6
Kingsholm Gdns	ELTH/MOT SE9	134	C3
Kings Keep	HAYES BR2 *	167	H2
	KUT/HW KT1 *	159	F3
Kingsland Gn	STNW/STAM N16	73	K5
Kingsland High St	HACK E8	74	B5
Kingsland Pas	HACK E8 *	74	A5
Kingsland Rd	BETH E2	7	K6
	PLSTW E13	95	G2
King's La	SUT SM1	175	H4
Kingslawn Cl	PUT/ROE SW15	126	E4
Kingsleigh Cl	BTFD TW8	104	E5
Kingsleigh Pl	MTCM CR4	162	E2
Kingsleigh Wk	HAYES BR2 *	167	J3
Kingsley Av	BORE WD6	24	B1
	CHEAM SM3	174	E4
	DART DA1	139	F5
	EDCW HA8	36	D4
	HSLW TW3	123	H1
	STHL UB1	84	A6
	SUT SM1	175	H3
	WEA W13	85	H5
Kingsley Cl	DAGE RM10	80	D3
	EFNCH N2	53	G4
Kingsley Ct	EDGW HA8	36	D1
	GPK RM2	63	K5
Kingsley Dr	WPK KT4	173	H1
Kingsley Gdns	CHING E4	43	J4
Kingsley Ms	CHST BR7	154	B5
	IL IG1	78	B1
	KENS W8	14	D4
	WAP E1W *	92	D6
Kingsley Pl	HGT N6	54	A7
Kingsley Rd	CROY/NA CRO	164	B7
	FSTGT E7	76	E6
	HSLW TW3	123	H1
	KIL/WHAMP NW6	70	D1
	ORP BR6	182	B7
	PIN HA5	47	K5
	PLMCR N13	41	G3
	PLSTW E13	95	F3
	WALTH E17	58	A1
	WIM/MER SW19	147	G4
Kingsley St	BTSEA SW11	128	E2
Kingsley Wood Dr	ELTH/MOT SE9	153	K2
Kingslyn Crs	NRWD SE19	150	A7
Kings MI	HMSMTH W6 *	107	F3
Kingsman Pde	WOOL/PLUM SE18	114	E2
Kingsman St	WOOL/PLUM SE18	114	E3
Kingsmead	BAR EN5	26	E3
Kingsmead Av	CDALE/KGS NW9	51	F6
	ED N9	30	D7
	MTCM CR4	163	H2
	ROM RM1	63	H5
	SUN TW16	156	B2
	SURB KT6	172	C1
	WPK KT4	173	K2
Kingsmead Cl	BFN/LL DA15	155	G1
	HOR/WEW KT19	173	F6
	TEDD TW11	143	H5
Kingsmead Dr	NTHLT UB5	65	K6
Kingsmead Pde	NTHLT UB5 *	65	K6
Kings Mead Pk	ESH/CLAY KT10	170	E6
Kingsmead Rd	BRXS/STRHM SW2	149	G1
Kingsmere Cl	PUT/ROE SW15	127	G2
Kingsmere Pk	CDALE/KGS NW9	50	E7
Kingsmere Pl	STNW/STAM N16 *	55	K7
Kingsmere Rd	WIM/MER SW19	146	B1
King's Ms	BMSBY WC1N	11	M1
	CLAP SW4	129	K4
Kingsmill Gdns	DAGW RM9	80	B4
Kingsmill Rd	DAGW RM9	80	B4
Kingsmill Ter	STJWD NW8	3	H5
Kingsnympton Pk	KUTN/CMB KT2	144	D6
Kings Oak	ROMW/RG RM7	62	C3
King's Orch	ELTH/MOT SE9	134	D5
King's Paddock	HPTN TW12	142	C7
Kings Pde	CAR SM5 *	175	J2
	SHB W12 *	106	D1
	TOTM N17 *	56	C1
	WLSDN NW10 *	70	A7
Kingspark Ct	SWFD E18	58	E2
Kings Pas	WAN E11 *	58	C6
Kings Pl	BKHH IG9	45	H1
	CHSWK W4	105	K4
King's Pl	STHWK SE1	18	E2
King's Quay	WBPTN SW10 *	108	B7
Kings Reach	EMB EC4Y *	12	B6
Kings Ride Ga	RCHPK/HAM TW10	125	H3
Kings Rd BAR EN5		26	A2
	EA W5	85	K4
	FELT TW13	122	B7
	MTCM CR4	163	F2
	RCHPK/HAM TW10	125	G5
	RYLN/HDSTN HA2	66	A1
	WDGN N22	41	F7
	WDR/YW UB7	100	B1
	WLSDN NW10	69	K6
	WPK KT4	173	H2
King's Rd BARK IG11		78	C6
	CHEL SW3	15	L7
	FUL/PGN SW6	108	B6
	KUTN/CMB KT2	144	B6
	MORT/ESHN SW14	126	A2
	PLSTW E13	77	F7
	ROM RM1	63	G5
	SNWD SE25	165	H2
	SURB KT6	158	D7
	TEDD TW11	142	E4
	TOTM N17	42	B7
	TWK TW1	124	C5
	WAN E11	58	C6
	WIM/MER SW19	146	E5
King St ACT W3		86	E7
	CITYW EC2V *	12	F5
	COVGDN WC2E	11	J6
	EFNCH N2	53	H2
	HMSMTH W6	106	D4
	NWDGN UB2	102	D3
	PLSTW E13	94	E4
	RCH/KEW TW9	124	E4
	STJS SW1Y	10	F9
	TWK TW1	124	B7
	WATW WD18	21	G3
	WHALL SW1A *	10	F9
King Street Cloisters	HMSMTH W6 *	106	E3
King Street Pde	TWK TW1 *	124	B7
Kingswater Pl	BTSEA SW11 *	108	D6
Kings Wy	CROY/NA CRO	177	G4
	HRW HA1	48	E3
Kingsway	HOL/ALD WC2B	11	L5
	HYS/HAR UB3	82	C7
	MORT/ESHN SW14	125	J2
	NFNCH/WDSPK N12	39	G6
	NWMAL KT3	161	G3
	PEND EN3	30	D4
	RCHPK/HAM TW10	125	G5
	STMC/STPC BR5	169	J4
	STWL/WRAY TW19	120	A7
	WBLY HA9	68	A3
	WWKM BR4	180	D2
Kingsway Av	SAND/SEL CR2	178	C6
Kingsway Crs	RYLN/HDSTN HA2	48	C3
Kingsway Pde	STNW/STAM N16 *	73	K2
Kingsway Pl	CLKNW EC1R *	6	B9
Kingswear Rd	KTTN NW5	72	B2
	RSLP HA4	64	E1
Kingswood Av	BELV DA17	117	G3
	HAYES BR2	167	H2
	HPTN TW12	142	B5
	HSLW TW3	122	E1
	KIL/WHAMP NW6	70	C7
	THHTH CR7	164	B4
Kingswood Cl	ASHF TW15	140	A3
	BAR EN5	27	G4
	EN EN1	30	A4
	NWMAL KT3	160	C5
	STNW/STAM N16 *	55	K7
	SURB KT6	159	F6
	VX/NE SW8	109	K6
Kingswood Ct	LEW SE13	133	F5
Kingswood Dr	BELMT SM2	175	F7
	CAR SM5	162	E7
	DUL SE21	150	A3
	FNCH N3	52	D1
Kingswood Pl	LEW SE13	133	H3
Kingswood Rd	BRXS/STRHM SW2	129	K5
	CHSWK W4	105	K2
	GDMY/SEVK IG3	61	G7
	HAYES BR2	167	H2
	PGE/AN SE20	150	E5
	WAN E11	58	C6
	WBLY HA9	68	C2
	WIM/MER SW19	146	C6
Kingswood Ter	CHSWK W4	105	K2
Kingswood Wy	WLGTN SM6	176	E4
Kingsworth Cl	BECK BR3	166	B4
Kingsworthy Cl	KUT/HW KT1	159	G1
Kings Yd	PUT/ROE SW15 *	127	G3
	SRTFD E15 *	75	J5
Kingthorpe Rd	WLSDN NW10	69	F6
Kingthorpe Ter	WLSDN NW10 *	69	F6
Kingweston Cl	CRICK NW2	70	C2
King William La	GNWCH SE10	113	H4
King William St	CANST EC4R	13	H6
King William Wk	GNWCH SE10	113	F5
Kingwood Rd	FUL/PGN SW6	107	H7
Kinlet Rd	WOOL/PLUM SE18	115	H6
Kinloch Dr	CDALE/KGS NW9	51	G6
Kinloch St	HOLWY N7	73	F2
Kinloss Gdns	FNCH N3	52	D2
Kinloss Rd	CAR SM5	162	B6
Kinnaird Av	BMLY BR1	152	D5
	CHSWK W4	105	K6
Kinnaird Cl	BMLY BR1	152	D5
Kinnaird Wy	WFD IG8	45	K5
Kinnear Rd	SHB W12	106	C1
Kinnerton Pl North	KTBR SW1X *	15	M2
Kinnerton Pl South	KTBR SW1X *	15	M2
Kinnerton St	KTBR SW1X	16	A2
Kinnerton Yd	KTBR SW1X *	16	A2
Kinnoul Rd	HMSMTH W6	107	H5
Kinross Av	WPK KT4	173	J1
Kinross Cl	KTN/HRWW/WS HA3	50	B4
	SUN TW16	140	B4
Kinross Dr	SUN TW16	140	B4
Kinross Ter	WALTH E17	57	H1
Kinsale Rd	PECK SE15	131	H2
Kinsella Gdns	WIM/MER SW19	145	K5
Kintyre Cl	STRHM/NOR SW16	164	A1
Kinveachy Gdns	CHARL SE7	114	D4
Kinver Rd	SYD SE26	150	E3
Kipling Dr	WIM/MER SW19	147	H5
Kipling Est	STHWK SE1	19	H2
Kipling Pl	STHWK SE1	19	H2
Kipling Ter	ED N9 *	41	E2
Kippington Dr	ELTH/MOT SE9	134	C7
Kirby Cl	HOR/WEW KT19	173	H4
	NTHWD HA6	32	D5
Kirby Est	BERM/RHTH SE16 *	111	J2
Kirby Gv	STHWK SE1	19	J1
Kirby St	HCIRC EC1N	12	B2
Kirchen Rd	WEA W13	85	H6
Kirkcaldy Gn	OXHEY WD19	33	G2
Kirkdale	SYD SE26	150	D1
Kirkdale Cnr	SYD SE26 *	150	E4
Kirkdale Rd	WAN E11	58	C7
Kirkfield Cl	WEA W13	85	H7
Kirkham Rd	EHAM E6	95	J5
Kirkham St	WOOL/PLUM SE18	115	K5
Kirkland Av	CLAY IG5	60	A1
Kirkland Cl	BFN/LL DA15	135	K5
Kirkland Ter	BECK BR3	151	J5
Kirkland Wk	HACK E8	74	B5
Kirk La	WOOL/PLUM SE18	115	H5
Kirkleas Rd	SURB KT6	159	F7
Kirklees Rd	BCTR RM8	79	J4
	THHTH CR7	164	B4
Kirkley Rd	WIM/MER SW19	146	E7
Kirkly Cl	SAND/SEL CR2	178	A7
Kirkmichael Rd	POP/IOD E14	94	A5
Kirk Rd	WALTH E17	57	H5
Kirkstall Av	TOTM N17	55	K3
Kirkstall Gdns	BRXS/STRHM SW2	129	J7
Kirkstall Rd	BRXS/STRHM SW2	129	J7
Kirksted Rd	MRDN SM4	162	A7
Kirkstone Wy	BMLY BR1	152	C5
Kirkton Rd	SEVS/STOTM N15	56	A3
Kirkwall Pl	BETH E2 *	92	E2
Kirkwood Rd	PECK SE15	131	H1
Kirn Rd	WEA W13	85	H6
Kirrane Cl	NWMAL KT3	160	C4
Kirtley Rd	SYD SE26	151	G3
Kirtling St	VX/NE SW8	109	H6
Kirton Cl	CHSWK W4	106	A3
Kirton Gdns	BETH E2	7	M8
Kirton Ldg	WAND/EARL SW18 *	128	A5
Kirton Rd	PLSTW E13	95	G1
Kirton Wk	EDGW HA8	36	E6
Kirwyn Wy	CMBW SE5	110	C6
Kitcat Ter	BOW E3	93	J2
Kitchener Rd	EFNCH N2	53	J2
	FSTGT E7	77	F5
	THHTH CR7	164	E2
	TOTM N17	56	A2
	WALTH E17	43	K7
Kite Pl	BETH E2 *	92	C2
Kite Yd	BTSEA SW11 *	108	E7
Kitley Gdns	NRWD SE19	150	B7
Kitson Rd	BARN SW13	106	D7

CMBW SE5 110 D6
Kittiwake Rd NTHLT UB5 83 H2
Kittiwake Wy YEAD UB4 83 H4
Kitto Rd NWCR SE14 132 A1
Kiver Rd ARCH N19 72 D1
Kiwi Ter EHAM E6 96 A2
Klea Av CLAP SW4 129 H5
Knapdale Cl FSTH SE23 150 D1
Knapmill Rd CAT SE6 151 J1
Knapmill Wy CAT SE6 151 J1
Knapp Cl WLSDN NW10 69 G5
Knapp Rd BOW E3 93 J3
Knapton Ms TOOT SW17 148 A5
Knaresborough Dr
WAND/EARL SW18 128 A7
Knaresborough Pl ECT SW5 14 C5
Knatchbull Rd CMBW SE5 130 C1
WLSDN NW10 69 F7
Knebworth Av WALTH E17 43 J7
Knebworth Cl BAR EN5 27 F3
Knebworth Pth BORE WD6 25 F3
Knebworth Rd
STNW/STAM N16 * 74 A3
Kneller Gdns ISLW TW7 123 J5
Kneller Rd BROCKY SE4 132 B3
NWMAL KT3 160 B6
WHTN TW2 123 H5
Knevett Ter HSLW TW3 123 F3
Knight Cl BCTR RM8 79 J1
Knighten St WAP E1W 92 D7
Knighthead Point
POP/IOD E14 * 112 D1
Knightland Rd CLPT E5 74 D1
Knighton Cl ROMW/RG RM7 63 F5
SAND/SEL CR2 177 H7
WFD IG8 45 F3
Knighton Dr WFD IG8 45 F3
Knighton La BKHH IG9 45 F1
Knighton Park Rd SYD SE26 151 F4
Knighton Rd FSTGT E7 76 E2
ROMW/RG RM7 62 E5
Knightrider Ct BLKFR EC4V * 12 D6
Knightrider St BLKFR EC4V 12 D6
Knight's Av EA W5 105 F1
Knightsbridge SKENS SW7 15 K2
Knightsbridge Gdns
ROMW/RG RM7 63 F4
Knightsbridge Gn
KTBR SW1X * 15 L2
Knights Chambers ED N9 * 42 C2
Knights Cl E/WMO/HCT KT8 156 E4
Knights Hl WNWD SE27 149 H4
Knight's Hill Sq WNWD SE27 149 H3
Knight's Pk KUT/HW KT1 159 F2
Knight's Pl WHTN TW2 123 K7
Knights Rd CAN/RD E16 94 E7
STAN HA7 35 J3
Knights Wk LBTH SE11 18 C6
Knightswood Cl EDGW HA8 36 E1
Knightswood Rd RAIN RM13 99 H1
Knightwood Crs NWMAL KT3 160 B5
Knivet Rd FUL/PGN SW6 107 K5
Knockholt Rd ELTH/MOT SE9 134 C4
Knole Cl CROY/NA CR0 * 165 K5
The Knole ELTH/MOT SE9 154 A3
Knoll Crs NTHWD HA6 46 C1
Knoll Dr STHGT/OAK N14 28 A6
Knollmead BRYLDS KT5 159 K7
Knoll Rd BXLY DA5 137 H6
SCUP DA14 155 H4
WAND/EARL SW18 128 A4
Knolls Cl WPK KT4 173 K2
The Knoll BECK BR3 151 K7
EA W5 85 J4
PIN HA5 * 47 H1
Knolly's Cl STRHM/NOR SW16 149 G2
Knolly's Rd STRHM/NOR SW16 149 G2
Knotley Wy WWKM BR4 179 K1
Knottisford St BETH E2 93 F2
Knotts Green Ms LEY E10 57 K5
Knotts Green Rd LEY E10 57 K5
Knowle Cl BRXN/ST SW9 130 B2
Knowle Rd HAYES BR2 181 J1
WHTN TW2 123 K7
Knowles Hill Crs LEW SE13 133 G4
Knowlton Gn HAYES BR2 167 J4
Knowl Wy BORE WD6 24 A4
Knowsley Av STHL UB1 84 B7
Knowsley Rd BTSEA SW11 128 E1
Knox Rd FSTGT E7 76 E5
Knox St CAMTN NW1 9 L2
Knoyle St NWCR SE14 112 B5
Kohat Rd WIM/MER SW19 147 F4
Koh-I-Noor Av BUSH WD23 22 A5
Kossuth St GNWCH SE10 113 H4
Kramer Ms ECT SW5 14 B8
Kreedman Wk HACK E8 * 74 C4
Kuala Gdns STRHM/NOR SW16 149 F7
Kydbrook Cl STMC/STPC BR5 169 H6
Kylemore Cl EHAM E6 95 H1
Kylemore Rd
KIL/WHAMP NW6 2 A1
Kymberley Rd HRW HA1 * 48 E5
Kyme Rd ROM RM1 63 H5
Kynance Gdns STAN HA7 35 J7
Kynance Ms SKENS SW7 14 D4
Kynance Pl KENS W8 14 E4
Kynaston Av THHTH CR7 164 D4
Kynaston Cl
KTN/HRWW/WS HA3 34 D6
Kynaston Crs THHTH CR7 164 D4
Kynaston Rd BMLY BR1 152 E4
STNW/STAM N16 74 A2
THHTH CR7 164 D4
Kynaston Wd
KTN/HRWW/WS HA3 34 D6
Kynersley Cl CAR SM5 175 K2
Kynoch Rd UED N18 42 E4
Kyrle Rd BTSEA SW11 129 F5
Kyverdale Rd
STNW/STAM N16 56 B6

L

Laburnum Av ED N9 42 A1
HCH RM12 81 J1
SUT SM1 175 J2
TOTM N17 41 K6
Laburnum Cl ALP/SUD HA0 68 C7
CHING E4 43 H5
FBAR/BDGN N11 40 A5
PECK SE15 111 K6
Laburnum Ct STAN HA7 35 J3
Laburnum Crs SUN TW16 141 F7
Laburnum Gdns
CROY/NA CR0 166 A6
Laburnum Gv
CDALE/KGS NW9 50 E6
HSLW TW3 122 E3
NWMAL KT3 160 A1
RSLP HA4 46 B5
STHL UB1 83 K3
WCHMH N21 41 J1
Laburnum Pl ELTH/MOT SE9 * 135 F4
Laburnum Rd HYS/HAR UB3 101 J3
MTCM CR4 163 F1
WIM/MER SW19 147 G6
Laburnum St BETH E2 7 L4
Laburnum Wy HAYES BR2 169 F6
STWL/WRAY TW19 120 C7
Lacebark Cl BFN/LL DA15 136 A6
Lacewing Cl PLSTW E13 94 E2
Lacey Cl ED N9 42 C1
Lacey Dr BCTR RM8 79 J2
EDGW HA8 36 A3
HPTN TW12 141 K7
Lacey Ms BOW E3 93 J1
Lackington St SDTCH EC2A 13 H2
Lacock Cl WIM/MER SW19 147 G5
Lacon Rd EDUL SE22 131 H3
Lacrosse Wy
STRHM/NOR SW16 148 D7
Lacy Rd PUT/ROE SW15 127 G3
Ladas Rd WNWD SE27 149 J4
Ladbroke Crs NTGHL W11 88 C5
Ladbroke Gdns NTGHL W11 88 D6
Ladbroke Gv NKENS W10 88 B3
Ladbroke Ms NTGHL W11 88 C7
Ladbroke Rd EN EN1 30 B5
NTGHL W11 88 D7
Ladbroke Sq NTGHL W11 88 D6
Ladbroke Ter NTGHL W11 88 D6
Ladbroke Wk NTGHL W11 88 D7
Ladbrook Cl PIN HA5 47 K4
Ladbrooke Crs SCUP DA14 155 K2
Ladbrook Rd SNWD SE25 164 E2
Ladderstile Ride
KUTN/CMB KT2 144 D4
Ladderswood Wy
FBAR/BDGN N11 40 C4
Lady Alesford Av STAN HA7 35 H4
Lady Booth Rd KUT/HW KT1 159 F1
Ladycroft Rd LEW SE13 132 E2
Ladycroft Wk STAN HA7 35 K7
Lady Forsdyke Wy
HOR/WEW KT19 172 C7
Ladygate La RSLP HA4 46 A5
Ladygrove CROY/NA CR0 179 G7
Lady Harewood Wy
HOR/WEW KT19 172 C7
Lady Hay WPK KT4 173 H1
Lady Margaret Rd KTTN NW5 72 C4
STHL UB1 84 A2
Ladymount WLGTN SM6 176 D3
Lady's Cl WATW WD18 21 G3
Ladyship Ter EDUL SE22 * 131 J6
Ladysmith Av EHAM E6 95 J1
GNTH/NBYPK IG2 60 D6
Ladysmith Cl MLHL NW7 37 J6
Ladysmith Rd CAN/RD E16 94 D2
ELTH/MOT SE9 135 F5
EN EN1 30 B1
KTN/HRWW/WS HA3 48 E1
TOTM N17 56 C1
Lady Somerset Rd KTTN NW5 72 B3
Ladywell Cl BROCKY SE4 132 D4
Ladywell Rd LEW SE13 132 D4
Ladywell St SRTFD E15 76 D7
Ladywell Water Tower
BROCKY SE4 * 132 C2
Ladywood Av
STMC/STPC BR5 169 K4
Ladywood Rd SURB KT6 172 C1
Lafone Av FELT TW13 122 B7
Lafone St STHWK SE1 19 L1
Lagado Ms BERM/RHTH SE16 93 F7
Laidlaw Dr WCHMH N21 29 F4
Laing Dean NTHLT UB5 65 G7
Laings Av MTCM CR4 162 E1
Lainlock Pl HSLW TW3 103 G7
Lainson St WAND/EARL SW18 127 K6
Lairdale Cl DUL SE21 130 D7
Lairs Cl HOLWY N7 * 72 E5
Laitwood Rd BAL SW12 129 G7
Lake Av BMLY BR1 152 E5
Lake Cl BCTR RM8 79 K2
Lakedale Rd
WOOL/PLUM SE18 115 K4
Lake Dr BUSH WD23 34 C1
Lakefield Rd WDGN N22 55 H1
Lake Gdns DAGE RM10 80 C4
RCHPK/HAM TW10 143 H2
WLGTN SM6 176 B2
Lakehall Gdns THHTH CR7 164 C4
Lakehall Rd THHTH CR7 164 C4
Lake House Rd WAN E11 76 E2
Lakehurst Rd HOR/WEW KT19 173 G4
Lakeland Cl
KTN/HRWW/WS HA3 34 D5
Lakenheath STHGT/OAK N14 28 D4
Lake Ri ROM RM1 63 H2
Lake Rd CHDH RM6 61 K3
CROY/NA CR0 179 H1
DAGW RM9 98 D2
LEY E10 57 K6
WIM/MER SW19 146 D4
Lakeside BECK BR3 166 E2
ENC/FH EN2 28 D3
HOR/WEW KT19 173 G5
WEA W13 85 J5
WLGTN SM6 176 B3
Lakeside Av REDBR IG4 59 H3
THMD SE28 97 G7
Lakeside Cl BFN/LL DA15 136 D4
RSLP HA4 46 B3
SNWD SE25 165 H1
Lakeside Crs EBAR EN4 27 K5
Lakeside Dr ESH/CLAY KT10 170 C5
HAYES BR2 181 J2
WLSDN NW10 86 B2
Lakeside Rd PLMGR N13 41 F3
WKENS W14 107 G2
Lakeside Wy WBLY HA9 68 C3
Lakes Rd HAYES BR2 181 G4
Lakeswood Rd
STMC/STPC BR5 169 G5
The Lake BUSH WD23 22 D7
Lake Vw EDGW HA8 36 B4
Lake View Est BOW E3 * 93 F1
Lakeview Rd WELL DA16 136 C3
WNWD SE27 149 G4
Lake View Ter UED N18 * 42 B3
Lakis Cl HAMP NW3 71 G3
Laleham Av MLHL NW7 37 F2
Laleham Ct SUT SM1 * 175 G4
Laleham Rd CAT SE6 133 F6
Lalor St FUL/PGN SW6 127 H1
Lambarde Av
ELTH/MOT SE9 154 A3
Lamb Cl NTHLT UB5 83 J2
Lamberhurst Rd BCTR RM8 62 A7
WNWD SE27 149 G3
Lambert Av RCH/KEW TW9 125 H2
Lambert Ct BUSH WD23 21 H3
Lambert Jones Ms
BARB EC2Y * 12 E2
Lambert Rd
BRXS/STRHM SW2 129 K4
CAN/RD E16 95 F5
NFNCH/WDSPK N12 39 H4
Lambert's Pl CROY/NA CR0 164 E7
Lambert's Rd BRYLDS KT5 159 F4
Lambert St IS N1 6 A2
Lambert Wy
NFNCH/WDSPK N12 39 G4
Lambeth Br WEST SW1P 17 K5
Lambeth High St STHWK SE1 17 L6
Lambeth Hl BLKFR EC4V 12 E6
Lambeth Palace Rd
STHWK SE1 17 L4
Lambeth Rd CROY/NA CR0 164 B7
STHWK SE1 18 A4
Lambeth Wk LBTH SE11 17 M5
PECK SE15 131 G1
Lambkins Ms WALTH E17 58 A3
Lamb La HACK E8 74 D6
Lamble St KTTN NW5 72 A3
Lambley Rd DAGW RM9 79 H5
Lambolle Pl HAMP NW3 71 J5
Lambolle Rd HAMP NW3 71 J5
Lambourn Cl HNWL W7 104 A1
KTTN NW5 * 72 C3
SAND/SEL CR2 177 H7
Lambourne Av
WIM/MER SW19 146 D3
Lambourne Gdns BARK IG11 79 F6
CHING E4 43 J1
EN EN1 30 B1
Lambourne Gv
BERM/RHTH SE16 112 A4
KUT/HW KT1 159 J1
Lambourne Pl BKHTH/KID SE3 134 A1
Lambourne Rd BARK IG11 78 E6
WAN E11 58 A6
Lambourn Rd VX/NE SW8 129 G2
Lambrook Ter FUL/PGN SW6 107 H7
Lambs Cl ED N9 42 C1
Lamb's Conduit Pas
FSBYW WC1X 11 L2
Lamb's Conduit St
BMSBY WC1N 11 L1
Lambscroft Av ELTH/MOT SE9 153 G2
Lambs Meadow WFD IG8 59 H1
Lambs Ms IS N1 6 C4
Lamb's Pas STLK EC1Y 13 G1
Lambs Ter ED N9 * 41 K1
Lamb St WCHPL E1 13 L2
Lambs Wk ENC/FH EN2 29 J1
Lambton Pl NTGHL W11 * 88 D6
Lambton Rd ARCH N19 54 E7
RYNPK SW20 146 A7
Lamb Wk STHWK SE1 19 J2
Lamerock Rd BMLY BR1 152 D3
Lamerton Rd BARK/HLT IG6 60 B1
Lamerton St DEPT SE8 112 D5
Lamford Cl TOTM N17 41 K6
Lamington St HMSMTH W6 106 E3
Lamlash St LBTH SE11 18 C5
Lammas Av MTCM CR4 163 F1
Lammas La ESH/CLAY KT10 170 A3
Lammas Park Gdns EA W5 85 J7
Lammas Rd HOM E9 75 F6
LEY E10 75 H1
RCHPK/HAM TW10 143 J3
WATW WD18 21 G4
Lammermoor Rd BAL SW12 * 129 G6
Lamont Rd WBPTN SW10 108 C5
Lamont Road Pas
WBPTN SW10 * 108 C5
Lamorbey Cl BFN/LL DA15 155 F1
Lamorbey Pk BFN/LL DA15 * 136 C7
Lamorna Cl WALTH E17 58 A1
Lamorna Gv STAN HA7 35 K7
Lampard Gv STNW/STAM N16 56 B7
Lampern Sq BETH E2 * 92 C2
Lampeter Sq HMSMTH W6 107 H5
Lamplighter Cl WCHPL E1 92 E3
Lampmead Rd
LEE/GVPK SE12 133 H4
Lamport Cl WOOL/PLUM SE18 114 E3
Lampton Av HSLW TW3 103 F7
Lampton House Cl
WIM/MER SW19 146 B3
Lampton Park Rd HSLW TW3 123 G1
Lampton Rd HEST TW5 103 G7
HSLW TW3 123 G1
Lamson Rd RAIN RM13 99 H3
Lanacre Av EDGW HA8 37 F7
Lanadron Cl ISLW TW7 124 A1
Lanark Cl EA W5 85 J4
Lanark Pl MV/WKIL W9 2 F9
Lanark Rd MV/WKIL W9 2 E7
Lanbury Rd PECK SE15 132 A3
Lancashire Ct
MYFR/PKLN W1K 10 C6
Lancaster Av BARK IG11 78 E6
MTCM CR4 163 K3
WAN E11 59 F3
WIM/MER SW19 146 B4
WNWD SE27 149 H1
Lancaster Cl CDALE/KGS NW9 37 H6
HAYES BR2 167 J3
IS N1 7 K2
STWL/WRAY TW19 120 B5
TOTM N17 * 42 C6
WPK KT4 160 E6
Lancaster Ct BAY/PAD W2 8 F6
Lancaster Dr HAMP NW3 71 J5
HCH RM12 81 K4
POP/IOD E14 94 A7
Lancaster Garde BMLY BR1 168 D4
Lancaster Gdn KUTN/CMB KT2 143 K4
Lancaster Gdns
KUTN/CMB KT2 144 A4
WIM/MER SW19 146 C4
Lancaster Ga BAY/PAD W2 8 E7
Lancaster Gv HAMP NW3 71 J5
Lancaster House
WOOL/PLUM SE18 * 114 D6
Lancaster Ms BAY/PAD W2 8 F6
RCHPK/HAM TW10 125 F6
WAND/EARL SW18 * 128 A4
Lancaster Pk
RCHPK/HAM TW10 125 F4
Lancaster Pl COVGDN WC2E 11 L7
TWK TW1 124 B5
WIM/MER SW19 146 B4
Lancaster Rd EBAR EN4 27 H3
FBAR/BDGN N11 40 D5
FSBYPK N4 55 G6
FSTGT E7 77 E6
NKENS W10 88 B5
NTHLT UB5 66 C5
RYLN/HDSTN HA2 48 A4
SNWD SE25 165 G1
STHL UB1 83 J6
UED N18 42 B4
WALTH E17 57 F1
WAN E11 76 C1
WIM/MER SW19 146 B4
WLSDN NW10 69 H4
Lancaster Stables
HAMP NW3 * 71 J5
Lancaster St STHWK SE1 18 C2
Lancaster Ter BAY/PAD W2 9 G6
Lancaster Wk HYS/HAR UB3 82 A5
Lancaster Wy WPK KT4 161 F6
Lancaster West NTGHL W11 * 88 C5
Lancastrian Rd WLGTN SM6 176 E6
Lancefield St NKENS W10 88 D2
Lancell St STNW/STAM N16 74 A1
Lancelot Av ALP/SUD HA0 67 K3
Lancelot Crs ALP/SUD HA0 67 K3
Lancelot Gdns EBAR EN4 28 A6
Lancelot Pde ALP/SUD HA0 * 68 A4
Lancelot Pl SKENS SW7 15 L2
Lancelot Rd ALP/SUD HA0 67 K3
WELL DA16 136 B3
Lance Rd HRW HA1 48 C6
Lancer Sq KENS W8 14 C1
Lancey Cl CHARL SE7 114 C3
Lanchester Rd HGT N6 53 K4
Lanchester Wy NWCR SE14 111 K7
Lancing Gdns ED N9 30 B7
Lancing Rd CROY/NA CR0 164 A5
FELT TW13 140 D1
GNTH/NBYPK IG2 60 D5
WEA W13 85 H6
Lancing St CAMTN NW1 5 G8
Landau Ter HAYES BR2 181 J3
Landau Wy ERITH DA8 119 G4
Landcroft Rd EDUL SE22 131 G5
Landells Rd EDUL SE22 131 G5
Landford Rd PUT/ROE SW15 127 F2
Landgrove Rd
WIM/MER SW19 146 E4
Landleys Flds HOLWY N7 * 72 D4
Landmann Wy NWCR SE14 112 A5
Landon Pl KTBR SW1X 15 L3
Landons Cl POP/IOD E14 94 A7
Landor Rd BRXN/ST SW9 129 K2
Landor Wk SHB W12 106 D1
Landra Gdns WCHMH N21 29 H5
Landridge Rd FUL/PGN SW6 127 H1
Landrock Rd CEND/HSY/T N8 54 E5
Landscape Rd WFD IG8 45 F6
Landseer Av MNPK E12 78 A4
Landseer Cl EDGW HA8 50 C1
EMPK RM11 63 K7
WIM/MER SW19 147 G7
Landseer Rd ARCH N19 72 E2
EN EN1 30 C4
NWMAL KT3 160 A6
SUT SM1 174 E5
Lands' End BORE WD6 23 K5
Landstead Rd
WOOL/PLUM SE18 115 J6
Lane Ap MLHL NW7 * 38 C4
Lane Cl CRICK NW2 69 K2
Lane Gdns BUSH WD23 22 E7
ESH/CLAY KT10 171 F6
Lane Ms MNPK E12 77 K2
Lanercost Gdns
STHGT/OAK N14 28 E5
Lanercost Rd
BRXS/STRHM SW2 149 G1
Laneside CHST BR7 154 B4
EDGW HA8 36 E4
Laneside Av BCTR RM8 62 B6
The Lane STJWD NW8 2 E6
Laneway PUT/ROE SW15 126 E4
Lanfranc Rd BOW E3 93 G1
Lanfrey Pl WKENS W14 107 J4
Langbourne Av HGT N6 72 A1
Langbourne Wy
ESH/CLAY KT10 171 F5
Langbrook Rd BKHTH/KID SE3 134 C2
Langcroft Cl CAR SM5 175 K2
Langdale Av MTCM CR4 162 E2
Langdale Cl BCTR RM8 61 J7
MORT/ESHN SW14 125 J3
WALW SE17 18 E9
Langdale Dr YEAD UB4 82 C1
Langdale Gdns HCH RM12 81 J4
Langdale Pde MTCM CR4 * 162 E1
Langdale Rd GNWCH SE10 113 F6
THHTH CR7 164 B3
Langdale St WCHPL E1 * 92 D5
Langdale Ter BORE WD6 * 25 F2
Langdon Ct WLSDN NW10 69 G7
Langdon Crs EHAM E6 96 A1
Langdon Dr CDALE/KGS NW9 50 E7
Langdon House
WOOL/PLUM SE18 * 114 D6
Langdon Pk TEDD TW11 143 J6
Langdon Park Rd HGT N6 54 B6
Langdon Pl MORT/ESHN SW14 125 J2
Langdon Rd EHAM E6 78 A7
HAYES BR2 168 A2
MRDN SM4 162 B4
Langdon Shaw SCUP DA14 155 F4
Langdon Wk MRDN SM4 162 B4
Langdon Wy STHWK SE1 111 H3
Langford Cl HACK E8 74 C4
SEVS/STOTM N15 56 A5
STJWD NW8 2 F5
Langford Crs EBAR EN4 27 K3
Langford Gn CMBW SE5 131 F2
Langford Pl SCUP DA14 155 G2
STJWD NW8 2 F6
Langford Rd EBAR EN4 27 K3
FUL/PGN SW6 128 A1
WFD IG8 45 G5
Langfords BKHH IG9 45 H1
Langham Ct RSLP HA4 * 65 F4
Langham Dr GDMY/SEVK IG3 61 H5
Langham Gdns ALP/SUD HA0 67 J1
EDGW HA8 36 E6
RCHPK/HAM TW10 143 J3
WCHMH N21 29 G4
WEA W13 85 H6
Langham House Cl
RCHPK/HAM TW10 143 K3
Langham Pde
SEVS/STOTM N15 * 55 H2
Langham Park Pl HAYES BR2 167 J3
Langham Pl CHSWK W4 106 B5
REGST W1B 10 D3
SEVS/STOTM N15 55 H2
Langham Rd EDGW HA8 36 E5
RYNPK SW20 146 A7
SEVS/STOTM N15 55 J3
TEDD TW11 143 H4
Langham St REGST W1B 10 D3
Langhedge Cl UED N18 42 B5
Langhedge La UED N18 42 B4
Langholm Cl BAL SW12 129 J6
Langholme BUSH WD23 22 C7
Langhorn Dr WHTN TW2 123 K6
Langhorne Rd DAGE RM10 80 C6
Langland Ct NTHWD HA6 32 A6
Langland Crs STAN HA7 49 K1
Langland Dr PIN HA5 33 J6
Langland Gdns CROY/NA CR0 179 H1
HAMP NW3 71 F4
Langler Rd WLSDN NW10 88 A1
Langley Av RSLP HA4 65 F1
SURB KT6 158 E7
WPK KT4 174 B1
Langley Ct BECK BR3 * 166 E3
COVGDN WC2E 11 J6
Langley Crs DAGW RM9 79 J6
EDGW HA8 36 E2
HYS/HAR UB3 101 J6
WAN E11 59 F6
Langley Dr ACT W3 105 J1
WAN E11 59 F6
Langley Gdns DAGW RM9 79 K6
STMC/STPC BR5 169 G5
Langley Gv NWMAL KT3 160 A1
Langley La VX/NE SW8 17 K9
Langley Pk MLHL NW7 37 G5
Langley Park Rd BELMT SM2 175 G5
Langley Pl WPK KT4 174 B1
Langley Rd BECK BR3 166 A3
ISLW TW7 124 A1
SAND/SEL CR2 179 F7
SURB KT6 159 F6
WIM/MER SW19 146 D7
Langley St LSQ/SEVD WC2H 11 J5
Langley Wy WWKM BR4 167 G7
Langley Wd BECK BR3 * 167 H4
Langmead Dr BUSH WD23 22 D7
Langmead St WNWD SE27 149 H3
Langport Ct WOT/HER KT12 156 B7
Langridge Ms HPTN TW12 141 K5
Langroyd Rd TOOT SW17 147 K1
Langside Av PUT/ROE SW15 126 D3
Langside Crs STHGT/OAK N14 40 D2
Langston Hughes Cl
HNHL SE24 * 130 C3
Lang St WCHPL E1 92 E3
Langthorn Ct LOTH EC2R * 13 H4
Langthorne Rd WAN E11 76 B2
Langthorne St FUL/PGN SW6 107 G7
Langton Av EHAM E6 96 A2
TRDG/WHET N20 27 G6
Langton Cl FSBYW WC1X 5 M8
Langton Gv NTHWD HA6 32 A4
Langton Ri EDUL SE22 131 J6
Langton Rd BRXN/ST SW9 110 C6
CRICK NW2 70 A2
E/WMO/HCT KT8 157 H4
KTN/HRWW/WS HA3 34 C6
Langton St WBPTN SW10 108 B5
Langton Vls TOTM N17 * 42 C7
Langton Wy CROY/NA CR0 178 A3
Langtry Rd KIL/WHAMP NW6 2 C4
NTHLT UB5 83 H1
Langtry Wk STJWD NW8 2 F2
Langwood Cha TEDD TW11 143 J5
Langworth Dr YEAD UB4 83 F5
Lanhill Rd MV/WKIL W9 2 A9
Lanier Rd LEW SE13 133 F5
Lanigan Dr HSLW TW3 123 G4
Lankaster Gdns EFNCH N2 39 H7
Lankers Dr RYLN/HDSTN HA2 47 K5
Lankton Cl BECK BR3 152 A7
Lannock Rd HYS/HAR UB3 82 D7
Lannoy Rd ELTH/MOT SE9 135 H7
Lanrick Rd POP/IOD E14 94 B4
Lanridge Rd ABYW SE2 116 E2
Lansbury Av BARK IG11 79 G6
CHDH RM6 62 A4
EBED/NFELT TW14 122 A5
UED N18 41 K4
Lansbury Cl WLSDN NW10 68 E4
Lansbury Dr YEAD UB4 82 D4
Lansbury Gdns POP/IOD E14 * 94 B5
Lansbury Wy UED N18 42 A4
Lanscombe Wk VX/NE SW8 * 109 K6
Lansdell Rd MTCM CR4 163 F1
Lansdown Cl WOT/HER KT12 156 B7
Lansdowne Av BXLYHN DA7 116 D6
ORP BR6 169 G7
Lansdowne Cl BRYLDS KT5 172 D1
TWK TW1 124 A7
Lansdowne Copse WPK KT4 * 173 J1
Lansdowne Ct WPK KT4 173 J1
Lansdowne Crs NTGHL W11 88 C6
Lansdowne Dr HACK E8 74 C6
Lansdowne Gdns VX/NE SW8 109 K7
Lansdowne Gn VX/NE SW8 109 K6
Lansdowne Gv WLSDN NW10 69 G3
Lansdowne Hl WNWD SE27 149 H2
Lansdowne La CHARL SE7 114 C4
Lansdowne Ms CHARL SE7 114 C4
NTGHL W11 88 D7
Lansdowne Pl NRWD SE19 150 B6
STHWK SE1 19 H3
Lansdowne Ri NTGHL W11 88 C6
Lansdowne Rd BMLY BR1 152 E6
CHING E4 43 J1
CROY/NA CR0 164 E7
FNCH N3 38 D6
GDMY/SEVK IG3 61 F7
HACK E8 74 C5
HOR/WEW KT19 172 E6
HSLW TW3 123 G2
MUSWH N10 54 C1
NTGHL W11 88 C6
RYNPK SW20 146 A6
STAN HA7 35 J5
SWFD E18 58 E2
TOTM N17 42 C7
WALTH E17 57 J5
WAN E11 76 D1
Lansdowne Ter BMSBY WC1N 11 K1
Lansdowne Wk NTGHL W11 88 C7
Lansdowne Wy VX/NE SW8 109 K7
Lansdowne Wood Cl
WNWD SE27 149 H2
Lansdown Rd FSTGT E7 77 G6
SCUP DA14 155 H2
Lansfield Av UED N18 42 C3
Lantern Cl ALP/SUD HA0 67 K4
PUT/ROE SW15 126 D3
Lanterns Ct POP/IOD E14 112 D2
Lantern Wy WDR/YW UB7 100 B1
Lant St STHWK SE1 18 E1
Lanvanor Rd PECK SE15 131 K1
Lapford Cl MV/WKIL W9 * 88 D3
Lapse Wood Wk FSTH SE23 131 J7
Lapstone Gdns
KTN/HRWW/WS HA3 49 J5
Lapwing Cl ERITH DA8 * 118 E6
Lapwing Ter FSTGT E7 77 H4
Lapwing Wy YEAD UB4 83 H5
Lapworth Ct BAY/PAD W2 8 D2
Lara Cl CHSGTN KT9 172 A6
LEW SE13 133 F5
Larbert Rd STRHM/NOR SW16 148 C7
Larch Av ACT W3 87 G7

Larch Cl BAL SW12 148 B1
DEPT SE8 112 C5
FBAR/BDGN N11 40 A6
Larch Crs HOR/WEW KT19 172 D5
YEAD UB4 83 G3
Larch Dr CHSWK W4 * 105 H4
Larches Av MORT/ESHN SW14 126 A3
The Larches BUSH WD23 21 J4
PLMGR N13 41 J2
Larch Gv BFN/LL DA15 136 A7
Larch Rd CRICK NW2 70 A3
LEY E10 75 J1
Larch Tree Wy CROY/NA CR0 179 J2
Larch Wy HAYES BR2 169 F6
Larchwood Rd ELTH/MOT SE9 154 B1
Larcombe Cl CROY/NA CR0 178 B3
Larcom St WALW SE17 18 F6
Larden Rd ACT W3 106 B1
Largewood Av SURB KT6 172 C1
Larkbere Rd SYD SE26 151 G3
Larken Cl BUSH WD23 22 C7
Larken Dr BUSH WD23 22 C7
Larkfield Av
KTN/HRWW/WS HA3 49 H2
Larkfield Rd RCH/KEW TW9 125 F3
SCUP DA14 155 F2
Larkhall La CLAP SW4 129 J1
Larkhall Ri CLAP SW4 129 H2
Larkham Cl FELT TW13 140 C2
Larkhill Ter
WOOL/PLUM SE18 * 115 F6
Lark Rw BETH E2 74 E7
Larks Gv BARK IG11 78 E6
Larkshall Crs CHING E4 44 A3
Larkshall Rd CHING E4 44 A4
Larkspur Cl CDALE/KGS NW9 50 D4
TOTM N17 41 K6
Larkspur Gv EDGW HA8 36 E3
Larkspur Wy HOR/WEW KT19 172 E4
Larkswood Ri PIN HA5 47 G3
Larkswood Rd CHING E4 43 J3
Lark Wy CAR SM5 162 D6
Larkway Cl CDALE/KGS NW9 51 F3
Larnach Rd HMSMTH W6 107 G5
Larne Rd RSLP HA4 46 D6
Larner Rd ERITH DA8 118 B6
Larpent Av PUT/ROE SW15 127 F4
Larwood Cl GFD/PVL UB6 66 D4
Lascelles Av HRW HA1 48 D6
Lascelles Cl WAN E11 76 B1
Lascott's Rd WDGN N22 41 F5
Lassa Rd ELTH/MOT SE9 134 D4
Lassell St GNWCH SE10 113 G4
Lasseter Pl BKHTH/KID SE3 113 H5
Latchett Rd SWFD E18 45 F7
Latchingdon Gdns WFD IG8 45 J5
Latchmere Cl
RCHPK/HAM TW10 144 A4
Latchmere La KUTN/CMB KT2 144 B5
Latchmere Rd BTSEA SW11 128 E1
KUTN/CMB KT2 144 A5
Latchmere St BTSEA SW11 128 E1
Lateward Rd BTFD TW8 104 E5
Latham Cl EHAM E6 95 J5
Latham Rd TWK TW1 124 A6
Latham's Wy CROY/NA CR0 164 A7
Lathkill Cl EN EN1 30 C6
Lathom Rd EHAM E6 77 K6
Latimer Av EHAM E6 77 K7
Latimer Cl PIN HA5 33 G7
WATW WD18 20 C4
WPK KT4 173 K3
Latimer Gdns PIN HA5 33 G7
Latimer Pl NKENS W10 88 A5
Latimer Rd BAR EN5 27 F2
CROY/NA CR0 * 177 H2
FSTGT E7 77 F3
NKENS W10 88 A4
SEVS/STOTM N15 56 A5
TEDD TW11 143 F4
WIM/MER SW19 147 F5
Latona Rd PECK SE15 111 H5
Lattimer Pl CHSWK W4 106 B6
Latton Cl ESH/CLAY KT10 170 B3
WOT/HER KT12 156 E6
Latymer Gdns FNCH N3 * 52 C1
Latymer Rd ED N9 42 B1
Latymer Wy ED N9 41 K1
Laubin Cl TWK TW1 124 C3
Lauder Cl NTHLT UB5 83 H1
Lauderdale Dr
RCHPK/HAM TW10 143 K2
Lauderdale Pde
MV/WKIL W9 * 2 C8
Lauderdale Pl BARB EC2Y * 12 F3
Lauderdale Rd MV/WKIL W9 2 D8
Laud St CROY/NA CR0 177 J2
LBTH SE11 17 L7
Laughton Rd NTHLT UB5 83 H1
Launcelot St STHWK SE1 18 A2
Launceston Gdns
GFD/PVL UB6 67 J7
Launceston Pl KENS W8 14 E3
Launceston Rd GFD/PVL UB6 67 J7
Launch St POP/IOD E14 113 F2
Launders Ga ACT W3 * 105 J1
Laundress La
STNW/STAM N16 74 C2
Laundry Ms FSTH SE23 132 A6
Laundry Rd HMSMTH W6 107 H5
Laura Cl EN EN1 30 A4
WAN E11 59 G4
Lauradale Rd EFNCH N2 53 K3
Laura Pl CLPT E5 74 E3
Laura Ter FSBYPK N4 * 73 H1
Laurel Av TWK TW1 124 A7
Laurel Bank
NFNCH/WDSPK N12 * 39 G3
Laurel Bank Gdns
FUL/PGN SW6 127 J1
Laurel Cl BFN/LL DA15 155 G2
OXHEY WD19 21 H6
TOOT SW17 147 J4
Laurel Crs CROY/NA CR0 179 J2
ROMW/RG RM7 63 G7
Laurel Dr WCHMH N21 29 G6
Laurel Gdns BMLY BR1 168 D3
CHING E4 31 K6
HNWL W7 84 E7
HSLWW TW4 122 D3
MLHL NW7 37 F2
Laurel Gv PGE/AN SE20 150 D6
SYD SE26 151 F4
Laurel La WDR/YW UB7 100 B3
Laurel Pk KTN/HRWW/WS HA3 35 F6
Laurel Rd BARN SW13 126 D1
HPTN TW12 142 D4
RYNPK SW20 145 K7
The Laurels BRXN/ST SW9 * 110 C6
BUSH WD23 * 34 E1
Laurel St HACK E8 74 B5
Laurel Vw NFNCH/WDSPK N12 39 F2
TRDG/WHET N20 39 F2
Laurel Vls HNWL W7 * 103 K1
Laurel Wy SWFD E18 58 D3
TRDG/WHET N20 38 E2
Laurence Ms SHB W12 106 D1
Laurence Pountney Hl
CANST EC4R 13 G6
Laurence Pountney La
CANST EC4R 13 G6
Laurie Gv NWCR SE14 112 B7
Laurie Rd HNWL W7 84 E4
Laurier Rd CROY/NA CR0 165 G6
KTTN NW5 72 B2
Laurimel Cl STAN HA7 35 H5
Laurino Pl BUSH WD23 34 C1
Lauriston Rd HOM E9 75 F6
WIM/MER SW19 146 B5
Lausanne Rd CEND/HSY/T N8 55 G3
PECK SE15 111 K7
Lavender Av CDALE/KGS NW9 50 E7
MTCM CR4 147 J7
WPK KT4 174 A2
Lavender Cl CAR SM5 176 A3
CHEL SW3 108 C5
CHING E4 43 J3
HAYES BR2 168 D5
Lavender Ct E/WMO/HCT KT8 157 G2
Lavender Gdns BTSEA SW11 128 E3
KTN/HRWW/WS HA3 34 E5
Lavender Gv HACK E8 74 C6
MTCM CR4 147 J7
Lavender Hl BTSEA SW11 128 E2
Lavender Pl IL IG1 78 B4
Lavender Ri WDR/YW UB7 100 D1
Lavender Rd
BERM/RHTH SE16 93 G7
BTSEA SW11 128 C2
CROY/NA CR0 164 A5
HOR/WEW KT19 172 D4
SUT SM1 175 H3
WLGTN SM6 176 A4
Lavender Sweep BTSEA SW11 128 E3
Lavender Ter BTSEA SW11 * 128 D2
Lavender V WLGTN SM6 176 D5
Lavender Wk BTSEA SW11 128 E3
Lavender Wy CROY/NA CR0 166 A5
Lavengro Rd WNWD SE27 149 J1
Lavenham Rd
WAND/EARL SW18 146 D1
Lavers Rd STNW/STAM N16 74 A2
Laverstoke Gdns
PUT/ROE SW15 126 C6
Laverton Ms ECT SW5 * 14 D6
Laverton Pl ECT SW5 14 D6
Lavidge Rd ELTH/MOT SE9 153 J1
Lavina Gv IS N1 5 L5
Lavington Cl HOM E9 75 H5
Lavington Rd CROY/NA CR0 177 F2
WEA W13 85 H7
Lavington St STHWK SE1 12 D9
Lawdon Gdns CROY/NA CR0 177 H3
Lawford Rd CHSWK W4 105 K6
IS N1 7 J2
KTTN NW5 72 C5
Lawless St POP/IOD E14 * 93 K6
Lawley Rd STHGT/OAK N14 28 B6
Lawley St CLPT E5 74 E3
Lawn Cl BMLY BR1 153 F6
EN EN1 30 B6
NWMAL KT3 160 B1
RSLP HA4 64 D2
Lawn Crs RCH/KEW TW9 125 H1
Lawn Farm Gv CHDH RM6 62 A3
Lawn Gdns HNWL W7 84 E7
Lawn House Cl POP/IOD E14 113 F1
Lawn La VX/NE SW8 17 K9
Lawn Rd BECK BR3 151 H6
HAMP NW3 71 K4
Lawns Ct WBLY HA9 * 68 C1
The Lawns BELMT SM2 174 C6
BKHTH/KID SE3 * 133 J2
CHING E4 43 J4
NRWD SE19 149 K7
PIN HA5 34 B6
SCUP DA14 155 H3
Lawnswood BAR EN5 * 26 C4
Lawn Ter BKHTH/KID SE3 133 J2
The Lawn NWDGN UB2 103 F4
Lawn V PIN HA5 47 H1
Lawrence Av MLHL NW7 37 G3
MNPK E12 78 A3
NWMAL KT3 160 A5
PLMGR N13 41 H3
WALTH E17 43 F7
WLSDN NW10 69 F7
Lawrence Blds
STNW/STAM N16 74 B2
Lawrence Campe Cl
TRDG/WHET N20 39 H2
Lawrence Cl SEVS/STOTM N15 56 A3
SHB W12 87 K6
Lawrence Ct MLHL NW7 37 G4
OXHEY WD19 * 33 H2
Lawrence Crs DAGE RM10 80 D2
EDGW HA8 50 C1
Lawrence Dr HGDN/ICK UB10 64 A3
Lawrence Gdns MLHL NW7 37 H2
Lawrence Hl CHING E4 43 J1
Lawrence La CITYW EC2V 12 F5
Lawrence Pde ISLW TW7 * 124 C2
Lawrence Pl IS N1 5 K3
Lawrence Rd EA W5 104 E3
EHAM E6 77 J7
ERITH DA8 117 J6
GPK RM2 63 K4
HPTN TW12 141 K6
HSLWW TW4 122 B3
PIN HA5 47 H4
PLSTW E13 77 F7
RCHPK/HAM TW10 143 J3
SEVS/STOTM N15 56 A2
SNWD SE25 165 G3
UED N18 42 D3
WWKM BR4 180 E3
YEAD UB4 82 A1
Lawrence St CAN/RD E16 94 D4
CHEL SW3 108 D5
MLHL NW7 37 H3
Lawrence Wy WLSDN NW10 68 E2
Lawrence Yd
SEVS/STOTM N15 56 A3
Lawrie Park Av SYD SE26 150 D4
Lawrie Park Crs SYD SE26 150 D4
Lawrie Park Gdns SYD SE26 150 D4
Lawrie Park Rd SYD SE26 150 E5
Laws Cl SNWD SE25 164 E3
Lawson Cl CAN/RD E16 95 G4
IL IG1 78 D4
WIM/MER SW19 146 B2
Lawson Gdns PIN HA5 46 E2
Lawson Rd STHL UB1 83 K3
Law St STHWK SE1 19 H3
Lawton Rd BOW E3 93 G2
EBAR EN4 27 H2
LEY E10 58 A7
Laxcon Cl WLSDN NW10 69 F4
Laxley Cl CMBW SE5 110 C6
Laxton Pl CAMTN NW1 4 D9
Layard Rd BERM/RHTH SE16 111 J3
THHTH CR7 164 E1
Layard Sq BERM/RHTH SE16 111 J3
Laycock St IS N1 73 G5
Layer Gdns ACT W3 86 C6
Layfield Cl HDN NW4 51 K6
Layfield Crs HDN NW4 51 K6
Layfield Rd HDN NW4 51 K6
Layhams Rd WWKM BR4 180 C3
Laymarsh Cl BELV DA17 117 G2
Laymead Cl NTHLT UB5 65 J5
Laystall St FSBYW WC1X 12 A1
Layton Crs CROY/NA CR0 177 G4
Layton Pl RCH/KEW TW9 105 H7
Layton Rd BTFD TW8 104 E4
HSLW TW3 123 G3
Layzell Wk ELTH/MOT SE9 134 C7
Lazenby Ct COVGDN WC2E * 11 J6
Leabank Cl HRW HA1 66 E2
Leabank Sq HOM E9 75 J5
Leabank Vw SEVS/STOTM N15 56 C5
Leabourne Rd
STNW/STAM N16 56 C5
Lea Bridge Rd LEY E10 75 F1
Lea Cl BUSH WD23 22 B4
WHTN TW2 122 C6
Lea Cots MTCM CR4 * 163 F1
Lea Crs RSLP HA4 64 D3
Leacroft Av BAL SW12 128 E6
Leacroft Cl WCHMH N21 41 H1
Leadale Av CHING E4 43 J1
Leadale Rd STNW/STAM N16 56 C5
Leadbeaters Cl
FBAR/BDGN N11 39 K4
Leadenhall Pl BANK EC3V 13 J5
Leadenhall St BANK EC3V 13 J5
Leader Av MNPK E12 78 A4
The Leadings WBLY HA9 68 E2
Leaf Cl NTHWD HA6 32 B6
THDIT KT7 157 K4
Leaf Gv WNWD SE27 149 G4
Leafield Cl STRHM/NOR SW16 149 H5
Leafield Rd RYNPK SW20 161 J2
SUT SM1 174 E1
Leafy Gv HAYES BR2 181 G4
Leafy Oak Rd LEE/GVPK SE12 153 G3
Leafy Wy CROY/NA CR0 178 B1
Lea Gdns WBLY HA9 68 B4
Leagrave St CLPT E5 74 E2
Lea Hall Gdns LEY E10 * 57 J7
Lea Hall Rd LEY E10 57 J7
Leahurst Rd LEW SE13 133 G4
Leake St STHWK SE1 17 M1
Lealand Rd SEVS/STOTM N15 56 B5
Leaming Cl MNPK E12 77 J4
Leamington Av BMLY BR1 153 G4
MRDN SM4 161 J3
WALTH E17 57 J4
Leamington Cl BMLY BR1 153 G3
HSLW TW3 123 H4
Leamington Crs
RYLN/HDSTN HA2 65 J2
Leamington Gdns
GDMY/SEVK IG3 79 F1
Leamington Pk ACT W3 87 F4
Leamington Pl YEAD UB4 82 D3
Leamington Rd NWDGN UB2 102 C3
Leamington Road Vls
NTGHL W11 88 D4
Leamore St HMSMTH W6 106 E3
Leamouth Rd POP/IOD E14 94 B5
Leander Rd BRXS/STRHM SW2 130 A5
NTHLT UB5 84 A1
THHTH CR7 164 A3
Learner Dr RYLN/HDSTN HA2 66 A1
Lea Rd BECK BR3 166 D1
NWDGN UB2 102 D3
Learoyd Gdns EHAM E6 96 A6
Leas Cl CHSGTN KT9 172 B6
Leas Dl ELTH/MOT SE9 154 A2
Leas Gn CHST BR7 155 F5
Leaside Av MUSWH N10 54 A2
Leaside Rd CLPT E5 56 E7
Leasowes Rd LEY E10 57 J7
The Leas BUSH WD23 21 K1
Leathart Cl HCH RM12 81 K6
Leatherbottle Gn
ERITH DA18 117 G2
Leather Cl MTCM CR4 163 F1
Leatherdale St WCHPL E1 * 93 F2
Leather Gdns SRTFD E15 76 C7
Leatherhead Cl
STNW/STAM N16 56 A7
Leatherhead Rd CHSGTN KT9 171 K6
Leather La HCIRC EC1N 12 A2
Leathermarket Ct STHWK SE1 19 J2
Leathermarket St STHWK SE1 19 J2
Leather Rd
BERM/RHTH SE16 * 112 A3
Leathersellers Cl BAR EN5 * 26 C2
Leather St WAP E1W 93 F6
Leathsale Rd
RYLN/HDSTN HA2 66 B2
Leathwaite Rd BTSEA SW11 128 E3
Leathwell Rd DEPT SE8 132 E1
Lea Valley Rd CHING E4 31 H5
Lea Valley Wk CLPT E5 56 E6
Leaveland Cl BECK BR3 166 D3
Leaver Gdns GFD/PVL UB6 84 D1
Leavesden Rd STAN HA7 35 G5
Leaway CLPT E5 * 56 E7
Lebanon Av FELT TW13 141 H4
Lebanon Gdns
WAND/EARL SW18 127 K5
Lebanon Pk TWK TW1 124 C6
Lebanon Rd CROY/NA CR0 165 F7
WAND/EARL SW18 127 K4
Lebrun Sq BKHTH/KID SE3 134 A3
Lechmere Ap WFD IG8 59 G1
Lechmere Rd CRICK NW2 69 K5
Leckford Rd
WAND/EARL SW18 147 G1
Leckhampton Pl
BRXS/STRHM SW2 130 B6
Leckwith Av ABYW SE2 117 F5
Lecky St SKENS SW7 15 G7
Leconfield Av BARN SW13 126 C2
Leconfield Rd HBRY N5 73 K3
Leda Rd WOOL/PLUM SE18 114 E2
Ledbury Ms North
NTGHL W11 8 A6
Ledbury Ms West NTGHL W11 8 A6
Ledbury Rd CROY/NA CR0 177 J3
NTGHL W11 88 D5
Ledbury St PECK SE15 111 H6
Ledrington Rd NRWD SE19 150 B5
Ledway Dr WBLY HA9 50 B7
Lee Av CHDH RM6 62 A5
Leechcroft Av BFN/LL DA15 136 A4
Leechcroft Rd WLGTN SM6 176 A2
Lee Church St LEW SE13 133 H3
Lee Cl WALTH E17 43 F7
Lee Conservancy Rd HOM E9 75 H4
Leecroft Rd BAR EN5 26 C3
Leeds Rd IL IG1 60 D7
Leeds St UED N18 42 C4
Lee High Rd LEW SE13 133 G3
Leeke St FSBYW WC1X 5 L7
Leeland Rd WEA W13 85 G7
Leeland Ter WEA W13 85 G7
Leeland Wy WLSDN NW10 69 G3
Leemount Cl HDN NW4 * 52 B3
Lee Pk BKHTH/KID SE3 133 J3
Lee Park Wy UED N18 43 F4
Lee Rd BKHTH/KID SE3 133 J2
EN EN1 30 C5
GFD/PVL UB6 67 J7
MLHL NW7 38 B6
WIM/MER SW19 147 F7
Lees Av NTHWD HA6 32 D7
Leeside BAR EN5 26 C4
Leeside Crs GLDGN NW11 52 C5
Leeside Rd TOTM N17 42 D5
Leeson Rd HNHL SE24 * 130 B4
Leesons Hl CHST BR7 169 K2
Lees Pl MYFR/PKLN W1K 10 A6
The Lees CROY/NA CR0 179 H1
Lee St HACK E8 7 L3
Lee Ter BKHTH/KID SE3 133 H2
The Lee NTHWD HA6 32 D4
Leeward Gdns
WIM/MER SW19 146 C5
Leeway DEPT SE8 112 C4
The Leeways CHEAM SM3 * 174 C5
Leewood Cl LEE/GVPK SE12 133 J5
Lefevre Wk BOW E3 75 H7
Leffern Rd SHB W12 106 D1
Lefroy Rd SHB W12 106 C1
Left Side STHGT/OAK N14 * 28 D6
Legard Rd HBRY N5 73 H2
Legatt Rd ELTH/MOT SE9 134 C4
Leggatt Rd SRTFD E15 94 A1
Legge St LEW SE13 133 F4
Leghorn Rd WLSDN NW10 87 J1
WOOL/PLUM SE18 115 J4
Legion Cl IS N1 6 B1
Legion Ct MRDN SM4 161 K5
Legion Ter BOW E3 75 J7
Legion Wy
NFNCH/WDSPK N12 39 J6
Legon Av ROMW/RG RM7 62 E7
Legrace Av HSLWW TW4 122 C1
Leicester Av MTCM CR4 163 K3
Leicester Cl WPK KT4 174 A3
Leicester Gdns
GDMY/SEVK IG3 60 E6
Leicester Pl LSQ/SEVD WC2H * 11 H6
Leicester Rd BAR EN5 27 F4
CROY/NA CR0 165 F6
EFNCH N2 53 J2
WAN E11 59 F4
WLSDN NW10 69 F6
Leicester Sq LSQ/SEVD WC2H 11 H7
Leicester St LSQ/SEVD WC2H 11 H6
Leigham Av
STRHM/NOR SW16 148 E2
Leigham Cl STRHM/NOR SW16 149 F2
Leigham Court Rd
STRHM/NOR SW16 149 F2
Leigham Dr ISLW TW7 103 K6
Leigham Hall Pde
STRHM/NOR SW16 * 148 E2
Leigham V STRHM/NOR SW16 149 G2
Leigh Av REDBR IG4 59 H3
Leigh Cl NWMAL KT3 160 A3
Leigh Ct BORE WD6 * 25 F1
RYLN/HDSTN HA2 * 48 E7
Leigh Crs CROY/NA CR0 179 K6
Leigh Gdns WLSDN NW10 88 A1
Leigh Hunt Dr
STHGT/OAK N14 28 D7
Leigh Orchard Cl
STRHM/NOR SW16 149 F2
Leigh Pl FELT TW13 122 B7
WELL DA16 136 B1
Leigh Rd EHAM E6 78 A6
HBRY N5 73 H3
HSLW TW3 123 J3
LEY E10 58 A6
Leigh Rodd OXHEY WD19 33 J2
Leigh St STPAN WC1H 5 J9
The Leigh KUTN/CMB KT2 145 G5
Leighton Av MNPK E12 78 A4
PIN HA5 47 J2
Leighton Cl EDGW HA8 50 C1
Leighton Crs KTTN NW5 72 C4
Leighton Gdns WLSDN NW10 88 A1
Leighton Gv KTTN NW5 72 C4
Leighton Pl KTTN NW5 72 C4
Leighton Rd EN EN1 30 B4
KTN/HRWW/WS HA3 48 D1
KTTN NW5 72 C4
WEA W13 104 B1
Leighton St CROY/NA CR0 164 C7
Leila Parnell Pl CHARL SE7 114 B5
Leinster Av MORT/ESHN SW14 125 K2
Leinster Gdns BAY/PAD W2 8 E5
Leinster Ms BAY/PAD W2 8 E7
Leinster Pl BAY/PAD W2 8 E5
Leinster Rd MUSWH N10 54 B3
Leinster Sq BAY/PAD W2 8 B5
Leinster Ter BAY/PAD W2 8 E6
Leisure Wy
NFNCH/WDSPK N12 39 H6
Leith Cl CDALE/KGS NW9 51 F7
Leithcote Gdns
STRHM/NOR SW16 149 F3
Leithcote Pth
STRHM/NOR SW16 149 F2
Leith Hl STMC/STPC BR5 155 G7
Leith Rd WDGN N22 41 H7
Leith Towers BELMT SM2 * 175 F6
Leith Yd KIL/WHAMP NW6 * 2 B3
Lela Av HSLWW TW4 122 A1
Lelitia Cl HACK E8 74 C7
Leman St WCHPL E1 13 M5
Lemark Cl STAN HA7 35 J5
Le May Av LEE/GVPK SE12 153 F2
Lemmon Rd GNWCH SE10 113 H5
Lemna Rd WAN E11 58 C6
Lemonwell Dr ELTH/MOT SE9 135 G4
Lemsford Cl SEVS/STOTM N15 56 C5
Lemsford Ct BORE WD6 25 F3
Lena Crs ED N9 42 E1
Lena Gdns HMSMTH W6 107 F2
Lena Kennedy Cl CHING E4 44 A5
Lendal Ter CLAP SW4 129 J2
Lenelby Rd SURB KT6 159 H7
Len Freeman Pl FUL/PGN SW6 107 J6
Lenham Rd BXLYHN DA7 117 G5
LEE/GVPK SE12 133 J3
SUT SM1 175 F3
THHTH CR7 164 E1
Lennard Av WWKM BR4 180 C1
Lennard Cl WWKM BR4 180 C1
Lennard Rd CROY/NA CR0 164 D7
HAYES BR2 168 E7
SYD SE26 150 E5
Lennard Ter PGE/AN SE20 * 151 F5
Lennon Rd CRICK NW2 70 A4
Lennox Cl ROM RM1 63 H5
Lennox Gdns CROY/NA CR0 177 H3
IL IG1 59 K7
KTBR SW1X 15 L4
WLSDN NW10 69 H3
Lennox Gardens Ms
KTBR SW1X 15 L5
Lennox Rd FSBYPK N4 73 F1
WALTH E17 57 H5
Lensbury Wy ABYW SE2 116 E2
Lens Rd FSTGT E7 77 G6
Lenthall Rd HACK E8 7 M1
Lenthorp Rd GNWCH SE10 113 J3
Lentmead Rd BMLY BR1 152 D2
Lenton Ri RCH/KEW TW9 125 F2
Lenton St WOOL/PLUM SE18 115 J3
Lenton Ter FSBYPK N4 * 73 G1
Leof Crs CAT SE6 151 K4
Leominster Rd MRDN SM4 162 B5
Leominster Wk MRDN SM4 162 B5
Leonard Av MRDN SM4 162 B4
ROMW/RG RM7 63 F7
Leonard Ct KENS W8 * 14 A3
Leonard Pl HAYES BR2 * 181 J2
STNW/STAM N16 74 A3
Leonard Rd CHING E4 43 J5
ED N9 42 B2
FSTGT E7 76 E3
NWDGN UB2 102 C2
STRHM/NOR SW16 148 C7
Leonard St CAN/RD E16 95 J7
SDTCH EC2A 7 H9
Leontine Cl PECK SE15 111 H6
Leopold Av WIM/MER SW19 146 D4
Leopold Ms HOM E9 74 E7
Leopold Rd EA W5 86 B7
EFNCH N2 53 H2
UED N18 42 D4
WALTH E17 57 J4
WIM/MER SW19 146 D3
WLSDN NW10 69 G6
Leopold St BOW E3 93 H4
Leo St PECK SE15 111 J6
Leppoc Rd CLAP SW4 129 J4
Leroy St STHWK SE1 19 J5
Lerry Cl WKENS W14 107 J5
Lescombe Cl FSTH SE23 151 G2
Lescombe Rd FSTH SE23 151 G2
Lesley Cl BXLY DA5 137 J6
Leslie Gdns BELMT SM2 174 E6
Leslie Gv CROY/NA CR0 164 E7
Leslie Grove Pl CROY/NA CR0 165 F7
Leslie Park Rd CROY/NA CR0 165 F7
Leslie Rd CAN/RD E16 95 F5
EFNCH N2 53 H2
WAN E11 76 B3
Lesney Pk ERITH DA8 118 A5
Lesney Park Rd ERITH DA8 118 A5
Lessar Av CLAP SW4 129 H4
Lessingham Av TOOT SW17 147 K3
Lessing St FSTH SE23 132 B6
Lessington Av ROMW/RG RM7 62 E5
Lessness Av BXLYHN DA7 116 E6
Lessness Pk BELV DA17 117 G4
Lessness Rd MRDN SM4 162 B5
Lester Av SRTFD E15 94 C3
Lestock Cl SNWD SE25 165 H2
Leston Cl RAIN RM13 99 K2
Leswin Pl STNW/STAM N16 74 B2
Leswin Rd STNW/STAM N16 74 B2
Letchford Gdns WLSDN NW10 87 J2
Letchford Ms WLSDN NW10 * 87 J2
Letchford Ter
KTN/HRWW/WS HA3 * 34 B7
Letchworth Av
EBED/NFELT TW14 121 J6
Letchworth Cl OXHEY WD19 33 H4
Letchworth St TOOT SW17 147 K3
Letterstone Rd FUL/PGN SW6 107 J6
Lettice St FUL/PGN SW6 127 J1
Lett Rd SRTFD E15 76 B6
Leucha Rd WALTH E17 57 G4
Levana Cl WIM/MER SW19 127 H7
Levehurst Wy CLAP SW4 129 K1
Leven Cl OXHEY WD19 * 33 H4
Levendale Rd FSTH SE23 151 G1
Leven Rd POP/IOD E14 94 A4
Leven Wy HYS/HAR UB3 82 C5
Leverett St CHEL SW3 15 K5
Leverholme Gdns
ELTH/MOT SE9 154 A3
Leverson St
STRHM/NOR SW16 148 C5
Lever St FSBYE EC1V 6 E8
Leverton Pl KTTN NW5 72 C4
Leverton St KTTN NW5 72 C4
Levett Gdns GDMY/SEVK IG3 79 F3
Levett Rd BARK IG11 78 E5
Levine Gdns BARK IG11 97 K1
Lewes Cl NTHLT UB5 66 A5
Lewesdon Cl WIM/MER SW19 127 G7
Lewes Rd BMLY BR1 168 C1
NFNCH/WDSPK N12 39 J4
Leweston Pl STNW/STAM N16 56 B6
Lewgars Av CDALE/KGS NW9 50 E5
Lewing Cl ORP BR6 169 K7
Lewin Rd MORT/ESHN SW14 126 A2
STRHM/NOR SW16 148 D5
Lewin Ter EBED/NFELT TW14 121 G6
Lewis Av WALTH E17 43 J7
Lewis Cl STHGT/OAK N14 28 C6
Lewis Crs WLSDN NW10 69 F4
Lewis Gdns EFNCH N2 53 H1
SEVS/STOTM N15 56 B6
Lewis Gv LEW SE13 133 F3
Lewisham High St LEW SE13 132 E5
Lewisham Hl LEW SE13 133 F1
Lewisham Pk LEW SE13 132 E5
Lewisham Rd LEW SE13 133 F1
Lewisham Wy BROCKY SE4 132 C1
Lewis Pl HACK E8 74 C4
Lewis Rd MTCM CR4 162 D1
RCH/KEW TW9 * 124 E4
SCUP DA14 155 J2
STHL UB1 102 D1
SUT SM1 175 F3
WELL DA16 136 D2
Lewis St CAMTN NW1 4 D1
Lewiston Cl WPK KT4 160 E6
Lewis Wy DAGE RM10 80 D5
Lexden Dr CHDH RM6 61 H5
Lexden Rd ACT W3 86 D6
MTCM CR4 163 J3
Lexham Gdns KENS W8 14 B5
Lexham Ms KENS W8 14 B5
Lexington Cl BORE WD6 24 B2

Lexington Pl KUT/HW KT1 143 K7
Lexington St SOHO/CST W1F 10 F5
Lexington Wy BAR EN5 26 B3
Lexton Gdns BAL SW12 129 J7
Leyborne Av WEA W13 104 D1
Leyborne Pk RCH/KEW TW9 105 H7
Leybourne Rd CAMTN NW1 4 D2
CDALE/KGS NW9 50 C4
HGDN/ICK UB10 64 A7
WAN E11 58 D7
Leybourne St CAMTN NW1 4 C2
Leyburn Cl WALTH E17 58 A3
Leyburn Gdns CROY/NA CR0 178 A1
Leyburn Gv UED N18 42 C5
Leyburn House CHARL SE7 * 114 D6
Leyburn Rd UED N18 42 C5
Leycroft Gdns ERITH DA8 118 E7
Leyden St WCHPL E1 13 L3
Leydon Cl BERM/RHTH SE16 93 F7
Leyes Rd CAN/RD E16 95 H6
Leyfield WPK KT4 173 G1
Leyland Av PEND EN3 31 G1
Leyland Gdns WFD IG8 45 G4
Leylang Rd NWCR SE14 112 A6
Leys Av DAGE RM10 80 E7
Leys Cl DAGE RM10 80 E6
HRW HA1 48 D3
Leysdown Rd ELTH/MOT SE9 153 J1
Leysfield Rd SHB W12 106 D1
Leys Gdns EBAR EN4 28 A4
Leyspring Rd WAN E11 58 D7
The Leys EFNCH N2 53 G3
KTN/HRWW/WS HA3 50 B5
Ley St IL IG1 78 B1
Leyswood Dr
GNTH/NBYPK IG2 60 E4
Leythe Rd ACT W3 105 K1
Leyton Gra LEY E10 75 J1
Leyton Green Rd LEY E10 58 A5
Leyton Park Rd LEY E10 76 A1
Leyton Rd SRTFD E15 76 A4
WIM/MER SW19 147 G6
Leytonstone Rd SRTFD E15 76 C5
Leywick St SRTFD E15 94 C1
Liardet St NWCR SE14 112 B5
Liberia Rd HBRY N5 73 H5
Liberty Av WIM/MER SW19 147 H7
Liberty Cl UED N18 42 B3
WPK KT4 161 F7
Liberty Ms WDGN N22 41 H7
Liberty St BRXN/ST SW9 110 A7
Libra Rd BOW E3 75 H7
PLSTW E13 94 E1
Library Pde WLSDN NW10 * 69 G7
Library St STHWK SE1 18 D2
Library Wy WHTN TW2 123 H6
Lichfield Cl EBAR EN4 27 K2
Lichfield Gdns
RCH/KEW TW9 * 125 F4
Lichfield Gv FNCH N3 38 E7
Lichfield Rd BCTR RM8 79 H3
BOW E3 93 G2
CRICK NW2 70 C3
ED N9 42 C1
EHAM E6 95 H2
HSLWW TW4 122 B2
NTHWD HA6 46 E2
RCH/KEW TW9 105 G7
WFD IG8 44 C3
Lichfield Ter RCH/KEW TW9 * 125 F4
Lidbury Rd MLHL NW7 38 C5
Lidcote Gdns BRXN/ST SW9 * 130 B1
Liddell Cl KTN/HRWW/WS HA3 49 K2
Liddell Gdns WLSDN NW10 88 A1
Liddell Rd KIL/WHAMP NW6 70 E5
Lidding Rd
KTN/HRWW/WS HA3 49 K4
Liddington Rd SRTFD E15 76 D7
Liddon Rd BMLY BR1 168 B2
PLSTW E13 95 F2
Liden Cl LEY E10 57 H6
Lidfield Rd STNW/STAM N16 73 K3
Lidgate Rd CMBW SE5 * 111 G6
Lidiard Rd WAND/EARL SW18 147 G1
Lidlington Pl CAMTN NW1 4 F6
Lido Sq TOTM N17 55 K1
Lidyard Rd ARCH N19 54 C7
Liffler Rd WOOL/PLUM SE18 115 K4
Lifford St PUT/ROE SW15 127 G3
Lightcliffe Rd PLMGR N13 41 G3
Lighter Cl BERM/RHTH SE16 112 B3
Lighterman Ms WCHPL E1 93 F5
Lighterman's Rd
POP/IOD E14 112 D1
Lightfoot Rd CEND/HSY/T N8 54 E4
Lightley Cl ALP/SUD HA0 68 B7
Ligonier St BETH E2 7 L9
Lilac Cl CHING E4 43 H5
Lilac Gdns CROY/NA CR0 179 J2
EA W5 104 E2
HYS/HAR UB3 82 C5
ROMW/RG RM7 63 G7
Lilac Pl LBTH SE11 17 L6
Lilac St SHB W12 87 J6
Lilah Ms HAYES BR2 167 J1
Lilburne Gdns ELTH/MOT SE9 134 D4
Lilburne Rd ELTH/MOT SE9 134 D4
Lile Crs HNWL W7 84 E4
Lilestone St STJWD NW8 3 J9
Lilford Rd CMBW SE5 130 C1
Lilian Board Wy GFD/PVL UB6 66 D4
Lilian Gdns WFD IG8 45 F7
Lilian Rd STRHM/NOR SW16 148 C7
Lillechurch Rd BCTR RM8 79 H5
Lilleshall Rd MRDN SM4 162 C4
Lilley Cl WAP E1W 92 C7
Lilley La MLHL NW7 * 37 G4
Lillian Av ACT W3 105 H1
Lillian Rd BARN SW13 106 D5
Lillie Rd FUL/PGN SW6 107 G5
Lillieshall Rd CLAP SW4 129 G2
Lillie Yd FUL/PGN SW6 14 A9
Lillington Gardens Est
PIM SW1V 16 F6
Lilliput Av NTHLT UB5 65 J7
Lilliput Rd ROMW/RG RM7 63 F6
Lily Cl WKENS W14 107 H3
Lily Dr WDR/YW UB7 100 A3
Lily Gdns ALP/SUD HA0 85 J1
Lily Pl FARR EC1M 12 B2
Lily Rd WALTH E17 57 J5
Lilyville Rd FUL/PGN SW6 107 J7
Limbourne Av BCTR RM8 62 B6
Limburg Rd BTSEA SW11 128 D3
Limeburner La STP EC4M 12 C4
Lime Cl BKHH IG9 45 H1
BMLY BR1 168 D3
KTN/HRWW/WS HA3 49 G1
OXHEY WD19 21 H6
PIN HA5 46 D2
ROMW/RG RM7 62 E3
WAP E1W 92 C7
Lime Crs SUN TW16 156 B1
Limecroft Cl HOR/WEW KT19 173 F6
Limedene Cl PIN HA5 33 H7
Lime Gv BFN/LL DA15 136 A5
CHING E4 43 H5
HYS/HAR UB3 82 B6
NWMAL KT3 160 A2
RSLP HA4 47 F5
SHB W12 107 F1
TRDG/WHET N20 26 C7
TWK TW1 124 A5
Limeharbour POP/IOD E14 112 E2
Limehouse POP/IOD E14 * 93 J6
Limehouse Cswy
POP/IOD E14 93 H6
Limehouse Link POP/IOD E14 93 G6
Limehouse Link (Tunnel)
POP/IOD E14 93 H6
Lime Kiln Dr CHARL SE7 114 A5
Limekiln Pl NRWD SE19 150 B6
Limerick Cl BAL SW12 129 H6
Limerston St WBPTN SW10 14 F9
Limes Av BARN SW13 126 C1
CAR SM5 162 E7
CROY/NA CR0 177 F2
GLDGN NW11 52 C6
MLHL NW7 37 G5
NFNCH/WDSPK N12 39 G3
PGE/AN SE20 150 D6
WAN E11 59 F3
The Limes Av FBAR/BDGN N11 40 B4
Limes Cl CAR SM5 175 K1
FBAR/BDGN N11 * 40 C4
Limesdale Gdns EDGW HA8 50 E1
Limes Field Rd
MORT/ESHN SW14 126 B2
Limesford Rd PECK SE15 132 A3
Limes Gdns WAND/EARL SW18 127 K5
Limes Gv LEW SE13 133 F3
Limes Rd BECK BR3 166 E1
CROY/NA CR0 164 E5
The Limes CMBW SE5 * 131 F2
WAND/EARL SW18 * 127 K5
Limestone Wk ERITHM DA18 116 E1
Lime St FENCHST EC3M 13 J6
WALTH E17 57 G3
Lime Street Pas BANK EC3V * 13 J5
Limes Wk EA W5 104 E1
PECK SE15 * 131 K3
Lime Tree Av ESH/CLAY KT10 157 J7
Limetree Cl BRXS/STRHM SW2 130 A7
Lime Tree Ct PIN HA5 * 34 A6
Lime Tree Gv CROY/NA CR0 179 H2
Limetree Pl MTCM CR4 148 B7
Lime Tree Rd HEST TW5 103 G7
Lime Tree Ter CAT SE6 * 132 C7
Lime Tree Wk BUSH WD23 22 E7
WWKM BR4 180 D3
Lime Wk SRTFD E15 * 76 C7
Limewood Cl BECK BR3 167 F4
WALTH E17 57 H3
WEA W13 85 H5
Limewood Rd ERITH DA8 117 K6
Limpsfield Av THHTH CR7 164 A4
WIM/MER SW19 146 B1
Linacre Cl PECK SE15 131 J2
Linacre Rd CRICK NW2 69 K5
Linchmere Rd LEE/GVPK SE12 133 J6
Lincoln Av ROMW/RG RM7 63 F7
STHGT/OAK N14 40 C2
WHTN TW2 142 C1
WIM/MER SW19 146 B2
Lincoln Cl GFD/PVL UB6 66 C7
RYLN/HDSTN HA2 47 K4
Lincoln Ct BORE WD6 25 F4
Lincoln Crs EN EN1 30 A4
Lincoln Dr OXHEY WD19 33 G2
Lincoln Est BOW E3 93 J3
Lincoln Gdns IL IG1 59 J6
Lincoln Ms KIL/WHAMP NW6 70 D7
SEVS/STOTM N15 55 J3
Lincoln Pde EFNCH N2 * 53 J2
Lincoln Rd ALP/SUD HA0 67 K5
EFNCH N2 53 J2
EN EN1 30 A3
ERITH DA8 138 C1
FELT TW13 141 K2
FSTGT E7 77 H5
MTCM CR4 163 K4
NTHWD HA6 46 D2
NWMAL KT3 159 K2
PEND EN3 30 D4
PLSTW E13 95 F3
RYLN/HDSTN HA2 47 K4
SCUP DA14 155 H4
SNWD SE25 165 J2
SWFD E18 44 D7
WPK KT4 160 E7
Lincoln's Inn Flds LINN WC2A 11 L4
The Lincolns MLHL NW7 37 H2
Lincoln St CHEL SW3 15 L6
WAN E11 76 C1
Lincoln Ter BELMT SM2 * 174 E6
Lincoln Wy EN EN1 30 D4
SUN TW16 140 C7
Lincombe Rd BMLY BR1 152 D2
Lindal Crs ENC/FH EN2 28 E4
The Lindales TOTM N17 42 C5
Lindal Rd BROCKY SE4 132 C4
Lindburgh Av WLGTN SM6 176 E7
Linden Av HSLW TW3 123 G4
RSLP HA4 46 E7
THHTH CR7 164 C3
WATW WD18 20 D3
WBLY HA9 68 B4
WLSDN NW10 88 B1
Linden Cl RSLP HA4 46 E7
STAN HA7 35 H4
STHGT/OAK N14 28 C5
THDIT KT7 158 B6
Linden Cots WIM/MER SW19 * 146 C5
Linden Crs GFD/PVL UB6 67 F5
KUT/HW KT1 159 G1
WFD IG8 45 F5
Lindenfield CHST BR7 169 G1
Linden Gdns BAY/PAD W2 8 B7
CHSWK W4 106 A4
Linden Gv NWMAL KT3 160 B2
PECK SE15 131 J2
SYD SE26 150 E5
TEDD TW11 143 F4
Linden Lea EFNCH N2 53 G4
PIN HA5 * 33 K6
Linden Leas WWKM BR4 180 B1
Linden Ms BAY/PAD W2 8 B7
IS N1 73 K4
Linden Pl MTCM CR4 162 D3
Linden Rd FBAR/BDGN N11 39 K1
HPTN TW12 142 A7
MUSWH N10 54 B3
The Lindens CHSWK W4 105 K7
CROY/NA CR0 180 A5
NFNCH/WDSPK N12 * 39 H4
WALTH E17 * 57 K3
Linden St ROMW/RG RM7 63 F3
Linden Wk ARCH N19 * 72 C1
Linden Wy STHGT/OAK N14 28 C5
Lindfield Gdns HAMP NW3 71 G4
Lindfield Rd CROY/NA CR0 165 G5
EA W5 85 J3
Lindfield St POP/IOD E14 93 J5
Lindhill Cl PEND EN3 31 F1
Lindisfarne Md HOM E9 75 G3
Lindisfarne Rd BCTR RM8 79 J2
RYNPK SW20 145 J6
Lindley Est PECK SE15 * 111 H6
Lindley Pl RCH/KEW TW9 105 H7
Lindley Rd LEY E10 76 A1
Lindley St WCHPL E1 92 E4
Lindore Rd BTSEA SW11 128 E3
Lindores Rd CAR SM5 162 B6
Lindo St PECK SE15 131 K1
Lind Rd SUT SM1 175 G4
Lindrop St FUL/PGN SW6 128 B1
Lindsay Cl CHSGTN KT9 172 A6
STWL/WRAY TW19 120 A4
Lindsay Dr
KTN/HRWW/WS HA3 50 A5
Lindsay Rd HPTN TW12 142 B3
WPK KT4 173 K1
Lindsay Sq PIM SW1V 17 H7
Lindsell St GNWCH SE10 113 F7
Lindsey Cl BMLY BR1 168 C2
MTCM CR4 163 K3
Lindsey Gdns
EBED/NFELT TW14 * 121 G6
Lindsey Ms IS N1 6 F1
Lindsey Rd BCTR RM8 79 J2
Lindsey St FARR EC1M 12 D2
Lind St DEPT SE8 132 E1
Lindum Rd TEDD TW11 143 J6
Lindway WNWD SE27 149 H4
Linfield Cl HDN NW4 52 A2
Linford Rd WALTH E17 58 A2
Linford St VX/NE SW8 109 H7
Lingards Rd LEW SE13 133 F3
Lingey Cl BFN/LL DA15 155 F1
Lingfield Av KUT/HW KT1 159 F3
Lingfield Cl EN EN1 30 A5
NTHWD HA6 32 C6
Lingfield Ct NTHLT UB5 * 84 A1
Lingfield Crs ELTH/MOT SE9 135 J3
Lingfield Gdns ED N9 30 D6
Lingfield Rd WIM/MER SW19 146 B5
WPK KT4 174 A2
Lingham St BRXN/ST SW9 129 K1
Lingholm Wy BAR EN5 26 B4
Ling Rd CAN/RD E16 94 E4
ERITH DA8 117 K5
Lingwell Rd TOOT SW17 147 J2
Lingwood Gdns ISLW TW7 103 K6
Lingwood Rd CLPT E5 56 C6
Linhope St CAMTN NW1 3 L9
Linkfield E/WMO/HCT KT8 157 F2
Linkfield Rd ISLW TW7 124 A1
Link La WLGTN SM6 176 D5
Linklea Cl CDALE/KGS NW9 37 G6
Link Rd DAGW RM9 98 D1
EBED/NFELT TW14 121 J6
FBAR/BDGN N11 40 A3
WATN WD24 21 H1
WLGTN SM6 163 F7
Links Av GPK RM2 63 K1
MRDN SM4 161 K3
Links Dr BORE WD6 24 B2
TRDG/WHET N20 26 E7
Links Gdns STRHM/NOR SW16 149 G6
Linkside NFNCH/WDSPK N12 38 D5
NWMAL KT3 160 B1
Linkside Cl ENC/FH EN2 29 F2
Linkside Gdns ENC/FH EN2 29 F2
Links Rd ACT W3 86 C5
CRICK NW2 69 H1
TOOT SW17 148 A5
WFD IG8 44 E4
WWKM BR4 167 F7
Links Side ENC/FH EN2 29 F2
The Links WALTH E17 57 G3
Link St HOM E9 74 E5
Links Vw FNCH N3 38 D6
Links View Cl STAN HA7 35 G5
Linksview Ct HPTN TW12 * 142 D3
Links View Rd CROY/NA CR0 179 J2
HPTN TW12 142 C4
Links Wy NTHWD HA6 32 A7
BECK BR3 166 D5
Linksway HDN NW4 52 B1
NTHWD HA6 32 B7
Links Wy RKW/CH/CXG WD3 20 A2
Links Yd WCHPL E1 13 M2
The Link ACT W3 86 D5
ALP/SUD HA0 49 J7
CRICK NW2 51 J7
NTHLT UB5 * 65 K4
PIN HA5 47 G5
TEDD TW11 143 F5
Linkway RYNPK SW20 160 E2
BCTR RM8 79 J3
FSBYPK N4 55 J6
Link Wy HAYES BR2 168 D6
Linkway NWMAL KT3 160 E3
PIN HA5 33 H7
Link Wy RCHPK/HAM TW10 143 H1
The Linkway BAR EN5 26 E5
BELMT SM2 175 G7
Linkwood Wk CAMTN NW1 5 H1
Linley Crs ROMW/RG RM7 62 D2
Linley Rd TOTM N17 56 A1
Linnell Cl GLDGN NW11 53 F5
Linnell Dr GLDGN NW11 53 F5
Linnell Rd CMBW SE5 131 F1
UED N18 42 C4
Linnet Cl BUSH WD23 22 C7
ED N9 31 F7
THMD SE28 97 J6
Linnet Ms BAL SW12 129 F6
Linnett Cl CHING E4 44 A3
Linom Rd CLAP SW4 129 K3
Linscott Rd CLPT E5 74 E3
Linsdell Rd BARK IG11 78 C7
Linsey St BERM/RHTH SE16 111 H2
Linslade Cl HSLWW TW4 122 D4
PIN HA5 47 F2
Linstead St KIL/WHAMP NW6 2 A1
Linstead Wy
WAND/EARL SW18 127 H6
Linster Gv BORE WD6 24 E4
Lintaine Cl HMSMTH W6 * 107 H5
Linthorpe Av ALP/SUD HA0 67 J5
Linthorpe Rd EBAR EN4 27 J2
STNW/STAM N16 56 A6
Linton Av BORE WD6 24 B1
Linton Cl CAR SM5 162 E6
CHARL SE7 114 B4
WELL DA16 116 B7
Linton Ct ROM RM1 63 G1
Linton Gdns EHAM E6 95 J5
Linton Gv WNWD SE27 149 H4
Linton Rd BARK IG11 78 C6
Linton St IS N1 6 F4
Lintott Ct STWL/WRAY TW19 120 A5
Linver Rd FUL/PGN SW6 127 J1
Linwood Cl CMBW SE5 131 G1
Linzee Rd CEND/HSY/T N8 54 E3
Lion Av TWK TW1 124 A7
Lion Cl BROCKY SE4 132 D5
Lionel Gdns ELTH/MOT SE9 134 C4
Lionel Ms NKENS W10 * 88 C4
Lionel Rd ELTH/MOT SE9 134 C4
Lionel Rd North BTFD TW8 105 F2
Lionel Rd South BTFD TW8 105 G4
Lion Gate Gdns RCH/KEW TW9 125 G2
Lion Gate Ms
WAND/EARL SW18 127 K6
Lion Mills BETH E2 * 92 C1
Lion Park Av CHSGTN KT9 172 C3
Lion Rd CROY/NA CR0 164 D4
ED N9 42 C1
EHAM E6 95 K4
TWK TW1 124 A7
Lions Cl LEE/GVPK SE12 153 G2
Lion Wy BTFD TW8 104 E6
Lion Wharf Rd ISLW TW7 124 C2
Liphook Cl HCH RM12 81 H3
Liphook Crs FSTH SE23 131 K6
Liphook Rd OXHEY WD19 33 H3
Lipton Rd WCHPL E1 93 F5
Lisbon Av WHTN TW2 142 C1
Lisbon Cl WALTH E17 57 H1
Lisburne Rd HAMP NW3 71 K3
Lisford St PECK SE15 111 G7
Lisgar Ter WKENS W14 107 J3
Liskeard Cl CHST BR7 154 C5
Lisle Cl TOOT SW17 148 B3
Lisle St LSQ/SEVD WC2H 11 H6
Lismore WIM/MER SW19 * 146 D4
Lismore Circ KTTN NW5 71 K4
Lismore Cl ISLW TW7 124 B1
Lismore Rd SAND/SEL CR2 178 A5
TOTM N17 55 K2
Lismore Wk IS N1 73 J5
Lissant Cl SURB KT6 158 D6
Lissenden Gdns KTTN NW5 72 A3
Lisson Gv STJWD NW8 3 H9
Lisson St CAMTN NW1 9 J2
Lister Cl ACT W3 87 F4
MTCM CR4 147 J6
Lister Gdns UED N18 41 J4
Lister Rd WAN E11 58 C7
Liston Rd CLAP SW4 129 H2
TOTM N17 42 C7
Liston Wy WFD IG8 45 G6
Listowel Cl BRXN/ST SW9 110 B6
Listowel Rd DAGE RM10 80 C2
Listria Pk STNW/STAM N16 74 A1
Litchfield Av MRDN SM4 161 J6
SRTFD E15 * 76 C5
Litchfield Gdns WLSDN NW10 69 J5
Litchfield Rd SUT SM1 175 G3
Litchfield St LSQ/SEVD WC2H 11 H6
Litchfield Wy GLDGN NW11 53 G4
Lithgow's Rd HTHAIR TW6 121 H3
Lithos Rd HAMP NW3 71 F5
Little Acre BECK BR3 166 D2
Little Albany St CAMTN NW1 4 D9
Little Argyll St REGST W1B * 10 E5
Little Benty WDR/YW UB7 100 A4
Little Birches BFN/LL DA15 154 E1
The Little Boltons
WBPTN SW10 14 D7
Little Bornes DUL SE21 150 A3
Little Britain STBT EC1A 12 D3
Littlebrook Cl CROY/NA CR0 166 A5
Little Brownings FSTH SE23 150 D1
Littlebury Rd CLAP SW4 * 129 J2
Little Bury St ED N9 30 A6
Little Bushey La BUSH WD23 22 A2
Little Cedars
NFNCH/WDSPK N12 39 G3
Little Chester St KTBR SW1X 16 C3
Little Cloisters WEST SW1P 17 J3
Littlecombe Cl
PUT/ROE SW15 * 127 G5
Little Common STAN HA7 35 G2
Littlecote Cl WIM/MER SW19 127 G6
Littlecote Pl PIN HA5 33 J7
Little Cottage Pl
GNWCH SE10 * 112 E6
Little Ct WWKM BR4 180 C1
Littlecroft ELTH/MOT SE9 135 F2
Littledale ABYW SE2 116 B5
Little Deans Yd WEST SW1P 17 J3
Little Dimocks BAL SW12 148 B1
Little Dorrit Ct STHWK SE1 18 F1
Little Ealing La EA W5 104 D3
Little Edward St
CAMTN NW1 * 4 D7
Little Elms HYS/HAR UB3 101 G6
Little Essex St
TPL/STR WC2R * 12 A6
Little Ferry Rd TWK TW1 * 124 C7
Littlefield Cl ARCH N19 72 C3
KUT/HW KT1 159 F1
Littlefield Rd EDGW HA8 36 E6
Little Friday Rd CHING E4 44 C1
Little Gearies BARK/HLT IG6 60 B3
Little George St WEST SW1P 17 J2
Little Green St KTTN NW5 * 72 B3
Little Gv BUSH WD23 22 B3
Littlegrove EBAR EN4 27 J5
Little Heath CHARL SE7 114 D5
CHDH RM6 61 H3
Littleheath Rd SAND/SEL CR2 178 D7
Little Ilford La MNPK E12 77 K3
Littlejohn Rd HNWL W7 85 F5
Little Marlborough St
REGST W1B * 10 E5
Little Martins BUSH WD23 22 B4
Littlemead ESH/CLAY KT10 170 D3
Littlemede ELTH/MOT SE9 153 K2
Littlemoor Rd IL IG1 78 D2
Littlemore Rd ABYW SE2 116 B1
Little Moss La PIN HA5 47 J1
Little Newport St
LSQ/SEVD WC2H 11 H6
Little New St
FLST/FETLN EC4A 12 B4
Little Orchard Cl PIN HA5 * 47 J1
Little Oxhey La OXHEY WD19 33 J4
Little Park Dr FELT TW13 141 H1
Little Park Gdns ENC/FH EN2 29 J2
Little Portland St REGST W1B 10 D4
Little Potters BUSH WD23 22 D6
Little Queens Rd TEDD TW11 143 F5
Little Redlands BMLY BR1 168 D1
Little Rd HYS/HAR UB3 101 J1
Littlers Cl WIM/MER SW19 147 H7
Little Russell St
NOXST/BSQ WC1A 11 J3
Little St James's St
WHALL SW1A 10 E9
Little St Leonards
MORT/ESHN SW14 125 K2
Little Smith St WEST SW1P 17 H3
Little Somerset St
TWRH EC3N 13 L5
Littlestone Cl BECK BR3 151 J5
Little Strd CDALE/KGS NW9 51 H1
Little Stream Cl NTHWD HA6 32 C4
Little Thrift STMC/STPC BR5 169 H3
Little Titchfield St
GTPST W1W 10 E3
Littleton Crs HRW HA1 67 F1
Littleton Rd ASHF TW15 140 A6
HRW HA1 67 F1
Littleton St WAND/EARL SW18 147 G1
Little Trinity La BLKFR EC4V 12 F6
Little Turnstile HHOL WC1V 11 L3
Littlewood LEW SE13 133 F4
Little Wood Cl
STMC/STPC BR5 155 G7
Littlewood Cl WEA W13 104 C2
Littleworth Av ESH/CLAY KT10 170 D4
Littleworth Common Rd
ESH/CLAY KT10 170 D2
Littleworth La ESH/CLAY KT10 170 D3
Littleworth Pl ESH/CLAY KT10 170 D3
Littleworth Rd
ESH/CLAY KT10 170 D4
Livermere Rd HACK E8 7 L3
Liverpool Gv WALW SE17 19 G8
Liverpool Rd CAN/RD E16 94 C4
EA W5 104 E1
IS N1 6 B3
KUTN/CMB KT2 144 C6
LEY E10 58 A5
THHTH CR7 164 D2
WATW WD18 21 F4
Liverpool St LVPST EC2M 13 J3
Livesey Cl KUT/HW KT1 159 G2
THMD SE28 115 H2
Livesey Pl STHWK SE1 111 H5
Livingstone Rd BTSEA SW11 128 C2
HSLW TW3 123 H3
PLMGR N13 40 E5
STHL UB1 83 H6
THHTH CR7 164 E1
WALTH E17 57 K5
Lizard St FSBYE EC1V 6 F8
Lizban St BKHTH/KID SE3 114 A6
Llanelly Rd CRICK NW2 70 D1
Llanover Rd WBLY HA9 67 K2
WOOL/PLUM SE18 115 F6
Llanthony Rd MRDN SM4 162 C5
Llanvanor Rd CRICK NW2 70 D1
Llewellyn St
BERM/RHTH SE16 111 H1
Lloyd Av STRHM/NOR SW16 148 E7
Lloyd Baker St FSBYW WC1X 6 A8
Lloyd Ct PIN HA5 47 H4
Lloyd Park Av CROY/NA CR0 178 B3
Lloyd Rd DAGW RM9 80 B5
EHAM E6 77 K7
WALTH E17 57 F3
WPK KT4 174 A2
Lloyd's Av FENCHST EC3M 13 K5
Lloyd's Pl BKHTH/KID SE3 * 133 H1
Lloyd Sq FSBYW WC1X 6 A7
Lloyd's Rw CLKNW EC1R 6 B8
Lloyd St FSBYW WC1X 6 A7
Lloyds Wy BECK BR3 166 B4
Lloyd Thomas Ct WDGN N22 * 41 F6
Lloyd Vls BROCKY SE4 132 D1
Loampit Hl LEW SE13 132 D1
Loampit V LEW SE13 132 E2
Loanda Cl HACK E8 7 L3
Loates La WAT WD17 21 G2
Loats Rd BRXS/STRHM SW2 129 K5
Local Board Rd WAT WD17 21 H4
Locarno Rd ACT W3 86 E7
GFD/PVL UB6 84 C3
Lochaber Rd LEW SE13 133 H3
Lochaline St HMSMTH W6 107 F5
Lochan Cl YEAD UB4 83 J3
Lochinvar St BAL SW12 129 G6
Lochmere Cl ERITH DA8 117 J5
Lochnagar St POP/IOD E14 94 A4
Lock Cha BKHTH/KID SE3 133 H2
Lock Cl NWDGN UB2 103 H1
Locke Cl RAIN RM13 81 H5
Lockesfield Pl POP/IOD E14 112 E3
Lockesley Sq SURB KT6 * 158 E5
Locket Rd
KTN/HRWW/WS HA3 49 F1
Locket Road Ms
KTN/HRWW/WS HA3 48 E1
Lockfield Av PEND EN3 31 G1
Lockgate Cl HOM E9 75 H4
Lockhart Cl HOLWY N7 73 F5
PEND EN3 30 D4
Lockhart St BOW E3 93 H3
Lockhurst St CLPT E5 75 F3
Lockington Rd VX/NE SW8 109 G7
Lock Keepers Cots
TOTM N17 * 56 D3
Lockmead Rd LEW SE13 133 F2
SEVS/STOTM N15 56 C5
Lock Rd RCHPK/HAM TW10 143 J2
Lock's La MTCM CR4 148 A7
Locksley Est POP/IOD E14 93 H5
Locksley St POP/IOD E14 93 H4
Locksmeade Rd
RCHPK/HAM TW10 143 H3
Lockton St NTGHL W11 * 88 B6
Lockwell Rd DAGE RM10 80 B2
Lockwood Cl EBAR EN4 27 K3
SYD SE26 151 F3
Lockwood Pl CHING E4 43 J5
Lockwood Sq
BERM/RHTH SE16 111 J2
Lockwood Wy CHSGTN KT9 172 C4
WALTH E17 57 F1
Lockyer St STHWK SE1 19 H2
Locomotive Dr
EBED/NFELT TW14 121 K6
Locton Gn BOW E3 * 75 H7
Loddiges Rd HOM E9 74 E6
Loder St PECK SE15 111 K6
Lodge Av BCTR RM8 79 H4
BORE WD6 24 B4
CROY/NA CR0 177 F2
DAGW RM9 79 G7
GPK RM2 63 J4
KTN/HRWW/WS HA3 50 A3
Lodge Cl EDGW HA8 * 36 B5
ISLW TW7 104 C7
UED N18 41 J4
WLGTN SM6 163 F7
Lodge Ct ALP/SUD HA0 * 68 A4
Lodge Dr PLMGR N13 41 G3
Lodge End RKW/CH/CXG WD3 20 B3
Lodge Gdns BECK BR3 166 C4

EN EN1 30 A3
FNCH N3 38 C7
GNTH/NBYPK IG2 60 D5
HAMP NW3 71 H4
PIN HA5 33 F7
Lyndhurst Gv CMBW SE5 131 F1
Lyndhurst Leys HAYES BR2 * 167 G1
Lyndhurst Prior SNWD SE25 * 165 F2
Lyndhurst Rd CHING E4 44 A6
GFD/PVL UB6 84 B3
HAMP NW3 71 H4
THHTH CR7 164 B3
UED N18 42 C3
WDGN N22 41 G5
Lyndhurst Sq PECK SE15 111 G7
Lyndhurst Ter HAMP NW3 71 H4
Lyndhurst Wy BELMT SM2 174 E7
PECK SE15 111 G7
Lyndon Av BFN/LL DA15 136 A4
PIN HA5 33 J5
WLGTN SM6 176 A2
Lyndon Rd BELV DA17 117 H3
Lyndon Yd TOOT SW17 147 F3
Lyne Crs WALTH E17 43 H7
Lynegrove Av ASHF TW15 140 A4
Lyneham Wk CLPT E5 * 75 G4
Lynette Av CLAP SW4 129 G5
Lynford Cl BAR EN5 25 H4
EDGW HA8 36 E7
Lynford Gdns EDGW HA8 36 D2
GDMY/SEVK IG3 79 F1
Lynford Ter ED N9 * 30 B7
Lynhurst Crs HGDN/ICK UB10 64 A6
Lynhurst Rd HGDN/ICK UB10 64 A6
Lynmere Rd WELL DA16 136 C1
Lyn Ms STNW/STAM N16 * 74 B3
Lynmouth Av EN EN1 30 B5
MRDN SM4 161 G6
Lynmouth Dr RSLP HA4 65 F1
Lynmouth Gdns GFD/PVL UB6 67 H7
HEST TW5 102 C7
Lynmouth Rd EFNCH N2 53 K2
GFD/PVL UB6 67 H7
STNW/STAM N16 56 B7
WALTH E17 57 G5
Lynn Cl ASHF TW15 140 B4
KTN/HRWW/WS HA3 48 D1
Lynnett Rd BCTR RM8 79 K1
Lynne Wk ESH/CLAY KT10 170 C4
Lynne Wy NTHLT UB5 83 H1
Lynn Ms WAN E11 76 C1
Lynn Rd BAL SW12 129 G6
GNTH/NBYPK IG2 60 D6
WAN E11 76 C1
Lynscott Wy SAND/SEL CR2 177 H7
Lynstead Cl BMLY BR1 168 B1
Lynsted Ct BECK BR3 166 B1
Lynsted Gdns ELTH/MOT SE9 134 C3
Lynton Av CDALE/KGS NW9 51 H3
NFNCH/WDSPK N12 39 H3
WEA W13 85 G5
Lynton Cl CHSGTN KT9 172 A3
ISLW TW7 124 A3
WLSDN NW10 69 G4
Lynton Crs GNTH/NBYPK IG2 60 B5
Lynton Est STHWK SE1 19 M6
Lynton Gdns EN EN1 30 A6
FBAR/BDGN N11 40 D5
Lynton Md TRDG/WHET N20 38 E2
Lynton Rd ACT W3 86 C6
CEND/HSY/T N8 54 D4
CHING E4 43 K4
CROY/NA CR0 164 B5
KIL/WHAMP NW6 70 D7
NWMAL KT3 160 A4
RYLN/HDSTN HA2 65 J1
STHWK SE1 19 M6
Lynton Ter ACT W3 * 86 E5
Lynwood Cl RYLN/HDSTN HA2 65 J2
SWFD E18 45 G7
Lynwood Dr NTHWD HA6 32 C7
WPK KT4 173 J1
Lynwood Gdns CROY/NA CR0 177 F3
STHL UB1 83 K5
Lynwood Gv ORP BR6 169 K6
WCHMH N21 29 G7
Lynwood Rd EA W5 85 K2
THDIT KT7 171 F1
TOOT SW17 147 K2
Lynwood Ter
WIM/MER SW19 * 146 D7
Lyon Meade STAN HA7 35 J7
Lyon Park Av ALP/SUD HA0 68 A5
Lyon Rd HRW HA1 49 F5
ROM RM1 63 H6
WIM/MER SW19 147 G7
Lyonsdown Av BAR EN5 27 G5
Lyonsdown Rd BAR EN5 27 G4
Lyons Pl STJWD NW8 9 G1
Lyon St IS N1 5 L2
Lyons Wk WKENS W14 107 H3
Lyon Wy GFD/PVL UB6 66 E7
Lyric Dr GFD/PVL UB6 84 B3
Lyric Ms SYD SE26 150 E3
Lyric Rd BARN SW13 106 C7
Lysander CDALE/KGS NW9 * 37 H7
Lysander Gdns SURB KT6 159 G5
Lysander Gv ARCH N19 54 D7
Lysander Ms ARCH N19 * 54 E7
Lysander Rd CROY/NA CR0 177 F5
RSLP HA4 64 B1
Lysias Rd BAL SW12 129 F5
Lysia St FUL/PGN SW6 107 G6
Lysons Wk PUT/ROE SW15 * 126 D4
Lytchet Rd BMLY BR1 152 E6
Lytchgate Cl SAND/SEL CR2 178 A6
Lytcott Dr E/WMO/HCT KT8 156 E2
Lytcott Gv EDUL SE22 131 G4
Lytham Av OXHEY WD19 33 H4
Lytham Cl THMD SE28 98 A5
Lytham St WALW SE17 19 G8
Lyttelton Rd EFNCH N2 53 G4
LEY E10 75 K2
Lyttleton Cl HAMP NW3 3 J2
Lyttleton Rd
CEND/HSY/T N8 * 55 G2
Lytton Av PLMGR N13 41 G1
Lytton Cl EFNCH N2 53 H4
NTHLT UB5 65 K6
Lytton Gdns WLGTN SM6 176 D3
Lytton Gv PUT/ROE SW15 127 G4
Lytton Rd BAR EN5 27 G3
GPK RM2 63 K4
PIN HA5 33 J6
WAN E11 58 C6
Lyveden Rd BKHTH/KID SE3 114 A6
TOOT SW17 147 J5

M

Maberley Crs NRWD SE19 150 C6
Maberley Rd BECK BR3 166 A2
NRWD SE19 150 B7
Mabledon Pl CAMTN NW1 5 H8
Mablethorpe Rd
FUL/PGN SW6 107 H6
Mabley St HOM E9 75 G4
Macaret Cl TRDG/WHET N20 27 F6
Macarthur Cl FSTGT E7 76 E5
WBLY HA9 68 D5
Macarthur Ter CHARL SE7 * 114 C5
Macaulay Av ESH/CLAY KT10 170 E1
Macaulay Rd CLAP SW4 129 G2
EHAM E6 95 H1
Macbean St
WOOL/PLUM SE18 115 F2
Macbeth St HMSMTH W6 106 E4
Macclesfield Br STJWD NW8 3 K5
Macclesfield Rd FSBYE EC1V 6 E7
SNWD SE25 165 J4
Macclesfield St
SOHO/SHAV W1D * 11 H6
Macdonald Av DAGE RM10 80 D2
Macdonald Rd ARCH N19 72 C1
FBAR/BDGN N11 39 K4
FSTGT E7 76 E3
WALTH E17 58 A1
Macduff Rd BTSEA SW11 109 F7
Mace Cl WAP E1W 92 D7
Mace St BETH E2 93 F1
Macfarlane La ISLW TW7 104 A5
Macfarlane Rd SHB W12 88 A7
Mac Farren Pl CAMTN NW1 10 B1
Macgregor Rd CAN/RD E16 95 G4
Machell Rd PECK SE15 131 K2
Mackay Rd VX/NE SW8 129 G2
Mackennal St STJWD NW8 3 K6
Mackenzie Cl SHB W12 87 K6
Mackenzie Rd BECK BR3 166 A1
HOLWY N7 73 F5
Mackeson Rd HAMP NW3 * 71 K3
Mackie Rd BRXS/STRHM SW2 130 B6
Mackintosh La HOM E9 75 F4
Macklin St HOL/ALD WC2B * 11 K4
Macks Rd BERM/RHTH SE16 111 H2
Mackworth St CAMTN NW1 4 E7
Maclean Rd FSTH SE23 132 B5
Macleod House CHARL SE7 * 114 D6
Macleod Rd WCHMH N21 28 E4
Macleod St WALW SE17 18 F8
Maclise Rd WKENS W14 107 H2
Macmillan Wy TOOT SW17 148 B3
Macoma Rd
WOOL/PLUM SE18 115 J5
Macoma Ter
WOOL/PLUM SE18 115 J5
Maconochies Rd
POP/IOD E14 * 112 E4
Macquarie Wy POP/IOD E14 112 E3
Macroom Rd MV/WKIL W9 88 D2
Maddams St BOW E3 93 K3
Maddison Cl EFNCH N2 53 G1
TEDD TW11 143 F5
Maddocks Cl SCUP DA14 155 K5
Maddock Wy WALW SE17 110 C5
Maddox St CONDST W1S 10 D6
Madeira Av BMLY BR1 152 C7
Madeira Gv WFD IG8 45 G5
Madeira Rd MTCM CR4 162 E3
PLMGR N13 41 H3
STRHM/NOR SW16 148 E4
WAN E11 58 B7
Madeleine Ct CHDH RM6 61 J5
Madeley Rd EA W5 85 K6
Madeline Gv IL IG1 78 D4
Madeline Rd PGE/AN SE20 150 C6
Madge Gill Wy EHAM E6 77 J7
Madge Hl HNWL W7 * 84 E6
Madinah Rd HACK E8 74 C4
Madison Cl BELMT SM2 175 H6
Madison Crs BXLYHN DA7 116 D6
Madison Gdns BXLYHN DA7 116 D6
Madras Pl HOLWY N7 73 G5
Madras Rd IL IG1 78 B3
Madrid Rd BARN SW13 106 D7
Madron St WALW SE17 19 K7
Mafeking Av BTFD TW8 105 F5
EHAM E6 95 H1
GNTH/NBYPK IG2 60 D6
Mafeking Rd CAN/RD E16 94 D3
EN EN1 30 B2
TOTM N17 56 C1
Magazine Ga BAY/PAD W2 * 9 K8
Magdala Av ARCH N19 72 C1
Magdala Rd ISLW TW7 124 B2
SAND/SEL CR2 177 K6
Magdalene Gdns EHAM E6 96 A3
Magdalen Rd
WAND/EARL SW18 128 B7
Magdalen St STHWK SE1 13 J9
Magee St LBTH SE11 18 A9
Magellan Bvd CAN/RD E16 96 C6
Magellan Pl POP/IOD E14 112 D3
Magnaville Rd BUSH WD23 22 E6
Magnet Rd WBLY HA9 67 K1
Magnin Cl HACK E8 74 C7
Magnolia Cl KUTN/CMB KT2 144 D5
LEY E10 75 J1
Magnolia Ct
KTN/HRWW/WS HA3 50 B6
Magnolia Gdns EDGW HA8 36 E3
Magnolia Pl CLAP SW4 * 129 K4
EA W5 * 85 K4
Magnolia Rd CHSWK W4 105 J5
Magnolia St WDR/YW UB7 100 A3
Magnolia Wy HOR/WEW KT19 172 E4
Magnolia Whf CHSWK W4 * 105 J5
Magpie Cl CDALE/KGS NW9 51 G1
FSTGT E7 76 D4
Magpie Hall Cl HAYES BR2 168 D5
Magpie Hall La HAYES BR2 168 D6
HAYES BR2 168 E4
Magpie Hall Rd STAN HA7 34 E1
Magpie Pl NWCR SE14 * 112 B5
Magri Wk WCHPL E1 92 E4
Maguire Dr RCHPK/HAM TW10 143 J3
Maguire St STHWK SE1 19 M1
Mahlon Av RSLP HA4 65 F4
Mahogany Cl
BERM/RHTH SE16 93 G7
Maida Av BAY/PAD W2 8 F2
CHING E4 31 K6
Maida Rd BELV DA17 117 H2
Maida V MV/WKIL W9 2 D6
STJWD NW8 3 G9
Maida Wy CHING E4 31 K6
Maiden Erlegh Av BXLY DA5 137 F7
Maiden La CAMTN NW1 5 H1
COVGDN WC2E 11 K6
DART DA1 138 D2
STHWK SE1 12 F9
Maiden Rd SRTFD E15 76 C6
Maidenstone Hl GNWCH SE10 113 F7
Maidstone Av CRW RM5 62 E1
Maidstone Buildings Ms
STHWK SE1 12 F9
Maidstone Rd
FBAR/BDGN N11 40 D5
SCUP DA14 155 K5
Main Av EN EN1 30 B4
NTHWD HA6 32 A2
Main Barracks
WOOL/PLUM SE18 * 114 E4
Main Dr GFD/PVL UB6 * 85 G2
WBLY HA9 67 K2
Mainridge Rd CHST BR7 154 A3
Main Rd ROM RM1 63 H3
SCUP DA14 154 E2
STMC/STPC BR5 155 J7
Main St FELT TW13 141 H4
Maise Webster Cl
STWL/WRAY TW19 * 120 A6
Maismore St PECK SE15 111 H5
The Maisonettes SUT SM1 * 174 D4
Maitland Cl GNWCH SE10 112 E6
HSLWW TW4 122 E2
Maitland Park Rd HAMP NW3 71 K5
Maitland Park Vls HAMP NW3 71 K5
Maitland Rd PGE/AN SE20 151 F5
SRTFD E15 76 D5
Majendie Rd
WOOL/PLUM SE18 115 J4
Major Cl BRXN/ST SW9 130 C2
Major Rd BERM/RHTH SE16 * 111 H2
SRTFD E15 76 A4
Makepeace Av HGT N6 72 A1
Makepeace Rd NTHLT UB5 83 J1
WAN E11 58 E3
Makins St CHEL SW3 15 K6
Malabar St POP/IOD E14 112 D1
Malam Gdns POP/IOD E14 93 K6
Malan Sq RAIN RM13 81 K5
Malbrook Rd PUT/ROE SW15 126 E3
Malcolm Cl PGE/AN SE20 * 150 E6
Malcolm Ct STAN HA7 35 J4
Malcolm Crs HDN NW4 51 J4
Malcolm Dr SURB KT6 158 E7
Malcolm Pl BETH E2 92 E3
Malcolm Rd PGE/AN SE20 150 E6
SNWD SE25 165 H5
WCHPL E1 92 E3
WIM/MER SW19 146 C5
Malcolms Wy
STHGT/OAK N14 * 28 C4
Malcolm Wy WAN E11 58 E4
Malden Av GFD/PVL UB6 66 E5
SNWD SE25 165 J3
Malden Flds BUSH WD23 21 H4
Malden Green Av WPK KT4 160 C7
Malden Hl NWMAL KT3 160 C3
Malden Hill Gdns NWMAL KT3 160 C2
Malden Pk NWMAL KT3 160 C5
Malden Pl KTTN NW5 72 A4
Malden Rd BORE WD6 24 C2
CHEAM SM3 174 B3
KTTN NW5 71 K4
NWMAL KT3 160 B4
WAT WD17 21 F1
Malden Wy NWMAL KT3 160 A5
Maldon Cl CMBW SE5 * 131 F2
IS N1 6 E3
Maldon Rd ACT W3 86 E6
ED N9 42 B2
ROMW/RG RM7 62 E6
WLGTN SM6 176 B4
Maldon Wk WFD IG8 45 G5
Malet St GWRST WC1E 11 G1
Maley Av WNWD SE27 149 H1
Malford Gv SWFD E18 58 D2
Malfort Rd CMBW SE5 131 F2
Malham Cl FBAR/BDGN N11 40 A5
Malham Rd FSTH SE23 132 A7
Malham Ter UED N18 * 42 D5
Malins Cl BAR EN5 * 25 K4
Malkin Wy WATW WD18 20 C3
Mallams Ms BRXN/ST SW9 130 B2
Mallard Cl BAR EN5 * 27 H5
HNWL W7 103 K1
KIL/WHAMP NW6 2 B4
WHTN TW2 123 F6
Mallard Ct WALTH E17 * 58 B2
Mallard Pl TWK TW1 143 G2
WDGN N22 * 55 F1
Mallards Ct OXHEY WD19 33 K2
Mallards Rd BARK IG11 97 G2
WFD IG8 45 F6
Mallard Wk BECK BR3 166 A4
Mallard Wy CDALE/KGS NW9 50 E6
NTHWD HA6 32 A6
WLGTN SM6 176 C7
Mall Chambers KENS W8 * 8 B8
Mallet Dr NTHLT UB5 65 K4
Mallet Rd LEW SE13 133 G5
Malling Cl CROY/NA CR0 * 165 K5
Malling Gdns MRDN SM4 162 B5
Malling Wy HAYES BR2 167 J6
Mallinson Rd BTSEA SW11 128 D4
CROY/NA CR0 176 D2
Mallord St CHEL SW3 15 H9
Mallory Cl BROCKY SE4 132 B3
POP/IOD E14 93 K3
Mallory Ct LEE/GVPK SE12 134 A6
Mallory Gdns EBAR EN4 28 A6
Mallory St STJWD NW8 9 K1
Mallow Cl CROY/NA CR0 166 A7
Mallow Md MLHL NW7 38 C6
Mallow St FSBYE EC1V 7 G9
Mall Rd HMSMTH W6 106 E4
The Mall BTFD TW8 * 104 E5
EA W5 86 A6
EMPK RM11 63 K7
KTN/HRWW/WS HA3 50 B5
MORT/ESHN SW14 125 K4
STHGT/OAK N14 40 E2
SURB KT6 158 E4
WHALL SW1A 16 E1
Mall Vls HMSMTH W6 * 106 E4
Malmains Cl BECK BR3 167 G4
Malmains Wy BECK BR3 167 F3
Malmesbury Cl PIN HA5 46 D3
Malmesbury Rd BOW E3 93 H1
CAN/RD E16 94 C4
MRDN SM4 162 B6
SWFD E18 44 D7
Malmesbury Ter CAN/RD E16 94 D4
Malmesbury West Est
BOW E3 93 H2
Malory Cl BECK BR3 166 B1
Malpas Dr PIN HA5 47 H4
Malpas Rd BROCKY SE4 132 C1
DAGW RM9 79 K5
HACK E8 74 D5
Malta Rd LEY E10 57 J7
Malta St FSBYE EC1V 6 C9
Maltby Rd CHSGTN KT9 172 C5
Maltby St STHWK SE1 19 L2
Malthouse Dr CHSWK W4 106 C5
FELT TW13 141 H4
Maltings Cl BOW E3 94 A2
Maltings Pl FUL/PGN SW6 108 A7
STHWK SE1 19 K1
The Maltings ROM RM1 63 H6
SNWD SE25 * 165 F2
Malting Wy ISLW TW7 124 A2
Malton Ms NKENS W10 * 88 C5
WOOL/PLUM SE18 115 K5
Malton Rd NKENS W10 88 C5
Malton St WOOL/PLUM SE18 115 K5
Maltravers St TPL/STR WC2R 11 M6
Malt St STHWK SE1 111 H5
Malva Cl WAND/EARL SW18 128 A4
Malvern Av CHING E4 44 B6
RYLN/HDSTN HA2 65 J2
Malvern Cl BUSH WD23 22 C5
MTCM CR4 163 H2
NKENS W10 88 D4
SURB KT6 159 F7
Malvern Dr FELT TW13 141 H4
GDMY/SEVK IG3 79 F3
WFD IG8 45 G4
Malvern Gdns CRICK NW2 70 C1
KTN/HRWW/WS HA3 50 A3
Malvern Ms KIL/WHAMP NW6 2 A8
Malvern Pl MV/WKIL W9 * 88 D2
Malvern Rd CEND/HSY/T N8 55 F2
EHAM E6 77 J7
HACK E8 74 C6
HPTN TW12 142 A7
HYS/HAR UB3 101 H6
KIL/WHAMP NW6 2 A7
SURB KT6 172 A1
THHTH CR7 164 B3
TOTM N17 56 C2
WAN E11 76 C1
Malvern Ter ED N9 30 B7
IS N1 6 A3
Malvern Wy WEA W13 85 H4
Malwood Rd BAL SW12 129 G5
Malyons Rd LEW SE13 132 E4
Malyons Ter LEW SE13 132 E4
Managers St POP/IOD E14 * 94 A7
Manaton Cl PECK SE15 131 J2
Manaton Crs STHL UB1 84 A5
Manbey Gv SRTFD E15 76 C5
Manbey Park Rd SRTFD E15 76 C5
Manbey Rd SRTFD E15 * 76 C5
Manbey St SRTFD E15 76 C5
Manbre Rd HMSMTH W6 107 F5
Manbrough Av EHAM E6 96 A2
Manchester Ct CAN/RD E16 95 F5
Manchester Dr NKENS W10 * 88 C3
Manchester Gv POP/IOD E14 113 F4
Manchester Ms MHST W1U 10 A3
Manchester Rd POP/IOD E14 113 F4
SEVS/STOTM N15 55 K5
THHTH CR7 164 D2
Manchester Sq MBLAR W1H 10 A4
Manchester St MHST W1U 10 A3
Manchester Wy DAGE RM10 * 80 D3
Manchuria Rd BTSEA SW11 129 F5
Manciple St STHWK SE1 19 H2
Mandalay Rd CLAP SW4 129 H4
Mandarin Wy YEAD UB4 83 H5
Mandela Cl WLSDN NW10 68 E6
Mandela Pl WATN WD24 21 H1
Mandela Rd CAN/RD E16 94 E5
Mandela St BRXN/ST SW9 110 B6
CAMTN NW1 4 F3
Mandela Wy STHWK SE1 19 K5
Mandeville Cl WIM/MER SW19 146 C6
Mandeville Ct CHING E4 43 G3
Mandeville Dr SURB KT6 158 E7
Mandeville Pl MHST W1U 10 B4
Mandeville Rd ISLW TW7 124 B1
NTHLT UB5 65 K6
STHGT/OAK N14 40 B1
Mandeville St CLPT E5 75 G2
Mandrake Rd TOOT SW17 147 K2
Mandrake Wy SRTFD E15 * 76 C6
Mandrell Rd
BRXS/STRHM SW2 129 K4
Manette St LSQ/SEVD WC2H 11 H5
Manfred Rd PUT/ROE SW15 127 J4
Manger Rd HOLWY N7 72 E5
Mangold Wy ERITHM DA18 116 E2
Manilla St POP/IOD E14 112 D1
Manister Rd ABYW SE2 116 B2
Manley Ct STNW/STAM N16 74 B2
Manley St CAMTN NW1 4 A3
Mann Cl CROY/NA CR0 177 J2
Manningford Cl FSBYE EC1V * 6 C7
Manning Gdns CROY/NA CR0 165 J6
KTN/HRWW/WS HA3 49 K6
Manning Pl
RCHPK/HAM TW10 125 G5
Manning Rd DAGE RM10 80 C5
WALTH E17 57 G3
Manningtree Cl
WIM/MER SW19 127 H7
Manningtree Rd RSLP HA4 65 F3
Manningtree St WCHPL E1 92 C5
Mannin Rd CHDH RM6 61 H6
Mannock Ms SWFD E18 45 F7
Mannock Rd WDGN N22 55 H2
Mann's Cl ISLW TW7 124 A4
Manns Rd EDGW HA8 36 C5
Manoel Rd WHTN TW2 142 C1
Manor Av BROCKY SE4 132 C1
HSLWW TW4 122 C2
NTHLT UB5 65 K6
Manor Cl BAR EN5 26 C3
CDALE/KGS NW9 50 D3
DAGE RM10 81 F5
DART DA1 138 A3
MLHL NW7 * 37 F4
ROM RM1 63 J4
RSLP HA4 46 D7
THMD SE28 97 J5
WPK KT4 160 B7
Manor Cots NTHWD HA6 32 D7
Manor Cottages Ap
EFNCH N2 53 G1
Manor Ct ACT W3 * 105 H3
E/WMO/HCT KT8 * 157 F3
HRW HA1 * 49 F5
KUTN/CMB KT2 * 144 C7
WBLY HA9 * 68 A4
Manor Court Rd HNWL W7 84 E6
Manor Crs BRYLDS KT5 159 H5
Manor Cft EDGW HA8 * 36 C5
Manordene Cl THDIT KT7 158 B7
Manordene Rd THMD SE28 97 J5
Manor Dr BRYLDS KT5 159 H5
ESH/CLAY KT10 171 F2
FELT TW13 141 H4
HOR/WEW KT19 173 G5
MLHL NW7 37 F4
STHGT/OAK N14 28 B6
TRDG/WHET N20 39 J2
WBLY HA9 68 B3
Manor Dr North NWMAL KT3 160 A6
The Manor Dr WPK KT4 160 B7
Manor Est BERM/RHTH SE16 111 J3
Manor Farm Cl WPK KT4 160 B7
Manor Farm Dr CHING E4 44 C1
Manor Farm Rd ALP/SUD HA0 85 K1
STRHM/NOR SW16 164 B1
Manorfield Cl ARCH N19 72 C3
Manor Gdns ACT W3 105 H3
CLAP SW4 * 129 H1
HOLWY N7 72 E2
HPTN TW12 142 B6
RCH/KEW TW9 125 G3
RSLP HA4 65 G4
RYNPK SW20 161 J1
SAND/SEL CR2 178 B5
SUN TW16 140 E7
Manor Ga NTHLT UB5 65 J6
Manorgate Rd KUTN/CMB KT2 144 C7
Manor Gv BECK BR3 166 E1
PECK SE15 111 K5
RCH/KEW TW9 125 H3
Manor Hall Av HDN NW4 52 A1
Manor Hall Dr HDN NW4 52 B1
Manor Hall Gdns LEY E10 57 J7
Manor House Dr
KIL/WHAMP NW6 70 B6
Manor House Wy ISLW TW7 124 C2
Manor La FELT TW13 140 E1
HYS/HAR UB3 101 G5
LEE/GVPK SE12 133 H5
SUN TW16 156 A1
SUT SM1 175 G4
Manor Lane Ter LEW SE13 133 H3
Manor Ms BROCKY SE4 132 C1
KIL/WHAMP NW6 2 B5
Manor Mt FSTH SE23 131 K7
Manor Pde HRW HA1 * 49 F5
STNW/STAM N16 * 74 B1
Manor Pk CHST BR7 169 J1
LEW SE13 133 G4
RCH/KEW TW9 125 G3
Manor Park Cl WWKM BR4 166 E7
Manor Park Crs EDGW HA8 36 C5
Manor Park Dr
RYLN/HDSTN HA2 48 B2
Manor Park Gdns EDGW HA8 36 C4
Manor Park Rd CHST BR7 154 C7
EFNCH N2 53 G2
MNPK E12 77 H3
SUT SM1 175 G4
WLSDN NW10 69 G7
WWKM BR4 166 E7
Manor Pl BORE WD6 * 24 E2
CHST BR7 169 J1
EBED/NFELT TW14 121 K7
MTCM CR4 163 H2
SUT SM1 175 F4
WALW SE17 18 D8
Manor Rd BAR EN5 26 C3
BARK IG11 79 F5
BECK BR3 166 D1
BELMT SM2 174 D6
BFN/LL DA15 155 F2
BXLY DA5 137 J7
CAN/RD E16 94 C4
CHDH RM6 61 K5
DAGE RM10 80 E5
DART DA1 138 B3
E/WMO/HCT KT8 157 J3
ENC/FH EN2 29 K1
HRW HA1 49 G5
HYS/HAR UB3 82 E5
LEY E10 57 J6
MTCM CR4 163 H2
RCH/KEW TW9 125 G2
ROM RM1 63 J4
RSLP HA4 46 B7
RYNPK SW20 161 J1
SNWD SE25 165 H3
SRTFD E15 94 C2
STNW/STAM N16 56 A7
TEDD TW11 143 G4
TOTM N17 42 C7
WDGN N22 40 E5
WEA W13 85 G6
WHTN TW2 142 C1
WLGTN SM6 176 B3
WWKM BR4 166 E7
Manor Rd North
ESH/CLAY KT10 171 F1
WLGTN SM6 176 B3
Manor Rd South
ESH/CLAY KT10 170 E3
Manorside BAR EN5 26 C3
Manor Sq BCTR RM8 79 J1
Manor V BTFD TW8 104 D4
Manor Vw FNCH N3 53 F1
Manor Wy MTCM CR4 163 H2
NWDGN UB2 102 C3
RAIN RM13 99 G3
RSLP HA4 46 C6
RYLN/HDSTN HA2 48 B3
SAND/SEL CR2 178 A5
WPK KT4 160 B7
BECK BR3 166 D2
BORE WD6 24 E3
BXLY DA5 137 H7
CDALE/KGS NW9 51 G3
CHING E4 44 B3
Manorway EN EN1 30 A6
Manor Wy HAYES BR2 168 D5
STMC/STPC BR5 169 H3
Manorway WFD IG8 45 G4
The Manor Wy WLGTN SM6 176 B3
Manresa Rd CHEL SW3 15 H7
Mansard Beeches TOOT SW17 148 A4
Mansard Cl HCH RM12 81 J1
PIN HA5 47 H2
Manse Cl HYS/HAR UB3 101 G5
Mansel Gv WALTH E17 43 J7
Mansell Rd ACT W3 87 F7
GFD/PVL UB6 84 B4
Mansell St WCHPL E1 13 M5
Mansel Rd WIM/MER SW19 146 C5
Mansergh Cl CHARL SE7 114 D6
Manse Rd STNW/STAM N16 74 B2
Manser Rd RAIN RM13 99 G2
Mansfield Av EBAR EN4 27 K5
RSLP HA4 47 F7
SEVS/STOTM N15 55 K3
Mansfield Cl ED N9 30 C5
Mansfield Dr YEAD UB4 82 C3
Mansfield Hl CHING E4 31 K7
Mansfield Ms CAVSQ/HST W1G 10 C3
Mansfield Rd ACT W3 86 D3
CHSGTN KT9 171 J4
HAMP NW3 71 K4
IL IG1 78 A1
SAND/SEL CR2 177 K5
WALTH E17 57 H3
WAN E11 59 F5
Mansfield St CAVSQ/HST W1G 10 C3

Column 1

Mansford St *BETH* E2............ 92 D2
Manship St *MTCM* CR4........ 148 A7
Mansion Cl *BRXN/ST* SW9.... 110 B3
Mansion Gdns *HAMP* NW3.... 71 F3
Mansion House Pl
 MANHO EC4N *............ 13 G5
Mansion House St
 MANHO EC4N............ 13 G5
Manson Ms *SKENS* SW7...... 14 E6
Manson Pl *SKENS* SW7...... 15 F6
Manstead Gdns *CHDH* RM6.. 61 J4
 RAIN RM13............ 99 K5
Manston Av *NWDGN* UB2.... 103 F3
Manston Cl *PGE/AN* SE20.... 150 E7
Manston Rd *CRICK* NW2...... 70 C4
Manston Gv *KUTN/CMB* KT2.. 143 K4
Mantle Wy *HCH* RM12........ 81 K5
Manthorpe Rd
 WOOL/PLUM SE18........ 115 H4
Mantilla Rd *TOOT* SW17...... 148 A3
Mantle Rd *BROCKY* SE4...... 132 B3
Mantlet Cl *STRHM/NOR* SW16 148 E7
Mantle Wy *SRTFD* E15........ 76 C6
Manton Av *HNWL* W7........ 104 A1
Manton Cl *HYS/HAR* UB3.... 82 C6
Manton Rd *ABYW* SE2........ 116 B3
Mantua St *BTSEA* SW11...... 128 C2
Mantus Cl *WCHPL* E1........ 92 E3
Mantus Rd *WCHPL* E1........ 92 E3
Manus Wy *TRDG/WHET* N20.. 39 G1
Manville Gdns *TOOT* SW17.. 148 B1
Manville Rd *TOOT* SW17...... 148 A1
Manwood Rd *BROCKY* SE4.. 132 B5
Manwood St *CAN/RD* E16.... 95 K7
Many Gates *BAL* SW12........ 148 B1
Mapesbury Ms
 CDALE/KGS NW9............ 51 J5
Mapesbury Rd *CRICK* NW2.. 70 C4
Mapeshill Pl *CRICK* NW2...... 70 B5
Mape St *BETH* E2............ 92 D3
Maple Av *ACT* W3............ 87 G7
 CHING E4.................. 43 H5
 RYLN/HDSTN HA2.......... 66 B1
Maple Cl *BKHH* IG9............ 45 H2
 BUSH WD23................ 21 J1
 CLAP SW4................ 129 J5
 FNCH N3.................. 38 E5
 HCH RM12................ 81 K2
 HPTN TW12.............. 141 H5
 MTCM CR4................ 148 B7
 RSLP HA4.................. 47 F5
 STMC/STPC BR5............ 169 J4
 STNW/STAM N16............ 56 C7
 YEAD UB4.................. 83 H4
Maple Ct *ASHF* TW15........ 140 B5
 HACK E8 *................ 74 C6
 NWMAL KT3.............. 160 A2
Maple Crs *BFN/LL* DA15.... 136 B5
Maplecroft Cl *EHAM* E6...... 95 H5
Mapledale Av *CROY/NA* CR0.. 178 D2
Mapledene Rd *HACK* E8...... 74 C6
 HACK E8 *................ 7 M1
Maple Gdns *EDGW* HA8...... 37 G7
Maple Gv *BTFD* TW8........ 104 C6
 CDALE/KGS NW9............ 50 E6
 EA W5...................... 104 E2
 STHL UB1.................. 83 K4
Maplehurst Cl *KUT/HW* KT1.. 159 F3
Maple Leaf Cl *BFN/LL* DA15.. 136 A7
Mapleleafe Gdns
 BARK/HLT IG6................ 60 B2
Maple Leaf Sq
 BERM/RHTH SE16 *........ 112 A1
Maple Ms *KIL/WHAMP* NW6 * 2 C5
 STRHM/NOR SW16........ 149 F6
Maple Pl *FITZ* W1T........ 10 F2
 TOTM N17................ 42 C6
Maple Rd *PGE/AN* SE20...... 150 D7
 SURB KT6.................. 158 E4
 WAN E11.................. 58 C4
 YEAD UB4.................. 83 G2
Maples Pl *WCHPL* E1 *...... 92 D4
Maplestead Rd
 BRXS/STRHM SW2.......... 130 A6
 DAGW RM9................ 79 H7
The Maples *ESH/CLAY* KT10 *.. 171 G6
 KUT/HW KT1.............. 143 H6
Maple St *BETH* E2............ 92 C1
 FITZ W1T.................. 10 E2
 ROMW/RG RM7............ 62 E3
Maplethorpe Rd *THHTH* CR7 164 B3
Mapleton Crs
 WAND/EARL SW18........ 128 A5
Mapleton Rd *CHING* E4...... 44 A2
 EN EN1.................... 30 D1
 WAND/EARL SW18........ 128 A5
Maple Tree Pl *BKHTH/KID* SE3.. 114 D5
Maple Wk *NKENS* W10 *...... 88 B3
Maple Wy *FELT* TW13........ 140 E2
Maplin Cl *WCHMH* N21...... 29 F5
Maplin Rd *CAN/RD* E16...... 94 E5
Maplin St *BOW* E3............ 93 H2
Mapperley Rd *WFD* IG8...... 44 C6
Marabou Cl *MNPK* E12...... 77 J4
Maran Wy *ERITHM* DA18.... 116 E2
Marathon Wy *THMD* SE28 *... 97 H2
 THMD SE28................ 116 A1
Marban Rd *MV/WKIL* W9.... 88 D2
Marble Cl *ACT* W3............ 105 J1
Marble Dr *CRICK* NW2........ 52 B6
Marble Hill Cl *TWK* TW1...... 124 C6
Marble Hill Gdns *TWK* TW1.. 124 C6
Marble Quay *WAP* E1W...... 18 M8
Marbrook Ct *LEE/GVPK* SE12 153 G3
Marcella Rd *BRXN/ST* SW9.. 130 B1
Marchant Rd *MLHL* NW7.... 37 G5
Marchant St *NWCR* SE14.... 112 B5
Marchbank Rd *WKENS* W14 107 J5
Marchmont Gdns
 RCHPK/HAM TW10.......... F4
Marchmont Rd
 RCHPK/HAM TW10........ 125 G4
 WLGTN SM6................ 176 C7
Marchmont St *BMSBY* WC1N.. 5 J9
March Rd *TWK* TW1.......... 124 A6
 WDSDE/HEL TW5............ 102 C7
Marchside Cl *HEST* TW5...... 102 C7
Marchwood Cl *CMBW* SE5.. 111 F6
Marchwood Crs *EA* W5...... 85 J6
Marcia Rd *STHWK* SE1...... 19 K6
Marcilly Rd *WAND/EARL* SW18 128 C4
Marconi Rd *LEY* E10.......... 57 J7
Marconi Wy *STHL* UB1...... 84 B5
Marcon Pl *HACK* E8.......... 74 D5
Marcus Garvey Ms *EDUL* SE22 131 J4
Marcus Garvey Wy
 HNHL SE24................ 130 B3
Marcus St *SRTFD* E15........ 76 C7
 WAND/EARL SW18........ 128 A5
Mardale Dr *CDALE/KGS* NW9 51 F4

Column 2

Mardell Rd *CROY/NA* CR0.... 166 A4
Marden Crs *CROY/NA* CR0.. 164 A5
Marden Rd *CROY/NA* CR0.. 164 A5
 ROM RM1.................. 63 G5
 TOTM N17.................. 56 A2
Marden Sq *BERM/RHTH* SE16 111 J3
Marder Rd *WEA* W13........ 104 B1
Mardyke Cl *RAIN* RM13...... 98 E1
Marechal Niel Av
 BFN/LL DA15.............. 154 D2
Marechal Niel Pde
 SCUP DA14 *.............. 154 D2
Maresfield *CROY/NA* CR0.... 178 A3
Maresfield Gdns *HAMP* NW3 71 G4
Mare St *HACK* E8............ 74 D7
Marfield Cl *WPK* KT4........ 160 D7
Marfleet Cl *CAR* SM5........ 175 J1
Margaret Av *CHING* E4...... 31 K5
Margaret Bondfield Av
 BARK IG11.................. 79 G5
Margaret Cl *GPK* RM2........ 63 K4
Margaret Gardner Dr
 ELTH/MOT SE9............ 153 K1
Margaret Ingram Cl
 FUL/PGN SW6 *............ 107 J5
Margaret Lockwood Cl
 KUT/HW KT1................ 159 G3
Margaret Rd *BXLY* DA5.... 136 E5
 EBAR EN4.................. 27 K3
 GPK RM2.................. 63 K4
 STNW/STAM N16............ 56 B7
Margaret Rutherford Pl
 BAL SW12................ 129 H7
Margaret St *REGST* W1B.. 10 D4
Margaretta Ter *CHEL* SW3 15 J9
Margaret Wy *REDBR* IG4.... 59 J5
Margate Rd
 BRXS/STRHM SW2.......... 129 K4
Margeholes *OXHEY* WD19.. 33 J1
Margery Park Rd *FSTGT* E7 76 E5
Margery Rd *BCTR* RM8........ 79 K2
Margery St *CLKNW* EC1R.... 6 A8
Margin Dr *WIM/MER* SW19.. 146 B4
Margravine Gdns
 HMSMTH W6.............. 107 G5
Margravine Rd *HMSMTH* W6 107 G5
Marguerite Vls *RYNPK* SW20 * 145 K6
Marham Dr *CDALE/KGS* NW9 51 G1
Marham Gdns *MRDN* SM4.. 162 B5
 WAND/EARL SW18........ 128 D7
Maria Cl *YEAD* UB4........ 111 H3
Marian Pl *BETH* E2............ 92 D1
Marian Rd *STRHM/NOR* SW16 148 C6
Marian St *BETH* E2 *........ 92 D1
Marian Wy *WLSDN* NW10.. 69 H6
Maria Ter *WCHPL* E1.......... 93 F4
Maria Theresa Cl *NWMAL* KT3 160 A4
Maricas Av
 KTN/HRWW/WS HA3...... 34 D7
Marie Curie *CMBW* SE5 *.. 111 F7
Marie Lloyd Wk *HACK* E8 *.. 74 C5
Mariette Wy *WLGTN* SM6.... 176 E7
Marigold Aly *STHWK* SE1.... 12 C7
Marigold Cl *STHL* UB1........ 83 J6
Marigold Rd *TOTM* N17...... 42 E6
Marigold St *BERM/RHTH* SE16 111 J1
Marigold Wy *CROY/NA* CR0 166 A7
Marina Ap *YEAD* UB4........ 83 J4
Marina Av *NWMAL* KT3.... 160 E5
Marina Dr *WELL* DA16...... 135 K1
Marina Gdns *ROMW/RG* RM7 62 E4
Marina Pl *KUT/HW* KT1...... 143 K7
Marina Wy *TEDD* TW11.... 143 K6
Marine Dr *BARK* IG11........ 97 J3
 WOOL/PLUM SE18........ 114 E3
Marinefield Rd *FUL/PGN* SW6 128 A1
Mariner Gdns
 RCHPK/HAM TW10........ 143 H2
Mariner Rd *MNPK* E12........ 78 A3
Mariners Ms *POP/IOD* E14.. 113 G3
Marine St *BERM/RHTH* SE16 * 111 H1
Marion Gv *WFD* IG8.......... 44 C4
Marion Ms *DUL* SE21........ 149 K2
Marion Rd *MLHL* NW7........ 37 J4
 THHTH CR7................ 164 D4
Marischal Rd *LEW* SE13.... 133 G2
Maritime Quay *POP/IOD* E14 112 D4
Maritime St *BOW* E3.......... 93 H3
Marius Rd *TOOT* SW17........ 148 A1
Marjorie Gv *BTSEA* SW11.... 128 E3
Mark Av *CHING* E4............ 31 K5
Mark Cl *HAYES* BR2.......... 181 J5
 STHL UB1.................. 84 A7
Markeston Gn *OXHEY* WD19 33 H3
Market Chambers
 ENC/FH EN2 *............ 29 K2
Market Est *HOLWY* N7........ 72 E5
Market La *EDGW* HA8........ 36 E7
Market Link *ROM* RM1...... 63 G3
Market Ms *MYFR/PICC* W1J 10 C9
Market Pde *BMLY* BR1 *.... 152 E7
 EW KT17 *................ 173 H7
 FELT TW13 *.............. 141 J1
 LEY E10 *.................. 57 K7
 SCUP DA14 *.............. 155 G3
 SNWD SE25 *.............. 165 H3
 STNW/STAM N16 *........ 56 C7
 WALTH E17 *.............. 57 F3
Market Pl *ACT* W3............ 86 E7
 BERM/RHTH SE16.......... 111 H4
 BTFD TW8.................. 104 D6
 EFNCH N2.................. 53 H3
GTPST W1W................ 10 E4
 KUT/HW KT1.............. 158 E1
 ROM RM1.................. 63 G4
 WAT WD17................ 21 G3
Market Rd *HOLWY* N7........ 72 E5
 RCH/KEW TW9............ 125 H2
Market Sq *ED* N9............ 42 D1
 EHAM E6.................. 95 K1
 BTFD TW8 *.............. 104 E5
Market Sq *EHAM* E6.......... 95 K1
 WATW WD18................ 21 F3
 WOOL/PLUM SE18........ 115 F3
Market Ter *BTFD* TW8 *...... 105 F6
The Market *HNWL* W7 *.... 104 A1
Market Yard Ms *STHWK* SE1 19 J3
Markfield Gdns *CHING* E4.. 31 K6
Markfield Rd
 SEVS/STOTM N15............ 56 C3
Markham Cl *BORE* WD6.... 24 A3
Markham Pl *CHEL* SW3...... 15 L7
Markham Sq *CHEL* SW3.. 15 L7
Markham St *CHEL* SW3.. 15 K7
Markhole Cl *HPTN* TW12.... 141 K6
Markhouse Av *WALTH* E17.. 57 G5
Markhouse Rd *WALTH* E17.. 57 H4
Mark La *MON* EC3R........ 13 K6
Markmanor Av *WALTH* E17 57 G6
Mark Rd *WDGN* N22.......... 55 H1
Marksbury Av *RCH/KEW* TW9 125 H2
Marks Rd *ROMW/RG* RM7.. 62 E4

Column 3

Mark St *SDTCH* EC2A...... 7 J9
 SRTFD E15................ 76 C6
Mark Ter *RYNPK* SW20 *.... 146 A6
The Markway *SUN* TW16 156 B1
Markwade Cl *MNPK* E12.... 59 H7
Markwell Cl *SYD* SE26........ 150 D3
Markyate Rd *BCTR* RM8...... 79 H4
Marlands Rd *CLAY* IG5...... 59 K1
Marlborough Av *EDGW* HA8 36 D2
 HACK E8.................... 74 C7
 RSLP HA4.................. 46 A5
 STHGT/OAK N14............ 40 C2
Marlborough Cl
 TRDG/WHET N20............ 39 K2
 WALW SE17................ 18 D6
 WIM/MER SW19............ 147 J5
Marlborough Ct *REGST* W1B 10 E6
Marlborough Crs *CHSWK* W4 106 A2
 HYS/HAR UB3.............. 101 H6
Marlborough Dr *BUSH* WD23 21 J2
 CLAY IG5.................... 59 J2
Marlborough Gdns
 TRDG/WHET N20............ 39 K2
Marlborough Ga *BAY/PAD* W2 9 G7
Marlborough Gv *STHWK* SE1 111 H4
Marlborough Hl *HRW* HA1 48 E3
 STJWD NW8................ 2 F4
Marlborough La *CHARL* SE7 114 B5
Marlborough Ms
 BRXS/STRHM SW2.......... 130 A3
Marlborough Pde
 FSBYPK N4 *.............. 55 J7
Marlborough Park Av
 BFN/LL DA15.............. 136 B7
Marlborough Pl *STJWD* NW8 2 E6
Marlborough Rd *ARCH* N19 72 E1
 BCTR RM8.................. 79 J3
 CHING E4.................. 43 K5
 CHSWK W4................ 105 K4
 DAGE RM10................ 80 B5
 ED N9........................ 30 B7
 FELT TW13................ 141 H1
 HAYES BR2................ 168 B3
 HPTN TW12.............. 142 A5
 NWDGN UB2................ 102 C2
 RCHPK/HAM TW10........ 125 G5
 ROMW/RG RM7............ 62 C3
 SAND/SEL CR2.............. 177 J6
 SRTFD E15.................. 76 C3
 SUT SM1.................... 174 E2
 SWFD E18.................. 58 E2
 WATW WD18................ 21 F3
 WDGN N22.................. 41 H7
 WELL DA16.............. 136 C2
 WHALL SW1A............ 10 F9
 WIM/MER SW19............ 147 J5
 WOOL/PLUM SE18........ 115 G2
Marlborough St *CHEL* SW3 15 J6
Marlborough Yd *ARCH* N19 72 D1
Marler Rd *FSTH* SE23........ 132 C7
Marley Av *BXLYHN* DA7.... 116 E5
Marley Cl *FUL/PGN* UB6.... 84 A2
 SEVS/STOTM N15............ 55 H4
Marlingdene Cl *HPTN* TW12 142 A5
Marlings Cl *CHST* BR7...... 169 K6
Marlings Park Av *CHST* BR7 169 K6
Marlins Cl *SUT* SM1 *........ 175 G4
Marlins Meadow *WATW* WD18 20 B5
The Marlins *NTHWD* HA6.. 32 D5
Marloes Cl *ALP/SUD* HA0.... 67 K3
Marloes Rd *KENS* W8...... 14 C5
Marlow Av *PUR* RM19........ 119 K5
Marlow Cl *PGE/AN* SE20.... 165 J2
Marlow Ct *CDALE/KGS* NW9 51 F4
Marlow Crs *TWK* TW1........ 124 A5
Marlow Dr *CHEAM* SM3.... 174 B2
Marlowe Cl *CHST* BR7...... 154 D5
Marlowe Rd *WALTH* E17.... 58 A3
Marlowe Sq *MTCM* CR4.... 163 H3
Marlowes *STJWD* NW8...... 2 E3
Marlow Gdns *HYS/HAR* UB3 101 H3
Marlow Rd *EHAM* E6........ 95 K2
 NWDGN UB2................ 102 E3
 PGE/AN SE20.............. 165 J2
Marlow Wy *BERM/RHTH* SE16 112 A1
Marl Rd *WAND/EARL* SW18 128 A3
Marlton St *GNWCH* SE10.... 113 J4
Marlwood Cl *BFN/LL* DA15 154 E1
Marmadon Rd
 WOOL/PLUM SE18........ 116 A3
Marmion Ap *CHING* E4...... 43 J3
Marmion Av *CHING* E4...... 43 H3
Marmion Cl *CHING* E4...... 43 H3
Marmion Ms *BTSEA* SW11 * 129 F2
Marmion Rd *BTSEA* SW11.. 129 F4
Marmont Rd *PECK* SE15.... 111 H7
Marmora Rd *EDUL* SE22.... 131 K5
Marmot Rd *HSLWW* TW4.. 122 C2
Marne Av *FBAR/BDGN* N11 40 B3
 WELL DA16................ 136 B2
Marnell Wy *HSLWW* TW4.. 122 C2
Marne St *NKENS* W10........ 88 C2
Marney Rd *BTSEA* SW11.... 129 F3
Marnfield Crs
 BRXS/STRHM SW2.......... 130 A7
Marnham Av *CRICK* NW2.... 70 C3
Marnham Crs *GFD/PVL* UB6 84 B1
Marnock Rd *BROCKY* SE4.. 132 C4
Maroon St *POP/IOD* E14.... 93 G4
Maroons Wy *CAT* SE6........ 151 J4
Marquess Rd North *IS* N1 * 73 K5
Marquess Rd South *IS* N1 * 73 K5
Marquis Cl *ALP/SUD* HA0.... 68 B6
Marquis Rd *CAMTN* NW1.. 72 E5
 FSBYPK N4.................. 55 F7
 WDGN N22.................. 41 F5
Marrabon Cl *BFN/LL* DA15 136 B7
Marrick Cl *PUT/ROE* SW15 126 D3
Married Quarters
 EDGW HA8 *.............. 36 D6
Marriner Ct *HYS/HAR* UB3 82 D6
Marriott Rd *MUSWH* N10.. 39 K7
Marriott Cl *EBED/NFELT* TW14 121 F5
Marriott Rd *BAR* EN5........ 26 B2
 FSBYPK N4.................. 55 F7
 LEY E10.................... 76 A2
 SRTFD E15................ 76 D3
Marryat Pl *WIM/MER* SW19 146 C3
Marryat Rd *WIM/MER* SW19 146 B4
Marryfields Wy *CAT* SE6.... 151 K4
Marsala Rd *LEW* SE13...... 132 E3
Marsden Rd *ED* N9............ 30 D7
 PECK SE15................ 131 G2
Marsden St *KTTN* NW5...... 72 A5
Marshall Cl *FBAR/BDGN* N11 40 D5

Column 4

 HRW HA1.................. 48 D6
 HSLWW TW4.............. 122 E4
 WAND/EARL SW18........ 128 B5
Marshall Dr *YEAD* UB4...... 82 D4
Marshall Est *MLHL* NW7 *.. 37 K3
Marshall Rd *LEY* E10.......... 75 K2
 TOTM N17.................. 41 K7
Marshalls Dr *ROM* RM1...... 63 F1
Marshall's Gv
 WOOL/PLUM SE18........ 114 D3
Marshall's Pl
 BERM/RHTH SE16.......... 19 M4
Marshall's Rd *SUT* SM1.... 175 F3
Marshall St *SOHO/CST* W1F 10 F5
Marshalsea Rd *STHWK* SE1 18 F1
Marsham St *WEST* SW1P 17 H5
Marsh Av *MTCM* CR4........ 162 E1
Marshbrook Cl
 BKHTH/KID SE3............ 134 C2
Marsh Cl *MLHL* NW7........ 37 J2
Marsh Dr *CDALE/KGS* NW9 51 H5
Marsh Farm Rd *WHTN* TW2 124 A7
Marshfield St *POP/IOD* E14 113 F2
Marsh Green Rd *DAGE* RM10 80 C7
Marsh Hl *HOM* E9............ 75 G4
Marsh La *LEY* E10.............. 75 H1
 MLHL NW7................ 37 G2
 STAN HA7.................. 35 J4
 TOTM N17.................. 42 D6
Marsh Rd *ALP/SUD* HA0.... 85 K2
 PIN HA5.................... 47 J3
Marshside Cl *ED* N9.......... 30 E7
Marsh St *DART* DA1.......... 139 K3
 POP/IOD E14 *............ 112 E3
Marsh Wall *POP/IOD* E14.. 112 E1
Marsh Wy *RAIN* RM13...... 99 H3
Marsland Cl *WALW* SE17.. 18 D8
Marston Av *CHSGTN* KT9.. 172 A5
Marston Cl *DAGE* RM10.... 80 C2
 KIL/WHAMP NW6............ 2 F1
Marston Rd *WOT/HER* KT12 156 E7
 CLAY IG5.................. 59 J1
 TEDD TW11................ 143 H4
Marston Wy *NRWD* SE19.. 149 H6
Marsworth Av *PIN* HA5.... 33 H7
Marsworth Cl *WATW* WD18 20 A4
 YEAD UB4.................. 83 J4
Martaban Rd
 STNW/STAM N16............ 74 A1
Martello St *HACK* E8........ 74 D6
Martell Rd *DUL* SE21........ 149 K2
Martel Pl *HACK* E8 *........ 74 B5
Marten Rd *WALTH* E17...... 43 J7
Martens Av *BXLYHN* DA7.. 137 K3
Martham Cl *THMD* SE28.... 97 K6
Martha Ct *BETH* E2 *........ 92 D1
Martha's Blds *FSBYE* EC1V 7 G9
Martha St *WCHPL* E1........ 92 D5
Marthorne Crs
 KTN/HRWW/WS HA3...... 48 D1
Martin Bowes Rd
 ELTH/MOT SE9.............. 134 E2
Martin Cl *ED* N9.............. 31 F7
Martin Crs *CROY/NA* CR0.. 164 A7
Martindale *MORT/ESHN* SW14 125 J4
Martindale Av *CAN/RD* E16 94 E6
Martindale Rd *BAL* SW12 129 G6
 HSLWW TW4.............. 122 D2
Martin Dr *NTHLT* UB5........ 65 K4
 RAIN RM13.................. 99 K4
Martineau Cl *ESH/CLAY* KT10 170 D3
Martineau Dr *TWK* TW1.... 124 C3
Martineau Ms *HBRY* N5.... 73 H3
Martineau Rd *HBRY* N5 *.. 73 H3
Martingales Cl
 RCHPK/HAM TW10........ 143 K2
Martin Gdns *BCTR* RM8...... 79 J3
Martin Gv *MRDN* SM4...... 161 K2
Martin La *CANST* EC4R.... 13 H6
Martin Rd *BCTR* RM8........ 79 J3
Martins Cl *WWKM* BR4.... 180 E1
Martins Mt *BAR* EN5.......... 26 E3
Martins Rd *THMD* SE28...... 96 E7
The Martins *SYD* SE26...... 150 D4
 WBLY HA9 *................ 68 B2
Martin St *THMD* SE28...... 96 E7
Martins Wk *MUSWH* N10 * 40 A7
 THMD SE28.................. 96 E7
Martin Wy *MRDN* SM4.... 161 K2
Martlet Gv *NTHLT* UB5...... 83 H2
Martlett Ct *HOL/ALD* WC2B 11 K5
Martley Dr *GNTH/NBYPK* IG2 60 B4
Martock Cl
 KTN/HRWW/WS HA3...... 49 G3
Martock Gdns
 FBAR/BDGN N11............ 39 K4
Marton Cl *CAT* SE6............ 151 J2
Marton Rd *STNW/STAM* N16 * 74 A1
Martys Yd *HAMP* NW3 *.... 71 H3
Marvell Av *YEAD* UB4........ 82 E4
Marvels Cl *LEE/GVPK* SE12 153 F1
Marvels La *LEE/GVPK* SE12 153 F1
Marville Rd *FUL/PGN* SW6 107 J6
Marvin St *HACK* E8.......... 74 D5
Marwell Cl *ROM* RM1........ 63 H5
 WWKM BR4................ 180 D1
Marwood Cl *WELL* DA16.. 136 C2
Marwood Dr *MLHL* NW7.. 38 B6
Mary Adelaide Cl
 PUT/ROE SW15.............. 145 G2
Mary Ann Blds *DEPT* SE8.. 112 D5
Maryat Rd *CAT* SE6............ 151 J1
Marybank *WOOL/PLUM* SE18 114 E3
Maryatt Av *RYLN/HDSTN* HA2 66 B1
Mary Cl *KTN/HRWW/WS* HA3 50 B6
Mary Datchelor Cl *CMBW* SE5 110 E7
Mary Gn *STJWD* NW8........ 2 D3
Maryland Pk *SRTFD* E15.... 76 C5
Maryland Rd *MV/WKIL* W9 8 B1
 SRTFD E15.................. 76 C5
 THHTH CR7.................. 149 H7
 WDGN N22.................. 41 G5
Marylands Rd *MV/WKIL* W9 88 E3
Maryland St *SRTFD* E15.... 76 C5
Maryland Wk *IS* N1 *........ 6 F2
Mary Lawrenson Pl
 BKHTH/KID SE3.............. 113 K6
Marylebone F/O *BAY/PAD* W2 9 J3
Marylebone High St
 CAVSQ/HST W1G............ 10 B3
Marylebone La *MHST* W1U 10 A4
Marylebone Ms
 CAVSQ/HST W1G............ 10 B3
Marylebone Pas *GTPST* W1W 10 F4
Marylebone Rd *MBLAR* W1H 9 K2
Marylebone St
 CAVSQ/HST W1G............ 10 B3
Marylee Wy *LBTH* SE11.. 17 M6
Maryon Gv *CHARL* SE7...... 114 D4
Maryon Ms *HAMP* NW3...... 71 J3
Maryon Rd *CHARL* SE7...... 114 D4

Column 5

Mary Peters Dr *GFD/PVL* UB6 66 D4
Mary Pl *NTGHL* W11........ 88 C6
Mary Rose Cl *HPTN* TW12 142 A7
Maryrose Wy
 TRDG/WHET N20............ 27 H7
Mary Seacole Cl *HACK* E8 * 7 L3
Mary Secole Cl *HACK* E8 *... 7 L3
Mary's Ter *TWK* TW1........ 124 B6
Mary St *CAN/RD* E16........ 94 D4
 IS N1.......................... 6 F4
Mary Ter *CAMTN* NW1...... 4 E4
Mary Wy *OXHEY* WD19...... 33 G3
Masbro' Rd *WKENS* W14.. 107 G2
Mascalls Rd *CHARL* SE7.... 114 B5
Mascotts Cl *CRICK* NW2.... 69 K2
Masefield Av *BORE* WD6.... 24 D4
 STAN HA7.................. 35 F4
 STHL UB1.................. 84 A6
Masefield Cl *ERITH* DA8.... 118 C6
Masefield Crs *STHGT/OAK* N14 28 C4
Masefield Gdns *EHAM* E6.. 96 A3
Masefield La *YEAD* UB4.... 83 F3
Masefield Rd *HPTN* TW12.. 141 K3
Masefield Wy
 STWL/WRAY TW19........ 120 C6
Mashie Rd *ACT* W3.......... 87 G5
Mashiters Wk *ROM* RM1.... 63 G2
Maskall Cl *BRXS/STRHM* SW2 130 B7
Maskell Rd *TOOT* SW17.... 147 G2
Maskelyne Cl *BTSEA* SW11 108 D7
Mason Cl *BERM/RHTH* SE16 111 H4
 BORE WD6.................. 25 F1
 CAN/RD E16................ 94 E6
 HPTN TW12.............. 141 K7
 RYNPK SW20.............. 146 B7
Mason Ct *WBLY* HA9 *...... 68 C1
Mason Rd *SUT* SM1.......... 175 F4
 WFD IG8.................... 44 C3
Mason's Arms Ms
 CONDST W1S *............ 10 D5
Masons Av
 KTN/HRWW/WS HA3...... 48 E2
Mason's Av *CITYW* EC2V 13 G4
 CROY/NA CR0............ 177 J2
Masons Ct *EW* KT17 *...... 173 J7
Masons Hl *BMLY* BR1........ 167 K2
 HAYES BR2................ 168 A3
 WOOL/PLUM SE18........ 115 G3
Mason's Pl *FSBYE* EC1V.. 6 D7
 MTCM CR4................ 147 K7
Masons Yd *FSBYE* EC1V *.. 6 E9
STJS SW1Y.................. 10 F8
Massey Cl *FBAR/BDGN* N11 40 B4
Massie Rd *HACK* E8.......... 74 C5
Massingberd Wy *TOOT* SW17 148 B3
Massinger St *WALW* SE17 19 J6
Massingham St *WCHPL* E1 93 F3
Masson Av *RSLP* HA4........ 65 G4
Masterman Rd *EHAM* E6.. 95 J2
Masters Cl *STRHM/NOR* SW16 148 C5
Masters Dr *BERM/RHTH* SE16 111 J4
Master's St *WCHPL* E1 *.... 93 F4
Mast House Ter
 POP/IOD E14.............. 112 D3
Mast Leisure Pk
 BERM/RHTH SE16 *...... 112 B2
Mastmaker Rd *POP/IOD* E14 112 D1
Mast Quay *WOOL/PLUM* SE18 114 E2
Maswell Park Crs *HSLW* TW3 123 H5
Maswell Park Rd *HSLW* TW3 123 G4
Matara Ms *WALW* SE17.... 18 E7
Matcham Rd *WAN* E11...... 76 C2
Matchless Dr
 WOOL/PLUM SE18........ 115 F6
Matfield Cl *BELV* DA17...... 117 H5
Matham Gv *EDUL* SE22.... 131 G3
Matham Rd *E/WMO/HCT* KT8 157 J4
Matheson Rd *WKENS* W14 107 J3
Mathews Av *EHAM* E6........ 96 A1
Mathews Park Av *SRTFD* E15 76 D5
Mathews Yd
 LSQ/SEVD WC2H *........ 11 J5
Mathiesson Ct *STHWK* SE1 18 E2
Matilda Cl *NRWD* SE19.... 149 K6
Matilda Gdns *BOW* E3........ 93 J1
Matilda St *IS* N1................ 5 M4
Matlock Cl *BAR* EN5.......... 26 B4
 HNHL SE24................ 130 D3
Matlock Crs *CHEAM* SM3.. 174 C3
 OXHEY WD19................ 33 G2
Matlock Gdns *CHEAM* SM3 174 C3
Matlock Pl *CHEAM* SM3.... 174 C3
Matlock Rd *LEY* E10.......... 58 A5
Matlock St *POP/IOD* E14.. 93 G5
Matlock Wy *NWMAL* KT3.. 145 F7
Matthew Cl *NKENS* W10 *.. 88 B3
Matthew Ct *MTCM* CR4.... 163 H4
Matthews Rd *GFD/PVL* UB6 66 D4
Matthews Rd *BTSEA* SW11 128 E1
Matthias Rd *STNW/STAM* N16 73 K4
Mattingley Wy *PECK* SE15 111 G6
Mattison Rd *FSBYPK* N4.... 55 G5
Mattock La *WEA* W13........ 85 H7
Maud Cashmore Wy
 WOOL/PLUM SE18........ 114 E3
Maude Rd *CMBW* SE5...... 131 F1
 WALTH E17.................. 57 G4
Maudesville Cots *HNWL* W7 * 84 E7
Maude Ter *WALTH* E17...... 57 G3
Maud Gdns *BARK* IG11...... 97 F1
 PLSTW E13................ 94 D7
Maudlins Gn *WAP* E1W.... 92 C7
Maud Rd *LEY* E10............ 76 A2
 PLSTW E13................ 94 D1
Maudslay Rd *ELTH/MOT* SE9 134 E2
Maud St *CAN/RD* E16........ 94 D4
Maud Wilkes Cl *KTTN* NW5 72 C4
Mauleverer Rd
 BRXS/STRHM SW2.......... 129 K4
Maundeby Wk
 WLSDN NW10................ 69 G5
Maunder Rd *HNWL* W7.... 84 F7
Maunsel St *WEST* SW1P.. 17 G5
Maurice Av *WDGN* N22...... 55 H1
Maurice Browne Cl
 MLHL NW7.................. 38 B5
Maurice St *SHB* W12........ 87 K5
Maurice Wk *GLDGN* NW11 53 G5
Maurier Cl *NTHLT* UB5...... 65 G7
Mauritius Rd *GNWCH* SE10 113 H3
Maury Rd *STNW/STAM* N16 74 C1
Mauveine Gdns *HSLW* TW3 123 F3
Maverton Rd *BOW* E3........ 75 J7
Mavis Av *HOR/WEW* KT19 173 G5
Mavis Cl *HOR/WEW* KT19 173 G5
Mawbey Pl *STHWK* SE1.... 19 M8
Mawbey Rd *STHWK* SE1.. 19 M8
Mawbey St *VX/NE* SW8.... 109 K6
Mawney Cl *ROMW/RG* RM7 62 D2
Mawney Rd *ROMW/RG* RM7 62 E3
Mawson Cl *RYNPK* SW20.. 161 H1
Mawson La *CHSWK* W4.... 106 C5

EMPK RM11 63 K7
WDR/YW UB7 100 C2
Napier Ct LEE/GVPK SE12 153 F1
Napier Dr BUSH WD23 21 J3
Napier Gv IS N1 6 F6
Napier Pl WKENS W14 107 J2
Napier Rd ALP/SUD HA0 67 K4
ASHF TW15 140 B6
BELV DA17 117 G3
EHAM E6 78 A7
HAYES BR2 168 A2
ISLW TW7 124 B3
PEND EN3 31 F4
SAND/SEL CR2 177 K6
SNWD SE25 165 J3
SRTFD E15 94 C1
TOTM N17 56 A2
WAN E11 76 C2
WKENS W14 107 J2
WLSDN NW10 87 K2
Napier Ter IS N1 6 C2
Napier Wk ASHF TW15 140 B6
Napoleon Rd CLPT E5 74 D2
TWK TW1 * 124 C6
Napton Cl YEAD UB4 83 J3
Narbonne Av CLAP SW4 129 H4
Narboro Ct ROM RM1 63 J5
Narborough Cl
HGDN/ICK UB10 64 A1
Narborough St FUL/PGN SW6 128 A1
Narcissus Rd
KIL/WHAMP NW6 70 E4
Narford Rd CLPT E5 74 C2
Narrow Boat Cl THMD SE28 115 J1
Narrow St ACT W3 86 D7
POP/IOD E14 93 G6
Narrow Wy HAYES BR2 168 D5
Nascot Pl WAT WD17 21 F1
Nascot Rd WAT WD17 21 F1
Nascot St SHB W12 88 A5
WAT WD17 21 F1
Naseby Cl ISLW TW7 103 K7
KIL/WHAMP NW6 2 F1
Naseby Rd CLAY IG5 45 K7
DAGE RM10 80 C2
NRWD SE19 149 K5
Nash Cl BORE WD6 24 B3
SUT SM1 175 H2
Nash Gn BMLY BR1 152 E6
Nash La HAYES BR2 180 E5
Nash Rd BROCKY SE4 132 B3
CHDH RM6 61 K3
ED N9 42 E1
Nash St CAMTN NW1 4 D7
Nash Wy KTN/HRWW/WS HA3 49 H5
Nasmyth St HMSMTH W6 106 E2
Nassau Rd BARN SW13 106 C7
Nassau St GTPST W1W 10 E3
Nassington Rd HAMP NW3 71 J3
Natalie Cl EBED/NFELT TW14 121 G6
Natalie Ms WHTN TW2 142 D2
Natal Rd FBAR/BDGN N11 40 E4
IL IG1 78 B3
STRHM/NOR SW16 148 D5
THHTH CR7 164 E2
Nathaniel Cl WCHPL E1 13 M3
Nathans Rd ALP/SUD HA0 67 J1
Nathan Wy ABYW SE2 116 B1
THMD SE28 116 A2
National Ter
BERM/RHTH SE16 * 111 J1
Naval Rw POP/IOD E14 94 A6
Navarino Gv HACK E8 74 C5
Navarino Rd HACK E8 74 C5
Navarre Rd EHAM E6 95 J1
Navarre St BETH E2 7 L9
Navestock Cl CHING E4 * 44 A2
Navestock Crs WFD IG8 45 G7
Navestock Ter WFD IG8 45 G6
Navigator Dr NWDGN UB2 103 H1
Navy St CLAP SW4 129 J2
Nayim Pl HACK E8 74 D5
Naylor Gv PEND EN3 31 F4
Naylor Rd PECK SE15 111 J6
TRDG/WHET N20 39 G1
Nazareth Cl PECK SE15 131 J1
Nazrul St BETH E2 7 L7
Neal Av STHL UB1 83 K3
Neal Cl NTHWD HA6 32 E7
Nealden St BRXN/ST SW9 130 A2
Neale Cl EFNCH N2 53 G2
Neal St LSQ/SEVD WC2H 11 J5
WATW WD18 21 G4
Neal Ter FSTH SE23 * 132 A7
Neal Yd LSQ/SEVD WC2H 11 J5
Near Acre CDALE/KGS NW9 37 H7
Neasden Cl WLSDN NW10 69 G4
Neasden La WLSDN NW10 69 F2
Neasham Rd BCTR RM8 79 H4
Neate St CMBW SE5 19 L9
Neath Gdns MRDN SM4 162 B5
Neathouse Pl PIM SW1V 16 E5
Neats Acre RSLP HA4 46 B6
Neatscourt Rd EHAM E6 95 H4
Neckinger BERM/RHTH SE16 19 M3
Neckinger Est
BERM/RHTH SE16 19 M3
Neckinger St STHWK SE1 19 M2
Nectarine Wy LEW SE13 132 E1
Needham Rd NTGHL W11 8 A5
Needleman St
BERM/RHTH SE16 112 A1
Neeld Crs HDN NW4 51 K4
WBLY HA9 68 C4
Neil Cl ASHF TW15 140 A4
Neils Yd LSQ/SEVD WC2H * 11 J5
Nelgarde Rd CAT SE6 132 D6
Nella Rd HMSMTH W6 107 G5
Nelldale Rd BERM/RHTH SE16 111 J3
Nello James Gdns
WNWD SE27 149 K3
Nelson Cl CROY/NA CR0 164 C7
EBED/NFELT TW14 * 121 J7
KIL/WHAMP NW6 2 A7
WOT/HER KT12 156 A7
Nelson Gdns BETH E2 92 C2
HSLW TW3 123 F5
Nelson Grove Rd
WIM/MER SW19 147 F7
Nelson Mandela Cl
MUSWH N10 53 K1
Nelson Mandela Rd
BKHTH/KID SE3 134 B2
Nelson Pl IS N1 6 D6
Nelson Rd BELV DA17 117 G4
CEND/HSY/T N8 55 F4
CHING E4 43 K5
ED N9 42 D2
GNWCH SE10 113 F5
HAYES BR2 168 B3
HRW HA1 48 D7
HTHAIR TW6 100 C7
NWMAL KT3 160 A4
PEND EN3 31 F5
RAIN RM13 99 H1
SCUP DA14 155 G3
SEVS/STOTM N15 56 A3
STAN HA7 35 J5
WAN E11 58 E3
WHTN TW2 123 F5
WIM/MER SW19 147 F6
Nelson Sq STHWK SE1 18 C1
Nelsons Rw CLAP SW4 129 J3
Nelson St CAN/RD E16 94 D6
EHAM E6 78 A7
WCHPL E1 92 D5
Nelson Ter FSBYE EC1V 6 D6
Nelson Wk HOR/WEW KT19 172 C7
Nemoure Rd ACT W3 86 E6
Nene Gdns FELT TW13 141 K1
Nene Rd HTHAIR TW6 100 E7
Nepaul Rd BTSEA SW11 128 D1
Nepean St PUT/ROE SW15 126 D5
Neptune Cl RAIN RM13 99 H1
Neptune Ct BORE WD6 * 24 C2
Neptune Rd HRW HA1 48 D5
HTHAIR TW6 * 101 F7
Neptune St BERM/RHTH SE16 111 K2
Nesbit Cl BKHTH/KID SE3 133 H2
Nesbit Rd ELTH/MOT SE9 134 C3
Nesbitts Aly BAR EN5 * 26 D2
Nesbitt Sq NRWD SE19 * 150 A6
Nesham St WAP E1W 92 C7
Ness Rd ERITH DA8 119 G5
Ness St BERM/RHTH SE16 111 H2
Nesta Rd WFD IG8 44 D5
Nestle's Av HYS/HAR UB3 101 J2
Nestor Av WCHMH N21 29 H5
Netheravon Rd CHSWK W4 106 C3
HNWL W7 85 F7
Netheravon Rd South
CHSWK W4 106 C5
Netherbury Rd EA W5 104 E2
Netherby Gdns ENC/FH EN2 28 E3
Netherby Rd FSTH SE23 131 K6
Nether Cl FNCH N3 38 E6
Nether Ct MLHL NW7 * 38 D5
Nethercourt Av FNCH N3 38 E5
Netherfield Gdns BARK IG11 78 D5
Netherfield Rd
NFNCH/WDSPK N12 39 F4
TOOT SW17 148 A2
Netherford Rd VX/NE SW8 129 H1
Netherhall Gdns HAMP NW3 71 G4
Netherhall Wy HAMP NW3 71 G4
Netherlands Rd BAR EN5 27 H5
Netherleigh Cl HGT N6 54 B7
Netherpark Dr GPK RM2 63 H1
Nether St FNCH N3 38 E6
Netherton Gv WBPTN SW10 108 B5
Netherton Rd
SEVS/STOTM N15 55 K5
TWK TW1 124 B4
Netherwood Pl
HMSMTH W6 * 107 G2
Netherwood Rd WKENS W14 107 G2
Netherwood St
KIL/WHAMP NW6 70 D6
Netley Cl CHEAM SM3 174 B4
CROY/NA CR0 180 A6
Netley Dr WOT/HER KT12 156 E6
Netley Gdns MRDN SM4 162 B6
Netley Rd BTFD TW8 105 F5
GNTH/NBYPK IG2 60 D4
MRDN SM4 162 B6
WALTH E17 57 H4
Netley St CAMTN NW1 4 E8
Nettlecombe Cl BELMT SM2 175 F7
Nettleden Av WBLY HA9 68 C5
Nettlefold Pl WNWD SE27 149 H2
Nettlestead Cl BECK BR3 151 H6
Nettleton Rd HTHAIR TW6 100 E7
NWCR SE14 112 A6
Nettlewood Rd
STRHM/NOR SW16 148 D6
Neuchatel Rd CAT SE6 151 H1
Nevada Cl NWMAL KT3 159 K3
Nevada St GNWCH SE10 113 F6
Nevern Pl ECT SW5 14 B6
Nevern Rd ECT SW5 14 A6
Nevern Sq ECT SW5 14 A6
Nevil Cl NTHWD HA6 32 B4
Neville Av NWMAL KT3 145 F7
Neville Cl ACT W3 105 K1
BFN/LL DA15 155 F3
CAMTN NW1 5 H6
HSLW TW3 123 F1
KIL/WHAMP NW6 88 D1
PECK SE15 111 H6
WAN E11 76 D2
Neville Dr EFNCH N2 53 G5
Neville Gdns BCTR RM8 79 K2
Neville Gill Cl
WAND/EARL SW18 127 K5
Neville Pl WDGN N22 41 F7
Neville Rd BCTR RM8 79 K1
CROY/NA CR0 164 E6
EA W5 85 K3
FSTGT E7 76 E6
KIL/WHAMP NW6 * 88 D1
KUT/HW KT1 159 H1
RCHPK/HAM TW10 143 J2
Neville St SKENS SW7 15 G7
Neville Ter SKENS SW7 * 15 G7
Neville Wk CAR SM5 162 D6
Nevill Rd STNW/STAM N16 74 A3
Nevil Wk CAR SM5 * 162 D6
Nevin Dr CHING E4 31 K7
Nevinson Cl
WAND/EARL SW18 128 C5
Nevis Rd TOOT SW17 148 A1
New Acres Rd THMD SE28 96 E7
THMD SE28 115 K1
Newall Rd HTHAIR TW6 101 F7
Newark Ct WOT/HER KT12 156 B7
Newark Crs WLSDN NW10 87 F2
Newark Gn BORE WD6 25 F2
Newark Knok EHAM E6 96 A5
Newark Rd SAND/SEL CR2 177 K5
Newark St WCHPL E1 92 D4
Newark Wy HDN NW4 51 J2
New Ash Cl EFNCH N2 53 H2
New Barn Cl WLGTN SM6 177 F5
New Barns Av MTCM CR4 163 J3
New Barn St PLSTW E13 94 E3
Newbery Rd ERITH DA8 118 C7
Newbiggin Pth OXHEY WD19 33 G3
Newbold Cots WCHPL E1 * 92 E5
Newbolt Av CHEAM SM3 174 A4
Newbolt Rd STAN HA7 35 F5
New Bond St MYFR/PICC W1J 10 D6
Newborough Gn NWMAL KT3 160 A3
New Brent St HDN NW4 52 A4
New Bridge St EMB EC4Y 12 C5
New Broad St LVPST EC2M 13 H3
New Broadway EA W5 85 J6
Newburgh Rd ACT W3 86 E7
Newburgh St SOHO/CST W1F 10 E5
New Burlington Ms
CONDST W1S 10 E6
New Burlington Pl
CONDST W1S 10 E6
New Burlington St
CONDST W1S 10 E6
Newburn St LBTH SE11 17 M7
Newbury Cl NTHLT UB5 65 K5
Newbury Gdns
HOR/WEW KT19 173 H3
Newbury Ms KTTN NW5 72 A5
Newbury Rd CHING E4 44 A5
GNTH/NBYPK IG2 60 D5
HAYES BR2 167 K2
HTHAIR TW6 100 C7
Newbury St STBT EC1A 12 E3
Newbury Wy NTHLT UB5 65 J5
New Butt La DEPT SE8 * 112 D6
Newby Cl EN EN1 30 A1
Newby Pl POP/IOD E14 94 A6
Newby St VX/NE SW8 129 G2
Newcastle Cl
FLST/FETLN EC4A 12 C4
Newcastle Pl BAY/PAD W2 9 H3
Newcastle Rw CLKNW EC1R 12 B1
New Cavendish St
CAVSQ/HST W1G 10 B3
New Change STP EC4M 12 E5
New Charles St FSBYE EC1V 6 D7
New Church Rd CMBW SE5 110 D6
New City Rd PLSTW E13 95 G2
New Cl FELT TW13 141 J4
WIM/MER SW19 162 B2
New College Ms IS N1 * 6 B1
New College Pde
HAMP NW3 * 71 G5
Newcombe Gdns HSLWW TW4 122 E3
Newcombe Pk ALP/SUD HA0 68 B7
MLHL NW7 37 G4
Newcombe St KENS W8 * 8 B8
Newcome Gdns
STRHM/NOR SW16 148 E3
Newcomen Rd BTSEA SW11 128 C2
WAN E11 * 76 D2
Newcomen St STHWK SE1 19 G1
New Compton St
LSQ/SEVD WC2H * 11 H5
New Ct EMB EC4Y * 12 A6
NTHLT UB5 66 B4
Newcourt St STJWD NW8 3 J6
New Crane Pl WAP E1W * 92 E7
New Crescent Yd
WLSDN NW10 * 87 H1
New Cross Rd NWCR SE14 111 K6
Newdales Cl ED N9 42 C1
Newdene Av NTHLT UB5 83 H1
Newdigate
STRHM/NOR SW16 * 149 G3
Newell St POP/IOD E14 93 H6
New End HAMP NW3 71 G3
New End Sq HAMP NW3 71 H3
Newent Cl CAR SM5 162 E7
PECK SE15 111 F6
New Era Est IS N1 7 J4
New Farm La NTHWD HA6 32 C7
New Ferry Ap
WOOL/PLUM SE18 115 F2
New Fetter La
FLST/FETLN EC4A 12 B4
Newfield Cl HPTN TW12 142 A7
Newfield Ri CRICK NW2 69 J2
Newgale Gdns EDGW HA8 36 B7
New Garden Dr WDR/YW UB7 100 B1
Newgate CROY/NA CR0 164 D7
Newgate Cl FELT TW13 141 J1
Newgate St CHING E4 44 C2
STBT EC1A 12 D4
New Globe Wk STHWK SE1 12 E8
New Goulston St WCHPL E1 13 L4
New Green Pl
BRXS/STRHM SW2 130 B6
NRWD SE19 150 A5
Newham's Rw STHWK SE1 19 K2
Newham Wy CAN/RD E16 94 D4
EHAM E6 95 J3
Newhaven Cl HYS/HAR UB3 101 J3
Newhaven Crs ASHF TW15 140 B4
Newhaven Gdns
ELTH/MOT SE9 134 C3
Newhaven La PLSTW E13 94 D4
Newhaven Rd SNWD SE25 164 E4
New Heston Rd HEST TW5 102 E6
Newhouse Av CHDH RM6 61 K2
Newhouse Cl NWMAL KT3 160 B6
Newhouse Wk MRDN SM4 162 B6
Newick Cl BXLY DA5 137 J5
Newick Rd CLPT E5 74 D2
Newing Gn BMLY BR1 153 H6
Newington Barrow Wy
HOLWY N7 73 F2
Newington Butts WALW SE17 18 D6
Newington Cswy STHWK SE1 18 E3
Newington Gn IS N1 73 K4
Newington Green Rd IS N1 73 K4
New Inn Broadway
SDTCH EC2A * 7 K9
New Inn Sq SDTCH EC2A * 7 K9
New Inn St SDTCH EC2A * 7 K9
New Inn Yd SDTCH EC2A 7 K9
New Kelvin Av TEDD TW11 142 E5
New Kent Rd WALW SE17 18 F5
New King's Rd FUL/PGN SW6 107 K7
New King St DEPT SE8 112 D5
Newland Cl PIN HA5 33 J5
Newland Ct WBLY HA9 68 C1
Newland Gdns WEA W13 104 B1
Newland Rd CEND/HSY/T N8 54 E2
Newlands Av THDIT KT7 157 K7
Newlands Cl ALP/SUD HA0 67 J5
EDGW HA8 36 A2
NWDGN UB2 102 D4
Newlands Pk SYD SE26 150 E5
Newlands Pl BAR EN5 26 B4
Newlands Quay WAP E1W 92 E6
Newlands Rd
STRHM/NOR SW16 163 K1
WFD IG8 44 D1
The Newlands WLGTN SM6 176 C6
Newland St CAN/RD E16 95 J7
Newlands Wy CHSGTN KT9 171 J4
Newlands Woods
CROY/NA CR0 179 H7
Newling Cl EHAM E6 95 K5
Newling Est BETH E2 7 M7
New London St MON EC3R * 13 K6
New Lydenburg St CHARL SE7 114 B2
Newlyn Gdns
RYLN/HDSTN HA2 47 K6
Newlyn Rd BAR EN5 26 D3
TOTM N17 42 B7
WELL DA16 136 A1
Newman Ms WDGN N22 41 F6
Newman Rd BMLY BR1 152 E7
CROY/NA CR0 164 A6
HYS/HAR UB3 83 F6
PLSTW E13 95 F2
WALTH E17 57 F4
Newmans La SURB KT6 158 E5
Newman's Rw LINN WC2A 11 M3
Newman St FITZ W1T 10 F3
Newman's Wy EBAR EN4 27 G1
Newmarket Av NTHLT UB5 66 A4
Newmarsh Rd THMD SE28 97 F7
New Mill Rd STMC/STPC BR5 155 J7
Newminster Ct ENC/FH EN2 * 29 H1
Newminster Rd MRDN SM4 162 B5
New Mount St SRTFD E15 76 B6
Newnham Av RSLP HA4 47 G7
Newnham Cl NTHLT UB5 66 C5
THHTH CR7 164 D1
Newnham Gdns NTHLT UB5 66 C5
Newnham Gn WDGN N22 * 41 G7
Newnham Rd WDGN N22 41 F7
Newnhams Cl BMLY BR1 168 E2
Newnham Ter STHWK SE1 18 A3
Newnham Wy
KTN/HRWW/WS HA3 50 A4
New North Pl SDTCH EC2A 7 J9
New North Rd IS N1 6 F3
New North St BMSBY WC1N 11 L2
Newnton Cl FSBYPK N4 55 K6
New Oak Rd EFNCH N2 53 G1
New Oxford St
NOXST/BSQ WC1A 11 H4
New Park Av PLMGR N13 41 J2
New Park Cl NTHLT UB5 65 J5
New Park Est UED N18 42 E4
New Park Rd ASHF TW15 140 A4
BRXS/STRHM SW2 129 K6
New Place Sq
BERM/RHTH SE16 * 111 J2
New Plaistow Rd SRTFD E15 76 C7
New Pond Pde RSLP HA4 * 64 E2
Newport Av POP/IOD E14 94 B6
Newport Ct LSQ/SEVD WC2H 11 H6
Newport Md OXHEY WD19 * 33 H3
Newport Pl
SOHO/SHAV W1D * 11 H6
Newport Rd HTHAIR TW6 100 D7
ACT W3 105 K1
LEY E10 76 B1
WALTH E17 * 57 G3
YEAD UB4 82 B4
Newport St LBTH SE11 17 L6
Newquay Crs
RYLN/HDSTN HA2 65 J1
Newquay Gdns OXHEY WD19 33 F1
Newquay Rd CAT SE6 151 K1
New Quebec St MBLAR W1H 9 M5
New River Av CEND/HSY/T N8 55 F2
New River Crs PLMGR N13 41 H3
New River Wy FSBYPK N4 55 K6
New Rd ABYW SE2 116 E3
BORE WD6 23 K5
BTFD TW8 * 104 E5
CEND/HSY/T N8 54 D4
CHING E4 43 K3
DAGE RM10 98 C1
E/WMO/HCT KT8 157 F2
EBED/NFELT TW14 121 G5
ED N9 42 D1
ESH/CLAY KT10 170 C3
FELT TW13 141 J4
GDMY/SEVK IG3 78 E1
HRW HA1 67 F3
HSLW TW3 123 G3
HYS/HAR UB3 101 F6
KUTN/CMB KT2 144 C6
MLHL NW7 38 C6
MTCM CR4 163 F7
RAIN RM13 98 E2
RCHPK/HAM TW10 143 J3
TOTM N17 42 B7
UX/CGN UB8 82 A3
WAT WD17 21 G3
WCHPL E1 92 C4
WDGN N22 41 J7
WELL DA16 136 C1
New Road Hl HAYES BR2 181 J7
New Rw CHCR WC2N 11 J6
Newry Rd TWK TW1 124 B3
Newsam Av SEVS/STOTM N15 55 K4
Newsholme Dr WCHMH N21 29 F4
New Spring Gardens Wk
STHWK SE1 * 17 K8
New Sq EBED/NFELT TW14 121 F7
LINN WC2A 11 M4
Newstead Cl
NFNCH/WDSPK N12 39 J5
Newstead Ct NTHLT UB5 * 83 J2
Newstead Rd LEE/GVPK SE12 133 J6
Newstead Wk CAR SM5 162 B6
Newstead Wy
WIM/MER SW19 146 B3
New St LVPST EC2M 13 K3
WAT WD17 * 21 G3
New Street Hl BMLY BR1 153 F4
New Street Sq
FLST/FETLN EC4A 12 B4
Newton Av ACT W3 105 K1
MUSWH N10 40 A7
Newton Cl RYLN/HDSTN HA2 66 A1
WALTH E17 57 G5
Newton Crs BORE WD6 24 E3
Newton Gv CHSWK W4 106 B2
Newton Park Pl CHST BR7 153 K6
Newton Pl POP/IOD E14 112 D3
Newton Rd ALP/SUD HA0 68 B6
BAY/PAD W2 8 B5
CRICK NW2 70 A3
HTHAIR TW6 100 B7
ISLW TW7 124 A1
KTN/HRWW/WS HA3 34 E7
SEVS/STOTM N15 56 B4
SRTFD E15 76 B4
WELL DA16 136 B2
WIM/MER SW19 146 C6
Newtons Cl RAIN RM13 81 G6
Newton St HOL/ALD WC2B 11 K4
Newton's Yd
WAND/EARL SW18 127 K4
Newton Ter HAYES BR2 168 C5
Newton Wk EDGW HA8 36 E7
Newton Wy UED N18 41 J4
New Tower Blds WAP E1W * 92 D7
Newtown St BTSEA SW11 109 G7
New Trinity Rd EFNCH N2 53 H2
New Union Cl POP/IOD E14 113 F2
New Union St BARB EC2Y 13 G3
New Vls TOTM N17 * 42 C7
New Wanstead WAN E11 58 E5
New Way Rd CDALE/KGS NW9 51 G3
New Wharf Rd IS N1 5 K5
New Zealand Wy RAIN RM13 99 H2
Niagara Av EA W5 104 D3
Niagara Cl IS N1 6 F5
Nibthwaite Rd HRW HA1 48 E4
Nicholas Cl GFD/PVL UB6 84 B1
Nicholas Gdns EA W5 85 K7
Nicholas La MANHO EC4N 13 H6
Nicholas Rd BCTR RM8 80 B1
BORE WD6 24 B5
CROY/NA CR0 176 E3
WCHPL E1 92 E3
Nicholas Wy NTHWD HA6 32 A7
Nicholay Rd ARCH N19 54 D7
Nichol Cl STHGT/OAK N14 28 D7
Nicholes Rd HSLW TW3 123 F3
Nichol La BMLY BR1 152 E6
Nichollsfield Wk HOLWY N7 72 E4
Nicholl St BETH E2 74 C7
Nichols Cl FSBYPK N4 * 55 G7
Nichols Gn EA W5 86 A4
Nicholson Dr BUSH WD23 22 C7
Nicholson House CHARL SE7 * 114 D6
Nicholson Ms KUT/HW KT1 159 F3
Nicholson Rd CROY/NA CR0 165 G7
Nicholson St STHWK SE1 12 C9
Nickelby Cl THMD SE28 97 J5
Nickols Wk WAND/EARL SW18 128 A3
Nicola Cl KTN/HRWW/WS HA3 48 D1
SAND/SEL CR2 177 J5
Nicol Cl TWK TW1 124 C5
Nicoll Pl HDN NW4 51 K5
Nicoll Rd WLSDN NW10 69 G7
Nicoll Wy BORE WD6 25 F4
Nicosia Rd WAND/EARL SW18 128 D6
Niederwald Rd SYD SE26 151 G3
Nield Rd HYS/HAR UB3 101 J1
Nigel Cl NTHLT UB5 65 J7
Nigel Fisher Wy CHSGTN KT9 171 J6
Nigel Ms IL IG1 78 B3
Nigel Playfair Av
HMSMTH W6 106 E3
Nigel Rd FSTGT E7 77 G4
PECK SE15 131 H2
Nigeria Rd CHARL SE7 114 B6
Nightingale Av CHING E4 44 C4
Nightingale Cl CAR SM5 176 A1
CHING E4 44 C3
CHSWK W4 105 K5
PIN HA5 47 G4
Nightingale Ct SUT SM1 175 G4
Nightingale Dr
HOR/WEW KT19 172 D5
Nightingale Gv LEW SE13 133 G4
Nightingale La BAL SW12 129 F5
BMLY BR1 168 B1
CEND/HSY/T N8 54 E3
RCHPK/HAM TW10 125 F6
WAN E11 59 F4
Nightingale Ms KUT/HW KT1 * 158 E2
LBTH SE11 18 B5
Nightingale Pl WBPTN SW10 14 F9
WOOL/PLUM SE18 115 F5
Nightingale Rd BUSH WD23 22 A4
CAR SM5 175 K2
CLPT E5 74 D2
E/WMO/HCT KT8 157 G4
ED N9 30 E6
HNWL W7 85 F7
HPTN TW12 142 A5
STMC/STPC BR5 169 H5
WDGN N22 40 E7
WLSDN NW10 87 H1
WOT/HER KT12 * 156 B6
Nightingale Sq BAL SW12 129 F6
The Nightingales
STWL/WRAY TW19 120 C7
Nightingale V
WOOL/PLUM SE18 115 F5
Nightingale Wk BAL SW12 129 G5
Nightingale Wy EHAM E6 95 J4
Nigntingale Av HRW HA1 49 H6
Nile Cl STNW/STAM N16 74 B2
Nile Dr ED N9 42 E1
Nile Rd PLSTW E13 95 G1
Nile St IS N1 7 G7
Nile Ter PECK SE15 19 M8
Nimmo Dr BUSH WD23 22 D6
Nimrod Cl NTHLT UB5 83 H2
Nimrod Pas IS N1 74 A5
Nimrod Rd STRHM/NOR SW16 148 B5
Nina Mackay Cl SRTFD E15 * 76 C7
Nine Acres Cl HYS/HAR UB3 101 F2
MNPK E12 77 J4
Nine Elms Cl
EBED/NFELT TW14 121 J7
Nine Elms La VX/NE SW8 17 H9
Nineteenth Rd MTCM CR4 163 K3
Ninth Av HYS/HAR UB3 82 E6
Nisbett Wk SCUP DA14 155 G3
Nithdale Rd
WOOL/PLUM SE18 115 G6
Nithsdale Gv HGDN/ICK UB10 64 A2
Niton Cl BAR EN5 26 B5
Niton Rd RCH/KEW TW9 * 125 H2
Niton St FUL/PGN SW6 107 G6
No1 St WOOL/PLUM SE18 115 G2
No2 St WOOL/PLUM SE18 115 G2
Nobel Dr HYS/HAR UB3 101 H6
Nobel Rd UED N18 42 E3
Noble Cnr HEST TW5 * 103 F7
Noble St CITYW EC2V 12 E4
Noel Rd ACT W3 86 C5
EHAM E6 95 J3
IS N1 6 C5
Noel St SOHO/CST W1F 10 F5
Nolan Wy CLPT E5 74 C3
Nolton Pl EDGW HA8 36 B7
Nonsuch Pl CHEAM SM3 * 174 B6
Norbiton Av KUT/HW KT1 159 H1
Norbiton Common Rd
KUT/HW KT1 159 J2
Norbiton Rd POP/IOD E14 93 H5
Norbreck Pde EA W5 86 A2
Norbroke St SHB W12 87 H6
Norburn St NKENS W10 88 C4
Norbury Av HSLW TW3 123 J4
STRHM/NOR SW16 149 F7
Norbury Cl STRHM/NOR SW16 149 G7
Norbury Court Rd
STRHM/NOR SW16 163 K1
Norbury Crs
STRHM/NOR SW16 164 B1
Norbury Cross
STRHM/NOR SW16 163 K2
Norbury Gdns CHDH RM6 61 K4
Norbury Gv MLHL NW7 37 G2
Norbury Hl STRHM/NOR SW16 149 G6
Norbury Ri STRHM/NOR SW16 163 K2
Norbury Rd CHING E4 43 J4
FELT TW13 140 D2
THHTH CR7 164 D1
Norbury Vls KUT/HW KT1 * 159 G1
Norcombe Gdns
KTN/HRWW/WS HA3 49 J5

Norcott Cl YEAD UB4 83 G3
Norcott Rd STNW/STAM N16 74 C1
Norcroft Gdns EDUL SE22 131 H6
Norcutt Rd WHTN TW2 123 K7
Norfolk Av PLMGR N13 41 H5
SEVS/STOTM N15 56 B5
Norfolk Cl EBAR EN4 28 A3
EFNCH N2 53 J2
PLMGR N13 41 H5
TWK TW1 * 124 C5
Norfolk Ct BAR EN5 * 26 C3
Norfolk Crs BAY/PAD W2 9 J4
BFN/LL DA15 135 K6
Norfolk Gdns BORE WD6 25 F3
Norfolk House Rd
STRHM/NOR SW16 148 D2
Norfolk Ms NKENS W10 88 C4
Norfolk Pl BAY/PAD W2 9 H4
WELL DA16 136 B1
Norfolk Rd BAR EN5 26 E2
BARK IG11 78 E6
DAGE RM10 80 D4
EHAM E6 77 K7
ESH/CLAY KT10 170 E4
FELT TW13 122 B7
GDMY/SEVK IG3 60 E7
HRW HA1 48 B4
PEND EN3 30 D4
ROMW/RG RM7 62 E5
STJWD NW8 3 H4
THHTH CR7 164 D2
WALTH E17 43 F7
WIM/MER SW19 147 J6
WLSDN NW10 69 G6
Norfolk Rw STHWK SE1 17 L5
Norfolk Sq BAY/PAD W2 9 H5
Norfolk Square Ms
BAY/PAD W2 9 H5
Norfolk St FSTGT E7 76 E4
Norgrove St BAL SW12 129 F7
Norhyrst Av SNWD SE25 165 G2
Norland Pl NTGHL W11 88 C7
Norland Rd NTGHL W11 88 B7
Norlands Crs CHST BR7 154 B7
Norlands Ga CHST BR7 * 154 B7
Norland Sq NTGHL W11 88 C7
Norley V PUT/ROE SW15 126 D7
Norlington Rd LEY E10 58 A7
Norman Av FELT TW13 141 J1
STHL UB1 83 J6
TWK TW1 124 C6
WDGN N22 41 J7
Normanby Cl PUT/ROE SW15 127 J4
Normanby Rd WLSDN NW10 69 H4
Norman Cl ROMW/RG RM7 62 D1
Norman Crs HEST TW5 102 C6
PIN HA5 33 G7
Normand Gdns WKENS W14 * 107 H5
Normand Ms WKENS W14 107 H5
Normand Rd WKENS W14 107 J5
Normandy Av BAR EN5 26 D4
Normandy Cl SYD SE26 151 G2
Normandy Dr HYS/HAR UB3 82 A5
Normandy Rd BRXN/ST SW9 110 B7
Normandy Ter CAN/RD E16 95 F5
Norman Gv BOW E3 93 G1
Normanhurst Av WELL DA16 116 E7
Normanhurst Dr TWK TW1 124 C4
Normanhurst Rd
BRXS/STRHM SW2 149 F1
Norman Rd ASHF TW15 140 B5
BELV DA17 98 D7
EHAM E6 95 K3
EMPK RM11 63 J6
GNWCH SE10 112 E6
IL IG1 78 B4
SEVS/STOTM N15 56 B4
SUT SM1 174 E4
THHTH CR7 164 C4
WAN E11 76 C1
WIM/MER SW19 147 G6
Normans Cl WDGN N22 * 41 J7
WLSDN NW10 69 F5
Normansfield Av KUT/HW KT1 143 J6
Normansfield Cl BUSH WD23 22 B6
Normanshire Dr CHING E4 43 J3
Normans Md WLSDN NW10 69 F5
Norman St FSBYE EC1V 6 E8
Norman Ter
KIL/WHAMP NW6 * 70 D4
Normanton Av
WAND/EARL SW18 146 E1
Normanton Pk CHING E4 44 C2
Normanton Rd SAND/SEL CR2 178 A5
Normanton St FSTH SE23 151 F1
Norman Wy ACT W3 86 D4
STHGT/OAK N14 40 E1
Normington Cl
STRHM/NOR SW16 149 G4
Norrice Lea EFNCH N2 53 H4
Norris St STJS SW1Y 11 G7
Norris Wy DART DA1 138 C2
Norroy Rd PUT/ROE SW15 127 G3
Norrys Cl EBAR EN4 27 K4
Norrys Rd EBAR EN4 27 K3
Norseman Cl GDMY/SEVK IG3 61 H7
Norseman Wy GFD/PVL UB6 66 B7
Norstead Pl PUT/ROE SW15 145 J1
North Access Rd WALTH E17 57 F5
North Acre CDALE/KGS NW9 37 G7
North Acton Rd WLSDN NW10 87 F1
Northall Rd BXLYHN DA7 137 K1
Northampton Gv IS N1 73 K4
Northampton Pk IS N1 73 J5
Northampton Rd
CLKNW EC1R 6 B9
CROY/NA CR0 178 C1
PEND EN3 31 G3
Northampton Rw
CLKNW EC1R * 6 B9
Northampton Sq FSBYE EC1V 6 C8
Northampton St IS N1 6 E1
Northanger Rd
STRHM/NOR SW16 148 E5
North Ap NTHWD HA6 32 A1
North Audley St
MYFR/PKLN W1K 10 A6
North Av CAR SM5 176 A6
HYS/HAR UB3 82 E6
RCH/KEW TW9 105 H7
RYLN/HDSTN HA2 48 B5
STHL UB1 83 K6
UED N18 42 C3
WEA W13 85 H5
North Bank STJWD NW8 3 J8
Northbank Rd WALTH E17 58 A1
North Birkbeck Rd WAN E11 76 B2
Northborough Rd
STRHM/NOR SW16 163 K1
Northbourne Rd CLAP SW4 129 J3
Northbrook Dr NTHWD HA6 32 C7
Northbrook Rd BAR EN5 26 C5
CROY/NA CR0 164 E4
IL IG1 78 A1
LEW SE13 133 G4
WDGN N22 40 E5
Northburgh St FSBYE EC1V 12 D1
North Carriage Dr
BAY/PAD W2 9 K6
Northchurch Rd IS N1 7 G1
WBLY HA9 68 C5
Northchurch Ter IS N1 7 J2
North Circular PLMGR N13 41 G4
WALTH E17 43 K7
North Circular Rd BARK IG11 78 A6
CHING E4 * 43 G5
EFNCH N2 53 G1
GLDGN NW11 52 C5
NFNCH/WDSPK N12 39 J6
REDBR IG4 59 G2
WLSDN NW10 86 B1
Northcliffe Cl WPK KT4 173 G2
Northcliffe Dr
TRDG/WHET N20 26 D7
North Cl BAR EN5 26 A4
BXLYHS DA6 136 E3
DAGE RM10 80 C7
EBED/NFELT TW14 121 G5
MRDN SM4 161 H3
The North Colonnade
POP/IOD E14 93 K7
North Common Rd EA W5 86 A6
Northcote Av BRYLDS KT5 159 H6
EA W5 86 A6
ISLW TW7 124 B4
STHL UB1 83 J6
Northcote Rd BTSEA SW11 128 D3
CROY/NA CR0 164 E5
NWMAL KT3 159 K2
SCUP DA14 154 E3
TWK TW1 124 B4
WALTH E17 57 G3
WLSDN NW10 69 G6
Northcott Av WDGN N22 40 E7
North Countess Rd
WALTH E17 57 H1
Northcourt FITZ W1T 10 F2
North Crs CAN/RD E16 94 B3
FNCH N3 52 D1
GWRST WC1E 11 G2
Northcroft Rd
HOR/WEW KT19 173 G6
WEA W13 104 C1
North Cross Rd BARK/HLT IG6 60 C3
EDUL SE22 131 G4
North Dene HSLW TW3 103 G7
MLHL NW7 37 F2
Northdene Gdns
SEVS/STOTM N15 56 A5
Northdown Cl RSLP HA4 64 D2
Northdown Gdns
GNTH/NBYPK IG2 60 E4
Northdown Rd EMPK RM11 63 K6
WELL DA16 136 C1
Northdown St IS N1 5 L6
North Dr BECK BR3 166 E3
HSLW TW3 123 H1
RSLP HA4 46 C6
STRHM/NOR SW16 148 C3
North End CROY/NA CR0 164 D7
HAMP NW3 71 G1
North End Av HAMP NW3 71 G1
North End Crs WKENS W14 107 J3
North End Rd FUL/PGN SW6 107 K6
GLDGN NW11 52 E7
WBLY HA9 68 C2
WKENS W14 107 H3
North End Wy HAMP NW3 71 G1
Northern Av ED N9 42 B1
Northernhay Wk MRDN SM4 161 H3
Northern Perimeter Rd
HTHAIR TW6 101 F7
Northern Perimeter Road
(West) HTHAIR TW6 100 B7
Northern Relief Rd BARK IG11 78 C6
North Eyot Gdns
HMSMTH W6 * 106 C4
Northey St POP/IOD E14 93 G6
Northfield Av PIN HA5 47 H3
WEA W13 104 C1
Northfield Cl BMLY BR1 153 J7
HYS/HAR UB3 101 J2
Northfield Crs CHEAM SM3 174 C3
Northfield Pde
HYS/HAR UB3 * 101 J2
Northfield Pk HYS/HAR UB3 101 H2
Northfield Recreation Gnd
EA W5 * 104 C3
Northfield Rd DAGW RM9 80 B3
EBAR EN4 27 J2
ED N9 * 30 D4
EHAM E6 77 K5
HEST TW5 102 C5
PEND EN3 30 D5
STNW/STAM N16 56 A6
WEA W13 104 C1
Northfields WAND/EARL SW18 127 K3
Northfields Rd ACT W3 86 E4
North Gdns WIM/MER SW19 147 H6
Northgate NTHWD HA6 32 A6
Northgate Dr
CDALE/KGS NW9 51 G5
North Gower St CAMTN NW1 4 E8
North Gv HGT N6 54 A6
SEVS/STOTM N15 55 K4
North Hl HGT N6 53 K5
North Hill Av HGT N6 53 K5
North Hyde Gdns
HYS/HAR UB3 101 K2
North Hyde La NWDGN UB2 102 D4
North Hyde Rd HYS/HAR UB3 101 H2
North Hyde Whf
NWDGN UB2 * 102 B3
Northiam NFNCH/WDSPK N12 38 E3
Northiam St HACK E8 74 D7
Northington St
BMSBY WC1N 11 L2
Northlands St CMBW SE5 130 D1
North La TEDD TW11 143 F5
North Lodge Cl
PUT/ROE SW15 * 127 G4
North Ms BMSBY WC1N 11 M1
North Mt TRDG/WHET N20 * 39 G1
Northolm EDGW HA8 37 F3
Northolme Gdns EDGW HA8 36 C7
Northolme Rd HBRY N5 73 J3
Northolt Av RSLP HA4 65 F4
Northolt Gdns GFD/PVL UB6 67 F4
Northolt Rd HTHAIR TW6 100 B7
RYLN/HDSTN HA2 66 B3
Northover BMLY BR1 152 D2
North Pde CHSGTN KT9 172 B4
EDGW HA8 * 50 C1
STHL UB1 * 84 A5
North Pk ELTH/MOT SE9 134 E5
North Pas WAND/EARL SW18 127 K4
North Peckham Est
PECK SE15 111 G6
North Pl MTCM CR4 147 K6
TEDD TW11 143 F5
Northpoint Cl SUT SM1 175 G2
North Pole La HAYES BR2 180 E5
North Pole Rd SHB W12 88 A5
Northport St IS N1 7 H4
North Ri BAY/PAD W2 * 9 K5
North Rd BELV DA17 117 J2
BMLY BR1 153 F7
BTFD TW8 105 F5
CHDH RM6 62 A4
EA W5 104 E2
EBED/NFELT TW14 121 G5
ED N9 30 D7
EDGW HA8 36 D7
GDMY/SEVK IG3 78 E1
HEST TW5 102 B5
HGT N6 54 A6
HOLWY N7 72 E5
HYS/HAR UB3 82 B4
RCH/KEW TW9 125 H1
STHL UB1 84 A6
SURB KT6 158 E5
WDR/YW UB7 100 C2
WIM/MER SW19 147 G5
WOOL/PLUM SE18 115 K3
WWKM BR4 166 E7
Northrop Rd HTHAIR TW6 101 H7
North Rw MYFR/PKLN W1K 9 M6
North Several
BKHTH/KID SE3 * 133 G1
Northside Rd BMLY BR1 152 E7
North Side Wandsworth
Common WAND/EARL SW18 128 B4
Northspur Rd SUT SM1 174 E2
North Sq ED N9 42 D1
GLDGN NW11 52 E4
Northstead Rd
BRXS/STRHM SW2 149 G1
North St BARK IG11 78 B6
BMLY BR1 152 E7
CAR SM5 175 K3
CLAP SW4 129 G2
HDN NW4 52 A4
ISLW TW7 124 B2
PLSTW E13 95 F1
ROM RM1 63 F3
North Tenter St WCHPL E1 13 M5
North Ter SKENS SW7 15 J5
Northumberland Aly
FENCHST EC3M * 13 K5
Northumberland Av
CHCR WC2N 11 J8
ISLW TW7 104 A7
MNPK E12 59 G7
WELL DA16 135 K3
Northumberland Cl
STWL/WRAY TW19 120 B5
Northumberland Crs
EBED/NFELT TW14 121 H5
Northumberland Gdns
BMLY BR1 169 F3
ED N9 42 B2
MTCM CR4 163 J4
Northumberland Gv
TOTM N17 42 D6
Northumberland Pk
ERITH DA8 117 K6
TOTM N17 42 C6
Northumberland Pl
BAY/PAD W2 8 A4
Northumberland Rd BAR EN5 27 G5
EHAM E6 95 J5
RYLN/HDSTN HA2 47 K4
WALTH E17 57 J6
Northumberland St
CHCR WC2N 11 J8
Northumberland Wy
ERITH DA8 117 K7
Northumbria St POP/IOD E14 93 J5
North Verbena Gdns
HMSMTH W6 * 106 D4
North Vw EA W5 85 J3
PIN HA5 47 G6
WIM/MER SW19 145 K4
Northview Crs WLSDN NW10 69 H3
Northview Dr WFD IG8 59 H1
Northview Pde HOLWY N7 * 72 E2
North View Rd
CEND/HSY/T N8 54 D2
North Vls CAMTN NW1 72 D5
North Wk CROY/NA CR0 179 K4
North Wy PIN HA5 47 G2
CDALE/KGS NW9 50 D2
ED N9 42 E1
FBAR/BDGN N11 40 C5
Northway GLDGN NW11 53 F4
MRDN SM4 161 H2
WLGTN SM6 176 C3
Northway Crs MLHL NW7 37 G3
Northway Rd CMBW SE5 130 D2
CROY/NA CR0 165 G5
Northways Pde HAMP NW3 3 G1
North Weald Cl HCH RM12 81 K6
North Weald La
KUTN/CMB KT2 143 J4
North Wharf Rd BAY/PAD W2 9 G3
Northwick Av
KTN/HRWW/WS HA3 49 G5
Northwick Cir
KTN/HRWW/WS HA3 49 J5
Northwick Cl STJWD NW8 3 G9
Northwick Park Rd HRW HA1 49 F5
Northwick Rd ALP/SUD HA0 67 K7
OXHEY WD19 33 G3
Northwick Ter STJWD NW8 3 G9
Northwold Dr PIN HA5 47 G2
Northwold Rd
STNW/STAM N16 74 C1
Northwood Av HCH RM12 81 J3
Northwood Gdns CLAY IG5 60 A3
GFD/PVL UB6 67 F4
NFNCH/WDSPK N12 39 H4
Northwood Pl ERITHM DA18 117 G2
Northwood Rd CAR SM5 176 A5
FSTH SE23 132 C7
HGT N6 54 B6
HTHAIR TW6 100 A7
THHTH CR7 164 D1
Northwood Wy NTHWD HA6 32 E6
North Woolwich Rd
CAN/RD E16 94 E7
CAN/RD E16 95 F7
North Worple Wy
MORT/ESHN SW14 126 A2
Norton Av BRYLDS KT5 159 J6
Norton Cl CHING E4 43 J4
Norton Folgate WCHPL E1 13 K1
Norton Gdns
STRHM/NOR SW16 163 K1
Norton Rd ALP/SUD HA0 67 K5
DAGE RM10 81 F5
LEY E10 57 H7
Norval Gn BRXN/ST SW9 * 130 B1
Norval Rd ALP/SUD HA0 67 H1
Norway Ga BERM/RHTH SE16 112 B2
Norway Pl POP/IOD E14 93 H5
Norway St GNWCH SE10 112 E5
Norwich Crs CHDH RM6 61 H4
Norwich Ms GDMY/SEVK IG3 61 G7
Norwich Rd FSTGT E7 76 E4
GFD/PVL UB6 66 B7
NTHWD HA6 46 D2
THHTH CR7 164 D2
Norwich St FLST/FETLN EC4A 12 A4
Norwich Wk EDGW HA8 36 E6
Norwood Av ALP/SUD HA0 68 B7
ROMW/RG RM7 63 F6
Norwood Cl CRICK NW2 70 C2
NWDGN UB2 103 F3
WHTN TW2 142 D1
Norwood Dr
RYLN/HDSTN HA2 47 K5
Norwood Gdns NWDGN UB2 102 E3
YEAD UB4 83 G3
Norwood Green Rd
NWDGN UB2 103 F3
Norwood High St
WNWD SE27 149 H2
Norwood Park Rd
WNWD SE27 149 J4
Norwood Rd NWDGN UB2 102 D2
WNWD SE27 149 H1
Notley St CMBW SE5 110 E6
Notson Rd SNWD SE25 165 J3
Notting Barn Rd NKENS W10 88 B3
Nottingdale Sq NTGHL W11 * 88 C7
Nottingham Av CAN/RD E16 95 G4
Nottingham Ct
LSQ/SEVD WC2H 11 J5
Nottingham Pl CAMTN NW1 10 A1
Nottingham Rd ISLW TW7 124 A1
LEY E10 58 A5
SAND/SEL CR2 177 J3
TOOT SW17 128 E7
Nottingham St MHST W1U 10 A2
Nottingham Ter CAMTN NW1 10 A1
Notting Hill Ga NTGHL W11 8 B8
Nova Ms CHEAM SM3 161 H6
Nova Rd CROY/NA CR0 164 C7
Novar Rd ELTH/MOT SE9 135 H7
Novello St FUL/PGN SW6 107 K7
Nowell Rd BARN SW13 106 D5
Nower Hl PIN HA5 47 K3
Noyna Rd TOOT SW17 147 K2
Nubia Wy BMLY BR1 152 C3
Nuding Cl LEW SE13 132 D2
Nugent Rd ARCH N19 54 E7
SNWD SE25 165 G2
Nugents Ct PIN HA5 * 33 J7
Nugent's Pk PIN HA5 33 J7
Nugent Ter STJWD NW8 2 F6
Nuneaton Rd DAGW RM9 79 K6
Nunhead Crs PECK SE15 131 J2
Nunhead Gv PECK SE15 131 J2
Nunhead La PECK SE15 131 J2
Nunnington Cl ELTH/MOT SE9 153 J2
Nunn's Rd ENC/FH EN2 29 J1
Nupton Dr BAR EN5 26 A5
Nurse Cl EDGW HA8 36 E7
Nursery Av CROY/NA CR0 179 F1
FNCH N3 53 F1
Nursery Cl BROCKY SE4 132 C1
CHDH RM6 61 K5
CROY/NA CR0 179 F1
EBED/NFELT TW14 122 A6
OXHEY WD19 21 F7
PUT/ROE SW15 127 G4
WFD IG8 45 F4
Nursery Gdns CHST BR7 154 B5
HPTN TW12 141 K3
HSLWW TW4 122 E4
Nursery La BETH E2 7 L4
FSTGT E7 76 E5
NKENS W10 88 A4
Nurserymans Rd
FBAR/BDGN N11 40 A1
Nursery Rd BRXN/ST SW9 130 A3
EFNCH N2 39 H7
HOM E9 74 E5
MTCM CR4 162 D2
PIN HA5 47 G2
STHGT/OAK N14 28 C6
SUN TW16 140 E7
SUT SM1 175 G3
THHTH CR7 164 E3
WIM/MER SW19 146 C6
Nursery Rw BAR EN5 * 26 C2
WALW SE17 19 G6
Nursery St TOTM N17 42 B6
The Nursery ERITH DA8 118 C6
Nursery Wk HDN NW4 51 K2
ROMW/RG RM7 63 F6
Nutbourne St NKENS W10 88 C2
Nutbrook St PECK SE15 131 G2
Nutbrowne Rd DAGW RM9 80 B7
Nutcroft Rd PECK SE15 111 J6
Nutfield Cl CAR SM5 175 J2
UED N18 42 C5
Nutfield Gdns GDMY/SEVK IG3 79 F1
NTHLT UB5 83 G1
Nutfield Rd CRICK NW2 69 J1
EDUL SE22 131 G4
SRTFD E15 76 A3
THHTH CR7 164 C3
Nutford Pl MBLAR W1H 9 K4
Nuthatch Cl
STWL/WRAY TW19 120 C7
Nuthatch Gdns THMD SE28 115 J1
Nuthurst Av
BRXS/STRHM SW2 149 F1
Nutley Ter HAMP NW3 71 H5
Nutmead Cl BXLY DA5 137 K7
Nutmeg Cl CAN/RD E16 94 C3
Nutmeg La POP/IOD E14 94 B5
Nuttall St IS N1 7 K5
Nutter La WAN E11 59 G4
Nutt Gv EDGW HA8 35 K1
Nutt St PECK SE15 111 G6
Nutwell St TOOT SW17 147 J4
Nuxley Rd BELV DA17 117 G5
Nyanza St WOOL/PLUM SE18 115 J5
Nylands Av RCH/KEW TW9 125 H1
Nymans Gdns RYNPK SW20 160 E2
Nynehead St NWCR SE14 112 B6
Nyon Gv CAT SE6 151 H1
Nyssa Cl WFD IG8 45 K5
Nyton Cl ARCH N19 54 E7

O

Oak Av CEND/HSY/T N8 54 E3
CROY/NA CR0 179 J1
HEST TW5 102 C6
HPTN TW12 141 J4
MUSWH N10 40 B6
TOTM N17 41 K6
WDR/YW UB7 100 D2
Oakbank CROY/NA CR0 180 A5
Oakbank Av WOT/HER KT12 156 E6
Oakbank Gv HNHL SE24 130 D3
Oakbrook Cl BMLY BR1 153 F3
Oakbury Rd FUL/PGN SW6 128 A1
Oak Cl STHGT/OAK N14 28 B6
Oakcombe Cl NWMAL KT3 145 G7
Oak Cottage Cl CAT SE6 133 H7
Oak Cots HNWL W7 * 103 K1
Oak Crs CAN/RD E16 94 C4
Oakcroft Cl PIN HA5 47 F1
Oakcroft Rd CHSGTN KT9 172 B3
LEW SE13 133 G1
Oakcroft Vls CHSGTN KT9 172 B3
Oakdale STHGT/OAK N14 28 B7
Oakdale Av
KTN/HRWW/WS HA3 50 A4
NTHWD HA6 46 E1
Oakdale Cl OXHEY WD19 33 G3
Oakdale Gdns CHING E4 44 A4
Oakdale Rd FSBYPK N4 55 J5
FSTGT E7 77 F6
HOR/WEW KT19 173 F7
OXHEY WD19 33 G2
PECK SE15 131 K2
STRHM/NOR SW16 148 E4
SWFD E18 59 F1
WAN E11 76 B1
Oakdale Wy MTCM CR4 163 F6
Oakdene WEA W13 85 H4
Oakdene Av CHST BR7 154 A4
ERITH DA8 117 K5
THDIT KT7 158 B7
Oak Dene Cl EMPK RM11 63 K5
Oakdene Cl PIN HA5 33 K6
Oakdene Dr BRYLDS KT5 159 K7
Oakdene Ms CHEAM SM3 161 J7
Oakdene Pk FNCH N3 38 D6
Oakden St LBTH SE11 18 B5
Oaken Dr ESH/CLAY KT10 171 F5
Oaken La ESH/CLAY KT10 170 E3
Oakenshaw Cl SURB KT6 159 F6
Oakeshott Av HGT N6 72 A1
Oakey La STHWK SE1 18 A3
Oak Farm BORE WD6 24 E4
Oakfield CHING E4 43 K4
Oakfield Av
KTN/HRWW/WS HA3 49 H2
Oakfield Cl NWMAL KT3 160 C4
RSLP HA4 46 D5
Oakfield Ct BORE WD6 * 24 D3
Oakfield Gdns BECK BR3 166 D4
CAR SM5 162 D7
GFD/PVL UB6 84 D3
UED N18 42 A3
Oakfield La HAYES BR2 181 G3
Oakfield Rd CROY/NA CR0 164 D7
EHAM E6 77 J7
FNCH N3 39 F7
FSBYPK N4 55 G5
IL IG1 78 B2
PGE/AN SE20 150 D6
STHGT/OAK N14 40 E1
WALTH E17 57 G1
WIM/MER SW19 146 B2
Oakfields Rd GLDGN NW11 52 C5
Oakfield St WBPTN SW10 14 E9
Oakford Rd KTTN NW5 72 C3
Oak Gdns CROY/NA CR0 179 J1
EDGW HA8 50 E1
Oak Gv CRICK NW2 70 B3
RSLP HA4 47 F7
SUN TW16 141 F6
WWKM BR4 180 A1
Oak Grove Rd PGE/AN SE20 150 E7
Oakhall Dr SUN TW16 140 D4
Oak Hall Rd WAN E11 59 F5
Oakham Cl CAT SE6 * 151 H1
Oakhampton Rd MLHL NW7 38 B7
Oakhill ESH/CLAY KT10 171 G5
Oak Hl SURB KT6 159 F6
WFD IG8 44 B6
Oakhill Av HAMP NW3 71 F3
PIN HA5 47 J1
Oak Hill Crs SURB KT6 159 F6
WFD IG8 44 C6
Oak Hill Gdns WFD IG8 44 C7
Oak Hill Gv SURB KT6 159 F5
Oak Hill Pk HAMP NW3 71 F3
Oak Hill Park Ms HAMP NW3 71 G3
Oakhill Pl PUT/ROE SW15 127 K4
Oak Hill Rd SURB KT6 * 159 F5
Oakhill Rd BECK BR3 167 F1
PUT/ROE SW15 127 J4
STRHM/NOR SW16 148 E7
SUT SM1 175 F2
Oak Hill Wy HAMP NW3 71 F3
Oakhurst Av EBAR EN4 27 J6
Oakhurst Cl CHST BR7 153 K7
TEDD TW11 142 E4
WALTH E17 58 C3
Oakhurst Gdns WALTH E17 58 C3
Oakhurst Gv EDUL SE22 131 H3
Oakhurst Pl WATW WD18 * 20 D3
Oakhurst Rd HOR/WEW KT19 172 E5
Oakington Av HYS/HAR UB3 101 G3
RYLN/HDSTN HA2 48 A6
WBLY HA9 68 B2
Oakington Cl SUN TW16 156 B1
Oakington Dr SUN TW16 156 B1
Oakington Manor Dr
WBLY HA9 68 C4
Oakington Rd MV/WKIL W9 2 B9
Oakington Wy
CEND/HSY/T N8 54 E5
Oakland Pl BKHH IG9 44 E1
Oakland Rd SRTFD E15 76 C3
Oaklands WCHMH N21 41 F1
Oaklands Av BFN/LL DA15 136 A6
ED N9 30 D5
ESH/CLAY KT10 157 J7
ISLW TW7 104 A5
OXHEY WD19 21 F7
ROM RM1 63 G2
THHTH CR7 164 B3
WWKM BR4 179 K2
Oaklands Cl ALP/SUD HA0 67 K4
CHSGTN KT9 171 J3
STMC/STPC BR5 169 K5
Oaklands Dr WHTN TW2 123 H6
Oaklands Ga NTHWD HA6 32 C5
Oaklands Gv SHB W12 87 J7
Oaklands La BAR EN5 25 K3
Oaklands Ms CRICK NW2 70 B3
Oaklands Park Av IL IG1 78 C1
Oaklands Pl CLAP SW4 129 J3
Oaklands Rd BMLY BR1 152 C6

Orpington Gdns UED N18 42 A2
Orpington Rd CHST BR7 169 K2
WCHMH N21 29 G7
Orpwood Cl HPTN TW12 141 K5
Orsett Ms BAY/PAD W2 8 D4
Orsett St LBTH SE11 17 M7
Orsett Ter BAY/PAD W2 8 E4
WFD IG8 45 G7
Orsman Rd IS N1 7 J4
Orton St WAP E1W 92 C7
Orville Rd BTSEA SW11 128 C1
Orwell Cl HYS/HAR UB3 82 C6
Orwell Ct WATN WD24 * 21 H2
Orwell Rd PLSTW E13 95 G1
Osbaldeston Rd
STNW/STAM N16 74 C1
Osbert St WEST SW1P 17 G6
Osborn Cl HACK E8 74 C7
Osborne Av STWL/WRAY TW19 120 B7
Osborne Cl BECK BR3 166 B3
EBAR EN4 27 K2
EMPK RM11 63 K5
FELT TW13 141 H4
Osborne Ct EA W5 * 86 A4
Osborne Gdns THHTH CR7 164 D1
Osborne Gv WALTH E17 57 H3
Osborne Ms WALTH E17 57 H4
Osborne Rd ACT W3 105 J1
BELV DA17 117 G4
CRICK NW2 69 K5
EMPK RM11 63 K5
FSBYPK N4 55 G7
FSTGT E7 77 F4
HOM E9 75 H5
HSLW TW3 122 E2
KUTN/CMB KT2 144 A6
LEY E10 75 K2
PEND EN3 31 G1
PLMGR N13 41 G2
STHL UB1 84 C5
THHTH CR7 164 D1
Osborne Sq DAGW RM9 80 B3
Osborne Ter TOOT SW17 * 148 A4
Osborne Wy CHSGTN KT9 172 B4
Osborn Gdns MLHL NW7 38 B6
Osborn La FSTH SE23 132 B6
Osborn St WCHPL E1 13 M3
Osborn Ter BKHTH/KID SE3 133 J3
Osbourne Ct
RYLN/HDSTN HA2 * 48 B3
Oscar Faber Pl IS N1 * 7 K2
Oscar St BROCKY SE4 132 D1
DEPT SE8 112 D7
Oseney Crs KTTN NW5 72 C5
Osidge La STHGT/OAK N14 28 A7
Osier Crs MUSWH N10 39 K7
Osiers Rd WAND/EARL SW18 127 K3
The Osiers RKW/CH/CXG WD3 20 A4
Osier St WCHPL E1 92 E3
Osier Wy LEY E10 75 K2
MTCM CR4 162 D4
Oslac Rd CAT SE6 151 K4
Oslo Sq BERM/RHTH SE16 112 B2
Osman Rd ED N9 42 C2
HMSMTH W6 * 107 F2
Osmond Cl RYLN/HDSTN HA2 66 C1
Osmond Gdns WLGTN SM6 176 C4
Osmund St SHB W12 87 H5
Osnaburgh St CAMTN NW1 4 D9
Osnaburgh Ter CAMTN NW1 4 D9
Osney Wk MRDN SM4 162 C5
Osprey Cl EHAM E6 95 J4
HAYES BR2 168 D7
SUT SM1 174 D4
WALTH E17 43 G6
WAN E11 58 E3
WDR/YW UB7 100 A1
Osprey Est BERM/RHTH SE16 112 A3
Osprey Ms PEND EN3 30 D4
Ospringe Cl PGE/AN SE20 150 E6
Ospringe Rd KTTN NW5 72 C3
Osram Rd WBLY HA9 67 K2
Ossian Rd FSBYPK N4 55 F6
Ossier Ms CHSWK W4 106 C5
Ossington Blds MHST W1U * 10 A2
Ossington Cl BAY/PAD W2 * 8 B7
Ossington St BAY/PAD W2 8 B6
Ossory Rd STHWK SE1 111 H4
Ossulston St CAMTN NW1 5 H6
Ossulton Pl EFNCH N2 * 53 G2
Ossulton Wy EFNCH N2 53 G3
Ostade Rd BRXS/STRHM SW2 130 A6
Osten Ms SKENS SW7 14 D4
Osterberg Rd DART DA1 139 J3
Osterley Av ISLW TW7 103 J6
Osterley Cl STMC/STPC BR5 155 G7
Osterley Crs ISLW TW7 103 K7
Osterley Gdns THHTH CR7 164 D1
Osterley La ISLW TW7 103 H3
NWDGN UB2 103 G4
Osterley Park Rd NWDGN UB2 102 E2
Osterley Park View Rd
HNWL W7 103 K1
Osterley Rd ISLW TW7 103 K6
STNW/STAM N16 74 A3
Ostlers Dr ASHF TW15 140 A4
Ostliffe Rd PLMGR N13 41 H4
Oswald Rd STHL UB1 83 J7
Oswald's Md HOM E9 75 G3
Oswald St CLPT E5 75 F2
Oswald Ter CRICK NW2 * 70 A2
Osward CROY/NA CR0 179 H7
Osward Pl ED N9 42 C1
Osward Rd BAL SW12 147 K1
Oswin St LBTH SE11 18 D5
Oswyth Rd CMBW SE5 131 F1
Otford Cl BMLY BR1 169 F2
BXLY DA5 137 J5
PGE/AN SE20 150 E7
Otford Crs BROCKY SE4 132 C5
Othello Cl LBTH SE11 18 C7
Otis St BOW E3 94 A2
Otley Ct FBAR/BDGN N11 40 A5
Otley Dr GNTH/NBYPK IG2 60 B5
Otley Rd CAN/RD E16 95 G5
Otley Ter CLPT E5 74 E1
Otley Wy OXHEY WD19 33 G2
Ottawa Gdns DAGE RM10 81 F6
Ottaway St CLPT E5 74 C2
Otterbourne Rd CHING E4 44 B2
CROY/NA CR0 177 J1
Otterburn Gdns ISLW TW7 104 B6
Otterburn St TOOT SW17 147 K5
Otter Cl SRTFD E15 76 A7
Otterden St CAT SE6 151 J3
Otter Rd GFD/PVL UB6 84 C3
Otto Cl CAT SE6 151 H2
SYD SE26 150 D1
Ottoman Ter WAT WD17 21 G2
Otto St WALW SE17 110 C5
Otway Gdns BUSH WD23 22 E6
Oulton Cl THMD SE28 97 J5
Oulton Crs BARK IG11 79 F5
Oulton Rd SEVS/STOTM N15 55 K4
Oulton Wy OXHEY WD19 33 K3
Oundle Av BUSH WD23 22 C5
Ouseley Rd BAL SW12 128 E7
Outer Cir CAMTN NW1 3 K6
Outgate Rd WLSDN NW10 69 H6
Outram Pl IS N1 5 K3
Outram Rd CROY/NA CR0 178 B1
EHAM E6 77 J7
WDGN N22 40 D7
Outwich St HDTCH EC3A * 13 K4
Oval Ct EDGW HA8 * 36 E6
Oval Pl VX/NE SW8 110 A6
Oval Rd CAMTN NW1 4 C3
CROY/NA CR0 177 K1
Oval Rd North DAGE RM10 80 D7
Oval Rd South DAGE RM10 98 D1
The Oval BETH E2 92 D1
BFN/LL DA15 136 B6
Oval Wy LBTH SE11 17 M8
Overbrae BECK BR3 151 J5
Overbrook Wk EDGW HA8 36 C6
Overbury Av BECK BR3 166 E2
Overbury Rd FSBYPK N4 55 K5
Overbury St CLPT E5 75 F3
Overcliff Rd BROCKY SE4 132 D2
Overcourt Cl BFN/LL DA15 136 C5
Overdale Av NWMAL KT3 159 K1
Overdale Rd EA W5 104 D2
Overdown Rd CAT SE6 151 J3
Overhill Cots MTCM CR4 * 163 F1
Overhill Rd EDUL SE22 131 H6
PUR/KEN CR8 177 G7
Overhill Wy BECK BR3 167 G4
Overlea Rd CLPT E5 56 C6
Overmead ELTH/MOT SE9 135 J6
Overstand Cl BECK BR3 166 D4
Overstone Gdns
CROY/NA CR0 166 C6
Overstone Rd HMSMTH W6 107 F3
Overton Cl ISLW TW7 104 A7
WLSDN NW10 68 E5
Overton Dr CHDH RM6 61 J6
WAN E11 59 F6
Overton Rd BELMT SM2 174 E5
BRXN/ST SW9 130 B1
LEY E10 57 G7
STHGT/OAK N14 28 E4
Overton's Yd CROY/NA CR0 177 J2
Ovesdon Av RYLN/HDSTN HA2 47 K7
Ovett Cl NRWD SE19 150 A5
Ovex Cl POP/IOD E14 113 F2
Ovington Gdns CHEL SW3 15 K4
Ovington Ms CHEL SW3 15 K4
Ovington Sq CHEL SW3 15 K4
Ovington St CHEL SW3 15 K4
Owen Cl CROY/NA CR0 164 E5
NTHLT UB5 65 J5
THMD SE28 97 J7
YEAD UB4 * 83 F2
Owen Gdns WFD IG8 45 J5
Owenite St ABYW SE2 116 C3
Owen Rd PLMGR N13 41 J4
Owens Ms WAN E11 76 C1
Owen's Rw FSBYE EC1V 6 C7
Owen St FSBYE EC1V 6 B6
Owens Wy FSTH SE23 132 B6
Owen Wk PGE/AN SE20 150 C6
Owen Wy WLSDN NW10 68 E5
Owgan Cl CMBW SE5 110 E6
Oxberry Av FUL/PGN SW6 127 H1
Oxendon St
SOHO/SHAV W1D * 11 G7
Oxenford St PECK SE15 131 G2
Oxenpark Av WBLY HA9 50 A6
Oxestalls Rd DEPT SE8 112 B4
Oxford Av HEST TW5 103 F4
HYS/HAR UB3 101 J6
RYNPK SW20 161 H1
STHGT/OAK N14 28 C7
Oxford Cl ASHF TW15 140 A6
ED N9 42 D1
GPK RM2 63 J4
MTCM CR4 163 H2
NTHWD HA6 32 A3
Oxford Ct MANHO EC4N 13 G6
Oxford Crs NWMAL KT3 160 A5
Oxford Dr RSLP HA4 65 G1
Oxford Gdns CHSWK W4 105 H4
NKENS W10 88 B5
TRDG/WHET N20 27 H7
WCHMH N21 29 J6
Oxford Ga HMSMTH W6 107 G3
Oxford Ms BXLY DA5 137 H7
Oxford Rd CAR SM5 175 J5
EA W5 85 K6
ED N9 42 D1
FSBYPK N4 55 G7
HRW HA1 48 C5
IL IG1 78 C3
KIL/WHAMP NW6 2 B5
KTN/HRWW/WS HA3 49 F2
NRWD SE19 149 K5
PEND EN3 30 D4
PUT/ROE SW15 127 H3
SCUP DA14 155 H4
SRTFD E15 76 B5
TEDD TW11 142 D4
WFD IG8 45 H4
WLGTN SM6 * 176 C4
Oxford Rd North CHSWK W4 105 J4
Oxford Rd South CHSWK W4 105 H4
Oxford Rw SUN TW16 * 156 B2
Oxford Sq BAY/PAD W2 9 J5
Oxford St OXSTW W1C 10 A5
SOHO/SHAV W1D 10 E4
WATW WD18 21 F4
Oxford Wk STHL UB1 83 K7
Oxford Wy FELT TW13 141 H3
Oxgate Court Pde
CRICK NW2 * 69 K1
Oxgate Gdns CRICK NW2 69 K2
Oxgate La CRICK NW2 69 K1
Oxhawth Crs HAYES BR2 169 F4
STMC/STPC BR5 169 G5
Oxhey Av OXHEY WD19 21 H6
Oxhey Dr NTHWD HA6 33 F4
OXHEY WD19 33 G2
Oxhey La OXHEY WD19 21 H6
PIN HA5 33 K3
Oxhey Ridge Cl NTHWD HA6 32 E4
Oxhey Rd OXHEY WD19 21 G6
Oxleas EHAM E6 96 B5
Oxleas Cl WELL DA16 135 J1
Oxleay Rd RYLN/HDSTN HA2 48 A7
Oxleigh Cl NWMAL KT3 160 B4
Oxley Cl STHWK SE1 19 M7
Oxleys Rd CRICK NW2 69 K2
Oxlow La DAGW RM9 80 B3
Oxonian St EDUL SE22 131 G3
Oxted Cl MTCM CR4 162 C2
Oxtoby Wy
STRHM/NOR SW16 148 D7
Oyster Catchers Cl
CAN/RD E16 95 F5
Oyster Rw WCHPL E1 92 E5
Ozolins Wy CAN/RD E16 94 D5

P

Pablo Neruda HNHL SE24 130 C3
Pace Pl WCHPL E1 92 D5
Pacific Cl EBED/NFELT TW14 121 J7
Pacific Rd CAN/RD E16 94 E5
Packington Sq IS N1 6 E4
Packington St IS N1 6 D4
Packmores Rd ELTH/MOT SE9 135 J4
Padbury Cl EBED/NFELT TW14 121 G7
Padbury Ct BETH E2 7 M8
Paddenswick Rd
HMSMTH W6 106 D2
Paddington Cl YEAD UB4 83 H3
Paddington Gn BAY/PAD W2 9 G3
Paddington St MHST W1U 10 A2
Paddock Cl NTHLT UB5 84 A1
OXHEY WD19 21 J5
SYD SE26 151 F3
WPK KT4 160 B7
Paddock Gdns NRWD SE19 150 A5
Paddock La BAR EN5 25 G3
Paddock Rd CRICK NW2 69 J2
RSLP HA4 65 H2
Paddocks Cl
RYLN/HDSTN HA2 66 B3
The Paddocks EA W5 * 104 E2
EBAR EN4 27 K2
MLHL NW7 * 38 D5
WBLY HA9 68 D1
Paddock Wy CHST BR7 154 D6
PUT/ROE SW15 127 F6
Padelford La STAN HA7 35 G1
Padfield Rd BRXN/ST SW9 130 D2
Padley Cl CHSGTN KT9 172 B4
Padnall Rd CHDH RM6 61 K2
Padstow Rd ENC/FH EN2 29 H1
Padstow Wk FELT TW13 140 D1
Padua Rd PGE/AN SE20 150 E7
Pagden St VX/NE SW8 109 G7
Pageant Crs
BERM/RHTH SE16 93 H7
Pageant Wk CROY/NA CR0 178 A2
Page Av WBLY HA9 68 E2
Page Cl DAGW RM9 80 A4
HPTN TW12 141 J5
KTN/HRWW/WS HA3 50 B5
Page Crs CROY/NA CR0 177 H4
Page Green Rd
SEVS/STOTM N15 * 56 C4
Page Green Ter
SEVS/STOTM N15 56 B4
Page Heath La BMLY BR1 168 C2
Page Heath Vls BMLY BR1 168 C2
Pagehurst Rd CROY/NA CR0 165 H6
Page Meadow MLHL NW7 37 J6
Page Rd EBED/NFELT TW14 121 G5
Page's Hl MUSWH N10 54 A1
Page's La MUSWH N10 54 A1
Page St MLHL NW7 37 J7
WEST SW1P 17 H5
Page's Wk STHWK SE1 19 J5
Page's Yd CHSWK W4 106 C5
Paget Av SUT SM1 175 H2
Paget Cl HPTN TW12 142 D3
Paget Gdns CHST BR7 154 B7
Paget La ISLW TW7 123 J2
Paget Pl KUTN/CMB KT2 * 144 E5
THDIT KT7 158 A7
Paget Ri WOOL/PLUM SE18 115 F6
Paget Rd HGDN/ICK UB10 82 A3
IL IG1 78 B3
STNW/STAM N16 55 K7
Paget St FSBYE EC1V 6 C7
Paget Ter WOOL/PLUM SE18 115 G5
Pagnell St NWCR SE14 112 C6
Pagoda Av RCH/KEW TW9 125 G2
Pagoda Gdns BKHTH/KID SE3 133 G1
Pagoda Gv WNWD SE27 149 J1
Paignton Rd RSLP HA4 64 E2
SEVS/STOTM N15 56 A5
Paines Cl PIN HA5 47 J2
Paine's La PIN HA5 47 J1
Pain's Cl MTCM CR4 163 G1
Painsthorpe Rd
STNW/STAM N16 74 A2
Painters Ms BERM/RHTH SE16 111 H3
Painters Rd GNTH/NBYPK IG2 61 G2
Paisley Rd CAR SM5 162 C7
WDGN N22 41 H7
Paisley Ter CAR SM5 162 C7
Pakeman St HOLWY N7 73 F2
Pakenham Cl BAL SW12 129 F7
Pakenham St FSBYW WC1X 5 M8
Palace Av KENS W8 8 D9
Palace Cl HOM E9 75 H5
Palace Ct BAY/PAD W2 8 C6
KTN/HRWW/WS HA3 50 A5
Palace Court Gdns
MUSWH N10 54 C2
Palace Gardens Ms KENS W8 8 C8
Palace Gardens Ter KENS W8 8 B8
Palace Ga KENS W8 14 E2
Palace Gates Rd WDGN N22 40 E7
Palace Gn CROY/NA CR0 179 H6
KENS W8 8 C9
Palace Gv BMLY BR1 153 F7
NRWD SE19 150 B6
Palace Ms FUL/PGN SW6 107 J6
WALTH E17 57 H3
Palace Pde WALTH E17 * 57 H3
Palace Pl BGVA SW1W 16 E3
Palace Rd BMLY BR1 153 F7
BRXS/STRHM SW2 130 A7
CEND/HSY/T N8 54 D4
E/WMO/HCT KT8 157 H2
FBAR/BDGN N11 40 E6
KUT/HW KT1 158 E3
NRWD SE19 150 B6
RSLP HA4 65 J3
Palace Sq NRWD SE19 150 B6
Palace St WESTW SW1E 16 D3
Palace Vw BMLY BR1 168 A2
CROY/NA CR0 179 H3
Palace View Rd CHING E4 43 K4
Palamos Rd LEY E10 57 J7
Palatine Av STNW/STAM N16 74 A3
Palatine Rd STNW/STAM N16 74 A3
Palemead Cl FUL/PGN SW6 107 G7
Palermo Rd WLSDN NW10 87 J1
Palestine Gv WIM/MER SW19 147 H7
Palewell Common Dr
MORT/ESHN SW14 126 A4
Palewell Pk
MORT/ESHN SW14 126 A4
Palfrey Pl VX/NE SW8 110 A6
Palgrave Av STHL UB1 84 A6
Palgrave Gdns CAMTN NW1 3 K9
Palgrave Rd SHB W12 106 C2
Palissy St BETH E2 7 L8
Pallet Wy WOOL/PLUM SE18 114 D7
Palliser Dr RAIN RM13 99 J4
Palliser Rd WKENS W14 107 H4
Pall Ml STJS SW1Y 11 G9
Pall Ml East STJS SW1Y 11 G8
Pall Mall Pl STJS SW1Y 10 F9
Palm Av SCUP DA14 155 K5
Palm Cl LEY E10 75 K2
Palmeira Rd BXLYHN DA7 136 E2
Palmer Av BUSH WD23 22 B5
CHEAM SM3 174 A3
Palmer Cl HEST TW5 103 F7
NTHLT UB5 65 J5
WWKM BR4 180 B1
Palmer Crs KUT/HW KT1 159 F2
Palmer Gdns BAR EN5 26 B4
Palmer Pl HOLWY N7 73 G4
Palmer Rd BCTR RM8 61 K7
PLSTW E13 95 F3
Palmers Gv E/WMO/HCT KT8 157 F3
Palmers Rd BETH E2 93 F1
MORT/ESHN SW14 125 K2
STRHM/NOR SW16 164 A1
Palmer's Rd FBAR/BDGN N11 40 C4
Palmerston Ct BKHH IG9 45 G1
Palmerston Crs PLMGR N13 41 F4
WOOL/PLUM SE18 115 H5
Palmerston Gv
WIM/MER SW19 146 E6
Palmerston Rd ACT W3 105 K2
BKHH IG9 45 G1
CAR SM5 175 K3
CROY/NA CR0 164 E4
FSTGT E7 77 F4
HSLW TW3 103 H7
KIL/WHAMP NW6 70 D6
KTN/HRWW/WS HA3 49 F2
MORT/ESHN SW14 125 K3
SUT SM1 175 G4
WALTH E17 57 H3
WDGN N22 41 F6
WHTN TW2 123 K5
WIM/MER SW19 146 E6
Palmerston Wy VX/NE SW8 * 109 G6
Palmer St STJSPK SW1H 16 F3
Palmers Whf KUT/HW KT1 * 158 E1
Palm Gv EA W5 105 F2
Palm Rd ROMW/RG RM7 62 E4
Pamela Ct
NFNCH/WDSPK N12 * 39 F5
Pamela Gdns PIN HA5 47 F4
Pampisford Rd SAND/SEL CR2 177 H7
Pams Wy HOR/WEW KT19 173 F4
Pancras La MANHO EC4N 12 F5
Pancras Rd CAMTN NW1 5 G5
Pancras Wy BOW E3 93 J1
Pandian Wy KTTN NW5 72 D5
Pandora Rd KIL/WHAMP NW6 70 E5
Panfield Ms GNTH/NBYPK IG2 60 A5
Panfield Rd ABYW SE2 116 B1
Pangbourne Av NKENS W10 * 88 A4
Pangbourne Dr STAN HA7 35 K4
Panhard Pl STHL UB1 84 B6
Pank Av BAR EN5 27 H4
Pankhurst Av CAN/RD E16 * 95 F7
Pankhurst Cl ISLW TW7 124 A2
NWCR SE14 112 A6
Pankhurst Pl WATN WD24 21 G2
Pankhurst Rd WOT/HER KT12 156 B6
Pankridge OXHEY WD19 * 33 H1
Panmuir Rd RYNPK SW20 145 K7
Panmure Cl HBRY N5 73 H3
Panmure Rd SYD SE26 150 D2
Pansy Gdns SHB W12 87 J6
Panther Dr WLSDN NW10 69 F4
Pantiles Cl PLMGR N13 41 H4
The Pantiles BMLY BR1 168 D2
BUSH WD23 22 D7
Panton Cl CROY/NA CR0 164 C7
Panton St STJS SW1Y 11 H7
Paper Blds EMB EC4Y * 12 B6
Papermill Cl CAR SM5 176 A3
Papworth Gdns HOLWY N7 73 F4
Papworth Wy
BRXS/STRHM SW2 130 B6
Parade Ms BRXS/STRHM SW2 149 H1
Parade Ter CDALE/KGS NW9 * 51 J5
The Parade BROCKY SE4 * 112 C7
BTSEA SW11 * 128 C3
CAR SM5 * 175 K4
CROY/NA CR0 * 163 K5
DART DA1 * 138 C4
EA W5 * 85 K5
EDUL SE22 * 131 F2
ESH/CLAY KT10 170 E5
FSBYPK N4 * 73 G1
GFD/PVL UB6 * 67 H5
KUT/HW KT1 * 159 F1
OXHEY WD19 33 H2
PGE/AN SE20 * 150 E7
RCH/KEW TW9 * 125 H2
SUN TW16 140 D6
SUT SM1 * 174 D2
SYD SE26 * 150 D3
WAT WD17 21 F2
WLGTN SM6 * 177 F4
Paradise Pas HOLWY N7 73 F4
Paradise Rd CLAP SW4 129 K1
RCH/KEW TW9 125 F4
Paradise Rw BETH E2 * 92 D2
Paradise St BERM/RHTH SE16 111 J1
Paradise Wk CHEL SW3 15 L9
Paragon Cl CAN/RD E16 94 E5
Paragon Gv BRYLDS KT5 159 G5
Paragon Ms STHWK SE1 19 H5
Paragon Pl BKHTH/KID SE3 133 J1
Paragon Rd HACK E8 74 D5
Parbury Ri CHSGTN KT9 172 A5
Parbury Rd FSTH SE23 132 B5
Parchmore Rd THHTH CR7 164 C1
Parchmore Wy THHTH CR7 164 C1
Pardoe Rd LEY E10 57 K6
Pardoner St STHWK SE1 19 H3
Pardon St FSBYE EC1V 6 D9
Parfett St WCHPL E1 92 C4
Parfitt Cl HAMP NW3 53 G7
Parfrey St HMSMTH W6 107 F5
Parham Dr GNTH/NBYPK IG2 60 B5
Paris Gdn STHWK SE1 12 C8
Parish Cl HCH RM12 81 K1
Parish Gate Dr BFN/LL DA15 135 K5
Parish La PGE/AN SE20 151 F5
Parish Whf WOOL/PLUM SE18 114 D3
Park Ap BERM/RHTH SE16 * 111 K2
WELL DA16 136 C3
Park Av BARK IG11 78 C5
BMLY BR1 152 E5
BUSH WD23 21 H1
CAR SM5 176 A5
CRICK NW2 69 K5
EHAM E6 78 A7
EN EN1 29 K4
FNCH N3 39 F7
GLDGN NW11 53 F7
HSLW TW3 123 G5
IL IG1 60 A7
MORT/ESHN SW14 126 A3
ORP BR6 181 K1
PLMGR N13 41 G2
RSLP HA4 46 C5
SRTFD E15 76 C5
STHL UB1 102 E1
UED N18 42 C3
WATW WD18 20 E2
WDGN N22 54 E1
WFD IG8 45 F4
WLSDN NW10 86 B2
WWKM BR4 180 A1
Park Av East EW KT17 173 J5
Park Avenue Ms MTCM CR4 148 B6
Park Av North
CEND/HSY/T N8 54 D3
WLSDN NW10 69 K4
Park Avenue Rd TOTM N17 42 D6
Park Av South
CEND/HSY/T N8 54 D3
Park Av West EW KT17 173 J5
Park Cha WBLY HA9 68 B3
Park Cl BUSH WD23 21 H2
CAR SM5 175 K5
CRICK NW2 69 J2
HOM E9 74 E7
HPTN TW12 142 C7
HSLW TW3 123 H4
KTN/HRWW/WS HA3 34 E7
KUTN/CMB KT2 144 C7
NFNCH/WDSPK N12 * 39 H3
SKENS SW7 * 15 L2
WKENS W14 107 J2
WLSDN NW10 86 B2
Park Cots FNCH N3 * 52 D1
Park Ct DUL SE21 * 149 K2
NWMAL KT3 160 A3
SYD SE26 * 150 D5
WBLY HA9 68 A4
Park Crs BORE WD6 24 B2
EMPK RM11 63 J6
ENC/FH EN2 29 K3
ERITH DA8 117 K5
FNCH N3 39 F6
KTN/HRWW/WS HA3 34 E7
REGST W1B 10 C1
WHTN TW2 123 J7
Park Crescent Ms East
GTPST W1W 10 D1
Park Crescent Ms West
CAVSQ/HST W1G 10 C1
Park Cft EDGW HA8 36 E7
Parkcroft Rd LEE/GVPK SE12 133 J6
Parkdale Crs WPK KT4 173 F2
Parkdale Rd
WOOL/PLUM SE18 115 K4
Park Dr ACT W3 105 H2
CHARL SE7 114 D4
DAGE RM10 80 E2
GLDGN NW11 53 F7
KTN/HRWW/WS HA3 34 D5
MORT/ESHN SW14 126 A4
ROM RM1 63 F3
RYLN/HDSTN HA2 48 A6
WCHMH N21 29 J5
Park End BMLY BR1 152 D7
HAMP NW3 71 J3
Park End Rd ROM RM1 63 G3
Parker Cl CAN/RD E16 95 J7
CAR SM5 175 K5
Parker Ms HOL/ALD WC2B * 11 K4
Parke Rd BARN SW13 106 D7
Parker Rd CROY/NA CR0 177 J3
Parker's Rw STHWK SE1 19 M2
Parker St CAN/RD E16 95 J7
HOL/ALD WC2B 11 K4
Parker Ter FSTH SE23 151 H1
Park Farm Cl EFNCH N2 53 G2
PIN HA5 47 F4
Park Farm Rd BMLY BR1 153 H7
KUTN/CMB KT2 144 A6
Parkfield Av FELT TW13 140 E2
MORT/ESHN SW14 126 B3
NTHLT UB5 83 H1
RYLN/HDSTN HA2 48 C1
Parkfield Cl EDGW HA8 36 D5
NTHLT UB5 83 J1
Parkfield Crs FELT TW13 140 E2
RSLP HA4 65 J1
RYLN/HDSTN HA2 48 C1
Parkfield Dr NTHLT UB5 83 H1
Parkfield Gdns
RYLN/HDSTN HA2 48 B2
Parkfield Pde FELT TW13 * 140 E2
Parkfield Rd FELT TW13 140 E2
NTHLT UB5 83 J1
NWCR SE14 112 C7
RYLN/HDSTN HA2 66 C2
WLSDN NW10 69 J6
Parkfields CROY/NA CR0 166 C7
PUT/ROE SW15 127 F3
Parkfields Av
CDALE/KGS NW9 51 F7
RYNPK SW20 145 K7
Parkfields Cl CAR SM5 176 A3
Parkfields Rd KUTN/CMB KT2 144 B4
Parkfield St IS N1 6 B5
Parkfield Wy HAYES BR2 168 E5
Park Gdns CDALE/KGS NW9 50 D2
ERITH DA8 118 A3
KUTN/CMB KT2 144 B4
Parkgate BKHTH/KID SE3 133 J2
Park Ga EA W5 85 K4
EFNCH N2 53 H2
WCHMH N21 29 F6
Parkgate Cl KUTN/CMB KT2 144 D5
Park Gate Ct HPTN TW12 * 142 C4
Parkgate Gdns
MORT/ESHN SW14 126 A4
Parkgate Ms HGT N6 54 C6
Parkgate Rd BTSEA SW11 108 D6
WLGTN SM6 176 A4
Park Gates
RYLN/HDSTN HA2 * 66 A3
Park Gv BMLY BR1 153 F7
EDGW HA8 36 B4
FBAR/BDGN N11 40 D6
SRTFD E15 76 E7
Park Grove Rd WAN E11 76 C1
Park Hall Rd DUL SE21 149 K1
EFNCH N2 53 J3
Parkham St BTSEA SW11 108 C7
Park Hl BMLY BR1 168 D3
CAR SM5 175 K5
CLAP SW4 129 J4
EA W5 85 K4

FSTH SE23 150 D1
RCHPK/HAM TW10 125 G5
Park Hill Cl CAR SM5 175 J4
Park Hill Ri CROY/NA CR0 178 A1
Park Hill Rd CROY/NA CR0 178 A3
HAYES BR2 167 H1
WLGTN SM6 176 B6
Parkhill Rd BFN/LL DA15 154 E2
BXLY DA5 137 G6
HAMP NW3 71 K4
Park Hill Wk HAMP NW3 71 K4
Parkholme Rd HACK E8 74 C5
Park House Gdns TWK TW1 124 D4
Parkhouse St CMBW SE5 110 E6
Parkhurst Gdns BXLY DA5 137 H6
Parkhurst Rd BXLY DA5 137 H6
FBAR/BDGN N11 40 A3
HOLWY N7 72 E3
MNPK E12 78 A3
SUT SM1 175 H3
TOTM N17 56 C1
WALTH E17 * 57 G3
WDGN N22 41 F6
Parkland Av ROM RM1 63 G1
Parkland Gv ISLW TW7 104 A7
Parkland Md BMLY BR1 169 F2
Parkland Rd WDGN N22 55 F1
WFD IG8 45 F6
Parklands BRYLDS KT5 159 G4
BUSH WD23 * 22 C5
HGT N6 54 B6
Parklands Cl GNTH/NBYPK IG2 60 C6
MORT/ESHN SW14 125 K4
Parklands Dr FNCH N3 52 C2
Parklands Pde HEST TW5 * 122 C1
Parklands Rd
STRHM/NOR SW16 148 B4
Parklands Wy WPK KT4 173 G1
Park La CAR SM5 176 A3
CHDH RM6 61 K5
CHEAM SM3 174 C5
CROY/NA CR0 177 K2
EMPK RM11 63 J6
HCH RM12 81 K5
HEST TW5 101 K6
OXSTW W1C 9 M6
RCH/KEW TW9 124 E3
RYLN/HDSTN HA2 66 B2
SRTFD E15 * 76 A7
STAN HA7 35 G2
TEDD TW11 143 F5
TOTM N17 42 B6
WBLY HA9 68 B3
YEAD UB4 82 C4
Park Lane Cl TOTM N17 42 C6
Parklea Cl CDALE/KGS NW9 37 G7
Parkleigh Rd WIM/MER SW19 162 A1
Parkleys RCHPK/HAM TW10 143 K3
Parkleys Pde
RCHPK/HAM TW10 * 143 K3
Park Lodge Av WDR/YW UB7 100 C1
Park Md BFN/LL DA15 136 B4
Parkmead PUT/ROE SW15 126 E5
Park Md RYLN/HDSTN HA2 66 B2
Parkmead Gdns MLHL NW7 37 H5
Park Ms GNWCH SE10 113 J4
NKENS W10 88 C1
RAIN RM13 81 J5
STWL/WRAY TW19 120 C6
Park Pde ACT W3 * 105 H2
HYS/HAR UB3 * 82 C5
WLSDN NW10 87 H1
Park Piazza LEW SE13 133 G5
Park Pl ACT W3 105 H3
BMLY BR1 * 153 F7
EA W5 85 K7
HPTN TW12 142 C5
IS N1 7 H3
POP/IOD E14 93 J7
WBLY HA9 68 B3
WHALL SW1A 10 E9
Park Place Vls BAY/PAD W2 8 F2
Park Ridings CEND/HSY/T N8 55 G2
Park Ri KTN/HRWW/WS HA3 34 E7
Park Rise Rd FSTH SE23 132 B7
Park Rd ALP/SUD HA0 68 A5
BAR EN5 26 D3
BECK BR3 151 H6
BMLY BR1 153 F7
BRYLDS KT5 159 G5
BUSH WD23 22 A5
CDALE/KGS NW9 51 F6
CEND/HSY/T N8 54 D4
CHEAM SM3 174 C5
CHST BR7 154 B5
CHSWK W4 106 A5
E/WMO/HCT KT8 157 H3
EBAR EN4 27 H3
EFNCH N2 53 H2
ESH/CLAY KT10 170 B3
FBAR/BDGN N11 40 D6
FELT TW13 141 H3
HDN NW4 51 K5
HNWL W7 85 F6
HPTN TW12 142 C4
HSLW TW3 123 H4
IL IG1 78 D2
ISLW TW7 104 C7
KUT/HW KT1 143 J7
LEY E10 57 J7
MNPK E12 77 H3
NWMAL KT3 160 A3
PLSTW E13 77 G7
RCHPK/HAM TW10 125 G5
SNWD SE25 165 F3
SRTFD E15 76 E7
STHGT/OAK N14 28 D6
STJWD NW8 3 K8
SUN TW16 141 F6
TEDD TW11 143 F5
TWK TW1 124 D5
UED N18 42 B3
WALTH E17 57 H4
WIM/MER SW19 147 H5
WLGTN SM6 176 B4
WLSDN NW10 * 69 G7
YEAD UB4 82 C4
Park Rd East ACT W3 105 K1
Park Rd North ACT W3 105 J1
Park Rw GNWCH SE10 113 G5
Park Royal Rd WLSDN NW10 86 E2
Parkshot RCH/KEW TW9 124 E3
Park Side BKHH IG9 45 F1
CRICK NW2 69 J2
HYS/HAR UB3 * 82 C6
Parkside BECK BR3 * 166 E1
BKHTH/KID SE3 * 113 J6
CHEAM SM3 174 C5
FNCH N3 39 F7
HPTN TW12 142 D4
MLHL NW7 37 J5
OXHEY WD19 * 21 G5
SCUP DA14 155 H1
WIM/MER SW19 146 B4
Parkside Av BMLY BR1 168 D3
BXLYHN DA7 138 A1
ROM RM1 63 F1
WIM/MER SW19 146 B4
Parkside Cl PGE/AN SE20 150 E6
Parkside Crs BRYLDS KT5 159 K5
HOLWY N7 73 G2
Parkside Dr EDGW HA8 36 C2
WAT WD17 20 C1
Parkside Est HOM E9 * 75 F7
Parkside Gdns EBAR EN4 27 K7
WIM/MER SW19 146 B3
Parkside Pde DART DA1 * 138 C1
Parkside Rd BELV DA17 117 J3
HSLW TW3 123 G4
NTHWD HA6 32 D4
Parkside St BTSEA SW11 109 F7
Parkside Ter UED N18 * 41 K3
Parkside Wy
RYLN/HDSTN HA2 48 B3
Park Sq East CAMTN NW1 4 C9
Park Square Ms CAMTN NW1 10 C1
Park Sq West CAMTN NW1 4 C9
Parkstead Rd PUT/ROE SW15 126 D4
Park Steps BAY/PAD W2 * 9 K6
Parkstone Av UED N18 42 B4
Parkstone Rd PECK SE15 * 131 H1
WALTH E17 58 A2
Park St CROY/NA CR0 177 J2
MYFR/PKLN W1K 10 A7
STHWK SE1 12 E8
TEDD TW11 142 E5
Park Ter CAR SM5 * 175 J2
WPK KT4 160 D7
The Park CAR SM5 175 K4
EA W5 85 K7
GLDGN NW11 53 F7
HGT N6 54 A6
SCUP DA14 155 F4
Parkthorne Cl
RYLN/HDSTN HA2 * 48 B5
Parkthorne Dr
RYLN/HDSTN HA2 48 A5
Parkthorne Rd BAL SW12 129 J6
Park Vw ACT W3 86 E4
NWMAL KT3 160 C2
PIN HA5 33 K7
WBLY HA9 68 D4
WCHMH N21 29 F6
Park View Cl CAR SM5 175 K6
Park View Ct
NFNCH/WDSPK N12 * 39 J3
Park View Crs
FBAR/BDGN N11 40 B3
Parkview Crs WPK KT4 161 F7
Park View Dr MTCM CR4 162 C1
Park View Est HBRY N5 * 73 J3
Parkview Gdns CLAY IG5 59 K3
Park View Gdns HDN NW4 52 A4
WDGN N22 * 41 G7
Parkview Ms RAIN RM13 99 K4
Park View Rd CRICK NW2 69 H3
Parkview Rd CROY/NA CR0 165 H7
Park View Rd EA W5 86 A4
ELTH/MOT SE9 135 G7
FNCH N3 39 F7
PIN HA5 33 F5
STHL UB1 84 A7
TOTM N17 56 C2
WELL DA16 136 D2
Park Village East CAMTN NW1 4 C5
Park Village West
CAMTN NW1 4 C5
Park Vls TOOT SW17 * 147 J4
Parkville Rd FUL/PGN SW6 107 J6
Park Vis GNWCH SE10 113 G5
Park Vista Apartments
CAN/RD E16 94 D2
Park Wk WBPTN SW10 14 F9
Parkwat Crs SRTFD E15 76 B4
Park Wy E/WMO/HCT KT8 157 G2
EBED/NFELT TW14 122 A6
EDGW HA8 36 D7
ENC/FH EN2 29 G1
GLDGN NW11 52 C4
RSLP HA4 46 E7
TRDG/WHET N20 39 K3
Parkway CAMTN NW1 4 D3
CROY/NA CR0 180 A7
ERITHM DA18 117 F2
GDMY/SEVK IG3 79 F2
GPK RM2 63 H1
RAIN RM13 99 J3
RYNPK SW20 161 G3
STHGT/OAK N14 40 E1
WFD IG8 45 G4
The Parkway HEST TW5 101 K5
NTHLT UB5 83 H2
NWDGN UB2 102 A2
Park West Pl BAY/PAD W2 9 K4
Parkwood BECK BR3 151 J6
Parkwood Av ESH/CLAY KT10 157 H7
Parkwood Ms HGT N6 54 B5
Parkwood Rd BXLY DA5 137 G6
ISLW TW7 104 A7
WIM/MER SW19 146 D4
Parliament Ct WCHPL E1 * 13 K3
Parliament Hl HAMP NW3 71 J3
Parliament Hill Flds
KTTN NW5 * 72 A2
Parliament Ms
MORT/ESHN SW14 125 K1
Parliament Sq WEST SW1P 17 J2
Parliament St WHALL SW1A 17 J1
Parma Crs BTSEA SW11 128 E3
Parmiter St BETH E2 92 D1
Parnell Cl EDGW HA8 36 D3
SHB W12 106 E2
Parnell Rd BOW E3 75 H7
Parnham Cl BMLY BR1 169 G2
Parnham St POP/IOD E14 * 93 G5
Parolles Rd ARCH N19 54 C7
Paroma Rd BELV DA17 117 H2
Parr Av EW KT17 173 K7
Parr Cl ED N9 42 D3
Parr Rd EHAM E6 77 H7
STAN HA7 35 K7
Parrs Cl SAND/SEL CR2 177 K7
Parr's Pl HPTN TW12 142 A6
Parr St IS N1 7 G5
Parry Av EHAM E6 95 K5
Parry Cl EW KT17 173 J6
Parry Pl WOOL/PLUM SE18 115 G3
Parry Rd NKENS W10 88 C2
SNWD SE25 165 F2
Parry St VX/NE SW8 17 K9
Parsifal Rd KIL/WHAMP NW6 70 E4
Parsloes Av DAGW RM9 80 A4
Parsonage Cl HYS/HAR UB3 82 D5
Parsonage Gdns
ENC/FH EN2 29 J1
Parsonage La ENC/FH EN2 29 K1
Parsonage Manorway
BELV DA17 117 H5
Parsonage St POP/IOD E14 113 F3
Parsons Crs EDGW HA8 36 C2
Parsons Gn FUL/PGN SW6 107 K7
Parsons Green La
FUL/PGN SW6 107 K7
Parsons Gv EDGW HA8 36 C2
Parsons Md E/WMO/HCT KT8 157 H2
Parson's Md CROY/NA CR0 164 C7
Parsons Rd PLSTW E13 95 G1
Parson St HDN NW4 52 A2
Parthenia Rd FUL/PGN SW6 107 K7
Partingdale La MLHL NW7 38 B4
Partington Cl ARCH N19 54 D7
Partridge Cl BAR EN5 26 A5
BUSH WD23 * 22 C7
CAN/RD E16 95 H4
STAN HA7 36 A3
Partridge Gn ELTH/MOT SE9 154 A2
Partridge Rd HPTN TW12 141 K5
SCUP DA14 154 E2
Partridge Sq EHAM E6 95 J4
Partridge Wy WDGN N22 40 E7
Pasadena Cl HYS/HAR UB3 101 K1
Pascal St VX/NE SW8 109 J6
Pascoe Rd LEW SE13 133 G4
Pasley Cl WALW SE17 18 D8
Pasquier Rd WALTH E17 57 G2
Passey Pl ELTH/MOT SE9 134 E5
Passfield Dr POP/IOD E14 93 K4
Passmore Gdns
FBAR/BDGN N11 40 D5
Passmore St BGVA SW1W 16 A6
Pasteur Cl CDALE/KGS NW9 51 G1
Pasteur Gdns UED N18 41 J4
Paston Cl WLGTN SM6 176 C2
Paston Crs LEE/GVPK SE12 134 A6
Pastor St LBTH SE11 18 D5
Pasture Cl ALP/SUD HA0 67 H2
BUSH WD23 22 C6
Pasture Rd ALP/SUD HA0 67 H1
CAT SE6 133 H7
DAGW RM9 80 B4
The Pastures OXHEY WD19 21 F6
TRDG/WHET N20 26 D7
Patcham Ter VX/NE SW8 109 G7
Patching Wy YEAD UB4 83 J4
Paternoster Sq STP EC4M 12 D5
Pater St KENS W8 14 A4
Pates Manor Dr
EBED/NFELT TW14 121 G6
Pathfield Rd
STRHM/NOR SW16 148 D5
The Path WIM/MER SW19 147 F7
The Pathway OXHEY WD19 21 H7
Patience Rd BTSEA SW11 128 D1
Patio Cl CLAP SW4 129 J5
Patmore St VX/NE SW8 109 H7
Patmos Rd BRXN/ST SW9 110 C6
Paton Cl BOW E3 93 J2
Patricia Ct WELL DA16 116 C6
Patricia Vls TOTM N17 * 42 D7
Patrick Rd PLSTW E13 95 G2
Patriot Sq BETH E2 92 D1
Patrol Pl CAT SE6 132 E5
Patshull Pl KTTN NW5 72 C5
Patshull Rd KTTN NW5 72 C5
Pattenden Rd CAT SE6 132 C7
Patten Rd WAND/EARL SW18 128 D6
Patterdale Cl BMLY BR1 152 C5
Patterdale Rd PECK SE15 111 K6
Patterson Rd NRWD SE19 150 B5
Pattina Wk BERM/RHTH SE16 93 G7
Pattison Rd CRICK NW2 70 E2
Paul Cl SRTFD E15 76 C6
Paulet Rd CMBW SE5 130 C1
Paulet Wy WLSDN NW10 * 69 G6
Paul Gdns CROY/NA CR0 178 B1
Paulhan Rd
KTN/HRWW/WS HA3 49 K3
Paulin Dr WCHMH N21 29 G6
Pauline Crs WHTN TW2 123 H7
Paul Julius Cl POP/IOD E14 94 B6
Paul Robeson Cl EHAM E6 96 A2
Paul St SDTCH EC2A 7 J9
SRTFD E15 76 C7
Paultons Sq CHEL SW3 15 H9
Paultons St CHEL SW3 108 C5
Pauntley St ARCH N19 54 C7
Paveley Dr BTSEA SW11 108 D6
Paveley St STJWD NW8 3 K8
Pavement Sq CROY/NA CR0 165 H7
The Pavement CLAP SW4 129 H3
EA W5 * 105 F2
TEDD TW11 * 143 H6
WAN E11 * 58 A7
WIM/MER SW19 * 146 D5
WNWD SE27 * 149 J3
Pavet Cl DAGE RM10 80 D5
Pavilion Ldg
RYLN/HDSTN HA2 * 48 D7
Pavilion Ms FNCH N3 52 E1
Pavilion Pde SHB W12 * 88 A5
Pavilion Rd IL IG1 59 K6
KTBR SW1X 15 M2
Pavilion St KTBR SW1X 15 M4
The Pavilion VX/NE SW8 * 109 J6
Pavilion Wy EDGW HA8 36 E6
RSLP HA4 65 G1
Pavillion Sq TOOT SW17 147 J2
Pavillion Ter SHB W12 * 88 A5
Pawleyne Cl PGE/AN SE20 150 E6
Pawsey Cl PLSTW E13 76 E7
Pawson's Rd THHTH CR7 164 D5
Paxford Rd ALP/SUD HA0 67 H1
Paxton Cl RCH/KEW TW9 125 G1
WOT/HER KT12 156 B6
Paxton Pl WNWD SE27 150 A3
Paxton Rd BMLY BR1 152 E6
CHSWK W4 106 B5
FSTH SE23 151 G2
TOTM N17 42 B6
Paxton Ter PIM SW1V 16 D9
Payne Cl BARK IG11 78 E6
Paynell Ct BKHTH/KID SE3 133 H2
Payne Rd BOW E3 93 K1
Paynesfield Av
MORT/ESHN SW14 126 A2
Paynesfield Rd BUSH WD23 23 F6
Payne St DEPT SE8 112 C5
Paynes Wk HMSMTH W6 107 H5
Payzes Gdns WFD IG8 * 44 D5
Peabody Av PIM SW1V 16 D8
Peabody Cl CROY/NA CR0 165 K7
GNWCH SE10 * 112 E7
PIM SW1V 16 D8
Peabody Cots HNHL SE24 * 130 D6
Peabody Est BTSEA SW11 * 128 D3
CHEL SW3 * 108 D5
CLKNW EC1R * 12 B1
CMBW SE5 * 110 E7
HMSMTH W6 * 107 F4
HNHL SE24 130 C6
NKENS W10 * 88 A4
STHWK SE1 * 12 B8
STLK EC1Y * 12 F1
TOTM N17 * 42 A7
Peabody Hl DUL SE21 130 C7
Peabody Sq IS N1 * 6 E3
Peabody Ter CLKNW EC1R * 12 B1
Peace Cl GFD/PVL UB6 66 D7
SNWD SE25 165 F3
STHGT/OAK N14 28 B4
Peace Dr WAT WD17 20 E2
Peace Gv WBLY HA9 68 D2
Peace St WOOL/PLUM SE18 115 F5
Peaches Cl BELMT SM2 174 C6
Peach Gv WAN E11 76 B2
Peach Rd FELT TW13 121 K7
NKENS W10 88 B2
Peachum Rd BKHTH/KID SE3 113 J5
Peachy Cl EDGW HA8 36 C5
Peacock Av
EBED/NFELT TW14 121 G7
Peacock Cl BCTR RM8 61 J7
CHING E4 43 H6
MLHL NW7 38 C4
Peacock St WALW SE17 18 D6
Peacock Yd WALW SE17 18 D6
Peaketon Av REDBR IG4 59 H4
Peak Hl SYD SE26 150 E3
Peak Hill Av SYD SE26 150 E3
Peak Hill Gdns SYD SE26 * 150 E3
The Peak SYD SE26 150 E2
Peal Gdns WEA W13 85 G2
Peall Rd CROY/NA CR0 164 A5
Pearce Cl MTCM CR4 163 F1
Pearcefield Av FSTH SE23 131 K7
Pear Cl CDALE/KGS NW9 51 F3
NWCR SE14 112 B6
Pearcroft Rd WAN E11 76 B1
Peardon St VX/NE SW8 129 G2
Peareswood Gdns STAN HA7 35 K7
Peareswood Rd ERITH DA8 118 C7
Pearfield Rd FSTH SE23 151 G2
Pearing Cl WPK KT4 174 B1
Pearl Cl CRICK NW2 52 B6
EHAM E6 96 A5
Pearl Rd WALTH E17 57 J2
Pearl St WAP E1W 92 D7
Pearman St STHWK SE1 18 B3
Pear Pl STHWK SE1 18 A1
Pear Rd WAN E11 76 B2
Pearscroft Ct FUL/PGN SW6 108 A7
Pearscroft Rd FUL/PGN SW6 128 A1
Pearse St PECK SE15 111 F5
Pearson Cl BAR EN5 27 F2
Pearson's NWCR SE14 112 D7
Pearson's Rd NWCR SE14 * 112 D7
Pearson St BETH E2 7 L5
Pearson Wy MTCM CR4 148 A7
Pears Rd HSLW TW3 123 H2
Peartree Av TOOT SW17 147 K5
Pear Tree Cl CHSGTN KT9 172 C4
Peartree Cl HAYES BR2 168 C4
Pear Tree Cl MTCM CR4 162 D1
Pear Tree Ct CLKNW EC1R 12 B1
Peartree Gdns BCTR RM8 79 H4
ROMW/RG RM7 62 D1
Peartree La WAP E1W * 92 E6
Pear Tree Rd ASHF TW15 140 A4
Peartree Rd EN EN1 30 A2
Pear Tree St FSBYE EC1V 6 D9
Pearwood Cots STAN HA7 * 35 J1
Peary Pl BETH E2 92 E2
Pease Cl HCH RM12 81 K6
Peasmead Ter CHING E4 * 44 A3
Peatfield Cl BFN/LL DA15 154 E2
Pebworth Rd HRW HA1 67 G1
Peckarmans Wd SYD SE26 150 C2
Peckett Sq HBRY N5 * 73 J3
Peckford Pl BRXN/ST SW9 130 B1
Peckham Gv PECK SE15 111 F6
Peckham High St PECK SE15 111 H7
Peckham Hill St PECK SE15 111 H6
Peckham Park Rd PECK SE15 111 H6
Peckham Rd CMBW SE5 111 F7
Peckham Rye EDUL SE22 131 H3
Pecks Yd WCHPL E1 * 13 L2
Peckwater St KTTN NW5 72 C4
Pedlars Wk HOLWY N7 * 72 E4
Pedley Rd BCTR RM8 61 J7
Pedley St WCHPL E1 13 M1
Pedro St CLPT E5 75 F2
Peek Crs WIM/MER SW19 146 B4
Peel Cl CHING E4 43 K1
ED N9 42 C2
Peel Dr CDALE/KGS NW9 51 H2
CLAY IG5 59 J2
Peel Gv BETH E2 92 E1
Peel Pas KENS W8 * 8 A9
Peel Pl CLAY IG5 59 J1
Peel Prec KIL/WHAMP NW6 88 D1
Peel Rd ALP/SUD HA0 67 J2
KTN/HRWW/WS HA3 49 F2
SWFD E18 44 D7
Peel St KENS W8 8 A9
Peerglow Est PEND EN3 * 30 E4
Peerless St FSBYE EC1V 7 G8
Pegamoid Rd UED N18 42 E2
Pegasus Cl STNW/STAM N16 * 73 K3
Pegasus Ct BTFD TW8 105 G4
Pegasus Pl FUL/PGN SW6 * 107 K7
LBTH SE11 18 A9
Pegasus Rd CROY/NA CR0 177 G5
Pegasus Wy FBAR/BDGN N11 40 B5
Pegg Rd HEST TW5 102 C6
Pegwell St WOOL/PLUM SE18 115 K6
Pekin St POP/IOD E14 93 J5
Peldon Wk IS N1 * 6 D3
Pelham Av BARK IG11 79 F7
Pelham Cl CMBW SE5 131 F2
Pelham Cots BXLY DA5 * 137 J7
Pelham Crs SKENS SW7 15 J6
Pelham Pl SKENS SW7 15 J5
Pelham Rd IL IG1 78 D1
PGE/AN SE20 165 K1
SEVS/STOTM N15 56 B3
SWFD E18 59 F2
WDGN N22 55 G1
WIM/MER SW19 146 E6
Pelhams Cl ESH/CLAY KT10 170 A4
Pelham St SKENS SW7 15 H5
Pelhams Wk ESH/CLAY KT10 170 A2
Pelier St WALW SE17 18 F9
Pelinore Rd CAT SE6 152 C1
Pellant Rd FUL/PGN SW6 107 H6
Pellatt Gv WDGN N22 41 G7
Pellatt Rd EDUL SE22 131 G4
WBLY HA9 68 A1
Pellerin Rd STNW/STAM N16 74 A4
Pellings Cl HAYES BR2 167 H2
Pelling St POP/IOD E14 93 H5
Pellipar Cl PLMGR N13 41 G2
Pellipar Rd WOOL/PLUM SE18 114 E4
Pellow Cl BAR EN5 26 D5
Pelly Rd PLSTW E13 94 E1
Pelter St BETH E2 7 L7
Pelton Rd GNWCH SE10 113 H4
Pembar Av WALTH E17 * 57 G2
Pemberley Cha
HOR/WEW KT19 172 D4
Pemberley Cl HOR/WEW KT19 172 D4
Pember Rd WLSDN NW10 88 B2
Pemberton Av GPK RM2 63 K2
Pemberton Cl
STWL/WRAY TW19 120 B7
Pemberton Gdns ARCH N19 72 C2
CHDH RM6 62 A4
Pemberton Pl ESH/CLAY KT10 170 C2
HACK E8 74 D6
Pemberton Rd
E/WMO/HCT KT8 157 H3
FSBYPK N4 55 H4
Pemberton Rw
FLST/FETLN EC4A 12 B4
Pemberton Ter ARCH N19 72 C2
Pembridge Av WHTN TW2 122 E7
Pembridge Crs NTGHL W11 88 D6
Pembridge Gdns BAY/PAD W2 8 A7
Pembridge Ms NTGHL W11 8 A6
Pembridge Pl NTGHL W11 8 B6
Pembridge Rd NTGHL W11 8 A7
Pembridge Sq BAY/PAD W2 8 A7
Pembridge Vls BAY/PAD W2 8 A6
Pembroke Av BRYLDS KT5 159 J4
IS N1 5 K3
KTN/HRWW/WS HA3 49 G2
PIN HA5 47 H7
Pembroke Cl ERITH DA8 117 K3
KTBR SW1X 16 B2
Pembroke Gdns DAGE RM10 80 D2
KENS W8 107 J2
Pembroke Gardens Cl
KENS W8 107 J2
Pembroke Ldg STAN HA7 * 35 J5
Pembroke Ms KENS W8 * 14 A4
MUSWH N10 40 A7
Pembroke Pde ERITH DA8 * 117 K4
Pembroke Pl EDGW HA8 36 C6
ISLW TW7 123 K1
KENS W8 * 14 A4
Pembroke Rd BMLY BR1 168 B1
CEND/HSY/T N8 54 E3
EHAM E6 95 K4
ERITH DA8 117 K4
GDMY/SEVK IG3 61 F7
GFD/PVL UB6 84 B3
MTCM CR4 163 F1
MUSWH N10 40 A7
NTHWD HA6 32 A2
PLMGR N13 41 J2
RSLP HA4 46 C7
SEVS/STOTM N15 56 B4
SNWD SE25 165 F3
WALTH E17 57 K4
WBLY HA9 67 K2
Pembroke Sq KENS W8 14 A4
Pembroke St IS N1 5 K2
Pembroke Ter STJWD NW8 * 3 G4
Pembroke Vls KENS W8 14 A4
Pembroke Wk KENS W8 14 A5
Pembrook Ms BTSEA SW11 * 128 C3
Pembry Cl BRXN/ST SW9 110 B7
Pembury Av WPK KT4 160 D6
Pembury Cl CLPT E5 * 74 D4
HAYES BR2 167 J6
Pembury Ct HYS/HAR UB3 101 G5
Pembury Rd CLPT E5 74 D4
SNWD SE25 165 H3
TOTM N17 42 B7
Pemdevon Rd CROY/NA CR0 164 B6
Pemell Cl WCHPL E1 92 E3
Pemerich Cl HYS/HAR UB3 * 101 J4
Pempath Pl WBLY HA9 67 K1
Penally Pl IS N1 7 H3
Penang St WAP E1W 92 D7
Penard Rd NWDGN UB2 103 F2
Penarth St PECK SE15 111 K5
Penates ESH/CLAY KT10 170 D3
Penberth Rd CAT SE6 133 F7
Penbury Rd NWDGN UB2 102 E4
Pencombe Ms NTGHL W11 88 D6
Pencraig Wy PECK SE15 111 J5
Pendall Cl EBAR EN4 27 J3
Pendarves Rd RYNPK SW20 146 A7
Penda's Md HOM E9 75 G3
Pendell Av HYS/HAR UB3 101 J6
Pendennis Rd
STRHM/NOR SW16 148 E3
TOTM N17 55 K2
Penderel Rd HSLW TW3 123 F4
Penderry Ri CAT SE6 152 B1
Penderyn Wy HOLWY N7 72 D3
Pendlebury House
CHARL SE7 * 114 D6
Pendle Rd STRHM/NOR SW16 148 B5
Pendlestone Rd WALTH E17 57 K4
Pendlewood Cl EA W5 85 J4
Pendrell Rd NWCR SE14 132 B2
Pendrell St WOOL/PLUM SE18 115 J5
Pendula Dr YEAD UB4 83 H3
Pendulum Ms HACK E8 * 74 B4
Penerley Rd CAT SE6 132 E7
RAIN RM13 99 K4
Penfold Cl CROY/NA CR0 177 G2
Penfold La BXLY DA5 136 E7
Penfold Pl BAY/PAD W2 9 J2
Penfold Rd ED N9 31 F7
Penfold St STJWD NW8 9 H1
Penford Gdns ELTH/MOT SE9 134 C3
Penford St CMBW SE5 130 C1
Pengarth Rd BXLY DA5 136 E4
Penge La PGE/AN SE20 150 E6
Penge Rd PLSTW E13 77 G6
SNWD SE25 165 H2
Penhall Rd CHARL SE7 114 C3
Penhill Rd BXLY DA5 136 D6
Penifather La GFD/PVL UB6 84 D2
Peninsular Cl
EBED/NFELT TW14 121 G5
Penistone Rd
STRHM/NOR SW16 148 E6
Penketh Dr HRW HA1 66 D2
Penmon Rd ABYW SE2 116 B2
Pennack Rd PECK SE15 111 G5
Pennant Ms KENS W8 14 C5
Pennant Ter WALTH E17 57 H1
Pennard Rd SHB W12 107 F1
The Pennards SUN TW16 156 B2
Penn Cl GFD/PVL UB6 84 B1
KTN/HRWW/WS HA3 49 J3
Penner Cl WIM/MER SW19 146 C1
Penners Gdns SURB KT6 159 F6
Pennethorne Cl HOM E9 74 E7
Pennethorne Rd PECK SE15 111 J6
Penn Gdns CHST BR7 169 G1
Pennine Dr CRICK NW2 70 B1

Pennine La CRICK NW2 70 C1
Pennine Pde CRICK NW2 * 70 C1
Pennine Wy HYS/HAR UB3 101 G6
Pennington Dr WCHMH N21 28 E4
Pennington St WAP E1W 92 D6
Pennington Wy
LEE/GVPK SE12 153 F1
Penniston Cl TOTM N17 55 J1
Penniwell Cl EDGW HA8 36 B3
Penn La BXLY DA5 136 E5
Penn Rd HOLWY N7 72 E4
Penn St IS N1 7 H4
Penny Cl RAIN RM13 99 K2
Pennycroft CROY/NA CR0 179 G7
Pennyfields POP/IOD E14 93 J6
Pennymead Pl
ESH/CLAY KT10 170 A5
Penny Ms WAND/EARL SW18 127 K4
Pennymoor Wk MV/WKIL W9 88 D3
Penny Rd WLSDN NW10 86 D2
Pennyroyal Av EHAM E6 96 A5
Penpoll Rd HACK E8 74 D5
Penpool La WELL DA16 136 C2
Penrhyn Av WALTH E17 43 J7
Penrhyn Crs
MORT/ESHN SW14 125 K3
WALTH E17 43 J7
Penrhyn Gdns KUT/HW KT1 158 E3
Penrhyn Gv WALTH E17 43 J7
Penrhyn Rd KUT/HW KT1 159 F2
Penrith Cl BECK BR3 151 K7
PUT/ROE SW15 127 H4
Penrith Crs HCH RM12 81 J4
Penrith Pl WNWD SE27 149 H1
Penrith Rd NWMAL KT3 160 A3
SEVS/STOTM N15 55 K4
THHTH CR7 164 D1
Penrith St STRHM/NOR SW16 148 C5
Penrose Av OXHEY WD19 33 J1
Penrose Gv WALW SE17 18 E8
Penrose St WALW SE17 18 E8
Penryn St CAMTN NW1 5 G5
Penry St STHWK SE1 19 K6
Pensbury Pl VX/NE SW8 129 H1
Pensbury St VX/NE SW8 129 H1
Penscroft Gdns BORE WD6 25 F3
Pensford Av RCH/KEW TW9 125 H1
Penshurst Av BFN/LL DA15 136 B5
Penshurst Gdns EDGW HA8 36 D4
Penshurst Gn HAYES BR2 167 J4
Penshurst Rd HOM E9 75 F6
THHTH CR7 164 C4
TOTM N17 42 B6
Penshurst Wy BELMT SM2 174 E6
Pensilver Cl EBAR EN4 * 27 J3
Penstemon Cl FNCH N3 38 E5
Penta Ct BORE WD6 * 24 C3
Pentelow Gdns
EBED/NFELT TW14 121 K5
Pentire Rd WALTH E17 44 B7
Pentland Av EDGW HA8 36 D1
Pentland Cl ED N9 42 E1
GLDGN NW11 70 C1
Pentland Pl NTHLT UB5 65 J7
Pentland Rd BUSH WD23 22 C5
KIL/WHAMP NW6 2 A7
Pentlands Cl MTCM CR4 163 G2
Pentland St
WAND/EARL SW18 128 B5
Pentland Wy HGDN/ICK UB10 64 A2
Pentlow St PUT/ROE SW15 127 F1
Pentney Rd BAL SW12 129 H7
RYNPK SW20 146 C7
Penton Gv IS N1 6 A6
Penton Pl WALW SE17 18 D6
Penton Ri FSBYW WC1X 5 M7
Penton St IS N1 6 A5
Pentonville Rd IS N1 5 L6
Pentridge St PECK SE15 111 G6
Pentyre Av UED N18 41 K4
Penwerris Av ISLW TW7 103 H6
Penwith Rd
WAND/EARL SW18 147 F1
Penwortham Rd
STRHM/NOR SW16 148 B5
Penylan Pl EDGW HA8 * 36 C7
Penywern Rd ECT SW5 14 B7
Penzance Pl NTGHL W11 88 C7
Penzance St NTGHL W11 88 C7
Peony Gdns SHB W12 87 J6
Pepler Ms CMBW SE5 19 L8
Peploe Rd KIL/WHAMP NW6 88 B1
Pepper Cl EHAM E6 95 K4
Peppercorn Cl THHTH CR7 164 E1
Peppermead Sq LEW SE13 132 D4
Peppermint Cl CROY/NA CR0 163 K6
Peppermint Pl WAN E11 76 C2
Pepper St POP/IOD E14 112 E2
STHWK SE1 18 E1
Peppie Cl STNW/STAM N16 74 A1
Pepys Crs BAR EN5 26 A4
CAN/RD E16 94 E7
Pepys Est DEPT SE8 112 B3
Pepys Park Est DEPT SE8 112 C3
Pepys Rd NWCR SE14 132 A1
RYNPK SW20 161 F1
Pepys St TWRH EC3N 13 K6
Perceval Av HAMP NW3 71 J4
Percheron Rd BORE WD6 25 F5
Perch St HACK E8 74 B3
Percival Ct TOTM N17 42 B6
Percival Gdns CHDH RM6 61 J5
Percival Rd EN EN1 30 B3
FELT TW13 140 D1
MORT/ESHN SW14 125 K4
Percival St FSBYE EC1V 6 C9
Percival Wy HOR/WEW KT19 172 E3
Percy Bryant Rd SUN TW16 140 C6
Percy Bush Rd WDR/YW UB7 100 C2
Percy Gdns PEND EN3 31 F4
WPK KT4 160 A7
YEAD UB4 82 C2
Percy Ms FITZ W1T 11 G3
Percy Rd CAN/RD E16 94 C4
GDMY/SEVK IG3 61 G6
HPTN TW12 142 A6
ISLW TW7 124 B3
MTCM CR4 163 F6
NFNCH/WDSPK N12 39 G4
PGE/AN SE20 151 F7
ROMW/RG RM7 62 E2
SHB W12 106 D1
SNWD SE25 165 G4
WAN E11 58 C6
WATW WD18 21 F3
WCHMH N21 29 J6
WHTN TW2 123 G7
Percy St FITZ W1T 11 G3
Percy Ter BMLY BR1 169 G2
Percy Wy WHTN TW2 123 H7
Peregrine Cl WLSDN NW10 69 F4
Peregrine Ct WELL DA16 116 A7
Peregrine Gdns CROY/NA CR0 179 G1
Peregrine Rd TOTM N17 41 J6
Peregrine Wy
WIM/MER SW19 146 A6
Perham Rd WKENS W14 107 H4
Peridot St EHAM E6 95 J4
Perifield DUL SE21 130 D7
Perimeade Rd GFD/PVL UB6 85 J1
Periton Rd ELTH/MOT SE9 134 C3
Perivale Gdns WEA W13 85 H3
Perivale La GFD/PVL UB6 85 G2
Perivale Village
GFD/PVL UB6 * 85 J2
Periwood Crs GFD/PVL UB6 67 G7
Perkin Cl ALP/SUD HA0 67 H4
HSLW TW3 123 G3
Perkin's Rents WEST SW1P 17 G3
Perkins Rd BARK/HLT IG6 60 D4
Perkins Sq STHWK SE1 12 F8
Perks Cl BKHTH/KID SE3 133 H1
Perpins Rd ELTH/MOT SE9 135 K5
Perran Rd BRXS/STRHM SW2 149 H1
Perrers Rd HMSMTH W6 106 E2
Perrin Rd ALP/SUD HA0 67 G3
Perrin's Ct HAMP NW3 * 71 G3
Perrin's Wk HAMP NW3 71 G3
Perry Av ACT W3 87 F5
Perry Cl RAIN RM13 99 F1
Perry Ct SEVS/STOTM N15 * 56 A5
Perryfield Wy
CDALE/KGS NW9 51 H5
RCHPK/HAM TW10 143 H1
Perry Gdns ED N9 42 A2
Perry Garth NTHLT UB5 65 G7
Perry Gv DART DA1 139 K3
Perry Hl CAT SE6 151 H1
Perry How WPK KT4 160 C7
Perry Mnr CHST BR7 154 E5
Perrymans Farm Rd
GNTH/NBYPK IG2 60 D5
Perry Md BUSH WD23 22 C5
ENC/FH EN2 29 H1
Perrymead St FUL/PGN SW6 107 K7
Perryn Rd ACT W3 87 F6
BERM/RHTH SE16 111 J2
Perry Ri FSTH SE23 151 G2
Perry Rd DAGW RM9 98 B4
Perry St CHST BR7 154 E5
Perry V FSTH SE23 150 E1
Persant Rd CAT SE6 152 C2
Perseverance Pl
BRXN/ST SW9 110 B6
Pershore Cl GNTH/NBYPK IG2 60 B4
Pershore Gv CAR SM5 162 C5
Pert Cl MUSWH N10 40 B6
Perth Av CDALE/KGS NW9 51 F6
YEAD UB4 83 G3
Perth Cl NTHLT UB5 66 A5
NWMAL KT3 160 C1
Perth Rd BARK IG11 96 D1
BECK BR3 167 F1
FSBYPK N4 55 G7
GNTH/NBYPK IG2 60 B5
LEY E10 57 G7
PLSTW E13 95 F1
WDGN N22 41 H7
Perth Ter GNTH/NBYPK IG2 60 C6
Perwell Av RYLN/HDSTN HA2 47 K7
Petavel Rd TEDD TW11 142 E5
Peter Av WLSDN NW10 69 K6
Peterboat Cl GNWCH SE10 113 H3
Peterborough Ms
FUL/PGN SW6 127 K1
Peterborough Rd CAR SM5 162 D5
FUL/PGN SW6 127 K1
HRW HA1 48 E7
LEY E10 58 A4
Peterborough Vls
FUL/PGN SW6 108 A7
Petergate BTSEA SW11 128 B3
Peters Cl BCTR RM8 61 K7
STAN HA7 35 K5
WELL DA16 135 K1
Petersfield Cl UED N18 41 J4
Petersfield Ri PUT/ROE SW15 126 E7
Petersfield Rd ACT W3 105 K1
Petersham Cl
RCHPK/HAM TW10 143 K1
SUT SM1 174 D4
Petersham La SKENS SW7 14 E3
Petersham Ms SKENS SW7 14 E4
Petersham Pl SKENS SW7 14 E4
Petersham Rd
RCHPK/HAM TW10 143 K2
Petersham Ter
CROY/NA CR0 * 176 E2
Peter's Hl BLKFR EC4V 12 E6
Peterstone Rd ABYW SE2 116 C1
Peterstow Cl WIM/MER SW19 146 C1
Peter St SOHO/CST W1F 11 G6
Peterwood Wy CROY/NA CR0 177 F1
Petherton Rd HBRY N5 73 J4
Petiver Cl HOM E9 * 74 E6
Petley Rd HMSMTH W6 107 F5
Peto Pl CAMTN NW1 4 D9
Peto St North CAN/RD E16 94 D5
Petrie Cl CRICK NW2 * 70 C5
Petros Gdns
KIL/WHAMP NW6 * 71 F4
Petro St South CAN/RD E16 94 D6
Pettacre Cl THMD SE28 115 H2
Pett Cl EMPK RM11 81 K1
Petticoat La WCHPL E1 13 K3
Petticoat Sq WCHPL E1 13 L4
Petticoat Tower WCHPL E1 * 13 L4
Pettits Bvd ROM RM1 63 G1
Pettits Cl ROM RM1 63 G1
Pettits La ROM RM1 63 G1
Pettit's Pl DAGE RM10 80 C4
Pettit's Rd DAGE RM10 80 C4
Pettiward Cl PUT/ROE SW15 127 F3
Pettley Gdns ROMW/RG RM7 63 F4
Pettman Crs THMD SE28 115 J2
Pettsgrove Av ALP/SUD HA0 67 J4
Pett's Hl NTHLT UB5 66 B4
Pett St WOOL/PLUM SE18 114 D3
Petts Wood Rd
STMC/STPC BR5 169 J4
Petty France WESTW SW1E 16 F3
Petty Wales MON EC3R 13 K7
Petworth Cl NTHLT UB5 65 K6
Petworth Gdns
HGDN/ICK UB10 64 A7
RYNPK SW20 160 E2
Petworth Rd
NFNCH/WDSPK N12 39 J4
Petworth St BTSEA SW11 108 D7
Petworth Wy HCH RM12 81 H3
Petyt Pl CHEL SW3 * 108 D5
Petyward CHEL SW3 15 K6
Pevensey Av EN EN1 30 A1
FBAR/BDGN N11 40 D4
Pevensey Cl ISLW TW7 103 H6
Pevensey Rd FELT TW13 122 D7
FSTGT E7 76 E3
TOOT SW17 147 H3
Peverel EHAM E6 96 A5
Peveret Cl FBAR/BDGN N11 * 40 B4
Peveril Dr TEDD TW11 142 D4
Pewsey Cl CHING E4 43 J4
Peyton Pl GNWCH SE10 113 F6
Pharaoh Cl MTCM CR4 162 E6
Pheasant Cl CAN/RD E16 95 F5
Phelp St WALW SE17 19 G8
Phelps Wy HYS/HAR UB3 101 J3
Phene St CHEL SW3 15 K9
Philbeach Gdns ECT SW5 14 A7
Philchurch Pl WCHPL E1 92 C5
Philimore Cl
WOOL/PLUM SE18 115 K4
Philip Av ROMW/RG RM7 63 F7
Philip Gdns CROY/NA CR0 179 H1
Philip La SEVS/STOTM N15 55 K3
Philippa Gdns ELTH/MOT SE9 134 C4
Philip Rd RAIN RM13 99 G2
Philips Cl CAR SM5 163 F7
Philip St PLSTW E13 94 E3
Philip Wk PECK SE15 131 H2
Phillimore Gdns KENS W8 14 A2
WLSDN NW10 70 A7
Phillimore Gardens Cl
KENS W8 * 14 A3
Phillimore Pl KENS W8 14 A2
Phillimore Wk KENS W8 14 A3
Phillipp St IS N1 7 K4
Philpot La FENCHST EC3M 13 J6
Philpot St WCHPL E1 * 92 D5
Phineas Pett Rd
ELTH/MOT SE9 134 D2
Phipp's Bridge Rd
WIM/MER SW19 162 B1
Phipp's Ms BGVA SW1W 16 C4
Phipp St SDTCH EC2A 7 J9
Phoebeth Rd LEW SE13 132 D4
Phoenix Cl HACK E8 * 7 L3
NTHWD HA6 32 D3
WALTH E17 57 H1
WWKM BR4 180 B1
Phoenix Ct BTFD TW8 105 F4
POP/IOD E14 112 D3
Phoenix Dr HAYES BR2 181 H2
Phoenix Pk BTFD TW8 * 104 E4
Phoenix Pl FSBYW WC1X 5 M9
Phoenix Rd CAMTN NW1 5 G7
PGE/AN SE20 150 E5
Phoenix St LSQ/SEVD WC2H 11 H5
Phoenix Wy HEST TW5 102 C5
Phoenix Wharf Rd
STHWK SE1 19 M2
Phyllis Av NWMAL KT3 160 E4
Picardy Manorway
BELV DA17 117 J1
Picardy Rd BELV DA17 117 H4
Picardy St BELV DA17 117 H2
Piccadilly MYFR/PICC W1J 10 E8
Piccadilly Ar STJS SW1Y 10 E8
Piccadilly Circ REGST W1B 10 F7
Pickard Cl STHGT/OAK N14 28 D7
Pickard St FSBYE EC1V 6 D7
Pickering Av EHAM E6 96 A1
Pickering Gdns CROY/NA CR0 165 G5
FBAR/BDGN N11 40 A5
Pickering Ms BAY/PAD W2 8 D4
Pickering Pl WHALL SW1A * 10 F9
Pickering St IS N1 6 D3
Pickets Cl BUSH WD23 22 D7
Pickets St BAL SW12 129 F6
Pickett Cft STAN HA7 35 K7
Pickett's Lock La ED N9 42 E1
Pickfords Whf IS N1 * 6 E6
Pickhurst Gn HAYES BR2 167 J6
Pickhurst La WWKM BR4 167 H5
Pickhurst Md HAYES BR2 167 J6
Pickhurst Pk HAYES BR2 167 H4
Pickhurst Ri WWKM BR4 167 G7
Pickwick Cl HSLWW TW4 122 D4
Pickwick Ms UED N18 42 A4
Pickwick Pl HRW HA1 48 E6
Pickwick Rd DUL SE21 130 E6
Pickwick St STHWK SE1 18 E2
Pickwick Wy CHST BR7 154 C5
Pickworth Cl VX/NE SW8 * 109 K6
Picton Pl MHST W1U 10 B5
SURB KT6 159 H7
Picton St CMBW SE5 110 E6
Pied Bull Yd IS N1 6 C4
Piedmont Rd
WOOL/PLUM SE18 115 J4
Pier Head WAP E1W * 92 D7
Piermont Pl BMLY BR1 168 C1
Piermont Rd EDUL SE22 131 J4
Pierrepoint Ar IS N1 * 6 C5
Pierrepoint Rd ACT W3 86 D6
Pierrepoint Rw IS N1 6 C5
Pier Rd CAN/RD E16 114 E1
EBED/NFELT TW14 122 A4
ERITH DA8 118 B5
Pier St POP/IOD E14 113 F3
Pier Ter WAND/EARL SW18 128 A3
Pier Wy THMD SE28 115 J2
Pigeon La HPTN TW12 142 A3
Pigott St POP/IOD E14 93 J5
Pike Cl BMLY BR1 153 F4
Pike Rd MLHL NW7 37 F3
Pike's End PIN HA5 47 F3
Pikestone Cl YEAD UB4 * 83 J3
Pilgrimage St STHWK SE1 19 G2
Pilgrim Cl MRDN SM4 162 A6
Pilgrim Hl WNWD SE27 149 J3
Pilgrims Cl NTHLT UB5 66 C4
PLMGR N13 41 F3
Pilgrim's La HAMP NW3 71 H3
Pilgrims Ms POP/IOD E14 94 B6
Pilgrim's Ri EBAR EN4 27 J4
Pilgrim St BLKFR EC4V * 12 C5
Pilgrims Wy ARCH N19 54 D7
WBLY HA9 50 D7
Pilgrim's Wy SAND/SEL CR2 178 B5
Pilkington Rd PECK SE15 131 J1
Pilot Cl DEPT SE8 112 C5
Pilsden Cl WIM/MER SW19 * 127 G7
Piltdown Rd OXHEY WD19 33 H3
Pilton Pl WALW SE17 18 F7
Pimlico Rd BGVA SW1W 16 A7
Pinchin & Johnsons Yd
WCHPL E1 * 92 C6
Pinchin St WCHPL E1 92 C6
Pincott Pl BROCKY SE4 132 A2
Pincott Rd WIM/MER SW19 147 G6
Pindar St SDTCH EC2A 13 J2
Pindock Ms MV/WKIL W9 8 D1
Pine Apple Ct WESTW SW1E * 16 E3
Pine Av SRTFD E15 76 B4
WWKM BR4 166 E7
Pine Cl LEY E10 75 J1
PGE/AN SE20 150 E7
STAN HA7 35 H3
STHGT/OAK N14 28 C6
Pine Coombe CROY/NA CR0 179 F3
Pinecroft
KTN/HRWW/WS HA3 50 B4
WOOL/PLUM SE18 116 B6
Pinecroft Crs BAR EN5 26 C3
Pinefield Cl POP/IOD E14 * 93 J6
Pine Gdns BRYLDS KT5 159 H5
RSLP HA4 47 F7
Pine Gld ORP BR6 181 K3
Pine Gv BUSH WD23 21 J1
FSBYPK N4 72 E1
TRDG/WHET N20 26 D7
WIM/MER SW19 146 D4
Pinelands Cl BKHTH/KID SE3 * 113 J6
Pinelees Ct
MORT/ESHN SW14 * 125 K3
Pinemartin Cl CRICK NW2 70 A2
Pine Rdg CAR SM5 176 A7
Pine Rd CRICK NW2 70 A3
FBAR/BDGN N11 40 A1
Pines Cl NTHWD HA6 32 C5
Pines Rd BMLY BR1 168 D1
The Pines BORE WD6 24 B1
NRWD SE19 * 149 H5
STHGT/OAK N14 28 C4
WFD IG8 44 D2
Pine St CLKNW EC1R 6 A9
Pine Tree Cl HEST TW5 102 A7
Pine Tree Wy LEW SE13 132 E2
Pine Wk BRYLDS KT5 159 H5
Pine Wd SUN TW16 140 E7
Pinewood Av BFN/LL DA15 135 K7
PIN HA5 34 B5
RAIN RM13 99 K3
Pinewood Cl CROY/NA CR0 179 G2
NTHWD HA6 32 E4
ORP BR6 169 J7
PIN HA5 34 B5
Pinewood Gv WEA W13 85 J5
Pinewood Ldg BUSH WD23 * 22 D7
Pinewood Ms
STWL/WRAY TW19 120 A5
Pinewood Rd ABYW SE2 116 E5
FELT TW13 141 F2
Pinfold Rd BUSH WD23 21 K1
STRHM/NOR SW16 148 E3
Pinglestone Cl WDR/YW UB7 100 B6
Pinkcoat Cl FELT TW13 141 F2
Pinkwell Av HYS/HAR UB3 101 G3
Pinkwell La HYS/HAR UB3 101 G3
Pinley Gdns DAGW RM9 79 H7
Pinnell Rd ELTH/MOT SE9 134 C3
Pinner Ct PIN HA5 48 A3
Pinner Gn PIN HA5 47 G1
Pinner Gv PIN HA5 47 J3
Pinner Hl PIN HA5 33 F6
Pinner Hill Rd PIN HA5 33 G7
Pinner Park Av
RYLN/HDSTN HA2 48 C1
Pinner Park Gdns
RYLN/HDSTN HA2 48 C1
Pinner Rd HRW HA1 48 B4
NTHWD HA6 32 D7
OXHEY WD19 21 H5
PIN HA5 47 K3
Pinner Vw HRW HA1 48 C4
Pinn Wy RSLP HA4 46 B6
Pintail Cl EHAM E6 95 J4
Pintail Rd WFD IG8 45 F6
Pintail Wy YEAD UB4 83 H4
Pinto Cl BORE WD6 * 25 F5
Pinto Wy BKHTH/KID SE3 134 A3
Pioneer Cl BOW E3 93 K4
SHB W12 87 K5
Pioneer St PECK SE15 111 H7
Pioneer Wy SHB W12 88 A5
WATW WD18 20 D5
Piper Cl HOLWY N7 73 F5
Piper Rd KUT/HW KT1 159 H2
Pipers Gdns CROY/NA CR0 166 B6
Pipers Gn CDALE/KGS NW9 50 E4
Pipers Green La STAN HA7 36 A2
Piper Wy IL IG1 60 D7
Pipewell Rd CAR SM5 162 D5
Pippin Cl CRICK NW2 69 J2
CROY/NA CR0 166 C7
Pippins Cl WDR/YW UB7 100 A2
Piquet Rd PGE/AN SE20 165 K1
Pirbright Crs CROY/NA CR0 180 A5
Pirbright Rd
WAND/EARL SW18 127 J7
Pirie St CAN/RD E16 95 F7
Pitcairn Cl ROMW/RG RM7 62 C3
Pitcairn Rd MTCM CR4 147 K6
Pitchford St SRTFD E15 76 B6
Pitfield Crs THMD SE28 97 G7
Pitfield St IS N1 7 J7
Pitfield Wy WLSDN NW10 68 E5
Pitlake CROY/NA CR0 177 H1
Pitman St CMBW SE5 110 D6
Pitsea Pl WCHPL E1 93 F5
Pitsea St WCHPL E1 93 F5
Pitshanger La EA W5 85 H3
Pitt Crs WIM/MER SW19 147 F3
Pittman Gdns IL IG1 78 C4
Pitt Rd RYLN/HDSTN HA2 66 C1
THHTH CR7 164 D4
Pitts Head Ms
MYFR/PICC W1J 10 B9
Pitt St KENS W8 14 B1
Pittville Gdns SNWD SE25 165 H2
Pixley St POP/IOD E14 93 H5
Pixton Wy CROY/NA CR0 179 G7
Place Farm Av ORP BR6 169 J7
Plaistow Gv BMLY BR1 153 F6
SRTFD E15 76 D7
Plaistow La BMLY BR1 153 G7
Plaistow Park Rd PLSTW E13 95 F1
Plaistow Rd SRTFD E15 76 D7
Plane St SYD SE26 150 D2
Plane Tree Crs FELT TW13 141 F2
Plantagenet Cl WPK KT4 173 F3
Plantagenet Gdns CHDH RM6 61 K6
Plantagenet Pl CHDH RM6 61 K6
Plantagenet Rd BAR EN5 27 G3
Plantain Gdns WAN E11 * 76 B2
Plantain Pl STHWK SE1 19 G1
Plantation La FENCHST EC3M 13 J6
Plantation Rd ERITH DA8 118 D7
Plashet Gv EHAM E6 77 G7
Plashet Rd PLSTW E13 76 E7
Plassy Rd CAT SE6 132 E6
Platina St SDTCH EC2A 7 H9
Plato Rd BRXS/STRHM SW2 129 K3
Platt's La HAMP NW3 70 E2
Platt St CAMTN NW1 5 G5
Plawsfield Rd BECK BR3 151 F7
Plaxtol Cl BMLY BR1 153 G7
Playfair St HMSMTH W6 * 107 F4
Playfield Crs EDUL SE22 131 F4
Playfield Rd EDGW HA8 50 E1
Playford Rd FSBYPK N4 73 F1
Playgreen Wy CAT SE6 151 J3
Playground Cl BECK BR3 166 A1
Playhouse Ct STHWK SE1 18 E1
Playhouse Yd BLKFR EC4V 12 C5
Plaza Pde ALP/SUD HA0 * 68 A5
Plaza Wk CDALE/KGS NW9 50 E2
Pleasance Rd PUT/ROE SW15 126 E4
The Pleasance PUT/ROE SW15 126 E3
Pleasant Gv CROY/NA CR0 179 H2
Pleasant Pl IS N1 6 D2
Pleasant Wy ALP/SUD HA0 85 J1
Plender St CAMTN NW1 4 E4
Pleshey Rd ARCH N19 72 D3
Plesman Wy WLGTN SM6 * 176 E7
Plevna Crs SEVS/STOTM N15 56 A5
Plevna Rd ED N9 42 C2
HPTN TW12 142 B7
Plevna St POP/IOD E14 113 F2
Pleydell Av HMSMTH W6 106 C2
NRWD SE19 150 B6
Pleydell Est FSBYE EC1V * 6 F8
Pleydell Gdns NRWD SE19 * 150 B5
Pleydell St EMB EC4Y 12 B5
Plimsoll Cl POP/IOD E14 93 K5
Plimsoll Rd FSBYPK N4 73 H2
Plough Farm Cl RSLP HA4 46 B5
Plough La EDUL SE22 131 G5
PUR/KEN CR8 176 E7
TEDD TW11 143 G4
WIM/MER SW19 147 F4
WLGTN SM6 176 E4
Plough Lane Cl WLGTN SM6 176 E4
Ploughmans Cl CAMTN NW1 5 G3
Ploughmans End ISLW TW7 123 J4
Plough Pl FLST/FETLN EC4A 12 B4
Plough Rd BTSEA SW11 128 C2
HOR/WEW KT19 173 F6
Plough St WCHPL E1 * 92 C5
Plough Ter BTSEA SW11 128 C3
Plough Wy BERM/RHTH SE16 112 A3
Plough Yd SDTCH EC2A 13 K1
Plover Wy BERM/RHTH SE16 112 B2
YEAD UB4 83 H5
Plowden Blds EMB EC4Y * 12 A6
Plowman Cl UED N18 41 K4
Plowman Wy BCTR RM8 61 J7
Plumbers Rw WCHPL E1 92 C4
Plumbridge St GNWCH SE10 * 113 F7
Plum Cl FELT TW13 121 K7
Plum Garth BTFD TW8 104 E3
Plum La WOOL/PLUM SE18 115 G6
Plummer La MTCM CR4 147 K7
Plummer Rd CLAP SW4 129 J6
Plumpton Wy CAR SM5 175 J2
Plumstead Common Rd
WOOL/PLUM SE18 115 H5
Plumstead High St
WOOL/PLUM SE18 115 J3
Plumstead Rd
WOOL/PLUM SE18 115 H3
Plumtree Cl DAGE RM10 80 D5
WLGTN SM6 176 D6
Plumtree Ct FLST/FETLN EC4A 12 B4
Plymouth Rd BMLY BR1 153 F7
CAN/RD E16 94 E4
Plymouth Whf POP/IOD E14 113 G3
Plympton Av
KIL/WHAMP NW6 70 D6
Plympton Cl BELV DA17 117 F2
Plympton Pl STJWD NW8 * 9 J1
Plympton Rd
KIL/WHAMP NW6 70 D6
Plympton St STJWD NW8 9 J1
Plymstock Rd WELL DA16 116 D6
Pocklington Cl
CDALE/KGS NW9 51 G1
Pocock Av WDR/YW UB7 100 C2
Pocock St STHWK SE1 18 C1
Podmore Rd
WAND/EARL SW18 128 B3
Poets Ms HNHL SE24 130 C4
Poet's Rd HBRY N5 73 K4
Poets Wy HRW HA1 48 E3
Pointalls Cl FNCH N3 53 G1
Point Cl GNWCH SE10 113 F7
Pointer Cl THMD SE28 97 K5
Pointers Cl POP/IOD E14 112 E4
Point Hl GNWCH SE10 113 F7
Point Pl WBLY HA9 68 D6
Point Pleasant
WAND/EARL SW18 127 K3
Point Wharf La BTFD TW8 104 E6
Poland St SOHO/SHAV W1D 10 F4
Polebrook Rd BKHTH/KID SE3 134 B2
Polecroft La CAT SE6 151 H1
Polesden Gdns RYNPK SW20 160 E2
Polesworth Rd DAGW RM9 98 B1
Polish War Memorial Rbt
RSLP HA4 65 G5
Pollard Cl CAN/RD E16 94 E6
HOLWY N7 73 F3
Pollard Rd MRDN SM4 162 C4
TRDG/WHET N20 39 J1
Pollard Rw BETH E2 92 C2
Pollards Crs
STRHM/NOR SW16 163 K2
Pollards Hl East
STRHM/NOR SW16 164 A2
Pollards Hl North
STRHM/NOR SW16 164 A2
Pollards Hl South
STRHM/NOR SW16 163 K2
Pollards Hl West
STRHM/NOR SW16 163 K2
Pollard St BETH E2 * 92 C2
Pollards Wood Rd
STRHM/NOR SW16 163 K1
Pollen St CONDST W1S 10 D5
Pollitt Dr STJWD NW8 3 G9
Polperro Ms LBTH SE11 18 B5
Polsted Rd CAT SE6 132 C6
Polthorne Gv
WOOL/PLUM SE18 115 H3
Polworth Rd
STRHM/NOR SW16 148 E4
Polygon Rd CAMTN NW1 5 G6
The Polygon CLAP SW4 * 129 H3
Polytechnic St
WOOL/PLUM SE18 115 F3
Pomell Wy WCHPL E1 13 M4
Pomeroy Cl TWK TW1 124 C3
Pomeroy St NWCR SE14 111 K6
Pomfret Rd CMBW SE5 130 C2
Pomoja La ARCH N19 72 E1
Pond Cl NFNCH/WDSPK N12 39 J5
Pond Cottage La BECK BR3 166 D7
Pond Cots DUL SE21 131 F7
Ponder St HOLWY N7 * 5 L1
Pond Farm Est CLPT E5 * 74 E2
Pondfield Rd DAGE RM10 80 D4
HAYES BR2 167 H7
Pond Gn RSLP HA4 64 C1
Pond Hill Gdns CHEAM SM3 * 174 C5

Pond Lees Cl DAGE RM10 81 F6
Pond Md DUL SE21 130 E5
Pond Pl CHEL SW3 15 J6
Pond Rd SRTFD E15 94 C1
Pondside Av WPK KT4 161 F7
Pondside Cl HYS/HAR UB3 101 G6
Pond St HAMP NW3 71 J4
Pond Wy TEDD TW11 143 J5
Pondwood Ri ORP BR6 169 K6
Ponler St WCHPL E1 92 D5
Ponsard Rd WLSDN NW10 87 K2
Ponsford St HOM E9 74 E5
Ponsonby Pl WEST SW1P 17 H7
Ponsonby Rd PUT/ROE SW15 126 E6
Ponsonby Ter WEST SW1P 17 H7
Pontefract Rd BMLY BR1 152 E4
Ponton Rd VX/NE SW8 109 J6
Pont St KTBR SW1X 15 L4
Pont Street Ms KTBR SW1X 15 L4
Pool Cl BECK BR3 151 J4
E/WMO/HCT KT8 156 E4
Pool Ct CAT SE6 151 J1
Poole Cl RSLP HA4 64 C1
Poole Court Rd HSLWW TW4 122 D1
Poole Rd HOM E9 75 F5
HOR/WEW KT19 173 F5
Pooles Blds FSBYW WC1X 12 A1
Pooles La WBPTN SW10 108 B6
Pooles Pk FSBYPK N4 73 G1
Poole St IS N1 7 G4
Poole Wy YEAD UB4 * 82 C2
Pooley Dr MORT/ESHN SW14 125 K2
Poolmans St
BERM/RHTH SE16 112 A1
Pool Rd E/WMO/HCT KT8 156 E4
HRW HA1 48 D6
Poolsford Rd CDALE/KGS NW9 51 G3
Poonah St WCHPL E1 92 E5
Pope Cl EBED/NFELT TW14 121 J7
WIM/MER SW19 * 147 H5
Pope Rd HAYES BR2 168 C4
Pope's Av WHTN TW2 142 E1
Popes Dr FNCH N3 38 E7
Popes Gv CROY/NA CR0 179 H2
Pope's Gv WHTN TW2 142 E1
Pope's La EA W5 104 E2
Pope's Rd BRXN/ST SW9 * 130 B3
Pope St STHWK SE1 19 K2
Popham Cl FELT TW13 141 J2
Popham Gdns
RCH/KEW TW9 * 125 J2
Popham Rd IS N1 6 E3
Popham St IS N1 6 D3
Popinjays Rw CHEAM SM3 * 174 B4
Poplar Av MTCM CR4 147 K7
NWDGN UB2 103 G2
Poplar Bath St POP/IOD E14 93 K6
Poplar Cl HOM E9 75 H4
PIN HA5 33 H7
Poplar Court Pde TWK TW1 * 124 D5
Poplar Crs HOR/WEW KT19 172 E5
Poplar Farm Cl
HOR/WEW KT19 172 E5
Poplar Gdns NWMAL KT3 160 A1
Poplar Gv FBAR/BDGN N11 40 A5
HMSMTH W6 107 F1
NWMAL KT3 160 A2
WBLY HA9 68 E2
Poplar High St POP/IOD E14 93 K6
Poplar La BECK BR3 166 E4
Poplar Ms SHB W12 88 A7
Poplar Mt BELV DA17 117 J3
Poplar Pl BAY/PAD W2 8 C6
HYS/HAR UB3 82 E6
THMD SE28 97 J6
Poplar Rd ASHF TW15 140 A4
CHEAM SM3 161 J7
HNHL SE24 130 D3
WIM/MER SW19 161 K1
Poplar Rd South
WIM/MER SW19 161 K2
Poplars Cl RSLP HA4 46 C7
Poplars Rd WALTH E17 57 K5
The Poplars STHGT/OAK N14 28 B4
Poplar St ROMW/RG RM7 62 E3
Poplar Vw WBLY HA9 * 67 K1
Poplar Wk CROY/NA CR0 177 J1
HNHL SE24 130 D3
Poplar Wy BARK/HLT IG6 60 C3
FELT TW13 140 E2
Poppins Ct FLST/FETLN EC4A 12 C5
Poppleton Rd WAN E11 58 C5
Poppy Cl BELV DA17 117 J2
NTHLT UB5 65 K5
WLGTN SM6 163 F7
Poppy La CROY/NA CR0 165 K6
Porchester Garden Ms
BAY/PAD W2 8 D5
Porchester Gdns BAY/PAD W2 8 D6
Porchester Ga BAY/PAD W2 * 8 E7
Porchester Md BECK BR3 151 K5
Porchester Pl BAY/PAD W2 9 K5
Porchester Rd BAY/PAD W2 8 D4
KUT/HW KT1 159 J1
Porchester Sq BAY/PAD W2 8 D4
Porchester Square Ms
BAY/PAD W2 8 D4
Porchester Ter BAY/PAD W2 8 E5
Porchester Ter North
BAY/PAD W2 8 D4
Porch Wy TRDG/WHET N20 39 K2
Porcupine Cl ELTH/MOT SE9 153 J1
Porden Rd BRXS/STRHM SW2 130 A3
Porlock Av RYLN/HDSTN HA2 48 C7
Porlock Rd EN EN1 30 B6
Porlock St STHWK SE1 19 H1
Porrington Cl CHST BR7 153 K7
Portal Cl RSLP HA4 64 E3
WNWD SE27 149 G2
Portal Wy ACT W3 87 F4
Portbury Cl PECK SE15 111 H7
Portchester Cl HNHL SE24 130 D3
Portchester Ga BAY/PAD W2 8 E7
Portcullis Lodge Rd EN EN1 29 K2
Portelet Rd WCHPL E1 93 F2
Porten Houses WKENS W14 * 107 H2
Porten Rd WKENS W14 107 H2
Porter Rd EHAM E6 95 K5
Porters Av DAGW RM9 79 H5
Porter Sq ARCH N19 54 E7
Porter St MHST W1U 9 M2
STHWK SE1 12 F8
Porters Wk WAP E1W * 92 D6
Porters Wy WDR/YW UB7 100 C2
Porteus Rd BAY/PAD W2 8 F3
Portgate Cl MV/WKIL W9 88 D3
Porthcawe Rd SYD SE26 151 G3
Porthkerry Av WELL DA16 136 B3
Portia Wy BOW E3 93 H3
The Porticos CHEL SW3 * 108 C5
Portinscale Rd
PUT/ROE SW15 127 H4
Portland Av BFN/LL DA15 136 B5
NWMAL KT3 160 C6
STNW/STAM N16 56 B7
Portland Cl CHDH RM6 62 A4
WPK KT4 160 E6
Portland Cots CROY/NA CR0 * 163 J6
Portland Crs ELTH/MOT SE9 153 J1
FELT TW13 140 B3
GFD/PVL UB6 84 B3
STAN HA7 49 K1
Portland Crs West STAN HA7 49 K2
Portland Gdns CHDH RM6 61 K4
FSBYPK N4 55 H5
Portland Gv VX/NE SW8 110 A7
Portland Ms SOHO/CST W1F 10 F5
Portland Pl REGST W1B 10 C1
SNWD SE25 165 H3
Portland Ri FSBYPK N4 55 H7
Portland Rd BMLY BR1 153 G3
ELTH/MOT SE9 153 J1
KUT/HW KT1 159 F2
MTCM CR4 162 D1
NTGHL W11 88 C6
NWDGN UB2 102 E2
SEVS/STOTM N15 56 A3
SNWD SE25 165 H3
YEAD UB4 82 C2
Portland Sq WAP E1W 92 D7
Portland St WALW SE17 19 G8
Portland Ter RCH/KEW TW9 * 124 E3
Portman Av
MORT/ESHN SW14 126 A2
Portman Cl BXLYHS DA6 136 E2
MBLAR W1H 10 A4
Portman Dr WFD IG8 59 H1
Portman Gdns
CDALE/KGS NW9 51 F2
Portman Ga CAMTN NW1 9 K1
Portman Ms South
MBLAR W1H 10 A5
Portman Pl BETH E2 92 E2
Portman Rd KUT/HW KT1 159 G1
Portman Sq MBLAR W1H 9 M4
Portman St MBLAR W1H 10 A5
Portmeadow Wk ABYW SE2 116 E1
Portmeers Cl WALTH E17 * 57 H5
Portnall Rd MV/WKIL W9 88 D2
Portnoi Cl ROM RM1 63 F1
Portobello Ct NTGHL W11 * 88 D6
Portobello Ms NTGHL W11 * 8 A7
Portobello Rd NKENS W10 88 C4
Portpool La FSBYW WC1X 12 A2
Portree St POP/IOD E14 94 B5
Portsdown Av GLDGN NW11 52 D5
Portsdown Ms GLDGN NW11 52 D5
Portsea Ms BAY/PAD W2 9 K5
Portsea Pl BAY/PAD W2 9 K5
Portslade Rd VX/NE SW8 129 H1
Portsmouth Av THDIT KT7 158 B6
Portsmouth Ms CAN/RD E16 95 F6
Portsmouth Rd
ESH/CLAY KT10 170 A5
KUT/HW KT1 158 E2
PUT/ROE SW15 126 E6
THDIT KT7 158 C6
Portsmouth St LINN WC2A 11 L4
Portsoken St TWRH EC3N 13 L6
Portugal Gdns WHTN TW2 * 142 C1
Portugal St LINN WC2A 11 M5
Portway RAIN RM13 81 J7
SRTFD E15 76 E7
Portway Crs EW KT17 173 J7
Portway Gdns
WOOL/PLUM SE18 114 C7
Postern Gn ENC/FH EN2 29 G1
The Postern BARB EC2Y * 12 F3
Post La WHTN TW2 123 J7
Postmill Cl CROY/NA CR0 178 E2
Post Office Ap FSTGT E7 77 F4
Post Office Wy VX/NE SW8 109 J6
Post Rd NWDGN UB2 103 G2
Postway Ms IL IG1 78 B2
Potier St STHWK SE1 19 H4
Potter Cl MTCM CR4 * 163 G1
The Potteries BAR EN5 * 26 E4
Potterne Cl WIM/MER SW19 127 G6
Potters Cl CROY/NA CR0 166 B7
PECK SE15 * 111 F6
Potters Fld EN EN1 * 30 A3
Potters Flds STHWK SE1 13 K9
Potters Gv NWMAL KT3 159 K3
Potters Heights Cl PIN HA5 33 F6
Potter's La BAR EN5 26 E3
STRHM/NOR SW16 * 148 D5
Potters Ms BORE WD6 23 K5
Potters Rd FUL/PGN SW6 128 B1
Potter's Rd BAR EN5 27 F3
Potter St NTHWD HA6 32 E7
Potter Street Hl PIN HA5 33 F5
Pottery La NTGHL W11 88 C7
Pottery Rd BTFD TW8 105 F5
Pottery St BERM/RHTH SE16 * 111 J1
Pott St BETH E2 92 D2
Poulett Gdns TWK TW1 143 F1
Poulett Rd EHAM E6 95 K1
Poulter Pk MRDN SM4 * 162 D5
Poulters Wd HAYES BR2 181 H4
Poulton Av SUT SM1 175 H2
Poultry LOTH EC2R 13 G5
Pound Cl SURB KT6 158 D7
Pound Farm Cl
ESH/CLAY KT10 157 J7
Pound La WLSDN NW10 69 J5
Pound Park Rd CHARL SE7 114 C3
Pound Pl ELTH/MOT SE9 135 F5
Pound St CAR SM5 175 K4
Pountney Rd BTSEA SW11 129 F2
Powder Mill La WHTN TW2 122 E7
Powell Cl EDGW HA8 36 B5
Powell Gdns DAGE RM10 80 C3
Powell Rd CLPT E5 74 D2
Power Rd CHSWK W4 105 H3
Powers Ct TWK TW1 124 E6
Powerscroft Rd CLPT E5 74 E3
SCUP DA14 155 J5
Powis Ct BUSH WD23 * 22 D7
Powis Gdns GLDGN NW11 52 D6
NTGHL W11 88 D5
Powis Ms NTGHL W11 88 D5
Powis Pl BMSBY WC1N 11 K1
Powis Rd BOW E3 93 K2
Powis Sq NTGHL W11 88 D5
Powis St WOOL/PLUM SE18 115 F2
Powis Ter NTGHL W11 88 D5
Powlett Pl CAMTN NW1 4 B1
Pownall Gdns HSLW TW3 123 G3
Pownall Rd HACK E8 74 C7
HSLW TW3 123 G3
Pownsett Ter IL IG1 * 78 C4
Powster Rd BMLY BR1 153 F4
Powys Cl BXLYHN DA7 116 E5
Powys Ct BORE WD6 25 F2
Powys La PLMGR N13 40 E3
Poynders Rd CLAP SW4 129 H6
Poynings Rd ARCH N19 72 C2
Poynings Wy
NFNCH/WDSPK N12 38 E4
Poyntell Crs CHST BR7 154 D7
Poynter Rd EN EN1 30 B4
Poynton Rd TOTM N17 56 C1
Poyntz Rd BTSEA SW11 128 E1
Poyser St BETH E2 92 D1
Praed Ms BAY/PAD W2 9 H4
Praed St BAY/PAD W2 9 H4
Pragel St PLSTW E13 95 F1
Pragnell Rd LEE/GVPK SE12 153 F1
Prague Pl BRXS/STRHM SW2 129 K4
Prah Rd FSBYPK N4 73 G1
Prairie St VX/NE SW8 129 F1
Pratt Ms CAMTN NW1 4 E4
Pratt St CAMTN NW1 4 E4
Pratt Wk LBTH SE11 17 M5
Prayle Gv CRICK NW2 52 B7
Prebend Gdns HMSMTH W6 106 C3
Prebend St IS N1 6 E4
Precinct Rd HYS/HAR UB3 82 E6
The Precinct IS N1 * 6 E4
Premiere Pl POP/IOD E14 93 J6
Premier Park Rd
WLSDN NW10 86 D1
Premier Pl WATW WD18 20 D4
Prendergast Rd
BKHTH/KID SE3 133 H2
Prentis Rd STRHM/NOR SW16 148 D3
Prentiss Ct CHARL SE7 114 C3
Presburg Rd NWMAL KT3 160 B4
Prescelly Pl EDGW HA8 36 B7
Prescot St WCHPL E1 13 M6
Prescott Av STMC/STPC BR5 169 G5
Prescott Cl EMPK RM11 63 K7
Prescott Pl CLAP SW4 129 J2
Presentation Ms
BRXS/STRHM SW2 149 F1
Presidents Dr WAP E1W 92 D7
President St FSBYE EC1V * 6 E7
Prespa Cl ED N9 42 E1
Press Rd WLSDN NW10 69 F2
Prestage Wy POP/IOD E14 94 A6
Prestbury Rd FSTGT E7 77 G6
Prestbury Sq ELTH/MOT SE9 153 K3
Prested Rd BTSEA SW11 128 D3
Preston Av CHING E4 44 B5
Preston Cl STHWK SE1 19 J5
WHTN TW2 142 E2
Preston Ct BAR EN5 27 G3
WOT/HER KT12 156 B7
Preston Dr BXLYHN DA7 116 E7
HOR/WEW KT19 173 G5
WAN E11 59 G4
Preston Gdns IL IG1 59 J5
WLSDN NW10 * 69 G5
Preston Hl
KTN/HRWW/WS HA3 50 A6
Preston Pl CRICK NW2 69 J5
Preston Rd
KTN/HRWW/WS HA3 50 A6
NRWD SE19 149 H5
RYNPK SW20 145 J6
WAN E11 58 C5
WBLY HA9 68 A1
Prestons Rd WWKM BR4 180 E2
Preston's Rd POP/IOD E14 94 A6
Preston Vls KUT/HW KT1 * 159 G1
Preston Waye
KTN/HRWW/WS HA3 50 A7
Prestwich Ter CLAP SW4 * 129 J4
Prestwick Cl NWDGN UB2 102 D4
Prestwick Rd OXHEY WD19 33 H1
Prestwood OXHEY WD19 * 33 J1
Prestwood Av
KTN/HRWW/WS HA3 49 H3
Prestwood Cl
KTN/HRWW/WS HA3 49 H3
WOOL/PLUM SE18 116 B6
Prestwood Gdns
CROY/NA CR0 164 D6
Prestwood St IS N1 * 6 F6
Pretoria Av WALTH E17 57 G3
Pretoria Pde BROCKY SE4 * 132 D1
Pretoria Rd CAN/RD E16 94 D2
IL IG1 78 B3
LEY E10 58 B7
ROMW/RG RM7 62 E3
STRHM/NOR SW16 148 B5
TOTM N17 42 B5
WATW WD18 20 E3
Pretoria Rd North UED N18 42 B5
Prevost Rd FBAR/BDGN N11 40 A1
Price Cl MLHL NW7 38 C5
TOOT SW17 147 K2
Price Rd CROY/NA CR0 177 H4
Price's St STHWK SE1 12 D9
Pricklers Hl BAR EN5 27 F4
Prickley Wd HAYES BR2 167 J7
Priddy's Yd CROY/NA CR0 177 J1
Prideaux Pl ACT W3 87 F6
FSBYW WC1X 5 M7
Prideaux Rd BRXN/ST SW9 129 K2
Pridham Rd THHTH CR7 164 E3
Priestfield Rd FSTH SE23 151 G2
Priestlands Park Rd
BFN/LL DA15 155 F2
SCUP DA14 155 F2
Priestley Cl STNW/STAM N16 * 56 B6
Priestley Gdns CHDH RM6 61 H5
Priestley Rd MTCM CR4 163 F1
Priestley Wy CRICK NW2 51 J7
WALTH E17 57 F2
Priest Park Av
RYLN/HDSTN HA2 66 A1
Priests Av ROM RM1 63 F1
Priests Br MORT/ESHN SW14 126 B2
Prima Rd BRXN/ST SW9 110 B6
Primrose Av GDMY/SEVK IG3 61 G6
Primrose Cl BOW E3 93 J1
CAT SE6 152 A4
FNCH N3 53 F1
RYLN/HDSTN HA2 65 K2
WLGTN SM6 163 G7
Primrose Dr WDR/YW UB7 100 A3
Primrose Gdns BUSH WD23 22 B6
HAMP NW3 71 J5
RSLP HA4 65 G4
Primrose Hl EMB EC4Y 12 B5
Primrose Hill Rd HAMP NW3 3 L2
Primrose Hill Studios
CAMTN NW1 4 A3
Primrose La CROY/NA CR0 165 K7
Primrose Ms CAMTN NW1 * 3 M2
Primrose Pl ISLW TW7 124 A1
Primrose Rd LEY E10 57 K7
SWFD E18 59 F1
Primrose Sq HOM E9 74 E6
Primrose St SDTCH EC2A 13 J2
Primrose Wk EW KT17 173 H6
NWCR SE14 112 B6
Primrose Wy ALP/SUD HA0 85 K1
Primula St SHB W12 87 J6
Prince Albert Rd STJWD NW8 3 J7
Prince Charles Dr HDN NW4 52 A6
Prince Charles Rd
BKHTH/KID SE3 113 J7
Prince Charles Wy
WLGTN SM6 176 B2
Prince Consort Dr CHST BR7 154 D7
Prince Consort Rd SKENS SW7 15 G3
Princedale Rd NTGHL W11 88 C7
Prince Edward Rd HOM E9 75 H5
Prince George Av
STHGT/OAK N14 28 E5
Prince George Rd
STNW/STAM N16 74 A3
Prince George's Av
RYNPK SW20 161 F1
Prince Georges Rd
WIM/MER SW19 147 H7
Prince Henry Rd CHARL SE7 114 C6
Prince Imperial Rd CHST BR7 154 B6
WOOL/PLUM SE18 114 E7
Prince John Rd
ELTH/MOT SE9 134 D4
Princelet St WCHPL E1 13 M2
Prince of Orange La
GNWCH SE10 * 113 F6
Prince of Wales Cl HDN NW4 51 K3
Prince of Wales Dr
BTSEA SW11 108 D7
VX/NE SW8 * 109 G6
Prince of Wales Ga
SKENS SW7 15 J1
Prince of Wales Pas
CAMTN NW1 * 4 E8
Prince of Wales Rd
BKHTH/KID SE3 113 J7
CAN/RD E16 95 G5
KTTN NW5 72 A5
Prince of Wales' Rd SUT SM1 175 H1
Prince of Wales Ter
CHSWK W4 106 B4
KENS W8 14 D2
Prince Regent La CAN/RD E16 95 G5
Prince Regent Ms
CAMTN NW1 4 E8
Prince Regent Rd HSLW TW3 123 G2
Prince Rd SNWD SE25 165 F4
Prince Rupert Rd
ELTH/MOT SE9 134 E3
Princes Ar MYFR/PICC W1J 10 F8
Princes Av ACT W3 105 H2
CAR SM5 175 K6
CDALE/KGS NW9 50 C3
FNCH N3 39 F7
MUSWH N10 54 A2
PLMGR N13 41 G4
STMC/STPC BR5 169 K4
SURB KT6 172 C1
WATW WD18 20 E4
WDGN N22 40 D7
WFD IG8 45 F3
Prince's Av GFD/PVL UB6 84 B5
Princes Cl CDALE/KGS NW9 50 C3
EDGW HA8 36 C4
FSBYPK N4 55 H7
SCUP DA14 155 K2
Prince's Cl HPTN TW12 142 D3
Princes Ct WAP E1W 92 D6
WBLY HA9 68 A4
Princes Dr HRW HA1 48 E2
Princes Gdns ACT W3 86 C5
EA W5 85 J3
SKENS SW7 15 H3
Princes Ga SKENS SW7 15 H3
Princes Gate Ct SKENS SW7 15 G2
Princes Gate Ms SKENS SW7 15 H3
Princes La MUSWH N10 54 A2
Princes Ms HMSMTH W6 * 106 E4
HSLW TW3 123 F3
Prince's Ms BAY/PAD W2 8 C6
Princes Pde GLDGN NW11 * 52 C5
Princes Pk RAIN RM13 81 J6
Princes Park Av GLDGN NW11 52 C5
HYS/HAR UB3 82 B6
Princes Park Cir
HYS/HAR UB3 82 B6
Princes Park Cl HYS/HAR UB3 82 B6
Princes Park La HYS/HAR UB3 82 B6
Princes Park Pde
HYS/HAR UB3 82 B6
Princes Pl NTGHL W11 88 C7
Prince's Pln HAYES BR2 168 D6
Princes Ri LEW SE13 133 F1
Princes Riverside Rd
BERM/RHTH SE16 93 F7
Princes Rd BARK/HLT IG6 60 D3
BKHH IG9 45 G1
FELT TW13 140 D2
KUTN/CMB KT2 144 C7
PGE/AN SE20 151 F5
RCHPK/HAM TW10 125 G4
ROM RM1 63 J4
TEDD TW11 142 D3
UED N18 42 E3
WEA W13 85 H7
Prince's Rd MORT/ESHN SW14 126 A2
TEDD TW11 142 D3
WIM/MER SW19 146 E5
Princess Alice Wy THMD SE28 115 J1
Princess Av WBLY HA9 68 A1
Princess Crs FSBYPK N4 73 H1
Princesses Pde DART DA1 * 138 C4
Princess La RSLP HA4 46 C7
Princess Louise Cl
BAY/PAD W2 9 H2
Princess May Rd
STNW/STAM N16 74 A3
Princess Ms HAMP NW3 71 H5
Prince's Sq BAY/PAD W2 8 B6
Princess Rd CAMTN NW1 4 A3
CROY/NA CR0 164 D5
KIL/WHAMP NW6 2 A6
Princess St STHWK SE1 18 D4
Princes St REGST W1B 10 D5
SUT SM1 175 H3
TOTM N17 42 A5
Prince's St LOTH EC2R 13 G5
RCH/KEW TW9 125 F3
Prince's Ter PLSTW E13 77 F7
Prince St DEPT SE8 112 C5
WAT WD17 21 G2
Princes Wy BKHH IG9 45 G1
CROY/NA CR0 177 F4
RSLP HA4 65 J3
WIM/MER SW19 127 G6
WWKM BR4 180 D3
Prince's Yd IS N1 5 M4
NTGHL W11 88 C7
Princethorpe Rd SYD SE26 151 F3
Princeton St GINN WC1R 11 L3
Pringle Gdns
STRHM/NOR SW16 148 C3
Printers Inn Ct
FLST/FETLN EC4A 12 A4
Printinghouse La
HYS/HAR UB3 101 H1
Printing House Yd BETH E2 * 7 K8
Priolo Rd CHARL SE7 114 B4
Prior Av BELMT SM2 175 J6
Prior Bolton St IS N1 73 H5
Prioress Rd WNWD SE27 149 H2
Prioress St STHWK SE1 19 H4
Prior Rd IL IG1 78 A2
Priors Cft WALTH E17 57 G1
Priors Fld NTHLT UB5 65 J5
Priors Gdns RSLP HA4 65 G4
Prior St GNWCH SE10 113 F6
Priory Av ALP/SUD HA0 67 F3
CEND/HSY/T N8 54 D3
CHEAM SM3 174 B3
CHING E4 43 H2
CHSWK W4 106 B2
STMC/STPC BR5 169 J5
WALTH E17 57 J4
Priory Cl ALP/SUD HA0 67 F3
BECK BR3 166 B2
CHING E4 43 H2
CHST BR7 153 K7
FNCH N3 38 D7
HPTN TW12 141 K7
HYS/HAR UB3 83 F6
RSLP HA4 46 D7
STAN HA7 35 F2
STHGT/OAK N14 28 B4
SUN TW16 140 E6
SWFD E18 44 E7
TRDG/WHET N20 26 D6
WIM/MER SW19 * 147 F7
Priory Cots EA W5 * 86 B4
Priory Ct BLKFR EC4V * 12 D5
VX/NE SW8 109 J7
WALTH E17 57 H1
Priory Crs ALP/SUD HA0 67 G2
CHEAM SM3 174 B3
NRWD SE19 149 J6
Priory Dr ABYW SE2 116 E4
STAN HA7 35 F2
Priory Field Dr EDGW HA8 36 D3
Priory Gdns ALP/SUD HA0 67 G3
ASHF TW15 140 B4
BARN SW13 126 C2
CHSWK W4 * 106 B3
HGT N6 54 B5
HPTN TW12 141 K7
SNWD SE25 165 G3
Priory Green Est IS N1 5 L5
Priory Gv VX/NE SW8 109 K7
Priory Hl ALP/SUD HA0 67 G3
Priory La E/WMO/HCT KT8 157 F3
PUT/ROE SW15 126 C4
Priory Leas ELTH/MOT SE9 * 134 D7
Priory Ms HCH RM12 63 K7
Priory Pk BKHTH/KID SE3 133 J2
Priory Park Rd ALP/SUD HA0 67 G3
KIL/WHAMP NW6 70 D7
Priory Rd BARK IG11 78 D6
CEND/HSY/T N8 54 D3
CHEAM SM3 174 B3
CHSGTN KT9 172 A2
CHSWK W4 106 A2
CROY/NA CR0 164 B6
EHAM E6 77 H7
HPTN TW12 141 K6
HSLW TW3 123 H4
KIL/WHAMP NW6 2 C2
MUSWH N10 54 C3
RCH/KEW TW9 105 H5
Priory St BOW E3 93 K2
Priory Ter KIL/WHAMP NW6 2 C3
The Priory BKHTH/KID SE3 133 J2
CROY/NA CR0 * 177 G2
Priory Vw BUSH WD23 22 E6
Priory Vls FBAR/BDGN N11 * 39 K5
Priory Wk WBPTN SW10 14 F8
Priory Wy NWDGN UB2 102 C2
RYLN/HDSTN HA2 48 B3
WDR/YW UB7 100 B5
Pritchard's Rd BETH E2 92 C1
Priter Rd BERM/RHTH SE16 * 111 H2
Private Rd EN EN1 29 K4
Probert Rd BRXS/STRHM SW2 130 B4
Probyn Rd BRXS/STRHM SW2 149 H1
Procter St GINN WC1R 11 L3
Proctor Cl MTCM CR4 148 A7
Proctors Cl EBED/NFELT TW14 121 K7
Progress Wy CROY/NA CR0 177 F1
EN EN1 30 C4
WDGN N22 41 G7
Promenade Approach Rd
CHSWK W4 106 B6
The Promenade CHSWK W4 106 B7
EDGW HA8 * 36 C4
Prospect Cl BELV DA17 117 H3
BUSH WD23 22 D6
HSLW TW3 102 E7
RSLP HA4 47 H6
SYD SE26 150 D3
Prospect Cots
WAND/EARL SW18 127 K3
Prospect Crs WHTN TW2 123 H5
Prospect Hl WALTH E17 57 K3
Prospect Pl CHSWK W4 106 A4
CRICK NW2 70 D2
CRW RM5 62 E1
EFNCH N2 53 H3
HAYES BR2 168 A2
RYNPK SW20 145 K6
WAP E1W 92 E7
Prospect Ring EFNCH N2 53 H2
Prospect Rd BAR EN5 26 E3
CRICK NW2 70 D2
SURB KT6 158 D5
WFD IG8 45 G4
Prospect St BERM/RHTH SE16 111 J1
Prospect V WOOL/PLUM SE18 114 D3
Prospero Rd ARCH N19 54 D7
Protea Cl CAN/RD E16 94 D3
Prothero Gdns HDN NW4 51 K4
Prothero Rd FUL/PGN SW6 107 H6
Prout Gv WLSDN NW10 69 G3
Prout Rd CLPT E5 74 D2
Provence St IS N1 6 E5
Providence Av
RYLN/HDSTN HA2 48 A7
Providence Cl HOM E9 * 75 F7
Providence Ct
MYFR/PKLN W1K 10 B6
Providence La HYS/HAR UB3 101 G6
Providence Pl IS N1 6 C4
Providence Row Cl BETH E2 92 D2
Providence Sq STHWK SE1 19 J1
Providence Yd BETH E2 * 92 C2
Provincial Ter PGE/AN SE20 * 151 F6
Provost Est IS N1 7 G7
Provost Rd HAMP NW3 3 M1

Provost St IS N1 7 G6
Prowse Av BUSH WD23 34 C1
Prowse Pl CAMTN NW1 4 E1
Pruden Cl STHGT/OAK N14 * 40 C1
Prusom St WAP E1W 92 D7
Pudding La MON EC3R 13 H6
Pudding Mill La SRTFD E15 75 K7
Puddle Dock BLKFR EC4V 12 D6
Puffin Cl BARK IG11 97 H2
BECK BR3 166 A4
Pulborough Rd
WAND/EARL SW18 127 J6
Pulborough Wy HSLWW TW4 122 B3
Pulford Rd SEVS/STOTM N15 55 K5
Pulham Av EFNCH N2 53 G3
Puller Rd BAR EN5 26 B1
Pulleyns Av EHAM E6 95 J2
Pullman Gdns PUT/ROE SW15 127 F5
Pullman Ms LEE/GVPK SE12 153 F2
Pullman Pl ELTH/MOT SE9 134 D4
Pulross Rd BRXN/ST SW9 130 A2
Pulteney Cl BOW E3 75 H7
ISLW TW7 124 B2
Pulteney Rd SWFD E18 59 F2
Pulton Pl FUL/PGN SW6 107 K6
Puma Ct WCHPL E1 13 L2
Pump Aly BTFD TW8 104 E6
Pump Cl NTHLT UB5 84 A1
Pump Ct EMB EC4Y * 12 A5
Pump House Cl HAYES BR2 167 J1
Pump House Ms WCHPL E1 * 92 C6
Pumping Station Rd
CHSWK W4 106 B6
Pump La HYS/HAR UB3 101 K1
NWCR SE14 111 K6
Punderson's Gdns BETH E2 92 D2
Purbeck Av NWMAL KT3 160 C5
Purbeck Dr CRICK NW2 70 B1
Purbeck Rd EMPK RM11 63 J6
Purbrook St STHWK SE1 19 K3
Purcell Crs FUL/PGN SW6 107 G6
Purcell Ms WLSDN NW10 * 69 G6
Purcell Rd GFD/PVL UB6 84 B4
Purcell St IS N1 7 J5
Purcers Cross Rd
FUL/PGN SW6 107 J7
Purchese St CAMTN NW1 5 G5
Purdy St BOW E3 93 K3
Purelake Ms LEW SE13 * 133 G2
Purkis Cl UX/CGN UB8 82 A6
Purland Cl BCTR RM8 62 B7
Purland Rd THMD SE28 116 A2
Purleigh Av WFD IG8 45 J5
Purley Av CRICK NW2 70 C1
Purley Cl CLAY IG5 60 A1
Purley Pl IS N1 6 C1
Purley Rd ED N9 41 K2
SAND/SEL CR2 177 K6
Purley Wy CROY/NA CR0 177 F1
Purlings Rd BUSH WD23 22 B4
Purneys Rd ELTH/MOT SE9 134 C3
Purrett Rd WOOL/PLUM SE18 116 A4
Pursers Cross Rd
FUL/PGN SW6 * 107 J7
Pursewardens Cl WEA W13 85 J7
Pursley Rd MLHL NW7 37 K6
Purves Rd WLSDN NW10 87 K2
Putney Br PUT/ROE SW15 127 H2
Putney Bridge Ap
FUL/PGN SW6 127 H2
Putney Bridge Rd
PUT/ROE SW15 127 H3
Putney Common
PUT/ROE SW15 127 F2
Putney Ex PUT/ROE SW15 * 127 G3
Putney Heath PUT/ROE SW15 126 E5
Putney Heath La
PUT/ROE SW15 127 G5
Putney High St
PUT/ROE SW15 127 H3
Putney Hl PUT/ROE SW15 127 F6
Putney Park Av
PUT/ROE SW15 126 D3
Putney Park La
PUT/ROE SW15 126 E3
Puttenham Cl OXHEY WD19 33 G2
Pycombe Cnr
NFNCH/WDSPK N12 38 D3
Pycroft Wy ED N9 42 C3
Pylbrook Rd SUT SM1 174 E2
Pylon Wy CROY/NA CR0 163 K7
Pym Cl EBAR EN4 27 H4
Pymers Md DUL SE21 130 D7
Pymmes Brook Trail
EBAR EN4 27 K6
Pymmes Cl PLMGR N13 41 F4
TOTM N17 42 D7
Pymmes Gdns North ED N9 42 B2
Pymmes Gdns South ED N9 42 B2
Pymmes Green Rd
FBAR/BDGN N11 40 B3
Pymmes Rd PLMGR N13 40 E5
Pymms Brook Dr EBAR EN4 27 J3
Pyne Rd SURB KT6 159 H7
Pynham Cl ABYW SE2 116 B2
Pynnacles Cl STAN HA7 35 H4
Pyrland Rd HBRY N5 73 K4
RCHPK/HAM TW10 125 G5
Pyrmont Gv WNWD SE27 149 H2
Pyrmont Rd CHSWK W4 105 H5
Pytchley Crs NRWD SE19 149 J5
Pytchley Rd EDUL SE22 131 F2

Q

The Quadrangle BAY/PAD W2 9 J4
HNHL SE24 * 130 D4
WBPTN SW10 * 108 B7
Quadrant Ar REGST W1B 10 F7
Quadrant Cl HDN NW4 * 51 K4
Quadrant Gv KTTN NW5 71 K4
Quadrant Rd RCH/KEW TW9 124 E3
THHTH CR7 164 C3
The Quadrant BELMT SM2 175 G5
BXLYHN DA7 116 E6
EDGW HA8 * 36 C5
NKENS W10 * 88 B2
RCH/KEW TW9 124 E4
RYLN/HDSTN HA2 * 48 D2
RYNPK SW20 146 C7
Quad Rd WBLY HA9 * 67 K2
Quainton St WLSDN NW10 69 F2
Quaker La NWDGN UB2 103 F2
Quakers Course
CDALE/KGS NW9 37 H7
Quakers La ISLW TW7 104 B6
Quakers Pl FSTGT E7 77 H4
Quaker St WCHPL E1 13 L1
Quakers Wk WCHMH N21 29 K5
Quality Ct LINN WC2A 12 A4
Quantock Cl HYS/HAR UB3 101 G6
Quantock Gdns CRICK NW2 * 70 B1
Quantock Ms PECK SE15 131 H1
Quarles Park Rd CHDH RM6 61 H5
Quarrendon St FUL/PGN SW6 107 K7
Quarr Rd CAR SM5 162 C5
Quarry Ms PUR RM19 119 K3
Quarry Park Rd SUT SM1 174 D5
Quarry Ri SUT SM1 174 D5
Quarry Rd WAND/EARL SW18 128 B5
Quatre Ports CHING E4 * 44 B4
Quay House POP/IOD E14 * 112 D1
Quebec Ms MBLAR W1H 9 M5
Quebec Rd GNTH/NBYPK IG2 60 C6
YEAD UB4 83 G6
Quebec Wy BERM/RHTH SE16 112 A1
Queen Adelaide Rd
PGE/AN SE20 150 E5
Queen Anne Av HAYES BR2 167 K2
Queen Anne Dr
ESH/CLAY KT10 170 E6
Queen Anne Ga BXLYHN DA7 136 E2
Queen Anne Ms
CAVSQ/HST W1G 10 D3
Queen Anne Rd HOM E9 75 F5
Queen Annes Cl WHTN TW2 142 D2
Queen Anne's Gdns
CHSWK W4 106 B2
EA W5 105 F1
EN EN1 30 A5
MTCM CR4 * 162 E2
Queen Anne's Ga
STJSPK SW1H 17 G2
Queen Anne's Gv CHSWK W4 106 B2
EA W5 105 F1
ED N9 29 K6
EN EN1 30 A5
Queen Anne's Pl EN EN1 30 A5
Queen Anne St
CAVSQ/HST W1G 10 C3
Queen Anne Ter WAP E1W * 92 D6
Queen Borough Gdns
CHST BR7 154 D5
Queenborough Gdns
GNTH/NBYPK IG2 60 A3
Queen Caroline Est
HMSMTH W6 107 F4
Queen Caroline St
HMSMTH W6 107 F4
Queen Elizabeth Blds
EMB EC4Y * 12 A6
Queen Elizabeth College
GNWCH SE10 * 113 F6
Queen Elizabeth Gdns
MRDN SM4 161 K3
Queen Elizabeth Rd
KUTN/CMB KT2 159 G1
WALTH E17 57 G2
Queen Elizabeth's Cl
STNW/STAM N16 73 K1
Queen Elizabeth's Dr
STHGT/OAK N14 28 E7
Queen Elizabeth St
STHWK SE1 19 K1
Queen Elizabeth's Wk
STNW/STAM N16 55 K7
WLGTN SM6 176 D3
Queen Elizabeth Wk
BARN SW13 106 D7
Queenhithe BLKFR EC4V 12 F7
Queen Isabella Wy STBT EC1A 12 D4
Queen Margaret's Gv IS N1 74 A4
Queen Mary Av RYNPK SW20 161 G4
Queen Mary Cl ROM RM1 63 H5
SURB KT6 172 C2
Queen Mary Rd NRWD SE19 149 H5
Queen Mary's Av CAR SM5 175 K6
WATW WD18 20 C3
Queen Mother Ga
MYFR/PICC W1J 10 B9
Queens Acre CHEAM SM3 174 B6
Queens Av FELT TW13 141 G3
KTN/HRWW/WS HA3 49 H2
MUSWH N10 54 A2
TRDG/WHET N20 39 H1
WATW WD18 20 D3
Queen's Av FNCH N3 39 G6
GFD/PVL UB6 84 B5
WCHMH N21 29 H7
WFD IG8 45 F4
Queensberry Ms West
SKENS SW7 * 15 G5
Queensberry Pl MNPK E12 77 H4
SKENS SW7 15 G5
Queensberry Wy
SKENS SW7 * 15 G5
Queensborough Ms
BAY/PAD W2 * 8 E6
Queensborough Pas
BAY/PAD W2 8 E6
Queensborough Studios
BAY/PAD W2 8 E6
Queensborough Ter
BAY/PAD W2 8 D6
Queensbridge Pk ISLW TW7 123 K5
Queensbridge Rd HACK E8 7 M4
Queensbury Rd ALP/SUD HA0 86 B1
CDALE/KGS NW9 51 F6
Queensbury St IS N1 6 F2
Queens Circ VX/NE SW8 109 G6
Queens Cl ESH/CLAY KT10 * 170 B3
Queen's Cl EDGW HA8 36 C4
WLGTN SM6 176 B4
Queen's Club Gdns
WKENS W14 107 H5
Queens Club Ter
WKENS W14 * 107 J5
Queenscourt WBLY HA9 68 A3
Queens Crs
RCHPK/HAM TW10 125 G4
Queen's Crs KTTN NW5 72 A4
Queenscroft Rd
ELTH/MOT SE9 134 C4
Queensdale Crs NTGHL W11 88 B7
Queensdale Pl NTGHL W11 88 C7
Queensdale Rd NTGHL W11 88 B7
Queensdale Wk NTGHL W11 88 C7
Queens Down Rd CLPT E5 74 D3
Queens Dr BRYLDS KT5 159 H6
LEY E10 57 J6
Queen's Dr EA W5 86 B5
FSBYPK N4 73 H1
THDIT KT7 158 B5
Queen's Elm Sq CHEL SW3 15 G8
Queens Gdns HDN NW4 52 A4
RAIN RM13 99 F1
Queen's Gdns BAY/PAD W2 8 E6
EA W5 85 J4
HEST TW5 102 D7
Queens Garth FSTH SE23 * 150 E1
Queens Ga SKENS SW7 14 F2
Queens Gate Gdns CHST BR7 154 D7
Queensgate Gdns
PUT/ROE SW15 126 E3
Queen's Gate Gdns
SKENS SW7 14 E4
Queen's Gate Ms SKENS SW7 14 E3
Queensgate Pl
KIL/WHAMP NW6 2 A2
Queen's Gate Pl SKENS SW7 14 F4
Queen's Gate Place Ms
SKENS SW7 14 F4
Queen's Gate Ter SKENS SW7 14 E3
Queen's Gv STJWD NW8 3 G4
Queen's Head St IS N1 6 D4
Queens Keep TWK TW1 * 124 D5
Queensland Av UED N18 41 J5
WIM/MER SW19 147 F7
Queensland Cl WALTH E17 57 H1
Queensland Rd HOLWY N7 73 G3
Queens La MUSWH N10 54 B2
Queens Md EDGW HA8 36 B5
Queensmead STJWD NW8 3 H3
Queen's Mead Rd HAYES BR2 167 J1
Queensmere Cl
WIM/MER SW19 146 B1
Queensmere Rd
WIM/MER SW19 146 B1
Queen's Ms BAY/PAD W2 8 C6
Queensmill Rd FUL/PGN SW6 107 G6
Queens Pde CEND/HSY/T N8 * 55 H3
CRICK NW2 * 70 A5
EA W5 * 86 B5
FBAR/BDGN N11 * 39 K4
HDN NW4 * 51 K4
Queens Parade Cl
FBAR/BDGN N11 39 K4
Queens Park Gdns
FELT TW13 * 140 D2
Queen's Pl MRDN SM4 161 K3
WAT WD17 21 G2
Queens Prom KUT/HW KT1 158 E3
Queen Sq BMSBY WC1N 11 K1
Queen's Ride PUT/ROE SW15 126 D3
Queen's Ri RCHPK/HAM TW10 125 G5
Queens Rd BAR EN5 26 B2
HYS/HAR UB3 82 C5
MRDN SM4 161 K3
WDR/YW UB7 100 C1
Queen's Rd BARK IG11 78 C6
BECK BR3 166 B1
BKHH IG9 45 F1
BMLY BR1 167 K1
CHST BR7 154 B5
CROY/NA CR0 164 C5
EA W5 86 A5
ED N9 42 D1
EN EN1 30 A3
FBAR/BDGN N11 40 E6
FELT TW13 122 A7
FNCH N3 39 G7
HDN NW4 52 A4
HPTN TW12 142 B3
HSLW TW3 123 G2
KUTN/CMB KT2 144 C6
MORT/ESHN SW14 126 A2
MTCM CR4 162 C2
NWDGN UB2 102 C1
NWMAL KT3 160 C3
PECK SE15 111 K7
PLSTW E13 77 F7
RCHPK/HAM TW10 144 C4
TEDD TW11 143 F5
THDIT KT7 158 A4
TWK TW1 124 A7
WALTH E17 57 H5
WAN E11 58 C6
WAT WD17 21 G2
WELL DA16 136 C1
WIM/MER SW19 146 E5
WLGTN SM6 176 B4
Queen's Rd West PLSTW E13 94 E1
Queen's Rw WALW SE17 19 G9
Queens Ter ISLW TW7 124 B3
PLSTW E13 77 F7
THDIT KT7 * 158 B5
WCHPL E1 * 92 E3
Queen's Ter ISLW TW7 124 B3
STJWD NW8 3 G4
Queens Terrace Cots
HNWL W7 * 103 K1
Queensthorpe Ms SYD SE26 * 151 F3
Queensthorpe Rd SYD SE26 151 F3
Queenstown Gdns RAIN RM13 99 H2
Queenstown Rd VX/NE SW8 129 G1
Queen St CROY/NA CR0 177 J3
ERITH DA8 * 118 B5
MYFR/PICC W1J 10 C8
ROMW/RG RM7 63 F5
STP EC4M 12 F5
TOTM N17 42 A5
Queen Street Pl CANST EC4R 12 F7
Queensville Rd BAL SW12 129 J6
Queens Wk CDALE/KGS NW9 68 E1
HRW HA1 48 E3
RSLP HA4 65 G2
Queen's Wk EA W5 85 J3
Queens Walk Ter RSLP HA4 * 65 G2
The Queens Wk STHWK SE1 13 K8
Queens Wy FELT TW13 141 G3
HDN NW4 52 A4
Queensway BAY/PAD W2 8 D4
CROY/NA CR0 177 F5
PEND EN3 30 E3
STMC/STPC BR5 169 H4
SUN TW16 156 A1
WWKM BR4 180 E3
Queens Well Av
TRDG/WHET N20 39 J3
Queen's Whf HMSMTH W6 107 F4
Queenswood Av HPTN TW12 142 B5
HSLW TW3 122 E1
THHTH CR7 164 B4
WALTH E17 44 A7
WLGTN SM6 176 D3
Queenswood Gdns WAN E11 58 E7
Queenswood Pk FNCH N3 52 C1
Queenswood Rd
BFN/LL DA15 136 A4
FSTH SE23 151 G2
Queen's Wood Rd HGT N6 54 B5
Queen's Yd FITZ W1T 10 F1
Queen Victoria Av
ALP/SUD HA0 67 K6
Queen Victoria St BLKFR EC4V 12 C6
Queen Victoria Ter
WAP E1W * 92 D6
Quemerford Rd HOLWY N7 73 F4
Quentin Pl LEW SE13 133 H2
Quentin Rd LEW SE13 133 H2
Quernmore Cl BMLY BR1 152 E5
Quernmore Rd BMLY BR1 152 E5
FSBYPK N4 55 G5
Querrin St FUL/PGN SW6 128 B1
Quex Ms KIL/WHAMP NW6 2 B3
Quex Rd KIL/WHAMP NW6 2 B3
Quick Rd CHSWK W4 106 B4
Quicks Rd WIM/MER SW19 147 F6
Quick St IS N1 6 D6
Quickswood HAMP NW3 3 K1
Quiet Nook HAYES BR2 181 H2
Quill St EA W5 86 A2
FSBYPK N4 73 G2
Quilp St STHWK SE1 18 E1
Quilters Pl ELTH/MOT SE9 135 H7
Quilter St BETH E2 92 C2
WOOL/PLUM SE18 116 A4
Quince Rd LEW SE13 132 E1
Quinnel Cl WOOL/PLUM SE18 116 A4
Quinnell Cl WOOL/PLUM SE18 116 A4
Quinta Dr BAR EN5 25 K4
Quintin Av RYNPK SW20 146 C7
Quinton Cl BECK BR3 167 F2
HEST TW5 102 A6
WLGTN SM6 176 B3
Quinton Rd THDIT KT7 158 B7
Quinton St WAND/EARL SW18 147 G1
Quixley St POP/IOD E14 94 B6
Quorn Rd EDUL SE22 131 F3

R

Rabbit Rw KENS W8 * 8 B8
Rabbits Rd MNPK E12 77 J3
Rabournmead Dr NTHLT UB5 65 J4
Raby Rd NWMAL KT3 160 A3
Raby St POP/IOD E14 * 93 G5
Raccoon Wy HSLWW TW4 122 B1
Rachel Cl BARK/HLT IG6 60 D3
Rackham Cl WELL DA16 136 C1
Rackham Ms
STRHM/NOR SW16 148 C5
Racton Rd FUL/PGN SW6 107 K5
Radbourne Av EA W5 104 D3
Radbourne Cl CLPT E5 75 F3
Radbourne Ct
KTN/HRWW/WS HA3 * 49 H5
Radbourne Crs WALTH E17 58 B2
Radbourne Rd BAL SW12 129 H6
Radcliffe Av WLSDN NW10 87 J1
Radcliffe Gdns CAR SM5 175 J6
Radcliffe Rd CROY/NA CR0 178 B1
KTN/HRWW/WS HA3 49 G1
STHWK SE1 19 K3
WCHMH N21 29 H7
Radcliffe Sq PUT/ROE SW15 127 G5
Radcliffe Wy NTHLT UB5 83 H2
Radcot St LBTH SE11 18 B8
Raddington Rd NKENS W10 88 C4
Radfield Wy BFN/LL DA15 135 J6
Radford Est WLSDN NW10 * 87 G2
Radford Rd LEW SE13 133 F5
Radford Wy BARK IG11 97 F2
Radipole Rd FUL/PGN SW6 107 J7
Radius Pk
EBED/NFELT TW14 * 121 J3
Radland Rd CAN/RD E16 94 E5
Radlet Av SYD SE26 150 D2
Radlett Cl FSTGT E7 76 D5
Radlett Pl STJWD NW8 3 J4
Radlett Rd WAT WD17 21 G2
Radley Av GDMY/SEVK IG3 79 F3
Radley Cl EBED/NFELT TW14 121 J7
Radley Ct BERM/RHTH SE16 112 A1
Radley Gdns
KTN/HRWW/WS HA3 50 A3
Radley Ms KENS W8 14 B4
Radley Rd TOTM N17 56 A1
Radley's La SWFD E18 58 E1
Radleys Md DAGE RM10 80 D5
Radley Sq CLPT E5 * 74 E1
Radley Ter CAN/RD E16 94 D4
Radlix Rd LEY E10 57 J7
Radnor Av HRW HA1 48 E4
WELL DA16 136 C4
Radnor Cl CHST BR7 154 E5
MTCM CR4 163 K4
Radnor Crs REDBR IG4 59 K4
WOOL/PLUM SE18 116 B6
Radnor Gdns TWK TW1 143 F1
Radnor Hall BORE WD6 * 24 A4
Radnor Ms BAY/PAD W2 9 H5
Radnor Pl BAY/PAD W2 9 J5
Radnor Rd HRW HA1 48 D4
KIL/WHAMP NW6 70 C7
PECK SE15 111 H6
TWK TW1 124 A7
Radnor St FSBYE EC1V 6 F8
Radnor Ter WKENS W14 107 J3
Radnor Wk CHEL SW3 15 K8
CROY/NA CR0 166 B6
Radnor Wy WLSDN NW10 86 D3
Radstock Av
KTN/HRWW/WS HA3 49 G2
Radstock Cl FBAR/BDGN N11 40 A4
Radstock St BTSEA SW11 * 108 D6
Raebarn Gdns BAR EN5 25 K4
Raeburn Av BRYLDS KT5 159 J6
Raeburn Cl GLDGN NW11 53 G5
KUT/HW KT1 143 K6
Raeburn Rd BFN/LL DA15 135 K5
EDGW HA8 50 C1
YEAD UB4 82 B1
Raeburn St BRXS/STRHM SW2 129 K3
Rafford Wy BMLY BR1 168 A1
Raggleswood CHST BR7 154 A7
Raglan Cl HSLWW TW4 122 D4
Raglan Ct SAND/SEL CR2 177 H4
Raglan Gdns OXHEY WD19 21 F7
Raglan Rd BELV DA17 117 G3
EN EN1 30 A6
HAYES BR2 168 B3
WALTH E17 58 A4
WOOL/PLUM SE18 115 H4
Raglan St KTTN NW5 72 B5
Raglan Ter
RYLN/HDSTN HA2 * 66 B3
Raglan Vls WALTH E17 * 58 A4
Raglan Wy NTHLT UB5 66 C5
Ragley Cl ACT W3 105 K1
Railey Ms KTTN NW5 72 C4
Railshead Rd ISLW TW7 124 C3
Railton Rd HNHL SE24 130 B4
Railway Ap FSBYPK N4 55 G5
HRW HA1 49 F3
STHWK SE1 13 G8
TWK TW1 124 B6
WLGTN SM6 * 176 B5
Railway Ar BRXN/ST SW9 * 130 B3
Railway Av BERM/RHTH SE16 111 K1
Railway Cots HMSMTH W6 * 107 F1
SRTFD E15 * 94 C1
WIM/MER SW19 * 147 F3
Railway Gv NWCR SE14 112 C6
Railway Pl BELV DA17 117 H2
Railway Ri EDUL SE22 131 F3
Railway Rd TEDD TW11 142 E3
Railway Side BARN SW13 126 B2
Railway Station Whf
LEY E10 * 57 G7
Railway St CHDH RM6 61 J7
IS N1 5 K6
Railway Ter FELT TW13 121 K7
LEW SE13 132 E4
WALTH E17 44 A7
Rainborough Cl WBLY HA9 68 E5
Rainbow Av POP/IOD E14 112 E4
Rainbow Ct OXHEY WD19 21 G5
Rainbow Quay
BERM/RHTH SE16 112 B2
Rainbow St CMBW SE5 111 F6
Raine St WAP E1W 92 D7
Rainham Cl BTSEA SW11 128 D5
ELTH/MOT SE9 135 K5
Rainham Rd RAIN RM13 99 J2
WLSDN NW10 88 A2
Rainham Rd North
DAGE RM10 80 D1
Rainham Rd South
DAGE RM10 80 E5
Rainhill Wy BOW E3 93 J2
Rainsborough Av DEPT SE8 112 B3
Rainsford Rd WLSDN NW10 86 C2
Rainsford St BAY/PAD W2 9 J4
Rainsford Wy HCH RM12 63 J7
Rainville Rd HMSMTH W6 107 F5
Raisins Hl PIN HA5 47 F2
Raith Av STHGT/OAK N14 40 D2
Raleigh Av WLGTN SM6 176 D3
YEAD UB4 83 F4
Raleigh Cl ERITH DA8 118 C5
HDN NW4 52 A4
PIN HA5 47 H6
RSLP HA4 64 D1
Raleigh Dr BRYLDS KT5 159 K7
ESH/CLAY KT10 170 D4
TRDG/WHET N20 39 J2
Raleigh Gdns
BRXS/STRHM SW2 130 A5
MTCM CR4 162 E1
Raleigh Ms IS N1 6 D4
Raleigh Rd CEND/HSY/T N8 55 G3
ENC/FH EN2 29 K3
FELT TW13 140 D1
NWDGN UB2 102 D4
PGE/AN SE20 151 F6
RCH/KEW TW9 125 G2
Raleigh St IS N1 6 D4
Raleigh Wy FELT TW13 141 G4
STHGT/OAK N14 28 D7
Ralph Perring Ct BECK BR3 166 D3
Ralston St CHEL SW3 15 L8
Ralston Wy OXHEY WD19 33 H1
Rama Cl STRHM/NOR SW16 148 E6
Ramac Wy CHARL SE7 114 A3
Rama La NRWD SE19 150 B6
Rambler Cl STRHM/NOR SW16 148 C3
Rame Cl TOOT SW17 148 A4
Ramilles Cl BRXS/STRHM SW2 129 K5
Ramillies Pl SOHO/CST W1F 10 E5
Ramillies Rd BFN/LL DA15 136 C5
CHSWK W4 106 A2
MLHL NW7 37 G1
Ramillies St SOHO/SHAV W1D 10 E5
Ramones Ter MTCM CR4 * 163 H3
Rampart St WCHPL E1 92 D5
Ram Pas KUT/HW KT1 158 E1
Rampayne St PIM SW1V 17 G7
Rampton Cl CHING E4 43 J2
Ramsay Rd ACT W3 105 K2
FSTGT E7 76 D3
Ramscroft Cl ED N9 30 A6
Ramsdale Rd TOOT SW17 148 A4
Ramsden Ga BAL SW12 * 129 G6
Ramsden Rd BAL SW12 129 F6
FBAR/BDGN N11 39 K4
Ramsey Cl CDALE/KGS NW9 51 H5
GFD/PVL UB6 66 D4
Ramsey Rd THHTH CR7 164 A5
Ramsey St BETH E2 92 C3
Ramsey Wk IS N1 73 K5
Ramsey Wy STHGT/OAK N14 28 C6
Ramsgate Cl CAN/RD E16 95 F7
Ramsgate St HACK E8 * 74 B5
Ramsgill Ap GNTH/NBYPK IG2 61 F3
Ramsgill Dr GNTH/NBYPK IG2 61 F4
Rams Gv CHDH RM6 62 A3
Ramulis Dr YEAD UB4 83 J3
Rancliffe Gdns ELTH/MOT SE9 134 D3
Rancliffe Rd EHAM E6 95 J1
Randall Av CRICK NW2 69 G1
Randall Cl BTSEA SW11 108 D7
ERITH DA8 117 K5
Randall Pl GNWCH SE10 113 F6
Randall Rd LBTH SE11 17 L7
Randell's Rd IS N1 5 K3
Randisbourne Gdns CAT SE6 * 151 K2
Randle Rd RCHPK/HAM TW10 143 J3
Randlesdown Rd CAT SE6 151 J3
Randolf Rd HAYES BR2 168 E7
Randolph Ap CAN/RD E16 95 G5
Randolph Av MV/WKIL W9 2 C6
Randolph Cl KUTN/CMB KT2 * 144 E4
Randolph Crs MV/WKIL W9 8 E1
Randolph Gdns
KIL/WHAMP NW6 2 C6
Randolph Gv CHDH RM6 61 J4
Randolph Ms MV/WKIL W9 8 F1
Randolph Rd MV/WKIL W9 8 E1
STHL UB1 * 102 E1
WALTH E17 * 57 K4
Randolph St CAMTN NW1 4 E2
Randon Cl RYLN/HDSTN HA2 48 B1
Ranelagh Av BARN SW13 126 D1
Ranelagh Cl EDGW HA8 36 C3
Ranelagh Dr EDGW HA8 36 C3
TWK TW1 124 C3
Ranelagh Gdns CHSWK W4 105 K6
FUL/PGN SW6 127 H2
IL IG1 60 A7
WAN E11 59 G4
Ranelagh Gv BGVA SW1W 16 B7
Ranelagh Pl NWMAL KT3 160 B4
Ranelagh Rd ALP/SUD HA0 67 K4
EA W5 104 E1
EHAM E6 78 A7
PIM SW1V 16 F8
SRTFD E15 76 C7
STHL UB1 83 H7
TOTM N17 56 A2
WAN E11 76 C3
WDGN N22 41 F7
WLSDN NW10 87 H1
Ranfurly Rd SUT SM1 174 E1
Rangefield Rd BMLY BR1 152 C4
Rangemoor Rd
SEVS/STOTM N15 56 B4
Rangeworth Pl BFN/LL DA15 155 F2
Rangoon St TWRH EC3N * 13 L5
Rankin Cl CDALE/KGS NW9 51 G2
Ranmere St BAL SW12 129 G7

Richmond Park Rd
KUTN/CMB KT2 144 A6
MORT/ESHN SW14 125 K4
Richmond Pl
WOOL/PLUM SE18 115 H3
Richmond Rd BAR EN5 27 F4
CROY/NA CR0 176 E2
EA W5 105 F1
EFNCH N2 * 53 G1
FBAR/BDGN N11 40 E5
FSTGT E7 77 F4
HACK E8 7 L1
IL IG1 78 C2
ISLW TW7 124 B2
KUTN/CMB KT2 143 K4
ROM RM1 63 H5
RYNPK SW20 145 K7
SEVS/STOTM N15 56 A5
THHTH CR7 164 C3
TWK TW1 124 B7
WAN E11 76 B1
Richmond St PLSTW E13 94 E1
Richmond Ter WHALL SW1A 17 J1
Richmond Vls WALTH E17 * 43 K7
Richmond Wy
RKW/CH/CXG WD3 20 A3
SHB W12 107 G1
WAN E11 76 E1
Rich St POP/IOD E14 93 H6
Rickard Cl BRXS/STRHM SW2 130 B7
HDN NW4 51 J3
WDR/YW UB7 100 A2
Rickards Cl SURB KT6 172 A1
Rickett St FUL/PGN SW6 14 B9
Rickman St WCHPL E1 92 E3
Rickmansworth Rd
NTHWD HA6 32 B6
WATW WD18 20 C3
Rick Roberts Wy SRTFD E15 76 B7
Rickthorne Rd ARCH N19 72 E1
Ridding La GFD/PVL UB6 67 F4
Riddons Rd LEE/GVPK SE12 153 G2
Rideout St WOOL/PLUM SE18 114 E3
Rider Cl BFN/LL DA15 135 K5
The Ride BTFD TW8 104 C4
PEND EN3 30 E2
Ridgdale St BOW E3 93 J1
Ridge Av WCHMH N21 29 J6
Ridgebrook Rd
BKHTH/KID SE3 134 B3
Ridge Cl CDALE/KGS NW9 51 F3
HDN NW4 52 B1
THMD SE28 115 J1
Ridgecroft Cl BXLY DA5 137 K7
Ridge Hl GLDGN NW11 52 C7
Ridgemead Cl
STHGT/OAK N14 40 E1
Ridgemont Gdns EDGW HA8 36 E3
Ridgemount Av CROY/NA CR0 179 F1
Ridgemount Cl PGE/AN SE20 150 D6
Ridgemount Gdns
ENC/FH EN2 29 H2
Ridge Rd CEND/HSY/T N8 55 F5
CHEAM SM3 161 J7
CRICK NW2 70 D2
MTCM CR4 148 B6
WCHMH N21 29 K7
Ridges Yd CROY/NA CR0 177 H2
Ridge Ter WCHMH N21 * 29 J6
The Ridge BAR EN5 * 26 D4
BRYLDS KT5 159 H4
BXLY DA5 137 G6
WHTN TW2 123 J6
Ridgeview Cl BAR EN5 26 B5
Ridgeview Rd
TRDG/WHET N20 39 F2
Ridge Wy FELT TW13 141 J2
Ridgeway WFD IG8 45 G3
Ridgeway Av EBAR EN4 27 K5
Ridgeway Dr BMLY BR1 153 F3
Ridgeway East BFN/LL DA15 136 A4
Ridgeway Gdns HGT N6 54 C6
REDBR IG4 59 J4
Ridgeway Rd ISLW TW7 103 K6
Ridgeway Rd North
ISLW TW7 103 K6
The Ridgeway ACT W3 105 H2
CDALE/KGS NW9 51 F3
CROY/NA CR0 177 F2
FNCH N3 39 F6
GLDGN NW11 52 D7
GPK RM2 63 J3
KTN/HRWW/WS HA3 49 J5
MLHL NW7 37 J3
RSLP HA4 46 D6
RYLN/HDSTN HA2 47 K4
STAN HA7 35 J5
STHGT/OAK N14 40 E1
Ridgeway West BFN/LL DA15 135 K4
Ridgewell Cl DAGE RM10 80 D7
IS N1 6 F3
SYD SE26 151 H3
Ridgmount Gdns
GWRST WC1E 11 G2
Ridgmount Rd
WAND/EARL SW18 128 A4
Ridgmount St GWRST WC1E 11 G2
Ridgway RCHPK/HAM TW10 * 125 F5
WIM/MER SW19 146 A6
Ridgway Gdns
WIM/MER SW19 146 B6
Ridgway Pl WIM/MER SW19 146 C5
Ridgway Rd BRXN/ST SW9 130 C2
The Ridgway BELMT SM2 175 H6
Ridgwell Rd CAN/RD E16 95 G4
Riding House St REGST W1B 10 D4
Ridings Av WCHMH N21 29 H3
Ridings Cl HGT N6 54 C6
The Ridings BRYLDS KT5 159 H4
EA W5 86 B3
EBAR EN4 * 27 J6
EW KT17 173 H7
SUN TW16 140 E7
The Riding GLDGN NW11 52 D6
Ridley Av WEA W13 104 C2
Ridley Cl BARK IG11 79 F6
Ridley Rd FSTGT E7 77 G3
HACK E8 74 B4
WELL DA16 116 C7
WIM/MER SW19 147 F6
WLSDN NW10 87 J1
Ridsdale Rd PGE/AN SE20 150 D7
Riefield Rd ELTH/MOT SE9 135 H3
Riesco Dr CROY/NA CR0 178 E5
Riffel Rd CRICK NW2 70 A4
Rifle Pl NTGHL W11 88 B7
Rifle Range La HRW HA1 49 F7
Rifle St POP/IOD E14 93 K4
Rigault Rd FUL/PGN SW6 127 H1
Rigby Cl CROY/NA CR0 177 G2
Rigby La HYS/HAR UB3 101 F1
Rigby Ms IL IG1 78 A1
Rigden St POP/IOD E14 93 K5
Rigeley Rd WLSDN NW10 87 J2
Rigg Ap LEY E10 57 F7
Rigge Pl CLAP SW4 129 J3
Riggindale Rd
STRHM/NOR SW16 148 D4
Right Side STHGT/OAK N14 * 28 D7
Riley Rd STHWK SE1 19 L3
Riley St WBPTN SW10 108 C6
Rinaldo Rd BAL SW12 129 G6
Ring Cl BMLY BR1 153 F6
Ringcroft St HOLWY N7 73 G4
Ringer's Rd BMLY BR1 167 K2
Ringford Rd
WAND/EARL SW18 127 J4
Ringlet Cl CAN/RD E16 95 F4
Ringlewell Cl EN EN1 30 D1
Ringmer Av FUL/PGN SW6 107 H7
Ringmer Pl WCHMH N21 29 K4
Ringmer Wy BMLY BR1 168 E4
Ringmore Ri FSTH SE23 131 J6
Ring Rd SHB W12 88 A7
Ringslade Rd WDGN N22 55 F1
Ringstead Rd CAT SE6 132 E6
SUT SM1 175 H3
Ring Wy FBAR/BDGN N11 40 C5
Ringway NWDGN UB2 102 C4
Ringwold Cl BECK BR3 151 G6
Ringwood Av CROY/NA CR0 163 K6
EFNCH N2 53 K2
Ringwood Cl PIN HA5 * 47 G2
Ringwood Gdns
PUT/ROE SW15 145 J1
Ringwood Rd WALTH E17 57 H5
Ringwood Wy HPTN TW12 142 A3
WCHMH N21 29 H6
Ripley Cl BMLY BR1 168 E4
CROY/NA CR0 180 A5
Ripley Gdns
MORT/ESHN SW14 126 A2
Ripley Ms WAN E11 58 C5
Ripley Rd BELV DA17 117 H3
CAN/RD E16 95 G5
GDMY/SEVK IG3 78 E1
HPTN TW12 142 A6
Ripleys Market DART DA1 * 139 H6
Ripley Vls EA W5 * 85 J5
Ripon Cl NTHLT UB5 66 A4
Ripon Gdns CHSGTN KT9 171 K4
IL IG1 59 J5
Ripon Rd ED N9 30 D6
TOTM N17 55 K2
WOOL/PLUM SE18 115 G5
Ripon Wy BORE WD6 24 E4
Rippersley Rd WELL DA16 116 B7
Ripple Rd BARK IG11 78 C6
DAGW RM9 98 A1
Ripplevale Gv IS N1 5 M2
Rippolson Rd
WOOL/PLUM SE18 116 A4
Ripston Rd ASHF TW15 140 B4
Risborough Cl MUSWH N10 * 54 B2
Risborough Dr WPK KT4 160 D6
Risborough St STHWK SE1 18 D1
Risdon St BERM/RHTH SE16 111 K1
Risebridge Rd GPK RM2 63 H1
Risedale Rd BXLYHN DA7 137 J2
Riseldine Rd FSTH SE23 132 B5
Rise Park Pde ROM RM1 63 G1
The Rise BORE WD6 24 B4
BXLY DA5 136 D6
EDGW HA8 36 D4
GFD/PVL UB6 67 G4
MLHL NW7 37 H5
PLMGR N13 41 G3
SAND/SEL CR2 178 E7
WAN E11 58 E4
WLSDN NW10 69 F2
Rising Hill Cl NTHWD HA6 * 32 A5
Risinghill St IS N1 6 A5
Risingholme Cl BUSH WD23 22 B6
KTN/HRWW/WS HA3 34 E7
Risingholme Rd
KTN/HRWW/WS HA3 48 E1
The Risings WALTH E17 58 B3
Risley Av TOTM N17 41 J7
Rita Rd VX/NE SW8 109 K6
Ritches Rd SEVS/STOTM N15 55 J4
Ritchie Rd CROY/NA CR0 165 J5
Ritchie St IS N1 6 B5
Ritchings Av WALTH E17 57 G3
Ritherdon Rd TOOT SW17 148 A1
Ritson Rd HACK E8 74 B5
Ritter St WOOL/PLUM SE18 115 F5
Rivaz Pl HOM E9 74 E5
Rivenhall Gdns SWFD E18 58 D3
River Av PLMGR N13 41 H2
THDIT KT7 158 B6
Riverbank E/WMO/HCT KT8 157 K2
River Bank THDIT KT7 158 A4
WCHMH N21 29 J6
Riverbank Wy BTFD TW8 104 D5
River Barge Cl POP/IOD E14 113 F1
River Cl NWDGN UB2 103 H1
RAIN RM13 99 K4
RSLP HA4 46 D5
WAN E11 59 G5
Rivercourt Rd HMSMTH W6 106 E3
Riverdale Dr
WAND/EARL SW18 128 A7
Riverdale Gdns TWK TW1 124 D4
Riverdale Rd BXLY DA5 137 G6
ERITH DA8 117 J4
FELT TW13 141 J3
TWK TW1 124 D5
WOOL/PLUM SE18 116 A4
Riverdene EDGW HA8 36 E3
Riverdene Rd IL IG1 78 A2
River Front EN EN1 29 K2
River Gdns CAR SM5 176 A1
EBED/NFELT TW14 122 A4
River Grove Pk BECK BR3 151 H7
Riverhead Cl WALTH E17 57 F1
Riverholme Dr
HOR/WEW KT19 173 F7
River La RCHPK/HAM TW10 124 E7
Rivermead E/WMO/HCT KT8 157 H2
KUT/HW KT1 * 158 D4
Rivermead Cl TEDD TW11 143 H4
Rivermead Rd UED N18 * 43 F4
River Meads Av WHTN TW2 142 B2
Rivernook Cl WOT/HER KT12 156 B4
Riverpark Gdns HAYES BR2 152 B6
River Park Rd WDGN N22 55 F1
River Pl IS N1 6 E2
River Reach TEDD TW11 143 J5
River Rd BARK IG11 96 E2
Riversdale Rd HBRY N5 73 H2
THDIT KT7 158 B4
Riversfield Rd EN EN1 30 A2
Riverside CHARL SE7 114 A2
HDN NW4 51 K6
RCH/KEW TW9 * 105 H5
RCH/KEW TW9 124 E4
SUN TW16 * 156 C1
TWK TW1 124 C7
Riverside Av E/WMO/HCT KT8 157 J4
Riverside Cl CLPT E5 56 E7
HNWL W7 84 E3
KUT/HW KT1 158 E3
ROMW/RG RM7 63 F3
WLGTN SM6 176 B2
Riverside Ct CHING E4 * 31 K5
Riverside Dr CHSWK W4 106 A6
ESH/CLAY KT10 170 A3
GLDGN NW11 * 52 C5
MTCM CR4 162 D4
RCHPK/HAM TW10 143 H2
Riverside Gdns ALP/SUD HA0 86 A1
ENC/FH EN2 29 J1
HMSMTH W6 106 E4
Riverside Ms CROY/NA CR0 * 176 E2
Riverside Pl
FBAR/BDGN N11 * 40 C2
STWL/WRAY TW19 120 A5
Riverside Rd IL IG1 78 B2
OXHEY WD19 21 F5
SEVS/STOTM N15 56 C5
SRTFD E15 94 A1
STWL/WRAY TW19 120 A4
TOOT SW17 147 F3
The Riverside
E/WMO/HCT KT8 157 J2
Riverside Vls SURB KT6 * 158 D5
Riverside Wk ISLW TW7 123 K2
KUT/HW KT1 158 E1
Riverside Wy DART DA1 139 H4
Riverside Yd TOOT SW17 147 F2
Riverstone Cl
RYLN/HDSTN HA2 66 D1
River St CLKNW EC1R 6 A7
River Ter HMSMTH W6 107 F4
Riverton Cl MV/WKIL W9 * 88 D2
Riverview Gdns BARN SW13 106 E5
River View Gdns TWK TW1 143 F1
Riverview Gv CHSWK W4 105 J5
Riverview Pk CAT SE6 151 J1
Riverview Rd CHSWK W4 105 J6
HOR/WEW KT19 172 E3
River Wk SUN TW16 156 C1
River Wy WHTN TW2 142 B1
GNWCH SE10 113 J2
HOR/WEW KT19 173 F4
Riverway PLMGR N13 41 G4
River Whf BELV DA17 * 118 A1
Riverwood La CHST BR7 169 J1
Rivington Av WFD IG8 59 H1
Rivington Crs MLHL NW7 37 G6
Rivington Pl FSBYE EC1V 7 K8
Rivington St SDTCH EC2A 7 K8
Rivington Wk HACK E8 * 74 C7
Rivulet Rd TOTM N17 41 J6
Rixon St HOLWY N7 73 G2
Rixsen Rd MNPK E12 77 J4
Roach Rd BOW E3 75 J6
Roads Pl ARCH N19 72 E1
Roan St GNWCH SE10 113 F5
Robarts Cl PIN HA5 47 F4
Robb Rd STAN HA7 35 G5
Robert Adam St MHST W1U 10 A4
Roberta St BETH E2 92 C2
Robert Cl MV/WKIL W9 8 F1
Robert Dashwood Wy
WALW SE17 18 E6
Robert Keen Cl PECK SE15 111 H7
Robert Lowe Cl NWCR SE14 112 A6
Roberton Dr BMLY BR1 168 B1
Robertsbridge Rd CAR SM5 162 B6
Roberts Cl CHEAM SM3 174 B6
DAGE RM10 80 C5
ELTH/MOT SE9 135 J7
THHTH CR7 164 E2
Roberts Ct CHSGTN KT9 171 K4
PGE/AN SE20 150 E7
WLSDN NW10 69 G5
Roberts House
WOOL/PLUM SE18 * 114 D6
Roberts Ms KTBR SW1X * 16 A4
Robertson St VX/NE SW8 129 G1
Robert's Pl CLKNW EC1R * 6 B9
Robert Sq LEW SE13 133 F3
Roberts Rd BELV DA17 117 H4
MLHL NW7 38 C4
WALTH E17 43 K7
WATW WD18 21 G4
Robert St CAMTN NW1 4 D8
CHCR WC2N 11 K7
CROY/NA CR0 177 J2
WOOL/PLUM SE18 115 J3
Robeson St BOW E3 93 H4
Robina Cl BXLYHS DA6 136 E3
NTHWD HA6 46 D1
Robin Cl FELT TW13 141 J4
MLHL NW7 37 G2
Robin Gv BTFD TW8 104 D5
HGT N6 72 A1
KTN/HRWW/WS HA3 50 B5
Robin Hill Dr CHST BR7 153 J5
Robinhood Cl MTCM CR4 163 H3
Robin Hood Dr
KTN/HRWW/WS HA3 35 F6
Robin Hood Gdns
POP/IOD E14 * 94 A6
Robinhood La MTCM CR4 163 H2
Robin Hood La POP/IOD E14 94 A6
PUT/ROE SW15 145 G2
SUT SM1 174 E4
Robin Hood Rd
PUT/ROE SW15 145 G3
Robin Hood Wy GFD/PVL UB6 67 F5
PUT/ROE SW15 145 G3
Robinia Cl PGE/AN SE20 150 C7
Robinia Crs LEY E10 75 K1
Robin La HDN NW4 52 B2
Robins Gv WWKM BR4 180 E2
Robinson Cl ENC/FH EN2 29 J2
HCH RM12 81 K6
WAN E11 76 C2
Robinson Crs BUSH WD23 22 C7
Robinson Rd BETH E2 92 E1
DAGE RM10 80 C3
TOOT SW17 147 J5
Robinson's Cl WEA W13 85 G4
Robinson St CHEL SW3 15 L9
Robinswood Ms HBRY N5 73 H4
Robinwood Pl PUT/ROE SW15 145 F3
Rob Pascoe La DAGW RM9 98 A2
Robsart St BRXN/ST SW9 130 A1
Robson Av WLSDN NW10 69 J6
Robson Cl EHAM E6 95 J5
ENC/FH EN2 29 H1
Robson Rd WNWD SE27 149 H2
Rocastle Rd BROCKY SE4 132 B4
Roch Av EDGW HA8 50 B1
Rochdale Rd ABYW SE2 116 C3
WALTH E17 57 J6
Rochdale Wy DEPT SE8 112 D6
Rochelle Cl BTSEA SW11 128 C3
Rochelle St BETH E2 7 L8
Rochemont Wk HACK E8 * 7 M4
Roche Rd STRHM/NOR SW16 148 E7
Rochester Av BMLY BR1 168 A1
FELT TW13 140 D1
PLSTW E13 77 G7
Rochester Cl BFN/LL DA15 136 C5
STRHM/NOR SW16 * 148 E6
Rochester Dr BXLY DA5 137 H5
PIN HA5 47 H4
Rochester Gdns
CROY/NA CR0 178 A2
IL IG1 59 K6
Rochester Ms CAMTN NW1 4 F1
EA W5 * 104 D3
Rochester Pde FELT TW13 * 140 E2
Rochester Pl CAMTN NW1 72 C5
Rochester Rd CAMTN NW1 72 C5
CAR SM5 175 K3
HCH RM12 81 K6
NTHWD HA6 46 D2
Rochester Rw WEST SW1P 16 F5
Rochester Sq CAMTN NW1 4 F1
Rochester St WEST SW1P 17 G4
Rochester Ter CAMTN NW1 72 C5
Rochester Wk STHWK SE1 * 13 G8
Rochester Wy BKHTH/KID SE3 114 A7
ELTH/MOT SE9 134 C2
ELTH/MOT SE9 134 E2
ELTH/MOT SE9 135 H2
Rochester Way Relief Rd
ELTH/MOT SE9 134 D4
ELTH/MOT SE9 135 G3
Roche Wk CAR SM5 162 C5
Rochford Av CHDH RM6 61 J4
Rochford Cl EHAM E6 95 H1
HCH RM12 81 K5
Rochford Wk HACK E8 * 74 C6
Rochford Wy CROY/NA CR0 163 K5
Rock Av MORT/ESHN SW14 126 A2
Rockbourne Rd FSTH SE23 132 A7
Rock Cl MTCM CR4 162 C1
Rockell's Pl EDUL SE22 131 J5
Rockford Av GFD/PVL UB6 85 H1
Rock Grove Wy
BERM/RHTH SE16 111 H3
Rockhall Rd CRICK NW2 70 B3
Rockhampton Rd
SAND/SEL CR2 178 A5
STRHM/NOR SW16 149 G3
Rock Hl DUL SE21 150 B3
Rockingham Av EMPK RM11 63 K5
Rockingham Cl
PUT/ROE SW15 126 C3
Rockingham Ga BUSH WD23 22 C5
Rockingham St STHWK SE1 18 E4
Rockland Rd PUT/ROE SW15 127 H3
Rocklands Dr
KTN/HRWW/WS HA3 49 H1
Rockley Rd SHB W12 107 G1
Rockmount Rd NRWD SE19 149 K5
WOOL/PLUM SE18 116 A4
Rocks La BARN SW13 126 D2
Rock St FSBYPK N4 73 G1
Rockware Av GFD/PVL UB6 66 E7
Rockways BAR EN5 25 H5
Rockwell Gdns NRWD SE19 150 A3
Rockwell Rd DAGE RM10 80 D4
Rocliffe St IS N1 6 D6
Rocombe Crs FSTH SE23 * 131 K6
Rocque La BKHTH/KID SE3 133 J2
Rodborough Rd GLDGN NW11 52 E7
Roden Gdns CROY/NA CR0 165 F5
Rodenhurst Rd CLAP SW4 129 H6
Roden St HOLWY N7 73 F2
IL IG1 78 A2
Roderick Rd HAMP NW3 71 K3
Rodgers Cl BORE WD6 23 K5
Roding La North WFD IG8 59 J1
Roding La South REDBR IG4 59 H3
Roding Ms WAP E1W 92 C7
Roding Rd CLPT E5 75 F3
EHAM E6 96 B4
Rodings Rw BAR EN5 * 26 C3
Rodmarton St MHST W1U 9 M3
Rodmell Cl YEAD UB4 83 J3
Rodmell Slope
NFNCH/WDSPK N12 38 D4
Rodmere St GNWCH SE10 113 H4
Rodney Cl CROY/NA CR0 164 C7
NWMAL KT3 160 B4
PIN HA5 47 J6
WOT/HER KT12 * 156 B7
Rodney Gdns PIN HA5 47 F4
WWKM BR4 180 E3
Rodney Pl STHWK SE1 18 F5
WALTH E17 57 G1
WIM/MER SW19 147 G7
Rodney Rd MTCM CR4 162 D1
NWMAL KT3 160 B4
WALW SE17 18 F6
WAN E11 59 F5
WHTN TW2 123 F6
Rodney St IS N1 5 M5
Rodway Rd BMLY BR1 153 F7
PUT/ROE SW15 126 D6
Rodwell Cl RSLP HA4 * 47 G7
Rodwell Rd EDUL SE22 131 G5
Roebuck Cl FELT TW13 141 F3
Roebuck Rd CHSGTN KT9 172 C4
Roedean Crs PUT/ROE SW15 126 B5
Roe End CDALE/KGS NW9 50 E3
Roe Gn CDALE/KGS NW9 50 E4
Roehampton Cl
PUT/ROE SW15 126 D3
Roehampton Dr CHST BR7 154 C5
Roehampton Ga
PUT/ROE SW15 126 B5
Roehampton High St
PUT/ROE SW15 126 D6
Roehampton La
PUT/ROE SW15 126 D6
Roehampton V
PUT/ROE SW15 145 H2
Roe La CDALE/KGS NW9 50 D3
Roe Rd WLGTN SM6 176 E5
Rofant Rd NTHWD HA6 32 C5
Roffey St POP/IOD E14 113 F1
Rogers Gdns DAGE RM10 80 C4
Rogers Rd CAN/RD E16 94 D5
DAGE RM10 80 C4
TOOT SW17 147 H3
Rogers Ruff NTHWD HA6 32 A7
Roger St BMSBY WC1N 11 M1
Rogers Wk
NFNCH/WDSPK N12 39 F2
Rojack Rd FSTH SE23 132 A7
Rokeby Gdns WFD IG8 44 E7
Rokeby Pl RYNPK SW20 145 K6
Rokeby Rd BROCKY SE4 * 132 C1
Rokeby St SRTFD E15 76 C7
Rokesby Cl WELL DA16 135 J1
Rokesby Pl ALP/SUD HA0 67 K4
Rokesly Av CEND/HSY/T N8 54 E4
Roland Gdns SKENS SW7 14 F7
Roland Ms WCHPL E1 * 93 F4
Roland Rd WALTH E17 58 B3
Roland Wy SKENS SW7 14 F7
WALW SE17 19 H8
WPK KT4 173 H1
Roles Gv CHDH RM6 61 K3
Rolfe Cl EBAR EN4 27 J3
Rolinsden Wy HAYES BR2 181 H3
Rollesby Rd CHSGTN KT9 172 C5
Rollesby Wy THMD SE28 97 J6
Rolleston Av STMC/STPC BR5 169 G5
Rolleston Cl STMC/STPC BR5 169 G6
Rolleston Rd SAND/SEL CR2 177 K6
Roll Gdns GNTH/NBYPK IG2 60 A4
Rollins St PECK SE15 111 K5
Rollit Crs HSLW TW3 123 F4
Rollit St HOLWY N7 73 G4
Rolls Blds FLST/FETLN EC4A 12 A4
Rollscourt Av HNHL SE24 130 D4
Rolls Park Av CHING E4 43 J5
Rolls Park Rd CHING E4 43 K4
Rolls Rd STHWK SE1 19 M7
Rolls Royce Cl WLGTN SM6 176 E6
Rolt St DEPT SE8 112 C5
NWCR SE14 112 B5
Rolvenden Gdns BMLY BR1 153 H7
Rolvenden Pl TOTM N17 42 C7
Roman Cl ACT W3 105 J1
EBED/NFELT TW14 122 B4
RAIN RM13 99 F1
Romanfield Rd
BRXS/STRHM SW2 130 A6
Romanhurst Av HAYES BR2 167 H3
Romanhurst Gdns HAYES BR2 167 H3
Roman Rd BORE WD6 23 K5
CAR SM5 175 K7
Roman Ri NRWD SE19 149 K5
Roman Rd BETH E2 93 F1
BOW E3 75 H7
CHSWK W4 106 B3
CRICK NW2 70 A2
EHAM E6 95 H3
IL IG1 78 B5
MUSWH N10 40 B6
Roman Sq THMD SE28 97 G7
Roman Wy CROY/NA CR0 177 H1
EN EN1 30 B4
HOLWY N7 73 F5
Romany Gdns CHEAM SM3 161 K6
Romany Ri STMC/STPC BR5 169 H7
Roma Rd WALTH E17 57 G2
Romberg Rd TOOT SW17 148 A2
Romborough Gdns LEW SE13 133 F4
Romborough Wy LEW SE13 133 F4
Rom Crs ROMW/RG RM7 63 G6
Romeland BORE WD6 23 K5
Romero Cl BRXN/ST SW9 130 A2
Romero Sq BKHTH/KID SE3 134 B3
Romeyn Rd
STRHM/NOR SW16 149 F2
Romford Rd SRTFD E15 76 D5
Romford St WCHPL E1 92 C4
Romilly Dr OXHEY WD19 33 J3
Romilly Rd FSBYPK N4 73 H1
Romilly St SOHO/SHAV W1D 11 H6
Rommany Rd WNWD SE27 149 K3
Romney Cl ASHF TW15 140 A4
CHSGTN KT9 172 A3
GLDGN NW11 53 G7
NWCR SE14 111 K6
RYLN/HDSTN HA2 48 K6
TOTM N17 42 D7
Romney Dr BMLY BR1 153 H6
RYLN/HDSTN HA2 48 A6
Romney Rd GNWCH SE10 113 F5
NWMAL KT3 160 A5
WOOL/PLUM SE18 115 H2
YEAD UB4 82 B1
Romney Rw CRICK NW2 * 70 B1
Romney St WEST SW1P 17 H4
Romola Rd HNHL SE24 130 C7
Romsey Rd DAGW RM9 79 K7
WEA W13 * 85 G6
Romside Pl ROMW/RG RM7 63 F3
Rom Valley Wy
ROMW/RG RM7 63 G5
Ronald Av SRTFD E15 94 C2
Ronald Cl BECK BR3 166 C4
Ronalds Rd BMLY BR1 152 E7
HBRY N5 73 G4
Ronaldstone Rd BFN/LL DA15 135 K5
Rona Rd HAMP NW3 72 A3
Ronart St
KTN/HRWW/WS HA3 49 F2
Rona Wk IS N1 73 K5
Rondu Rd CRICK NW2 70 C4
Ronelean Rd SURB KT6 172 B1
Roneo Cnr ROMW/RG RM7 63 H7
Roneo Link HCH RM12 63 H7
Ron Leighton Wy EHAM E6 77 J7
Ronnie La BCTR RM8 79 J1
Ron Todd Cl DAGE RM10 80 C7
Rood La FENCHST EC3M 13 J6
Rookby Ct WCHMH N21 41 H1
Rook Cl WBLY HA9 68 D2
Rookeries Cl FELT TW13 141 F2
Rookery Dr CHST BR7 154 A7
Rookery La HAYES BR2 168 C5
Rookery Rd CLAP SW4 129 H3
The Rookery
STRHM/NOR SW16 * 149 F5
Rookery Wy CDALE/KGS NW9 51 H4
Rookfield Av MUSWH N10 54 C3
Rookfield Cl MUSWH N10 54 C3
Rooksley Cl BELMT SM2 175 F7
Rooks Ter WDR/YW UB7 * 100 B1
Rookstone Rd TOOT SW17 147 K4
Rookwood Av NWMAL KT3 160 D3
WLGTN SM6 176 D3
Rookwood Gdns CHING E4 * 44 D1
Rookwood Rd
STNW/STAM N16 56 C6
Roosevelt Wy DAGE RM10 81 F5
Rootes Dr NKENS W10 88 B3
Ropemaker Rd
BERM/RHTH SE16 112 B1
Ropemaker's Flds
POP/IOD E14 * 93 H6
Ropemaker St BARB EC2Y 13 G2
Roper La STHWK SE1 19 K2
Ropers Av CHING E4 44 A4
Ropers Orch CHEL SW3 * 108 D5
Roper St ELTH/MOT SE9 134 E4
Roper Wy MTCM CR4 163 F1
Ropery St BOW E3 93 H3
Rope St BERM/RHTH SE16 112 B2
Ropewalk Gdns WCHPL E1 92 C5
Rope Yard Rails
WOOL/PLUM SE18 115 G2
Ropley St BETH E2 92 C1

Rosa Alba Ms HBRY N5 73 J3
Rosaline Rd FUL/PGN SW6 107 H6
Rosaline Ter FUL/PGN SW6 * 107 H6
Rosamond St SYD SE26 150 D2
Rosamond Vls
MORT/ESHN SW14 * 126 A3
Rosamund Cl SAND/SEL CR2 177 K3
Rosamun Rd NWDGN UB2 102 D3
Rosary Cl HSLW TW3 122 D1
Rosary Gdns BUSH WD23 22 E6
SKENS SW7 14 F6
Rosary Ga BTSEA SW11 109 G6
Rosaville Rd FUL/PGN SW6 107 J6
Roscoe St STLK EC1Y 12 F1
Roscoff Cl EDGW HA8 36 D7
Roseacre Cl WEA W13 85 H4
Roseacre Rd WELL DA16 136 C2
Rose Aly LVPST EC2M 13 K3
STHWK SE1 12 F8
Roseary Cl WDR/YW UB7 100 A3
Rose Av MRDN SM4 162 B4
MTCM CR4 147 K7
SWFD E18 59 F1
Rosebank PGE/AN SE20 150 D6
Rosebank Av ALP/SUD HA0 67 F3
Rose Bank Cl
NFNCH/WDSPK N12 39 J4
Rosebank Cl TEDD TW11 143 G5
Rosebank Est BOW E3 93 H1
Rosebank Gdns ACT W3 * 87 F5
BOW E3 * 93 G1
Rosebank Gv WALTH E17 57 H2
Rosebank Rd HNWL W7 103 K1
WALTH E17 57 J5
Rosebank Wk CAMTN NW1 5 H2
Rosebank Wy ACT W3 87 F5
Roseberry Gdns FSBYPK N4 55 H5
Roseberry Pl HACK E8 74 B5
Roseberry St
BERM/RHTH SE16 111 J3
Rosebery Av BFN/LL DA15 135 K6
CLKNW EC1R 12 A1
MNPK E12 77 J5
NWMAL KT3 160 C1
RYLN/HDSTN HA2 65 J3
THHTH CR7 164 D1
TOTM N17 56 C1
Rosebery Cl MRDN SM4 161 G5
Rosebery Ct CLKNW EC1R 6 A9
Rosebery Gdns
CEND/HSY/T N8 * 54 E4
SUT SM1 175 F3
WEA W13 85 G5
Rosebery Ms MUSWH N10 54 C1
Rosebery Pde EW KT17 * 173 H6
Rosebery Rd BUSH WD23 22 B7
CLAP SW4 129 K5
HSLW TW3 123 H4
KUT/HW KT1 159 J1
MUSWH N10 54 C1
SUT SM1 174 D5
Rosebine Av WHTN TW2 123 J6
Rosebriars ESH/CLAY KT10 170 C4
Rosebury Rd FUL/PGN SW6 128 A1
Rosebury V RSLP HA4 64 E1
Rose Ct WCHPL E1 13 L3
Rosecourt Rd CROY/NA CR0 164 A5
Rosecroft Av HAMP NW3 70 E2
Rosecroft Ct NTHWD HA6 * 32 A5
Rose Croft Gdns CRICK NW2 69 J2
Rosecroft Gdns WHTN TW2 123 J7
Rosecroft Rd STHL UB1 84 A3
Rosecroft Wk ALP/SUD HA0 67 K4
PIN HA5 47 H4
Rose & Crown Yd STJS SW1Y * 10 F9
Rosedale Av HYS/HAR UB3 82 B4
Rosedale Cl ABYW SE2 116 C2
HNWL W7 104 A1
STAN HA7 35 H5
Rosedale Dr DAGW RM9 79 H7
Rosedale Gdns DAGW RM9 79 H6
Rosedale Pl CROY/NA CR0 166 A6
Rosedale Rd DAGW RM9 79 H6
EW KT17 173 J4
FSTGT E7 77 G4
RCH/KEW TW9 125 F3
ROM RM1 62 E2
Rosedene Av CROY/NA CR0 163 K6
GFD/PVL UB6 84 A2
MRDN SM4 161 K4
STRHM/NOR SW16 149 F2
Rosedene Gdns
GNTH/NBYPK IG2 60 A3
Rosedene Ter LEY E10 75 K1
Rosedew Rd HMSMTH W6 107 G5
Rose End WPK KT4 161 G7
Rosefield POP/IOD E14 93 J6
Rosefield Cl CAR SM5 175 J4
Rosefield Gdns POP/IOD E14 93 J6
Rose Garden Cl EDGW HA8 36 A5
Rose Gdns EA W5 104 E2
FELT TW13 140 E1
STHL UB1 84 A3
STWL/WRAY TW19 120 A6
WATW WD18 20 E4
Rose Gln CDALE/KGS NW9 51 F3
ROMW/RG RM7 63 G7
Rosehart Ms NTGHL W11 8 A5
Rosehatch Av CHDH RM6 61 K2
Roseheath Rd HSLWW TW4 122 E4
Rosehill ESH/CLAY KT10 171 G5
HPTN TW12 142 A7
Rose Hl SUT SM1 175 F1
Rosehill Av SUT SM1 162 B7
Rosehill Court Pde
MRDN SM4 * 162 B6
Rosehill Gdns GFD/PVL UB6 67 F4
SUT SM1 175 F1
Rose Hill Pk West SUT SM1 162 B7
Rosehill Rd WAND/EARL SW18 128 B5
Rose Joan Ms
KIL/WHAMP NW6 70 E3
Roseland Cl TOTM N17 41 K6
Rose La CHDH RM6 62 A3
Rose Lawn BUSH WD23 22 C7
Roseleigh Av HBRY N5 73 H3
Roseleigh Cl TWK TW1 124 E5
Rosemary Av
E/WMO/HCT KT8 157 F2
ED N9 30 D7
FNCH N3 53 F1
HSLWW TW4 122 C1
ROM RM1 63 H2
Rosemary Cl CROY/NA CR0 163 K6
Rosemary Dr POP/IOD E14 94 B5
REDBR IG4 59 H4
Rosemary Gdns BCTR RM8 62 B7
CHSGTN KT9 172 A3
Rosemary La
MORT/ESHN SW14 125 K2
Rosemary Rd PECK SE15 111 G6
TOOT SW17 147 G2
WELL DA16 116 A7
Rosemary St IS N1 7 G3
Rosemead CDALE/KGS NW9 51 H6
Rosemead Av FELT TW13 140 D1
MTCM CR4 163 H2
WBLY HA9 68 A4
Rose Ms UED N18 42 D3
Rosemont Av
NFNCH/WDSPK N12 39 G5
Rosemont Rd ACT W3 86 D6
HAMP NW3 71 G5
NWMAL KT3 159 K2
RCHPK/HAM TW10 125 F5
Rosemoor St CHEL SW3 15 L6
Rosemount Cl WFD IG8 45 K5
Rosemount Dr BMLY BR1 168 E3
Rosemount Rd ALP/SUD HA0 68 A7
WEA W13 85 G5
Rosenau Crs BTSEA SW11 108 E7
Rosenau Rd BTSEA SW11 108 D7
Rosendale Rd DUL SE21 149 J1
Roseneath Av WCHMH N21 29 H7
Roseneath Pl
STRHM/NOR SW16 149 G3
Roseneath Rd BTSEA SW11 129 F5
Roseneath Wk EN EN1 30 A3
Rosens Wk EDGW HA8 36 D2
Rosenthal Rd CAT SE6 132 E5
Rosenthorpe Rd PECK SE15 132 A4
Rose Park Cl YEAD UB4 83 G4
Roserton St POP/IOD E14 113 F1
The Rosery CROY/NA CR0 166 A5
The Roses WFD IG8 * 44 D6
Rose St COVGDN WC2E 11 J6
Rosethorn Cl BAL SW12 129 H6
Rosetree Pl HPTN TW12 142 A6
Rosetta Cl VX/NE SW8 109 K6
Roseveare Rd LEE/GVPK SE12 153 G3
Roseville WCHMH N21 29 G7
Roseville Av HSLW TW3 123 F4
Roseville Rd HYS/HAR UB3 101 K4
Rosevine Rd RYNPK SW20 146 A7
Rose Wk BRYLDS KT5 159 J4
WWKM BR4 180 A1
Roseway DUL SE21 130 E5
EDGW HA8 36 E3
Rosewell Cl PGE/AN SE20 150 D6
Rosewood Av GFD/PVL UB6 67 G4
HCH RM12 81 J4
Rosewood Cl SCUP DA14 155 J2
Rosewood Ct KUTN/CMB KT2 144 C6
Rosewood Gv SUT SM1 175 G1
Rosewood Ter PGE/AN SE20 * 150 E6
Rosher Cl SRTFD E15 76 B6
Rosina St HOM E9 75 F5
Roskell Rd PUT/ROE SW15 127 G2
Roslin Rd ACT W3 105 J2
Roslin Wy BMLY BR1 152 E4
Roslyn Cl MTCM CR4 162 C1
Roslyn Gdns GPK RM2 63 H1
Roslyn Ms SEVS/STOTM N15 * 56 A4
Roslyn Rd SEVS/STOTM N15 55 K4
Rosmead Rd NTGHL W11 88 C6
Rosoman Pl CLKNW EC1R 6 B9
Rosoman St CLKNW EC1R 6 B8
Rossall Cl EMPK RM11 63 J5
Rossall Crs WLSDN NW10 86 B2
Ross Av BCTR RM8 80 B1
Ross Cl HYS/HAR UB3 101 G3
KTN/HRWW/WS HA3 34 C6
NTHLT UB5 66 D3
Rossdale SUT SM1 175 J4
Rossdale Dr CDALE/KGS NW9 50 E7
ED N9 30 E5
Rossdale Rd PUT/ROE SW15 127 F3
Rosse Ms BKHTH/KID SE3 114 A7
Rossendale St CLPT E5 74 D1
Rossendale Wy CAMTN NW1 4 F2
Rossetti Ms STJWD NW8 3 G4
Rossetti Rd BERM/RHTH SE16 111 J4
Ross House CHARL SE7 * 114 D6
Rossignol Gdns CAR SM5 176 A1
Rossindel Rd HSLW TW3 123 F4
Rossington St CLPT E5 74 C1
Rossiter Cl NRWD SE19 149 J6
Rossiter Flds BAR EN5 26 C5
Rossiter Rd BAL SW12 129 G7
Rosslyn Av BARN SW13 126 B2
BCTR RM8 62 B6
CHING E4 44 D1
EBAR EN4 27 J5
EBED/NFELT TW14 121 K5
Rosslyn Cl HYS/HAR UB3 82 B4
SUN TW16 140 C5
WWKM BR4 180 D2
Rosslyn Crs HRW HA1 49 F3
WBLY HA9 68 A2
Rosslyn Hl HAMP NW3 71 H4
Rosslyn Park Ms HAMP NW3 71 H4
Rosslyn Rd BARK IG11 78 D6
TWK TW1 124 D5
WALTH E17 * 58 A3
WATW WD18 21 F2
Rossmore Cl CAMTN NW1 * 9 K1
PEND EN3 31 F3
Rossmore Rd CAMTN NW1 3 K9
Ross Pde WLGTN SM6 176 B5
Ross Rd SNWD SE25 165 F2
WHTN TW2 123 H7
WLGTN SM6 176 C5
Ross Wy ELTH/MOT SE9 134 D2
NTHWD HA6 32 D3
Rossway Dr BUSH WD23 22 C4
Rosswood Gdns WLGTN SM6 176 B5
Rostella Rd TOOT SW17 147 H3
Rostrever Gdns HYS/HAR UB3 82 C7
Rostrevor Av
SEVS/STOTM N15 56 B5
Rostrevor Gdns NWDGN UB2 102 D4
Rostrevor Rd FUL/PGN SW6 107 J7
WIM/MER SW19 146 E4
Rotary St STHWK SE1 18 C3
Rothbury Av RAIN RM13 99 K4
Rothbury Cots GNWCH SE10 113 H3
Rothbury Gdns ISLW TW7 104 B6
Rothbury Rd HOM E9 75 H6
Rotherfield Rd CAR SM5 176 A3
Rotherfield St IS N1 6 F2
Rotherham Wk STHWK SE1 * 12 D9
Rotherhill Av
STRHM/NOR SW16 148 D5
Rotherhithe New Rd
BERM/RHTH SE16 111 J4
Rotherhithe Old Rd
BERM/RHTH SE16 112 A3
Rotherhithe St
BERM/RHTH SE16 111 J1
Rotherhithe Tnl
BERM/RHTH SE16 111 K1
Rothermere Rd
CROY/NA CR0 177 F4
Rotherwick Hl EA W5 86 B3
Rotherwick Rd GLDGN NW11 52 E6
Rotherwood Cl RYNPK SW20 146 C7
Rotherwood Rd
PUT/ROE SW15 127 G2
Rothery St IS N1 * 6 D3
Rothery Ter BRXN/ST SW9 * 110 C6
Rothesay Av GFD/PVL UB6 66 D5
RCHPK/HAM TW10 125 J3
RYNPK SW20 161 H1
Rothesay Rd SNWD SE25 164 E3
Rothsay Rd FSTGT E7 77 G6
Rothsay St STHWK SE1 19 J3
Rothschild Rd CHSWK W4 105 K3
Rothschild St WNWD SE27 149 H3
Rothwell Gdns DAGW RM9 79 J6
Rothwell Rd DAGW RM9 79 J7
Rothwell St CAMTN NW1 3 M3
Rotten Rw BAY/PAD W2 15 K1
Rotterdam Dr POP/IOD E14 113 F2
Rouel Rd BERM/RHTH SE16 111 H2
Rougemont Av MRDN SM4 161 K5
The Roughs NTHWD HA6 32 C2
Roundaway Rd CLAY IG5 59 K1
Roundel Cl BROCKY SE4 132 C3
Round Gv CROY/NA CR0 166 A6
Roundhay Cl FSTH SE23 151 F1
Round Hl SYD SE26 150 D1
Roundhill Dr ENC/FH EN2 29 F3
Roundtree Rd ALP/SUD HA0 67 H4
Roundways RSLP HA4 64 D2
The Roundway
ESH/CLAY KT10 171 F5
TOTM N17 41 J7
WATW WD18 20 D5
Roundwood CHST BR7 169 G1
Roundwood Av STKPK UB11 82 A7
Roundwood Cl RSLP HA4 * 46 B6
Roundwood Pk
WLSDN NW10 * 69 J7
Roundwood Rd WLSDN NW10 69 G5
Roundwood Ter
STNW/STAM N16 56 A6
Rounton Rd BOW E3 93 J3
Roupell Rd BRXS/STRHM SW2 130 A7
Roupell St STHWK SE1 12 B9
Rousden St CAMTN NW1 4 E2
Rousebarn La
RKW/CH/CXG WD3 20 A2
Rouse Gdns DUL SE21 150 A3
Routemaster Cl PLSTW E13 95 F2
Routh Ct EBED/NFELT TW14 121 G7
Routh Rd WAND/EARL SW18 128 D6
Routh St EHAM E6 95 K4
Rowallan Rd FUL/PGN SW6 107 H6
Rowan Av CHING E4 43 H5
Rowan Cl ALP/SUD HA0 67 G2
EA W5 105 F1
IL IG1 78 D4
NWMAL KT3 160 B1
STAN HA7 35 F5
STRHM/NOR SW16 148 C7
Rowan Crs STRHM/NOR SW16 148 C7
Rowan Dr CDALE/KGS NW9 51 J2
Rowan Gdns CROY/NA CR0 178 B2
Rowan Pl HYS/HAR UB3 82 D6
Rowan Rd BTFD TW8 104 C6
HMSMTH W6 107 G3
STRHM/NOR SW16 163 H1
WDR/YW UB7 100 A3
The Rowans PLMGR N13 41 J2
SUN TW16 140 D4
Rowan Ter HMSMTH W6 107 G3
PGE/AN SE20 * 150 C7
WIM/MER SW19 * 146 C6
Rowantree Cl WCHMH N21 29 K7
Rowantree Ms ENC/FH EN2 29 H1
Rowantree Rd ENC/FH EN2 29 H1
WCHMH N21 29 K7
Rowan Wk EFNCH N2 53 G5
HAYES BR2 181 K2
NKENS W10 * 88 C3
Rowan Wy CHDH RM6 61 J2
Rowanwood Av BFN/LL DA15 136 B7
Rowben Cl TRDG/WHET N20 27 F7
Rowberry Cl FUL/PGN SW6 107 G6
Rowcross St STHWK SE1 19 L7
Rowdell Rd NTHLT UB5 66 A7
Rowden Pde CHING E4 * 43 J5
Rowden Rd BECK BR3 151 G7
CHING E4 43 K5
HOR/WEW KT19 172 E3
Rowditch La BTSEA SW11 129 F1
Rowdon Av WLSDN NW10 69 K6
Rowdown Crs CROY/NA CR0 180 B7
Rowdowns Rd DAGW RM9 80 B7
Rowe Gdns BARK IG11 97 F1
Rowe La HOM E9 74 E4
Rowena Crs BTSEA SW11 128 D1
Rowe Wk RYLN/HDSTN HA2 66 A2
Rowfant Rd TOOT SW17 148 A1
Rowhill Rd CLPT E5 74 D3
Rowington Cl BAY/PAD W2 8 C2
Rowland Av
KTN/HRWW/WS HA3 49 J2
Rowland Gv SYD SE26 150 D2
Rowland Hill Av TOTM N17 41 J6
Rowland Hill St HAMP NW3 71 J4
Rowland Pl NTHWD HA6 * 32 C6
Rowlands Av PIN HA5 34 A5
Rowlands Cl HGT N6 * 54 A5
MLHL NW7 37 J6
Rowlands Rd BCTR RM8 80 B1
Rowland Wy ASHF TW15 140 A6
WIM/MER SW19 147 F7
Rowley Av BFN/LL DA15 136 C6
Rowley Cl ALP/SUD HA0 68 B6
OXHEY WD19 21 J5
Rowley Cots WKENS W14 * 107 J3
Rowley Gdns FSBYPK N4 55 J6
Rowley Green Rd BAR EN5 25 J4
Rowley La BORE WD6 25 F1
Rowley Rd SEVS/STOTM N15 55 J4
Rowley Wy STJWD NW8 2 F3
Rowlheys Pl WDR/YW UB7 100 B2
Rowlls Rd KUT/HW KT1 159 G2
Rowney Gdns DAGW RM9 79 J5
Rowney Rd DAGW RM9 79 H5
Rowntree Clifford Cl
PLSTW E13 95 F3
Rowntree Cl
KIL/WHAMP NW6 * 70 E5
Rowntree Rd WHTN TW2 123 K7
Rowse Cl SRTFD E15 76 A7
Rowsley Av HDN NW4 52 A2
Rowstock Gdns HOLWY N7 72 D5
Rowton Rd
WOOL/PLUM SE18 115 H6
Roxborough Av HRW HA1 48 D6
ISLW TW7 104 A6
Roxborough Pk HRW HA1 48 E6
Roxborough Rd HRW HA1 48 D4
Roxbourne Cl NTHLT UB5 65 H5
Roxburgh Rd WNWD SE27 149 H4
Roxburn Wy RSLP HA4 64 D2
Roxby Pl FUL/PGN SW6 14 B9
Roxeth Green Av
RYLN/HDSTN HA2 66 B2
Roxeth Gv RYLN/HDSTN HA2 66 B3
Roxeth Hl RYLN/HDSTN HA2 66 D1
Roxley Rd LEW SE13 132 E5
Roxton Gdns CROY/NA CR0 179 H5
Roxwell Rd BARK IG11 97 G1
SHB W12 106 D1
Roxwell Wy WFD IG8 45 G6
Roxy Av CHDH RM6 61 J6
Royal Albert Wy CAN/RD E16 95 H6
Royal Ar CONDST W1S 10 E7
Royal Arsenal West
WOOL/PLUM SE18 * 115 F4
Royal Av CHEL SW3 15 L7
WPK KT4 173 G1
Royal Circ WNWD SE27 149 G2
Royal Cl DEPT SE8 112 C5
GDMY/SEVK IG3 61 G6
STNW/STAM N16 56 A7
WIM/MER SW19 146 B1
WPK KT4 173 G1
Royal College St CAMTN NW1 4 F3
Royal Connaught Dr
BUSH WD23 21 K3
Royal Ct BANK EC3V 13 H5
ELTH/MOT SE9 * 134 E7
EN EN1 * 30 A5
Royal Crs GNTH/NBYPK IG2 60 D5
NTGHL W11 107 G1
RSLP HA4 65 J3
Royal Crescent Ms
NTGHL W11 107 G1
Royal Docks Rd EHAM E6 96 B4
Royal Dr FBAR/BDGN N11 40 A4
Royal Herbert Pavilions
WOOL/PLUM SE18 * 114 E7
Royal Hl GNWCH SE10 113 F6
Royal Hospital Rd CHEL SW3 15 L9
Royal Ms BAL SW12 129 G6
Royal Mint Pl WCHPL E1 13 M6
Royal Mint St WCHPL E1 13 M6
Royal Naval Pl NWCR SE14 112 C6
Royal Oak Ms TEDD TW11 143 G4
Royal Oak Pl EDUL SE22 131 J5
Royal Oak Rd HACK E8 74 D5
Royal Oak Yd STHWK SE1 19 J2
Royal Opera Ar STJS SW1Y * 11 G8
Royal Orchard Cl
WAND/EARL SW18 127 H6
Royal Pde BKHTH/KID SE3 133 J1
CHST BR7 154 C6
FUL/PGN SW6 * 107 H6
Royal Pl GNWCH SE10 113 F6
Royal Rd CAN/RD E16 95 H5
LBTH SE11 18 C9
SCUP DA14 155 K2
TEDD TW11 142 D4
Royal Route WBLY HA9 68 B3
Royal St STHWK SE1 17 M3
Royal Victor Pl BOW E3 93 F1
Roycraft Av BARK IG11 97 F1
Roycroft Cl
BRXS/STRHM SW2 * 130 B7
SWFD E18 45 F7
Roydene Rd
WOOL/PLUM SE18 115 K5
Roy Gdns GNTH/NBYPK IG2 60 E3
Roy Gv HPTN TW12 142 B5
Royle Cl GPK RM2 63 K4
Royle Crs WEA W13 85 G3
Roy Rd NTHWD HA6 32 D6
Roy Sq POP/IOD E14 93 G6
Royston Av CHING E4 43 J4
SUT SM1 175 H2
WLGTN SM6 176 D3
Royston Cl HEST TW5 102 A7
Royston Gdns IL IG1 59 H5
Royston Gv PIN HA5 33 K5
Royston Park Rd PIN HA5 33 K5
Royston Rd PGE/AN SE20 151 F7
RCHPK/HAM TW10 125 F4
The Roystons BRYLDS KT5 159 J4
Royston St BETH E2 92 E1
Rozel Rd VX/NE SW8 129 H1
Rubastic Rd NWDGN UB2 102 B2
Rubens Rd NTHLT UB5 83 G1
Rubens St CAT SE6 151 H1
Ruby Ms WALTH E17 * 57 J2
Ruby Rd WALTH E17 57 J2
Ruby St PECK SE15 111 J5
WLSDN NW10 68 E6
Ruby Triangle PECK SE15 * 111 J5
Ruckholt Cl LEY E10 75 K2
Ruckholt Rd LEY E10 75 K3
Rucklidge Av WLSDN NW10 87 H1
Rudall Crs HAMP NW3 71 H3
Ruddington Cl CLPT E5 75 G3
Ruddock Cl EDGW HA8 36 E6
Ruddstreet Cl
WOOL/PLUM SE18 115 G3
Rudgwick Ter STJWD NW8 * 3 K4
Rudloe Rd BAL SW12 129 H6
Rudolf Pl VX/NE SW8 109 K5
Rudolph Rd BUSH WD23 22 A5
KIL/WHAMP NW6 2 B6
PLSTW E13 94 D1
Rudyard Gv EDGW HA8 36 E5
Ruffetts Cl SAND/SEL CR2 178 D6
The Ruffetts SAND/SEL CR2 178 D6
Ruffle Cl WDR/YW UB7 100 B1
Rufford Cl
KTN/HRWW/WS HA3 49 G5
Rufford St IS N1 5 K3
Rufford Street Ms IS N1 5 K2
Rufus Cl RSLP HA4 65 H2
Rufus St FSBYE EC1V 7 J8
Rugby Av ALP/SUD HA0 67 J3
ED N9 30 B7
GFD/PVL UB6 66 D5
Rugby Cl HRW HA1 48 E3
Rugby Gdns DAGW RM9 79 J5
Rugby La BELMT SM2 174 B7
Rugby Rd CDALE/KGS NW9 50 C3
CHSWK W4 106 B1
DAGW RM9 79 H6
TWK TW1 123 K5
Rugby St BMSBY WC1N 11 L1
Rugg St POP/IOD E14 93 J6
Ruislip Cl GFD/PVL UB6 84 B3
Ruislip Ct RSLP HA4 * 64 D1
Ruislip Rd GFD/PVL UB6 84 A2
NTHLT UB5 65 G7
Ruislip Rd East GFD/PVL UB6 84 C3
Ruislip St TOOT SW17 147 K3
Rumbold Rd FUL/PGN SW6 108 A6
Rum Cl WAP E1W 92 D6
Rumsey Cl HPTN TW12 141 K5
Rumsey Rd BRXN/ST SW9 130 A2
Runbury Cir CDALE/KGS NW9 69 F1
Runcorn Cl TOTM N17 56 D3
Runcorn Pl NTGHL W11 88 C6
Rundell Crs HDN NW4 51 K4
Runes Cl MTCM CR4 162 C3
Runnelfield HRW HA1 66 E2
Runnymede WIM/MER SW19 147 H7
Runnymede Cl WHTN TW2 123 G5
Runnymede Crs
STRHM/NOR SW16 148 D7
Runnymede Gdns
GFD/PVL UB6 84 D1
HSLW TW3 123 G5
Runnymede Rd WHTN TW2 123 G5
Runway Cl CDALE/KGS NW9 51 H1
The Runway RSLP HA4 65 F4
Rupack St BERM/RHTH SE16 * 111 K1
Rupert Av WBLY HA9 68 A4
Rupert Ct E/WMO/HCT KT8 * 157 F3
SOHO/SHAV W1D 11 G6
Rupert Gdns BRXN/ST SW9 130 C1
Rupert Rd ARCH N19 72 D2
CHSWK W4 106 B2
KIL/WHAMP NW6 88 D1
Rupert St SOHO/SHAV W1D 11 G6
Rural Cl EMPK RM11 63 K7
Rural Wy STRHM/NOR SW16 148 B6
Rusbridge Cl HACK E8 74 C4
Ruscoe Rd CAN/RD E16 94 D5
Ruscombe Wy
EBED/NFELT TW14 121 J6
Rusham Rd BAL SW12 128 E5
Rushbridge Cl CROY/NA CR0 164 D5
Rushbrook Crs WALTH E17 43 H7
Rushbrook Rd ELTH/MOT SE9 154 C1
Rush Common Ms
BRXS/STRHM SW2 129 K6
Rushcroft Rd
BRXS/STRHM SW2 130 B3
CHING E4 43 K6
Rushden Cl NRWD SE19 149 K6
Rushdene Av EBAR EN4 27 J6
Rushdene Cl NTHLT UB5 83 G1
Rushdene Crs NTHLT UB5 83 F1
Rushdene Rd PIN HA5 47 G5
Rushden Gdns CLAY IG5 60 A2
MLHL NW7 38 A5
Rushdon Cl ROM RM1 63 J4
Rushett Cl THDIT KT7 158 C7
Rushett Rd THDIT KT7 158 C6
Rushey Cl NWMAL KT3 160 A3
Rushey Gn CAT SE6 132 E6
Rushey Hl ENC/FH EN2 29 F3
Rushey Md BROCKY SE4 132 D4
Rushford Rd BROCKY SE4 132 C5
Rush Green Gdns
ROMW/RG RM7 62 E7
Rush Green Rd
ROMW/RG RM7 62 E7
Rushgrove Av
CDALE/KGS NW9 51 H3
Rushgrove Pde
CDALE/KGS NW9 * 51 H4
Rushgrove St
WOOL/PLUM SE18 114 E3
Rush Hill Ms BTSEA SW11 129 F2
Rush Hill Rd BTSEA SW11 129 F2
Rushley Cl HAYES BR2 181 H3
Rushmead BETH E2 92 D2
RCHPK/HAM TW10 143 H2
Rushmead Cl CROY/NA CR0 178 B3
Rushmere Ct WPK KT4 173 J1
Rushmere Pl WIM/MER SW19 146 B4
Rushmon Pl CHEAM SM3 * 174 C5
Rushmon Vls NWMAL KT3 * 160 C3
Rushmoor Cl PIN HA5 47 F3
Rushmore Cl BMLY BR1 168 D2
Rushmore Ct WATW WD18 * 20 B5
Rushmore Rd CLPT E5 74 E3
Rusholme Av DAGE RM10 80 C2
Rusholme Gv NRWD SE19 150 A4
Rusholme Rd PUT/ROE SW15 127 G5
Rushout Av
KTN/HRWW/WS HA3 49 H5
Rushton St IS N1 7 H5
Rushworth St STHWK SE1 18 D1
Rushy Meadow La CAR SM5 175 J1
Ruskin Av EBED/NFELT TW14 121 J6
MNPK E12 77 J5
RCH/KEW TW9 105 H6
WELL DA16 136 B2
Ruskin Cl GLDGN NW11 53 F5
Ruskin Dr WELL DA16 136 B2
WPK KT4 173 K1
Ruskin Gdns EA W5 85 K3
KTN/HRWW/WS HA3 50 B4
Ruskin Gv WELL DA16 136 B1
Ruskin Rd BELV DA17 117 H3
CAR SM5 176 A4
CROY/NA CR0 177 H1
ISLW TW7 124 A2
STHL UB1 83 J6
TOTM N17 42 B7
Ruskin Wk ED N9 42 C1
HAYES BR2 168 D5
HNHL SE24 130 D4
Ruskin Wy WIM/MER SW19 162 C1
Rusland Park Rd HRW HA1 48 E3
Rusper Cl CRICK NW2 70 A2
STAN HA7 35 J3
Rusper Rd DAGW RM9 79 J5
WDGN N22 55 H1
Russel Cl BECK BR3 166 E2
Russell Av WDGN N22 55 H1
Russell Cl BKHTH/KID SE3 114 B6
CHSWK W4 106 C5
DART DA1 138 D2
NTHWD HA6 32 A4
RSLP HA4 65 G1
WLSDN NW10 68 E6
Russell Ct BAR EN5 * 27 G3
WHALL SW1A 10 F9
Russell Dr STWL/WRAY TW19 120 A5
Russell Gdns GLDGN NW11 52 C5
RCHPK/HAM TW10 143 J1
TRDG/WHET N20 39 J1
WDR/YW UB7 100 D4
WKENS W14 * 107 H2
Russell Gardens Ms
WKENS W14 107 H1
Russell Gv BRXN/ST SW9 110 B7
MLHL NW7 37 G4
Russell Kerr Cl CHSWK W4 * 105 K6
Russell La TRDG/WHET N20 39 K1
Russell Pde GLDGN NW11 * 52 C5
Russell Pl HAMP NW3 71 J4
Russell Rd CAN/RD E16 94 E5
CDALE/KGS NW9 51 H5
CEND/HSY/T N8 54 D5
CHING E4 43 H3
MTCM CR4 162 D2
NTHLT UB5 66 C4
NTHWD HA6 32 A2
SEVS/STOTM N15 56 A4
TRDG/WHET N20 39 J1
WALTH E17 57 K5
WDGN N22 41 F5

WHTN TW2 124 A5
WIM/MER SW19 146 E6
WKENS W14 107 H2
Russell Sq *RSQ* WC1B 11 H2
Russell St *HOL/ALD* WC2B 11 K6
Russell Wy *OXHEY* WD19 21 F6
SUT SM1 175 F4
Russell Yd *PUT/ROE* SW15 127 H3
Russet Cl *HGDN/ICK* UB10 82 A3
Russet Crs *HOLWY* N7 * 73 F4
Russet Dr *CROY/NA* CR0 166 B7
Russets Cl *CHING* E4 44 B3
Russia Dock Rd
BERM/RHTH SE16 * 93 G7
Russia La *BETH* E2 92 E1
Russia Rw *CITYW* EC2V 12 F5
Rusthall Av *CHSWK* W4 106 A2
Rusthall Cl *CROY/NA* CR0 165 K5
Rustic Av *STRHM/NOR* SW16 148 B6
Rustic Pl *ALP/SUD* HA0 67 K3
Rustington Wk *CHEAM* SM3 161 J6
Ruston Av *BRYLDS* KT5 159 J6
Ruston Gdns *STHGT/OAK* N14 28 A5
Ruston Ms *NTGHL* W11 * 88 C5
Ruston Rd *WOOL/PLUM* SE18 114 D2
Ruston St *BOW* E3 75 H7
Rust Sq *CMBW* SE5 110 E6
Rutford Rd *STRHM/NOR* SW16 148 E4
Ruth Cl *STAN* HA7 50 B3
Rutherford Cl *BELMT* SM2 175 H5
BORE WD6 24 E1
Rutherford St *WEST* SW1P 17 G5
Rutherford Wy *BUSH* WD23 22 D7
WBLY HA9 68 C2
Rutherglen Rd *ABYW* SE2 116 B5
Rutherwyke Cl *EW* KT17 173 J5
Ruthin Cl *CDALE/KGS* NW9 51 G5
Ruthven St *HOM* E9 75 F7
Rutland Av *BFN/LL* DA15 136 B6
Rutland Cl *BXLY* DA5 136 E7
CHSGTN KT9 172 B5
MORT/ESHN SW14 125 J2
WIM/MER SW19 147 J5
Rutland Ct *CHST* BR7 154 A7
SKENS SW7 15 K2
Rutland Dr *MRDN* SM4 161 K6
RCHPK/HAM TW10 124 E7
Rutland Gdns *BCTR* RM8 79 J4
CROY/NA CR0 178 A3
FSBYPK N4 55 H5
SKENS SW7 15 K2
WEA W13 * 85 G4
Rutland Gardens Ms
SKENS SW7 15 K2
Rutland Ga *BELV* DA17 117 J4
HAYES BR2 167 J3
SKENS SW7 15 J2
Rutland Gate Ms *SKENS* SW7 * 15 J2
Rutland Gv *HMSMTH* W6 106 E4
Rutland Ms *STJWD* NW8 2 D4
Rutland Ms South
SKENS SW7 * 15 J3
Rutland Pk *CAT* SE6 151 H1
CRICK NW2 70 A5
Rutland Pl *BUSH* WD23 * 22 D7
FARR EC1M * 12 D2
Rutland Rd *FSTGT* E7 77 H6
HOM E9 75 F7
HRW HA1 48 C5
HYS/HAR UB3 101 G3
IL IG1 78 B3
STHL UB1 84 A3
WALTH E17 57 J5
WAN E11 59 F4
WHTN TW2 142 D1
Rutland St *SKENS* SW7 15 K3
Rutland Wk *CAT* SE6 151 H1
Rutley Cl *WALW* SE17 18 C9
Rutlish Rd *WIM/MER* SW19 146 E7
Rutter Gdns *MTCM* CR4 162 C3
Rutters Cl *WDR/YW* UB7 100 D1
Rutt's Ter *NWCR* SE14 112 A7
The Rutts *BUSH* WD23 22 D7
Ruvigny Gdns *PUT/ROE* SW15 127 G2
Ruxley Cl *HOR/WEW* KT19 172 D4
SCUP DA14 155 K5
Ruxley Crs *ESH/CLAY* KT10 171 H6
Ruxley La *HOR/WEW* KT19 172 E4
Ruxley Ms *HOR/WEW* KT19 172 D4
Ruxley Rdg *ESH/CLAY* KT10 171 G6
Ruxley Towers
ESH/CLAY KT10 * 171 G6
Ryan Cl *BKHTH/KID* SE3 134 A3
RSLP HA4 47 F7
Ryan Ct *OXHEY* WD19 * 21 J6
Ryan Dr *BTFD* TW8 104 B5
Rycroft Wy *TOTM* N17 * 56 B2
Ryculff Sq *BKHTH/KID* SE3 133 J1
Rydal Cl *HDN* NW4 38 C7
Rydal Crs *GFD/PVL* UB6 85 H2
Rydal Dr *WWKM* BR4 180 C1
Rydal Gdns *CDALE/KGS* NW9 51 G4
HSLW TW3 123 G5
PUT/ROE SW15 145 G4
WBLY HA9 49 J7
Rydal Mt *HAYES* BR2 * 167 J3
Rydal Rd *STRHM/NOR* SW16 148 D4
Rydal Wy *PEND* EN3 30 E5
RSLP HA4 65 G3
Ryde Pl *TWK* TW1 124 D5
Ryder Cl *BUSH* WD23 22 B5
Ryder Dr *BERM/RHTH* SE16 111 J4
Ryder Gdns *RAIN* RM13 81 H5
Ryder St *WHALL* SW1A 10 E8
Ryder Yd *STJS* SW1Y 10 F8
Ryde Vale Rd *BAL* SW12 148 B1
Rydon Ms *WIM/MER* SW19 146 A6
Rydon St *IS* N1 6 F3
Rydston Cl *HOLWY* N7 5 K1
Rye Cl *BORE* WD6 25 F3
BXLY DA5 137 J5
Ryecotes Md *DUL* SE21 131 F7
Ryecroft Av *CLAY* IG5 60 B1
WHTN TW2 123 G7
Ryecroft Crs *BAR* EN5 25 K4
Ryecroft Rd *LEW* SE13 133 F4
STMC/STPC BR5 169 J5
STRHM/NOR SW16 149 G5
Ryecroft St *FUL/PGN* SW6 108 A7
Ryedale *EDUL* SE22 131 J5
Ryefield Av *HGDN/ICK* UB10 64 A7
Ryefield Crs *PIN* HA5 * 46 E1
Ryefield Pde *NTHWD* HA6 * 46 E1
Ryefield Rd *NRWD* SE19 149 J5
Rye Hill Pk *PECK* SE15 131 K3
Ryelands Crs *LEE/GVPK* SE12 134 B5
Rye La *PECK* SE15 131 H1
Rye Rd *PECK* SE15 132 A3
The Rye *STHGT/OAK* N14 28 C6
Rye Wk *PUT/ROE* SW15 127 G4
Rye Wy *EDGW* HA8 36 B5
Ryfold Rd *WIM/MER* SW19 146 E2
Ryhope Rd *FBAR/BDGN* N11 40 B3
Ryland Cl *FELT* TW13 140 D3
Rylandes Rd *CRICK* NW2 69 J2
SAND/SEL CR2 178 D7
Ryland Rd *KTTN* NW5 * 72 B5
Rylett Crs *SHB* W12 106 C2
Rylett Rd *SHB* W12 106 C1
Rylston Rd *FUL/PGN* SW6 107 J5
PLMGR N13 41 K2
Rymer Rd *CROY/NA* CR0 165 F6
Rymer St *HNHL* SE24 130 C5
Rymill St *CAN/RD* E16 96 A7
Rysbrack St *CHEL* SW3 15 L3
Rythe Cl *CHSGTN* KT9 171 J6
Rythe Ct *THDIT* KT7 158 B6
Rythe Rd *ESH/CLAY* KT10 170 D4
Ryves Cots *MTCM* CR4 * 163 F1

S

Sabbarton St *CAN/RD* E16 94 D5
Sabine Rd *BTSEA* SW11 128 E2
Sable Cl *HSLWW* TW4 122 B2
Sable St *IS* N1 6 D1
Sach Rd *CLPT* E5 74 D1
Sackville Cl *RYLN/HDSTN* HA2 66 D2
Sackville Est
STRHM/NOR SW16 148 E2
Sackville Gdns *IL* IG1 59 K7
Sackville Rd *BELMT* SM2 174 E6
Sackville St *CONDST* W1S 10 E7
Saddlebrook Pk *SUN* TW16 140 C6
Saddlers Cl *BAR* EN5 25 K4
PIN HA5 34 A4
Saddlers Ms *KUT/HW* KT1 143 J7
Saddlescombe Wy
NFNCH/WDSPK N12 38 E4
Sadler Cl *MTCM* CR4 162 E1
Sadlers Gate Ms
PUT/ROE SW15 127 F2
Sadlers Ride *E/WMO/HCT* KT8 157 H1
Saffron Av *POP/IOD* E14 94 B6
Saffron Cl *CROY/NA* CR0 163 K5
GLDGN NW11 52 D4
Saffron Hl *HCIRC* EC1N 12 B2
Saffron Rd *CRW* RM5 63 F1
Saffron St *HCIRC* EC1N 12 B2
Saffron Wy *SURB* KT6 158 E7
Sage Cl *EHAM* E6 95 K4
Sage Ms *EDUL* SE22 131 G4
Sage St *WCHPL* E1 92 E6
Sage Wy *FSBYW* WC1X 5 L8
Sage Yd *SURB* KT6 159 G7
Saigasso Cl *CAN/RD* E16 95 H5
Sail St *LBTH* SE11 17 M5
Sainfoin Rd *TOOT* SW17 148 A1
Sainsbury Rd *NRWD* SE19 150 A4
St Agatha's Dr *KUTN/CMB* KT2 144 B5
St Agatha's Gv *CAR* SM5 162 E7
St Agnes Cl *HOM* E9 * 74 E7
St Agnes Pl *LBTH* SE11 110 C5
St Agnes Well *STLK* EC1Y 7 H9
St Aidan's Rd *EDUL* SE22 131 J5
WEA W13 104 C1
St Albans Av *CHSWK* W4 106 A2
FELT TW13 141 H4
St Alban's Av *EHAM* E6 95 K2
St Albans Crs *WDGN* N22 41 G7
St Albans Farm
EBED/NFELT TW14 * 122 B4
St Alban's Gdns *TEDD* TW11 143 G4
St Alban's Gv *CAR* SM5 162 D6
KENS W8 14 D3
St Albans La *GLDGN* NW11 52 E7
St Alban's Ms *BAY/PAD* W2 9 H2
St Alban's Pl *IS* N1 6 C4
St Albans Rd *GDMY/SEVK* IG3 61 F7
KUTN/CMB KT2 144 A5
SUT SM1 174 D3
WAT WD17 21 F1
St Alban's Rd *KTTN* NW5 72 A2
WFD IG8 44 E6
WLSDN NW10 69 G7
St Alban's St *STJS* SW1Y 11 G7
St Albans Ter *HMSMTH* W6 107 H5
St Alfege Pas *GNWCH* SE10 113 F5
St Alfege Rd *CHARL* SE7 114 C5
St Alphage Gdns *BARB* EC2Y 12 F3
St Alphage Highwalk
BARB EC2Y 12 F3
St Alphage Wk *EDGW* HA8 * 50 E1
St Alphege Rd *ED* N9 30 E6
St Alphonsus Rd *CLAP* SW4 129 H3
St Amunds Cl *CAT* SE6 151 J3
St Andrews Av *ALP/SUD* HA0 67 G3
HCH RM12 81 H4
St Andrews Cl
BERM/RHTH SE16 * 111 J4
RSLP HA4 65 H1
STAN HA7 * 49 J1
THDIT KT7 158 C7
THMD SE28 97 K5
WIM/MER SW19 147 F5
St Andrew's Cl *CRICK* NW2 * 69 K2
ISLW TW7 103 J7
NFNCH/WDSPK N12 * 39 G3
St Andrew's Ct
WAND/EARL SW18 147 G1
St Andrews Dr *STAN* HA7 35 J7
St Andrew's Gv
STNW/STAM N16 55 K7
St Andrew's Hl *BLKFR* EC4V 12 D5
St Andrews Ms *BAL* SW12 129 J7
St Andrew's Ms
STNW/STAM N16 56 A7
St Andrew's Pl *CAMTN* NW1 4 C9
St Andrews Rd *CAR* SM5 175 J2
CDALE/KGS NW9 51 F7
ED N9 30 E6
ROMW/RG RM7 63 F5
SCUP DA14 155 K2
St Andrew's Rd *ACT* W3 87 G5
CROY/NA CR0 177 J3
EN EN1 29 K2
GLDGN NW11 52 D5
HNWL W7 103 K1
IL IG1 59 K6
PLSTW E13 95 F2
SURB KT6 158 E5
WALTH E17 57 F1
WAN E11 58 C5
WKENS W14 107 H5
WLSDN NW10 69 K5
St Andrew's Sq *NTGHL* W11 * 88 C5
SURB KT6 158 E5
St Andrews Ter
OXHEY WD19 * 33 G4
St Andrew St *HCIRC* EC1N 12 B3
St Andrews Wy *BOW* E3 93 K3
St Anna Rd *BAR* EN5 * 26 B4
St Anne's Av
STWL/WRAY TW19 120 A6
St Annes Cl *OXHEY* WD19 33 G3
St Anne's Cl *HGT* N6 72 A2
St Annes Ct *SOHO/CST* W1F 11 G5
St Annes Gdns *WLSDN* NW10 86 B2
St Anne's Pas *POP/IOD* E14 * 93 H5
St Anne's Rd *ALP/SUD* HA0 67 K4
LEY E10 76 B1
St Anne's Rw *POP/IOD* E14 93 H5
St Anne St *POP/IOD* E14 93 H5
St Ann's *BARK* IG11 78 C7
St Anns Ct *HDN* NW4 * 51 K2
St Ann's Crs
WAND/EARL SW18 128 A5
St Ann's Gdns *KTTN* NW5 72 A5
St Ann's Hl *WAND/EARL* SW18 128 A4
St Ann's Park Rd
WAND/EARL SW18 128 B5
St Anns Rd *BARN* SW13 * 126 C1
St Ann's Rd *BARK* IG11 78 C7
ED N9 42 B1
HRW HA1 48 E5
NTGHL W11 88 B6
SEVS/STOTM N15 55 J4
St Ann's St *WEST* SW1P 17 H3
St Ann's Ter *STJWD* NW8 3 H5
St Ann's Vls *NTGHL* W11 88 B7
St Ann's Wy *CROY/NA* CR0 177 H5
St Anselms Rd *HYS/HAR* UB3 101 J1
St Anthony's Av *WFD* IG8 45 G5
St Anthonys Cl *TOOT* SW17 147 J1
St Anthony's Cl *WAP* E1W * 92 C7
St Anthony's Ct *ORP* BR6 169 G7
St Anthony's Wy
EBED/NFELT TW14 121 J3
St Antony's Rd *FSTGT* E7 77 F6
St Arvans Cl *CROY/NA* CR0 178 A2
St Asaph Rd *BROCKY* SE4 132 A2
St Aubyn's Av *HSLW* TW3 123 F4
WIM/MER SW19 146 D4
St Aubyn's Rd *NRWD* SE19 150 B5
St Augustine's Av *EA* W5 86 A1
HAYES BR2 168 D4
SAND/SEL CR2 177 J6
WBLY HA9 68 A2
St Augustine's Rd *BELV* DA17 117 G3
CAMTN NW1 5 G1
St Austell Cl *EDGW* HA8 50 B1
St Austell Rd *LEW* SE13 133 F1
St Awdry's Rd *BARK* IG11 78 D6
St Barnabas Cl *BECK* BR3 167 F1
EDUL SE22 131 F3
St Barnabas' Gdns
E/WMO/HCT KT8 157 F4
St Barnabas Rd *MTCM* CR4 148 A6
SUT SM1 175 H4
WALTH E17 57 J5
WFD IG8 45 F7
St Barnabas St *BGVA* SW1W 16 B7
St Barnabas Ter *HOM* E9 75 F4
St Barnabas Vls *VX/NE* SW8 109 K7
St Bartholomew's Cl
SYD SE26 150 E3
St Bartholomew's Rd
EHAM E6 77 J7
St Benets Cl *TOOT* SW17 147 J1
St Benet's Gv *CAR* SM5 162 B6
St Bernards *CROY/NA* CR0 178 A2
St Bernards Cl *WNWD* SE27 149 K3
St Bernard's Rd *EHAM* E6 77 H7
St Blaise Av *BMLY* BR1 168 A1
St Botolph St *TWRH* EC3N 13 L4
St Bride's Av *EDGW* HA8 36 B7
St Brides Cl *ERITHM* DA18 116 E1
St Bride St *FLST/FETLN* EC4A 12 C4
St Catherines Cl *CHSGTN* KT9 171 K5
TOOT SW17 * 147 J1
St Catherines Ct *FELT* TW13 121 K7
St Catherine's Dr *NWCR* SE14 132 A1
St Catherines Ms *CHEL* SW3 15 L5
St Catherines Rd *CHING* E4 43 J1
RSLP HA4 46 A4
St Chads Cl *SURB* KT6 158 D6
St Chad's Gdns *CHDH* RM6 62 A6
St Chad's Pl *FSBYW* WC1X 5 K7
St Chad's Rd *CHDH* RM6 62 A5
St Chad's St *STPAN* WC1H 5 K7
St Charles Pl *NKENS* W10 88 C4
St Charles Sq *NKENS* W10 88 B4
St Christopher's Cl *ISLW* TW7 103 K7
St Christophers Dr
HYS/HAR UB3 83 F6
St Christopher's Ms
WLGTN SM6 176 C4
St Christopher's Pl *MHST* W1U 10 B5
St Clair Cl *CLAY* IG5 59 K1
St Clair Dr *WPK* KT4 173 K2
St Clair Rd *PLSTW* E13 95 F1
St Clair's Rd *CROY/NA* CR0 178 A1
St Clare St *TWRH* EC3N 13 L5
St Clement's La *LINN* WC2A 11 M5
St Clements Yd *EDUL* SE22 * 131 G4
St Cloud Rd *WNWD* SE27 149 J3
St Crispins Cl *HAMP* NW3 71 J3
St Crispin's Cl *STHL* UB1 83 K5
St Cross St *HCIRC* EC1N 12 B2
St Cuthberts Gdns *PIN* HA5 * 33 K6
St Cuthberts Rd *PLMGR* N13 41 G5
St Cuthbert's Rd *CRICK* NW2 70 D5
St Cyprian's St *TOOT* SW17 147 K3
St Davids Cl
BERM/RHTH SE16 * 111 J4
WBLY HA9 68 E2
St David's Cl *WWKM* BR4 166 E6
St David's Dr *EDGW* HA8 36 B7
St Davids Ms *BOW* E3 * 93 G2
St David's Pl *HDN* NW4 51 K6
St Davids Sq *POP/IOD* E14 112 E4
St Denis Rd *WNWD* SE27 149 J3
St Dionis Rd *FUL/PGN* SW6 127 J1
MNPK E12 77 J2
St Donatt's Rd *NWCR* SE14 112 C7
St Dunstan's Av *ACT* W3 87 F6
St Dunstans Cl *HYS/HAR* UB3 101 J3
St Dunstan's Gdns *ACT* W3 87 F6
St Dunstan's Hl *MON* EC3R * 13 J7
SUT SM1 174 C5
St Dunstan's La *MON* EC3R * 13 J7
St Dunstans Rd *FSTGT* E7 77 F5
St Dunstan's Rd *FELT* TW13 140 D2
HMSMTH W6 107 G4
HNWL W7 103 K1
HSLWW TW4 122 A1
SNWD SE25 165 G3
St Edmunds Av *RSLP* HA4 46 B5
St Edmunds Cl *ERITHM* DA18 116 E1
TOOT SW17 147 J1
St Edmund's Cl *STJWD* NW8 3 L4
St Edmunds Dr *STAN* HA7 35 G7
St Edmund's La *WHTN* TW2 123 G6
St Edmunds Rd *DART* DA1 139 J3
ED N9 30 C6
St Edmund's Rd *IL* IG1 59 K5
St Edmunds Sq *BARN* SW13 107 F5
St Edmund's Ter *STJWD* NW8 3 K4
St Edward's Cl *GLDGN* NW11 52 E5
St Edwards Wy *ROM* RM1 63 F4
St Elmo Rd *SHB* W12 106 C1
St Elmos Rd
BERM/RHTH SE16 112 B1
St Erkenwald Ms *BARK* IG11 78 D7
St Erkenwald Rd *BARK* IG11 78 D7
St Ervans Rd *NKENS* W10 88 C4
St Faith's Rd *DUL* SE21 130 C7
St Fidelis' Rd *ERITH* DA8 118 A3
St Fillans Rd *CAT* SE6 133 F7
St Francis Cl *ORP* BR6 169 K5
OXHEY WD19 21 F7
St Francis Rd *EDUL* SE22 131 F3
St Francis Wy *IL* IG1 78 D3
St Gabriel's Cl *WAN* E11 59 F7
St Gabriel's Rd *CRICK* NW2 70 B4
St George's Av
CDALE/KGS NW9 50 E3
EA W5 104 E1
FSTGT E7 77 F6
HOLWY N7 72 D3
STHL UB1 83 K6
St George's Circ *STHWK* SE1 18 C2
St Georges Cl *HRW* HA1 67 G2
THMD SE28 97 K5
VX/NE SW8 109 H7
St George's Cl *GLDGN* NW11 52 D5
St Georges Dr *PIM* SW1V 16 D7
St George's Dr *OXHEY* WD19 33 J2
PIM SW1V 16 D6
St Georges Flds *BAY/PAD* W2 9 K6
St George's Gdns *SURB* KT6 172 D1
St George's Gv *TOOT* SW17 147 H2
St George's Industrial Est
KUTN/CMB KT2 143 K4
St George's La *MON* EC3R * 13 H6
St Georges Ms *CHSWK* W4 * 105 K5
DEPT SE8 112 C3
St George's Ms *HAMP* NW3 3 M2
St Georges Pde *CAT* SE6 * 151 H1
St Georges Rd *BMLY* BR1 168 E1
CHSWK W4 106 A1
DAGW RM9 80 A4
STMC/STPC BR5 169 J5
St George's Rd *BECK* BR3 151 K7
FELT TW13 141 H3
FSTGT E7 77 F6
GLDGN NW11 52 D5
HNWL W7 85 F7
IL IG1 59 K6
KUTN/CMB KT2 144 B6
LEY E10 76 A2
MTCM CR4 163 G2
PLMGR N13 41 F1
RCH/KEW TW9 125 G2
SCUP DA14 155 K5
STHWK SE1 18 C4
TWK TW1 124 C4
WIM/MER SW19 146 D5
WLGTN SM6 176 B4
St Georges Rd West
BMLY BR1 168 D1
St Georges's Ct *STP* EC4M * 12 C4
St Georges Sq *NWMAL* KT3 * 160 B2
St George's Sq *FSTGT* E7 77 F6
PIM SW1V 17 G7
St George's Square Ms
PIM SW1V 17 G8
St Georges Ter *PECK* SE15 * 111 H6
St George's Ter *CAMTN* NW1 3 M2
St George St *CONDST* W1S 10 D6
St George's Wk *CROY/NA* CR0 177 J1
St George's Wy *PECK* SE15 111 F5
St Gerards Cl *CLAP* SW4 129 H4
St German's Rd *FSTH* SE23 132 B7
St Giles Av *DAGE* RM10 80 D6
HGDN/ICK UB10 64 A3
St Giles Churchyard
BARB EC2Y * 12 F3
St Giles Circ *SOHO/SHAV* W1D 11 H4
St Giles Cl *DAGE* RM10 80 D6
HEST TW5 102 D6
St Giles Ct *LSQ/SEVD* WC2H 11 H4
St Giles High St
LSQ/SEVD WC2H 11 H4
St Giles Pas *LSQ/SEVD* WC2H 11 H5
St Giles Rd *CMBW* SE5 111 F7
St Gothard Rd *WNWD* SE27 149 K3
St Gregory Cl *RSLP* HA4 65 G3
St Helena Rd
BERM/RHTH SE16 112 A3
St Helena St *FSBYW* WC1X * 6 A8
St Helena Ter *RCH/KEW* TW9 * 124 E4
St Helens *THDIT* KT7 * 157 K6
St Helens Ct *RAIN* RM13 99 J3
St Helen's Crs
STRHM/NOR SW16 149 F7
St Helen's Gdns *NKENS* W10 88 B5
St Helens Pl *LEY* E10 57 G6
St Helen's Pl *HDTCH* EC3A 13 J4
St Helens Rd *ERITHM* DA18 116 E1
St Helen's Rd *IL* IG1 59 K5
STRHM/NOR SW16 164 A1
WEA W13 85 H7
St Helier Av *MRDN* SM4 162 B6
St Heliers Av *HSLWW* TW4 123 F4
St Helier's Rd *LEY* E10 57 K5
St Hildas Cl
KIL/WHAMP NW6 * 70 B7
TOOT SW17 147 J1
St Hilda's Rd *BARN* SW13 106 E5
St Hughes Cl *TOOT* SW17 * 147 J1
St Hugh's Rd *PGE/AN* SE20 * 150 D7
St Ivians Dr *GPK* RM2 63 J2
St James Av *SUT* SM1 174 E4
TRDG/WHET N20 39 J2
St James' Av *WEA* W13 85 G7
St James Cl *EBAR* EN4 27 H2
STJWD NW8 3 L5
TRDG/WHET N20 39 J2
St James' Cl *NWMAL* KT3 160 C4
RSLP HA4 65 G1
St James' Ct *WESTW* SW1E * 16 F3
St James Gdns *CHDH* RM6 61 H3
St James' Gdns *ALP/SUD* HA0 67 K6
St James Ms *POP/IOD* E14 * 113 F2
St James Rd *CAR* SM5 175 J2
WATW WD18 21 F4
St James' Rd *ED* N9 42 D1
MTCM CR4 148 A6
SRTFD E15 76 D4
SURB KT6 158 E5
SUT SM1 174 E5
St James's *NWCR* SE14 112 B7
St James's Av *BECK* BR3 166 B2
BETH E2 92 E1
HPTN TW12 142 C4
St James's Chambers
STJS SW1Y * 10 F8
St James's Cl *TOOT* SW17 * 147 K1
WOOL/PLUM SE18 115 H4
St James's Cots
RCH/KEW TW9 * 124 E4
St James's Ct *KUT/HW* KT1 * 159 F2
WESTW SW1E 16 F3
St James's Crs *BRXN/ST* SW9 130 B2
St James's Dr *BAL* SW12 128 E7
St James's Gdns
CAMTN NW1 * 4 E8
NTGHL W11 88 B7
St James's Gv *BTSEA* SW11 128 E1
St James's La *MUSWH* N10 54 B3
St James's Market
STJS SW1Y * 11 G7
St James's Ms *WALTH* E17 57 G4
St James's Pk *CROY/NA* CR0 164 D6
St James's Pl *WHALL* SW1A 10 E9
St James Sq *SURB* KT6 158 D6
St James's Rd
BERM/RHTH SE16 111 H4
CROY/NA CR0 164 D6
HPTN TW12 142 B4
KUT/HW KT1 158 E1
St James's Rw *CHSGTN* KT9 * 171 K5
St James's Sq *STJS* SW1Y 11 G8
St James's St *WALTH* E17 57 G4
WHALL SW1A 10 E8
St James's Ter *STJWD* NW8 3 L4
St James's Terrace Ms
STJWD NW8 3 L4
St James St *HMSMTH* W6 107 F4
St James Ter *BAL* SW12 * 129 F7
St James Wk *CLKNW* EC1R 6 C9
St Jerome's Gv *UX/CGN* UB8 82 A5
St Joan's Rd *ED* N9 42 B1
St John Cl *FUL/PGN* SW6 * 107 K6
St John's Av *FBAR/BDGN* N11 39 K4
PUT/ROE SW15 127 G4
WLSDN NW10 69 H7
St John's Church Rd
HOM E9 * 74 E4
St Johns Cl *STHGT/OAK* N14 28 C5
St John's Cl *FUL/PGN* SW6 * 107 K6
RAIN RM13 81 J6
TRDG/WHET N20 * 39 G1
WBLY HA9 68 A4
St Johns Cots *PGE/AN* SE20 * 150 E6
St John's Ct *ISLW* TW7 124 A1
St John's Crs *BRXN/ST* SW9 130 B2
St Johns Dr *WOT/HER* KT12 156 B7
St John's Dr
WAND/EARL SW18 128 A7
St John's Gdns *NTGHL* W11 88 C6
St John's Gv *ARCH* N19 72 C1
BARN SW13 * 126 C1
RCH/KEW TW9 124 E3
St John's Hl *BTSEA* SW11 128 D3
St John's Hill Gv *BTSEA* SW11 128 C3
St John's La *FARR* EC1M 12 C1
St Johns Pde *SCUP* DA14 * 155 H3
WEA W13 * 85 H7
St John's Pl *FARR* EC1M 12 C1
St Johns Rd *GNTH/NBYPK* IG2 60 E6
NWMAL KT3 159 K2
STMC/STPC BR5 169 J5
St John's Rd *BARK* IG11 78 E7
BTSEA SW11 128 D3
CAN/RD E16 94 E5
CAR SM5 175 J2
CHING E4 43 K2
CROY/NA CR0 177 H2
E/WMO/HCT KT8 157 J3
EHAM E6 77 J7
FELT TW13 141 J3
GLDGN NW11 52 D5
HRW HA1 49 F5
ISLW TW7 124 A1
KUT/HW KT1 158 D1
NWDGN UB2 102 D2
PGE/AN SE20 150 E6
RCH/KEW TW9 125 F3
SCUP DA14 155 H3
SEVS/STOTM N15 56 A5
SUT SM1 174 E1
WALTH E17 57 K1
WAT WD17 21 F1
WBLY HA9 67 K3
WELL DA16 136 C2
WIM/MER SW19 146 C6
St John's Sq *FARR* EC1M 12 C1
St John's Ter *FSTGT* E7 77 F5
NKENS W10 88 B3
WOOL/PLUM SE18 115 H5
St John St *FSBYE* EC1V 6 B6
St John's V *BROCKY* SE4 132 D1
St Johns Vls *KENS* W8 14 D4
St John's Vls *ARCH* N19 72 D1
St John's Wy *ARCH* N19 54 D7
St John's Wood High St
STJWD NW8 3 H6
St John's Wood Pk
STJWD NW8 3 G4
St John's Wood Rd
STJWD NW8 3 G9
St John's Wood Ter
STJWD NW8 3 J5
St Josephs Cl *NKENS* W10 88 C4
St Joseph's Dr *STHL* UB1 83 J7
St Josephs Gv *HDN* NW4 51 K3
St Joseph's Rd *ED* N9 30 D6
St Joseph's St *VX/NE* SW8 * 109 G7
St Joseph's V *BKHTH/KID* SE3 133 G1
St Jude's Rd *BETH* E2 92 D1
St Jude St *STNW/STAM* N16 74 A4
St Julian's Cl
STRHM/NOR SW16 * 149 G3
St Julian's Farm Rd
WNWD SE27 149 G3
St Julian's Rd
KIL/WHAMP NW6 70 D6
St Katharine's Prec
CAMTN NW1 * 4 C5
St Katharine's Wy *WAP* E1W 13 M8
St Katherines Rd
ERITHM DA18 116 E1
St Katherines Wk
NTGHL W11 * 88 B6
St Keverne Rd
ELTH/MOT SE9 134 E6
ELTH/MOT SE9 153 J3
St Kilda Rd *WEA* W13 104 B1
St Kilda's Rd *HRW* HA1 48 E5
STNW/STAM N16 55 K7
St Kitts Ter *NRWD* SE19 150 A4
St Laurence's Cl
KIL/WHAMP NW6 70 B7
St Lawrence Cl *EDGW* HA8 36 B6
St Lawrence Cots
POP/IOD E14 * 94 A7
St Lawrence Dr *PIN* HA5 47 F4
St Lawrence St *POP/IOD* E14 94 A7
St Lawrence Ter *NKENS* W10 88 C4
St Lawrence Wy
BRXN/ST SW9 130 B1

Sangora Rd BTSEA SW11 128 C3
Sansom Rd WAN E11 * 76 D1
Sansom St CMBW SE5 110 E6
Sans Wk CLKNW EC1R 6 C9
Santley St CLAP SW4 129 K3
Santos Rd WAND/EARL SW18 127 K4
Saperton Wk LBTH SE11 17 M5
Sapphire Cl BCTR RM8 61 J7
Sapphire Rd DEPT SE8 112 B3
WLSDN NW10 68 E6
Saracen Cl CROY/NA CR0 164 E5
Saracen's Head Yd
FENCHST EC3M 13 K5
Saracen St POP/IOD E14 93 J5
Saratoga Rd CLPT E5 74 E3
Sardinia St HOL/ALD WC2B 11 L5
Sarita Cl KTN/HRWW/WS HA3 48 D1
Sark Cl HEST TW5 103 F6
Sarnesfield Rd ENC/FH EN2 * 29 K3
Sarre Rd CRICK NW2 70 D4
Sarsen Av HSLW TW3 122 E1
Sarsfeld Rd BAL SW12 128 E7
Sarsfield Rd GFD/PVL UB6 85 H1
Sartor Rd PECK SE15 132 A3
Sarum Ter BOW E3 * 93 H3
Satanita Cl CAN/RD E16 95 H5
Satchell Md CDALE/KGS NW9 37 H7
Satchwell Rd BETH E2 92 C2
Sattar Ms STNW/STAM N16 * 73 K2
Sauls Gn WAN E11 76 C2
Saunders Cl IL IG1 60 D7
POP/IOD E14 * 93 H6
Saunders Ness Rd
POP/IOD E14 113 G3
Saunders Rd
WOOL/PLUM SE18 116 A4
Saunders St LBTH SE11 18 A5
Saunders Wy THMD SE28 97 H6
Saunderton Rd ALP/SUD HA0 67 H4
Saunton Av HYS/HAR UB3 101 J6
Saunton Rd HCH RM12 81 J1
Savage Gdns EHAM E6 95 K5
TWRH EC3N 13 K6
Savanah Cl PECK SE15 111 G6
Savera Cl NWDGN UB2 102 B2
Savernake Ct STAN HA7 * 35 J5
Savernake Rd ED N9 30 C5
HAMP NW3 71 K3
Savery Dr SURB KT6 158 C6
Savile Cl NWMAL KT3 160 B4
THDIT KT7 158 A7
Savile Gdns CROY/NA CR0 178 B1
Savile Rw CONDST W1S 10 E6
Saville Crs ASHF TW15 140 B5
Saville Rd CAN/RD E16 95 J7
CHDH RM6 62 B5
CHSWK W4 106 A2
TWK TW1 124 A7
Saville Rw HAYES BR2 167 J7
PEND EN3 31 F1
Savill Gdns RYNPK SW20 160 D2
Savill Rw WFD IG8 44 D5
Savona Cl WIM/MER SW19 146 B6
Savona St VX/NE SW8 109 H6
Savoy Av HYS/HAR UB3 101 H4
Savoy Cl EDGW HA8 36 C4
SRTFD E15 76 C7
Savoy Ct TPL/STR WC2R * 11 K7
Savoy Hl TPL/STR WC2R 11 L7
Savoy Ms BRXN/ST SW9 129 K2
Savoy Pde EN EN1 * 30 A2
Savoy Pl CHCR WC2N 11 K7
Savoy Rw TPL/STR WC2R 11 L6
Savoy Steps TPL/STR WC2R * 11 L7
Savoy St TPL/STR WC2R 11 L6
Savoy Wy TPL/STR WC2R 11 L7
Sawbill Cl YEAD UB4 83 H4
Sawkins Cl WIM/MER SW19 146 B1
Sawley Rd SHB W12 87 J7
Sawtry Cl CAR SM5 162 C6
Sawyer Cl ED N9 42 C1
Sawyers Cl DAGE RM10 80 E5
Sawyer's Hl
MORT/ESHN SW14 125 K6
RCHPK/HAM TW10 125 G6
Sawyers Lawn WEA W13 85 G5
Sawyer St STHWK SE1 18 E1
Saxby Rd BRXS/STRHM SW2 129 K6
Saxham Rd BARK IG11 78 E7
Saxlingham Rd CHING E4 44 B2
Saxon Av FELT TW13 141 J1
Saxonbury Av SUN TW16 156 A2
Saxonbury Cl MTCM CR4 162 C2
Saxonbury Gdns SURB KT6 158 D7
Saxon Cl SURB KT6 158 E5
WALTH E17 57 J6
Saxon Dr ACT W3 86 D5
Saxonfield Cl
BRXS/STRHM SW2 130 A6
Saxon Rd ASHF TW15 140 B5
BOW E3 93 H1
EHAM E6 95 K3
IL IG1 78 B5
KUTN/CMB KT2 144 A7
SNWD SE25 164 E4
STHL UB1 83 J6
WBLY HA9 68 E2
WDGN N22 41 H7
Saxon Wy STHGT/OAK N14 28 D5
Saxony Pde HYS/HAR UB3 82 A4
Saxton Cl LEW SE13 133 G2
Sayesbury La UED N18 42 C4
Sayes Court St DEPT SE8 112 C4
Scala St FITZ W1T 10 F2
Scales Rd TOTM N17 56 B2
Scammell Wy WATW WD18 20 D5
Scampton Rd
STWL/WRAY TW19 120 C5
Scandrett St WAP E1W * 92 D7
Scarba Wk IS N1 73 K5
Scarborough Rd ED N9 30 E6
FSBYPK N4 55 G6
HTHAIR TW6 121 F5
WAN E11 58 B7
Scarborough St WCHPL E1 13 M5
Scarbrook Rd CROY/NA CR0 177 J2
Scarle Rd ALP/SUD HA0 67 K5
Scarlet Rd CAT SE6 152 C2
Scarsbrook Rd
BKHTH/KID SE3 134 C2
Scarsdale Pl KENS W8 * 14 C3
Scarsdale Rd
RYLN/HDSTN HA2 66 C2
Scarsdale Vls KENS W8 14 B4
Scarth Rd BARN SW13 126 C2
Scawen Cl CAR SM5 176 A3
Scawen Rd DEPT SE8 112 B4
Scawfell St BETH E2 7 M6
Scaynes Link
NFNCH/WDSPK N12 38 E3
Sceptre Rd BETH E2 92 E2
Scholars Cl BAR EN5 26 C3
Scholars Rd BAL SW12 129 H7
Scholars Wy GPK RM2 63 K4
Scholefield Rd ARCH N19 72 D1
Schonfeld Sq
STNW/STAM N16 73 K1
Schoolbank Rd GNWCH SE10 113 J3
School House La TEDD TW11 143 H6
Schoolhouse La WAP E1W * 93 F6
School La BUSH WD23 22 B7
KUT/HW KT1 143 J7
PIN HA5 * 47 J3
SURB KT6 159 G7
School Pas KUT/HW KT1 159 G1
STHL UB1 83 K7
School Rd CHST BR7 154 C7
DAGE RM10 80 C7
E/WMO/HCT KT8 157 J3
HPTN TW12 142 C5
HSLW TW3 123 H2
KUT/HW KT1 * 143 J7
MNPK E12 77 K3
WDR/YW UB7 100 A5
WLSDN NW10 87 F3
School Road Av HPTN TW12 142 C5
School Sq GNWCH SE10 113 J2
School Wy BCTR RM8 79 H2
Schoolway
NFNCH/WDSPK N12 39 H5
Schooner Cl BARK IG11 97 H2
BERM/RHTH SE16 112 A1
POP/IOD E14 113 G2
Schubert Rd BORE WD6 23 K5
PUT/ROE SW15 127 J4
Sclater St WCHPL E1 7 L9
Scoble Pl STNW/STAM N16 74 B3
Scoles Crs BRXS/STRHM SW2 130 B7
Scope Wy KUT/HW KT1 159 F3
Scoresby St STHWK SE1 12 C9
Scorton Av GFD/PVL UB6 85 G1
Scotch Common WEA W13 85 G4
Scoter Cl WFD IG8 45 F6
Scot Gv PIN HA5 33 H6
Scotia Rd BRXS/STRHM SW2 130 B6
Scotland Gn TOTM N17 56 B1
Scotland Green Rd PEND EN3 31 F4
Scotland Green Rd North
PEND EN3 31 F3
Scots Cl STWL/WRAY TW19 120 A7
Scotsdale Cl CHEAM SM3 174 C6
STMC/STPC BR5 169 K3
Scotsdale Rd LEE/GVPK SE12 134 A4
Scotswood St CLKNW EC1R * 6 B9
Scotswood Wk TOTM N17 * 42 D6
Scott Av PUT/ROE SW15 127 H5
Scott Cl HOR/WEW KT19 172 E4
STRHM/NOR SW16 149 F7
WDR/YW UB7 100 C3
Scott Crs RYLN/HDSTN HA2 48 B7
Scott Ellis Gdns STJWD NW8 3 G8
Scottes La BCTR RM8 61 K7
Scott Farm Cl THDIT KT7 158 C7
Scott Gdns HEST TW5 102 C6
Scott Lidgett Crs
BERM/RHTH SE16 111 H1
Scott Rd EDGW HA8 50 D1
Scotts Av HAYES BR2 167 G1
SUN TW16 140 C6
Scotts Dr HPTN TW12 142 B6
Scotts Farm Rd
HOR/WEW KT19 172 E5
Scott's La HAYES BR2 167 G2
Scotts Pas
WOOL/PLUM SE18 * 115 G3
Scotts Rd BMLY BR1 152 E6
NWDGN UB2 102 B2
Scott's Rd LEY E10 58 A7
SHB W12 106 E1
Scott St WCHPL E1 92 D3
Scotts Wy SUN TW16 140 C6
Scottswood Cl BUSH WD23 21 J1
Scottswood Rd BUSH WD23 21 J1
Scott's Yd MANHO EC4N 13 G6
Scott Trimmer Wy HSLW TW3 122 D1
Scottwell Dr CDALE/KGS NW9 51 H4
Scoulding Rd CAN/RD E16 94 D5
Scouler St POP/IOD E14 94 B6
Scout Ap WLSDN NW10 69 G3
Scout Wy MLHL NW7 37 F3
Scovell Crs STHWK SE1 * 18 E2
Scovell Rd STHWK SE1 18 E2
Scrattons Ter BARK IG11 97 K1
Scriven St HACK E8 7 M3
Scrooby St CAT SE6 132 E5
Scrubs La WLSDN NW10 87 J2
Scrutton Cl BAL SW12 129 J6
Scrutton St SDTCH EC2A 13 J1
Scutari Rd EDUL SE22 131 J4
Scylla Crs HTHAIR TW6 120 E6
Scylla Rd HTHAIR TW6 120 E5
PECK SE15 131 J2
Seabright St BETH E2 92 D2
Seabrook Dr WWKM BR4 180 C1
Seabrook Gdns
ROMW/RG RM7 62 C6
Seabrook Rd BCTR RM8 79 K2
Seaburn Cl RAIN RM13 99 G2
Seacole Cl ACT W3 87 F5
Seacourt Rd ABYW SE2 116 E1
Seacroft Gdns OXHEY WD19 33 H2
Seafield Rd FBAR/BDGN N11 40 D3
Seaford Cl RSLP HA4 64 B1
Seaford Rd EN EN1 30 A3
HTHAIR TW6 120 A4
SEVS/STOTM N15 55 K4
WALTH E17 57 K2
WEA W13 85 H7
Seaford St STPAN WC1H 5 K8
Seaforth Av NWMAL KT3 160 E4
Seaforth Crs HBRY N5 73 J4
Seaforth Gdns
HOR/WEW KT19 173 H3
WCHMH N21 29 F6
WFD IG8 45 G4
Seaforth Pl WESTW SW1E 16 F3
Seager Blds DEPT SE8 * 112 D7
Seager Pl BOW E3 93 H4
Seagrave Cl WCHPL E1 * 93 F4
Seagrave Rd FUL/PGN SW6 14 B9
Seagry Rd WAN E11 58 E5
Seagull La CAN/RD E16 94 E6
Sealand Rd HTHAIR TW6 120 D4
Seal St HACK E8 74 B3
Searles Cl BTSEA SW11 108 D6
Searles Dr EHAM E6 96 B4
Searles Rd STHWK SE1 19 H5
Sears St CMBW SE5 110 E6
Seasons Cl HNWL W7 85 F7
Seasprite Cl NTHLT UB5 83 H2
Seaton Av GDMY/SEVK IG3 78 E4
Seaton Cl LBTH SE11 18 B7
PLSTW E13 94 E3
PUT/ROE SW15 126 E6
WHTN TW2 123 J5
Seaton Gdns RSLP HA4 64 E2
Seaton Rd ALP/SUD HA0 * 86 A1
HYS/HAR UB3 101 G3
MTCM CR4 162 D1
WELL DA16 116 D6
WHTN TW2 123 H5
Seaton St UED N18 42 C4
Sebastian St FSBYE EC1V 6 D8
Sebastopol Rd ED N9 42 C3
Sebbon St IS N1 6 D2
Sebergham Gv MLHL NW7 37 J6
Sebert Rd FSTGT E7 77 F4
Sebright Rd BAR EN5 26 B1
Secker Crs
KTN/HRWW/WS HA3 34 C7
Secker St STHWK SE1 12 A9
Second Av ACT W3 87 H7
CHDH RM6 61 J4
DAGE RM10 98 D1
EN EN1 30 B4
HDN NW4 52 B3
HYS/HAR UB3 82 D7
MNPK E12 77 J3
MORT/ESHN SW14 126 B2
NKENS W10 88 C3
PLSTW E13 94 E2
UED N18 42 E3
WALTH E17 57 J4
WBLY HA9 67 K1
WOT/HER KT12 156 A5
Second Cl E/WMO/HCT KT8 157 G3
Second Cross Rd WHTN TW2 142 D1
Second Wy WBLY HA9 68 D3
Sedan Wy WALW SE17 19 J7
Sedcombe Cl SCUP DA14 155 H3
Sedcote Rd PEND EN3 30 E4
Sedding St KTBR SW1X 16 A5
Seddon Rd MRDN SM4 162 C4
Seddon St FSBYW WC1X 5 L8
Sedgebrook Rd
BKHTH/KID SE3 134 C1
Sedgecombe Av
KTN/HRWW/WS HA3 49 J4
Sedgeford Rd SHB W12 87 H7
Sedgehill Rd CAT SE6 151 J4
Sedgemere Av EFNCH N2 53 G2
Sedgemoor Dr DAGE RM10 80 C3
Sedge Rd TOTM N17 42 E6
Sedgeway CAT SE6 133 J7
Sedgewood Cl HAYES BR2 167 J6
Sedgmoor Pl CMBW SE5 111 F6
Sedgwick Rd LEY E10 76 A1
Sedgwick St HOM E9 75 F4
Sedleigh Rd
WAND/EARL SW18 127 J5
Sedlescombe Rd
FUL/PGN SW6 107 J5
Sedley Pl OXSTW W1C 10 C5
Sednem Ct PECK SE15 131 H1
Sedum Cl CDALE/KGS NW9 50 D4
Seeley Dr DUL SE21 150 A3
Seelig Av CDALE/KGS NW9 51 J6
Seely Rd TOOT SW17 148 A5
Seething La TWRH EC3N 13 K6
Seething Wells La SURB KT6 158 D5
Sefton Av
KTN/HRWW/WS HA3 34 D7
MLHL NW7 37 F4
Sefton Ct ENC/FH EN2 * 29 H1
Sefton Rd CROY/NA CR0 165 H7
Sefton St PUT/ROE SW15 127 F1
Sekforde St CLKNW EC1R 12 C1
Sekhon Ter FELT TW13 142 A2
Selan Gdns YEAD UB4 83 F4
Selbie Av WLSDN NW10 69 H4
Selborne Av BXLY DA5 137 F7
MNPK E12 78 A3
Selborne Gdns GFD/PVL UB6 85 G1
HDN NW4 51 J3
Selborne Rd CMBW SE5 130 E1
CROY/NA CR0 178 A2
IL IG1 78 A1
NWMAL KT3 160 B1
SCUP DA14 155 H3
STHGT/OAK N14 40 E2
WALTH E17 57 H4
WDGN N22 41 F7
Selbourne Av SURB KT6 172 B1
Selby Cha RSLP HA4 65 F1
Selby Cl CHSGTN KT9 172 A6
CHST BR7 154 A5
Selby Gdns STHL UB1 84 A3
Selby Gn CAR SM5 162 D6
Selby Rd ASHF TW15 140 A5
CAR SM5 162 D6
EA W5 85 H3
PGE/AN SE20 165 H1
PLSTW E13 95 F4
TOTM N17 42 A5
WAN E11 76 C2
Selby St WCHPL E1 92 C3
Selden Rd PECK SE15 131 K1
Selhurst Cl WIM/MER SW19 127 G7
Selhurst New Rd SNWD SE25 165 F5
Selhurst Pl SNWD SE25 165 F5
Selhurst Rd ED N9 41 K2
SNWD SE25 165 F4
Selinas La BCTR RM8 62 A6
Selkirk Dr ERITH DA8 118 B7
Selkirk Rd TOOT SW17 147 J3
WHTN TW2 142 C1
Sellers Hall Cl FNCH N3 38 E6
Sellincourt Rd TOOT SW17 147 J4
Sellindge Cl BECK BR3 151 H6
Sellons Av WLSDN NW10 69 H7
Sellwood Dr BAR EN5 26 B4
Selsdon Av SAND/SEL CR2 177 K5
Selsdon Cl SURB KT6 159 F4
Selsdon Park Rd
SAND/SEL CR2 179 F7
Selsdon Rd CRICK NW2 69 H1
PLSTW E13 77 G7
SAND/SEL CR2 177 K5
WAN E11 58 E6
WNWD SE27 149 H2
Selsdon Wy POP/IOD E14 112 E2
Selsea Pl STNW/STAM N16 74 A4
Selsey Crs WELL DA16 116 E7
Selsey St BOW E3 93 J4
Selvage La MLHL NW7 37 F4
Selway Cl PIN HA5 47 F3
Selwood Pl SKENS SW7 15 G7
Selwood Rd CHEAM SM3 161 J7
CHSGTN KT9 171 K3
CROY/NA CR0 178 D1
Selwood Ter SKENS SW7 15 G7
Selworthy Cl WAN E11 58 E4
Selworthy Rd CAT SE6 151 H2
Selwyn Av CHING E4 44 A5
GDMY/SEVK IG3 61 F5
RCH/KEW TW9 125 G2
Selwyn Cl HSLWW TW4 122 D3
Selwyn Ct EDGW HA8 36 D6
Selwyn Crs WELL DA16 136 C2
Selwyn Rd BOW E3 93 H1
NWMAL KT3 160 A4
PLSTW E13 77 F7
WLSDN NW10 69 G6
Semley Pl BGVA SW1W 16 B6
STRHM/NOR SW16 164 A1
Semley Rd STRHM/NOR SW16 163 K1
Senate St PECK SE15 131 K1
Seneca Rd THHTH CR7 164 D3
Senga Rd WLGTN SM6 163 F7
Senhouse Rd CHEAM SM3 174 B2
Senior St BAY/PAD W2 8 C2
Senlac Rd LEE/GVPK SE12 134 A7
Sennen Rd EN EN1 30 B6
Senrab St WCHPL E1 93 F5
Sentamu Cl HNHL SE24 130 C7
Sentinel Cl NTHLT UB5 83 J3
September Wy STAN HA7 35 H5
Sequoia Cl BUSH WD23 22 D7
Sequoia Pk PIN HA5 34 B5
Serbin Cl LEY E10 58 A6
Serenaders Rd BRXN/ST SW9 130 B1
Serjeant's Inn EMB EC4Y * 12 B5
Serle St LINN WC2A 11 M4
Sermon La BLKFR EC4V 12 E5
Serpentine Rd BAY/PAD W2 9 K9
Service Route No 1
SRTFD E15 76 B6
Service Route No 2
SRTFD E15 76 B6
Service Route No 3
SRTFD E15 76 B5
Serviden Dr BMLY BR1 153 H7
Setchell Est STHWK SE1 19 L5
Setchell Rd STHWK SE1 19 L5
Setchell Wy STHWK SE1 19 L5
Seth St BERM/RHTH SE16 111 K1
Seton Gdns DAGW RM9 79 J6
Settles St WCHPL E1 92 C5
Settrington Rd FUL/PGN SW6 128 A1
Seven Acres CAR SM5 175 J1
NTHWD HA6 32 E5
Seven Dials LSQ/SEVD WC2H 11 J5
Sevenex Pde WBLY HA9 * 68 A4
Seven Kings Rd
GDMY/SEVK IG3 60 E7
Seven Kings Wy
KUTN/CMB KT2 143 K7
Sevenoaks Rd BROCKY SE4 132 C5
Seven Seas Rd HTHAIR TW6 121 F5
Seven Sisters Rd HOLWY N7 73 F2
SEVS/STOTM N15 55 K5
Seven Stars Yd WCHPL E1 13 M2
Seventh Av HYS/HAR UB3 82 E7
MNPK E12 77 K3
Severnake Cl POP/IOD E14 112 D3
Severn Av GPK RM2 63 K2
NKENS W10 88 C2
Severn Dr ESH/CLAY KT10 171 G1
Severn Wy WLSDN NW10 69 H4
Severus Rd BTSEA SW11 128 D3
Seville Ms IS N1 7 J2
Seville St KTBR SW1X 15 M2
Sevington Rd HDN NW4 51 K5
Sevington St MV/WKIL W9 8 C1
Seward Rd BECK BR3 166 A1
HNWL W7 104 B1
Sewardstone Rd BETH E2 92 E1
CHING E4 31 K3
Seward St FSBYE EC1V 6 D9
Sewdley St CLPT E5 75 F2
Sewell Rd ABYW SE2 116 B1
Sewell St PLSTW E13 94 E2
Sextant Av POP/IOD E14 113 G3
Sexton Cl RAIN RM13 81 H7
Seymer Rd ROM RM1 63 F2
Seymour Av EW KT17 173 K7
MRDN SM4 161 G6
TOTM N17 56 C1
Seymour Cl E/WMO/HCT KT8 157 H4
PIN HA5 33 K7
Seymour Dr HAYES BR2 168 E7
Seymour Gdns BROCKY SE4 132 B2
BRYLDS KT5 159 G4
FELT TW13 141 F3
IL IG1 59 K7
RSLP HA4 47 H7
TWK TW1 124 C6
Seymour Ms MBLAR W1H 10 A4
Seymour Pl MBLAR W1H 9 L3
SNWD SE25 165 J3
Seymour Rd CAR SM5 176 A4
CEND/HSY/T N8 55 H4
CHING E4 31 K7
CHSWK W4 105 K3
E/WMO/HCT KT8 157 H4
ED N9 42 D1
EHAM E6 77 H7
FNCH N3 39 F6
HPTN TW12 142 C4
KUT/HW KT1 143 K7
LEY E10 57 H7
MTCM CR4 163 F6
WAND/EARL SW18 127 J6
WIM/MER SW19 146 B2
Seymour St BAY/PAD W2 9 L5
WOOL/PLUM SE18 115 H2
Seymour Ter PGE/AN SE20 150 D7
Seymour Vls PGE/AN SE20 150 D7
Seymour Wk WBPTN SW10 14 E9
Seymour Wy SUN TW16 140 C5
Seyssel St POP/IOD E14 113 F3
Shaa Rd ACT W3 87 F6
Shacklegate La TEDD TW11 142 E3
Shackleton Cl FSTH SE23 150 D1
Shackleton Rd STHL UB1 83 K6
Shacklewell La HACK E8 74 B3
Shacklewell Rd
STNW/STAM N16 74 B3
Shacklewell Rw HACK E8 74 B3
Shacklewell St BETH E2 7 M9
Shadbolt Av CHING E4 43 G4
Shadbolt Cl WPK KT4 173 H1
Shad Thames STHWK SE1 13 L9
Shadwell Dr NTHLT UB5 83 K2
Shadwell Gdns WCHPL E1 * 92 E6
Shadwell Pierhead WAP E1W 92 E6
Shady Bush Cl BUSH WD23 22 C6
Shady La WAT WD17 21 F1
Shaef Wy TEDD TW11 143 G6
Shafter Rd DAGE RM10 80 E5
Shaftesbury Av BAR EN5 27 G3
EBED/NFELT TW14 121 K5
KTN/HRWW/WS HA3 49 K5
LSQ/SEVD WC2H 11 J4
NWDGN UB2 103 F3
PEND EN3 31 F1
RYLN/HDSTN HA2 48 B7
SOHO/SHAV W1D 11 G6
Shaftesbury Cir
RYLN/HDSTN HA2 * 48 C7
Shaftesbury Ct
RKW/CH/CXG WD3 * 20 A4
Shaftesbury Gdns
WLSDN NW10 87 G3
Shaftesbury Ms CLAP SW4 129 H4
KENS W8 * 14 B4
Shaftesbury Pde
RYLN/HDSTN HA2 * 48 C7
Shaftesbury Pl BARB EC2Y * 12 E3
Shaftesbury Rd ARCH N19 54 E7
BECK BR3 166 C1
CAR SM5 162 C6
FSTGT E7 77 G6
LEY E10 57 J7
RCH/KEW TW9 125 F2
ROM RM1 63 H5
UED N18 42 A5
WALTH E17 57 K4
WAT WD17 21 G2
The Shaftesburys BARK IG11 96 C1
Shaftesbury St IS N1 6 F6
Shaftesbury Ter
HMSMTH W6 * 106 C3
Shaftesbury Wy WHTN TW2 142 D2
Shaftesbury Waye YEAD UB4 83 F4
Shafteswood Ct TOOT SW17 147 K2
Shafto Ms KTBR SW1X 15 L4
Shafton Ms HOM E9 * 75 F7
Shafton Rd HOM E9 75 F7
Shakespeare Av
EBED/NFELT TW14 121 K5
FBAR/BDGN N11 40 C4
WLSDN NW10 68 E7
YEAD UB4 82 E5
Shakespeare Crs MNPK E12 77 K6
WLSDN NW10 69 F7
Shakespeare Dr BORE WD6 24 C3
KTN/HRWW/WS HA3 50 B5
Shakespeare Gdns EFNCH N2 53 K3
Shakespeare Rd ACT W3 86 E7
DART DA1 139 K3
FNCH N3 * 38 E7
HNHL SE24 130 C4
HNWL W7 85 F6
MLHL NW7 37 J3
ROM RM1 63 H5
WALTH E17 57 F1
Shakespeare Ter
RCH/KEW TW9 * 125 H2
Shakespeare Wy FELT TW13 141 G3
Shakspeare Ms
STNW/STAM N16 74 A3
Shakspeare Wk
STNW/STAM N16 74 A3
Shalbourne Sq HOM E9 75 H5
Shalcomb St WBPTN SW10 108 B5
Shaldon Dr MRDN SM4 161 H4
RSLP HA4 65 G2
Shaldon Rd EDGW HA8 50 B1
Shalfleet Dr NKENS W10 88 B6
Shalford Ct IS N1 * 6 C5
Shalimar Gdns ACT W3 86 E6
Shalimar Rd ACT W3 86 E6
Shallons Rd ELTH/MOT SE9 154 B3
Shalstone Rd
MORT/ESHN SW14 125 J2
Shalston Vls SURB KT6 159 G5
Shamrock Rd CROY/NA CR0 164 A5
Shamrock St CLAP SW4 129 J2
Shamrock Wy
STHGT/OAK N14 28 B7
Shandon Rd CLAP SW4 129 H5
Shand St STHWK SE1 19 K1
Shandy St WCHPL E1 93 F4
Shanklin Gdns OXHEY WD19 33 G3
Shanklin Rd CEND/HSY/T N8 54 D4
SEVS/STOTM N15 56 C3
Shannon Cl CRICK NW2 70 B2
NWDGN UB2 102 C4
Shannon Gv BRXN/ST SW9 130 A3
Shannon Pl STJWD NW8 3 K5
Shannon Wy BECK BR3 151 K5
Shap Crs CAR SM5 162 E7
Shapland Wy PLMGR N13 41 F4
Shapwick Cl FBAR/BDGN N11 39 K4
Shardcroft Av HNHL SE24 130 C4
Shardeloes Rd NWCR SE14 132 C1
Shard's Sq PECK SE15 111 H5
Sharland Cl THHTH CR7 164 B5
Sharman Ct SCUP DA14 155 G3
Sharnbrooke Cl WELL DA16 136 D2
Sharon Cl SURB KT6 158 D7
Sharon Gdns HOM E9 74 E7
Sharon Rd CHSWK W4 106 A4
PEND EN3 31 G1
Sharples Hall St CAMTN NW1 3 M2
Sharps La RSLP HA4 46 B6
Sharp Wy DART DA1 139 J2
Sharratt St PECK SE15 111 K5
Sharsted St WALW SE17 18 C8
Sharvel La YEAD UB4 64 E7
Shavers Pl MYFR/PICC W1J 11 G7
Shaw Av BARK IG11 98 A1
Shawbrooke Rd
ELTH/MOT SE9 134 C3
Shawbury Cl CDALE/KGS NW9 37 G7
Shawbury Rd EDUL SE22 131 G4
Shaw Cl BUSH WD23 34 E1
EMPK RM11 63 K7
THMD SE28 97 H7
Shaw Crs POP/IOD E14 93 G5
Shaw Dr WOT/HER KT12 156 B6
Shawfield Pk BMLY BR1 168 C1
Shawfield St CHEL SW3 15 K8
Shawford Rd HOR/WEW KT19 173 F5
Shaw Gdns BARK IG11 98 A1
Shaw Rd BMLY BR1 152 D2
EDUL SE22 131 F3
Shaw's Cots FSTH SE23 151 G2
Shaw Sq WALTH E17 43 G7
The Shaw CHST BR7 * 154 C6
Shaw Wy WLGTN SM6 176 E6
Shaxton Crs CROY/NA CR0 180 A7
Sheaf Cots THDIT KT7 * 157 K7
Shearing Dr CAR SM5 162 B6
Shearling Wy HOLWY N7 72 E5
Shearman Rd BKHTH/KID SE3 133 J3
Shearwater Cl BARK IG11 97 G2
Shearwater Rd SUT SM1 174 D4
Shearwater Wy YEAD UB4 83 H5
Sheaths Cots THDIT KT7 * 158 C6
Sheaveshill Av
CDALE/KGS NW9 51 G2
Sheaveshill Pde
CDALE/KGS NW9 * 51 G3
Sheen Common Dr
RCHPK/HAM TW10 125 H3
Sheen Court Rd
RCHPK/HAM TW10 125 H3
Sheendale Rd RCH/KEW TW9 125 G3
Sheenewood SYD SE26 150 D4
Sheen Ga MORT/ESHN SW14 126 A5
Sheen Gate Gdns
MORT/ESHN SW14 125 K3
Sheen Gv IS N1 6 A3

Sheen La MORT/ESHN SW14 125 K3
Sheen Pk RCH/KEW TW9 125 F3
Sheen Rd RCH/KEW TW9 125 F3
Sheen Wy WLGTN SM6 177 F4
Sheen Wd MORT/ESHN SW14 125 K4
Sheepcote Cl HEST TW5 101 K6
Sheepcote La BTSEA SW11 128 E1
Sheepcote Rd HRW HA1 49 F5
Sheepcotes Rd CHDH RM6 61 K3
Sheephouse Wy NWMAL KT3 160 A7
Sheep La HACK E8 74 D7
Sheep Walk Ms
WIM/MER SW19 146 B5
Sheerwater Rd CAN/RD E16 95 H4
Sheffield Rd HTHAIR TW6 121 F5
Sheffield St LINN WC2A * 11 L5
Sheffield Ter KENS W8 14 A1
Shefton Ri NTHWD HA6 32 E6
Shelbourne Cl PIN HA5 47 K2
Shelbourne Rd TOTM N17 42 D7
Shelburne Dr HSLWW TW4 123 F5
Shelburne Rd HOLWY N7 73 F3
Shelbury Cl SCUP DA14 155 G2
Shelbury Rd EDUL SE22 131 J4
Sheldon Av CLAY IG5 60 B1
HGT N6 53 K6
Sheldon Cl LEE/GVPK SE12 134 A4
PGE/AN SE20 150 D7
Sheldon Pl BETH E2 92 C1
Sheldon Rd CRICK NW2 70 B3
DAGW RM9 80 A6
UED N18 42 A3
Sheldon Sq BAY/PAD W2 8 F3
Sheldon St CROY/NA CR0 177 J2
Sheldrake Cl CAN/RD E16 95 K7
Sheldrake Pl KENS W8 107 J1
Sheldrick Cl MTCM CR4 162 C1
Shelduck Cl SRTFD E15 76 D4
Sheldwich Ter HAYES BR2 * 168 D5
Shelford Pl STNW/STAM N16 73 K2
Shelford Ri NRWD SE19 150 A6
Shelford Rd BAR EN5 26 A5
Shelgate Rd BTSEA SW11 128 E4
Shell Cl HAYES BR2 168 D5
Shellduck Cl CDALE/KGS NW9 51 G1
Shelley Av GFD/PVL UB6 84 D2
HCH RM12 81 H1
MNPK E12 77 J5
Shelley Cl EDGW HA8 36 C3
GFD/PVL UB6 84 D2
NTHWD HA6 32 D4
PECK SE15 131 J1
YEAD UB4 82 E4
Shelley Crs HEST TW5 102 C7
STHL UB1 83 K5
Shelley Dr WELL DA16 115 K7
Shelley Gdns ALP/SUD HA0 67 J1
Shelley Rd WLSDN NW10 69 F7
Shelley Wy WIM/MER SW19 147 H5
Shellgrove Rd
STNW/STAM N16 * 74 A4
Shellness Rd CLPT E5 74 D4
Shell Rd LEW SE13 132 E2
Shellwood Rd BTSEA SW11 128 E1
Shelly Cl BORE WD6 24 C3
Shelmerdine Cl BOW E3 93 J4
Shelson Av FELT TW13 140 D2
Shelson Pde FELT TW13 * 140 D2
Shelton Rd WIM/MER SW19 146 E7
Shelton St LSQ/SEVD WC2H * 11 J5
Shenfield Rd WFD IG8 45 F6
Shenfield St IS N1 7 K6
Shenley Av RSLP HA4 64 D1
Shenley Rd BORE WD6 24 C2
CMBW SE5 111 F7
HEST TW5 102 D7
Shepherd Cl FELT TW13 141 J3
Shepherdess Pl FSBYE EC1V 6 F7
Shepherdess Wk IS N1 6 F5
Shepherd Market
MYFR/PICC W1J 10 C9
Shepherd's Bush Gn SHB W12 107 F1
Shepherd's Bush Market
SHB W12 107 F1
Shepherd's Bush Pl
SHB W12 * 107 G1
Shepherd's Bush Rd
HMSMTH W6 107 F2
Shepherds Cl CHDH RM6 61 K4
STAN HA7 35 G4
Shepherd's Cl HGT N6 54 B5
Shepherds Gn CHST BR7 154 D6
Shepherd's Hl HGT N6 54 B5
Shepherds La THMD SE28 96 E7
Shepherd's La HOM E9 75 F4
Shepherd's Leas
ELTH/MOT SE9 * 135 J3
Shepherds Pl
MYFR/PKLN W1K 10 A6
Shepherds Rd WATW WD18 20 D2
Shepherd St MYFR/PICC W1J 10 C9
Shepherds Wk BUSH WD23 34 D1
CRICK NW2 69 J1
Shepherd's Wk HAMP NW3 71 H4
Shepherds Wy SAND/SEL CR2 179 F6
Shepiston La HYS/HAR UB3 100 E3
Shepley Cl CAR SM5 176 A2
Sheppard Cl KUT/HW KT1 159 F3
Sheppard Dr
BERM/RHTH SE16 111 J4
Sheppard St CAN/RD E16 94 D3
Shepperton Rd IS N1 6 F3
STMC/STPC BR5 169 H5
Sheppey Cl ERITH DA8 118 E6
Sheppey Gdns DAGW RM9 79 J6
Sheppey Rd DAGW RM9 79 H6
Sheppey Wk IS N1 6 F1
Shepton Houses BETH E2 * 92 E2
Sherard Rd ELTH/MOT SE9 134 D4
Sheraton Cl BORE WD6 24 B4
Sheraton Ms WATW WD18 20 C3
Sheraton St SOHO/CST W1F * 11 G5
Sherborne Av NWDGN UB2 103 F3
PEND EN3 30 E1
Sherborne Cl YEAD UB4 83 G5
Sherborne Crs CAR SM5 162 D6
Sherborne Gdns
CDALE/KGS NW9 50 C2
WEA W13 85 H5
Sherborne La MANHO EC4N 13 G6
Sherborne Pl NTHWD HA6 32 B5
Sherborne Rd CHEAM SM3 174 E1
CHSGTN KT9 172 A4
EBED/NFELT TW14 121 G6
Sherborne St IS N1 7 G3
Sherborne Vls WEA W13 * 85 H4
Sherboro Rd
SEVS/STOTM N15 56 B5
Sherbrooke Rd FUL/PGN SW6 107 H6
Sherbrooke Ter
FUL/PGN SW6 * 107 H6
Sherbrooke Wy WPK KT4 160 E6
Sherbrook Gdns WCHMH N21 29 H6
Shere Cl CHSGTN KT9 171 K4
Sheredan Rd CHING E4 44 B4
Shere Rd GNTH/NBYPK IG2 60 A4
Sherfield Cl NWMAL KT3 159 J3
Sherfield Gdns
PUT/ROE SW15 126 C5
Sheridan Ct DART DA1 139 K3
HSLWW TW4 122 D4
Sheridan Crs CHST BR7 169 G1
Sheridan Gdns
KTN/HRWW/WS HA3 49 K5
Sheridan Ms WAN E11 59 F5
Sheridan Pl BMLY BR1 168 C1
HPTN TW12 142 B7
Sheridan Rd BELV DA17 117 H3
FSTGT E7 76 D2
MNPK E12 77 J4
OXHEY WD19 21 H6
RCHPK/HAM TW10 143 J2
WIM/MER SW19 146 D7
Sheridan Ter NTHLT UB5 * 66 B4
Sheridan Wk CAR SM5 175 K4
GLDGN NW11 52 E5
Sheridan Wy BECK BR3 151 H7
Sheringham Av MNPK E12 77 K3
ROMW/RG RM7 62 E5
STHGT/OAK N14 28 D4
WHTN TW2 122 E7
Sheringham Dr BARK IG11 79 F4
Sheringham Rd HOLWY N7 73 G5
PGE/AN SE20 165 J1
Sherington Av PIN HA5 34 A6
Sherington Rd
BKHTH/KID SE3 114 A5
Sherland Rd TWK TW1 124 A7
Sherlock Ms MHST W1U 10 A2
Shermanbury Cl ERITH DA8 118 C6
Sherman Gdns CHDH RM6 61 J5
Sherman Rd BMLY BR1 152 E7
Shernhall St WALTH E17 58 A4
Sherrard Rd FSTGT E7 77 G5
Sherrards Wy BAR EN5 26 E4
Sherrick Green Rd
WLSDN NW10 69 K4
Sherriff Cl ESH/CLAY KT10 170 B1
Sherriff Rd KIL/WHAMP NW6 70 E5
Sherringham Av FELT TW13 140 E2
TOTM N17 56 C1
Sherrock Gdns HDN NW4 51 J3
Sherry Ms BARK IG11 78 D6
Sherwin Rd NWCR SE14 112 A7
Sherwood SURB KT6 171 K1
Sherwood Av GFD/PVL UB6 66 E5
RSLP HA4 46 C5
STRHM/NOR SW16 148 D6
SWFD E18 59 F2
YEAD UB4 83 F3
Sherwood Cl BXLY DA5 136 D5
WALTH E17 57 H1
WEA W13 85 H7
Sherwood Ct MBLAR W1H * 9 L3
Sherwood Gdns BARK IG11 78 D6
BERM/RHTH SE16 111 H4
POP/IOD E14 112 D3
Sherwood House
RYLN/HDSTN HA2 * 66 C2
Sherwood Park Av
BFN/LL DA15 136 B6
Sherwood Park Rd
MTCM CR4 163 H3
SUT SM1 174 E4
Sherwood Rd BARK/HLT IG6 60 D3
CROY/NA CR0 165 J6
HDN NW4 52 A2
HPTN TW12 142 C4
RYLN/HDSTN HA2 66 C1
WELL DA16 135 K2
WIM/MER SW19 146 D6
Sherwoods Rd OXHEY WD19 21 J6
Sherwood St SOHO/CST W1F 10 F6
TRDG/WHET N20 39 H2
Sherwood Ter
TRDG/WHET N20 39 H2
Sherwood Wy WWKM BR4 180 A1
Shetland Cl BORE WD6 25 F5
Shetland Rd BOW E3 93 H1
Shield Dr BTFD TW8 104 B5
Shield Rd ASHF TW15 140 A3
Shifford Pth FSTH SE23 151 F2
Shillibeer Pl MBLAR W1H 9 K3
Shillingford Cl MLHL NW7 38 B6
Shillingford St IS N1 * 6 D3
Shilling Pl HNWL W7 * 85 G7
Shinfield St SHB W12 88 A5
Shinners Cl SNWD SE25 165 H4
Shipka Rd BAL SW12 129 G7
Ship La MORT/ESHN SW14 125 K2
Shipman Rd CAN/RD E16 95 F5
FSTH SE23 151 F1
Ship & Mermaid Rw
STHWK SE1 * 19 H1
Ship St DEPT SE8 112 D7
Ship Tavern Pas BANK EC3V 13 J6
Shipton Cl BCTR RM8 79 K2
Shipton St BETH E2 7 M7
Shipwright Rd
BERM/RHTH SE16 112 B1
Shipwright Yd STHWK SE1 * 13 J9
Shirburn Cl FSTH SE23 131 K6
Shirbutt St POP/IOD E14 93 J6
Shirebrook Rd
BKHTH/KID SE3 134 C1
Shire Ct EW KT17 173 H6
Shirehall Cl HDN NW4 52 B5
Shirehall Gdns HDN NW4 52 B5
Shirehall La HDN NW4 52 B5
Shirehall Pk HDN NW4 52 B5
Shire Horse Wy ISLW TW7 124 A2
Shire La ORP BR6 181 K6
Shiremeade BORE WD6 24 B4
Shire Ms WHTN TW2 123 H5
Shire Pl WAND/EARL SW18 128 B6
The Shires RCHPK/HAM TW10 144 A3
Shirland Ms MV/WKIL W9 88 D2
Shirland Rd MV/WKIL W9 2 B9
Shirley Av BXLY DA5 136 E6
CROY/NA CR0 165 K7
SUT SM1 175 J3
Shirley Church Rd
CROY/NA CR0 179 F2
Shirley Cl HSLW TW3 123 H4
WALTH E17 * 57 K4
Shirley Crs BECK BR3 166 B3
Shirley Dr HSLW TW3 123 H4
Shirley Gdns BARK IG11 78 E5
HNWL W7 85 F7
Shirley Gv BTSEA SW11 129 F2
ED N9 30 E6
Shirley Hills Rd CROY/NA CR0 179 F3
Shirley Oaks Rd CROY/NA CR0 166 A7
Shirley Park Rd CROY/NA CR0 165 J7
Shirley Rd BFN/LL DA15 154 E2
CHSWK W4 106 A1
CROY/NA CR0 165 J7
ENC/FH EN2 29 J2
SRTFD E15 76 C6
WLGTN SM6 176 C7
Shirley Rw SNWD SE25 * 165 H1
Shirley St CAN/RD E16 94 D5
Shirley Wy CROY/NA CR0 179 H2
Shirlock Rd HAMP NW3 71 K3
Shirwell Cl MLHL NW7 38 B6
Shobden Rd TOTM N17 41 K7
Shobroke Cl CRICK NW2 70 A2
Shoebury Rd EHAM E6 77 K6
Shoe La FLST/FETLN EC4A 12 B4
Shooters Av
KTN/HRWW/WS HA3 49 J3
Shooters Hill Rd
BKHTH/KID SE3 114 B6
GNWCH SE10 113 H7
Shoot-Up Hl CRICK NW2 70 C5
Shore Cl EBED/NFELT TW14 121 K6
HPTN TW12 141 J4
Shoreditch High St
FSBYE EC1V 7 K8
WCHPL E1 13 K2
Shore Gv FELT TW13 142 A1
Shoreham Cl CROY/NA CR0 165 K5
WAND/EARL SW18 128 A4
Shoreham Rd STMC/STPC BR5 155 H7
Shoreham Road (East)
HTHAIR TW6 120 B4
Shoreham Road (West)
HTHAIR TW6 120 B4
Shore Pl HOM E9 74 E6
Shore Rd HOM E9 74 E6
Shore Wy BRXN/ST SW9 130 B1
Shorncliffe Rd STHWK SE1 19 L8
Shorndean St CAT SE6 133 F7
Shorne Cl BFN/LL DA15 136 C5
Shornefield Cl BMLY BR1 169 F2
Shorrolds Rd FUL/PGN SW6 107 K6
Shortcroft Rd EW KT17 173 H6
Shortcrofts Rd DAGW RM9 80 B5
Shorter St TWRH EC3N 13 L6
Shortgate
NFNCH/WDSPK N12 38 D3
Shortlands HMSMTH W6 107 G3
HYS/HAR UB3 101 G5
Shortlands Cl BELV DA17 117 G2
UED N18 41 K2
Shortlands Gdns HAYES BR2 167 H1
Shortlands Gv HAYES BR2 167 G2
Shortlands Rd HAYES BR2 167 G2
KUTN/CMB KT2 144 B6
LEY E10 57 K6
Short La STWL/WRAY TW19 120 C6
Short Rd CHSWK W4 106 B5
WAN E11 76 C1
Shorts Cft CDALE/KGS NW9 50 D3
Shorts Gdns
LSQ/SEVD WC2H * 11 J5
Shorts Rd CAR SM5 175 J3
Short St HDN NW4 52 A3
STHWK SE1 18 B1
Shortway ELTH/MOT SE9 134 D2
Short Wy NFNCH/WDSPK N12 39 J5
WHTN TW2 123 H6
Shotfield WLGTN SM6 176 B5
Shott Cl SUT SM1 175 G4
Shottendane Rd
FUL/PGN SW6 * 107 K7
Shottery Cl ELTH/MOT SE9 153 J2
Shottfield Av
MORT/ESHN SW14 126 B3
Shoulder of Mutton Aly
POP/IOD E14 93 G6
Shouldham St MBLAR W1H 9 K3
Showers Wy HYS/HAR UB3 82 E7
Shrapnel Cl WOOL/PLUM SE18 114 E6
Shrapnel Rd ELTH/MOT SE9 134 E2
Shrewsbury Av
KTN/HRWW/WS HA3 50 A3
MORT/ESHN SW14 125 K3
Shrewsbury Cl SURB KT6 172 A1
Shrewsbury Crs WLSDN NW10 69 F7
Shrewsbury La
WOOL/PLUM SE18 115 G7
Shrewsbury Ms BAY/PAD W2 8 A4
Shrewsbury Rd BAY/PAD W2 8 A3
BECK BR3 166 B2
CAR SM5 162 D6
FBAR/BDGN N11 40 D5
FSTGT E7 77 H5
HTHAIR TW6 121 F5
Shrewsbury St NKENS W10 88 A3
Shrewton Rd TOOT SW17 * 147 K6
Shroffold Rd BMLY BR1 152 C3
Shropshire Cl MTCM CR4 163 K3
Shropshire Rd WDGN N22 41 F6
Shroton St CAMTN NW1 9 J2
The Shrubberies SWFD E18 58 E1
Shrubbery Gdns WCHMH N21 29 H6
Shrubbery Rd ED N9 42 C2
STHL UB1 83 K7
STRHM/NOR SW16 148 E3
The Shrubbery SURB KT6 * 159 F7
Shrubland Cl
TRDG/WHET N20 * 39 H1
Shrubland Gv WPK KT4 174 A2
Shrubland Rd HACK E8 74 C7
LEY E10 57 J6
Shrublands Av CROY/NA CR0 179 J3
Shrublands Cl SYD SE26 150 E2
TRDG/WHET N20 27 H7
Shrubsall Cl ELTH/MOT SE9 134 D7
Shubbery Cl IS N1 6 F3
Shuna Wk IS N1 * 73 K5
Shurland Av EBAR EN4 27 H5
Shurland Gdns PECK SE15 * 111 G6
Shuters Sq WKENS W14 * 107 J4
Shuttle Cl BFN/LL DA15 136 A6
Shuttlemead BXLY DA5 137 G6
Shuttle Rd DART DA1 138 D2
Shuttle St WCHPL E1 92 C3
Shuttleworth Rd BTSEA SW11 128 C1
Sibella Rd CLAP SW4 129 J1
Sibley Cl BMLY BR1 168 D4
Sibley Ct UX/CGN UB8 82 A4
Sibley Gv EHAM E6 77 J6
Sibthorpe Rd LEE/GVPK SE12 134 A6
Sibthorp Rd MTCM CR4 * 162 E1
Sibton Rd CAR SM5 162 D6
Sicilian Av NOXST/BSQ WC1A * 11 K3
Sidbury St FUL/PGN SW6 107 H7
Sidcup By-Pass Rd
SCUP DA14 154 E3
SCUP DA14 155 G5
Sidcup Hl SCUP DA14 155 H4
Sidcup Hill Gdns SCUP DA14 * 155 J4
Sidcup Pl SCUP DA14 155 G4
Sidcup Rd ELTH/MOT SE9 153 K1
ELTH/MOT SE9 154 B1
LEE/GVPK SE12 134 A4
LEE/GVPK SE12 134 B6
Siddeley Dr HSLWW TW4 122 D2
Siddons La CAMTN NW1 9 M1
Siddons Rd CROY/NA CR0 177 G2
FSTH SE23 151 G1
TOTM N17 42 C7
Side Rd WALTH E17 57 H4
Sidewood Rd ELTH/MOT SE9 135 J7
Sidford Pl STHWK SE1 17 M4
Sidings Ms HOLWY N7 73 G3
The Sidings WAN E11 58 A7
Sidmouth Av ISLW TW7 123 K1
Sidmouth Cl OXHEY WD19 33 F1
Sidmouth Dr RSLP HA4 64 E2
Sidmouth Pde CRICK NW2 * 70 A6
Sidmouth Rd CRICK NW2 70 A6
LEY E10 76 A1
PECK SE15 111 G7
WELL DA16 116 D6
Sidmouth St STPAN WC1H 5 K8
Sidney Av PLMGR N13 41 F4
Sidney Elson Wy EHAM E6 96 A1
Sidney Gdns BTFD TW8 104 E5
Sidney Gv FSBYE EC1V 6 C6
Sidney Rd BECK BR3 166 B1
BRXN/ST SW9 130 A1
FSTGT E7 76 E2
RYLN/HDSTN HA2 48 C2
SNWD SE25 165 H4
TWK TW1 124 B5
WDGN N22 41 F6
WOT/HER KT12 156 A7
Sidney Sq WCHPL E1 * 92 E4
Sidney St WCHPL E1 92 D4
Sidworth St HACK E8 74 D6
Siemens Rd
WOOL/PLUM SE18 114 C2
Sienna Cl CHSGTN KT9 171 K5
Sienna Ter CRICK NW2 * 69 J1
Sierra Dr DAGE RM10 98 D1
Sigdon Rd HACK E8 74 C4
The Sigers PIN HA5 47 F5
Signmakers Yd CAMTN NW1 * 4 D4
Sigrist Sq KUTN/CMB KT2 144 A7
Silbury Av MTCM CR4 147 J7
Silbury St IS N1 * 7 G7
Silesia Blds HACK E8 74 D6
Silex St STHWK SE1 18 D2
Silkfield Rd CDALE/KGS NW9 51 G4
Silkin Ms PECK SE15 111 H6
Silk Mill Rd OXHEY WD19 21 F6
Silk Mills Pth LEW SE13 133 F2
Silkstream Pde EDGW HA8 * 36 E7
Silkstream Rd EDGW HA8 36 E7
Silk St BARB EC2Y 12 F2
Silsoe Rd WDGN N22 55 F2
Silver Birch Av CHING E4 43 H4
Silver Birch Cl CAT SE6 151 H2
FBAR/BDGN N11 40 A5
THMD SE28 97 G7
Silverbirch Wk HAMP NW3 * 71 K5
Silvercliffe Gdns EBAR EN4 27 J3
Silver Cl KTN/HRWW/WS HA3 34 D6
NWCR SE14 * 112 B6
Silver Crs CHSWK W4 105 J3
Silverdale ENC/FH EN2 28 E3
SYD SE26 150 E3
Silverdale Cl HNWL W7 84 E7
NTHLT UB5 65 K4
SUT SM1 174 D3
Silverdale Dr ELTH/MOT SE9 153 J1
HCH RM12 81 K4
SUN TW16 156 A1
Silverdale Gdns HYS/HAR UB3 101 K1
Silverdale Rd BUSH WD23 21 J4
CHING E4 44 B5
HYS/HAR UB3 101 K1
STMC/STPC BR5 169 H3
Silverdene
NFNCH/WDSPK N12 * 39 F5
Silver Dene PUT/ROE SW15 * 127 F4
Silvergate HOR/WEW KT19 172 E4
Silverhall St ISLW TW7 124 B2
Silverholme Cl
KTN/HRWW/WS HA3 50 A6
Silver La WWKM BR4 180 B1
Silverleigh Rd THHTH CR7 164 A3
Silvermere Dr UED N18 * 43 F4
Silvermere Rd CAT SE6 132 D5
Silvermere Rw SNWD SE25 * 165 H1
Silver Pl SOHO/CST W1F 10 F5
Silver Rd LEW SE13 132 E2
NKENS W10 88 B6
Silver Spring Cl ERITH DA8 117 J5
Silverston Wy STAN HA7 35 J5
Silver St EN EN1 29 K2
UED N18 41 K3
Silverthorne Rd VX/NE SW8 129 G1
Silverthorn Gdns CHING E4 43 J1
Silverton Rd HMSMTH W6 107 G6
Silvertown Wy CAN/RD E16 94 D6
Silvertree La GFD/PVL UB6 84 D2
Silver Wk BERM/RHTH SE16 93 H7
Silver Wy ROMW/RG RM7 62 D2
Silverwood Cl BECK BR3 151 J6
CROY/NA CR0 179 H7
NTHWD HA6 32 A7
Silvester Rd EDUL SE22 131 G4
Silvester St STHWK SE1 19 G2
Silwood Estate Regeneration
Area BERM/RHTH SE16 112 A4
Silwood St BERM/RHTH SE16 112 A4
Simmil Rd ESH/CLAY KT10 170 E4
Simmons Cl TRDG/WHET N20 27 J7
Simmons Dr BCTR RM8 80 A2
Simmons Ga ESH/CLAY KT10 170 C4
Simmons La CHING E4 44 B1
Simmons Rd
WOOL/PLUM SE18 115 G4
Simmons' Wy
TRDG/WHET N20 39 J1
Simms Cl CAR SM5 175 J1
Simms Gdns EFNCH N2 53 G1
Simms Rd STHWK SE1 111 H3
Simnel Rd LEE/GVPK SE12 134 A6
Simon Cl NTGHL W11 88 D6
Simonds Rd LEY E10 75 J1
Simone Cl BMLY BR1 153 H7
Simons Wk SRTFD E15 76 B4
Simpson Cl CROY/NA CR0 164 D5
WCHMH N21 29 F4
Simpson Dr ACT W3 87 F5
Simpson Rd HSLWW TW4 122 E5
RAIN RM13 81 H5
RCHPK/HAM TW10 143 J3
Simpson's Rd HAYES BR2 167 K2
POP/IOD E14 93 K6
Simpson St BTSEA SW11 128 D1
Simpson Wy SURB KT6 158 D5
Simrose Ct WAND/EARL SW18 127 K4
Sims Cl ROM RM1 63 H3
Sinclair Dr BELMT SM2 175 F7
Sinclair Gdns WKENS W14 107 G1
Sinclair Gv GLDGN NW11 52 B5
Sinclair Rd CHING E4 43 H4
WKENS W14 107 H2
Singapore Rd WEA W13 85 G7
Singer St FSBYE EC1V 7 H8
Singleton Cl CROY/NA CR0 164 D6
HCH RM12 81 H3
TOOT SW17 147 K6
Singleton Rd DAGW RM9 80 B4
Singleton Scarp
NFNCH/WDSPK N12 38 E4
Sinnott Rd WALTH E17 43 F7
Sion Rd TWK TW1 124 C7
Sipson Cl WDR/YW UB7 100 D5
Sipson La WDR/YW UB7 100 E5
Sipson Rd WDR/YW UB7 100 D6
Sipson Wy WDR/YW UB7 100 D6
Sir Abraham Dawes Cots
PUT/ROE SW15 * 127 H3
Sir Alexander Cl ACT W3 87 H7
Sir Cyril Black Wy
WIM/MER SW19 146 D6
Sirdar Rd MTCM CR4 148 A5
NTGHL W11 88 B6
WDGN N22 55 H2
Sir John Kirk Cl CMBW SE5 110 D6
Sir Thomas More Est
CHEL SW3 108 C5
Sirus Rd NTHWD HA6 32 E4
Sise La MANHO EC4N * 13 G5
Siskin Cl BORE WD6 24 C3
BUSH WD23 21 J3
Sisley Rd BARK IG11 78 E7
Sispara Gdns
WAND/EARL SW18 127 J5
Sissinghurst Cl BMLY BR1 152 C4
Sissinghurst Rd CROY/NA CR0 165 H6
Sister Mabels Wy PECK SE15 * 111 H6
Sisters Av BTSEA SW11 128 E3
Sistova Rd BAL SW12 129 G7
Sisulu Pl BRXN/ST SW9 130 B2
Sittingbourne Av EN EN1 29 K5
Sitwell Gv STAN HA7 35 F4
Siverst Cl NTHLT UB5 66 B5
Siviter Wy DAGE RM10 80 D6
Siward Rd HAYES BR2 168 A2
TOOT SW17 147 G2
TOTM N17 41 K7
Sixth Av HYS/HAR UB3 82 D7
MNPK E12 77 K3
NKENS W10 88 C3
Sixth Cross Rd WHTN TW2 142 C2
Skardu Rd CRICK NW2 70 C4
Skeena Hl WAND/EARL SW18 127 H6
Skeffington Rd EHAM E6 77 K7
Skeffington St
WOOL/PLUM SE18 115 H2
Skelbrook St
WAND/EARL SW18 147 F1
Skelgill Rd PUT/ROE SW15 127 J3
Skelley Rd SRTFD E15 76 D6
Skelton Cl HACK E8 * 74 B5
Skelton Rd FSTGT E7 76 E5
Skelton's La LEY E10 57 K6
Skelwith Rd HMSMTH W6 107 F5
Skerne Rd KUTN/CMB KT2 143 K7
Skerne Wk KUTN/CMB KT2 143 K7
Sketchley Gdns
BERM/RHTH SE16 112 A4
Sketty Rd EN EN1 30 B2
Skiers St SRTFD E15 76 C7
Skiffington Cl
BRXS/STRHM SW2 130 B7
Skinner Pl BGVA SW1W * 16 A6
Skinners La BLKFR EC4V 12 F6
HEST TW5 103 G7
Skinner St CLKNW EC1R 6 C9
Skipsey Av EHAM E6 95 K2
Skipton Cl FBAR/BDGN N11 40 A5
Skipton Dr HYS/HAR UB3 101 F2
Skipworth Rd HOM E9 74 E7
Skylines POP/IOD E14 113 F1
Skylines Village
POP/IOD E14 * 113 F1
Sky Peals Rd WFD IG8 44 B6
Skyport Dr WDR/YW UB7 100 A6
Sladebrook Rd
BKHTH/KID SE3 134 C2
Sladedale Rd
WOOL/PLUM SE18 115 K4
Slade Gdns ERITH DA8 118 C7
Sladen Pl CLPT E5 74 D3
Slades Cl ENC/FH EN2 29 G2
Slades Dr CHST BR7 154 C2
ELTH/MOT SE9 154 C3
Slades Gdns ENC/FH EN2 29 G1
Slades Hl ENC/FH EN2 29 G2
Slades Ri ENC/FH EN2 29 G2
The Slade WOOL/PLUM SE18 115 K5
Slade Wk WALW SE17 110 C5
Slade Wy MTCM CR4 148 A7
Slagrove Pl LEW SE13 132 D4
Slaidburn St WBPTN SW10 108 B5
Slaithwaite Rd LEW SE13 133 F3
Slaney Pl HOLWY N7 73 G4
Slaney Rd ROM RM1 63 G4
Slattery Rd FELT TW13 122 B7
Sleaford Gn OXHEY WD19 33 H2
Sleaford St VX/NE SW8 109 H6
Sledmere Ct
EBED/NFELT TW14 121 H7
Slievemore Cl CLAP SW4 129 J2
Slingsby Pl LSQ/SEVD WC2H 11 J6
Slippers Pl BERM/RHTH SE16 111 J2
Sloane Av CHEL SW3 15 K6
Sloane Ct East CHEL SW3 16 A7
Sloane Ct West CHEL SW3 15 M7
Sloane Gdns BGVA SW1W 16 A6
Sloane Sq BGVA SW1W 15 M6
Sloane St KTBR SW1X 15 M2
Sloane Ter KTBR SW1X 15 M5
Sloane Wk CROY/NA CR0 166 C5
Slocum Cl THMD SE28 97 J6
Slough La CDALE/KGS NW9 50 E5
Sly St WCHPL E1 * 92 D5
Smaldon Cl WDR/YW UB7 100 D2
Smallberry Av ISLW TW7 124 A1
Smallbrook Ms BAY/PAD W2 9 G5
Smalley Cl STNW/STAM N16 74 B2
Smallwood Rd TOOT SW17 147 H3
Smarden Cl BELV DA17 117 H4
Smart's Pl NOXST/BSQ WC1A 11 K4
UED N18 42 C4
Smart St BETH E2 93 F2
Smeaton Rd
WAND/EARL SW18 127 K6
WFD IG8 45 K4
Smeaton St WAP E1W 92 D7
Smedley St VX/NE SW8 129 J1
Smeed Rd BOW E3 75 J6
Smiles Pl LEW SE13 133 F1
Smith Cl BERM/RHTH SE16 93 F7
Smithfield St STBT EC1A 12 C3
Smithies Rd ABYW SE2 116 C3

Smith's Ct SOHO/SHAV W1D * 11 G6
Smithson Rd TOTM N17 41 K7
Smith Sq WEST SW1P 17 J4
Smith St BRYLDS KT5 159 G5
CHEL SW3 15 L7
WATW WD18 21 G3
Smith's Yd CROY/NA CR0 177 J2
Smith Ter CHEL SW3 15 L8
Smithwood Cl
WIM/MER SW19 127 H7
Smithy St WCHPL E1 92 E4
Smtyhe Cl ED N9 42 C2
Smugglers Wy
WAND/EARL SW18 128 A3
Smyrk's Rd WALW SE17 19 K8
Smyrna Rd KIL/WHAMP NW6 2 A2
Smythe St POP/IOD E14 93 K6
Snakes La EBAR EN4 28 B2
Snakes La East WFD IG8 45 G5
Snakes La West WFD IG8 44 E5
Snakey La FELT TW13 140 E3
Snaresbrook Dr STAN HA7 35 K3
Snaresbrook Rd WALTH E17 58 C3
Snarsgate St NKENS W10 88 A4
Sneath Av GLDGN NW11 52 D6
Snell's Pk UED N18 42 B5
Sneyd Rd CRICK NW2 70 A4
Snowberry Cl SRTFD E15 76 B3
Snowbury Rd FUL/PGN SW6 128 A1
Snowden Dr CDALE/KGS NW9 51 G5
Snowdon Crs HYS/HAR UB3 101 F2
Snowdon Rd HTHAIR TW6 121 F5
Snowdown Cl PGE/AN SE20 150 E7
Snowdrop Cl HPTN TW12 142 A5
Snow Hl STBT EC1A 12 C3
Snowsfields STHWK SE1 19 H1
Snowshill Rd MNPK E12 77 J4
Snowy Fielder Waye
ISLW TW7 124 C1
Soames St PECK SE15 131 G2
Soames Wk NWMAL KT3 145 G7
Soane Cl EA W5 104 E1
Soaphouse La BTFD TW8 105 F6
Soho Sq SOHO/SHAV W1D 11 G4
Soho St SOHO/SHAV W1D 11 G4
Sojourner-Truth Cl HACK E8 74 D5
Solander Gdns WCHPL E1 92 D6
Solar Ct WATW WD18 * 20 D4
Solebay St WCHPL E1 93 G3
Solent Ri PLSTW E13 94 E2
Solent Rd KIL/WHAMP NW6 70 E4
Solna Av PUT/ROE SW15 127 F4
Solna Rd WCHMH N21 29 K7
Solomon Av UED N18 42 C3
Solomon's Pas PECK SE15 131 J3
Solon New Rd CLAP SW4 129 K3
Solon Rd BRXS/STRHM SW2 129 K3
Solway Cl HACK E8 74 B5
HSLWW TW4 122 D2
Solway Rd EDUL SE22 131 H3
WDGN N22 41 H7
Somaford Gv EBAR EN4 27 H5
Somali Rd CRICK NW2 70 D3
Somerby Rd BARK IG11 78 D6
Somercoates Cl EBAR EN4 27 J2
Somerfield Rd FSBYPK N4 73 H1
Somerfield St
BERM/RHTH SE16 112 A4
Somerford Cl PIN HA5 46 E3
Somerford Gv
STNW/STAM N16 74 B3
TOTM N17 42 C6
Somerford St WCHPL E1 * 92 D3
Somerford Wy
BERM/RHTH SE16 112 B1
Somerhill Av BFN/LL DA15 136 C6
Somerhill Rd WELL DA16 136 C1
Somerleyton Rd
BRXN/ST SW9 130 B3
Somersby Gdns REDBR IG4 59 K4
Somers Cl CAMTN NW1 5 G5
Somers Crs BAY/PAD W2 9 J5
Somerset Av CHSGTN KT9 171 K3
RYNPK SW20 160 E1
WELL DA16 136 A4
Somerset Cl CHEAM SM3 174 A2
NWMAL KT3 160 B5
TOTM N17 55 K1
WFD IG8 44 E7
Somerset Gdns HGT N6 54 A6
LEW SE13 132 E1
STRHM/NOR SW16 164 A2
TEDD TW11 142 E4
TOTM N17 * 42 A6
Somerset Rd BAR EN5 27 F4
BTFD TW8 104 D5
CHSWK W4 106 A2
HDN NW4 52 A3
HRW HA1 48 C5
KUT/HW KT1 159 G1
STHL UB1 84 A4
TEDD TW11 142 E4
TOTM N17 56 B2
WALTH E17 57 J4
WEA W13 85 H7
WIM/MER SW19 146 B2
Somerset Sq WKENS W14 * 107 H2
Somerset Waye HEST TW5 102 D5
Somers Pl BRXS/STRHM SW2 130 A6
Somers Rd BRXS/STRHM SW2 130 A5
WALTH E17 57 H3
Somers Wy BUSH WD23 22 C6
Somerton Av RCH/KEW TW9 125 J2
Somerton Rd CRICK NW2 70 B2
PECK SE15 131 J3
Somertrees Av
LEE/GVPK SE12 153 F1
Somervell Rd
RYLN/HDSTN HA2 65 K4
Somerville Av BARN SW13 107 F5
Somerville Cl BRXN/ST SW9 110 A7
Somerville Rd CHDH RM6 61 J4
PGE/AN SE20 151 F6
Sonderburg Rd HOLWY N7 73 F1
Sondes St WALW SE17 19 G8
Songhurst Cl CROY/NA CR0 164 A5
Sonia Cl OXHEY WD19 21 G6
Sonia Gdns HEST TW5 103 F6
NFNCH/WDSPK N12 39 G3
WLSDN NW10 69 H3
Sonning Gdns HPTN TW12 141 J5
Sonning Rd SNWD SE25 165 H5
Soper Cl CHING E4 43 H4
FSTH SE23 132 A7
Sophia Cl HOLWY N7 73 F5
Sophia Rd CAN/RD E16 95 F4
LEY E10 57 K7
Sophia Sq BERM/RHTH SE16 93 G6
Sopwith Av CHSGTN KT9 172 A4
Sopwith Cl KUTN/CMB KT2 144 B4
Sopwith Rd HEST TW5 102 B6
Sopwith Wy KUTN/CMB KT2 144 A7
VX/NE SW8 109 G6
Sorrel Bank CROY/NA CR0 * 179 G7
Sorrel Cl THMD SE28 97 G7
Sorrel Gdns EHAM E6 95 J4
Sorrel La POP/IOD E14 94 B5
Sorrell Cl BRXN/ST SW9 * 130 B1
NWCR SE14 112 B6
Sorrel Wk ROM RM1 63 H2
Sorrento Rd SUT SM1 175 F2
Sotheby Rd HBRY N5 73 J3
Sotheran Cl HACK E8 74 C7
Sotheron Rd WAT WD17 21 G1
Soudan Rd BTSEA SW11 108 E7
Souldern Rd WKENS W14 * 107 G2
Souldern St WATW WD18 21 F4
South Access Rd LEY E10 57 F6
South Africa Rd SHB W12 87 K6
Southall Ct STHL UB1 * 83 K6
Southall La HEST TW5 102 A5
Southall Pl STHWK SE1 19 G2
Southampton Blds
LINN WC2A * 12 A3
Southampton Gdns
MTCM CR4 163 K4
Southampton Ms
CAN/RD E16 95 F7
Southampton Pl
NOXST/BSQ WC1A 11 K3
Southampton Rd HAMP NW3 71 K4
Southampton Rd East
HTHAIR TW6 120 C5
Southampton Rd West
HTHAIR TW6 120 C5
Southampton Rw RSQ WC1B 11 J2
Southampton St
COVGDN WC2E 11 K6
Southampton Wy CMBW SE5 110 E6
Southam St NKENS W10 88 C3
South Ap NTHWD HA6 32 B2
South Audley St
MYFR/PKLN W1K 10 B7
South Av CAR SM5 176 A6
CHING E4 31 K6
RCH/KEW TW9 * 125 H1
STHL UB1 83 K6
South Avenue Gdns STHL UB1 83 K6
South Bank STHWK SE1 12 B7
SURB KT6 159 F5
Southbank THDIT KT7 158 C6
South Bank Ter SURB KT6 * 159 F5
South Birkbeck Rd WAN E11 76 B2
South Black Lion La
HMSMTH W6 106 D4
South Bolton Gdns
WBPTN SW10 14 D7
Southborough Cl SURB KT6 158 E7
Southborough La HAYES BR2 168 D4
HAYES BR2 169 F4
Southborough Rd BMLY BR1 168 D2
HOM E9 74 E7
SURB KT6 159 F7
Southborough Road (The
Lane) SURB KT6 * 159 F7
Southbourne Av
CDALE/KGS NW9 50 E1
Southbourne Cl PIN HA5 47 J6
Southbourne Crs HDN NW4 52 C3
Southbourne Gdns IL IG1 78 C4
LEE/GVPK SE12 134 A4
RSLP HA4 47 F7
Southbridge Pl CROY/NA CR0 177 J3
Southbridge Rd
CROY/NA CR0 177 J3
Southbridge Wy NWDGN UB2 102 D1
Southbrook Rd
LEE/GVPK SE12 133 H5
STRHM/NOR SW16 148 E7
Southbury Av EN EN1 30 C3
RAIN RM13 99 K4
Southbury Rd EN EN1 30 B3
South Carriage Dr SKENS SW7 15 J2
Southchurch Rd EHAM E6 95 K1
South Cl BAR EN5 26 D2
BXLYHS DA6 136 E3
DAGE RM10 80 C7
HGT N6 54 B5
PIN HA5 47 K6
WDR/YW UB7 100 C2
WHTN TW2 142 A2
The South Colonnade
POP/IOD E14 93 J7
Southcombe St WKENS W14 107 H3
Southcote Av BRYLDS KT5 159 J6
FELT TW13 140 D1
Southcote Ri RSLP HA4 46 B6
Southcote Rd ARCH N19 72 C3
SNWD SE25 165 J4
WALTH E17 57 F4
South Countess Rd
WALTH E17 57 H2
South Crs CAN/RD E16 94 B3
Southcroft Av WELL DA16 135 K2
WWKM BR4 180 A1
Southcroft Rd TOOT SW17 148 A5
South Cross Rd BARK/HLT IG6 60 C4
South Croxted Rd DUL SE21 149 K2
Southdean Gdns
WIM/MER SW19 146 D1
South Dene MLHL NW7 37 F2
Southdown Av HNWL W7 104 B2
Southdown Crs
GNTH/NBYPK IG2 60 E4
RYLN/HDSTN HA2 48 C7
Southdown Dr RYNPK SW20 146 B6
Southdown Rd CAR SM5 176 A7
EMPK RM11 63 K6
RYNPK SW20 146 B7
Southdown Vls
SEVS/STOTM N15 * 55 H4
South Dr RSLP HA4 46 C7
South Ealing Rd EA W5 104 E1
South Eastern Av ED N9 42 B2
South Eaton Pl BGVA SW1W 16 B5
South Eden Park Rd
BECK BR3 166 E4
South Edwardes Sq KENS W8 107 J2
South End CROY/NA CR0 177 J3
KENS W8 14 D3
Southend Cl ELTH/MOT SE9 135 G5
Southend Crs ELTH/MOT SE9 135 F5
Southend La SYD SE26 151 H3
Southend Rd BECK BR3 151 J7
CLAY IG5 59 J2
EHAM E6 77 K6
South End Rd HAMP NW3 71 J3
RAIN RM13 81 J7
Southend Road (North
Circular) WALTH E17 44 B7
South End Rw KENS W8 14 D3
Southern Av
EBED/NFELT TW14 121 K7
SNWD SE25 165 G2
Southern Down FELT TW13 * 122 B7
Southerngate Wy NWCR SE14 112 B6
Southern Gv BOW E3 93 H2
Southern Perimeter Rd
HTHAIR TW6 121 F4
STWL/WRAY TW19 120 C5
Southern Rd EFNCH N2 53 K3
PLSTW E13 95 F1
Southern Rw NKENS W10 88 B3
Southern St IS N1 5 L5
Southern Wy GNWCH SE10 113 H3
ROMW/RG RM7 62 C5
Southerton Rd HMSMTH W6 * 107 F3
South Esk Rd FSTGT E7 77 G5
Southey Rd BRXN/ST SW9 110 B7
SEVS/STOTM N15 56 A4
WIM/MER SW19 146 E6
Southey St PGE/AN SE20 151 F6
Southfield BAR EN5 26 B5
Southfield Gdns TWK TW1 143 F3
Southfield Pk
RYLN/HDSTN HA2 48 B3
Southfield Rd CHSWK W4 106 A1
PEND EN3 30 D5
Southfields E/WMO/HCT KT8 157 K5
HDN NW4 51 K2
Southfields Ms
WAND/EARL SW18 * 127 K5
Southfields Rd
WAND/EARL SW18 127 K5
South Gdns WBLY HA9 * 68 C1
WIM/MER SW19 147 H6
South Gate Av FELT TW13 140 B3
Southgate Gv IS N1 7 H2
Southgate Rd IS N1 7 H2
South Gate Rd MNPK E12 77 H2
South Gipsy Rd WELL DA16 136 E2
South Gv HGT N6 54 A7
SEVS/STOTM N15 55 K4
WALTH E17 57 H4
South Hall Dr RAIN RM13 99 K4
South Hl CHST BR7 153 K5
NTHWD HA6 * 32 C7
South Hill Av
RYLN/HDSTN HA2 66 C2
South Hill Gv HRW HA1 66 E3
South Hill Pk HAMP NW3 71 J3
South Hill Park Gdns
HAMP NW3 71 J3
South Hill Rd HAYES BR2 167 H2
Southholme Cl NRWD SE19 150 A7
Southill La PIN HA5 46 E3
Southill Rd CHST BR7 153 J6
Southill St POP/IOD E14 93 K5
South Island Pl BRXN/ST SW9 110 A6
South Kensington Station Ar
SKENS SW7 15 H5
South Lambeth Pl VX/NE SW8 17 K9
South Lambeth Rd
VX/NE SW8 17 K9
Southland Rd
WOOL/PLUM SE18 116 A6
Southlands Dr
WIM/MER SW19 146 B1
Southlands Gv BMLY BR1 168 D2
Southlands Rd HAYES BR2 168 C3
Southland Wy HSLW TW3 123 J4
South La KUT/HW KT1 158 E2
NWMAL KT3 160 A3
South La West NWMAL KT3 160 A3
South Lodge Av MTCM CR4 163 K3
South Lodge Crs ENC/FH EN2 28 D3
South Lodge Dr
STHGT/OAK N14 28 D3
South Md CDALE/KGS NW9 37 H7
HOR/WEW KT19 173 H6
Southmead Rd
WIM/MER SW19 127 H7
South Molton La
MYFR/PKLN W1K 10 C5
South Molton Rd CAN/RD E16 94 E5
South Molton St
MYFR/PKLN W1K 10 C5
Southmont Rd
ESH/CLAY KT10 170 E1
Southmoor Wy HOM E9 75 H5
South Mt TRDG/WHET N20 * 39 G1
South Norwood Hl
SNWD SE25 150 A7
South Oak Rd
STRHM/NOR SW16 149 F3
Southold Ri ELTH/MOT SE9 153 K2
Southolm St BTSEA SW11 109 G7
Southover BMLY BR1 152 E4
NFNCH/WDSPK N12 38 E3
South Pde CHEL SW3 15 H7
CHSWK W4 106 A3
EDGW HA8 * 50 C1
WLGTN SM6 * 176 C5
South Park Crs CAT SE6 133 H7
IL IG1 78 D2
South Park Dr
GDMY/SEVK IG3 78 E4
South Park Gv NWMAL KT3 159 K3
South Park Hill Rd
SAND/SEL CR2 177 K4
South Park Ms FUL/PGN SW6 128 A2
South Park Rd IL IG1 78 D3
WIM/MER SW19 147 F5
South Park Ter IL IG1 78 D2
South Park Wy RSLP HA4 65 G5
South Pl BRYLDS KT5 159 G6
LVPST EC2M 13 H3
PEND EN3 30 E4
South Place Ms LVPST EC2M 13 H3
Southport Rd
WOOL/PLUM SE18 115 J3
Southridge Pl RYNPK SW20 146 B6
South Ri BAY/PAD W2 * 9 K6
CAR SM5 175 J7
South Rd CHDH RM6 61 J4
EA W5 104 E3
ED N9 30 C7
EDGW HA8 36 D7
FELT TW13 141 H4
FSTH SE23 151 F1
HPTN TW12 141 J5
STHL UB1 83 K7
WDR/YW UB7 100 D2
WHTN TW2 142 D2
WIM/MER SW19 147 H5
Southsea Av WATW WD18 20 E3
Southsea Rd KUT/HW KT1 159 F3
South Sea St
BERM/RHTH SE16 112 C2
South Side HMSMTH W6 106 C2
SEVS/STOTM N15 * 56 B3
Southside Common
WIM/MER SW19 146 B5
Southspring BFN/LL DA15 135 J6
South Sq GINN WC1R 12 A3
GLDGN NW11 52 E5
South St BMLY BR1 167 K1
EMPK RM11 63 J5
ISLW TW7 124 B2
MYFR/PKLN W1K 10 B8
PEND EN3 31 F4
RAIN RM13 98 E1
ROM RM1 63 G5
South Tenter St WCHPL E1 13 M6
South Ter SKENS SW7 15 J5
SURB KT6 159 F5
WDGN N22 54 E1
South V HRW HA1 66 E3
NRWD SE19 150 A5
Southvale Rd BKHTH/KID SE3 133 H1
South Vale Rd SURB KT6 172 A1
South Vw BMLY BR1 168 B1
Southview Av WLSDN NW10 69 H4
South View Cl BXLY DA5 137 G5
Southview Cl TOOT SW17 148 A4
South View Ct NRWD SE19 * 149 J6
South View Crs
GNTH/NBYPK IG2 60 B5
Southview Dr SWFD E18 59 F2
Southview Gdns WLGTN SM6 176 C6
Southview Rd BMLY BR1 152 B3
South View Rd
CEND/HSY/T N8 54 D2
PIN HA5 33 F5
Southviews SAND/SEL CR2 179 F7
South Vls CAMTN NW1 72 D5
Southville VX/NE SW8 109 J7
Southville Cl
EBED/NFELT TW14 121 H6
HOR/WEW KT19 173 F7
Southville Crs
EBED/NFELT TW14 121 H7
Southville Rd
EBED/NFELT TW14 121 H7
THDIT KT7 158 B6
South Wk WWKM BR4 180 C2
Southwark Br CANST EC4R 12 F7
Southwark Bridge Rd
STHWK SE1 18 D3
Southwark Park Est
BERM/RHTH SE16 * 111 J3
Southwark Park Rd
BERM/RHTH SE16 19 M5
Southwark Pl BMLY BR1 168 E2
Southwark St STHWK SE1 12 D8
Southwater Cl BECK BR3 151 K6
POP/IOD E14 93 H5
South Wy RYLN/HDSTN HA2 48 A3
WBLY HA9 68 C4
CROY/NA CR0 179 G2
ED N9 42 E1
FBAR/BDGN N11 40 C5
Southway GLDGN NW11 53 F5
RYNPK SW20 161 G3
TRDG/WHET N20 38 E1
WLGTN SM6 176 C3
Southway Cl SHB W12 106 E1
Southwell Av NTHLT UB5 66 A5
Southwell Gdns SKENS SW7 14 E5
Southwell Grove Rd WAN E11 76 C1
Southwell Rd CMBW SE5 130 D2
CROY/NA CR0 164 B5
KTN/HRWW/WS HA3 49 K5
South Western Rd TWK TW1 124 B5
South West India Dock
Entrance POP/IOD E14 113 F1
Southwest Rd WAN E11 58 B7
South Wharf Rd BAY/PAD W2 9 G4
Southwick Ms BAY/PAD W2 9 H4
Southwick Pl BAY/PAD W2 9 J5
Southwick St BAY/PAD W2 9 J4
Southwick Yd BAY/PAD W2 * 9 K5
Southwold Dr BARK IG11 79 G4
Southwold Rd BXLY DA5 137 J5
CLPT E5 74 D1
Southwood Av HGT N6 54 B6
KUTN/CMB KT2 144 E7
Southwood Cl BMLY BR1 168 E3
WPK KT4 161 G7
Southwood Dr BRYLDS KT5 159 K6
South Woodford SWFD E18 58 E1
Southwood Gdns
ESH/CLAY KT10 171 G2
GNTH/NBYPK IG2 60 B3
Southwood La HGT N6 54 A6
Southwood Lawn Rd HGT N6 54 A6
Southwood Pk HGT N6 * 54 B6
Southwood Rd
ELTH/MOT SE9 154 B1
THMD SE28 97 H7
South Worple Wy
MORT/ESHN SW14 126 A2
Southy Ms CAN/RD E16 94 E7
Sovereign Cl EA W5 85 J4
RSLP HA4 46 C7
WAP E1W 92 D6
Sovereign Ct E/WMO/HCT KT8 156 E3
Sovereign Crs
BERM/RHTH SE16 93 G6
Sovereign Gv ALP/SUD HA0 67 K2
Sovereign Ms BETH E2 * 7 L5
EBAR EN4 27 K2
Sovereign Pk WLSDN NW10 * 86 D3
Sovereign Pl HRW HA1 49 F4
Sovereign Rd BARK IG11 97 J2
Sowerby Cl ELTH/MOT SE9 134 E4
Sowrey Av RAIN RM13 81 H5
Space Waye
EBED/NFELT TW14 122 A4
Spafield St CLKNW EC1R 6 A9
Spa Green Est CLKNW EC1R * 6 B7
Spa Hl NRWD SE19 149 K7
Spalding Cl EDGW HA8 37 G6
Spalding Rd HDN NW4 52 A5
TOOT SW17 148 B4
Spanby Rd BOW E3 93 J3
Spaniards Cl GLDGN NW11 53 G7
Spaniards End HAMP NW3 53 G7
Spaniards Rd HAMP NW3 71 G1
Spanish Pl MHST W1U * 10 B4
Spanish Rd WAND/EARL SW18 128 B4
Sparkbridge Rd HRW HA1 48 E3
Sparkes Cl HAYES BR2 168 A3
Sparke Ter CAN/RD E16 * 94 D5
Sparkford Gdns
FBAR/BDGN N11 40 A4
Sparks Cl ACT W3 87 F5
BCTR RM8 79 K1
HPTN TW12 141 J5
Spa Rd BERM/RHTH SE16 19 L4
Sparrow Cl HPTN TW12 141 J5
Sparrow Dr STMC/STPC BR5 169 H7
Sparrow Farm Dr
EBED/NFELT TW14 122 B6
Sparrow Farm Rd EW KT17 173 J3
Sparrow Gn DAGE RM10 80 D2
Sparrows Herne BUSH WD23 22 B6
Sparrows La ELTH/MOT SE9 135 H6
Sparrows Wy BUSH WD23 * 22 C6
Sparrows Wick BUSH WD23 * 22 C7
Sparsholt Rd ARCH N19 55 F7
BARK IG11 78 E7
Spartan Cl WLGTN SM6 176 E6
Sparta St GNWCH SE10 113 F7
Speakers Ct CROY/NA CR0 * 164 E7
Spearman St
WOOL/PLUM SE18 * 115 F5
Spear Ms ECT SW5 14 B6
Spears Rd ARCH N19 54 E7
Speart La HEST TW5 102 D6
Spectrum Pl WALW SE17 19 G8
Spedan Cl HAMP NW3 71 F2
Speedwell St DEPT SE8 112 D6
Speedy Pl STPAN WC1H 5 J8
Speer Rd THDIT KT7 158 A5
Speirs Cl NWMAL KT3 160 C5
Spekehill ELTH/MOT SE9 153 K2
Speke Rd THHTH CR7 164 E1
Speldhurst Cl HAYES BR2 167 J4
Speldhurst Rd CHSWK W4 106 A2
HOM E9 75 F6
Spellbrook Wk IS N1 * 6 F3
Spelman St WCHPL E1 92 C4
Spelthorne Gv SUN TW16 140 D6
Spelthorne La ASHF TW15 140 A6
Spence Cl BERM/RHTH SE16 112 C1
Spencer Av PLMGR N13 41 F5
YEAD UB4 82 E4
Spencer Cl FNCH N3 52 D1
WFD IG8 45 G4
WLSDN NW10 86 B2
Spencer Dr EFNCH N2 53 G5
Spencer Gdns
MORT/ESHN SW14 125 K4
Spencer Hl WIM/MER SW19 146 C5
Spencer Hill Rd
WIM/MER SW19 146 C6
Spencer House SURB KT6 * 159 F4
Spencer Ms CLAP SW4 109 K7
HMSMTH W6 107 H5
Spencer Pk WAND/EARL SW18 128 C4
Spencer Pl CROY/NA CR0 164 E6
IS N1 6 C1
WEST SW1P 16 F4
Spencer Ri KTTN NW5 72 B3
Spencer Rd ACT W3 86 E7
ALP/SUD HA0 67 J1
BMLY BR1 152 D6
BTSEA SW11 128 C3
CEND/HSY/T N8 55 F4
CHSWK W4 105 K6
E/WMO/HCT KT8 157 H3
EHAM E6 77 H7
FBAR/BDGN N11 40 B3
GDMY/SEVK IG3 61 F7
ISLW TW7 103 J7
KTN/HRWW/WS HA3 48 E1
MTCM CR4 162 E6
RAIN RM13 99 F2
RYNPK SW20 145 K7
SAND/SEL CR2 178 A4
TOTM N17 42 C7
WALTH E17 58 A1
WHTN TW2 142 E2
Spencer St FSBYE EC1V 6 C8
NWDGN UB2 102 C2
Spencer Wk PUT/ROE SW15 127 G3
Spencer Wy WCHPL E1 92 D5
Spenser Gv STNW/STAM N16 74 A3
Spenser Ms DUL SE21 130 E7
Spenser Rd HNHL SE24 130 C4
Spenser St WESTW SW1E 16 F3
Spensley Wk STNW/STAM N16 73 K2
Speranza St
WOOL/PLUM SE18 116 A4
Sperling Rd TOTM N17 56 B1
Spert St POP/IOD E14 93 G6
Speyside STHGT/OAK N14 28 C5
Spey St POP/IOD E14 94 A4
Spezia Rd WLSDN NW10 87 J1
Spicer Cl BRXN/ST SW9 130 C1
WOT/HER KT12 156 B5
Spices Yd CROY/NA CR0 177 J3
Spielman Rd DART DA1 139 J3
Spigurnell Rd TOTM N17 41 K7
Spikes Bridge Rd STHL UB1 83 J5
Spindle Cl WOOL/PLUM SE18 114 D2
Spindlewood Gdns
CROY/NA CR0 178 A3
Spindrift Av POP/IOD E14 112 E3
Spinel Cl WOOL/PLUM SE18 116 A4
Spinnaker Cl BARK IG11 97 H2
Spinnells Rd
RYLN/HDSTN HA2 47 K7
Spinney Cl BECK BR3 166 E3
NWMAL KT3 160 B4
RAIN RM13 99 G1
WPK KT4 173 H2
Spinney Dr EBED/NFELT TW14 121 F6
Spinney Gdns DAGW RM9 80 A4
NRWD SE19 150 B4
Spinney Oak BMLY BR1 168 D1
The Spinneys BMLY BR1 168 E1
The Spinney ALP/SUD HA0 67 G2
BAR EN5 27 F1
BARN SW13 * 106 E5
CHEAM SM3 174 A3
NFNCH/WDSPK N12 * 39 G6
STAN HA7 36 A3
STRHM/NOR SW16 148 C2
SUN TW16 140 E7
WCHMH N21 29 G6
Spirit Quay WAP E1W 92 C7
Spital Sq WCHPL E1 13 K2
Spital St WCHPL E1 92 C4
Spital Yd WCHPL E1 * 13 K2
Spitfire Est HEST TW5 * 102 B4
Spitfire House
WOOL/PLUM SE18 * 114 D6
Spitfire Rd WLGTN SM6 177 F6
Spitfire Wy HEST TW5 102 B4
Spode Wk KIL/WHAMP NW6 * 71 F4
Spondon Rd SEVS/STOTM N15 56 C3
Spoonbill Wy YEAD UB4 83 H4
Spooner Wk WLGTN SM6 176 D4
Sportsbank St CAT SE6 133 F6
Sportsman Pl BETH E2 74 C7
Spottons Gv TOTM N17 41 J7
Spout Hl CROY/NA CR0 179 J4
Spratt Hall Rd WAN E11 58 E5
Spray St WOOL/PLUM SE18 115 G3
Spreighton Rd
E/WMO/HCT KT8 157 G3
Sprimont Pl CHEL SW3 15 L7
Springall St PECK SE15 111 J6
Springbank WCHMH N21 29 F5
Springbank Rd LEW SE13 133 H5
Springbank Wk CAMTN NW1 5 G2
Springbourne Ct BECK BR3 152 A7
Spring Bridge Rd EA W5 85 K6
Spring Cl BAR EN5 26 B4
BCTR RM8 61 K6
BORE WD6 24 C1
Springclose La CHEAM SM3 174 C5
Spring Cnr FELT TW13 * 140 E2

Spring Cots SURB KT6 * 158 E4
Springcroft Av EFNCH N2 53 K2
Spring Crofts BUSH WD23 22 A4
Springdale Rd
STNW/STAM N16 73 K3
Spring Dr PIN HA5 46 E5
Springfield BUSH WD23 22 D7
CLPT E5 56 D7
Springfield Av HPTN TW12 142 B5
MUSWH N10 54 C2
RYNPK SW20 161 J2
Springfield Cl
NFNCH/WDSPK N12 39 F4
STAN HA7 35 G2
Springfield Dr
GNTH/NBYPK IG2 60 C4
Springfield Gdns BMLY BR1 168 E3
CDALE/KGS NW9 51 F4
CLPT E5 56 D7
RSLP HA4 47 F7
WFD IG8 45 G6
WWKM BR4 179 K1
Springfield Gv CHARL SE7 114 B5
SUN TW16 140 E7
Springfield La
KIL/WHAMP NW6 2 B4
Springfield Mt
CDALE/KGS NW9 51 G4
Springfield Parade Ms
PLMGR N13 41 G3
Springfield Pl NWMAL KT3 159 K3
Springfield Ri SYD SE26 150 D2
Springfield Rd BMLY BR1 168 E3
EHAM E6 77 K6
FBAR/BDGN N11 40 C4
HNWL W7 84 E7
HRW HA1 48 E5
KUT/HW KT1 159 F3
SEVS/STOTM N15 56 C3
SRTFD E15 * 94 C2
STJWD NW8 2 E4
SYD SE26 150 D4
TEDD TW11 143 G4
THHTH CR7 149 J7
WALTH E17 57 H5
WELL DA16 136 C2
WHTN TW2 123 F7
WIM/MER SW19 146 D4
WLGTN SM6 176 B4
YEAD UB4 83 G7
Springfield Wk
KIL/WHAMP NW6 2 C4
Spring Gdns E/WMO/HCT KT8 157 H4
HBRY N5 73 J4
HCH RM12 81 K3
ROMW/RG RM7 62 E4
WFD IG8 45 G6
WHALL SW1A 11 J8
WLGTN SM6 176 C4
Spring Gv CHSWK W4 105 H4
HPTN TW12 142 B7
MTCM CR4 148 A7
Spring Grove Crs HSLW TW3 103 H7
Spring Grove Rd HSLW TW3 103 H7
RCHPK/HAM TW10 125 G4
Spring Hl CLPT E5 56 C6
SYD SE26 150 E3
Springhill Cl CMBW SE5 130 E2
Springhurst Cl CROY/NA CR0 179 H3
Spring Lake STAN HA7 35 H3
Spring La CLPT E5 56 D7
MUSWH N10 54 A2
SNWD SE25 165 J5
Spring Ms MHST W1U * 9 M2
Spring Park Av CROY/NA CR0 179 F1
Springpark Dr BECK BR3 167 F2
FSBYPK N4 55 J7
Spring Park Rd CROY/NA CR0 179 F1
Spring Pl BARK IG11 96 C1
KTTN NW5 72 A4
Springpond Rd DAGW RM9 80 A4
Springrice Rd LEW SE13 133 F5
Spring Rd FELT TW13 140 D2
Spring Shaw Rd
STMC/STPC BR5 155 G7
Spring St BAY/PAD W2 9 G5
EW KT17 173 H7
Spring Tide Cl PECK SE15 * 111 H7
Springvale Av BTFD TW8 104 E4
Spring V South DART DA1 * 139 G6
Springvale Ter WKENS W14 107 G2
Spring Villa Rd EDGW HA8 36 C6
Spring Vls WEA W13 * 85 H7
Spring Wk WCHPL E1 92 C4
Springwater Cl
WOOL/PLUM SE18 * 115 F7
Springwell Av WLSDN NW10 69 H7
Springwell Rd HEST TW5 102 C7
STRHM/NOR SW16 149 F3
Springwood Cl BOW E3 93 J1
Springwood Crs EDGW HA8 36 E1
Springwood Wy ROM RM1 63 J4
Sprowston Ms FSTGT E7 76 E4
Sprowston Rd FSTGT E7 76 E4
Sprucedale Gdns
CROY/NA CR0 179 F3
WLGTN SM6 176 E7
Spruce Hills Rd WALTH E17 57 K1
Sprules Rd BROCKY SE4 132 B1
Spurfield E/WMO/HCT KT8 157 G2
Spurgeon Av NRWD SE19 149 K7
Spurgeon Rd NRWD SE19 149 K6
Spurgeon St STHWK SE1 19 G4
Spurling Rd DAGW RM9 80 B5
EDUL SE22 * 131 G3
Spur Rd BARK IG11 96 C2
EBED/NFELT TW14 122 A4
EDGW HA8 36 A3
ISLW TW7 104 B6
SEVS/STOTM N15 * 55 K3
STHWK SE1 18 A1
WHALL SW1A 16 E2
Spurstowe Rd HACK E8 74 D5
Spurstowe Ter HACK E8 74 C4
The Square CAR SM5 176 A4
HMSMTH W6 107 F4
IL IG1 60 A6
RCH/KEW TW9 125 F4
STKPK UB11 82 B7
WFD IG8 44 E4
Squarey St TOOT SW17 147 G2
Squire Gdns STJWD NW8 3 G8
Squires Ct WIM/MER SW19 146 E3
Squires La FNCH N3 39 F7
Squire's Mt HAMP NW3 71 H2
Squires Wk ASHF TW15 140 B6
Squires Wood Dr CHST BR7 * 153 K6
Squirrel Cl HSLWW TW4 122 B2
Squirrel Ms WEA W13 * 85 G6
Squirrels Cl
NFNCH/WDSPK N12 39 G3
Squirrels Gn WPK KT4 173 H1
Squirrel's Heath Av GPK RM2 63 K2
The Squirrels BUSH WD23 22 D5
LEW SE13 133 G2
PIN HA5 47 K2
Squirries St BETH E2 92 C2
Stable Cl KUTN/CMB KT2 144 B5
NTHLT UB5 84 A1
Stable Ms TWK TW1 124 A7
WNWD SE27 149 J4
Stables Wy LBTH SE11 18 A7
Stable Wk EFNCH N2 39 H7
IS N1 5 K5
Stable Wy NKENS W10 88 A5
Stable Yard Rd WHALL SW1A 16 F1
Stacey Av UED N18 42 E3
Stacey Cl LEY E10 58 B4
Stacey St HOLWY N7 73 G2
LSQ/SEVD WC2H 11 H5
Stackhouse St KTBR SW1X 15 L3
Stacy Pth CMBW SE5 * 111 F6
Staddon Cl BECK BR3 166 B3
Staddon Ct BECK BR3 166 B3
Stadium Rd HDN NW4 51 K6
WOOL/PLUM SE18 114 E6
Stadium St WBPTN SW10 108 B6
Stadium Wy WBLY HA9 68 B3
Staffa Rd LEY E10 57 G7
Stafford Av CLAY IG5 60 A1
Stafford Cl CHEAM SM3 174 C5
KIL/WHAMP NW6 2 A8
STHGT/OAK N14 28 C4
WALTH E17 57 H5
Stafford Cross CROY/NA CR0 177 F4
Stafford Gdns CROY/NA CR0 177 F4
Stafford Pl RCHPK/HAM TW10 125 G6
WESTW SW1E 16 E3
Stafford Rd BOW E3 93 H1
CROY/NA CR0 177 G3
FSTGT E7 77 G6
KIL/WHAMP NW6 2 A7
KTN/HRWW/WS HA3 34 C6
NWMAL KT3 159 K2
RSLP HA4 64 D3
SCUP DA14 154 E3
WLGTN SM6 176 C5
Staffordshire St PECK SE15 111 H7
Stafford St CONDST W1S 10 E8
Stafford Ter KENS W8 14 A3
Stag Cl EDGW HA8 50 D1
Stag La BKHH IG9 45 F1
EDGW HA8 50 D1
PUT/ROE SW15 145 H2
Stag Pl WESTW SW1E 16 E3
Stags Wy ISLW TW7 104 A5
Stainbank Rd MTCM CR4 163 G2
Stainby Cl WDR/YW UB7 100 B2
Stainby Rd TOTM N17 56 B2
Stainer St STHWK SE1 13 H9
Staines Av CHEAM SM3 174 B1
Staines Rd EBED/NFELT TW14 120 E7
EBED/NFELT TW14 122 C4
IL IG1 78 D3
WHTN TW2 142 C2
Staines Rd East SUN TW16 140 E6
Staines Rd West ASHF TW15 140 A6
Stainford Cl ASHF TW15 140 B4
Stainforth Rd
GNTH/NBYPK IG2 60 D6
WALTH E17 57 J3
Staining La CITYW EC2V 12 F4
Stainmore Cl CHST BR7 154 D7
Stainsbury St BETH E2 92 E1
Stainsby Pl POP/IOD E14 * 93 J5
Stainsby Rd POP/IOD E14 93 J5
Stainton Rd CAT SE6 133 G6
Stalbridge St CAMTN NW1 9 K2
Stalham St BERM/RHTH SE16 111 J2
Stambourne Wy NRWD SE19 150 A6
WWKM BR4 180 A2
Stambourne Woodland Wk
NRWD SE19 150 A6
Stamford Brook Av
HMSMTH W6 106 C2
Stamford Brook Gdns
HMSMTH W6 106 C2
Stamford Brook Rd
HMSMTH W6 106 C2
Stamford Cl HAMP NW3 * 71 G2
KTN/HRWW/WS HA3 34 E6
SEVS/STOTM N15 56 C3
STHL UB1 84 A6
Stamford Cots WBPTN SW10 * 108 A6
Stamford Dr HAYES BR2 167 J3
Stamford Gdns DAGW RM9 79 J6
Stamford Gv East
STNW/STAM N16 56 C7
Stamford Gv West
STNW/STAM N16 56 C7
Stamford Hl STNW/STAM N16 56 B7
Stamford Rd DAGW RM9 79 H6
EHAM E6 77 J7
IS N1 7 K1
SEVS/STOTM N15 56 C4
WAT WD17 21 F1
Stamford St STHWK SE1 12 A8
Stamp Pl BETH E2 7 L6
Stanborough Cl HPTN TW12 141 K5
Stanborough Pas HACK E8 74 B5
Stanborough Rd HSLW TW3 123 J2
Stanbridge Pl WCHMH N21 41 H1
Stanbridge Rd
PUT/ROE SW15 127 F2
Stanbrook Rd ABYW SE2 116 C1
Stanbury Ct HAMP NW3 71 K5
Stanbury Rd PECK SE15 111 J7
Stancroft CDALE/KGS NW9 51 G3
Standale Gv RSLP HA4 46 A4
Standard Pl SDTCH EC2A 7 K8
Standard Rd BELV DA17 117 H4
HSLWW TW4 122 D2
WLSDN NW10 86 E3
Standen Rd
WAND/EARL SW18 127 K6
Standfield Rd DAGE RM10 80 C4
Standish Rd HMSMTH W6 106 D3
Stane Cl WIM/MER SW19 147 F6
Stane Gv VX/NE SW8 129 J1
Stane Wy WOOL/PLUM SE18 114 C6
Stanford Cl HPTN TW12 141 K5
ROMW/RG RM7 62 D5
RSLP HA4 46 A5
WFD IG8 45 J4
Stanford Pl WALW SE17 19 J6
Stanford Rd FBAR/BDGN N11 39 K4
KENS W8 14 D4
STRHM/NOR SW16 163 K1
Stanford St PIM SW1V 17 G6
Stanford Wy
STRHM/NOR SW16 163 J1
Stangate Crs BORE WD6 25 G4
Stangate Gdns STAN HA7 35 H3
Stanger Rd SNWD SE25 165 H3
Stanhope Av FNCH N3 52 D2
KTN/HRWW/WS HA3 34 D7
Stanhope Cl
BERM/RHTH SE16 * 112 A1
Stanhope Gdns BCTR RM8 80 B2
FSBYPK N4 55 H5
HGT N6 54 B5
IL IG1 59 K7
MLHL NW7 37 H4
SKENS SW7 14 F5
Stanhope Ga BAY/PAD W2 9 L6
MYFR/PKLN W1K 10 B9
Stanhope Gv BECK BR3 166 C4
Stanhope Ms East SKENS SW7 14 F5
Stanhope Ms South
SKENS SW7 14 F6
Stanhope Ms West
SKENS SW7 14 F5
Stanhope Pde CAMTN NW1 4 D7
Stanhope Park Rd
GFD/PVL UB6 84 C3
Stanhope Pl BAY/PAD W2 9 L5
Stanhope Rd BAR EN5 26 B5
BCTR RM8 80 B1
BFN/LL DA15 155 G3
CAR SM5 176 A6
CROY/NA CR0 178 A2
GFD/PVL UB6 84 C4
HGT N6 54 C5
NFNCH/WDSPK N12 39 G4
RAIN RM13 99 J1
WALTH E17 57 K4
Stanhope Rw
MYFR/PICC W1J * 10 C9
Stanhope St CAMTN NW1 4 E7
Stanhope Ter BAY/PAD W2 9 H6
WHTN TW2 * 124 A6
Stanier Cl WKENS W14 107 J4
Stanlake Rd SHB W12 88 A7
Stanlake Vls SHB W12 88 A7
Stanley Av ALP/SUD HA0 68 A6
BARK IG11 97 F2
BCTR RM8 62 B7
BECK BR3 167 F2
GFD/PVL UB6 66 C7
GPK RM2 63 J3
NWMAL KT3 160 D4
Stanley Cl ALP/SUD HA0 68 A6
ELTH/MOT SE9 135 H7
GPK RM2 63 J3
VX/NE SW8 110 A5
Stanley Crs NTGHL W11 88 D6
Stanleycroft Cl ISLW TW7 103 K7
Stanley Gdns ACT W3 106 B1
CRICK NW2 70 A4
MTCM CR4 * 148 A5
NTGHL W11 88 D6
WLGTN SM6 176 C5
Stanley Gardens Rd
TEDD TW11 142 E4
Stanley Gv CROY/NA CR0 164 B5
VX/NE SW8 129 F1
Stanley Park Dr ALP/SUD HA0 68 B6
Stanley Park Rd CAR SM5 175 K6
Stanley Pas CAMTN NW1 5 H6
Stanley Rd ACT W3 105 J2
BELMT SM2 175 F5
CROY/NA CR0 164 B6
ED N9 30 B7
EFNCH N2 53 H3
EN EN1 30 A2
FBAR/BDGN N11 40 D5
HAYES BR2 168 B2
HSLW TW3 123 H3
IL IG1 78 D1
MNPK E12 77 J4
MORT/ESHN SW14 125 J3
MRDN SM4 161 K3
MTCM CR4 148 A6
MUSWH N10 40 B6
NTHWD HA6 32 E7
RYLN/HDSTN HA2 66 C1
SCUP DA14 155 G2
SEVS/STOTM N15 55 H3
STHL UB1 83 J6
SWFD E18 44 D7
TEDD TW11 142 E4
WALTH E17 57 K5
WAT WD17 21 G2
WBLY HA9 68 B5
WHTN TW2 142 D2
WIM/MER SW19 146 E6
Stanley Rd North RAIN RM13 81 G7
Stanley Rd South RAIN RM13 99 H1
Stanley Sq CAR SM5 175 K7
Stanley St DEPT SE8 112 C6
Stanley Ter ARCH N19 * 72 E1
Stanmer St BTSEA SW11 108 D7
Stanmore Gdns
RCH/KEW TW9 125 G2
SUT SM1 175 G2
Stanmore Hl STAN HA7 35 H3
Stanmore Rd BELV DA17 117 K3
RCH/KEW TW9 125 G2
SEVS/STOTM N15 55 H3
WAN E11 58 D7
Stanmore St IS N1 5 L3
Stanmore Ter BECK BR3 166 D1
Stannard Ms HACK E8 * 74 C5
Stannard Rd HACK E8 74 C5
Stannary Pl LBTH SE11 18 B8
Stannary St LBTH SE11 18 B9
Stannet Wy WLGTN SM6 176 C3
Stansbury Sq NKENS W10 88 C2
Stansfeld Rd CAN/RD E16 95 H5
Stansfield Rd BRXN/ST SW9 130 A2
HSLWW TW4 122 A1
Stansgate Rd DAGE RM10 80 C1
Stanstead Cl HAYES BR2 167 J4
Stanstead Gv CAT SE6 132 C7
Stanstead Rd FSTH SE23 132 A7
WAN E11 59 F4
Stansted Cl HCH RM12 81 K5
Stansted Crs BXLY DA5 136 E7
Stanswood Gdns CMBW SE5 111 F6
Stanthorpe Cl
STRHM/NOR SW16 * 148 E4
Stanthorpe Rd
STRHM/NOR SW16 148 E4
Stanton Av TEDD TW11 142 E5
Stanton Cl HOR/WEW KT19 172 D4
WPK KT4 161 G7
Stanton Rd BARN SW13 126 C1
CROY/NA CR0 164 D6
RYNPK SW20 161 G1
Stanton St PECK SE15 * 111 H7
Stanton Wy SYD SE26 151 H3
Stanway Gdns ACT W3 86 C7
EDGW HA8 36 E5
Stanway St IS N1 7 K5
Stanwell Cl STWL/WRAY TW19 120 A5
Stanwell Gdns
STWL/WRAY TW19 120 A5
Stanwick Rd WKENS W14 107 J3
Stanworth St STHWK SE1 19 L2
Stapenhill Rd ALP/SUD HA0 67 H2
Staplefield Cl
BRXS/STRHM SW2 * 129 K7
PIN HA5 33 J6
Stapleford Av
GNTH/NBYPK IG2 60 E4
Stapleford Cl CHING E4 44 A2
KUT/HW KT1 159 H1
WIM/MER SW19 127 H6
Stapleford Rd ALP/SUD HA0 67 K6
Stapleford Wy BARK IG11 97 H2
Staplehurst Rd CAR SM5 175 J6
LEW SE13 133 G4
Staple Inn HHOL WC1V 12 A3
Staples Cl BERM/RHTH SE16 93 G7
Staple St STHWK SE1 19 H2
Stapleton Crs RAIN RM13 81 J5
Stapleton Gdns CROY/NA CR0 177 G4
Stapleton Hall Rd FSBYPK N4 55 F6
Stapleton Rd TOOT SW17 148 A2
Stapleton Vls
STNW/STAM N16 * 74 A3
Stapley Rd BELV DA17 117 H4
Stapylton Rd BAR EN5 26 C2
Starboard Wy POP/IOD E14 112 D2
Starbuck Cl ELTH/MOT SE9 135 F6
Starch House La
BARK/HLT IG6 60 D1
Star Cl PEND EN3 30 E5
Starcross St CAMTN NW1 4 F8
Starfield Rd SHB W12 106 D1
Star & Garter Hl
RCHPK/HAM TW10 125 F7
Star La CAN/RD E16 94 C3
Starling Cl PIN HA5 47 G2
Starling Rd CROY/NA CR0 166 B5
Starmans Cl DAGW RM9 80 A7
Star Pl WAP E1W 13 M7
Star Rd HGDN/ICK UB10 82 A3
ISLW TW7 123 J1
WKENS W14 107 J5
Star St BAY/PAD W2 9 H4
Starveall Cl WDR/YW UB7 100 C2
Star Yd LINN WC2A 12 A4
Staten Gdns TWK TW1 124 A7
Statham Gv STNW/STAM N16 73 K2
UED N18 42 A4
Station Ap ALP/SUD HA0 67 H5
BAR EN5 27 G3
BECK BR3 151 G7
BELMT SM2 174 C6
BKHH IG9 * 45 H3
BKHTH/KID SE3 134 A2
CAMTN NW1 * 10 A1
CHST BR7 153 J5
CHST BR7 154 A7
CROY/NA CR0 * 177 K1
ESH/CLAY KT10 171 F2
FBAR/BDGN N11 40 B4
FSTGT E7 77 F3
FUL/PGN SW6 * 127 H2
GFD/PVL UB6 66 C6
GLDGN NW11 * 52 B6
HOR/WEW KT19 173 H4
HPTN TW12 142 A7
HYS/HAR UB3 101 J2
KUT/HW KT1 159 H1
NFNCH/WDSPK N12 39 F3
NTHWD HA6 32 C6
OXHEY WD19 33 H2
PIN HA5 47 J2
RCH/KEW TW9 105 H7
RSLP HA4 46 C7
RSLP HA4 65 F4
SAND/SEL CR2 177 K7
STRHM/NOR SW16 148 D4
SUN TW16 140 E7
SURB KT6 158 E5
SWFD E18 * 59 F1
SYD SE26 151 H4
WALTH E17 57 J4
WAN E11 58 E4
WAN E11 * 76 C3
WATW WD18 * 20 D3
WELL DA16 136 A1
WFD IG8 * 45 G5
WLSDN NW10 87 H2
Station Approach Rd
CHSWK W4 105 K6
Station Ar GTPST W1W * 10 D1
Station Av HOR/WEW KT19 173 G7
NWMAL KT3 160 B2
RCH/KEW TW9 105 H7
Station Chambers EA W5 * 86 C3
Station Cl HPTN TW12 142 B7
Station Cots WDGN N22 * 54 E1
Station Crs ALP/SUD HA0 67 H5
SEVS/STOTM N15 55 K3
Stationers Hall Ct STP EC4M * 12 D5
Station Est BECK BR3 166 A3
Station Estate Rd
EBED/NFELT TW14 122 A7
Station Garage Ms
STRHM/NOR SW16 * 148 D5
Station Gdns CHSWK W4 105 K6
Station Gv ALP/SUD HA0 68 A5
Station House Ms ED N9 42 C3
Station Pde ACT W3 * 86 C5
BAL SW12 * 129 F7
BARK IG11 78 C6
BECK BR3 * 166 A3
BELMT SM2 * 175 G5
BMLY BR1 * 152 E7
CHSWK W4 * 105 K6
CLPT E5 * 74 D2
CRICK NW2 70 A5
EA W5 * 86 B7
EBAR EN4 * 28 A3
EBED/NFELT TW14 * 122 A6
EDGW HA8 * 36 A6
EHAM E6 * 77 J6
HCH RM12 81 K3
KTN/HRWW/WS HA3 * 49 H1
NTHLT UB5 * 66 A6
PLSTW E13 * 77 G7
RCH/KEW TW9 105 H7
ROM RM1 * 63 G5
RSLP HA4 * 64 A1
RYLN/HDSTN HA2 * 66 B3
STHGT/OAK N14 28 D7
Station Pas PECK SE15 111 K7
SWFD E18 59 F1
Station Pl FSBYPK N4 73 G1
Station Ri WNWD SE27 149 H1
Station Rd BAR EN5 27 F4
BARK/HLT IG6 60 D2
BARN SW13 126 C1
BCTR RM8 61 K7
BELV DA17 117 H2
BFN/LL DA15 155 G1
BMLY BR1 152 E7
BORE WD6 24 C3
CAR SM5 175 K3
CHSGTN KT9 172 A4
CROY/NA CR0 164 D7
EA W5 86 B5
EDGW HA8 36 C5
ESH/CLAY KT10 170 D4
FBAR/BDGN N11 40 B4
FNCH N3 38 E7
GPK RM2 63 K3
HAYES BR2 167 H1
HDN NW4 51 J5
HNWL W7 84 E7
HOLWY N7 72 C2
HPTN TW12 142 B7
HRW HA1 48 B4
HSLW TW3 123 G3
HYS/HAR UB3 101 H3
IL IG1 78 B1
KUT/HW KT1 143 K7
LEW SE13 133 F2
MLHL NW7 37 G5
MNPK E12 77 H3
NWMAL KT3 160 E4
PGE/AN SE20 150 E5
RYLN/HDSTN HA2 48 B4
SCUP DA14 155 G2
SNWD SE25 165 G3
SUN TW16 140 E6
TEDD TW11 143 G5
THDIT KT7 158 A6
TOTM N17 56 C2
TWK TW1 124 A7
WALTH E17 57 G5
WAT WD17 21 F1
WCHMH N21 29 H7
WDGN N22 54 E1
WDR/YW UB7 100 B1
WIM/MER SW19 147 G7
WLSDN NW10 87 H1
WWKM BR4 167 F7
Station Rd North BELV DA17 117 J2
Station Sq STMC/STPC BR5 169 H4
Station St SRTFD E15 76 B6
Station Ter CMBW SE5 110 D7
WLSDN NW10 88 B1
Station Vw GFD/PVL UB6 66 D7
Station Wy BKHH IG9 45 H3
CHEAM SM3 174 C6
ESH/CLAY KT10 170 E5
Station Yd RSLP HA4 * 64 B1
STHL UB1 * 102 E1
TWK TW1 124 B6
Staunton Rd KUTN/CMB KT2 144 B6
Staunton St DEPT SE8 112 C5
Staveley Cl HOLWY N7 * 72 E3
PECK SE15 111 K7
Staveley Gdns CHSWK W4 106 A7
Staveley Rd ASHF TW15 140 B5
CHSWK W4 105 K5
Staverton Rd CRICK NW2 70 A6
Stave Yard Rd
BERM/RHTH SE16 93 G7
Stavordale Rd CAR SM5 162 B6
HBRY N5 73 H3
Stayner's Rd WCHPL E1 93 F3
Stayton Rd SUT SM1 174 E2
Steadfast Rd KUT/HW KT1 143 K7
Stead St WALW SE17 19 G6
Steam Farm La
EBED/NFELT TW14 121 J3
Stean St HACK E8 7 L3
Stebbing Wy BARK IG11 97 G1
Stebondale St POP/IOD E14 113 F4
Stedly SCUP DA14 * 155 G3
Steed Cl EMPK RM11 81 K1
Steedman St WALW SE17 18 E6
Steeds Rd MUSWH N10 39 K7
Steel Ap BARK IG11 97 H1
Steele Rd CHSWK W4 105 K2
ISLW TW7 124 B3
TOTM N17 56 A2
WAN E11 76 C3
WLSDN NW10 86 E1
Steele's Ms North
HAMP NW3 * 71 K5
Steele's Ms South HAMP NW3 71 K5
Steele's Rd HAMP NW3 71 K5
Steeles Studios HAMP NW3 * 71 K5
Steel's La WCHPL E1 92 E5
Steep Hl CROY/NA CR0 178 A3
STRHM/NOR SW16 148 D2
Steeplands BUSH WD23 22 B6
Steeple Cl FUL/PGN SW6 127 H2
WIM/MER SW19 146 C3
Steeplestone Cl UED N18 41 J4
Steeple Wk IS N1 6 F3
Steerforth St
WAND/EARL SW18 147 F1
Steering Cl ED N9 30 E7
Steers Md MTCM CR4 147 K7
Steers Wy BERM/RHTH SE16 112 B1
Stella Rd TOOT SW17 147 K5
Stelling Rd ERITH DA8 118 A6
Stellman Cl CLPT E5 74 C2
Stembridge Rd PGE/AN SE20 165 J1
Stephan Cl HACK E8 74 C7
Stephen Av RAIN RM13 81 J5
Stephendale Rd
FUL/PGN SW6 128 A2
Stephen Ms FITZ W1T 11 G3
Stephen Pl CLAP SW4 129 H2
Stephen Rd BXLYHN DA7 137 K2
Stephenson Cl WELL DA16 136 A1
Stephenson Rd HNWL W7 85 F5
WALTH E17 57 G4
WHTN TW2 123 F6
Stephenson St CAN/RD E16 94 C3
WLSDN NW10 87 G2
Stephenson Wy BUSH WD23 21 H2
CAMTN NW1 4 F9
Stephen's Rd SRTFD E15 76 C7
Stephen St FITZ W1T 11 G4
Stepney Cswy WCHPL E1 93 F5
Stepney Gn WCHPL E1 92 E4
Stepney High St WCHPL E1 93 F4
Stepney Wy MTCM CR4 148 A7
WCHPL E1 92 D4
Sterling Av EDGW HA8 36 B3
Sterling Cl WLSDN NW10 69 J6
Sterling Gdns NWCR SE14 112 B5
Sterling Pl EA W5 105 F3
Sterling St SKENS SW7 15 K2
Sterling Way (North Circular)
UED N18 41 K4
Stern Cl BARK IG11 97 J1
Sterndale Rd WKENS W14 * 107 G2
Sterne St SHB W12 107 G1
Sternhall La PECK SE15 131 H2
Sternhold Av
BRXS/STRHM SW2 148 D1
Sterry Crs DAGE RM10 80 C4
Sterry Dr HOR/WEW KT19 173 G3
THDIT KT7 157 K5
Sterry Gdns DAGE RM10 80 C5

- Sterry Rd BARK IG11 ... 79 F7
- Sterry St STHWK SE1 ... 19 G2
- Steucers La FSTH SE23 ... 132 B7
- Steve Biko La CAT SE6 ... 151 K1
- Steve Biko Wy HSLW TW3 ... 123 H4
- Stevedale Rd WELL DA16 ... 136 H1
- Stevedore St WAP E1W ... 92 D3
- Stevenage Rd FUL/PGN SW6 ... 107 G7
- Stevens Av HOM E9 ... 74 E5
- Stevens Cl BECK BR3 ... 151 H4
- Stevens St STHWK SE1 ... 19 K3
- Stewart Cl CDALE/KGS NW9 ... 50 E2
- Stewart Quay SRTFD E15 ... 76 B3
- Stewart Rd WAN E11 ... 58 B7
- Stewart's Gv CHEL SW3 ... 15 H7
- Stillingfleet Rd BARN SW13 ... 106 D6
- Stillington St WEST SW1P ... 16 B6

PUT/ROE SW15 126 E4
Sunnymede Av
HOR/WEW KT19 173 G7
Sunnymede Dr BARK/HLT IG6 60 B3
Sunny Nook Gdns
SAND/SEL CR2 177 K5
Sunny Pl HDN NW4 52 A3
Sunnyside CAT SE6 * 132 C6
CRICK NW2 70 D2
WOT/HER KT12 156 B4
Sunnyside Pl WIM/MER SW19 146 C5
Sunnyside Rd ARCH N19 54 D6
EA W5 85 K7
IL IG1 78 C2
LEY E10 57 J7
TEDD TW11 142 D3
Sunnyside Rd East ED N9 42 C2
Sunnyside Rd North ED N9 42 B2
Sunnyside Rd South ED N9 42 B2
Sunny Vw CDALE/KGS NW9 51 F4
Sunny Wy
NFNCH/WDSPK N12 39 J6
Sun Pas BERM/RHTH SE16 111 H2
Sunray Av BRYLDS KT5 172 D1
HAYES BR2 168 D5
HNHL SE24 130 E3
WDR/YW UB7 100 A1
Sunrise Cl FELT TW13 141 K2
Sun Rd WKENS W14 107 J4
Sunset Av CHING E4 31 K7
WFD IG8 44 E4
Sunset Gdns SNWD SE25 165 F1
Sunset Rd HNHL SE24 130 D3
THMD SE28 97 G7
THMD SE28 116 B1
WIM/MER SW19 145 K4
Sunset Vw BAR EN5 26 C1
Sunshine Wy MTCM CR4 162 E1
Sun St SDTCH EC2A 13 H2
Sun Street Pas LVPST EC2M 13 J3
Surbiton Ct SURB KT6 158 D5
Surbiton Court Ms SURB KT6 158 E5
Surbiton Crs KUT/HW KT1 159 F3
Surbiton Hall Cl KUT/HW KT1 159 F3
Surbiton Hill Pk BRYLDS KT5 159 G4
Surbiton Hill Rd SURB KT6 159 F3
Surbiton Rd KUT/HW KT1 158 E3
Surlingham Cl THMD SE28 97 K6
Surma Cl WCHPL E1 92 C3
Surmans Cl DAGW RM9 79 J7
Surrendale Pl MV/WKIL W9 8 B1
Surrey Canal Rd PECK SE15 111 K5
Surrey Cl FNCH N3 52 C2
Surrey Crs CHSWK W4 105 H4
Surrey Gdns FSBYPK N4 55 J5
Surrey Gv SUT SM1 175 H2
WALW SE17 19 J8
Surrey La BTSEA SW11 108 D7
Surrey Ms WNWD SE27 150 A3
Surrey Mt FSTH SE23 131 J7
Surrey Quays Rd
BERM/RHTH SE16 111 K2
Surrey Rd BARK IG11 78 E6
DAGE RM10 80 D4
HRW HA1 48 C5
PECK SE15 132 A4
WWKM BR4 166 E7
Surrey Rw STHWK SE1 18 C1
Surrey Sq WALW SE17 19 J7
Surrey St CROY/NA CR0 177 J2
PLSTW E13 95 F2
TPL/STR WC2R 11 M6
Surrey Ter WALW SE17 19 K6
Surrey Water Rd
BERM/RHTH SE16 93 F7
Surridge Gdns NRWD SE19 149 K5
Surr St HOLWY N7 72 E4
Sury Basin KUTN/CMB KT2 144 A7
Susan Cl ROMW/RG RM7 62 E2
Susannah St POP/IOD E14 93 K5
Susan Rd BKHTH/KID SE3 134 A1
Susan Wd CHST BR7 154 A7
Sussex Av ISLW TW7 123 K2
Sussex Cl ARCH N19 * 72 E1
NWMAL KT3 160 B3
REDBR IG4 59 K5
TWK TW1 124 C5
Sussex Crs NTHLT UB5 66 A5
Sussex Gdns BAY/PAD W2 9 H4
CHSGTN KT9 171 K5
FSBYPK N4 55 J4
HGT N6 53 K4
Sussex Ga HGT N6 53 K4
Sussex Ms East BAY/PAD W2 * 9 H6
Sussex Ms West BAY/PAD W2 9 H6
Sussex Pl BAY/PAD W2 9 H5
CAMTN NW1 3 L9
HMSMTH W6 107 F4
NWMAL KT3 160 B3
Sussex Ring
NFNCH/WDSPK N12 38 E4
Sussex Rd CAR SM5 175 K5
EHAM E6 96 A1
HGDN/ICK UB10 64 A3
HRW HA1 48 C4
MTCM CR4 * 163 K4
NWDGN UB2 102 C2
NWMAL KT3 160 B3
SAND/SEL CR2 177 K5
SCUP DA14 155 H4
WWKM BR4 166 E7
Sussex Sq BAY/PAD W2 9 H6
Sussex St PIM SW1V 16 D8
PLSTW E13 95 F2
Sussex Ter PGE/AN SE20 * 150 E6
Sussex Wy ARCH N19 54 D7
EBAR EN4 28 B4
Sutcliffe Cl BUSH WD23 22 C3
GLDGN NW11 53 F4
Sutcliffe Rd WELL DA16 136 D1
WOOL/PLUM SE18 115 K5
Sutherland Av HYS/HAR UB3 101 K3
MV/WKIL W9 2 E8
MV/WKIL W9 8 B1
WEA W13 85 H5
WELL DA16 135 J3
WELL DA16 136 A4
Sutherland Cl BAR EN5 26 C3
Sutherland Ct
CDALE/KGS NW9 50 D3
Sutherland Dr
WIM/MER SW19 147 H7
Sutherland Gdns
MORT/ESHN SW14 126 B2
WPK KT4 160 E7
Sutherland Gv TEDD TW11 142 E4
WAND/EARL SW18 127 J6
Sutherland House
WALTH E17 * 57 G2
Sutherland Pl BAY/PAD W2 8 A4
Sutherland Rd BELV DA17 117 H2
BOW E3 93 H1
CHSWK W4 106 A5
CROY/NA CR0 164 B6
ED N9 30 C7
STHL UB1 83 K5
TOTM N17 42 C6
WEA W13 85 G5
Sutherland Rw PIM SW1V 16 D7
Sutherland Sq WALW SE17 18 E8
Sutherland St PIM SW1V 16 D7
Sutherland Vls WEA W13 * 85 G6
Sutherland Wk WALW SE17 18 F8
Sutlej Rd CHARL SE7 114 B6
Sutterton St HOLWY N7 73 F5
Sutton Cl BECK BR3 151 K7
CHSWK W4 * 105 K5
PIN HA5 46 E4
Sutton Common Rd
CHEAM SM3 161 J6
Sutton Ct BELMT SM2 175 G6
CHSWK W4 * 105 K5
EA W5 * 86 A7
Sutton Court Rd CHSWK W4 105 K5
PLSTW E13 95 G2
SUT SM1 175 G5
Sutton Crs BAR EN5 26 B4
Sutton Dene HSLW TW3 103 G7
Sutton Dwelling Est
CHEL SW3 15 J7
Sutton Est IS N1 * 6 C1
The Sutton Est IS N1 6 C2
Sutton Gdns CROY/NA CR0 165 G4
Sutton Gv SUT SM1 175 H4
Sutton Hall Rd HEST TW5 103 F6
Sutton La FARR EC1M 12 D1
HSLW TW3 122 E1
Sutton La North CHSWK W4 105 K4
Sutton La South CHSWK W4 105 K5
Sutton Park Rd SUT SM1 175 F5
Sutton Pl HOM E9 74 E4
Sutton Rd BARK IG11 96 E1
HEST TW5 103 F7
MUSWH N10 40 A7
PLSTW E13 94 D3
WALTH E17 43 F7
WAT WD17 21 G2
Sutton Rw SOHO/SHAV W1D 11 G4
Sutton Sq HEST TW5 102 E7
HOM E9 * 74 E4
Sutton St WCHPL E1 92 E5
Sutton Wy HEST TW5 102 E7
NKENS W10 88 A4
STLK EC1Y 12 F1
Swaby Rd WAND/EARL SW18 147 G1
Swaffield Rd
WAND/EARL SW18 128 B6
Swain Cl STRHM/NOR SW16 148 B5
Swain Rd THHTH CR7 164 D4
Swains Cl WDR/YW UB7 100 B1
Swain's La HGT N6 72 A2
Swainson Rd ACT W3 106 C1
Swains Rd MTCM CR4 147 K6
Swain St STJWD NW8 9 H1
Swaislands Dr DART DA1 138 C4
Swaledale Cl FBAR/BDGN N11 40 A5
Swale Rd DART DA1 138 D2
Swallands Rd CAT SE6 151 J2
Swallow Cl BUSH WD23 22 B7
NWCR SE14 111 K7
Swallow Ct RSLP HA4 * 47 G7
Swallowdale SAND/SEL CR2 179 F7
Swallow Dr NTHLT UB5 84 A1
WLSDN NW10 69 F5
Swallowfield Rd CHARL SE7 114 A4
Swallowfield Wy
HYS/HAR UB3 101 G1
Swallow Gdns
STRHM/NOR SW16 148 D4
Swallow Pl REGST W1B 10 D5
Swallow St EHAM E6 95 J4
REGST W1B 10 F7
Swanage Rd CHING E4 44 A6
WAND/EARL SW18 128 B5
Swanage Waye YEAD UB4 83 G5
Swan Ap EHAM E6 95 J4
Swan Cl CROY/NA CR0 * 165 F6
FELT TW13 141 J3
WALTH E17 43 G7
Swandon Wy
WAND/EARL SW18 128 A3
Swan Dr CDALE/KGS NW9 51 G1
Swanfield St BETH E2 7 L8
Swan Island TWK TW1 * 143 G2
Swan La CANST EC4R 13 G7
TRDG/WHET N20 39 G2
Swanley Rd WELL DA16 116 D7
Swan Md STHWK SE1 19 J4
Swan Ms BRXN/ST SW9 130 A1
Swan Pas WCHPL E1 13 M7
Swan Pl BARN SW13 126 C1
Swan Rd BERM/RHTH SE16 111 K1
FELT TW13 141 J3
STHL UB1 84 B5
WDR/YW UB7 100 A1
WOOL/PLUM SE18 114 C2
Swanscombe Rd CHSWK W4 106 B4
NTGHL W11 88 B7
Swansea Rd HTHAIR TW6 121 F5
PEND EN3 30 E3
Swanston Pth OXHEY WD19 33 G2
Swan St ISLW TW7 124 C2
STHWK SE1 18 F2
Swanton Gdns
WIM/MER SW19 127 G7
Swan Wk CHEL SW3 15 L9
Swan Wy PEND EN3 31 F1
Swanwick Cl PUT/ROE SW15 126 C6
Swan Yd IS N1 73 H5
Swaton Rd BOW E3 93 J3
Swaylands Rd BELV DA17 117 H5
Swaythling Cl UED N18 42 D3
Swedenbourg Gdns
WCHPL E1 92 C6
Sweden Ga BERM/RHTH SE16 112 B3
Sweeney Crs STHWK SE1 19 M2
Sweet Briar Gn ED N9 42 B2
Sweet Briar Gv ED N9 42 B2
Sweet Briar Wk UED N18 42 B3
Sweetmans Av PIN HA5 47 H2
Sweets Wy TRDG/WHET N20 39 H1
Swete St PLSTW E13 94 E1
Swift Cl HYS/HAR UB3 82 D5
RYLN/HDSTN HA2 66 B1
THMD SE28 97 H5
WALTH E17 43 G6
Swift Rd FELT TW13 141 H3
NWDGN UB2 102 E2
Swiftsden Wy BMLY BR1 152 C5
Swift St FUL/PGN SW6 107 H7
Swinbrook Rd NKENS W10 88 C4
Swinburne Crs CROY/NA CR0 165 K5
Swinburne Rd PUT/ROE SW15 126 D3
Swinderby Rd ALP/SUD HA0 68 A5
Swindon Cl GDMY/SEVK IG3 78 E1
Swindon Rd HTHAIR TW6 121 F4
Swindon St SHB W12 * 87 K7
Swinfield Cl FELT TW13 141 J3
Swinford Gdns BRXN/ST SW9 130 C2
Swingate La
WOOL/PLUM SE18 115 K6
Swinnerton St HOM E9 75 G4
Swinton Cl WBLY HA9 50 D7
Swinton Pl FSBYW WC1X 5 L7
Swinton St FSBYW WC1X 5 L7
Swires Shaw HAYES BR2 181 H3
Swiss Av WATW WD18 20 C3
Swiss Cl WATW WD18 20 C2
Swithland Gdns
ELTH/MOT SE9 153 K3
Swyncombe Av EA W5 104 C3
Swynford Gdns HDN NW4 51 J3
Sybil Ms FSBYPK N4 55 H5
Sybil Phoenix Cl DEPT SE8 112 A4
Sybourn St WALTH E17 57 H6
Sycamore Ap
RKW/CH/CXG WD3 20 A4
Sycamore Av BFN/LL DA15 136 A5
BOW E3 75 H7
EA W5 104 E2
HYS/HAR UB3 82 C6
Sycamore Cl ACT W3 87 G7
BUSH WD23 21 J1
CAN/RD E16 94 C3
CAR SM5 175 K3
EBAR EN4 27 H5
ED N9 42 C3
EDGW HA8 36 E3
FELT TW13 140 E2
NTHLT UB5 65 J7
SAND/SEL CR2 178 A4
Sycamore Gdns MTCM CR4 162 C1
SHB W12 106 E1
Sycamore Gv CAT SE6 133 F5
CDALE/KGS NW9 50 E6
GPK RM2 63 J1
NWMAL KT3 160 B2
PGE/AN SE20 150 C7
Sycamore Hl FBAR/BDGN N11 40 A5
Sycamore Ms CLAP SW4 129 H2
ERITH DA8 * 118 A4
Sycamore Rd
RKW/CH/CXG WD3 20 A4
WIM/MER SW19 146 A5
Sycamore St FSBYE EC1V 12 E1
Sycamore Wk NKENS W10 88 C3
Sycamore Wy TEDD TW11 143 J5
Sydcote DUL SE21 * 149 J1
Sydenham Av SYD SE26 150 D4
Sydenham Cl ROM RM1 63 H3
Sydenham Cots
LEE/GVPK SE12 * 153 G1
Sydenham Hl FSTH SE23 150 D1
SYD SE26 150 C2
Sydenham Pk SYD SE26 150 E2
Sydenham Park Rd
SYD SE26 150 E2
Sydenham Ri FSTH SE23 150 D1
Sydenham Rd CROY/NA CR0 177 J1
SYD SE26 151 F4
Sydenham Station Ap
SYD SE26 150 E3
Sydmons Ct FSTH SE23 * 131 K6
Sydner Rd STNW/STAM N16 74 B3
Sydney Chapman Wy
BAR EN5 26 D1
Sydney Cl SKENS SW7 15 H6
Sydney Gv HDN NW4 52 A4
Sydney Ms CHEL SW3 15 H6
Sydney Pl SKENS SW7 15 H6
Sydney Rd ABYW SE2 116 E2
BARK/HLT IG6 60 C1
BXLYHS DA6 136 E3
CEND/HSY/T N8 55 G3
EBED/NFELT TW14 121 K7
ENC/FH EN2 29 K3
MUSWH N10 40 B7
RCH/KEW TW9 125 F3
RYNPK SW20 161 G1
SCUP DA14 154 E3
SUT SM1 174 E3
TEDD TW11 143 F4
WAN E11 59 F5
WATW WD18 20 C4
WEA W13 85 G7
WFD IG8 44 E3
Sydney St CHEL SW3 15 J7
Sydney Ter ESH/CLAY KT10 * 171 F5
Sylvan Av CHDH RM6 62 B5
MLHL NW7 37 G5
WDGN N22 41 G6
Sylvan Gdns SURB KT6 158 E6
Sylvan Gv CRICK NW2 70 B3
PECK SE15 111 J5
Sylvan Hl NRWD SE19 150 A7
Sylvan Rd FSTGT E7 76 E5
IL IG1 78 C1
NRWD SE19 150 B7
WALTH E17 * 57 J4
WAN E11 58 E4
Sylvan Ter PECK SE15 * 111 J6
Sylvan Wk BMLY BR1 168 E2
Sylvan Wy BCTR RM8 79 H2
WWKM BR4 180 C3
Sylverdale Rd CROY/NA CR0 177 H2
Sylvester Av CHST BR7 153 K5
Sylvester Pth HACK E8 * 74 D5
Sylvester Rd ALP/SUD HA0 67 J4
EFNCH N2 53 G1
HACK E8 * 74 D5
WALTH E17 * 57 H6
Sylvia Av PIN HA5 33 K5
Sylvia Gdns WBLY HA9 68 D6
Symes Ms CAMTN NW1 4 E5
Symington Ms HOM E9 75 F4
Symister Ms IS N1 7 J8
Symons Cl PECK SE15 131 K1
Symons St CHEL SW3 15 M6
Symphony Cl EDGW HA8 36 D6
Symphony Ms NKENS W10 88 C2
Syon Gate Wy BTFD TW8 104 B6
Syon La ISLW TW7 104 B6
Syon Pk ISLW TW7 * 124 C2
Syon Park Gdns ISLW TW7 104 A6

T

Tabard Garden Est
STHWK SE1 19 G1
Tabard St STHWK SE1 19 G2
Tabernacle Av PLSTW E13 94 E3
Tabernacle St SDTCH EC2A 13 H1
Tableer Av CLAP SW4 129 H4
Tabley Rd HOLWY N7 72 E3
Tabor Gdns CHEAM SM3 174 C5
Tabor Gv WIM/MER SW19 146 C6
Tabor Rd HMSMTH W6 106 E2
Tachbrook Rd
EBED/NFELT TW14 121 J6
NWDGN UB2 102 C3
Tachbrook St PIM SW1V 16 F6
Tack Ms BROCKY SE4 132 D2
Tadema Rd WBPTN SW10 108 B6
Tadmor St SHB W12 88 B7
Tadworth Av NWMAL KT3 160 C3
Tadworth Pde HCH RM12 81 K3
Tadworth Rd CRICK NW2 69 J1
Taeping St POP/IOD E14 112 E3
Taffy's How MTCM CR4 162 D2
Tait Ct BOW E3 75 H7
Tait Rd CROY/NA CR0 165 F6
Tait St WCHPL E1 92 D5
Takeley Cl CRW RM5 63 F1
Talacre Rd KTTN NW5 72 A5
Talbot Av EFNCH N2 53 H2
OXHEY WD19 21 J6
Talbot Cl SEVS/STOTM N15 56 B3
Talbot Ct BANK EC3V 13 H6
Talbot Crs HDN NW4 51 J4
Talbot Gdns GDMY/SEVK IG3 79 G1
Talbot Pl BKHTH/KID SE3 133 H1
Talbot Rd ALP/SUD HA0 67 K4
BAY/PAD W2 8 B4
CAR SM5 176 A4
DAGW RM9 80 B6
EDUL SE22 131 F3
EHAM E6 95 K1
FSTGT E7 76 E3
HGT N6 54 A5
ISLW TW7 124 B3
KTN/HRWW/WS HA3 49 F1
NTGHL W11 88 D5
NWDGN UB2 102 D3
SEVS/STOTM N15 56 B3
THHTH CR7 164 E3
WDGN N22 54 C1
WEA W13 * 85 G6
WHTN TW2 123 K7
Talbot Sq BAY/PAD W2 9 G5
Talbot Wk NTGHL W11 88 C5
WLSDN NW10 * 69 G5
Talbot Yd STHWK SE1 13 G9
Talcott Pth
BRXS/STRHM SW2 * 130 B7
Talehangers Cl BXLYHS DA6 136 E3
Talfourd Pl PECK SE15 111 G7
Talfourd Rd PECK SE15 111 G7
Talgarth Rd WKENS W14 107 H4
Talgarth Wk CDALE/KGS NW9 51 G4
Talisman Cl GDMY/SEVK IG3 61 H7
Talisman Sq SYD SE26 150 C3
Talisman Wy WBLY HA9 68 B2
Tallack Cl KTN/HRWW/WS HA3 34 E6
Tallack Rd LEY E10 57 H7
Tall Elms Cl HAYES BR2 167 J4
Tallis Cl CAN/RD E16 95 F5
Tallis Gv CHARL SE7 114 A5
Tallis St EMB EC4Y 12 B6
Tallis Vw WLSDN NW10 69 F5
Tallow Cl DAGW RM9 79 K5
Tallow Rd BTFD TW8 104 D5
Tall Trees STRHM/NOR SW16 164 A2
Talma Gdns WHTN TW2 123 K6
Talmage Cl FSTH SE23 131 K6
Talman Gv STAN HA7 35 K5
Talma Rd BRXS/STRHM SW2 130 B3
Talwin St BOW E3 93 K2
Tamar Cl BOW E3 * 75 H7
Tamarind Yd WAP E1W 92 C7
Tamarisk Sq SHB W12 87 H6
Tamar St CHARL SE7 114 D3
Tamesis Gdns WPK KT4 173 G1
Tamian Wy HSLWW TW4 122 B3
Tamworth Av WFD IG8 44 C5
Tamworth La MTCM CR4 163 G2
Tamworth Pk MTCM CR4 163 G3
Tamworth Pl CROY/NA CR0 * 177 J1
Tamworth Rd CROY/NA CR0 177 J1
Tamworth St FUL/PGN SW6 14 A9
Tancred Rd FSBYPK N4 55 H5
Tandridge Dr ORP BR6 169 J7
Tanfield Av CRICK NW2 69 H3
Tanfield Rd CROY/NA CR0 177 J3
Tangier Rd RCHPK/HAM TW10 125 H3
Tangleberry Cl BMLY BR1 168 E3
Tangle Tree Cl FNCH N3 53 F1
Tanglewood Cl CROY/NA CR0 178 E2
STAN HA7 34 E1
Tanglewood Wy FELT TW13 141 F2
Tangley Gv PUT/ROE SW15 126 C6
Tangley Park Rd HPTN TW12 * 141 K4
Tangmere Crs HCH RM12 81 K5
Tangmere Gdns NTHLT UB5 83 G1
Tangmere Gv KUTN/CMB KT2 143 K4
Tangmere Wy
CDALE/KGS NW9 51 G1
Tanhouse Fld KTTN NW5 * 72 D4
Tankerton Houses
STPAN WC1H * 5 K8
Tankerton Rd SURB KT6 172 B1
Tankerton St STPAN WC1H 5 K8
Tankerton Ter CROY/NA CR0 * 164 A6
Tankerville Rd
STRHM/NOR SW16 148 D6
Tankridge Rd CRICK NW2 69 K1
The Tanneries WCHPL E1 * 92 E3
Tanners Cl WOT/HER KT12 156 A5
Tanners End La UED N18 42 A3
Tanner's Hl DEPT SE8 112 D7
Tanners La BARK/HLT IG6 60 C2
Tanners Ms DEPT SE8 112 C7
Tanner St BARK IG11 78 C5
STHWK SE1 19 K2
Tannery Cl CROY/NA CR0 166 A4
DAGE RM10 80 D2
Tannington Ter HBRY N5 73 G2
Tannsfeld Rd SYD SE26 151 F4
Tansley Cl HOLWY N7 72 D4
Tanswell St STHWK SE1 * 18 A2
Tansy Cl EHAM E6 96 A5
Tantallon Rd BAL SW12 129 F7
Tant Av CAN/RD E16 94 D5
Tantony Gv CHDH RM6 61 K2
Tanworth Cl NTHWD HA6 32 A5
Tanworth Gdns PIN HA5 47 F1
Tan Yard La BXLY DA5 * 137 H6
Tanza Rd HAMP NW3 71 K3
Tapestry Cl BELMT SM2 175 F6
Taplow Ct MTCM CR4 162 D3
Taplow Rd PLMGR N13 41 J3
Taplow St IS N1 6 F6
Tappesfield Rd PECK SE15 131 K2
Tapping Cl KUTN/CMB KT2 * 144 C6
Tapp St WCHPL E1 92 D3
Tapster St BAR EN5 26 D2
Tara Ms CEND/HSY/T N8 54 E5
Taransay Wk IS N1 73 K5
Tara Ter BROCKY SE4 * 132 B2
Tarbert Rd EDUL SE22 131 F4
Tarbert Wk WCHPL E1 92 E6
Target Cl EBED/NFELT TW14 121 H5
Tariff Rd UED N18 42 C5
Tarleton Gdns FSTH SE23 131 J7
Tarling Cl SCUP DA14 155 H2
Tarling Rd CAN/RD E16 94 D5
EFNCH N2 39 G7
Tarling St WCHPL E1 92 D5
Tarnbank ENC/FH EN2 28 E4
Tarn St STHWK SE1 18 E4
Tarnwood Pk ELTH/MOT SE9 134 E7
Tarragon Cl NWCR SE14 112 B6
Tarragon Gv SYD SE26 151 F5
Tarrant Pl MBLAR W1H 9 L3
Tarriff Crs DEPT SE8 112 C3
Tarrington Cl
STRHM/NOR SW16 148 D3
Tarver Rd WALW SE17 18 D8
Tarves Wy GNWCH SE10 112 E6
Tash Pl FBAR/BDGN N11 * 40 B4
Tasker Cl HYS/HAR UB3 101 F6
Tasker Rd HAMP NW3 71 K4
Tasmania Ter UED N18 41 J5
Tasman Rd BRXN/ST SW9 129 K2
Tasso Rd HMSMTH W6 107 H5
Tate Gdns BUSH WD23 22 E6
Tate Rd CAN/RD E16 95 K7
SUT SM1 174 E4
Tatham Pl STJWD NW8 3 H5
Tatnell Rd FSTH SE23 132 B5
Tattersall Cl ELTH/MOT SE9 134 D4
Tatton Cl CAR SM5 163 F7
Tatton Crs CLPT E5 56 B6
Tatum Rd WLSDN NW10 68 E6
Tatum St WALW SE17 19 H6
Tauber Cl BORE WD6 24 B3
Tauheed Cl FSBYPK N4 73 J1
Taunton Av HSLW TW3 123 H1
RYNPK SW20 160 E1
Taunton Cl BXLYHN DA7 138 A2
CHEAM SM3 161 K7
Taunton Dr EFNCH N2 53 G1
ENC/FH EN2 29 G2
Taunton Ms CAMTN NW1 9 L1
Taunton Pl CAMTN NW1 3 L9
Taunton Rd GFD/PVL UB6 66 B6
LEE/GVPK SE12 133 H4
Taunton Wy STAN HA7 50 A1
Tavern Cl CAR SM5 162 D6
Taverners Cl NTGHL W11 88 C7
Taverner Sq HBRY N5 * 73 J3
Tavistock Av GFD/PVL UB6 85 G1
MLHL NW7 38 B6
WALTH E17 57 F2
Tavistock Cl
STNW/STAM N16 * 74 A4
Tavistock Ct COVGDN WC2E * 11 K6
Tavistock Crs MTCM CR4 163 K3
NTGHL W11 88 D4
Tavistock Gdns
GDMY/SEVK IG3 78 E3
Tavistock Gv CROY/NA CR0 164 E6
Tavistock Ms NTGHL W11 * 88 D5
Tavistock Pl
STHGT/OAK N14 * 28 B5
STPAN WC1H 5 H9
Tavistock Rd CAR SM5 162 C7
CROY/NA CR0 164 E7
EDGW HA8 36 B7
FSBYPK N4 55 K5
HAYES BR2 167 J3
HGDN/ICK UB10 64 B4
NTGHL W11 88 D4
SRTFD E15 76 D5
SWFD E18 58 E2
WELL DA16 116 D7
WLSDN NW10 87 H1
Tavistock Sq STPAN WC1H 5 H9
Tavistock St COVGDN WC2E 11 K6
Tavistock Ter ARCH N19 72 D2
Taviton St STPAN WC1H 5 G9
Tavy Cl LBTH SE11 18 B7
Tawney Rd THMD SE28 97 H6
Tawny Cl FELT TW13 140 E2
WEA W13 85 H7
Tawny Wy BERM/RHTH SE16 112 A3
Tayben Av WHTN TW2 123 K5
Taybridge Rd BTSEA SW11 129 F2
Tayburn Cl POP/IOD E14 94 A5
Tayfield Cl HGDN/ICK UB10 64 A2
Taylor Av RCH/KEW TW9 125 J1
Taylor Cl DEPT SE8 112 C5
HPTN TW12 142 C4
HSLW TW3 103 H7
TOTM N17 42 C6
Taylor Rd MTCM CR4 147 J6
WLGTN SM6 176 B4
Taylor's Blds
WOOL/PLUM SE18 115 G3
Taylors Cl SCUP DA14 155 F3
Taylors Ct FELT TW13 140 E1
Taylor's Gn ACT W3 * 87 G5
Taylor's La SYD SE26 150 D3
WLSDN NW10 69 G6
Taylors Md MLHL NW7 * 37 J4
Taymount Ri FSTH SE23 150 E1
Tayport Cl IS N1 5 L2
Tayside Dr EDGW HA8 36 D2
Taywood Rd NTHLT UB5 83 J3
Teak Cl BERM/RHTH SE16 93 G7
Teal Cl CAN/RD E16 95 H4
Teal Dr NTHWD HA6 32 A6
Teale St BETH E2 92 C1
Tealing Dr HOR/WEW KT19 173 F3
Teal Pl SUT SM1 174 D4
Teasel Cl CROY/NA CR0 166 A7
Teasel Crs THMD SE28 96 E7
Teasel Wy SRTFD E15 94 C2
Tebworth Rd TOTM N17 42 B6
Technology Pk
CDALE/KGS NW9 * 51 F2
Teck Cl ISLW TW7 124 B1
Tedder Cl CHSGTN KT9 171 J4
RSLP HA4 64 E4
Tedder Rd SAND/SEL CR2 179 F6
Teddington Pk TEDD TW11 143 F4
Teddington Park Rd
TEDD TW11 143 F3
Tedworth Gdns CHEL SW3 15 L8
Tedworth Sq CHEL SW3 15 L8
Tees Av GFD/PVL UB6 84 E1
Teesdale Av ISLW TW7 104 B7
Teesdale Cl BETH E2 92 C1
Teesdale Gdns ISLW TW7 104 B7
SNWD SE25 165 F1
Teesdale Rd WAN E11 58 D5
Teesdale St BETH E2 92 D1
Teesdale Yd BETH E2 * 92 D1
The Tee ACT W3 87 G5
Teevan Cl CROY/NA CR0 165 H6
Teevan Rd CROY/NA CR0 165 H6
Teign Ms ELTH/MOT SE9 153 J1
Teignmouth Cl CLAP SW4 129 J3
EDGW HA8 50 B1

Teignmouth Gdns
GFD/PVL UB6 85 G1
Teignmouth Rd CRICK NW2 70 B4
WELL DA16 136 D1
Telcote Wy RSLP HA4 * 47 G6
Telegraph Hl HAMP NW3 71 F2
Telegraph La ESH/CLAY KT10 171 F3
Telegraph Ms GDMY/SEVK IG3 61 F7
Telegraph Pas
BRXS/STRHM SW2 129 K6
Telegraph Pl POP/IOD E14 112 E3
Telegraph Rd PUT/ROE SW15 126 E6
Telegraph St LOTH EC2R 13 G4
Telephone Pl WKENS W14 * 107 J5
Telferscot Rd BAL SW12 129 J7
Telford Av BRXS/STRHM SW2 129 J7
Telford Cl NRWD SE19 150 B5
WALTH E17 57 G6
Telford Dr WOT/HER KT12 156 B6
Telford Rd CDALE/KGS NW9 51 H5
ELTH/MOT SE9 154 D1
NKENS W10 88 C4
STHL UB1 84 B6
WHTN TW2 123 F6
Telford Road North Circular Rd
FBAR/BDGN N11 40 C4
Telfords Yd WAP E1W * 92 C6
Telford Ter PIM SW1V 16 E9
Telford Wy ACT W3 87 G4
YEAD UB4 83 J4
Telham Rd EHAM E6 96 A1
Tell Gv EDUL SE22 131 G3
Tellisford ESH/CLAY KT10 170 B3
Tellson Av WOOL/PLUM SE18 114 D7
Temeraire Pl BTFD TW8 105 G4
Temeraire St
BERM/RHTH SE16 111 K1
Tempelhof Av HDN NW4 52 A6
Temperley Rd BAL SW12 129 F6
Tempest Wy RAIN RM13 81 J5
Templar Dr THMD SE28 97 K5
Templar Pl HPTN TW12 142 A6
Templars Av GLDGN NW11 52 D5
Templars Ct DART DA1 * 139 K4
Templars Crs FNCH N3 52 E1
Templars Dr
KTN/HRWW/WS HA3 * 34 D5
Templar St CMBW SE5 130 C1
Temple Av BCTR RM8 62 C7
CROY/NA CR0 179 H2
EMB EC4Y 12 B6
TRDG/WHET N20 27 H6
Temple Cl FNCH N3 52 D1
THMD SE28 115 H2
WAN E11 58 C6
WAT WD17 20 D1
Templecombe Rd HOM E9 74 E7
Templecombe Wy MRDN SM4 161 H4
Temple Dwellings BETH E2 * 92 D1
Temple Fortune Hl
GLDGN NW11 52 E4
Temple Fortune La
GLDGN NW11 52 D5
Temple Gdns BCTR RM8 79 K2
EMB EC4Y * 12 A6
GLDGN NW11 52 D5
WCHMH N21 * 41 H1
Temple Gv ENC/FH EN2 29 H2
GLDGN NW11 52 E5
Temple La EMB EC4Y 12 B5
Templeman Rd HNWL W7 85 F4
Templemead Cl ACT W3 87 G5
Temple Mead Cl STAN HA7 35 H5
Temple Mills La LEY E10 75 K3
Temple Pde BAR EN5 * 27 H6
Temple Pl TPL/STR WC2R 11 M6
Temple Rd CEND/HSY/T N8 55 F3
CHSWK W4 105 K2
CRICK NW2 70 A3
CROY/NA CR0 177 K3
EA W5 104 E2
EHAM E6 77 J7
HSLW TW3 123 G3
RCH/KEW TW9 125 G1
Temple Sheen Rd
MORT/ESHN SW14 125 K3
Temple St BETH E2 92 D1
Temple Ter WDGN N22 * 55 G1
Templeton Av CHING E4 43 J3
Templeton Cl NRWD SE19 149 K7
STNW/STAM N16 * 74 A4
Templeton Pl ECT SW5 14 B6
Templeton Rd FSBYPK N4 55 K5
Temple Wy SUT SM1 175 H2
Templewood WEA W13 85 H4
Templewood Av HAMP NW3 71 F2
Templewood Gdns
HAMP NW3 71 F2
Temple Yd BETH E2 92 C2
Tempsford Av BORE WD6 25 F3
Tempsford Cl ENC/FH EN2 29 J2
Temsford Cl RYLN/HDSTN HA2 48 C1
Tenbury Cl FSTGT E7 77 H4
Tenbury Ct BAL SW12 129 J7
Tenby Av KTN/HRWW/WS HA3 49 H1
Tenby Cl CHDH RM6 62 A5
SEVS/STOTM N15 56 B3
Tenby Gdns NTHLT UB5 66 A5
Tenby Rd CHDH RM6 62 A5
EDGW HA8 36 B7
PEND EN3 30 E2
WALTH E17 57 G4
WELL DA16 116 E7
Tench St WAP E1W * 92 D7
Tenda Rd STHWK SE1 111 J3
Tendring Wy CHDH RM6 61 J4
Tenham Av BRXS/STRHM SW2 148 D1
Tenison Wy STHWK SE1 12 A9
Tenniel Cl BAY/PAD W2 8 E5
Tennison Av BORE WD6 24 D4
Tennison Rd SNWD SE25 165 G3
Tennis St STHWK SE1 19 G1
Tennyson Av CDALE/KGS NW9 50 E2
MNPK E12 77 J6
NWMAL KT3 160 E4
TWK TW1 124 A7
WAN E11 58 E6
Tennyson Cl
EBED/NFELT TW14 121 K5
PEND EN3 31 F4
WELL DA16 115 K7
Tennyson Rd HNWL W7 85 F6
HSLW TW3 123 H1
KIL/WHAMP NW6 70 D7
MLHL NW7 37 H4
PGE/AN SE20 151 F6
SRTFD E15 76 C6
WALTH E17 57 H5
WIM/MER SW19 147 G5
Tennyson St VX/NE SW8 129 G1
Tennyson Wy HCH RM12 63 H7
Tensing Rd NWDGN UB2 103 F2
Tentelow La NWDGN UB2 103 G2
Tenterden Cl ELTH/MOT SE9 153 K3
HDN NW4 52 B2
Tenterden Dr HDN NW4 52 B2
Tenterden Gdns
CROY/NA CR0 165 H6
HDN NW4 52 B2
Tenterden Gv HDN NW4 52 A3
Tenterden Rd BCTR RM8 80 B1
CROY/NA CR0 165 H6
TOTM N17 42 B6
Tenterden St CONDST W1S 10 D5
Tenter Gnd WCHPL E1 13 L3
Tent Peg La STMC/STPC BR5 169 H4
Tent St WCHPL E1 92 D3
Teredo St LEW SE13 132 E1
Terling Cl WAN E11 76 D2
Terling Rd BCTR RM8 80 C1
Terling Wk IS N1 * 6 E3
Terminus Pl BGVA SW1W 16 D4
Terrace Gdns BARN SW13 126 C1
WAT WD17 21 F1
Terrace Rd HOM E9 75 F6
PLSTW E13 76 E7
WOT/HER KT12 156 A5
The Terrace BARN SW13 126 B1
BETH E2 * 92 E2
CHING E4 * 44 C2
DEPT SE8 * 112 C3
EFNCH N2 * 54 A3
FNCH N3 * 52 D1
FSTH SE23 * 132 B6
KIL/WHAMP NW6 2 A3
Terrace Vls HMSMTH W6 * 106 D4
Terrace Wk DAGW RM9 80 A4
Terrac St RCH/KEW TW9 125 G3
Terrapin Rd TOOT SW17 148 B2
Terretts Pl IS N1 6 C2
Terrick Rd WDGN N22 40 E7
Terrick St SHB W12 87 K5
Terrilands PIN HA5 47 K2
Terront Rd SEVS/STOTM N15 55 J4
Tessa Sanderson Wy
GFD/PVL UB6 66 D4
Testerton Rd NTGHL W11 * 88 B6
Testerton Wk NTGHL W11 * 88 B6
Tetbury Pl IS N1 6 C4
Tetcott Rd WBPTN SW10 108 B6
Tetherdown MUSWH N10 54 A2
Tetty Wy BMLY BR1 167 K1
Teversham La VX/NE SW8 109 K7
Teviot Cl WELL DA16 116 C7
Teviot St POP/IOD E14 94 A4
Tewkesbury Av FSTH SE23 131 J7
PIN HA5 47 J4
Tewkesbury Gdns
CDALE/KGS NW9 50 D2
Tewkesbury Rd CAR SM5 162 C7
SEVS/STOTM N15 55 K6
WEA W13 85 G7
Tewkesbury Ter
FBAR/BDGN N11 40 C5
Tewson Rd WOOL/PLUM SE18 115 K4
Teynham Av EN EN1 29 K5
Teynton Ter TOTM N17 41 J7
Thackeray Av TOTM N17 56 C1
Thackeray Cl ISLW TW7 124 B1
WIM/MER SW19 146 B6
Thackeray Dr CHDH RM6 61 H6
Thackeray Ms HACK E8 74 C5
Thackeray Rd EHAM E6 95 H1
VX/NE SW8 129 G1
Thackeray St KENS W8 14 D3
Thakeham Cl SYD SE26 150 D4
Thalia Cl GNWCH SE10 113 G5
Tham Cl HNHL SE24 130 C2
Thame Rd BERM/RHTH SE16 112 A1
Thames Av DAGW RM9 98 D3
GFD/PVL UB6 85 F1
WBPTN SW10 108 B7
WPK KT4 161 F7
Thames Bank
MORT/ESHN SW14 125 K1
Thamesbank Pl THMD SE28 97 J5
Thames Cir POP/IOD E14 112 D3
Thames Cl HPTN TW12 157 G1
RAIN RM13 99 K5
Thames Crs CHSWK W4 106 B6
Thames Down Link
BRYLDS KT5 159 K4
HOR/WEW KT19 172 C6
Thames Dr RSLP HA4 46 A5
Thames Eyot TWK TW1 * 143 G1
Thamesgate Cl
RCHPK/HAM TW10 143 H3
Thameside TEDD TW11 143 K6
Thames Meadow
E/WMO/HCT KT8 157 F2
Thamesmere Dr THMD SE28 97 G6
Thames Pth CHARL SE7 114 B2
ISLW TW7 124 C1
PIM SW1V 17 H8
POP/IOD E14 112 D2
STHWK SE1 17 K7
SUN TW16 156 D1
THDIT KT7 158 C5
TPL/STR WC2R 12 A6
TWRH EC3N 13 K8
VX/NE SW8 109 J5
WAND/EARL SW18 127 J3
WEST SW1P 17 K4
Thames Pl PUT/ROE SW15 127 G2
Thamespoint TEDD TW11 * 143 K6
Thames Quay WBPTN SW10 * 108 B7
Thames Reach KUT/HW KT1 * 143 K7
Thames Rd BARK IG11 97 G2
CAN/RD E16 95 H7
CHSWK W4 105 H5
DART DA1 138 D2
Thames Side KUT/HW KT1 143 K7
THDIT KT7 158 C5
Thames St GNWCH SE10 112 E5
KUT/HW KT1 158 E1
SUN TW16 156 A2
Thamesvale Cl HSLW TW3 123 F1
Thames Village CHSWK W4 105 K7
Thamley PUR RM19 119 K3
Thanescroft Gdns
CROY/NA CR0 178 A2
Thanet Dr HAYES BR2 181 H2
Thanet Pl CROY/NA CR0 177 J3
Thanet Rd BXLY DA5 137 H6
Thanet St STPAN WC1H 5 J8
Thane Vls HOLWY N7 73 F2
Thant Cl LEY E10 75 K2
Tharp Rd WLGTN SM6 176 D4
Thatcham Gdns
TRDG/WHET N20 27 G6
Thatcher Cl WDR/YW UB7 100 B1
Thatchers Wy ISLW TW7 123 J4
Thatches Gv CHDH RM6 62 A2
Thavies Inn FLST/FETLN EC4A 12 B4
Thaxted Pl RYNPK SW20 146 B6
Thaxted Rd ELTH/MOT SE9 154 C1
Thaxton Rd WKENS W14 107 J5
Thayers Farm Rd BECK BR3 151 G7
Thayer St MHST W1U 10 B4
Theatre Sq SRTFD E15 76 B5
Theatre St BTSEA SW11 128 E2
Theberton St IS N1 6 B3
The Beverly MRDN SM4 161 G5
The Courtyard HAYES BR2 181 J5
Theed St STHWK SE1 12 A9
The Green WIM/MER SW19 146 B4
Thelma Gv TEDD TW11 143 G5
Theobald Crs
KTN/HRWW/WS HA3 34 B7
Theobald Rd CROY/NA CR0 177 H1
WALTH E17 57 H6
Theobald's Rd GINN WC1R 11 L2
Theobald St BORE WD6 24 B2
STHWK SE1 19 G4
Theodora Wy PIN HA5 46 D2
Theodore Rd LEW SE13 133 G5
Therapia La CROY/NA CR0 163 J6
Therapia Rd EDUL SE22 131 K5
Theresa Rd HMSMTH W6 106 D3
Theresa's Wk SAND/SEL CR2 177 K7
Thermopylae Ga
POP/IOD E14 112 E3
Theseus Wk IS N1 6 D6
Thesiger Rd PGE/AN SE20 151 F6
Thessaly Rd VX/NE SW8 109 J7
Thetford Cl PLMGR N13 41 H5
Thetford Rd DAGW RM9 79 K6
NWMAL KT3 160 A5
Theydon Gdns RAIN RM13 81 G6
Theydon Gv WFD IG8 45 G5
Theydon Rd CLPT E5 74 E1
Theydon St WALTH E17 57 H6
Thicket Crs SUT SM1 175 G3
Thicket Gv DAGW RM9 79 J5
PGE/AN SE20 150 C6
Thicket Rd PGE/AN SE20 150 D6
SUT SM1 175 G3
Thicket Ter PGE/AN SE20 * 150 C6
Third Av ACT W3 87 H7
CHDH RM6 61 J5
DAGE RM10 80 D7
EN EN1 30 B4
HYS/HAR UB3 82 D7
MNPK E12 77 J3
NKENS W10 88 C2
PLSTW E13 94 E2
WALTH E17 57 J4
WBLY HA9 67 K1
Third Cl E/WMO/HCT KT8 157 G3
Third Cross Rd WHTN TW2 142 D1
Thirleby Rd EDGW HA8 37 F7
WEST SW1P 16 F4
Thirlmere Av GFD/PVL UB6 85 J2
Thirlmere Gdns WBLY HA9 49 J7
Thirlmere Ri BMLY BR1 152 D5
Thirlmere Rd BXLYHN DA7 137 K1
MUSWH N10 40 B7
STRHM/NOR SW16 148 D3
Thirsk Cl NTHLT UB5 66 A5
Thirsk Rd BTSEA SW11 129 F2
MTCM CR4 148 A6
SNWD SE25 164 E3
Thisilefield Cl BXLY DA5 136 E7
Thistlecroft Gdns STAN HA7 35 K7
Thistledene THDIT KT7 157 K5
Thistledene Av
RYLN/HDSTN HA2 65 J2
Thistle Gv WBPTN SW10 14 F8
Thistlemead CHST BR7 169 G1
Thistlewaite Rd CLPT E5 74 D2
Thistlewood Cl HOLWY N7 73 F1
Thistleworth Cl ISLW TW7 103 J6
Thistley Cl
NFNCH/WDSPK N12 39 J5
Thomas A Beckett Cl
HRW HA1 67 F3
Thomas Baines Rd
BTSEA SW11 128 C2
Thomas Cribb Ms EHAM E6 95 K5
Thomas Dean Rd SYD SE26 * 151 H3
Thomas Dinwiddy Rd
LEE/GVPK SE12 153 F1
Thomas Doyle St STHWK SE1 18 C3
Thomas' La CAT SE6 132 E6
Thomas Moore Wy EFNCH N2 53 G2
Thomas More St WAP E1W * 92 C6
Thomas North Ter
CAN/RD E16 * 94 D4
Thomas Pl KENS W8 14 C4
Thomas Rd POP/IOD E14 93 H5
Thomas St WOOL/PLUM SE18 115 F3
Thomas Wall Cl SUT SM1 175 F4
Thompson Av CMBW SE5 110 D6
RCH/KEW TW9 125 J2
Thompson Cl CHEAM SM3 161 K7
IL IG1 78 C1
Thompson Rd DAGW RM9 80 B2
EDUL SE22 131 G5
HSLW TW3 123 G3
Thompson's Av CMBW SE5 * 110 D6
Thomson Crs CROY/NA CR0 164 B7
Thomson Rd
KTN/HRWW/WS HA3 48 E2
Thorburn Sq STHWK SE1 111 H3
Thorburn Wy
WIM/MER SW19 * 147 H7
Thoresby St IS N1 6 F7
Thorkhill Gdns THDIT KT7 158 B7
Thorkhill Rd THDIT KT7 158 C7
Thornaby Gdns UED N18 42 C5
Thorn Av BUSH WD23 22 C7
Thornbury Av ISLW TW7 103 J6
Thornbury Cl
STNW/STAM N16 74 A4
Thornbury Gdns BORE WD6 24 E3
Thornbury Rd CLAP SW4 129 K5
ISLW TW7 123 J1
Thornbury Sq HGT N6 54 C7
Thornby Rd CLPT E5 74 E2
Thorncliffe Rd CLAP SW4 129 J5
NWDGN UB2 102 E4
Thorn Cl HAYES BR2 169 F5
NTHLT UB5 83 K2
Thorncombe Rd EDUL SE22 131 F4
Thorn Ct BELMT SM2 * 175 F6
Thorncroft EMPK RM11 63 K5
Thorncroft Rd SUT SM1 175 F3
Thorncroft St VX/NE SW8 109 K6
Thorndean St
WAND/EARL SW18 147 G1
Thorndene Av
TRDG/WHET N20 28 A7
Thorndike Av NTHLT UB5 65 H7
Thorndike Cl WBPTN SW10 108 B6
Thorndike Rd IS N1 73 K5
Thorndike St PIM SW1V * 17 G6
Thorndon Gdns
HOR/WEW KT19 173 G3
Thorndyke Ct PIN HA5 33 K6
Thorne Cl ASHF TW15 140 A6
CAN/RD E16 94 E5
ERITH DA8 117 J5
ESH/CLAY KT10 171 G6
WAN E11 76 C3
Thorneloe Gdns
CROY/NA CR0 177 H4
Thorne Rd VX/NE SW8 109 K6
Thorne's Cl BECK BR3 167 F2
Thorne St BARN SW13 126 B2
Thornet Wood Rd BMLY BR1 169 F2
Thorney Crs BTSEA SW11 * 108 C6
Thorneycroft Cl
WOT/HER KT12 156 B5
Thorney Hedge Rd
CHSWK W4 105 J3
Thorney St WEST SW1P 17 J5
Thornfield Av MLHL NW7 38 C7
Thornfield Pde MLHL NW7 * 38 C6
Thornfield Rd SHB W12 106 E1
Thornford Rd LEW SE13 133 F4
Thorngate Rd MV/WKIL W9 2 B9
Thorngrove Rd PLSTW E13 77 F7
Thornham Gv SRTFD E15 76 B4
Thornham St GNWCH SE10 112 E5
Thornhaugh St STPAN WC1H 11 H1
Thornhill Av SURB KT6 172 A1
WOOL/PLUM SE18 115 K6
Thornhill Bridge Whf IS N1 5 L4
Thornhill Crs IS N1 5 M2
Thornhill Gdns BARK IG11 78 E6
LEY E10 75 K1
Thornhill Gv IS N1 6 A2
Thornhill Rd CROY/NA CR0 164 D6
IS N1 6 A1
LEY E10 75 K1
NTHWD HA6 32 A3
SURB KT6 172 A1
Thornhill Sq IS N1 5 M2
Thornlaw Rd WNWD SE27 149 G3
Thornley Cl TOTM N17 42 C6
Thornley Dr RYLN/HDSTN HA2 66 B1
Thornsbeach Rd CAT SE6 133 F7
Thornsett Pl PGE/AN SE20 165 J1
Thornsett Rd PGE/AN SE20 165 J1
WAND/EARL SW18 147 F1
Thornsett Ter PGE/AN SE20 * 165 J1
Thornton Av
BRXS/STRHM SW2 129 J7
CHSWK W4 106 B3
CROY/NA CR0 164 A5
WDR/YW UB7 100 C2
Thornton Cl WDR/YW UB7 100 C2
Thornton Dene BECK BR3 166 D1
Thornton Gdns BAL SW12 129 J7
Thornton Gv PIN HA5 34 A5
Thornton Hl WIM/MER SW19 146 C6
Thornton Pl MBLAR W1H 9 L2
Thornton Rd BAL SW12 129 J6
BAR EN5 26 C2
BELV DA17 * 117 J3
BMLY BR1 152 E4
CAR SM5 162 C7
IL IG1 78 B3
MORT/ESHN SW14 126 A2
THHTH CR7 164 B4
UED N18 42 E2
WAN E11 76 B1
WIM/MER SW19 146 B5
Thornton Rw THHTH CR7 164 B4
Thorntons Farm Av
ROMW/RG RM7 80 E1
Thornton St BRXN/ST SW9 130 B1
Thornton Wy GLDGN NW11 53 F4
Thorntree Rd CHARL SE7 114 C4
Thornville Gv MTCM CR4 162 B1
Thornville St DEPT SE8 112 D7
Thornwood Cl SWFD E18 59 F1
Thornwood Rd LEW SE13 133 H4
Thorogood Gdns SRTFD E15 76 C4
Thorogood Wy RAIN RM13 81 G7
Thorold Rd IL IG1 78 B1
WDGN N22 40 E6
Thorparch Rd VX/NE SW8 109 J7
Thorpebank Rd SHB W12 87 J7
Thorpe Cl NKENS W10 88 C5
SYD SE26 * 151 F3
Thorpe Ct TOOT SW17 147 J3
Thorpe Crs OXHEY WD19 21 F6
WALTH E17 57 H1
Thorpedale Gdns
GNTH/NBYPK IG2 60 A3
Thorpedale Rd FSBYPK N4 55 F7
Thorpe Hall Rd WALTH E17 44 A7
Thorpe Rd BARK IG11 78 D6
EHAM E6 77 K7
FSTGT E7 76 E2
KUTN/CMB KT2 144 A6
SEVS/STOTM N15 56 A5
WALTH E17 58 A1
Thorpewood Av SYD SE26 150 D1
Thorpland Av HGDN/ICK UB10 64 A2
Thorsden Wy NRWD SE19 * 150 A4
Thorverton Rd CRICK NW2 70 C2
Thoydon Rd BOW E3 93 G1
Thrale Rd STRHM/NOR SW16 148 C4
Thrale St STHWK SE1 12 F9
Thrasher Cl HACK E8 * 7 L3
Thrawl St WCHPL E1 13 M3
Threadneedle St LOTH EC2R 13 H5
Three Colts La BETH E2 92 D3
Three Colt St POP/IOD E14 * 93 H6
Three Kings Yd
MYFR/PKLN W1K 10 C6
Three Meadows Ms
KTN/HRWW/WS HA3 35 F7
Three Mill La BOW E3 94 A2
Three Oak La STHWK SE1 19 L1
Three Valleys Wy
BUSH WD23 21 H4
Threshers Pl NTGHL W11 88 C6
Thriffwood SYD SE26 150 E2
Thrift Farm La BORE WD6 24 E1
Thrigby Rd CHSGTN KT9 172 B5
Throckmorten Rd
CAN/RD E16 95 F5
Throgmorton Av OBST EC2N 13 H4
Throgmorton St OBST EC2N 13 H4
Throwley Rd SUT SM1 175 F4
Throwley Wy SUT SM1 175 F3
Thrupp Cl MTCM CR4 163 G1
Thrush Gn RYLN/HDSTN HA2 48 A3
Thrush St WALW SE17 18 E7
Thunderer Rd DAGW RM9 98 A3
Thurbarn Rd CAT SE6 151 K4
Thurland Rd
BERM/RHTH SE16 111 H2
Thurlby Cl WFD IG8 45 K4
Thurlby Rd ALP/SUD HA0 67 K5
WNWD SE27 149 G3
Thurleigh Av BAL SW12 129 F5
Thurleigh Rd BAL SW12 128 E5
Thurleston Av MRDN SM4 161 H4
Thurlestone Av
GDMY/SEVK IG3 79 F3
NFNCH/WDSPK N12 39 K5
Thurlestone Rd WNWD SE27 149 G2
Thurloe Cl SKENS SW7 15 J5
Thurloe Gdns ROM RM1 63 G5
Thurloe Pl SKENS SW7 15 H5
Thurloe Place Ms
SKENS SW7 * 15 H5
Thurloe Sq SKENS SW7 15 H5
Thurloe St SKENS SW7 15 H5
Thurlow Cl CHING E4 43 K5
Thurlow Gdns ALP/SUD HA0 * 67 K4
Thurlow Hl DUL SE21 130 D7
Thurlow Park Rd DUL SE21 149 H1
Thurlow Rd HAMP NW3 71 H4
HNWL W7 104 B1
Thurlow St WALW SE17 19 J8
Thurlow Ter KTTN NW5 71 K4
Thurlow Wk WALW SE17 19 J7
Thurlston Rd RSLP HA4 64 E2
Thursley Crs CROY/NA CR0 180 B6
Thursley Gdns
WIM/MER SW19 146 B1
Thursley Rd ELTH/MOT SE9 153 K2
Thurso St TOOT SW17 147 H3
Thurstan Rd RYNPK SW20 145 K6
Thurston Rd DEPT SE8 132 E1
STHL UB1 83 K5
Thurtle Rd BETH E2 7 M4
Thwaite Cl ERITH DA8 117 K5
Thyra Gv NFNCH/WDSPK N12 39 F5
Tibbatt's Rd BOW E3 93 K3
Tibbenham Pl CAT SE6 151 J1
Tibberton Sq IS N1 6 E2
Tibbets Cl WIM/MER SW19 127 G7
Tibbet's Ride PUT/ROE SW15 127 G6
Tiber Cl BOW E3 75 J7
Tiber Gdns IS N1 5 K4
Ticehurst Cl STMC/STPC BR5 155 G6
Ticehurst Rd FSTH SE23 151 G1
Tidal Basin Rd CAN/RD E16 94 D6
Tide Cl MTCM CR4 148 A7
Tidenham Gdns CROY/NA CR0 178 A2
Tideswell Rd CROY/NA CR0 179 J2
PUT/ROE SW15 127 F3
Tideway Cl RCHPK/HAM TW10 143 H3
Tideway Wk VX/NE SW8 * 109 H5
Tidey St BOW E3 93 J4
Tidford Rd WELL DA16 136 A1
Tidworth Rd BOW E3 93 J2
Tiepigs La WWKM BR4 180 C1
Tierney Rd BRXS/STRHM SW2 129 K7
Tierney Ter
BRXS/STRHM SW2 * 129 K7
Tiger La HAYES BR2 168 A3
Tiger Wy CLPT E5 74 D3
Tigres Cl ED N9 42 E1
Tilbrook Rd BKHTH/KID SE3 134 B2
Tilbury Cl PECK SE15 111 G6
PIN HA5 * 33 K6
Tilbury Rd EHAM E6 95 K1
LEY E10 58 A6
Tildesley Rd PUT/ROE SW15 127 F5
Tilehouse Cl BORE WD6 24 B2
Tilehurst Rd CHEAM SM3 174 C4
WAND/EARL SW18 128 C7
Tile Kiln La HGT N6 54 B7
PLMGR N13 41 J4
Tileyard Rd HOLWY N7 5 J1
Tilford Av CROY/NA CR0 180 A6
Tilford Gdns WIM/MER SW19 127 G7
Tilia Cl SUT SM1 174 D4
Tilia Rd CLPT E5 74 D3
Tilia Wk BRXN/ST SW9 130 C3
Tiller Rd POP/IOD E14 112 D2
Tillett Cl WLSDN NW10 68 E5
Tillet Wy BETH E2 92 C2
Tilley Rd FELT TW13 121 K7
Tillingbourne Gdns FNCH N3 52 D2
Tillingbourne Wy FNCH N3 52 D3
Tillingham Wy
NFNCH/WDSPK N12 38 E3
Tilling Rd CRICK NW2 51 K7
Tilling Wy WBLY HA9 * 67 K2
Tillman St WCHPL E1 92 D5
Tilloch St IS N1 * 5 L2
Tillotson Rd ED N9 42 B1
IL IG1 60 A6
KTN/HRWW/WS HA3 34 B6
Tilney Gdns IS N1 73 K5
Tilney Rd DAGW RM9 80 B5
NWDGN UB2 102 B3
Tilney St MYFR/PKLN W1K 10 B8
Tilson Cl CMBW SE5 111 F6
Tilson Gdns BRXS/STRHM SW2 129 K6
Tilson Rd TOTM N17 42 C7
Tilston Cl WAN E11 76 D2
Tilton St FUL/PGN SW6 107 H5
The Tiltwood ACT W3 86 E6
Tilt Yard Ap ELTH/MOT SE9 134 E5
Timber Cl CHST BR7 169 F1
Timbercroft HOR/WEW KT19 173 G3
Timbercroft La
WOOL/PLUM SE18 115 K5
Timberland Cl PECK SE15 * 111 H6
Timberland Rd WCHPL E1 * 92 D5
Timber Mill Wy CLAP SW4 129 J2
Timber Pond Rd
BERM/RHTH SE16 112 A1
Timberslip Dr WLGTN SM6 176 D7
The Timbers CHEAM SM3 * 174 C5
Timber St FSBYE EC1V * 6 E9
Timberwharf Rd
SEVS/STOTM N15 56 C5
Time Sq HACK E8 * 74 B4
Times Sq SUT SM1 * 175 F4
Timms Cl BMLY BR1 168 E3
Timothy Cl CLAP SW4 129 H4
Tindal St BRXN/ST SW9 110 C7
Tinniswood Cl HBRY N5 73 G4
Tinsley Cl SNWD SE25 165 J2
Tinsley Rd WCHPL E1 92 E4
Tintagel Crs EDUL SE22 131 G3
Tintagel Dr STAN HA7 35 K4
Tintern Av CDALE/KGS NW9 50 D2
Tintern Cl PUT/ROE SW15 127 H4
WIM/MER SW19 147 G6
Tintern Gdns STHGT/OAK N14 28 E6
Tintern Rd CAR SM5 162 C7
WDGN N22 41 J7
Tintern St CLAP SW4 129 K3
Tintern Wy RYLN/HDSTN HA2 48 B7
Tinto Rd CAN/RD E16 94 E4
Tinwell Ms BORE WD6 25 F4
Tinworth St LBTH SE11 17 K7
Tipthorpe Rd BTSEA SW11 129 F2
Tipton Dr CROY/NA CR0 178 A3
Tiptree Cl CHING E4 44 A2
Tiptree Crs CLAY IG5 60 A1
Tiptree Dr ENC/FH EN2 29 K3
Tiptree Rd RSLP HA4 65 F3
Tirlemont Rd SAND/SEL CR2 177 J6

Tirrell Rd CROY/NA CR0 164 D5
Tisbury Rd STRHM/NOR SW16 163 K1
Tisdall Pl WALW SE17 19 H6
Titan Ct BTFD TW8 105 G4
Titchborne Rw BAY/PAD W2 9 K5
Titchfield Rd CAR SM5 162 C7
STJWD NW8 3 K4
Titchfield Wk CAR SM5 162 C6
Titchwell Rd WAND/EARL SW18 128 C6
Tite St CHEL SW3 15 L9
Tithe Barn Cl KUTN/CMB KT2 144 B7
Tithe Barn Wy NTHLT UB5 83 F1
Tithe Cl MLHL NW7 37 J7
WOT/HER KT12 156 A5
YEAD UB4 82 D4
Tithe Ct HDN NW4 * 37 J7
Tithe Farm Av RYLN/HDSTN HA2 66 A2
Tithe Farm Cl RYLN/HDSTN HA2 66 A2
Tithe Wk MLHL NW7 37 J7
Titian Av BUSH WD23 22 E6
Titley Cl CHING E4 43 J4
Titmus Cl UX/CGN UB8 82 A5
Titmuss Av THMD SE28 97 H6
Titmuss St SHB W12 * 106 E1
Tiverton Av CLAY IG5 60 A2
Tiverton Cl CROY/NA CR0 165 G6
Tiverton Rd ALP/SUD HA0 86 A1
EDGW HA8 50 B1
HSLW TW3 123 G1
RSLP HA4 64 E2
SEVS/STOTM N15 55 K5
UED N18 42 A4
WLSDN NW10 70 B7
Tiverton St STHWK SE1 18 E3
Tiverton Wy CHSGTN KT9 171 J4
MLHL NW7 38 B6
Tivoli Gdns WOOL/PLUM SE18 114 D3
Tivoli Rd CEND/HSY/T N8 54 D4
HSLWW TW4 122 D3
WNWD SE27 149 J4
Toad La HSLWW TW4 122 E3
Tobago St POP/IOD E14 112 D1
Tobin Cl HAMP NW3 3 K1
Toby La WCHPL E1 93 G3
Toby Wy SURB KT6 172 D1
Tokenhouse Yd LOTH EC2R 13 G4
Token Yd PUT/ROE SW15 127 H3
Tokyngton Av WBLY HA9 68 C5
Toland Sq PUT/ROE SW15 126 D4
Tolcarne Dr PIN HA5 46 E1
Toley Av KTN/HRWW/WS HA3 50 A6
Tollbridge Cl NKENS W10 88 C3
Tollesbury Gdns BARK/HLT IG6 60 D2
Tollet St WCHPL E1 93 F3
Tollgate Dr DUL SE21 150 A1
YEAD UB4 83 H6
Tollgate Gdns KIL/WHAMP NW6 2 C5
Tollgate Rd CAN/RD E16 95 G4
Tollhouse La WLGTN SM6 176 C7
Tollhouse Wy ARCH N19 72 C1
Tollington Pk FSBYPK N4 73 F1
Tollington Pl FSBYPK N4 73 F1
Tollington Rd HOLWY N7 73 F3
Tollington Wy HOLWY N7 72 E2
Tolmer's Sq CAMTN NW1 4 F9
Tolpits Cl WATW WD18 20 D4
Tolpits La WATW WD18 20 A7
Tolpuddle Av PLSTW E13 77 G7
Tolpuddle St IS N1 6 A5
Tolsford Rd HACK E8 74 D4
Tolson Rd ISLW TW7 124 B2
Tolverne Rd RYNPK SW20 146 A7
Tolworth Broadway SURB KT6 159 H7
Tolworth Cl SURB KT6 159 J7
Tolworth Gdns CHDH RM6 61 K4
Tolworth Park Rd SURB KT6 172 B1
Tolworth Ri North BRYLDS KT5 159 K6
Tolworth Rise North (Kingston By-Pass) BRYLDS KT5 159 J7
Tolworth Ri South BRYLDS KT5 159 K6
Tolworth Rd SURB KT6 172 A1
Tolworth Underpass (Kingston By-Pass) SURB KT6 172 C2
Tom Cribb Rd THMD SE28 115 J2
WOOL/PLUM SE18 115 H2
Tom Groves Cl SRTFD E15 76 B4
Tom Hood Cl SRTFD E15 76 B4
Tom Jenkinson Rd CAN/RD E16 94 E7
Tomlin's Gv BOW E3 93 J2
Tomlinson Cl BETH E2 7 M8
CHSWK W4 105 J4
Tomlins Orch BARK IG11 78 C7
Tomlin's Ter POP/IOD E14 93 H5
Tom Mann Cl BARK IG11 78 E7
Tom Nolan Cl SRTFD E15 94 C1
Tompion St FSBYE EC1V 6 C8
Tom Smith Cl GNWCH SE10 113 H5
Tonbridge Crs KTN/HRWW/WS HA3 50 A3
Tonbridge Rd E/WMO/HCT KT8 156 D3
Tonbridge St STPAN WC1H 5 J8
Tonfield Rd CHEAM SM3 161 J7
Tonge Cl BECK BR3 166 D4
Tonsley Hl WAND/EARL SW18 128 A4
Tonsley Pl WAND/EARL SW18 128 A4
Tonsley Rd WAND/EARL SW18 128 A4
Tonsley St WAND/EARL SW18 128 A4
Tonstall Rd MTCM CR4 163 F1
Tooke Cl PIN HA5 33 J7
Tookey Cl KTN/HRWW/WS HA3 50 B6
Took's Ct FLST/FETLN EC4A 12 A4
Tooley St STHWK SE1 19 L1
Toorack Rd KTN/HRWW/WS HA3 48 D1
Tooting Bec Gdns STRHM/NOR SW16 148 D3
Tooting Bec Rd TOOT SW17 148 A2
Tooting Gv TOOT SW17 147 J4
Tooting High St TOOT SW17 147 J5
Tootswood Rd HAYES BR2 167 H4
Topham Sq TOTM N17 41 J7
Topham St CLKNW EC1R * 6 A9
Topiary Sq RCH/KEW TW9 125 G2
Topley St ELTH/MOT SE9 134 B3
Topmast Point POP/IOD E14 * 112 D1
Top Pk BECK BR3 167 H4
Topsfield Cl CEND/HSY/T N8 54 D4
Topsfield Pde CEND/HSY/T N8 * 54 E4
Topsfield Rd CEND/HSY/T N8 54 E4
Topsham Rd TOOT SW17 147 K2
Torbay Rd KIL/WHAMP NW6 70 D6
RYLN/HDSTN HA2 65 J1
Torbay St CAMTN NW1 4 D1
Torbitt Wy GNTH/NBYPK IG2 61 F4
Torbridge Cl EDGW HA8 36 A6
Torcross Dr FSTH SE23 150 E1
Torcross Rd RSLP HA4 65 F2
Tor Gdns KENS W8 14 A1
Tor Gv THMD SE28 96 E7
Tormead Cl SUT SM1 174 E5
Tormount Rd WOOL/PLUM SE18 115 K5
Toronto Av MNPK E12 77 K3
Toronto Rd IL IG1 60 B7
Torquay Gdns REDBR IG4 59 H3
Torquay St BAY/PAD W2 8 C3
Torrens Rd BRXS/STRHM SW2 130 A4
SRTFD E15 76 D5
Torrens Sq SRTFD E15 76 D5
Torrens St FSBYE EC1V 6 C6
Torres Sq POP/IOD E14 112 D4
Torrey Dr BRXN/ST SW9 130 B1
Torriano Av KTTN NW5 72 D4
Torriano Cots KTTN NW5 72 D4
Torriano Ms KTTN NW5 72 C4
Torridge Gdns PECK SE15 131 K3
Torridge Rd THHTH CR7 164 C4
Torridon Rd CAT SE6 133 G7
Torrington Av NFNCH/WDSPK N12 39 H4
Torrington Cl ESH/CLAY KT10 170 E5
Torrington Dr RYLN/HDSTN HA2 66 B3
Torrington Gdns FBAR/BDGN N11 40 C5
GFD/PVL UB6 67 J7
Torrington Gv NFNCH/WDSPK N12 39 J4
Torrington Pk NFNCH/WDSPK N12 39 H3
Torrington Pl FITZ W1T 10 F2
GWRST WC1E 11 G1
WAP E1W 92 C7
Torrington Rd BCTR RM8 62 B7
ESH/CLAY KT10 170 E5
GFD/PVL UB6 67 J7
RSLP HA4 64 E2
Torrington Sq CROY/NA CR0 * 164 E6
STPAN WC1H 11 H1
Torrington Wy MRDN SM4 161 K6
Tor Rd WELL DA16 116 D7
Torr Rd PGE/AN SE20 151 F6
Torver Rd HRW HA1 48 E3
Torwood Rd PUT/ROE SW15 126 D4
Tothill St STJSPK SW1H 17 G2
Totnes Rd WELL DA16 116 C6
Totnes Vls FBAR/BDGN N11 * 40 C4
Totnes Wk EFNCH N2 53 H3
Tottan Ter WCHPL E1 * 93 F5
Tottenhall Rd PLMGR N13 41 G5
Tottenham Court Rd FITZ W1T 10 F1
Tottenham Gn East SEVS/STOTM N15 56 B3
Tottenham Green East South Side SEVS/STOTM N15 56 B3
Tottenham La CEND/HSY/T N8 54 E4
Tottenham Ms FITZ W1T * 10 F2
Tottenham Rd IS N1 74 A5
Tottenham St FITZ W1T 10 F3
Totterdown St TOOT SW17 147 K3
Totteridge Common TRDG/WHET N20 37 J1
Totteridge La TRDG/WHET N20 38 E1
Totteridge Village TRDG/WHET N20 26 C7
Totternhoe Cl KTN/HRWW/WS HA3 49 J4
Totton Rd THHTH CR7 164 B2
Toucan Cl WLSDN NW10 86 C2
Toulmin St STHWK SE1 18 E2
Toulon St CMBW SE5 110 D6
Tournay Rd FUL/PGN SW6 107 J6
Toussaint Wk BERM/RHTH SE16 111 H2
Tovil Cl PGE/AN SE20 165 H1
Towcester Rd BOW E3 93 K3
Tower Br WAP E1W 13 L8
Tower Bridge Ap TWRH EC3N 13 L8
Tower Bridge Ms ALP/SUD HA0 67 F3
Tower Bridge Rd STHWK SE1 19 J4
Tower Blds WAP E1W * 92 D7
Tower Cl HAMP NW3 71 H4
PGE/AN SE20 150 D6
Tower Ct LSQ/SEVD WC2H * 11 J5
Tower Gdns ESH/CLAY KT10 171 G6
Tower Gardens Rd TOTM N17 41 J7
Tower Hamlets Rd FSTGT E7 76 D3
WALTH E17 57 J2
Tower Hl TWRH EC3N 13 L7
Tower Hill Ter MON EC3R 13 K7
Tower La WBLY HA9 * 67 K2
Tower Ms CLPT E5 75 G3
WALTH E17 57 J3
Tower Mill Rd CMBW SE5 * 111 F6
Tower Pl MON EC3R 13 K7
Tower Ri RCH/KEW TW9 125 F2
Tower Rd BELV DA17 117 K3
TWK TW1 143 F2
WLSDN NW10 69 J6
Tower Royal MANHO EC4N * 12 F6
Towers Av HGDN/ICK UB10 82 A2
Towers Ct HGDN/ICK UB10 * 82 A2
Towers Pl RCH/KEW TW9 125 F4
Towers Rd PIN HA5 33 J7
STHL UB1 84 A3
Tower St LSQ/SEVD WC2H 11 J5
Tower Ter WDGN N22 55 F1
Tower Vw BUSH WD23 22 E6
CROY/NA CR0 166 B7
Towfield Rd FELT TW13 141 K1
Towncourt Crs STMC/STPC BR5 169 H4
Towncourt La STMC/STPC BR5 169 J5
Towncourt Pth FSBYPK N4 55 J7
Town End Pde KUT/HW KT1 * 158 E2
Towney Md NTHLT UB5 83 K1
Town Farm Wy STWL/WRAY TW19 * 120 A6
Townfield Rd HYS/HAR UB3 82 D7
Townfield Sq HYS/HAR UB3 82 D7
Town Field Wy ISLW TW7 124 B1
Town Hall Approach Rd SEVS/STOTM N15 56 B3
Townhall Av CHSWK W4 106 A4
Town Hall Pde BRXS/STRHM SW2 * 130 A3
Town Hall Rd BTSEA SW11 128 E2
Townholm Crs HNWL W7 104 A2
Town La STWL/WRAY TW19 120 A5
Townley Ct SRTFD E15 76 D5
Townley Rd EDUL SE22 131 F4
Townley St WALW SE17 19 G7
Town Meadow BTFD TW8 104 E6
Townmead Rd FUL/PGN SW6 128 A2
RCH/KEW TW9 125 J1
Town Quay BARK IG11 78 B7
Town Rd ED N9 42 D1
Townsend Av STHGT/OAK N14 40 D3
Townsend La CDALE/KGS NW9 51 F6
Townsend Ms WAND/EARL SW18 147 G1
Townsend Rd SEVS/STOTM N15 56 B4
STHL UB1 83 J7
STJWD NW8 3 K5
WOOL/PLUM SE18 115 G2
Townsend St WALW SE17 19 H6
Townsend Wy NTHWD HA6 32 D6
Townsend Yd HGT N6 54 A7
Townshend Cl SCUP DA14 155 H5
Townshend Est STJWD NW8 3 J5
Townshend Rd CHST BR7 154 B4
RCH/KEW TW9 125 G3
STJWD NW8 3 J4
Townshend Ter RCH/KEW TW9 125 G3
Townson Av NTHLT UB5 83 F1
Townson Wy NTHLT UB5 82 E1
Town Whf ISLW TW7 * 124 C2
Towpath WOT/HER KT12 * 156 A3
Towpath Rd UED N18 43 F5
Towpath Wy CROY/NA CR0 165 G5
Towton Rd WNWD SE27 149 J1
Toynbec Cl CHST BR7 154 B3
Toynbee Rd RYNPK SW20 146 C7
Toynbee St WCHPL E1 13 L3
Toyne Wy HGT N6 53 K5
Tracey Av CRICK NW2 * 70 A4
Trade Cl PLMGR N13 41 G3
Trader Rd EHAM E6 96 B5
Tradescant Rd VX/NE SW8 109 K6
Trading Estate Rd WLSDN NW10 * 86 E3
Trafalgar Av PECK SE15 19 M8
TOTM N17 42 A5
WPK KT4 161 G7
Trafalgar Gdns WCHPL E1 93 F4
Trafalgar Gv GNWCH SE10 113 G5
Trafalgar Ms HOM E9 * 75 H5
Trafalgar Pl UED N18 42 C4
WAN E11 58 E3
Trafalgar Rd GNWCH SE10 113 H4
RAIN RM13 99 H1
WHTN TW2 142 D1
WIM/MER SW19 147 F6
Trafalgar Sq STJS SW1Y * 11 H8
Trafalgar St WALW SE17 19 G7
Trafalgar Wy CROY/NA CR0 177 F1
POP/IOD E14 94 A6
Trafford Rd THHTH CR7 164 A4
Trahorn Cl WCHPL E1 92 C3
Tramway Av ED N9 30 D6
Tramway Cl PGE/AN SE20 150 E7
Tramway Pth MTCM CR4 162 D3
Tranby Ms HOM E9 75 F4
Tranley Ms HAMP NW3 * 71 J3
Tranmere Rd ED N9 30 B6
WAND/EARL SW18 147 G1
WHTN TW2 123 G6
Tranquil Pas BKHTH/KID SE3 * 133 J1
Tranquil V BKHTH/KID SE3 133 H1
Transept St CAMTN NW1 9 J3
Transmere Rd STMC/STPC BR5 169 H5
Transom Cl BERM/RHTH SE16 112 B3
Transom Sq POP/IOD E14 112 E4
Transport Av BTFD TW8 104 B4
Tranton Rd BERM/RHTH SE16 111 J2
Traps La NWMAL KT3 160 B1
Travellers Site CHING E4 * 43 H6
Travellers Wy HSLWW TW4 122 B1
Travers Cl WALTH E17 43 F7
Travers Rd HOLWY N7 73 G2
Treacy Cl BUSH WD23 34 C1
Treadgold St NTGHL W11 88 B6
Treadway St BETH E2 92 D1
Treaty St IS N1 5 L4
Trebeck St MYFR/PICC W1J 10 C8
Trebovir Rd ECT SW5 14 B7
Treby St BOW E3 93 H3
Trecastle Wy HOLWY N7 72 D3
Tredegar Rd BOW E3 93 H1
FBAR/BDGN N11 40 D6
Tredegar Sq BOW E3 93 H2
Trederwen Rd HACK E8 74 C7
Tredown Rd SYD SE26 150 E4
Tredwell Cl HAYES BR2 168 C3
Tredwell Rd WNWD SE27 149 H3
Tree Cl RCHPK/HAM TW10 124 E7
Treen Av BARN SW13 126 B2
Tree Rd CAN/RD E16 95 G5
Treeside Cl WDR/YW UB7 100 A3
Tree Top Ms DAGE RM10 81 F5
Treetops Cl ABYW SE2 117 F4
NTHWD HA6 32 B4
Tree View Cl NRWD SE19 150 A7
Treewall Gdns BMLY BR1 153 F3
Trefgarne Rd DAGE RM10 80 C1
Trefoil Rd WAND/EARL SW18 128 B4
Tregaron Av CEND/HSY/T N8 54 E6
Tregaron Gdns NWMAL KT3 160 B3
Tregarvon Rd BTSEA SW11 129 F3
Tregenna Av RYLN/HDSTN HA2 66 A3
Tregenna Cl STHGT/OAK N14 28 C4
Trego Rd HOM E9 75 J6
Tregothnan Rd BRXN/ST SW9 129 K2
Tregunter Rd WBPTN SW10 14 E9
Treherne Ct BRXN/ST SW9 * 110 C7
Trehern Rd MORT/ESHN SW14 126 A2
Trehurst St CLPT E5 75 G4
Trelawney Est HOM E9 * 74 E5
Trelawn Rd BRXS/STRHM SW2 130 B4
LEY E10 76 A2
Trelawny Cl WALTH E17 57 K3
Trellis Sq BOW E3 93 H2
Treloar Gdns NRWD SE19 149 K5
Trelwney Est HOM E9 * 74 E5
Tremadoc Rd CLAP SW4 129 J3
Tremaine Cl BROCKY SE4 132 D1
Tremaine Rd PGE/AN SE20 165 J1
Trematon Pl TEDD TW11 143 J6
Tremlett Gv ARCH N19 72 C2
Tremlett Ms ARCH N19 * 72 C2
Trenance Gdns GDMY/SEVK IG3 79 G2
Trenchard Av RSLP HA4 65 F4
Trenchard Cl CDALE/KGS NW9 37 G7
STAN HA7 35 H5
Trenchard St GNWCH SE10 113 G4
Trenchold St VX/NE SW8 * 109 K5
Trenholme Rd PGE/AN SE20 150 D6
Trenholme Ter PGE/AN SE20 150 D6
Trenmar Gdns WLSDN NW10 87 K2
Trent Av EA W5 104 D2
Trent Ct WAN E11 58 E4
Trent Gdns STHGT/OAK N14 28 B5
Trentham St WAND/EARL SW18 127 K7
Trent Pk EBAR EN4 * 28 C1
Trent Rd BRXS/STRHM SW2 130 A4
Trent Wy WPK KT4 174 A2
YEAD UB4 82 C2
Trentwood Side ENC/FH EN2 29 F2
Treport St WAND/EARL SW18 128 A6
Tresco Cl BMLY BR1 152 C5
Trescoe Gdns RYLN/HDSTN HA2 47 J6
Tresco Gdns GDMY/SEVK IG3 79 F1
Tresco Rd PECK SE15 131 J3
Tresham Crs STJWD NW8 3 J9
Tresham Rd BARK IG11 79 F6
Tresilian Av WCHMH N21 29 F4
Tressel Cl IS N1 6 D2
Tressillian Crs BROCKY SE4 132 D2
Tressillian Rd BROCKY SE4 132 D2
Trestis Cl YEAD UB4 83 H3
Treswell Rd DAGW RM9 80 A7
Tretawn Gdns MLHL NW7 37 G3
Tretawn Pk MLHL NW7 37 G3
Trevanion Rd WKENS W14 * 107 H4
Treve Av HRW HA1 48 C6
Trevelyan Av MNPK E12 77 K3
Trevelyan Crs KTN/HRWW/WS HA3 49 K6
Trevelyan Gdns WLSDN NW10 * 70 A7
Trevelyan Rd SRTFD E15 76 C3
TOOT SW17 147 K5
Treveris St STHWK SE1 12 D9
Treverton St NKENS W10 88 B3
Treves Cl WCHMH N21 29 F4
Treville St PUT/ROE SW15 126 E6
Treviso Rd FSTH SE23 151 F1
Trevithick Cl EBED/NFELT TW14 121 J7
Trevithick St DEPT SE8 112 D5
Trevone Gdns PIN HA5 47 J5
Trevor Cl EBAR EN4 27 H5
ISLW TW7 124 A4
KTN/HRWW/WS HA3 35 F6
NTHLT UB5 83 G1
Trevor Crs RSLP HA4 64 D3
Trevor Gdns EDGW HA8 37 F7
Trevor Pl SKENS SW7 15 K2
Trevor Rd EDGW HA8 37 F7
HYS/HAR UB3 101 H1
WFD IG8 44 E6
WIM/MER SW19 146 C6
Trevor Sq SKENS SW7 15 K2
Trevor St SKENS SW7 15 K2
Trevose Rd WALTH E17 44 B7
Trevose Wy OXHEY WD19 33 G2
Trewenna Dr CHSGTN KT9 171 K4
Trewince Rd RYNPK SW20 146 A7
Trewint St WAND/EARL SW18 147 G1
Trewsbury Rd SYD SE26 151 F4
Triandra Wy YEAD UB4 83 H4
Triangle Pas EBAR EN4 * 27 G3
Triangle Pl CLAP SW4 129 J3
Triangle Rd HACK E8 74 D7
The Triangle BFN/LL DA15 * 136 B6
HACK E8 74 D7
KUT/HW KT1 159 K1
Triangle Wy ACT W3 105 H2
Trident St BERM/RHTH SE16 112 A3
Trident Wy NWDGN UB2 102 A2
Trigon Rd VX/NE SW8 110 A6
Trilby Rd FSTH SE23 151 F1
Trim St NWCR SE14 112 C5
Trinder Rd ARCH N19 54 E7
BAR EN5 26 A4
Tring Av EA W5 86 B7
STHL UB1 83 K5
WBLY HA9 68 C5
Tring Cl GNTH/NBYPK IG2 60 C4
Trinidad Gdns DAGE RM10 81 F6
Trinidad St POP/IOD E14 93 H6
Trinity Av EFNCH N2 53 H2
EN EN1 30 B5
Trinity Buoy Whf POP/IOD E14 * 94 B4
Trinity Church Rd BARN SW13 106 E5
Trinity Church Sq STHWK SE1 18 F3
Trinity Cl CLAP SW4 * 129 H3
HACK E8 * 74 B5
HAYES BR2 168 D7
HSLWW TW4 122 D3
LEW SE13 133 G3
NTHWD HA6 32 C5
SAND/SEL CR2 178 A7
WAN E11 76 C1
Trinity Ct ELTH/MOT SE9 135 G5
Trinity Crs TOOT SW17 147 K1
Trinity Dr UX/CGN UB8 82 A5
Trinity Est DEPT SE8 112 C4
Trinity Gdns BRXN/ST SW9 130 A3
CAN/RD E16 94 D4
Trinity Gn WCHPL E1 * 92 E4
Trinity Gv GNWCH SE10 113 F7
Trinity Hall Cl WATN WD24 21 G1
Trinity Ms PGE/AN SE20 165 J1
Trinity Pde HSLW TW3 * 123 G2
Trinity Pk CHING E4 * 43 H5
Trinity Ri BRXS/STRHM SW2 130 C6
Trinity Rd BARK/HLT IG6 60 C2
EFNCH N2 53 H2
RCH/KEW TW9 * 125 G2
STHL UB1 83 J7
WAND/EARL SW18 128 C5
WDGN N22 40 E6
WIM/MER SW19 146 E5
Trinity Sq TWRH EC3N 13 K7
Trinity St CAN/RD E16 94 D4
ENC/FH EN2 29 J1
STHWK SE1 18 F2
Trinity Wy ACT W3 87 G6
CHING E4 43 H5
Trio Pl STHWK SE1 18 F2
Tristan Ldg BUSH WD23 * 21 J3
Tristan Sq BKHTH/KID SE3 133 H2
Tristram Cl WALTH E17 58 B2
Tristram Dr ED N9 42 B2
Tristram Rd BMLY BR1 152 D3
Tritton Av CROY/NA CR0 176 E3
Tritton Rd DUL SE21 149 K2
Triumph Cl HYS/HAR UB3 101 F7
Triumph Rd EHAM E6 95 K5
Trojan Wy CROY/NA CR0 177 F2
Troon Cl BERM/RHTH SE16 * 111 J4
THMD SE28 97 K5
Troon St WCHPL E1 93 G5
Trosley Rd BELV DA17 117 H5
Trossachs Rd EDUL SE22 131 F4
Trothy Rd STHWK SE1 111 H3
Trott Rd MUSWH N10 40 A6
Trott St BTSEA SW11 108 C7
Troughton Rd CHARL SE7 114 A4
Troutbeck Rd NWCR SE14 112 B7
Trouville Rd CLAP SW4 129 H5
Trowbridge Rd HOM E9 75 H5
Trowlock Av TEDD TW11 143 J5
Trowlock Wy TEDD TW11 143 J5
Troy Ct KENS W8 14 A3
Troy Rd NRWD SE19 149 K5
Troy Town PECK SE15 131 H2
Trubshaw Rd NWDGN UB2 103 F2
Trueman Cl EDGW HA8 * 36 D6
Trulock Rd TOTM N17 42 C6
Truman's Rd STNW/STAM N16 74 A4
Trumpers Wy HNWL W7 104 A2
Trumpington Rd FSTGT E7 76 D3
Trump St CITYW EC2V 12 F5
Trundlers Wy BUSH WD23 22 E7
Trundle St STHWK SE1 18 E1
Trundley's Rd DEPT SE8 112 A4
Trundley's Ter DEPT SE8 112 A3
Truro Gdns IL IG1 59 J6
Truro Rd WALTH E17 57 H3
WDGN N22 40 E6
Truro St KTTN NW5 72 A5
Truro Wy YEAD UB4 82 C2
Trusedale Rd EHAM E6 95 K5
Truslove Rd WNWD SE27 149 G4
Trussley Rd HMSMTH W6 107 F2
Trustons Gdns EMPK RM11 63 J6
Tryfan Cl REDBR IG4 59 H4
Tryon Crs HOM E9 74 E7
Tryon St CHEL SW3 15 L7
Trystings Cl ESH/CLAY KT10 171 G5
Tuam Rd WOOL/PLUM SE18 115 J5
Tubbs Rd WLSDN NW10 87 H1
Tucker St WATW WD18 21 G4
Tuck Rd RAIN RM13 81 J5
Tudor Av GPK RM2 63 J2
HPTN TW12 142 A5
WPK KT4 173 K2
Tudor Cl BRXS/STRHM SW2 * 130 A5
CDALE/KGS NW9 68 E1
CHEAM SM3 174 B4
CHSGTN KT9 172 A4
CHST BR7 153 K7
HAMP NW3 71 J4
HGT N6 54 C6
HPTN TW12 142 C4
MLHL NW7 37 J5
PIN HA5 46 E4
WFD IG8 45 F4
WLGTN SM6 176 C6
Tudor Ct BORE WD6 24 A1
ELTH/MOT SE9 * 134 D3
WALTH E17 57 H6
Tudor Ct North WBLY HA9 68 C4
Tudor Ct South WBLY HA9 68 C4
Tudor Dr GPK RM2 63 J3
KUTN/CMB KT2 144 A4
MRDN SM4 161 G5
WOT/HER KT12 156 C7
Tudor Est WLSDN NW10 * 86 D1
Tudor Gdns ACT W3 86 C5
BARN SW13 126 B2
CDALE/KGS NW9 68 E1
GPK RM2 63 J3
TWK TW1 124 A7
WWKM BR4 180 A2
Tudor Gv HOM E9 74 E6
Tudor Ms WLSDN NW10 69 J5
Tudor Pde ELTH/MOT SE9 * 134 D3
Tudor Pl MTCM CR4 147 J6
NRWD SE19 * 150 B6
Tudor Rd ASHF TW15 140 B5
BAR EN5 26 E2
BARK IG11 79 F6
BECK BR3 167 F2
CHING E4 43 K5
ED N9 30 D6
HACK E8 74 D7
HPTN TW12 142 A6
HSLW TW3 123 J3
HYS/HAR UB3 82 B5
KTN/HRWW/WS HA3 48 D1
KUTN/CMB KT2 144 C6
NRWD SE19 150 B6
PIN HA5 47 G1
PLSTW E13 77 G7
SNWD SE25 165 J4
STHL UB1 83 J6
Tudor Sq HYS/HAR UB3 82 B4
Tudor St EMB EC4Y 12 B6
Tudor Wy ACT W3 105 H1
STHGT/OAK N14 28 D7
STMC/STPC BR5 169 J5
Tudor Well Cl STAN HA7 35 H4
Tudway Rd BKHTH/KID SE3 134 B3
Tufnell Park Rd HOLWY N7 72 D3
Tufton Gdns E/WMO/HCT KT8 157 G1
Tufton Rd CHING E4 43 J3
Tufton St WEST SW1P 17 J4
Tugboat St THMD SE28 115 K1
Tugela Rd CROY/NA CR0 164 E5
Tugela St CAT SE6 151 H1
Tulip Cl CROY/NA CR0 166 A7
EHAM E6 95 J4
HPTN TW12 141 K5
NWDGN UB2 103 H1
Tulip Gdns CHING E4 * 44 B2
IL IG1 78 B5
Tulip Wy WDR/YW UB7 100 A3
Tull St CAR SM5 162 E6
Tulse Cl BECK BR3 167 F2
Tulse Hl BRXS/STRHM SW2 130 B6
Tulsemere Rd WNWD SE27 149 J1
Tummons Gdns SNWD SE25 165 F1
Tuncombe Rd UED N18 42 A3
Tunis Rd SHB W12 88 A7
Tunley Gn POP/IOD E14 93 H4
Tunley Rd TOOT SW17 148 A1
WLSDN NW10 69 G7
Tunmarsh La PLSTW E13 95 F2
Tunnan Leys EHAM E6 96 A5
Tunnel Av GNWCH SE10 113 G1
Tunnel Gdns FBAR/BDGN N11 40 C6
Tunnel Link Rd HTHAIR TW6 120 D4
Tunnel Rd BERM/RHTH SE16 111 K1
Tunnel Rd East WDR/YW UB7 100 E6
Tunnel Rd West WDR/YW UB7 100 D7
Tunstall Rd BRXN/ST SW9 130 A3
CROY/NA CR0 165 F7
Tunstock Wy BELV DA17 117 F2
Tunworth Cl CDALE/KGS NW9 50 E5
Tunworth Crs PUT/ROE SW15 126 C5
Tupelo Rd LEY E10 75 K1
Tuppy St THMD SE28 115 H2
Turene Cl WAND/EARL SW18 128 B3
Turin Rd ED N9 30 E6
Turin St BETH E2 92 C2
Turkey Oak Cl NRWD SE19 150 A7
Turks Rw CHEL SW3 15 M7
Turle Rd FSBYPK N4 * 73 F1

STRHM/NOR SW16 163 K1
Turlewray Cl FSBYPK N4 55 F7
Turley Cl SRTFD E15 76 C7
Turnagain La
FLST/FETLN EC4A * 12 C4
Turnage Rd BCTR RM8 62 A7
Turnant Rd TOTM N17 41 J7
Turnberry Cl
BERM/RHTH SE16 * 111 J4
HDN NW4 52 B1
Turnberry Ct OXHEY WD19 * 33 G2
Turnberry Wy ORP BR6 169 J7
Turnbury Cl THMD SE28 97 K5
Turnchapel Ms CLAP SW4 129 G2
Turner Av MTCM CR4 147 K7
SEVS/STOTM N15 56 A3
WHTN TW2 142 C2
Turner Cl ALP/SUD HA0 67 K4
BRXN/ST SW9 110 C7
GLDGN NW11 53 F5
Turner Ct CMBW SE5 * 130 E3
Turner Crs THHTH CR7 164 D5
Turner Dr GLDGN NW11 53 F5
Turner Ms BELMT SM2 175 F6
Turner Rd BUSH WD23 22 C3
EDGW HA8 50 A1
NWMAL KT3 160 A6
WALTH E17 58 A3
Turners Cl TRDG/WHET N20 39 K2
Turners Meadow Wy
BECK BR3 151 H7
Turner's Rd BOW E3 93 H4
Turner St CAN/RD E16 94 D5
WCHPL E1 92 D4
Turners Wy CROY/NA CR0 177 G1
Turner's Wd GLDGN NW11 53 G7
Turneville Rd WKENS W14 107 J5
Turney Rd DUL SE21 130 D6
Turnham Green Ter
CHSWK W4 106 B3
Turnham Rd BROCKY SE4 132 B4
Turnmill St FARR EC1M 12 B1
Turnpike Cl DEPT SE8 112 C6
Turnpike La CEND/HSY/T N8 55 G3
SUT SM1 175 G4
Turnpike Link CROY/NA CR0 178 A1
Turnpike Ms
CEND/HSY/T N8 * 55 G2
Turnpike Pde
SEVS/STOTM N15 * 55 H2
Turnpike Wy ISLW TW7 104 B7
Turnstone Cl
CDALE/KGS NW9 * 51 G1
PLSTW E13 94 E2
Turnstone Ter WEA W13 * 85 F3
Turpentine La PIM SW1V 16 D7
Turpin Cl WAP E1W 93 F6
Turpington Cl HAYES BR2 168 D5
Turpington La HAYES BR2 168 D4
Turpin La ERITH DA8 118 D5
Turpin Rd EBED/NFELT TW14 121 J5
Turpin's La WFD IG8 45 K4
Turpins Yd CRICK NW2 * 69 K1
GNWCH SE10 113 F6
Turpin Wy WLGTN SM6 176 B6
Turquand St WALW SE17 18 F6
Turret Gv CLAP SW4 129 H2
Turton Rd ALP/SUD HA0 68 A4
Turville St BETH E2 7 L9
Tuscan Rd WOOL/PLUM SE18 115 J4
Tuskar St GNWCH SE10 113 H4
Tweeddale Gv
HGDN/ICK UB10 64 A2
Tweeddale Rd CAR SM5 162 C7
Tweedmouth Rd PLSTW E13 95 F1
Tweedy Rd BMLY BR1 152 E7
Twelvetrees Crs BOW E3 94 A3
Twentyman Cl WFD IG8 44 E4
Twickenham Br TWK TW1 124 D4
Twickenham Cl CROY/NA CR0 177 F2
Twickenham Gdns
GFD/PVL UB6 67 G4
KTN/HRWW/WS HA3 34 E6
Twickenham Rd FELT TW13 141 J3
ISLW TW7 124 A3
TEDD TW11 143 G3
WAN E11 76 B1
Twig Folly Cl BETH E2 93 F1
Twig Folly Whf BETH E2 * 93 F1
Twigg Cl ERITH DA8 118 B6
Twilley St WAND/EARL SW18 128 A6
Twine Cl BARK IG11 97 H2
Twine Ct WCHPL E1 92 E6
Twineham Gn
NFNCH/WDSPK N12 38 E3
Twine Ter BOW E3 * 93 H3
Twining Av WHTN TW2 142 C2
Twinn Rd MLHL NW7 38 C5
Twin Tumps Wy THMD SE28 97 G6
Twisden Rd KTTN NW5 72 B3
Twybridge Wy WLSDN NW10 68 E6
Twycross Ms GNWCH SE10 113 H3
Twyford Abbey Rd
WLSDN NW10 86 B2
Twyford Av ACT W3 86 C6
EFNCH N2 53 K2
Twyford Crs ACT W3 86 C7
Twyford Rd CAR SM5 162 C7
IL IG1 78 C4
RYLN/HDSTN HA2 48 B6
Twyford St IS N1 5 L3
Tyas Rd CAN/RD E16 94 D3
Tybenham Rd
WIM/MER SW19 161 K2
Tyberry Rd PEND EN3 30 D2
Tyburn La HRW HA1 48 E6
Tyburn Wy MBLAR W1H 9 M6
Tyers Ga STHWK SE1 19 J2
Tyers St LBTH SE11 17 L7
Tyers Ter LBTH SE11 17 L8
Tyeshurst Cl ABYW SE2 117 F4
Tylecroft Rd
STRHM/NOR SW16 163 K1
Tylehurst Gdns IL IG1 78 C4
Tyler Cl BETH E2 7 L5
Tylers Ga
KTN/HRWW/WS HA3 50 A5
Tyler St GNWCH SE10 113 H4
Tylney Av NRWD SE19 150 B4
Tylney Rd BMLY BR1 168 C1
FSTGT E7 77 G3
Tynan Cl EBED/NFELT TW14 121 K7
Tyndale La IS N1 6 C1
Tyndale Ter IS N1 6 C1
Tyndall Rd LEY E10 76 A1
WELL DA16 136 A2
Tyneham Cl BTSEA SW11 * 129 F2
Tyneham Rd BTSEA SW11 129 F1
Tynemouth Cl EHAM E6 96 B5
Tynemouth Rd MTCM CR4 148 A6
SEVS/STOTM N15 56 B3
WOOL/PLUM SE18 115 K4
Tynemouth St FUL/PGN SW6 128 B1
Tynemouth Ter
SEVS/STOTM N15 * 56 B3
Tyne St WCHPL E1 13 M4
Tynsdale Rd WLSDN NW10 69 G6
Type St BETH E2 93 F1
Tyrawley Rd FUL/PGN SW6 108 A7
Tyre La CDALE/KGS NW9 * 51 G3
Tyrell Cl HRW HA1 66 E3
Tyrone Rd EHAM E6 95 K1
Tyron Wy SCUP DA14 154 E3
Tyrrell Av WELL DA16 136 B4
Tyrrell Rd EDUL SE22 131 H3
Tyrrel Wy CDALE/KGS NW9 51 H6
Tyrwhitt Rd BROCKY SE4 132 D2
Tysoe St FSBYW WC1X 6 A8
Tyson Gdns FSTH SE23 * 131 K6
Tyson Rd FSTH SE23 131 K6
Tyssen Rd STNW/STAM N16 * 74 B2
Tyssen St HACK E8 74 B5
IS N1 7 K5
Tytherton Rd ARCH N19 72 D2

U

Uamvar St POP/IOD E14 93 K4
Uckfield Gv MTCM CR4 148 A7
Udall St WEST SW1P 16 F6
Udney Park Rd TEDD TW11 143 G4
Uffington Rd WLSDN NW10 69 J7
WNWD SE27 149 G3
Ufford Cl KTN/HRWW/WS HA3 34 B6
Ufford Rd
KTN/HRWW/WS HA3 34 B6
Ufford St STHWK SE1 18 B1
Ufton Rd IS N1 7 J1
Uhura Sq STNW/STAM N16 * 74 A2
Ullathorne Rd
STRHM/NOR SW16 148 C3
Ulleswater Rd
STHGT/OAK N14 40 E3
Ulleswater Vls
STHGT/OAK N14 * 40 E3
Ullin St POP/IOD E14 94 A4
Ullswater Cl BMLY BR1 152 C5
PUT/ROE SW15 * 145 F3
YEAD UB4 82 C1
Ullswater Ct
RYLN/HDSTN HA2 * 48 A6
Ullswater Crs PUT/ROE SW15 145 F3
Ullswater Rd BARN SW13 106 D6
WNWD SE27 149 H2
Ullswater Wy HCH RM12 81 J4
Ulster Gdns PLMGR N13 41 J3
Ulster Pl CAMTN NW1 10 C1
Ulundi Rd BKHTH/KID SE3 113 H5
Ulva Rd PUT/ROE SW15 127 G3
Ulverscroft Rd EDUL SE22 131 H4
Ulverston Rd WALTH E17 58 B1
Ulysses Rd KIL/WHAMP NW6 70 D4
Umberston St WCHPL E1 * 92 C5
Umbria St PUT/ROE SW15 126 D5
Umfreville Rd FSBYPK N4 55 H5
Undercliff Rd LEW SE13 132 D2
Underhill BAR EN5 26 E4
Underhill Ct BAR EN5 * 26 E4
Underhill Rd EDUL SE22 131 H4
Underhill St CAMTN NW1 4 D4
Underne Av STHGT/OAK N14 40 B1
Undershaft HDTCH EC3A 13 J5
Undershaw Rd BMLY BR1 152 C2
Underwood CROY/NA CR0 180 A5
Underwood Rd CHING E4 43 K4
WCHPL E1 92 C3
WFD IG8 45 H6
Underwood Rw IS N1 6 F7
Underwood St IS N1 6 F7
The Underwood
ELTH/MOT SE9 153 K1
Undine Rd POP/IOD E14 112 E3
Undine St TOOT SW17 147 K4
Uneeda Dr GFD/PVL UB6 66 D7
Union Cl WAN E11 76 B3
Union Ct CLAP SW4 129 K1
OBST EC2N 13 J4
Union Dr WCHPL E1 * 93 G3
Union Gv VX/NE SW8 129 J1
Union Pk GNWCH SE10 113 J4
Union Rd ALP/SUD HA0 68 A5
CLAP SW4 129 J1
CROY/NA CR0 164 D6
FBAR/BDGN N11 40 D5
HAYES BR2 168 C4
NTHLT UB5 84 A1
Union Sq IS N1 6 E4
Union St BAR EN5 26 C3
KUT/HW KT1 158 E1
STHWK SE1 12 D9
Union Wk BETH E2 7 L7
Unity Cl CROY/NA CR0 179 K7
NRWD SE19 149 J4
WLSDN NW10 69 J5
Unity Ms CAMTN NW1 5 G5
Unity Wy WOOL/PLUM SE18 114 C2
University Cl BUSH WD23 21 K3
MLHL NW7 37 H6
University Gdns BXLY DA5 137 G6
University Rd WIM/MER SW19 147 H5
University St FITZ W1T 10 F1
University Wy CAN/RD E16 96 A6
Unwin Av EBED/NFELT TW14 121 G4
Unwin Cl PECK SE15 111 H5
Unwin Rd ISLW TW7 123 K2
SKENS SW7 15 H3
Upbrook Ms BAY/PAD W2 8 F5
Upcerne Rd WBPTN SW10 108 B6
Upcroft Av EDGW HA8 36 E4
Updale Rd SCUP DA14 155 F3
Upfield CROY/NA CR0 178 D1
Upfield Rd HNWL W7 85 F3
Uphall Rd IL IG1 78 B4
Upham Park Rd CHSWK W4 106 B3
Uphill Dr CDALE/KGS NW9 50 E4
MLHL NW7 37 G4
Uphill Gv MLHL NW7 37 G3
Uphill Rd MLHL NW7 37 G3
Upland Rd BELMT SM2 175 H6
EDUL SE22 131 H6
PLSTW E13 94 E3
SAND/SEL CR2 177 K4
Uplands BECK BR3 166 D1
Uplands Cl MORT/ESHN SW14 125 J4
WOOL/PLUM SE18 115 G4
Uplands Park Rd ENC/FH EN2 29 G1
Uplands Rd CEND/HSY/T N8 55 F4
CHDH RM6 61 K2
EBAR EN4 28 A7
WFD IG8 45 J6
The Uplands RSLP HA4 46 E7
Uplands Wy WCHMH N21 29 G4
Upminster Rd South
RAIN RM13 99 J3
Upney La BARK IG11 79 F6
Upnor Wy WALW SE17 19 K7
Uppark Dr GNTH/NBYPK IG2 60 C5
Upper Abbey Rd BELV DA17 117 G3
Upper Addison Gdns
WKENS W14 107 H1
Upper Bank St POP/IOD E14 93 K7
Upper Bardsey Wk IS N1 * 73 J5
Upper Belgrave St
KTBR SW1X 16 B3
Upper Berenger Wk
WBPTN SW10 * 108 C6
Upper Berkeley St
MBLAR W1H 9 L5
Upper Beulah Hl NRWD SE19 150 A7
Upper Blantyre Wk
WBPTN SW10 * 108 C6
Upper Brighton Rd SURB KT6 158 E5
Upper Brockley Rd
BROCKY SE4 132 C1
Upper Brook St
MYFR/PKLN W1K 10 A6
Upper Butts BTFD TW8 104 D5
Upper Caldy Wk IS N1 * 73 J5
Upper Camelford Wk
NTGHL W11 * 88 C5
Upper Cavendish Av FNCH N3 52 E2
Upper Cheyne Rw CHEL SW3 108 D5
Upper Clapton Rd CLPT E5 74 D1
Upper Clarendon Wk
NTGHL W11 * 88 C5
Upper Dartrey Wk
WBPTN SW10 * 108 B6
Upper Dengie Wk IS N1 * 6 E3
Upper Elmers End Rd
BECK BR3 166 B3
Upper Farm Rd
E/WMO/HCT KT8 156 E3
Upper Gn East MTCM CR4 162 E1
Upper Gn West MTCM CR4 162 E1
Upper Grosvenor St
MYFR/PKLN W1K 10 A7
Upper Grotto Rd TWK TW1 143 F1
Upper Gnd STHWK SE1 12 A8
Upper Gv SNWD SE25 165 F3
Upper Grove Rd BELV DA17 117 G5
Upper Gulland Wk IS N1 * 73 J5
Upper Ham Rd
RCHPK/HAM TW10 143 K3
Upper Handa Wk IS N1 * 73 K5
Upper Harley St CAMTN NW1 10 B1
Upper Hawkwell Wk IS N1 * 6 F3
Upper Hitch OXHEY WD19 21 J7
Upper Holly Hill Rd
BELV DA17 117 J4
Upper John St SOHO/CST W1F 10 F6
Upper Lismore Wk IS N1 * 73 J5
Upper Ldg KENS W8 * 8 D9
Upper Ml HMSMTH W6 106 D4
Upper Marsh STHWK SE1 17 M3
Upper Montagu St
MBLAR W1H 9 L2
Upper Mulgrave Rd
BELMT SM2 174 C6
Upper North St POP/IOD E14 93 J4
Upper Paddock Rd
OXHEY WD19 21 J5
Upper Park Rd BELV DA17 117 J3
BMLY BR1 153 F7
FBAR/BDGN N11 40 B4
HAMP NW3 71 K5
KUTN/CMB KT2 144 C5
Upper Phillimore Gdns
KENS W8 14 A2
Upper Rainham Rd HCH RM12 81 H3
Upper Ramsey Wk IS N1 73 K5
Upper Rawreth Wk IS N1 * 6 F3
Upper Richmond Rd
PUT/ROE SW15 126 E3
Upper Richmond Rd West
RCHPK/HAM TW10 125 H3
Upper Rd PLSTW E13 94 E2
WLGTN SM6 176 D4
Upper St Martin's La
LSQ/SEVD WC2H 11 J5
Upper Selsdon Rd
SAND/SEL CR2 178 B7
Upper Sheppey Wk IS N1 73 J5
Upper Sheridan Rd
BELV DA17 117 H3
Upper Shirley Rd
CROY/NA CR0 178 E2
Upper Sq ISLW TW7 124 B2
Upper St IS N1 6 B5
Upper Sunbury Rd
HPTN TW12 141 K7
Upper Sutton La HEST TW5 103 F7
Upper Tachbrook St
PIM SW1V 16 E5
Upper Tail OXHEY WD19 33 J2
Upper Talbot Wk
NTGHL W11 * 88 C5
Upper Teddington Rd
KUT/HW KT1 143 J7
Upper Ter HAMP NW3 71 G2
Upper Thames St BLKFR EC4V 12 E6
Upper Tollington Pk
FSBYPK N4 55 G7
Upperton Rd SCUP DA14 155 F4
Upperton Rd East PLSTW E13 95 G2
Upperton Rd West
PLSTW E13 95 G2
Upper Tooting Pk TOOT SW17 147 K1
Upper Tooting Rd TOOT SW17 147 K3
Upper Town Rd STHL UB1 84 B3
Upper Tulse Hl
BRXS/STRHM SW2 130 A6
Upper Vernon Rd SUT SM1 175 H4
Upper Walthamstow Rd
WALTH E17 58 B3
Upper Whistler Wk
WBPTN SW10 * 108 B6
Upper Wickham La
WELL DA16 136 C1
Upper Wimpole St
CAVSQ/HST W1G 10 B2
Upper Woburn Pl
STPAN WC1H 5 H9
Uppingham Av STAN HA7 49 J2
Upsdell Av PLMGR N13 41 G5
Upstall St CMBW SE5 110 C7
Upton Av FSTGT E7 76 E6
Upton Cl BXLY DA5 137 G5
CRICK NW2 70 C2
Upton Dene BELMT SM2 175 F6
Upton Gdns
KTN/HRWW/WS HA3 49 J5
Upton La FSTGT E7 77 F5
Upton Lodge Cl BUSH WD23 22 C6
Upton Park Rd FSTGT E7 77 F6
Upton Rd HSLW TW3 123 F2
THHTH CR7 164 E1
UED N18 42 C4
WATW WD18 21 F3
WOOL/PLUM SE18 115 H5
Upton Rd South BXLY DA5 137 G5
Upway NFNCH/WDSPK N12 39 J6
Upwood Rd
STRHM/NOR SW16 148 E7
Urban Ms FSBYPK N4 55 H6
Urlwin St CMBW SE5 110 D5
Urlwin Wk BRXN/ST SW9 110 B7
Urmston Dr WIM/MER SW19 127 H7
Ursula Ms FSBYPK N4 55 H7
Ursula St BTSEA SW11 108 D7
Urswick Gdns DAGW RM9 80 A6
Urswick Rd CLPT E5 74 E4
DAGW RM9 80 A6
Usborne Ms VX/NE SW8 110 A6
Usher Rd BOW E3 93 H1
Usk Rd BTSEA SW11 128 B3
Usk St BETH E2 93 F2
Uvedale Rd DAGE RM10 80 C2
ENC/FH EN2 29 K4
Uverdale Rd WBPTN SW10 108 B6
Uxbridge Rd EA W5 86 A6
FELT TW13 141 H1
HGDN/ICK UB10 82 A3
HNWL W7 84 E7
HPTN TW12 142 B4
KUT/HW KT1 158 E3
SHB W12 87 J7
STHL UB1 84 A7
YEAD UB4 82 E5
Uxbridge Road (Harrow Weald) KTN/HRWW/WS HA3 34 C6
Uxbridge Road (Hatch End)
PIN HA5 33 J7
Uxbridge Road High St
STHL UB1 83 K7
Uxbridge Road (Pinner)
PIN HA5 47 H1
Uxbridge Road (Stanmore)
STAN HA7 35 F5
Uxbridge Road The Broadway
YEAD UB4 83 H6
Uxbridge St KENS W8 8 A8
Uxendon Crs WBLY HA9 50 A7
Uxendon Hl WBLY HA9 50 B7

V

Valan Leas HAYES BR2 167 H2
Vale Av BORE WD6 24 D4
Vale Cl EFNCH N2 53 K2
MV/WKIL W9 2 E8
TWK TW1 * 143 G2
Vale Cots PUT/ROE SW15 * 145 G2
Vale Ct ACT W3 * 87 H7
Vale Crs PUT/ROE SW15 145 G3
Vale Cft ESH/CLAY KT10 171 F6
PIN HA5 47 J4
Vale Dr BAR EN5 26 D3
Vale End EDUL SE22 131 G3
Vale Gv ACT W3 87 F7
FSBYPK N4 55 J6
Vale La ACT W3 86 C4
Valence Av BCTR RM8 61 K7
Valence Circ BCTR RM8 79 K2
Valence Rd ERITH DA8 118 A6
Valence Wood Rd BCTR RM8 79 K2
Valencia Rd STAN HA7 35 J3
Valency Cl NTHWD HA6 32 D3
Valentia Pl BRXN/ST SW9 130 B3
Valentine Pl STHWK SE1 18 C1
Valentine Rd HOM E9 * 75 F5
RYLN/HDSTN HA2 66 B2
Valentines Rd IL IG1 60 B7
Valentines Wy
ROMW/RG RM7 81 G1
Vale of Health HAMP NW3 71 G2
Valerian Wy SRTFD E15 94 C2
Vale Ri GLDGN NW11 52 D7
Vale Rd BMLY BR1 169 F1
BUSH WD23 21 J4
ESH/CLAY KT10 170 E7
FSBYPK N4 55 J6
FSTGT E7 77 F5
HOR/WEW KT19 173 H3
MTCM CR4 163 J2
SUT SM1 175 F3
Vale Rw HBRY N5 73 H2
Vale Royal HOLWY N7 5 J2
Vale St DUL SE21 149 K2
Valeswood Rd BMLY BR1 152 D4
Vale Ter FSBYPK N4 55 J5
The Vale ACT W3 87 F7
CHEL SW3 15 G9
CROY/NA CR0 179 F1
EBED/NFELT TW14 122 A5
GLDGN NW11 70 B2
HEST TW5 102 D5
MUSWH N10 40 A7
RSLP HA4 65 G3
SHB W12 87 H7
STHGT/OAK N14 28 E6
SUN TW16 * 140 E5
WFD IG8 44 E6
Valetta Gv PLSTW E13 94 E1
Valetta Rd ACT W3 106 B1
Valette St HACK E8 * 74 D5
Valiant Cl NTHLT UB5 83 H2
ROMW/RG RM7 62 C1
Valiant Wy EHAM E6 95 K4
Vallance Rd MUSWH N10 54 C1
WCHPL E1 92 C3
Vallentin Rd WALTH E17 58 A3
Valley Av NFNCH/WDSPK N12 39 H3
Valley Cl PIN HA5 47 F1
Valley Dr CDALE/KGS NW9 50 D4
Valleyfield Rd
STRHM/NOR SW16 149 F4
Valley Fields Crs ENC/FH EN2 29 G1
Valley Gdns ALP/SUD HA0 68 B6
WIM/MER SW19 147 H6
Valley Gv CHARL SE7 114 B4
Valley Pk WATW WD18 20 A6
Valley Rd ERITH DA8 117 K3
HAYES BR2 167 H1
STMC/STPC BR5 155 H7
STRHM/NOR SW16 149 F3
Valley Side CHING E4 31 J7
Valley Vw BAR EN5 26 C5
Valley Wk CROY/NA CR0 178 E1
RKW/CH/CXG WD3 20 A4
Valliere Rd WLSDN NW10 87 J2
Valliers Wood Rd
BFN/LL DA15 135 J7
Vallis Wy CHSGTN KT9 171 K3
WEA W13 85 G4
Valmar Rd CMBW SE5 110 D7
Val McKenzie Av HOLWY N7 73 G2
Valnay St TOOT SW17 147 K4
Valognes Av WALTH E17 43 G7
Valonia Gdns
WAND/EARL SW18 127 J5
Vambery Rd
WOOL/PLUM SE18 115 H5
Vanbrough Crs NTHLT UB5 83 G1
Vanbrugh Dr WOT/HER KT12 156 B6
Vanbrugh Flds
BKHTH/KID SE3 113 J5
Vanbrugh Hl GNWCH SE10 113 H4
Vanbrugh Pk BKHTH/KID SE3 113 J6
Vanbrugh Park Rd
BKHTH/KID SE3 113 J6
Vanbrugh Park Rd West
BKHTH/KID SE3 113 J6
Vanbrugh Rd CHSWK W4 106 A2
Vanbrugh Ter BKHTH/KID SE3 113 J7
Vanburgh Cl CAN/RD E16 95 H4
ORP BR6 169 K7
Vancouver Man EDGW HA8 * 36 D7
Vancouver Rd EDGW HA8 36 D7
FSTH SE23 151 G1
RCHPK/HAM TW10 143 J3
YEAD UB4 83 F3
Vanderbilt Rd
WAND/EARL SW18 128 A7
Vanderbilt Vls SHB W12 * 107 G1
Vanderville Gdns EFNCH N2 53 G1
Vandome Cl CAN/RD E16 95 F5
Vandon St STJSPK SW1H 16 F3
Van Dyck Av NWMAL KT3 160 A6
Vandyke Cl PUT/ROE SW15 127 G5
Vandyke Cross ELTH/MOT SE9 134 D4
Vandy St SDTCH EC2A 13 J1
Vane Cl HAMP NW3 71 H4
KTN/HRWW/WS HA3 50 B5
Vanessa Cl BELV DA17 117 H4
Van Gogh Cl ISLW TW7 124 B2
Vanguard CDALE/KGS NW9 * 37 G6
Vanguard Cl CAN/RD E16 94 E4
CROY/NA CR0 164 C7
ROMW/RG RM7 62 D1
Vanguard St DEPT SE8 112 D7
Vanguard Wy CROY/NA CR0 178 B3
HTHAIR TW6 121 H1
SAND/SEL CR2 178 C4
WLGTN SM6 176 E6
Vanneck Sq PUT/ROE SW15 * 126 D4
Vanquish Cl WHTN TW2 123 F6
Vansittart Rd FSTGT E7 76 E3
Vansittart St NWCR SE14 112 B6
Vanston Pl FUL/PGN SW6 107 K6
Vantage Pl KENS W8 14 B4
Vant Rd TOOT SW17 147 K4
Varcoe Rd BERM/RHTH SE16 111 J4
Vardens Rd BTSEA SW11 128 C3
Varden St WCHPL E1 92 D5
Vardon Cl ACT W3 87 F5
Varley Dr TWK TW1 124 C3
Varley Rd CAN/RD E16 95 F5
Varley Wy MTCM CR4 162 C1
Varna Rd FUL/PGN SW6 107 H6
HPTN TW12 * 142 B7
Varndell St CAMTN NW1 4 E7
Varsity Dr TWK TW1 123 K4
Varsity Rw MORT/ESHN SW14 125 K1
Vartry Rd SEVS/STOTM N15 56 A5
Vassall Rd BRXN/ST SW9 110 B6
Vauban Est BERM/RHTH SE16 19 M4
Vauban St BERM/RHTH SE16 19 M4
Vaughan Av HDN NW4 51 J4
HMSMTH W6 106 C3
Vaughan Est BETH E2 * 7 L7
Vaughan Gdns IL IG1 59 K6
Vaughan Rd CMBW SE5 130 D1
HRW HA1 48 C6
SRTFD E15 76 D5
THDIT KT7 158 C6
WELL DA16 136 A1
Vaughan St BERM/RHTH SE16 112 C1
Vaughan Wy WAP E1W 92 C6
Vaughan Williams Cl
DEPT SE8 112 D6
Vauxhall Br STHWK SE1 17 J8
Vauxhall Bridge Rd PIM SW1V 16 E4
WEST SW1P 17 H7
Vauxhall Gdns SAND/SEL CR2 177 J5
Vauxhall Gv VX/NE SW8 17 K9
Vauxhall St LBTH SE11 17 M7
Vauxhall Wk LBTH SE11 17 L7
Vawdrey Cl WCHPL E1 92 E3
Veals Md MTCM CR4 147 J7
Vectis Gdns TOOT SW17 148 B5
Vectis Rd TOOT SW17 148 B5
Veda Rd LEW SE13 132 D3
Vega Crs NTHWD HA6 32 D4
Vega Rd BUSH WD23 22 C6
Veitch Cl EBED/NFELT TW14 121 J6
Veldene Wy RYLN/HDSTN HA2 65 K2
Vellum Dr CAR SM5 176 A2
Venables Cl DAGE RM10 80 D3
Venables St STJWD NW8 9 H1
Vencourt Pl HMSMTH W6 106 D3
Venetian Rd CMBW SE5 130 D1
Venetia Rd EA W5 104 E1
FSBYPK N4 55 H5
Venette Cl RAIN RM13 99 K4
Venice Av WATW WD18 20 C3
Venner Rd SYD SE26 150 E5
Venners Cl BXLYHN DA7 138 B1
Venn St CLAP SW4 129 H3
Ventnor Av STAN HA7 35 H7
Ventnor Dr TRDG/WHET N20 39 F2
Ventnor Gdns BARK IG11 78 E5
Ventnor Rd BELMT SM2 175 F6
NWCR SE14 112 A6
Ventnor Ter
SEVS/STOTM N15 * 56 C3
Venture Cl BXLY DA5 137 F6
Venue St POP/IOD E14 93 K4
Venus Ms MTCM CR4 162 D2
Venus Rd WOOL/PLUM SE18 114 E2
Vera Av WCHMH N21 29 G4
Vera Ct OXHEY WD19 21 H6
Vera Lynn Cl FSTGT E7 76 E3
Vera Rd FUL/PGN SW6 107 H7
Verbena Cl CAN/RD E16 94 C3
Verbena Gdns HMSMTH W6 106 D4
Ver-Colne Valley Wk
WAT WD17 21 H2
Verdant La CAT SE6 133 H7
Verdayne Av CROY/NA CR0 166 A7
Verdun Rd BARN SW13 106 D6
WOOL/PLUM SE18 116 B5
Vereker Rd WKENS W14 * 107 H4
Vere St CAVSQ/HST W1G 10 C5
Vermont Cl ENC/FH EN2 29 H3
Vermont Rd NRWD SE19 149 K5
SUT SM1 175 F2
WAND/EARL SW18 128 A5
Verney Gdns DAGW RM9 80 A3
Verney Rd BERM/RHTH SE16 111 J4
DAGW RM9 80 A3
Verney St WLSDN NW10 69 F2

Verney Wy BERM/RHTH SE16....111 J4
Vernham Rd
WOOL/PLUM SE18.......115 H5
Vernon Av MNPK E12........77 K3
RYNPK SW20.........161 G1
WFD IG8.........45 F5
Vernon Cl HOR/WEW KT19.......172 E5
STWL/WRAY TW19.......120 B7
Vernon Crs EBAR EN4.......28 A4
Vernon Dr STAN HA7.......35 G7
Vernon Pl FSBYW WC1X.......11 K3
Vernon Ri FSBYW WC1X.......5 M7
GFD/PVL UB6.......66 D4
Vernon Rd BOW E3.......93 H1
BUSH WD23.......21 J4
CEND/HSY/T N8 *.......55 G2
FELT TW13.......140 D1
GDMY/SEVK IG3.......61 F6
MORT/ESHN SW14.......126 A2
SRTFD E15.......76 C6
SUT SM1.......175 G4
WALTH E17.......57 H3
WAN E11.......58 C7
Vernon Sq FSBYW WC1X.......5 M7
Vernon St WKENS W14.......107 H3
Vernon Yd NTGHL W11.......88 D6
Verona Ct CHSWK W4.......106 B4
Verona Dr SURB KT6.......172 A1
Veronica Gdns
STRHM/NOR SW16.......148 C7
Veronica Rd TOOT SW17.......148 B2
Veronique Gdns
BARK/HLT IG6.......60 C4
Verran Rd BAL SW12 *.......129 G6
Versailles Rd PGE/AN SE20.......150 C6
Verulam Av WALTH E17.......57 H5
Verulam Ct CDALE/KGS NW9 *.......51 J6
Verulam Rd GFD/PVL UB6.......84 A3
Verulam St FSBYW WC1X.......12 A2
Verwood Dr EBAR EN4.......27 K2
Verwood Rd
RYLN/HDSTN HA2.......48 C1
Vespan Rd SHB W12.......106 D1
Vesta Rd BROCKY SE4.......132 B1
Vestris Rd FSTH SE23.......151 F1
Vestry Ms CMBW SE5.......111 F7
Vestry Rd CMBW SE5.......111 F7
WALTH E17.......57 K4
Vestry St IS N1.......7 G7
Vevey St CAT SE6.......151 H1
Viaduct Pl BETH E2.......92 D2
Viaduct St BETH E2.......92 D2
The Viaduct MUSWH N10 *.......54 B3
SWFD E18.......58 E1
Vian St LEW SE13.......132 E3
Vibart Gdns
BRXS/STRHM SW2.......130 A6
Vibart Wk IS N1.......5 K3
Vibia Cl STWL/WRAY TW19.......120 A6
Vicarage Cl ERITH DA8.......117 K5
NTHLT UB5.......65 K7
RSLP HA4.......46 B6
WPK KT4.......160 B7
Vicarage Ct BECK BR3 *.......166 B2
Vicarage Crs BTSEA SW11.......128 C1
Vicarage Dr BARK IG11.......78 C6
BECK BR3.......151 J7
MORT/ESHN SW14.......126 A4
Vicarage Farm Rd
HSLWW TW4.......122 D1
Vicarage Flds WOT/HER KT12.......156 B5
Vicarage Gdns KENS W8 *.......14 B1
MTCM CR4.......162 D2
Vicarage Ga KENS W8.......8 C9
Vicarage Gv CMBW SE5.......110 E7
Vicarage La EHAM E6.......95 K2
IL IG1.......60 D7
SRTFD E15.......76 C5
Vicarage Ms CHSWK W4 *.......106 B5
Vicarage Pde
SEVS/STOTM N15 *.......55 J3
Vicarage Pk
WOOL/PLUM SE18.......115 H4
Vicarage Rd BXLY DA5.......137 J7
CROY/NA CR0.......177 G2
DAGE RM10.......80 D6
HCH RM12.......63 J7
HDN NW4.......51 J5
KUT/HW KT1.......143 J7
LEY E10.......57 K6
MORT/ESHN SW14.......125 K4
SRTFD E15.......76 D6
SUN TW16.......140 D5
SUT SM1.......174 E3
TEDD TW11.......143 G4
TOTM N17.......42 C6
WATW WD18.......20 E6
WFD IG8.......45 J6
WHTN TW2.......123 H5
WOOL/PLUM SE18.......115 H4
Vicarage Wk BTSEA SW11 *.......108 C7
Vicarage Wy
RYLN/HDSTN HA2.......48 A6
WLSDN NW10.......69 F2
Vicars Bridge Cl ALP/SUD HA0.......86 A1
Vicar's Cl EN EN1.......30 A1
HOM E9.......74 E7
SRTFD E15.......77 E7
Vicars Hl LEW SE13.......132 E3
Vicars Moor La WCHMH N21.......29 G6
Vicars Oak Rd NRWD SE19.......150 A5
Vicar's Rd KTTN NW5.......72 A4
Viceroy Ct EFNCH N2 *.......53 J3
Viceroy Pde EFNCH N2 *.......53 J3
Viceroy Rd VX/NE SW8.......109 K7
Vickers Cl WLGTN SM6.......177 F6
Vickers Rd ERITH DA8.......118 A4
Victor Gv ALP/SUD HA0.......68 A6
Victoria Ar WESTW SW1E.......16 D4
Victoria Av E/WMO/HCT KT8.......157 G2
EHAM E6.......77 H7
FNCH N3.......38 D7
HSLW TW3.......123 F4
SURB KT6.......158 E5
WBLY HA9.......68 D5
WLGTN SM6.......176 A2
Victoria Cl E/WMO/HCT KT8.......157 F2
EBAR EN4.......27 H3
HRW HA1.......49 F5
HYS/HAR UB3.......82 B5
Victoria Cots RCH/KEW TW9.......105 G7
WCHPL E1 *.......92 C4
Victoria Ct WBLY HA9.......68 C5
Victoria Crs NRWD SE19.......150 A5
SEVS/STOTM N15.......56 A4
WIM/MER SW19 *.......146 D6
Victoria Dock Rd CAN/RD E16.......94 D5
Victoria Dr WIM/MER SW19.......146 C1
Victoria Emb TPL/STR WC2R.......11 L7
WHALL SW1A.......17 K2
Victoria Embankment Gdns
CHCR WC2N *.......11 K7
Victoria Gdns HEST TW5.......102 D7
Victoria Ga BAY/PAD W2.......9 H6
Victoria Gv KENS W8.......14 E3
NFNCH/WDSPK N12.......39 H4
Victoria Grove Ms
BAY/PAD W2 *.......8 C7
Victoria La BAR EN5.......26 D3
HYS/HAR UB3.......101 G4
Victoria Ms KIL/WHAMP NW6.......2 A4
WAND/EARL SW18.......128 B7
Victorian Gv STNW/STAM N16.......74 A2
Victorian Rd STNW/STAM N16.......74 A2
Victoria Pde RCH/KEW TW9 *.......105 H7
Victoria Park Rd HOM E9.......74 E7
Victoria Park Sq BETH E2.......92 E2
Victoria Park Studios
HOM E9 *.......74 E5
Victoria Pas WATW WD18.......21 F3
Victoria Pl RCH/KEW TW9.......124 E4
Victoria Ri CLAP SW4.......129 G2
Victoria Rd ACT W3.......87 F4
BARK IG11.......78 B5
BFN/LL DA15.......155 F2
BKHH IG9.......45 H1
BUSH WD23.......22 B7
CHST BR7.......154 A4
DAGE RM10.......80 E4
EA W5.......85 H4
EBAR EN4.......27 H3
ED N9.......42 B2
ERITH DA8.......118 B5
FELT TW13.......122 A7
FSBYPK N4.......55 F6
HAYES BR2.......168 C4
HDN NW4.......52 A3
KENS W8.......14 E4
KIL/WHAMP NW6.......2 A3
KUT/HW KT1.......159 G1
MLHL NW7.......37 H4
MORT/ESHN SW14.......126 A2
MTCM CR4.......147 J6
NWDGN UB2.......102 E2
PLSTW E13.......94 E1
ROM RM1.......63 H4
RSLP HA4.......65 F3
SEVS/STOTM N15 *.......56 C3
SURB KT6.......158 E5
SUT SM1.......175 H4
SWFD E18.......59 F2
TEDD TW11.......143 G5
TWK TW1.......124 C6
UED N18.......42 B3
WALTH E17.......58 A1
WAN E11.......76 B1
WDGN N22.......40 D7
WIM/MER SW19.......147 J6
WLSDN NW10.......87 G3
Victoria Sq BGVA SW1W.......16 D3
Victoria St BELV DA17.......117 G4
SRTFD E15.......76 C6
WESTW SW1E.......16 D4
Victoria Ter EA W5 *.......85 K7
FSBYPK N4.......55 G7
HRW HA1.......48 E7
Victoria Vls RCH/KEW TW9.......125 G2
Victoria Wy CHARL SE7.......114 A4
Victoria Works
STMC/STPC BR5.......169 H4
Victoria Yd WCHPL E1 *.......92 C5
Victor Rd PGE/AN SE20.......151 F6
RYLN/HDSTN HA2.......48 C2
TEDD TW11.......142 E4
WLSDN NW10.......87 K2
Victors Dr HPTN TW12 *.......141 J5
Victors Wy BAR EN5.......26 D2
Victor Vls ED N9 *.......41 K2
Victory Av MRDN SM4.......162 B4
Victory Cl STWL/WRAY TW19.......120 B7
Victory Pk WBLY HA9 *.......67 K2
Victory Pl NRWD SE19 *.......150 A5
WALW SE17.......18 F6
Victory Rd RAIN RM13.......99 J1
WAN E11.......58 E3
WIM/MER SW19.......147 G6
Victory Road Ms
WIM/MER SW19.......147 G6
Victory Wy BERM/RHTH SE16.......112 B1
HEST TW5.......102 B4
ROMW/RG RM7.......62 D1
Vienna Cl WFD IG8.......59 H1
View Cl HGT N6.......53 K6
HRW HA1.......48 D3
View Crs CEND/HSY/T N8.......54 D4
Viewfield Cl
KTN/HRWW/WS HA3.......50 A6
Viewfield Rd BFN/LL DA15.......136 D7
WAND/EARL SW18.......127 J5
Viewland Rd
WOOL/PLUM SE18.......116 A4
View Rd HGT N6.......53 K6
The View ABYW SE2.......117 F4
Viga Rd WCHMH N21.......29 G5
Vigilant Cl SYD SE26.......150 C3
Vignoles Rd ROMW/RG RM7.......62 C6
Vigo St CONDST W1S.......10 E7
Viking Cl BOW E3.......93 G1
Viking Gdns EHAM E6.......95 J4
Viking Pl LEY E10.......57 H7
Viking Rd STHL UB1.......83 J6
Viking Wy ERITH DA8.......117 K2
Villacourt Rd
WOOL/PLUM SE18.......116 B6
Village Cl CHING E4.......44 A4
HAMP NW3 *.......71 H4
Village Ms CDALE/KGS NW9 *.......69 F1
Village Mt HAMP NW3 *.......71 G3
Village Park Cl EN EN1.......30 A5
Village Rd EN EN1.......29 K5
FNCH N3.......52 C1
Village Rw BELMT SM2.......174 E6
The Village CHARL SE7.......114 B5
HAMP NW3 *.......71 G1
Village Wy BARK/HLT IG6.......60 C2
BECK BR3.......166 D2
DUL SE21.......130 E5
PIN HA5.......47 K5
WLSDN NW10.......69 F3
Village Wy East PIN HA5.......47 K6
Villa Rd BRXN/ST SW9.......130 B2
Villas Rd WOOL/PLUM SE18.......115 H3
Villa St WALW SE17.......19 H8
Villiers Av BRYLDS KT5.......159 G4
WHTN TW2.......122 E7
Villiers Cl BRYLDS KT5.......159 G3
LEY E10.......75 J1
Villiers Gv BELMT SM2.......174 B7
Villiers Rd BECK BR3.......166 A1
CRICK NW2.......69 J5
ISLW TW7.......123 K1
KUT/HW KT1.......159 G2
OXHEY WD19.......21 J5
STHL UB1.......83 K7
Villiers St CHCR WC2N.......11 K8
Vimy Cl HSLWW TW4.......122 E4
Vincam Cl WHTN TW2.......123 F6
Vincennes Est WNWD SE27 *.......149 K3
Vincent Av BRYLDS KT5.......159 J7
Vincent Cl BAR EN5.......26 E2
BFN/LL DA15.......135 K7
ESH/CLAY KT10.......170 B2
HAYES BR2.......168 A4
WDR/YW UB7.......100 D5
Vincent Gdns CRICK NW2.......69 H2
Vincent Rd FSBYPK N4 *.......54 E7
Vincent Rd ACT W3.......105 K2
ALP/SUD HA0.......68 B6
CHING E4.......44 B5
CROY/NA CR0.......165 F6
DAGW RM9.......80 A6
HSLWW TW4.......122 C2
ISLW TW7.......103 J7
KUT/HW KT1.......159 H2
WDGN N22.......55 G1
WOOL/PLUM SE18.......115 G3
Vincent Rw HPTN TW12.......142 C5
Vincents Cl BERM/RHTH SE16.......112 B1
Vincent Sq WDGN N22 *.......55 G1
WEST SW1P.......16 F6
Vincent St CAN/RD E16.......94 E4
WEST SW1P.......17 G5
Vincent Ter IS N1.......6 C5
Vincent Vls
SEVS/STOTM N15 *.......55 J3
Vince St FSBYE EC1V.......7 H8
Vine Cl BRYLDS KT5.......159 G5
CLPT E5.......74 C3
SUT SM1.......175 G2
WDR/YW UB7.......100 D3
Vine Cots HNWL W7 *.......84 E7
WCHPL E1 *.......92 E5
Vine Ct KTN/HRWW/WS HA3.......50 A5
WCHPL E1.......92 C4
Vine Gdns IL IG1.......78 C4
Vinegar St WAP E1W.......92 D7
Vinegar Yd STHWK SE1.......19 J1
Vine Hl CLKNW EC1R.......12 A1
Vine La STHWK SE1.......13 K9
Vine Pl HSLW TW3.......123 G3
Vineries Cl WDR/YW UB7.......100 D5
The Vineries CAT SE6 *.......132 D7
EN EN1.......30 A2
STHGT/OAK N14.......28 C5
Vine Rd BARN SW13.......126 C2
E/WMO/HCT KT8.......157 H3
SRTFD E15.......76 D6
Vine Rw RCHPK/HAM TW10 *.......125 F4
Viners Cl WOT/HER KT12.......156 B5
Vines Av FNCH N3.......39 F7
Vine Sq WKENS W14 *.......107 J4
Vine St MYFR/PICC W1J.......10 F7
ROMW/RG RM7.......62 E4
TWRH EC3N.......13 L5
Vine Street Br FARR EC1M.......12 B1
Vine Yd STHWK SE1.......18 F1
Vineyard Av MLHL NW7.......38 C6
Vineyard Cl CAT SE6.......132 D7
KUT/HW KT1.......159 G2
Vineyard Gv FNCH N3.......39 F7
Vineyard Hill Rd
WIM/MER SW19.......146 E3
Vineyard Ms CLKNW EC1R *.......6 A9
Vineyard Pth
MORT/ESHN SW14.......126 A2
Vineyard Rd FELT TW13.......140 E2
Vineyard Rw KUT/HW KT1.......143 J7
The Vineyard
RCHPK/HAM TW10.......124 E4
Vineyard Wk CLKNW EC1R.......6 A9
Viney Bank CROY/NA CR0.......179 H7
Viney Rd LEW SE13.......132 E2
Vining St BRXS/STRHM SW2.......130 B3
Vinries Bank MLHL NW7.......37 K4
Vintage Ms CHING E4.......43 J3
Vintry Ms WALTH E17.......57 J3
Viola Av ABYW SE2.......116 C3
EBED/NFELT TW14.......122 B5
STWL/WRAY TW19.......120 B7
Viola Sq SHB W12.......87 H6
Violet Cl CAN/RD E16.......94 C3
CHEAM SM3.......161 H7
DEPT SE8.......112 C5
WLGTN SM6.......163 F7
Violet Gdns CROY/NA CR0.......177 H4
Violet Hl STJWD NW8.......2 E6
Violet La SAND/SEL CR2.......177 H4
Violet Rd BOW E3.......93 K3
SWFD E18.......59 F1
WALTH E17.......57 J5
Violet St BETH E2.......92 D3
Virgil St STHWK SE1.......17 M3
Virginia Cl HAYES BR2.......167 H2
NWMAL KT3.......159 K3
Virginia Gdns BARK/HLT IG6.......60 D1
Virginia Rd BETH E2.......7 L8
THHTH CR7.......149 H7
Virginia St WCHPL E1 *.......92 C6
Viscount Cl FBAR/BDGN N11.......40 B4
Viscount Dr EHAM E6.......95 K4
Viscount Gv NTHLT UB5.......83 H2
Viscount Rd
STWL/WRAY TW19.......120 A6
Viscount St BARB EC2Y.......12 E1
Viscount Wy HTHAIR TW6.......121 H3
Vista Av PEND EN3.......31 F1
Vista Dr REDBR IG4.......59 H4
The Vista ELTH/MOT SE9.......134 C5
Vista Wy KTN/HRWW/WS HA3.......50 A5
Viveash Cl HYS/HAR UB3.......101 J2
Vivian Av HDN NW4.......51 K4
WBLY HA9.......68 C5
Vivian Cl OXHEY WD19.......32 E1
Vivian Gdns OXHEY WD19.......20 E7
WBLY HA9.......68 C4
Vivian Rd BOW E3.......93 G1
Vivian Sq PECK SE15.......131 J2
Vivian Wy EFNCH N2.......53 H4
Vivien Cl CHSGTN KT9.......172 A6
Vivienne Cl TWK TW1.......124 E5
Vixen Ms HACK E8 *.......7 L3
Voce Rd WOOL/PLUM SE18.......115 J6
Voewood Cl NWMAL KT3.......160 C5
Voltaire Rd CLAP SW4.......129 J2
Volt Av WLSDN NW10.......87 F2
Volta Wy CROY/NA CR0.......164 A7
Voluntary Pl WAN E11.......58 E5
Vorley Rd ARCH N19.......72 C1
Voss Ct STRHM/NOR SW16.......148 E5
Voss St BETH E2.......92 C2
Voyagers Cl THMD SE28.......97 J5
Vulcan Cl EHAM E6.......96 A5
Vulcan Ga ENC/FH EN2.......29 G1
Vulcan Rd BROCKY SE4.......132 C1
Vulcan Ter BROCKY SE4.......132 C1
Vulcan Wy HOLWY N7.......73 F5
WLGTN SM6.......176 E7
Vyner Rd ACT W3.......87 F6
Vyner St BETH E2.......92 D1
Vyse Cl BAR EN5.......26 A3

W

Wadbrook St KUT/HW KT1.......158 E1
Wadding St WALW SE17.......19 G6
Waddington Cl EN EN1.......30 A3
Waddington Rd SRTFD E15.......76 B4
Waddington St SRTFD E15.......76 B5
Waddington Wy NRWD SE19.......149 J7
Waddon Cl CROY/NA CR0.......177 G2
Waddon Court Rd
CROY/NA CR0.......177 G3
Waddon Marsh Wy
CROY/NA CR0.......164 A7
Waddon New Rd
CROY/NA CR0.......177 H2
Waddon Park Av
CROY/NA CR0.......177 G3
Waddon Rd CROY/NA CR0.......177 G2
Waddon Wy CROY/NA CR0.......177 G5
Wade House STHWK SE1 *.......111 H1
Wade's Gv WCHMH N21.......29 G6
Wade's Hl WCHMH N21.......29 G5
Wade's La TEDD TW11.......143 G4
Wadeson St BETH E2.......92 D1
Wade's Pl POP/IOD E14.......93 K6
Wadeville Av CHDH RM6.......62 A5
Wadeville Cl BELV DA17.......117 H4
Wadham Av WALTH E17.......43 K6
Wadham Gdns GFD/PVL UB6.......66 D5
HAMP NW3.......3 J2
Wadham Rd CHING E4.......44 A7
PUT/ROE SW15.......127 H3
WALTH E17.......43 K7
Wadhurst Cl PGE/AN SE20.......165 J1
Wadhurst Rd CHSWK W4.......106 A2
Wadley Rd WAN E11.......58 C6
Wadsworth Cl GFD/PVL UB6.......85 J1
PEND EN3.......31 F4
Wadsworth Rd GFD/PVL UB6.......85 H1
Wager St BOW E3.......93 H3
Waghorn Rd
KTN/HRWW/WS HA3.......49 K2
PLSTW E13.......77 G7
Waghorn St PECK SE15.......131 H2
Wagner St PECK SE15.......111 K6
Wagstaff Gdns DAGW RM9.......79 J6
Wagtail Cl CDALE/KGS NW9.......51 G1
Wagtail Wk BECK BR3.......167 F4
Waights Ct KUTN/CMB KT2.......144 A7
Wainfleet Av CRW RM5.......62 E1
Wainford Cl WIM/MER SW19.......127 G7
Wainwright Gv ISLW TW7.......123 J3
Waite Davies Rd
LEE/GVPK SE12.......133 J6
Waite St CMBW SE5.......19 L9
Waithman St STP EC4M.......12 C5
Wakefield Gdns IL IG1.......59 J5
NRWD SE19.......150 A6
Wakefield Ms STPAN WC1H.......5 J8
Wakefield Rd
FBAR/BDGN N11.......40 D4
RCHPK/HAM TW10.......124 E4
SEVS/STOTM N15.......56 B4
Wakefield St BMSBY WC1N.......5 K9
EHAM E6.......77 J7
STPAN WC1H.......5 K8
UED N18.......42 C4
Wakehams Hl PIN HA5.......47 K2
Wakeham St IS N1.......73 K5
Wakehurst Rd BTSEA SW11.......128 D4
Wakeling La ALP/SUD HA0.......67 H2
Wakeling Rd HNWL W7.......85 F4
Wakeling St WCHPL E1 *.......93 G5
Wakelin Rd SRTFD E15.......94 C1
Wakeman Rd WLSDN NW10.......88 A2
Wakemans Hill Av
CDALE/KGS NW9.......51 F4
Wakering Rd BARK IG11.......78 C5
Wakerly Cl EHAM E6.......95 K5
Wakley St FSBYE EC1V.......6 C7
Walberswick St VX/NE SW8.......109 K6
Walbrook MANHO EC4N.......13 G6
Walburgh St WCHPL E1.......92 D5
Walcorde Av WALW SE17.......18 F6
Walcot Rd PEND EN3.......31 H1
Walcot Sq LBTH SE11.......18 B5
Walcott St WEST SW1P *.......16 F5
Waldeck Gv WNWD SE27.......149 H2
Waldeck Rd CHSWK W4.......105 H5
MORT/ESHN SW14.......125 K2
SEVS/STOTM N15.......55 H2
WEA W13.......85 H5
Waldegrave Gdns TWK TW1.......143 F1
Waldegrave Pk TWK TW1.......143 F3
Waldegrave Rd BCTR RM8.......79 J1
BMLY BR1.......168 D4
CEND/HSY/T N8 *.......55 G2
EA W5.......86 B6
NRWD SE19.......150 B6
TWK TW1.......143 F3
Waldegrove CROY/NA CR0.......178 B2
Waldemar Av FUL/PGN SW6.......107 H7
WEA W13.......85 J7
Waldemar Rd
WIM/MER SW19.......146 E4
Walden Av CHST BR7.......153 K3
PLMGR N13.......41 J3
RAIN RM13.......99 F1
Walden Cl BELV DA17.......117 G4
Walden Gdns THHTH CR7.......164 A3
Walden Pde CHST BR7 *.......153 K5
Walden Rd CHST BR7.......153 K5
TOTM N17.......41 K7
Waldenshaw Rd FSTH SE23.......131 K7
Walden St WCHPL E1 *.......92 D5
Walden Wy MLHL NW7.......38 B5
Waldo Cl CLAP SW4.......129 H4
Waldo Pl MTCM CR4.......147 J6
Waldorf Cl SAND/SEL CR2.......177 H7
Waldo Rd BMLY BR1.......168 B2
WLSDN NW10.......87 J2
Waldram Crs FSTH SE23.......131 K7
Waldram Park Rd FSTH SE23.......132 A7
Waldrist Wy ERITHM DA18.......117 G1
Waldron Gdns HAYES BR2.......167 G2
Waldronhyrst CROY/NA CR0.......177 H3
Waldron Ms CHEL SW3.......15 H9
Waldron Rd RYLN/HDSTN HA2.......48 E7
WAND/EARL SW18.......147 G2
The Waldrons CROY/NA CR0.......177 J3
Waldron's Yd
RYLN/HDSTN HA2.......66 D1
Waldstock Rd THMD SE28.......97 G6
Waleran Cl STAN HA7.......35 F5
Walerand Rd LEW SE13.......133 F1
Wales Av CAR SM5.......175 J4
Wales Cl PECK SE15.......111 J6
Wales Farm Rd ACT W3.......87 F4
Waleton Acres WLGTN SM6 *.......176 C5
Waley St WCHPL E1 *.......93 F4
Walfield Av TRDG/WHET N20.......27 F6
Walford Rd STNW/STAM N16.......74 A3
Walfrey Gdns DAGW RM9.......80 A6
Walham Green Ct
FUL/PGN SW6 *.......108 A6
Walham Gv FUL/PGN SW6.......107 K6
Walham Ri WIM/MER SW19.......146 C5
Walham Yd FUL/PGN SW6.......107 K6
Walkden Rd CHST BR7.......154 A3
Walker Cl DART DA1.......138 C2
EBED/NFELT TW14.......121 J6
FBAR/BDGN N11.......40 C3
HNWL W7.......84 E7
HPTN TW12.......141 K5
WOOL/PLUM SE18.......115 H3
Walker's Ct SOHO/CST W1F.......11 G6
Walkerscroft Md CAT SE6.......151 K1
DUL SE21.......130 D7
Walker's Pl PUT/ROE SW15.......127 H3
The Walks EFNCH N2.......53 H2
The Walk PLMGR N13 *.......41 G2
Wallace Cl THMD SE28.......97 K6
Wallace Crs CAR SM5.......175 K4
Wallace Rd IS N1.......73 J5
Wallbutton Rd BROCKY SE4.......132 B1
Wallcote Av CRICK NW2.......52 B7
Walled Garden Cl BECK BR3.......166 E3
Wall End Rd EHAM E6.......78 A6
Wallenger Av GPK RM2.......63 K2
Waller Dr NTHWD HA6.......32 E7
Waller Rd NWCR SE14.......112 A7
Wallers Cl DAGW RM9.......80 A7
WFD IG8.......45 K5
Wallflower St SHB W12.......87 H6
Wallgrave Rd ECT SW5.......14 B5
Wallingford Av NKENS W10.......88 B4
Wallington Cl RSLP HA4.......46 A5
Wallington Rd
GDMY/SEVK IG3.......61 F6
Wallis Cl BTSEA SW11.......128 C2
EMPK RM11.......63 K7
Wallis Rd HOM E9.......75 H5
STHL UB1.......84 B5
Wallman Pl WDGN N22.......41 F7
Wallorton Gdns
MORT/ESHN SW14.......126 A3
Wallside BARB EC2Y *.......12 F3
Wall St IS N1.......73 K5
Wallwood Rd WAN E11.......58 B6
Wallwood St POP/IOD E14.......93 H4
Walmer Cl CHING E4.......43 K1
ROMW/RG RM7.......62 D1
Walmer Gdns WEA W13.......104 B1
Walmer Pl MBLAR W1H *.......9 L2
Walmer Rd NTGHL W11.......88 C6
Walmer Ter WOOL/PLUM SE18.......115 H3
Walmgate Rd GFD/PVL UB6.......67 H7
Walmington Fold
NFNCH/WDSPK N12.......38 E5
Walm La CRICK NW2.......70 B4
Walney Wk IS N1 *.......73 J5
Walnut Av WDR/YW UB7.......100 D2
Walnut Cl BARK/HLT IG6.......60 C3
CAR SM5.......175 K4
DEPT SE8.......112 C5
HYS/HAR UB3.......82 C6
Walnut Ct EA W5 *.......105 F1
Walnut Gdns SRTFD E15.......76 C4
Walnut Gn BUSH WD23.......21 K1
Walnut Gv EN EN1.......29 K4
Walnut Ms BELMT SM2.......175 G6
Walnut Rd LEY E10.......75 J1
Walnut Tree Av MTCM CR4 *.......162 D2
Walnut Tree Cl BARN SW13.......106 C7
CHST BR7.......154 C7
Walnut Tree Rd BCTR RM8.......79 K1
BTFD TW8.......105 F5
GNWCH SE10 *.......113 H4
HEST TW5.......102 E5
Walnut Tree Wk LBTH SE11.......18 A5
Walnut Wy BKHH IG9.......45 H2
RSLP HA4.......65 G5
Walpole Av RCH/KEW TW9.......125 G1
Walpole Cl PIN HA5.......34 A5
WEA W13.......104 D1
Walpole Crs TEDD TW11.......143 F4
Walpole Gdns CHSWK W4.......105 K4
WHTN TW2.......142 E1
Walpole Ms STJWD NW8.......3 G4
Walpole Pl TEDD TW11.......143 F4
Walpole Rd CROY/NA CR0.......177 K1
EHAM E6.......77 G6
HAYES BR2.......168 C4
SURB KT6.......159 F6
SWFD E18.......44 D7
TEDD TW11.......143 F4
TOTM N17.......55 J1
WALTH E17.......57 G3
WHTN TW2.......142 E1
WIM/MER SW19.......147 H5
Walpole St CHEL SW3.......15 L7
Walrond Av WBLY HA9.......68 A4
Walsham Cl STNW/STAM N16.......56 C7
THMD SE28.......97 K6
Walsham Rd
EBED/NFELT TW14.......122 A6
NWCR SE14.......132 A1
Walsingham Gdns
HOR/WEW KT19.......173 G3
Walsingham Pk CHST BR7.......169 J1
Walsingham Rd CLAP SW4.......129 F5
CLPT E5.......74 C2
ENC/FH EN2.......29 K3
MTCM CR4.......162 E4
STMC/STPC BR5.......155 H7
WEA W13 *.......85 G7
Walsingham Wk BELV DA17.......117 H5
Walter Rodney Cl MNPK E12.......77 K5
Walters Cl HYS/HAR UB3.......101 J1
Walters Rd PEND EN3.......30 E4
Walter's Rd SNWD SE25.......165 F3
Walter St BETH E2.......93 F2
KUTN/CMB KT2 *.......144 A7
Walters Wy FSTH SE23.......132 A5
Walters Yd BMLY BR1.......167 K1
Walter Ter WCHPL E1.......93 F5
Walterton Rd MV/WKIL W9.......88 D3
Walter Wk EDGW HA8.......36 E5
Waltham Av CDALE/KGS NW9.......50 C5
HYS/HAR UB3.......101 F2
Waltham Dr EDGW HA8.......50 C1
Waltham Pk WALTH E17.......43 J6
Waltham Park Wy CHING E4 *.......43 J6
Waltham Rd CAR SM5.......162 C7
NWDGN UB2.......102 D2
WFD IG8.......45 J5
Walthamstow Av CHING E4.......43 J6
Walthamstow Avenue (North
Circular) CHING E4.......43 G4
Waltham Wy CHING E4.......43 H2
Waltheof Av TOTM N17.......41 K7
Waltheof Gdns TOTM N17.......41 K7

WHTN TW2 142 D3
Wellington Gv GNWCH SE10 113 G6
Wellington Ms CHARL SE7 114 B5
EDUL SE22 131 H3
HOLWY N7 73 F5
STRHM/NOR SW16 148 D2
Wellington Pde
BFN/LL DA15 * 136 B4
Wellington Park Est
CRICK NW2 * 69 J1
Wellington Pas WAN E11 58 E4
Wellington Pl EFNCH N2 * 53 J4
STJWD NW8 3 H7
Wellington Rd BELV DA17 117 G4
BXLY DA5 136 E5
CROY/NA CR0 164 C6
EA W5 104 D3
EBED/NFELT TW14 121 H4
EHAM E6 77 K7
EN EN1 30 A6
FSTGT E7 76 D3
HAYES BR2 168 B3
HPTN TW12 142 D3
KTN/HRWW/WS HA3 48 E2
LEY E10 57 G7
NKENS W10 * 88 B2
PIN HA5 33 K7
STJWD NW8 3 H6
WALTH E17 57 G2
WAN E11 58 E4
WAT WD17 21 F1
WIM/MER SW19 146 E1
Wellington Rd North
HSLWW TW4 122 E2
Wellington Rd South
HSLWW TW4 122 E3
Wellington Rw BETH E2 7 M7
Wellington Sq CHEL SW3 15 L7
IS N1 5 K3
Wellington St COVGDN WC2E 11 K6
WOOL/PLUM SE18 115 F3
Wellington Ter BAY/PAD W2 8 B7
CEND/HSY/T N8 * 55 G2
HRW HA1 48 D7
WAP E1W * 92 D7
Wellington Wy BOW E3 93 J2
Welling Wy ELTH/MOT SE9 135 J2
WELL DA16 135 K2
Well La MORT/ESHN SW14 125 K4
Wellmeadow Rd CAT SE6 133 H7
HNWL W7 104 B3
Well Rd BAR EN5 26 A4
HAMP NW3 71 H2
Wells Cl NTHLT UB5 83 G2
SAND/SEL CR2 178 A4
Wells Dr CDALE/KGS NW9 51 F7
Wellsfield BUSH WD23 21 J4
Wells Gdns IL IG1 59 J6
RAIN RM13 81 H5
Wells House Rd WLSDN NW10 87 G4
Wellside Cl BAR EN5 26 A3
Wellside Gdns
MORT/ESHN SW14 125 K3
Wells Ms FITZ W1T * 10 F3
Wellsmoor Gdns BMLY BR1 169 F2
Wells Park Rd SYD SE26 150 C2
Wells Pl CMBW SE5 111 F6
WAND/EARL SW18 128 B6
Wellspring Crs WBLY HA9 68 D1
Wells Ri STJWD NW8 3 L4
Wells Rd BMLY BR1 168 E1
SHB W12 107 F1
Wells Sq FSBYW WC1X 5 L8
Wells St GTPST W1W 10 E3
Wellstead Av ED N9 30 E6
Wellstead Rd EHAM E6 96 A1
Wells Ter FSBYPK N4 73 G1
The Wells STHGT/OAK N14 28 D7
Wellstones WAT WD17 * 21 F3
Well St HOM E9 74 E6
SRTFD E15 76 C5
Wells Wy SKENS SW7 15 G3
Well Wk HAMP NW3 71 H2
Wellwood Rd GDMY/SEVK IG3 61 G7
Welsford St STHWK SE1 111 H4
Welsh Cl PLSTW E13 94 E2
Welshpool St HACK E8 * 74 C7
Welshside CDALE/KGS NW9 * 51 G4
Welstead Wy CHSWK W4 106 C2
Weltje Rd HMSMTH W6 106 D4
Welton Rd WOOL/PLUM SE18 115 K6
Welwyn Av EBED/NFELT TW14 121 J5
Welwyn St BETH E2 92 E2
Welwyn Wy YEAD UB4 82 C3
Wembley Hill Rd WBLY HA9 68 B4
Wembley Park Dr WBLY HA9 68 B3
Wembley Rd HPTN TW12 142 A7
Wembley Wy WBLY HA9 68 D5
Wemborough Rd STAN HA7 35 H7
Wembury Ms HGT N6 54 B6
Wembury Rd HGT N6 54 B6
Wemyss Rd BKHTH/KID SE3 133 J1
Wendela Ct HRW HA1 66 E2
Wendell Rd SHB W12 106 C1
Wendling Rd SUT SM1 162 C7
Wendon St BOW E3 75 H7
Wendover Cl YEAD UB4 83 H3
Wendover Dr NWMAL KT3 160 C5
Wendover Rd ELTH/MOT SE9 134 C2
HAYES BR2 168 A3
WLSDN NW10 87 H1
Wendover Wy BUSH WD23 22 C5
WELL DA16 136 B4
Wendy Cl EN EN1 30 B5
Wendy Wy ALP/SUD HA0 68 A7
Wenlock Gdns HDN NW4 * 51 J3
Wenlock Rd EDGW HA8 36 D5
IS N1 6 E6
Wenlock St IS N1 6 F6
Wennington Rd BOW E3 93 F1
RAIN RM13 99 K4
Wensley Av WFD IG8 44 E6
Wensley Cl ELTH/MOT SE9 134 E5
FBAR/BDGN N11 40 A5
Wensleydale Av CLAY IG5 59 J1
Wensleydale Gdns
HPTN TW12 142 B6
Wensleydale Rd HPTN TW12 142 A7
Wensley Rd UED N18 42 D5
Wentland Cl CAT SE6 152 B1
Wentland Rd CAT SE6 152 B1
Wentworth Av BORE WD6 24 B4
FNCH N3 38 E6
Wentworth Cl FNCH N3 39 F6
MRDN SM4 161 K6
SURB KT6 171 K1
THMD SE28 97 K5
Wentworth Crs HYS/HAR UB3 101 G2
PECK SE15 111 H6
Wentworth Dr OXHEY WD19 33 H4
PIN HA5 46 E4
Wentworth Gdns PLMGR N13 41 H2
Wentworth Hl WBLY HA9 50 B7
Wentworth Ms BOW E3 93 G3
Wentworth Pk FNCH N3 39 F6
Wentworth Pl STAN HA7 * 35 H5
Wentworth Rd BAR EN5 26 B1
CROY/NA CR0 164 B6
GLDGN NW11 52 D5
MNPK E12 77 H3
NWDGN UB2 102 B3
Wentworth St WCHPL E1 13 L4
Wentworth Wy PIN HA5 47 H3
RAIN RM13 99 K2
Wepham Cl YEAD UB4 83 H4
Wernbrook St
WOOL/PLUM SE18 115 H5
Werndee Rd SNWD SE25 165 H3
Werneth Hall Rd CLAY IG5 59 K2
Werrington St CAMTN NW1 4 F6
Werter Rd PUT/ROE SW15 127 H3
Wesleyan Pl KTTN NW5 72 B3
Wesley Av CAN/RD E16 94 E7
CAN/RD E16 95 F7
HSLW TW3 122 D1
WLSDN NW10 87 F2
Wesley Cl HOLWY N7 73 F1
RYLN/HDSTN HA2 66 C1
WALW SE17 18 D6
Wesley Rd HYS/HAR UB3 82 E6
LEY E10 58 A6
WLSDN NW10 68 E7
Wesley Sq NTGHL W11 88 B5
Wesley St CAVSQ/HST W1G 10 B3
Wessex Av WIM/MER SW19 161 K1
Wessex Cl GDMY/SEVK IG3 60 E5
KUT/HW KT1 144 D7
THDIT KT7 171 F1
Wessex Ct BECK BR3 * 151 G7
Wessex Dr PIN HA5 33 J6
Wessex Gdns GLDGN NW11 52 C7
Wessex La GFD/PVL UB6 84 D1
Wessex St BETH E2 92 E2
Wessex Ter MTCM CR4 * 162 D4
Wessex Wy GLDGN NW11 52 C6
Wesson Md CMBW SE5 * 110 D6
Westacott YEAD UB4 82 C4
Westacott Cl ARCH N19 54 D7
West Ap STMC/STPC BR5 169 H4
West Arbour St WCHPL E1 92 E5
West Av FNCH N3 38 E5
HDN NW4 52 B4
HYS/HAR UB3 82 D6
PIN HA5 47 K5
STHL UB1 83 K6
WALTH E17 57 K4
WLGTN SM6 176 E4
West Avenue Rd WALTH E17 57 J3
West Bank BARK IG11 78 B7
ENC/FH EN2 29 J2
STNW/STAM N16 56 A6
Westbank Rd HPTN TW12 142 C5
West Barnes La NWMAL KT3 160 D4
Westbeech Rd WDGN N22 55 G2
Westbere Dr STAN HA7 35 K4
Westbere Rd CRICK NW2 70 C3
Westbourne Av ACT W3 87 F5
CHEAM SM3 174 C1
Westbourne Cl YEAD UB4 83 G3
Westbourne Crs BAY/PAD W2 9 G6
Westbourne Crescent Ms
BAY/PAD W2 9 G6
Westbourne Dr FSTH SE23 132 A7
Westbourne Gdns
BAY/PAD W2 8 C4
Westbourne Ga BAY/PAD W2 9 H6
Westbourne Gv NTGHL W11 8 A5
Westbourne Grove Ms
NTGHL W11 8 A5
Westbourne Grove Ter
BAY/PAD W2 8 C4
Westbourne Park Rd
NTGHL W11 8 A4
Westbourne Park Vls
BAY/PAD W2 8 B3
Westbourne Pl ED N9 42 D2
Westbourne Rd BXLYHN DA7 116 E6
CROY/NA CR0 165 G5
FELT TW13 140 D2
HOLWY N7 73 F5
SYD SE26 151 F5
Westbourne St BAY/PAD W2 9 G6
Westbourne Ter BAY/PAD W2 8 E3
Westbourne Terrace Ms
BAY/PAD W2 8 E4
Westbourne Terrace Rd
BAY/PAD W2 8 E3
Westbridge Cl SHB W12 87 J7
Westbridge Rd BTSEA SW11 108 C7
Westbrook Av HPTN TW12 141 K6
Westbrook Cl EBAR EN4 27 H2
Westbrook Crs EBAR EN4 27 H2
Westbrooke Crs WELL DA16 136 D2
Westbrooke Rd BFN/LL DA15 154 D1
WELL DA16 136 D2
Westbrook Rd
BKHTH/KID SE3 114 A7
HEST TW5 102 E6
THHTH CR7 149 K7
Westbury Ar WDGN N22 * 55 H2
Westbury Av ALP/SUD HA0 68 A6
ESH/CLAY KT10 171 F5
SEVS/STOTM N15 55 H2
STHL UB1 84 A3
WDGN N22 55 H1
Westbury Cl RSLP HA4 46 E6
Westbury Gv
NFNCH/WDSPK N12 38 E5
Westbury La BKHH IG9 45 G1
Westbury Lodge Cl PIN HA5 47 H2
Westbury Pl BTFD TW8 104 E5
Westbury Rd ALP/SUD HA0 68 A6
BARK IG11 78 D7
BECK BR3 166 B2
BMLY BR1 153 H7
CROY/NA CR0 164 E5
EA W5 86 A5
FBAR/BDGN N11 40 E5
FELT TW13 122 C7
FSTGT E7 77 F4
IL IG1 78 A1
NFNCH/WDSPK N12 38 E5
NTHWD HA6 32 C3
NWMAL KT3 160 A3
PGE/AN SE20 151 F7
WALTH E17 57 J3
WATW WD18 21 F4
Westbury Ter FSTGT E7 77 F5
West Carriage Dr
BAY/PAD W2 15 H1
West Central St
LSQ/SEVD WC2H 11 J4
West Chantry
KTN/HRWW/WS HA3 34 B7
Westchester Dr HDN NW4 52 B2
Westcliffe Vls KUT/HW KT1 * 159 G1
West Cl BAR EN5 25 K4
EBAR EN4 28 A3
ED N9 42 B2
GFD/PVL UB6 84 C1
RAIN RM13 99 K3
WBLY HA9 50 B7
Westcombe Av CROY/NA CR0 163 K5
Westcombe Dr BAR EN5 26 E4
Westcombe Lodge Dr
YEAD UB4 82 B4
Westcombe Park Rd
BKHTH/KID SE3 113 H5
West Common Rd HAYES BR2 181 F3
Westcoombe Av RYNPK SW20 145 H7
Westcote Ri RSLP HA4 46 A6
Westcote Rd
STRHM/NOR SW16 148 C4
Westcott Cl BMLY BR1 168 D4
CROY/NA CR0 179 K7
SEVS/STOTM N15 56 B5
Westcott Crs HNWL W7 84 E4
Westcott House
POP/IOD E14 * 93 J6
Westcott Rd WALW SE17 18 D9
West Ct ALP/SUD HA0 67 J1
Westcroft Cl CRICK NW2 70 C3
Westcroft Gdns MRDN SM4 161 J2
Westcroft Ms HMSMTH W6 * 106 D3
Westcroft Rd CAR SM5 176 A3
Westcroft Sq HMSMTH W6 106 D3
Westcroft Wy CRICK NW2 70 C3
West Cross Route NTGHL W11 88 B7
West Cross Wy BTFD TW8 104 C5
Westdale Rd
WOOL/PLUM SE18 115 G5
Westdean Av LEE/GVPK SE12 134 A7
Westdean Cl
WAND/EARL SW18 128 A5
Westdown Rd CAT SE6 132 D6
SRTFD E15 76 A3
West Drayton Park Av
WDR/YW UB7 100 B2
West Drayton Rd
UX/CGN UB8 82 A4
West Dr BELMT SM2 174 B7
KTN/HRWW/WS HA3 34 D5
STRHM/NOR SW16 148 B3
West Drive Gdns
KTN/HRWW/WS HA3 34 D5
West Eaton Pl BGVA SW1W 16 A5
West Eaton Place Ms
KTBR SW1X 16 A5
West Ella Rd WLSDN NW10 69 G6
West End Av LEY E10 58 A4
PIN HA5 47 H3
West End Cl WLSDN NW10 68 E6
West End Ct PIN HA5 * 47 H3
West End Gdns NTHLT UB5 83 G1
West End La BAR EN5 26 B3
HYS/HAR UB3 101 F6
KIL/WHAMP NW6 2 B4
PIN HA5 47 H3
West End Rd NTHLT UB5 65 G6
RSLP HA4 64 D2
STHL UB1 83 J7
Westerfield Rd
SEVS/STOTM N15 * 56 B4
Westergate Rd ABYW SE2 117 F5
Westerham Av ED N9 41 K2
Westerham Dr BFN/LL DA15 136 D5
Westerham Rd HAYES BR2 181 H5
LEY E10 57 K5
Westerley Crs SYD SE26 * 151 H4
Western Av DAGE RM10 80 E5
EA W5 86 A2
GFD/PVL UB6 66 A7
GLDGN NW11 52 B5
RSLP HA4 65 F6
Western Ct FNCH N3 * 38 E5
Western Gdns EA W5 86 C6
Western Gtwy CAN/RD E16 94 E6
Western La BAL SW12 129 F6
Western Man BAR EN5 * 27 F4
Western Ms MV/WKIL W9 88 D3
Western Pde BAR EN5 26 E4
Western Pl BERM/RHTH SE16 111 K1
Western Rd BRXN/ST SW9 130 B2
EA W5 85 K6
EFNCH N2 53 K2
MTCM CR4 147 J7
NWDGN UB2 102 B3
PLSTW E13 77 F7
ROM RM1 63 G4
SUT SM1 174 E4
WALTH E17 58 A4
WDGN N22 55 F1
WLSDN NW10 86 E3
Western Ter HMSMTH W6 * 106 D4
Western Vw HYS/HAR UB3 101 J1
Westernville Gdns
GNTH/NBYPK IG2 60 C6
Western Wy BAR EN5 26 E5
THMD SE28 115 J2
Westferry Circ POP/IOD E14 93 J7
Westferry Rd POP/IOD E14 112 D2
Westfield Cl CDALE/KGS NW9 50 E2
PEND EN3 31 G2
SUT SM1 174 D3
WBPTN SW10 108 B6
Westfield Dr
KTN/HRWW/WS HA3 49 K4
Westfield Gdns CHDH RM6 61 J5
KTN/HRWW/WS HA3 49 K3
Westfield Pk PIN HA5 33 K6
Westfield Park Dr WFD IG8 45 J5
Westfield Rd BECK BR3 166 C1
CROY/NA CR0 177 H1
DAGW RM9 80 A3
MLHL NW7 37 F2
MTCM CR4 162 D1
SURB KT6 158 E4
SUT SM1 174 D3
WEA W13 85 G7
WOT/HER KT12 156 D6
Westfields BARN SW13 126 C2
Westfields Av BARN SW13 126 B2
Westfields Rd ACT W3 86 D4
Westfield St
WOOL/PLUM SE18 114 C2
Westfield Wy RSLP HA4 64 C2
WCHPL E1 93 G2
West Gdns TOOT SW17 147 J5
WAP E1W 92 D6
West Ga EA W5 86 A2
Westgate Est
EBED/NFELT TW14 * 120 E7
West Gate Ms WATW WD18 20 C4
Westgate Rd BECK BR3 152 A7
SNWD SE25 165 J3
Westgate St HACK E8 74 D7
Westgate Ter WBPTN SW10 14 D8
Westglade Ct
KTN/HRWW/WS HA3 49 K4
West Green Pl GFD/PVL UB6 66 D7
West Green Rd
SEVS/STOTM N15 55 H3
West Gv GNWCH SE10 113 F7
WFD IG8 45 G5
Westgrove La GNWCH SE10 113 F7
West Halkin St KTBR SW1X 16 A3
West Hallowes ELTH/MOT SE9 134 C7
West Ham La SRTFD E15 76 B6
West Hampstead Ms
KIL/WHAMP NW6 71 F5
West Harding St
FLST/FETLN EC4A * 12 B4
West Hatch Mnr RSLP HA4 46 D7
Westhay Gdns
MORT/ESHN SW14 125 J4
West Heath Av GLDGN NW11 52 E7
West Heath Cl DART DA1 * 138 C5
HAMP NW3 70 E2
West Heath Dr GLDGN NW11 52 E7
West Heath Gdns HAMP NW3 70 E1
West Heath Rd ABYW SE2 116 E5
HAMP NW3 70 E1
West Hl PUT/ROE SW15 127 H5
RYLN/HDSTN HA2 66 E1
SAND/SEL CR2 178 A7
WAND/EARL SW18 127 K4
WBLY HA9 50 B7
WIM/MER SW19 127 G6
Westhill Pk HGT N6 71 K1
West Hill Rd
WAND/EARL SW18 127 J5
West Hill Wy TRDG/WHET N20 27 F7
Westholm GLDGN NW11 53 F3
West Holme ERITH DA8 117 K7
Westholme ORP BR6 169 K6
Westholme Gdns RSLP HA4 46 E7
Westhorne Av ELTH/MOT SE9 134 B5
Westhorpe Gdns HDN NW4 52 A2
Westhorpe Rd PUT/ROE SW15 127 F2
West House Cl
WIM/MER SW19 127 H7
Westhurst Dr CHST BR7 154 B4
West India Av POP/IOD E14 93 J7
West India Dock Rd
POP/IOD E14 93 K6
Westlake Cl PLMGR N13 41 G2
YEAD UB4 83 J3
Westland Cl
STWL/WRAY TW19 * 120 B5
Westland Dr HAYES BR2 180 D1
Westland Pl FSBYE EC1V 7 G7
Westland Rd WAT WD17 * 21 F1
Westlands Cl HYS/HAR UB3 101 K3
Westlands Ter BAL SW12 129 H5
West La BERM/RHTH SE16 111 J1
Westlea Rd HNWL W7 104 B2
Westleigh Av PUT/ROE SW15 127 F4
Westleigh Dr BMLY BR1 168 D1
Westleigh Gdns EDGW HA8 36 C7
West Links ALP/SUD HA0 85 K2
Westlinton Cl MLHL NW7 38 C5
West Lodge Av ACT W3 86 C7
West Lodge Ct ACT W3 * 86 C7
Westmacott Dr
EBED/NFELT TW14 121 J6
West Malling Wy HCH RM12 81 K4
West Md HOR/WEW KT19 173 G5
Westmead PUT/ROE SW15 126 E6
West Md RSLP HA4 65 G3
Westmead Rd SUT SM1 175 H3
Westmere Dr MLHL NW7 37 F2
West Mersea Cl CAN/RD E16 95 F7
West Ms PIM SW1V 16 D6
TOTM N17 * 42 D6
Westminster Av THHTH CR7 164 C1
Westminster Br WHALL SW1A 17 K2
Westminster Bridge Rd
WHALL SW1A 17 K2
Westminster Cl
EBED/NFELT TW14 121 K7
TEDD TW11 143 G4
Westminster Dr PLMGR N13 40 E4
Westminster Gdns BARK IG11 96 E1
BARK/HLT IG6 60 D1
Westminster Rd ED N9 30 D7
HNWL W7 84 E7
SUT SM1 175 H1
Westmoat Cl BECK BR3 152 A6
Westmont Rd ESH/CLAY KT10 170 E1
Westmoor Gdns PEND EN3 31 F1
Westmoor Rd PEND EN3 31 F1
Westmoor St CHARL SE7 114 C3
Westmoreland Av WELL DA16 135 K2
Westmoreland Dr BELMT SM2 175 F7
Westmoreland Pl BMLY BR1 * 167 K2
EA W5 * 85 K4
PIM SW1V 16 D8
Westmoreland Rd
BARN SW13 106 C7
CMBW SE5 18 F9
HAYES BR2 167 H4
KTN/HRWW/WS HA3 50 B3
WWKM BR4 167 H4
Westmoreland St
CAVSQ/HST W1G 10 B3
Westmoreland Ter
PGE/AN SE20 * 150 D6
PIM SW1V 16 D7
Westmorland Cl MNPK E12 77 H1
TWK TW1 124 C5
Westmorland Rd HRW HA1 48 B4
WALTH E17 57 J5
Westmorland Wy MTCM CR4 163 J3
Westmount Ct EA W5 * 86 B4
Westmount Rd
ELTH/MOT SE9 134 E1
ELTH/MOT SE9 135 F4
West Oak BECK BR3 152 B7
Westoe Rd ED N9 42 D1
Weston Av E/WMO/HCT KT8 156 D3
THDIT KT7 157 K6
Weston Dr STAN HA7 35 H7
Weston Gdns ISLW TW7 103 J7
Weston Gn DAGW RM9 80 A3
THDIT KT7 170 E1
Weston Green Rd
ESH/CLAY KT10 157 J7
Weston Gv BMLY BR1 152 D6
Weston Pk CEND/HSY/T N8 54 E5
KUT/HW KT1 159 F1
THDIT KT7 157 K7
Weston Park Cl THDIT KT7 * 157 K7
Weston Ri FSBYW WC1X 5 M7
Weston Rd BMLY BR1 152 D7
CHSWK W4 105 K2
DAGW RM9 80 A3
ENC/FH EN2 29 K1
THDIT KT7 157 K7
Weston St STHWK SE1 19 H3
Weston Wk HACK E8 74 D6
Westover Cl BELMT SM2 175 F7
Westover Hl HAMP NW3 70 E1
Westover Rd
WAND/EARL SW18 128 B5
Westow Hl NRWD SE19 150 A5
Westow St NRWD SE19 150 A5
West Pk ELTH/MOT SE9 153 J1
West Park Av RCH/KEW TW9 105 H7
West Park Cl CHDH RM6 61 K4
HEST TW5 102 E5
West Park Rd NWDGN UB2 84 C7
RCH/KEW TW9 105 H7
West Parkside GNWCH SE10 113 H1
West Pl NWDGN UB2 * 103 G3
WIM/MER SW19 146 A4
Westpole Av EBAR EN4 28 B3
Westport Rd PLSTW E13 95 F3
Westport St WCHPL E1 93 F5
West Poultry Av FARR EC1M 12 C3
West Quarters SHB W12 87 J5
West Quay Dr YEAD UB4 83 J4
West Ridge Gdns
GFD/PVL UB6 84 C1
West Ri BAY/PAD W2 * 9 K6
West Rd CHDH RM6 62 A5
CHEL SW3 15 M9
CLAP SW4 129 J4
EA W5 86 A4
EBAR EN4 28 A7
EBED/NFELT TW14 121 G6
KUTN/CMB KT2 144 E7
ROMW/RG RM7 63 F6
SRTFD E15 76 D7
TOTM N17 42 D5
WDR/YW UB7 100 C2
West Rw NKENS W10 88 C3
Westrow Dr BARK IG11 79 F5
Westrow Gdns
GDMY/SEVK IG3 79 F1
West Sheen V RCH/KEW TW9 125 G3
Westside HDN NW4 51 K1
West Side Common
WIM/MER SW19 146 A4
West Smithfield STBT EC1A 12 C3
West Sq LBTH SE11 18 C4
West St BETH E2 92 D1
BMLY BR1 152 E7
CAR SM5 175 K2
CROY/NA CR0 177 J3
HRW HA1 48 D7
LSQ/SEVD WC2H 11 H5
SUT SM1 175 F4
WALTH E17 57 K4
WAN E11 76 C2
WAT WD17 21 F1
West Street La CAR SM5 175 K3
West Street Pl CROY/NA CR0 * 177 J3
West Temple Sheen
MORT/ESHN SW14 125 J4
West Tenter St WCHPL E1 13 M5
West Ter BFN/LL DA15 * 135 K7
West Towers PIN HA5 47 H5
West Vw EBED/NFELT TW14 121 F7
Westview HNWL W7 84 E5
Westview Cl NKENS W10 88 A5
WLSDN NW10 69 H4
Westview Ct BORE WD6 23 K5
Westview Crs ED N9 30 A6
Westview Dr WFD IG8 59 H1
West View Gdns BORE WD6 23 K5
Westville Rd SHB W12 106 D1
THDIT KT7 158 B6
West Wk EBAR EN4 28 A7
HYS/HAR UB3 82 E7
Westward Rd CHING E4 43 H4
Westward Wy
KTN/HRWW/WS HA3 50 A5
West Warwick Pl PIM SW1V * 16 E6
West Wy CROY/NA CR0 179 G1
EDGW HA8 36 D5
HEST TW5 102 E7
PIN HA5 47 H2
RSLP HA4 46 D7
STMC/STPC BR5 169 J4
UED N18 41 K3
WLSDN NW10 69 F3
WWKM BR4 167 G5
Westway BAY/PAD W2 8 E3
NKENS W10 88 D4
RYNPK SW20 160 E3
SHB W12 87 J6
Westway Cl RYNPK SW20 160 E2
West Way Gdns CROY/NA CR0 179 F1
Westways HOR/WEW KT19 173 H3
Westwell Rd
STRHM/NOR SW16 148 E5
Westwell Road Ap
STRHM/NOR SW16 148 E5
Westwick Gdns HMSMTH W6 107 G1
HSLWW TW4 122 A1
Westwood Av NRWD SE19 149 J7
RYLN/HDSTN HA2 66 B3
Westwood Cl BMLY BR1 168 C2
ESH/CLAY KT10 170 C2
Westwood Gdns BARN SW13 126 C2
Westwood Hl SYD SE26 150 C4
Westwood La WELL DA16 136 B3
Westwood Pk FSTH SE23 131 J6
Westwood Pl SYD SE26 * 150 C4
Westwood Rd BARN SW13 126 C2
GDMY/SEVK IG3 61 F7
West Woodside BXLY DA5 137 F7
Wetheral Dr STAN HA7 35 H7
Wetherby Cl NTHLT UB5 66 B5
Wetherby Gdns ECT SW5 14 E6
Wetherby Ms ECT SW5 14 D7
Wetherby Pl SKENS SW7 14 E6
Wetherby Wy CHSGTN KT9 172 A6
Wetherden St WALTH E17 57 H6
Wetherell Rd HOM E9 75 F7
Wetherill Rd MUSWH N10 40 A7
Wexford Rd BAL SW12 128 E6
Weybourne St
WAND/EARL SW18 147 G1
Weybridge Ct
BERM/RHTH SE16 * 111 J4
Weybridge Rd THHTH CR7 164 B3
Wey Ct HOR/WEW KT19 172 E3
Weydown Cl WIM/MER SW19 127 H7
Weyhill Rd WCHPL E1 * 92 C5
Weylond Rd BCTR RM8 80 B2
Weyman Rd BKHTH/KID SE3 114 B7
Weymouth Av EA W5 104 D2
MLHL NW7 37 G4
Weymouth Cl EHAM E6 96 B5
Weymouth Ct BELMT SM2 * 175 F6
Weymouth Ms
CAVSQ/HST W1G 10 C2
Weymouth Rd YEAD UB4 82 C2
Weymouth St
CAVSQ/HST W1G 10 B2
Weymouth Ter BETH E2 7 M5
Weymouth Vls FSBYPK N4 * 73 F1
Weymouth Wk STAN HA7 35 G5
Whadcoat St FSBYPK N4 73 G1

Whalebone Av CHDH RM6 62 B5
Whalebone Gv CHDH RM6 62 B5
Whalebone La North
CHDH RM6 62 A3
Whalebone La South
BCTR RM8 62 B6
Whales Yd SRTFD E15 * 76 C6
Wharfdale Cl FBAR/BDGN N11 40 A5
Wharfdale Rd IS N1 5 K5
Wharfedale Gdns THHTH CR7 164 A3
Wharfedale St WBPTN SW10 14 C8
Wharf La POP/IOD E14 93 H5
TWK TW1 124 B7
Wharf Pl BETH E2 74 C7
Wharf Rd CAMTN NW1 5 H4
PEND EN3 31 G5
SRTFD E15 76 B7
Wharfside Rd POP/IOD E14 94 C5
Wharf St CAN/RD E16 94 C4
Wharf Ter PUT/ROE SW15 127 H2
Wharncliffe Dr STHL UB1 84 D7
Wharncliffe Gdns SNWD SE25 165 F1
Wharncliffe Rd SNWD SE25 164 E1
Wharton Cl WLSDN NW10 69 G5
Wharton Cots FSBYW WC1X * 5 M8
Wharton Rd BMLY BR1 153 F7
Wharton St FSBYW WC1X 5 M8
Whateley Rd EDUL SE22 131 G4
PGE/AN SE20 151 F6
Whatley Av RYNPK SW20 161 G2
Whatman Rd FSTH SE23 132 A6
Wheastone Rd NKENS W10 * 88 C4
Wheatfield Wy KUT/HW KT1 159 F1
Wheathill Rd PGE/AN SE20 165 J1
Wheatlands HEST TW5 103 F5
Wheatlands Rd TOOT SW17 148 A2
Wheatley Cl HDN NW4 51 J1
Wheatley Crs HYS/HAR UB3 82 E6
Wheatley Gdns ED N9 42 A1
Wheatley Rd ISLW TW7 124 A2
Wheatley St CAVSQ/HST W1G 10 B3
Wheatsheaf Cl NTHLT UB5 65 J4
Wheat Sheaf Cl POP/IOD E14 112 D3
Wheatsheaf La FUL/PGN SW6 107 F6
VX/NE SW8 109 K6
Wheatsheaf Rd ROM RM1 63 H5
Wheatsheaf Ter
FUL/PGN SW6 * 107 J6
Wheatstone Cl
WIM/MER SW19 147 H7
Wheatstone Rd NKENS W10 88 C4
Wheeler Gdns IS N1 5 K3
Wheeler La WCHPL E1 13 L2
Wheeler Pl HAYES BR2 168 A3
Wheelers Cross BARK IG11 96 D1
Wheelers Dr RSLP HA4 46 A5
Wheelers's St SUT SM1 174 E2
Wheel Farm Dr DAGE RM10 80 E2
Wheelright Cl BUSH WD23 22 B5
Wheelwright St HOLWY N7 5 L1
Whelan Wy WLGTN SM6 176 D2
Wheler St WCHPL E1 13 L1
Whellock Rd CHSWK W4 106 B2
Whetstone Cl
TRDG/WHET N20 39 H1
Whetstone Pk LINN WC2A 11 L4
Whetstone Rd
BKHTH/KID SE3 134 B1
Whewell Rd ARCH N19 72 E1
Whichcote St STHWK SE1 * 12 A9
Whidborne Cl DEPT SE8 132 D1
Whidborne St STPAN WC1H 5 K8
Whimbrel Wy YEAD UB4 83 H5
Whinchat Rd THMD SE28 115 J2
Whinfell Cl STRHM/NOR SW16 148 D4
Whinyates Rd ELTH/MOT SE9 134 D2
Whippendell Cl
STMC/STPC BR5 155 H7
Whippendell Rd WATW WD18 20 C4
Whippendell Wy
STMC/STPC BR5 155 H7
Whipps Cross Rd WAN E11 58 C4
Whiskin St CLKNW EC1R 6 C8
Whistler Gdns EDGW HA8 50 B1
Whistlers Av BTSEA SW11 * 108 C6
Whistler St HBRY N5 73 H3
Whistler Wk WBPTN SW10 * 108 B6
Whiston Rd BETH E2 7 L5
Whitacre Ms LBTH SE11 18 B8
Whitbread Cl TOTM N17 42 C7
Whitbread Rd BROCKY SE4 132 B3
Whitburn Rd LEW SE13 132 E4
Whitby Av WLSDN NW10 86 D2
Whitby Gdns CDALE/KGS NW9 50 C2
SUT SM1 175 H1
Whitby Pde RSLP HA4 * 65 G1
Whitby Rd RSLP HA4 65 G1
RYLN/HDSTN HA2 66 C2
SUT SM1 175 H1
WOOL/PLUM SE18 114 E3
Whitby St WCHPL E1 7 L9
Whitcher Cl NWCR SE14 112 B5
Whitcher Pl CAMTN NW1 72 C5
Whitchurch Av EDGW HA8 36 B6
Whitchurch Cl EDGW HA8 36 B5
Whitchurch Gdns EDGW HA8 36 B5
Whitchurch La EDGW HA8 35 A6
Whitchurch Pde EDGW HA8 * 36 C6
Whitchurch Rd NKENS W10 88 B6
Whitcomb St
SOHO/SHAV W1D 11 G6
Whitcome Ms RCH/KEW TW9 105 J7
Whiteadder Wy POP/IOD E14 112 E3
Whitear Wk SRTFD E15 76 B5
Whitebarn La DAGE RM10 80 C7
Whitebeam Av HAYES BR2 169 F6
Whitebeam Cl VX/NE SW8 * 110 A6
White Bear Pl HAMP NW3 * 71 H3
White Bear Yd CLKNW EC1R * 12 A1
White Bridge Av MTCM CR4 162 C3
White Bridge Cl
EBED/NFELT TW14 121 J5
White Butts Rd RSLP HA4 65 H2
Whitechapel High St
TWRH EC3N 13 M4
Whitechapel Rd WCHPL E1 92 C5
White Church La WCHPL E1 92 C5
White City Cl SHB W12 88 A6
White City Rd SHB W12 87 K6
White Conduit St IS N1 6 B5
Whitecote Rd STHL UB1 84 C5
White Craig Cl PIN HA5 34 A4
Whitecroft Cl BECK BR3 167 G3
Whitecroft Wy BECK BR3 167 F3
Whitecross St STLK EC1Y 6 F9
Whitefield Av CRICK NW2 52 A6
Whitefield Cl PUT/ROE SW15 127 H5
Whitefoot La BMLY BR1 152 B3
Whitefoot Ter BMLY BR1 152 D2
Whitefriars Av
KTN/HRWW/WS HA3 48 E1
Whitefriars Dr
KTN/HRWW/WS HA3 48 E1
Whitefriars St EMB EC4Y 12 B5
White Gdns DAGE RM10 80 C5
White Gate Gdns
KTN/HRWW/WS HA3 34 E6
White Gates THDIT KT7 158 B6
Whitehall WHALL SW1A 11 J9
Whitehall Cl BORE WD6 24 C3
Whitehall Ct WHALL SW1A 11 J9
Whitehall Crs CHSGTN KT9 171 K4
Whitehall Gdns ACT W3 86 C7
CHSWK W4 105 J5
WHALL SW1A 11 J9
Whitehall La BKHH IG9 44 E1
ERITH DA8 138 C1
Whitehall Pk ARCH N19 54 C7
Whitehall Park Rd CHSWK W4 105 J5
Whitehall Pl WHALL SW1A 11 J9
WLGTN SM6 176 B3
Whitehall Rd CHING E4 44 C1
HAYES BR2 168 C4
HNWL W7 104 B1
HRW HA1 48 E6
THHTH CR7 164 B4
WFD IG8 44 E2
Whitehall St TOTM N17 42 B6
White Hart Av
WOOL/PLUM SE18 116 A2
White Hart La BARN SW13 126 B1
WDGN N22 41 G7
White Hart Rd
WOOL/PLUM SE18 115 K3
White Hart St LBTH SE11 18 B7
White Hart Ter TOTM N17 * 42 B6
White Hart Yd STHWK SE1 13 G9
Whitehaven St STJWD NW8 9 J1
Whitehead Cl UED N18 41 K4
WAND/EARL SW18 128 B6
Whiteheads Gv CHEL SW3 15 K6
Whitehead's Gv CHEL SW3 15 K7
White Heart Av UX/CGN UB8 82 A4
Whiteheath Av RSLP HA4 46 A6
White Heron Ms TEDD TW11 * 143 F5
White Horse Hl CHST BR7 154 A3
Whitehorse La SNWD SE25 165 F3
White Horse La WCHPL E1 93 F3
Whitehorse Rd CROY/NA CR0 164 D6
White Horse Rd EHAM E6 95 K2
White Horse Rd WCHPL E1 93 G4
White Horse Rd WCHPL E1 93 G5
White Horse St
MYFR/PICC W1J 10 D9
Whitehouse Av BORE WD6 24 D3
White House Dr STAN HA7 35 J3
Whitehouse Wy
STHGT/OAK N14 40 B1
Whitehurst Dr UED N18 * 43 F4
White Kennett St
HDTCH EC3A 13 K4
Whitelands Crs
WAND/EARL SW18 127 H6
White Ledges WEA W13 85 J5
Whitelegg Rd PLSTW E13 94 D1
Whiteley Rd NRWD SE19 149 K4
Whiteleys Wy FELT TW13 142 A2
White Lion Ct LOTH EC2R 13 J5
PECK SE15 * 111 K5
White Lion Hl BLKFR EC4V 12 D6
White Lion St IS N1 6 A6
White Ldg NRWD SE19 149 H6
White Lodge Cl BELMT SM2 175 G6
EFNCH N2 53 H5
ISLW TW7 124 B1
The White Ldg BAR EN5 * 26 C2
White Lyon Ct STBT EC1A 12 E2
White Oak Dr BECK BR3 167 F1
White Oak Gdns BFN/LL DA15 136 A6
Whiteoaks La GFD/PVL UB6 84 D1
White Orchards STAN HA7 35 G4
TRDG/WHET N20 26 D6
White Post La HOM E9 75 H6
White Post St NWCR SE14 111 K6
White Rd SRTFD E15 76 C6
Whites Av GNTH/NBYPK IG2 60 E5
White's Grounds STHWK SE1 19 K1
Whites Grounds Est
STHWK SE1 19 K1
Whites Meadow BMLY BR1 * 169 F3
White's Rw WCHPL E1 13 L3
White's Sq CLAP SW4 129 J3
Whitestile Rd BTFD TW8 104 D4
Whitestone La HAMP NW3 71 G2
Whitestone Wk HAMP NW3 71 G2
White St STHL UB1 102 C1
Whitethorn Gdns
CROY/NA CR0 178 D1
ENC/FH EN2 29 K4
Whitethorn St BOW E3 93 J3
White Tower Wy WCHPL E1 93 G4
Whitewebbs Wy
STMC/STPC BR5 155 F7
Whitfield Ct RYNPK SW20 161 G1
Whitfield Pl FITZ W1T 10 E1
Whitfield Rd EHAM E6 77 G6
GNWCH SE10 113 G7
Whitfield St FITZ W1T 10 F2
Whitford Gdns MTCM CR4 162 E2
Whitgift Av SAND/SEL CR2 177 J4
Whitgift St CROY/NA CR0 177 J2
STHWK SE1 17 L5
Whitings Rd BAR EN5 26 A4
Whitings Wy EHAM E6 96 A4
Whitland Rd CAR SM5 162 C7
Whitley Cl STWL/WRAY TW19 120 B5
Whitley Rd TOTM N17 56 A1
Whitlock Dr WIM/MER SW19 127 H6
Whitman Rd WCHPL E1 93 G3
Whitmead Cl SAND/SEL CR2 177 K5
Whitmore Cl FBAR/BDGN N11 40 B4
Whitmore Est IS N1 7 K4
Whitmore Gdns WLSDN NW10 88 A1
Whitmore Rd BECK BR3 166 C2
HRW HA1 48 C6
IS N1 7 J4
Whitnell Wy PUT/ROE SW15 * 127 F4
Whitney Av REDBR IG4 59 H3
Whitney Rd LEY E10 57 J6
Whitstable Cl BECK BR3 151 H7
Whitstable Pl CROY/NA CR0 177 J3
Whittaker Av RCH/KEW TW9 * 124 E4
Whittaker Rd CHEAM SM3 174 D2
EHAM E6 77 G6
Whittaker St BCVA SW1W 16 A6
Whitta Rd MNPK E12 77 H3
Whittell Gdns SYD SE26 150 E2
Whittingstall Rd
FUL/PGN SW6 107 J7
Whittington Av BANK EC3V 13 J5
YEAD UB4 82 D4
Whittington Ms
NFNCH/WDSPK N12 39 G3
Whittington Rd WDGN N22 40 E6
Whittington Wy PIN HA5 47 J4
Whittlebury Cl CAR SM5 175 K6
Whittle Cl STHL UB1 84 B5
WALTH E17 57 G5
Whittle Rd HEST TW5 102 B6
NWDGN UB2 103 G1
Whittlesea Rd
KTN/HRWW/WS HA3 34 C6
Whittlesey St STHWK SE1 12 B9
Whitton Av East
GFD/PVL UB6 67 F4
Whitton Av West NTHLT UB5 66 B4
Whitton Cl GFD/PVL UB6 67 H5
Whitton Dene HSLW TW3 123 G4
Whitton Dr GFD/PVL UB6 67 G5
Whitton Manor Rd
WHTN TW2 123 H5
Whitton Rd HSLW TW3 123 G4
Whitton Waye HSLW TW3 123 F5
Whitwell Rd PLSTW E13 94 E2
Whitworth Rd SNWD SE25 165 F2
WOOL/PLUM SE18 115 F6
Whitworth St GNWCH SE10 113 H4
Whorlton Rd PECK SE15 131 H2
Whybridge Cl RAIN RM13 81 G7
Whymark Av WDGN N22 55 G2
Whytecroft HEST TW5 102 C6
Whyteville Rd FSTGT E7 77 F5
Wickersley Rd BTSEA SW11 129 F1
Wickers Oake NRWD SE19 150 B3
Wicker St WCHPL E1 * 92 D5
Wicket Rd GFD/PVL UB6 85 G2
The Wicket CROY/NA CR0 179 J4
Wickford St WCHPL E1 92 E3
Wickford Wy WALTH E17 57 F3
Wickham Av CHEAM SM3 174 A4
CROY/NA CR0 179 G1
Wickham Cha WWKM BR4 167 G6
Wickham Cl NWMAL KT3 160 C4
PEND EN3 30 D2
WCHPL E1 92 E4
Wickham Ct WWKM BR4 * 180 B3
Wickham Court Rd
WWKM BR4 180 A1
Wickham Crs WWKM BR4 180 A1
Wickham Gdns BROCKY SE4 132 C2
Wickham La ABYW SE2 116 B5
Wickham Ms BROCKY SE4 132 C1
Wickham Rd BECK BR3 166 E2
BROCKY SE4 132 C2
CHING E4 44 A6
CROY/NA CR0 178 E1
KTN/HRWW/WS HA3 48 D1
Wickham St LBTH SE11 17 L7
WELL DA16 116 B7
WELL DA16 135 K1
Wickham Wy BECK BR3 167 F4
Wick La BOW E3 93 J1
Wickliffe Av FNCH N3 52 C1
Wickliffe Gdns WBLY HA9 68 C1
Wicklow St FSBYW WC1X 5 L7
Wick Rd HOM E9 75 F5
TEDD TW11 143 H6
Wicks Cl LEE/GVPK SE12 153 H3
Wickstead Est CMBW SE5 130 C1
Widdenham Rd HOLWY N7 73 F3
Widdicombe Av
RYLN/HDSTN HA2 65 J1
Widdin St SRTFD E15 76 C6
Widecombe Gdns REDBR IG4 59 J3
Widecombe Rd
ELTH/MOT SE9 153 J2
Widecombe Wy EFNCH N2 53 H4
Widegate St WCHPL E1 13 K3
Widenham Cl PIN HA5 47 G4
Wide Wy MTCM CR4 163 J2
Widgeon Cl CAN/RD E16 95 F5
Widley Rd MV/WKIL W9 2 B8
Widmore Lodge Rd BMLY BR1 168 C1
Widmore Rd BMLY BR1 168 A1
Wieland Rd NTHWD HA6 32 E6
Wigeon Wy YEAD UB4 83 H5
Wiggenhall Rd WATW WD18 21 F4
Wiggins La RCHPK/HAM TW10 143 J1
Wiggins Md CDALE/KGS NW9 37 H6
Wigginton Av WBLY HA9 68 C5
Wightman Rd
CEND/HSY/T N8 55 G3
Wigley Rd FELT TW13 122 C7
Wigmore Pl MHST W1U * 10 C4
Wigmore Rd CAR SM5 175 H1
Wigmore St MHST W1U 10 B4
Wigram Rd WAN E11 59 G5
Wigram Sq WALTH E17 58 A2
Wigston Cl UED N18 42 A4
Wigston Rd PLSTW E13 95 F3
Wigton Gdns STAN HA7 36 A7
Wigton Pl LBTH SE11 18 B8
Wigton Rd WALTH E17 43 H7
Wilberforce Ms CLAP SW4 129 J3
Wilberforce Rd
CDALE/KGS NW9 51 J5
FSBYPK N4 73 H1
Wilberforce Wy
WIM/MER SW19 146 B5
Wilbraham Pl KTBR SW1X 16 A5
Wilbury Wy UED N18 41 K4
Wilby Ms NTGHL W11 88 D6
Wilcot Av OXHEY WD19 21 J6
Wilcot Cl OXHEY WD19 21 J6
Wilcox Cl VX/NE SW8 109 K6
Wilcox Rd SUT SM1 * 175 F3
TEDD TW11 142 D3
VX/NE SW8 109 K6
Wildacres NTHWD HA6 32 D3
Wild Ct HOL/ALD WC2B 11 L4
Wildcroft Gdns STAN HA7 35 K5
Wildcroft Rd PUT/ROE SW15 127 F6
Wilde Cl HACK E8 74 C7
Wilde Pl PLMGR N13 41 H5
WAND/EARL SW18 128 C6
Wilder Cl RSLP HA4 47 F7
Wilderness Ms CLAP SW4 129 G3
Wilderness Rd CHST BR7 154 B6
The Wilderness
E/WMO/HCT KT8 157 H4
HPTN TW12 * 142 B3
Wilderton Rd
STNW/STAM N16 56 A6
Wildfell Rd CAT SE6 132 E6
Wild Goose Dr NWCR SE14 111 K7
Wild Hatch GLDGN NW11 52 E5
Wild Oaks Cl NTHWD HA6 32 D5
Wild's Rents STHWK SE1 19 J3
Wild St HOL/ALD WC2B 11 K5
Wildwood NTHWD HA6 32 B5
Wildwood Cl LEE/GVPK SE12 133 J6
Wildwood Gv HAMP NW3 53 G7
Wildwood Ri GLDGN NW11 53 G7
Wildwood Rd GLDGN NW11 53 F5
Wildwood Ter HAMP NW3 53 G7
Wilford Cl ENC/FH EN2 * 29 K2
NTHWD HA6 32 B6
Wilfred Av RAIN RM13 99 J4
Wilfred Owen Cl
WIM/MER SW19 147 G5
Wilfred St WESTW SW1E 16 E3
Wilfrid Gdns ACT W3 86 E4
Wilkes Rd BTFD TW8 105 F5
Wilkes St WCHPL E1 13 M2
Wilkins Cl HYS/HAR UB3 101 J4
MTCM CR4 147 J7
Wilkinson Gdns SNWD SE25 150 A7
Wilkinson Rd CAN/RD E16 95 G5
Wilkinson St VX/NE SW8 110 A6
Wilkinson Wy CHSWK W4 106 A1
Wilkin St KTTN NW5 72 A5
Wilkin Street Ms KTTN NW5 72 A5
Wilks Gdns CROY/NA CR0 166 B7
Wilks Pl IS N1 7 K6
Willan Rd TOTM N17 55 K1
Willan Wall CAN/RD E16 94 D6
Willard St VX/NE SW8 129 G2
Willcocks Cl CHSGTN KT9 172 A2
Willcott Rd ACT W3 86 D7
Will Crooks Gdns
ELTH/MOT SE9 134 C3
Willenfield Rd WLSDN NW10 86 D1
Willenhall Av BAR EN5 27 G5
Willenhall Dr HYS/HAR UB3 82 C6
Willenhall Rd
WOOL/PLUM SE18 115 G4
Willersley Av BFN/LL DA15 136 A7
Willersley Cl BFN/LL DA15 136 A7
Willesden La
KIL/WHAMP NW6 70 B6
Willes Rd KTTN NW5 72 B5
Willett Cl NTHLT UB5 83 G2
STMC/STPC BR5 169 K5
Willett Rd THHTH CR7 164 B4
Willett Wy STMC/STPC BR5 169 J4
William Ash Cl DAGW RM9 79 H5
William Barefoot Dr
ELTH/MOT SE9 154 A1
ELTH/MOT SE9 154 A3
William Booth Rd
PGE/AN SE20 150 C7
William Carey Wy HRW HA1 48 E5
William Cl EFNCH N2 53 H1
LEW SE13 133 F2
NWDGN UB2 103 H1
William Dr STAN HA7 35 G5
William Ellis Wy
BERM/RHTH SE16 * 111 H2
William Foster La WELL DA16 116 B7
William Gdns PUT/ROE SW15 126 E4
William Guy Gdns BOW E3 93 K2
William IV St CHCR WC2N 11 J7
William Margrie Cl
PECK SE15 * 131 H1
William Ms KTBR SW1X 15 M2
William Morley Cl EHAM E6 77 H7
William Morris Cl WALTH E17 57 H2
William Morris Wy
FUL/PGN SW6 128 B2
William Rd CAMTN NW1 4 E8
SUT SM1 175 G4
WIM/MER SW19 146 C6
Williams Av WALTH E17 43 H7
William's Blds WCHPL E1 * 92 E3
Williams Cl CEND/HSY/T N8 * 54 D5
FUL/PGN SW6 107 H6
Williams Dr HSLW TW3 123 F3
Williams Gv SURB KT6 158 D5
WDGN N22 41 G7
Williams La MORT/ESHN SW14 125 K1
MRDN SM4 162 B5
Williamson Cl GNWCH SE10 113 J4
Williamson Rd FSBYPK N4 55 H5
Williamson St HOLWY N7 * 72 E3
Williamson Wy MLHL NW7 38 C5
William Sq BERM/RHTH SE16 93 G7
Williams Rd NWDGN UB2 102 D3
William's Rd WEA W13 * 85 G7
Williams Ter CROY/NA CR0 177 G5
William St BARK IG11 78 C6
BUSH WD23 21 H2
CAR SM5 175 J2
KTBR SW1X 15 M2
LEY E10 57 K5
TOTM N17 42 B6
Willifield Wy GLDGN NW11 52 E4
Willingdon Rd WDGN N22 55 H1
Willingham Cl KTTN NW5 72 C4
Willingham Ter KTTN NW5 * 72 C4
Willingham Wy KUT/HW KT1 159 H1
Willington Rd BRXN/ST SW9 129 K2
Willis Av BELMT SM2 175 J5
Willis Rd CROY/NA CR0 164 D6
ERITH DA8 117 K3
SRTFD E15 76 D7
Willis St POP/IOD E14 93 K5
Willmore End WIM/MER SW19 147 F7
Willoughby Av CROY/NA CR0 177 F3
Willoughby Dr RAIN RM13 81 G6
Willoughby Gv TOTM N17 42 D6
Willoughby La TOTM N17 42 D6
Willoughby Ms TOTM N17 42 D6
Willoughby Park Rd
TOTM N17 42 D6
Willoughby Rd
CEND/HSY/T N8 55 G2
HAMP NW3 71 H3
KUTN/CMB KT2 144 B7
TWK TW1 124 D4
Willoughby Wy CHARL SE7 114 A3
Willow Av BARN SW13 126 C1
BFN/LL DA15 136 B5
Willow Bank
RCHPK/HAM TW10 143 H2
Willowbay Cl BAR EN5 26 B5
Willow Bridge Rd IS N1 73 J5
Willowbrook HPTN TW12 142 B4
Willowbrook Est PECK SE15 * 111 G6
Willowbrook Rd NWDGN UB2 102 E2
PECK SE15 111 G5
STWL/WRAY TW19 120 B7
The Willow Centre MTCM CR4 162 E4
Willow Cl BKHH IG9 45 H2
BTFD TW8 104 D5
BXLY DA5 137 G5
CAT SE6 133 J7
HAYES BR2 168 E4
HCH RM12 81 K2
Willow Ct STAN HA7 * 35 K6
Willowcourt Av
KTN/HRWW/WS HA3 49 H4
Willow Dean PIN HA5 * 47 H1
Willow Dene PIN HA5 47 H1
BUSH WD23 22 E6
Willowdene HGT N6 * 53 K6
Willowdene Cl WHTN TW2 123 H6
Willow Dr BAR EN5 26 C3
Willow End NTHWD HA6 32 E5
SURB KT6 159 F7
TRDG/WHET N20 38 E1
Willowfields Cl
WOOL/PLUM SE18 115 K4
Willow Gdns HSLW TW3 * 103 F7
RSLP HA4 64 D1
Willow Gv CHST BR7 154 A5
RSLP HA4 64 D1
Willowhayne Dr
WOT/HER KT12 156 A6
Willowhayne Gdns WPK KT4 174 A3
Willow La MTCM CR4 162 E4
WATW WD18 20 E4
WOOL/PLUM SE18 114 E3
Willowmead Cl EA W5 85 K4
Willowmere ESH/CLAY KT10 170 C3
Willow Mt CROY/NA CR0 178 A3
Willow Pl WEST SW1P 16 F5
Willow Rd CHDH RM6 62 A5
EA W5 105 F1
EN EN1 30 A1
ERITH DA8 118 D7
HAMP NW3 71 H3
NWMAL KT3 159 K3
WLGTN SM6 176 B6
Willows Av MRDN SM4 162 A4
Willows Cl PIN HA5 47 G1
Willows Ter WLSDN NW10 * 87 H1
The Willows BECK BR3 * 151 J7
EBAR EN4 * 27 J5
ESH/CLAY KT10 170 E5
OXHEY WD19 21 F6
Willow St ROMW/RG RM7 62 E3
SDTCH EC2A 7 J9
Willow Ter PGE/AN SE20 * 150 D7
Willow Tree Cl NTHLT UB5 65 J5
WAND/EARL SW18 128 A7
YEAD UB4 83 G3
BOW E3 75 G7
Willowtree Cl HGDN/ICK UB10 64 A2
Willow Tree La YEAD UB4 83 G3
Willow Tree Rd YEAD UB4 83 H4
Willow Tree Wk BMLY BR1 153 F7
Willowtree Wy THHTH CR7 149 G7
Willow V CHST BR7 154 A5
SHB W12 87 J7
Willow Vw WIM/MER SW19 147 H7
Willow Wk CHEAM SM3 174 D2
DART DA1 * 139 H4
SEVS/STOTM N15 55 H3
STHWK SE1 19 K5
WALTH E17 57 H4
WCHMH N21 29 F5
Willow Wy ALP/SUD HA0 * 67 G2
FNCH N3 39 F6
HOR/WEW KT19 173 F5
NTGHL W11 88 B6
SYD SE26 150 D2
WHTN TW2 142 B1
Willow Wood Crs SNWD SE25 165 F5
Willow Wren Whf
NWDGN UB2 * 102 A3
Will Rd KTTN NW5 72 B5
Willrose Crs ABYW SE2 116 C4
Wills Crs HSLW TW3 123 G5
Wills Gv MLHL NW7 37 J4
Wilman Gv HACK E8 74 C6
Wilmar Cl YEAD UB4 82 B3
Wilmar Gdns WWKM BR4 166 E7
Wilmer Cl KUTN/CMB KT2 144 B4
Wilmer Crs KUTN/CMB KT2 144 B4
Wilmer Gdns IS N1 7 J4
Wilmer Lea Cl SRTFD E15 76 A6
Wilmer Pl STNW/STAM N16 74 B1
Wilmer Wy FBAR/BDGN N11 40 D4
Wilmington Av CHSWK W4 106 A6
Wilmington Gdns BARK IG11 78 D6
Wilmington Sq FSBYW WC1X 6 A8
Wilmington St FSBYW WC1X 6 A8
Wilmot Cl PECK SE15 * 111 H6
Wilmot Pl CAMTN NW1 4 E1
HNWL W7 84 E7
Wilmot Rd CAR SM5 * 175 K4
LEY E10 75 K1
TOTM N17 55 K2
Wilmot St BETH E2 92 D3
Wilmount St
WOOL/PLUM SE18 115 G3
Wilna Rd WAND/EARL SW18 128 B6
Wilsham St NTGHL W11 88 B7
Wilshaw Cl HDN NW4 51 J2
Wilshaw St NWCR SE14 112 D7
Wilsmere Dr
KTN/HRWW/WS HA3 34 E6
NTHLT UB5 65 J5
Wilson Av MTCM CR4 147 J6
Wilson Cl SAND/SEL CR2 177 K4
WBLY HA9 50 B6
Wilson Dr WBLY HA9 50 B6
Wilson Gdns HRW HA1 48 C6
Wilson Gv BERM/RHTH SE16 111 J1
Wilson Rd CHSGTN KT9 172 B5
CMBW SE5 110 E7
IL IG1 59 K6
PLSTW E13 95 H2
Wilson's Av TOTM N17 56 B1
Wilson's Pl POP/IOD E14 93 H5
Wilson's Rd HMSMTH W6 107 G4
Wilson St LVPST EC2M 13 H2
WALTH E17 58 A4
WCHMH N21 29 G6
Wilson Wk CHSWK W4 * 106 C3
Wilstone Cl YEAD UB4 83 J3
Wilthorne Gdns DAGE RM10 80 D6
Wilton Av CHSWK W4 106 B4
Wilton Cl WDR/YW UB7 100 A5
Wilton Crs KTBR SW1X 16 A2
WIM/MER SW19 146 D7
Wilton Est HACK E8 * 74 C5
Wilton Gdns E/WMO/HCT KT8 157 F2
WOT/HER KT12 156 C7
Wilton Gv NWMAL KT3 160 C5
WIM/MER SW19 146 D6
Wilton Ms HACK E8 * 74 D5
KTBR SW1X 16 B3
Wilton Pl KTBR SW1X 16 A1
Wilton Rd EBAR EN4 27 K3
HSLWW TW4 122 C2
MUSWH N10 54 A1
PIM SW1V 16 D4
WIM/MER SW19 147 J6
Wilton Rw KTBR SW1X 16 A2
Wilton Sq IS N1 7 G3
Wilton St KTBR SW1X 16 C3
Wilton Ter KTBR SW1X 16 A3
Wilton Vls IS N1 7 G4
Wilton Wk FELT TW13 * 141 F1
Wilton Wy HACK E8 74 C5
Wiltshire Cl CHEL SW3 15 K6
MLHL NW7 * 37 H4
Wiltshire Gdns FSBYPK N4 55 J5
WHTN TW2 123 H7
Wiltshire La PIN HA5 46 D2
Wiltshire Rd BRXN/ST SW9 130 B2
THHTH CR7 164 B2

Wiltshire Rw IS N1 7 G4
Wilverley Crs NWMAL KT3 160 B5
Wimbart Rd
BRXS/STRHM SW2 * 130 A6
Wimbledon Br
WIM/MER SW19 146 D5
Wimbledon Hill Rd
WIM/MER SW19 146 C5
Wimbledon Park Rd
WIM/MER SW19 146 C2
Wimbledon Park Side
PUT/ROE SW15 126 E7
Wimbledon Rd TOOT SW17 147 G3
Wimbolt St BETH E2 92 C2
Wimborne Av NWDGN UB2 103 F3
YEAD UB4 83 F5
Wimborne Cl BKHH IG9 45 G1
LEE/GVPK SE12 133 J4
WPK KT4 161 F7
Wimborne Dr EDGW HA8 50 C2
PIN HA5 47 H6
Wimborne Gdns WEA W13 85 H5
Wimborne Rd ED N9 42 C1
TOTM N17 56 A1
Wimborne Wy BECK BR3 166 A2
Wimbourne St IS N1 7 G5
Wimpole Cl HAYES BR2 168 B3
KUT/HW KT1 159 G1
Wimpole Ms CAVSQ/HST W1G 10 C2
Wimpole St CAVSQ/HST W1G 10 C3
Wimshurst Cl CROY/NA CR0 163 K7
Winans Wk BRXN/ST SW9 130 B1
Wincanton Crs NTHLT UB5 66 A4
Wincanton Gdns
BARK/HLT IG6 60 B2
Wincanton Rd
WAND/EARL SW18 127 J6
Winchcombe Rd CAR SM5 175 H1
Winchcomb Gdns
ELTH/MOT SE9 134 C2
Winchelsea Cl PUT/ROE SW15 127 G4
Winchelsea Rd FSTGT E7 76 E3
TOTM N17 56 A2
WLSDN NW10 69 F7
Winchelsey Ri SAND/SEL CR2 178 B5
Winchendon Rd
FUL/PGN SW6 107 J6
TEDD TW11 142 D3
Winchester Av
CDALE/KGS NW9 50 B2
HEST TW5 102 E5
KIL/WHAMP NW6 70 C6
Winchester Cl EN EN1 * 30 A4
ESH/CLAY KT10 170 A3
HAYES BR2 167 J2
KUTN/CMB KT2 144 D6
LBTH SE11 * 18 D6
Winchester Dr PIN HA5 47 H4
Winchester Ms WPK KT4 174 B1
Winchester Pk HAYES BR2 167 J2
Winchester Pl HACK E8 74 B4
HGT N6 54 B7
Winchester Rd BXLYHN DA7 136 E1
CHING E4 44 A6
ED N9 30 B7
FELT TW13 141 K2
HAMP NW3 3 H1
HAYES BR2 167 J2
HGT N6 54 B7
HYS/HAR UB3 101 H6
IL IG1 78 D2
KTN/HRWW/WS HA3 50 A3
TWK TW1 124 C5
Winchester Sq STHWK SE1 13 G8
Winchester St ACT W3 86 E7
PIM SW1V 16 D7
Winchester Wk STHWK SE1 13 G8
Winchfield Cl
KTN/HRWW/WS HA3 49 J5
Winchfield Rd SYD SE26 151 G4
Winchilsea Crs
E/WMO/HCT KT8 157 H1
Winchmore Hill Rd
STHGT/OAK N14 28 D7
Winchmore Vls WCHMH N21 * 29 F6
Winckley Cl
KTN/HRWW/WS HA3 50 B4
Wincott St LBTH SE11 18 B5
Wincrofts Dr ELTH/MOT SE9 135 J3
Windall Cl NRWD SE19 150 C7
Windborough Rd CAR SM5 176 A6
Windermere Av FNCH N3 52 E1
HCH RM12 81 J4
KIL/WHAMP NW6 70 C7
RSLP HA4 47 G6
WBLY HA9 49 J7
WIM/MER SW19 162 A2
Windermere Cl
EBED/NFELT TW14 121 H7
Windermere Gdns REDBR IG4 59 J4
Windermere Gv WBLY HA9 49 J7
Windermere Hall EDGW HA8 * 36 B4
Windermere Rd ARCH N19 * 72 C1
BXLYHN DA7 137 K1
CROY/NA CR0 165 G7
EA W5 104 D2
MUSWH N10 40 B7
PUT/ROE SW15 145 G3
STHL UB1 83 K4
STRHM/NOR SW16 148 C7
WWKM BR4 180 C1
Winders Rd BTSEA SW11 128 D1
Windfield Cl SYD SE26 151 F3
Windham Rd RCH/KEW TW9 125 G2
Winding Wy BCTR RM8 79 J2
Windlass Pl DEPT SE8 112 B3
Windlesham Gv
WIM/MER SW19 127 G7
Windley Cl FSTH SE23 150 E1
Windmill Cl LEW SE13 * 133 F1
STHWK SE1 * 111 H3
SUN TW16 140 C6
SURB KT6 158 D7
Windmill Dr CLAP SW4 129 G4
CRICK NW2 70 C2
Windmill Gdns ENC/FH EN2 29 G1
Windmill Gv CROY/NA CR0 164 D6
Windmill Hl ENC/FH EN2 29 H2
HAMP NW3 * 71 G2
RSLP HA4 46 D6
Windmill La BAR EN5 25 H5
BUSH WD23 22 E7
GFD/PVL UB6 84 C4
HAYES BR2 181 G3
NWDGN UB2 103 H1
SRTFD E15 76 B5
SURB KT6 158 C6
Windmill Pas CHSWK W4 * 106 B3
Windmill Ri KUTN/CMB KT2 144 D6
Windmill Rd CHSWK W4 106 B3
CROY/NA CR0 164 D6
EA W5 104 D3
HPTN TW12 142 B4
MTCM CR4 163 H4
SUN TW16 140 C7
UED N18 41 K3
WAND/EARL SW18 128 C5
WIM/MER SW19 145 K4
Windmill Rd West SUN TW16 140 C7
Windmill Rw LBTH SE11 18 A8
Windmill St BUSH WD23 22 E7
FITZ W1T 11 G3
Windmill Wk STHWK SE1 * 12 B9
Windmill Wy RSLP HA4 46 D7
Windover Av CDALE/KGS NW9 51 F3
Windrose Cl
BERM/RHTH SE16 112 A1
Windrush NWMAL KT3 159 J3
Windrush Cl BTSEA SW11 * 128 C3
CHSWK W4 * 105 K6
HACK E8 74 C6
TOTM N17 42 A7
Windrush La FSTH SE23 151 F2
Windrush Rd WLSDN NW10 69 F7
Windsor Av CHEAM SM3 174 C2
E/WMO/HCT KT8 157 F2
EDGW HA8 36 D3
NWMAL KT3 159 K4
WALTH E17 57 G1
WIM/MER SW19 147 G7
Windsor Cl CHST BR7 154 B4
FNCH N3 52 C1
NTHWD HA6 46 E1
RYLN/HDSTN HA2 66 A2
WNWD SE27 149 J3
Windsor Ct NTHLT UB5 65 K4
PIN HA5 * 47 H2
STHGT/OAK N14 28 C6
Windsor Crs RYLN/HDSTN HA2 66 A2
WBLY HA9 68 C2
Windsor Dr EBAR EN4 27 K5
Windsor Gdns CROY/NA CR0 176 E2
HYS/HAR UB3 101 G2
MV/WKIL W9 8 A1
Windsor Gv WNWD SE27 149 J3
Windsor Ms CAT SE6 133 F7
Windsor Park Rd
HYS/HAR UB3 101 J6
Windsor Rd BAR EN5 26 B5
BCTR RM8 80 A2
CHING E4 43 K3
CRICK NW2 69 K5
EA W5 86 A6
FNCH N3 52 C1
FSTGT E7 77 F4
HOLWY N7 72 E2
HSLWW TW4 122 A1
IL IG1 78 C3
KTN/HRWW/WS HA3 34 C7
KUTN/CMB KT2 144 A6
LEY E10 75 K1
NWDGN UB2 102 E2
PLMGR N13 41 G2
RCH/KEW TW9 125 G1
SUN TW16 140 E6
TEDD TW11 142 D4
THHTH CR7 164 C1
TOTM N17 56 C1
WAN E11 58 E7
WPK KT4 173 J1
The Windsors BKHH IG9 45 J1
Windsor St IS N1 6 D3
Windsor Ter IS N1 6 F7
Windsor Wk CMBW SE5 130 E1
Windsor Wy WKENS W14 107 G3
Windspoint Dr PECK SE15 111 J5
Windstock Cl
BERM/RHTH SE16 112 C2
Windus Rd STNW/STAM N16 56 B7
Windy Rdg BMLY BR1 153 J7
Windy Ridge Cl
WIM/MER SW19 146 B4
Wine Cl WAP E1W 92 E6
Wine Office Ct
FLST/FETLN EC4A 12 B4
Winery La KUT/HW KT1 159 G2
Winey Cl CHSGTN KT9 171 J6
Winforton St GNWCH SE10 113 F7
Winfrith Rd WAND/EARL SW18 128 B6
Wingate Crs CROY/NA CR0 163 K5
Wingate Rd HMSMTH W6 106 E2
IL IG1 78 B4
SCUP DA14 155 J4
Wingfield Ct WATW WD18 * 20 B5
Wingfield Ms PECK SE15 131 H2
Wingfield Rd KUTN/CMB KT2 144 B5
SRTFD E15 76 C4
WALTH E17 57 K4
Wingfield St PECK SE15 131 H2
Wingfield Wy RSLP HA4 65 F5
Wingford Rd
BRXS/STRHM SW2 129 K5
Wingmore Rd HNHL SE24 130 D2
Wingrave Rd HMSMTH W6 107 F5
Wingrove Rd CAT SE6 152 C1
Wings Cl SUT SM1 174 E3
Winifred Cl BAR EN5 25 H5
Winifred Pl
NFNCH/WDSPK N12 39 G4
Winifred Rd BCTR RM8 80 A1
ERITH DA8 118 B4
HPTN TW12 142 A3
WIM/MER SW19 146 E7
Winifred St CAN/RD E16 95 K7
Winifred Ter EN EN1 30 B6
PLSTW E13 94 E1
Winkfield Rd WDGN N22 41 G7
Winkley St BETH E2 92 D1
Winkworth Cots WCHPL E1 * 92 E3
Winlaton Rd BMLY BR1 152 B3
Winmill Rd BCTR RM8 80 B2
Winn Common Rd
WOOL/PLUM SE18 115 K5
Winnett St SOHO/SHAV W1D 11 G6
Winnington Cl EFNCH N2 53 H5
Winnington Rd EFNCH N2 53 H6
Winns Av WALTH E17 57 H2
Winns Ms SEVS/STOTM N15 56 A3
Winns Ter WALTH E17 57 J1
Winsbeach WALTH E17 58 B2
Winscombe Crs EA W5 85 K3
Winscombe St KTTN NW5 72 B2
Winscombe Wy STAN HA7 35 G4
Winsford Rd CAT SE6 151 H2
Winsford Ter UED N18 * 41 K4
Winsham Gv BTSEA SW11 129 F4
Winslade Rd
BRXS/STRHM SW2 129 K4
Winsland Ms BAY/PAD W2 9 G4
Winsland St BAY/PAD W2 9 G4
Winsley St GTPST W1W 10 E4
Winslow Cl PIN HA5 47 F5
WLSDN NW10 69 G2
Winslow Gv CHING E4 44 C1
Winslow Rd HMSMTH W6 107 F5
Winslow Wy FELT TW13 141 H2
Winsor Ter EHAM E6 96 A4
Winstanley Rd BTSEA SW11 128 C2
Winstead Gdns DAGE RM10 80 E4
Winston Av CDALE/KGS NW9 51 G6
Winston Cl
KTN/HRWW/WS HA3 35 F5
ROMW/RG RM7 62 D3
Winston Ct
KTN/HRWW/WS HA3 34 B6
Winston House SURB KT6 * 159 F4
Winston Rd STNW/STAM N16 73 K3
Winston Wy IL IG1 78 B2
Winter Av EHAM E6 77 J7
Winterbourne Rd BCTR RM8 79 J1
CAT SE6 132 C7
THHTH CR7 164 B3
Winter Box Wk
RCHPK/HAM TW10 125 G4
Winterbrook Rd HNHL SE24 130 D5
Winterburn Cl
FBAR/BDGN N11 40 A5
Winterfold Cl WIM/MER SW19 146 C1
Winters Rd THDIT KT7 158 C6
Winterstoke Rd FSTH SE23 132 C7
Winterton Pl WBPTN SW10 14 F9
Winterwell Rd
BRXS/STRHM SW2 129 K4
Winthorpe Rd PUT/ROE SW15 127 H3
Winthorpe St WCHPL E1 92 D4
Winthrop St WCHPL E1 * 92 D4
Winton Ap RKW/CH/CXG WD3 20 A4
Winton Av FBAR/BDGN N11 40 C6
Winton Cl ED N9 31 F6
Winton Dr RKW/CH/CXG WD3 20 A4
Winton Gdns EDGW HA8 36 B6
The Wintons BUSH WD23 * 22 D7
Winton Wy STRHM/NOR SW16 149 G4
Wirral Wood Cl CHST BR7 154 A5
Wisbeach Rd CROY/NA CR0 164 E4
Wisborough Rd
SAND/SEL CR2 178 B7
Wisdons Cl DAGE RM10 62 D7
Wise La MLHL NW7 37 J5
WDR/YW UB7 100 A3
Wiseman Rd LEY E10 * 75 J1
Wise Rd SRTFD E15 76 A7
Wiseton Rd TOOT SW17 128 D7
Wishart Rd BKHTH/KID SE3 114 C7
Wishaw Wk FBAR/BDGN N11 40 E5
Wisley Rd BTSEA SW11 128 E4
STMC/STPC BR5 155 G6
Wisteria Cl IL IG1 78 B4
MLHL NW7 37 H5
Wisteria Rd LEW SE13 133 G3
Witanhurst La HGT N6 54 A7
Witan St BETH E2 92 D2
Witham Rd DAGE RM10 80 C4
GPK RM2 63 K4
ISLW TW7 103 J7
PGE/AN SE20 165 K2
WEA W13 85 G7
Witherby Cl CROY/NA CR0 178 A4
Witherington Rd HBRY N5 * 73 G4
Withers Md CDALE/KGS NW9 37 H7
Witherston Wy
ELTH/MOT SE9 154 A1
Withycombe Rd
WIM/MER SW19 127 G6
Withy La RSLP HA4 46 A4
Withy Md CHING E4 44 B2
Witley Crs CROY/NA CR0 180 A5
Witley Gdns NWDGN UB2 102 E3
Witley Rd ARCH N19 72 C1
Witney Cl PIN HA5 33 K5
Witney Pth FSTH SE23 151 F2
Wittenham Wy CHING E4 44 B2
Wittering Cl KUTN/CMB KT2 143 K4
Wittersham Rd BMLY BR1 152 D4
Wivenhoe Cl PECK SE15 131 H2
Wivenhoe Ct HSLW TW3 122 E3
Wivenhoe Rd BARK IG11 97 G1
Wiverton Rd SYD SE26 150 E5
Wix Rd DAGW RM9 79 K7
Wix's La CLAP SW4 129 G3
Woburn WEA W13 * 85 H4
Woburn Av HCH RM12 81 J3
Woburn Cl BUSH WD23 22 C5
THMD SE28 97 K5
WIM/MER SW19 147 G5
Woburn Pl STPAN WC1H 5 J9
Woburn Rd CAR SM5 162 D7
CROY/NA CR0 164 D7
Woburn Sq STPAN WC1H 11 H1
Woburn Wk STPAN WC1H * 5 H8
Wodeham Gdns WCHPL E1 92 C4
Wodehouse Av CMBW SE5 111 G7
Wodehouse Rd DART DA1 139 K3
Woffington Cl TEDD TW11 143 J6
Woking Cl PUT/ROE SW15 126 C3
Woldham Pl HAYES BR2 168 B3
Woldham Rd HAYES BR2 168 B3
Wolfe Cl YEAD UB4 83 F2
Wolfe Crs BERM/RHTH SE16 112 A1
CHARL SE7 114 C4
Wolferton Rd MNPK E12 77 K3
Wolfington Rd WNWD SE27 149 H3
Wolfram Cl LEW SE13 133 H4
Wolftencroft Cl BTSEA SW11 128 D2
Wollaston Cl STHWK SE1 18 D5
Wolmer Cl EDGW HA8 36 C3
Wolmer Gdns EDGW HA8 36 C2
Wolseley Av
WAND/EARL SW18 146 E1
Wolseley Gdns CHSWK W4 105 J5
Wolseley Rd CEND/HSY/T N8 54 D5
CHSWK W4 105 K3
FSTGT E7 77 F6
KTN/HRWW/WS HA3 48 E2
MTCM CR4 163 F6
ROMW/RG RM7 63 F6
WDGN N22 41 F7
Wolseley St STHWK SE1 19 M2
Wolsey Av EHAM E6 96 A2
THDIT KT7 158 A4
WALTH E17 57 H2
Wolsey Cl HSLW TW3 123 H3
KUTN/CMB KT2 144 D7
NWDGN UB2 103 H2
RYNPK SW20 145 K6
WPK KT4 173 J3
Wolsey Ct ELTH/MOT SE9 * 134 E5
Wolsey Crs CROY/NA CR0 180 A7
MRDN SM4 161 J6
Wolsey Dr KUTN/CMB KT2 144 A4
WOT/HER KT12 156 C7
Wolsey Gv EDGW HA8 37 F6
ESH/CLAY KT10 170 B3
Wolsey Ms KTTN NW5 72 C5
Wolsey Rd E/WMO/HCT KT8 157 J3
EN EN1 30 D1
ESH/CLAY KT10 170 B3
HPTN TW12 142 B5
IS N1 73 K4
NTHWD HA6 32 A1
SUN TW16 140 D6
Wolsey St WCHPL E1 92 E4
Wolsey Wy CHSGTN KT9 172 C4
Wolstonbury
NFNCH/WDSPK N12 38 E4
Wolvercote Rd ABYW SE2 116 E1
Wolverley St BETH E2 * 92 D2
Wolverton Av KUTN/CMB KT2 144 C7
Wolverton Gdns EA W5 86 B6
HMSMTH W6 107 G3
Wolverton Rd STAN HA7 35 H5
Wolverton Wy
STHGT/OAK N14 28 C4
Wolves La WDGN N22 41 G6
Womersley Rd
CEND/HSY/T N8 55 F5
Wonersh Wy BELMT SM2 174 B7
Wonford Cl KUTN/CMB KT2 145 G7
Wontner Cl IS N1 6 E2
Wontner Rd BAL SW12 147 K1
Woodall Cl CHSGTN KT9 171 J6
Woodall Rd PEND EN3 31 F4
Woodbank Rd BMLY BR1 152 D2
Woodbastwick Rd SYD SE26 151 F5
Woodberry Av
RYLN/HDSTN HA2 48 C3
WCHMH N21 41 G1
Woodberry Cl MLHL NW7 38 B6
SUN TW16 140 E5
Woodberry Crs MUSWH N10 54 B2
Woodberry Down FSBYPK N4 55 J7
Woodberry Gdns
NFNCH/WDSPK N12 39 G5
Woodberry Gv FSBYPK N4 55 J6
NFNCH/WDSPK N12 39 G5
Woodberry Wy
NFNCH/WDSPK N12 39 G5
Woodbine Cl WHTN TW2 142 D1
Woodbine Gv PGE/AN SE20 150 D6
Woodbine La WPK KT4 173 K2
Woodbine Pl WAN E11 58 E5
Woodbine Rd BFN/LL DA15 135 K7
Woodbines Av KUT/HW KT1 158 E2
Woodbine Ter HOM E9 74 E5
Woodborough Rd
PUT/ROE SW15 126 E3
Woodbourne Av
STRHM/NOR SW16 148 D2
Woodbourne Dr
ESH/CLAY KT10 171 F5
Woodbourne Gdns
WLGTN SM6 176 B6
Woodbridge Cl HOLWY N7 73 F1
Woodbridge Rd BARK IG11 79 F4
Woodbridge St CLKNW EC1R 6 C9
Woodbrook Rd ABYW SE2 116 B5
Woodburn Cl HDN NW4 52 B4
Woodbury Cl CROY/NA CR0 178 B1
WAN E11 59 F3
Woodbury Gdns
LEE/GVPK SE12 153 F2
Woodbury Park Rd WEA W13 85 H3
Woodbury Rd WALTH E17 57 K3
Woodbury St TOOT SW17 147 J4
Woodchester Sq BAY/PAD W2 8 C2
Woodchurch Cl SCUP DA14 154 D2
Woodchurch Dr BMLY BR1 153 H6
Woodchurch Rd
KIL/WHAMP NW6 2 B2
Wood Cl BETH E2 92 C3
CDALE/KGS NW9 51 F6
HRW HA1 48 D6
Woodclyffe Dr CHST BR7 169 F1
Woodcock Dell Av
KTN/HRWW/WS HA3 49 J6
Woodcock Hl
KTN/HRWW/WS HA3 49 J5
Woodcocks CAN/RD E16 95 G4
Woodcombe Crs FSTH SE23 131 K7
Woodcot Cl PEND EN3 30 E5
Woodcote Av HCH RM12 81 J3
MLHL NW7 38 A5
THHTH CR7 164 C3
WLGTN SM6 176 B7
Woodcote Cl KUTN/CMB KT2 144 B4
Woodcote Dr ORP BR6 169 J6
Woodcote Gn WLGTN SM6 176 C7
Woodcote Ms WLGTN SM6 176 B5
Woodcote Pl WNWD SE27 * 149 H4
Woodcote Rd WAN E11 58 E6
WLGTN SM6 176 B5
Wood Crest BELMT SM2 * 175 G6
Woodcroft ELTH/MOT SE9 153 K2
GFD/PVL UB6 67 G5
WCHMH N21 29 F7
Woodcroft Av MLHL NW7 37 G6
STAN HA7 35 G7
Woodcroft Ms DEPT SE8 112 B3
Woodcroft Rd THHTH CR7 164 C4
Wood Dene PECK SE15 * 111 J7
Wood Dr CHST BR7 153 J5
Wooden Bridge Ter
WNWD SE27 * 149 H2
Wood End HYS/HAR UB3 82 C5
Woodend ESH/CLAY KT10 170 C1
NRWD SE19 149 J5
SUT SM1 175 G1
Wood End Av
RYLN/HDSTN HA2 66 B3
Wood End Cl NTHLT UB5 66 D4
Woodend Gdns ENC/FH EN2 28 E3
Wood End Gdns NTHLT UB5 66 C4
Wood End Gn YEAD UB4 82 D4
Wood End Green Rd
HYS/HAR UB3 82 B4
Wood End La NTHLT UB5 66 B5
Wood End Rd HRW HA1 66 D3
Woodend Rd WALTH E17 58 A1
The Wood End WLGTN SM6 176 B7
Wood End Wy NTHLT UB5 66 C4
Wooder Gdns FSTGT E7 76 D3
Wooderson Cl SNWD SE25 165 F3
Woodfall Av BAR EN5 26 D4
Woodfall Dr DART DA1 138 C3
Woodfall Rd FSBYPK N4 55 G7
Woodfall St CHEL SW3 15 L8
Woodfarrs CMBW SE5 130 E3
Wood Fld HAMP NW3 * 71 K4
Woodfield Av ALP/SUD HA0 67 J2
CAR SM5 176 A5
CDALE/KGS NW9 51 G3
EA W5 85 J3
NTHWD HA6 32 C3
STRHM/NOR SW16 148 D2
Woodfield Cl EN EN1 30 A3
NRWD SE19 149 J6
Woodfield Crs EA W5 85 K3
Woodfield Dr EBAR EN4 28 A7
GPK RM2 63 J3
Woodfield Gdns NWMAL KT3 160 C4
Woodfield Gv
STRHM/NOR SW16 148 D2
Woodfield La
STRHM/NOR SW16 148 D2
Woodfield Pl MV/WKIL W9 88 D4
Woodfield Ri BUSH WD23 22 D6
Woodfield Rd EA W5 85 J3
HSLWW TW4 122 A1
MV/WKIL W9 88 D4
THDIT KT7 171 F1
Woodfields WATW WD18 * 21 G3
Woodfield Wy
FBAR/BDGN N11 40 D6
Woodford Av
GNTH/NBYPK IG2 59 K4
Woodford Bridge Rd
REDBR IG4 59 H2
Woodford Crs PIN HA5 47 F1
Woodford New Rd
WALTH E17 58 C2
Woodford Pl WBLY HA9 50 A7
Woodford Rd FSTGT E7 77 F3
SWFD E18 58 E3
WAT WD17 21 F1
Woodgate Av CHSGTN KT9 171 K4
Woodgate Crs NTHWD HA6 32 E5
Woodgate Dr
STRHM/NOR SW16 148 D6
Woodger Rd SHB W12 107 F1
Woodget Cl EHAM E6 95 J5
Woodgrange Av EA W5 86 B7
EN EN1 30 C5
KTN/HRWW/WS HA3 49 J4
NFNCH/WDSPK N12 39 H5
Woodgrange Cl
KTN/HRWW/WS HA3 49 K4
Woodgrange Gdns EN EN1 30 C5
Woodgrange Rd FSTGT E7 76 E4
Woodgrange Ter EN EN1 * 30 C5
Woodhall Av DUL SE21 150 B2
PIN HA5 33 J7
Woodhall Dr DUL SE21 150 B2
PIN HA5 33 H7
Woodhall Ga PIN HA5 33 H6
Woodhall La OXHEY WD19 33 H2
Woodham Ct SWFD E18 58 D3
Woodham Rd CAT SE6 152 A2
Woodhatch Cl EHAM E6 95 J4
Woodhaven Gdns
BARK/HLT IG6 60 C3
Woodhayes Rd
WIM/MER SW19 146 A5
Woodheyes Rd WLSDN NW10 69 G4
Woodhill WOOL/PLUM SE18 114 D3
Woodhill Crs
KTN/HRWW/WS HA3 49 K5
Woodhouse Av GFD/PVL UB6 85 F1
Woodhouse Cl EDUL SE22 131 H3
GFD/PVL UB6 85 F1
HYS/HAR UB3 101 H2
Woodhouse Eaves
NTHWD HA6 32 E4
Woodhouse Gv FSTGT E7 77 J5
Woodhouse Rd
NFNCH/WDSPK N12 39 G5
WAN E11 76 D2
Woodhurst Av
STMC/STPC BR5 169 H5
Woodhurst Rd ABYW SE2 116 B4
ACT W3 86 E7
Woodington Cl
ELTH/MOT SE9 135 F5
Woodknoll Dr CHST BR7 153 K7
Woodland Ap GFD/PVL UB6 67 G5
Woodland Cl CDALE/KGS NW9 50 E5
HOR/WEW KT19 * 173 G5
NRWD SE19 150 A5
WFD IG8 45 F2
Woodland Ct GLDGN NW11 * 52 C4
Woodland Crs
BERM/RHTH SE16 112 A1
GNWCH SE10 113 H5
Woodland Gdns ISLW TW7 123 K2
MUSWH N10 54 B4
Woodland Gv CROY/NA CR0 177 G6
GNWCH SE10 113 H4
Woodland Hl NRWD SE19 150 A5
Woodland Ms
STRHM/NOR SW16 148 E2
Woodland Ri GFD/PVL UB6 67 G5
MUSWH N10 54 B3
Woodland Rd
FBAR/BDGN N11 40 B4
NRWD SE19 150 A4
THHTH CR7 164 B3
Woodlands GLDGN NW11 52 C4
RYLN/HDSTN HA2 48 A3
RYNPK SW20 161 F3
Woodlands Av ACT W3 86 D7
BFN/LL DA15 135 K7
CHDH RM6 62 A5
FNCH N3 39 G6
NWMAL KT3 145 F7
RSLP HA4 47 G7
WAN E11 59 F7
WPK KT4 173 H1
Woodlands Cl BMLY BR1 168 E1
BORE WD6 24 D3
ESH/CLAY KT10 171 F6
GLDGN NW11 52 C4
Woodlands Dr STAN HA7 35 F5
SUN TW16 156 B1
Woodlands Gdns WALTH E17 * 58 C3
Woodlands Gv ISLW TW7 123 K1
Woodlands Pde ASHF TW15 140 A5
Woodlands Park Rd
GNWCH SE10 113 H5
SEVS/STOTM N15 55 J4
Woodlands Rd BARN SW13 126 C2
BMLY BR1 168 E1
BUSH WD23 21 J3
ED N9 30 E7
HRW HA1 49 F4
IL IG1 78 C2
ISLW TW7 123 K2
ROM RM1 63 H2
STHL UB1 83 H7
SURB KT6 158 E6
WALTH E17 58 A2
WAN E11 76 C1
Woodlands St LEW SE13 133 G6
The Woodlands
BRXN/ST SW9 * 110 C6
ESH/CLAY KT10 170 C1
HRW HA1 * 66 E1
ISLW TW7 124 A1
LEW SE13 133 G6
NRWD SE19 149 J6
STAN HA7 * 35 H4
STHGT/OAK N14 28 B7
WLGTN SM6 176 B7
Woodland St HACK E8 * 74 B5
Woodlands Wy
PUT/ROE SW15 127 J4
Woodland Ter CHARL SE7 114 D3

2 Willow Road (NT) HAMP NW3 71 J3
30 St Mary Axe HDTCH EC3A 13 K5
41 Hotel BGVA SW1W 16 D3
51 Buckingham Gate (Hotel) WESTW SW1E 16 F3
7/7 Memorial MYFR/PKLN W1K 10 B9
Aarotya Medical Centre SEVS/STOTM N15 55 J3
Abbey Business Centre VX/NE SW8 109 H7
Abbey Christian School for the English Language STJWD NW8 2 F6
The Abbey Clinic BELV DA17 117 G4
Abbey College London BAY/PAD W2 8 B5
Abbey Industrial Estate
ALP/SUD HA0 68 B7
MTCM CR4 162 E4
Abbey Lane Commercial Estate SRTFD E15 94 B1
Abbey Medical Centre STJWD NW8 2 D4
Abbey Mills WIM/MER SW19 147 G7
Abbey Park Industrial Estate BARK IG11 96 B1
Abbey Primary School
ABYW SE2 116 D2
MRDN SM4 161 K6
Abbey Road SRTFD E15 94 B1
Abbey Road Health Centre SRTFD E15 76 C7
Abbey Road Studios STJWD NW8 2 F6
Abbey Sports Centre BARK IG11 78 C7
Abbey Trading Estate SYD SE26 151 G4
Abbey Wharf Industrial Estate BARK IG11 96 D2
Abbey Wood ABYW SE2 116 D2
Abbey Wood School ABYW SE2 116 B2
Abbotsbury Primary School MRDN SM4 161 K4
Abbs Cross School & Arts College HCH RM12 81 K2
ABC Cinema PUT/ROE SW15 127 H2
Abercorn Place School CAMTN NW1 9 K2
Abercorn School
MBLAR W1H 9 L3
STJWD NW8 2 F6
Aberdeen Wharf WAP E1W 92 D7
Aberglen Industrial Estate HYS/HAR UB3 101 G1
Abingdon House School KENS W8 14 B3
Abney Park Cemetery STNW/STAM N16 74 A1
Acacia Business Centre WAN E11 76 C2
The Academy at Peckham PECK SE15 111 G7
The Academy School HAMP NW3 71 H3
Acland Burghley School KTTN NW5 72 B3
Acorn Industrial Park DART DA1 138 D4
Acorn Medical Centre TWK TW1 124 B7
Acre Road Health Clinic KUTN/CMB KT2 144 B6
Acton Business Centre WLSDN NW10 87 F3
Acton Central ACT W3 87 F7
Acton Central Industrial Estate ACT W3 86 D6
Acton Health Centre ACT W3 86 E7
Acton High School ACT W3 105 H1
Acton Hospital ACT W3 105 H1
Acton Lane Medical Centre CHSWK W4 105 K1
Acton Main Line ACT W3 86 E5
Acton Park Industrial Estate ACT W3 106 A1
Acton Superbowl ACT W3 86 C4
Acton Swimming Baths ACT W3 86 E7
Acton Town ACT W3 105 H1
Acton & West London College ACT W3 86 D7
Acumen (Anglo School) NRWD SE19 150 A7
Adams Bridge Business Centre WBLY HA9 68 D4
Adamsrill Primary School SYD SE26 151 G2
Addey & Stanhope School NWCR SE14 112 C7
Addington Court Golf Club CROY/NA CR0 179 H7
Addington Golf Club CROY/NA CR0 179 H3
Addington Palace Golf Club CROY/NA CR0 179 G5
Addington Village CROY/NA CR0 179 J5
Addiscombe CROY/NA CR0 165 H7
Addiscombe CC CROY/NA CR0 178 C2
Addison Primary School WKENS W14 107 G2
Adelphi Theatre COVGDN WC2E 11 K7
Adler Industrial Estate HYS/HAR UB3 101 G1
Admiral Hyson Industrial Estate STHWK SE1 111 J3
Admiralty Arch STJS SW1Y 11 H8
The Adult College of Barking & Dagenham BARK IG11 78 E5
Aerodrome Hotel CROY/NA CR0 177 G5
Africa Centre COVGDN WC2E 11 K6
Aga Khan University
CAN/RD E16 94 D4
RSQ WC1B 11 H3
Agency of Jewish Education HDN NW4 52 B3
Agnew's CONDST W1S 10 E8
Agora Shopping Centre PECK SE15 131 H1
AHA International London Centre BMSBY WC1N 11 M2
Ainslie Wood Primary School CHING E4 43 K4
Airbase Unity Elementary School RSLP HA4 64 A1
Airbus Coach Station HTHAIR TW6 120 C2
Air Call Business Centre CDALE/KGS NW9 51 F2
Airedale Physiotherapy Clinic CHSWK W4 106 C4
Airlinks Golf Club NWDGN UB2 102 B3
Air Links Industrial Estate HEST TW5 102 B4
Airport Gate Business Centre WDR/YW UB7 100 C6
Akiva School FNCH N3 52 E1
Aksaray Sports Club STNW/STAM N16 73 K3
Albany Centre & Theatre DEPT SE8 112 C6
Albany Clinic
BFN/LL DA15 155 G3
WIM/MER SW19 147 F6
Albany Park SCUP DA14 155 K1
Albany Park Canoe & Sailing Club KUTN/CMB KT2 143 K5
The Albany School HCH RM12 81 K1
Albemarle Primary School WIM/MER SW19 146 C1
Albert Memorial SKENS SW7 15 G1
Albion College RSQ WC1B 11 J3
Albion Health Centre WCHPL E1 92 D4
Albion J & I School BERM/RHTH SE16 111 K1
Albion Street Health Centre BERM/RHTH SE16 111 K1
Albright Industrial Estate RAIN RM13 99 H4
Alchemea IS N1 6 D3
The Alchemy Gallery CLKNW EC1R 6 A9
Aldenham Country Park BORE WD6 23 H4
Aldenham Preparatory School BORE WD6 23 F1
Alderbrook Primary School BAL SW12 129 G6
Aldersbrook County Secondary School MNPK E12 59 G7
Aldersbrook Primary School MNPK E12 59 F7
Alderwood Primary School ELTH/MOT SE9 135 J5
Aldgate TWRH EC3N 13 L5
Aldgate Bus Station WCHPL E1 13 L4
Aldgate East WCHPL E1 13 M4
Aldwych Theatre HOL/ALD WC2B 11 L5
Alexander McLeod Primary School ABYW SE2 116 C4
Alexandra Avenue Clinic RYLN/HDSTN HA2 65 K1
Alexandra Business Centre PEND EN3 31 F3
Alexandra Infant School
KUTN/CMB KT2 144 C6
PGE/AN SE20 151 F6
Alexandra Junior School
HSLW TW3 123 G1
SYD SE26 151 F5
Alexandra Palace
WDGN N22 54 D2
WDGN N22 54 E1
Alexandra Palace Ice Rink WDGN N22 54 D1
Alexandra Park School FBAR/BDGN N11 40 C6
Alexandra Primary School WDGN N22 55 F1
Alexandra School RYLN/HDSTN HA2 65 K1
Al Falah Boys School CLPT E5 74 D2
Alfred Salter Primary School BERM/RHTH SE16 112 A1
Alfreds Way Industrial Estate BARK IG11 79 G7
Al-Khair Primary & Secondary School CROY/NA CR0 164 E7
Allenby Primary School STHL UB1 84 A5
Allen Edwards Primary School CLAP SW4 109 K7
The All England Lawn Tennis & Croquet Club WIM/MER SW19 146 B2
Alleyns Junior School EDUL SE22 131 F4
Allfarthing JMI School WAND/EARL SW18 128 B5
All Saints POP/IOD E14 94 A5
All Saints Benhilton CE Primary School SUT SM1 175 F2
All Saints Catholic School & Technology College BCTR RM8 62 C7
All Saints CE Junior School NRWD SE19 150 A7
All Saints CE Primary School
BKHTH/KID SE3 133 H1
CAR SM5 176 A4
CRICK NW2 70 D2
FUL/PGN SW6 127 H1
PUT/ROE SW15 127 F2
TRDG/WHET N20 39 H1
WIM/MER SW19 147 G6
All Souls CE Primary School GTPST W1W 10 E3
Allum Lane Cemetery BORE WD6 24 A4
Allum Medical Centre WAN E11 58 B6
Alma Primary School
BERM/RHTH SE16 111 H3
PEND EN3 31 G4
Almeida Theatre IS N1 6 C2
Al-Noor Primary School GDMY/SEVK IG3 61 H7
Alperton ALP/SUD HA0 67 K7
Alperton Cemetery ALP/SUD HA0 67 K7
Alperton Community School ALP/SUD HA0 68 A6
Alperton High School ALP/SUD HA0 67 K7
Alperton Sports Ground ALP/SUD HA0 85 K1
Alpha Business Centre WALTH E17 57 H4
Alpha Preparatory School HRW HA1 48 E4
Alpine Business Centre EHAM E6 96 A4
Al-Risaala Boys Secondary School BAL SW12 129 G7
Al Sadiq & Al-Zahra High School KIL/WHAMP NW6 70 C7
Alscot Road Industrial Estate STHWK SE1 19 M5
Altmore Infant School EHAM E6 77 K6
The Alton School PUT/ROE SW15 126 C6
Ambler Primary School FSBYPK N4 73 H2
Ambleside Junior School WOT/HER KT12 156 B7
Ambulance Centre STRHM/NOR SW16 149 F2
AMC Business Centre WLSDN NW10 86 D2
American Intercontinental University MHST W1U 10 B3
AMF Bowling LEW SE13 133 F2
Amida Golf FELT TW13 142 A2
Ampere Way CROY/NA CR0 164 A7
Ampthill Square Medical Centre CAMTN NW1 4 F6
Anchorage Point Industrial Estate CHARL SE7 114 B2
Anchor Bay Industrial Estate ERITH DA8 118 C6
Anchor Retail Park WCHPL E1 92 E3
Andaz Hotel LVPST EC2M 13 J3
Andover Medical Centre HOLWY N7 73 F2
The Andrew Ewing Primary School HEST TW5 102 E6
Anerley PGE/AN SE20 150 C7
Anerley School NRWD SE19 150 C7
Angel IS N1 6 C5
Angel Centre DART DA1 139 H5
Angel Road UED N18 42 E4
Angerstein Business Park GNWCH SE10 113 K3
Anglian Industrial Estate BARK IG11 97 F3
Animal Cemetery REDBR IG4 59 H2
Annemount School EFNCH N2 53 G5
Annunciation RC Infant School EDGW HA8 37 F7
The Annunciation RC Junior School MLHL NW7 37 F5
Anson Primary School CRICK NW2 70 B4
Apex Hotel MON EC3R 13 K6
Apex Industrial Estate WLSDN NW10 87 H3
Apex Primary School IL IG1 60 A7
Apex Retail Park FELT TW13 141 K2
Apollo Theatre SOHO/SHAV W1D 11 G6
Apollo Victoria Theatre PIM SW1V 16 E4
Apostolic Nuncio WIM/MER SW19 146 A2
Applegarth Primary School CROY/NA CR0 179 K5
Apsley House, The Wellington Museum KTBR SW1X 16 A1
Aquarius Business Park CRICK NW2 51 J7
Aquarius Golf Club EDUL SE22 131 K4
Aragon Primary School MRDN SM4 161 H6
Arcadia Shopping Centre EA W5 85 K6
Arcadia University BAY/PAD W2 8 C7
The Archbishop Lanfranc School CROY/NA CR0 163 K5
Archbishop Sumners CE Primary School LBTH SE11 18 B6
Archbishop Tenisons CE School CROY/NA CR0 178 B2
Archbishop Tenison's School VX/NE SW8 110 A5
Archdale Business Centre RYLN/HDSTN HA2 66 C1
Archdeacon Cambridge's CE Primary School WHTN TW2 142 E1
Arches Business Centre NWDGN UB2 102 E1
Arches Leisure Centre GNWCH SE10 113 G5
Archgate Business Centre NFNCH/WDSPK N12 39 G3
Architectural Association School of Architecture RSQ WC1B 11 G3
Archway ARCH N19 72 C1
Archway Business Centre ARCH N19 72 D2
Archway Leisure Centre ARCH N19 72 C1
Arena SNWD SE25 165 K4
Arena Estate FSBYPK N4 55 H5
Argent Centre Industrial Estate HYS/HAR UB3 101 K1
Argyle Primary School STPAN WC1H 5 K8
Arkley Golf Club BAR EN5 25 H4
Arklow Trading Estate NWCR SE14 112 B5
Armourers & Braziers' Hall LOTH EC2R 13 G3
Arndale Health Centre WAND/EARL SW18 127 K5
Arnhem Wharf Primary School POP/IOD E14 112 C2
Arnold House School STJWD NW8 3 G5
Arnos Grove FBAR/BDGN N11 40 C3
Arnos Pool FBAR/BDGN N11 40 D4
Arsenal HBRY N5 73 G2
Arsenal FC (Emirates Stadium) HOLWY N7 73 G3
Artsdepot NFNCH/WDSPK N12 39 G4
The Arts Educational School CHSWK W4 106 B3
Arts Theatre LSQ/SEVD WC2H 11 H6
Ashburnham Primary School WBPTN SW10 108 C6
Ashburton Community School CROY/NA CR0 165 J6
Ashburton Primary School CROY/NA CR0 165 J5
Ashby Mill BRXS/STRHM SW2 129 K5
Ashby Mill School CLAP SW4 129 K4
Ashcroft Technology Academy PUT/ROE SW15 127 J4
Ashfield Junior School BUSH WD23 22 B6
Ashford Industrial Estate ASHF TW15 140 A3
Ashford Sports Club STWL/WRAY TW19 120 C7
Ashgrove College WALTH E17 57 J2
Ashgrove Trading Estate BMLY BR1 152 B5
Ashleigh Commercial Estate CHARL SE7 114 B3
Ashmead Primary School BROCKY SE4 132 D1
Ashmole Centre STHGT/OAK N14 28 C7
Ashmole Primary School VX/NE SW8 110 A5
Ashmole School STHGT/OAK N14 28 C7
Ashmount Primary School ARCH N19 54 D6
Ashton House School ISLW TW7 103 J7
Ashton Playing Fields Track WFD IG8 45 J5
Aspen House School LBTH SE11 110 C5
Aspen House Secondary & Primary School BRXS/STRHM SW2 129 K7
Asquith Court School
HPTN TW12 142 B7
KTN/HRWW/WS HA3 49 H5
Asquith School PEND EN3 30 E3
Assembly Rooms SURB KT6 159 F3
Associated Newspapers Offices BERM/RHTH SE16 112 A2
Assunah School TOTM N17 56 B1
Aston Clinic NWMAL KT3 160 B3
Aston House School EA W5 85 K5
Asylum Medical Centre CEND/HSY/T N8 55 G2
Athelney Primary School CAT SE6 151 J2
Athelstan House School HPTN TW12 142 A7
Athenaeum Hotel MYFR/PICC W1J 10 C9
Athena Medical Centre CLPT E5 74 E3
Atherton Leisure Centre SRTFD E15 76 D5
Athlone House Hospital HGT N6 53 K7
Athlon Industrial Estate ALP/SUD HA0 85 K1
Atkinson Morley Hospital RYNPK SW20 145 K6
Atlantic House (Richmond American International University) KENS W8 14 E3
Atlas Business Centre CRICK NW2 69 K1
Atlas Transport Estate BTSEA SW11 128 B1
Attlee Youth & Community Centre WCHPL E1 13 M3
Auriol Junior School HOR/WEW KT19 173 H3
Australia House HOL/ALD WC2B 11 M5
Avenue House Museum FNCH N3 52 D1
Avenue House School WEA W13 85 H5
Avenue Industrial Estate CHING E4 43 H5
Avenue Pre-Preparatory School HGT N6 54 B6
Avenue Primary School MNPK E12 77 J3
Avenue Road BECK BR3 166 A1
Avery Hill Park ELTH/MOT SE9 135 H5
Avondale Park Primary School NTGHL W11 88 B6
Avon House School WFD IG8 44 E3
Avon Trading Estate WKENS W14 107 J3
Axis Business Centre SRTFD E15 75 K7
The Aylesham Centre PECK SE15 111 H7
Ayloff Primary School HCH RM12 81 K3
Aylward First & Middle Schools STAN HA7 35 K4
Azhar Academy FSTGT E7 76 E5
B6 Sixth Form College CLPT E5 74 D2
BAA Heathrow Visitor Centre HTHAIR TW6 100 E7
Babington House School CHST BR7 153 K5
BackCare Clinic WPK KT4 160 D7
Bacon's College BERM/RHTH SE16 93 G7
Baden Powell House SKENS SW7 14 F5
Baglioni Hotel KENS W8 14 E2
Bakers Hall MON EC3R 13 K7
Baker Street CAMTN NW1 9 M1
Balaam Leisure Centre PLSTW E13 94 E3
Bales College NKENS W10 88 B2
Balfour Business Centre NWDGN UB2 102 C2
Balgowan Primary School BECK BR3 166 B1
Balham BAL SW12 129 G7
Balham Girls Preparatory Secondary School TOOT SW17 147 K2
Balham Health Centre BAL SW12 148 B1
Balham Leisure Centre TOOT SW17 148 A1
Balmoral Trading Estate BARK IG11 97 F3
Baltic Exchange HDTCH EC3A 13 K4
Bancrofts School WFD IG8 44 E2
Bandon Hill Cemetery WLGTN SM6 176 D4
Bandon Hill Primary School WLGTN SM6 176 D5
Bangabandhu Primary School BETH E2 92 E2
Bank LOTH EC2R 13 G5
Bank of England Extension CITYW EC2V 12 E5
Bank of England (& Museum) LOTH EC2R 13 G5
Bankside Gallery STHWK SE1 12 D7
Bankside Jetty STHWK SE1 12 E7
Bankside Park Industrial Estate BARK IG11 97 G2
Bannister Stadium KTN/HRWW/WS HA3 34 C5
Bannockburn Primary School WOOL/PLUM SE18 116 A3
The Banqueting House, Whitehall WHALL SW1A 11 J9
Barbara Speake Theatre School ACT W3 87 G6
Barber Surgeons' Hall BARB EC2Y 12 F3
Barbican FARR EC1M 12 D2
Barbican Cinema BARB EC2Y 12 E2
Barbican Exhibition Halls BARB EC2Y 12 F2
The Barbican BARB EC2Y 12 E2
Barbican Theatre BARB EC2Y 12 F2
Barclay Primary School LEY E10 58 B5
Barham Primary School ALP/SUD HA0 67 J5
Baring Primary School LEE/GVPK SE12 133 K6
Baring Road Medical Centre BMLY BR1 152 E1
Barkantine Clinic POP/IOD E14 112 D1
Barking BARK IG11 78 C6
Barking Abbey Comprehensive School (Lower) IL IG1 78 D4
Barking Abbey Comprehensive School (Upper) BARK IG11 79 F5
Barking Abbey Industrial Estate BARK IG11 78 B7
Barking Abbey Leisure Centre BARK IG11 79 G5
Barking Abbey School BARK IG11 79 F5
Barking College ROMW/RG RM7 81 F1

Barking FC BCTR RM8 79 H4
Barking Hospital BARK IG11 79 F6
Barking Industrial Park BARK IG11 79 F7
Barking RUFC DAGW RM9 79 K7
Barkingside ⊖ BARK/HLT IG6 60 D3
Barkingside Cemetery BARK/HLT IG6 60 B2
Barkingside FC BARK/HLT IG6 60 D3
Barlby Primary School NKENS W10 88 B3
Barley Lane Primary School GDMY/SEVK IG3 61 G6
Barnabas Medical Centre NTHLT UB5 66 C5
Barn Croft Primary School WALTH E17 57 G5
Barnehurst ⇌ BXLYHN DA7 137 K1
Barnehurst Primary School ERITH DA8 117 K7
Barnehurst Public Golf Club BXLYHN DA7 138 A2
Barn Elms Athletics Track BARN SW13 126 E1
Barn Elms Sports Centre BARN SW13 107 F7
Barn Elms Water Sports Centre PUT/ROE SW15 127 F1
Barnes ⇌ BARN SW13 126 D2
Barnes Bridge ⇌ BARN SW13 126 B1
Barnes Cray Primary School DART DA1 138 D3
Barnes Hospital MORT/ESHN SW14 126 B2
Barnes Primary School BARN SW13 126 B2
Barnes Sports Club BARN SW13 106 C7
Barnet College
BAR EN5 26 D3
CDALE/KGS NW9 37 H7
EBAR EN4 27 K7
FBAR/BDGN N11 39 K2
HDN NW4 51 J5
NFNCH/WDSPK N12 39 G4
Barnet Copthall Pool HDN NW4 37 K6
Barnet Copthall Stadium HDN NW4 38 A7
Barnet FC (Underhill) BAR EN5 26 E4
Barnet General Hospital BAR EN5 26 B3
Barnet Health Centre BAR EN5 26 E4
Barnet Hill JMI School BAR EN5 26 D4
Barnet Hospital Chest Clinic BAR EN5 26 B3
Barnet Museum BAR EN5 26 C3
Barnet Trading Estate BAR EN5 26 D2
Barnfield Primary School EDGW HA8 36 E7
Barnhill Community High School YEAD UB4 83 F2
Barn Hotel RSLP HA4 64 C1
Barnsbury Complex IS N1 6 A1
Barnsbury School for Girls IS N1 73 G5
Barons Court ⊖ HMSMTH W6 107 G4
Barons Court Theatre WKENS W14 107 H4
Barratt Industrial Park BOW E3 94 A3
Barrett Industrial Park STHL UB1 84 A7
Barrett Way Industrial Estate RYLN/HDSTN HA2 48 D2
Barrington Primary School WELL DA16 136 E1
Barrow Hedges Primary School CAR SM5 175 J6
Barrow Hill Junior School STJWD NW8 3 J6
Barton House Health Centre STNW/STAM N16 73 K2
Barwell Business Park CHSGTN KT9 171 K6
Bassett House School NKENS W10 88 B5
Baston School HAYES BR2 181 F1
Bath Factory Estate HNHL SE24 130 D5
Battersea Arts Centre (BAC) BTSEA SW11 128 E2
Battersea Business Centre BTSEA SW11 129 F2
Battersea Dogs' Home VX/NE SW8 109 G6
Battersea Park ⇌ BTSEA SW11 109 G6
Battersea Power Station (disused) VX/NE SW8 109 G5
Battersea Sports Centre BTSEA SW11 128 C2
Battersea Technology College BTSEA SW11 108 E7
Battersea Tutorial College TOOT SW17 148 A1
Bayswater ⊖ BAY/PAD W2 8 C6
BBC Broadcasting House REGST W1B 10 D3
BBC Media Village SHB W12 88 A6
BBC Studios MV/WKIL W9 2 C9
BBC Television Centre SHB W12 88 A6
BBC Worldwide SHB W12 88 A5
Beal High School REDBR IG4 59 J2
Beam Primary School DAGE RM10 98 E1
Beatrice Tate School BETH E2 92 D2
Beatrix Potter Primary School WAND/EARL SW18 128 B7
Beauclerc Infant School SUN TW16 156 B2
The Beaufort Hotel CHEL SW3 15 L4
Beaumont Primary School LEY E10 57 K6
Beaver College BAY/PAD W2 8 C7
The Beavers Community Primary School HSLWW TW4 122 B2
Beaverwood School for Girls CHST BR7 154 E5
Beckenham Business Centre BECK BR3 151 G5
Beckenham Crematorium BECK BR3 165 K2
Beckenham CC BECK BR3 151 K6
Beckenham Hill ⇌ CAT SE6 152 A4
Beckenham Hospital BECK BR3 166 C1
Beckenham Junction ⇌ Ⓣ BECK BR3 151 J7
Beckenham Leisure Centre BECK BR3 151 G7
Beckenham Place Park Golf Course BECK BR3 151 K5
Beckenham RFC BECK BR3 166 B3
Beckenham Road Ⓣ BECK BR3 151 F7
Beckenham School of Art BECK BR3 166 B4
Beckenham Theatre Centre BECK BR3 166 E1
Beckenham Town FC BECK BR3 166 D4
Becket Sports Centre DART DA1 139 F5
Beckford Primary School KIL/WHAMP NW6 70 D4
Beckmead School BECK BR3 166 D7
The Beck Theatre HYS/HAR UB3 82 D5
Beckton ⊖ EHAM E6 96 A4
Beckton Park ⊖ EHAM E6 95 K6
Beckton Ski Centre EHAM E6 96 A3
Beckton Triangle Retail Park EHAM E6 96 B2
Becontree ⊖ DAGW RM9 79 J5
Becontree Day Hospital BCTR RM8 80 A1
Becontree Primary School BCTR RM8 79 H2
Bective House Clinic PUT/ROE SW15 127 J3
Beddington Infants School WLGTN SM6 176 C2
Beddington Lane Ⓣ CROY/NA CR0 163 H5
Beddington Medical Centre CROY/NA CR0 176 E3
Beddington Park Primary School CROY/NA CR0 176 D2
Beddington Trading Estate CROY/NA CR0 163 K7
Bedelsford School KUT/HW KT1 159 F2
Bedfont Cemetery EBED/NFELT TW14 121 F7
Bedfont Health Clinic EBED/NFELT TW14 121 H6
Bedfont Industrial Park ASHF TW15 140 B2
Bedfont J & I School EBED/NFELT TW14 121 H5
Bedfont Lakes Country Park EBED/NFELT TW14 140 A1
Bedfont Lakes Office Park EBED/NFELT TW14 121 F7
Bedford Hotel RSQ WC1B 11 K2
Bedington Infant School WLGTN SM6 176 C3
Bedonwell Clinic ABYW SE2 117 F5
Bedonwell Medical Centre BELV DA17 117 G4
Bedonwell Primary School BXLYHN DA7 117 F5
Beecholme Primary School MTCM CR4 148 B7
Beechwood School STRHM/NOR SW16 148 E2
Beehive Preparatory School REDBR IG4 59 K3
The Beehive School ARCH N19 54 D6
Beis Hamedrash Elyon GLDGN NW11 52 C6
Beis Malka Girls School STNW/STAM N16 56 B7
Beis Rochel D'Satmar Girls School STNW/STAM N16 56 A6
Beis Yaakov Primary School CDALE/KGS NW9 51 F2
Belgrave Walk Ⓣ MTCM CR4 162 C3
Bellamy's Wharf BERM/RHTH SE16 93 F7
Bellenden Primary School PECK SE15 131 H2
Bellenden Road Business Centre PECK SE15 131 G1
Bellenden Road Retail Park PECK SE15 111 G7
Bellerbys College DEPT SE8 112 E5
Belleville Primary School BTSEA SW11 128 E4
Belle Vue Cinema WLSDN NW10 69 K6
Bell Industrial Estate CHSWK W4 105 K3
Bellingham ⇌ CAT SE6 151 K2
Bellingham Trading Estate CAT SE6 151 K2
Bell Lane JMI School HDN NW4 52 B3
Belmont Bowling Club STRHM/NOR SW16 148 E2
Belmont First School KTN/HRWW/WS HA3 49 F1
Belmont Infant School TOTM N17 55 J2
Belmont (Mill Hill Preparatory School) MLHL NW7 37 J2
Belmont Park School LEY E10 58 A5
Belmont Primary School
CHSWK W4 106 A3
ERITH DA8 117 H6
Belmore Primary School YEAD UB4 83 F2
Belsize Park ⊖ HAMP NW3 71 J4
Belvedere ⇌ BELV DA17 117 J2
Belvedere Day Hospital WLSDN NW10 69 J7
Belvedere Industrial Estate BELV DA17 99 F7
Belvedere Link Business Park ERITH DA8 117 K2
Belvedere Primary School BELV DA17 117 J3
Belvue Business Centre NTHLT UB5 66 B6
Belvue School NTHLT UB5 66 A7
Benedict House Preparatory School BFN/LL DA15 155 F3
Benedict Primary School MTCM CR4 162 C2
Ben Jonson Primary School WCHPL E1 93 G3
Bensham Manor School THHTH CR7 164 D4
Benson Primary School CROY/NA CR0 179 G2
Bentalls Shopping Centre KUT/HW KT1 158 E1
Benthal Primary School STNW/STAM N16 74 C2
The Bentley Kempinski Hotel SKENS SW7 14 E6
Bentley Wood Girls School STAN HA7 35 F4
Bentworth Primary School SHB W12 87 K5
Ben Uri Gallery, London Jewish Museum of Art STJWD NW8 2 D4
Beormund School STHWK SE1 19 G2
Berger Primary School HOM E9 75 F5
The Berkeley Hotel KTBR SW1X 16 A1
Berkeley Primary School HEST TW5 102 C5
Berlitz School of Languages HHOL WC1V 11 M3
Bermondsey ⊖ ⊖ BERM/RHTH SE16 111 H2
Bermondsey Town Hall STHWK SE1 19 L4
Bermondsey Trading Estate BERM/RHTH SE16 111 K3
Berrylands ⇌ BRYLDS KT5 159 J3
Berrymede Infant School ACT W3 105 J1
Berrymede Junior School ACT W3 105 J1
Bertram House School TOOT SW17 148 A1
Bessemer Grange J & I School HNHL SE24 130 E4
Bessemer Park Industrial Estate BRXN/ST SW9 130 C3
Best Western Bromley Court Hotel BMLY BR1 152 C5
Best Western Cumberland Hotel HRW HA1 49 F5
Best Western Lodge Hotel PUT/ROE SW15 127 J4
Best Western Master Robert Hotel HEST TW5 102 E7
Best Western Mostyn Hotel MBLAR W1H 9 M5
Best Western Phoenix Hotel BAY/PAD W2 8 C6
Best Western White House Hotel WATW WD18 20 E3
Bethlem Royal Hospital BECK BR3 166 D6
Bethnal Green ⇌ WCHPL E1 92 D3
Bethnal Green ⊖ BETH E2 92 E2
Bethnal Green Technology College BETH E2 7 M8
Beths Grammar School for Boys BXLY DA5 137 H5
The Betty Layward School STNW/STAM N16 73 K2
Beulah Infant School THHTH CR7 164 D1
Beverley School NWMAL KT3 160 D4
Beverley Trading Estate MRDN SM4 161 G6
Bevington Primary School NKENS W10 88 C4
Bexley ⇌ BXLY DA5 137 H7
Bexley College BELV DA17 117 K3
Bexley CC BXLY DA5 137 H7
Bexley Grammar School WELL DA16 136 C3
Bexleyheath ⇌ BXLYHN DA7 137 F1
Bexleyheath Cemetery BXLYHN DA7 137 G2
Bexleyheath Centre BXLYHS DA6 137 F3
Bexleyheath Golf Club BXLYHS DA6 137 F4
Bexleyheath Marriott Hotel BXLYHS DA6 137 J3
Bexleyheath School BXLYHN DA7 137 G2
Bexleyheath Superbowl BXLYHS DA6 137 G3
Bexley RFC BXLY DA5 137 H6
BFI London IMAX Cinema STHWK SE1 11 M9
Bickerly School of Dance HAYES BR2 168 D4
Bickley ⇌ BMLY BR1 168 D2
Bickley Park CC BMLY BR1 168 D1
Bickley Park Pre-Preparatory School BMLY BR1 168 D2
Bickley Park Preparatory School BMLY BR1 168 C2
Big Ben WHALL SW1A 17 K2
Bigland Green Primary School WCHPL E1 92 D5
Billingsgate Fish Market POP/IOD E14 93 K7
Bingham Hotel TWK TW1 124 E5
Birchmere Business Park THMD SE28 116 B1
Bird College SCUP DA14 155 G2
Birkbeck ⇌ Ⓣ BECK BR3 165 K1
Birkbeck College
GWRST WC1E 11 H1
RSQ WC1B 11 H3
Birkbeck Primary School SCUP DA14 155 H2
Bishop Challoner Catholic Collegiate School WCHPL E1 92 E6
Bishop Challoner Girls School WCHPL E1 92 C6
Bishop Challoner School HAYES BR2 167 G1
Bishop Douglass RC School EFNCH N2 53 G1
Bishop Gilpin Primary School WIM/MER SW19 146 D4
Bishop John Robinson CE Primary School THMD SE28 97 J6
Bishop Justus CE (Secondary) School HAYES BR2 168 D6
Bishop Perrin CE Primary School WHTN TW2 123 G6
Bishop Ramsey CE School (Upper) RSLP HA4 46 E6
Bishop Ramsey CE School RSLP HA4 46 D6
Bishopsgate Institute LVPST EC2M 13 K3
Bishop Thomas Grant School STRHM/NOR SW16 149 F4
Bishop Winnington-Ingram CE Primary School RSLP HA4 46 B6
Bittacy Business Centre MLHL NW7 38 C5
Blackburn Trading Estate STWL/WRAY TW19 120 C5
Blackfen Medical Centre BFN/LL DA15 136 A4
Blackfen School for Girls BFN/LL DA15 136 C5
Blackfriars ⇌ BLKFR EC4V 12 C7
Blackfriars Millennium Pier EMB EC4Y 12 B6
Blackfriars Pier BLKFR EC4V 12 D7
Blackheath ⇌ BKHTH/KID SE3 133 J2
Blackheath Bluecoat School BKHTH/KID SE3 114 A6
Blackheath Business Estate GNWCH SE10 113 F7
The Blackheath Clinic BKHTH/KID SE3 133 K3
Blackheath High School GDST BKHTH/KID SE3 133 J1
Blackheath High Senior School BKHTH/KID SE3 113 K6
Blackheath Hospital BKHTH/KID SE3 133 J2
Blackheath Preparatory School BKHTH/KID SE3 113 K7
Blackheath RFC (The Rectory Field) BKHTH/KID SE3 114 A6
Blackhorse Lane Ⓣ CROY/NA CR0 165 H6
Blackhorse Road ⊖ ⊖ WALTH E17 57 F3
Blackwall ⊖ POP/IOD E14 94 A6
Blackwall Trading Estate POP/IOD E14 94 B4
Blair Peach Primary School STHL UB1 83 H7
Blake College GTPST W1W 10 E2
Blanche Nevile School
HGT N6 53 K5
MUSWH N10 54 A2
Blenheim Business Centre MTCM CR4 147 K7
Blenheim Shopping Centre PGE/AN SE20 150 E6
Blessed Dominic RC Primary School CDALE/KGS NW9 51 G1
Blessed Sacrament RC Primary School IS N1 5 K4
Blood Transfusion Centre EDGW HA8 36 D6
Bloomfield Clinic Guys STHWK SE1 19 H1
Bloomsbury International NOXST/BSQ WC1A 11 K3
Bloomsbury Theatre GWRST WC1E 5 G9
Blossom House School RYNPK SW20 146 A6
Blossoms Inn Medical Centre BLKFR EC4V 12 F6
Blue Gate Fields Infant School WCHPL E1 92 E6
The Blue School ISLW TW7 124 B2
Blyth's Wharf POP/IOD E14 93 G6
BMI Medical Centre CAVSQ/HST W1G 10 B3
Bnois Jerusalem Girls School STNW/STAM N16 55 K6
The Bob Hope Theatre ELTH/MOT SE9 134 E5
Bodywise Natural Health Centre BETH E2 92 E2
Boleyn Cinema EHAM E6 95 H1
Bolingbroke Hospital BTSEA SW11 128 D4
Bolingbroke Primary School BTSEA SW11 108 C7
Bond First School MTCM CR4 162 E1
Bond Primary School MTCM CR4 162 E1
Bond Street ⊖ OXSTW W1C 10 B5
Bonner Primary School BETH E2 93 F1
Bonneville Primary School CLAP SW4 129 H5
Bonnington Hotel RSQ WC1B 11 K2
Bonus Pastor Catholic College BMLY BR1 152 B3
Boomes Industrial Estate RAIN RM13 99 H3
Booster Cushion Theatre WDGN N22 55 F1
Borehamwood FC BORE WD6 24 D1
Borehamwood Industrial Park BORE WD6 25 F1
Borough ⊖ STHWK SE1 18 F2
Borough Cemetery HSLWW TW4 123 F6
Borough Market STHWK SE1 13 G8
Borthwick Wharf DEPT SE8 112 D4
Boston Business Park HNWL W7 103 K2
Boston Manor ⊖ HNWL W7 104 B3
Botwell RC Primary School HYS/HAR UB3 101 J1
Boulevard 25 Retail Park BORE WD6 24 C2
Boundary Business Park MTCM CR4 162 C1
Bounds Green ⊖ FBAR/BDGN N11 40 D6
Bounds Green Health Centre FBAR/BDGN N11 40 D6
Bounds Green Industrial Estate FBAR/BDGN N11 40 B5
Bounds Green Infant School FBAR/BDGN N11 40 D6
Bourne CP School RSLP HA4 65 G4
Bourne Hall Health Centre EW KT17 173 H7
Bournehall J & I School BUSH WD23 22 A4
Bourne Hall Museum EW KT17 173 H7
Bourne Road Industrial Park DART DA1 138 A4
Bourneside Sports Club STHGT/OAK N14 28 E7
Bousfield Primary School ECT SW5 14 E7
Boutcher CE Primary School STHWK SE1 19 L4
Bowater House SKENS SW7 15 L2
Bow Church ⊖ BOW E3 93 J2
Bowden House Clinic HRW HA1 66 E1
Bowes Park ⇌ WDGN N22 40 E6
Bowes Primary School FBAR/BDGN N11 40 D4
Bowes Road Clinic FBAR/BDGN N11 40 C4
Bow Junior & Youth Centre BOW E3 93 H4
Ealing Conservative Bowling Club EA W5 85 J6
Bowman Trading Estate CDALE/KGS NW9 50 C2
Bow Road ⊖ BOW E3 93 J2
Bow Secondary School BOW E3 93 J1
Bow Triangle Business Centre BOW E3 93 J3
Boxgrove Primary School ABYW SE2 116 D2
BPP Law School HHOL WC1V 11 L3
Brackenbury Health Centre HMSMTH W6 106 E2
Brackenbury Primary School HMSMTH W6 106 E2
Brady Recreation Centre WCHPL E1 92 C4
Braincroft Primary School CRICK NW2 69 H2
Braintree Road Industrial Estate RSLP HA4 65 F3
Bramah's Tea & Coffee Museum STHWK SE1 12 F9
Brampton College HDN NW4 52 A3
Brampton Manor School EHAM E6 95 H3
Brampton Primary School
BXLYHN DA7 136 E1
EHAM E6 95 J2
Brandlehow Primary School PUT/ROE SW15 127 J3
Branollys Health Centre PLSTW E13 94 E3
Breakspear Crematorium RSLP HA4 46 A4
Breaside Preparatory School BMLY BR1 153 G7
Brecknock Primary School HOLWY N7 72 D5

Bredinghurst School *PECK* SE15 131 K3
Brent Adult College *WLSDN* NW10 69 F7
Brent Arts Council *CRICK* NW2 69 J2
Brent Child & Family Clinic *WLSDN* NW10 69 H4
Brent Cross ⊖ *GLDGN* NW11 52 B6
Brent Cross Shopping Centre *HDN* NW4 52 A6
Brentfield Medical Centre *WLSDN* NW10 69 F5
Brentfield Primary School *WLSDN* NW10 69 F5
Brentford ⇌ *BTFD* TW8 104 E5
Brentford Business Centre *BTFD* TW8 104 D6
Brentford FC (Griffin Park) *BTFD* TW8 104 E5
Brentford Fountain Leisure Centre *BTFD* TW8 105 G4
Brentford Health Centre *BTFD* TW8 104 D5
Brentford School for Girls *BTFD* TW8 104 E5
Brent Knoll School *FSTH* SE23 151 F2
Brent Park Industrial Estate *NWDGN* UB2 102 A2
Brentside First School *HNWL* W7 84 E4
Brentside High School *HNWL* W7 84 E3
Brentside Primary School *HNWL* W7 84 E3
Brent Trading Estate *WLSDN* NW10 69 G4
Brent Valley Golf Club *HNWL* W7 84 E6
Brentwaters Business Park *BTFD* TW8 104 D6
Brettenham Primary School *ED* N9 42 C3
Brewers' Hall *CITYW* EC2V 12 F3
Brewery Industrial Estate *IS* N1 6 E6
Brewery Mews Business Centre *ISLW* TW7 124 A2
The Brewery *ROMW/RG* RM7 63 G5
Brick Lane Music Hall *CAN/RD* E16 95 H7
Brick Lane Music House *WCHPL* E1 13 M1
Bricklayer Arms Industrial Estate *STHWK* SE1 19 L6
The Bridewell Theatre *EMB* EC4Y 12 C5
The Bridge Academy *BETH* E2 7 L4
The Bridge Business Centre *NWDGN* UB2 103 F1
Bridge Lane Theatre *BTSEA* SW11 108 D7
The Bridge Leisure Centre *SYD* SE26 151 H4
Bridge Park Business & Leisure Centre *WLSDN* NW10 68 D6
The Bridge School *ARCH* N19 72 C1
HOLWY N7 72 D5
Brigham Young University *BAY/PAD* W2 8 C7
Bright Sparks Montessori School *WKENS* W14 107 G1
Brigstock Medical Centre *THHTH* CR7 164 C4
Brimsdown ⇌ *PEND* EN3 31 G1
Brimsdown Industrial Estate *PEND* EN3 30 E1
Brimsdown Infant School *PEND* EN3 31 F2
Brindishe Primary School *LEE/GVPK* SE12 133 J4
Britain & London Visitor Centre *STJS* SW1Y 11 G8
Britannia Business Centre *CRICK* NW2 70 B3
Britannia Leisure Centre *IS* N1 7 H4
Britannia Sports Ground *WALTH* E17 43 J6
Britannia Village Primary School *CAN/RD* E16 95 F7
British Airways Museum *HTHAIR* TW6 121 H3
The British American Drama Academy *CAMTN* NW1 4 B4
SRTFD E15 94 B1
British Cartoon Centre *BMSBY* WC1N 11 K1
British College of Osteopathy *HAMP* NW3 71 G5
British Dental Association *CAVSQ/HST* W1G 10 C3
The British Hernia Centre *HDN* NW4 51 K4
British Library *CAMTN* NW1 5 H7
British Library Newspaper Library *CDALE/KGS* NW9 51 G2
British Medical Association *STPAN* WC1H 5 H9
British Museum *RSQ* WC1B 11 J3
British Telecom Tower *GTPST* W1W 10 E2
BRIT School for Performing Arts *CROY/NA* CR0 164 E5
Brittons School Technology College *RAIN* RM13 81 H6
Brixton ⇌ ⊖ *BRXN/ST* SW9 130 B3
Brixton Academy *BRXN/ST* SW9 130 B2
Brixton Recreation Centre *BRXN/ST* SW9 130 B2
Broadfields Primary School *EDGW* HA8 36 C1
Broadgate *LVPST* EC2M 13 H2
Broadgate Ice Arena *LVPST* EC2M 13 H3
Broadhurst School *KIL/WHAMP* NW6 2 E1
Broadmead J & I School *CROY/NA* CR0 164 E5
Broadreach College *THMD* SE28 116 A2
Broadwalk Shopping Centre *EDGW* HA8 36 C5
Broadwater Farm Primary School *TOTM* N17 55 K1
Broadwater Primary School *TOOT* SW17 147 H3
Broadway Clinic *EDGW* HA8 36 D7
Broadway Retail Park *CRICK* NW2 70 B3
Broadway Shopping Centre *HMSMTH* W6 107 F4
Broadway Square *BXLYHS* DA6 137 H3
Broadway Squash & Fitness Centre *HMSMTH* W6 107 G3
Brocklebank Health Centre *WAND/EARL* SW18 128 A6
Brocklebank Industrial Estate *GNWCH* SE10 113 K3
Brockley ⇌ ⊖ *BROCKY* SE4 132 C2
Brockley Cross Business Centre *BROCKY* SE4 132 B2
Brockley Primary School *BROCKY* SE4 132 C4
Brockwell Lido *HNHL* SE24 130 C5
Bromet Primary School *OXHEY* WD19 21 H6
Bromley by Bow ⊖ *BOW* E3 93 K2
Bromley Cemetery *BMLY* BR1 152 D6
Bromley Civic Centre *BMLY* BR1 168 A1
Bromley College of Further & Higher Education *BMLY* BR1 152 E7
HAYES BR2 168 C5
Bromley FC *HAYES* BR2 168 A4
Bromley Golf Club *HAYES* BR2 168 D6
Bromley High School GDST *BMLY* BR1 169 F3
Bromley Industrial Centre *BMLY* BR1 168 C2
Bromley Mall Indoor Market *BMLY* BR1 167 K1
Bromley North ⇌ *BMLY* BR1 152 E7
Bromley Road Infant School *BECK* BR3 151 K7
Bromley Road Retail Park *CAT* SE6 151 K1
Bromley Ski Centre *STMC/STPC* BR5 155 K7
Bromley South ⇌ *BMLY* BR1 168 A2
Bromley Wendover Lawn Tennis Club *HAYES* BR2 168 A3
Brompton Medical Centre *ECT* SW5 14 D7
Brompton Oratory *SKENS* SW7 15 J4
Bromyard Leisure Centre *ACT* W3 87 G7
Brondesbury ⊖ *KIL/WHAMP* NW6 70 D6
Brondesbury College for Boys *KIL/WHAMP* NW6 70 B6
Brondesbury Park ⊖ *KIL/WHAMP* NW6 70 C7
Brook Community Primary School *HACK* E8 74 C4
Brooke Trading Estate *ROM* RM1 63 H6
Brookfield House School *WFD* IG8 44 C5
Brookfield Primary School *CHEAM* SM3 161 H7
HGT N6 72 B1
Brook House FC *YEAD* UB4 82 D2
Brook Industrial Estate *YEAD* UB4 83 H7
Brookland Junior School *GLDGN* NW11 53 F3
Brooklands Primary School *BKHTH/KID* SE3 133 K2
Brook Lane Business Centre *BTFD* TW8 104 E4
Brookmarsh Trading Estate *DEPT* SE8 112 E6
Brookmead Industrial Estate *CROY/NA* CR0 163 H5
Brookside Primary School *YEAD* UB4 83 G2
Broomfield House School *RCH/KEW* TW9 105 G7
Broomfield School *FBAR/BDGN* N11 40 D4
Broomsleigh Business Park *SYD* SE26 151 H4
Broomwood Hall Lower School *BAL* SW12 128 E5
STRHM/NOR SW16 148 D2
Brownlow Medical Centre *FBAR/BDGN* N11 40 E4
Brown's Hotel *MYFR/PICC* W1J 10 D7
Bruce Castle Museum *TOTM* N17 42 A7
Bruce Grove ⇌ *TOTM* N17 56 B1
Bruce Grove Primary School *TOTM* N17 56 B1
Brunei Gallery *STPAN* WC1H 11 H1
Brunel Engine House *BERM/RHTH* SE16 111 K1
Brunel University *GLDGN* NW11 52 B5
ISLW TW7 103 K6
TWK TW1 124 C3
Brunel University (Osterley Campus) Track *ISLW* TW7 103 K6
Brunswick Health Centre *FBAR/BDGN* N11 40 A1
Brunswick Housing & Shopping Centre *BMSBY* WC1N 5 K9
Brunswick Industrial Park *FBAR/BDGN* N11 40 B3
Brunswick Medical Centre *BMSBY* WC1N 5 J9
Brunswick Park JMI School *STHGT/OAK* N14 28 A7
Brunswick Park Primary School *CMBW* SE5 110 E6
BT Centre *STBT* EC1A 12 E4
Buckhurst Hill ⊖ *BKHH* IG9 45 H1
Buckhurst Hill Primary School *BKHH* IG9 45 J1
Buckingham College Preparatory School *PIN* HA5 47 K6
Buckingham Palace *WHALL* SW1A 16 E2
Buckingham Primary School *HPTN* TW12 141 K4
Buckingham Road Cemetery *IL* IG1 78 D1
Building Centre *GWRST* WC1E 11 G3
Bullers Wood School *CHST* BR7 153 K7
Bullsbridge Industrial Estate *NWDGN* UB2 102 A3
The Bull Theatre *BAR* EN5 26 D3
BUPA Roding Hospital *REDBR* IG4 59 H2
Burbage School *IS* N1 7 J5
Burdett Coutts CE Primary School *WEST* SW1P 17 G4
Burgess Business Park *CMBW* SE5 110 E6
Burgess Park Tennis Centre *CMBW* SE5 110 D5
Burlington Danes School *SHB* W12 87 K5
Burlington Infant School *NWMAL* KT3 160 C3
Burney Street Clinic *GNWCH* SE10 113 F6
Burnham Trading Estate *DART* DA1 139 G3
Burnhill Business Centre *BECK* BR3 166 D1
Burnley Road Clinic *WLSDN* NW10 69 J4
Burns Hotel *ECT* SW5 14 C6
Burnt Ash Primary School *BMLY* BR1 152 E4
Burnt Oak ⊖ *EDGW* HA8 36 E7
Burnt Oak Junior School *BFN/LL* DA15 136 B7
Burntwood School *TOOT* SW17 147 H1
Bursted Wood Primary School *BXLYHN* DA7 137 J1
Burwell Industrial Estate *LEY* E10 57 G7
Bushey ⇌ ⊖ *OXHEY* WD19 21 H5
Bushey Golf & Country Club *BUSH* WD23 22 A5
Bushey Grove Leisure Centre *BUSH* WD23 21 K3
Bushey Hall Golf Club *BUSH* WD23 21 J2
Bushey Hall School *BUSH* WD23 21 K5
Bushey Hall Swimming Pool *BUSH* WD23 21 K4
Bushey Health Centre *BUSH* WD23 21 K5
Bushey Heath Primary School *BUSH* WD23 22 D7
Bushey Jewish Cemetery *BUSH* WD23 22 B2
Bushey Manor Junior School *BUSH* WD23 21 K4
Bushey Meads School *BUSH* WD23 22 C4
Bushey Museum & Art Gallery *BUSH* WD23 22 A5
Bushey & Oxhey Infant School *BUSH* WD23 21 J4
Bush Hill Park ⇌ *EN* EN1 30 B5
Bush Hill Park Golf Club *WCHMH* N21 29 J4
Bush Hill Park Medical Centre *EN* EN1 30 B5
Bush Hill Park Primary School *EN* EN1 30 C4
BBC Bush House *HOL/ALD* WC2B 11 L5
Bush Industrial Estate *ARCH* N19 72 C2
WLSDN NW10 87 F3
The Business Academy Bexley *ERITHM* DA18 117 F1
The Business Centre *CEND/HSY/T* N8 54 E1
IL IG1 78 B1
The Business Design Centre *IS* N1 6 B4
Business Training & Solutions *CDALE/KGS* NW9 37 H7
Bute House Preparatory School for Girls *HMSMTH* W6 107 F3
Butlers Wharf *STHWK* SE1 13 M9
Butler's Wharf Business Centre *STHWK* SE1 19 M1
Butler's Wharf Pier *STHWK* SE1 13 M9
Butterfly Sports Club *ELTH/MOT* SE9 135 G5
Buxlow Preparatory School *WBLY* HA9 68 A2
Buzzard Creek Industrial Estate *BARK* IG11 97 F4
Byam Shaw School of Art *ARCH* N19 72 C1
Byfleet Industrial Estate *WATW* WD18 20 A7
Bygrove Prim School *POP/IOD* E14 93 K5
Byron Court Primary School *ALP/SUD* HA0 67 J1
Cabot Place *POP/IOD* E14 93 J7
The Cadogan Hotel *KTBR* SW1X 15 M4
Cadogan Pier *CHEL* SW3 108 D5
Caledonian Market *STHWK* SE1 19 K3
Caledonian Road ⊖ *HOLWY* N7 72 E4
Caledonian Road & Barnsbury ⊖ *HOLWY* N7 5 M1
Cally Pool *IS* N1 5 L3
Calverton Primary School *CAN/RD* E16 95 H5
Cambell Primary School *DAGW* RM9 79 K6
Camberwell Business Centre *CMBW* SE5 110 E6
Camberwell College of Arts *CMBW* SE5 111 F7
Camberwell Leisure Centre *CMBW* SE5 110 E7
Camberwell New Cemetery *PECK* SE15 132 A5
Camberwell Trading Estate *CMBW* SE5 130 C1
Cambridge Heath ⇌ *BETH* E2 92 D1
Cambridge Park Bowling & Sports Club *TWK* TW1 124 D5
Cambridge School *HMSMTH* W6 106 E3
Cambridge Theatre *LSQ/SEVD* WC2H 11 J5
Camden Arts Centre *HAMP* NW3 71 F4
Camden House Clinic *BKHTH/KID* SE3 133 H1
Camden Junior School *CAR* SM5 175 K3
Camden Market *CAMTN* NW1 4 B2
Camden Mews Day Hospital *CAMTN* NW1 4 F1
Camden People's Theatre *CAMTN* NW1 4 E8
Camden Road ⊖ *CAMTN* NW1 4 E1
Camden School for Girls *KTTN* NW5 72 C5
Camden Theatre *CAMTN* NW1 4 E5
Camden Town ⊖ *CAMTN* NW1 4 D3
Camden Town Hall & St Pancras Library *CAMTN* NW1 5 J7
Camelot Primary School *PECK* SE15 111 J6
Cameron House School *CHEL* SW3 15 H9
Camperdown House *WCHPL* E1 13 M5
Campion House College *ISLW* TW7 103 J6
Campsbourne School *CEND/HSY/T* N8 54 E2
Canada House *STJS* SW1Y 11 H8
Canada House Business Centre *RSLP* HA4 47 G7
Canada Place *POP/IOD* E14 93 J7
Canada Square *POP/IOD* E14 93 K7
Canada Water ⊖ ⊖ *BERM/RHTH* SE16 111 K2
Canada Water Retail Park *BERM/RHTH* SE16 112 A2
Canada Wharf Museum *BERM/RHTH* SE16 93 H7
Canal Cafe Theatre *BAY/PAD* W2 8 D2
Canary Riverside *BERM/RHTH* SE16 93 H7
Canary Wharf ⊖ *POP/IOD* E14 93 J7
Canary Wharf Pier *POP/IOD* E14 93 H7
Canberra Primary School *SHB* W12 87 K6
Canbury 2000 Business Park *KUTN/CMB* KT2 144 A7
Canbury Business Centre *KUTN/CMB* KT2 144 A7
Canbury Medical Centre *KUTN/CMB* KT2 144 B7
Canbury School *KUTN/CMB* KT2 144 D5
Cann Hall Primary School *WAN* E11 76 D2
The Canning School *ECT* SW5 14 C5
KENS W8 14 A3
Canning Town ⊖ ⊖ *POP/IOD* E14 94 C5
Cannizaro House Hotel *WIM/MER* SW19 146 A5
Cannon Hill Clinic *STHGT/OAK* N14 40 E2
Cannon Lane First School *PIN* HA5 47 H5
Cannon Sports Club *CANST* EC4R 12 F6
Cannon Street ⇌ ⊖ *CANST* EC4R 13 G7
Cannon Trading Estate *WBLY* HA9 68 D3
Cannon Wharf Business Centre *DEPT* SE8 112 B3
Canon Barnett Primary School *WCHPL* E1 13 M4
Canonbury ⊖ *HBRY* N5 73 J4
Canonbury Business Centre *IS* N1 6 F3
Canonbury Primary School *IS* N1 73 H5
Canon Palmer RC High School *IL* IG1 60 E7
Canons High School *EDGW* HA8 50 B1
The Canons Leisure Centre *MTCM* CR4 162 E3
Canons Park ⊖ *EDGW* HA8 36 A6
Canterbury Industrial Estate *NWCR* SE14 112 A5
Cantium Retail Park *STHWK* SE1 111 H5
Capital Business Centre *ALP/SUD* HA0 85 K1
MTCM CR4 162 E4
SAND/SEL CR2 177 K5
Capital City Academy *WLSDN* NW10 69 K7
The Capital Hotel *CHEL* SW3 15 L2
Capital Industrial Estate *BELV* DA17 98 E7
Capital Radio *LSQ/SEVD* WC2H 11 H7
Capital Wharf *WAP* E1W 92 C7
Capitol Industrial Park *CDALE/KGS* NW9 50 E2
Caplan Estate *MTCM* CR4 148 C7
Cardiff Road Industrial Estate *WATW* WD18 21 F5
Cardinal Hinsley College *WLSDN* NW10 69 J7
Cardinal Pole RC School *HOM* E9 75 G5
Cardinal Pole RC Secondary Lower School *HOM* E9 75 F6
Cardinal Road Infant School *FELT* TW13 122 A7
The Cardinal Vaughan Memorial School *WKENS* W14 107 H1
Cardinal Wiseman RC School (Technology & Art College) *GFD/PVL* UB6 84 C4
Cardwell Primary School *WOOL/PLUM* SE18 114 E3
Carew Manor School *WLGTN* SM6 176 D2
Carlisle Infant School *HPTN* TW12 142 B5
Carlton House *STJS* SW1Y 11 G9
The Carlton Mitre Hotel *E/WMO/HCT* KT8 157 K2
Carlton Primary School *KTTN* NW5 72 A4
Carlton Vale Infant School *MV/WKIL* W9 88 D2
Carlyle's House (NT) *CHEL* SW3 108 D5
Carnwath Road Industrial Estate *FUL/PGN* SW6 128 A2
Carpenders Park ⊖ *OXHEY* WD19 33 H2
Carpenders Park Cemetery *OXHEY* WD19 33 K3
Carpenters' Hall *OBST* EC2N 13 H3
Carpenters Primary School *SRTFD* E15 76 A7
Carshalton ⇌ *CAR* SM5 175 J3
Carshalton AFC *SUT* SM1 175 J2
Carshalton Beeches ⇌ *CAR* SM5 175 K5
Carshalton College *CAR* SM5 175 K2
Carshalton High School for Boys *CAR* SM5 175 H1
Carshalton High School for Girls *CAR* SM5 175 J2
Carshalton War Memorial Hospital *CAR* SM5 175 K4
The Cartoon Museum *RSQ* WC1B 11 J3
Caryl Thomas Clinic *HRW* HA1 48 E3
The Cassel Hospital *RCHPK/HAM* TW10 143 K3
Cassidy Medical Centre *FUL/PGN* SW6 107 K6
Castilion Primary School *THMD* SE28 97 J5
Castle Bar Park ⇌ *HNWL* W7 85 F4
Castlebar School *HNWL* W7 85 F4
Castlebar Special School *WEA* W13 85 G4
Castlecombe Primary School *ELTH/MOT* SE9 153 J4
Castle Hill Primary School *CROY/NA* CR0 180 A5
Castle Industrial Estate *WALW* SE17 18 E5
Casualty Plus Clinic *BTFD* TW8 104 D4
Caterham High School *CLAY* IG5 59 K1
Catford ⇌ *CAT* SE6 132 D6
Catford Bridge ⇌ *CAT* SE6 132 D6
Catford Cricket & Sports Club *CAT* SE6 132 E7
Catford Cyphers CC *CAT* SE6 151 H1
Catford High School *CAT* SE6 152 B2
Catford Trading Estate *CAT* SE6 151 K1
Catford Wanderers Sports Club *CAT* SE6 152 A3
Cathall Leisure Centre *WAN* E11 76 B2
The Cathedral School of St Saviour & St Mary Overy *STHWK* SE1 18 F1
Cator Park School for Girls *BECK* BR3 151 G6
Cavendish College *FITZ* W1T 11 G2
Cavendish Hotel *STJS* SW1Y 10 F8
Cavendish Primary School *CHSWK* W4 106 B6
Cavendish School *BERM/RHTH* SE16 111 K3
The Cavendish School *CAMTN* NW1 4 C3
Cavendish Special School *HNWL* W7 85 F5
Caxton Hall *STJSPK* SW1H 17 G3

Caxton Trading Estate HYS/HAR UB3 101 H1
Cayley Primary School WCHPL E1 93 G4
Cecil Park Clinic PIN HA5 47 J3
Cecil Sharpe House CAMTN NW1 4 B3
The Cedar School FSTGT E7 77 G5
Cedars Manor School KTN/HRWW/WS HA3 34 C7
The Cedars Primary School HEST TW5 101 K6
Cedar Way Industrial Estate CAMTN NW1 5 G2
Cenotaph WHALL SW1A 17 J1
Centaurs Business Centre ISLW TW7 104 B5
Centaurs RFC ISLW TW7 104 A5
Central Business Centre WLSDN NW10 69 G4
Centrale ⊖ CROY/NA CR0 177 J1
Centrale Shopping Centre CROY/NA CR0 177 J1
Central Foundation Boys School SDTCH EC2A 7 H9
Central Foundation Girls School (Lower) BOW E3 93 G2
Central Foundation Girls School (Upper) BOW E3 93 H2
Central Hall STJSPK SW1H 17 H2
Central Hendon Clinic HDN NW4 51 K3
Central London Golf Club TOOT SW17 147 H1
Central London Markets STBT EC1A 12 C3
Central Medical Centre MRDN SM4 162 B3
Central Middlesex Hospital WLSDN NW10 86 E2
Central Park Arena DART DA1 139 H7
Central Park Primary School EHAM E6 95 H1
Central Primary School WAT WD17 21 G3
Central St Martins College of Art & Design RSQ WC1B 11 L3
Central School of Ballet CLKNW EC1R 12 B1
Central School of Fashion GTPST W1W 10 E3
Central School of Speech & Drama HAMP NW3 3 G1
Central Square Shopping Centre WBLY HA9 68 A5
Centre Court Shopping Centre WIM/MER SW19 146 D5
The Centre Performing Arts College CHARL SE7 114 C2
Centre Point LSQ/SEVD WC2H 11 H4
Chadwell Heath ⇌ CHDH RM6 61 K6
The Chadwell Heath Foundation School CHDH RM6 61 H5
Chadwell Heath Industrial Park BCTR RM8 62 A7
Chadwell Heath Leisure Centre CHDH RM6 61 K5
Chadwell Infant & Primary School CHDH RM6 61 J6
Chaffinch Business Park BECK BR3 166 A2
Chailey Industrial Estate HYS/HAR UB3 101 K1
Chalcot School CAMTN NW1 4 C1
CAMTN NW1 72 B5
Chalgrove Primary School FNCH N3 52 C2
Chalk Farm ⊖ HAMP NW3 4 A1
Chalkhill Primary School WBLY HA9 68 D2
The Chamberlain Hotel TWRH EC3N 13 L6
Chambers Business Park WDR/YW UB7 100 D5
Chambers Wharf BERM/RHTH SE16 111 H1
Chancery Court Hotel HHOL WC1V 11 L3
Chancery Lane ⊖ FSBYW WC1X 12 A3
Chandlers Field Primary School E/WMO/HCT KT8 157 F4
Chandos Business Centre WLGTN SM6 176 C5
Channelsea Business Centre SRTFD E15 94 B1
Channing School HGT N6 54 B7
Chapel End Infant School WALTH E17 57 K1
Chapel End Junior School WALTH E17 43 K7
Chapman Park Industrial Estate WLSDN NW10 69 H5
Charing Cross ⇌ ⊖ CHCR WC2N 11 J8
Charing Cross Hospital HMSMTH W6 107 G5
Charing Cross Hotel CHCR WC2N 11 J7
The Charles Dickens Museum BMSBY WC1N 11 L1
Charles Dickens Primary School STHWK SE1 18 E2
Charles Edward Brooke School (Lower School) CMBW SE5 110 C7
Charles Edward Brooke School (Upper School) BRXN/ST SW9 110 C7
Charlotte Sharman Primary School LBTH SE11 18 C4
Charlotte Turner Primary School DEPT SE8 112 D5
Charlton ⇌ CHARL SE7 114 B4
Charlton Athletic FC (The Valley) CHARL SE7 114 B4
Charlton Cemetery CHARL SE7 114 D5
Charlton Health & Fitness Centre CHARL SE7 114 B4
Charlton House CHARL SE7 114 C5
Charlton Manor Junior School CHARL SE7 114 C6
Charlton RFC ELTH/MOT SE9 135 G6
Charlton School CHARL SE7 114 D5
Charrington Bowl SURB KT6 172 D1
Charrville Primary School YEAD UB4 82 C1
Charter Clinic CHEL SW3 15 L8
Charterhouse FARR EC1M 12 D1
Charteris Road Sports Centre HAMP NW3 71 J4
KIL/WHAMP NW6 70 D7
Charter Nightingale Hospital & Counselling Centre CAMTN NW1 9 K2
The Charter School HNHL SE24 130 E4
Chartwell Business Centre BMLY BR1 168 C2
Chase Bridge Primary School WHTN TW2 123 K5
Chase Lane Primary School CHING E4 43 H3
Chase Road Trading Estate WLSDN NW10 87 F3
Chase Side Primary School ENC/FH EN2 29 J1
Chaseville Clinic WCHMH N21 29 F5
Chater Infant School WATW WD18 20 E3
Chater Junior School WATW WD18 20 E3
Chatsworth Infant School BFN/LL DA15 136 B7
Chatsworth J & I School HSLW TW3 123 H3
Chaucer Clinic NWDGN UB2 103 J1
Cheam ⇌ BELMT SM2 174 D6
Cheam Common J & I School WPK KT4 173 K1
Cheam Fields Primary School CHEAM SM3 174 C4
Cheam High School CHEAM SM3 174 C3
Cheam Leisure Centre CHEAM SM3 174 B3
Cheam Park Farm Junior School CHEAM SM3 174 C2
Cheam Sports Club CHEAM SM3 174 C6
Chelsea Bridge Business Centre VX/NE SW8 109 G6
Chelsea Centre & Theatre WBPTN SW10 108 B6
Chelsea Cinema CHEL SW3 15 K8
The Chelsea Club Leisure Centre FUL/PGN SW6 108 A5
Chelsea College of Art & Design CHEL SW3 15 J8
FUL/PGN SW6 128 B1
SHB W12 106 E1
WEST SW1P 17 H7
Chelsea FC (Stamford Bridge) FUL/PGN SW6 108 A6
Chelsea Fields Industrial Estate WIM/MER SW19 147 H7
Chelsea Group of Children WBPTN SW10 108 B6
Chelsea Independent College FUL/PGN SW6 108 A6
Chelsea Leisure Centre CHEL SW3 15 K8
Chelsea Old Town Hall CHEL SW3 15 K8
Chelsea Physic Garden CHEL SW3 15 L9
CHEL SW3 108 E5
Chelsea & Westminster Hospital WBPTN SW10 108 B5
Chelsea Wharf WBPTN SW10 108 C6
Chennestone Community School SUN TW16 156 A1
Cherington House Health Centre HNWL W7 85 F7
Cherry Garden Pier BERM/RHTH SE16 111 J1
Cherry Garden School BERM/RHTH SE16 111 H3
Cherry Lane Primary School WDR/YW UB7 100 C3
Cherry Orchard Primary School CHARL SE7 114 B6
Chessington CC CHSGTN KT9 171 J6
Chessington Community College & Sports Centre CHSGTN KT9 171 K6
Chessington Golf Club CHSGTN KT9 171 K6
Chessington North ⇌ CHSGTN KT9 172 A4
Chessington South ⇌ CHSGTN KT9 171 K6
The Chesterfield Mayfair Hotel MYFR/PICC W1J 10 C8
Chesterton Primary School BTSEA SW11 109 F7
Chestnut Grove School BAL SW12 129 F7
Chestnuts Primary School SEVS/STOTM N15 55 J4
Cheyne Centre CHEL SW3 108 C5
Chicken Shed Theatre STHGT/OAK N14 28 A4
Childeric Primary School NWCR SE14 112 B6
Childs Hill Clinic CRICK NW2 70 D1
Childs Hill Primary School CRICK NW2 70 C2
Childs Welfare Clinic BCTR RM8 79 J4
Chiltonian Industrial Estate LEE/GVPK SE12 133 J5
Chimnocks Wharf POP/IOD E14 93 G6
Chingford Foundation School CHING E4 31 K7
Chingford Hall Primary School CHING E4 43 H5
Chingford Health Centre CHING E4 43 J3
Chingford Industrial Centre CHING E4 43 G4
Chingford Mount Cemetery CHING E4 43 K2
Chingford RFC CHING E4 31 J7
Chisenhale Primary School BOW E3 93 G1
Chislehurst ⇌ BMLY BR1 169 F1
Chislehurst Caves CHST BR7 154 A7
Chislehurst Cemetery CHST BR7 154 E4
Chislehurst Golf Club CHST BR7 154 B6
Chislehurst Natural Health Centre CHST BR7 154 B5
Chislehurst & Sidcup Grammar School BFN/LL DA15 155 H1
Chiswick ⇌ CHSWK W4 105 K6
Chiswick & Bedford Park Preparatory School CHSWK W4 106 B3
Chiswick Business Park CHSWK W4 105 J3
Chiswick Community School CHSWK W4 106 A6
Chiswick House CHSWK W4 106 A5
Chiswick Moran Hotel CHSWK W4 105 J4
Chiswick Park ⊖ CHSWK W4 105 K3
Chrisp Street Health Centre POP/IOD E14 93 K5
Christ Church Bentinck CE Primary School CAMTN NW1 9 J2
Christ Church Brondesbury CE J & I School KIL/WHAMP NW6 70 D7
Christ Church CE Junior School EA W5 85 K6
Christ Church CE Primary School BAR EN5 26 B1
BRXN/ST SW9 110 B7
BRXS/STRHM SW2 130 A7
BRYLDS KT5 159 H5
BTSEA SW11 128 D2
FSTH SE23 151 F1
WOOL/PLUM SE18 115 F7
CHEL SW3 15 K9
Christchurch CE Primary School HAMP NW3 71 H2
WCHPL E1 13 M3
Christchurch Industrial Centre STHWK SE1 12 C8
Christ Church Malden CE Primary School NWMAL KT3 160 B2
Christ Church Primary School ERITH DA8 118 A5
NWMAL KT3 160 A2
Christ Church School CAMTN NW1 4 D6
Christian Meeting Hall BECK BR3 151 J7
Christopher Hatton Primary School FSBYW WC1X 12 A1
Christs College Finchley FNCH N3 53 F2
Christs College School EFNCH N2 53 F2
Christs School RCHPK/HAM TW10 125 G4
Christ the King RC Primary School FSBYPK N4 55 F7
Christ the King Sixth Form College LEW SE13 133 G2
Chrysalis Theatre BAL SW12 129 F7
Chrysanthemum Clinic CHSWK W4 105 K6
Chrysolyte Independent Christian School STHWK SE1 19 H3
Church Down Adult School LEE/GVPK SE12 152 E1
Church End Medical Centre WLSDN NW10 69 G5
Church Farm House Museum HDN NW4 51 K2
Church Farm Swimming Pool EBAR EN4 27 K7
Churchfield Primary School ED N9 30 B7
Churchfields J & I School SWFD E18 44 E7
Churchfields Primary School BECK BR3 166 A2
Church Hill Primary School EBAR EN4 27 K6
Church House WEST SW1P 17 H3
Churchill Clinic STHWK SE1 18 B3
Churchill College RYNPK SW20 161 F1
Churchill Gardens Primary School PIM SW1V 16 E8
Churchill Museum & Cabinet War Rooms STJSPK SW1H 17 H1
Churchill Theatre BMLY BR1 167 K1
Church Stairs BERM/RHTH SE16 111 J1
Church Street ⊖ CROY/NA CR0 177 J1
Church Trading Estate ERITH DA8 118 D6
Cineworld BXLYHS DA6 137 J3
CHEL SW3 15 H9
CRICK NW2 51 K7
EA W5 85 K6
EN EN1 30 C3
FELT TW13 141 F1
HMSMTH W6 106 E3
SOHO/SHAV W1D 11 G7
WBPTN SW10 14 F8
WDGN N22 55 G1
Citigroup Tower POP/IOD E14 93 K7
City Business Centre BERM/RHTH SE16 111 K1
City Business College FSBYE EC1V 6 D8
City Central Estate FSBYE EC1V 6 E8
City College of Higher Education IS N1 7 H7
City & Guilds of London Art School LBTH SE11 18 B8
City Health Centre FSBYE EC1V 7 G9
City & Islington College FSBYE EC1V 6 F8
FSBYPK N4 73 H1
HBRY N5 73 G5
HOLWY N7 72 E3
IS N1 7 G3
STLK EC1Y 13 G1
City & Islington Sixth Form College FSBYE EC1V 6 C6
City Literary College HHOL WC1V 11 K4
City of East London College WCHPL E1 92 C5
The City of London Academy Islington IS N1 6 E4
The City of London Academy EDUL SE22 131 H4
STHWK SE1 111 H4
City of London Business College SEVS/STOTM N15 56 A4
SEVS/STOTM N15 56 C4
City of London Cemetery MNPK E12 77 J1
City of London Club OBST EC2N 13 J4
City of London College WCHPL E1 92 C5
City of London Crematorium MNPK E12 77 J2
City of London School BLKFR EC4V 12 D6
City of London School for Girls BARB EC2Y 12 E2
City of London School Sports Ground LEE/GVPK SE12 153 G1
City of Westminster Cemetery HNWL W7 85 F7
City of Westminster College BAY/PAD W2 9 G2
MV/WKIL W9 2 B8
City of Westminster Vehicle Pound MYFR/PKLN W1K 9 M7
City Thameslink ⇌ FLST/FETLN EC4A 12 C4
City University CLKNW EC1R 6 C8
STBT EC1A 12 E3
City University Business School BARB EC2Y 12 F2
Civil Service Sports Ground CHSWK W4 106 B7
LEE/GVPK SE12 134 B5
Clapham Common ⊖ CLAP SW4 129 H3
Clapham Common Clinic CLAP SW4 129 J3
Clapham High Street ⇌ ⊖ CLAP SW4 129 J2
Clapham Junction ⇌ ⊖ BTSEA SW11 128 D3
Clapham Manor Primary School CLAP SW4 129 H2
Clapham Manor Street Public Baths CLAP SW4 129 J2
Clapham North ⊖ CLAP SW4 129 K2
Clapham North Business Centre CLAP SW4 129 J2
Clapham Picture House CLAP SW4 129 H3
Clapham South ⊖ CLAP SW4 129 G5
Clapton ⇌ CLPT E5 74 D1
Clapton Girls Technology College CLPT E5 74 E3
Clara Grant Primary School BOW E3 93 J3
Clare House Primary School BECK BR3 167 F1
Claremont Clinic FSTGT E7 77 G4
Claremont Fan Court School ESH/CLAY KT10 170 B5
Claremont High School KTN/HRWW/WS HA3 50 A4
Claremont Landscape Garden (NT) ESH/CLAY KT10 170 A6
Claremont Primary School CRICK NW2 70 B1
Claremont Way Industrial Estate CRICK NW2 52 A7
Clarence House WHALL SW1A 16 F1
Clarendon Special School HPTN TW12 142 B5
Claridge's Hotel MYFR/PKLN W1K 10 C6
Claverings Industrial Estate ED N9 42 E1
Claygate ⇌ ESH/CLAY KT10 170 D5
Claygate Primary School ESH/CLAY KT10 170 E6
Clayhall Clinic CLAY IG5 59 J2
Claypond Hospital BTFD TW8 105 F3
Cleeve Park School SCUP DA14 155 J2
Clementine Churchill Hospital HRW HA1 66 E2
Cleopatra's Needle CHCR WC2N 11 L8
Clerkenwell Heritage Centre FARR EC1M 12 C1
Clerkenwell Parochial CE Primary School CLKNW EC1R 6 A8
Cleveland Primary School IL IG1 78 B3
Cleves Primary School EHAM E6 77 H7
C & L Golf & Country Club NTHLT UB5 65 F6
Clifton Lodge School EA W5 85 J6
Clifton Primary School NWDGN UB2 102 D3
Clink Exhibition STHWK SE1 13 G8
Clissold Leisure Centre STNW/STAM N16 73 K2
Clissold Park Natural Health Centre STNW/STAM N16 74 A1
C & L Leisure Centre RSLP HA4 65 F6
Clock House ⇌ BECK BR3 166 B1
Clockhouse Industrial Estate EBED/NFELT TW14 120 E7
Clock Museum CITYW EC2V 12 F4
Cloisters Business Centre VX/NE SW8 109 G6
Clore Gallery WEST SW1P 17 J6
Clore Tikva School BARK/HLT IG6 60 C1
Clothworkers' Hall FENCHST EC3M 13 K6
Clouster's Green WAP E1W 92 C7
Cobbold Estate WLSDN NW10 69 H5
Cobourg Primary School CMBW SE5 19 L9
Cochrane Theatre GINN WC1R 11 L3
Cockfosters ⊖ EBAR EN4 28 A3
Cockfosters Sports Ground EBAR EN4 27 K2
The Cockpit Theatre STJWD NW8 9 J1
Coldharbour Industrial Estate CMBW SE5 130 D1
Coldharbour Leisure Centre ELTH/MOT SE9 153 K1
Coldharbour Sports Ground ELTH/MOT SE9 154 A1
Colebrooke Primary School IS N1 6 C5
Colegrave School SRTFD E15 76 B4
Coleraine Park Primary School TOTM N17 42 D7
Coleridge Primary School HGT N6 54 D6
Colfe's Preparatory School LEE/GVPK SE12 133 K5
Colfe's Senior School LEE/GVPK SE12 133 K5
Colindale ⊖ CDALE/KGS NW9 51 G2
Colindale Business Park CDALE/KGS NW9 50 E2
Colindale Hospital CDALE/KGS NW9 51 G2
Colindale Primary School CDALE/KGS NW9 51 H3
Coliseum Theatre CHCR WC2N 11 J7
College Fields Business Centre WIM/MER SW19 147 J7
College of Arms BLKFR EC4V 12 E5
College of Business & Technology FSTGT E7 76 E4
College of Central London SDTCH EC2A 7 J9
College of Fuel Technology HGT N6 54 A5
The College of Law FITZ W1T 11 G3
LINN WC2A 12 A4
College of North East London CEND/HSY/T N8 55 G3
SEVS/STOTM N15 56 B3
WDGN N22 40 C7
College of North West London KIL/WHAMP NW6 2 A3
WBLY HA9 68 C2
WLSDN NW10 69 H4
College of Organists FLST/FETLN EC4A 12 B3
College of Osteopathy BORE WD6 24 D2
College Park School BAY/PAD W2 8 B5
Collier's Wood ⊖ WIM/MER SW19 147 H6
Collingwood Business Centre ARCH N19 72 E2
Collingwood Preparatory School WLGTN SM6 176 B4
Collins Method School CRICK NW2 70 A5
Collis Primary School TEDD TW11 143 H5
Colnbrook School OXHEY WD19 33 G1
Colne Bridge Retail Park WAT WD17 21 H4
Colne Valley Retail Park WAT WD17 21 H4
Coloma Convent Girls School CROY/NA CR0 179 F2
Colonnades Leisure Park CROY/NA CR0 177 G5

The Colonnades Shopping Centre BGVA SW1W 16 C5
Colours Sports Club SUT SM1 175 G4
Columbia Primary School BETH E2 7 M7
Colvestone Primary School HACK E8 74 B4
Colville Primary School NTGHL W11 88 D5
Colyers Lane Medical Centre ERITH DA8 118 A7
Comber Grove Primary School CMBW SE5 110 D6
Comedy Theatre STJS SW1Y 11 G7
Comelle House Trading Estate DEPT SE8 112 B4
Comfort Hotel ENC/FH EN2 29 H1
Comfort Inn HYS/HAR UB3 101 H4
Commonwealth Institute WKENS W14 107 J2
Community Arts Centre GNWCH SE10 112 E6
Community Centre (Island History Trust) POP/IOD E14 113 F3
Community College & School GNWCH SE10 113 F6
The Community College HACK E8 74 D7
Compass Theatre HGDN/ICK UB10 64 A2
Complementary Health Centre LEE/GVPK SE12 133 H5
Compton Leisure Centre NTHLT UB5 65 J7
The Compton School NFNCH/WDSPK N12 39 J5
Compton Sports Centre NFNCH/WDSPK N12 39 J5
Concord Business Centre ACT W3 86 D4
Conductive Education Centre MUSWH N10 54 B2
Conduit House GNWCH SE10 113 G6
Coney Hill School HAYES BR2 180 D1
Connaught Business Centre CDALE/KGS NW9 51 H4
CROY/NA CR0 177 F5
MTCM CR4 162 E4
The Connaught Hotel MYFR/PKLN W1K 10 B7
Connaught House School BAY/PAD W2 9 K5
Connaught School for Girls WAN E11 58 C7
Consort Clinic PECK SE15 131 J2
Consulate General of Monaco SKENS SW7 15 G5
Consulate General of the Republic of Guinea Bissau KENS W8 14 E3
Consulate of Burkina Faso BTSEA SW11 128 B2
Consulate of Chile CAVSQ/HST W1G 10 C1
Consulate of Colombia GTPST W1W 10 E4
Consulate of Eritrea IS N1 6 B5
Consulate of Guinea MYFR/PKLN W1K 10 A7
Consulate of Panama MYFR/PICC W1J 10 C9
Convent of Jesus & Mary Infant School CRICK NW2 70 A5
Convent of Jesus & Mary Language College WLSDN NW10 69 H7
Convoy's Wharf DEPT SE8 112 C4
Conway Medical Centre WOOL/PLUM SE18 115 J4
Conway Primary School WOOL/PLUM SE18 115 K3
Coombe Girls School NWMAL KT3 160 A1
Coombe Hill Golf Club KUTN/CMB KT2 145 F6
Coombe Hill J & I School NWMAL KT3 145 F7
Coombe Lane CROY/NA CR0 178 E4
Coombe Wood Golf Club KUTN/CMB KT2 144 D6
Coopers' Hall LVPST EC2M 13 K3
Coopers Lane Primary School LEE/GVPK SE12 152 E1
Coopers Technology College CHST BR7 154 C7
Copenhagen Primary School IS N1 5 K4
Copland Specialist Science College WBLY HA9 68 B4
Coppermill Primary School WALTH E17 57 F4
Coppetts Wood Hospital MUSWH N10 39 K7
Coppetts Wood Primary School MUSWH N10 40 A7
Copthall School MLHL NW7 37 K6
Copthorne Tara Hotel KENS W8 14 C3
Cordwainers College HACK E8 74 E6
Corinthian Casuals FC SURB KT6 172 C2
Coronet Cinema NTGHL W11 8 A8
SEVS/STOTM N15 55 H2
Corpus Christi RC Primary School BRXS/STRHM SW2 130 A4
Corus Hotel BAY/PAD W2 9 G6
BORE WD6 24 A6
Cosmopolitan College IS N1 5 L6
Coston Primary School GFD/PVL UB6 84 C2
Coteford Infant School PIN HA5 46 E4
Courtauld Institute of Art TPL/STR WC2R 11 M7
Court Farm Industrial Estate STWL/WRAY TW19 120 C5
Courtfield Medical Centre ECT SW5 14 D6
Courtland JMI School MLHL NW7 37 G1
Covent Garden ⊖ COVGDN WC2E 11 J6
Covent Garden Flower Market VX/NE SW8 109 J5
Covent Garden Medical Centre LSQ/SEVD WC2H 11 J5
Crafts Council IS N1 6 B6
Crampton Primary School WALW SE17 18 D6
Cranbrook College IL IG1 78 A1
Cranbrook Primary School IL IG1 59 K6
Crane Park Island Nature Reserve WHTN TW2 141 K1
Cranford Community College HEST TW5 102 A5
Cranford Infant School HSLWW TW4 121 K1
Cranford Junior School HSLWW TW4 122 A1
Cranford Park Junior School HYS/HAR UB3 101 J3
Cranford Park Primary School HYS/HAR UB3 101 J1
Cranleigh Gardens Industrial Estate STHL UB1 83 K4
Cranmer Primary School MTCM CR4 162 E3
The Craven Clinic HMSMTH W6 106 E3
Craven Park Medical Centre WLSDN NW10 69 F7
Crawford Primary School CMBW SE5 110 D7
Crayfields Business Park STMC/STPC BR5 155 J7
Crayford ⇌ DART DA1 138 B5
Crayford Commercial Centre DART DA1 138 B4
Crayford Industrial Estate DART DA1 138 C4
Crayford Leisure Centre & Greyhound Stadium DART DA1 138 B5
Crayford Medical Centre DART DA1 138 C4
Crayside Industrial Estate DART DA1 138 D2
Creekmouth Industrial Estate BARK IG11 97 F3
Creek Road Health Centre DEPT SE8 112 D5
Creek Road Industrial Estate DEPT SE8 112 E5
Crescent Hotel HRW HA1 48 E5
Crewe House MYFR/PICC W1J 10 C8
Cricket Green School MTCM CR4 162 D2
Cricklefield Stadium IL IG1 78 E1
Cricklewood ⇌ CRICK NW2 70 B2
Cricklewood Trading Estate CRICK NW2 70 C2
Crispin Industrial Centre UED N18 42 E4
Criterion Theatre MYFR/PICC W1J 10 F7
Crofton Leisure Centre BROCKY SE4 132 D5
Crofton Park ⇌ BROCKY SE4 132 C4
Croham Hurst Golf Club SAND/SEL CR2 178 B5
Cromer Road Primary School BAR EN5 27 F2
Cromwell Business Centre BARK IG11 96 E2
Cromwell Hospital ECT SW5 14 C5
Crook Log Primary School BXLYHS DA6 136 E3
Crook Log Sports Centre WELL DA16 136 E2
Crossharbour ⊖ POP/IOD E14 112 E2
Crossways Academy BROCKY SE4 132 B1
Crouch End Art School CEND/HSY/T N8 54 E4
Crouch End Health Centre CEND/HSY/T N8 54 E4
Crouch Hill ⊖ FSBYPK N4 55 F6
Crouch Hill Recreation Centre CEND/HSY/T N8 54 E6
Crowland Primary School SEVS/STOTM N15 56 C4
Crowlands Primary School ROMW/RG RM7 62 E5
Crown Close Business Centre BOW E3 75 J7
Crowndale Health Centre CAMTN NW1 4 F5
Crowne Plaza CAN/RD E16 94 E6
EA W5 86 A2
WDR/YW UB7 100 D3
Crownfield Primary School ROMW/RG RM7 62 C1
Crown Lane Clinic STHGT/OAK N14 28 C7
Crown Lane Primary School WNWD SE27 149 J3
Crown Moran Hotel CRICK NW2 70 B3
Crown Trading Centre HYS/HAR UB3 101 H1
Crown Woods School ELTH/MOT SE9 135 H4
Croydon Airport Industrial Estate CROY/NA CR0 177 G6
Croydon Bowling Club SAND/SEL CR2 177 J4
Croydon Cemetery CROY/NA CR0 164 A4
Croydon Clocktower Cinema CROY/NA CR0 177 J2
Croydon College CROY/NA CR0 177 K2
Croydon Crematorium THHTH CR7 163 K4
Croydon Fairfield Halls Cinema CROY/NA CR0 177 K2
Croydon FC SNWD SE25 165 K4
Croydon Road Industrial Estate BECK BR3 165 K3
Croydon Sports Arena SNWD SE25 165 K4
Crusader Industrial Estate FSBYPK N4 55 J5
Crystal Palace ⇌ ⊖ PGE/AN SE20 150 C5
Crystal Palace FC (Selhurst Park) SNWD SE25 165 F3
Crystal Palace FC Soccer & Sports Centre BRXN/ST SW9 130 A2
Crystal Palace Museum NRWD SE19 150 B5
Cuaco Sports Ground BECK BR3 151 J5
Cubitt Town Infants School POP/IOD E14 113 F2
Cuddington Cemetery WPK KT4 173 K1
Cuddington CP School WPK KT4 173 H2
Cuddington Croft Primary School BELMT SM2 174 B7
Culloden Primary School POP/IOD E14 94 B5
Culvers House Primary School MTCM CR4 163 F7
Cumberland Business Park WLSDN NW10 86 D2
The Cumberland Hotel FITZ W1T 11 G4
OXSTW W1C 9 M5
Cumberland Park Industrial Estate WLSDN NW10 87 J2
The Cumming Museum WALW SE17 18 E6
Cumnor House School SAND/SEL CR2 177 H7
Curwen Primary School PLSTW E13 94 E1
Curzon Mayfair Cinema MYFR/PICC W1J 10 C9
Curzon Soho Cinema SOHO/SHAV W1D 11 H6
Custom House MON EC3R 13 J7
Custom House for ExCeL ⊖ CAN/RD E16 95 F6
Cutlers' Hall STP EC4M 12 D4
Cutty Sark ⊖ GNWCH SE10 113 F5
Cutty Sark Clipper Ship GNWCH SE10 113 F5
Cygnet Clinic Beckton EHAM E6 96 B4
Cygnus Business Centre WLSDN NW10 69 H4
Cypress Infant School SNWD SE25 165 F1
Cypress Junior School SNWD SE25 165 F1
Cyprus ⊖ CAN/RD E16 96 A6
Cyprus College of Art WNWD SE27 149 H3
Cyril Jackson Primary School POP/IOD E14 93 H6
Dagenham Chest Clinic BCTR RM8 80 B2
Dagenham Civic Centre DAGE RM10 80 D1
Dagenham Dock ⇌ DAGW RM9 98 B1
Dagenham East ⊖ DAGE RM10 80 E5
Dagenham Heathway ⊖ DAGW RM9 80 B5
Dagenham Priory Comprehensive School & Performing Arts College DAGE RM10 80 D6
Dagenham & Redbridge FC DAGE RM10 80 D4
Dagenham Superbowl DAGE RM10 98 D1
Dagenham Swimming Pool DAGE RM10 80 C1
Daily Telegraph Newspaper Offices POP/IOD E14 112 D2
Dairy Meadow Primary School NWDGN UB2 102 E2
D'Albiac House HTHAIR TW6 120 D1
Dali Universe STHWK SE1 17 L1
Dallington School FSBYE EC1V 6 D9
Dalmain Primary School FSTH SE23 132 B7
Dalston Junction ⊖ HACK E8 74 B5
Dalston Kingsland ⊖ IS N1 74 A5
Damilola Taylor Centre PECK SE15 111 G6
Danegrove Primary School EBAR EN4 27 J5
Danetree School HOR/WEW KT19 172 E6
Danson House BXLYHS DA6 136 D3
Danson Primary School WELL DA16 136 C3
Danson Watersports Centre BXLYHS DA6 136 D4
Darell Primary School RCH/KEW TW9 125 H2
Darent Industrial Park ERITH DA8 119 G4
Dartford ⇌ DART DA1 139 H4
Dartford Adult Education Centre DART DA1 139 F6
Dartford Grammar School for Boys DART DA1 139 F5
Dartford Grammar School for Girls DART DA1 139 F6
Dartford Museum & Library DART DA1 139 H6
Dartford Natural Health Centre DART DA1 139 H6
Dartford Technology College DART DA1 139 F6
Dartford West Health Centre DART DA1 139 F5
Darwin Centre SKENS SW7 15 G4
Datapoint Business Centre BOW E3 94 B3
Daubeney Primary School CLPT E5 75 G3
The David Beckham Academy GNWCH SE10 113 J1
David Game College KENS W8 8 A8
David Livingstone Primary School THHTH CR7 149 J7
David Lloyd Leisure NFNCH/WDSPK N12 39 H6
SKENS SW7 14 D5
David Lloyd Sports Centre EN EN1 30 C1
David Lloyd Tennis Centre SCUP DA14 155 J4
Davidson Primary School CROY/NA CR0 165 G6
Davies Laing & Dick College BAY/PAD W2 8 C7
Davies Lane Primary School WAN E11 76 D1
Davies's College STHWK SE1 19 G1
Dawlish Primary School LEY E10 76 A1
Days Hotel BAY/PAD W2 9 H5
MLHL NW7 36 E1
RSLP HA4 65 G4
STHWK SE1 18 A4
Days Hotel London South Ruislip RSLP HA4 65 G3
Days Inn PIM SW1V 16 F7
Days Lane Primary School BFN/LL DA15 136 A5
Dean College of London HOLWY N7 73 F2
Deanesfield Primary School RSLP HA4 65 H3
Deansbrook Infant School MLHL NW7 36 E5
Deansfield Primary School ELTH/MOT SE9 135 F2
De Bohun Primary School STHGT/OAK N14 28 B4
Delta Wharf GNWCH SE10 113 G1
Denmark Hill ⇌ ⊖ CMBW SE5 130 E2
Denmead School HPTN TW12 142 A6
Denver Industrial Estate RAIN RM13 99 H5
Department for Environment, Food & Rural Affairs CHCR WC2N 11 J8
Department for Transport WEST SW1P 17 H5
Department of Art & Design (London Metropolitan University) WCHPL E1 13 M4
Department of Economics (London Metropolitan University) TWRH EC3N 13 L5
Department of Education STJSPK SW1H 17 H2
Department of Health WHALL SW1A 17 J1
Department of Trade & Industry STJSPK SW1H 17 H3
Deptford ⇌ DEPT SE8 112 D6
Deptford Bridge ⊖ DEPT SE8 112 D7
Deptford Business Centre NWCR SE14 112 A4
Deptford Green School NWCR SE14 112 C6
Deptford Park Business Centre DEPT SE8 112 B4
Deptford Park Primary School DEPT SE8 112 B4
Deptford Trading Estate DEPT SE8 112 B4
Dersingham Infant School MNPK E12 77 K4
Derwentwater Primary School ACT W3 86 E7
Design Centre Chelsea Harbour FUL/PGN SW6 108 B7
Design Museum STHWK SE1 13 M9
Deutsche Schule RCHPK/HAM TW10 124 E7
Devonshire Hospital MHST W1U 10 B2
Devonshire House Preparatory School HAMP NW3 71 G4
Devonshire Primary School BELMT SM2 175 G6
Devons Road ⊖ BOW E3 93 K3
Diamond College SOHO/SHAV W1D 11 H4
Diana Fountain E/WMO/HCT KT8 158 A1
Diana Princess of Wales Memorial Fountain BAY/PAD W2 9 H9
Diane Matthews Clinic ROMW/RG RM7 63 F3
Dilloway Industrial Estate NWDGN UB2 102 D1
Discovery Business Park BERM/RHTH SE16 111 H2
Discovery Primary School THMD SE28 97 F7
Docklands Medical Centre POP/IOD E14 112 D3
Docklands Sailing & Watersports Centre POP/IOD E14 112 D2
Dockmaster's House POP/IOD E14 93 J6
Dock Offices BERM/RHTH SE16 111 K2
Dockwell's Industrial Estate EBED/NFELT TW14 122 A4
Dockyard Industrial Estate WOOL/PLUM SE18 114 D2
Dog Kennel Hill Primary School EDUL SE22 131 F2
Dokal Industrial Estate NWDGN UB2 102 D1
Dollis Hill ⊖ WLSDN NW10 69 J4
Dollis Infant School MLHL NW7 38 A6
The Dolphin Leisure Centre ROM RM1 63 H3
Dolphin School BTSEA SW11 128 D4
The Dominie BTSEA SW11 108 E7
Dominion Business Park ED N9 43 F1
Dominion Theatre RSQ WC1B 11 H4
Donhead (Wimbledon College Preparatory School) WIM/MER SW19 146 B6
Donmar Warehouse Theatre LSQ/SEVD WC2H 11 J5
Donnington Primary School WLSDN NW10 69 K6
The Dorchester Hotel MYFR/PKLN W1K 10 B8
Dorchester Primary School WPK KT4 161 F7
Dorma Trading Park LEY E10 57 F7
Dormers Wells High School STHL UB1 84 A5
Dormers Wells Junior School STHL UB1 84 B6
Dormers Wells Leisure Centre STHL UB1 84 B5
Dormers Wells Medical Centre STHL UB1 84 A5
Dorothy Barley Primary School BCTR RM8 79 H4
Dorset Road Infant School ELTH/MOT SE9 153 J1
Dorset Square Hotel CAMTN NW1 9 L2
Douglas Bader Foundation PUT/ROE SW15 126 D5
Dovers Corner Industrial Estate RAIN RM13 99 H2
Downderry Primary School BMLY BR1 152 C3
Downe Manor Primary School NTHLT UB5 83 F2
Downham Health Centre BMLY BR1 152 C3
Downhills Primary School TOTM N17 55 K3
Downsell Primary School SRTFD E15 76 B3
Downshall Primary School GNTH/NBYPK IG2 60 E6
Downsview Primary School NRWD SE19 149 J6
Downsview School CLPT E5 74 D3
Drapers Hall LOTH EC2R 13 H4
Drapers Sports Ground SRTFD E15 76 A3
The Draycott Hotel CHEL SW3 15 M5
Drayton Green ⇌ HNWL W7 85 F6
Drayton Green Primary School WEA W13 85 G6
Drayton Manor High School HNWL W7 85 F6
Drayton Park ⇌ HOLWY N7 73 G4
Drayton Park Primary School HBRY N5 73 G4
DRCA Business Centre BTSEA SW11 109 F7
Drew Primary School CAN/RD E16 95 J7
The Drill Hall GWRST WC1E 11 G2
The Drizen School EDGW HA8 36 C6
Dr Johnson's House FLST/FETLN EC4A 12 B4
Dr Tripletts CE J & I School HYS/HAR UB3 82 D5
Drury Way Industrial Estate WLSDN NW10 69 F3
Duchess Theatre COVGDN WC2E 11 L6
Duff Miller College SKENS SW7 14 F5
Duke of York Column STJS SW1Y 11 H9
Duke of York Theatre CHCR WC2N 11 J7
Dukes Hotel WHALL SW1A 10 E9
Dulverton Primary School ELTH/MOT SE9 154 D1
Dulwich College DUL SE21 131 F7
Dulwich College Track DUL SE21 150 A1
Dulwich Hamlet FC EDUL SE22 131 F3
Dulwich Hamlet Junior School HNHL SE24 130 E5
Dulwich Hospital EDUL SE22 131 F3
Dulwich Leisure Centre EDUL SE22 131 H3
Dulwich Medical Centre EDUL SE22 131 H4
Dulwich Picture Gallery DUL SE21 131 F6
Dulwich & Sydenham Hill Golf Club DUL SE21 150 C1
Dulwich Village CE Infant School DUL SE21 131 F5

Dunbar Wharf POP/IOD E14 93 H6
Duncombe Primary School ARCH N19 54 E7
Dundee Wharf POP/IOD E14 93 H6
Dundonald Primary School WIM/MER SW19 146 D6
Dundonald Road WIM/MER SW19 146 D6
Dunningford Primary School HCH RM12 81 H4
Dunraven School STRHM/NOR SW16 149 F2
Duppas Junior School CROY/NA CR0 177 H4
Durand Primary School BRXN/ST SW9 110 A7
Durands Wharf BERM/RHTH SE16 112 C1
Durdans Park Primary School STHL UB1 83 K4
Durston House School EA W5 85 K5
Dysart School KUTN/CMB KT2 143 K3
SURB KT6 159 F6
Eaglesfield School WOOL/PLUM SE18 115 F7
Eagle Trading Estate MTCM CR4 162 E5
Ealdham Primary School ELTH/MOT SE9 134 B3
Ealing Abbey EA W5 85 J5
Ealing Abbey Scriptorium WEA W13 85 J5
Ealing Broadway EA W5 85 K6
The Ealing Broadway Centre EA W5 85 K6
Ealing Central Sports Ground GFD/PVL UB6 85 G1
Ealing Civic Centre EA W5 85 J6
Ealing College Upper School WEA W13 85 H5
Ealing Common EA W5 86 B7
Ealing CC EA W5 86 A5
Ealing Film Studios EA W5 85 J7
Ealing Golf Club GFD/PVL UB6 85 H2
Ealing Hammersmith & West London College WKENS W14 107 G3
Ealing Hospital NWDGN UB2 103 J1
Ealing Independent College EA W5 85 J6
Ealing Northern Sports Centre GFD/PVL UB6 66 D3
Ealing Park Health Centre EA W5 104 E3
Ealing Road Trading Estate BTFD TW8 104 E4
Ealing Snooker Club WEA W13 85 H7
Ealing Sports Centre EA W5 86 A6
Ealing & West London College EA W5 85 J7
Eardley Primary School STRHM/NOR SW16 148 C5
Earlham Primary School FSTGT E7 76 D4
WDGN N22 41 F6
Earl's Court ECT SW5 14 B6
Earl's Court Exhibition Centre ECT SW5 14 A8
Earlsfield WAND/EARL SW18 128 B7
Earlsfield Primary School WAND/EARL SW18 147 G1
Earlsmead First & Middle School RYLN/HDSTN HA2 65 K3
Earlsmead Primary School SEVS/STOTM N15 56 B3
Earth Galleries SKENS SW7 15 H4
East Acton SHB W12 87 H5
East Acton Primary School ACT W3 87 G6
East Barking Centre BCTR RM8 79 J4
East Barnet Health Centre EBAR EN4 27 H4
East Barnet School EBAR EN4 27 H2
EBAR EN4 27 K5
East Beckton District Centre EHAM E6 95 K5
Eastbrook Comprehensive School DAGE RM10 80 E3
Eastbrook End Cemetery ROMW/RG RM7 81 G2
Eastbrookend Country Park ROMW/RG RM7 81 F3
Eastbury Comprehensive School BARK IG11 79 F7
Eastbury Farm JMI School NTHWD HA6 32 D3
Eastbury Primary School BARK IG11 79 F6
Eastcote RSLP HA4 47 G6
Eastcote CC PIN HA5 47 F4
Eastcote Health Centre PIN HA5 47 G6
Eastcote Industrial Estate RSLP HA4 47 G6
Eastcote Lane Cemetery RYLN/HDSTN HA2 66 B2
Eastcote Primary School WELL DA16 135 J2
Eastcourt Independent School GDMY/SEVK IG3 61 G7
East Croydon CROY/NA CR0 177 K1
East Dulwich EDUL SE22 131 F3
East End Computing & Business College WCHPL E1 92 D5
Eastern Business Park HTHAIR TW6 121 J1
East Finchley EFNCH N2 53 J3
East Finchley Cemetery EFNCH N2 53 F2
East Finchley Medical Centre EFNCH N2 53 J3
East Finchley School of English EFNCH N2 53 J2
Eastgate Business Park LEY E10 57 G7
East Greenwich Christ Church CE Primary School GNWCH SE10 113 H3
East Ham EHAM E6 77 J6
East Ham Industrial Estate EHAM E6 95 H4
East Ham Jewish Cemetery EHAM E6 95 J2
East Ham Leisure Centre EHAM E6 77 K7
East Ham Memorial Hospital EHAM E6 77 H6
East Ham Nature Reserve EHAM E6 95 K3
East Hill Cemetery DART DA1 139 K6
East India POP/IOD E14 94 B6
Eastlea Community Centre CAN/RD E16 94 D3
Eastlea Community School CAN/RD E16 94 C3
East London Business College WAN E11 58 C7
East London Cemetery PLSTW E13 94 D2
East London Crematorium SRTFD E15 94 D2
East London RFC EHAM E6 95 K4
East London RUFC SRTFD E15 94 D1
Eastman Dental Hospital FSBYW WC1X 5 L9
East Molesey CC E/WMO/HCT KT8 157 H2
East Putney PUT/ROE SW15 127 H4
East Sheen Cemetery RCHPK/HAM TW10 125 H4
East Sheen Primary School MORT/ESHN SW14 126 B3
East Thamesmead Business Park ERITHM DA18 117 G1
East Wickham Primary School WELL DA16 116 A7
Eaton Manor RFC WAN E11 59 G4
Eaton Square Preparatory School BGVA SW1W 16 C5
Eaton Square School PIM SW1V 16 E6
Ecclesbourne Primary School THHTH CR7 164 D4
Eden College STHWK SE1 18 D3
Edenham High School CROY/NA CR0 166 B6
Eden High School FUL/PGN SW6 107 J7
Eden Medical Centre WKENS W14 107 J3
Eden Park BECK BR3 166 D4
Edenvale Child Health Clinic MTCM CR4 148 A6
Eden Walk Shopping Centre KUT/HW KT1 159 F1
Edes Business Park WLGTN SM6 176 A1
Edgebury Primary School CHST BR7 154 C3
Edge Business Centre CRICK NW2 69 K1
Edgware EDGW HA8 36 D5
Edgwarebury Cemetery EDGW HA8 36 C1
Edgware Clinic EDGW HA8 36 C5
Edgware College KIL/WHAMP NW6 71 G5
Edgware Community Hospital EDGW HA8 36 D6
Edgware FC & Wealdstone FC EDGW HA8 36 C6
Edgware Infant School EDGW HA8 36 C5
Edgware Jewish Primary School EDGW HA8 36 D4
Edgware Junior School EDGW HA8 36 D5
Edgware Road BAY/PAD W2 9 H3
Edinburgh Primary School WALTH E17 57 H4
Edith Neville Primary School CAMTN NW1 5 G6
Edmonton Cemetery WCHMH N21 41 K1
Edmonton Green ED N9 42 C1
Edmonton Green Shopping Centre ED N9 42 D1
Edmonton Leisure Centre ED N9 42 C2
Edmonton Lower School ED N9 30 A7
Edmonton Upper School EN EN1 30 B6
Edmund Waller Primary School NWCR SE14 132 A1
Education Centre WOOL/PLUM SE18 115 G4
Edward Betham CE Primary School GFD/PVL UB6 84 D2
Edward Pauling School FELT TW13 140 C1
Edward Wilson Primary School BAY/PAD W2 8 C2
Edwin Lambert School EMPK RM11 63 J5
Effra Road Retail Park BRXS/STRHM SW2 130 B4
The Egerton House Hotel CHEL SW3 15 K4
Eglinton Junior School WOOL/PLUM SE18 115 F5
Eglinton Primary School WOOL/PLUM SE18 115 F6
Elbourne Trading Estate BELV DA17 117 J2
Eldenwall Industrial Estate BCTR RM8 62 A7
Eldon Infant School ED N9 30 D7
Eldon Junior School ED N9 30 E7
Eleanor Palmer Primary School KTTN NW5 72 C3
Eleanor Smith Special School PLSTW E13 94 E1
Electrical Trades Union College ESH/CLAY KT10 170 A3
Electric Cinema NTGHL W11 88 D5
Elephant & Castle WALW SE17 18 E5
Elephant & Castle Leisure Centre LBTH SE11 18 D5
Elephant & Castle Shopping Centre STHWK SE1 18 D4
Elers Clinic HYS/HAR UB3 101 G3
Elfrida Primary School CAT SE6 151 K3
Eliot Bank Primary School FSTH SE23 150 D1
Elizabeth Garrett Anderson Hospital CAMTN NW1 5 H8
Elizabeth Selby Infant School BETH E2 92 C2
Elizabeth Trading Estate NWCR SE14 112 A5
Ellen Wilkinson Primary School CAN/RD E16 95 H4
Ellen Wilkinson School for Girls ACT W3 86 B5
Ellern Mede School TRDG/WHET N20 26 B7
Ellerslie Square Industrial Estate BRXS/STRHM SW2 129 K3
Ellingham Primary School CHSGTN KT9 171 K6
Elmbridge Leisure Centre WOT/HER KT12 156 A4
Elm Court School WNWD SE27 149 H1
Elmers End BECK BR3 166 A3
The Elmgreen School WNWD SE27 149 H1
Elmgrove Middle School KTN/HRWW/WS HA3 49 G3
Elmhurst Primary School FSTGT E7 77 F6
Elmhurst School SAND/SEL CR2 177 K4
Elm Lea Trading Estate TOTM N17 42 C6
Elm Park HCH RM12 81 J3
The Elms Football & Tennis Club STAN HA7 35 H4
Elmstead Woods CHST BR7 153 J5
Elmwood J & I School CROY/NA CR0 164 C6
Elm Wood Primary School DUL SE21 149 K2
Elsdale Street Health Centre HOM E9 74 E6
Elsley Primary School WBLY HA9 68 B5
Elsley School BTSEA SW11 129 F2
Elstree Aerodrome BORE WD6 23 F2
Elstree & Borehamwood BORE WD6 24 B3
Elstree Golf & Country Club BORE WD6 23 K2
Elstree Studios BORE WD6 24 C2
Elstree Way Clinic BORE WD6 24 D1
Eltham ELTH/MOT SE9 134 E3
Eltham Bus Station ELTH/MOT SE9 134 E4
Eltham CE Primary School ELTH/MOT SE9 134 E4
Eltham College Junior School ELTH/MOT SE9 134 C7
Eltham College Senior School ELTH/MOT SE9 153 H1
Eltham Crematorium ELTH/MOT SE9 135 J3
Eltham Green School ELTH/MOT SE9 134 C5
Eltham Health Clinic ELTH/MOT SE9 134 D4
Eltham Health & Fitness Centre ELTH/MOT SE9 135 F5
Eltham Hill Technology College ELTH/MOT SE9 134 D5
Eltham Palace ELTH/MOT SE9 134 D6
Eltham Pools ELTH/MOT SE9 134 D4
Eltham Warren Golf Club ELTH/MOT SE9 135 G4
Elthorne Park High School HNWL W7 104 A2
Elthorne Sports Centre HNWL W7 104 A2
Elverson Road LEW SE13 132 E1
Elystan Business Centre YEAD UB4 83 G6
Emanuel School BTSEA SW11 128 C4
Embankment CHCR WC2N 11 K8
Embankment Pier CHCR WC2N 11 L8
Embassy of Afghanistan SKENS SW7 15 G2
Embassy of Albania BGVA SW1W 16 D4
Embassy of Algeria NTGHL W11 88 C7
Embassy of Angola MYFR/PKLN W1K 10 A7
Embassy of Argentina MYFR/PKLN W1K 10 C6
Embassy of Armenia KENS W8 14 C3
Embassy of Austria KTBR SW1X 16 A3
Embassy of Bahrain SKENS SW7 14 E4
Embassy of Belarus KENS W8 14 D2
Embassy of Belgium KTBR SW1X 16 B4
Embassy of Bolivia BGVA SW1W 16 B4
Embassy of Bosnia-Herzegovina CAVSQ/HST W1G 10 D4
Embassy of Brazil MYFR/PKLN W1K 10 A6
Embassy of Bulgaria SKENS SW7 14 F3
Embassy of Cameroon NTGHL W11 88 C7
Embassy of China CAVSQ/HST W1G 10 C2
Embassy of Costa Rica BAY/PAD W2 8 F6
Embassy of Cote d'Ivoire KTBR SW1X 16 B3
Embassy of Croatia GTPST W1W 10 D1
Embassy of Cuba LSQ/SEVD WC2H 11 J4
Embassy of Democratic Republic of the Congo KTBR SW1X 15 M4
Embassy of Denmark KTBR SW1X 15 L3
Embassy of Dominican Republic BAY/PAD W2 8 D5
Embassy of Ecuador KTBR SW1X 15 L3
Embassy of Egypt MYFR/PICC W1J 10 C8
Embassy of Estonia SKENS SW7 14 F2
Embassy of Ethiopia SKENS SW7 15 H2
Embassy of Finland KTBR SW1X 16 A3
Embassy of France KTBR SW1X 15 M1
Embassy of Gabon SKENS SW7 14 F4
Embassy of Georgia KENS W8 14 C2
Embassy of Germany KTBR SW1X 16 A3
Embassy of Ghana HGT N6 54 B7
Embassy of Greece NTGHL W11 88 D7
Embassy of Guatemala WBPTN SW10 14 E9
Embassy of Honduras MBLAR W1H 9 M2
Embassy of Hungary KTBR SW1X 16 B4
Embassy of Iceland KTBR SW1X 16 A5
Embassy of Indonesia MYFR/PKLN W1K 10 B7
Embassy of Iran SKENS SW7 15 H2
Embassy of Iraq SKENS SW7 14 F3
Embassy of Ireland KTBR SW1X 16 C2
Embassy of Israel KENS W8 14 D1
Embassy of Italy MYFR/PKLN W1K 10 B6
Embassy of Japan MYFR/PICC W1J 10 D9
Embassy of Jordan KENS W8 14 A2
Embassy of Korea WESTW SW1E 16 F3
Embassy of Krygyzstan MBLAR W1H 9 L3
Embassy of Kuwait KTBR SW1X 15 M1
Embassy of Latvia CAMTN NW1 10 A1
Embassy of Lebanon KENS W8 8 C8
Embassy of Liberia BAY/PAD W2 8 B6
Embassy of Lithuania MBLAR W1H 9 L3
Embassy of Luxembourg KTBR SW1X 16 A2
Embassy of Mexico MYFR/PICC W1J 10 C9
Embassy of Mongolia KENS W8 14 D2
Embassy of Morocco SKENS SW7 14 E5
Embassy of Mozambique FITZ W1T 10 E1
Embassy of Myanmar MYFR/PICC W1J 10 C8
Embassy of Nepal KENS W8 8 C8
Embassy of Netherlands SKENS SW7 14 F2
Embassy of Norway KTBR SW1X 16 B3
Embassy of Paraguay SKENS SW7 14 D4
Embassy of Peru KTBR SW1X 15 M3
Embassy of Philippines KENS W8 8 C9
Embassy of Poland CAVSQ/HST W1G 10 C2
Embassy of Portugal KTBR SW1X 16 A2
Embassy of Qatar MYFR/PKLN W1K 10 B8
Embassy of Romania KENS W8 14 C1
Embassy of Russian Federation KENS W8 8 C9
Embassy of Saudi Arabia MYFR/PICC W1J 10 C8
Embassy of Senegal CRICK NW2 70 A6
Embassy of Slovak Republic KENS W8 8 C8
Embassy of Slovenia MHST W1U 10 C4
Embassy of Spain KTBR SW1X 16 B3
Embassy of Sudan WHALL SW1A 10 E9
Embassy of Sweden MBLAR W1H 9 L3
Embassy of Switzerland MBLAR W1H 9 L3
Embassy of Syria KTBR SW1X 16 A2
Embassy of Thailand SKENS SW7 14 F4
Embassy of the Holy See WIM/MER SW19 146 A2
Embassy of the United States MYFR/PKLN W1K 10 A6
Embassy of Tunisia SKENS SW7 15 H2
Embassy of Turkey KTBR SW1X 16 B2
Embassy of Turkmenistan FITZ W1T 10 F3
Embassy of Ukraine NTGHL W11 88 C7
Embassy of United Arab Emirates BAY/PAD W2 15 H1
Embassy of Uruguay SKENS SW7 15 K3
Embassy of Uzbekistan NTGHL W11 88 D7
Embassy of Venezuela SKENS SW7 15 H4
Embassy of Vietnam KENS W8 14 D3
Embassy of Yemen SKENS SW7 15 G5
Emberhurst School ESH/CLAY KT10 157 J6
Ember Sports Club ESH/CLAY KT10 157 H7
Embroidery World Business Centre WFD IG8 59 H1
EMD Walthamstow Cinema WALTH E17 57 J3
Emery Theatre POP/IOD E14 93 K5
Emmanuel CE Primary School KIL/WHAMP NW6 70 E4
Empire Cinema LSQ/SEVD WC2H 11 H6
Endsleigh Industrial Estate NWDGN UB2 102 D3
Enfield Business Centre PEND EN3 30 E1
Enfield CC EN EN1 30 A3
Enfield Chase ENC/FH EN2 29 J2
Enfield College PEND EN3 30 E2
Enfield County School ENC/FH EN2 29 K2
Enfield FC ED N9 42 E1
Enfield Golf Club ENC/FH EN2 29 H3
Enfield Grammar School (Upper) ENC/FH EN2 29 K2
Enfield Town EN EN1 29 K3
English Martyrs RC Primary School WALW SE17 19 G6
WCHPL E1 13 M5
Ensham Secondary School TOOT SW17 147 K4
Enterprise Business Park POP/IOD E14 112 E1
Enterprise Industrial Estate BERM/RHTH SE16 111 K4
Epsom & Ewell High School HOR/WEW KT19 172 E5
Eric Liddell Sports Centre ELTH/MOT SE9 153 H1
Eridge House Preparatory School FUL/PGN SW6 127 J1
Erith ERITH DA8 118 A4
Erith & District Hospital ERITH DA8 118 A5
Erith Health Centre ERITH DA8 118 B5
Erith Library & Museum ERITH DA8 118 B4
Erith Playhouse ERITH DA8 118 C4
Erith School ERITH DA8 117 K6
Erith School Community Sports Centre ERITH DA8 117 K6
Erith Small Business Centre ERITH DA8 118 C5
Erith Sports Centre ERITH DA8 118 B5
Erith Stadium ERITH DA8 118 B5
Ernest Bevin College TOOT SW17 147 J2
Eros MYFR/PICC W1J 11 G7
Esher ESH/CLAY KT10 170 D1
Esher CE High School ESH/CLAY KT10 170 A2
Esher Church Primary School ESH/CLAY KT10 170 C5
Esher College THDIT KT7 157 K6
Essendine Primary School KIL/WHAMP NW6 2 B8
Essex Primary School MNPK E12 77 J5
Ethelburga GM School BTSEA SW11 108 D7
Euro Business Centre SRTFD E15 76 D7
Euro Freightliner Terminal WLSDN NW10 87 G2
Eurolink Business Centre BRXS/STRHM SW2 130 B3
Europa Trading Estate ERITH DA8 118 A4
European Business Centre CDALE/KGS NW9 51 F2
European Business School London CAMTN NW1 4 A9

European College of Business Management SDTCH EC2A 7 J9
European School of Economics KTBR SW1X 16 B2
European Vocational College HDTCH EC3A 13 K5
Euro Way School CEND/HSY/T N8 55 G2
Euro Way School London FSBYPK N4 55 H6
Euston ⇌ ⊖ ⊖ CAMTN NW1 5 G8
Euston Centre University of Westminster CAMTN NW1 4 D9
Euston Square ⊖ CAMTN NW1 4 F9
Euston Tower CAMTN NW1 4 E9
Evans Business Centre CRICK NW2 69 J2
Eveline Day School TOOT SW17 147 K1
Evendine College SOHO/SHAV W1D 11 G4
Eversley Medical Centre CROY/NA CR0 164 B5
Eversley Primary School WCHMH N21 28 E4
Everyman Belsize Park HAMP NW3 71 J4
Everyman Cinema HAMP NW3 71 G3
Evolution House, Kew Gardens RCH/KEW TW9 125 F1
Ewell Athletics Track HOR/WEW KT19 173 F5
Ewell Castle Junior School EW KT17 173 H7
Ewell Castle School EW KT17 173 J7
Ewell Grove Infant School EW KT17 173 H7
Ewell West ⇌ HOR/WEW KT19 173 G7
ExCeL Exhibition Centre CAN/RD E16 95 F6
Excelsior College UED N18 42 A5
Exchange Square SDTCH EC2A 13 J2
The Exchange IL IG1 78 B1
Executive Medical & Occupational Health Centre CROY/NA CR0 177 K2
Exhibition Halls WBLY HA9 68 C3
Express by Holiday Inn
CAN/RD E16 94 D5
CHING E4 43 J6
CROY/NA CR0 177 J1
GNTH/NBYPK IG2 60 D5
HMSMTH W6 106 E3
PIM SW1V 16 F7
SDTCH EC2A 7 J8
STHWK SE1 12 D8
WAND/EARL SW18 128 A3
WAP E1W 93 F6
WIM/MER SW19 147 H6
The Eye Clinic NOXST/BSQ WC1A 11 H4
Faculty of Engineering & Science (University of Westminster) FITZ W1T 10 F2
Fairbrook Medical Centre BORE WD6 24 D1
Faircharm Trading Estate
DEPT SE8 112 E6
IS N1 6 E5
The Faircross Complementary Medical Centre BARK IG11 78 E5
Fairfield Pool & Leisure Centre DART DA1 139 H6
Fairfield Trade Park KUT/HW KT1 159 G2
Fairholme Primary School EBED/NFELT TW14 121 G7
Fairlawn Primary School FSTH SE23 131 K6
Fairley House School PIM SW1V 17 G6
Fairview Industrial Centre RAIN RM13 99 F5
Fairview Industrial Estate HYS/HAR UB3 101 J1
Fairview Medical Centre STRHM/NOR SW16 148 E7
Fairway Primary School MLHL NW7 37 F1
Fairways Business Park LEY E10 75 G1
Falconbrook Primary School BTSEA SW11 128 C1
Falcon Business Centre BTSEA SW11 128 D3
Falconer Special School BUSH WD23 21 K4
Falcon Park Industrial Estate WLSDN NW10 69 G4
The Falcons Preparatory School for Boys RCH/KEW TW9 124 E2
The Falcons School for Girls EA W5 86 B7
Falconwood ⇌ ELTH/MOT SE9 135 J2
Falkner House School SKENS SW7 14 F7
Family Records Centre FSBYW WC1X 6 A8
Fanmakers' Hall LVPST EC2M 13 J3
The Fan Museum GNWCH SE10 113 F6
Faraday Building BLKFR EC4V 12 D5
Farm Lane Trading Estate FUL/PGN SW6 107 K5
Farnell House Medical Centre HSLW TW3 103 G7
Farnham Green Primary School GDMY/SEVK IG3 61 G5
Farringdon ⇌ ⊖ FARR EC1M 12 B2
Farrington & Stratford House School CHST BR7 154 D6
Featherstone Industrial Estate NWDGN UB2 102 D1
Featherstone Primary School NWDGN UB2 102 C3
Featherstone Road Health Clinic NWDGN UB2 102 D2
Federation St Elpheges RC School WLGTN SM6 176 E5
Felnex Trading Estate WLGTN SM6 176 A1
Feltham ⇌ FELT TW13 122 A7
Feltham Airparcs Leisure Centre FELT TW13 141 H1
Feltham Athletics Arena EBED/NFELT TW14 121 K6
Felthambrook Industrial Estate FELT TW13 141 F2
Feltham Cemetery FELT TW13 140 D2
Feltham Community College FELT TW13 141 G1
Feltham Hill Infant School FELT TW13 140 D2
Feltham Hill Junior School FELT TW13 140 D2
Feltham & Hounslow Borough FC EBED/NFELT TW14 121 K6
Feltham Superbowl FELT TW13 141 F1
Fenchurch Street ⇌ FENCHST EC3M 13 K6
Fenstanton J & I School BRXS/STRHM SW2 130 B7
Fenton House (NT) HAMP NW3 71 G2
Ferrier Industrial Estate WAND/EARL SW18 128 A3
Ferry Island Retail Park TOTM N17 56 B2
Ferry Lane Industrial Estate
RAIN RM13 99 J4
WALTH E17 56 E2
Ferry Lane Primary School TOTM N17 56 D3
Festival Pier STHWK SE1 11 M8
Field End J & I Schools RSLP HA4 65 H1
Field Infant School WATW WD18 21 G4
Fielding Primary School WEA W13 104 C2
Field Junior School WATW WD18 21 G4
Fieldway ◆ CROY/NA CR0 179 K6
Film House Cinema RCH/KEW TW9 124 E4
Financial Times STHWK SE1 12 F8
Financial Times Newspaper Offices POP/IOD E14 94 A5
Finchley Catholic High School NFNCH/WDSPK N12 39 G2
Finchley Central ⊖ FNCH N3 38 E7
Finchley CC FNCH N3 53 F1
Finchley Golf Club MLHL NW7 38 D5
Finchley Industrial Centre NFNCH/WDSPK N12 39 G3
Finchley Lawn Tennis Club FNCH N3 38 D5
Finchley Lido Leisure Centre NFNCH/WDSPK N12 39 H6
Finchley Memorial Hospital NFNCH/WDSPK N12 39 G6
Finchley Road ⊖ KIL/WHAMP NW6 71 G5
Finchley Road & Frognal ⊖ KIL/WHAMP NW6 71 F4
Finchley Youth Theatre EFNCH N2 53 J2
Finsbury Circus Medical Centre LVPST EC2M 13 H3
Finsbury Health Centre CLKNW EC1R 6 A9
Finsbury Leisure Centre FSBYE EC1V 6 F8
Finsbury Park ⇌ ⊖ FSBYPK N4 73 G1
Finsbury Park Track FSBYPK N4 55 H6
Finton House School TOOT SW17 147 K1
Fircroft Primary School TOOT SW17 147 K1
Fire Brigade HQ STHWK SE1 17 L5
Fire Brigade Museum STHWK SE1 18 E1
Firepower Royal Artillery Museum WOOL/PLUM SE18 115 G2
Firs Farm Primary School PLMGR N13 41 K2
Fisher Athletic FC BERM/RHTH SE16 93 F7
Fisher Industrial Estate WATW WD18 21 G4
Fishmonger's Hall CANST EC4R 13 G7
Fitness Unlimited Leisure Centre BOW E3 93 J1
Fitzrovia Medical Centre FITZ W1T 10 E1
Fitzroy Nuffield Hospital MBLAR W1H 9 L4
Five Bridges LBTH SE11 17 M8
Five Elms Primary School DAGW RM9 80 B2
Five Ways Business Centre FELT TW13 141 F2
Flamsteed House Museum GNWCH SE10 113 G6
Flaxman Sports Centre CMBW SE5 130 D1
Fleecefield Primary School ED N9 42 C3
Fleet Primary School HAMP NW3 71 K4
Fleetway Business Park GFD/PVL UB6 85 H1
Fleming Lab Museum BAY/PAD W2 9 H4
Flora Gardens Primary School HMSMTH W6 106 E3
Florence Nightingale Museum STHWK SE1 17 L2
Flutters Leisure Centre FUL/PGN SW6 107 K6
Follys End Christian High School SNWD SE25 165 F5
Follys End Christian School SAND/SEL CR2 178 A3
The Foot Clinic WIM/MER SW19 146 C5
The Ford College CONDST W1S 10 D5
Fordgate Business Park BELV DA17 117 K1
Ford Industrial Park DAGW RM9 98 D2
Fordview Industrial Estate RAIN RM13 99 F2
Foreign & Commonwealth Office WHALL SW1A 17 H1
Foreland Medical Centre NTGHL W11 88 C6
Forest Business Park LEY E10 57 F6
Forestdale Primary School CROY/NA CR0 179 G7
Foresters Primary School WLGTN SM6 176 D5
Forest Gate ⇌ FSTGT E7 76 E4
Forest Gate Community School FSTGT E7 76 E4
Forest Hill ⇌ ⊖ FSTH SE23 150 E1
Forest Hill Business Centre FSTH SE23 150 E1
Forest Hill Industrial Estate FSTH SE23 150 E1
Forest Hill Pools SYD SE26 150 E1
Forest Hill School FSTH SE23 151 F2
Forest House Business Centre WAN E11 58 D6
Forest Preparatory School WALTH E17 58 C3
Forest Road Medical Centre WALTH E17 57 H2
Forest Trading Estate WALTH E17 57 F2
Forge Close Clinic HAYES BR2 167 K7
Forge Lane Primary School FELT TW13 141 J5
The Former Health Centre CHARL SE7 114 C3
Forster Park Primary School CAT SE6 152 C2
Fortismere School EFNCH N2 53 K1
Fortune Theatre HOL/ALD WC2B 11 K5
The Forum EDGW HA8 36 C5
Fossdene Primary School CHARL SE7 114 A4
Foster's Primary School WELL DA16 136 D2
Foulds School BAR EN5 26 B2
The Foundling Museum BMSBY WC1N 5 K9
The Fountain Studios WBLY HA9 68 C2
Fountayne Business Centre SEVS/STOTM N15 56 C3
Fountayne Road Health Centre STNW/STAM N16 74 C1
Four Seasons Hotel
BERM/RHTH SE16 93 H7
MYFR/PKLN W1K 16 C1
Foxfield Primary School WOOL/PLUM SE18 115 H4
Fox Primary School KENS W8 8 A9
Frances Bardsley School for Girls ROM RM1 63 J4
Franciscan Primary School TOOT SW17 148 A3
Francis Holland School
BGVA SW1W 16 B6
CAMTN NW1 9 L1
Frank Barnes Primary School STJWD NW8 3 H2
Franklin Industrial Estate PGE/AN SE20 150 E7
Frederick Bremer Secondary School WALTH E17 58 A1
Freehold Industrial Centre HSLWW TW4 122 B4
Free Trade Wharf WAP E1W 93 F6
Freightliners City Farm HOLWY N7 73 F5
The French Institute SKENS SW7 15 G5
Fresh Wharf Estate BARK IG11 78 B7
Freuchen Medical Centre WLSDN NW10 87 H1
Freud Museum HAMP NW3 71 H5
Friars Primary Foundation School STHWK SE1 18 C1
Friends House CAMTN NW1 5 G8
Friern Barnet School FBAR/BDGN N11 39 K4
Friern Bridge Retail Park FBAR/BDGN N11 40 B5
Frithwood Primary School NTHWD HA6 32 D5
Frogmore Industrial Estate
HBRY N5 73 J3
HYS/HAR UB3 101 H1
WLSDN NW10 86 E2
Fryent Country Park KTN/HRWW/WS HA3 50 C6
Fryent Medical Centre CDALE/KGS NW9 50 E6
Fryent Primary School CDALE/KGS NW9 50 E6
Fulham Broadway ⊖ FUL/PGN SW6 107 K6
Fulham Cemetery FUL/PGN SW6 107 G6
Fulham Clinic HMSMTH W6 107 H5
Fulham Cross Girls Secondary School FUL/PGN SW6 107 G6
Fulham FC (Craven Cottage) PUT/ROE SW15 107 F7
Fulham Medical Centre FUL/PGN SW6 108 A6
Fulham Palace FUL/PGN SW6 127 G1
Fulham Pools FUL/PGN SW6 107 J5
Fulham Preparatory School WKENS W14 107 H5
Fulham Pre-Preparatory School FUL/PGN SW6 127 H1
Fulham Primary School FUL/PGN SW6 107 K5
Fuller Smith & Turner Sports Club CHSWK W4 106 B7
Fullwell Cross Health Centre BARK/HLT IG6 60 C1
Fullwell Cross Swimming Pool & Recreation Centre BARK/HLT IG6 60 C1
Fullwood Primary School BARK/HLT IG6 60 C3
Fulwell ⇌ WHTN TW2 142 D3
Fulwell Golf Club HPTN TW12 142 D3
Furness Primary School WLSDN NW10 87 J1
Furzedown Primary School TOOT SW17 148 B5
Furze Infant School CHDH RM6 62 A5
Future Business College CONDST W1S 10 D5
Gaflac Sports Ground Pavilion SUN TW16 140 E7
Gainsborough Clinic PLMGR N13 41 F3
Gainsborough Primary School
HOM E9 75 H5
SRTFD E15 94 C2
Galliard Primary School ED N9 30 C5
Gallions Mount Primary School WOOL/PLUM SE18 116 A4
Gallions Primary School EHAM E6 96 B5
Gallions Reach ⊖ EHAM E6 96 B6
Gallions Reach Shopping Park EHAM E6 96 B4
Gants Hill ⊖ GNTH/NBYPK IG2 60 A5
Gants Hill Medical Centre GNTH/NBYPK IG2 60 A5
Gardener Industrial Estate SYD SE26 151 G4
Garden House School BGVA SW1W 16 A7
Garden Primary School MTCM CR4 163 J2
Garden Suburb Infant School GLDGN NW11 52 D4
Garfield Primary School
FBAR/BDGN N11 40 B4
WIM/MER SW19 147 G5
Garratt Park Secondary Special School WAND/EARL SW18 147 G2
Garrick Industrial Centre CDALE/KGS NW9 51 H4
Garrick Theatre LSQ/SEVD WC2H 11 J7
Garth Primary School MRDN SM4 162 C4
The Garth Road Industrial Centre MRDN SM4 161 F6
Gascoigne Primary School BARK IG11 78 C7
Gate Cinema KENS W8 8 A8
Gatehouse School BETH E2 93 F1
The Gatehouse Theatre HGT N6 54 A6
The Gate Theatre NTGHL W11 8 A8
Gateway EHAM E6 96 B3
Gateway Business Centre
SYD SE26 151 G5
WOOL/PLUM SE18 115 H2
Gateway Industrial Estate WLSDN NW10 87 H2
Gatton School TOOT SW17 147 J3
Gayhurst Primary School HACK E8 74 C6
Gazelda Industrial Estate WAT WD17 21 G4
Gearies Infant School GNTH/NBYPK IG2 60 A4
Gearies Junior School GNTH/NBYPK IG2 60 B4
Geffrye Museum BETH E2 7 K6
Gemini Business Estate NWCR SE14 112 A4
General Medical Clinics WCHPL E1 13 L2
Genesis Cinema WCHPL E1 92 E3
Geoffrey Chaucer Technology College STHWK SE1 19 G4
The Geoffrey Lloyd Foulkes Clinic IL IG1 78 A1
Geoffrey Whitworth Theatre DART DA1 138 D3
George Eliot Infant School STJWD NW8 2 F3
George Eliot Junior School STJWD NW8 2 F3
George Greens School POP/IOD E14 113 F4
George Mitchell School LEY E10 57 K7
George Spicer Primary School EN EN1 30 B2
George Street ◆ CROY/NA CR0 177 J1
George Tomlinson Primary School WAN E11 58 C7
Germal College FSBYPK N4 55 G7
Gibbs Green Special School WKENS W14 107 J4
Gibson Business Centre TOTM N17 42 B5
The Gibson Business Centre TOTM N17 42 B6
Gidea Park ⇌ GPK RM2 63 K3
Gidea Park College GPK RM2 63 J2
Gidea Park Primary School GPK RM2 63 H3
The Gielgud Theatre SOHO/CST W1F 11 G6
Giffin Business Centre DEPT SE8 112 D6
Gifford Primary School NTHLT UB5 83 K1
Gilbert Collection TPL/STR WC2R 11 M6
Gilbert Scott Primary School SAND/SEL CR2 179 G6
Gillespie Primary School HBRY N5 73 H2
Gipsy Hill ⇌ NRWD SE19 150 A4
Girdlers' Hall CITYW EC2V 12 F3
Glade Primary School CLAY IG5 45 K7
The Glades Shopping Centre BMLY BR1 167 K1
Gladstone Medical Centre CRICK NW2 69 H3
Gladstone Park Primary School WLSDN NW10 69 J4
The Gladys Aylward School UED N18 41 K3
Glaziers/Scientific Instrument Makers Hall STHWK SE1 13 G8
Glebe First & Middle School KTN/HRWW/WS HA3 49 K3
Glebe Primary School HGDN/ICK UB10 64 B3
Glebe School WWKM BR4 167 G7
Gleen Lecky Health Centre PUT/ROE SW15 127 G3
Glenbrook Primary School CLAP SW4 129 J5
Glencairn Sports Club FBAR/BDGN N11 40 C6
Glenham College IL IG1 78 B1
Glenlyn Medical Centre E/WMO/HCT KT8 157 H4
Glenthorne High Specialist Arts CHEAM SM3 161 K7
Globe Academy STHWK SE1 19 G4
Globe Primary School BETH E2 92 E2
Globe Wharf BERM/RHTH SE16 93 F6
Gloucester Primary School PECK SE15 111 F6
Gloucester Road ⊖ SKENS SW7 14 E5
Godolphin & Latymer School HMSMTH W6 106 E3
Godwin Junior School FSTGT E7 77 F3
Goethe Institute SKENS SW7 15 H3
Golborne Medical Centre NKENS W10 88 D3
Goldbeaters Primary School EDGW HA8 37 F7
Golden Hinde Educational Trust STHWK SE1 13 G7
Golders Green ⊖ GLDGN NW11 52 E6
Golders Green Crematorium GLDGN NW11 52 E6
Golders Green Health Centre GLDGN NW11 53 F7
Golders Hill Health Centre GLDGN NW11 53 G5
Golders Hill School GLDGN NW11 52 E6
Goldhawk Industrial Estate SHB W12 106 E2
Goldhawk Road ⊖ SHB W12 107 F1
Goldsmiths Hall STBT EC1A 12 E4
Goldsmiths University of London
DEPT SE8 112 D5
LEW SE13 133 H3
NWCR SE14 112 B7
Gonville Primary School THHTH CR7 164 A4
Goodge St ⊖ FITZ W1T 10 F2
Goodinge Health Centre HOLWY N7 72 E5
Goodmayes ⇌ GDMY/SEVK IG3 61 G7
Goodmayes Retail Park CHDH RM6 61 H6
Goodrich J & I School EDUL SE22 131 H5
Good Shepherd RC Primary School
BMLY BR1 152 D3
CROY/NA CR0 179 K6
The Good Shepherd RC Primary School SHB W12 106 C1
Goodwyn School MLHL NW7 37 J4
Goose Green Primary School EDUL SE22 131 G3
Goose Green Trading Estate EDUL SE22 131 H3
Gordonbrock Primary School BROCKY SE4 132 D4
Gordon Hospital WEST SW1P 17 G6
Gordon House Health Centre WEA W13 85 H7
Gordon Infant School IL IG1 78 D2
Gordon Primary School ELTH/MOT SE9 134 E3
Goresbrook Leisure Centre DAGW RM9 79 K7
Goresbrook Sports Centre DAGW RM9 79 K7

The Goring Hotel *BGVA* SW1W 16 D3
Gorringe Park Primary School *MTCM* CR4 148 A7
Gosai Cinema *WEA* W13 85 H7
Gosbury Hill Health Centre *CHSGTN* KT9 172 A3
Gosford Primary School *REDBR* IG4 59 K4
Gospel Oak *HAMP* NW3 72 A3
Gove Farm Retail Park *CHDH* RM6 61 J6
Government Offices *WHALL* SW1A 11 J8
Gower House School *CDALE/KGS* NW9 68 E1
Grace Business Centre *MTCM* CR4 162 E5
Grace Theatre at the Latchmere *BTSEA* SW11 128 E1
Graduate School of Management *TOTM* N17 42 B7
Grafton Primary School *BCTR* RM8 80 A1
HOLWY N7 72 E2
Grahame Park Health Centre *CDALE/KGS* NW9 37 G7
Grahame Park J & I School *CDALE/KGS* NW9 37 G7
Granard Business Centre *MLHL* NW7 37 G5
Granard Primary School *PUT/ROE* SW15 126 E5
Granby Sports Club *CHST* BR7 153 J4
Grand Avenue Primary School *BRYLDS* KT5 159 K5
Grande Vitesse Industrial Centre *STHWK* SE1 12 D9
Grand Union Industrial Estate *WLSDN* NW10 86 D2
The Grange City Hotel *TWRH* EC3N 13 L6
Grange First School *RYLN/HDSTN* HA2 48 B7
The Grange Museum *CRICK* NW2 69 H3
Grange Park *WCHMH* N21 29 H4
Grange Park Clinic *YEAD* UB4 82 D3
Grange Park Junior School *YEAD* UB4 82 D3
Grange Park Preparatory School *WCHMH* N21 29 H5
Grange Park Primary School *WCHMH* N21 29 G3
Grange Primary School *CAN/RD* E16 94 D3
EA W5 104 E1
STHWK SE1 19 J4
Grange Whitehall Hotel *RSQ* WC1B 11 J3
Grangewood Independent School *FSTGT* E7 77 H6
Grangewood School *PIN* HA5 46 E4
Granton Primary School *STRHM/NOR* SW16 148 C6
Granville Road Industrial Estate *CRICK* NW2 70 D1
Grasmere Primary School *STNW/STAM* N16 73 K3
Grasshoppers RFC *ISLW* TW7 104 A5
Grassroots School *HPTN* TW12 142 A7
Grasvenor Avenue Infant School *BAR* EN5 26 E5
Gravel Hill *CROY/NA* CR0 179 G6
Gravel Hill Primary School *BXLYHS* DA6 137 J4
Graveney School *TOOT* SW17 148 B5
Graves Yard Industrial Estate *WELL* DA16 136 B1
Grays Farm Primary School *STMC/STPC* BR5 155 H7
Grazebrook Primary School *STNW/STAM* N16 74 A1
Great Cambridge Industrial Estate *EN* EN1 30 D4
Great Chapel Street Medical Centre *SOHO/SHAV* W1D 11 G4
Greater London Authority Headquarters (City Hall) *STHWK* SE1 13 K9
Greatham Road Industrial Estate *BUSH* WD23 21 J3
Great Jubilee Wharf *WAP* E1W 92 E7
Great Ormond Street Hospital for Children *BMSBY* WC1N 11 K1
Great Portland Street *GTPST* W1W 10 D1
Great Scotland Yard *WHALL* SW1A 11 J8
Great Western Industrial Park *NWDGN* UB2 103 G1
Great West Trading Estate *BTFD* TW8 104 C5
Greek School of London *ACT* W3 86 D6
Greenacres Primary School *ELTH/MOT* SE9 154 A1
The Green CE Primary School *TOTM* N17 56 B2
Green Dragon Primary School *BTFD* TW8 105 F4
Greenfield Medical Centre *CRICK* NW2 70 C2
Greenfields Junior School *SHB* W12 87 H6
Greenfields Primary School *OXHEY* WD19 33 G4
Greenfields Special School *MUSWH* N10 39 K7
Greenford *GFD/PVL* UB6 66 D7
Greenford Avenue Medical Centre *HNWL* W7 84 E4
Greenford Green Clinic *GFD/PVL* UB6 66 E4
Greenford High School *STHL* UB1 84 A2
Greenford Industrial Estate *GFD/PVL* UB6 66 B7
Greenford Park Cemetery Greenford Park Cemetery *GFD/PVL* UB6 84 B4
Greenford Road Medical Centre *GFD/PVL* UB6 84 D1
Greenford Sports Centre *STHL* UB1 84 A2
Greengate Medical Centre *PLSTW* E13 95 F2
Greengrove College *STHGT/OAK* N14 40 E1
Greenheath Business Centre *BETH* E2 92 D2
Greenhill College *HRW* HA1 49 F4
Greenhill Park Medical Centre *WLSDN* NW10 69 G7
Greenland Pier *BERM/RHTH* SE16 112 C2
Green Lane Business Park *ELTH/MOT* SE9 154 A1
Green Lane Primary School *WPK* KT4 160 E6
Greenleaf Primary School *WALTH* E17 57 H2
Greenmead Primary School *PUT/ROE* SW15 126 E4
Green Park *MYFR/PICC* W1J 10 D9
The Green School *ISLW* TW7 104 B6
Greenshaw High School *SUT* SM1 175 G1
Greenshields Industrial Estate *CAN/RD* E16 94 E7
Greenside Primary School *SHB* W12 106 D1
Greenslade Primary School *WOOL/PLUM* SE18 115 J5
Greenvale School *FSTH* SE23 151 G2
Greenwich *GNWCH* SE10 112 E6
Greenwich Centre Business Park *DEPT* SE8 112 E6
Greenwich Cinema *GNWCH* SE10 113 F6
Greenwich Community College *WOOL/PLUM* SE18 115 G3
Greenwich Industrial Estate *CHARL* SE7 114 A3
GNWCH SE10 112 E6
Greenwich Natural Health Centre *GNWCH* SE10 113 F6
Greenwich Odeon Cinema *GNWCH* SE10 113 J3
Greenwich Pier *GNWCH* SE10 113 F4
Greenwich School of Management *GNWCH* SE10 113 F6
Greenwich Theatre & Art Gallery *GNWCH* SE10 113 G6
Greenwood Primary School *NTHLT* UB5 66 C4
Greenwood Theatre *STHWK* SE1 19 H1
Green Wrythe Primary School *CAR* SM5 162 C5
Gresham College *HCIRC* EC1N 12 A3
Gresham Way Industrial Estate *WIM/MER* SW19 147 F2
Grey Coat Hospital School for Girls *WEST* SW1P 17 G4
The Greycoat Hospital *WEST* SW1P 17 G6
Grey Court School *RCHPK/HAM* TW10 143 K2
Griffen Manor School *WOOL/PLUM* SE18 115 K7
Grimsdyke First & Middle School *PIN* HA5 33 K5
Grims Dyke Golf Club *PIN* HA5 34 A4
Grim's Dyke Hotel *KTN/HRWW/WS* HA3 34 C3
Grinling Gibbons Primary School *DEPT* SE8 112 C5
Grist Memorial Sports Club *E/WMO/HCT* KT8 157 K4
Grocers' Hall *CITYW* EC2V 13 G5
Grosvenor House Hotel *MYFR/PKLN* W1K 10 A7
Grove Health Centre *KENS* W8 8 B8
The Grove Health Centre *SHB* W12 106 E1
Grove House (Froebel College) *PUT/ROE* SW15 126 C5
Grove House Primary School for Deaf Children *WNWD* SE27 149 H1
Grovelands Priory Hospital *STHGT/OAK* N14 28 E7
Grovelands School *WOT/HER* KT12 156 A5
Grove Medical Centre *DEPT* SE8 112 B3
The Grove Medical Centre *ARCH* N19 72 D1
Grove Park *BMLY* BR1 152 E2
Grove Park Cemetery *LEE/GVPK* SE12 153 H3
Grove Park Industrial Estate *CDALE/KGS* NW9 51 F3
Grove Park Primary School *CHSWK* W4 105 K5
Grove Park School *CDALE/KGS* NW9 50 E3
Grove Primary School *CHDH* RM6 61 H4
Grove Road Primary School *HSLW* TW3 123 F3
The Groves Medical Centre *NWMAL* KT3 160 B2
Grove Village Medical Centre *EBED/NFELT* TW14 121 H7
Guardian Angels RC Primary School *BOW* E3 93 G3
Guardian Newspapers *POP/IOD* E14 112 E1
Guards' Chapel & Museum *STJSPK* SW1H 16 F2
Gumley House Convent School *ISLW* TW7 124 B2
Gunnersbury *CHSWK* W4 105 J4
Gunnersbury Catholic School *BTFD* TW8 104 D4
Gunnersbury Cemetery *BTFD* TW8 105 H3
Gunnersbury Park Museum *ACT* W3 105 H2
Gurnell Leisure Centre *WEA* W13 85 F2
Guru Nanak Medical Centre *STHL* UB1 83 H7
Guru Nanak Sikh Primary School *YEAD* UB4 83 G7
Guru Nanak Sikh Secondary School *YEAD* UB4 83 G7
Guy's Hospital *STHWK* SE1 13 H9
Guys Kings & Thomas Medical School (Kings College London) *STHWK* SE1 12 E8
Gwyn Jones Primary School *WAN* E11 58 B6
GX Superbowl *EHAM* E6 96 A4
Gypsy Moth IV *GNWCH* SE10 113 F5
Haberdashers Askes Hatcham College *NWCR* SE14 132 A1
Haberdashers Askes Knights Academy *BMLY* BR1 152 E3
The Haberdashers Askes School *BORE* WD6 23 H2
Haberdashers' Hall *STBT* EC1A 12 C3
Haberdashers RUFC *BORE* WD6 24 B1
Hackbridge *WLGTN* SM6 176 B1
Hackbridge Primary School *WLGTN* SM6 163 F7
Hackney Business Centre *HACK* E8 74 D5
Hackney Central *HACK* E8 74 D5
Hackney City Farm *BETH* E2 92 C1
Hackney Community College *IS* N1 7 J6
Hackney Downs *HACK* E8 74 C4
Hackney Empire Variety Theatre *HACK* E8 74 D5
Hackney Free & Parochial CE School *HOM* E9 74 E5
The Hackney Museum *HACK* E8 74 D5
Hackney Sports Centre *HOM* E9 75 J3
Hackney Wick *HOM* E9 75 J5
The Haelan Clinic *CEND/HSY/T* N8 54 E5
Haggerston *HACK* E8 7 L2
Haggerston School *BETH* E2 7 M5
Haggerston Swimming Pool *BETH* E2 7 M4
Hague Primary School *BETH* E2 92 D3
Hailey Road Business Park *ERITHM* DA18 117 H1
Haimo Primary School *ELTH/MOT* SE9 134 C4
Hakim Qureshi Clinic *NWDGN* UB2 102 D2
The Hale Clinic *CAMTN* NW1 10 D1
Half Moon Theatre *WCHPL* E1 93 F3
Haling Manor High School *SAND/SEL* CR2 177 H6
The Halkin Hotel *KTBR* SW1X 16 B2
Halley Primary School *POP/IOD* E14 93 G4
Hallfield Clinic *BAY/PAD* W2 8 E5
Hallfield Infant School *BAY/PAD* W2 8 D5
Hallmark Trading Estate *WBLY* HA9 68 E3
Hall Place & Gardens *BXLY* DA5 137 K5
The Hall Pre-Preparatory School *NTHWD* HA6 32 B5
Halls Business Centre *HYS/HAR* UB3 101 K2
The Hall School *HAMP* NW3 71 H5
Hall School Wimbledon *RYNPK* SW20 146 B7
Hall School Wimbledon Junior Department *PUT/ROE* SW15 145 J2
Hallsville Primary School *CAN/RD* E16 94 E5
Halstow Primary School *GNWCH* SE10 113 J4
Hambledon Clinic *CMBW* SE5 130 E2
Hambrough Primary School *STHL* UB1 83 J7
Hamer Indoor Market *BOW* E3 93 H1
Ham Health Clinic *RCHPK/HAM* TW10 143 J2
Ham House & Garden (NT) *RCHPK/HAM* TW10 124 D7
Hamilton Road Industrial Estate *WNWD* SE27 149 K3
Ham Lands Nature Reserve *RCHPK/HAM* TW10 143 H3
Hamlet International Industrial Estate *ERITH* DA8 118 A4
Hammersmith *HMSMTH* W6 107 F3
Hammersmith Apollo *HMSMTH* W6 107 F4
Hammersmith Cemetery *HMSMTH* W6 107 G4
Hammersmith Hospital *SHB* W12 87 J5
Hammersmith Industrial Estate *HMSMTH* W6 107 F5
Hammersmith New Cemetery *RCH/KEW* TW9 125 J1
Hammersmith Physio & Sports Injury Clinic *HMSMTH* W6 107 F3
Hammersmith & West London College *WKENS* W14 107 H3
Hampden Gurney School *MBLAR* W1H 9 K4
Ham & Petersham CC *RCHPK/HAM* TW10 143 K3
The Hampshire School *SKENS* SW7 15 J2
Hampstead *HAMP* NW3 71 G3
Hampstead Cemetery *CRICK* NW2 70 D3
Hampstead College of Fine Art & Humanities *HAMP* NW3 71 J5
Hampstead CC *KIL/WHAMP* NW6 71 F5
Hampstead Golf Club *GLDGN* NW11 53 G6
Hampstead Heath *HAMP* NW3 71 J3
Hampstead Medical Centre *HAMP* NW3 71 G3
Hampstead Parochial CE School *HAMP* NW3 71 G3
Hampstead School *CRICK* NW2 70 C3
The Hampstead School of Art *HAMP* NW3 70 E3
Hampstead School of English *KIL/WHAMP* NW6 70 E3
Hampstead Theatre *HAMP* NW3 3 G1
Hampton *HPTN* TW12 142 A7
Hampton Cemetery *HPTN* TW12 142 A6
Hampton Community College *HPTN* TW12 142 A4
Hampton Court *E/WMO/HCT* KT8 157 K3
Hampton Court House School *E/WMO/HCT* KT8 157 K1
Hampton Court Palace *E/WMO/HCT* KT8 158 A2
Hampton Court Palace Golf Club *SURB* KT6 158 D4
Hampton Farm Industrial Estate *FELT* TW13 141 J2
Hampton FC *HPTN* TW12 142 B7
Hampton Hill Junior School *HPTN* TW12 142 C4
Hampton Infant School *HPTN* TW12 141 K6
Hampton Junior School *HPTN* TW12 142 A7
The Hampton Medical Centre *HPTN* TW12 142 A6
Hampton Open Air Pool *HPTN* TW12 142 C6
Hampton Road Industrial Park *CROY/NA* CR0 164 D5
Hampton School *HPTN* TW12 142 A4
Hampton Wick *KUT/HW* KT1 143 K7
Hampton Wick Infants School *TEDD* TW11 143 J6
Handel's House *MYFR/PKLN* W1K 10 C6
Handsworth Health Clinic *CHING* E4 44 B5
Hanger Lane *EA* W5 86 B2
Hanover Primary School *IS* N1 6 D5
Hanover Trading Estate *HOLWY* N7 72 E4
Hanover West Industrial Estate *WLSDN* NW10 86 E2
Hanwell *HNWL* W7 84 E6
Hanworth Trading Estate *FELT* TW13 141 J2
Harbinger Primary School *POP/IOD* E14 112 D3
Harborough School *ARCH* N19 72 D1
Harefield Manor Hotel *ROM* RM1 63 H3
Harenc School *SCUP* DA14 155 J4
Hargrave Park Primary School *ARCH* N19 72 C1
Haringey Arts Council *ED* N9 42 C1
Haringey Community Health Clinic *SEVS/STHAM* N15 56 B3
Haringey Sixth Form Centre *TOTM* N17 42 B6
Harkness Industrial Estate *BORE* WD6 24 C3
The Harlequin Shopping Centre *WAT* WD17 21 G3
Harlequins RFC & Harlequins RL (The Stoop) *WHTN* TW2 123 K6
Harlesden *WLSDN* NW10 87 F1
Harlesden Primary School *WLSDN* NW10 87 G1
Harley Medical Centre *CAVSQ/HST* W1G 10 D4
The Harley Medical Centre *CANST* EC4R 12 F6
Harley Street Clinic *CAVSQ/HST* W1G 10 C3
The Harley Street Clinic *CAVSQ/HST* W1G 10 C2
Harlington Community School *HYS/HAR* UB3 101 G3
Harlyn Primary School *PIN* HA5 47 F2
The Harold Macmillan Medical Centre *HRW* HA1 48 D6
Harp Business Centre *CRICK* NW2 69 J1
Harringay *FSBYPK* N4 55 G5
Harringay Green Lanes *FSBYPK* N4 55 H5
Harrington Hill Primary School *CLPT* E5 56 D7
Harrington Road *SNWD* SE25 165 K2
Harris Academy Bermondsey *STHWK* SE1 19 M5
Harris Academy Falconwood *WELL* DA16 135 J3
Harris Academy Merton School *STRHM/NOR* SW16 163 J2
Harris Academy South Norwood *SNWD* SE25 165 G2
Harris City Academy Crystal Palace *NRWD* SE19 150 B7
Harris Girls Academy *EDUL* SE22 131 K4
Harrodian School *BARN* SW13 106 C6
Harrods Store *CHEL* SW3 15 L3
Harrovian Business Village *HRW* HA1 48 D6
Harrow Arts Centre *PIN* HA5 34 A6
Harrow Borough FC *RYLN/HDSTN* HA2 66 A3
Harrow Cemetery *HRW* HA1 48 D5
Harrow College *HRW* HA1 48 E6
KTN/HRWW/WS HA3 34 E5
Harrow CC *HRW* HA1 66 E3
Harrow Driving Cycling & Road Safety Centre *KTN/HRWW/WS* HA3 49 G2
Harrow Heritage Museum *RYLN/HDSTN* HA2 48 C2
Harrow High School *HRW* HA1 49 G5
Harrow Leisure Centre *KTN/HRWW/WS* HA3 49 F2
Harrow-on-the-Hill *HRW* HA1 48 E5
Harrow RFC *STAN* HA7 35 H2
Harrow Road Health Centre *BAY/PAD* W2 8 B2
Harrow School *RYLN/HDSTN* HA2 66 E1
Harrow Town CC *RYLN/HDSTN* HA2 48 A7
Harrow Weald Cemetery *KTN/HRWW/WS* HA3 34 E5
Harrow & Wealdstone *HRW* HA1 48 E3
Harry Gosling Primary School *WCHPL* E1 92 C5
Hartley Primary School *EHAM* E6 77 J7
Hartsbourne Primary School *BUSH* WD23 34 D1
Hartspring Industrial Park *BUSH* WD23 22 A1
Hartspring Sports Centre *BUSH* WD23 22 A1
Harvington School *EA* W5 85 J5
Haseltine Primary School *SYD* SE26 151 H3
Haslemere Business Centre *EN* EN1 30 D3
Haslemere Industrial Estate *EBED/NFELT* TW14 121 K4
WAND/EARL SW18 147 F1
Haslemere Primary School *MTCM* CR4 162 C1
Hasmonean High School Boys Site *HDN* NW4 52 B1
Hasmonean High School Girls Site *MLHL* NW7 37 J7
Hasmonean Primary School *HDN* NW4 52 B4
Haste Hill Golf Club *NTHWD* HA6 46 C1
Hastings Clinic *BRXS/STRHM* SW2 130 A4
Hastingwood Trading Estate *UED* N18 43 G5
Hatcham Mews Business Centre *NWCR* SE14 112 A6
Hatch End *PIN* HA5 34 A6
Hatch End High School *KTN/HRWW/WS* HA3 34 B6
Hatch End Swimming Pool *PIN* HA5 34 A6
Hatfield Primary School *MRDN* SM4 161 H5
Hatton Cross *HTHAIR* TW6 121 J3
Hatton School *WFD* IG8 59 H2
Havelock Primary School *NWDGN* UB2 102 E2
Haven Green Clinic *EA* W5 85 K5
Havering College of Further & Higher Education *EMPK* RM11 63 K6
Haverstock School *HAMP* NW3 4 A1
HAMP NW3 72 A5
Hawes Down Clinic *WWKM* BR4 180 B1
Hawes Down Primary School *WWKM* BR4 167 G7
The Hawker Centre *KUTN/CMB* KT2 143 K4
Hawkesdown House School *KENS* W8 8 B9
Hawkins Clinic *PUT/ROE* SW15 127 G3
RYNPK SW20 145 H7
Hawksmoor Primary School *THMD* SE28 97 H6

Hawley Infant School *CAMTN* NW1 4 D2
Haydon School *PIN* HA5 46 E2
Haydons Road *WIM/MER* SW19 147 G4
Hayes *HAYES* BR2 167 J7
Hayes Bridge Middle School *STHL* UB1 102 D1
Hayes Bridge Retail Park *YEAD* UB4 83 G6
Hayes CC *HYS/HAR* UB3 82 D5
Hayes FC *HYS/HAR* UB3 82 D6
Hayes Grove Priory Hospital *HAYES* BR2 180 E1
Hayes & Harlington *HYS/HAR* UB3 101 J2
The Hayes Manor School *HYS/HAR* UB3 82 B5
Hayes Park J & I School *YEAD* UB4 82 D3
Hayes Pool *HYS/HAR* UB3 82 D7
Hayes Primary School *HAYES* BR2 168 A7
Hayes School *HAYES* BR2 181 F1
Hayes Social & Sports Club *HYS/HAR* UB3 82 D6
Hayes Stadium Sports Centre *HYS/HAR* UB3 82 B5
Hay Lane School *CDALE/KGS* NW9 50 E3
Haymerle School *PECK* SE15 111 H5
Hays Galleria *STHWK* SE1 13 J8
Hayward Gallery *STHWK* SE1 11 M9
Hazelbury Junior School *ED* N9 42 A2
Hazeldene Medical Centre *WBLY* HA9 68 D5
Hazelwood Infant School *PLMGR* N13 41 H3
Hazelwood Junior School *PLMGR* N13 41 G3
Headstart Montessori School *TOOT* SW17 147 G2
Headstone Lane *RYLN/HDSTN* HA2 34 B7
Health & Vitality Osteopathic Clinic *HOR/WEW* KT19 173 F4
The Heart Hospital *CAVSQ/HST* W1G 10 B3
Heathbrook Primary School *VX/NE* SW8 129 H1
Heath Business Centre *HSLW* TW3 123 H3
Heathcote School *CHING* E4 44 C1
Heathfield College *HAYES* BR2 181 G5
Heathfield House School *CHSWK* W4 105 K4
Heathfield Primary School *WHTN* TW2 123 F7
Heathfield School *PIN* HA5 47 H6
Heath House Preparatory School *BKHTH/KID* SE3 133 J1
The Heathland School *HSLWW* TW4 122 E5
Heathmere Primary School *PUT/ROE* SW15 126 D7
Heathrow Airport Central Bus & Coach Station *HTHAIR* TW6 120 D2
Heathrow Airport Terminal 4 *HTHAIR* TW6 120 E4
Heathrow Airport (Terminals 1 & 3) *HTHAIR* TW6 120 E1
Heathrow Air Traffic Control Tower *HTHAIR* TW6 120 E2
Heathrow International Trading Estate *HSLWW* TW4 122 A2
Heathrow Medical Centre *HYS/HAR* UB3 101 G4
Heathrow Primary School *WDR/YW* UB7 100 C5
Heathrow Terminal 4 *HTHAIR* TW6 121 F4
Heathrow Terminals 1 & 3 *HTHAIR* TW6 120 E2
Heathrow Viewing Area *HTHAIR* TW6 120 E2
Heathrow World Cargo Centre *HTHAIR* TW6 120 C4
Heathside Preparatory School *HAMP* NW3 71 G3
Heathside Preparatory School (Lower) *HAMP* NW3 71 G3
Heathside Preparatory School (Upper) *HAMP* NW3 71 G3
Heathway Industrial Estate *DAGE* RM10 80 D3
Heathway Medical Centre *DAGW* RM9 80 B3
Heavers Farm Primary School *SNWD* SE25 165 G4
Heber Primary School *EDUL* SE22 131 G5
Heckford Street Business Centre *WAP* E1W 93 F6
Hedges & Butler Estate *SRTFD* E15 94 A1
Hedgewood School *YEAD* UB4 82 C2
Helena Road Clinic *WLSDN* NW10 69 K3
Heliport Industrial Estate *BTSEA* SW11 128 C1
Helston Court Business Centre *WIM/MER* SW19 145 K4
Henderson Hospital *BELMT* SM2 174 E7
Hendon *HDN* NW4 51 J5
Hendon Cemetery *MLHL* NW7 38 B7
Hendon Central *HDN* NW4 51 K4
Hendon Crematorium *MLHL* NW7 38 B6
Hendon FC *CRICK* NW2 70 B1
Hendon Golf Club *MLHL* NW7 38 A6
Hendon Hall Hotel *HDN* NW4 52 A2
Hendon Preparatory School *HDN* NW4 52 B2
Hendon School *HDN* NW4 52 B4
Hendon Secretarial College *HDN* NW4 51 K4
Hendon Youth Sports Centre *CRICK* NW2 52 B6
Henrietta Barnett School *GLDGN* NW11 53 F4
Henry Cavendish Primary School *BAL* SW12 129 H7
Henry Compton School *FUL/PGN* SW6 107 G7
Henry Fawcett Primary School *LBTH* SE11 18 A9
Henry Green Primary School *BCTR* RM8 61 K7
Henry Maynard J & I School *WALTH* E17 58 A4
Henwick Primary School *ELTH/MOT* SE9 134 C2
Herbert Morrison Primary School *VX/NE* SW8 109 K6
Hereward House School *HAMP* NW3 71 J5
Her Majestys' Theatre *STJS* SW1Y 11 H8
Hermitage Primary School *WAP* E1W 92 C7
Herne Hill *HNHL* SE24 130 C4
Herne Hill School *HNHL* SE24 130 D4
Herne Hill Stadium (Cycle Centre) *HNHL* SE24 130 E5
Heron Industrial Estate *SRTFD* E15 93 K1
Heron Quays *POP/IOD* E14 93 J7
Heronsgate Primary School *THMD* SE28 115 J2
Heron Trading Estate *ACT* W3 86 D4
Heston Community School *HEST* TW5 103 F6
Heston Community Sports Hall *HEST* TW5 103 F6
Heston Industrial Mall *HEST* TW5 102 E6
Heston Infant School *HEST* TW5 103 F6
Heston Junior School *HEST* TW5 103 F6
Heston Park CC *HEST* TW5 102 E5
Heston Swimming Baths *HEST* TW5 102 E5
Heythrop College *KENS* W8 14 C3
Higgs Industrial Estate *HNHL* SE24 130 C2
Highams Lodge Business Centre *WALTH* E17 57 F2
Highams Park *CHING* E4 44 A5
Highams Park Primary School *CHING* E4 44 B5
High Barnet *BAR* EN5 26 E3
Highbury Fields School *HBRY* N5 73 H3
Highbury Grove School *HBRY* N5 73 J4
Highbury & Islington *IS* N1 73 G5
Highbury Park Clinic *HBRY* N5 73 H2
Highbury Pool *HBRY* N5 73 H5
Highbury Quadrant Primary School *HBRY* N5 73 J3
Highbury Square Development *HBRY* N5 73 H2
High Commission of Angola *MHST* W1U 9 M3
High Commission of Antigua & Barbuda *MHST* W1U 10 A4
High Commission of Bahamas *MYFR/PICC* W1J 10 B8
High Commission of Bangladesh *SKENS* SW7 14 F3
High Commission of Barbados *FITZ* W1T 11 G4
High Commission of Belize *CAVSQ/HST* W1G 10 D4
High Commission of Botswana *OXSTW* W1C 10 C5
High Commission of Brunei *KTBR* SW1X 16 A3
High Commission of Canada *MYFR/PKLN* W1K 10 B6
High Commission of Cyprus *MYFR/PKLN* W1K 10 A6
High Commission of Dominica *ECT* SW5 14 D6
High Commission of Fiji *SKENS* SW7 14 E2
High Commission of Guyana *BAY/PAD* W2 8 C7
High Commission of Jamaica *SKENS* SW7 15 G2
High Commission of Kenya *CAVSQ/HST* W1G 10 C2
High Commission of Lesotho *KTBR* SW1X 16 A3
High Commission of Malawi *MYFR/PKLN* W1K 10 C6
High Commission of Malaysia *KTBR* SW1X 16 B2
High Commission of Maldives *MHST* W1U 10 A2
High Commission of Malta *CONDST* W1S 10 F7
High Commission of Mauritius *SKENS* SW7 14 F4
High Commission of Namibia *CAVSQ/HST* W1G 10 D3
High Commission of New Zealand *STJS* SW1Y 11 G8
High Commission of Nigeria *CHCR* WC2N 11 J8
EMB EC4Y 12 B5
High Commission of Pakistan *KTBR* SW1X 15 M3
High Commission of Papua New Guinea *STJS* SW1Y 10 F8
High Commission of St Vincent & the Grenadines *KENS* W8 14 D2
High Commission of Seychelles *MHST* W1U 9 M2
High Commission of Sierra Leone *REGST* W1B 10 E4
High Commission of Singapore *KTBR* SW1X 15 M2
High Commission of South Africa *CHCR* WC2N 11 J8
High Commission of Sri Lanka *BAY/PAD* W2 9 H6
High Commission of Swaziland *WESTW* SW1E 16 E3
High Commission of the Gambia *KENS* W8 14 D2
High Commission of Tonga *MBLAR* W1H 9 K3
High Commission of Trinidad & Tobago *KTBR* SW1X 16 A3
High Commission of Uganda *CHCR* WC2N 11 H8
High Commission of Zambia *KENS* W8 14 E2
High Commission of Zimbabwe *CHCR* WC2N 11 J7
High Cross Centre *SEVS/STOTM* N15 56 C3
Highfield Infant School *HAYES* BR2 167 J3
Highfield Junior School *HAYES* BR2 167 H3
Highfield Primary School *WCHMH* N21 29 H7
Highfield School *WAND/EARL* SW18 128 D6
Highgate *HGT* N6 54 B5
Highgate Cemetery *HGT* N6 54 A7
Highgate Golf Club *EFNCH* N2 53 J5
Highgate Junior School *HGT* N6 53 K6
Highgate Private Hospital *HGT* N6 53 K5
Highgate School *HGT* N6 53 K6
Highgate Wood School *MUSWH* N10 54 C4
Highgrove Pool *RSLP* HA4 46 E6
Highlands J & I School *IL* IG1 59 K7
Highlands Primary School *IL* IG1 59 J7
Highshore School *PECK* SE15 111 G7
High Street Kensington *KENS* W8 14 C2
High View Primary School *BTSEA* SW11 128 C3
Highview Primary School *WLGTN* SM6 176 E4
The Highway Trading Centre *WAP* E1W 93 F6
Hillbrook Primary School *TOOT* SW17 147 K3
Hill Crest London School *CROY/NA* CR0 165 G7
Hillcross Primary School *MRDN* SM4 161 J3
Hill House International Junior School *KTBR* SW1X 15 M4
Hill House School *CHEL* SW3 15 K9
KTBR SW1X 15 L4
Hill Mead Infant School *BRXN/ST* SW9 130 C3
Hillmead Primary School *BRXN/ST* SW9 130 C3
Hills Grove Primary School *WELL* DA16 116 D6
Hillside Infant School *NTHWD* HA6 32 E6
Hillyfield Primary School *WALTH* E17 57 G2
Hilly Fields Medical Centre *BROCKY* SE4 132 D4
Hilton Docklands Pier *BERM/RHTH* SE16 93 H7
The Hiltongrove Business Centre *WALTH* E17 57 J3
Hinchley Wood *ESH/CLAY* KT10 171 F2
Hinchley Wood Primary School *ESH/CLAY* KT10 171 G1
Hinchley Wood School & Sixth Form Centre *ESH/CLAY* KT10 171 G1
Hinley Clinic *LBTH* SE11 18 B6
Hispaniola *WHALL* SW1A 11 K9
Hitherfield Primary School *STRHM/NOR* SW16 149 G1
Hither Green *LEW* SE13 133 H5
Hither Green Cemetery *CAT* SE6 152 D1
Hither Green Primary School *LEW* SE13 133 G5
HM Customs & Excise *HTHAIR* TW6 100 E7
HM Prison *BRXS/STRHM* SW2 129 K5
HOLWY N7 72 E3
SHB W12 87 J5
THMD SE28 115 J3
WAND/EARL SW18 128 C6
HMS Belfast *STHWK* SE1 13 K8
HMS President *EMB* EC4Y 12 B6
HM Young Offenders Institution *FELT* TW13 140 B2
Hobbayne First & Middle School *HNWL* W7 85 F5
Hobbayne Primary School *HNWL* W7 84 E5
Hogarth Business Park *CHSWK* W4 106 B5
Hogarth Industrial Estate *WLSDN* NW10 87 J3
Hogarth's House *CHSWK* W4 106 A5
Holbeach Primary School *CAT* SE6 132 D6
Holborn *HHOL* WC1V 11 K4
Holborn College *WOOL/PLUM* SE18 114 C3
Holborn College Independent School *HMSMTH* W6 107 F4
Holborn Medical Centre *BMSBY* WC1N 11 L1
Holborn Town Hall *HHOL* WC1V 11 K4
Holiday Inn *BORE* WD6 25 G2
BTFD TW8 104 D6
BXLY DA5 137 J5
CAMTN NW1 4 C2
CHSGTN KT9 171 J7
FSBYW WC1X 5 M8
HYS/HAR UB3 101 G7
SUT SM1 175 F4
WDR/YW UB7 100 D7
Holland House *WKENS* W14 107 J1
Holland House School *EDGW* HA8 36 C3
Holland Park *NTGHL* W11 88 D7
Holland Park Pre-Preparatory School *WKENS* W14 107 J2
Holland Park School *KENS* W8 107 J1
Holland Park Theatre *WKENS* W14 107 J1
Holland Street Clinic *KENS* W8 14 B2
Hollickwood JMI School *MUSWH* N10 40 B6
Holloway Road *HOLWY* N7 73 F4
Holloway School *HOLWY* N7 72 D4
Hollydale Primary School *PECK* SE15 131 K1
The Hollyfield School *SURB* KT6 159 F4
Holly House Private Hospital *BKHH* IG9 45 F1
Hollymount Primary School *RYNPK* SW20 146 A7
Holly Park JMI School *FBAR/BDGN* N11 40 A4
Hollywood Bowl *BERM/RHTH* SE16 112 A2
The Holme *CAMTN* NW1 3 M8
Holmleigh Primary School *STNW/STAM* N16 56 B7
Holmshill School *BORE* WD6 24 E1
Holocaust Memorial Garden *KTBR* SW1X 15 M1
The Holy Cross Catholic Girls School *NWMAL* KT3 160 A3
Holy Cross Preparatory School *KUTN/CMB* KT2 144 E6
Holy Cross RC Primary School *CAT* SE6 133 F7
Holy Family RC Primary School *BKHTH/KID* SE3 134 A3
POP/IOD E14 93 J6
Holy Family Technology College *WALTH* E17 57 K3
Holy Ghost RC Primary School *BAL* SW12 128 E6
Holy Trinity CE Junior School *WLGTN* SM6 176 C3
Holy Trinity CE Primary School *BRXS/STRHM* SW2 130 A6
DART DA1 139 F4
EFNCH N2 53 H2
KIL/WHAMP NW6 71 G5
KTBR SW1X 16 A5
NTHWD HA6 32 A5
RCHPK/HAM TW10 125 H3
SYD SE26 150 E1
Holy Trinity College *BMLY* BR1 153 G7
Holy Trinity in St Silas *CAMTN* NW1 4 C1
Holy Trinity Lamorbey CE Primary School *BFN/LL* DA15 136 B7
Holy Trinity Primary School *HACK* E8 74 B5
WIM/MER SW19 146 E5
Holy Trinity School *CHEL* SW3 15 M5
Holywell School *WATW* WD18 20 D5
Homefield Preparatory School *SUT* SM1 174 E4
Home Office *WEST* SW1P 17 H4
Homerton *HOM* E9 75 F5
Homerton University Hospital *HOM* E9 75 F4
Homoeopathic Health Centre *PLSTW* E13 94 E3
The Homoeopathic Health Centre *MLHL* NW7 37 H4
Honeypot Business Centre *STAN* HA7 36 A7
Honeypot Lane Centre *STAN* HA7 35 K7
Honeypot Medical Centre *STAN* HA7 50 A1
Honeywell Primary School *BTSEA* SW11 128 E5
Honor Oak Crematorium *FSTH* SE23 132 A4
Honor Oak Gallery *FSTH* SE23 132 A5
Honor Oak Health Centre *BROCKY* SE4 132 B3
Honor Oak Park *FSTH* SE23 132 A5
Honourable Artillery Company *STLK* EC1Y 13 G1
Hook Lane Primary School *WELL* DA16 136 B2
Hook Rise South Industrial Park *CHSGTN* KT9 172 B2
Hopewell School *BARK* IG11 78 D5
Horizon Business Centre *ED* N9 43 F1
Horizon Industrial Estate *PECK* SE15 111 H5
Horizon School *STNW/STAM* N16 74 A3
The Horniman Museum & Gardens *FSTH* SE23 131 J7
Horniman Primary School *FSTH* SE23 131 J7
Horn Park Primary School *LEE/GVPK* SE12 134 A6
Hornsby House School *BAL* SW12 129 F7
Hornsey *CEND/HSY/T* N8 55 F3
Hornsey Central Hospital *CEND/HSY/T* N8 54 C4
Hornsey Rise Health Centre *ARCH* N19 54 D6
Hornsey Secondary School for Girls *CEND/HSY/T* N8 55 F4
Horn Stairs *BERM/RHTH* SE16 93 H7
Horse Guards Parade *WHALL* SW1A 11 H9
Horsenden Hill Golf Club *GFD/PVL* UB6 67 H5
Horsenden Primary School *GFD/PVL* UB6 66 E5
Horton Country Park *HOR/WEW* KT19 172 C7
Horton Park Golf & Country Club *HOR/WEW* KT19 172 E6
Hortus Cemetery *NWDGN* UB2 102 E1
Hospital of St John & St Elizabeth *STJWD* NW8 3 G6
The Hotel Russell *RSQ* WC1B 11 J1
Hotham Primary School *PUT/ROE* SW15 127 G3
Hotspur Industrial Estate *TOTM* N17 42 D5
Houndsfield Primary School *ED* N9 30 C6
Hounslow *HSLW* TW3 123 H3
Hounslow Business Park *HSLW* TW3 123 F3
Hounslow CC *HSLW* TW3 122 E1
Hounslow Cemetery *HSLWW* TW4 122 E6
Hounslow Central *HSLW* TW3 123 G1
Hounslow East *HSLW* TW3 123 H1
Hounslow Heath Golf Club *HSLWW* TW4 122 C4
Hounslow Heath Infant School *HSLWW* TW4 122 D2
Hounslow Heath Junior School *HSLWW* TW4 122 D2
Hounslow Manor School *HSLW* TW3 123 G2
Hounslow Manor Sports Hall *HSLW* TW3 123 G2
Hounslow Town Primary School *HSLW* TW3 123 H2
Hounslow West *HSLWW* TW4 122 D1
House of Detention *CLKNW* EC1R 6 B9
House of St Barnabus *SOHO/SHAV* W1D 11 G5
Houses of Parliament *WHALL* SW1A 17 K2
Houston Business Park *YEAD* UB4 83 G7
Howard Primary School *SAND/SEL* CR2 177 J3
Howbury Centre *ERITH* DA8 118 D6
Howland Quay *BERM/RHTH* SE16 112 A2
Hoxton *BETH* E2 7 L6
Hoxton Hall Community Theatre *IS* N1 7 J5
HQS Wellington (Master Mariners) *TPL/STR* WC2R 12 A7
HSBC Sports Club *BECK* BR3 151 G5
HSBC Tower *POP/IOD* E14 93 K7
Hubbinet Industrial Estate *ROMW/RG* RM7 62 E2
Hugh Myddelton Primary School *CLKNW* EC1R 6 B8
The Humana Wellington Hospital *STJWD* NW8 3 H7
Humber Trading Estate *CRICK* NW2 69 K1
Hunterian Museum *LINN* WC2A 11 M4
Hunters Hall Primary School *DAGE* RM10 80 D4
Hunter Street Health Centre *STPAN* WC1H 5 J9
Huntsman Sports Club *BKHTH/KID* SE3 133 K3
Hurlingham Business Park *FUL/PGN* SW6 127 K2
Hurlingham House *FUL/PGN* SW6 127 K2
Hurlingham Private School *PUT/ROE* SW15 127 J3
Huron University *RSQ* WC1B 11 J2
Hurricane Trading Centre *CDALE/KGS* NW9 37 H7
Hurstmere School *BFN/LL* DA15 136 C7

Hurst Park Primary School
E/WMO/HCT KT8 157 F2
Hurst Primary School
BXLY DA5 136 E7
Hyatt Carlton Tower Hotel
KTBR SW1X 15 M4
Hyatt Regency, The Churchill
MBLAR W1H 9 M4
The Hyde Industrial Estate
CDALE/KGS NW9 51 H4
Hyde Park Corner ⊖
KTBR SW1X 16 A1
The Hyde School
CDALE/KGS NW9 51 H4
Hyland House School
WALTH E17 58 B1
Hyleford Leavers Unit School
BARK/HLT IG6 60 D1
Hythe Road Industrial Estate
WLSDN NW10 87 J3
Ian Mikardo High School
BOW E3 93 K2
Ibis Hotel
CAMTN NW1 4 F8
CAN/RD E16 95 F6
FUL/PGN SW6 14 A9
GNWCH SE10 113 F5
HYS/HAR UB3 101 H7
POP/IOD E14 94 A6
SRTFD E15 76 C5
WBLY HA9 68 C4
Ibstock Place School
PUT/ROE SW15 126 B5
ICA Cinema
STJS SW1Y 11 H8
Ickburgh School
CLPT E5 74 D2
Ickenham ⊖
HGDN/ICK UB10 64 A3
Ickenham Clinic
HGDN/ICK UB10 64 A2
Ihlara Sport FC
HBRY N5 73 J3
Ilderton Primary School
PECK SE15 111 K5
Ilford ⇌
IL IG1 78 A2
Ilford County High School
BARK/HLT IG6 60 C1
Ilford Golf Club
IL IG1 59 K7
Ilford Jewish Primary School
BARK/HLT IG6 60 D2
Ilford Medical Centre
IL IG1 78 B2
Ilford Preparatory School
GDMY/SEVK IG3 61 F7
Ilford Retail Park
IL IG1 78 C1
Ilford Swimming Pool
IL IG1 78 D1
Ilford Ursuline High School
IL IG1 78 B1
Ilford Ursuline Preparatory School
IL IG1 78 B1
Iman Zakaria Academy
FSTGT E7 77 F4
Imber Court Trading Estate
E/WMO/HCT KT8 157 J5
Immanuel CE Primary School
STRHM/NOR SW16 148 E5
Immanuel College
BUSH WD23 22 E6
Imperial College
PUT/ROE SW15 127 G1
SKENS SW7 15 G3
SKENS SW7 15 G8
Imperial College Athletic Ground
HYS/HAR UB3 101 F5
Imperial College of London
SKENS SW7 15 G2
Imperial College of Science
FUL/PGN SW6 14 A9
Imperial College of Science & Technology
SKENS SW7 15 H2
Imperial College of Science Technology & Medicine
SKENS SW7 14 F3
Imperial College School of Medicine
PIM SW1V 17 G6
Imperial War Museum
STHWK SE1 18 B4
Imperial War Museum Annexe
LBTH SE11 18 B4
Imperial Wharf ⇌ ⊖
FUL/PGN SW6 108 B7
Inchbald School of Design
BGVA SW1W 16 B5
PIM SW1V 16 E6
Independent Jewish School
HDN NW4 52 B4
India House
HOL/ALD WC2B 11 L6
The Infirmary Royal Hospital
CHEL SW3 16 A8
Innellan House School
PIN HA5 47 J2
Innholders Hall
CANST EC4R 13 G6
Innkeeper's Lodge
BECK BR3 166 D5
BORE WD6 24 E1
CHEAM SM3 161 K7
NTHLT UB5 66 A5
SAND/SEL CR2 177 J7
STHGT/OAK N14 40 E1
WAN E11 58 E3
WFD IG8 45 K5
Inns of Court & Chancery
TPL/STR WC2R 12 A5
Inns of Court Law School
GINN WC1R 11 M2
Institute of Cancer Research
ECT SW5 14 F7
Institute of Education University of London
RSQ WC1B 11 H1
Instituto Espanol Canada Blanch
NKENS W10 88 C4
Intercontinental Hotel
MYFR/PICC W1J 16 B1
International Community School
CAMTN NW1 10 A1
International Medical Centre
ECT SW5 14 B6
International School of Business Studies (ISBS)
PIN HA5 48 A6
International School of London
ACT W3 105 H3
International Trading Estate
NWDGN UB2 102 A2
International University
BUSH WD23 21 K3
Invicta Industrial Estate
SRTFD E15 94 A2
Invicta Primary School
BKHTH/KID SE3 113 K5
Invicta Sports Club
DART DA1 139 G4
Inwood Business Centre
HSLW TW3 123 G3
IQRA Independent School
BRXN/ST SW9 130 B2
Ironmonger Row Baths
FSBYE EC1V 6 E8
Ironmongers Hall
STBT EC1A 12 E3
Islamia Girls School
KIL/WHAMP NW6 70 C7
Islamic College for Advanced Studies
WLSDN NW10 69 K6
The Islamic Grammar School
WAND/EARL SW18 127 J6
Islamic Shaksiyah Foundation School
WALTH E17 57 G4
Island Clinic
POP/IOD E14 113 F1
Island Gardens ⊖
POP/IOD E14 113 F3
Isleworth ⇌
ISLW TW7 124 A1
Isleworth Cemetery
ISLW TW7 124 B1
Isleworth Recreation Centre
ISLW TW7 124 A3
Isleworth & Syon School for Boys
ISLW TW7 103 K6
Isleworth Town Primary School
ISLW TW7 124 A1
Islington Arts & Media School
FSBYPK N4 55 F7
Islington Business Centre
IS N1 6 F3
Islington Crematorium
MUSWH N10 39 K7
Islington Green Medical Centre
IS N1 6 C3
Islington Tennis Centre
HOLWY N7 72 E5
Islington Town Hall
IS N1 6 C1
Ismaili Centre
SKENS SW7 15 H5
Italia Conti Academy of Theatre Art
FARR EC1M 12 E1
Italia Conti Academy of Theatre Arts
BRXN/ST SW9 129 K2
Italian Hospital
PIM SW1V 16 E5
Ivybridge Primary School
TWK TW1 124 A5
Ivybridge Retail Park
ISLW TW7 124 A4
Ivydale Primary School
PECK SE15 132 A3
Jack & Jill School
HPTN TW12 142 A5
WHTN TW2 142 E1
Jack Taylor School
STJWD NW8 2 E3
Jack Tizard School
FUL/PGN SW6 107 G7
SHB W12 88 A6
Jacques Prevert School
HMSMTH W6 107 G3
James Allens Preparatory Girls School
HNHL SE24 130 E4
James Dixon Primary School
PGE/AN SE20 150 C7
Jamestown Mental Health Centre
HAMP NW3 3 L1
James Wolfe Primary School
GNWCH SE10 112 E6
Jamiatul Ummah School
WCHPL E1 92 D5
Janet Adegoke Leisure Centre
SHB W12 87 J6
The Japanese School
ACT W3 86 C6
Japan Green Medical Centre
ACT W3 86 D7
Jenner Health Centre
FSTH SE23 132 B7
Jenny Hammond Primary School
WAN E11 76 C3
Jermyn Street Theatre
MYFR/PICC W1J 10 F7
Jessop Primary School
HNHL SE24 130 C3
Jewel Tower
WEST SW1P 17 J3
Jewish Cemetery
GLDGN NW11 52 E5
Jewish Community Theatre
HNHL SE24 130 E2
Jewish Free School
KTN/HRWW/WS HA3 50 C5
KTTN NW5 72 D5
The Jewish Museum
CAMTN NW1 4 C4
FNCH N3 53 F1
Johanna Primary School
STHWK SE1 18 A2
John Ball Primary School
BKHTH/KID SE3 133 H1
John Betts Primary School
HMSMTH W6 106 D2
John Burns Primary School
BTSEA SW11 129 F1
John Chilton School
NTHLT UB5 65 J6
John Dixon Clinic
BERM/RHTH SE16 111 J2
John Donne Primary School
PECK SE15 111 J7
John F Kennedy School
CAN/RD E16 95 H4
John F Kennedy Special School
SRTFD E15 76 C7
John Keble CE Primary School
WLSDN NW10 87 H1
John Kelly Girls Technology College
CRICK NW2 69 H2
The John Loughborough School
TOTM N17 56 B1
John Lyon School
RYLN/HDSTN HA2 48 D7
John Nightingale School
E/WMO/HCT KT8 156 E2
John Orwell Sports Centre
WAP E1W 92 C7
John Paul II RC School
WIM/MER SW19 127 G6
John Perryn Primary School
ACT W3 87 G5
John Perry Primary School
DAGE RM10 81 F5
John Roan Lower School
BKHTH/KID SE3 113 J6
John Roan School
BKHTH/KID SE3 113 H6
John Ruskin College
SAND/SEL CR2 179 G6
John Ruskin Primary School
WALW SE17 18 E9
John Scott Health Centre
FSBYPK N4 55 J7
John Scurr Primary School
WCHPL E1 92 E3
John Smith House
WALW SE17 18 E6
Johnsons Industrial Estate
HYS/HAR UB3 101 K2
John Stainer Primary School
BROCKY SE4 132 B2
The Jo Richardson Community School
DAGW RM9 79 K7
Joseph Clarke Special School
CHING E4 44 B5
Joseph Hood Primary School
RYNPK SW20 161 H1
Joseph Lancaster Primary School
STHWK SE1 18 F4
Jubilee Country Park
BMLY BR1 169 G3
Jubilee Market
COVGDN WC2E 11 K6
Jubilee Primary School
BRXS/STRHM SW2 130 B5
THMD SE28 97 J6
Jubilee Sports Ground
CHING E4 44 B3
Julians Primary School
STRHM/NOR SW16 149 G3
Jumeirah Carlton Tower Hotel
KTBR SW1X 15 M3
Jumeirah Lowndes Hotel
KTBR SW1X 15 M3
Juno Way Industrial Estate
NWCR SE14 112 A5
Jurys Clifton-Ford Hotel
MHST W1U 10 B3
Jurys Great Russell Street
RSQ WC1B 11 H4
Jurys Inn
CROY/NA CR0 177 J1
Jurys Inn Chelsea
FUL/PGN SW6 108 B7
Jurys Inn Hotel
HTHAIR TW6 121 J2
Jurys Inn Islington
IS N1 6 A6
Jurys Kensington Hotel
SKENS SW7 15 G6
JVC Business Park
CRICK NW2 51 J7
Kaizen Primary School
PLSTW E13 95 F3
Kangley Business Centre
SYD SE26 151 H4
Katella Trading Estate
BARK IG11 96 E2
Katherine Road Medical Centre
FSTGT E7 77 G5
Keats House
HAMP NW3 71 H3
Keble Preparatory School
WCHMH N21 29 G6
Keen Students Supplementary School
WCHPL E1 92 C4
Keir Hardie Primary School
CAN/RD E16 94 E4
Keith Davis Cue Sports Club
DAGW RM9 79 K6
Kelmscott Community Centre
WALTH E17 57 H5
Kelmscott Leisure Centre
WALTH E17 57 H5
Kelmscott School
WALTH E17 57 H5
Kelsey Park Sports College
BECK BR3 166 D2
Kelvin Industrial Estate
GFD/PVL UB6 66 B7
Kemnal Technology College
STMC/STPC BR5 155 H6
Kempton Park ⇌
SUN TW16 141 F6
Kempton Park Racecourse
SUN TW16 141 F6
Ken Barrington Centre
LBTH SE11 110 A5
Kender Primary School
NWCR SE14 111 K7
Kenilworth Primary School
BORE WD6 25 F2
Kenmont Primary School
WLSDN NW10 87 J2
Kenmore Park First School
KTN/HRWW/WS HA3 49 K2
Kenneth More Theatre
IL IG1 78 C2
Kennington ⊖
LBTH SE11 18 C7
Kensal Green ⊖ ⊖
WLSDN NW10 88 A2
Kensal Green Cemetery
WLSDN NW10 87 K2
Kensal Rise ⊖
WLSDN NW10 88 A1
Kensal Rise Primary School
KIL/WHAMP NW6 88 B1
Kensington & Chelsea College
NKENS W10 88 C3
Kensington & Chelsea Town Hall
KENS W8 14 B2
Kensington Avenue Primary School
THHTH CR7 149 G7
Kensington Business Centre
SKENS SW7 15 K3
Kensington & Chelsea College
CHEL SW3 15 H9
KENS W8 14 A1
NTGHL W11 107 J1
WBPTN SW10 108 B6
The Kensington Clinic
KENS W8 14 C4
Kensington House Hotel
KENS W8 14 E2
Kensington Leisure Centre
NTGHL W11 88 B6
Kensington Market
KENS W8 14 C2
Kensington (Olympia) ⇌ ⊖ ⊖
WKENS W14 107 H2
Kensington Palace State Apartments & Royal Ceremonial Dress Collection
KENS W8 8 D9
Kensington Park School
REGST W1B 10 D2
Kensington Preparatory School
FUL/PGN SW6 107 J7
Kensington Primary School
MNPK E12 77 K5
Kensington School of Business
HCIRC EC1N 12 B2
Kensington Wharf
WBPTN SW10 108 C6
Kensit Memorial College
FNCH N3 52 C1
Kent House ⇌
BECK BR3 151 G7
Kentish Town ⇌ ⊖
KTTN NW5 72 C4
Kentish Town CE Primary School
KTTN NW5 72 C4
Kentish Town Health Centre
KTTN NW5 72 C5
Kentish Town Industrial Estate
KTTN NW5 72 B4
Kentish Town Sports Centre
KTTN NW5 72 A5
Kentish Town West ⊖
KTTN NW5 72 B5
Kenton ⊖ ⊖
KTN/HRWW/WS HA3 49 H5
Kenton CC
KTN/HRWW/WS HA3 49 J3
Kenton Clinic
KTN/HRWW/WS HA3 50 A4
Kent Park Industrial Estate
PECK SE15 111 J5
Kenwood House
HAMP NW3 53 J7
Kenyngton Manor Primary School
SUN TW16 140 E4
The Kerem School
EFNCH N2 53 H4
Keston CE Primary School
HAYES BR2 181 H4
Kew Bridge ⇌
BTFD TW8 105 G4
Kew Bridge Steam Museum
BTFD TW8 105 G4
Kew College
RCH/KEW TW9 105 H6
Kew Gardens ⊖ ⊖
RCH/KEW TW9 105 H7
Kew Palace
RCH/KEW TW9 105 F6
Kew Retail Park
RCH/KEW TW9 105 J7
Kew Riverside Primary School
RCH/KEW TW9 125 J1
Keyplan & Roxburghe College
FITZ W1T 10 F1
Keyworth Primary School
WALW SE17 18 C8
Khalsa College London
HRW HA1 49 F5
Kidbrooke ⇌
BKHTH/KID SE3 134 B2
Kidbrooke Park Primary School
BKHTH/KID SE3 134 B1
Kidbrooke School
BKHTH/KID SE3 134 C1
Kilburn ⊖
CRICK NW2 70 C5
Kilburn High Road ⊖
KIL/WHAMP NW6 2 B4
Kilburn Park ⊖
KIL/WHAMP NW6 2 B5
Kilburn Park Junior School
KIL/WHAMP NW6 2 A6
KIL/WHAMP NW6 88 D2
Killick Street Medical Centre
IS N1 5 L5
Kilmorie Primary School
FSTH SE23 151 G1
Kimberley Industrial Estate
WALTH E17 43 H6
Kimpton Industrial Estate
CHEAM SM3 174 D1
Kinetic Business Centre
BORE WD6 24 B2
King Alfred School
GLDGN NW11 53 F7
King Athelstan Primary School
KUT/HW KT1 159 G2
King Edwards Road Clinic
RSLP HA4 46 B7
King Edward VII Hospital for Officers
MHST W1U 10 B2
King Fahad Academy
ACT W3 87 G6
King Fahad Academy (Girls Upper School)
EA W5 104 D3
The Kingfisher Medical Centre
DEPT SE8 112 C5
The Kingfisher Sports Centre
KUT/HW KT1 159 F1
King George Hospital
GNTH/NBYPK IG2 61 G4
King George V ⊖
CAN/RD E16 96 A7
King George VI Youth Hostel
KENS W8 107 J1
Kingham Industrial Estate
WLSDN NW10 87 F2
King Henry VIII Mound
RCHPK/HAM TW10 125 G7
King Henry's Drive (tram)
CROY/NA CR0 179 K7
King & Queen Wharf
BERM/RHTH SE16 93 F6
Kings Avenue Medical Centre
STHL UB1 84 C5
Kings Avenue School
CLAP SW4 129 K4
Kingsbury ⊖
CDALE/KGS NW9 50 C4
Kingsbury Green Primary School
CDALE/KGS NW9 50 D4
Kingsbury High School
CDALE/KGS NW9 50 D3
Kingsbury Hospital
CDALE/KGS NW9 50 C3
Kingsbury Trading Estate
CDALE/KGS NW9 50 E5
Kings College (Hampstead Campus)
HAMP NW3 70 E3
King's College Hospital
CMBW SE5 130 D2
Kings College London
HOL/ALD WC2B 11 K5
STHWK SE1 12 C8
WEST SW1P 16 F5
Kings College London - Humanities
TPL/STR WC2R 11 L6
Kings College London - Law
TPL/STR WC2R 11 M6
Kings College London (Waterloo Campus)
STHWK SE1 12 A9
Kings College School
WIM/MER SW19 146 A5
Kings College School of Medicine & Dentistry
CMBW SE5 130 E1
DUL SE21 130 E5
Kings College Sports Ground
RSLP HA4 46 C5
King's Cross ⇌ ⊖
CAMTN NW1 5 J6
King's Cross St Pancras ⊖
CAMTN NW1 5 J7
Kingsdale School
DUL SE21 150 A2
Kings Estate
HCH RM12 81 J3
Kingsford Community School
PLSTW E13 95 G3
Kingsgate Business Centre
KUTN/CMB KT2 144 A7
Kingsgate Primary School
KIL/WHAMP NW6 2 A1
Kings Hall Leisure Centre
CLPT E5 74 E4
Kings Head Theatre
IS N1 6 C3
Kings House School
RCHPK/HAM TW10 125 G4
Kingsland College of Business Studies
SRTFD E15 94 B1
Kingsland Health Centre
IS N1 7 K1
Kingsland Shopping Centre
HACK E8 74 B5
Kingsley Primary School
CROY/NA CR0 164 A7
Kings Mall Shopping Centre
HMSMTH W6 107 F3
Kingsmeadow Athletics Centre
KUT/HW KT1 159 H2
Kingsmead Primary School
CLPT E5 75 G3
Kingsmead School
EN EN1 30 C2
King Solomon High School
BARK/HLT IG6 60 D1
Kings Private Clinic
GDMY/SEVK IG3 61 F7
MHST W1U 10 A2
Kings School of English
BECK BR3 166 C1
Kings Stairs
BERM/RHTH SE16 111 J1
Kingston ⇌
KUTN/CMB KT2 144 A7
Kingston Business Centre
CHSGTN KT9 172 A2
Kingston Cemetery
KUT/HW KT1 159 G2
Kingston College of Further Education
KUT/HW KT1 159 F2
Kingston College Theatre
KUT/HW KT1 158 E2
Kingston Crematorium
KUT/HW KT1 159 H2
Kingston Grammar School
KUT/HW KT1 159 G1
Kingston Hospital
KUTN/CMB KT2 144 C7
Kingstonian FC
NWMAL KT3 159 J2
Kingston University
KUT/HW KT1 159 F2
KUTN/CMB KT2 145 F6
PUT/ROE SW15 145 H1
King Street College
HMSMTH W6 107 F3
Kingsway Business Park
HPTN TW12 141 K7
Kingsway College
CAMTN NW1 4 E9
STPAN WC1H 5 L8
Kingswood Primary School
WNWD SE27 149 K3
Kisharon School
GLDGN NW11 52 D5
K+K Hotel George
ECT SW5 14 B6
KLC School of Design
WBPTN SW10 108 B7
Knightsbridge ⊖
CHEL SW3 15 K3
Knightsbridge Barracks
SKENS SW7 15 K2
Knightsbridge Medical Centre
KTBR SW1X 15 M3
Knightsbridge School
KTBR SW1X 15 L4
Knollmead Primary School
BRYLDS KT5 172 E1
Knowledge Point School
HOLWY N7 73 F5
Kobi Nazrul Primary School
WCHPL E1 92 C5
KP Estate
RAIN RM13 99 G6

Krishna-Avanti Primary School *EDGW* HA8 36 C7
Kubrick Business Estate *FSTGT* E7 77 F3
Laban Centre for Movement & Dance *DEPT* SE8 112 E6
Laburnum Health Centre *DAGE* RM10 80 C1
Ladbroke Grove ⊖ *NKENS* W10 88 C5
Lady Bankes Junior School *RSLP* HA4 64 E1
The Lady Eleanor Holles School *HPTN* TW12 142 B4
Lady Margaret Primary School *STHL* UB1 83 K4
Lady Margaret School *FUL/PGN* SW6 107 K7
Ladywell ≠ *LEW* SE13 132 E4
Ladywell Arena *LEW* SE13 132 E5
Ladywell Cemetery *BROCKY* SE4 132 C4
Ladywell Leisure Centre *LEW* SE13 133 F4
Laings Sports Ground *BAR* EN5 25 G3
Lake Business Centre *TOTM* N17 42 C5
Laker Industrial Estate *BECK* BR3 151 H4
Lambeth Academy *CLAP* SW4 129 H4
Lambeth Cemetery *TOOT* SW17 147 G4
Lambeth College
BRXS/STRHM SW2 130 A4
CLAP SW4 129 H4
STHWK SE1 13 K9
STRHM/NOR SW16 148 E1
VX/NE SW8 109 J7
Lambeth Crematorium *TOOT* SW17 147 G3
Lambeth Hospital *BRXN/ST* SW9 129 K2
Lambeth North ⊖ *STHWK* SE1 18 A3
Lambeth Palace *STHWK* SE1 17 L4
Lambs Court *POP/IOD* E14 93 G6
Lammas School *LEY* E10 57 H7
Lamont Business Centre *CROY/NA* CR0 163 K6
Lamorbey Swimming Centre *BFN/LL* DA15 155 G1
Lampton School *HSLW* TW3 103 F7
The Lanark Medical Centre *MV/WKIL* W9 2 D7
Lancaster Gate ⊖ *BAY/PAD* W2 9 G6
Lancaster House *WHALL* SW1A 16 E1
Lancasterian Primary School *TOTM* N17 42 A7
Lancaster Road Industrial Estate *EBAR* EN4 27 H4
Lancelot Medical Centre *ALP/SUD* HA0 67 K4
The Landmark Hotel *CAMTN* NW1 9 L2
The Lanesborough Hotel *KTBR* SW1X 16 A1
Lanford Obesity Clinic *ED* N9 30 D6
Langbourne Primary School *DUL* SE21 150 A2
Langdon Down Centre *TEDD* TW11 143 J6
Langdon Park *POP/IOD* E14 93 K4
Langdon Park School *POP/IOD* E14 93 K5
Langdon School *EHAM* E6 96 B1
Langford Primary School *FUL/PGN* SW6 128 A1
Langham Hotel *CAVSQ/HST* W1G 10 D4
Langhedge Lane Industrial Estate *UED* N18 42 B5
Langley Park Girls School & Sports Centre *BECK* BR3 166 E4
Langley Park Golf Club *BECK* BR3 167 G5
Langley Park School for Boys *BECK* BR3 166 E5
Langthorne Health Centre *WAN* E11 76 B2
Langthorne Hospital *WAN* E11 76 B3
Lansbury Lawrence Primary School *POP/IOD* E14 93 K5
Lansdowne College *BAY/PAD* W2 8 C7
Lansdowne School *BRXN/ST* SW9 130 A2
La Retraite RC Girls School *BAL* SW12 129 H6
Lark Hall Primary School *CLAP* SW4 129 J1
Larkshall Business Centre *CHING* E4 44 B1
Larkswood Primary School *CHING* E4 43 K3
Larmenier & Sacred Catholic Primary School *HMSMTH* W6 107 G3
La Sainte Union Catholic Secondary School *HGT* N6 72 A2
La Sainte Union Convent School *KTTN* NW5 72 B2
La Salette RC Primary School *RAIN* RM13 99 J2
Latchmere Leisure Centre *BTSEA* SW11 128 E1
Latchmere Primary School *KUTN/CMB* KT2 144 B5
Lathom Junior School *EHAM* E6 77 J6
Latimer Road ⊖ *NTGHL* W11 88 B6
Latymer All Saints CE Primary School *ED* N9 42 B1
The Latymer Preparatory School *HMSMTH* W6 106 D4
The Latymer School *ED* N9 42 A1
Latymer Upper School *HMSMTH* W6 106 D3
Launcelot Primary School *BMLY* BR1 152 E3
Laurance Haines School *WATW* WD18 20 E5
Laurel Clinic *EA* W5 104 D3
Lauriston Primary School *HOM* E9 75 F7
Lawdale Junior School *BETH* E2 92 C2
Lawrence Trading Estate *GNWCH* SE10 113 H3
Lawrence University *SKENS* SW7 14 F6
Lawrence Wharf *BERM/RHTH* SE16 93 H7
Laycock Primary School *IS* N1 73 G5
Lazards Sports Club *SUN* TW16 141 F7
Leadenhall Market *BANK* EC3V 13 J5
Lea Park Trading Estate *LEY* E10 57 H6
Leaside Business Centre *PEND* EN3 31 H1
Leathermarket Gardens *STHWK* SE1 19 J2
Leathersellers Sports Ground *LEE/GVPK* SE12 134 B6
Leathers Hall *HDTCH* EC3A 13 J4
Lea Valley Primary School *TOTM* N17 42 C6
Lea Valley Trading Estate
UED N18 42 E3
UED N18 43 F5
Lebanon Road *CROY/NA* CR0 178 A1
L'Ecoles Des Petits School *FUL/PGN* SW6 128 A1
Lee ≠ *LEE/GVPK* SE12 133 K5
Lee Manor Primary School *LEW* SE13 133 H5
Leeside Court *BERM/RHTH* SE16 93 F7
Leeside Trading Estate *TOTM* N17 42 E6
Lee Valley Camping & Caravan Park *ED* N9 31 G7
Lee Valley Campsite *CHING* E4 31 K1
Lee Valley Ice Centre *LEY* E10 75 F1
Lee Valley Leisure Complex, Athletics Centre & Golf Club *ED* N9 31 G6
Lee Valley Watersports Centre *CHING* E4 43 G5
Leicester Square ⊖ *LSQ/SEVD* WC2H 11 H6
Leigh Close Industrial Estate *NWMAL* KT3 160 A3
Leigh Technology Academy *DART* DA1 139 K7
Leighton House Museum *WKENS* W14 107 J2
Lena Gardens Primary School *HMSMTH* W6 107 F2
Leopold Primary School *WLSDN* NW10 69 H6
Leopold Street Clinic *BOW* E3 93 H4
Lesnes Abbey *BELV* DA17 116 E3
Lesnes Abbey (remains of) *ABYW* SE2 116 C5
Lessness Heath Primary School *BELV* DA17 117 H4
The Levin Hotel *KTBR* SW1X 15 L3
Lewin Mead Community Mental Health Centre *STRHM/NOR* SW16 148 D5
Lewis Clinic *CAR* SM5 176 A3
Lewisham ≠ *DEPT* SE8 132 E1
Lewisham Bridge Primary School *LEW* SE13 132 E2
Lewisham Business Centre *NWCR* SE14 112 A5
Lewisham Centre *LEW* SE13 133 F3
Lewisham College *BROCKY* SE4 132 D1
Lewisham Crematorium *CAT* SE6 152 D1
Lewisham Lions Centre *BERM/RHTH* SE16 111 K4
The Leys Primary School *DAGE* RM10 80 E6
Leyton ⊖ *WAN* E11 76 A2
Leyton Business Centre *LEY* E10 75 H1
Leyton FC *LEY* E10 57 H7
Leyton Industrial Village *LEY* E10 57 F6
Leyton Leisure Centre *LEY* E10 57 K6
Leyton Midland Road ⊖ *LEY* E10 58 A7
Leyton Orient FC (Matchroom Stadium) *LEY* E10 75 K2
Leyton Sixth Form College *LEY* E10 58 B5
Leytonstone ⊖ *WAN* E11 58 C7
Leytonstone High Road ⊖ *WAN* E11 76 C1
Leytonstone School *WAN* E11 58 C5
Leyton Youth Sports Ground *LEY* E10 57 K7
The Liberty City Clinic *SDTCH* EC2A 7 J9
Liberty II Centre *ROM* RM1 63 G3
Liberty Middle School *MTCM* CR4 162 D1
The Liberty *ROM* RM1 63 G4
Library & Community Centre *BTSEA* SW11 128 C2
L'Ile Aux Enfants *KTTN* NW5 72 A4
Lilian Baylis School *VX/NE* SW8 17 L9
Lilian Baylis Technology School *VX/NE* SW8 17 L9
Lillian Baylis School *LBTH* SE11 17 M6
Lillian Baylis Theatre *CLKNW* EC1R 6 C7
Lillian Bishop School of English *SKENS* SW7 15 G5
Limehouse ≠ *WCHPL* E1 93 G5
Limehouse Hole Stairs *BERM/RHTH* SE16 93 H7
Lime Trees Park Golf Club *NTHLT* UB5 65 G7
Lincoln Road Clinic *EN* EN1 30 C4
Lincoln's Inn *LINN* WC2A 11 M4
Linden Bridge School *WPK* KT4 173 G2
Linden Lodge School *WIM/MER* SW19 127 H7
Lindon Bennett School *FELT* TW13 141 H4
Linford Christie Stadium *SHB* W12 87 J4
The Link Day Primary School *CROY/NA* CR0 176 E3
The Link Secondary School *CROY/NA* CR0 177 F3
Links Primary School *TOOT* SW17 148 A5
Linley House School *BRYLDS* KT5 159 G5
Linley Sambourne House
KENS W8 14 A2
WKENS W14 107 J1
Linnet House Clinic *STJWD* NW8 3 J6
Linton Mead Primary School *THMD* SE28 97 H6
Lionel Road Primary School *BTFD* TW8 105 F3
Liongate Hotel *E/WMO/HCT* KT8 158 A2
Lion House School *PUT/ROE* SW15 127 G3
Lismarrine Industrial Park *BORE* WD6 23 H5
Lisson Grove Health Centre *STJWD* NW8 3 J9
Lister Community School *PLSTW* E13 95 F1
The Lister Hospital *BGVA* SW1W 16 C8
Lister House Clinic *CAVSQ/HST* W1G 10 C4
Little Danson Welfare Clinic *WELL* DA16 136 B3
Little Davids School *CROY/NA* CR0 179 K5
Little Hands Theatre *HDN* NW4 52 A3
Little Heath School *CHDH* RM6 61 H3
Little Ilford School *MNPK* E12 77 K4
Little Reddings Primary School *BUSH* WD23 22 B4
Little St Helens School *NTHWD* HA6 32 C5
Little Stanmore First & Middle School *EDGW* HA8 36 A7
Little Venice Medical Centre *MV/WKIL* W9 8 F1
Little Wandsworth School *TOOT* SW17 148 A1
Liverpool Street ≠ ⊖ *LVPST* EC2M 13 J3
Livesey Museum for Children *PECK* SE15 111 J5
Livingstone Hospital *DART* DA1 139 J6
Livingstone Primary School *EBAR* EN4 27 H2
The Livity School *BRXS/STRHM* SW2 129 K4
Lloyd Park *CROY/NA* CR0 178 B3
Lloyd Park Centre *WALTH* E17 57 J1
Lloyd's *FENCHST* EC3M 13 J5
Lloyds Register CC *DUL* SE21 130 E7
Locks View Court *POP/IOD* E14 93 G6
Lockwood Industrial Park *TOTM* N17 56 D2
Lombard Business Centre *BTSEA* SW11 128 C1
Lombard Business Park
CROY/NA CR0 164 A6
WAND/EARL SW18 128 C5
WIM/MER SW19 162 B1
Lombard Trading Estate *CHARL* SE7 114 A3
Lombardy Retail Park *HYS/HAR* UB3 83 F6
London Academy *EDGW* HA8 36 B3
London Academy of Music & Dramatic Art *KENS* W8 14 A5
London Allergy Clinic *CAVSQ/HST* W1G 10 C3
London Bridge ≠ ⊖ *STHWK* SE1 13 H9
London Bridge City Pier *STHWK* SE1 13 J8
London Bridge Hospital *STHWK* SE1 13 H8
London Bridge Hotel *STHWK* SE1 13 G9
London Bridge Sports Centre *CANST* EC4R 13 G7
London Brookes College *HDN* NW4 51 K3
London Business School *CAMTN* NW1 3 L9
London Butterfly House *BTFD* TW8 104 D7
The London Canal Museum *IS* N1 5 K5
London Capital College *CAMTN* NW1 4 D3
London Centre of Contemporary Music *STHWK* SE1 12 F9
London Chest Hospital *BETH* E2 92 E1
London Chinese Dance School
CAN/RD E16 94 B4
REGST W1B 10 D2
London City Airport *CAN/RD* E16 95 J7
London City College (English Language Institute) & Schiller International University *STHWK* SE1 11 M9
London City Mission *STHWK* SE1 19 K1
The London Clinic *CAVSQ/HST* W1G 10 B1
London College of Business & Computer Services *CLAP* SW4 129 J3
London College of Business & Computing *BETH* E2 92 D1
London College of Communication *LBTH* SE11 18 D4
London College of Fashion
CAVSQ/HST W1G 10 D4
MHST W1U 10 B4
SDTCH EC2A 7 K9
London College of Further Education *LBTH* SE11 18 C6
London College of Higher Education *CLAP* SW4 129 G2
London College of International Business Studies *HHOL* WC1V 11 K3
London College of Science & Technology *GDMY/SEVK* IG3 61 G7
London Commodity Exchange *WAP* E1W 13 M7
London Contemporary Dance School
CAMTN NW1 5 H8
PLSTW E13 94 D2
London Cornish RFC *PUT/ROE* SW15 145 H2
The London Dungeon *STHWK* SE1 13 H9
London Esthetique *POP/IOD* E14 94 C5
London Eye *STHWK* SE1 17 L1
London Eye Clinic *CAVSQ/HST* W1G 10 C3
London Fields ≠ *HACK* E8 74 D6
London Fields Lido *HACK* E8 74 D6
London Fields Primary School *HACK* E8 74 D7
London Film Academy *FUL/PGN* SW6 107 K6
London Film School *LSQ/SEVD* WC2H 11 J5
London Financial Training College *FSBYPK* N4 55 H4
London Foot Hospital *FITZ* W1T 10 E1
London Gender Clinic *HDN* NW4 51 K5
London Group Business Park *CRICK* NW2 51 H7
London Heart Clinic *CAVSQ/HST* W1G 10 C3
The London Industrial Estate *EHAM* E6 96 A4
London Industrial Park *EHAM* E6 96 B4
London International College
POP/IOD E14 94 C5
SOHO/SHAV W1D 10 F4
London Irish RFC *SUN* TW16 140 E7
The London Irish Youth Theatre *HGT* N6 54 B7
London Islamic School / Madrasah *WCHPL* E1 92 D5
London Jewish Girls High School *HDN* NW4 52 A4
London Ladies & Girls FC *CAT* SE6 151 K4
London Lane Clinic *BMLY* BR1 152 D6
London Lighthouse *NTGHL* W11 88 C5
London Living Theatre *SYD* SE26 151 F3
The London Make-up Academy *UED* N18 42 D4
London Marriott Hotel
HAMP NW3 3 H2
MYFR/PKLN W1K 10 B6
OXSTW W1C 9 M6
STHWK SE1 17 L1
London Marriott West India Quay Hotel *POP/IOD* E14 93 J6
London Metrocity College *BOW* E3 93 J2
London Metropolitan University
HBRY N5 73 J4
HOLWY N7 73 F4
LVPST EC2M 13 H3
WCHPL E1 13 L4
WCHPL E1 92 C5
London Natural Therapy School
POP/IOD E14 94 C6
SOHO/CST W1F 10 F6
London Nautical School *STHWK* SE1 12 B8
London Open College *FSBYE* EC1V 6 D7
London Oratory School *FUL/PGN* SW6 107 K6
London Road Medical Centre *CROY/NA* CR0 164 B5
London School of Economics
CLKNW EC1R 6 B8
HHOL WC1V 11 J4
HOL/ALD WC2B 11 L5
STHWK SE1 12 E8
London School of Hygiene & Tropical Medicine *GWRST* WC1E 11 H2
London School of Theology *NTHWD* HA6 32 B5
London Scottish Golf Club *WIM/MER* SW19 145 K2
London Silver Vaults *LINN* WC2A 12 A3
London South Bank University *STHWK* SE1 18 D3
London Stock Exchange *STBT* EC1A 12 D4
London's Transport Museum *HOL/ALD* WC2B 11 K6
The London Television Centre *STHWK* SE1 12 A8
London Tourist Board & Convention Centre *BGVA* SW1W 16 C3
London Toy & Model Museum *BAY/PAD* W2 8 F6
London Transport Bus Depot *BXLYHN* DA7 137 J2
London Underwriting Centre *MON* EC3R 13 J6
London Wall *BARB* EC2Y 12 E3
London Weather Centre *HCIRC* EC1N 12 A2
The London Welbeck Hospital *CAVSQ/HST* W1G 10 B3
London Welsh FC *RCH/KEW* TW9 125 F2
London Welsh School *CRICK* NW2 70 A5
London West Crematorium *WLSDN* NW10 87 K3
London Wetland Centre *BARN* SW13 106 E7
Lonesome Primary School *MTCM* CR4 163 G1
Long Ditton Cemetery *SURB* KT6 171 J1
Long Ditton County Infant School *SURB* KT6 158 D7
Long Ditton St Marys CE Junior School *THDIT* KT7 158 C7
Longfield Primary School *RYLN/HDSTN* HA2 48 A5
Longford Community School *EBED/NFELT* TW14 121 J6
Longford Industrial Estate *HPTN* TW12 142 B5
Longlands Primary School *BFN/LL* DA15 154 E2
Long Lane AFC *BKHTH/KID* SE3 134 B1
Longmead Primary School *WDR/YW* UB7 100 A3
Longshaw Primary School *CHING* E4 44 B2
Longwood School *BUSH* WD23 21 J3
Lord Chancellors Department *WEST* SW1P 17 H4
Lord Lister Health Centre *FSTGT* E7 76 E3
Lordship Lane Clinic *TOTM* N17 56 A1
Lordship Lane Primary School *WDGN* N22 41 J7
Lord's Tour & MCC Museum *STJWD* NW8 3 G8
Lord Williamson School *NKENS* W10 88 C4
Lorimar Business Centre *RAIN* RM13 99 G5
Loughborough Junction ≠ *CMBW* SE5 130 C1
Loughborough Primary School *CMBW* SE5 130 C1
Lovelace Primary School *CHSGTN* KT9 171 J4
Lovell's Wharf *GNWCH* SE10 113 G4
Lower Clapton Health Centre *CLPT* E5 74 E4
Lower Place Business Centre *WLSDN* NW10 86 E1
Lower Sydenham ≠ *SYD* SE26 151 H4
Lower Sydenham Industrial Estate *SYD* SE26 151 H4
Lowfield Medical Centre *DART* DA1 139 H6
Low Hall Sports Ground *LEY* E10 57 F5
Lowther Primary School *BARN* SW13 106 D5
Loxford School of Science & Technology *IL* IG1 78 D4
LSE Sports Club *NWMAL* KT3 160 A5
Lubavitch Boys Primary School *CLPT* E5 56 B6
Lubavitch House School (Senior Girls) *STNW/STAM* N16 56 A6
Lucas Vale Primary School *DEPT* SE8 112 D7
Lutomer House Business Centre *POP/IOD* E14 93 K7
Lux Cinema *IS* N1 7 J8
Lycee Francais *SKENS* SW7 15 G5
Lycee Francais Charles De Gaulle *BTSEA* SW11 129 G3
The Lyceum Theatre *COVGDN* WC2E 11 L6
Lyndean Industrial Estate *ABYW* SE2 116 D2
Lyndhurst House Preparatory School *HAMP* NW3 71 H4
Lyndhurst Primary School *CMBW* SE5 130 E1
Lyon Business Park *BARK* IG11 96 E1
Lyon Park Infant School *ALP/SUD* HA0 68 B6
Lyonsdown School *BAR* EN5 27 G4
Lyric Theatre *SOHO/SHAV* W1D 11 G6

Lyric Theatre Hammersmith *HMSMTH* W6 107 F3
Mabwin Supplementary School *ED* N9 42 D1
Macaulay CE Primary School *CLAP* SW4 129 G2
Madame Tussauds & the London Auditorium *CAMTN* NW1 9 M1
Madeira Grove Clinic *WFD* IG8 45 F4
Madison Bowl *NTHWD* HA6 32 C6
Madni Girls School *WCHPL* E1 92 D5
Madrasah-E-Darue Qirat Majidiah School *WCHPL* E1 92 D6
Mahatma Gandhi Industrial Estate *BRXN/ST* SW9 130 C2
Maida Vale ⊖ *MV/WKIL* W9 2 D8
Maida Vale Medical Centre *MV/WKIL* W9 2 C8
Malcolm Primary School *PGE/AN* SE20 150 E6
The Malden Centre *NWMAL* KT3 160 C3
Malden Golf Club *NWMAL* KT3 160 B1
Malden Manor ⇌ *NWMAL* KT3 160 B6
Malden Manor Primary School *NWMAL* KT3 160 B6
Malden Parochial Primary School *WPK* KT4 160 B7
Malden Road Baths *CHEAM* SM3 174 B3
Malham Road Industrial Estate *FSTH* SE23 132 A7
The Mall Bexleyheath *BXLYHS* DA6 137 H3
Mall Galleries *STJS* SW1Y 11 H8
The Mall School *WHTN* TW2 142 D2
Malmaison Charterhouse Square Hotel *FARR* EC1M 12 D2
Malmesbury Primary School *BOW* E3 93 H2
MRDN SM4 162 B6
Malorees Junior School *KIL/WHAMP* NW6 70 B6
Malvern Way Infant School *RKW/CH/CXG* WD3 20 A4
Mandarin Oriental Hotel *KTBR* SW1X 15 M1
The Mandeville Hotel *MHST* W1U 10 B4
Mandeville Primary School *CLPT* E5 75 G2
Mandeville Special School *NTHLT* UB5 65 K5
Manford Industrial Estate *ERITH* DA8 118 E5
Manor Brook Medical Centre *BKHTH/KID* SE3 134 A1
Manor Drive Health Centre *WPK* KT4 160 C7
Manorfield Primary School *POP/IOD* E14 93 K4
Manor House ⊖ *FSBYPK* N4 55 J7
Manor Infant School *BARK* IG11 79 F5
Manor Park ⇌ *MNPK* E12 77 H3
Manor Park Cemetery *FSTGT* E7 77 H3
Manor Park Crematorium *FSTGT* E7 77 G3
Manor Park Methodist School *MNPK* E12 77 J3
Manor Park Primary School *SUT* SM1 175 G4
Manor Place Industrial Estate *BORE* WD6 24 E2
Manor Primary School *SRTFD* E15 94 C1
The Manor Primary School *ROM* RM1 63 H4
Manorside Primary School *FNCH* N3 39 F7
Manor Special School *WLSDN* NW10 88 B1
Manor Way Business Centre *RAIN* RM13 99 F4
Mansfield Infant College *IL* IG1 78 A1
Mansion House ⊖ *STP* EC4M 12 F5
Mapledown School *CRICK* NW2 52 B6
Maple Grove Business Centre *HSLWW* TW4 122 B3
Maple House Independant Montessori School *THHTH* CR7 164 C2
Maple Industrial Estate *FELT* TW13 140 E1
Maples Business Centre *IS* N1 6 B3
Marble Arch ⊖ *MBLAR* W1H 9 M5
Marble Arch *MBLAR* W1H 9 M6
Marble Hill House *TWK* TW1 124 D6
Maria Fidelis Convent School *CAMTN* NW1 4 F8
Maria Montessori Childrens House *HAMP* NW3 71 H4
Mariner Business Centre *CROY/NA* CR0 177 F4
Marion Richardson Primary School *WCHPL* E1 93 F5
Marion Vian Primary School *BECK* BR3 166 A4
Maritime Greenwich College *DEPT* SE8 112 D6
Maritime Industrial Estate *CHARL* SE7 114 A3
Maritime Museum *GNWCH* SE10 113 H3
Marjorie McClure School *CHST* BR7 154 C7
The Marjory Kinnon School *EBED/NFELT* TW14 121 H4
The Market *COVGDN* WC2E 11 K6
Market Trading Estate *NWDGN* UB2 102 A3
Marks Gate Junior School *CHDH* RM6 62 A2
Marlborough CC *DUL* SE21 131 H7
Marlborough Day Hospital *STJWD* NW8 2 E5
Marlborough First & Middle School *HRW* HA1 48 E3
Marlborough House *STJS* SW1Y 10 F9
Marlborough Primary School *CHEL* SW3 15 K6
ISLW TW7 104 B7
Marlborough School *BFN/LL* DA15 136 B7
Marlborough Trading Estate *RCH/KEW* TW9 105 J7
Marlowe Business Centre *NWCR* SE14 112 B6
Marner Primary School *BOW* E3 93 K3
Marriott Hotel *ECT* SW5 14 C5
HYS/HAR UB3 101 G6
KIL/WHAMP NW6 2 C5
MBLAR W1H 9 K4
Marshalls Park School *ROM* RM1 63 G1
Marsh Gate Business Centre *SRTFD* E15 94 A1
Marshgate Primary School *RCHPK/HAM* TW10 125 G4
Marsh Green School *DAGW* RM9 98 C1
Martan College *HOL/ALD* WC2B 11 K4
Martinbridge Industrial Estate *EN* EN1 30 C4
Martindale Industrial Estate *EN* EN1 30 A4
Martin Primary School *EFNCH* N2 53 J3
Marvels Lane Primary School *LEE/GVPK* SE12 153 G3
Mary Boone School *WKENS* W14 107 H3
Maryland ⇌ *SRTFD* E15 76 C4
Maryland Industrial Estate *SRTFD* E15 76 C4
Maryland Primary School *SRTFD* E15 76 C4
Marylebone ⇌ ⊖ *CAMTN* NW1 9 K1
Marylebone Health Centre *CAMTN* NW1 10 B1
Marymount International School *KUTN/CMB* KT2 144 E6
Mary Wallace Theatre *TWK* TW1 124 B7
Maswell Park Health Centre *HSLW* TW3 123 H4
Mathilda Marks Kennedy Primary School *MLHL* NW7 37 F4
Matrix Business Centre *DART* DA1 139 H4
Maudlin's Green *WAP* E1W 13 M8
The Maudsley Hospital *CMBW* SE5 130 E1
Maughan Library (Kings College) *LINN* WC2A 12 A4
Mawbrey Brough Health Centre *VX/NE* SW8 109 K6
The Mawney School *ROMW/RG* RM7 63 F4
Mayday University Hospital *THHTH* CR7 164 C5
Mayesbrook Park Arena *BARK* IG11 79 G4
Mayespark Primary School *GDMY/SEVK* IG3 79 G2
Mayfield Primary School *HNWL* W7 84 D5
Mayfield School *PIN* HA5 47 J2
Mayflower Primary School *POP/IOD* E14 93 J5
Mayplace Primary School *BXLYHN* DA7 138 A3
Maytime School *IL* IG1 78 A2
Mayville J & P School *WAN* E11 76 C2
Maze Hill ⇌ *GNWCH* SE10 113 H5
McKay Trading Estate *NKENS* W10 88 C3
McMillan Clinic *HYS/HAR* UB3 82 A6
MDQ Majidiah School *WCHPL* E1 92 D6
The Mead Infant School *WPK* KT4 173 H2
Meadlands Primary School *RCHPK/HAM* TW10 143 J3
Meadowgate School *BROCKY* SE4 132 A2
Meadowside Leisure Centre *BKHTH/KID* SE3 134 B3
The Meadow Special School *STMC/STPC* BR5 155 G6
Meadow Wood School *BUSH* WD23 22 C4
Mead Road Infant School *CHST* BR7 154 C5
The Medical Centre *WAT* WD17 21 F1
Medical Express Clinic *CAVSQ/HST* W1G 10 C2
Mednurs Clinic *SEVS/STOTM* N15 55 K5
Megabowl *KUTN/CMB* KT2 159 F1
Melcombe Primary School *HMSMTH* W6 107 G5
Melia White House Hotel *CAMTN* NW1 4 D9
Mellish Industrial Estate *WOOL/PLUM* SE18 114 C2
Mellow Lane School *HGDN/ICK* UB10 82 A3
Melrose Special School *MTCM* CR4 162 D2
Memorial Hospital *WOOL/PLUM* SE18 135 F1
Menorah Grammar School *EDGW* HA8 36 E6
GLDGN NW11 52 C6
Menorah High School for Girls *CRICK* NW2 69 H2
Menorah Primary School *GLDGN* NW11 52 C6
MERC Education *WOOL/PLUM* SE18 115 G2
Mercers' Hall *CITYW* EC2V 12 F5
The Merchant Taylors Hall *BANK* EC3V 13 H5
Merchant Taylors School *NTHWD* HA6 20 C7
Mercure London City Bankside Hotel *STHWK* SE1 12 E9
Meridian Clinic *BRXN/ST* SW9 130 A2
Meridian Locality Mental Health Centre *CHARL* SE7 114 B5
Meridian Primary School *GNWCH* SE10 113 G4
Meridian Sports Club *CHARL* SE7 114 D6
Meridian Trading Estate *CHARL* SE7 114 A3
Merlin Primary School *BMLY* BR1 152 E2
Merlin School *PUT/ROE* SW15 127 G4
Mermaid Theatre *BLKFR* EC4V 12 D6
Merrielands Retail Park *DAGW* RM9 80 B7
Merry Hill Infant School *BUSH* WD23 22 B6
Merryhills Clinic *ENC/FH* EN2 29 F2
Merryhills Primary School *ENC/FH* EN2 29 F3
Merton Abbey Primary School *WIM/MER* SW19 147 F7
Merton Adult College *RYNPK* SW20 161 H2
Merton College *MRDN* SM4 161 J5
Merton Court Preparatory School *SCUP* DA14 155 J3
Merton Industrial Park *WIM/MER* SW19 147 G7
Merton Park ◓ *WIM/MER* SW19 146 E7
Merton Park Primary School *WIM/MER* SW19 161 J1
Merton Road Industrial Estate *WAND/EARL* SW18 127 K6
The Method Studio *FSBYW* WC1X 11 L2
Metro Business Centre *SYD* SE26 151 H5
The Metro Golf Centre *HDN* NW4 38 A7
Metro Industrial Centre *ISLW* TW7 123 K1
Metropolis Centre *BORE* WD6 24 C2
Metropolitan Business Centre *HACK* E8 7 K2
Metropolitan Hospital *STHWK* SE1 18 B3
The Metropolitan Hotel *MYFR/PKLN* W1K 10 C9
Metropolitan Police Bushey Sports Ground *BUSH* WD23 22 A2
Metropolitan Police FC *E/WMO/HCT* KT8 157 J5
Metropolitan Police Hayes Sports Club *HAYES* BR2 180 D1
Metropolitan Police (Hendon) Track *CDALE/KGS* NW9 51 H2
Metropolitan Police Training School, Hendon *CDALE/KGS* NW9 51 H2
Metropolitan Tabernacle *STHWK* SE1 18 D5
Metro Trading Centre *WBLY* HA9 68 D3
Michael Faraday Primary School *WALW* SE17 19 H8
Michael Manley Industrial Estate *VX/NE* SW8 109 H7
Michael Sobell Sinai School *KTN/HRWW/WS* HA3 50 C5
The Michael Tippett School *LBTH* SE11 18 B6
Midas Business Centre *DAGE* RM10 80 C3
Midas Industrial Estate *DAGE* RM10 80 C3
Middle Park Primary School *ELTH/MOT* SE9 134 C6
Middle Row Primary School *NKENS* W10 88 C3
Middlesex Business Centre *NWDGN* UB2 103 F1
Middlesex CCC (Lord's Cricket Ground) *STJWD* NW8 3 H7
Middlesex Hospital Medical School *FITZ* W1T 10 F2
Middlesex Hospital Nurses Home *GTPST* W1W 10 E2
Middlesex Hospital School of Physiotherapy *FITZ* W1T 10 F2
Middlesex Hospital Sports Ground *CHST* BR7 155 F4
Middlesex School of Complementary Medicine *STAN* HA7 36 A7
Middlesex University *ARCH* N19 54 C7
GLDGN NW11 53 F7
PEND EN3 31 F4
WDGN N22 54 E1
Middlesex University (Cat Hill Campus) *EBAR* EN4 28 A5
Middlesex University (Enfield Campus) *PEND* EN3 30 D4
Middlesex University (Hendon Campus) *HDN* NW4 51 K3
Middlesex University (Trent Park Campus) *EBAR* EN4 28 C1
Midfield Primary School *STMC/STPC* BR5 155 G6
Midway Mission Hospital *BETH* E2 7 L8
Milbourne Lodge Junior School *ESH/CLAY* KT10 170 C4
Milbourne Lodge School *ESH/CLAY* KT10 170 D5
Mile End ⊖ *BOW* E3 93 H3
Mile End & Bow Business Centre *WCHPL* E1 92 D4
Mile End Hospital *WCHPL* E1 93 F2
Mile End Stadium *POP/IOD* E14 93 H4
Milehams Industrial Estate *PUR* RM19 119 K2
Miles Coverdale Primary School *SHB* W12 107 F1
Milestone Hotel *KENS* W8 14 D2
Military Barracks *WOOL/PLUM* SE18 115 F4
Millbank Millennium Pier *WEST* SW1P 17 J6
Millbank Primary School *WEST* SW1P 17 H6
Millbank Tower *WEST* SW1P 17 J6
Millennium Arena *BTSEA* SW11 109 F6
Millennium Bailey's Hotel *SKENS* SW7 14 E5
Millennium Balloon *STHWK* SE1 13 K9
Millennium & Copthorne Hotels at Chelsea FC *FUL/PGN* SW6 108 A6
Millennium Dance 2000 Theatre School *HAMP* NW3 71 J4
Millennium Gloucester Hotel *ECT* SW5 14 D6
Millennium Harbour *POP/IOD* E14 112 C1
Millennium Hotel *KTBR* SW1X 15 M2
Millennium Hotel London Mayfair *MYFR/PKLN* W1K 10 B7
Millennium Primary School *GNWCH* SE10 113 J2
Millennium Quay *DEPT* SE8 112 E5
Millennium Wharf *POP/IOD* E14 113 G2
Mill Farm Business Park *HSLWW* TW4 122 D6
Millfields Primary School *CLPT* E5 74 E3
Millfield Theatre *UED* N18 41 K3
Mill Green Business Park *MTCM* CR4 162 E6
Mill Hill Broadway ⇌ *MLHL* NW7 37 G5
Mill Hill Cemetery *MLHL* NW7 38 A5
Mill Hill County High School *MLHL* NW7 37 G1
The Mill Hill CC *MLHL* NW7 38 A2
Mill Hill East ⊖ *MLHL* NW7 38 B6
Mill Hill Golf Club *MLHL* NW7 37 G1
Mill Hill Industrial Estate *MLHL* NW7 37 H5
Mill Hill School *MLHL* NW7 37 K3
Mill Lane Medical Centre *KIL/WHAMP* NW6 70 E4
Mill Lane Trading Estate *CROY/NA* CR0 177 F2
Mill River Trading Estate *PEND* EN3 31 G3
Millside Industrial Estate *DART* DA1 139 G3
Mill Street Clinic *STHWK* SE1 19 M1
Mill Trading Estate *WLSDN* NW10 86 D1
The Mill Trading Estate *WLSDN* NW10 86 E2
Millwall FC (The New Den) *BERM/RHTH* SE16 111 K4
Milmead Industrial Centre *TOTM* N17 56 D1
Milton Natural Health Centre *HGT* N6 54 C6
Minet Clinic *HYS/HAR* UB3 82 E7
Minet J & I Schools *HYS/HAR* UB3 83 F7
Ministry of Defence *WHALL* SW1A 11 J9
Mint Business Park *CAN/RD* E16 94 E4
Mirravale Trading Estate *CHDH* RM6 62 A6
Mission Grove Primary School *WALTH* E17 57 H4
Mitcham ◓ *MTCM* CR4 162 D3
Mitcham CC *MTCM* CR4 162 D3
Mitcham Eastfields ⇌ *MTCM* CR4 163 F1
Mitcham Golf Club *MTCM* CR4 163 F4
Mitcham Industrial Estate *MTCM* CR4 148 A7
Mitcham Junction ⇌ ◓ *MTCM* CR4 163 F4
Mitcham Vale High School *STRHM/NOR* SW16 163 H1
Mitchell Brook Primary School *WLSDN* NW10 69 F5
Mitre Bridge Industrial Park *NKENS* W10 87 K3
Mitre House Hotel *BAY/PAD* W2 9 G5
Moatbridge School *ELTH/MOT* SE9 134 C5
The Moat School *FUL/PGN* SW6 127 H1
Moberly Sports & Education Centre *WLSDN* NW10 88 B2
Molesey Cemetery *E/WMO/HCT* KT8 157 F2
Molesey Hospital *E/WMO/HCT* KT8 157 F4
Mollison Drive Health Centre *WLGTN* SM6 176 E6
Monega Primary School *MNPK* E12 77 H4
Monkfrith Primary School *EBAR* EN4 28 A6
Monks Hill Sports Centre *SAND/SEL* CR2 179 F6
Monksmead School *BORE* WD6 24 E2
Monks Orchard Primary School *CROY/NA* CR0 166 A4
The Montague on the Gardens Hotel *RSQ* WC1B 11 J2
Montbelle Primary School *ELTH/MOT* SE9 154 A3
The Montcalm-Hotel Nikko *MBLAR* W1H 9 M5
Monteagle Primary School *DAGW* RM9 79 H7
Montem Primary School *HOLWY* N7 73 F2
Montpelier Primary School *EA* W5 85 K4
Monument ⊖ *MANHO* EC4N 13 H6
The Monument *CANST* EC4R 13 H6
Moore Place Golf Club *ESH/CLAY* KT10 170 A4
Moorfields Eye Hospital *FSBYE* EC1V 7 G8
Moorgate ⇌ ⊖ *BARB* EC2Y 13 G3
Moor Lane Junior School *CHSGTN* KT9 172 B4
Moor Park ⊖ *NTHWD* HA6 32 B2
Moor Park Industrial Estate *WATW* WD18 20 A6
Mora Primary School *CRICK* NW2 70 A3
Morden ⊖ *WIM/MER* SW19 162 A2
Morden Cemetery *MRDN* SM4 161 F5
Morden College Homes *BKHTH/KID* SE3 133 K1
Morden First School *MRDN* SM4 161 K4
Morden Hall Medical Centre *WIM/MER* SW19 162 A2
Morden Hall Park (NT) *MRDN* SM4 162 B3
Morden Mount Primary School *LEW* SE13 132 E1
Morden Park Pool *MRDN* SM4 161 J4
Morden Road ◓ *WIM/MER* SW19 162 A1
Morden Road Clinic *WIM/MER* SW19 162 A2
Morden South ⇌ *MRDN* SM4 161 K4
Moreland Primary School *FSBYE* EC1V 6 D7
Moriah Jewish Day School *PIN* HA5 47 J7
Morley College *STHWK* SE1 18 B3
Morningside Primary School *HOM* E9 74 E5
Mornington Crescent ⊖ *CAMTN* NW1 4 E5
Mornington Sports & Fitness Centre *CAMTN* NW1 4 D3
Morpeth School *BETH* E2 92 E2
Mortimer Road Clinic *WLSDN* NW10 88 A2
Mortimer School *STRHM/NOR* SW16 148 D1
Mortlake ⇌ *MORT/ESHN* SW14 125 K2
Mortlake Cemetery *MORT/ESHN* SW14 126 B2
Mortlake Crematorium *RCH/KEW* TW9 125 J1
Moselle School *TOTM* N17 56 A1
Moselle Special School *TOTM* N17 55 K1
Mosiah Foundation Supplementary School *STNW/STAM* N16 56 A7
Mossbourne Community Academy *HACK* E8 74 C3
Mossford Green Primary School *BARK/HLT* IG6 60 C1
Moss Hall Junior School *FNCH* N3 39 F5
The Mother & Baby Clinic *HOM* E9 74 E5
Motspur Park ⇌ *NWMAL* KT3 160 E4
Mottingham ⇌ *ELTH/MOT* SE9 134 E7
Mottingham Community Health Clinic *ELTH/MOT* SE9 153 J3
Mottingham Primary School *ELTH/MOT* SE9 153 K2
Mount Carmel RC Primary School *EA* W5 104 D2
Mount Carmel RC Technical College for Girls *ARCH* N19 54 D7
The Mount Infant School *NWMAL* KT3 159 J2
Mount Medical Centre *FELT* TW13 141 J1
Mount School *MLHL* NW7 37 K4
Mount Stewart Infant School *KTN/HRWW/WS* HA3 49 K5
The Movieum of London *STHWK* SE1 17 L1

Mowlem Primary School BETH E2 92 E1
Mowlem Trading Estate TOTM N17 42 E6
MPR Eurotots School KIL/WHAMP NW6 70 B6
MS Business Centre PIN HA5 47 H2
MSP Business Centre WBLY HA9 68 D3
Mudchute ⊖ POP/IOD E14 112 E3
Mudchute City Farm POP/IOD E14 113 F3
Mudlands Estate RAIN RM13 99 G2
Mulberry Business Centre BERM/RHTH SE16 112 A1
Mulberry House School CRICK NW2 70 C4
Mulberry Primary School TOTM N17 56 B1
Mulberry School for Girls WCHPL E1 92 D5
Mulgrave Primary School WOOL/PLUM SE18 115 F3
Munroe Centre STHWK SE1 19 H1
Murky Puddle Theatre NWMAL KT3 160 C2
Muschamp Primary School CAR SM5 175 J1
Museum in Docklands POP/IOD E14 93 J6
Museum of Domestic Design & Architecture EBAR EN4 27 K4
Museum of Fulham Palace FUL/PGN SW6 127 G1
Museum of Garden History STHWK SE1 17 K4
Museum of London BARB EC2Y 12 E3
Museum of London Archaeology IS N1 6 F4
Museum of Richmond TWK TW1 124 E4
Museum of the Artillery in the Rotunda CHARL SE7 114 D4
Museum of the Order of St John FARR EC1M 12 D1
Musical Museum BTFD TW8 105 F5
Muswell Hill Bowling Club MUSWH N10 54 A2
Muswell Hill Golf Club MUSWH N10 40 B7
Muswell Hill Primary School MUSWH N10 54 B2
Myatt Garden Primary School BROCKY SE4 132 C1
Myatts Field Clinic BRXN/ST SW9 110 C7
N1 Shopping Centre IS N1 6 B5
Nagi Business Centre ALP/SUD HA0 85 K1
Nags Head Shopping Centre HOLWY N7 72 E2
Naima Jewish Preparatory School KIL/WHAMP NW6 2 C5
Nancy Rueben Primary School HDN NW4 52 B3
Nash College of Further Education WWKM BR4 180 D2
The National Archives RCH/KEW TW9 105 H6
National Army Museum CHEL SW3 15 M9
National Film Theatre STHWK SE1 11 M8
National Gallery LSQ/SEVD WC2H 11 H7
National Hospital for Neurology & Neurosurgery RSQ WC1B 11 J1
National Maritime Museum GNWCH SE10 113 G5
National Physical Laboratory TEDD TW11 142 E5
National Portrait Gallery LSQ/SEVD WC2H 11 H7
National Sports Centre NRWD SE19 150 C5
National Temperance Hospital CAMTN NW1 4 E7
National Tennis Centre PUT/ROE SW15 126 B4
National Youth Theatre Great Britain HOLWY N7 72 E2
The Natural History Museum SKENS SW7 15 G4
Natural Therapy Clinic TOOT SW17 148 B4
Natwest Sports Club BECK BR3 151 H5
Navigation College CANST EC4R 12 F6
Neasden ⊖ WLSDN NW10 69 G4
Negus Sixth Form Centre WOOL/PLUM SE18 115 J5
Nelson Dock Museum BERM/RHTH SE16 93 H7
Nelson Hospital RYNPK SW20 161 J1
Nelson Primary School EHAM E6 96 A1
WHTN TW2 123 G5
Nelson's Column STJS SW1Y 11 H8
Nelson Trading Estate WIM/MER SW19 147 F7
Neo Clinic PIM SW1V 16 E5
The New Ambassadors Theatre LSQ/SEVD WC2H 11 H5
New Atlas Wharf POP/IOD E14 112 C2
The New Aylesbury Medical Centre WALW SE17 19 H7
New Barnet ⇌ BAR EN5 27 G4
New Beckenham ⇌ BECK BR3 151 G6
New Brentford Cemetery HSLW TW3 122 E1
Newbridge School CHDH RM6 61 H4
Newbury Park ⊖ GNTH/NBYPK IG2 60 D5
Newbury Park Health Centre GNTH/NBYPK IG2 60 D5
The New Business Centre WLSDN NW10 87 H2
New Caledonian Wharf BERM/RHTH SE16 112 C2
New Chiswick Pool CHSWK W4 106 B6
New City Primary School PLSTW E13 95 G2
New Connaught Rooms HOL/ALD WC2B 11 K5
New Covent Garden Market VX/NE SW8 109 J6
New Crane Wharf WAP E1W 92 E7
New Cross ⇌ ⊖ NWCR SE14 112 C6
New Cross Gate ⇌ ⊖ NWCR SE14 112 B6
New Cross Sports Arena NWCR SE14 112 B6
New Eltham ⇌ ELTH/MOT SE9 135 G7
New End Primary School HAMP NW3 71 G3
New End Theatre HAMP NW3 71 G2
New England Industrial Estate BARK IG11 96 C1
Newfield Primary School WLSDN NW10 69 H6
Newham City Farm CAN/RD E16 95 H5
Newham College of Further Education EHAM E6 95 K1
SRTFD E15 76 C6
Newham General Hospital PLSTW E13 95 G3
Newham Leisure Centre PLSTW E13 95 G4
Newham Medical Centre PLSTW E13 95 G1
Newham Sixth Form College PLSTW E13 95 F3
Newham Training & Education Centre SRTFD E15 76 C5
New Hope Christian School EDUL SE22 131 G3
New Horizons Computer Learning Centre FSBYE EC1V 7 G8
Newington Court Business Centre STHWK SE1 18 E4
Newington Green Primary School STNW/STAM N16 74 A4
Newington Industrial Estate WALW SE17 18 D6
New Kings Primary School FUL/PGN SW6 127 J1
Newland House School TWK TW1 143 F3
New London Theatre LSQ/SEVD WC2H 11 K4
New Malden ⇌ NWMAL KT3 160 B2
Newnham Junior School RSLP HA4 47 G7
New North Community School IS N1 7 G1
Newport School LEY E10 76 A1
New River Sports Centre WDGN N22 41 H6
New River Village CEND/HSY/T N8 55 F2
New Rush Hall School IL IG1 78 C1
New School FUL/PGN SW6 107 J7
New Scotland Yard STJSPK SW1H 17 G3
News International Offices WAP E1W 92 D6
New Southgate ⇌ FBAR/BDGN N11 40 A4
New Southgate Cemetery FBAR/BDGN N11 40 B2
New Southgate Crematorium FBAR/BDGN N11 40 B2
New Southgate Industrial Estate FBAR/BDGN N11 40 C4
New Southgate Pain Clinic & Medical Centre FBAR/BDGN N11 40 C4
New Spitalfields Market LEY E10 75 J3
Newton Farm First & Middle School RYLN/HDSTN HA2 65 K1
Newton Industrial Estate CHDH RM6 61 K3
Newton Medical Centre BAY/PAD W2 8 C4
Newton Preparatory School VX/NE SW8 109 G6
Newtons Primary School RAIN RM13 99 F1
New Victoria Hospital KUTN/CMB KT2 145 G7
New Woodlands School BMLY BR1 152 C3
N H Harrington Hall Hotel SKENS SW7 14 E6
Nightingale Clinic PLSTW E13 95 G1
Nightingale Primary School CLPT E5 74 C2
SWFD E18 59 G3
WDGN N22 41 F7
WOOL/PLUM SE18 115 G5
Nightingale School TOOT SW17 147 J1
Noam Primary School NFNCH/WDSPK N12 39 F4
Noel Coward Theatre CHCR WC2N 11 J6
Noel Park Primary School WDGN N22 55 H1
Nonsuch High School for Girls CHEAM SM3 174 B6
Nonsuch Park Hotel EW KT17 174 A4
Nonsuch Primary School EW KT17 173 K4
Noor Ul Islam Primary School LEY E10 76 A1
Norbiton ⇌ KUTN/CMB KT2 144 C7
Norbury ⇌ STRHM/NOR SW16 149 F7
Norbury Business & Enterprise College STRHM/NOR SW16 149 G7
Norbury Complementary Therapy Clinic STRHM/NOR SW16 149 F7
Norbury First & Middle School HRW HA1 48 E4
Norbury Health Centre STRHM/NOR SW16 164 A1
Norbury Manor Primary School STRHM/NOR SW16 148 E7
Norbury Trading Estate STRHM/NOR SW16 164 A1
Norland Place School NTGHL W11 88 C7
Norlington School LEY E10 58 B7
Normand Croft Community School WKENS W14 107 J5
Normandy Primary School BXLYHN DA7 118 A7
Norman Park Athletics Track HAYES BR2 168 A5
Norman Shaw Building (MP's Offices) WHALL SW1A 17 J1
North Acton ⊖ WLSDN NW10 87 F3
North Acton Business Park ACT W3 87 F5
North Beckton Primary School EHAM E6 95 K3
North Bridge House HAMP NW3 71 G5
North Bridge House Preparatory School CAMTN NW1 4 C4
North Bridge House School HAMP NW3 71 H5
Northbrook CE School LEE/GVPK SE12 133 H4
Northbury Primary School BARK IG11 78 B5
North Clinic BMLY BR1 152 E7
North Croydon Medical Centre THHTH CR7 164 C5
North Dulwich ⇌ HNHL SE24 130 E4
North Ealing ⊖ ACT W3 86 B5
North Ealing Primary School WEA W13 85 H3
North East Surrey Crematorium NWMAL KT3 161 F5
Northend Primary School ERITH DA8 118 C7
North End Trading Estate ERITH DA8 118 B6
North Feltham Trading Estate EBED/NFELT TW14 122 A3
Northfields ⊖ WEA W13 104 D2
Northfields Industrial Estate ALP/SUD HA0 68 C7
Northfields Prospect Business Centre PUT/ROE SW15 127 J3
Northgate Business Centre EN EN1 30 D2
Northgate Clinic CDALE/KGS NW9 51 G5
Northgate Industrial Park CRW RM5 62 B1
North Greenwich ⊖ GNWCH SE10 113 H1
North Harringay Primary School CEND/HSY/T N8 55 G3
North Harrow ⊖ RYLN/HDSTN HA2 48 A4
North Havering College of Adult Education ROM RM1 63 G3
North Kensington Video-Drama Project NKENS W10 88 C5
North London College SEVS/STOTM N15 56 B2
North London Collegiate School EDGW HA8 36 A5
The North London Hospice NFNCH/WDSPK N12 39 F2
North London International School (Diploma Centre) NFNCH/WDSPK N12 39 J4
North London International School (Lower School) NFNCH/WDSPK N12 39 F2
North London International School (Upper School) FBAR/BDGN N11 39 K4
North London Nuffield Hospital ENC/FH EN2 29 G1
North London School of Physiotherapy ARCH N19 54 C7
North London Tutorial College HDN NW4 52 A5
North Middlesex Golf Club NFNCH/WDSPK N12 39 H2
North Middlesex Hospital UED N18 42 A4
Northolt ⊖ NTHLT UB5 66 A6
Northolt Aerodrome RSLP HA4 64 E5
Northolt High School NTHLT UB5 65 K5
Northolt Park ⇌ RYLN/HDSTN HA2 66 B3
Northolt Primary School NTHLT UB5 65 H6
Northolt Road Clinic RYLN/HDSTN HA2 66 C2
Northolt Swimarama NTHLT UB5 66 A5
North Pole Depot WLSDN NW10 87 H3
North Primary School STHL UB1 83 K6
North Sheen ⇌ RCH/KEW TW9 125 H3
Northside Primary School NFNCH/WDSPK N12 39 G4
The North Street Health Centre CLAP SW4 129 H2
Northumberland Heath Medical Centre ERITH DA8 118 A6
Northumberland Heath Primary School ERITH DA8 117 J6
Northumberland Park ⇌ TOTM N17 42 D7
Northumberland Park Industrial Estate TOTM N17 42 D5
Northumberland Park School TOTM N17 42 C6
Northview Primary School WLSDN NW10 69 G3
Northway School MLHL NW7 37 F1
North Wembley ⊖ ⊖ ALP/SUD HA0 67 K2
North West London Jewish Primary School CRICK NW2 70 C6
North West London Medical Centre MV/WKIL W9 2 E6
North Westminster Community Secondary School MV/WKIL W9 2 B9
Northwick Park ⊖ KTN/HRWW/WS HA3 49 H6
Northwick Park Hospital & Clinical Research Centre HRW HA1 49 H6
Northwold Primary School CLPT E5 74 C1
Northwood ⊖ NTHWD HA6 32 C6
Northwood Cemetery NTHWD HA6 46 D1
Northwood College NTHWD HA6 32 B6
Northwood FC NTHWD HA6 46 D1
Northwood Golf Club NTHWD HA6 32 B6
Northwood Hills ⊖ NTHWD HA6 46 E1
Northwood & Pinner Community Hospital NTHWD HA6 32 E7
Northwood Preparatory School RKW/CH/CXG WD3 32 A1
Northwood Primary School ERITHM DA18 117 F2
Northwood School NTHWD HA6 33 F7
Northwood Sports Centre NTHWD HA6 33 F7
Norwegian/British Monument BAY/PAD W2 9 J8
The Norwegian School WIM/MER SW19 146 A6
Norwood Green Infant School NWDGN UB2 102 D4
Norwood Green Junior School NWDGN UB2 102 D4
Norwood Heights Shopping Centre NRWD SE19 150 A5
Norwood Junction ⇌ ⊖ SNWD SE25 165 H3
Norwood School NRWD SE19 149 J4
Notre Dame RC Girls School STHWK SE1 18 C3
Notre Dame RC Primary School WOOL/PLUM SE18 115 G5
Notre Dame University LSQ/SEVD WC2H 11 H7
Notting Hill & Ealing High School WEA W13 85 H4
Notting Hill Gate ⊖ NTGHL W11 8 A8
Novello Theatre HOL/ALD WC2B 11 L6
Novotel CAMTN NW1 5 H7
CAN/RD E16 95 F6
GNWCH SE10 112 E6
STHWK SE1 12 F9
STHWK SE1 17 L5
TWRH EC3N 13 K6
WDR/YW UB7 100 D3
Novotel London West HMSMTH W6 107 G4
Nower Hill High School PIN HA5 48 A3
NTGB Sports Ground EHAM E6 78 A5
Number 10 Bowling ROM RM1 63 G4
Nunhead ⇌ PECK SE15 131 K2
NutriLife Clinic MHST W1U 10 A2
The O2 POP/IOD E14 94 B7
Oakdale Infant School SWFD E18 59 F1
Oakdale Junior School SWFD E18 59 G1
Oakfield Preparatory School DUL SE21 149 K1
Oakfield Road Industrial Estate PGE/AN SE20 150 D6
Oak Heights Independent School HSLW TW3 123 G2
Oak Hill Health Centre SURB KT6 159 F5
Oakington Manor School WBLY HA9 68 D4
Oakland CP School EBAR EN4 27 K5
Oaklands College BORE WD6 24 E1
Oaklands Primary School HNWL W7 104 A1
Oaklands School ISLW TW7 123 J2
Oaklands Secondary School BETH E2 92 C2
Oak Lane Cemetery TWK TW1 124 B6
Oak Lane Medical Centre TWK TW1 124 C6
Oakleigh Park ⇌ TRDG/WHET N20 27 H6
Oakleigh School TRDG/WHET N20 39 J2
Oak Lodge JMI School WWKM BR4 166 E6
Oak Lodge Medical Centre EDGW HA8 36 D6
Oak Lodge School BAL SW12 128 E6
EFNCH N2 53 G2
Oaks Park High School GNTH/NBYPK IG2 60 D4
Oakthorpe Primary School UED N18 41 J4
Oak Tree Medical Centre GDMY/SEVK IG3 78 E1
Oakwood ⊖ STHGT/OAK N14 28 C3
Oakwood Business Park WLSDN NW10 87 F2
Oakwood Medical Centre STHGT/OAK N14 28 C4
Oakwood School BXLYHN DA7 138 A3
Oasis Sports Centre LSQ/SEVD WC2H 11 J4
Odeon Cinema BAR EN5 26 E4
BAY/PAD W2 9 L5
BECK BR3 166 D1
BERM/RHTH SE16 112 A2
CAMTN NW1 4 D3
ED N9 31 F6
ELTH/MOT SE9 134 D3
ESH/CLAY KT10 170 B3
FITZ W1T 11 G3
HAMP NW3 3 G2
HAYES BR2 167 K1
HOLWY N7 72 E2
KENS W8 14 A4
KUT/HW KT1 159 F1
MUSWH N10 54 A3
RCH/KEW TW9 124 E4
ROM RM1 63 H4
STJS SW1Y 11 G7
STRHM/NOR SW16 148 E2
SWFD E18 58 E1
WIM/MER SW19 146 E6
Odeon Covent Garden Cinema LSQ/SEVD WC2H 11 H5
Odeon Wardour Street Cinema SOHO/SHAV W1D 11 G6
Odessa Infant School FSTGT E7 76 E4
Odyssey Business Park RSLP HA4 65 F4
Old Abbotstonians RFC YEAD UB4 82 B1
Old Actonians Sports Club EA W5 105 G1
Old Admiralty STJS SW1Y 11 H9
Old Bancroftians FC BKHH IG9 45 H3
Old Barnes Cemetery BARN SW13 126 E1
Old Beckenhamian RFC WWKM BR4 180 B2
Old Bellgate Wharf POP/IOD E14 112 C2
Old Bexley Business Park BXLY DA5 137 J6
Old Bexley CE Primary School BXLY DA5 137 G7
Old Brockleians Sports Ground LEE/GVPK SE12 134 B5
Old Bromlians CC HAYES BR2 168 A4
Old Cemetery EDUL SE22 131 J5
Old Colfeian Sports Club LEE/GVPK SE12 133 K4
Old Curiosity Shop LINN WC2A 11 L4
Old Elthamians Sports Club CHST BR7 154 E5
Oldfield House Special School HPTN TW12 141 K7
Oldfield Primary School GFD/PVL UB6 84 D1
Oldfields Trading Estate SUT SM1 174 E2
Old Ford Primary School BOW E3 93 H1
Oldhill Medical Centre STNW/STAM N16 56 B7
Old Jamaica Business Estate BERM/RHTH SE16 19 M3
Old Lyonian Sports Ground RYLN/HDSTN HA2 48 C4
Old Millhillians Sports Ground RYLN/HDSTN HA2 34 A7
Old Oak Primary School SHB W12 87 H5
Old Operating Theatre & Herb Garret Museum STHWK SE1 13 G9
Old Owens Sports Ground TRDG/WHET N20 27 H7
Old Palace Primary School BOW E3 93 K2
Old Palace School CROY/NA CR0 177 H2
Old Royal Naval College GNWCH SE10 113 G4
Old Royal Observatory Greenwich GNWCH SE10 113 G6
Old Spitalfields Market Hall WCHPL E1 13 L2
Old Street ⇌ ⊖ FSBYE EC1V 7 G8
Old Sun Wharf POP/IOD E14 93 G6
Old Tiffinians Sports Ground E/WMO/HCT KT8 157 K4
Old Treasury WHALL SW1A 17 J1
Old Vicarage School RCHPK/HAM TW10 125 F5
Old Vic Theatre STHWK SE1 18 B1
Old War Office WHALL SW1A 11 J9
Old Wilsonians Sports Club WWKM BR4 167 H7
Olga Primary School BOW E3 93 G1
Oliver Business Park WLSDN NW10 86 E1

Oliver Goldsmith Primary School
CDALE/KGS NW9 51 F4
CMBW SE5 111 G7
Oliver House Preparatory School
CLAP SW4 129 G5
Olympia
WKENS W14 107 H2
Olympia Industrial Estate
WDGN N22 55 F1
Olympic Industrial Estate
WBLY HA9 68 D3
Olympic Retail Park
WBLY HA9 68 C3
Olympic site (under development)
SRTFD E15 75 K6
Olympic Trading Estate
WBLY HA9 68 D3
One Aldwych Hotel
COVGDN WC2E 11 L6
The One Stanley Medical Centre
ALP/SUD HA0 68 A6
On Sai Clinic
ECT SW5 14 C6
The Open University
FSBYW WC1X 5 L7
HAMP NW3 70 E3
Ophaboom Theatre
WLSDN NW10 87 K1
Optimax Laser Eye Clinic
HAMP NW3 71 G5
Orange Tree Theatre
RCH/KEW TW9 125 F3
Orchard Business Centre
BECK BR3 151 H4
The Orchard Health Centre
BARK IG11 96 C1
Orchard Hill College
WLGTN SM6 176 B5
Orchard House School
CHSWK W4 106 A3
Orchard J & I School
HOM E9 74 E6
The Orchard Junior School
HSLWW TW4 123 F3
Orchard Primary School
SCUP DA14 155 H4
The Orchard School
BRXS/STRHM SW2 130 A7
E/WMO/HCT KT8 157 J4
Orchard Shopping Centre
DART DA1 139 H5
The Orchard Theatre
DART DA1 139 H5
Orchard Way Primary School
CROY/NA CR0 166 B6
Oriel Primary School
FELT TW13 141 J2
Orient Industrial Park
LEY E10 75 J1
Orion Business Centre
NWCR SE14 112 A4
The Orion Primary School
CDALE/KGS NW9 37 G7
Orleans House Gallery
TWK TW1 124 C7
Orleans Infant School
TWK TW1 124 C6
Orley Farm School
HRW HA1 66 D2
Osidge JMI School
STHGT/OAK N14 28 C7
Osier Industrial Estate
WAND/EARL SW18 127 K3
Osmani Primary School
WCHPL E1 92 C4
Osterley
ISLW TW7 103 J6
Osterley Park & House (NT)
ISLW TW7 103 H5
Osterley RFC
NWDGN UB2 103 G2
Our Lady Immaculate RC Primary School
BRYLDS KT5 159 J7
Our Lady of Dolours RC Primary School
BAY/PAD W2 8 C2
Our Lady of Grace RC Junior School
CRICK NW2 69 K2
Our Lady of Grace RC Primary School
CHARL SE7 114 A5
Our Lady of Lourdes RC Primary School
FBAR/BDGN N11 40 B4
NFNCH/WDSPK N12 39 G6
WAN E11 58 D5
WLSDN NW10 68 E7
Our Lady of Muswell RC Primary School
MUSWH N10 54 A1
Our Lady of the Rosary RC School
ELTH/MOT SE9 135 K5
Our Lady of the Sacred Heart School
HOLWY N7 73 F4
Our Lady of the Visitation RC Primary School
GFD/PVL UB6 84 C3
Our Lady of Victories RC Primary School
PUT/ROE SW15 127 G3
SKENS SW7 14 F6
Our Lady Queen of Heaven RC Primary School
PUT/ROE SW15 127 G6
Our Lady RC Primary School
CAMTN NW1 4 F3
POP/IOD E14 93 H5
Our Lady & St Johns RC Primary School
BTFD TW8 104 D4
Our Lady & St Joseph Primary School
IS N1 74 A5
Our Lady & St Philip Neri Infants School
FSTH SE23 151 F2
Our Lady & St Philip Neri RC Primary School
SYD SE26 151 G3
Our Ladys Catholic Primary School
DART DA1 139 G5
Oval
LBTH SE11 110 B5
Oval Business Centre
LBTH SE11 17 M8
Oval House Theatre
LBTH SE11 110 B5
Oval Primary School
CROY/NA CR0 165 F7
Overton Grange School
BELMT SM2 175 F7
Oxford Circus
REGST W1B 10 D4
Oxford Gardens Primary School
NKENS W10 88 B5
Oxford House College
SOHO/SHAV W1D 11 G4
Oxhey Park Golf Centre
OXHEY WD19 21 H7
Oxhey Wood Primary School
OXHEY WD19 33 G3
Oxo Tower Wharf
STHWK SE1 12 B7
Paddington
BAY/PAD W2 9 G4
Paddington Academy
MV/WKIL W9 8 B1
Paddington Bowling & Sports Club
MV/WKIL W9 2 C9
Paddington Community Hospital
MV/WKIL W9 8 A2
Paddington Green Primary School
BAY/PAD W2 9 G1
Paddington Recreation Ground Athletics Track
KIL/WHAMP NW6 2 B7
Paddock Primary School
BTSEA SW11 129 F3
Paddock School
PUT/ROE SW15 126 C3
Paines Lane Cemetery
PIN HA5 47 J2
Pain Relief Clinic
HDN NW4 51 K5
Paint Pots Montessori School
WBPTN SW10 108 B5
Pakeman Primary School
HOLWY N7 73 F2
Palace Gardens Shopping Centre
ENC/FH EN2 29 K2
Palace of Westminster
WHALL SW1A 17 K2
Palace Theatre
SOHO/SHAV W1D 11 H6
WAT WD17 21 F2
Palladium Theatre
SOHO/CST W1F 10 E5
Palmers Green
PLMGR N13 41 F3
Palmers Green High School
WCHMH N21 41 G1
Palmerston Business Centre
SUT SM1 175 G4
Palm House, Kew Gardens
RCH/KEW TW9 105 G7
Panorama Pier
STHWK SE1 12 E7
Paradise Swimming Pools
MLHL NW7 37 G4
Paray House School
FUL/PGN SW6 127 J1
Parayhouse School
WBPTN SW10 108 B6
Parchmore Medical Centre
THHTH CR7 164 D2
Pardes House & Beis Yaakov School
FNCH N3 52 D1
Parent Infant Clinic
HAMP NW3 71 G4
Parish CE Primary School
BMLY BR1 152 E6
Park Avenue Clinic
WAT WD17 20 E1
Park Business Centre
KIL/WHAMP NW6 2 A8
Parkes Hotel
CHEL SW3 15 K3
Parkfield Industrial Estate
BTSEA SW11 129 F1
Parkfield JMI School
HDN NW4 51 K6
Parkgate House School
CLAP SW4 129 F3
Park Hall Trading Estate
WNWD SE27 149 J2
Park High School
STAN HA7 49 K1
Park Hill Junior School
CROY/NA CR0 177 K2
Parkhill Primary School
CLAY IG5 59 K2
Park Hill School
KUTN/CMB KT2 144 C6
Park House Medical Centre
KIL/WHAMP NW6 88 C1
Park House RFC
HAYES BR2 181 G1
Parklands Primary School
ROM RM1 63 F2
Park Lane Primary School
WBLY HA9 68 A3
Park Medical Centre
BERM/RHTH SE16 112 A3
Park Mews Small Business Centre
HNHL SE24 130 D5
Park Plaza County Hall Hotel
STHWK SE1 17 M1
Park Primary School
SRTFD E15 76 D6
Park Road Clinic
CEND/HSY/T N8 54 D4
Park Road Swimming Centre
CEND/HSY/T N8 54 D4
Park Royal
EA W5 86 C3
Park Royal Business Centre
WLSDN NW10 87 F3
Park School for Girls
IL IG1 78 A1
Parkside Business Estate
DEPT SE8 112 C5
Parkside Clinic
NTGHL W11 88 C5
Parkside Health
NTGHL W11 88 C5
Parkside Hospital
WIM/MER SW19 146 B2
Park View Academy
SEVS/STOTM N15 55 J3
Park Walk Primary School
WBPTN SW10 108 C5
Parkway Primary School
ERITHM DA18 117 F2
Parkway Trading Estate
HEST TW5 102 B5
Parkwood Primary School
FSBYPK N4 73 H1
Parliament Hill Fields Athletics Track
HAMP NW3 71 K3
Parliament Hill Lido
HAMP NW3 72 A3
Parliament Hill School
KTTN NW5 72 A3
Parmiter Industrial Centre
BETH E2 92 D1
Parnells Sports Ground
KTN/HRWW/WS HA3 50 B5
Parsloes Primary School
DAGW RM9 80 B5
Parsons Green
FUL/PGN SW6 107 K7
Parsons Green Health Clinic
FUL/PGN SW6 107 K7
Pascals College
BECK BR3 166 D1
Passport Language Schools
BMLY BR1 153 F7
Pastoria Hotel
LSQ/SEVD WC2H 11 H7
Patent Office
FLST/FETLN EC4A 12 A3
The Patrick Doody Clinic & Health Centre
WIM/MER SW19 146 E6
Pattinson Clinic
RCH/KEW TW9 124 E4
The Paul Robeson Theatre
HSLW TW3 123 G2
Pavilion Barclays Sports Ground
EA W5 86 A4
The Pavilion Leisure Centre
BMLY BR1 167 K1
Pavilion Restaurant
RCH/KEW TW9 125 F1
Paxton Primary School
NRWD SE19 150 B5
PCMS London
SRTFD E15 94 B1
PDSA Hospital
REDBR IG4 59 H2
Peace Pagoda
CHEL SW3 108 E6
Peacock Estate
TOTM N17 42 B5
Peacock Industrial Estate
TOTM N17 42 B6
The Peacock Theatre
HOL/ALD WC2B 11 L5
Peall Road Industrial Estate
CROY/NA CR0 164 A5
Peckham Park Primary School
PECK SE15 111 H6
The Peckham Pulse Health & Leisure Centre
PECK SE15 111 H7
Peckham Rye
PECK SE15 131 H1
Pelham Primary School
BXLYHN DA7 137 H2
WIM/MER SW19 146 E6
Pembridge Hall Preparatory School for Girls
BAY/PAD W2 8 B6
Pendragon School
BMLY BR1 152 E2
Penge East
SYD SE26 150 E5
Penge West
PGE/AN SE20 150 D6
Pentavia Retail Park
MLHL NW7 37 H6
Penwortham Primary School
STRHM/NOR SW16 148 B5
Percival David Foundation of Chinese Art
STPAN WC1H 5 H9
Perivale
GFD/PVL UB6 85 G1
Perivale Industrial Park
GFD/PVL UB6 85 G1
Perivale New Business Centre
GFD/PVL UB6 85 J1
Perivale Park Athletics Track
GFD/PVL UB6 84 E2
Perivale Park Golf Course
GFD/PVL UB6 84 E2
Perrin Road Clinic
ALP/SUD HA0 67 H3
Perrymount Primary School
FSTH SE23 151 F1
The Petchy Academy
HACK E8 74 B4
Peterborough Primary School
FUL/PGN SW6 127 K1
Peterborough & St Margaret's School
STAN HA7 34 E2
Peter Hills School
BERM/RHTH SE16 93 F7
Peter James Business Centre
HYS/HAR UB3 101 K1
Peterley Business Centre
BETH E2 92 D1
Peter Pan Statue
BAY/PAD W2 9 G8
The Petersham Hotel
RCHPK/HAM TW10 125 F6
Petrie Museum of Egyptian Archaeology
FITZ W1T 10 F1
Petts Hill Primary School
NTHLT UB5 66 B4
Petts Wood
STMC/STPC BR5 169 H4
Pewterers' Hall
CITYW EC2V 12 F3
Pheasantry Welcome Centre
TEDD TW11 143 F7
Phipps Bridge
WIM/MER SW19 162 B2
Phoenix Academy
ED N9 30 D7
Phoenix Business Centre
POP/IOD E14 93 J4
Phoenix Cinema
EFNCH N2 53 J3
Phoenix College
MRDN SM4 162 A4
Phoenix High School
SHB W12 87 J6
Phoenix Industrial Estate
HRW HA1 49 F3
Phoenix Leisure Centre
CAT SE6 132 E6
Phoenix School
HAMP NW3 71 H5
Phoenix Secondary & Primary School
BOW E3 93 H2
Phoenix Theatre
LSQ/SEVD WC2H 11 H5
Phoenix Trading Estate
GFD/PVL UB6 67 J7
Physical Energy Statue
BAY/PAD W2 9 G9
Piccadilly Circus
MYFR/PICC W1J 11 G7
Piccadilly Theatre
SOHO/SHAV W1D 11 G6
Pickford Lane Medical Centre
BXLYHN DA7 117 F7
Pickhurst Infant School
WWKM BR4 167 H5
Pickhurst Junior School
WWKM BR4 167 J5
Picture House Cinema
SRTFD E15 76 B5
Pilgrims Way J & I School
PECK SE15 111 K5
Pilot Industrial Centre
WLSDN NW10 87 G3
Pilton Estate
CROY/NA CR0 177 H1
Pimlico
PIM SW1V 17 G7
Pimlico Academy
PIM SW1V 16 F8
Pinkwell Primary School
HYS/HAR UB3 101 F3
Pinnacles Cricket & Squash Club
SUT SM1 174 E5
Pinner
PIN HA5 47 J3
Pinner Hill Golf Club
PIN HA5 33 F5
Pinner Medical Centre
PIN HA5 47 J3
Pinner New Cemetery
PIN HA5 48 A2
Pinner Park Primary School
PIN HA5 48 B2
Pinner View Medical Centre
HRW HA1 48 C4
Pinner Wood School
PIN HA5 33 G7
Pioneers Industrial Park
CROY/NA CR0 163 K7
Pitshanger Manor Museum
EA W5 85 J7
Plaisterers Hall
STBT EC1A 12 E3
Plaistow
SRTFD E15 94 D1
Plaistow Hospital
PLSTW E13 95 F1
Plaistow Primary School
PLSTW E13 95 F1
Plantation House Medical Centre
LOTH EC2R 13 H4
Plashet Jewish Cemetery
MNPK E12 77 H5
Plashet Road Medical Centre
FSTGT E7 77 F6
Plashet School
EHAM E6 77 J6
Players Theatre
CHCR WC2N 11 K8
Playgolf Northwick Park
HRW HA1 49 G7
The Playhouse
CHCR WC2N 11 K8
Plaza Business Centre
PEND EN3 31 H1
Pleasance Theatre
HOLWY N7 72 E5
Plumcroft Primary School
WOOL/PLUM SE18 115 H5
Plumstead
WOOL/PLUM SE18 115 J3
Plumstead Cemetery
ABYW SE2 116 C6
Plumstead Leisure Centre
WOOL/PLUM SE18 116 A4
Plumstead Manor School
WOOL/PLUM SE18 115 J4
The Pointer School
BKHTH/KID SE3 113 K7
Police Cadet School
WAN E11 58 E7
The Polish Institute & Sikorski Museum
SKENS SW7 15 H2
Polish War Memorial
RSLP HA4 65 F5
Polka Theatre for Children
WIM/MER SW19 147 F5
Ponders End
PEND EN3 31 G4
Ponders End Industrial Estate
PEND EN3 31 H3
Pontoon Dock
CAN/RD E16 95 G7
Pooles Park Primary School
FSBYPK N4 73 F1
Pools on the Park
RCH/KEW TW9 124 E3
Pope John Primary School
SHB W12 87 K6
Pop In Business Centre
WBLY HA9 68 D4
Poplar
POP/IOD E14 93 K6
Poplar Business Park
POP/IOD E14 112 D1
Poplar Primary School
WIM/MER SW19 161 K2
Pop Up Theatre
CLKNW EC1R 6 B6
Porchester Leisure Centre
BAY/PAD W2 8 C4
Portcullis House
WHALL SW1A 17 K2
Portico City Learning Centre
CLPT E5 74 E3
The Portland Hospital
REGST W1B 10 D1
Portland House Medical Centre
GFD/PVL UB6 84 B3
Portland Medical Centre
SNWD SE25 165 J4
Portland Place School
REGST W1B 10 D2
The Portman Clinic
HAMP NW3 71 H5
Portobello Market
NKENS W10 88 C4
Portobello Medical Centre
NTGHL W11 88 C5
Portway Primary School
SRTFD E15 76 E7
Pound Park Nursery School
CHARL SE7 114 C4
The Pountney Clinic
HSLW TW3 123 F2
Powergate Business Park
WLSDN NW10 87 F2
Power Industrial Estate
ERITH DA8 118 C7
Premier Cinema
PECK SE15 131 H1
Prendergast Ladywell Fields College
BROCKY SE4 132 D5
Prendergast School
BROCKY SE4 132 D3
Preston Manor School
WBLY HA9 68 B1
Preston Medical Centre
WBLY HA9 68 A2
Preston Park Primary School
WBLY HA9 49 K7
Preston Road
WBLY HA9 50 A7
Priestmead Middle School
KTN/HRWW/WS HA3 49 H2
Primrose Hill School
CAMTN NW1 4 B3
Primrose Montessori School
HBRY N5 73 J2
Prince Charles Cinema
LSQ/SEVD WC2H 11 H6
Prince Edward Theatre
SOHO/SHAV W1D 11 G5
Prince of Wales Theatre
STJS SW1Y 11 G7
Prince Regent
CAN/RD E16 95 G6
Princes College
NOXST/BSQ WC1A 11 J4
Princes Court Business Centre
WAP E1W 92 D6
Princes Park Stadium
DART DA1 139 K7
Princes Plain Primary School
HAYES BR2 168 D6
Princess Avenue School
MUSWH N10 54 B2
Princess Frederica CE J & I School
WLSDN NW10 87 K1
Princess Grace Hospital
MHST W1U 10 A1
Princess Louise Hospital
NKENS W10 88 A4
Princess May Primary School
STNW/STAM N16 74 A4
Princess of Wales Conservatory
RCH/KEW TW9 105 G6
The Princess Royal Distribution Centre
WLSDN NW10 68 D7
Prior Weston Primary School
STLK EC1Y 12 F1
Priory CE Primary School
WIM/MER SW19 147 F4
Priory Retail Park
WIM/MER SW19 147 H6
Priory Shopping Centre
DART DA1 139 G5
Priory Special School
SNWD SE25 165 G3
Privy Council
STJS SW1Y 11 G9
Privy Council Office
WHALL SW1A 11 J9
Progress Business Park
CROY/NA CR0 177 F1
Pronto Trading Estate
YEAD UB4 82 C4
Prospect House School
PUT/ROE SW15 127 G6
Proud Gallery
CHCR WC2N 11 J7
Provident Industrial Estate
HYS/HAR UB3 101 K1
PS Tattershall Castle
WHALL SW1A 11 K9
Pudding Mill Lane
SRTFD E15 75 K7
Pumphouse Educational Museum
BERM/RHTH SE16 93 G7
Pump House Theatre
WATW WD18 21 G4
Pump Lane Industrial Estate
HYS/HAR UB3 102 A1
The Purcell School
HRW HA1 66 D2
Purdy Hicks Gallery
STHWK SE1 12 C8
Purfleet
PUR RM19 119 K4
Purfleet Primary School
PUR RM19 119 K3
Purley Oaks
SAND/SEL CR2 177 K7
Purley Oaks Primary School
SAND/SEL CR2 177 K6
Pursuit Centre
WAP E1W 92 E6
Putney
PUT/ROE SW15 127 G3
Putney Animal Hospital
PUT/ROE SW15 127 G3
Putney Arts Theatre
PUT/ROE SW15 127 G3
Putney Bridge
FUL/PGN SW6 127 H2
Putney Exchange Shopping Centre
PUT/ROE SW15 127 G3
Putney High School
PUT/ROE SW15 127 G4
Putney Leisure Centre
PUT/ROE SW15 127 F3
Putney Lower Common Cemetery
BARN SW13 126 E1
Putneymead Medical Centre
PUT/ROE SW15 127 F3
Putney Park School
PUT/ROE SW15 126 E3
Putney School of Art
PUT/ROE SW15 127 H3
Putney Town Social & Bowls Club
PUT/ROE SW15 127 F1

Putney Vale Cemetery *PUT/ROE* SW15 ....145 J1
Putney Vale Crematorium *PUT/ROE* SW15 ....145 J1
Pylon Trading Estate *CAN/RD* E16 ....94 B3
Quadrant Business Park *KIL/WHAMP* NW6 ....70 C7
Quality Hotel *HRW* HA1 ....48 D5
WBLY HA9 ....68 C3
Quebec Industrial Estate *BERM/RHTH* SE16 ....112 B1
Queen Charlotte's & Chelsea Hospital *SHB* W12 ....87 K5
Queen Charlotte's Cottage, Kew Gardens *RCH/KEW* TW9 ....124 E1
Queen Elizabeth College *KENS* W8 ....14 A1
Queen Elizabeth Conference Centre *WEST* SW1P 17 H2
Queen Elizabeth Hall *STHWK* SE1 ....11 L8
Queen Elizabeth Hospital *WOOL/PLUM* SE18 ....114 E5
Queen Elizabeth II School *MV/WKIL* W9 ....88 D3
Queen Elizabeth Leisure Centre *BAR* EN5 ....26 D3
Queen Elizabeths Boys School *BAR* EN5 ....26 B2
Queen Elizabeths Girls School *BAR* EN5 ....26 D3
Queen Elizabeth Stadium *EN* EN1 ....30 B1
Queenhithe Stairs *BLKFR* EC4V 12 E7
Queen Mary College *WCHPL* E1 ....93 F3
Queen Mary's Hospital *HAMP* NW3 ....71 G2
Queen Marys Hospital *SCUP* DA14 ....155 G4
Queen Mary's Hospital for Children *SUT* SM1 ....162 B7
Queen Mary's University Hospital *PUT/ROE* SW15 ....126 D5
Queen Mary & Westfield College *SWFD* E18 ....44 E7
Queen Mother Sports Centre *PIM* SW1V 16 E5
Queensbridge Primary School *HACK* E8 ....7 M2
Queensbridge Sports Centre *HACK* E8 ....7 M1
Queen's Building *HTHAIR* TW6 ....120 E2
Queensbury *STAN* HA7 ....50 B2
Queens Business & Secretarial College *SKENS* SW7 ....15 G5
The Queens CE Primary School *RCH/KEW* TW9 ....105 G6
Queen's Club *WKENS* W14 ....107 H4
Queens College London *CAVSQ/HST* W1G 10 C3
Queens College Preparatory School *CAVSQ/HST* W1G 10 C2
The Queen's Gallery *BGVA* SW1W 16 D2
Queens Gate School *SKENS* SW7 ....15 G5
Queens Hospital *ROMW/RG* RM7 ....63 G6
The Queens House *GNWCH* SE10 ....113 G5
Queens Ice Rink & Bowl *BAY/PAD* W2 ....8 D7
Queens Manor Primary School *FUL/PGN* SW6 ....107 F6
Queensmead School *RSLP* HA4 ....65 H3
Queensmead Sports Centre *RSLP* HA4 ....65 H4
Queens Medical Centre *RCHPK/HAM* TW10 ....125 G4
Queensmill School *FUL/PGN* SW6 ....127 K1
Queens Park *KIL/WHAMP* NW6 ....88 D1
Queens Park Community School *WLSDN* NW10 ....70 A7
Queens Park Health Centre *NKENS* W10 ....88 C2
Queens Park Primary School *NKENS* W10 ....88 C2
Queens Park Rangers FC (Loftus Road Stadium) *SHB* W12 ....87 K7
Queen's Road Cemetery *CROY/NA* CR0 ....164 D5
Queen's Road Peckham *PECK* SE15 ....111 J7
Queens School *BUSH* WD23 ....21 K2
Queens Theatre *SOHO/SHAV* W1D 11 G6
Queenstown Road Battersea *VX/NE* SW8 ....109 G7
Queensway *BAY/PAD* W2 ....8 D7
Queensway Business Centre *PEND* EN3 ....30 E3
Queenswell J & I School *TRDG/WHET* N20 ....39 H1
Queen Victoria Memorial *WHALL* SW1A 16 E2
The Questors Theatre *EA* W5 ....85 J6
Quintin Kynaston School Technology College *STJWD* NW8 ....2 F4
Quwwat UL Islam Girl's School *FSTGT* E7 ....76 E5
Radcliffe College *SOHO/SHAV* W1D 10 E5
Radisson Edwardian Berkshire Hotel *OXSTW* W1C 10 C5
Radisson Edwardian Grafton Hotel *CAMTN* NW1 ....4 E9
Radisson Edwardian Hampshire Hotel *LSQ/SEVD* WC2H 11 H7
Radisson Edwardian Hotel *HYS/HAR* UB3 ....101 F6
Radisson Edwardian Kenilworth Hotel *RSQ* WC1B 11 H3
Radisson Edwardian Marlborough Hotel *NOXST/BSQ* WC1A 11 H4
Radisson Edwardian Mayfair Hotel *MYFR/PICC* W1J 10 D7
Radisson Edwardian Mountbatten Hotel *LSQ/SEVD* WC2H 11 J5
Radisson Edwardian Vanderbilt Hotel *SKENS* SW7 ....14 F5
Radisson SAS Portman Hotel *MBLAR* W1H 9 M4
RAF West Ruislip (University of Maryland) *HGDN/ICK* UB10 ....64 A1
Raglan Infant School *EN* EN1 ....30 A5
Raglan Junior School *EN* EN1 ....30 A6
Raglan Primary School *HAYES* BR2 ....168 B3
Railton Road Clinic *HNHL* SE24 ....130 C4
Rainbow Industrial Estate *RYNPK* SW20 ....160 E1
Rainbow Quay *BERM/RHTH* SE16 ....112 B2
Rainbow School for Autistic Children *WAND/EARL* SW18 ....147 G1
Raines Foundation School *BETH* E2 ....92 D2
Rainham *RAIN* RM13 ....99 H3
Rainham Hall (NT) *RAIN* RM13 ....99 J3
Rainham Marshes RSPB Reserve *RAIN* RM13 ....99 K6
Rainham Trading Estate *RAIN* RM13 ....99 G2
Rainham Village Primary School *RAIN* RM13 ....99 J3
Ramac Industrial Estate *CHARL* SE7 ....113 K4
Ramada Encore Hotel *ACT* W3 ....87 F4
Ramada Hotel *BAY/PAD* W2 ....8 C7
EA W5 ....86 B6
GSTN WD25 ....22 C2
Rambert School *TWK* TW1 ....124 C4
Randal Cremer Primary School *BETH* E2 ....7 L5
Ranelagh Gardens (site of Chelsea Flower Show) *BGVA* SW1W 16 B8
Ranelagh Primary School *SRTFD* E15 ....94 C1
Rangefield Primary School *BMLY* BR1 ....152 C4
Ransomes Dock Business Centre *BTSEA* SW11 ....108 D6
Raphael Independent School *EMPK* RM11 ....63 J5
The Rathbone Education Centre *CAN/RD* E16 ....94 D4
Rathbone Clinic *BAY/PAD* W2 ....9 H1
Rathfern Primary School *FSTH* SE23 ....132 C7
Ravenor Primary School *GFD/PVL* UB6 ....84 A2
Ravensbourne *BECK* BR3 ....152 A6
Ravensbourne College of Design & Communication *CHST* BR7 ....154 A4
The Ravensbourne School *HAYES* BR2 ....168 A3
Ravenscourt Park *HMSMTH* W6 ....106 D3
Ravenscourt Park Preparatory School *HMSMTH* W6 ....106 D3
Ravenscroft Medical Centre *GLDGN* NW11 ....52 D6
Ravenscroft Primary School *CAN/RD* E16 ....94 E3
Ravenscroft School *TRDG/WHET* N20 ....26 D6
Ravenside Retail Park *UED* N18 ....43 F5
Ravens Lawn Tennis Club *NFNCH/WDSPK* N12 ....39 H3
Ravenstone Preparatory School *SKENS* SW7 ....14 F4
Ravenstone Primary School *BAL* SW12 ....129 F7
Ravenswood Industrial Estate *WALTH* E17 ....58 A3
Ravens Wood School *HAYES* BR2 ....181 H2
Ray Lodge Primary School *WFD* IG8 ....45 H5
Rayners Lane *RYLN/HDSTN* HA2 ....47 K7
Raynes Park *RYNPK* SW20 ....161 F1
Raynes Park High School *RYNPK* SW20 ....160 E2
Raynes Park Sports Ground *RYNPK* SW20 ....160 D1
Raynes Park Vale FC *RYNPK* SW20 ....161 G4
Raynham Primary School *UED* N18 ....42 C4
Reay Primary School *BRXN/ST* SW9 ....110 B6
Records Office *CLKNW* EC1R 6 B9
Rectory Business Centre *SCUP* DA14 ....155 H3
Rectory Road *STNW/STAM* N16 ....74 C2
Redbridge *REDBR* IG4 ....59 H5
Redbridge College *CHDH* RM6 ....61 H4
Redbridge Drama Centre *SWFD* E18 ....44 E7
Redbridge Museum *IL* IG1 ....78 B2
Redbridge Primary School *REDBR* IG4 ....59 J4
Redburn Industrial Estate *PEND* EN3 ....31 F5
Redcliffe School *WBPTN* SW10 ....14 E9
Reddiford School *PIN* HA5 ....47 J3
Redford Lodge Psychiatric Hospital *ED* N9 ....42 C1
Red Gates School *CROY/NA* CR0 ....177 G4
Redhill Primary School *CHST* BR7 ....154 B5
Red House (NT) *BXLYHS* DA6 ....137 F3
Redlands Primary School *WCHPL* E1 ....92 E4
Red Lion Business Park *SURB* KT6 ....172 B1
Redriff Primary School *BERM/RHTH* SE16 ....112 B1
Red Rose Trading Estate *EBAR* EN4 ....27 H4
Reeves Corner *CROY/NA* CR0 ....177 H1
Regal International College *ALP/SUD* HA0 ....68 A4
Regent Business Centre *HYS/HAR* UB3 ....102 A1
Regent Clinic *CAVSQ/HST* W1G 10 C3
Regent College London *PIN* HA5 ....47 K6
Regent's Park *CAMTN* NW1 ....10 C1
Regent's Park Barracks *CAMTN* NW1 ....4 C6
Regent's Park Clinic *CAMTN* NW1 ....3 L9
Regent's Park Medical Centre *CAMTN* NW1 ....4 D7
Regent's Park Open Air Theatre *CAMTN* NW1 ....4 A8
Regent's Park Track *STJWD* NW8 ....3 L5
Regina Coeli RC Primary School *SAND/SEL* CR2 ....177 H6
Renaissance Hotel *HTHAIR* TW6 ....100 E7
Renoir Cinema *BMSBY* WC1N 5 K9
Renwick Industrial Estate *BARK* IG11 ....97 H1
Rewards Centre *HSLW* TW3 ....123 H2
Reynard Mills Trading Estate *BTFD* TW8 ....104 D4
Reynolds Sports Centre *ACT* W3 ....105 H1
Rhodes Avenue Primary School *WDGN* N22 ....40 C7
Rhodes Farm Clinic *MLHL* NW7 ....38 A3
Rhyl Primary School *KTTN* NW5 ....72 A5
RIBA Library Drawings & Manuscript Collection *MBLAR* W1H 9 M4
Ricards Lodge High School *WIM/MER* SW19 ....146 D3
Richard Alibon Primary School *DAGE* RM10 ....80 C4
Richard Atkins Primary School *BRXS/STRHM* SW2 ....129 K6
Richard Cloudesley School *STLK* EC1Y 12 E1
Richard Cobden Primary School *CAMTN* NW1 ....4 F4
Richdales Institute *ALP/SUD* HA0 ....67 K7
Rich Industrial Estate *STHWK* SE1 ....19 K4
Richmond *RCH/KEW* TW9 ....125 F3
Richmond Adult & Community College *RCH/KEW* TW9 ....124 E3
Richmond American International University *KENS* W8 ....14 C2
RCHPK/HAM TW10 ....125 F5
The Richmond Clinic *RCH/KEW* TW9 ....125 G3
Richmond Community College *TWK* TW1 ....124 A7
Richmond FC *RCH/KEW* TW9 ....124 E3
Richmond Gate Hotel *RCHPK/HAM* TW10 ....125 F6
The Richmond Golf Club *RCHPK/HAM* TW10 ....144 A1
The Richmond Green Medical Centre *RCH/KEW* TW9 ....124 E4
Richmond Hill Hotel *RCHPK/HAM* TW10 ....125 F6
Richmond House School *HPTN* TW12 ....141 K4
Richmond Park Golf Club *PUT/ROE* SW15 ....126 B6
Richmond Park National Nature Reserve *RCHPK/HAM* TW10 ....145 G1
Richmond Road Medical Centre *KUTN/CMB* KT2 ....144 A6
Richmond Theatre *RCH/KEW* TW9 ....124 E3
Richmond upon Thames College *WHTN* TW2 ....123 K6
Ridge House Clinic *WCHMH* N21 ....29 K6
Ridgeway Hotel *CHING* E4 ....43 K1
Ridgeway Primary School *SAND/SEL* CR2 ....178 A7
Rio Cinema *HACK* E8 ....74 B4
Ripley Arts Centre *BMLY* BR1 ....153 H7
Ripple Infant School *BARK* IG11 ....78 E7
Rippleside Cemetery *BARK* IG11 ....79 G7
Risley Avenue Primary School *TOTM* N17 ....42 A7
The Ritz Hotel *WHALL* SW1A 10 E8
Ritzy Cinema *BRXN/ST* SW9 ....130 B3
Riverbank Park Plaza Hotel *STHWK* SE1 ....17 L6
River Brent Business Park *HNWL* W7 ....103 K2
River Gardens Business Centre *EBED/NFELT* TW14 ....122 A3
River House Montessori School *POP/IOD* E14 ....93 J7
Riverley Primary School *LEY* E10 ....57 J7
River Mole Business Park *ESH/CLAY* KT10 ....157 F7
River Place Health Centre *IS* N1 ....6 E2
River Road Business Park *BARK* IG11 ....96 E2
Riversdale Primary School *WAND/EARL* SW18 ....127 K7
Riverside Business Centre *WAND/EARL* SW18 ....128 A7
Riverside Business Park *WIM/MER* SW19 ....147 G7
Riverside Community Health Care *WKENS* W14 ....107 G2
Riverside Golf Club *THMD* SE28 ....98 A5
Riverside Industrial Estate *BARK* IG11 ....97 G2
DART DA1 ....139 H4
Riverside Primary School *BERM/RHTH* SE16 ....111 H1
Riverside Quarter *WAND/EARL* SW18 ....127 K3
Riverside Studios Cinema *HMSMTH* W6 ....107 F4
Riverside Swimming Centre *ERITH* DA8 ....118 B4
Riverside Wandle Trading Estate *MTCM* CR4 ....162 E6
Riverston School *LEE/GVPK* SE12 ....133 K4
Riverview C E Primary School *HOR/WEW* KT19 ....172 E3
The RJ Mitchell Primary School *HCH* RM12 ....81 K5
RNLI Lifeboat Station *TWRH* EC3N 13 K8
Roan Industrial Estate *MTCM* CR4 ....147 J7
Robert Blair Primary School *HOLWY* N7 ....72 E5
Robert Browning Primary School *WALW* SE17 ....18 F7
Robin Hood Infant School *SUT* SM1 ....174 E4
Robin Hood Junior School *SUT* SM1 ....175 F4
Robin Hood Lane Health Centre *SUT* SM1 ....174 E4
Robin Hood Primary School *KUTN/CMB* KT2 ....145 F4
Robinsfield Infant School *STJWD* NW8 ....3 H5
The Roche School *WAND/EARL* SW18 ....127 K4
Rockliffe Manor Primary School *WOOL/PLUM* SE18 ....116 A5
Rockmount Primary School *NRWD* SE19 ....149 J5
Rockware Business Centre *GFD/PVL* UB6 ....66 D7
The Rockwell Hotel *ECT* SW5 ....14 C5
Roding Lane Cemetery *WFD* IG8 ....45 J7
Roding Primary School *BCTR* RM8 ....79 J3
WFD IG8 ....45 J6
Roding Valley *BKHH* IG9 ....45 H3
Roe Green Junior School *CDALE/KGS* NW9 ....50 D3
Roehampton Church School *PUT/ROE* SW15 ....126 E6
The Roehampton Priory Hospital *PUT/ROE* SW15 ....126 C3
Roehampton Recreation Centre *PUT/ROE* SW15 ....126 C6
Roehampton University (Digby Stuart College) *PUT/ROE* SW15 ....126 C4
Roehampton University (Froebel College) *PUT/ROE* SW15 ....126 C5
Roehampton University (Southlands College) *PUT/ROE* SW15 ....126 C4
Roehampton University (Whitelands College) *PUT/ROE* SW15 ....126 C6
Roger Ascham Primary School *WALTH* E17 ....43 H7
Roger Bannister Sports Ground *KTN/HRWW/WS* HA3 ....34 C5
Rokeby School *KUTN/CMB* KT2 ....144 E6
SRTFD E15 ....76 B6
Rokesly Junior School *CEND/HSY/T* N8 ....54 E4
Roman Bath *TPL/STR* WC2R 11 M6
Roman Industrial Estate *CROY/NA* CR0 ....165 F6
Roman Road Primary School *EHAM* E6 ....95 H3
Romford *ROM* RM1 ....63 G5
Romford Cemetery *ROMW/RG* RM7 ....62 E6
Romford Clinic *ROM* RM1 ....63 H3
Romford Golf Club *GPK* RM2 ....63 J2
Romford Ice Arena *ROMW/RG* RM7 ....63 G6
Romford IT Learning Centre *ROM* RM1 ....63 G4
Romford Shopping Hall *ROM* RM1 ....63 G3
Ronald Rose Primary School *PUT/ROE* SW15 ....127 G6
Rood Lane Medical Centre *FENCHST* EC3M 13 J6
Rooks Heath College for Business & Enterprise *RYLN/HDSTN* HA2 ....66 A2
Roosevelt Memorial *MYFR/PKLN* W1K 10 B6
Ropery Business Park *CHARL* SE7 ....114 B3
Rosary Priory High School *BUSH* WD23 ....22 E5
Rosary RC Infant School *HEST* TW5 ....102 E5
Rosary RC Primary School *HAMP* NW3 ....71 J4
Rosebery Industrial Park *TOTM* N17 ....56 D1
Rose Bruford College *BFN/LL* DA15 ....136 C7
Rosedale College *HYS/HAR* UB3 ....82 B5
Roselands Clinic *NWMAL* KT3 ....159 K3
Rose McAndrew Clinic *BRXN/ST* SW9 ....130 A1
Rosemead Preparatory School *DUL* SE21 ....149 J1
Rosendale Primary School *DUL* SE21 ....130 D6
Rose of Kingston (Kingston Theatre) *KUT/HW* KT1 ....158 E1
Rose Theatre Exhibition *STHWK* SE1 ....12 E8
Rosetta Primary School *CAN/RD* E16 ....95 F4
Rosewood Medical Centre *HCH* RM12 ....81 K4
Rosh Pinah Primary School *EDGW* HA8 ....36 D1
Rosslyn Park RFC *PUT/ROE* SW15 ....126 C3
Rotherfield Primary School *IS* N1 ....6 F3
Rotherhithe *BERM/RHTH* SE16 ....111 K1
Rotherhithe Civic Centre *BERM/RHTH* SE16 ....111 K1
Rotherhithe Primary School *BERM/RHTH* SE16 ....111 K3
The Rotunda *KUT/HW* KT1 ....159 F1
The Roundhouse Theatre *CAMTN* NW1 ....4 A1
Roundshaw J & I School *WLGTN* SM6 ....176 E6
Rowan Preparatory School *ESH/CLAY* KT10 ....171 F6
Rowans School *RYNPK* SW20 ....145 J6
Rowley Industrial Park *ACT* W3 ....105 J2
Roxbourne First School *RYLN/HDSTN* HA2 ....65 J1
Roxbourne Medical Centre *RYLN/HDSTN* HA2 ....66 B1
Roxeth First & Middle School *RYLN/HDSTN* HA2 ....66 D1
Roxeth Mead School *RYLN/HDSTN* HA2 ....66 D1
Roxwell Trading Park *LEY* E10 ....57 G6
Royal Academy of Arts *MYFR/PICC* W1J 10 E7
Royal Academy of Dance *BTSEA* SW11 ....108 D7
Royal Academy of Dramatic Art *GWRST* WC1E 11 G2
Royal Academy of Music *CAMTN* NW1 ....10 B1
Royal Air Force Museum London *CDALE/KGS* NW9 ....51 J1
Royal Albert *CAN/RD* E16 ....95 J6
Royal Albert Hall *SKENS* SW7 ....15 G2
Royal Arsenal *WOOL/PLUM* SE18 ....115 G2
The Royal Ballet School *RCHPK/HAM* TW10 ....126 A7
Royal Ballet Upper School *COVGDN* WC2E 11 K5
Royal Blackheath Golf Club *ELTH/MOT* SE9 ....134 E6
Royal Botanic Gardens, Kew *BTFD* TW8 ....105 F6
Royal Botanic Gardens Kew School *RCH/KEW* TW9 ....105 G6
Royal Brompton Hospital *CHEL* SW3 ....15 J7
Royal College of Anaesthetists *RSQ* WC1B 11 J2
Royal College of Art *SKENS* SW7 ....14 F2
SKENS SW7 ....14 F4
Royal College of Art Sculpture School *BTSEA* SW11 ....108 D6
Royal College of Music *SHB* W12 ....106 D2
SKENS SW7 ....15 G3
Royal College of Nursing *CAMTN* NW1 ....4 F9
IS N1 ....6 C4
Royal College of Obstetricians & Gynaecologists *CAMTN* NW1 ....3 L9
Royal College of Ophthalmologists *CAMTN* NW1 ....10 A1
Royal College of Paediatrics & Child Health *GTPST* W1W 10 D2
The Royal College of Pathology *STJS* SW1Y 11 G9
Royal College of Physicians *CAMTN* NW1 ....4 C9
Royal College of Surgeons *LINN* WC2A 11 M4
Royal College of Veterinary Surgeons *WEST* SW1P 17 J5
Royal Courts of Justice *LINN* WC2A 11 M5
Royal Court Theatre *BGVA* SW1W 16 A6
Royal Court Young Peoples Theatre *NKENS* W10 ....88 C4
The Royal Docks Community School *CAN/RD* E16 ....95 G5
Royal Docks Medical Centre *EHAM* E6 ....96 A5
Royal Exchange *BANK* EC3V 13 H5

Royal Festival Hall STHWK SE1 11 L9
Royal Free Hospital HAMP NW3 71 J4
Royal Garden Hotel KENS W8 14 D1
Royal Geographical Society SKENS SW7 15 G2
The Royal Horseguards Hotel WHALL SW1A 11 K9
Royal Horticultural Society New Hall WEST SW1P 17 G4
Royal Horticultural Society Old Hall WEST SW1P 17 G5
Royal Hospital RCH/KEW TW9 125 F2
Royal Hospital Chelsea CHEL SW3 16 A9
Royal Hospital for Neuro-disability PUT/ROE SW15 127 H5
Royal Hospital & Home PUT/ROE SW15 126 E6
Royal Hospital Museum CHEL SW3 16 A8
Royal Institute of British Architects REGST W1B 10 D2
Royal Institution's Faraday Museum MYFR/PICC W1J 10 D7
Royal Lancaster Hotel BAY/PAD W2 9 H7
The Royal London Estate TOTM N17 42 D6
Royal London Homeopathic Hospital BMSBY WC1N 11 K2
Royal Marsden Hospital CHEL SW3 15 H7
The Royal Mews BGVA SW1W 16 D3
Royal Mid-Surrey Golf Club RCH/KEW TW9 124 E2
Royal Military School of Music WHTN TW2 123 J5
Royal Mint Court TWRH EC3N 13 M7
Royal National Orthopaedic Hospital
GTPST W1W 10 D1
STAN HA7 23 H7
Royal National Theatre STHWK SE1 12 A8
Royal National Throat Nose & Ear Hospital FSBYW WC1X 5 L7
Royal Oak ⊖ BAY/PAD W2 8 D3
Royal Opera House COVGDN WC2E 11 K5
Royal Russell Preparatory School CROY/NA CR0 178 D5
The Royal School HAMP NW3 71 H3
Royal Society of Arts CHCR WC2N 11 K7
Royal Society of Medicine CAVSQ/HST W1G 10 C4
Royal Veterinary College CAMTN NW1 5 G4
Royal Victoria ⊖ CAN/RD E16 94 E6
Royal Victoria Docks Watersports Centre CAN/RD E16 94 E6
Royal Wimbledon Golf Club WIM/MER SW19 145 K4
Royston Primary School PGE/AN SE20 151 F7
RSPCA Animal Hospital FSBYPK N4 73 F1
Rudolph Steiner Hall CAMTN NW1 3 L9
Rufus Business Centre WIM/MER SW19 147 F1
Ruislip ⊖ RSLP HA4 64 C1
Ruislip Gardens ⊖ RSLP HA4 64 E3
Ruislip Gardens Primary School RSLP HA4 64 C3
Ruislip Golf Club HGDN/ICK UB10 64 A1
Ruislip High School RSLP HA4 64 E2
Ruislip Manor ⊖ RSLP HA4 46 E7
Ruislip Manor FC RSLP HA4 64 D1
Ruislip RFC RSLP HA4 64 C1
Ruislip Woods National Nature Reserve
NTHWD HA6 46 A2
RSLP HA4 46 C4
Rushcroft School CHING E4 43 K6
Rushey Green Primary School CAT SE6 132 E7
Rush Green Primary School ROMW/RG RM7 63 F7
Rushmore Primary School CLPT E5 74 E3
Ruskin House School HNHL SE24 130 D4
The Russell JMI School RCHPK/HAM TW10 143 K1
The Russell School RCHPK/HAM TW10 124 E7
Russell Square ⊖ STPAN WC1H 11 J1
Rutlish School RYNPK SW20 161 J1
Ruxley Corner Industrial Estate SCUP DA14 155 K5
Ruxley Park Golf Centre STMC/STPC BR5 155 K7
Ryefield Primary School HGDN/ICK UB10 64 B7
Ryelands Primary School SNWD SE25 165 J4
Rye Oak Primary School PECK SE15 131 J2
Saatchi Gallery CHEL SW3 15 M7
Sacred Heart Catholic Primary School PUT/ROE SW15 126 D4
Sacred Heart High School HMSMTH W6 107 F3
Sacred Heart Language College KTN/HRWW/WS HA3 48 E1
Sacred Heart RC Infant School BTSEA SW11 128 D1
Sacred Heart RC JMI School TRDG/WHET N20 39 J1
Sacred Heart RC Primary School
NWMAL KT3 160 D3
OXHEY WD19 21 K5
RSLP HA4 64 C1
TEDD TW11 143 H6
Sacred Heart RC School CMBW SE5 110 D7
Sacred Heart School HOLWY N7 73 F4
Saddlers Hall CITYW EC2V 12 F4
Sadler's Wells Theatre CLKNW EC1R 6 B7
Safari Cinema CROY/NA CR0 164 C7
Safari Cinema & Bingo HRW HA1 49 F4
Saffron Green Primary School BORE WD6 25 F3
Sai Medical Centre POP/IOD E14 94 A6
St Agathas RC Primary School KUTN/CMB KT2 144 B5
St Agnes RC Primary School
BOW E3 93 J2
CRICK NW2 70 C2
St Aidans Primary School FSBYPK N4 55 G6
St Aidans RC Primary School IL IG1 60 D7
St Albans CE Primary School HCIRC EC1N 12 A2
St Albans Health Clinic HGT N6 72 A2
St Albans RC Aided Primary School E/WMO/HCT KT8 157 G4
St Albans RC Church & School Presbytery HCH RM12 81 J4
St Albans RC JMI School HCH RM12 81 K6
St Albans Road Infant School DART DA1 139 J5
St Alfege with St Peter CE Primary School GNWCH SE10 113 F5
St Aloysius College HGT N6 54 C7
St Aloysius RC Infant School CAMTN NW1 5 G7
St Aloysius RC Junior School CAMTN NW1 4 F6
St Andrew & St Francis CE JMI School CRICK NW2 69 J5
St Andrews CE JMI School TRDG/WHET N20 38 D1
St Andrews CE Primary School
EN EN1 29 K1
STHGT/OAK N14 28 C6
St Andrews CE VA High School CROY/NA CR0 177 H2
St Andrews Greek School CAMTN NW1 72 B5
St Andrews Primary School
BRXN/ST SW9 130 A1
IS N1 5 M3
St Andrews School
RYLN/HDSTN HA2 48 B4
WLSDN NW10 69 K6
St Angelas Ursuline School FSTGT E7 77 F5
St Annes Catholic High School for Girls ENC/FH EN2 29 K3
St Annes Catholic High School PLMGR N13 41 G3
St Annes CE Primary School WAND/EARL SW18 128 A4
St Annes CP School STWL/WRAY TW19 120 B6
St Annes RC Primary School VX/NE SW8 17 L9
St Anne's Special School MRDN SM4 161 K4
St Anne's Trading Estate POP/IOD E14 93 H5
St Anns CE Primary School SEVS/STOTM N15 55 K4
St Ann's General Hospital FSBYPK N4 55 J4
St Anns School HNWL W7 84 E7
St Ann's Shopping Centre HRW HA1 48 E5
St Anselms RC Primary School
DART DA1 139 J4
HRW HA1 48 E6
NWDGN UB2 102 E2
TOOT SW17 148 A2
St Anthonys Hospital WPK KT4 161 G7
St Anthonys RC Primary School
EDUL SE22 131 H5
PGE/AN SE20 150 D7
WATW WD18 20 C4
St Anthony's School (Junior House) HAMP NW3 71 H4
St Anthony's School (Senior House) HAMP NW3 71 G4
St Antonys RC Primary School
FSTGT E7 76 E6
WFD IG8 44 E3
St Aubyns School WFD IG8 44 D6
St Augustines CE High School KIL/WHAMP NW6 2 B6
St Augustines Primary School
BELV DA17 117 G2
KIL/WHAMP NW6 2 B5
St Augustines Priory School EA W5 86 A4
St Augustines RC Infant School GNTH/NBYPK IG2 60 B4
St Augustines RC Primary School
CAT SE6 151 K4
GNTH/NBYPK IG2 60 B4
WKENS W14 107 H5
St Barnabas CE Primary School BGVA SW1W 16 B7
St Barnabas & St Philip's CE Primary School KENS W8 14 A4
St Bartholomews CE Primary School SYD SE26 150 E3
St Bartholomews Hospital STBT EC1A 12 D3
St Bartholomews Medical School FARR EC1M 12 D1
St Bartholomews & Royal London School of Medicine FARR EC1M 12 E2
St Bartholomew's the Great STBT EC1A 12 D3
St Barts Hospital Sports Ground CHST BR7 154 D5
St Barts & the Royal London Hospital WCHPL E1 92 D4
St Bedes RC Infant School BAL SW12 129 J7
St Bedes RC Primary School CHDH RM6 61 J4
St Benedicts Junior School EA W5 85 J4
St Benedicts School EA W5 85 K4
St Bernadette Catholic Junior School BAL SW12 129 H6
St Bernadettes RC Primary School KTN/HRWW/WS HA3 50 B3
St Bonaventures School FSTGT E7 76 E6
St Boniface RC Primary School TOOT SW17 147 K4
St Catherines RC Girls School BXLYHS DA6 137 J4
St Catherines RC J & I School WDR/YW UB7 100 A1
St Catherines RC School BAR EN5 26 D3
St Catherines School TWK TW1 143 F1
St Cecilias CE School WAND/EARL SW18 127 J6
St Cecilias RC Primary School WPK KT4 174 B1
St Chads RC Primary School SNWD SE25 165 F4
St Charles Hospital NKENS W10 88 B4
St Charles Primary School NKENS W10 88 B4
St Christinas RC Preparatory School STJWD NW8 3 K5
St Christophers School
BECK BR3 167 F1
HAMP NW3 71 H4
WBLY HA9 68 B2
St Clare Business Park HPTN TW12 142 C5
St Clement Danes CE Primary School HOL/ALD WC2B 11 L5
St Clement & St James CE Primary School NTGHL W11 88 B7
St Clements Hospital BOW E3 93 H2
St Clements Primary School EW KT17 173 H7
St Columbas RC Boys School BXLYHS DA6 137 J4
St Cuthbert with St Mattias CE Primary School ECT SW5 14 B7
St Cyprians Greek Orthodox Primary School THHTH CR7 164 D1
St Davids College WWKM BR4 166 E6
St Davids Health Centre STWL/WRAY TW19 120 A6
St Dominics RC Primary School
HAMP NW3 71 K4
HOM E9 75 G5
St Dominics Sixth Form College HRW HA1 66 E1
St Dunstans CE Primary School CHEAM SM3 174 C5
St Dunstans College CAT SE6 132 C7
St Ebba's Hospital HOR/WEW KT19 172 E7
St Edmunds RC Primary School
ED N9 30 D7
POP/IOD E14 112 D3
WHTN TW2 123 G6
St Edwards CE Comprehensive School CHDH RM6 62 C5
St Edwards CE Primary School ROM RM1 63 F3
St Edwards RC JMI School STJWD NW8 9 J1
St Elizabeths RC Primary School
BETH E2 92 E1
RCHPK/HAM TW10 125 G5
St Eugene de Mazenod RC Primary School KIL/WHAMP NW6 2 B2
St Faiths CE School WAND/EARL SW18 128 A4
St Fidelis Catholic Primary School ERITH DA8 117 K5
St Francesca Cabrini Primary School FSTH SE23 131 K5
St Francis de Sales RC J & I School TOTM N17 42 B6
St Francis of Assisi Primary School NKENS W10 88 B6
St Francis RC Primary School
PECK SE15 111 H5
SRTFD E15 76 C4
St Francis Xavier College BAL SW12 129 G5
St Gabriels CE Primary School PIM SW1V 16 E8
St George's Cathedral STHWK SE1 18 B3
St Georges CE Primary School
BMLY BR1 168 B1
CMBW SE5 111 F6
VX/NE SW8 109 H7
St Georges College HOLWY N7 73 G2
St Georges Elizabethan Theatre HOLWY N7 72 D3
St Georges Hanover Square CE Primary School MYFR/PKLN W1K 10 B7
St Georges Hospital TOOT SW17 147 J4
St Georges Industrial Estate
KUTN/CMB KT2 143 K4
PLMGR N13 41 H6
St Georges Medical Centre HDN NW4 51 K2
St Georges RC Primary School
ENC/FH EN2 29 K1
HRW HA1 67 F2
St Georges RC School MV/WKIL W9 2 D6
St Georges Shopping Centre & Cinema HRW HA1 48 D5
St Georges University of London TOOT SW17 147 H4
St George the Martyr CE Primary School BMSBY WC1N 11 L1
St George Wharf VX/NE SW8 17 J9
St Gildas RC Junior School CEND/HSY/T N8 54 E6
St Giles College London Central RSQ WC1B 11 K2
St Giles School SAND/SEL CR2 177 H5
St Gregorys High School KTN/HRWW/WS HA3 49 K4
St Gregorys RC Primary School EA W5 85 J3
St Helens Catholic Infant School WALTH E17 58 A4
St Helens RC Primary School
BRXN/ST SW9 130 B2
CAN/RD E16 94 D3
St Helens School NTHWD HA6 32 C5
St Helier ⇌ MRDN SM4 161 K5
St Helier Hospital CAR SM5 162 B7
St Hildas School BUSH WD23 22 B6
St Ignatius RC Primary School
SEVS/STOTM N15 56 A5
SUN TW16 140 E7
St James CE J & I School BERM/RHTH SE16 111 H2
St James CE Primary School
MUSWH N10 54 A3
NWCR SE14 112 B7
PEND EN3 30 E1
St James CE Junior School FSTGT E7 76 D4
St James Independent School for Girls NTGHL W11 8 A6
St James Independent School for Senior Boys TWK TW1 143 G1
St James Independent School for Senior Girls WKENS W14 107 H3
St James Independent Schools for Juniors & Girls WKENS W14 107 H3
St James & Lucie Clayton College SKENS SW7 14 D6
St James Medical Centre CROY/NA CR0 164 E6
St James RC Primary School
HAYES BR2 169 G4
WHTN TW2 142 E2
St James St ⇌ WALTH E17 57 G4
St James's Health Centre WALTH E17 57 G4
St James's Palace WHALL SW1A 10 F9
St James's Park ⊖ STJSPK SW1H 17 G3
St James the Great RC Primary School
PECK SE15 111 G7
THHTH CR7 164 C1
St Joachims RC Primary School CAN/RD E16 95 G5
St Joan of Arc RC Primary School HBRY N5 73 H3
St John Fisher RC First & Middle School PIN HA5 48 A3
St John Fisher RC Primary School
ERITH DA18 117 F2
GFD/PVL UB6 85 J2
RYNPK SW20 161 F4
St John of Jerusalem CE Primary School HOM E9 74 E6
St Johns ⇌ DEPT SE8 132 D1
St Johns & St James CE School UED N18 42 B4
St Johns Angell Town CE Primary School BRXN/ST SW9 130 B1
St Johns CE Primary School
BETH E2 92 E1
CROY/NA CR0 179 F2
FBAR/BDGN N11 39 K3
KUT/HW KT1 159 F2
PGE/AN SE20 150 E6
TRDG/WHET N20 39 G1
St Johns CE School CDALE/KGS NW9 51 G4
St John's CE Walham Green Primary School FUL/PGN SW6 107 H7
St Johns Church of England School STAN HA7 35 G3
St John's Concert Hall WEST SW1P 17 J4
St Johns Highbury Vale CE Primary School HBRY N5 73 H3
St John's Hospital Day Centre BTSEA SW11 128 C3
St John's Lodge CAMTN NW1 4 A7
St Johns Primary School WEA W13 85 G6
St Johns RC Primary School BERM/RHTH SE16 112 B1
St Johns & St Clements CE J & I School PECK SE15 131 H2
St Johns School NTHWD HA6 33 F5
St Johns Upper Holloway CE Primary School ARCH N19 72 C1
St Johns Walworth CE Primary School WALW SE17 18 E6
St Johns Way Medical Centre ARCH N19 54 D7
St John's Wood ⊖ STJWD NW8 3 G5
St Johns Wood Pre-Preparatory School STJWD NW8 3 J7
St John the Baptist CE Junior School KUT/HW KT1 143 K6
St John the Baptist CE Primary School BMLY BR1 152 A3
St John the Baptist VA CE Primary School IS N1 7 J6
St John the Divine CE Primary School CMBW SE5 110 C6
St John the Evangelist RC Primary IS N1 6 C5
St John Vianney RC Primary School SEVS/STOTM N15 55 H3
St Joseph's Annexe ABYW SE2 116 D5
St Josephs Catholic Infant School LEY E10 57 H7
St Josephs Catholic Junior School CMBW SE5 110 D6
St Josephs Catholic Primary School
BMLY BR1 153 G6
DAGW RM9 80 B3
St Josephs College STRHM/NOR SW16 149 H5
St Josephs Convent School WAN E11 58 E5
St Josephs Primary School WAND/EARL SW18 127 K4
St Joseph's RC College MLHL NW7 37 H3
St Josephs RC First & Middle School KTN/HRWW/WS HA3 49 G1
St Josephs RC Infant School NRWD SE19 149 J5
St Josephs RC J & I School HDN NW4 51 K3
St Josephs RC Junior School
LEY E10 57 J7
NRWD SE19 149 J5
WBLY HA9 68 B4
St Josephs RC Primary School
ARCH N19 54 B7
BARK IG11 78 C7
BERM/RHTH SE16 111 K2
CHEL SW3 15 L6
DART DA1 138 A3
DEPT SE8 112 D6
GNWCH SE10 113 H4
HNWL W7 84 E7
HOL/ALD WC2B 11 K4
KUT/HW KT1 159 F1
MV/WKIL W9 2 E9
OXHEY WD19 33 F2
STHWK SE1 18 F1
STHWK SE1 111 H1
WLSDN NW10 69 G6
St Judes CE Primary School
HNHL SE24 130 C5
STHWK SE1 18 C4
St Judes & St Pauls CE Primary School IS N1 74 A4
St Katharine Pier WAP E1W 13 M8
St Katherine TPL/STR WC2R 11 M7
St Lawrence Business Centre FELT TW13 141 F1
St Lawrence Catholic School FELT TW13 141 F1
St Lawrence Junior School E/WMO/HCT KT8 157 J2
St Lawrence University BMSBY WC1N 11 M1
St Leonards CE Primary School STRHM/NOR SW16 148 D4
St Leonards Hospital IS N1 7 K5
St Luke's Catholic Sixth Form College SCUP DA14 155 F4
St Lukes Cemetery HAYES BR2 168 E5
St Lukes CE Primary School
CAN/RD E16 94 D5
FSBYE EC1V 6 F8
KUTN/CMB KT2 144 B7
MV/WKIL W9 88 D1
POP/IOD E14 113 G3
WNWD SE27 149 J4
St Luke's Health Centre CAN/RD E16 94 D5
St Lukes Hospital for the Clergy FITZ W1T 10 E1
St Lukes School THHTH CR7 164 B3
St Lukes Woodside Hospital MUSWH N10 54 A3
St Margaret Clitherow RC Primary THMD SE28 97 H7
St Margaret's ⇌ TWK TW1 124 C5
St Margarets Business Centre TWK TW1 124 B6
St Margarets CE Primary School WOOL/PLUM SE18 115 H5
St Margarets Clitherow RC Primary WBLY HA9 68 E2
St Margarets Primary School BARK IG11 78 B7

St Margarets School
BUSH WD23 22 A6
HAMP NW3 71 F3
St Marks Catholic School
HSLW TW3 122 E2
St Marks CE Academy
MTCM CR4 163 G1
St Marks CE Primary School
ARCH N19 72 E1
HAYES BR2 167 K2
LBTH SE11 17 M9
SNWD SE25 165 H3
St Marks Industrial Estate
CAN/RD E16 95 H7
St Marks Primary School
HNWL W7 103 K1
MTCM CR4 162 E1
St Marthas Junior School
BAR EN5 26 C2
St Martin-in-the-Fields
CHCR WC2N 11 J7
St Martin in the Fields High School
BRXS/STRHM SW2 130 C7
St Martin of Porres RC Primary School
FBAR/BDGN N11 40 C5
St Martins Hospital
MYFR/PKLN W1K 10 A6
St Martins Medical Centre
RSLP HA4 46 C6
St Martins School
MLHL NW7 37 G4
St Martins School of Art
SOHO/SHAV W1D 11 H5
St Martins Theatre
LSQ/SEVD WC2H 11 H6
St Mary Abbots CE Primary School
KENS W8 14 C2
St Mary Abbots Church Hall
KENS W8 14 C1
The St Marylebone CE School
MHST W1U 10 B2
St Marylebone Crematorium
FNCH N3 53 F2
St Mary Magdalene CE Primary School
MV/WKIL W9 8 C1
WOOL/PLUM SE18 114 E3
St Mary Magdalen RC Junior School
CRICK NW2 69 K5
St Mary Magdalens Catholic Primary School
BROCKY SE4 132 B3
St Mary Magdalens Primary School
MORT/ESHN SW14 126 A2
St Mary of the Angels RC Primary School
NTGHL W11 8 A4
St Marys Abbey
MLHL NW7 37 J2
St Mary & St Michael Primary School
WCHPL E1 92 E5
St Mary & St Peters CE Primary School
TEDD TW11 142 E4
St Marys Bryanston Square CE Primary School
MBLAR W1H 9 K2
St Marys Catholic Primary School
HCH RM12 63 J7
St Marys CE Junior School
CEND/HSY/T N8 54 E3
STWL/WRAY TW19 120 B5
St Mary's Cemetery
BTSEA SW11 128 D4
St Marys CE Primary School
CHSGTN KT9 172 A5
EBAR EN4 27 J5
FNCH N3 38 D7
IS N1 6 D2
LEW SE13 132 E4
PUT/ROE SW15 127 G2
STNW/STAM N16 73 K1
TWK TW1 124 B6
WALTH E17 57 K3
WLSDN NW10 69 G5
St Mary's CE School
HDN NW4 51 K2
St Marys Greek Cathedral
WDGN N22 41 F7
St Marys High School
CROY/NA CR0 164 D7
St Marys Hospital
BAY/PAD W2 9 H4
St Marys Hospital Medical School
BAY/PAD W2 9 H4
St Marys Infant School
CAR SM5 175 J3
St Mary's Junior School
TWK TW1 124 C6
St Marys Kilburn Primary School
KIL/WHAMP NW6 2 B3
St Marys Primary School
WKENS W14 107 G2
St Marys RC Infant School
CAR SM5 175 K4
St Marys RC J & I School
CROY/NA CR0 164 E7
St Marys RC Junior School
FSBYPK N4 55 K4
WALTH E17 58 A2
St Marys RC Primary School
BECK BR3 152 A6
CHSWK W4 106 B4
CLAP SW4 129 H4
ELTH/MOT SE9 135 F4
ISLW TW7 124 B2
KIL/WHAMP NW6 2 A5
NKENS W10 88 C3
PEND EN3 31 F3
VX/NE SW8 109 G7
WIM/MER SW19 146 E6
St Marys & St Johns CE Primary School
HDN NW4 51 K4
St Marys School
CEND/HSY/T N8 55 F4
HAMP NW3 71 G4
St Mary's Western Eye Hospital
MBLAR W1H 9 L2
St Matthew Academy
LEW SE13 133 G2
St Matthews CE Primary School
PEND EN3 30 E4
RYNPK SW20 145 J7
SURB KT6 159 F6
St Matthias CE Primary School
BETH E2 7 M9
STNW/STAM N16 74 A4
St Meryl JMI School
OXHEY WD19 33 J2
St Michael & All Angels CE Academy
CMBW SE5 110 C6
St Michael at Bowes Junior School
PLMGR N13 41 G5
St Michaels & St Martins RC Primary School
HSLWW TW4 122 E2
St Michaels Catholic Grammar School
NFNCH/WDSPK N12 39 F4
St Michaels CE Primary School
CAMTN NW1 4 E3
HGT N6 54 A6
WAND/EARL SW18 127 J6
WDGN N22 41 F7
WELL DA16 116 D7
St Michaels RC Primary School
EHAM E6 95 K1
St Michaels RC Secondary School
BERM/RHTH SE16 111 H1
St Michaels Sydenham CE Primary School
SYD SE26 151 G3
The St Michael Steiner School
WAND/EARL SW18 127 K4
St Monica's RC Primary School
IS N1 7 J7
St Monicas RC Primary School
STHGT/OAK N14 40 E2
St Nicholas Centre
SUT SM1 175 F4
St Nicholas Preparatory School
SKENS SW7 15 H2
St Nicholas School
BORE WD6 24 A5
CDALE/KGS NW9 68 E1
CHST BR7 154 C6
St Olaves Preparatory School
ELTH/MOT SE9 154 B1
St Pancras Hospital
CAMTN NW1 5 G4
St Pancras International
CAMTN NW1 5 J6
St Pancras International Youth Hostel
CAMTN NW1 5 H7
St Pancras & Islington Cemetery
EFNCH N2 39 J7
St Patricks Church School
STHWK SE1 12 A9
St Patricks Infants School
WAP E1W 92 D7
St Patricks International School
SOHO/SHAV W1D 10 F4
St Patricks Primary School
KTTN NW5 72 B5
St Patricks RC Primary School
WALTH E17 57 G3
WOOL/PLUM SE18 115 J3
St Paulinus CE Primary School
DART DA1 138 B3
St Paul's
STP EC4M 12 E4
St Pauls & All Hallows Infant School
TOTM N17 42 C6
St Pauls & All Hallows Junior School
TOTM N17 42 C6
St Paul's Cathedral
STP EC4M 12 E5
St Paul's Cathedral School
STP EC4M 12 E5
St Pauls Catholic College
SUN TW16 140 E7
St Pauls CE Primary School
BTFD TW8 104 E5
CHSGTN KT9 172 A3
FBAR/BDGN N11 40 A4
HAMP NW3 3 K2
MLHL NW7 37 K3
WALW SE17 18 D8
WCHMH N21 29 H6
WCHPL E1 92 C6
St Pauls CE Junior School
KUTN/CMB KT2 144 C6
St Pauls Girls School
HMSMTH W6 107 G3
St Paul's Primary School
HMSMTH W6 107 F4
St Pauls RC Primary School
THDIT KT7 157 K6
WDGN N22 55 F1
St Pauls RC School
ABYW SE2 116 B5
St Pauls Road Medical Centre
IS N1 73 H5
St Pauls School
BARN SW13 106 E4
St Pauls Steiner School
IS N1 73 K5
St Pauls Way Community School
BOW E3 93 J4
St Pauls with St Lukes CE Primary School
BOW E3 93 H4
St Pauls with St Michaels CE School
HACK E8 74 C7
St Peter Chanel RC Primary School
SCUP DA14 155 J4
St Peter & Paul RC Primary School
STMC/STPC BR5 169 K1
St Peter & St Pauls Primary School
FSBYE EC1V 6 C9
St Peters Catholic Primary School
ROM RM1 63 F2
St Peters CE Primary School
HMSMTH W6 106 D4
MV/WKIL W9 8 A1
WALW SE17 19 G8
WAP E1W 92 E7
St Peter's Church
KTBR SW1X 16 C3
St Peters Eaton Square CE Primary School
BGVA SW1W 16 C4
St Peter's Hospital
COVGDN WC2E 11 K6
St Peters Primary School
SAND/SEL CR2 177 K5
St Peters RC Primary School
DAGW RM9 80 B7
WOOL/PLUM SE18 115 G4
St Philips School
CHSGTN KT9 171 K5
SKENS SW7 14 F6
St Phillips Infant School
SYD SE26 150 D3
St Philomenas Catholic High School
CAR SM5 175 J4
St Quintins Health Centre
NKENS W10 88 A4
St Raphaels Hospice
WPK KT4 174 B1
St Raphaels RC Primary School
NTHLT UB5 83 F1
St Raphaels Way Medical Centre
WLSDN NW10 68 E4
St Richards with St Andrews CE Primary School
RCHPK/HAM TW10 143 H2
St Robert Southwell RC Primary School
CDALE/KGS NW9 50 E5
St Saviour & St Olaves School
STHWK SE1 19 H4
St Saviours CE Primary School
HNHL SE24 130 D2
MV/WKIL W9 8 D1
POP/IOD E14 93 K4
WALTH E17 57 H6
St Saviours CE Infant School
EA W5 85 K7
St Saviours RC Primary School
LEW SE13 133 F3
St Scholasticas RC Primary School
CLPT E5 74 C2
St Stephens CE Junior School
TWK TW1 124 B5
St Stephens CE Primary School
BAY/PAD W2 8 B3
DEPT SE8 132 D1
SHB W12 87 K7
St Stephens CE School
VX/NE SW8 109 K6
St Stephens Primary School
EHAM E6 77 G6
St Stephens RC Primary School
WELL DA16 136 B2
St Swithun Wells RC Primary School
RSLP HA4 65 G2
St Teresa RC First & Middle School
KTN/HRWW/WS HA3 34 C7
St Teresa RC Primary School
BCTR RM8 79 J3
St Teresa's RC Primary School
BORE WD6 24 D1
St Theresas RC Primary School
FNCH N3 52 E2
St Thomas a' Becket RC Primary School
ABYW SE2 116 B2
St Thomas Becket RC Primary School
SNWD SE25 165 H5
St Thomas CE Primary School
NKENS W10 88 C3
St Thomas Childrens Day Hospital
LBTH SE11 17 M7
St Thomas' Hospital
STHWK SE1 17 L3
St Thomas More RC Primary School
BXLYHN DA7 137 G1
ELTH/MOT SE9 134 D2
St Thomas More RC School
CHEL SW3 15 L5
ELTH/MOT SE9 135 F5
WDGN N22 41 G6
St Thomas of Canterbury
MTCM CR4 163 F2
St Thomas of Canterbury RC Primary School
FUL/PGN SW6 107 J6
St Thomas the Apostle College
PECK SE15 111 K7
St Ursulas Convent School
GNWCH SE10 113 G6
St Vincent de Paul RC Primary
WEST SW1P 16 E4
St Vincents Catholic Primary School
ELTH/MOT SE9 153 J3
St Vincents Hospital
PIN HA5 46 C2
St Vincents RC Primary School
BCTR RM8 79 J1
St Vincent's RC Primary School
MHST W1U 10 A3
St Vincents RC Primary School
MLHL NW7 37 K3
St Walter & St John Sports Ground
TOOT SW17 128 D7
St William of York Primary School
FSTH SE23 132 B6
St Winefrides Catholic Primary School
MNPK E12 77 K4
St Winifreds Catholic Junior School
LEE/GVPK SE12 133 J5
St Winifreds RC Infant School
LEW SE13 133 H4
SS Andrews & Marks CE Junior School
SURB KT6 158 E4
SS Mary & Pancras CE Primary School
CAMTN NW1 5 G6
SS Peter & Paul RC Primary School
MTCM CR4 162 E3
SS Peter & Pauls RC Primary School
IL IG1 78 D2
Salcombe Preparatory School (Infants)
STHGT/OAK N14 28 B5
Salcombe Preparatory School (Juniors)
STHGT/OAK N14 28 B6
Salisbury Primary School
MNPK E12 77 H4
Salisbury School
ED N9 30 E7
Salters' Hall
BARB EC2Y 12 F3
Salusbury Primary School
KIL/WHAMP NW6 70 C7
Salvatorian College
KTN/HRWW/WS HA3 48 D1
Samuel Jones Industrial Estate
PECK SE15 111 F6
Samuel Rhodes School
IS N1 6 A3
Sanderstead
SAND/SEL CR2 177 K7
Sanderstead Junior School
SAND/SEL CR2 177 K7
Sandgate Trading Estate
BERM/RHTH SE16 111 J4
Sandhurst Primary School
CAT SE6 133 H6
Sandilands
CROY/NA CR0 178 B1
Sandown Grandstand & Exhibition Centre
ESH/CLAY KT10 170 B2
Sandown Industrial Park
ESH/CLAY KT10 170 A1
Sandown Park Racecourse
ESH/CLAY KT10 170 B2
Sandown Sports Club & Dry Ski Slope
ESH/CLAY KT10 170 B2
Sandringham Primary School
FSTGT E7 77 G5
Sandy Lodge Golf Club
NTHWD HA6 32 B1
Sapcote Trading Centre
WLSDN NW10 69 H4
Sarah Bonnell School
SRTFD E15 76 C5
Sarum Hall School
HAMP NW3 3 K1
Satmer Trust School
STNW/STAM N16 74 C1
Savoy Pier
TPL/STR WC2R 11 L7
The Savoy
TPL/STR WC2R 11 K7
Savoy Theatre
TPL/STR WC2R 11 L7
Saxon Business Centre
WIM/MER SW19 162 B1
Sayer Clinic
CROY/NA CR0 177 F3
Sayer Clinics
MBLAR W1H 9 M5
Scargill Infant School
RAIN RM13 81 J6
Scargill Junior School
RAIN RM13 81 J5
Scarsdale Place Medical Centre
KENS W8 14 C3
School of Oriental & African Studies
GWRST WC1E 11 H1
Schomberg House
STJS SW1Y 10 F9
School of English
GLDGN NW11 52 E7
School of Islamic Republic Iran
KIL/WHAMP NW6 2 A6
School of Oriental & African Studies
STPAN WC1H 11 H1
The School of Pharmacy
BMSBY WC1N 5 K9
The School of St David & St Katharine
CEND/HSY/T N8 54 E3
Science Museum
SKENS SW7 15 H4
Science Museum IMAX Cinema
SKENS SW7 15 G4
The Science Museum Library
SKENS SW7 15 G3
Scotts Park Primary School
BMLY BR1 153 G7
Scott Wilkie Primary School
CAN/RD E16 95 G5
Screen on Baker Street Cinema
MHST W1U 9 M2
Screen on the Green Cinema
IS N1 6 C4
Sealife London Aquarium
WHALL SW1A 17 L2
Sebright Primary School
BETH E2 92 C1
Secombe Centre
SUT SM1 175 F5
Sedgehill School
CAT SE6 151 K4
Sedgewick Centre
WCHPL E1 13 M4
Selborne Primary School
GFD/PVL UB6 85 F1
The Selfridge Hotel
MBLAR W1H 10 B5
Selhurst
SNWD SE25 165 F4
The Selhurst Medical Centre
SNWD SE25 165 F5
Sellincourt School
TOOT SW17 147 J5
Selsdon High School
SAND/SEL CR2 179 F6
Selsdon Primary School
SAND/SEL CR2 178 E7
Selsdon Road Industrial Estate
SAND/SEL CR2 177 K6
Selwyn Primary School
CHING E4 44 A6
PLSTW E13 76 E7
Sergeant Industrial Estate
WAND/EARL SW18 128 A5
Serpentine Gallery
BAY/PAD W2 9 H9
Serpentine Lido & Cafe
SKENS SW7 15 J1
Servite RC Primary School
WBPTN SW10 14 E9
Seven Islands Leisure Centre
BERM/RHTH SE16 111 K2
Seven Kings
GDMY/SEVK IG3 60 E7
Seven Kings Health Centre
GDMY/SEVK IG3 60 E7
Seven Kings High School
GNTH/NBYPK IG2 60 D6
Seven Mills Primary School
POP/IOD E14 112 D1
Seven Sisters
SEVS/STOTM N15 56 A4
Seven Sisters Primary School
SEVS/STOTM N15 55 K4
Seymour Gardens Medical Centre
IL IG1 59 K7
Seymour Leisure Centre
MBLAR W1H 9 L3
Shaare Zedek Medical Centre
GLDGN NW11 52 D5
Shacklewell Primary School
HACK E8 74 B3
Shadwell
WCHPL E1 92 D5
Shadwell Dock Stairs
WAP E1W 93 F6
Shaftesbury High School
KTN/HRWW/WS HA3 34 B7
Shaftesbury Hospital
LSQ/SEVD WC2H 11 J5
Shaftesbury Medical Centre
RYLN/HDSTN HA2 48 C7
Shaftesbury Park Primary School
BTSEA SW11 129 F2
Shaftesbury Primary School
FSTGT E7 77 G6
Shaftesbury Theatre
LSQ/SEVD WC2H 11 J4
Shahjalal Medical Centre
WCHPL E1 92 C5
Shakespeare Business Centre
BRXN/ST SW9 130 C2
Shakespeare's Globe Theatre & Exhibition
STHWK SE1 12 E8
The Shamrock Sports Club
ACT W3 86 E5
Shannon Corner Retail Park
NWMAL KT3 160 D3
Shapla Primary School
WCHPL E1 92 C6
Sharp Sports Centre
EDGW HA8 36 C5
Sheen Lane Health Centre
MORT/ESHN SW14 125 K2
Sheen Lawn Tennis & Squash Club
MORT/ESHN SW14 125 K4
Sheen Mount Primary School
RCHPK/HAM TW10 125 J4
Sheen Sports Centre
MORT/ESHN SW14 126 B3
Shell Centre
STHWK SE1 11 M9
Shelley School
CLAP SW4 129 H2
Shene School
MORT/ESHN SW14 126 B3
Shenstone School
DART DA1 138 A4
Shepherd's Bush
SHB W12 107 G1
Shepherd's Bush CC
ACT W3 87 G6
Shepherd's Bush Empire
SHB W12 107 F1
Shepherd's Bush Market
SHB W12 88 A7
Sheraton Belgravia Hotel
KTBR SW1X 16 A4
Sheraton Business Centre
GFD/PVL UB6 85 J1
Sheraton Park Tower Hotel
KTBR SW1X 15 M1
Sheraton Skyline Hotel
HYS/HAR UB3 101 G6
Sheringdale Primary School
WAND/EARL SW18 127 J7
Sheringham Junior School
MNPK E12 77 K3
Sherington Primary School
CHARL SE7 114 A5
Sherlock Holmes Hotel
MHST W1U 9 M2
Sherlock Holmes Museum
CAMTN NW1 9 M1
Sherwood Park Primary School
BFN/LL DA15 136 C5
Sherwood Park School
WLGTN SM6 176 D2
Sherwood School
MTCM CR4 163 H3
Shirley Clinic
CROY/NA CR0 165 K7
Shirley High School
CROY/NA CR0 179 F2
Shirley Oaks Hospital
CROY/NA CR0 165 K6
Shirley Park Golf Club
CROY/NA CR0 178 D1
Shirley Wanderers RFC
WWKM BR4 180 A3
Shirley Windmill
CROY/NA CR0 178 E2
Shooters Hill Golf Club
WOOL/PLUM SE18 115 H7
Shooters Hill Post 16 Campus
WOOL/PLUM SE18 115 F6
Shooting Star House (Childrens Hospice)
HPTN TW12 141 K5
Shopping City
WDGN N22 55 F1
Shore Business Centre
HOM E9 74 E6
Shoreditch Comprehensive School
IS N1 7 K6
Shoreditch High Street
WCHPL E1 13 L1
Shortlands
HAYES BR2 167 H1
Shotfield Health Clinic
WLGTN SM6 176 B5
Showcase Cinema
WDGN N22 55 G1
Showcase Newham Cinema
BARK IG11 96 C2
Shrewsbury House School
SURB KT6 171 K1
Shrewsbury Road Health Centre
FSTGT E7 77 H6
Sidcup
BFN/LL DA15 155 G1
Sidcup Cemetery
BXLY DA5 155 K1
Sidcup Golf Club
BFN/LL DA15 155 G1
Sidcup Health Centre
SCUP DA14 155 G2

Sidcup Sports Club *SCUP* DA14 155 F3
Sidney Russell School *DAGW* RM9 80 A3
Silicon Business Centre *GFD/PVL* UB6 85 J1
Silverdale Industrial Estate *HYS/HAR* UB3 101 K1
Silver Industrial Estate *TOTM* N17 56 B1
Silver Street ⇌ *UED* N18 42 B3
Silver Street Medical Centre *UED* N18 42 A3
Silver Wing Industrial Estate *CROY/NA* CR0 177 F5
Simon Marks Jewish Primary School *STNW/STAM* N16 56 B7
Singlegate Primary School *WIM/MER* SW19 147 H6
Sion College *EMB* EC4Y 12 B6
Sion Manning RC Girls School *NKENS* W10 88 B4
Sir Francis Drake Primary School *DEPT* SE8 112 B4
Sir George Monoux College *WALTH* E17 57 K1
Sir James Altham Swimming Pool *OXHEY* WD19 33 J4
Sir James Barrie School *VX/NE* SW8 109 H7
Sir John Cass Foundation School *HDTCH* EC3A 13 K5
Sir John Cass Found/ Redcoat School *WCHPL* E1 93 F4
Sir John Heron Primary School *MNPK* E12 77 K3
Sir John Lillie Primary School *HMSMTH* W6 107 H5
Sir John Soane's Museum *LINN* WC2A 11 L4
Sir Thomas Abney Primary School *STNW/STAM* N16 55 K6
Sir Thomas Lipton Memorial Hospital *STHGT/OAK* N14 28 B6
Sir William Burrough Primary School *POP/IOD* E14 93 G5
Site of Greenwich Hospital *GNWCH* SE10 113 J4
Six Bridges Trading Estate *STHWK* SE1 111 H4
Skillion Business Park *BARK* IG11 97 F2
Skinners Company Lower Girls School *CLPT* E5 56 D7
Skinners Company School for Girls *STNW/STAM* N16 56 A6
Slade Green ⇌ *ERITH* DA8 118 D7
Slade Green FC *ERITH* DA8 118 E7
Slade Green Primary School *ERITH* DA8 118 D6
Slade School of Fine Art *STPAN* WC1H 5 H8
Sleaford Industrial Estate *VX/NE* SW8 109 H6
Sloane Hospital *BECK* BR3 152 B7
Sloane Square ⊖ *BGVA* SW1W 16 A6
Smallberry Green Primary School *ISLW* TW7 124 B1
Smallwood Primary School *TOOT* SW17 147 H3
SMA Medical Centre *LEY* E10 57 K6
Smithy Street School *WCHPL* E1 92 E4
Snaresbrook ⊖ *WAN* E11 58 E4
Snaresbrook College Preparatory School *SWFD* E18 58 E1
Snaresbrook Primary School *SWFD* E18 58 E3
Snowsfields Primary School *STHWK* SE1 19 J1
Sobell Leisure Centre *HOLWY* N7 73 F2
Sobell Medical Centre *HOLWY* N7 73 G3
Sofitel St James Hotel *STJS* SW1Y 11 G8
Soho Parish CE Primary School *SOHO/CST* W1F 11 G6
Solent Road Health Centre *KIL/WHAMP* NW6 70 E5
Somerset House *COVGDN* WC2E 11 L6
Somers Town Community Sports Centre *CAMTN* NW1 4 F6
Sorsby Health Centre *CLPT* E5 75 F3
South Acton ⊖ *ACT* W3 105 K2
Southall ⇌ *STHL* UB1 102 E1
Southall & West London College *STHL* UB1 102 D1
South Bank Business Centre *VX/NE* SW8 109 J5
Southbank International School Hampstead *HAMP* NW3 71 G5
Southbank International School Kensington *NTGHL* W11 88 D6
Southbank International School Westminster *BAY/PAD* W2 8 B7
South Bank University *STHWK* SE1 18 C3
South Bermondsey ⇌ *BERM/RHTH* SE16 111 K4
Southborough Primary School *HAYES* BR2 169 F4
Southborough School *SURB* KT6 172 A2
Southbury ⇌ *EN* EN1 30 D3
Southbury Primary School *PEND* EN3 30 D3
South Camden Community School *CAMTN* NW1 4 F5
South Chelsea College *BRXN/ST* SW9 130 A3
South Croydon ⇌ *SAND/SEL* CR2 177 K4
South Croydon Medical Centre *SAND/SEL* CR2 177 J6
South Croydon Sports Club *CROY/NA* CR0 178 A4
South Ealing ⊖ *EA* W5 104 E2
South Ealing Cemetery *EA* W5 104 E3
South Eastern University *HOLWY* N7 73 F2
Southern Road Primary School *PLSTW* E13 95 F1
Southfield First & Middle School *CHSWK* W4 106 B1
Southfield Medical Centre *CHSWK* W4 106 A1
Southfields ⊖ *WAND/EARL* SW18 127 J7
The Southfields Clinic *WAND/EARL* SW18 127 K5
Southfields Community College *WAND/EARL* SW18 127 K7
Southgate ⊖ *STHGT/OAK* N14 28 D7
Southgate Cemetery *STHGT/OAK* N14 40 C1
Southgate College *STHGT/OAK* N14 40 C1
Southgate Compton CC *EBAR* EN4 27 K3
Southgate Leisure Centre *STHGT/OAK* N14 28 D6
Southgate Road Medical Centre *IS* N1 7 H1
Southgate School *EBAR* EN4 28 B4
South Greenford ⇌ *GFD/PVL* UB6 84 E2
South Grove Primary School *WALTH* E17 57 G5
South Hampstead ⊖ *KIL/WHAMP* NW6 2 F2
South Hampstead CC *CRICK* NW2 70 A6
South Hampstead High School *HAMP* NW3 71 H5
South Haringay Infant School *FSBYPK* N4 55 H4
South Harrow ⊖ *RYLN/HDSTN* HA2 66 C2
South Herts Golf Club *TRDG/WHET* N20 26 E7
South Kensington ⊖ *SKENS* SW7 15 H5
South Kenton ⊖ ⊖ *ALP/SUD* HA0 49 J7
Southlake Primary School *ABYW* SE2 116 E1
South Lewisham Health Centre *CAT* SE6 152 A3
South London Crematorium *MTCM* CR4 163 H1
South London Gallery *CMBW* SE5 111 F7
The South London Natural Health Centre *CLAP* SW4 129 H3
South London Tamil School *CROY/NA* CR0 164 D6
South London Theatre *WNWD* SE27 149 J2
Southmead Primary School *WIM/MER* SW19 127 H7
South Merton ⇌ *RYNPK* SW20 161 J2
South Norwood Country Park *SNWD* SE25 165 K3
South Norwood Hill Medical Centre *SNWD* SE25 165 F1
South Norwood Medical Centre *SNWD* SE25 165 F3
South Norwood Pools & Fitness Centre *SNWD* SE25 165 H4
South Norwood Primary School *SNWD* SE25 165 H4
South Park Business Centre *IL* IG1 78 E1
South Park Clinic *IL* IG1 78 D3
South Park Hotel *SAND/SEL* CR2 178 A3
South Park Primary School *GDMY/SEVK* IG3 78 E2
South Quay ⊖ *POP/IOD* E14 112 E1
South Quay Plaza *POP/IOD* E14 112 E1
South Rise Primary School *WOOL/PLUM* SE18 115 J4
South Ruislip ⇌ ⊖ *RSLP* HA4 65 G3
Southside Industrial Estate *VX/NE* SW8 109 H6
Southside Shopping Centre *WAND/EARL* SW18 128 A5
South Thames College *PUT/ROE* SW15 126 C5
PUT/ROE SW15 127 G4
TOOT SW17 147 J4
WAND/EARL SW18 128 A4
South Tottenham ⊖ *SEVS/STOTM* N15 56 B4
Southville Infant School *EBED/NFELT* TW14 121 J7
Southwark ⊖ *STHWK* SE1 12 C9
Southwark Bridge Stairs *BLKFR* EC4V 12 E7
Southwark Cathedral *STHWK* SE1 13 G8
Southwark College *BERM/RHTH* SE16 111 J2
CMBW SE5 111 F6
STHWK SE1 18 B1
Southwark Park Primary School *BERM/RHTH* SE16 111 J2
Southwark Park Sports Centre *BERM/RHTH* SE16 111 K3
Southwark Sports Ground *DUL* SE21 131 G7
South West Middlesex Crematorium *FELT* TW13 122 D7
South Wimbledon ⊖ *WIM/MER* SW19 147 F6
Southwold Primary School *CLPT* E5 74 E1
South Woodford ⊖ *SWFD* E18 58 E1
South Woodford Health Centre *SWFD* E18 44 E7
Southwood Hospital *HGT* N6 54 A6
Southwood Primary School *DAGW* RM9 80 A3
Sovereign Business Centre *PEND* EN3 31 H2
The Space Arts Centre Cinema *DEPT* SE8 112 C3
Sparrow Farm Community Junior School *EW* KT17 173 K4
Sparrow Farm Infant School *EBED/NFELT* TW14 122 B6
Sparrow Farm Junior School *EBED/NFELT* TW14 122 B6
Spa School *STHWK* SE1 111 H3
Speakers Corner *BAY/PAD* W2 9 M6
The Speech Centre *CAMTN* NW1 5 H7
Speedway Industrial Estate *HYS/HAR* UB3 101 G1
Speke's Monument *BAY/PAD* W2 8 F8
Spelthorne Clinic *ASHF* TW15 140 B5
Spelthorne Infant School *ASHF* TW15 140 B5
Spelthorne Sports Club *ASHF* TW15 140 B6
Spencer House *WHALL* SW1A 10 E9
The Spires Shopping Centre *BAR* EN5 26 C2
Spitalfields Community Farm *WCHPL* E1 92 C3
Spitalfields Health Centre *WCHPL* E1 13 M3
Spitfire Business Park *CROY/NA* CR0 177 G5
Splashworld Swimming Centre *BXLYHS* DA6 136 D3
Springfield Christian School *CAT* SE6 151 H2
Springfield Community Primary School *SEVS/STOTM* N15 56 C5
Springfield Hospital *TOOT* SW17 147 J2
Springfield Primary School *SUN* TW16 140 C7
VX/NE SW8 109 J6
Spring Grove Primary School *ISLW* TW7 123 J1
Springhallow School *HNWL* W7 85 F5
Spring Park Primary School *CROY/NA* CR0 179 J2
Springwell Infant School *HEST* TW5 102 D6
Springwell Junior School *HEST* TW5 102 D6
Squirrels Heath Infant School *GPK* RM2 63 K4
Squirrels Heath Junior School *GPK* RM2 63 K4
Squirrels Trading Estate *HYS/HAR* UB3 101 J2
The Stables Gallery & Art Centre *CRICK* NW2 69 J3
Stadium Business Centre *WBLY* HA9 68 D2
Stadium Industrial Estate *WBLY* HA9 68 D4
Stadium Retail Park *WBLY* HA9 68 C2
Stafford Cross Business Park *CROY/NA* CR0 177 F4
The Stafford Hotel *WHALL* SW1A 10 E9
Stag Lane First School *EDGW* HA8 50 C1
Stag Lane Medical Centre *CDALE/KGS* NW9 50 E2
Staines RFC *FELT* TW13 140 E4
Stamford Brook ⊖ *CHSWK* W4 106 C3
Stamford Clinic *HMSMTH* W6 106 D3
Stamford Hill ⇌ *SEVS/STOTM* N15 56 A5
Stamford Hill Primary School *SEVS/STOTM* N15 55 K5
Stanburn First School *STAN* HA7 35 J6
Standard Industrial Estate *CAN/RD* E16 114 C1
Stanford Primary School *STRHM/NOR* SW16 148 D7
Stanhope Primary School *GFD/PVL* UB6 84 C3
Stanley Infant School *TEDD* TW11 142 E3
Stanley Park High School *CAR* SM5 176 A5
Stanley Park Primary School *CAR* SM5 175 K6
Stanmore ⊖ *STAN* HA7 35 K3
Stanmore College *STAN* HA7 35 H5
Stanmore Golf Club *STAN* HA7 35 H6
Stanton Square Industrial Estate *SYD* SE26 151 H3
Staple Inn Buildings *HHOL* WC1V 12 A3
Staples Corner Business Park *CRICK* NW2 51 J7
Star Business Centre *RAIN* RM13 99 F4
Starksfield Primary School *ED* N9 30 A7
Star Lane ⊖ *CAN/RD* E16 94 C3
Star Primary School *CAN/RD* E16 94 C3
Stationers Hall *STP* EC4M 12 D5
Stationery Office *HOL/ALD* WC2B 11 L4
Stebon Primary School *POP/IOD* E14 93 H4
Stephen Hawking Primary Special School *POP/IOD* E14 93 G5
Stepney Day Hospital *WCHPL* E1 92 E5
Stepney Green ⊖ *WCHPL* E1 93 F3
Stepney Greencoat CE Primary School *POP/IOD* E14 93 H5
Stepney Green College *WCHPL* E1 93 F4
Sterling Industrial Estate *DAGE* RM10 80 D3
Sterling Way Clinic *UED* N18 42 B4
Stewart Fleming Primary School *PGE/AN* SE20 165 K2
Stewart Headlam Primary School *WCHPL* E1 92 D3
Stillness Primary School *FSTH* SE23 132 B5
Stirling Industrial Centre *BORE* WD6 25 F4
Stirling Retail Park *BORE* WD6 25 F5
Stirling Way Industrial Estates *CROY/NA* CR0 163 K6
Stockley Park Business Centre *STKPK* UB11 82 A7
Stockley Park Golf Club *STKPK* UB11 82 A6
Stockwell ⊖ *CLAP* SW4 129 K1
Stockwell Park School *BRXN/ST* SW9 110 A7
Stockwell Primary School *BRXN/ST* SW9 130 A2
Stoke Newington ⇌ *STNW/STAM* N16 74 B1
Stonebridge Park ⊖ ⊖ *ALP/SUD* HA0 68 C6
The Stonebridge Primary School (London Welsh School) *WLSDN* NW10 68 E7
Stonebridge Shopping Centre *WLSDN* NW10 69 F7
Stonehill Business Centre *UED* N18 43 F5
Stonehill Business Park *UED* N18 43 F4
Stone Lake Retail Park *CHARL* SE7 114 B3
Stoneleigh ⇌ *HOR/WEW* KT19 173 H4
Stoneleigh First School *EW* KT17 173 K3
Stoneydown Park Primary School *WALTH* E17 57 G3
Stowford College *BELMT* SM2 175 G6
Strand on the Green J & I School *CHSWK* W4 105 H5
Strand Palace Hotel *COVGDN* WC2E 11 K6
Stratford College *SRTFD* E15 76 C6
Stratford High Street ⊖ *SRTFD* E15 76 B6
Stratford International ⇌ ⊖ *SRTFD* E15 76 A5
Stratford ⇌ ⊖ ⊖ ⊖ *SRTFD* E15 76 A5
Stratford School *FSTGT* E7 76 E6
Stratford Shopping Centre *SRTFD* E15 76 B6
Strathmore School *RCHPK/HAM* TW10 124 E7
Strawberry Fields School *NTGHL* W11 8 B5
Strawberry Hill ⇌ *WHTN* TW2 142 E2
Strawberry Hill Golf Club *WHTN* TW2 142 E2
Streatham ⇌ *STRHM/NOR* SW16 148 D4
Streatham Cemetery *TOOT* SW17 147 J2
Streatham & Clapham High School *STRHM/NOR* SW16 148 C2
BRXS/STRHM SW2 130 A7
Streatham Common ⇌ *STRHM/NOR* SW16 148 D5
Streatham & Croydon RFC *THHTH* CR7 164 B4
Streatham Hill ⇌ *STRHM/NOR* SW16 148 E1
Streatham Ice Rink *STRHM/NOR* SW16 148 E4
Streatham Leisure Centre *STRHM/NOR* SW16 148 E1
Streatham Modern School *STRHM/NOR* SW16 148 E5
Streatham Park Cemetery *MTCM* CR4 163 H1
Streatham Swimming Pool *STRHM/NOR* SW16 148 E4
Streatham Vale Sports Club *STRHM/NOR* SW16 148 C6
Streatham Wells Primary School *BRXS/STRHM* SW2 149 F1
Stroud Green Primary School *FSBYPK* N4 55 G7
The Study Preparatory School *WIM/MER* SW19 146 B4
The Study School *NWMAL* KT3 160 B4
Sudbourne Primary School *BRXS/STRHM* SW2 130 A4
Sudbury Court Sports Club *ALP/SUD* HA0 67 J2
Sudbury Golf Club *GFD/PVL* UB6 67 J5
Sudbury & Harrow Road ⇌ *ALP/SUD* HA0 67 H4
Sudbury Hill ⇌ ⊖ *HRW* HA1 66 E3
Sudbury Primary School *ALP/SUD* HA0 67 H3
Sudbury Town ⊖ *GFD/PVL* UB6 67 H5
Suffolks Primary School *EN* EN1 30 D1
Sulivan Primary School *FUL/PGN* SW6 127 K1
Summerside JMI School *NFNCH/WDSPK* N12 39 H5
Summerswood Primary School *BORE* WD6 24 D3
Summit Business Park *SUN* TW16 140 E6
Sunbury ⇌ *SUN* TW16 140 E7
Sunbury Business Centre *SUN* TW16 140 C7
Sunbury Court *SUN* TW16 156 C1
Sunbury Leisure Centre *SUN* TW16 140 D7
Sunbury Manor School *SUN* TW16 140 D7
Sundridge Park ⇌ *BMLY* BR1 153 F6
Sundridge Park Golf Club *BMLY* BR1 153 G5
Sun Life Trading Estate *EBED/NFELT* TW14 121 K2
Sunnyfields Primary School *HDN* NW4 51 K2
Sunnyhill Primary School *STRHM/NOR* SW16 149 F3
Sunrise School *TOTM* N17 42 C5
Sunshine House School *NTHWD* HA6 32 B5
Surbiton ⇌ *SURB* KT6 159 F5
Surbiton Business Centre *SURB* KT6 158 E5
Surbiton Cemetery *KUT/HW* KT1 159 H3
Surbiton Golf Club *CHSGTN* KT9 171 H3
Surbiton High School *KUT/HW* KT1 159 F3
Surbiton Hospital *SURB* KT6 159 F5
Surbiton Natural Health Centre *SURB* KT6 159 F5
Surrey County CC (The Oval) *LBTH* SE11 17 M9
Surrey Docks Farm *BERM/RHTH* SE16 112 C1
Surrey Docks Health Centre *BERM/RHTH* SE16 112 B1
Surrey Docks Watersports Centre *BERM/RHTH* SE16 112 B2
Surrey Quays ⊖ *BERM/RHTH* SE16 112 A3
Surrey Quays Leisure Park *BERM/RHTH* SE16 112 A2
Surrey Quays Shopping Centre *BERM/RHTH* SE16 112 A2
Surrey Square Infant School *WALW* SE17 19 J7
Susi Earnshaw Theatre School *BAR* EN5 26 D2
Sussex Hotel *OXSTW* W1C 10 A5
Sussex House School *KTBR* SW1X 15 L5
Sutcliffe Park Athletics Track *LEE/GVPK* SE12 134 A4
Sutton ⇌ *SUT* SM1 175 G5
Sutton Alternative Health Centre *SUT* SM1 175 F4
Sutton Arena *CAR* SM5 162 C6
Sutton Bowling Club *BELMT* SM2 174 E7
Sutton Cemetery *CHEAM* SM3 174 D1
Sutton Civic Centre *SUT* SM1 175 F4
Sutton College of Learning for Adults *SUT* SM1 175 F4
Sutton Common ⇌ *SUT* SM1 174 E1
Sutton Grammar School for Boys *SUT* SM1 175 G4
Sutton High Junior School *SUT* SM1 175 F5
Sutton High School for Girls GDST *SUT* SM1 174 E5
Sutton House *HACK* E8 74 E4
Suttons Business Park *RAIN* RM13 99 F2
Sutton Superbowl *SUT* SM1 175 F4
Sutton United FC *SUT* SM1 174 E3
Sutton West Centre *SUT* SM1 174 E4
Swaffield Primary School *WAND/EARL* SW18 128 B5
Swaminarayan School *WLSDN* NW10 69 F5
Swan Business Centre *CHSWK* W4 106 A3
Swan Business Park *DART* DA1 139 G3
Swan Lane Pier *CANST* EC4R 13 G7
Swanlea School *WCHPL* E1 92 D3
Swansmere School *WOT/HER* KT12 156 B7
Swedish School *BARN* SW13 106 D5
Swiss Cottage ⊖ *KIL/WHAMP* NW6 3 G1
Swiss Cottage Hotel *HAMP* NW3 3 H1
Swiss Cottage Leisure Centre *HAMP* NW3 3 H2
Swiss Cottage School *STJWD* NW8 3 H2
Swissotel The Howard *TPL/STR* WC2R 11 M6
Sybil Elgar School *EA* W5 86 A6
NWDGN UB2 102 E2
Sybourn Infant School *LEY* E10 57 G7

The Sybourn Junior School
WALTH E17 57 H6
Sydenham
SYD SE26 150 E4
Sydenham Girls School
SYD SE26 150 D2
Sydenham High Junior School
SYD SE26 150 D3
Sydenham High School Sports Ground
CAT SE6 151 J4
Sydenham High Senior School
SYD SE26 150 D4
Sydenham Hill
DUL SE21 150 A2
The Sydney Russell School
DAGW RM9 79 K4
Syon House
BTFD TW8 104 D7
Syon Lane
ISLW TW7 104 B6
Syon Park
BTFD TW8 124 D1
Syracuse University
NTGHL W11 88 D6
Tabard Theatre
CHSWK W4 106 B3
Tabernacle School
NTGHL W11 88 B7
Taberner House
CROY/NA CR0 177 J2
TA Centre
EDGW HA8 36 D6
HRW HA1 49 F4
NFNCH/WDSPK N12 39 H7
Tait Road Industrial Estate
CROY/NA CR0 165 F5
Talmud Torah School
STNW/STAM N16 55 K6
Tamian Industrial Estate
HSLWW TW4 122 B3
Tandem Centre
WIM/MER SW19 147 H7
Tashbar of Edgware Primary School
EDGW HA8 36 C3
Tate Britain
WEST SW1P 17 J6
Tate Modern
STHWK SE1 12 D8
Tavistock Clinic
HAMP NW3 71 H5
TAVR Centre
KUT/HW KT1 158 E3
Tavy Clinic
ABYW SE2 116 D1
Tawhid Boys School
STNW/STAM N16 74 B1
Tayyibah Girls School
STNW/STAM N16 56 C7
Teddington
TEDD TW11 143 G5
Teddington Business Park
TEDD TW11 143 F4
Teddington Cemetery
TEDD TW11 142 E3
Teddington Clinic
TEDD TW11 142 E5
Teddington Memorial Hospital
TEDD TW11 142 E5
Teddington Pool & Fitness Centre
TEDD TW11 143 G4
Teddington School
TEDD TW11 143 K5
The Teddington Theatre Club
E/WMO/HCT KT8 157 J4
Telferscot Primary School
BAL SW12 129 H7
Temperate House, Kew Gardens
RCH/KEW TW9 125 G1
Temple
TPL/STR WC2R 12 A6
Temple Grove Hatcham School
NWCR SE14 112 A6
Temple Hill Primary School
DART DA1 139 K4
Temple of Bacchus
CMBW SE5 130 D1
Temple of Mithras
MANHO EC4N 13 G5
Tenby Road Clinic
EDGW HA8 50 B1
Tenterden Sports Ground
KTN/HRWW/WS HA3 50 A6
Terence McMillan Stadium
PLSTW E13 95 G3
Tetherdown Primary School
MUSWH N10 54 A3
Thames Barrier
CAN/RD E16 114 C1
Thames Barrier Information & Learning Centre
CHARL SE7 114 C2
Thames Christian College
BTSEA SW11 128 C2
Thames Ditton
THDIT KT7 157 K6
Thames Ditton & Esher Golf Club
ESH/CLAY KT10 170 D1
Thames Ditton Infant School
THDIT KT7 158 A5
Thames Ditton Junior School
THDIT KT7 158 A6
Thames Gateway Park
DAGW RM9 98 B2
Thames House
WEST SW1P 17 J5
Thameside Industrial Estate
CAN/RD E16 95 H7
Thamesmead Leisure Centre
THMD SE28 97 H6
Thamesmead Shopping Centre
THMD SE28 97 G6
Thames Valley University
EA W5 85 J7
Thamesview Business Centre
RAIN RM13 99 G4
Thames View Clinic
BARK IG11 97 F1
Thames View J & I School
BARK IG11 97 G1
Thames Water Tower
NTGHL W11 107 G1
Theatre de l'Ange Fou International School of Corporeal Mime
ARCH N19 54 E7
Theatre for Mankind
FSBYPK N4 55 F7
Theatre Museum Library & Archive
COVGDN WC2E 11 K6
Theatre of the Dispossessed
WIM/MER SW19 127 G7
Theatre Royal
HOL/ALD WC2B 11 K5
SRTFD E15 76 B5
Theatre Royal Haymarket
STJS SW1Y 11 H7
Theodore McLeary Primary School
EDUL SE22 131 G3
Therapia Lane
CROY/NA CR0 163 K6
Therapia Trading Estate
CROY/NA CR0 163 J6
Thistlebrook Industrial Estate
ABYW SE2 116 D2
Thistle Hotel
BAY/PAD W2 8 E7
BGVA SW1W 16 D4
CAMTN NW1 4 F8
FITZ W1T 10 F4
FSBYE EC1V 6 E8
NOXST/BSQ WC1A 11 J3
WESTW SW1E 16 D4
Thistle Marble Arch Hotel
MBLAR W1H 9 M5
Thistle Piccadilly Hotel
SOHO/SHAV W1D 11 H7
Thomas Arnold Primary School
DAGW RM9 80 B6
Thomas Buxton Infant School
WCHPL E1 92 C3
Thomas Fairchild Primary School
IS N1 7 G5
Thomas Francis Academy
BRXN/ST SW9 130 C3
Thomas Gamuel Primary School
WALTH E17 57 J5
Thomas Jones Primary School
NTGHL W11 88 C5
Thomas London Independent Day School
KENS W8 14 D3
Thomas Road Industrial Estate
POP/IOD E14 93 J4
Thomas's Fulham
FUL/PGN SW6 128 A2
Thomas's Preparatory School
BTSEA SW11 108 C7
BTSEA SW11 128 E4
Thomas Tallis School
BKHTH/KID SE3 134 A2
Thornhill Primary School
IS N1 6 A2
Thornton Heath
THHTH CR7 164 D3
Thornton Heath Health Centre
THHTH CR7 164 D3
Thornton Heath Pools & Fitness Centre
THHTH CR7 164 D3
Thornton Road Industrial Estate
CROY/NA CR0 163 K5
Thorntree Primary School
CHARL SE7 114 C4
Thorpe Hall Primary School
WALTH E17 44 A7
Three Bridges Business Centre
NWDGN UB2 103 H1
Three Bridges Primary School
NWDGN UB2 103 G2
Three Mills Heritage Centre
BOW E3 94 A2
Thurston Industrial Estate
LEW SE13 132 E2
Tibetan Buddhist Centre
WALW SE17 18 E7
Tidemill Primary School
DEPT SE8 112 D6
Tideway Industrial Estate
VX/NE SW8 109 H5
Tiffin Girls School
KUTN/CMB KT2 144 A5
Tiffin School & Sports Centre
KUTN/CMB KT2 159 G1
Tiller Centre (Swimming Baths)
POP/IOD E14 112 D2
Tiller Leisure Centre
POP/IOD E14 112 D2
Timbercroft Primary School
WOOL/PLUM SE18 115 K6
Timbers Clinic
KTN/HRWW/WS HA3 34 D5
Timebridge Youth & Community Centre
CROY/NA CR0 179 K4
Times Square Shopping Centre
SUT SM1 175 F4
Tiverton Primary School
SEVS/STOTM N15 55 K5
Tobacco Dock
WAP E1W 92 D6
Tokyngton Community Centre
WBLY HA9 68 D4
Toldos School
STNW/STAM N16 55 K7
Tollgate
DUL SE21 150 A1
Tollgate Primary School
PLSTW E13 95 G3
Tolworth
BRYLDS KT5 172 D1
Tolworth CP School
SURB KT6 159 G7
Tolworth Girls School
SURB KT6 172 B2
Tolworth Recreation Centre
SURB KT6 172 B2
Tom Hood School
WAN E11 76 D2
Tooting
TOOT SW17 147 K5
Tooting Bec
TOOT SW17 148 A2
Tooting Bec Athletics Track
TOOT SW17 148 B3
Tooting Broadway
TOOT SW17 147 J4
Tooting Leisure Centre
TOOT SW17 147 H3
Tooting & Mitcham United FC
MTCM CR4 148 A7
Torah Temimah Primary School
CRICK NW2 69 K3
Torah Vodaas
GLDGN NW11 70 D1
Torriano Junior School
KTTN NW5 72 C4
Torridon Primary School
CAT SE6 152 B1
Torrington Clinic
NFNCH/WDSPK N12 39 G4
Torrington Park Health Centre
NFNCH/WDSPK N12 39 G3
Total Health Clinic
SHB W12 106 E1
Tottenham Cemetery
TOTM N17 42 A6
Tottenham Court Road
SOHO/SHAV W1D 11 G4
Tottenham Green Leisure Centre
SEVS/STOTM N15 56 A3
Tottenham Hale
TOTM N17 56 D2
Tottenham Hale Retail Park
SEVS/STOTM N15 56 C3
Tottenham Hotspur FC (White Hart Lane)
TOTM N17 42 B6
Tottenham Park Cemetery
ED N9 42 D2
Tottenham Sports Centre
TOTM N17 42 B7
Totteridge CC
TRDG/WHET N20 38 E1
Totteridge & Whetstone
TRDG/WHET N20 39 F1
Tower 42
OBST EC2N 13 J4
The Tower Bridge Exhibition
STHWK SE1 13 L9
Tower Bridge Primary School
STHWK SE1 19 L1
Tower Bridge Wharf
WAP E1W 92 C7
Tower Gateway
TWRH EC3N 13 L6
Tower Hamlets College
POP/IOD E14 93 K6
WCHPL E1 92 E4
Tower Hill
TWRH EC3N 13 L7
The Tower Hotel
WAP E1W 13 M8
Tower Industrial Estate
SNWD SE25 165 H3
Tower Medical Centre
WCHPL E1 92 C5
Tower Millennium Pier
TWRH EC3N 13 K8
Tower of London
TWRH EC3N 13 L7
Tower Retail Park
DART DA1 138 C4
Towers Business Park
WBLY HA9 68 D3
Tower Stairs
MON EC3R 13 J7
Town Farm Primary School
STWL/WRAY TW19 120 A6
Townley Grammar School for Girls
BXLYHS DA6 137 G5
Townmead Business Centre
FUL/PGN SW6 128 B1
Townsend Industrial Estate
WLSDN NW10 68 E7
Townsend Primary School
WALW SE17 19 H5
Toynbee Hall & Curtain Theatre
WCHPL E1 13 L3
Trade Union Congress
NOXST/BSQ WC1A 11 H4
Trafalgar Business Centre
BARK IG11 97 F3
Trafalgar Infant & Junior School
WHTN TW2 142 D1
Trafalgar Infant School
WHTN TW2 123 J7
Trafalgar Square
STJS SW1Y 11 H8
Trafalgar Trading Estate
PEND EN3 31 H3
Tramshed Theatre
WOOL/PLUM SE18 115 G3
Trans Atlantic College
BETH E2 7 K5
Transport for London Lost Property Office
CAMTN NW1 9 M1
Transport House
WEST SW1P 17 J4
Travelodge
ACT W3 86 C3
BTFD TW8 105 F5
BTSEA SW11 128 B2
CAMTN NW1 9 K2
CAN/RD E16 95 H7
FELT TW13 121 K7
FSBYW WC1X 5 M7
HEST TW5 102 B5
IL IG1 78 B2
KUTN/CMB KT2 159 F1
LSQ/SEVD WC2H 11 J4
POP/IOD E14 94 B5
REDBR IG4 59 K5
STPAN WC1H 5 K7
SUN TW16 140 E6
SURB KT6 159 J7
WCHPL E1 13 L4
WLSDN NW10 86 C1
Travelodge Croydon Central
CROY/NA CR0 177 K1
Travelodge Watford Central
WATW WD18 21 F3
Treasury
WHALL SW1A 17 J2
The Treaty Centre
HSLW TW3 123 G2
Treehouse School
MUSWH N10 54 A3
The Treehouse School
BMSBY WC1N 5 L9
Trent CE Primary School
EBAR EN4 27 K3
Trent Country Park
EBAR EN4 28 A1
Trent Park Cemetery
EBAR EN4 28 A2
Trent Park Golf Club
STHGT/OAK N14 28 C3
Trevor Roberts School
HAMP NW3 3 H1
Tricycle Theatre
KIL/WHAMP NW6 70 D6
Trident Business Centre
TOOT SW17 147 K4
Trinity Business Centre
BERM/RHTH SE16 112 C1
Trinity Catholic Lower High School
WFD IG8 44 E3
Trinity College Centre
PECK SE15 111 F6
Trinity College of Music
GNWCH SE10 113 F5
MHST W1U 10 B3
Trinity Hospital
GNWCH SE10 113 G4
Trinity House
TWRH EC3N 13 K6
Trinity RC High School (Upper)
WFD IG8 44 E3
Trinity St Marys Primary School
BAL SW12 129 F7
Trinity School
CROY/NA CR0 178 E1
DAGE RM10 80 C2
Trinity School Belvedere
BELV DA17 117 K3
Trinity Trading Estate
HYS/HAR UB3 101 K2
Tripcock Point Development Site
THMD SE28 97 F6
Triumph Trading Estate
TOTM N17 42 C5
Trocadero
SOHO/SHAV W1D 11 G7
Trojan Business Centre
WLSDN NW10 69 H5
Troy Industrial Estate
HRW HA1 49 F4
True Buddha School
IS N1 5 L4
TS Queen Mary
TPL/STR WC2R 11 L7
TTMH Belz Day School
STNW/STAM N16 56 C6
Tudor Enterprise Park
KTN/HRWW/WS HA3 48 D2
Tudor Lodge Health Centre
WIM/MER SW19 127 G7
Tudor Lodge Hotel
PIN HA5 47 F5
Tudor Primary School
FNCH N3 39 G7
STHL UB1 83 J6
Tufnell Park
KTTN NW5 72 B3
Tufnell Park Primary School
HOLWY N7 72 D3
Tuke School
PECK SE15 111 J7
Tulse Hill
WNWD SE27 149 H1
Tunnel Avenue Trading Estate
GNWCH SE10 113 G1
Turin Grove School
ED N9 30 E6
Turney School
DUL SE21 130 D6
Turnham Green
CHSWK W4 106 B3
Turnham Primary School
BROCKY SE4 132 B3
Turnpike Lane
SEVS/STOTM N15 55 H2
Turtle Key Arts Centre
FUL/PGN SW6 107 K5
Tutorial College of West London
STHL UB1 84 A7
Tweeddale Primary School
CAR SM5 162 C6
Twenty Nevern Square Hotel
ECT SW5 14 B6
Twickenham
TWK TW1 124 B6
Twickenham Cemetery
WHTN TW2 123 G7
Twickenham Park Health Centre
TWK TW1 124 D5
Twickenham Preparatory School
HPTN TW12 142 B7
Twickenham Stadium
ISLW TW7 123 K5
Twickenham Trading Estate
TWK TW1 124 A5
Two Bridges Business Park
SAND/SEL CR2 177 K5
Twyford CE High School
ACT W3 86 C7
Twyford Sports Centre
ACT W3 86 D7
Tyburn Infant School
STJWD NW8 3 H9
Tynemouth Road Health Centre
SEVS/STOTM N15 56 B3
The Type Museum
BRXN/ST SW9 110 A7
Tyssen Primary School
STNW/STAM N16 56 C7
UCI Cinema
BAY/PAD W2 8 D5
SUT SM1 175 F4
UCI Empire Cinema
LSQ/SEVD WC2H 11 H7
UK Passport Office
PIM SW1V 16 D5
Underhill Infant School
BAR EN5 26 C4
Unicorn Primary School
BECK BR3 166 E4
Unicorn School
RCH/KEW TW9 105 G7
Unicorn Theatre
STHWK SE1 19 K1
United Medical & Dental Schools
STHWK SE1 17 L3
Unity College
KTTN NW5 72 B3
Unity Trading Estate
WFD IG8 59 H2
University Church of Christ the King
STPAN WC1H 11 G1
University College Hospital
CAMTN NW1 4 F9
HAMP NW3 71 H5
University College London
FITZ W1T 10 F2
GWRST WC1E 11 G1
STPAN WC1H 5 G9
University College London, Astor College
FITZ W1T 10 F2
University College London Medical School
FITZ W1T 10 E2
University College London Obstetrics Hospital
GWRST WC1E 10 F1
University College School
HAMP NW3 71 G3
University Hospital Lewisham
LEW SE13 132 E4
University of California
WHALL SW1A 10 E9
University of East London
BARK IG11 79 G3
CAN/RD E16 96 A6
PLSTW E13 95 F2
SRTFD E15 76 B7
University of Greenwich
GNWCH SE10 113 G4
WOOL/PLUM SE18 115 F3
University of Greenwich (Mansion Site)
ELTH/MOT SE9 135 H5
University of Greenwich (Southwood Site)
ELTH/MOT SE9 135 H6
University of Greenwich Sports Ground
ELTH/MOT SE9 134 D3
ELTH/MOT SE9 135 H6
University of London
BAY/PAD W2 9 G5
BMSBY WC1N 11 K1
CLKNW EC1R 6 B9
FITZ W1T 11 G4
MBLAR W1H 9 K4
STHWK SE1 13 G9
STPAN WC1H 5 H9
University of London Athletics Ground
NWMAL KT3 160 D4
University of the Arts London
MYFR/PKLN W1K 10 C5
University of Westminster
CAMTN NW1 4 E9
CAVSQ/HST W1G 10 D4
CHSWK W4 105 K7
GTPST W1W 10 D2
HRW HA1 49 G6
University of Westminster, Environment
MHST W1U 10 A2
Uphall Primary School
IL IG1 78 B4
Upland Primary School
BXLYHN DA7 137 G2
Uplands Business Park
WALTH E17 57 F1
Upney
BARK IG11 79 F6
Upper Holloway
ARCH N19 72 D1
Upper Montagu Street Clinic
CAMTN NW1 9 L2
Upper Tooting Independent High School
TOOT SW17 147 J1
Upton Cross Primary School
PLSTW E13 77 F7
Upton Day Hospital
BXLYHS DA6 137 F3
Upton Lane Medical Centre
FSTGT E7 77 F5
Upton Park
PLSTW E13 77 G7
Upton Primary School
BXLY DA5 137 F4
Upton Road School
BXLYHS DA6 137 F4
The Urdang Academy
LSQ/SEVD WC2H 11 J5
Ursuline High School
RYNPK SW20 146 B6
Ursuline Preparatory School
RYNPK SW20 146 B6
Uxbridge College
HYS/HAR UB3 82 E6
Uxendon Manor JM&I School
KTN/HRWW/WS HA3 50 A4
Vale Farm Sports Centre
ALP/SUD HA0 67 H3
Vale Industrial Estate
WATW WD18 20 A7
The Vale Medical Centre
FSTH SE23 151 G1
Valence House Museum & Library
BCTR RM8 79 K1
Valence Primary School
BCTR RM8 79 K1
Valentine High School
GNTH/NBYPK IG2 60 A5
Valentines High Lower School
GNTH/NBYPK IG2 60 B4
Vale Park Industrial
ACT W3 106 B1
Vale Resource Base
TOTM N17 42 A7
The Vale School
SKENS SW7 14 E4
Valley Link Business Centre
PEND EN3 31 G5
Valley Link Business Estate
PEND EN3 31 G5
Valley Primary School
HAYES BR2 167 J1
Valmar Trading Estate
CMBW SE5 110 D7
V & A Museum of Childhood
BETH E2 92 E2
Vanbrugh Theatre
GWRST WC1E 11 G1
Vanguard Trading Estate
SRTFD E15 76 A7
Vaudeville Theatre
COVGDN WC2E 11 K6
Vaughan First & Middle School
RYLN/HDSTN HA2 48 C5
Vauxhall
VX/NE SW8 17 K8
Vauxhall Primary School
LBTH SE11 17 L7
Vernon House Special School
WLSDN NW10 68 E4
Vestry Hall
MTCM CR4 162 E2
Vestry House Museum
WALTH E17 57 K3
Vicarage Fields Health Clinic
BARK IG11 78 C6
The Vicarage Field Shopping Centre
BARK IG11 78 C6

Vicarage Primary School EHAM E6 95 K2
Vicarage Road Cemetery WATW WD18 20 E3
Vicars Green Primary School GFD/PVL UB6 85 J1
V I Components Industrial Park ERITH DA8 118 B4
Victoria PIM SW1V 16 D5
Victoria & Albert Museum SKENS SW7 15 H4
Victoria Business Centre WELL DA16 136 B1
Victoria Bus Station PIM SW1V 16 D4
Victoria Chiropractic Clinic SKENS SW7 15 L2
Victoria Coach Station BGVA SW1W 16 C6
Victoria Hall FNCH N3 38 D7
Victoria Industrial Estate ACT W3 87 F4
Victoria Industrial Park DART DA1 139 G4
Victoria Junior School FELT TW13 122 A7
Victoria Medical Centre PIM SW1V 16 F6
Victoria Palace Theatre BGVA SW1W 16 D4
Victoria Park Industrial Centre HOM E9 75 H6
Victoria Park Plaza Hotel PIM SW1V 16 E5
Victoria Place Shopping Centre BGVA SW1W 16 D5
Victoria Rail/Air Terminal PIM SW1V 16 D5
Victoria Retail Park RSLP HA4 65 H4
Victoria Wharf POP/IOD E14 93 G6
Victoria Wharf Industrial Estate DEPT SE8 112 B4
Victor Seymour Infant School CAR SM5 175 K2
Victory Business Centre ISLW TW7 124 A3
Victory Day School THHTH CR7 164 D3
Victory Primary School WALW SE17 18 F5
Viking Business Centre ROMW/RG RM7 62 E6
Viking Primary School NTHLT UB5 83 H2
Village Infant School DAGE RM10 80 C6
The Village School HAMP NW3 71 K5
Villiers High School STHL UB1 84 A7
The Vine Clinic KUTN/CMB KT2 144 A5
Vine Medical Centre E/WMO/HCT KT8 157 H2
The Vines School BTSEA SW11 129 F3
The Vineyard Primary School RCHPK/HAM TW10 125 F5
Vinopolis, City of Wine STHWK SE1 12 F8
Vinters' Hall BLKFR EC4V 12 F6
V I P Trading Estate CHARL SE7 114 B3
Virginia Primary School BETH E2 7 L8
Virgo Fidelis Convent Schools NRWD SE19 149 J5
Visage School of Hair & Beauty ELTH/MOT SE9 135 F5
Vision College of Technology HOM E9 75 J5
Vita et Pax School STHGT/OAK N14 28 B4
Vittoria Primary School IS N1 5 M4
Voyager Business Estate BERM/RHTH SE16 111 H2
Vue Cinema
ACT W3 86 C3
CROY/NA CR0 177 F1
DAGW RM9 80 A7
FUL/PGN SW6 107 K6
HAMP NW3 71 G5
HRW HA1 48 E5
LSQ/SEVD WC2H 11 H6
NFNCH/WDSPK N12 39 H6
ROMW/RG RM7 63 G4
SHB W12 107 G1
Vulcan Business Centre CROY/NA CR0 180 C7
Waddon CROY/NA CR0 177 G3
Waddon Clinic CROY/NA CR0 177 G4
Waddon Infant School CROY/NA CR0 177 G4
Waddon Marsh CROY/NA CR0 177 G1
Wadham Lodge Sports Centre WALTH E17 43 K7
Wadsworth Business Centre GFD/PVL UB6 85 J1
The Waldegrave Clinic TEDD TW11 143 F4
Waldegrave Girls School WHTN TW2 142 D2
Waldo Industrial Estate BMLY BR1 168 B2
Waldorf School of South West London BAL SW12 148 C1
Waldron Health Centre & Surgery NWCR SE14 112 C6
Walker Primary School STHGT/OAK N14 40 D1
The Wallace Centre DEPT SE8 112 E5
The Wallace Collection MHST W1U 10 A4
Wallbrook Business Centre HSLWW TW4 122 A2
Wallington WLGTN SM6 176 B5
Wallington County Grammar School WLGTN SM6 176 B2
Wallington High School for Girls WLGTN SM6 176 B7
Walmer Road Clinic NTGHL W11 88 C6
Walm Lane Clinic CRICK NW2 70 B4
Walnut Tree Walk Primary School LBTH SE11 18 A5
Waltham Forest College
WALTH E17 56 E2
WALTH E17 57 K2
Waltham Forest Pool & Track WALTH E17 57 K1
Waltham Forest Theatre WALTH E17 57 H2
Walthamstow Academy WALTH E17 43 H7
Walthamstow Business Centre WALTH E17 58 A1
Walthamstow Central WALTH E17 57 J4
Walthamstow Marsh Nature Reserve CLPT E5 56 D6
Walthamstow Queens Road WALTH E17 57 J4
Walthamstow School for Girls WALTH E17 57 K3
Walton Business Centre WOT/HER KT12 156 A6
Walton Casuals FC WOT/HER KT12 156 A4
Walton Swimming Pool WOT/HER KT12 156 A7
Walworth Academy STHWK SE1 19 K8
Walworth Lower Secondary School WALW SE17 19 H7
Walworth Town Hall WALW SE17 18 E6
Wandle Park CROY/NA CR0 177 G1
Wandle Recreation Centre WAND/EARL SW18 128 A5
Wandle Trading Estate MTCM CR4 162 E6
Wandle Valley School CAR SM5 162 D6
Wandsworth Adult College
BTSEA SW11 109 F7
TOOT SW17 147 J1
Wandsworth Cemetery WAND/EARL SW18 128 B7
Wandsworth Common TOOT SW17 128 D6
Wandsworth Road VX/NE SW8 129 H1
Wandsworth Town WAND/EARL SW18 128 A3
Wandsworth Trading Estate WAND/EARL SW18 128 A6
Wanstead WAN E11 59 F5
Wanstead CC WAN E11 59 F6
Wanstead CE Primary School WAN E11 58 E4
Wanstead Golf Club WAN E11 59 G6
Wanstead High School WAN E11 59 G5
Wanstead Hospital WAN E11 59 F3
Wanstead Leisure Centre WAN E11 59 G5
Wanstead Park FSTGT E7 77 F3
Wapping WAP E1W 92 E7
Wapping Wharf WAP E1W 92 E7
War Memorial Sports Ground SUT SM1 175 J3
Warnford Industrial Estate HYS/HAR UB3 101 H1
Warren Comprehensive School CHDH RM6 62 B4
Warren Dell Primary School OXHEY WD19 33 G2
Warrender School RSLP HA4 46 D6
Warren Junior School CHDH RM6 62 B4
The Warren Medical Centre YEAD UB4 83 F5
Warren Sports Centre CHDH RM6 62 B4
Warren Street CAMTN NW1 4 E9
Warwick Avenue MV/WKIL W9 8 E1
Warwick Dubbing Theatre SOHO/CST W1F 11 G5
Warwick Estate BAY/PAD W2 8 D3
Warwick Leadlay Gallery GNWCH SE10 113 F5
Warwick School for Boys WALTH E17 58 A3
The Washington Mayfair Hotel MYFR/PICC W1J 10 D8
Waterfields Retail Park WAT WD17 21 H3
Waterfront Leisure Centre WOOL/PLUM SE18 115 F2
Watergate School
CAT SE6 151 K4
LEW SE13 132 E3
Waterloo STHWK SE1 18 A1
Waterloo East STHWK SE1 12 B9
Waterloo Health Centre STHWK SE1 18 A2
Waterloo School of English NOXST/BSQ WC1A 11 J3
Watermans Arts, Cinema & Theatre Centre BTFD TW8 105 F5
The Watermans Hall MON EC3R 13 J7
Watermeads High School MRDN SM4 162 C5
Watermill Business Centre PEND EN3 31 H1
Water Rats Theatre STPAN WC1H 5 K7
Waterside Business Centre ISLW TW7 124 C3
Waterside Primary School WOOL/PLUM SE18 115 J4
The Waterside Trading Centre HNWL W7 103 K2
Watersports Centre STNW/STAM N16 55 J7
Watford WATW WD18 20 D2
Watford Arches Retail Park WAT WD17 21 G4
Watford Business Centre WAT WD17 21 F2
Watford County Court WAT WD17 21 F1
Watford FC & Saracens RFC (Vicarage Road Stadium) WATW WD18 21 F4
Watford General Hospital WATW WD18 21 F4
Watford Grammar School for Boys WATW WD18 20 D3
Watford Grammar School for Girls WATW WD18 21 G4
Watford High Street WATW WD18 21 G3
Watford Junction WAT WD17 21 G1
Watford Museum WATW WD18 21 G4
Watling Boys' Club EDGW HA8 36 C6
Watling Clinic EDGW HA8 37 F6
Watling Medical Centre EDGW HA8 36 E7
Wavelengths Leisure Pool & Library DEPT SE8 112 D6
Waverley Industrial Estate HRW HA1 48 D2
Waverley Lower Secondary School EDUL SE22 131 J4
Waverley School PEND EN3 30 E3
Waxchandlers' Hall CITYW EC2V 12 F4
Weald Middle School KTN/HRWW/WS HA3 35 F6
Wealdstone Cemetery KTN/HRWW/WS HA3 49 G2
Webber Douglas Academy of Dramatic Art SKENS SW7 14 F6
Webster Graduate Studies Center CAMTN NW1 3 M9
Welbeck Clinic CRICK NW2 70 E2
Welbourne Primary School SEVS/STOTM N15 56 C3
Wellcome Institute CAMTN NW1 5 G9
Welldon Park Middle School RYLN/HDSTN HA2 66 C3
Wellesley Road CROY/NA CR0 177 J1
Welling WELL DA16 136 B1
The Welling Clinic WELL DA16 136 B1
Welling Medical Centre WELL DA16 136 A3
Welling School WELL DA16 116 C7
Wellington Arch MYFR/PICC W1J 16 B1
Wellington Barracks WESTW SW1E 16 F2
Wellington Primary School
BOW E3 93 J2
CHING E4 43 K1
HSLW TW3 122 E1
Welling United FC WELL DA16 136 D2
Wells Primary School WFD IG8 45 F3
Wembley Arena WBLY HA9 68 C3
Wembley Central WBLY HA9 68 A4
Wembley Commercial Centre WBLY HA9 67 K1
Wembley Conference Centre WBLY HA9 68 B3
Wembley FC ALP/SUD HA0 67 H3
Wembley High Technology College ALP/SUD HA0 67 J2
Wembley Hospital ALP/SUD HA0 67 K5
Wembley Park WBLY HA9 68 C2
Wembley Park Business Centre WBLY HA9 68 D2
Wembley Primary School WBLY HA9 68 A2
Wembley Stadium WBLY HA9 68 C4
Wembley Stadium Industrial Estate
WBLY HA9 68 C2
WBLY HA9 68 E2
Wendell Park Primary School SHB W12 106 C1
Wentworth Tutorial College GLDGN NW11 52 B5
The Wernher Collection at Ranger's House GNWCH SE10 113 G7
Wesley's Chapel, House & Museum STLK EC1Y 7 G9
Wessex Gardens Primary School GLDGN NW11 52 C7
West 12 Shopping & Leisure Centre SHB W12 107 G1
West Acton ACT W3 86 C5
West Acton Primary School ACT W3 86 D5
West Beckton Health Centre CAN/RD E16 95 G4
Westbourne Green Sports Complex BAY/PAD W2 8 B3
Westbourne Park NKENS W10 88 D4
Westbourne Primary School SUT SM1 174 E2
Westbridge College BTSEA SW11 108 D7
West Brompton ECT SW5 14 B8
Westbrooke School WELL DA16 136 E2
The Westbury Hotel CONDST W1S 10 D6
Westbury Medical Centre WDGN N22 55 J1
Westcombe Park BKHTH/KID SE3 113 K4
Westcroft Leisure Centre CAR SM5 176 A3
West Croydon CROY/NA CR0 164 D7
West Drayton Cemetery WDR/YW UB7 100 B2
West Drayton Primary School WDR/YW UB7 100 B1
West Dulwich DUL SE21 130 E7
West Ealing WEA W13 85 H6
West Ealing Business Centre WEA W13 85 G6
Western Avenue Business Park ACT W3 86 D3
Western International Market NWDGN UB2 102 A3
Western Trading Estate WLSDN NW10 86 E3
West Ewell Infant School HOR/WEW KT19 173 F4
Westferry POP/IOD E14 93 H6
Westfield Community Technical College WATW WD18 20 D4
Westfield London SHB W12 88 A7
Westfield Stratford City development SRTFD E15 76 A5
Westfields Primary School BARN SW13 126 C1
West Finchley FNCH N3 39 F5
Westgate Business Centre NKENS W10 88 C3
Westgate Primary School DART DA1 139 G6
West Green Primary School SEVS/STOTM N15 55 J3
West Grove Primary School STHGT/OAK N14 28 D6
West Ham SRTFD E15 94 C2
West Ham Church Primary School SRTFD E15 76 D7
West Ham Lane Clinic SRTFD E15 76 C7
West Hampstead KIL/WHAMP NW6 70 E5
West Hampstead KIL/WHAMP NW6 71 F5
West Hampstead Clinic KIL/WHAMP NW6 2 B1
West Hampstead Thameslink KIL/WHAMP NW6 70 E5
West Ham United FC (Upton Park) PLSTW E13 95 H1
West Harrow HRW HA1 48 C5
West Hatch High School WFD IG8 45 K4
West Hendon Clinic CDALE/KGS NW9 51 H5
West Herts Business Centre BORE WD6 24 D2
West Herts College (Watford Campus) WAT WD17 20 E1
West Herts Golf Club RKW/CH/CXG WD3 20 B2
West Hill Primary School
DART DA1 139 F5
WAND/EARL SW18 127 K4
West India Pier POP/IOD E14 112 C1
West India Quay POP/IOD E14 93 J6
West India Shopping Centre POP/IOD E14 93 J7
West Kensington WKENS W14 107 J4
Westland Heliport BTSEA SW11 128 C2
West Lea School ED N9 42 A2
West Lodge Middle School PIN HA5 47 H3
West Lodge Preparatory School BFN/LL DA15 155 F2
West London Academy NTHLT UB5 65 H7
West London Academy Primary NTHLT UB5 65 H6
West London Tamil School WLSDN NW10 87 H1
West Mead Clinic RSLP HA4 65 G2
West Middlesex Golf Club STHL UB1 84 C6
West Middlesex University Hospital ISLW TW7 124 B1
Westminster WHALL SW1A 17 K2
Westminster Abbey WEST SW1P 17 J3
Westminster Abbey Choir School WEST SW1P 17 H3
Westminster Academy BAY/PAD W2 8 B3
Westminster Bridge Park Plaza Hotel STHWK SE1 17 L2
Westminster Business Square LBTH SE11 17 L8
Westminster Cathedral WESTW SW1E 16 E4
Westminster Cathedral Choir School WEST SW1P 16 F4
Westminster Cathedral RC Primary School PIM SW1V 17 H7
Westminster City Hall WESTW SW1E 16 F4
Westminster City School WESTW SW1E 16 F3
Westminster Hall WHALL SW1A 17 K2
Westminster Industrial Estate WOOL/PLUM SE18 114 C2
Westminster Kingsway College
CAMTN NW1 4 E8
WEST SW1P 16 F5
Westminster Natural Health Centre PIM SW1V 16 E6
Westminster Pier WHALL SW1A 17 K2
Westminster School WEST SW1P 17 J3
Westminster Theatre WESTW SW1E 16 E3
Westminster Under School WEST SW1P 17 G6
Westmoor Community Clinic PUT/ROE SW15 126 D6
West Norwood WNWD SE27 149 H3
West Norwood Clinic WNWD SE27 149 J1
West Norwood Crematorium WNWD SE27 149 J2
West One Shopping Centre MYFR/PKLN W1K 10 B5
Weston Green School THDIT KT7 157 K7
Weston Park Clinic CEND/HSY/T N8 54 E4
Weston Park Primary School CEND/HSY/T N8 55 F4
Westpoint Trading Estate ACT W3 86 D4
West Ramp Coach Park HTHAIR TW6 100 D7
West Ruislip RSLP HA4 64 A1
West Silvertown CAN/RD E16 94 E7
West Sutton SUT SM1 174 E3
West Thames College ISLW TW7 103 K7
West Thamesmead Business Park THMD SE28 116 A2
West Thornton Primary School CROY/NA CR0 164 A6
West Twyford Primary School WLSDN NW10 86 C1
Westway Business Centre BAY/PAD W2 8 C3
Westway Sports Centre NKENS W10 88 B5
West Wickham WWKM BR4 167 F6
West Wickham Swimming Baths WWKM BR4 167 F7
West Wimbledon Primary School RYNPK SW20 160 E2
Westwood Language College for Girls NRWD SE19 149 J6
Westwood Primary School WELL DA16 135 K3
Westwood School BUSH WD23 34 D1
Wetherby Preparatory School BAY/PAD W2 8 B6
Whaddon House Clinic CMBW SE5 131 F2
Whipps Cross Hospital LEY E10 58 B5
Whitchurch Middle School STAN HA7 35 J6
Whitechapel WCHPL E1 92 D4
Whitechapel Art Gallery WCHPL E1 13 M4
Whitechapel Sports Centre WCHPL E1 92 C4
White City SHB W12 88 A6
Whitefield School CRICK NW2 52 B6
Whitefield School & Leisure Centre WALTH E17 44 B7
Whitefriars First & Middle School KTN/HRWW/WS HA3 48 E1
Whitefriars Trading Estate KTN/HRWW/WS HA3 48 D1
Whitehall Theatre WHALL SW1A 11 H8
White Hart Lane TOTM N17 42 B6
Whiteheath Junior School RSLP HA4 46 A5
Whitehorse Manor Primary School THHTH CR7 164 E4
The White House Preparatory School BAL SW12 129 J7
Whiteleys Shopping Centre BAY/PAD W2 8 C5
Whiterose Trading Estate EBAR EN4 27 J6
Whitgift Almshouses CROY/NA CR0 177 J1
Whitgift School SAND/SEL CR2 177 J4
Whitgift Shopping Centre CROY/NA CR0 177 J1
Whitings Hill Primary School BAR EN5 26 A4
Whitmore High School RYLN/HDSTN HA2 48 C7
Whitmore Primary School IS N1 7 H5
Whittingham Community Primary School WALTH E17 43 G7
Whittington Hospital ARCH N19 72 B1
Whitton WHTN TW2 123 H6
Whitton Health Centre WHTN TW2 123 H7
Whitton Health Clinic WHTN TW2 123 G7
Whitton School WHTN TW2 142 B1

Whitton Sports & Fitness Centre *WHTN* TW2 142 B1
Whybridge Infant School *RAIN* RM13 81 J7
Whybridge Junior School *RAIN* RM13 81 H7
Wickham Theatre *WWKM* BR4 180 B2
Wide Way Health Clinic *MTCM* CR4 163 J2
Widmore Centre *BMLY* BR1 168 B1
Wigmore Hall *CAVSQ/HST* W1G 10 C4
Wigram House (University of Westminster) *WEST* SW1P 17 G4
Wilberforce Primary School *NKENS* W10 88 C2
Wilbury Primary School *UED* N18 41 K4
Willesden Centre for Health & Care *WLSDN* NW10 69 J6
Willesden Green ⊖ *CRICK* NW2 70 A5
Willesden Junction ⊖ ⊖ *WLSDN* NW10 87 H1
Willesden Medical Centre *CRICK* NW2 69 K5
Willesden New Cemetery *WLSDN* NW10 69 H6
Willesden Sports Centre *WLSDN* NW10 69 K7
Willesden Sports Stadium *WLSDN* NW10 69 K7
William Bellamy J & I School *DAGE* RM10 80 C1
William Byrd School *HYS/HAR* UB3 101 F5
William Davies Primary School *FSTGT* E7 77 H5
William Ellis School *KTTN* NW5 72 A2
William Ellis Sports Ground *EDGW* HA8 36 C7
William Ford CE Junior School *DAGE* RM10 80 C6
William Hogarth School *CHSWK* W4 106 B5
William Morris Academy *HMSMTH* W6 107 G4
William Morris Gallery *WALTH* E17 57 J2
William Morris Primary School *MTCM* CR4 163 J2
William Morris School *WALTH* E17 43 G7
William Patten Primary School *STNW/STAM* N16 74 B1
William Torbitt J & I School *GNTH/NBYPK* IG2 60 E4
William Tyndale Primary School *IS* N1 6 D1
Willington School *WIM/MER* SW19 146 D5
Willow Brook Primary *LEY* E10 57 J7
Willow Business Centre *MTCM* CR4 162 E4
Willow Business Park *SYD* SE26 150 E2
Willowfield Adult Education Centre *WALTH* E17 57 F2
Willowfield School *WALTH* E17 57 G2
The Willows Clinic *CHST* BR7 154 A5
The Willows School *YEAD* UB4 83 H3
Willow Tree Primary School *NTHLT* UB5 65 J5
Wilson's School *WLGTN* SM6 176 E5
Wimbledon ⇌ ⊖ ⊕ *WIM/MER* SW19 146 D5
Wimbledon Chase ⇌ *RYNPK* SW20 161 H1
Wimbledon Chase Primary School *RYNPK* SW20 146 C7
Wimbledon Common Golf Club *WIM/MER* SW19 145 K4
Wimbledon Common Pre-Preparatory School *WIM/MER* SW19 146 B6
Wimbledon (Gap Road) Cemetery *WIM/MER* SW19 147 F3
Wimbledon High School *WIM/MER* SW19 146 C5
Wimbledon House School *WIM/MER* SW19 146 D7
Wimbledon Lawn Tennis Museum *WIM/MER* SW19 146 C2
Wimbledon Park ⊖ *WIM/MER* SW19 146 E2
Wimbledon Park Athletics Track *WIM/MER* SW19 146 D1
Wimbledon Park Golf Club *WIM/MER* SW19 146 D2
Wimbledon Park Primary School *WIM/MER* SW19 146 E1
Wimbledon Recreation Centre *WIM/MER* SW19 147 F5
Wimbledon RFC *RYNPK* SW20 145 H6
Wimbledon School of Art *WIM/MER* SW19 146 C7
Wimbledon Squash & Badminton Club *WIM/MER* SW19 146 C6
Wimbledon Stadium *WIM/MER* SW19 147 F3
Wimbledon Stadium Business Centre *WIM/MER* SW19 147 F2
Wimbledon Theatre *WIM/MER* SW19 146 E6
Wimbledon Windmill *WIM/MER* SW19 146 A2
Winchcombe Business Centre *PECK* SE15 111 F5
Winchmore Hill ⇌ *WCHMH* N21 29 H6
Winchmore Hill Clinic *WCHMH* N21 29 H7
Winchmore Hill CC *WCHMH* N21 29 J7
Winchmore School *WCHMH* N21 41 J1
Windmill Business Centre *NWDGN* UB2 84 C7
Windmill Trading Estate *MTCM* CR4 163 H4
SUN TW16 140 B7
Windrush Primary School *THMD* SE28 97 H7
Winfield House *CAMTN* NW1 3 K7
Wingate & Finchley FC *NFNCH/WDSPK* N12 39 H6
Wingate Trading Estate *TOTM* N17 42 B6
Wingfield Primary School *BKHTH/KID* SE3 133 K2
Winns Primary School *WALTH* E17 57 H1
Winsor Primary School *EHAM* E6 96 A5
Winston Churchill's Britain at War Experience *STHWK* SE1 13 H9
Winston House Preparatory School *SWFD* E18 44 E7
Winston Way Primary School *IL* IG1 78 A2
Winterbourne Infant School *THHTH* CR7 164 B3
Winton Primary School *IS* N1 5 L6
Witley Industrial Estate *NWDGN* UB2 102 E3
Wolf Fields Primary School *NWDGN* UB2 102 E3
Wolfson Hillel Primary School *STHGT/OAK* N14 28 D5
Wolfson Medical Centre *RYNPK* SW20 145 J6
Wolsey Business Park *WATW* WD18 20 B6
Wolsey Junior School *CROY/NA* CR0 180 B6
The Women's Library *WCHPL* E1 13 L4
The Woodberry Clinic *MUSWH* N10 54 B2
Woodberry Down Centre *FSBYPK* N4 55 J7
Woodberry Down Community Primary *FSBYPK* N4 55 J6
Woodbridge High School & Language College *WFD* IG8 45 F6
Woodcroft Primary School *EDGW* HA8 37 F6
Wood End J & I Schools *GFD/PVL* UB6 66 D4
Wood End Park Junior School *UX/CGN* UB8 82 A6
Woodfield School *CDALE/KGS* NW9 51 G7
Woodford ⊖ *WFD* IG8 45 F5
Woodford County High School Girls *WFD* IG8 44 D5
Woodford Golf Club *WFD* IG8 44 D4
Woodford Green Preparatory School *WFD* IG8 44 E5
Woodford Green Primary School *WFD* IG8 44 D4
Woodford Trading Estate *WFD* IG8 59 G1
Woodgrange Infant School *FSTGT* E7 77 F3
Woodgrange Park ⊖ *FSTGT* E7 77 H4
Woodgrange Park Cemetery *MNPK* E12 77 H4
Wood Green ⊖ *WDGN* N22 55 G1
Wood Green Health Centre *WDGN* N22 41 F7
Wood Green Old Boys FC *WDGN* N22 41 G6
Woodhall School *OXHEY* WD19 33 J3
Woodhill Primary School *CHARL* SE7 114 D3
Woodhouse College *NFNCH/WDSPK* N12 39 H5
Woodlands First & Middle School *KTN/HRWW/WS* HA3 34 C6
Woodlands J & I School *IL* IG1 78 D3
Woodlands Medical Centre *LEW* SE13 133 G5
Wood Lane ⊖ *SHB* W12 88 A6
Wood Lane Medical Centre *RSLP* HA4 46 C7
Wood Lane School *FUL/PGN* SW6 108 B7
Wood Lane Sports Centre *BCTR* RM8 62 D7
Woodmansterne Primary School *STRHM/NOR* SW16 148 D7
Woodridge Primary School *NFNCH/WDSPK* N12 38 E2
Woodside ⊕ *SNWD* SE25 165 J5
Woodside Health Centre *SNWD* SE25 165 J4
Woodside High School *WDGN* N22 41 H6
Woodside Infant School *CROY/NA* CR0 165 H6
Woodside Park ⊖ *NFNCH/WDSPK* N12 38 E3
Woodside Park Golf Club *NFNCH/WDSPK* N12 38 E3
Woodside Park International School *NFNCH/WDSPK* N12 39 F3
Woodside Primary School *WALTH* E17 58 A2
Woodside School *BELV* DA17 117 J3
Wood Street ⇌ *WALTH* E17 58 B3
Wood Wharf *POP/IOD* E14 93 K7
Wood Wharf Business Park *POP/IOD* E14 113 F1
Woolmore Primary School *POP/IOD* E14 94 A6
Woolwich Arsenal ⇌ ⊖ *WOOL/PLUM* SE18 115 G3
Woolwich Cemetery *WOOL/PLUM* SE18 116 A6
Woolwich Dockyard ⇌ *WOOL/PLUM* SE18 114 E3
Woolwich Polytechnic School *THMD* SE28 97 G7
Worcester Park ⇌ *WPK* KT4 160 D7
World Business Centre Heathrow *HTHAIR* TW6 101 F7
World Rugby Museum & Twickenham Stadium Tours *WHTN* TW2 123 K5
Worlds End Place *WBPTN* SW10 108 B6
World Spiritual University *WLSDN* NW10 69 J6
World University Service *STLK* EC1Y 13 G1
Wormholt Park Primary School *SHB* W12 87 J6
Worple Primary School *ISLW* TW7 124 B3
Worsley Bridge Junior School *BECK* BR3 151 J6
Worton Hall Industrial Estate *ISLW* TW7 123 K3
Wren Academy *NFNCH/WDSPK* N12 39 H4
Wrencote House *CROY/NA* CR0 177 J2
Wyborne Primary School *ELTH/MOT* SE9 135 G7
Wyke Green Golf Club *ISLW* TW7 104 A5
Wykeham Primary School *HCH* RM12 63 J7
WLSDN NW10 69 F2
Wyndham Grand Hotel *WBPTN* SW10 108 B7
Wyndhams Theatre *CHCR* WC2N 11 H6
Wyvil Primary School *VX/NE* SW8 109 K6
Yale University Press *HAMP* NW3 71 J3
Yardley Primary School *CHING* E4 31 K5
Yavneh College *BORE* WD6 24 D3
Yeading FC *YEAD* UB4 83 G7
Yeading Junior School *YEAD* UB4 83 G4
Yeading Medical Centre *NTHLT* UB5 83 G2
Yeading Primary School *YEAD* UB4 83 G4
Yerbury Primary School *ARCH* N19 72 D2
Yeshivo Horomo Talmudical College *STNW/STAM* N16 55 K7
Yesodey Hatorah Jewish Boys School *SEVS/STOTM* N15 56 B6
Yesodey Hatorah School For Girls *STNW/STAM* N16 56 B6
Yetev Lev Day School for Boys *STNW/STAM* N16 56 C7
YMCA Leisure Centre *RSQ* WC1B 11 H4
York Clinic *STHWK* SE1 13 G9
York Hall *BETH* E2 92 D1
York Road Junior School & Language Unit *DART* DA1 139 J6
York Water Gate *CHCR* WC2N 11 K8
Young Actors Theatre *IS* N1 6 A4
Young England RFC *VX/NE* SW8 110 A6
Young Vic Theatre *STHWK* SE1 18 B1
Zennor Road Industrial Estate *BAL* SW12 129 H7
Zephyr Business Centre *SEVS/STOTM* N15 56 A3
The Zetter Hotel *FARR* EC1M 12 C1
Ziam Trading Estate *CLPT* E5 56 E7
ZSL London Zoo *CAMTN* NW1 4 A5

Acknowledgements

Schools address data provided by Education Direct.

Petrol station information supplied by Johnsons.

Garden centre information provided by:

Garden Centre Association Britains best garden centres

Wyevale Garden Centres

The boundary of the London Congestion Charging Zone and Low Emission Zone supplied by Transport for London

The statement on the front cover of this atlas is sourced, selected and quoted from a reader comment and feedback form received in 2004

Notes

AA **Street by Street** QUESTIONNAIRE

Dear Atlas User
Your comments, opinions and recommendations are very important to us. So please help us to improve our street atlases by taking a few minutes to complete this simple questionnaire.

You do not need a stamp (unless posted outside the UK). If you do not want to remove this page from your street atlas, then photocopy it or write your answers on a plain sheet of paper.

Send to: Marketing Assistant, AA Publishing, 14th Floor Fanum House, Freepost SCE 4598, Basingstoke RG21 4GY

ABOUT THE ATLAS...

Please state which city / town / county street atlas you bought:

____

____

Where did you buy the atlas? (City, Town, County)

____

For what purpose? (please tick all applicable)

To use in your own local area ☐ **To use on business or at work** ☐

Visiting a strange place ☐ **In the car** ☐ **On foot** ☐

Other (please state)

____

Have you ever used any street atlases other than AA Street by Street?

Yes ☐ **No** ☐

If so, which ones?

____

Is there any aspect of our street atlases that could be improved?
(Please continue on a separate sheet if necessary)

____

____

____

____

____

continued overleaf

Please list the features you found most useful:

Please list the features you found least useful:

LOCAL KNOWLEDGE...

Local knowledge is invaluable. Whilst every attempt has been made to make the information contained in this atlas as accurate as possible, should you notice any inaccuracies, please detail them below (if necessary, use a blank piece of paper) or e-mail us at *streetbystreet@theAA.com*

ABOUT YOU...

Name (Mr/Mrs/Ms)

Address

Postcode

Daytime tel no

E-mail address

Which age group are you in?

Under 25 ☐ **25-34** ☐ **35-44** ☐ **45-54** ☐ **55-64** ☐ **65+** ☐

Are you an AA member? **Yes** ☐ **No** ☐

Do you have Internet access? **Yes** ☐ **No** ☐

Thank you for taking the time to complete this questionnaire. Please send it to us as soon as possible, and remember, you do not need a stamp (unless posted outside the UK).

We may use information we hold about you to, telephone or email you about other products and services offered by the AA, we do NOT disclose this information to third parties.

Please tick here if you do not wish to hear about products and services from the AA. ☐